WEBSTER'S ENGLISH DICTIONARY

FOR HOME, SCHOOL OR OFFICE

GEDDES & GROSSET

This edition published 2003 by Geddes & Grosset,
David Dale House, New Lanark, ML11 9DJ, Scotland

© 2003 Geddes & Grosset

This book is not published by the original publishers
of *Webster's Dictionary* or by their successors.

ISBN 1 84205 366 3

Printed and bound in the USA

A

A *abbr* = ampere(s).

a *adj* the indefinite article; one; any; per.

A[1] *adj* (*inf*) in perfect condition; physically fit; excellent.

AA *abbr* = Alcoholics Anonymous; anti-aircraft; Automobile Association.

aardvark *n* a nocturnal African mammal with a long snout that feeds on termites.

aback *adv* **taken aback** startled.

abacus *n* (*pl* **abaci, abacuses**) a frame with sliding beads for doing arithmetic.

abandon *vt* to leave behind; to desert; to yield completely to an emotion or urge. * *n* freedom from inhibitions.–**abandonment** *n*.

abandoned *adj* (*behavior*) showing abandon, unrestrained.–**abandonedly** *adv*.

abase *vt* to degrade, humiliate.–**abasement** *n*.

abash *vt* to cause a feeling of shame, embarrassment or confusion.–**abashment** *n*.–**abashed** *adj*.

abate *vti* to make or become less; (*law*) to end.–**abatement** *n*.

abattoir *n* a slaughterhouse.

abbess *n* the woman who heads a convent of nuns.

abbey *n* a building occupied by monks or nuns; a church built as part of such a building; the community of monks or nuns.

abbot *n* the head of an abbey of monks.

abbreviate *vt* to make shorter, esp to shorten (a word) by omitting letters.–**abbreviation** *n*. **abdicate** *vti* to renounce an official position or responsibility, etc.–**abdication** *n*.

abdomen *n* the region of the body below the chest containing the digestive organs; the belly; (*insects, etc*) the section of the body behind the thorax.–**abdominal** *adj*.–**abdominally** *adv*.

abduct *vt* to carry off (a person) by force; (*anat*) to draw (a limb, etc) from its natural position.–**abduction** *n*.–**abductor** *n*.

aberration *n* a deviation from the normal; a mental or moral lapse.–**aberrant** *adj*.–**aberrance, aberrancy** *n*.

abet *vt* (**abetting, abetted**) to encourage or assist, esp to do wrong.–**abetment** *n*.–**abetter**, (*esp law*) **abettor** *n*.

abhor *vt* (**abhorring, abhorred**) to detest, despise.–**abhorrence** *n*.–**abhorrent** *adj*.

abide *vt* (**abiding, abode** *or* **abided**) to endure; to put up with.

abiding *adj* permanent.–**abidingly** *adv*.

ability *n* (*pl* **abilities**) the state of being able; power to do; talent; skill.

abject *adj* wretched; dejected.–**abjection** *n*.–**abjectly** *adv*.

abjure *vt* to renounce.–**abjuration** *n*.–**abjurer** *n*.

ablaze *adj* burning, on fire.

able *adj* having the competence or means (to do); talented; skilled.–**ably** *adv*.

able-bodied *adj* fit, strong.

ablution *n* (*usu pl*) a washing or cleansing of the body by water; the ritual cleansing of vessels or hands.–**ablutionary** *adj*.

abnegate *vt* to deny oneself (a right, etc); to renounce.–**abnegation** *n*.

abnormal *adj* unusual, not average or typical; irregular.–**abnormality** *n*.–**abnormally** *adv*.

abnormality *n* (*pl* **abnormalities**) deformity; irregularity; difference or departure from a regular type or rule.

aboard *adv* on or in an aircraft, ship, train, etc.–*also prep*.

abode[1] *n* a home, residence.

abode[2] *see* **abide**.

abolish *vt* to bring to an end, do away with.–**abolisher** *n*.–**abolition** *n*.– **abolitionist** *n*.–**abolishment** *n*.

A-bomb *n* atomic bomb.

abominable *adj* despicable, detestable; (*inf*) very unpleasant.–**abominably** *adv*.

abominate *vt* to abhor; to regard with feelings of disgust or hatred.–**abominator** *n*.

abomination *n* detestation; a loathsome person or thing.

aboriginal *adj* existing in a place from the earliest times; of aborigines. * *n* the species of animals or plants presumed to have originated within a given area.

aborigine *n* any of the first known inhabitants of a region; (*with cap*) one of the original inhabitants of Australia before the arrival of European settlers.

abort *vti* to undergo or cause an abortion; to terminate or cause to terminate prematurely. * *n* the premature termination of a rocket flight, etc.

abortion *n* the premature expulsion of a fetus, esp if induced on purpose.–**abortionist** *n*.

abortive *adj* failing in intended purpose; fruitless; causing abortion.–**abortively** *adv*.

abound *vi* to be in abundance; to have in great quantities.

about *prep* on all sides of; near to; with; on the point of; concerning. * *adv* all around; near; to face the opposite direction.

above *prep* over, on top of; better or more than; beyond the reach of; too complex to understand. * *adv* in or to a higher place; in addition; (*text*) mentioned earlier.

aboveboard *adj, adv* without trickery; in open sight.

abrade *vt* to wear or rub away; to remove as by friction or abrasion; to corrode, as by acids.–**abrader** *n*.–**abrasion** *n*.

abrasive *adj* causing abrasion; harsh, irritating. * *n* a substance or tool used for grinding or polishing, etc. –**abrasively** *adv*.

abreast *adv* side by side and facing the same way; informed (of); aware.

abridge *vt* to shorten by using fewer words but keeping the substance.

abridgment, abridgement *n* the state of being contracted or curtailed; a shortened version of a text; an epitome.

abroad *adv* in or to a foreign country; over a wide area; out in the open; in circulation, current.

abrogate *vt* to repeal, cancel.–**abrogator** *n*.–**abrogation** *n*.

abrupt *adj* sudden; unexpected; curt.–**abruptly** *adv*.–**abruptness** *n*.

abscess *n* an inflamed area of the body containing pus.

abscond *vi* to hide, run away, esp to avoid punishment for a wrongdoing.

abseil *vi* to descend a rock face by means of a double rope attached to a higher point.–**abseiling** *n*.

absence *n* the state of not being present; the time of this; a lack; inattention.

absent[1] *adj* not present; not existing; inattentive.–**absently** *adv*.

absent[2] *vt* to keep (oneself) away.

absentee *n* a person who is absent, as from work or school.–**absenteeism** *n*.

absently *adv* in an abstracted manner.

absent-minded *adj* inattentive; forgetful.

absinthe, absinth *n* a potent, green, brandy-based liqueur flavored with wormwood.

absolute *adj* unrestricted, unconditional; complete; positive; perfect, pure; not relative; (*monarch, ruler, etc*) authoritarian, despotic; (*inf*) utter, out-and-out.

absolutely *adv* completely; unconditionally; (*inf*) I completely agree, certainly.

absolution *n* forgiveness; remission of sin or its penalty.

absolutism *n* the state of being absolute; the principle or system of absolute government.–**absolutist** *n, adj*.

absolve *vt* to clear from guilt or blame; to give religious absolution to; to free from a duty, obligation, etc.

absorb *vt* to take in; to soak up; to incorporate; to pay for (costs, etc); to take in (a shock) without recoil; to occupy one's attention or interest completely.–**absorbency** *n*.–**absorbent** *adj*.

absorbing adj engrossing.–**absorbingly** adv.

absorption n the process or act of absorbing; the state of being absorbed; entire preoccupation of the mind.

absorptivity n the power of absorption; (physics) the rate of absorption of radiation by a material.–**absorptive** adj.

abstain vi to keep oneself from some indulgence, esp from drinking alcohol; to refrain from using one's vote.

abstemious adj sparing in consuming food or alcohol.–**abstemiously** adv.–**abstemiousness** n.

abstention n the act of holding off or abstaining; the withholding of a vote.–**abstentious** adj.–**abstentionist** n.

abstinence n an abstaining or refraining, esp from food or alcohol.

abstinent adj refraining from over-indulgence, esp with regard to food and drink. * n an abstainer.–**abstinently** adv.

abstract adj having no material existence; theoretical; (art) non-representational. * n (writing, speech) a summary or condensed version. * vt to remove or extract; to separate; to summarize.

abstracted adj not paying attention.–**abstractedly** adv.–**abstractedness** n.

abstraction n preoccupation, inattention; an abstract concept.–**abstractive** adj.

abstract noun n the name of a state or quality considered apart from the object to which it belongs.

abstruse adj obscure; hidden; difficult to comprehend; profound.–**abstrusely** adv.–**abstruseness** n.

absurd adj against reason or common sense; ridiculous.–**absurdly** adv.

absurdity n (pl **absurdities**) the state of being absurd; that which is absurd.

abundance n a plentiful supply; a considerable amount.–**abundant** adj.–**abundantly** adv.

abuse vt to make wrong use of; to mistreat; to insult, attack verbally. * n misuse; mistreatment; insulting language; immoderate or illegal use of drugs or other stimulants.–**abuser** n.

abusive adj insulting.–**abusively** adv.–**abusiveness** n.

abut vi (**abutting, abutted**) to adjoin, border or lean (on, against).

abutment, abuttal n that which borders upon something else; the solid structure that supports the extremity of a bridge or arch.

abysmal adj extremely bad, deplorable.–**abysmally** adv.

abyss n a bottomless depth; anything too deep to measure; hell.

AC, ac abbr = alternating current.

a/c abbr = account; account current.

acacia n a genus of shrubby or arboreous leguminous plants of warmer regions with white or yellow flowers, several species of which yield gum.

academic adj pertaining to a school, college or university; scholarly; purely theoretical in nature. * n a member of a college or university; a scholarly person.

academically adv theoretically, unpractically.

academy n (pl **academies**) a school for specialized training; (Scot) a secondary school; (with cap) a society of scholars, writers, scientists, etc.

acc. abbr = according; account; accusative.

accede vi to take office; to agree or assent to (a suggestion).

accelerate vti to move faster; to happen or cause to happen more quickly; to increase the velocity of (a vehicle, etc).–**accelerative, acceleratory** adj.

acceleration n the act of accelerating or condition of being accelerated; the rate of increase in speed or change in velocity; the power of accelerating.

accelerator n a device for increasing speed; a throttle; (physics) an apparatus that imparts high velocities to elementary particles.

accent n emphasis on a syllable or word; a mark used to indicate this; any way of speaking characteristic of a region, class, or an individual; the emphasis placed on something; rhythmic stress in music or verse. * vt to express the accent, or denote the vocal division of a word by stress or modulation of the voice; to pronounce; to mark or accent a word in writing by use of a sign; to dwell upon or emphasize, as a passage of music.

accentuate vt to emphasize.

accentuation n the act of accentuating by stress or accent; speaking or writing with emphasis or distinction.

accept vt to receive, esp willingly; to approve; to agree to; to believe in; to agree to pay.

acceptable adj satisfactory; welcome; tolerable.–**acceptability** n.–**acceptably** adv.

acceptance n the act of accepting; the act of being accepted or received with approbation; agreement; the subscription to a bill of exchange; the bill accepted or the sum contained in it.

access n approach, or means of approach; the right to enter, use, etc. * vt (comput) to retrieve (information) from a storage device; to gain access to.

accessible adj able to be reached; open (to).–**accessibility** n.–**accessibly** adv.

accession n the act of reaching or assuming a rank or position.–**accessional** adj.

accessory adj additional; extra. * n (pl **accessories**) a supplementary part or item, esp of clothing; a person who aids another in a crime.–**accessorial** adj.

accident n an unexpected event; a mishap or misfortune, esp one resulting in death or injury; chance.

accidental adj occurring or done by accident; non-essential; (mus) a sign prefixed to a note indicating a departure from the key signature.–**accidentally** adv.

acclaim vt to praise publicly (the merits of a person or thing); to welcome enthusiastically. * vi to shout approval. * n a shout of welcome or approval.

acclamation n a shout of applause or other demonstration of hearty approval, loud united assent; an outburst of joy or praise; the adoption of a resolution viva voce; a mode of papal election.–**acclamatory** adj.

acclimatize vt to adapt to a new climate or environment * vi to become acclimatized.–**acclimatization** n.

accolade n praise; approval; an award.

accommodate vt to provide lodging for; to oblige, supply; to adapt, harmonize.

accommodating adj obliging, willing to help.–**accommodatingly** adv.

accommodation n lodgings; the process of adapting; willingness to help.

accompaniment n an instrumental part supporting a solo instrument, a voice, or a choir; something that accompanies.

accompanist, accompanyist n one who plays a musical accompaniment.

accompany vt (**accompanying, accompanied**) (person) to go with; (something) to supplement.

accomplice n a partner, esp in committing a crime.

accomplish vt to succeed in carrying out; to fulfill.

accomplished adj done; completed; skilled, expert; polished.

accomplishment n a skill or talent; the act of accomplishing; something accomplished.

accord vi to agree; to harmonize (with). * vt to grant. * n consent; harmony.–**accordance** n. –**accordant** adj.

according prep as stated by or in; (with **to**) in conformity with; (with **as**) depending on whether. * adj agreeing, harmonious.

accordingly adv consequently; therefore; suitably.

accordion n a portable keyboard instrument with manually operated folding bellows that force air through metal reeds.–**accordionist** n.

accost vt to approach and speak to, often to accuse of crime or to solicit sexually.

account n a description; an explanatory statement; a business record or statement; a credit arrangement with a bank, department store, etc; importance, consequence. * vt to think of as; consider. * vi to give a financial reckoning (to); (with **for**) to give reasons (for); (with **for**) to kill, dispose of.

accountable adj liable; responsible; explainable.–**accountability** n.–**accountably** adv.

accountant n one whose profession is auditing business accounts.–**accountancy** n.

accounting n the maintaining or auditing of detailed business accounts; accountancy.

accouterments, accoutrements npl equipage; dress; military equipment.

accredit vt to give credit or authority to; to have confidence in; to authorize; to stamp with authority; to believe and accept as true.–**accreditation** n.–**accredited** adj.

accrete vi to adhere, to grow together; to be added. * vt to cause to grow or unite. * adj (bot) grown into one.–**accretion** n.–**accretive, accretionary** adj.

accrue vi (**accruing, accrued**) to come as a natural increase or addition; (money, etc) to accumulate or be added periodically.–**accrual, accrument** n.

accumulate vti to collect together in increasing quantities, to amass.–**accumulation** n.–**accumulative** adj.

accumulator n a rechargeable battery; (horseracing) a bet that accumulates in value over successive races; (comput) a storage register.

accurate adj conforming with the truth or an accepted standard; done with care, exact.–**accuracy** n.–**accurately** adv.

accursed, accurst adj under or subject to a curse; ill-fated, doomed to destruction; detestable; execrable.

accusation n the act of accusing or being accused; an allegation; the charge of guilt brought against a person.

accuse vt to charge with a crime, fault, etc; to blame.–**accuser** n.–**accusingly** adv.

accused n (law) (with **the**) the defendant in court facing a criminal charge.

accustom vt to make used (to) by habit, use, or custom.

accustomed adj usual, customary; used to.

ace n the one spot in dice, playing cards, dominoes, etc; a point won by a single stroke, as in tennis; an expert. * adj (inf) excellent.

acerbic adj bitter and harsh to the taste; astringent.

acetate n a salt or ester of acetic acid; a fabric made from cellulose acetate.

acetic acid n a clear liquid with a strong acid taste and sharp smell, present in a dilute form in vinegar.

acetone n a clear flammable liquid used as a solvent.

acetylene n a gas that burns with a hot flame, used for welding, etc.

ache n a dull, continuous pain. * vi to suffer a dull, continuous mental or physical pain; (inf) to yearn.–**achy** adj.

achieve vt to perform successfully, accomplish; to gain, win.–**achievable** adj.–**achiever** n.

achievement n a thing achieved, esp by great effort, courage, determination, etc; accomplishment; (her) an escutcheon in memory of a distinguished feat.

Achilles' tendon n a tendon attaching the heel to the calf muscles.

achromatic adj colorless; transmitting light without decomposing it.–**achromatically** adv.–**achromaticity, achromatism** n.

acid adj sharp or sour to the taste. * n a sour substance; one that with certain other substances forms salts.–**acidic** adj.

acidify vti (**acidifying, acidified**) to make or become acid.–**acidification** n.

acidity n (pl **acidities**) the quality or condition of being acid.

acidosis n an acid condition of the blood.–**acidotic** adj.

acid rain n rain made acidic by air pollution from power stations, etc.

acid test n a crucial or conclusive test.

acknowledge vt to admit that something is true and valid; to show that one has noticed or recognized.

acknowledgment, acknowledgement n the act of acknowledging; the admission or recognition of a truth; confession; the expression of appreciation of a favor or benefit conferred; a printed recognition by an author of others' works used or referred to; a receipt.

acme n the peak or highest point; the height of perfection.

acne n inflammation of the skin glands producing pimples.

acolyte n an assistant or follower, esp of a priest.

acorn n the nut of the oak tree.

acoustic, acoustical adj of the sense of hearing or sound; of acoustics; (mus) not amplified, eg a guitar.–**acoustically** adv.

acoustics npl (room, concert hall, etc) properties governing how clearly sounds can be heard in it; (in sing) the physics of sound.–**acoustician** n.

acquaint vt to make (oneself) familiar (with); to inform; (with **with**) to introduce (to).

acquaintance n a person whom one knows only slightly.

acquainted adj having personal knowledge; (with **of, with**) familiar, known.

acquiesce vi (with **in**) to comply with readily, or put up no opposition to.–**acquiescence** n.–**acquiescent** adj.

acquire vt to gain by one's own efforts; to obtain.–**acquirable** adj.

acquirement n the act of acquiring; that which is acquired; mental attainment.

acquisition n the act of gaining, acquiring; someone or something that is acquired, often of special worth or talent.

acquisitive adj eager or greedy for possessions.–**acquisitively** adv.–**acquisitiveness** n.

acquit vt (**acquitting, acquitted**) to free from an obligation; to behave or conduct (oneself); to declare innocent.

acquittal n the act of releasing or acquitting, the state of being acquitted; a judicial discharge from accusation; the performance (of duty).

acre n land measuring 4840 square yards.

acreage n area measured in acres.

acrid adj sharp and bitter of taste or smell; caustic, critical in attitude or speech.–**acridity** n.–**acridly** adv.

acrimony n (pl **acrimonies**) bitterness of manner or language.–**acrimonious** adj.–**acrimoniously** adv.

acrobat n a skillful performer of spectacular gymnastic feats.–**acrobatic** adj.–**acrobatically** adv.

acrobatics npl acrobatic feats.

acronym n a word formed from the initial letters of other words (as laser).

acrophobia n dread of heights.–**acrophobe** n.–**acrophobic** adj, n.

across prep from one side to the other of; on or at an angle; on the other side of. * adv crosswise; from one side to the other.

acrostic n a poem or word puzzle in which certain letters of each line spell a complete word, etc.–**acrostically** adv.

acrylic adj of or derived from acrylic acid. * n an acrylic fiber or resin.

act vi to perform or behave in a certain manner; to perform a specific function; to have an effect; to perform on the stage; (with **up**) (inf) to misbehave; to malfunction. * vt to portray by actions, esp on the stage; to pretend, simulate; to take the part of, as a character in a play. * n something done, a deed; an exploit; a law; a main division of a play or opera; the short repertoire of a comic, etc; something done merely for effect or show.

acting n the art of an actor. * adj holding an office or position temporarily.

action n the process of doing something; an operation; a movement of the body, gesture; a land or sea battle; a lawsuit; the unfolding of events in a play, novel, etc; (inf) (with **the**) the center of (social) activity.

actionable adj providing grounds for legal action.–**actionably** adv.

activate vt to make active; to set in motion; to make radioactive.–**activation** n.–**activator** n.

active adj lively, physically mobile; engaged in practical activities; energetic, busy; (volcano) liable to erupt; capable of producing an effect; radioactive; (armed forces) in full-time service. * n (gram) the verb form having as its subject the doer of the action.–**actively** adv.–**activeness** n.

activist n an advocate of direct or militant action, esp in politics.–**activism** n.

activity n (pl **activities**) the state of being active; energetic, lively action; specific occupations (indoor activities).

act of God n a direct and unforeseeable act of nature that could not reasonably have been guarded against.

actor n a person who acts in a play, film, etc.–**actress** nf.

actual adj real; existing in fact or reality.

actuality n (pl **actualities**) the state of being real or actual; that which is in full existence; reality

actualize vt to realize in action; to describe realistically; to make actual.–**actualization** n.

actually adv as an existing fact, really; strange though it seems.

actuary n (pl **actuaries**) a person who calculates insurance risks, premiums, etc.–**actuarial** adj.

actuate vt to move or incite to action; to put in motion; to impel, influence.–**actuation** n.–**actuator** n.

acuity n sharpness of thought or vision.

acumen n sharpness of mind, perception.

acupuncture n the insertion of the tips of fine needles into the skin at certain points to treat various common ailments.–**acupuncturist** n.

acute adj perceptive; sharp-witted; (hearing) sensitive; (pain) severe; very serious; (angles) less than 90 degrees; (disease) severe but not long lasting.–**acutely** adv.–**acuteness** n.

acute accent n a mark (") over a vowel in certain languages to indicate emphasis or special quality.

ad abbr = advertisement.

ad abbr = anno domini (in the year of Our Lord) in dates of the Christian era, indicating the number of years since the birth of Christ.

adage n a proverb, old saying.

adagio adv (mus) slowly, gracefully. * n (pl **adagios**) a slow movement.

adamant adj inflexible, unyielding. * n adamantine, an extremely hard substance.

adamantine adj made of adamantine; impenetrable, very hard. * n an extremely hard substance; the diamond (–also **adamant**).

Adam's apple n the hard projection of cartilage in the front of the neck.

adapt vti to make or become fit; to adjust to a new purpose or circumstances.–**adaptability** n.–**adaptable** adj.–**adapter** n.

adaptation n the process or condition of being adapted; something produced by modification; a version of a literary composition rewritten for a different medium.

adapter n a device that allows an item of equipment to be put to new use; a device for connecting parts of differing size and shape; an electrical plug using one socket for different appliances.–also **adaptor**.

ADC abbr = aide-de-camp.

add vt to combine (two or more things together); to combine numbers or amounts in a total; to remark or write further. * vi to perform or come together by addition.

addendum n (pl **addenda**) a thing to be added; supplementary text appended to a book, etc.

adder n the venomous viper.

addict n a person who is dependent upon a drug. * vt to devote or give oneself up to.–**addiction** n.–**addictive** adj.

addition n the act or result of adding; something to be added; an extra part.

additional adj added, extra; supplementary.–**additionally** adv.

additive adj produced by addition. * n a substance added (to food, etc) to improve texture, flavor, etc.

address vt to write directions for delivery on (a letter, etc); to speak or write directly to; to direct one's skills or attention (to); (golf) to adjust one's stance and aim before hitting the ball; * n a place where a person or business resides, the details of this on a letter for delivery; a speech, esp a formal one; (comput) a specific memory location where information is stored.–**addressable** adj.

addressee n a person or company to whom a letter is addressed.

adduce vt to offer as an example or evidence.

adenoids npl enlarged masses of tissue in the throat behind the nose.–**adenoidal** adj.

adept adj highly proficient. * n a highly skilled person.–**adeptly** adv.–**adeptness** n.

adequate adj sufficient for requirements; barely acceptable.–**adequacy** n.–**adequately** adv.

adhere vi to stick, as by gluing or suction; to give allegiance or support (to); to follow.

adherence n the act or state of adhering; unwavering attachment.

adherent adj sticking, attached. * n a supporter of a political party, idea, etc.

adhesion n the action or condition of adhering; the attachment of normally separate tissues in the body.

adhesive adj sticky; causing adherence. * n a substance used to stick, such as glue, paste, etc.–**adhesiveness** n.

ad hoc adj for a particular purpose.

adieu n (pl **adieux, adieus**) farewell, goodbye; good wishes at parting.

adipose adj of, like or containing animal fat; fatty.–**adiposity** n.

adjacent adj nearby; adjoining, contiguous.–**adjacency** n.

adjective n a word used to add a characteristic to a noun or pronoun.–**adjectival** adj.–**adjectivally** adv.

adjoin vt to unite or join. * vi to lie next to.–**adjoining** adj.

adjourn vt to suspend (a meeting) temporarily. * vi (inf) to retire (to another room, etc).–**adjournment** n.

adjudge vt (**adjudging, adjudged**) to decide or award judicially; to sentence; to determine in a controversy, to adjudicate.–**adjudgment, adjudgement** n.

adjudicate vt (law) to hear and decide (a case). * vi to serve as a judge (in or on).–**adjudication** n.–**adjudicator** n.

adjunct n something joined or added but inessential.–**adjunctive** adj.

adjure vt to command on oath under pain of a penalty; to charge solemnly, request earnestly.–**adjuration** n.

adjust vt to arrange in a more proper or satisfactory manner; to regulate or modify by minor changes; to decide the amount to be paid in settling (an insurance claim). * vi to adapt oneself.–**adjustable** adj.–**adjuster** n.

adjustment n the act of adjusting; arrangement.

adjutant n a military staff officer who assists the commanding officer.–**adjutancy** n.

ad-lib vti (**ad-libbing, ad-libbed**) (speech, etc) to improvise. * n an ad-libbed remark. * adv spontaneously, freely.–**ad-libber** n.

admin n (inf) administration.

administer vt to manage, direct; to give out as a punishment; to dispense (medicine, punishment, etc); to tender (an oath, etc).

administrate vti to manage or control the affairs of a business, institution, etc.

administration n management; the people who administer an organization; the government; (with cap) the executive officials of a government, their policies, and term of office.

administrative adj of management; executive.—**administratively** adv.

administrator n a person who manages or supervises; (law) one appointed to settle an estate.

admirable adj deserving of admiration or approval.—**admirably** adv.

admiral n the commanding officer of a fleet; a naval officer of the highest rank.

admiralty n (pl **admiralties**) the department of a government having authority over naval affairs; the building in which naval affairs are transacted; the office of an admiral.

admiration n a feeling of pleasurable and often surprised respect or approval; an admired person or thing.

admire vt to regard with honor, approval and pleasure; to express admiration for.—**admirer** n.—**admiring** adj.—**admiringly** adv.

admissible adj that may be admitted or allowed.—**admissibility, admissibleness** n.

admission n an entrance fee; a conceding, confessing, etc; a thing conceded, confessed, etc.—**admissive** adj.

admit vb (**admitting, admitted**) vt to allow to enter or join; to concede or acknowledge as true. * vi to give access; (with **of**) to allow or permit.

admittance n the act of admitting; the right to enter.

admittedly adv acknowledged as fact, willingly conceded.

admonish vt to remind or advise earnestly; to reprove gently.

admonition n a friendly reproof or warning.—**admonitory** adj.

ado n fuss, excitement, esp over trivial matters.

adobe n a brick made of sun-dried clay; clay for making adobe bricks; a building using such bricks.

adolescence n the period of life between puberty and maturity; youth.

adolescent adj pertaining to the stage between childhood and maturity; (inf) immature. * n an adolescent person.

adopt vt to take legally into one's family and raise as one's child; to select and pursue, eg a course of action; to take as one's own.—**adoption** n.—**adoptive** adj.

adoration n worship, homage; profound regard.

adore vt to worship; to love deeply.—**adorable** adj.— **adorably, adoringly** adv.

adorn vt to decorate; to make more pleasant or attractive.—**adornment** n.

adrenal adj of or near the kidney. * n an adrenal gland.

adrenal gland n one of two glands situated above the kidneys that secretes adrenaline.

adrenaline n a hormone that stimulates the heart rate, blood pressure, etc in response to stress and that is secreted by the adrenal glands or manufactured synthetically.

adrift adj, adv afloat without mooring, drifting; loose; purposeless.

adroit adj skillful and clever, sharp-witted.—**adroitly** adv.—**adroitness** n.

adulation n excessive flattery.—**adulatory** adj.

adult adj fully grown; mature; suitable only for adults, as in pornography, etc. * n a mature person, etc.—**adulthood** n.

adulterate vt to make impure or inferior, etc by adding an improper substance.—**adulteration** n.—**adulterator** n.

adultery n (pl **adulteries**) sexual intercourse between a married person and someone other than their legal partner.—**adulterer** n. —**adulteress** nf.— **adulterous** adj.

advance vt to bring or move forward; to promote; to raise the rate of; (money) to lend. * vi to go forward; to make progress; to rise in rank, price, etc. * n progress; improvement; a rise in value; payment beforehand; (pl) friendly approaches, esp to please. * adj in front; beforehand.

advanced adj in front; old; superior in development or progress.

advancement n promotion to a higher rank; progress in development.

advantage n superiority of position or condition; a gain or benefit; (tennis) the first point won after deuce. * vt to produce a benefit or favor to.—**advantageous** adj.—**advantageously** adv.

advent n an arrival or coming; (with cap) (Christianity) the coming of Christ; the four-week period before Christmas.

adventitious adj happening by chance; casual; fortuitous; accidental; produced out of normal and regular order; growing in an abnormal position.—**adventitiously** adv.—**adventitiousness** n.

adventure n a strange or exciting undertaking; an unusual, stirring, often romantic, experience.

adventurer n a person who seeks adventure; someone who seeks money or power by unscrupulous means.—**adventuress** nf.

adventurous adj inclined to incur risk; full of risk; rash; enterprising; daring.—**adventurously** adv.

adverb n a word that modifies a verb, adjective, another adverb, phrase, clause or sentence and indicates how, why, where, etc.—**adverbial** adj.—**adverbially** adv.

adversary n (pl **adversaries**) an enemy or opponent.

adverse adj hostile; contrary or opposite; unfavorable.—**adversely** adv.

adversity n (pl **adversities**) trouble, misery, misfortune.

advert[1] vt to refer (to); to turn attention (to).

advert[2] n (inf) an advertisement.

advertise, advertize vt to call public attention to, esp in order to sell something, by buying space or time in the media, etc. * vi to call public attention to things for sale; to ask (for) by public notice.—**advertiser, advertizer** n.—**advertising, advertizing** n.

advertisement, advertizement n advertising; a public notice, usu paid for by the provider of a good or service.

advice n recommendation with regard to a course of action; formal notice or communication.

advisable adj prudent, expedient.—**advisability** n.

advise vt to give advice to; to caution; to recommend; to inform. * vi to give advice.—**adviser, advisor** n.—**advisory** adj.

advised adj acting with caution; deliberate; judicious.—**advisedly** adv.

advocacy n (pl **advocacies**) the function of an advocate; a pleading in support (of).

advocate n a person who argues or defends the cause of another, esp in a court of law; a supporter. * vt to plead in favor of, to recommend.

adz, adze n a type of ax with a blade at right angles to the handle for cutting and shaping wood.

aegis n protection, sponsorship.—also **egis**.

aeon n a period of immense duration; an age.—also **eon**.

aerate vt to supply (blood) with oxygen by respiration; to supply or impregnate with air; to combine or charge a liquid with gas.—**aeration** n.

aerial adj belonging to or existing in the air; of aircraft or flying. * n a radio or TV antenna.

aerie see **eyrie**.

aerobatics npl stunts performed while flying an aircraft.

aerobe, aerobium n (pl **aerobes, aerobia**) a microbe that cannot live without air.

aerobic adj (exercise) that conditions the heart and lungs by increasing the efficient intake of oxygen by the body.

aerobics npl aerobic exercises.

aerodynamics n the study of the forces exerted by air or other gases in motion, esp around solid bodies such as aircraft.—**aerodynamic** adj.—**aerodynamically** adv.

aerofoil n a wing, the lifting surface of an aircraft.

aeronaut n an aviator; the pilot or navigator of an aircraft.

aeronautics n the science dealing with the operation of aircraft; the art or science of flight.— **aeronautical, aeronautic** adj.—**aeronautically** adv.

aerosol n a suspension of fine solid or liquid particles in gas, esp as held in a container under pressure, with a device for releasing it in a fine spray.

aerospace n the earth's atmosphere and the space beyond. * adj technology for flight in aerospace.

aesthetic, aesthetical adj of or pertaining to aesthetics; concerned with beauty rather than practicality.–also **esthetic, esthetical.–aesthetically, esthetically** adv.

aestheticism n the cult of the beautiful, esp a fantastic art movement at the end of the 19th century.–also **estheticism**.

aesthetics n the philosophy of art and beauty.–also **esthetics**.

aetiology, aetiological, aetiologist see **etiology**.

afar adv at, to, or from a great distance.

affable adj friendly; approachable.–**affability** n.–**affably** adv.

affair n a thing done or to be done; (pl) public or private business; (inf) an event; a temporary romantic or sexual relationship.

affect[1] vt to have an effect on; to produce a change in; to act in a way that alters or affects the feelings of.

affect[2] vt to pretend or feign (an emotion); to incline to or show a preference for.

affectation n a striving after or an attempt to assume what is not natural or real; pretence.

affected adj (manner, etc) assumed artificially.–**affectedly** adv.–**affectedness** n.

affecting adj having power to excite the emotions; moving; pathetic.–**affectingly** adv.

affection n tender feeling; liking.–**affectional** adj.

affectionate adj showing affection, loving.–**affectionately** adv.

affective adj arousing the emotions, emotional.–**affectivity** adv.–**affectiveness** n.

affidavit n a statement written on oath.

affiliate vt to connect as a subordinate member or branch; to associate (oneself with). * vi to join. * n an affiliated person, club, etc.–**affiliation** n.

affinity n (pl **affinities**) attraction, liking; a close relationship, esp by marriage; similarity, likeness.

affirm vt to assert confidently or positively; to confirm or ratify; (law) to make an affirmation.

affirmation n affirming; an assertion; a solemn declaration made by those declining to swear an oath, eg on religious grounds.

affirmative adj confirming; indicating agreement. * n a positive word or statement, eg yes.–**affirmatively** adv.

affix vt to fasten; to add, esp in writing; to attach.

afflict vt to cause persistent pain or suffering to; to trouble greatly.–**afflictive** adj.

affliction n persistent pain, suffering; a cause of this.

affluence n an abundant supply, as of thoughts, words, riches; wealth.–**affluent** adj.–**affluently** adv.

afford vt to be in a position to do or bear without much inconvenience; to have enough time, money, or resources for; to supply, produce.

afforest vt to plant trees to cover with forest.–**afforestation** n.

affranchise vt to free from an obligation or slavery; to enfranchise.–**affranchisement** n.

affray n a noisy fight.

affront vi to insult or offend openly or deliberately. * n such an insult or offence.

aficionado n (pl **aficionados**) a devotee of a particular sport, activity, etc.

afield adv far away from home; to or at a distance; astray.

aflame adj, adv flaming, ablaze, in a glow.

afloat adj floating; at sea, on board a ship; debt-free; flooded.–also adv.

afoot adj, adv on foot; astir; on the move; in operation.

aforementioned adj mentioned previously.

aforesaid adj referred to previously.

aforethought adj premeditated.

afraid adj full of fear or apprehension; regretful.

afresh adv anew, starting again.

African adj pertaining to Africa. * n a native of Africa.

Afro-American n a Black American. * adj of or relating to Black Americans, or their culture, history, etc.

aft adv at, near, or towards the stern of a ship or rear of an aircraft.

after prep behind in place or order; following in time, later than; in pursuit of; in imitation of; in view of, in spite of; according to; about, concerning; subsequently. * adv later; behind. * conj at a time later than. * adj later, subsequent; nearer the stern of a ship or aircraft.

afterbirth n the placenta expelled from the womb after giving birth.

aftercare n care following hospital treatment, etc.

aftereffect n an effect that occurs some time after its cause.

afterlife n life after death.

aftermath n the result, esp an unpleasant one.

aftermost adj hindmost; farthest aft, nearest to the stern.

afternoon n the time between noon and sunset or evening.–also adj.

aftertaste n the taste that remains after eating or drinking.

afterthought n a thought or reflection occurring later.

afterwards, afterward adv at a later time.

Ag (chem symbol) silver.

again adv once more; besides; on the other hand.

against prep in opposition to; unfavorable to; in contrast to; in preparation for; in contact with; as a charge on.

agate n stone with striped or clouded coloring used as a gemstone.

age n the period of time during which someone or something has lived or existed; a stage of life; later years of life; a historical period; a division of geological time; (inf: often pl) a long time. * vti (**ageing** or **aging, aged**) to grow or make old, ripe, mature, etc.

aged adj very old; of a specified age. * n (with **the**) the elderly.

ageism n discrimination on grounds of age.–also **agism**.–**ageist, agist** adj.

ageless adj timeless; appearing never to grow old.

agency n (pl **agencies**) action; power; means; a firm, etc empowered to act for another; an administrative government division.

agenda, agendum n (pl **agendas, agendums**) a list of items or matters of business that need to be attended to.

agent n a person or thing that acts or has an influence; a substance or organism that is active; one empowered to act for another; a government representative; a spy.

agent provocateur n (pl **agents provocateurs**) a person hired to tempt or provoke suspected persons into illegal acts so as to incriminate themselves.

age-old adj ancient.–also **age-long**.

agglomerate vti to gather into a heap; to accumulate; to collect into a mass. * n a heap or mass; a rock consisting of volcanic fragments.–**agglomeration** n.–**agglomerative** adj.

agglutinate vti to stick or fuse together; to form words into compounds. * adj glued together.–**agglutination** n.–**agglutinative** adj.

aggrandize vt to increase the power, rank, wealth, or reputation of.–**aggrandizement** n.

aggravate vt to make worse; (inf) to annoy, irritate.–**aggravating** adj.–**aggravation** n.

aggravated adj (law) denoting a grave form of a specified offense.

aggregate adj formed of parts combined into a mass or whole; taking all units as a whole. * n a collection or sum of individual parts; sand, stones, etc mixed with cement to form concrete. * vt to collect or form into a mass or whole; to amount to (a total).–**aggregation** n.

aggression n an unprovoked attack; a hostile action or behavior.

aggressive adj boldly hostile; quarrelsome; self-assertive, enterprising.–**aggressively** adv.–**aggressiveness** n.

aggressor n a person or country that attacks first.

aggrieve vt to pain; to injure; to have a grievance; to bear heavily upon; to oppress.–**aggrieved** adj.–**aggrievedly** adv.

aghast adj utterly horrified.

agile adj quick and nimble in movement; mentally acute.–**agility** n.

agism see **ageism**.

agitate vt to shake, move; to disturb or excite the emotions of. * vi to stir up public interest for a cause, etc.–**agitation** n.– **agitator** n.

aglow adj radiant with warmth or excitement.

agnostic n one who believes that knowledge of God is impossible. * adj pertaining to the agnostics or their teachings; expressing ignorance.–**agnostically** adv.–**agnosticism** n.

ago adv in the past. * adj gone by; past.

agog adj, adv in agitation or expectation; eager, on the lookout.

agonize vti to suffer or cause to suffer agony; to strive.–**agonizingly** adv.

agony n (pl **agonies**) extreme mental or physical suffering.

agoraphobia n abnormal fear of crossing open places.–**agoraphobic** adj, n.

agrarian adj of or relating to fields, or their cultivation; of or relating to farmers or agricultural life. * n an advocate of redistribution of property in land.

agrarianism n the principle of a uniform division of land; agitation with respect to land tenure.

agree vb (**agreeing, agreed**) vi to be of similar opinion; to consent or assent (to); to come to an understanding about; to be consistent; to suit a person's digestion; (gram) to be consistent in gender, number, case, or person. * vt to concede, grant; to bring into harmony; to reach terms on.

agreeable adj likeable, pleasing; willing to agree.–**agreeableness** n.–**agreeably** adv.

agreement n harmony in thought or opinion, correspondence; an agreed settlement between two people, etc.

agriculture n the science or practice of producing crops and raising livestock; farming.–**agricultural** adj.–**agriculturally** adv.– **agriculturist, agriculturalist** n.

aground adj, adv on or onto the shore.

ague n malaria, an intermittent fever; the cold fit of the intermittent fever.–**aguish** adj.

ah interj an exclamation of sudden emotion.

AH abbr = anno Hegira (in the year of the Hegira) used in dates of the Muslim era.

aha interj an exclamation of satisfaction, triumph or mockery.

ahead adj in or to the front; forward; onward; in advance; winning or profiting.–also adv.

ahem interj an exclamation to call attention.

ahoy interj a term used in hailing a vessel.

AI abbr = artificial insemination; artificial intelligence.

AID abbr = Agency for International Development; artificial insemination (by) donor.

aid vti to help, give assistance to. * n anything that helps; a specific means of assistance, eg money, equipment; a helper.

aide n an aide-de-camp; assistant.

aide-de-camp n (pl **aides-de-camp**) a military officer serving as an assistant to a senior officer.

AIDS, Aids n (acronym for acquired immune deficiency syndrome) a condition caused by a virus, in which the body loses its immunity to infection.

AIDS-related complex n a condition in which mild symptoms of AIDS (e.g. fever, weight loss) precede development of the full-blown disease.

ail vt to give or cause pain. * vi to feel pain; to be afflicted with pain.

aileron n a hinged section on the wing of an aircraft used for lateral control.

ailing adj unwell.

ailment n a slight illness.

aim vti to point or direct towards a target so as to hit; to direct (one's efforts); to intend. * n the act of aiming; purpose, intention.

aimless adj without purpose or object.–**aimlessly** adv.–**aimlessness** n.

ain't = am not, is not, are not, has not, have not.

air n the mixture of invisible gases surrounding the earth; the earth's atmosphere; empty, open space; a light breeze; aircraft, aviation; outward appearance, demeanor; a pervading influence; (mus) a melody; (pl) an affected manner. * vt to expose to the air for drying, etc; to expose to public notice; (clothes) to place in a warm place to finish drying.

airbag n a safety device in a motor vehicle that automatically inflates to protect the occupants in the event of an accident.

air base n a base for military aircraft.

air bed n an inflatable mattress usu of plastic or rubber.

airborne adj carried by or through the air; aloft or flying.

airbrush n a device for spraying paint by compressed air.

airbus n a jet aircraft designed for short-distance intercity flights.

air conditioning n regulation of air humidity and temperature in buildings, etc.

air cover n protection for ground forces given by fighter aircraft; the aircraft giving this protection.

aircraft n (pl **aircraft**) any machine for traveling through air.

aircraft carrier n a warship with a large flat deck, for the carrying, taking off and land of aircraft.

air drop n a dropping by parachute of troops and supplies.

airfield n a field where aircraft can take off and land.

air force n the aviation branch of a country's armed forces.

airgun n a gun that fires pellets by compressed air.

air hostess n a stewardess on a passenger aircraft.

airing n exposure to the open air for drying or freshening; exercise in the open air; exposure to public view.

airless adj stuffy; sultry.–**airlessness** n.

airlift n the transport of cargo, troops, passengers, etc by air, esp in an emergency.–also vt.

airline n a system or company for transportation by aircraft; a beeline.

airliner n a large passenger aircraft.

airlock n a blockage in a pipe caused by an air bubble; an airtight compartment giving access to a pressurized chamber.

airmail n mail transported by aircraft.

airman n (pl **airmen**) a male civilian or military pilot, etc.–**airwoman** nf (pl **airwomen**).

airmiss n the near collision of aircraft in flight.

airplane n a power-driven aircraft.

airplay n the playing of a recording over radio or TV.

air pocket n a patch of rarefied air causing aircraft to drop abruptly.

airport n a place where aircraft can land and take off, with facilities for repair, etc.

air raid n an attack by military aircraft on a surface target.

airs npl affected behavior for the purpose of impressing others.

airship n a self-propelled steerable aircraft that is lighter than air.

airsick adj nauseated due to the motion of an aircraft.

airspace n the space above a nation over which it maintains jurisdiction.

airspeed n the speed of an aircraft relative to the outside air.

airstrip n an area of land cleared for aircraft to land on; a runway.

airtight adj too tight for air or gas to enter or escape; (alibi, etc) invulnerable.

airtime n (radio, TV) the time allotted to a program, item, commercial, etc; the time at which the broadcast begins.

air-to-air adj (weaponry, communications, etc) activated between aircraft in flight.

airway n an aircraft route; a ventilation passage, as in a mine; a passage for air into the lungs; (med) a device to maintain the airway of an unconscious person.

airworthy adj safe to fly.–**airworthiness** n.

airy adj (**airier, airiest**) open to the air; breezy; light as air; graceful; lighthearted; flippant.–**airily** adv.–**airiness** n.

aisle n a passageway, as between rows of seats; a side part of a church.

ajar adv partly open, as a door.

AK abbr = Alaska.

aka, a.k.a or **AKA** abbr = also known as.

akimbo adv having the hands on the hips and the elbows bent outwards.

akin adj related; essentially similar, compatible.

AL abbr = Alabama.

Al (chem symbol) = aluminum.

Ala. abbr = Alabama.

à la prep in the style of.

alabaster n a type of soft, chalky stone used in ornaments.– **alabastrine** adj.

à la carte adj (menu) with dishes listed and priced as separate items.

alacrity n promptness, eager readiness.–**alacritous** adj.

alarm n a signal warning of danger; an automatic device to arouse from sleep or to attract attention; the fear arising from the apprehension of danger. * vt to give warning of danger; to fill with apprehension or fear.– **alarming** adj.– **alarmingly** adv.

alarm clock n a clock with an apparatus that can be set to ring loudly at a particular time.

alas interj expressive of misery, unhappiness, grief, etc.

albatross n any of various large web-footed seabirds; a heavy burden, as of debt, guilt, etc.

albeit conj although, even though, notwithstanding.

albino n (pl **albinos**) a person lacking normal coloration, so that they have white skin and pink eyes; an animal or plant with abnormal pigmentation.

album n a book with blank pages for the insertion of photographs, autographs, etc; a long-playing record, cassette, or CD.

albumen n the white of an egg.

alchemy n (pl **alchemies**) chemistry as practiced during medieval times, with the aim of transmuting base metals into gold.–**alchemic, alchemical** adj.–**alchemist** n.

alcohol n a liquid, generated by distillation and fermentation, that forms the intoxicating agent in wine, beer and spirits; a liquid containing alcohol; a chemical compound of this nature.

alcoholic adj of or containing alcohol; caused by alcohol. * n a person suffering from alcoholism.

alcoholism n a disease caused by excessive consumption of alcohol.

alcove n a recess off a larger room.

aldehyde n a volatile fluid with a suffocating smell, obtained from alcohol.

al dente adj cooked but still firm to the teeth.

alder n a genus of plants growing in moist land and related to the birch.

alderman n (pl **aldermen**) in US, a member of certain municipal councils; (formerly) in England and Wales, a senior councilor.– **aldermanic** adj.

ale n beer.

alert adj watchful; active, brisk. * n a danger signal. * vt to warn of impending danger, put in a state of readiness.–**alertly** adv.– **alertness** n.

alfalfa n a deep-rooted leguminous plant grown widely for hay and forage.–also **lucerne**.

alfresco adj taking place outside in the open.–also adv.

alga n (pl **algae**) any of a group of chiefly aquatic lower plants classified according to color.–**algal** adj.

algebra n the branch of mathematics dealing with the properties and relations of numbers; the generalization and extension of arithmetic.–**algebraic, algebraical** adj.–**algebraist** n. **algid** adj cold, chilly.

algorithm n (math) any method or procedure for computation.–**algorithmic** adj.–**algorithmically** adv.

alias adv otherwise called. * n (pl **aliases**) an assumed name.

alibi n (pl **alibis**) (law) the plea that a person charged with a crime was elsewhere when it was committed; (inf) any excuse.

alien adj foreign; strange; distasteful to, counter to. * n a person from another country, place, etc; a person of foreign birth who has not been naturalized; a being from outer space.

alienate vt to render hostile or unfriendly; to make less affection-ate or interested.

alienation n estrangement; transference; diversion to another purpose; mental derangement.

alight[1] vi (**alighting, alighted** or **alit**) to come down, as from a bus; to land after a flight.

alight[2] adj on fire; lively.

align vt to place in a straight line, to bring into agreement, etc. * vi to line up.–**alignment** n.

alike adj like one another. * adv equally; similarly.

aliment n food; the necessaries of life generally; an allowance for support by decree of court. * vt to make provision for the main-tenance of; to make provision for the support of parents or chil-dren respectively.–**alimental** adj .

alimentary adj pertaining to nourishment, food.

alimentary canal n the tube extending within the body from the mouth to the anus through which food passes and is absorbed.

alimony n (pl **alimonies**) an allowance for support made by one spouse to the other, esp a man to his wife or former wife, pending or after a legal separation or divorce.–also **mainte-nance**.

alive adj having life; active, alert; in existence, operation, etc.

alkali n (pl **alkalis, alkalies**) (chem) any salt or mixture that neutralizes acids.–**alkaline** adj.–**alkalinity** n.

alkaloid n a body or substance containing alkaline properties; (pl) nitrogenous compounds met with in plants incombination with organic acids. * adj resembling an alkali in its properties.

all adj the whole amount or number of; every one of. * adv wholly; supremely, completely; entirely. * n the whole number, quantity; everyone; everything.

Allah n the Muslim name of God.

all along adv throughout.

allay vt to lighten, alleviate; to pacify or make calm.

all but adv almost.

all clear n a signal indicating that a danger has passed or that it is safe to proceed.

allegation n the act of alleging; assertion; declaration; that which is asserted or alleged; that which is offered as a plea, an excuse, or justification; the statement as yet unproved of a party to a suit.

allege vt to assert or declare, esp without proof; to offer as an excuse.

allegedly adv asserted without proof.

allegiance n the obligation of being loyal to one's country, etc; devotion, as to a cause.

allegorical, allegoric adj pertaining to, consisting of, or in the nature of allegory; figurative.–**allegorically** adv.

allegory n (pl **allegories**) a fable, story, poem, etc in which the events depicted are used to convey a deeper, usu moral or spiri-tual, meaning.–**allegorist** n.

allegro adv (mus) fast. * n (pl **allegros**) a piece of music played in this way.

allergen n a substance inducing an allergic reaction.–**allergenic** adj.

allergy n (pl **allergies**) an abnormal reaction of the body to substances (certain foods, pollen, etc) normally harmless; antipa-thy.–**allergic** adj.

alleviate vt to lessen or relieve (pain, worry, etc).–**alleviation** n.–**alleviator** n.

alley n a narrow street between or behind buildings; a bowling lane.

all fours *adv* on hands and knees.

alliance *n* a union by marriage or treaty for a common purpose; an agreement for this; the countries, groups, etc in such an association.

allied *see* ally.

alligator *n* a large reptile similar to the crocodile but having a short, blunt snout.

all in *adj* (*price, etc*) all-inclusive.

all-inclusive *adj* including everything.

alliteration *n* the repetition of the same sound at the beginning of two or more words in a phrase, etc.–**alliterative** *adj*.

allocate *vt* to distribute or apportion in shares; to set apart for a specific purpose.

allocation *n* the act of alloting, allocating, or assigning; an allotment or assignment; an allowance made on an account.

all one *adj, n* in effect the same.

allopath, allopathist *n* one who favors or practices allopathy.

allopathy *n* the orthodox medical practice of treating disease by inducing an action opposite to the disease it is sought to cure, opposite of homoeopathy.–**allopathic** *adj*.–**allopathically** *adv*.

allot *vt* (**allotting, allotted**) to distribute, allocate.

allotment *n* allotting; a share allotted; a small area of land rented for cultivation.

all out *adv* with maximum capacity.

all-out *adj* using maximum effort.

all-over *adj* covering the whole surface.

allow *vt* to permit; to acknowledge, admit as true; (*money*) to give, grant as an allowance at regular intervals; to estimate as an addition or deduction. * *vi* to admit the possibility (of).

allowable *adj* permissible.–**allowably** *adv*.

allowance *n* an amount or sum allowed or given at regular times; a discount; a portion of income not subject to income tax; permission; admission, concession.

alloy *n* a solid substance comprising a mixture of two or more metals; something that degrades the substance to which it is added. * *vt* to make into an alloy; to degrade or spoil by mixing with an inferior substance.

all-purpose *adj* suitable for many uses.

all right *adv* good enough, acceptable; without doubt. * *adj* satisfactory; safe, well; agreeable. * *interj* (*used to express consent*).–*also* **alright**.

all-round *adj* efficient in all respects, esp sport.

allspice *n* an aromatic spice made from the berry of a West Indian tree.

all-time *adj* unsurpassed until now.

all told *adv* with all counted; all in all.

allude *vi* to refer indirectly to.

allure *vt* to entice, charm. * *n* fascination; charm.–**allurement** *n*.

alluring *adj* attractive.

allusion *n* alluding; an implied or indirect reference.–**allusive** *adj*.–**allusively** *adv*.–**allusiveness** *n*.

alluvium *n* (*pl* **alluviums, alluvia**) earth, sand, gravel, etc deposited by moving water.–**alluvial** *adj*.

ally *vti* (**allying, allied**) to join or unite for a specific purpose; to relate by similarity of structure, etc. * *n* (*pl* **allies**) a country or person joined with another for a common purpose.

almanac *n* a calendar with astronomical data, weather forecasts, etc.

almighty *adj* all-powerful. * *n* (*with cap*) God, the all-powerful.–**almightily** *adv*.–**almightiness** *n*.

almond *n* the edible kernel of the fruit of a tree of the rose family; the tree bearing this fruit. * *adj* (*eyes, etc*) oval and pointed at one or both ends.

almost *adv* all but, very nearly but not quite all.

alms *npl* money, food, etc given to the poor.

aloe *n* (*pl* **aloes**) a succulent plant with tall spikes of flowers.

aloft *adv* in the air, flying; high up.

alone *adj* isolated; without anyone or anything else; unassisted; unique. * *adv* exclusively.

along *adv* onward, forward; over the length of; in company and together with; in addition. * *prep* in the direction of the length of; in accordance with.

alongside *prep* close beside. * *adv* at the side.

aloof *adv* at a distance; apart. * *adj* cool and reserved.–**aloofness** *n*.

alopecia *n* baldness; loss of hair through skin disease.

aloud *adv* with a normal voice; loudly; spoken.

alp *n* a mountain peak.

alpaca *n* a Peruvian llama with long fine wool; a fabric made of this wool.

alpha *n* the first letter of the Greek alphabet.

alphabet *n* the characters used in a language arranged in conventional order.

alphabetical, alphabetic *adj* pertaining to an alphabet; in the order of the alphabet.–**alphabetically** *adv*.

alphabetize *vt* to arrange in alphabetical order.–**alphabetization** *n*.

alpine *adj* (*with cap*) of the Alps; of high mountains. * *n* a mountain plant, esp a small herb.

already *adv* by or before the time specified; before the time expected.

alright *adv* a frequent spelling of all right.

also *adv* in addition, besides.

also-ran *n* a defeated contestant in a race, an election, etc.

altar *n* a table, etc for sacred purposes in a place of worship.

alter *vti* to make or become different in a small way; to change.–**alterable** *adj*.–**alterability** *n*.

alteration *n* the act of altering or changing; the change or modification effected.

altercation *n* an angry or heated quarrel.

alter ego *n* one's other self; a constant companion.

alternate[1] *vt* to do or use by turns. * *vi* to act, happen, etc by turns; to take turns regularly.–**alternation** *n*.

alternate[2] *adj* occurring or following in turns.–**alternately** *adv*.

alternating current *n* an electric current that reverses its direction at regular intervals.

alternative *adj* presenting a choice between two things. * *n* either of two possibilities.–**alternatively** *adv*.

alternative comedy *n* a form of comedy that avoids conventional humor (e.g. racist and sexist jokes), characterized by aggressively delivered and blackly humorous stand-up routines that usu challenge political and social orthodoxy.

alternative medicine *n* any technique of medical treatment without use of drugs, eg osteopathy, acupuncture, dieting.

alternator *n* an electric generator that produces alternating current.

although *conj* though; in spite of that.

altimeter *n* an instrument for measuring altitude.

altitude *n* height, esp above sea level.–**altitudinal** *adj*.

alto *n* (*pl* **altos**) the range of the highest male voice; a singer with this range; a contralto. * *adj* high.

alto clef *n* the C clef placed on the third line of the staff.

altogether *adv* in all; on the whole; completely.

altruism *n* unselfish concern for or dedication to the interests or welfare of others.–**altruist** *n*.–**altruistic** *adj*.–**altruistically** *adv*.

alum *n* a double sulfate formed of aluminum and some other element, usually an alkali metal.

aluminum, aluminium *n* a silvery-white malleable metallic element notable for its lightness.

alumna *n* (*pl* **alumnae**) a female graduate or pupil of a university or college.

alumnus n (pl **alumni**) a former pupil or student.–**alumna** nf (pl **alumnae**).

always adv at all times; in all cases; repeatedly; forever.

Alzheimer's disease n a degenerative disorder of the brain resulting in progressive senility.

am see **be**.

a.m. abbr = ante meridiem, before noon.

amalgam n an alloy of mercury and another metal; a mixture.

amalgamate vt to combine, unite.

amalgamation n the act or process of compounding mercury with another metal; the blending or mixing of different elements or things; the union or consolidation of two or more companies or businesses into one concern, a merger.

amaryllis n a genus of bulbous flowering plants to which the belladonna lily and narcissus belong.

amass vt to bring together in a large quantity; to accumulate.–**amasser** n.–**amassment** n.

amateur n one who engages in a particular activity as a hobby, and not as a profession. * adj of or done by amateurs.–**amateurism** n.

amateurish adj lacking expertise.–**amateurishly** adv.–**amateurishness** n.

amaze vt to fill with wonder, astonish.–**amazing** adj.–**amazingly** adv.

amazement n the state of being amazed; astonishment; perplexity arising from sudden surprise.

ambassador n the highest-ranking diplomatic representative from one country to another; an authorized messenger.–**ambassadorial** adj.–**ambassadress** nf.

amber n a hard yellowish fossil resin, used for jewellery and ornaments, etc; the color of amber; a yellow traffic light used to signal "caution".

ambergris n a waxy substance found in tropical seas, which is secreted by sperm whales and is used in perfumery as a fixative.

ambidextrous adj able to use the left and the right hand equally well.–**ambidexterity** n.

ambience, ambiance n surrounding influence, atmosphere.

ambient adj surrounding.

ambiguity n (pl **ambiguities**) double or dubious significance; vagueness.

ambiguous adj capable of two or more interpretations; indistinct, vague.–**ambiguously** adv.–**ambiguousness** n.

ambit n a circuit or compass; the line or sum of the lines by which a figure is bounded; the perimeter; sphere of action.

ambition n desire for power, wealth and success; an object of ambition.

ambitious adj having or governed by ambition; resulting from or showing ambition; requiring considerable effort or ability.–**ambitiously** adv.

ambivalent adj having mixed feelings toward the same object.–**ambivalence** n.

amble vi to walk in a leisurely way. * n an easy pace. –**ambler** n.

ambulance n a special vehicle for transporting the sick or injured.

ambulance chaser n one who attempts to profit from disaster.

ambulant adj (patient) able to walk, not bed-ridden; moving from place to place.

ambulate vi to walk about; to move about; to wander.–**ambulation** n.

ambuscade n a strategic disposition of troops in ambush.

ambush n the concealment of soldiers, etc to make a surprise attack; the bushes or other cover in which they are hidden. * vti to lie in wait; to attack from an ambush.

ameba see **amoeba**.

ameliorate vti to make or become better.–**ameliorative** adj.–**ameliorator** n.

amelioration n the making or growing better; improvement.

amen interj may it be so!

amenable adj easily influenced or led, tractable; answerable to legal authority.–**amenability** n.–**amenably** adv.

amend vt to remove errors, esp in a text; to modify, improve; to alter in minor details.–**amendable** adj.–**amender** n.

amendment n the act of amending, correction; an alteration to a document, etc.

amends npl (used as sing) compensation or recompense for some loss, harm, etc.

amenity n (pl **amenities**) pleasantness, as regards situation, convenience, or service.

American adj belonging to or characteristic of America. * n an inhabitant of the US.

Americanism n a form of expression peculiar to the US; a custom peculiar to the US; attachment to the US.

Americanize vt to render American; to assimilate to the political and social institutions of the US.–**Americanization** n.

Amerindian, Amerind n an American Indian.–**Amerindic** adj.

amethyst n a gemstone consisting of bluish-violet quartz; the color of an amethyst.–**amethystine** adj.

amiable adj friendly in manner, congenial.–**amiability** n.–**amiably** adv.

amicable adj friendly; peaceable.–**amicability, amicableness** n.–**amicably** adv.

amid, amidst prep in or to the middle of; during.

amidships adv in the middle of a ship.

amino acid n any of a group of organic acids that occur in proteins.

amiss adj wrong, improper. * adv in an incorrect manner.

ammeter n an instrument for measuring electric current in amperes.

ammonia n a pungent colorless gas composed of nitrogen and hydrogen.

ammonite n a fossil shell, twisted like a ram's horn; snakestone.–**ammonitic** adj.

ammunition n bullets, shells, rockets, etc; any means of attack or defense; facts and reasoning used to prove a point in an argument.

amnesia n a partial or total loss of memory.–**amnesiac, amnesic** n, adj.

amnesty n (pl **amnesties**) a general pardon, esp of political prisoners; a pardon granted for a limited time. * vt (**amnestying, amnestied**) to pardon (an offense).

amniocentesis n the extraction by hollow needle of a sample of amniotic fluid from the womb to test for fetal abnormalities.

amnion n (pl **amnions, amnia**) the thin innermost membrane surrounding the fetus in the womb of mammals, birds, and reptiles.–**amniotic** adj.

amoeba n (pl **amoebae, amoebas**) a unicellular microorganism found in water, damp soil and the digestive tracts of animals.–also **ameba**.–**amoebic, amebic** adj.

amok adj, adv **run amok** to run about armed, in a state of frenzy, attacking all that come in the way; indiscriminate slaughter; headstrong violence.–also **amuck**.

among, amongst prep in the number of, surrounded by; in the group or class of; within a group, between; by the joint efforts of.

amoral adj neither moral nor immoral; without moral sense.–**amorality** n.–**amorally** adv.

amorous adj displaying or feeling love or desire.–**amorously** adv.–**amorousness** n.

amorphous adj lacking a specific shape, shapeless; unrecognizable, indefinable.–**amorphism** n.

amortize vt to put money aside at intervals for gradual payment of (a debt, etc).–**amortization** n.

amount vi to be equivalent (to) in total, quantity or significance. * n the total sum; the whole value or effect; a quantity.

amp n an ampere; (inf) an amplifier.

amperage n the strength of an electric current measured in amperes.

ampere n the standard SI unit by which an electric current is measured.

ampersand *n* the sign (&) meaning "and".

amphetamine *n* a drug used esp as a stimulant and to suppress appetite.

amphibian *n* an animal living on land but breeding in water; an aircraft that can take off and land on water or land; a vehicle that can travel on land and through water.

amphibious *adj* living on both land and in water; (*mil*) involving both sea and land forces.

amphitheater, amphitheatre *n* an oval or circular building with rising rows of seats around an open arena.

ample *adj* large in size, scope, etc; plentiful.–**amply** *adv*.

amplification *n* the act of amplifying or expanding; enlargement.

amplifier *n* a device that increases electric voltage, current, or power, or the loudness of sound.

amplify *vt* (**amplifying, amplified**) to expand more fully, add details to; (*electrical signals, etc*) to strengthen.

amplitude *n* largeness of extent, scope; abundance; the maximum deviation of an oscillation from the mean or zero.

ampoule, ampul, ampule *n* a small sealed glass vessel containing liquid, esp for injection.

amputate *vt* to cut off, esp by surgery.–**amputation** *n*.

amuck *see* **amok**.

amulet *n* something worn as a charm against evil.

amuse *vt* to entertain or divert in a pleasant manner; to cause to laugh or smile.–**amusing** *adj*.

amusement *n* that which amuses; the state of being amused; an entertainment; a pastime.

amylase *n* an enzyme that breaks down starch and glycogen.

an *adj* the indefinite article ("a"), used before words beginning with the sound of a vowel except "u".

anabolic steroid *n* any of various synthetic steroid hormones that promote rapid muscle growth.

anabolism *n* constructive metabolism, in which simple molecules synthesize into more complex ones.–**anabolic**.

anachronism *n* a person, custom, or idea regarded as out of date or out of its period.–**anachronistic** *adj*.–**anachronistically** *adv*.

anaconda *n* a large South American semiaquatic snake that kills its prey by constriction.

anaemia *see* **anemia**.

anaemic *see* **anemic**.

anaerobe, anaerobium *n* (*pl* **anaerobes, anaerobia**) a microbe that can live without air.

anaesthesia *see* **anesthesia**.

anaesthetic *see* **anesthetic**.

anaesthetist *see* **anesthetist**.

anaesthetize *see* **anesthetize**.

anagram *n* a word or sentence formed by rearranging another word or sentence.–**anagrammatic, anagrammatical** *adj*.–**anagrammatically** *adv*.

anal *adj* of or situated near the anus.

analeptic *adj* restorative. * *n* a restorative drug.

analgesia *n* insensibility to pain without loss of consciousness.

analgesic *adj* relieving pain. * *n* a pain-relieving drug.

analogize *vt* to reason or expound by reference to analogy, to draw comparisons. * *vi* to treat or investigate by use of analogy.

analogous *adj* corresponding in certain respects (to).–**analogously** *adv*.–**analogue, analog** *n*.

analogy *n* (*pl* **analogies**) a similarity or correspondence in certain respects between two things.–**analogical, analogic** *adj*.

analysis *n* (*pl* **analyses**) the process of analyzing; a statement of the results of this; psychoanalysis.–**analytic, analytical** *adj*.–**analytically** *adv*.

analyst *n* a person who analyzes; a psychoanalyst.

analyze *vt* to separate (something) into its constituent parts to investigate its structure and function, etc; to examine in detail; to psychoanalyze.

anaphylaxis *n* excessive sensitivity to a substance or germ due to prior inoculation with it, an allergy.–**anaphylactic** *adj*.–**anaphylactically** *adv*.

anarchist *n* a person who believes that all government is unnecessary and should be abolished.–**anarchistic** *adj*.–**anarchism** *n*.

anarchy *n* the absence of government; political confusion; disorder, lawlessness.–**anarchic, anarchical** *adj*.

anathema *n* (*pl* **anathemas**) anything greatly detested; an ecclesiastical curse or denunciation accompanied by excommunication.

anatomist *n* one possessing a knowledge of anatomy by dissection.

anatomize *vt* to dissect; to study the structure of; to analyze.–**anatomization** *n*.

anatomy *n* (*pl* **anatomies**) the science of the physical structure of plants and animals; the structure of an organism.–**anatomical** *adj*.–**anatomically** *adv*.

ancestor *n* one from whom a person is descended, a forefather; an early animal or plant from which existing types are descended; something regarded as a forerunner.–**ancestress** *nf*.

ancestral *adj* belonging to, or connected with, one's ancestors; derived from one's progenitors; lineal.

ancestry *n* (*pl* **ancestries**) ancestors collectively; lineage.

anchor *n* a heavy metal implement that lodges at the bottom of the sea or a river to hold a ship in position; something that gives support or stability. * *vt* to fix by an anchor; to secure firmly.

anchorage *n* a safe anchoring place for ships; the charge for anchoring.

anchorman *n* (*pl* **anchormen**) (*sport*) the last man in a team to compete and whose contribution is vital; the compere of a television broadcast.

anchovy *n* (*pl* **anchovies, anchovy**) a small Mediterranean fish resembling a herring with a very salty taste.

anchylose, anchylosis *see* **ankylose, ankylosis**.

ancient *adj* very old; dating from the distant past; of the period and civilizations predating the fall of the Roman Empire; old-fashioned. * *n* a person who lived in the ancient period; (*pl*) the members of the classical civilizations of antiquity, esp of Greece and Rome.

ancillary *adj* subordinate (to); auxiliary; supplementary. * *n* (*pl* **ancillaries**) a subordinate or auxiliary person or thing.

and *conj* in addition to; together with; plus; increasingly; as a consequence, afterwards; expressing contrast.

androgen *n* a male sex hormone.–**androgenic** *adj*.

androgenous *adj* (*biol*) having only male offspring.

androgynous *adj* combining both sexes or bearing both male and female organs; hermaphroditical.–**androgyne** *n*.–**androgyny** *n*.

android *n* (*science fiction*) a robot in human form.–*also adj*.

anecdotal *adj* relating to anecdotes; (*evidence, etc*) obtained from experience, not scientific.

anecdote *n* a short entertaining account about an amusing or interesting event or person.

anemia *n* a condition in which the blood is low in red cells or in hemoglobin, resulting in paleness, weakness, etc.–*also* **anaemia**.

anemic *adj* suffering from anemia; weak; pale; listless.–*also* **anaemic**.

anemography *n* the scientific description of winds, and the measurement and registration of their force and direction.–**anemographic** *adj*.–**anemographically** *adv*.

anemone *n* a plant of the buttercup family.

aneroid *adj* having no liquid, as quicksilver. * *n* a barometer shaped like a watch, the action depending on the varying pressure of the atmosphere on the top of an elastic metal box.

anesthesia *n* a partial or total loss of the sense of pain, touch, etc.–*also* **anaesthesia**.

anesthetic *n* a drug, gas, etc used to produce anesthesia, as before surgery. * *adj* of or producing anesthesia.–*also* **anaesthetic**.

anesthetist *n* a person trained to give anesthetics.–*also* **anaesthetist**.

anesthetize *vt* to administer an anesthetic.–*also* **anaesthetize.–anesthetization, anaesthetization** *n*.

aneurysm, aneurism *n* the permanent abnormal swelling of an artery.

anew *adv* afresh; again, once more; in a new way or form.

angel *n* a messenger of God; an image of a human figure with wings and a halo; a very beautiful or kind person; (*inf*) one who gives financial backing to an enterprise.

angelfish *n* (*pl* **angelfish, angelfishes**) a species of shark with large pectoral fins, which give to it a winged appearance.

angelic, angelical *adj* belonging to or resembling an angel in nature or function.–**angelically** *adv*.

angelica *n* the candied stalks of a fragrant plant used esp in cake decoration.

anger *n* strong displeasure, often because of opposition, a hurt, etc. * *vti* to make or become angry.

angina *n* sharp stabbing pains in the chest, usu caused by angina pectoris.

angina pectoris *n* a heart disease causing a spasmodic gripping pain in the chest.

angle[1] *n* a corner; the point from which two lines or planes extend or diverge; a specific viewpoint; an individual method or approach (eg to a problem). * *vt* to bend at an angle; to move or place at an angle; to present information, news, etc from a particular point of view.

angle[2] *vi* to fish with a hook and line; to use hints or artifice to get something.–**angler** *n*.

angler *n* one who fishes with rod and line; the name of a fish with filamentary appendage that attracts smaller fish on which it feeds.

Anglicism *n* a form of speech, an English idiom; a principle or mannerism peculiar to England.

anglicize *vt* to make or to render into English; to accord with English manners and customs.–**anglicization** *n*.

angling *n* the art or act of fishing with rod and line.

Anglo-American *adj* pertaining to England and the United States conjointly, as to commerce or population. * *n* an American citizen of English descent.

Anglophile *n* a person who loves England or anything English.–*also* **Anglophil**.

Anglophobe *n* one who hates or fears England and the English.–**Anglophobia** *n*.

angora *n* a long-haired variety of cat, rabbit or goat; fabric made from the hair of angora goats or rabbits.

angry *adj* (**angrier, angriest**) full of anger; inflamed.–**angrily** *adv*.

angst *n* a feeling of anxiety, fear or remorse.

angstrom, ångström *n* one hundred millionth of a centimetre, a unit used in measuring the length of light waves.

anguish *n* agonizing physical or mental distress.

angular *adj* having one or more angles; forming an angle; measured by an angle; stiff and clumsy in manner, thin and bony.

angularity *n* (*pl* **angularities**) the quality of being angular in any sense.

anil *n* the indigo plant; a dye yielded by it.

animal *n* any living organism except a plant or bacterium, typically able to move about; a lower animal as distinguished from man, esp mammals; a brutish or bestial person. * *adj* of or like an animal; bestial; sensual.

animal liberation *n* freeing animals from captivity and exploitation (eg in laboratories) by humans, action esp associated with organizations such as the Animal Liberation Front.

animal magnetism *n* another name for mesmerism; attractiveness, esp to the opposite sex.

animal rights *n* a movement that seeks to extend certain rights, such as freedom from captivity and exploitation by humans, to animals.

animate *vt* to give life to; to liven up; to inspire, encourage. * *adj* alive; lively.

animated *adj* lively, full of spirit.

animated cartoon *n* a film made by photographing a series of drawings, giving the illusion of movement.

animation *n* liveliness; movement; the skill of making animated films.

animator, animater *n* an artist who draws and produces animated cartoons.

animism *n* in primitive religion, the belief that natural effects are due to spirits and that inanimate objects have spirits; the belief in a human apparitional soul, having the form and appearance of the body, existing after death as semi-human.–**animist** *n*.–**animistic** *adj*.

animosity *n* (*pl* **animosities**) strong dislike; hostility.

animus *n* an actuating spirit; a bitter or hostile feeling (against); hostility.

anise *n* the common name for a plant (indigenous in Egypt) yielding the seeds used in aniseed.

aniseed *n* the seed of the anise plant, used as a flavoring.

ankh *n* an Egyptian cross with a loop or handle at the top, the symbol of life.–*also* **crux ansata**.

ankle *n* the joint between the foot and leg, the part of the leg between the foot and calf.

anklet *n* an ornamental chain worn round the ankle.

ankylose *vt* to consolidate or join by bony growth; to stiffen as a joint. * *vi* to grow together; to become stiff.–*also* **anchylose**.

ankylosis *n* (*zool*) the joining or consolidation of parts formerly or normally separate or movable by means of bony growth; (*med*) the stiffening of a joint by fibrous bands or union of bones.–*also* **anchylosis.–ankylotic, anchylotic**.

annals *npl* a written account of events year by year; historical records; periodical reports or records of a society.–**annalist** *n*.–**annalistic** *adj*.

anneal *vt* to fix by heat; to temper and render malleable; to bake or fuse.–**annealer** *n*.

annex[1] *n* an extension to a main building; something added, a supplement.

annex[2] *vt* to attach, esp to something larger; to incorporate into a state the territory of (another state).

annihilate *vt* to destroy completely; (*inf*) to defeat convincingly, as in an argument.–**annihilable** *adj*.–**annihilative** *adj*.–**annihilator** *n*.

annihilation *n* the act of annihilating; nonexistence.

anniversary *n* (*pl* **anniversaries**) the yearly return of the date of some event; a celebration of this.–*also* **adj**.

anno Domini *adv* (*abbr* AD) in the year of our Lord, dating from the birth of Christ. * *n* (*inf*) advancing age.

annotate *vti* to provide with explanatory notes.–**annotative** *adj*.–**annotator** *n*.

annotation *n* the act of noting or commenting upon; a note, remark, or criticism made in a book.

announce *vt* to bring to public attention; to give news of the arrival of; to be an announcer for. * *vi* to serve as an announcer.

announcement *n* the act of announcing; that which is announced; a proclamation.

announcer *n* a person who reads the news, etc on the radio or TV.

annoy *vt* to vex, tease, irritate, as by a repeated action.–**annoyingly** *adv*.

annoyance *n* the act of annoying or causing vexation; the state of being annoyed; the thing or act that annoys.

annual *adj* of or measured by a year; yearly; coming every year; living only one year or season. * *n* a plant that lives only one year; a periodical published once a year.–**annually** *adv*.

annuity *n* (*pl* **annuities**) an investment yielding fixed payments, esp yearly; such a payment.

annul *vt* (**annulling, annulled**) to do away with; to deprive of legal force, nullify.

annular adj ring-like; in the form of a ring or annulus. * n the ring of light surrounding the moon's body in an annular eclipse of the sun.

annulment n the act of reducing to nothing; abolition; invalidation.

annunciate vt to make known officially or publicly; to announce, proclaim.–**annunciation** n.–**annunciative, annunciatory** adj.

anode n the positive electrode by which electrons enter an electric circuit.

anodyne n a drug that relieves pain; anything that relieves pain or soothes.

anoint vt to rub with oil; to apply oil in a sacred ritual as a sign of consecration.–**anointment** n.

anomaly n (pl **anomalies**) abnormality; anything inconsistent or odd. **anomalous** adj.

anonymous adj having or providing no name; written or provided by an unnamed person; lacking individuality.–**anonymity** n.–**anonymously** adv.

anorak n a waterproof jacket with a hood.

anorexia n loss of appetite.–**anorexic** adj.

anorexia nervosa n the psychological condition causing fear of becoming overweight and reluctance to eat even to the point of starvation and death.

another adj a different or distinct (thing or person); an additional one of the same kind; some other.–also pron.

answer n a spoken or written reply or response; the solution to a problem; a reaction, response. * vt to speak or write in reply; to satisfy or correspond to (eg a specific need); to justify, offer a refutation of. * vi to reply; to act in response (to); to be responsible (for); to conform (to).

answerable adj capable of being refuted; (with for or to) responsible, accountable.–**answerability** n.–**answerableness** n.

answering machine n an apparatus that records incoming telephone calls.

ant n any of a family of small, generally wingless insects of many species, all of which form and live in highly organized groups.

antacid n a substance that counters excessive acidity.

antagonism n antipathy, hostility; an opposing force, principle, etc.–**antagonistic** adj.–**antagonistically** adv.

antagonist n an adversary; an opponent.

antagonize vt to arouse opposition in.–**antagonization** n.

antalkali n (pl **antalkalis, antalkalies**) a substance that counteracts the presence of alkali in the system; an acid.–**antalkaline** adj, n.

Antarctic adj of the South Pole or its surroundings. * n the Antarctic regions; the Antarctic Ocean.

ante n a player's stake in poker; (inf) money contributed as a share in a joint project.

anteater n an ant-eating animal, as the pangolin.

antecedent adj prior in time, previous. * n a preceding event or happening; (pl) ancestry; (pl) the previous events of a person's life.

antedate vt to carry back to an earlier period; to anticipate. * n a date esp on a document earlier than the actual date.

antelope n (pl **antelopes, antelope**) any of the family of fast-running and graceful deer-like animals of Africa and Asia.

ante meridiem n (abbr a.m.) the period between midnight and noon.–**antemeridian** adj.

antenatal adj occurring or present before birth.

antenna n (pl **antennae**) either of a pair of feelers on the head of an insect, crab, etc; (pl **antennas**) a metal device for transmitting and receiving radio waves.

antepenult n the last but two, usu of syllables.

antepenultimate adj pertaining to the last but two. * n that which is last but two, antepenult.

anterior adj at or towards the front; earlier; previous.

anteroom n an outer room leading into a larger or main room.

anthem n a religious choral song; a song of praise or devotion, as to a nation.

anther n the part of a flower's stamen containing pollen.–**antheral** adj.

anthill n a mound thrown up by ants or termites in digging their nests.

anthology n (pl **anthologies**) a collection of poetry or prose.–**anthological** adj.–**anthologist** n.

anthracite n a hard coal that gives off a lot of heat and little smoke.–**anthracitic** adj.

anthrax n (pl **anthraces**) a contagious bacterial disease of cattle and sheep, etc that can be transmitted to people.

anthropoid adj resembling man. * n one of the higher apes resembling man.–**anthropoidal** adj.

anthropology n the scientific study of human beings, their origins, distribution, physical attributes and culture.–**anthropological** adj.–**anthropologist** n.

anti-aircraft adj for use against aircraft.

antibiotic n any of various chemical, fungal or synthetic substances used against bacterial or fungal infections.

antibody n (pl **antibodies**) a protein produced by an organism in response to the action of a foreign body, such as the toxin of a parasite, that neutralizes its effects.

antic n a ludicrous action intended to amuse.

anticipate vt to give prior thought and attention to; to use, spend, act on in advance; to foresee and take action to thwart another; to expect. * vi to speak, act, before the appropriate time.

anticipation n the act of taking beforehand; expectation; hope; preconception.

anticlimax n a sudden drop from the important to the trivial; an ending to a story or series of events that disappoints one's expectations.–**anticlimactic** adj.–**anticlimactically** adv.

anticlockwise see **counterclockwise**.

anticoagulant n a substance that inhibits blood clotting.

anticyclone n a body of air rotating about an area of high atmospheric pressure.–**anticyclonic** adj.

antidepressant n any of various drugs used to alleviate mental depression.–also adj.

antidote n a remedy that counteracts a poison; something that counteracts harmful effects.

antifreeze n a substance used, as in a car radiator, to prevent freezing up.

antigen n a substance introduced into the blood to stimulate production of antibodies.–**antigenic** adj.–**antigenically** adv.

antihero n (pl **antiheroes**) a leading character in a book, film, etc who lacks the conventional heroic attributes.

antihistamine n any of a group of drugs that inhibit the action of histamines, used in treating allergic conditions.

antimatter n matter composed of antiparticles.

antimony n (pl **antimonies**) a brittle metallic element used in making alloys.–**antimonial** adj, n.

antipathy n (pl **antipathies**) a fixed dislike; aversion; an object of this.–**antipathetic, antipathetical** adj.–**antipathetically** adv.

antipersonnel adj (weapon) used to destroy people rather than objects.

antiperspirant n a substance used to stem excessive perspiration.

antipodes npl the regions on the earth's surface opposite each other; (with cap preceded by the) Australia and New Zealand.–**antipodean** adj.

antiquarian adj connected with the study of antiquities. * n an antiquary.

antiquary n (pl **antiquaries**) a person who studies or collects antiquities.

antiquated adj old-fashioned; obsolete.

antique adj from the distant past; old-fashioned. * n a relic of the distant past; a piece of furniture, pottery, etc dating from an earlier historical period and sought after by collectors.

antiquity n (pl **antiquities**) the far distant past, esp before the Middle Ages; (pl) relics dating from the far distant past.

anti-Semite n one who is hostile toward or discriminates against Jews as a religious or racial group.–**anti-Semitic** adj.–**anti-Semitism** n.

antiseptic n a substance that destroys or prevents the growth of disease-producing microorganisms. * adj destroying harmful organisms; very clean; (inf) unexciting.–**antiseptically** adv.

antisocial adj avoiding the company of other people, unsocial; contrary to the interests of society in general.

antispasmodic adj counteractive to or curative of spasms. * n a medicine having such an effect.

antistatic adj (material, agent) counteracting the effects of static electricity.

antithesis n (pl **antitheses**) a contrast or opposition, as of ideas; the exact opposite.–**antithetical, antithetic** adj.

antitoxin n a substance that acts against a specific toxin in the body; a serum containing an antitoxin, injected into a person to prevent disease.–**antitoxic** adj.

antivivisectionist n a person who opposes scientific experimentation on live animals.

antler n the branched horn of a deer or related animal.–**antlered** adj.

antonym n a word that has the opposite meaning to another.

anus n the excretory opening of the alimentary canal.

anvil n the heavy iron block on which metal objects are shaped with a hammer.

anxiety n (pl **anxieties**) the condition of being anxious; eagerness, concern; a cause of worry.

anxious adj worried; uneasy; eagerly wishing; causing anxiety.–**anxiously** adv.–**anxiousness** n.

any adj one out of many, some; every.

anybody pron any person; an important person.

anyhow adv in any way whatever; in any case.

any more, anymore adv now; nowadays.

anyone pron any person; anybody.

anything pron any object, event, fact, etc. * n a thing, no matter what kind.

anyway adv in any manner; at any rate; haphazardly.

anywhere adv in, at, or to any place.

aorta n (pl **aortas, aortae**) the main artery that carries blood from the heart to be distributed through the body.–**aortic, aortal** adj.

apace adv at a swift pace.

apart adv at a distance, separately, aside; into two or more pieces.

apartheid n a policy of racial segregation implemented in South Africa.

apartment n a room or set of rooms in a building.

apathy n lack of feeling; lack of concern, indifference.–**apathetic** adj.–**apathetically** adv.

ape n a chimpanzee, gorilla, orangutan, or gibbon; any monkey; a mimic. * vt to imitate.

aperient adj gently laxative; opening the bowels. * n a mild laxative medicine.

aperitif, apéritif n an alcoholic drink taken before a meal as an appetizer.

aperture n an opening; a hole; a slit; in optical instruments, the (diameter of the) opening allowing or controlling the amount of light or radiation to enter.

apex n (pl **apexes, apices**) the highest point, the tip; the culminating point; the vertex of a triangle.–**apical** adj.–**apically** adv.

aphid n any of various small insects, such as the greenfly, that suck the juice of plants.

aphorism n a brief, wise saying; an adage.–**aphoristic** adj.

aphrodisiac adj arousing sexually. * n a food, drug, etc that excites sexual desire.

apiarist n a beekeeper.

apiary n (pl **apiaries**) a place with hives where bees are kept.

apiculture n beekeeping.–**apicultural** adj.–**apiculturist** n.

apiece adv to, by, or for each one.

apish adj like an ape in manners; foolish; imitative.–**apishness** n.

aplomb n poise; self-possession.

apnea, apnoea n partial suspension of breathing; suffocation.–**apnoeic** adj.

apocalypse n a cataclysmic event, the end of the world; revelation, esp that of St John; (with cap) the last book of the New Testament.–**apocalyptic** adj.–**apocalyptically** adv.

apocryphal adj doubtful; untrue; invented.–**apocryphally** adv.

apogee n the point in the orbit of the moon or any planet where it is most distant from the earth; the highest point.

apolitical adj uninterested or uninvolved in politics.

apologetic adj expressing an apology; contrite; presented in defence.–**apologetically** adv.

apologetics n (used as sing) the defense and vindication of the principles and laws of Christian belief.

apologia n a written defense of one's principles or conduct.

apologist n a person who makes an apology; a defender of a cause.

apologize vi to make an apology.

apology n (pl **apologies**) an expression of regret for wrongdoing; a defence or justification of one's beliefs, etc; (with **for**) a poor substitute.

apoplectic adj of, causing, or exhibiting symptoms of apoplexy; (inf) furious.

apoplexy n a sudden loss of consciousness and subsequent partial paralysis, usu caused by a broken or blocked artery in the brain.

apostasy n (pl **apostasies**) abandonment of one's religion, principles or political party.

apostle n the first or principal supporter of a new belief or cause; (with cap) one of the twelve disciples of Christ.–**apostolic** adj.

apostrophe n a mark (') showing the omission of letters or figures, also a sign of the possessive case or the plural of letters and figures–**apostrophic** adj.

apotheosis n (pl **apotheoses**) deification; glorification of a person or thing; the supreme or ideal example.

appall, appal vt (or **appalls, appals, appalling, appalled**) to fill with terror or dismay.

appalling adj shocking, horrifying.–**appallingly** adv.

apparatus n (pl **apparatus, apparatuses**) the equipment used for a specific task; any complex machine, device, or system.

apparel n clothing, dress. * vt (**apparelling, apparelled** or **appareling, appareled**) to dress; to clothe.

apparent adj easily seen, evident; seeming, but not real.–**apparently** adv.

apparition n an appearance or manifestation, esp something unexpected or unusual; a ghost.

appeal vi to take a case to a higher court; to make an earnest request; to refer to a witness or superior authority for vindication, confirmation, etc; to arouse pleasure or sympathy. * n the referral of a lawsuit to a higher court for rehearing; an earnest call for help; attraction, the power of arousing sympathy; a request for public donations to a charitable cause.–**appealable** adj.–**appealer** n.–**appealing** adj.

appear vi to become or be visible; to arrive, come in person; to be published; to present oneself formally (before a court, etc); to seem, give an impression of being.

appearance n the act or occasion of appearing; that which appears; external aspect of a thing or person; outward show, semblance.

appease vt to pacify; to allay; to conciliate by making concessions.–**appeasement** n.

appellation *n* the name, title or designation by which a person or thing is called or known; the act of appealing.

append *vt* to attach; to add, esp to the end as a supplement, etc.

appendage *n* something appended; an external organ or part, as a tail.

appendectomy, appendicectomy *n* (*pl* **appendectomies, appendicectomies**) surgical removal of the appendix that grows from the intestine.

appendicitis *n* inflammation of the appendix that grows from the intestine.

appendix *n* (*pl* **appendixes, appendices**) a section of supplementary information at the back of a book, etc; a small tube of tissue that forms an outgrowth of the intestine (–*also* **vermiform appendix**).

appertain *vi* to belong or pertain to, as by relation or custom.

appetite *n* sensation of bodily desire, esp for food; (*with* **for**) a strong desire or liking, a craving.

appetizer *n* a food or drink that stimulates the appetite; something that whets one's interest.

appetizing *adj* stimulating the appetite.–**appetizingly** *adv.*

applaud *vt* to show approval, esp by clapping the hands; to praise.

applause *n* approval expressed by clapping; acclamation.

apple *n* a round, firm, fleshy, edible fruit.

appliance *n* a device or machine, esp for household use.

applicable *adj* that may be applied; appropriate, relevant (to).–**applicability** *n.*

applicant *n* a person who applies, esp for a job.

application *n* the act of applying; the use to which something is put; a petition, request; concentration, diligent effort; relevance or practical value.

applicator *n* a device for applying something.

applied *adj* practical.

appliqué *n* ornamental fabricwork applied to another fabric. * *vt* (**appliquéing, appliquéed**) to decorate with appliqué.

apply *vb* (**applying, applied**) *vt* to bring to bear; to put to practical use; to spread, lay on; to devote (oneself) with close attention. * *vi* to make a formal, esp written, request; to be relevant.

appoint *vt* to fix or decide officially; to select for a job; to prescribe.

appointed *adj* equipped; furnished.

appointee *n* a person appointed.

appointment *n* an appointing; a job or position for which someone has been selected; an arrangement to meet.

apportion *vt* to divide into shares; allot.–**apportionable** *adj.*–**apportioner** *n.*–**apportionment** *n.*

apposite *adj* (*remarks*) especially pertinent, appropriate.–**appositely** *adv.*

appraisal, appraisement *n* the act of appraising or valuing, esp the putting of a price upon with a view to sale; a valuation.

appraise *vt* to estimate the value or quality of.–**appraiser** *n.*

appreciable *adj* capable of being perceived or measured; fairly large.–**appreciably** *adv.*

appreciate *vt* to value highly; to recognize gratefully; to understand, be aware of; to increase the value of. * *vi* to rise in value.

appreciation *n* gratitude, approval; sensitivity to aesthetic values; an assessment or critical evaluation of a person or thing; a favorable review; an increase in value.–**appreciative** *adj.*

apprehend *vt* to arrest, capture; to understand, to perceive.

apprehension *n* anxiety; the act of arresting; understanding; an idea.

apprehensive *adj* uneasy; anxious.–**apprehensively** *adv.*

apprentice *n* one being taught a trade or craft; a novice. * *vt* to take on as an apprentice.–**apprenticeship** *n.*

apprise, apprize *vt* to give notice to; to inform.

approach *vi* to draw nearer. * *vt* to make a proposal to; to set about dealing with; to come near to. * *n* the act of approaching; a means of entering or leaving; a move to establish relations; the final descent of an aircraft.

approachable *adj* within approaching distance; easy to approach; inviting friendship.–**approachability** *n.*–**approachably** *adv.*

approbation *n* formal approval; sanction.

appropriate *adj* fitting, suitable. * *vt* to take for one's own use, esp illegally; (*money, etc*) to set aside for a specific purpose.–**appropriately** *adv.*–**appropriateness** *n.*

appropriation *n* the act of setting apart or reserving for one's own use; a sum of money set aside for a particular purpose.

approval *n* the act of approving; favorable opinion; official permission.

approve *vt* to express a good opinion of; to authorize. * *vi* (*with* **of**) to consider to be favorable or satisfactory.

approx. *abbr* = approximate(ly).

approximate *adj* almost exact or correct. * *vt* to come near to; to be almost the same as. * *vi* to come close.–**approximately** *adv.*

approximation *n* a close estimate; a near likeness.

appurtenance *n* that which belongs or relates to something else; an adjunct or appendage; that which belongs it, is accessory to; an estate or property.–**appurtenant** *adj, n.*

APR *abbr* = annual percentage rate.

Apr. *abbr* = April.

après-ski *n* social activity after skiing.–*also adj.*

apricot *n* a small, oval, orange-pink fruit resembling the plum and peach.

April *n* the fourth month of the year, having 30 days.

apron *n* a garment worn to protect clothing; anything resembling the shape of an apron used for protection; the paved surface on an airfield where aircraft are parked, etc.

apropos *adv* at the right time; opportunely; appropriately. * *adj* appropriate. * *prep* (*with* **of**) regarding, in reference to.

apse *n* a domed or vaulted recess, esp in a church.

apt *adj* ready or likely (to); suitable, relevant; able to learn easily.–**aptness** *n.*

aptitude *n* suitability; natural talent, esp for learning.

aqua *n* (*pl* **aquae, aquas**) water as used in pharmacy.

aquaculture *n* the cultivation and breeding of fish and other marine organisms.–*also* **aquiculture**.–**aquacultural** *adj.*–**aquaculturist** *n.*

aqualung *n* portable diving gear comprising air cylinders connected to a face mask.

aquamarine *n* a variety of bluish-green beryl used as a gemstone; its color.

aquaplane *n* a plank towed at high speed. * *vi* to ride on one.

aquarium *n* (*pl* **aquariums, aquaria**) a tank, pond, etc for keeping aquatic animals or plants; a building where collections of aquatic animals are exhibited.

Aquarius *n* (*astrol*) the eleventh sign of the zodiac, the water-carrier, operative 20 January–18 February.–**Aquarian** *adj, n.*

aquatic *adj* of or taking place in water; living or growing in water.

aqueduct *n* a large pipe or conduit for carrying water; an elevated structure supporting this.

aqueous *adj* of, like, or formed by water.

aquiline *adj* of or like an eagle; (*nose*) hooked, like an eagle's beak.

AR *abbr* = Arkansas.

Arab *n* a native of Arabia; one of the Arabic races spread over the African and Syrian deserts. * *adj* pertaining to Arabia or the Arabs.–**Arabian** *adj, n.*

arabesque *n* a decorative design incorporating organic motifs, such as leaves and flowers, in an intricate pattern; (*ballet*) a posture in which the dancer balances on one leg with one arm extending forwards and the other arm and leg extending backwards.

Arabic n the Arabian language. * adj of or pertaining to the Arabic language and the countries in which it is spoken.

Arabic numeral n one of the numbers 0, 1, 2, 3, 4, 5, etc.

arable adj (land) suitable for plowing or planting crops.–also n.

arachnid n any of a class of animals including spiders, scorpions, mites and ticks.–**arachnidan** adj, n.

arbiter n a person having absolute power of decision or absolute control.

arbitrary adj not bound by rules; despotic, absolute; capricious, unreasonable.–**arbitrarily** adv.–**arbitrariness** n.

arbitrate vi to act as an arbitrator. * vt to submit to an arbiter; to act as an arbiter upon.

arbitration n the settlement of disputes by arbitrating.

arbor n a place shaded by trees, foliage, etc; a bower.–also **arbour**.

arboreal adj of or living in trees.

arboretum n (pl **arboreta, arboretums**) a botanical tree garden where rare trees are cultivated and exhibited.

arboriculture n the cultivation of trees and shrubs, forestry.

arbour see **arbor**.

ARC abbr = AIDS-related complex.

arc n a portion of the circumference of a circle or other curve; a luminous discharge of electricity across a gap between two electrodes or terminals. * vi to form an electric arc.

arcade n a series of arches supported on columns; an arched passageway; a covered walk or area lined with shops.

arcane adj secret or esoteric.

arch[1] n a curved structure spanning an opening; the curved underside of the foot. * vti to span or cover with an arch; to curve, bend into an arch.

arch[2] adj (criminal, etc) principal, expert; clever, sly; mischievous.–**archly** adv.–**archness** n.

archaeology see **archeology**.

archaic adj belonging to ancient times; (language) no longer in common use.

archaism n an archaic word or phrase.–**archaistic** adj.

archangel n a principal angel.–**archangelic** adj.

archbishop n a bishop of the highest rank.

archdeacon n a clergyman ranking next under a bishop.

archdiocese n the diocese of an archbishop.–**archdiocesan** adj.

archeology n the study of past human societies through their extant remains.–also **archaeology**.–**archeological, archaeological** adj.–**archeologist, archaeologist** n.

archer n a person who shoots with a bow and arrow.

archery n the art or sport of shooting arrows from a bow.

archetype n the original pattern or model; a prototype.–**archetypal, archetypical** adj.

archipelago n (pl **archipelagoes, archipelagos**) a sea filled with small islands; a group of small islands.–**archipelagic, archipelagian** adj.

architect n a person who designs buildings and supervises their erection; someone who plans something.

architecture n the art, profession, or science of designing and constructing buildings; the style of a building or buildings; the design and organization of a computer's parts.–**architectural** adj.–**architecturally** adv.

architrave n an epistyle, the lowest division of an entablature, the part resting immediately on a column; the parts round a door or window.

archives npl the location in which public records are kept; the public records themselves.–**archival** adj.

archivist n a keeper of public records.

archway n an arched or vaulted passage, esp that leading into a castle.

arc light n light produced by a current of electricity passing between two carbon points placed a short distance from each other.

arctic adj (often with cap) of, near, or relating to the North Pole or its surroundings; (inf) very cold, icy.

Arctic Circle n an imaginary circle around the arctic regions parallel to the equator.

Arctic Ocean n the ocean that washes the northern coasts of Europe, Asia and North America.

arc welding n welding using an electric arc.

ardent adj passionate; zealous.–**ardency** n.–**ardently** adv.

ardor, ardour n warmth of feeling; extreme intensity.

arduous adj difficult, laborious; steep, difficult to climb.–**arduously** adv.–**arduousness** n.

are[1] see **be**.

are[2] n a metric unit of measure equal to 100 square meters.

area n an expanse of land; a total outside surface, measured in square units; a specific part of a house, district, etc; scope or extent.

arena n an area within a sports stadium, etc where events take place; a place or sphere of contest or activity.

aren't = are not.

areola n (pl **areolae, areolas**) a very small area; an interstice in tissue; the colored circle or halo surrounding the nipple of the breast.–**areolar, areolate** adj.–**areolation** n.

argon n an inert gaseous element.

argot n the special vocabulary of any set of persons, as of lawyers, criminals, etc.–**argotic** adj.

arguable adj debatable; able to be asserted; plausible.–**arguably** adv.

argue vb (**arguing, argued**) vt to try to prove by reasoning; to debate, dispute; to persuade (into, out of). * vi to offer reasons for or against something; to disagree, exchange angry words.–**arguer** n.

argument n a disagreement; a debate, discussion; a reason offered in debate; an abstract, summary.

argumentative adj prone to arguing.–**argumentatively** adv.–**argumentativeness** n.

aria n a song for one voice accompanied by instruments, eg in opera.

arid adj very dry, parched; uninteresting; dull.–**aridity** n.–**aridly** adv.

Aries n (astrol) the first sign of the zodiac, the Ram, operative 21 March–21 April.–**Arian** adj, n.

arise vi (**arising, arose, pp arisen**) to get up, as from bed; to rise, ascend; to come into being, to result (from).

aristocracy n (pl **aristocracies**) (a country with) a government dominated by a privileged minority class; the privileged class in a society, the nobility; those people considered the best in their particular sphere.

aristocrat n a member of the aristocracy; a supporter of aristocratic government; a person with the manners or taste of a privileged class.–**aristocratic** adj.–**aristocratically** adv.

arithmetic n (math) computation (addition, subtraction, etc) using real numbers; calculation.–**arithmetic, arithmetical** adj.–**arithmetically** adv.

arithmetician n one skilled in the science of numbers.

Ariz. abbr = Arizona.

ark n (Bible) the boat in which Noah and his family and two of every kind of creature survived the Flood; a place of safety; an enclosure in a synagogue for the scrolls of the Torah.

Ark. abbr = Arkansas.

arm[1] n the upper limb from the shoulder to the wrist; something shaped like an arm, as a support on a chair; a sleeve; power, authority; an administrative division of a large organization.

arm[2] n (usu pl) a weapon; a branch of the military service; (pl) heraldic bearings. * vt to provide with weapons, etc; to provide with something that protects or strengthens, etc; to set a fuse ready to explode. * vi to prepare for war or any struggle.

armada n a fleet of warships or aircraft.

pls ch
end
priod
no
priod
after
abbre
in oth
places

armadillo n (pl **armadillos**) a small animal from South America with a body covering of small bony plates.

armament n (often pl) all the military forces and equipment of a nation; all the military equipment of a warship, etc; the process of arming or being armed for war.

armature n a piece of iron connecting the poles of a magnet or electromagnet to preserve and increase the magnetic force; the revolving part of a dynamo; arms, armor, that which serves as a means of defense; iron bars or framework used to strengthen a building; a framework supporting clay, etc, in sculpture or modeling.

armchair n a chair with side rests for the arms. * adj lacking practical experience.

armed forces npl the military forces of a nation.–also **armed services**.

armful n as much as the arms can hold.

armhole n an opening for the arm in an item of clothing.

armistice n a truce, preliminary to a peace treaty.

armlet n an ornamental or protective band worn around the arm; a badge worn on the arm; a small arm of the sea.

armor, armour n any defensive or protective covering.

armored, armoured adj covered or protected with armor; equipped with tanks and armor vehicles.

armor plate, armour plate n a plate of iron or steel affixed to a ship or tank as part of a casing for protection against shellfire.

armory, armoury n (pl **armories, armouries**) an arsenal; a place where armor or ammunition is stored.

armpit n the hollow underneath the arm at the shoulder.

arms see **arm**[2].

army n (pl **armies**) a large organized body of soldiers for waging war, esp on land; any large number of persons, animals, etc.

arnica n a genus of perennial herbs, esp mountain tobacco, whose roots and flowers are used to make a tincture for treating bruises.

aroma n a pleasant smell; a fragrance.

aromatherapy n the massage of fragrant oils into the skin to relieve tension and promote well-being.

aromatic adj giving out an aroma; fragrant, spicy; odoriferous. * n a plant, herb or drug yielding a fragrant smell.–**aromatically** adv.

arose see **arise**.

around prep on all sides of; on the border of; in various places in or on; approximately, about. * adv in a circle; in every direction; in circumference; to the opposite direction.

arousal n the act of awakening or stimulating; the state of being awakened or stimulated.

arouse vt to wake from sleep; to stir, as to action; to evoke.

arpeggio n (pl **arpeggios**) (mus) the playing of notes of a chord in rapid succession, instead of simultaneously; a passage or chord so played.

arraign vt to put on trial; to indict, accuse; to censure publicly; to impeach.–**arraigner** n.–**arraignment** n.

arrange vt to put in a sequence or row; to settle, make preparations for; (mus) to prepare a composition for different instruments other than those intended.* vi to come to an agreement; to make plans.–**arranger** n.

arrangement n the act of putting in proper form or order; that which is ordered or disposed; the method or style of disposition; a preparatory measure; preparation; settlement; classification; adjustment; adaptation; (pl) plans.

arrant adj notorious; unmitigated; downright, thorough; shameless.

array n an orderly grouping, esp of troops; an impressive display; fine clothes; (comput) an ordered data structure that allows information to be easily indexed. * vt to set in order, to arrange; to dress, decorate.–**arrayal** n.

arrears npl overdue debts; work, etc still to be completed.

arrest vt to stop; to capture, apprehend esp by legal authority; to check the development of a disease; to catch and hold the attention of. * n a stoppage; seizure by legal authority.

arresting adj striking or attracting to the mind or eye; impressive.–**arrestingly** adv.

arrival n arriving; a person or thing that has arrived.

arrive vi to reach any destination; to come; (with **at**) to reach agreement, a decision; to achieve success, celebrity.

arriviste n an ambitious person, a self-seeker.

arrogance n an exaggerated assumption of importance.

arrogant adj overbearing; aggressively self-important.–**arrogantly** adv.

arrogate vt to assume or lay claim to unduly or presumptuously.–**arrogation** n.–**arrogative** adj.–**arrogator** n.

arrow n a straight, pointed weapon, made to be shot from a bow; a sign used to indicate direction or location.

arrowhead n the head or barb of an arrow.

arrowroot n a starch obtained from the rootstocks of several species of West Indian plants.

arroyo n a watercourse or rivulet; the dry bed of a small stream.

arsenal n a workshop or store for weapons and ammunition.

arsenic n a soft grey metallic element, highly poisonous.

arson n the crime of using fire to destroy property deliberately.–**arsonist** n.

art n human creativity; skill acquired by study and experience; any craft and its principles; the making of things that have form and beauty; any branch of this, as painting, sculpture, etc; drawings, paintings, statues, etc; (pl) the creative and nonscientific branches of knowledge, esp as studied academically.

artefact see **artifact**.

arterial adj pertaining to an artery or the arteries; contained in an artery; (blood) oxygenated, of a lighter red color than venous blood; (road) major, with many branches.

arteriosclerosis n (med) hardening of the walls of the arteries due to the action of fatty deposits, which impairs blood circulation.–**arteriosclerotic** adj.

artery n (pl **arteries**) a tubular vessel that conveys blood from the heart; any main channel of transport or communication.

artesian well n a well in which water rises to the surface by internal pressure.

artful adj skillful at attaining one's ends; clever, crafty.–**artfully** adv.–**artfulness** n.

arthritis n painful inflammation of a joint.–**arthritic** adj.

arthropod n a member of the largest group of invertebrate animals with jointed legs, such as the butterfly, spider, crab, centipede.

artichoke n a thistle-like plant with a scaly flower head, parts of which are eaten as a vegetable.

article n a separate item or clause in a written document; an individual item on a particular subject in a newspaper, magazine, etc; a particular or separate item; (gram) a word placed before a noun to identify it as definite or indefinite.

articulate adj capable of distinct, intelligible speech, or expressing one's thoughts clearly; jointed. * vti to speak or express clearly; to unite or become united (as) by a joint.–**articulately** adv.–**articulateness** n.

articulated truck, articulated lorry n a large vehicle composed of a tractor and one or more trailers connected by flexible joints for greater maneuverability.–also **trailer truck**.

articulation n the act of jointing; the act of speaking distinctly; a distinct utterance; the state of being articulated; a joint or juncture between bones; the point of separation of organs or parts of a plant; a node or joint of the stem, or the space between two nodes.–**articular, articulatory** adj.

artifact n a product of human craftsmanship, esp a simple tool or ornament.–also **artefact**.

artifice n a clever contrivance or stratagem; a trick, trickery.

artificer n a skilled or artistic worker; a maker or constructor; an inventor.

artificial adj lacking natural qualities; man-made.–**artificiality** n.–**artificially** adv.

artificial insemination n injection of semen into the womb by artificial means so that conception takes place without sexual intercourse.

artificial intelligence n (comput) the ability to imitate intelligent human behavior.

artificial respiration n the forcing of air into and out of the lungs of somebody whose breathing has stopped.

artillery n (pl **artilleries**) large, heavy guns; the branch of the army that uses these.

artisan n a skilled workman.

artist n one who practices fine art, esp painting; one who does anything very well.–**artistic** adj.–**artistically** adv.

artiste n a professional, usu musical or theatrical, entertainer.

artistry n artistic quality, ability, work, etc.

artless adj simple, natural; without art or skill.–**artlessly** adv.–**artlessness** n.

arty adj (**artier, artiest**) (inf) having a pretentious or affected interest in art.

arum n a genus of plants with small flowers within a hood-shaped leaf.

Aryan n a member of the Indo-European race; according to Nazi belief, a Caucasian, esp of the Nordic type, with no Jewish blood. * adj pertaining to the Aryans, or to their language.

as adv equally; for instance; when related in a certain way. * conj in the same way that; while; when; because. * prep in the role or function of.

ASAP, a.s.a.p. abbr = as soon as possible.

asbestos, asbestus n a fine fibrous mineral used for making incombustible and chemical-resistant materials.

asbestosis n (med) a disease of the lungs caused by the inhalation of asbestos fibers.

ascend vti to go up; to succeed to (a throne).

ascendancy, ascendency n governing or dominating influence; power; sway.

ascendant, ascendent adj rising upwards; dominant.

ascension n the act of ascending or rising.–**ascensional** adj.

ascent n an ascending; an upward slope; the means of, the way of ascending.

ascertain vt to acquire definite knowledge of, to discover positively.–**ascertainable** adj.

ascetic adj self-denying, austere. * n a person who practices rigorous self-denial as a religious discipline; any severely abstemious person.–**ascetically** adv.–**asceticism** n.

ASCII acronym (comput) = American Standard Code for Information Interchange, a standard code of 128 alphanumeric characters for storing and exchanging information.

ascorbic acid n vitamin C, found esp in citrus fruit and fresh green vegetables.

ascribe vt to attribute, impute or refer; to assign.–**ascribable** adj.–**ascription, adscription** n.

asexual adj lacking sex or sexual organs; (reproduction) produced without the union of male and female germ cells.–**asexuality** n.–**asexually** adv.

ash[1] n a tree with silver-gray bark; the wood of this tree.

ash[2] n powdery residue of anything burnt; fine, volcanic lava.

ashamed adj feeling shame or guilt.–**ashamedly** adv.

ash can n a container for household refuse, a garbage can.

ashen adj like ashes, esp in color; pale.

ashore adv to or on the shore; to or on land.–also adj.

ashram n a Hindu religious retreat.

ashtray n a small receptacle for tobacco ash and cigarette stubs.

Asian adj of or relating to the continent of Asia, its inhabitants or languages.–also n.

aside adv on or to the side; in reserve; away from; notwithstanding. * n words uttered and intended as inaudible, esp as spoken by an actor to the audience.

asinine adj silly, stupid.–**asininity** n.

ask vt to put a question to, inquire of; to make a request of or for; to invite; to demand, expect. * vi to inquire about.–**asker** n.

askance, askant adv with a sideways glance; with distrust.

askew adv to one side; awry.–also adj.

asleep adj sleeping; inactive; numb. * adv into a sleeping condition.

asocial adj not capable of or avoiding social contact; antisocial.

asp n a small poisonous snake.

asparagus n a plant cultivated for its edible young shoots.

aspartame n an artificial sweetener derived from an amino acid.

aspect n the look of a person or thing to the eye; a particular feature of a problem, situation, etc; the direction something faces; view; (astrol) the position of the planets with respect to one another, regarded as having an influence on human affairs.

aspen n a species of poplar with leaves that tremble in the slightest breeze. * adj (arch) quivering.

asperity n (pl **asperities**) hardship, severity; sharpness of temper.

aspersions npl slander; an attack on a person's reputation.

asphalt n a hard, black bituminous substance, used for paving roads, etc. * vt to surface with asphalt.–**asphaltic** adj.

asphyxia n unconsciousness due to lack of oxygen or excess of carbon dioxide in the blood.

asphyxiate vt to suffocate.–**asphyxiation** n.–**asphyxiator** n.

aspic n a savory jelly used to coat fish, game, etc.

aspidistra n an Asian plant with broad leaves, grown as a house plant.

aspirant n someone who aspires to something.

aspirate[1] n the sound of h.

aspirate[2] vt to pronounce with an h; to suck out using an aspirator.

aspiration n strong desire; ambition; the act of aspirating; the act of breathing; the withdrawal of air or fluid from a body cavity.–**aspiratory** adj.

aspirator n a device used to suck (air, fluid, etc) from a (body) cavity.

aspire vi to desire eagerly; to aim at high things.–**aspirer** n.–**aspiring** adj.

aspirin n (pl **aspirin, aspirins**) acetylsalicylic acid, a pain-relieving drug.

ass[1] n a donkey; a silly, stupid person.

assail vt to attack violently either physically or verbally.–**assailable** adj.–**assailer** n.–**assailment** n.

assailant n an attacker.

assassin n a murderer, esp one hired to kill a leading political figure, etc.

assassinate vt to kill a political figure, etc; to harm (a person's reputation, etc).–**assassination** n.

assault n a violent attack; (law) an unlawful threat or attempt to harm another physically. * vti to make an assault (on); to rape.–**assaulter** n.

assault course n an obstacle course used for military training .

assay n the analysis of the quantity of metal in an ore or alloy, esp the standard purity of gold or silver; a test. * vt (**assaying, assayed**) to subject to analysis; to determine the quantity or proportion of one or more of the constituents of a metal.–**assayable** adj.–**assayer** n.

assemblage n a gathering of persons or things; (art) a form of collage.

assemble vti to bring together; to collect; to fit together the parts of; (comput) to translate using an assembler.

assembly n (pl **assemblies**) assembling or being assembled; a gathering of persons, esp for a particular purpose; the fitting together of parts to make a whole machine, etc.

assembly line n a series of machines, equipment and workers through which a product passes in successive stages to be assembled.

assemblyman n (pl **assemblymen**) a member of a legislative assembly.–**assemblywoman** nf (pl **assemblywomen**).

assent vi to express agreement to something. * n consent or agreement.–**assentor, assenter** n.

assert vt to declare, affirm as true; to maintain or enforce (eg rights).–**assertible** adj.

assertion n asserting; a statement that something is a fact, usu without evidence.

assertive adj self-assured, positive, confident; dogmatic.–**assertively** adv.–**assertiveness** n.

assess vt to establish the amount of, as a tax; to impose a tax or fine; to value, for the purpose of taxation; to estimate the worth, importance, etc of.–**assessable** adj.

assessment n the act of assessing or determining an amount to be paid; an official valuation of property, or income, for the purpose of taxation; the specific sum levied as tax, or assessed for damages.

assessor n a person appointed to assess property or persons for taxation; an expert appointed to assist a judge or magistrate as an adviser on special points of law.–**assessorial** adj.

asset n anything owned that has value; a desirable thing; (pl) all the property, accounts receivable, etc of a person or business; (pl) (law) property usable to pay debts.

asset-stripping n the practice of buying a company in order to sell off its assets at a profit.–**asset-stripper** n.

assiduity n (pl **assiduities**) close application, steady attention; diligence; (usu pl) constant attentions.

assiduous adj persistent or persevering; diligent.–**assiduously** adv.–**assiduousness** n.

assign vt to allot; to appoint to a post or duty; to ascribe; (law) to transfer (a right, property, etc).–**assignable** adj.–**assigner** n.

assignation n the act of assigning; a meeting, esp one made secretly by lovers.

assignment n the act of assigning; something assigned to a person, such as a share, task, etc.

assimilate vt to absorb; to digest; to take in and understand fully; to be ascribed; to be like.–**assimilable** adj.–**assimilation** n.

assist vti to support or aid.–**assister** n.

assistance n help; furtherance; aid; succor; support.

assistant n one who or that which assists; a helper; an auxiliary; a subordinate. * adj helping; lending aid; auxiliary.

associate vt to join as a friend, business partner or supporter; to bring together; to unite; to connect in the mind. * vi to combine or unite with others; to come together as friends, business partners or supporters. * adj allied or connected; having secondary status or privileges. * n a companion, business partner, supporter, etc; something closely connected with another; a person admitted to an association as a subordinate member.

association n an organization of people joined together for a common aim; the act of associating or being associated; a connection in the mind, memory, etc.–**associative** adj.

assonance n a correspondence in sound between words or syllables.–**assonant** adj, n.–**assonantal** adj.

assorted adj distributed according to sorts; miscellaneous.

assortment n a collection of people or things of different sorts.

asst abbr = assistant.

assuage vt to soften the intensity of; to soothe.–**assuager** n.–**assuagement** n.–**assuasive** adj.

assume vt to take on, to undertake; to usurp; to take as certain or true; to pretend to possess.–**assumable** adj.–**assumer** n.

assuming adj presumptuous.

assumption n something taken for granted; the taking on of a position, esp of power.–**assumptive** adj.

assurance n a promise, guarantee; a form of life insurance; a feeling of certainty, self-confidence.

assure vt to make safe or certain; to give confidence to; to state positively; to guarantee, ensure.–**assurable** adj.–**assurer** n.

assured adj certain; convinced; self-confident.–**assuredness** n.

assuredly adv certainly.

aster n a kind of plant with round composite flowers; a Michaelmas daisy.

asterisk n a sign (*) used in writing or printing to mark omission of words, a footnote or other reference, etc. * vt to mark with an asterisk.

asteroid n any of the small planets between Mars and Jupiter. * adj star-like; star-shaped (–also **asteroidal**).

asthma n a chronic respiratory condition causing difficulty with breathing.–**asthmatic** adj.–**asthmatically** adv.

astigmatism n a defective condition of the eye or lens causing poor focusing.–**astigmatic** adj.–**astigmatically** adv.

astir adv moving or bustling about; out of bed.

astonish vt to fill with sudden or great surprise.–**astonishing** adj.–**astonishment** n.

astound vt to astonish greatly.–**astounding** adj.–**astoundingly** adv.

astragal n (archit) a small molding or bead of semicircular form; a ring of molding round the top or bottom of a column.

astrakhan n the dark curly fleece of lambs from Astrakhan in Russia; a cloth with a curled pile made from or imitating this.

astral adj of or from the stars.

astray adv off the right path; into error.

astride adv with a leg on either side. * prep extending across.

astringent adj that contracts body tissues; stopping blood flow, styptic; harsh; biting. * n an astringent substance–**astringency** n.

astrology n the study of planetary positions and motions to determine their supposed influence on human affairs.–**astrologer, astrologist** n.–**astrological** adj.–**astrologically** adv.

astronaut n one trained to make flights in outer space.

astronautics npl (used as sing) the scientific study of space flight and technology.

astronomical, astronomic adj enormously large; of or relating to astronomy.–**astronomically** adv.

astronomical clock n a clock that keeps sidereal time.

astronomical year n a year the length of which is determined by astronomical observations.

astronomy n the scientific investigation of the stars and other planets.–**astronomer** n.

astrophysics n (used as sing) the branch of astronomy that deals with the physical and chemical constitution of the stars.–**astrophysical** adj.–**astrophysicist** n.

astute adj clever, perceptive; crafty, shrewd.–**astutely** adv.–**astuteness** n.

asunder adv apart in direction or position; into pieces.

asylum n a place of safety, a refuge; (formerly) an institution for the blind, the mentally ill, etc.

asymmetric, asymmetrical adj lacking symmetry.–**asymmetrically** adv.

asymmetry n a lack of symmetry or proportion between the parts of a thing.

at prep on; in; near; by; used to indicate location or position.

atavism n the appearance in plants or animals of characteristics typical in more remote ancestors; reversion to a more primitive type.–**atavistic** adj.–**atavistically** adv.

ataxia n irregularities in the functions of the body, esp muscular coordination, or in the course of a disease.–**ataxic, atactic** adj.

ate see **eat**.

atheism n belief in the nonexistence of God.–**atheist** n.–**atheistic, atheistical** adj.

atherosclerosis n (pl **atheroscleroses**) a degenerative disease of the arteries characterized by deposition of fatty material on the inner arterial walls.–**atherosclerotic** adj.

athlete n a person trained in games or exercises requiring skill, speed, strength, stamina, etc.–**athletic** adj.–**athletically** adv.–**athleticism** n.

athlete's foot n a fungal infection of the feet.

athletics n (used as sing or pl) running, jumping, throwing sports, games, etc.

Atlantic *adj* of, near or relating to the Atlantic Ocean.

atlas *n* a book containing maps, charts and tables.

atmosphere *n* the gaseous mixture that surrounds the earth or the other stars and planets; a unit of pressure equal to the pressure of the atmosphere at sea level; any dominant or surrounding influence; special mood or aura.–**atmospheric, atmospherical** *adj*.

atmospherics *npl* interference in radio reception, etc caused by atmospheric disturbances.

atoll *n* a coral reef enclosing a central lagoon.

atom *n* the smallest particle of a chemical element; a tiny particle, bit.

atomic *adj* pertaining to or consisting of atoms; extremely minute.–**atomically** *adv*.

atomic bomb *n* a bomb whose explosive power derives from the atomic energy released during nuclear fission or fusion.–*also* **A-bomb.**

atomic energy *n* the energy derived from nuclear fission.

atomize *vt* to reduce to a fine spray or minute particles.–**atomization** *n*.

atomizer *n* a device for atomizing liquids, usu perfumes or cleaning agents.

atonal *adj* (*mus*) avoiding traditional tonality; not written in any established key.–**atonality** *n*.–**atonally** *adv*.

atone *vi* to give satisfaction or make amends (for).–**atonable, atoneable** *adj*.–**atoner** *n*.

atonement *n* satisfaction, reparation; (*Christianity: with cap*) the reconciliation of humankind with God through Christ's self-sacrifice.

atrium *n* (*pl* **atria, atriums**) an auricle of the heart; the unroofed courtyard of a Roman house; an entrance hall that rises up several storeys, often with a glass roof.

atrocious *adj* extremely brutal or wicked; (*inf*) very bad, of poor quality.–**atrociously** *adv*.

atrocity *n* (*pl* **atrocities**) a cruel act; something ruthless, wicked, repellent.

atrophy *n* (*pl* **atrophies**) a wasting away or failure to grow of a bodily organ. * *vti* (**atrophying, atrophied**) to cause or undergo atrophy.

atropine, atropin *n* a crystalline alkaloid of a very poisonous nature extracted from the deadly nightshade (belladonna).

attach *vt* to fix or fasten to something; to appoint to a specific group; to ascribe, attribute. * *vi* to become attached; to adhere.–**attachable** *adj*.–**attacher** *n*.

attaché *n* a technical expert on a diplomatic staff.

attaché case *n* a flat case for carrying documents, etc.

attached *adj* fixed; feeling affection for.

attachment *n* a fastening; affection, devotion; something attached; a device or part fixed to a machine, implement, etc; the act of attaching or being attached.

attack *vt* to set upon violently; to assault in speech or writing; to invade, as of a disease. * *vi* to make an assault. * *n* an assault; a fit of illness; severe criticism; an enthusiastic beginning of a performance, task, undertaking, etc.–**attacker** *n*.

attain *vt* to succeed in getting or arriving at; to achieve. * *vi* to come to or arrive at by growth or effort.–**attainable** *adj*.–**attainability** *n*.

attainment *n* something attained; an accomplishment.

attempt *vt* to try to accomplish, get, etc. * *n* an endeavor or effort to accomplish; an attack, assault.–**attemptable** *adj*.–**attempter** *n*.

attend *vt* to take care of; to go with, accompany; to be present at. * *vi* to apply oneself (to); to deal with, give attention to.–**attender** *n*.

attendance *n* attending; the number of people present; the number of times a person attends.

attendant *n* a person who serves or accompanies another; someone employed to assist or guide. * *adj* accompanying, following as a result; being in attendance.

attention *n* the application of the mind to a particular purpose, aim, etc; awareness, notice; care, consideration; (*usu. pl*) an act of civility or courtesy; (*usu. pl*) indications of admiration or love; (*mil*) a soldier's formal erect posture.

attention deficit disorder *n phr* any of a wide range of behavioral problems, ie learning difficulties, hyperactivity etc. esp. in children.

attentive *adj* observant, diligent; courteous.–**attentively** *adv*.–**attentiveness** *n*.

attenuate *vt* to make thin; to weaken; to reduce the force or severity of. * *vi* to become thin; to weaken.–**attenuation** *n*.

attest *vt* to state as true; to certify, as by oath; to give proof of. * *vi* to testify, bear witness (to).–**attestable** *adj*.–**attestation** *n*.–**attester, attestor** *n*.

attestation *n* the act of attesting; testimony or evidence given on oath or by official declaration; swearing in.

attic *n* the room or space just under the roof; a garret.

attire *vt* to clothe; to dress up. * *n* dress, clothing.

attitude *n* posture, position of the body; a manner of thought or feeling; behavior; the position of an aircraft or spacecraft in relation to certain reference points.–**attitudinal** *adj*.

attorney *n* (*pl* **attorneys**) one legally authorized to act for another; a lawyer.

attorney general *n* (*pl* **attorneys general, attorneys generals**) the chief law officer of of a state or nation acting as its legal representative and advising the chief executive on legal matters.

attract *vt* to pull towards oneself; to get the admiration, attention, etc of. * *vi* to be attractive.–**attractable** *adj*.–**attractor** *n*.

attraction *n* the act of attraction; the power of attracting, esp charm; (*physics*) the mutual action by which bodies tend to be drawn together.

attractive *adj* pleasing in appearance, etc; arousing interest; able to draw or pull.–**attractively** *adv*.–**attractiveness** *n*.

attribute *vt* to regard as belonging to; to ascribe, impute (to). * *n* a quality, a characteristic of.–**attributable** *adj*.

attribution *n* the act of attributing, esp a work of art, etc to a particular creator; a designation; a function.–**attributional** *adj*.

attributive *adj* expressing an attribute; (*gram*) qualifying. * *n* a word joined to and describing a noun; an adjective or adjective phrase.–**attributively** *adv*.

attrition *n* a grinding down by or as by friction; a relentless wearing down and weakening.–**attritional** *adj*.–**attritive** *adj*.

attune *vt* to bring (a person or thing) into harmony with; to adapt.

atypical *adj* not according to type; without definite typical character.–**atypically** *adv*.

Au (*chem symbol*) gold.

auburn *adj* reddish brown.

auction *n* a public sale of items to the highest bidder. * *vt* to sell by or at an auction.

auctioneer *n* one who conducts an auction.

audacity *n* (*pl* **audacities**) boldness; daring; spirit; presumptuousness; impudence; effrontery.–**audacious** *adj*.–**audaciously** *adv*.–**audaciousness** *n*.

audible *adj* heard or able to be heard.–**audibility** *n*.–**audibly** *adv*.

audience *n* a gathering of listeners or spectators; the people addressed by a book, play, film, etc; a formal interview or meeting, esp one in which one's views are heard.

audio *n* sound; the reproduction, transmission or reception of sound.

audio frequency *n* a frequency audible to the human ear.

audiovisual *adj* using both sound and vision, as in teaching aids.

audit *n* the inspection and verification of business accounts by a qualified accountant. * *vt* to make such an inspection.

audition *n* a trial to test a performer. * *vti* to test or be tested by audition.

auditor *n* a person qualified to audit business accounts.–**auditorial** *adj*.

auditorium n (pl **auditoriums, auditoria**) the part of a building allotted to the audience; a building or hall for speeches, concerts, etc.

auditory adj of or relating to the sense of hearing.

au fait adj fully informed about; competent.

auger n a tool for boring holes, a large gimlet.

augment vti to increase.–**augmentable** adj.–**augmenter, augmentor** n.

augmentation n enlargement, addition, increase; (mus) the increase in time value of the notes of a theme; (her) an additional charge to a coat of arms bestowed as a mark of honor.

au gratin adj topped with breadcrumbs or breadcrumbs and cheese, and cooked until crisp.

augur vti to prophesy; to be an omen (of).–**augural** adj.

augury n (pl **auguries**) the art or practice of foretelling events by reference to natural signs or omens; an omen; prediction; presage.

August n the eighth month of the year, having 31 days.

august adj imposing; majestic.

auk n a northern sea bird with short wings used as paddles.

aunt n a father's or mother's sister; an uncle's wife.

au pair n a person, esp a girl, from abroad who performs domestic chores, child-minding, etc in return for board and lodging.

aura n (pl **auras, aurae**) a particular quality or atmosphere surrounding a person or thing.

aural adj of the ear or the sense of hearing.–**aurally** adv.

aureole, aureola n (art) a halo, radiance, or luminous cloud encircling the figures of Christ, the virgin and the saints in sacred pictures; anything resembling an aureole.

auric adj of or pertaining to gold.

auricle n the external part of the ear; either of the two upper chambers of the heart.

aurora n (pl **auroras, aurorae**) either of the luminous bands seen in the night sky in the polar regions.–also **northern lights**.

aurora Australis n the aurora seen at the South Pole.

aurora borealis n the aurora seen at the North Pole.

auspice n (pl **auspices**) an omen; (pl) sponsorship; patronage.

auspicious adj showing promise, favorable.–**auspiciously** adv.

Aussie n (sl) an Australian.

austere adj stern, forbidding in attitude or appearance; abstemious; severely simple, plain.–**austerely** adv.–**austereness** n.

austerity n (pl **austerities**) being austere; economic privation.

Austral adj southern; (with cap) Australian.

Australasian adj of or pertaining to Australasia (Australia, New Zealand and adjacent islands). * n a native or inhabitant of Australasia.

Australian adj of or pertaining to Australia. * n a native or inhabitant of Australia.

autarchy n (pl **autarchies**) absolute or autocratic rule or sovereignty; a country governed in such a way; autarky.–**autarchic, autarchical** adj.

authentic adj genuine, conforming to truth or reality; trustworthy, reliable.–**authentically** adv.–**authenticity** n.

authenticate vt to demonstrate the authenticity of; to make valid; to verify.–**authentication** n.–**authenticator** n.

author n a person who brings something into existence; the writer of a book, article, etc. * vt to be the author of.–**authoress** nf.–**authorial** adj.

authoritarian adj favoring strict obedience; dictatorial. * n a person advocating authoritarian principles.–**authoritarianism** n.

authoritative adj commanding or possessing authority; accepted as true; official.–**authoritatively** adv.

authority n (pl **authorities**) the power or right to command; (pl) officials with this power; influence resulting from knowledge, prestige, etc; a person, writing, etc cited to support an opinion; an expert.

authorize vt to give authority to, to empower; to give official approval to, sanction.–**authorization** n.

authorship n the writing profession; origin (of book).

autism n (psychiatry) a mental state, usu of children, marked by disregard of external reality–**autistic** adj.

auto n (pl **autos**) (inf) an automobile.

autobiography n (pl **autobiographies**) the biography of a person written by himself or herself.–**autobiographer** n.–**autobiographical** adj.

autoclave n a strong container used for chemical reactions at high temperatures and pressures; a device for sterilizing implements using steam at high pressure.

autocracy n (pl **autocracies**) government by one person with absolute power.

autocrat n an absolute ruler; any domineering person.–**autocratic** adj.–**autocratically** adv.

Autocue n (trademark) a prompting device used in TV, etc, which provides speakers with a script that remains invisible to the audience.–also **Teleprompter**.

autogenesis, autogeny n spontaneous generation.–**autogenetic** adj.

autogenous adj self-generated; produced independently.

autograph n a person's signature. * vt to write one's signature in or on.–**autographic** adj.–**autographically** adv.

automat n a restaurant equipped with slot machines for dispensing food and drink; a vending machine.

automate vt to control by automation; to convert to automatic operation.

automated telling machine n a device that provides cash and other banking services automatically when activated by a plastic card issued to customers; a cash dispenser.–also **autoteller**.

automatic adj involuntary or reflexive; self-regulating; acting by itself. * n an automatic pistol or rifle.–**automatically** adv.

automatic pilot n a device that can maintain an aircraft or ship on a previously set course.–also **autopilot**.

automatic transmission n a system in a motor vehicle for changing gears automatically.

automation n the use of automatic methods, machinery, etc in industry.

automaton n (pl **automatons, automata**) any automatic device, esp a robot; a human being who acts like a robot.

automobile n a usu four-wheeled vehicle powered by an internal combustion engine.–also **motor car**.

automotive adj relating to motor vehicles.

autonomy n (pl **autonomies**) freedom of self-determination; independence, self-government.–**autonomous** adj.

autopilot n automatic pilot.

autopsy n (pl **autopsies**) a post-mortem examination to determine the cause of death.

autosuggestion n (psychoanal) self-applied suggestion.–**autosuggestive** adj.

autoteller see **automated telling machine**.

autumn n the season between summer and winter.–also **fall**.

autumnal adj belonging or peculiar to autumn or fall; produced or gathered in autumn; pertaining to the period of life when middle age is past. * n a plant that flowers in autumn.

auxiliary adj providing help, subsidiary; supplementary. * n (pl **auxiliaries**) a helper; (gram) a verb that helps form tenses, moods, voices, etc of other verbs, as have, be, may, shall, etc.

AV abbr = audiovisual.

avail vti to be of use or advantage to. * n benefit, use or help.

available adj ready for use; obtainable, accessible.–**availability** n.–**availably** adv.

avalanche n a mass of snow, ice, and rock tumbling down a mountainside; a sudden overwhelming accumulation or influx.

avant-garde n (arts) those ideas and practices regarded as in advance of those generally accepted. * adj pertaining to such ideas and practices and their creators.–**avant-gardism** n.

avarice *n* greed for wealth.–**avaricious** *adj*.–**avariciously** *adv*.

Ave, ave *abbr* = avenue.

avenge *vt* to get revenge for.–**avenger** *n*.

avenue *n* a street, drive, etc, esp when broad; means of access; the way to an objective.

aver *vt* (**averring, averred**) to state as true; to assert.–**averment** *n*.

average *n* the result of dividing the sum of two or more quantities by the number of quantities; the usual kind, amount, quality, etc. * *vt* to calculate the average of; to achieve an average number of.

averse *adj* unwilling; opposed (to).

aversion *n* antipathy; hatred; something arousing hatred or repugnance.

avert *vt* to turn away or aside from; to prevent, avoid.–**avertible, avertable** *adj*.

aviary *n* (*pl* **aviaries**) a building or large cage for keeping birds.

aviation *n* the art or science of flying aircraft.

aviator *n* a pilot, esp in the early history of flying.

avid *adj* eager, greedy.–**avidly** *adv*.–**avidity** *n*.

avocado *n* (*pl* **avocados**) a thick-skinned, pear-shaped fruit with yellow buttery flesh.

avoid *vt* to keep clear of, shun; to refrain from.–**avoider** *n*.

avoidable *adj* able to be avoided.

avoidance *n* the act of annulling or making void; the act of shunning; the state of being vacant.

avoirdupois *n* the system of weights based on the pound of 16 ounces; (*inf*) excess weight.

avow *vt* to declare confidently; to acknowledge.–**avowed** *adj*.–**avowedly** *adv*.–**avower** *n*.

avowal *n* an open declaration; a frank acknowledgment; a confession.

avuncular *adj* like an uncle.

await *vti* to wait for; to be in store for.

awake *vb* (**awaking, awoke** *or* **awaked, pp awoken** *or* **awaked**) *vi* to wake; to become aware. * *vt* to rouse from sleep; to rouse from inaction. * *adj* roused from sleep, not asleep; active; aware.

awaken *vti* to awake.

awakening *n* the act of rousing from sleep; a revival of religion, or activity of a particular religious sect. * *adj* rousing; exciting; alarming.

award *vt* to give, as by a legal decision; to give (a prize, etc); to grant. * *n* a decision, as by a judge; a prize.

aware *adj* realizing, having knowledge; conscious; fully conversant with and sympathetic towards (*ecologically aware*).–**awareness** *n*.

awash *adj* filled or overflowing with water.

away *adv* from a place; in another place or direction; off, aside; far. * *adj* absent; at a distance.

awe *n* a mixed feeling of fear, wonder and dread. * *vt* to fill with awe.

awesome *adj* inspiring awe; (*inf*) marvelous, terrific.

awestricken, awestruck *adj* struck with awe.

awful *adj* very bad; unpleasant. * *adv* (*inf*) very.–**awfulness** *n*.

awfully *adv* in an awful manner; excessively; (*inf*) very.

awhile *adv* for a short time.

awkward *adj* lacking dexterity, clumsy; graceless; embarrassing; embarrassed; inconvenient; deliberately obstructive or difficult to deal with.–**awkwardly** *adv*.–**awkwardness** *n*.

awl *n* a small pointed tool for boring or piercing, used by shoemakers, etc.

awning *n* a structure, as of canvas, extended above or in front of a window, door, etc to provide shelter against the sun or rain.

awoke *see* **awake**.

AWOL *abbr* = absent without leave.

awry *adv* twisted to one side. * *adj* contrary to expectations, wrong.

ax, axe *n* (*pl* **axes**) a tool with a long handle and bladed head for chopping wood, etc. * *vt* to trim, split, etc with an ax.

axiom *n* a widely held or accepted truth or principle.

axiomatic *adj* pertaining to, or of the nature of, an axiom.–**axiomatically** *adv*.

axis *n* (*pl* **axes**) a real or imaginary straight line about which a body rotates; the centre line of a symmetrical figure; a reference line of a coordinate system.–**axial** *adj*.

axle *n* a rod on or with which a wheel turns; a bar connecting two opposite wheels, as of a car.

ayatollah *n* a Shiite Muslim leader; a title of respect.

aye, ay *adv, interj* yes; even so; indeed. * *n* (*pl* **ayes**) an affirmative answer or vote in a parliamentary division; the members so voting.

AZ *abbr* = Arizona.

azalea *n* a flowering shrub-like plant.

azure *adj* sky-blue.

B

B *abbr* = boron.

b *abbr* = born; billion.

BA *abbr* = Bachelor of Arts.

Ba *abbr* = barium.

babble *vi* to make sounds like a baby; to talk incoherently, endlessly or senselessly; to give away secrets; to murmur, as a brook. * *n* incoherent talk; chatter; a murmuring sound.–**babbler** *n*.

babe *n* a baby; a naive person; (*sl*) a girl or young woman.

baboon *n* a large, short-tailed monkey.

baby *n* (*pl* **babies**) a newborn child or infant; a very young animal; a personal project. * *vt* (**babying, babied**) to pamper.–*also adj*.–**babyish** *adj*.

baby boom *n* a sharp rise in the birth rate.

baby-boomer *n* a person born in the period immediately after World War II when the birth rate increased sharply (*baby boom*).

baby carriage *n* a small four-wheeled carriage, usually with a folding top for pushing a baby around in.

baby-sit *vti* (**baby-sitting, baby-sat**) to look after a baby or child while the parents are out.–**baby-sitter** *n*.

bacchanalia *npl* drunken revels.

bachelor *n* an unmarried man; a person who holds a degree from a college or university.–**bachelorhood** *n*.

bacillus *n* (*pl* **bacilli**) any of a genus of rod-shaped bacteria; (*loosely*) bacteria in general.

back *n* the rear surface of the human body from neck to hip; the corresponding part in animals; a part that supports or fits or makes firm the back of anything; the part farthest from the front; (*sport*) a player or position behind the front line. * *adj* at the rear; (*streets, etc*) remote or inferior; (*pay, etc*) of or for the past; backward. * *adv* at or towards the rear; to or towards a former condition, time, etc; in return or requital; in reserve or concealment. * *vti* to move or go backwards; to support; to bet on; to provide or be a back for; to supply a musical backing for a singer; (*with* **down**) to withdraw from a position or claim; (*with* **off**) to move back (or away, etc); (*with* **out**) to withdraw from an enterprise; to evade keeping a promise, etc; (*with* **up**) to support; to move backwards; to accumulate because of restricted movement; (*comput*) to make a copy (of a data file, etc) for safekeeping.

backbite *vt* (**backbiting, backbit**, *pp* **backbitten** *or* **backbit**) to talk spitefully or ill of behind a person's back.–**backbiter** *n*.–**backbiting** *n*.

backbone n the spinal column; main support; strength, courage.

backbreaking adj arduous; physically exhausting.

backdate vt to declare valid from some previous date.

backdoor adj indirect, concealed, devious.

backdrop n a curtain, often scenic, at the back of a stage; background.

backer n a patron; one who bets on a contestant.

backfire vi (cars) to ignite prematurely causing a loud bang from the exhaust; to have the opposite effect from that intended, usu with unfortunate consequences.–also n.

backgammon n a board game played by two people with pieces moved according to throws of the dice.

background n the distant part of a scene or picture; an inconspicuous position; social class, education, experience; circumstances leading up to an event.

backhand n (tennis, etc) a stroke played with the hand turned outwards.

backhanded adj backhand; (compliment) indirect, ambiguous.–also adv.–**backhandedly** adv.

backhander n a backhanded stroke; (inf) a backhanded remark; (sl) a bribe.

backing n support; supporters; a lining to support or strengthen the back of something; musical accompaniment to a (esp pop) singer.

backlash n a violent and adverse reaction; a recoil in machinery.

backlist n books published in past years that are still in print.

backlog n an accumulation of work, etc still to be done.

back number n a former issue (of a magazine, etc); an out-of-date person.

backpack n a rucksack; an equipment pack carried on the back of an astronaut, etc. * vi to travel, hike, etc wearing a backpack.

back-pedal vi (back-pedaling, back-pedaled or back-pedalling, back-pedalled) to work the pedals of a bicycle backwards; to modify or withdraw one's original argument or action.

backslide vi (backsliding, backslid, pp backslid or backslidden) to return to one's (bad) old ways.–**backslider** n.

backspin n (sport) a backward spin in a ball to slow it down.

backstage adv behind the stage of a theater in areas hidden from the audience; (inf) away from public view.–also adj.

backstroke n (swimming) a stroke using backward circular sweeps of the arms whilst lying face upwards.

back-to-back adj facing in opposite directions, often with the backs touching.

backtrack vi to return along the same path; to reverse or recant one's opinion, action, etc.

backup n an alternate or auxiliary; support, reinforcement; (comput) a copy of a data file, etc.

backward adj turned toward the rear or opposite way; shy; slow or retarded. * adv backwards.–**backwardness** n.

backwards adv towards the back; with the back foremost; in a way opposite the usual; into a less good or favourable state or condition; into the past.

backwash n water receding from the action of an oar, propeller, etc; the consequences of an event.

backwoods npl uncleared forest land; an isolated, thinly populated area.–**backwoodsman** n (pl **backwoodsmen**).

backyard n a yard at the back of a house.

bacon n salted and smoked meat from the back or sides of a pig; **to bring home the bacon** to succeed; to help materially; **to save one's bacon** to have a narrow escape.

bacteria npl (sing **bacterium**) microscopic unicellular organisms usu causing disease.–**bacterial** adj.

bacteriology n the scientific study of bacteria.–**bacteriological** adj.–**bacteriologist** n.

bacterium see **bacteria**.

bad[1] adj (**worse, worst**) not good; not as it should be; inadequate or unfit; rotten or spoiled; incorrect or faulty; wicked; immoral; mischievous; harmful; ill; sorry, distressed.–**badness** n.

bad[2] see **bid**.

bad blood n enmity, hostility.

bad debt n a debt that is not recoverable.

bad hair day n phr term used to describe a day when nothing seems to go as planned.

baddie, baddy n (pl **baddies**) (inf) a villain.

bade see **bid**.

badge n an emblem, symbol or distinguishing mark.

badger n a hibernating, burrowing black and white mammal related to the weasel. * vt to pester or annoy persistently.

badly adv (**worse, worst**) poorly; inadequately; unsuccessfully; severely; (inf) very much.

badminton n a court game for two or four players played with light rackets and a shuttlecock volleyed over a net.

baffle vt to bewilder or perplex; to frustrate; to make ineffectual. * n a plate or device used to restrict the flow of sound, light or fluid.–**bafflement** n.–**baffling** adj.

bag n a usu flexible container of paper, plastic, etc that can be closed at the top; a satchel, suitcase, etc; a handbag; a purse; game taken in hunting; a bag-like shape or part; (inf: in pl) plenty (of). * vti (**bagging, bagged**) to place in a bag; to kill in hunting; (inf) to get; to make a claim on; to hang loosely.

bagatelle n something of little value; a piece of light music usu for piano; a board game in which balls struck with a cue or by a spring are aimed at holes or pinned spaces.

bagel n a ring-shaped bread roll, hard and glazed on the outside, soft in the centre.

baggage n suitcases; luggage; **bag and baggage** with one's entire possessions; entirely.

baggy adj (**baggier, baggiest**) hanging loosely in folds.–**baggily** adv.–**bagginess** n.

bagpipe n (often pl) a musical instrument consisting of an air-filled bag fitted with pipes.

bail[1] n money lodged as security that a prisoner, if released, will return to court to stand trial; such a release; the person pledging such money. * vt to free a person by providing bail; (with **out**) to help out of financial or other difficulty; (government, bank, etc) to assist a floundering business.–**bailable** adj.

bail[2] vti (usu with **out**) to scoop out (water) from (a boat).

bait n food attached to a hook to entice fish or make them bite; any lure or enticement. * vt to put food on a hook to lure; to set dogs upon (a badger, etc); to persecute, worry or tease, esp by verbal attacks; to lure, to tempt; to entice.

baize n a coarse, green woolen fabric used to cover snooker tables.

bake vt (pottery) to dry and harden by heating in the sun or by fire; (food) to cook by dry heat in an oven. * vi to do a baker's work; to dry and harden in heat; (inf) to be very hot. * n all the food baked at one time or baking; a party or picnic featuring one baked item, eg a clambake.

baked beans npl cooked haricot beans canned in tomato sauce.

baker n a person who bakes and sells bread, cakes, etc.

bakery n (pl **bakeries**) a room or building for baking; a shop that sells bread, cakes, etc; baked goods.

baking powder n a leavening agent containing sodium bicarbonate and an acid-forming substance.

baking soda n sodium bicarbonate.

balaclava (helmet) n a woolen hood that covers the ears and neck.

balalaika n a Russian, three-stringed guitar with a triangular body.

balance n a device for weighing, consisting of two dishes or pans hanging from a pivoted horizontal beam; equilibrium; mental stability; the power to influence or control; a remainder.–**in the balance** a state of uncertainty.–**on balance** having considered all aspects or factors. * vt to weigh; to compare; to equalize the debit and credit sides of an account. * vi to be equal in power or weight, etc; to have the debits and credits equal.–**balanceable** adj.–**balancer** n.

balance of payments n the difference between a country's total receipts from abroad and total payments abroad over a given period.

balance sheet n a statement of assets and liabilities.

balcony n (pl **balconies**) a projecting platform from an upper story enclosed by a railing; an upper floor of seats in a theater, etc, often projecting over the main floor.–**balconied** adj.

bald adj lacking a natural or usual covering, as of hair, vegetation, or nap; (tire) having little or no tread; (truth) plain or blunt; bare, unadorned.–**baldly** adv.–**baldness** n.

balderdash n nonsense.

bale n a large bundle of goods, as raw cotton, compressed and bound. * vt (hay etc) to make into bales. * vi (with out) to parachute from an aircraft, usu in an emergency.

baleful adj evil; harmful; deadly; ominous.–**balefully** adv.–**balefulness** n.

balk vt to obstruct or foil. * vi to stop and refuse to move and act.–also **baulk**.

ball¹ n a spherical or nearly spherical body or mass; a round object for use in tennis, football, etc; a throw or pitch of a ball; a missile for a cannon, rifle, etc. * vti to form into a ball.

ball² n a formal social dance; (inf) a good time.–**ballroom** n.–**ballroom dancing** n.

ballad n a narrative song or poem; a slow, sentimental, esp pop, song.–**balladeer** n.–**balladry** n.

ballast n heavy material carried in a ship or vehicle to stabilize it when it is not carrying cargo; crushed rock or gravel, etc used in railway tracks.

ball bearing n a device for lessening friction by having a rotating part resting on small steel balls; one of these balls.

ballcock n a device that uses a floating ball to regulate the flow of water in a cistern, tank, etc.

ballerina n a female ballet dancer.

ballet n a theatrical representation of a story, set to music and performed by dancers; the troupe of dancers.

ballistic adj relating to the flight of projectiles.

ballistic missile n a missile whose trajectory is initially guided then ballistic.

ballistics n (used as sing) the scientific study of projectiles and firearms.

balloon n a large airtight envelope that rises up when filled with hot air or light gases, often fitted with a basket or gondola for carrying passengers; a small inflatable rubber pouch used as a toy or for decoration. * vti to inflate; to swell, expand; to travel in a balloon.–**balloonist** n.

ballot n a paper used in voting; the process of voting; the number of votes cast; the candidates offering themselves for election. * vi (**balloting, balloted**) to vote.–**balloter** n.

ballpoint pen n a pen with a tiny ball, which rotates against an inking cartridge, as its writing tip.

ballyhoo n vulgar, noisy publicity or advertisement.

balm n a fragrant ointment used in healing and soothing; anything comforting and soothing.

balmy adj (**balmier, balmiest**) having a pleasant fragrance; soothing; (weather) mild, warm.

baloney n (inf) foolish talk; nonsense.–also **boloney**.

balsa n lightweight wood from a tropical American tree.

balsam n a fragrant, resinous substance; the tree yielding it.–**balsamic** adj.

bamboo n (pl **bamboos**) any of various, often tropical, woody grasses, used for furniture.

bamboozle vt (inf) to deceive; to mystify.–**bamboozlement** n.–**bamboozler** n.

ban n a condemnation, an official prohibition. * vt (**banning, banned**) to prohibit, esp officially; to forbid.

banal adj trite, commonplace.–**banally** adv.

banality n (pl **banalities**) anything trite or trivial; a commonplace remark, etc.

banana n a herbaceous plant bearing its fruit in compact, hanging bunches.

band¹ n a strip of material used for binding; a stripe; (radio) a range of wavelengths.

band² n a group of people with a common purpose; a group of musicians playing together, an orchestra. * vti to associate together for a particular purpose.

bandage n a strip of cloth for binding wounds and fractures. * vt to bind a wound.

bandanna, bandana n a large colored handkerchief.

bandit n (pl **bandits, banditti**) a robber.–**banditry** n.

bandstand n a platform for a musical band.

bandwagon n a wagon for carrying a band in a parade; a movement, idea, etc that is (thought to be) heading for success.

bandwidth n the range of frequencies within a given waveband for radio or other types of transmission.

bandy¹ vt (**bandying, bandied**) to pass to and fro; (often with about) (rumors, etc) to spread freely; to exchange words, esp angrily.

bandy² adj (**bandier, bandiest**) having legs curved outwards at the knee.

bane n a person causing distress or misery; something bringing destruction or death; a poison.–**baneful** adj.

bang¹ n a hard blow; a sudden loud sound. * vt to hit or knock with a loud noise; (door) to slam. * vi to make a loud noise; to hit noisily or sharply. * adv with a bang, abruptly; successfully; (inf) precisely.

bang² n (pl) hair cut straight across the forehead to form a fringe; false hair so worn. * vt to cut the hair across the forehead to form a fringe.

bangle n a bracelet worn on the arm or ankle.

banian see **banyan**.

banish vt to exile from a place; to drive away; to get rid of.–**banishment** n.

banister n the railing or supporting balusters in a staircase.–also **bannister**.

banjo n (pl **banjos, banjoes**) a stringed musical instrument with a drum-like body and a long fretted neck.–**banjoist** n.

bank¹ n a mound or pile; the sloping side of a river; elevated ground in a lake or the sea; a row or series of objects, as of dials, switches. * vti to form into a mound; to cover (a fire) with fuel so that it burns more slowly; (aircraft) to curve or tilt sideways.

bank² n an institution that offers various financial services, such as the safekeeping, lending and exchanging of money; the money held by the banker or dealer in a card game; any supply or store for the future, such as a blood bank. * vti (checks, cash, etc) to deposit in a bank; to work as a banker.–**banking** n, adj.

banker n a person who runs a bank; the keeper of the bank at a gaming table.

bankrupt n a person, etc legally declared unable to pay his debts; one who becomes insolvent. * adj judged to be insolvent; financially ruined; devoid of resources, ideas, etc. * vt to make bankrupt.–**bankruptcy** n.

banner n a flag or ensign; a headline running across a newspaper page; a strip of cloth bearing a slogan or emblem carried between poles in a parade.

bannister see **banister**.

banns npl public declaration of intention, esp in church, to marry.

banquet n a feast; an elaborate and sometimes formal dinner in honor of a person or occasion. * vt (**banqueting, banqueted**) to hold a banquet.–**banqueter** n.

banshee n (folklore) a female fairy whose wail portends a death in the family.

bantam n a dwarf breed of domestic fowl; a small, aggressive person.

banter vt to tease good-humouredly.–**banterer** n.

banyan n an Indian fig tree with vast, rooting branches.–also **banian**.

baptism n the sprinkling of water on the forehead, or complete immersion in water, as a rite of admitting a person to a Christian church; any initiating experience.–**baptismal** adj.–**baptismally** adv.

baptize vt to christen, to name.–**baptizer** n.

bar[1] n a straight length of wood or metal; a counter where alcoholic drinks or other refreshments are served; a place with such a counter; an oblong piece, as of soap; anything that obstructs or hinders; a band or strip; a strip or bank of sand or mud near and in line with the shore or across a river or harbor; (mil) a badge signifying a second award; (with cap) barristers or lawyers collectively; the legal profession; (mus) a vertical line dividing a staff into measures; (mus) a measure. * vt (**barring, barred**) to secure or fasten as with a bar; to exclude or prevent; to oppose. * prep except for.

bar[2] n a unit of atmospheric pressure.

barb n the sharp backward point of a fish-hook, etc; one of the sharp parts combined to form barbed wire; a pointed or critical remark; a beard-like growth. * vt to provide with a barb.– **barbed** adj.

barbarian n an uncivilized, primitive person; a cruel vicious person.–also adj.

barbaric adj of or suitable for barbarians.–**barbarically** adv.

barbarism n a barbarous act; the state of being a barbarian; an expression or word that is tasteless or not standard; an object or act that offends.

barbarity n (pl **barbarities**) savage cruelty; a vicious act.

barbecue n a metal frame for grilling food over an open fire; an open-air party where barbecued food is served. * vt (**barbecuing, barbecued**) to cook on a barbecue.

barb wire n wire with barbs at close intervals.–also **barbwire**.

barber n a person who cuts hair and shaves beards.

barbiturate n a sedative drug.

barbwire see **barbed wire**.

bar code n a striped pattern on a package, book cover, etc, containing information about the price that can be read by a computer for stock control, etc.

bard n a poet.–**bardic** adj.

bare adj without covering; unclothed, naked; simple, unadorned; mere; without furnishings. * vt to uncover; to reveal.–**bareness** n.

bareback adj on a horse with no saddle.–also adv.

barefaced adj with the face shaven or uncovered; shameless.– **barefacedly** adv.

barely adv openly; merely; scarcely.

bargain n an agreement laying down the conditions of a transaction; something sold at a price favorable to the buyer; **into the bargain** as well; in addition. * vt to make a bargain, to haggle; (with **for**) to expect or hope for.

barge n a flat-bottomed vessel, used to transport freight along rivers and canals; a large boat for excursions or pleasure trips. * vi to lurch clumsily; (with **in**) to interrupt (a conversation) rudely; (with **into**) to enter abruptly.

baritone n the adult male voice ranging between bass and tenor; a singer with such a voice.–also adj.

barium n (chem) a white metallic element.

bark[1] n the harsh or abrupt cry of a dog, wolf, etc; a similar sound, such as one made by a person. * vi to make a loud cry like a dog; to speak or shout sharply or angrily.

bark[2] n the outside covering of a tree trunk. * vt to remove the bark from; to scrape; to skin (the knees, etc).

bark[3] see **barque**.

barker n one who or that which barks; a person who shouts his wares, etc, usu at a fairground.

barley n a grain used in making beer and whisky, and for food.

bar mitzvah n (Judaism) the ceremony marking the thirteenth birthday of a boy, who then assumes full religious obligations; the boy himself.

barn n a farm building used for storing grain, hay, etc, and sheltering animals.

barnacle n a marine crustacean that attaches itself to rocks and ship bottoms.

barn owl n any of a genus of owl with brownish plumage above and white plumage below.

barnstorm vi to tour (rural areas) as an actor, or making speeches in a political campaign, or demonstrating flying stunts.–**barnstormer** n.

barometer n an instrument for measuring atmospheric pressure and imminent changes in the weather; anything that marks change.–**barometric** adj.–**barometrically** adv.

baron n a member of a rank of nobility, the lowest in the British peerage; a powerful businessman.–**baroness** nf.

baroque adj extravagantly ornamented, esp in architecture and decorative art.

barque n a three-masted vessel with the foremast and main mast square-rigged and the mizzen fore-and-aft.–also **bark**.

barrack vti to shout or protest at.–**barracker** n.

barracks n (used as sing) a building for housing soldiers.

barracuda n (pl **barracuda, barracudas**) a fierce fish with edible flesh.

barrage n a man-made dam across a river; heavy artillery fire; (of protests, questions, etc) continuous and heavy delivery.

barre n a horizontal rail used for ballet practice.

barred see **bar**[1].

barrel n a cylindrical container, usu wooden, with bulging sides held together with hoops; the amount held by a barrel; a tubular structure, as in a gun. * vt (**barreling, barreled** or **barrelling, barrelled**) to put into barrels.

barren adj infertile; incapable of producing offspring; unable to bear crops; unprofitable; (with **of**) lacking in.

barricade n a barrier or blockade used in defence to block a street; an obstruction. * vt to block with a barricade.

barrier n anything that bars passage, prevents access, controls crowds, etc, such as a fence; obstruction; hindrance.

barring prep excepting; leaving out of account.

barrister n a qualified lawyer who has been called to the bar in England.

barrow n a wheelbarrow or hand-cart used for carrying loads.

barter vt to trade commodities or services without exchanging money. * vi to haggle or bargain. * n trade by the exchanging of commodities.–**barterer** n.

basalt n hard, compact, dark-colored igneous rock.–**basaltic** adj.

base[1] n the bottom part of anything; the support or foundation; the fundamental principle; the center of operations (eg military); (baseball) one of the four corners of the diamond. * vt to use as a basis; to found (on); (with **at, in**) to place, to station.– **basal** adj.

base[2] adj low in morality or honor; worthless; menial.–**basely** adv.–**baseness** n.

baseball n the US national game, involving two teams that score runs by hitting a ball and running round four bases arranged in a diamond shape on the playing area.

baseline n the line at each end of a games court marking the limit of play; (baseball) the line between any two consecutive bases; a measured line in a survey area from which triangulations are calculated.

basement n the part of a building that is partly or wholly below ground level.

bash vt (inf) to hit hard; to dent by striking. * n (inf) a heavy blow; (inf) a try or attempt; (sl) a party.

bashful adj easily embarrassed, shy.–**bashfully** adv.–**bashfulness** n.

BASIC n (comput) a simple programming language: Beginners' All-purpose Symbolic Instruction Code.

basic adj fundamental; simple. * n (often pl) a basic principle, factor, etc; the rudiments.–**basically** adv.

basil n a plant with aromatic leaves used for seasoning food.

basilica n a church with a broad nave, side aisles, and an apse.– **basilican** adj.

basin n a wide shallow container for liquid; its contents; any large hollow, often with water in it; a tract of land drained by a river.

basis n (pl **bases**) a base or foundation; a principal constituent; a fundamental principle or theory.

bask vi to lie in sunshine or warmth; to enjoy someone's approval.

basket n a container made of interwoven cane, wood strips, etc; the hoop through which basketball players throw the ball to score.

basketball n a game in which two teams compete to score by throwing the ball through an elevated net basket or hoop; this ball.

basque n a woman's jacket with a short skirt.

bass[1] n (mus) the range of the lowest male voice; a singer or instrument with this range. * adj of, for or in the range of a bass.

bass[2] n (pl **bass**) any of numerous freshwater food and game fishes.

bass clef n (mus) the character C placed at the beginning of the bass staff.

basset, basset hound n a smooth-haired hound with short legs.

bassoon n an orchestral, deep-toned woodwind instrument.– **bassoonist** n.

bastard n a person born of unmarried parents. * adj illegitimate (by birth); false; not genuine.–**bastardy** n.

baste[1] vt to drip fat over (roasting meat, etc).

baste[2] vt to sew with long loose stitches as a temporary seam.

bastion n a tower at the corner of a fortification; any strong defence; one who strongly upholds or supports a principle, etc.–**bastioned** adj.

bat[1] n a wooden club used in baseball, cricket, etc; a batsman; a paddle used in table tennis. * vb (**batting, batted**) vt to hit as with a bat. * vi to take one's turn at bat.

bat[2] n a nocturnal, mouse-like flying mammal with forelimbs modified to form wings.

bat[3] vt (**batting, batted**) (one's eyelids) to wink or flutter.

batch n the quantity of bread, etc produced at one time; one set, group, etc; an amount of work for processing by a computer in a single run.

bate vt to lessen or reduce; to deduct.

bath n water for washing the body; a bathing; a bathtub; (pl) a building with baths for public use; a municipal swimming pool.

bathe vt to dampen with any liquid. * vi to take a bath; to go swimming; to become immersed.–**bather** n.

bathos n anticlimax; descent from the elevated to the ordinary in speech or writing.

bathrobe n a loose-fitting garment of absorbent fabric for use after bathing or as a dressing gown.

bathroom n a room with a bath or shower and usually a lavatory and washbasin.–also **lavatory**.

bathtub n a usu fixed tub for bathing.

batik n a method of printing colored designs on fabric; fabric produced by this method.

baton n a staff serving as a symbol of office; a thin stick used by the conductor of an orchestra to beat time; a hollow cylinder carried by each member of a relay team in succession; a policeman's truncheon.

battalion n an army unit consisting of three or more companies; a large group.

batten n a strip of wood or metal; a strip of wood put over a seam between boards. * vt to fasten or supply with battens.

batter vt to beat with repeated blows; to wear out with heavy use; to criticize strongly and at length. * vi to strike heavily and repeatedly. * n a mixture of flour, egg, and milk or water used in cooking.–**batterer** n.

battery n (pl **batteries**) a set of heavy guns; a small unit of artillery; an electric cell that supplies current; an unlawful beating; an arrangement of hens' cages designed to increase egg laying.

battle n a combat or fight between two opposing individuals or armies; a contest; any struggle towards a goal. * vti to fight; to struggle.–**battler** n.

battle-ax, battle-axe n (pl **battle-axes**) an old-fashioned two-headed ax; (inf) a domineering woman.

battle cry n a war cry; a slogan used to rally supporters of a political campaign, etc.

battlefield n the land on which a battle is fought.

battlement n a parapet or wall with indentations, from which to shoot.

batty adj (**battier, battiest**) (inf) crazy; eccentric.–**battiness** n.

bauble n a showy toy; a shining ball hung on a Christmas tree as a decoration; a worthless trifle or ornament.

baud n (comput) a unit used in measuring the speed of electronic data transmissions.

baulk see **balk**.

bauxite n aluminum ore.

bawdy adj (**bawdier, bawdiest**) humorously indecent; obscene, lewd.–**bawdily** adv.–**bawdiness** n.

bawl vti to shout; to weep loudly. * n a loud shout; a noisy weeping.–**bawler** n.–**bawling** n.

bay[1] n a type of laurel tree.

bay[2] n a wide inlet of a sea or lake; an inward bend of a shore.

bay[3] n an alcove or recess in a wall; a compartment used for a special purpose.

bay[4] vti to bark (at). * n the cry of a hound or a pursuing pack.–**at bay** the position of one forced to turn and fight.

bay[5] adj reddish brown. * n a horse of this color.

bayonet n a blade for stabbing attached to the muzzle of a rifle. * vt (**bayoneting, bayoneted** or **bayonetting, bayonetted**) to kill or stab with a bayonet.

bayou n in the southern US, the marshy inlet or outlet of a lake or river.

bazaar n a marketplace; a street full of small shops; a benefit sale for a church, etc.

bazooka n a portable anti-tank weapon that fires rockets from a long tube.

BC abbr = Before Christ; British Columbia.

BD abbr = Bachelor of Divinity.

be vi (pr t **am, are, is**, pt **was, were**, pp **been**) to exist; to live; to take place.

beach n a flat, sandy shore of the sea. * vi to bring (a boat) up on the beach from the sea.

beachcomber n a person who hangs about the shore on the lookout for wreckage or plunder; a long curling wave rolling in from the ocean.–**beachcombing** n.

beacon n a light, esp on a high place, tower, etc, for warning or guiding. * vi to guide, to act as a beacon.

bead n a small ball pierced for stringing; (pl) a string of beads; (pl) a rosary; a bubble or droplet of liquid; the sight of a rifle.–**beaded** adj.

beading n molding or edging in the form of a series of beads; a wooden strip, rounded on one side, used for trimming.–also **beadwork**.

beady adj (**beadier, beadiest**) (eyes) small, round and bright, sometimes calculating or unfriendly.–**beadily** adv.–**beadiness** n.

beagle n a small hound with short legs and drooping ears.

beak n a bird's bill; any projecting part; the nose.–**beaked** adj.

beaker n a large drinking cup, or the amount it holds; a cylindrical vessel with a pouring lip used by chemists and pharmacists.

beam n a long straight piece of timber or metal; the crossbar of a balance; a ship's breadth at its widest point; a slender shaft of light, etc; a radiant look, smile, etc; a steady radio or radar signal for guiding aircraft or ships. * vt (light, etc) to send out; to smile with great pleasure.

bean n a plant bearing kidney-shaped seeds; a seed or pod of such a plant; any bean-like seed.

bean sprout n the shoot of the mung bean used in Chinese cooking.

bear[1] vb (**bearing, bore**, pp **borne**) vt to carry; to endure; to support, to sustain; to conduct (oneself); to produce or bring forth; (with **out**) to show to be true, confirm. * vi to be productive; (with **down**) to press or weigh down; to overwhelm; (with **on** or **upon**) to have reference to, be relevant to; (with **out**) to confirm the truth of; (with **up**) to endure with courage; (with **with**) to listen to patiently.

bear[2] n (pl **bears, bear**) a large mammal with coarse black, brown or white fur, short legs, strong claws and feeding mainly on fruit and insects; a gruff or ill-mannered person; a teddy bear; a speculator who sells stock in anticipation of a fall in price so that he may buy them back at a lower price.

bearable adj endurable.–**bearably** adv.

beard n hair covering a man's chin; similar bristles on an animal or plant. * vt to defy, oppose openly.–**bearded** adj.

bearing n demeanor; conduct; a compass direction; (with **on, upon**) relevance; a machine part on which another part slides, revolves, etc; (usu pl) one's position, orientation.

beast n a large, wild, four-footed animal; a brutal, vicious person; (inf) something difficult, an annoyance.–**beastly** adj.

beat vb (**beating, beaten**, pp **beat**) vt to strike, dash or pound repeatedly; to flog; to overcome or counteract; to win against, to arrive first; to find too difficult for; (mus) to mark (time) with a baton, etc; (eggs, etc) to mix by stirring vigorously; (esp wings) to move up and down; (a path, way, etc) to form by repeated trampling; (sl) to baffle; (with **up**) (inf) to cause grievous bodily harm to by severe and repeated blows and kicks. * vi to hit, pound, etc repeatedly; to throb; (naut) to sail against the wind. * n a recurrent stroke, pulsation, as in a heartbeat or clock ticking; rhythm in music or poetry; the area patrolled by a police officer.– **beatable** adj.

beaten adj defeated; (metal) shaped or formed by pounding; (a path) formed by constant trampling.

beatitude n blessedness; heavenly happiness; (with cap) (Bible) one of Christ's eight sayings in the Sermon on the Mount (Matthew 5).

beau n (pl **beaus, beaux**) a woman's suitor or sweetheart.

Beaufort scale n an international system of indicating wind strength, from 0 (calm) to 12 (hurricane).

beautician n one who works in a beauty salon offering cosmetic treatments.

beautify vti (**beautifying, beautified**) to make or become beautiful.–**beautification** n.

beauty n (pl **beauties**) the combination of qualities in a person or object that cause delight or pleasure; a very attractive woman or girl; good looks; a very fine specimen.–**beautiful** adj.–**beautifully** adv.

beauty parlor, beauty salon, beauty shop n an establishment that offers cosmetic beauty treatments.

beaver n a large semi-aquatic dam-building rodent; its fur; a hat made from beaver fur. * vi (often with **away**) to work hard (at).

bebop see **bop**.

becalm vt to make calm; to make (a ship) motionless from lack of wind.–**becalmed** adj.

became see **become**.

because conj since; for the reason that.

beckon vti to summon by a gesture.–**beckoner** n.–**beckoning** adj.

become vb (**becoming, became**, pp **become**) vi to come or grow to be. * vt to be suitable for.

becoming adj appropriate; seemly; suitable to the wearer.– **becomingly** adv.

becquerel n the SI unit of radiation activity.

bed n a piece of furniture for sleeping on; the mattress and covers for this; a plot of soil where plants are raised; the bottom of a river, lake, etc; any flat surface used as a foundation; a stratum. * vt (**bedding, bedded**) to put to bed; to embed; to plant in a bed of earth; to arrange in layers.

bedbug n a bloodsucking wingless insect that infests dirty bedding.

bedclothes npl sheets, blankets, etc for a bed.

bedding n bedclothes; litter (straw, etc) for animals; a bottom layer, foundation.

bedeck vt to cover with finery, to adorn.

bedevil vt (**bedeviling, bedeviled** or **bedevilling, bedevilled**) to plague or bewilder.–**bedevilment** n.

bedfellow n a sharer of a bed; an associate, ally, etc, esp a temporary one.

bedlam n (arch) a madhouse; uproar.

Bedouin n (pl **Bedouins, Bedouin**) an Arab desert nomad; a gypsy.

bedraggle vt to make untidy or dirty by dragging in the wet or dirt.–**bedraggled** adj.

bedridden adj confined to bed through illness.

bedrock n solid rock underlying soil, etc; the base or bottom; fundamentals.

bedroom n a room for sleeping in. * adj suggestive of sexual relations; (area, suburb, etc) inhabited by commuters.

bedside n the space beside a bed. * adj situated or conducted at the bedside; suitable for someone bedridden.

bedsore n an ulcerous sore caused by pressure, common in bedridden persons.

bee[1] n a social, stinging four-winged insect that is often kept in hives to make honey; any of numerous insects that also feed on pollen and nectar and are related to wasps.

bee[2] n a social meeting for work on behalf of a neighbor or a charitable object.

beech n a tree with smooth silvery-gray bark; its wood.

beef n the meat of a full-grown cow, steer, etc; (inf) muscular strength; (inf) a complaint, grudge. * vt (with **up**) to add weight, strength or power to.

beefy adj (**beefier, beefiest**) brawny, muscular.

beehive n a container for keeping honeybees; a scene of crowded activity.

beeline n the straight course pursued by a bee returning laden to the hive; a direct line or course.

been see **be**.

beep n the brief, high-pitched sound of a horn or electronic signal. * vti to make or cause to make this sound.

beeper n a small portable electronic radio receiver that emits a bleep to convey a message.

beer n an alcoholic drink made from malt, sugar, hops and water fermented with yeast.

beeswax n wax secreted by bees, refined and used for polishing.

beet n a red, edible root used as a vegetable, in salads, etc; a source of sugar.

beetle[1] n any of an order of insects having hard wing covers.

beetle[2] vi to be prominent; to jut out, overhang, as a cliff.– **beetling** adj.

beetroot n (pl **beetroot**) the fleshy root of beet used as a vegetable, in salads, etc.–also **red beet**.

befall vti (**befalling, befell**, pp **befallen**) to happen or occur to.

befit vt (**befitting, befitted**) to be suitable or appropriate for; to be right for.–**befittingly** adv.

before prep ahead of; in front of; in the presence of; preceding in space or time; in preference to; rather than. * adv beforehand; previously; until now. * conj earlier than the time that; rather than.

beforehand adv ahead of time; in anticipation.

befriend vt to be a friend to, to favor.

befuddle *vt* to confuse, stupefy, often with drink.

beg *vti* (**begging, begged**) to ask for money or food; to ask earnestly; to implore.

began *see* **begin**.

beget *vt* (**begetting, begot** *or* **begat**, *pp* **begotten** *or* **begot**) to become the father of; to cause.—**begetter** *n*.

beggar *n* a person who begs or who lives by begging; a pauper. * *vt* to reduce to poverty; (*description*) to render inadequate.

begin *vti* (**beginning, began**, *pp* **begun**) to start doing, acting, etc; to originate.

beginner *n* one who has just started to learn or do something; a novice.

beginning *n* source or origin; commencement.

begot, begotten *see* **beget**.

begrudge *vt* to grudge; to envy.—**begrudgingly** *adv*.

beguile *vt* (**beguiling, beguiled**) to cheat or deceive; to charm; to fascinate.—**beguilement** *n*.—**beguiler** *n*.—**beguilingly** *adv*.

begun *see* **begin**.

behalf *n* in or **on behalf of** in the interest of; for.

behave *vti* to act in a specified way; to conduct (oneself) properly.

behavior, behaviour *n* way of behaving; conduct or action.—**behavioral, behavioural** *adj*.

behead *vt* to cut the head off.

beheld *see* **behold**.

behest *n* a command; a precept.

behind *prep* at the rear of; concealed by; later than; supporting. * *adv* in the rear; slow; late.

behindhand *adj, adv* late, in arrears.

behold *vb* (**beholding, beheld**) *vt* to look at; to observe. * *vi* to see.—**beholder** *n*.

beholden *adj* indebted to; bound under an obligation.

beige *n* a very light brown.

being *n* life; existence; a person or thing that exists; nature or substance.

belated *adj* coming late.—**belatedly** *adv*.

belch *vti* to expel gas from the stomach by the mouth; to eject violently from inside.—*also n*.

beleaguer *vt* to besiege, to blockade; to harass.

belfry *n* (*pl* **belfries**) the upper part of a tower, in which bells are hung.

belie *vt* (**belying, belied**) to show to be a lie; to misrepresent; to fail to live up to (a hope, promise).—**belier** *n*.

belief *n* a principle or idea considered to be true; religious faith.

believe *vt* to accept as true; to think; to be convinced of. * *vi* to have religious faith.—**believable** *adj*.—**believer** *n*.

belittle *vt* (*a person*) to make feel small; to disparage.—**belittlement** *n*.—**belittler** *n*.—**belittlingly** *adv*.

bell *n* a hollow metal object which rings when struck; anything bell-shaped; the sound made by a bell.

belladonna *n* the deadly nightshade plant, whose flowers, leaves and stalk are poisonous.

bellhop, bellboy *n* one who carries luggage, runs errands, etc in a hotel or club.

bellicose *adj* war-like; ready to fight.—**bellicosity** *n*.

belligerent *adj* at war; of war; war-like; ready to fight or quarrel.—**belligerence** *n*.—**belligerently** *adv*.

bellow *vi* to roar; to make an outcry. * *vt* to utter loudly. * *n* the roar of a bull; any deep roar.

bellows *n* (*used as pl or sing*) a device for creating and directing a stream of air by compression of its collapsible sides.

belly *n* (*pl* **bellies**) the lower part of the body between the chest and the thighs; the abdomen; the stomach; the underside of an animal's body; the deep interior, as of a ship. * *vti* (**bellying, bellied**) to swell out; to bulge.

belly dance *n* a solo dance performed by a woman with sinuous, provocative movements of the belly and hips.—**belly dancer** *n*.

belly-flop *vt* (**belly-flopping, belly-flopped**) to dive in such a way that the body lands almost flat against the water.—**belly flop** *n*.

belong *vi* to have a proper place; to be related (to); (*with* **to**) to be a member; to be owned; (*inf*) to fit in socially.

belongings *npl* personal effects, possessions.

beloved *adj* dearly loved. * *n* one who is dearly loved.

below *prep* lower than; unworthy of. * *adv* in or to a lower place; south of; beneath; later (in a book, etc).

belt *n* a band of leather, etc worn around the waist; any similar encircling thing; a belt as an award for skill, eg in boxing, judo; a continuous moving strap passing over pulleys and so driving machinery; a distinctive region or strip; (*sl*) a hard blow. * *vt* to surround, attach with a belt; to thrash with a belt; (*sl*) to deliver a hard blow; (*sl*) to hurry; (*with* **out**) (*sl*) to sing or play loudly; (*with* **up**) to fasten with a belt. * *vi* (*with* **up**) (*inf*) to wear a seat belt; (*sl: often imper*) to be quiet.

beluga *n* a large sturgeon; its caviar; a white whale.

bemoan *vti* to lament.

bemuse *vt* to muddle; to preoccupy.—**bemused** *adj*.—**bemusement** *n*.

bench *n* a long hard seat for two or more persons; a long table for working at; the place where judges sit in a court of law; the status of a judge; judges collectively; (*sport*) the place where reserves, etc, sit during play.

bench mark *n* a surveyor's mark for making measurements; something that serves as a standard.

bend *vb* (**bending, bent**) *vt* to form a curve; to make crooked; to turn, esp from a straight line; to adapt to one's purpose, distort. * *vi* to turn, esp from a straight line; to yield from pressure to form a curve; (*with* **over** *or* **down**) to curve the body; to give in. * *n* a curve, turn; a bent part; (*pl: used as sing or pl*) decompression sickness in divers.—**bendable** *adj*.

beneath *prep* underneath; below; unworthy. * *adv* in a lower place; underneath.—*also adj*.

benediction *n* a blessing; an invocation of a blessing, esp at the end of a church service.—**benedictory** *adj*.

benefactor *n* a patron.—**benefactress** *nf*.

beneficent *adj* generous; conferring blessings.—**beneficence** *n*.—**beneficently** *adv*.

beneficial *adj* advantageous.—**beneficially** *adv*.

beneficiary *n* (*pl* **beneficiaries**) a person who receives or will receive benefit, as from a will, etc.

benefit *n* advantage; anything contributing to improvement; (*often pl*) allowances paid by a government, insurance company, etc; a public performance, bazaar, etc, the proceeds of which are to help some person or cause. * *vb* (**benefiting, benefited**) *vt* to help. * *vi* to receive advantage.

benevolence *n* inclination to do good; kindness; generosity.—**benevolent** *adj*.—**benevolently** *adv*.

benign *adj* favorable; kindly; gentle or mild; (*med*) not malignant.—**benignly** *adv*.

bent[1] *see* **bend**.

bent[2] *n* aptitude; inclination of the mind. * *adj* curved or crooked; (*with* **on**) strongly determined; (*sl*) dishonest.

benumb *vt* to make numb.—**benumbed** *adj*.

bequeath *vt* (*property, etc*) to leave by will; to pass on to posterity.—**bequeathal** *n*.—**bequeather** *n*.

bequest *n* act of bequeathing; something that is bequeathed, a legacy.

berate *vt* to scold severely.

bereave *vt* to deprive (of) a loved one through death.—**bereaved** *adj*.—**bereavement** *n*.

bereft *adj* deprived; bereaved.

beret *n* a flat, round, brimless, soft cap.

bergamot *n* a variety of lemon, the rind of which yields a valuable oil used in perfumery; the oil of the bergamot.

beriberi *n* a disease of the nervous system, due to lack of vitamin B.

berry *n* (*pl* **berries**) any small, juicy, stoneless fruit (eg black-berry, holly berry). * *vti* (**berrying, berried**) to bear, produce or gather berries.

berserk *adj* frenzied; destructively violent.–*also adv*.

berth *n* a place in a dock for a ship at mooring; a built-in bed, as in a ship or train; (*inf*) a job. * *vt* to put into or furnish with a berth; to moor a ship. * *vi* to occupy a berth.

beryl *n* a (usu green) precious stone.

beryllium *n* a hard lightweight silvery-white metallic element used in making alloys.

beseech *vt* (**beseeching, beseeched** *or* **besought**) to implore, to entreat; to beg earnestly for.

beset *vt* (**besetting, beset**) to surround or hem in; to attack from all sides; to harass.

beside *prep* at, by the side of, next to; in comparison with; in addition to; aside from; **beside oneself** extremely agitated.

besides *prep* other than; in addition; over and above. * *adv* in addition; also; except for that mentioned; moreover.

besiege *vt* to hem in with armed forces; to close in on; to over-whelm, harass, etc.

besmirch *vt* to sully; to make dirty, to soil.

besotted *adj* muddled with drunkenness or infatuation; dull, stupid.–**besottedly** *adv*.

besought *see* **beseech**.

bespatter *vt* to soil by spattering; to spot with mud.

bespeak *vt* (**bespeaking, bespoke,** *pp* **bespoken** *or* **bespoke**) to speak for beforehand; to order or arrange in advance; to be evidence of; to indicate, as by signs or marks.

bespoke *adj* (*clothes*) custom-made; (*tailor*) making such clothes.

besprinkle *vt* to sprinkle over (with).

best *adj* (*superl of* **good**) most excellent; most suitable, desir-able, etc; largest; above all others. * *n* one's utmost effort; the highest state of excellence. * *adv* (*superl of* **well**) in or to the highest degree. * *vt* to defeat, outdo.

bestial *adj* brutal; savage.–**bestially** *adv*.

bestiality *n* (*pl* **bestialities**) brutal or brutish behavior; a bru-tal or savage action or practice; sexual intercourse by a person with an animal.

best man *n* the principal attendant of the bridegroom at a wed-ding.

bestow *vt* to present as a gift or honor.–**bestowal** *n*.–**bestower** *n*.

bestride *vt* (**bestriding, bestrode,** *pp* **bestridden**) to stand, sit on or mount with the legs astride.

best seller *n* a book or other commodity that sells in vast num-bers; the author of such a book.–**best-selling** *adj*.

bet *n* a wager or stake; the thing or sum staked; a person or thing likely to bring about a desired result; (*inf*) belief, opinion. * *vti* (**betting, bet** *or* **betted**) to declare as in a bet; to stake (money, etc) in a bet (with someone).

beta *n* the second letter of the Greek alphabet.

beta blocker *n* a drug that subdues cardiac activity, used in the treatment of high blood pressure.

betel palm *n* a palm tree of tropical Asia with feathery leaves and scarlet or orange fruit.

bête noire *n* (*pl* **bêtes noires**) pet hate.

betide *vt* to happen to, to befall. * *vi* to come to pass.

betoken *vt* to signify, to indicate by signs; to augur, to foreshadow.

betray *vt* to aid an enemy; to expose treacherously; to be a traitor to; to reveal unknowingly.–**betrayal** *n*.–**betrayer** *n*.

betroth *vt* to promise in marriage.–**betrothed** *adj*.–**betrothal** *n*.

better *adj* (*compar of* **good**) more excellent; more suitable; improved in health; larger. * *adv* (*compar of* **well**) in a more excellent manner; in a higher degree; more. * *n* a person superior in position, etc; a more excellent thing, condition, etc. * *vt* to outdo; to surpass.

between *prep* the space, time, etc separating (two things); (*bond, etc*) connecting from one or the other.

bevel *n* an angle other than a right angle; the inclination that one surface makes with another when not at right angles; a tool for setting of angles. * *vb* (**beveling, beveled** *or* **bevelling, bevelled**) *vt* to cut on the slant. * *vi* to slant or incline.

beverage *n* a drink, esp one other than water.

bevy *n* (*pl* **bevies**) a flock of quails; a large group (esp of girls).

bewail *vt* to mourn or weep aloud for, to lament. * *vi* to express grief.–**bewailer** *n*.–**bewailing** *n*.

beware *vti* to be wary or careful (of).

bewilder *vt* to perplex; to confuse hopelessly.–**bewilderingly** *adv*.–**bewilderment** *n*.

bewitch *vt* to cast a spell over; to fascinate or enchant. –**bewitching**.–**bewitchingly** *adv*.

beyond *prep* further on than; past; later than; outside the reach of (*beyond help*). * *adv* further away. * *n* (*with* **the**) life after death.

biannual *adj* occurring twice a year.–**biannually** *adv*.

bias *n* a slanting or diagonal line, cut or sewn across the grain in cloth; a weight inside a bowl in a game of bowls slanting its course when rolled; partiality; prejudice. * *vt* (**biasing, biased** *or* **biassing, biassed**) to prejudice.

bib *n* a cloth or plastic cover tied around a baby or child to prevent food spillage on clothes; the upper part of dungarees or an apron.

Bible *n* the sacred book of the Christian Church; the Old and New Testaments; (*without cap*) an authoritative book on a particu-lar subject.

biblical *adj* of or referring to the Bible.–**biblically** *adv*.

bibliography *n* (*pl* **bibliographies**) a list of writings on a given subject or by a given author; the study of the history of books and book production. –**bibliographer** *n*.–**bibliographic** *adj*.–**bibliographical** *adj*.

bicentenary *adj* occurring every two hundred years. * *n* (*pl* **bicentenaries**) a two hundredth anniversary or its celebration.

bicentennial *adj* lasting or occurring every two hundred years. * *n* a bicentenary, the two hundredth anniversary of an event, or its celebration.

biceps *n* (*pl* **biceps, bicepses**) the muscle with two points of origin, esp the large muscle in the upper arm.

bicker *vi* to squabble, quarrel.–*also n*.–**bickerer** *n*.

bicuspid *adj* having two points or prominences (–*also* **bicuspi-date**). * *n* one of the two double-pointed teeth forming the first pair of molars on either side of the jaw, above and below.

bicycle *n* a vehicle consisting of a metal frame on two wheels, driven by pedals and having handlebars and a seat. * *vti* to ride or travel on a bicycle.–**bicyclist, bicycler** *n*.

bid[1] *n* an offer of an amount one will pay or accept; (*cards*) a statement of the number of tricks that a player intends to win. * *vi* (**bidding, bid**) to make a bid.–**bidder** *n*.

bid[2] *vt* (**bidding, bade** *or* **bid,** *pp* **bidden** *or* **bid**) to com-mand or ask; to summon; (*farewell, etc*) to express.

biddable *adj* docile, obedient; worth bidding on.–**biddability** *n*.–**biddably** *adv*.

bidding *n* an order; command; an invitation; the act of offering a price at auction.

bidet *n* a low, bowl-shaped bathroom fixture with running water for bathing the crotch and anus.

biennial *adj* lasting two years; occurring every two years. * *n* a plant that lasts for two years.–**biennially** *adv*.

bier *n* a portable framework on which a coffin is put.

bifocal *adj* (*spectacles*) having two different focuses.

bifocals *npl* spectacles with bifocal lenses for near and distant vision.

big adj (**bigger, biggest**) large; of great size; important; influential; grown-up; pregnant; generous; boastful.–**bigness** n.

bigamy n (pl **bigamies**) the act of marrying a second time when one is already legally married.–**bigamist** n.–**bigamous** adj.–**bigamously** adv.

big bang theory n (astron) the theory that the universe originated in a cataclysmic explosion and is still expanding.

big brother n an older brother; a person who fills that protective role; (with caps) a ruthless and sinister dictator, corporation, etc that wields absolute power.

big game n large animals or fish hunted for sport; an important, usu risky objective.

bighead n (inf) a boastful or conceited person.–**bigheaded** adj.

bight n a loop or bend of a rope, in distinction from the ends; a bend in a coastline forming an open bay; a small bay between two headlands.

bigmouth n (inf) a loud-mouthed, bragging or indiscreet person.

big name n a famous person, esp in entertainment.

bigot n an intolerant person who blindly supports a particular political view or religion.–**bigoted** adj.

bigotry n (pl **bigotries**) the state or condition of a narrow-minded, intolerant person; blind and obstinate attachment to a particular creed, party or opinion; intolerance; fanaticism.

big screen n (inf) the cinema (industry).

big shot n (inf) an important person.

big top n a large circus tent.

bigwig n (inf) an important person.

bike n (inf) a bicycle; a motorcycle.

bikini n (pl **bikinis**) a scanty two-piece swimsuit for women.

bilateral adj having two sides; affecting two parties reciprocally.–**bilaterally** adv.

bile n a gall, a thick bitter fluid secreted by the liver; bad temper.

bilge n the lowest part of a ship's hull; filth that collects there.

bilingual adj written in two languages; able to speak two languages.–**bilingualism** n.–**bilingually** adv.

bilious adj suffering from or caused by disorder of the bile; peevish.–**biliously** adv.–**biliousness** n.

bilk vt to deceive or defraud, as by evading a payment; to leave in the lurch. * n a swindler.–**bilker** n.

bill[1] n a bird's beak.

bill[2] n a statement for goods supplied or services rendered, the money due for this; a list, as a menu or theater program; a poster or handbill; a draft of a proposed law, to be discussed by a legislature; a piece of paper money; (law) an written declaration of charges and complaints filed. * vt to make out a bill of (items); to present a statement of charges to; to advertise by bills; (a performer) to book.

billboard n a large panel designed to carry outdoor advertising; a hoarding.

billet n a written order to provide lodging for military personnel; the lodging; a position or job. * vt (**billeting, billeted**) to assign to lodging by billet.

billet-doux n (pl **billets-doux**) a love letter.

bill fold n a notecase or wallet.

billhook n a small curved cutting tool with a hooked point.

billiards n a game in which hard balls are driven by a cue on a felt-covered table with raised, cushioned edges.

billing n the order in which actors' names are listed.

billion n (pl **billions, billion**) a thousand millions, the numeral 1 followed by 9 zeros; in UK, a million million, a trillion.–**billionaire** n.–**billionth** adj, n.

bill of fare n a menu.

bill of rights n a charter or summary of basic human rights.

billow n a large wave; any large swelling mass or surge, as of smoke. * vi to surge or swell in a billow.–**billowy** adj.

billy-goat n a male goat.

bimonthly adj every two months; loosely twice a month.

bin n a box or enclosed space for storing grain, coal, etc; a dustbin. * vt (**binning, binned**) to put or store in a bin; (inf) to discard, throw away.

binary adj made up of two parts; double; denoting or of a number system in which the base is two, each number being expressed by using only two digits, specifically 0 and 1.

bind vb (**binding, bound**) vt to tie together, as with rope; to hold or restrain; to encircle with a belt, etc; to fasten together the pages of (a book) and protect with a cover; to obligate by duty, love, etc; (with **over**) to compel, as by oath or legal restraint; (often with **up**) to bandage. * vi to become tight or stiff; to stick together; to be obligatory; (sl) to complain. * n anything that binds; (inf) a difficult situation.

binder n a folder for keeping loose papers together; a bookbinder; something used to bind; a sheaf-binding machine.

binding n the covering of a book holding the pages together.

binge n (inf) a heavy drinking session; immoderate indulgence in anything.

bingo n a game of chance in which players cover numbers on their cards according to the number called aloud. * interj, n a cry of delight, surprise or success.

binoculars npl a viewing device for use with both eyes, consisting of two small telescope lenses joined together.

biochemistry n the chemistry of living organisms.–**biochemical** adj.–**biochemist** n.

biodegradable adj readily decomposed by bacterial action.

bioengineering n the application of engineering principles in the biological and medical sciences.–**bioengineer** n.

biogenesis n the theory that only living matter can produce living matter; the science of life development.–**biogenetic** adj.–**biogenetically** adv.

biography n (pl **biographies**) an account of a person's life written by another; biographical writings in general.–**biographer** n.–**biographical** adj.

biology n the study of living organisms.–**biological** adj.–**biologically** adv.–**biologist** n.

bionics n the study of electronically operated mechanical systems that function like living organisms.–**bionic** adj.

bionomics n (used as sing) ecology.–**bionomic, bionomical** adj.–**bionomist** n.

biophysics n the application of physics to biology.–**biophysical** adj.–**biophysicist** n.

biopsy n (n **biopsies**) the removal of parts of living tissue for medical diagnosis.

biorhythm n a cyclical pattern in physiological activity said to determine a person's intellectual, emotional and physical moods and behavior.–**biorhythmic** adj.

biosphere n the regions of the earth's surface and atmosphere inhabited by living things.

biosynthesis n (pl **biosyntheses**) the formation of chemical compounds by living organisms.–**biosynthetic** adj.–**biosynthetically** adv.

biotechnology n the commercial and industrial application of biological processes, such as the use of microorganisms to dye cloth.

biped n an animal having two feet.–also adj.–**bipedal** adj.

biplane n an airplane with two sets of wings.

bipolar adj having two poles or opposite extremities; of or affecting both the earth's poles; having or expressing two directly opposite ideas or qualities.–**bipolarity** n.

birch n a tree with a smooth white bark and hard wood; a bundle of birch twigs used for thrashing. * vt to flog.–**birchen** adj.

bird n any class of warm-blooded, egg-laying vertebrates with a feathered body, scaly legs, and forelimbs modified to form wings.

birdlime n a viscous substance used for snaring small birds; a thing that snares. * vt to smear or trap with birdlime.

bird of passage n a migratory bird; a transient person.

bird of prey n a meat-eating bird (as a hawk, owl, falcon, etc) that hunts other animals for food.

bird's-eye *adj* seen from above.

bird watcher *n* one who makes a study of birds in the wild.–**bird watching** *n*.

birth *n* the act of being born; childbirth; the origin of something; lineage, ancestry.

birth control *n* the use of contraceptive drugs or devices to limit reproduction.

birthday *n* the day of birth; the anniversary of the day of birth.

birthmark *n* a patch or blemish on the body dating from birth.

birth rate *n* the number of births per thousand of population per year.

birthright *n* privileges or property that a person is believed entitled to by birth.

birthstone *n* a gem symbolizing the month of one's birth.

biscuit *n* (*Brit*) a cookie * *adj* pale brown in color.

bisect *vt* to split into two equal parts; (*geom*) to divide into two equal parts.–**bisection** *n*.

bisexual *adj* sexually attracted to both sexes; having the characteristics of both sexes. * *n* a person sexually attracted to both sexes.–**bisexualism, bisexuality** *n*.

bishop *n* a high-ranking clergyman governing a diocese or church district; a chessman that can move in a diagonal direction.

bismuth *n* one of the elements, a light reddish-colored metal of brittle texture.–**bismuthal, bismuthic** *adj*.

bison *n* (*pl* **bison**) a wild ox of Europe and America.–*also* **buffalo**.

bistro *n* (*pl* **bistros**) a small restaurant.

bit[1] *n* a small amount or piece; in US, a small coin worth one eighth of a dollar; a small part in a play, film, etc, a bit part.–**a bit** slightly, rather.

bit[2] *n* a metal mouthpiece in a bridle used for controlling a horse; a cutting or boring attachment for use in a brace, drill, etc. * *vt* (**bitting, bitted**) to put a bridle upon; to put the bit in the mouth of.

bit[3] *n* (*comput*) a unit of information in binary notation equivalent to either of two digits, 0 or 1.

bit[4] *see* **bite**.

bitch *n* a female dog or wolf. * *vi* (*inf*) to grumble; to act spitefully; (*with* **up**) to make a mess of, to ruin.

bite *vb* (**biting, bit**, *pp* **bitten**) *vt* to grip or tear with the teeth; to sting or puncture, as an insect; to cause to smart; to take the bait. * *vi* to press or snap the teeth (into, at, etc); (*with* **back**) to stop oneself from saying something offensive, embarrassing, etc. * *n* the act of biting with the teeth; a sting or puncture by an insect.

biting *adj* severe; critical, sarcastic.–**bitingly** *adv*.–**bitingness** *n*.

bit part *n* a small acting role in a play, film, etc.

bitter *adj* having an acrid or sharp taste; sorrowful; harsh; resentful; cynical; (*weather*) extremely cold.–**bitterly** *avj*.–**bitterness** *n*.

bittern *n* a wading bird of the heron family, with a booming cry.

bittersweet *n* the woody nightshade, the roots and leaves of which when chewed produce first a bitter then a sweet taste; a variety of apple. * *adj* simultaneously sweet and bitter; pleasantly sad.

bitty *adj* (**bittier, bittiest**) small, tiny; made up of scraps of something.

bitumen *n* any of several substances obtained as residue in the distillation of coal tar, petroleum, etc, or occurring naturally as asphalt.–**bituminous** *adj*.

bivalve *n* any mollusk having two valves or shells hinged together, as a clam.–**bivalvular** *adj*.

bivouac *n* a temporary camp, esp one without tents or other cover. * *vi* (**bivouacking, bivouacked**) to spend the night in a bivouac.

biweekly *adj* every two weeks; twice a week. * *n* (*pl* **biweeklies**) a periodical published every two weeks.

bizarre *adj* odd, unusual.

blab *vti* (**blabbing, blabbed**) to reveal (a secret); to gossip. * *n* a gossip.–**blabber** *n*.

black *adj* of the darkest color, like coal or soot; having dark-colored skin and hair; without light; dirty; evil, wicked; sad, dismal; sullen; angry; (*coffee, etc*) without milk. * *n* black color; (*often with cap*) a Negro, Australian Aborigine; black clothes, esp when worn in mourning; (*chess, draughts*) black pieces.–**in the black** without debts, in credit. * *vt* to make black; to blacken; (*shoes*) to polish with blacking; to boycott; (*with* **out**) (*lights*) to extinguish, obliterate; (*broadcast*) to prevent transmission. * *vi* (*with* **out**) to lose consciousness or vision.–**blackly** *adv*.–**blackness** *n*.

black-and-blue *adj* livid with bruises.

black and white *n* writing, print; a line drawing; a photograph not in color. * *adj* black-and-white.

black-and-white *adj* (*film, photography*) in black and white, not color; (*ideas, etc*) highly simplistic.

blackball *vt* to ostracize.

blackberry *n* (*pl* **blackberries**) a woody bush with thorny stems and berry-like fruit; its black or purple edible fruit (–*also* **bramble**). * *vt* to gather blackberries.

blackbird *n* any of various birds, the male of which is almost all black.

blackboard *n* a black or dark green board written on with chalk.

black box *n* a flight recorder on an aircraft.

black comedy *n* a comedy with a tragic theme.

black economy *n* undeclared economic activity.

blacken *vt* to make black; to defame.

black eye *n* (*inf*) discoloration around the eye caused by a blow; (*sl*) shame.

blackguard *n* a villain, scoundrel.–**blackguardism** *n*.–**blackguardly** *adj*.

blackhead *n* a small spot or pimple clogging a pore in the skin.

black hole *n* a hypothetical, invisible region in space.

black ice *n* a thin transparent coating of ice on roads or other surfaces.

blackjack[1] *n* a gambling game with cards in which players try to obtain points better than the banker's but not more than 21.–*also* **pontoon, twenty-one**.

blackjack[2] *n* a large leather vessel or drinking cup; a short leather club with a flexible handle. * *vt* to hit with a blackjack.

blackleg *n* a person who takes a striker's place, a scab; a person who endeavors to obtain money by cheating at races or cards, a rook; a disease affecting sheep and cattle. * *vti* (**blacklegging, blacklegged**) to act or injure, as a blackleg.

blacklist *n* a list of those censored, refused employment, regarded as suspicious politically or generally not to be trusted. * *vt* to put on such a list.

black magic *n* sorcery, witchcraft.

blackmail *vt* to extort money by threatening to disclose discreditable facts. * *n* the crime of blackmailing.–**blackmailer** *n*.

black market *n* the illegal buying and selling of goods, esp banned goods, eg drugs, or when rationing is in force.–**black marketeer, black marketer** *n*.

blackout *n* the darkness when all lights are switched off; temporary loss of consciousness or electricity.

black power *n* a movement of black people whose goal is political, social and economic equality with whites.

black sheep *n* a person regarded as disreputable or a disgrace by their family.

blacksmith *n* a metal worker, esp one who shoes horses.

black spot *n* an area where traffic accidents frequently happen; a difficult or dangerous place; a disease affecting leaves, esp of roses.

bladder *n* a sac that fills with fluid, esp one that holds urine flowing from the kidneys; any inflatable bag.

blade *n* the cutting edge of a tool or knife; the broad, flat surface of a leaf; a straight, narrow leaf of grass; the flat part of an oar or paddle; the runner of an ice skate.–**bladed** *adj*.

blame *vt* to hold responsible for; to accuse. * *n* responsibility for an error; reproof.–**blamable, blameable** *adj*.

blameless adj innocent; free from blame.–**blamelessly** adv.–
blamelessness n.

blameworthy adj deserving blame.–**blameworthiness** n.

blanch vt to whiten or bleach; to make pale; (vegetables, almonds, etc) to scald. * vi to turn pale.

blancmange n a dessert made from gelatinous or starchy ingredients (as cornflour) and milk.

bland adj mild; gentle; insipid.–**blandly** adv.–**blandness** n.

blandish vti to flatter in order to coax; to cajole.–**blandishment** n (usu pl).

blank adj (paper) bearing no writing or marks; vacant; (mind) empty of thought; (look) without expression; (denial, refusal) utter, complete; (check) signed but with no amount written in. * n an empty space, esp one to be filled out on a printed form; an empty place or time.–**blankly** adv.–**blankness** n.

blank (cartridge) n a powder-filled cartridge without a bullet.

blanket n a large, soft piece of cloth used for warmth, esp as a bed cover; (of snow, smoke) a cover or layer. * adj applying to a wide variety of cases or situations. * vt to cover.

blare vti to sound harshly or loudly. * n a loud, harsh sound.

blarney n wheedling talk, flattery. * vt (**blarneying, blarneyed**) to influence or talk over by soft wheedling speeches; to humbug with flattery.

blasé adj bored, indifferent; sated with pleasure.

blaspheme vt to speak irreverently of (God, a divine being or sacred things). * vi to utter blasphemy.–**blasphemer** n.

blasphemy n (pl **blasphemies**) impious speaking; speaking irreverently of God, a divine being or sacred things.–**blasphemous** adj.

blast n a sharp gust of air; the sound of a horn; an explosion; an outburst of criticism. * vt to wither; to blow up, explode; to criticize sharply. * vi to make a loud, harsh sound; to set off explosives, etc; (with **off**) to be launched.

blasted adj withered; (inf) damned.

blastoff n the launch of a space vehicle or rocket; the time when this takes place.

blatant adj noisy; glaringly conspicuous.–**blatancy** n.–**blatantly** adv.

blaze[1] n an intensive fire; a bright light; splendor; an outburst (of emotion). * vi to burn brightly; to shine with a brilliant light; to be excited, as with anger.

blaze[2] n a white mark on the face of a horse or other quadruped; a white mark cut on a tree to serve as a guide. * vt to mark, as trees, by removing a portion of the bark; to indicate, as a path or boundary, by blazing trees; **blaze a trail** to act as a pioneer.

blazer n a lightweight jacket, often in a bright color representing membership of a sports club, school, etc.

bleach vti to make or become white or colorless. * n a substance for bleaching.–**bleachable** adj.–**bleacher** n.

bleak adj cold; exposed; bare; harsh; gloomy; not hopeful.–**bleakly** adv.–**bleakness** n.

bleary adj (**blearier, bleariest**) (eyesight) dim with water or tears; obscure, indistinct.–**blearily** adv.–**bleariness** n.

bleat vi to cry as a sheep, goat or calf; to complain. * n a bleating cry or sound.–**bleater** n.–**bleatingly** adv.

bleed vb (**bleeding, bled**) vi to lose blood; to ooze sap, color or dye; to die for a country or an ideal; to sympathize (often ironically). * vt to remove blood or sap from; (inf) to extort money or goods from.

blemish n a flaw or defect, as a spot. * vt to mar; to spoil.

blench vi to flinch; to blanch.

blend vt (varieties of tea, etc) to mix or mingle; to mix so that the components cannot be distinguished. * vi to mix, merge; to shade gradually into each other, as colors; to harmonize. * n a mixture.

blender n something or someone that blends; an electrical device for preparing food.–also **liquidizer**.

bless vt (**blessing, blessed** or **blest**) to consecrate; to praise; to call upon God's protection; to grant happiness; to make the sign of the cross over.

blessed adj holy, sacred; fortunate; blissful; beatified.–**blessedly** adv.–**blessedness** n.

blessing n a prayer or wish for success or happiness; a cause of happiness; good wishes or approval; a grace said before or after eating.

blether vi (inf) to talk foolishly. * n (inf) foolish talk; one who talks it.–also **blather**.

blew see **blow**[2].

blight n any insect, disease, etc that destroys plants; anything that prevents growth or destroys; someone or something that spoils. * vt to destroy; to frustrate.

blind adj sightless; unable to discern or understand; not directed by reason; (exit) hidden, concealed; closed at one end. * n something that deceives. * vti to make sightless, to deprive of insight; to dazzle (with facts, a bright light, etc); to deceive.–**blindly** adv.–**blindness** n.

blind date n a date between two individuals who have never met before; either individual on a blind date.

blindfold n a cloth or bandage used to cover the eyes. * adj having the eyes covered, so as not to see; reckless. * vt to cover the eyes with a strip of cloth, etc; to hamper sight or understanding; to mislead.

blind spot n a point on the retina of the eye that is insensitive to light; a place where vision is obscured; a subject on which someone is ignorant.

blini, blinis npl (sing **blin**) buckwheat pancakes.

blink vi to open and close the eyes rapidly; (light) to flash on and off; (with **at**) to ignore. * vt (with **at**) to be amazed or surprised. * n a glance, a glimpse; a momentary flash.

blinker n one who blinks; that which obscures the sight or mental perception; (pl) a screen for a horse's eye, to prevent it from seeing sideways; (sl) the eyes.

blip n a trace on a radar screen; a recurring sound; a temporary setback. * vi (**blipping, blipped**) to make a blip.

bliss n supreme happiness; spiritual joy.–**blissful** adj.–**blissfully** adv.

blister n a raised patch on the skin, containing water, as caused by burning or rubbing; a raised bubble on any other surface. * vti to cause or form blisters; to lash with words.

blithe adj happy, cheerful, gay.–**blithely** adv.–**blitheness** n.

blitz n heavy aerial bombing; any sudden destructive attack; a determined effort. * vt to subject to a blitz.

blizzard n a severe storm of wind and snow.

bloat vti to swell as with water or air; to puff up, as with pride.–**bloated** adj.

bloater n a herring or mackerel smoked and partially dried, but not split open.

blob n a drop of liquid; a round spot (of color, etc).

bloc n a group of parties, nations, etc united to achieve a common purpose.

block n a solid piece of stone or wood, etc; a piece of wood used as a base (for chopping, etc); a group or row of buildings; a number of things as a unit; the main body of an internal combustion engine; a building divided into offices; an obstruction; a child's building brick; (sl) the head. * vt to impede or obstruct; to shape; (often with **out**) to sketch roughly. * vi to obstruct an opponent in sports.–**blocker** n.

blockade n (mil) the obstruction of an enemy seaport by warships; any strategic barrier. * vt to obstruct in this way.–**blockader** n.

blockage n an obstruction.

blockbuster n (sl) a very heavy bomb of great penetrative power; a conspicuously powerful or effective person or thing; one who engages in blockbusting.

blockhead n a dolt, a stupid person.

block vote n at a conference, a total vote represented by one delegate.

blond, blonde adj having light-colored hair and skin; light-colored. * n a blond person.–**blondness, blondeness** n.

blood n the red fluid that circulates in the arteries and veins of animals; the sap of a plant; the essence of life; kinship; descent; hatred; anger; bloodshed; guilt of murder.

blood bank n a place where blood is taken from blood donors and stored.

blood bath n a massacre.

blood count n the determination of the numbers of red and white corpuscles in a sample of blood.

bloodcurdling adj exciting terror, horrifying, chilling.

blood donor n a person who donates his or her blood for transfusion.

blood group n any of the classes of human blood.–also **blood type**.

bloodhound n a large breed of hound used for tracking; a detective.

blood poisoning n septicemia.

blood pressure n the pressure of the blood in the arterial system.

blood relation, blood relative n a person related by descent, not marriage.

bloodshed n killing.

bloodshot adj (eye) suffused with blood, red and inflamed.

blood sport n any sport in which an animal is hunted and killed.

bloodstream n the flow of blood through the blood vessels in the human body.

bloodsucker n an animal that sucks blood, a leech; a person who sponges or preys on another, an extortionist.–**bloodsucking** adj, n.

bloodthirsty adj (**bloodthirstier, bloodthirstiest**) eager for blood, cruel, warlike.–**bloodthirstiness** n.

blood vessel n in the body, a vein, artery, or capillary.

bloody adj (**bloodier, bloodiest**) stained with or covered in blood; bloodthirsty; cruel, murderous. * vt (**bloodying, bloodied**) to cover with blood.–**bloodily** adv.–**bloodiness** n.

bloody-minded adj (inf) deliberately obstructive.–**bloodymindedness** n.

bloom n a flower or blossom; the period of being in flower; a period of most health, vigor, etc; a youthful, healthy glow; the powdery coating on some fruit and leaves. * vi to blossom; to be in one's prime; to glow with health etc.

blooming adj blossoming, flowering; flourishing.–**bloomingly** adv.

blossom n a flower, esp one that produces edible fruit; a state or time of flowering. * vi to flower; to begin to develop.–**blossomy** adj.

blot n a spot or stain, esp of ink; something that diminishes or spoils the beauty of; a blemish in reputation. * vt (**blotting, blotted**) to spot or stain; to obscure; to disgrace; to absorb with blotting paper.

blotch n a spot or discoloration on the skin; any large blot or stain. * vt to cover with blotches.–**blotched** adj.–**blotchily** adv.–**blotchy** adj.

blotting paper n absorbent paper used to dry freshly written ink.

blouse n a shirt-like garment worn by women.

blow[1] n a hard hit, as with the fist; a sudden attack; a sudden misfortune; a setback.

blow[2] vb (**blowing, blew**, pp **blown**) vi to cause a current of air; to be moved or carried (by air, the wind, etc); (mus) to make a sound by forcing in air with the mouth; (often with **out**) to burst suddenly; to breathe hard; (with **out**) to become extinguished by a gust of air; (gas or oil well) to erupt out of control; (with **over**) to pass without consequence. * vt to move along with a current of air; to make a sound by blowing; to inflate with air; (a fuse, etc) to melt; (inf) to spend (money) freely; (sl) to leave; (sl) to divulge a secret; (sl) to bungle;

(often with **up**) to burst by an explosion; (with **out**) to extinguish by a gust; (storm) to dissipate (itself) by blowing; (with **over**) to pass over or pass by; (with **up**) to enlarge a photograph; (with **up**) (inf) to lose one's temper.

blowhole n a nostril of a whale; a vent for the escape of gas, air, etc; a hole in ice used for breathing by whales, seals, etc.

blowlamp, blowtorch n a gas-powered torch that produces a hot flame for welding, etc.

blowpipe n a tube through which a current of air or gas is driven upon a flame to concentrate its heat on a substance, eg glass, to fuse it; a long tube of cane or reed used to discharge arrows by the force of the breath.

blowy adj (**blowier, blowiest**) breezy, windy.

blubber[1] vi to weep loudly.

blubber[2] n whale fat; excessive fat on the body.

bludgeon n a short, heavy stick used for striking. * vti to strike with a bludgeon; to bully or coerce.

blue adj (**bluer, bluest**) of the color of the clear sky; depressed; (film) indecent, obscene. * n the color of the spectrum lying between green and violet; (with **the**) the sky, the sea. * vt (**blueing** or **bluing, blued**) to make or dye blue; to dip in blue liquid.

bluebell n any of several plants with a one-sided cluster of blue bell-shaped flowers.

bluebird n any of various small songbirds prevalent in North America.

blue blood n royal or aristocratic descent.

bluebottle n a large fly.

blue chip adj (stocks, shares) providing a reliable return.

blue-collar adj of or pertaining to manual workers.

bluegrass n any of several rich pasture grasses with bluish green blades, esp in Kentucky; improvisatory country music played on unamplified instruments.

blue mold n a minute fungus that attacks bread and other foodstuffs.

blueprint n a blue photographic print of plans; a detailed scheme, template of work to be done; basis or prototype for future development.

blues npl (used as sing or pl) depression, melancholy; a type of melancholy folk music originating among Black Americans.

blue whale n a rorqual, the largest mammal known.

bluff[1] adj rough in manner; abrupt, outspoken; ascending steeply with a flat front. * n a broad, steep bank or cliff.–**bluffness** n.

bluff[2] vti to mislead or frighten by a false, bold front.* n deliberate deception.–**bluffer** n.

blunder vi to make a foolish mistake; to move about clumsily. * n a foolish mistake.–**blunderer** n.–**blundering** adj.–**blunderingly** adv.

blunt adj not having a sharp edge or point; rude, outspoken, unsubtle. * vti to make or become dull.–**bluntly** adv.–**bluntness** n.

blur n a stain, smear; an ill-defined impression. * vti (**blurring, blurred**) to smear; to make or become indistinct in shape, etc; to dim.–**blurred** adj.–**blurredly** adv.–**blurry** adj.

blurb n a promotional description, as on a book cover; an exaggerated advertisement.

blurt vt (with **out**) to utter impulsively.

blush n a red flush of the face caused by embarrassment or guilt; any rosy color. * vi (with **for, at**) to show embarrassment, modesty, joy, etc involuntarily, by blushing; to become rosy.

bluster vi to make a noise like the wind; to bully. * n a blast, as of the wind; bullying or boastful talk, often to hide shame or embarrassment.–**blusterer** n.–**blustery** adj.–**blusteringly, blusterously** adv.

BMus abbr = Bachelor of Music.

boa n any of various large South American snakes that crush their prey; a long fluffy scarf of feathers.

boa constrictor n the largest boa, remarkable for its length and power of destroying its prey by constriction.

boar n a male pig, a wild hog.

board n meals, esp when provided regularly for pay; a long, flat piece of sawed wood, etc; a flat piece of wood, etc for some special purpose; pasteboard; a council; a group of people who supervise a company; the side of a ship (overboard). * vt to provide with meals and lodging at fixed terms; to come onto the deck of (a ship); to get on (a train, bus, etc). * vi to provide with meals, or room and meals, regularly for pay; (with up) to cover with boards; **to take on board** to appoint to a position; to adopt new ideas.

board game n a game as chess, chequers, etc, played by moving pieces on a marked board.

boardroom n a room where meetings of a company's board are held.

boardwalk n a footway of boards, esp by the sea.

boast vi to brag. * vt to speak proudly of; to possess with pride. * n boastful talk.–**boaster** n.–**boastingly** adv.

boastful adj given to boasting.–**boastfully** adv.–**boastfulness** n.

boat n a small, open, waterborne craft; (inf) a ship. * vi to travel in a boat, esp for pleasure.

boat people npl refugees fleeing by boat.

boatswain n a ship's officer in charge of hull maintenance and related work.–also **bosun.**

boat train n a train for steamer or ferry passengers.

bob vb (**bobbing, bobbed**) vi to move abruptly up and down, often in water; to nod the head; to curtsey. * vt (hair) to cut short. * n a jerking motion up and down; the weight on a pendulum, plumb line, etc; a woman's or girl's short haircut.

bobbin n a reel or spool on which yarn or thread is wound.

bobble n a small woolly ball used for ornament or trimming; a bobbing movement; (inf) a mistake; a fumble. * vti to bob up and down; to make a mistake; to fumble with (a ball).

bobby pin n a clip for holding hair in position; a hairgrip.

bobcat n (pl **bobcats, bobcat**) a medium-sized feline of eastern North America with a black-spotted reddish-brown coat and a short tail.

bobsled, bobsleigh n a long racing sled. * vi (**bobsledding, bobsledded**) to ride or race on a bobsled.

bode vt to be an omen of.

bodice n the upper part of a woman's dress.

bodily adj physical; relating to the body. * adv in the flesh; as a whole; altogether.

body n (pl **bodies**) the whole physical substance of a person, animal, or plant; the trunk of a person or animal; a corpse; the principal part of anything; a distinct mass; substance or consistency, as of liquid; a richness of flavor; a person; a distinct group of people. * vt (**bodying, bodied**) to give shape to.

body bag n a large plastic sack, usu zipped, to carry a corpse from the scene of a disaster.

bodybuilding n strengthening and enlarging the muscles through exercise and diet for competitive display.–**bodybuilder** n.

bodyguard n a person or persons assigned to guard someone.

body language n gestures, unconscious bodily movements, etc, that function as a means of communication.

bodywork n the outer shell of a motor vehicle.

bog n wet, spongy ground; quagmire. * vb (**bogging, bogged**) vt to sink or submerge in a bog or quagmire. * vi to sink or stick in a bog.–**boggy** adj.

bogeyman n (pl **bogeymen**) an imaginary monster commonly used to frighten children.

boggle vi to be surprised; to hesitate (at). * vt to confuse (the imagination, mind, etc).

bogus adj counterfeit, spurious.

bohemian n a person who disregards social conventions or evinces a wild or roving disposition.–also adj.

boil[1] vi to change rapidly from a liquid to a vapor by heating; to bubble when boiling; to cook in boiling liquid; to be aroused with anger; (with **down**) to reduce by boiling; to condense; (with **over**) to overflow when boiling; to burst out in anger. * vt to heat to boiling point; to cook in boiling water.–**boilable** adj.

boil[2] n an inflamed, pus-filled, painful swelling on the skin.

boiler n a container in which to boil things; a storage tank in which water is heated and steam generated; a device for providing central heating and hot water.

boiling point n the temperature at which a liquid boils; the point at which a person loses his temper; the point of crisis.

boisterous adj wild, noisy; stormy; loud and exuberant.–**boisterously** adv.

bold adj daring or courageous; fearless; impudent; striking to the eye. * n boldface type.–**boldly** adv.–**boldness** n.

bolero n (pl **boleros**) a lively Spanish dance; the music accompanying such a dance; a short jacket-shaped bodice.

boll n the pod of a plant, esp of cotton or flax.

bollard n a strong post on a wharf around which mooring lines are secured; one of a line of posts closing off a street to traffic; an illuminated marker on a traffic island.

boll weevil n an American weevil that infests cotton bolls.

boloney see **baloney.**

Bolshevik n (pl **Bolsheviks, Bolsheviki**) a Russian communist; a revolutionary; an opponent of an existing social order.–**Bolshevism** n.–**Bolshevist** adj, n.

bolster n a long narrow pillow; any bolster-like object or support. * vt (often with **up**) to support or strengthen.–**bolsterer** n.–**bolsteringly** adv.

bolt[1] n a bar used to lock a door, etc; an arrow for a crossbow; a flash of lightning; a threaded metal rod used with a nut to hold parts together; a roll (of cloth, paper, etc); a sudden dash. * vt to lock with a bolt; to eat hastily; to say suddenly; to blurt (out); to abandon (a party, group, etc). * vi (horse) to rush away suddenly * adv erectly upright.–**bolter** n.

bolt[2] vt to sift or separate coarser from finer particles; to examine with care, to investigate; to separate.–also **boult.**–**bolter** n.

bomb n a projectile containing explosives, incendiary material, or chemicals used for destruction; (with **the**) the hydrogen or atomic bomb; (sl) a lot of money. * vt to attack with bombs. * vi to fail, to flop.

bombard vt to attack with bombs or artillery; to attack verbally.–**bombardment** n.

bombardier n the crew member who releases the bombs in a bomber.

bombast n pretentious or boastful language.–**bombastic** adj.–**bombastically** adv.

bomber n a person who bombs; an aircraft that carries bombs.

bombshell n a shocking surprise.

bona fide adj in good faith; genuine or real.

bonanza n a rich vein of ore; any source of wealth; unexpected good fortune or luck.

bond n anything that binds, fastens, or unites; (pl) shackles; an obligation imposed by a contract, promise, etc; the status of goods in a warehouse until taxes are paid; an interest-bearing certificate issued by the government or business, redeemable on a specified date; surety against theft, absconding, etc. * vt to join, bind, or otherwise unite; to provide a bond for; to place or hold (goods) in bond; to put together bricks or stones so that they overlap to give strength. * vi to hold together by means of a bond.–**bondable** adj.–**bonder** n.

bondage n slavery, captivity.

bone n the hard material making up the skeleton; any constituent part of the skeleton; (pl) the skeleton; the essentials or basics of anything. * vti to remove the bones from, as meat; (with **up**) (inf) to study hard.–**boneless** adj.

bone china n china made from clay mixed with bone ash.

bone meal *n* fertilizer or feed made of crushed or ground bone.

bonfire *n* an outdoor fire.

bongo *n* (*pl* **bongos**) either of a pair of small drums of different pitch struck with the fingers.

bonhomie *n* good-heartedness; a frank good-natured manner.–**bonhomous** *adj.*

bonnet *n* a hat with a chin ribbon, worn by women and children.

bonsai *n* (*pl* **bonsai**) a miniature tree or shrub that has been dwarfed by selective pruning; the art of cultivating bonsai.

bonus *n* (*pl* **bonuses**) an amount paid over the sum due as interest, dividend, or wages.

bon voyage *n, interj* an expression used to wish travelers a pleasant trip.

bony *adj* (**bonier, boniest**) of or resembling bones; having large or prominent bones; full of bones.

boo *interj* an expression of disapproval. * *n* (*pl* **boos**) hooting. * *vb* (**booing, booed**) *vi* to low like an ox; to groan. * *vt* to hoot at.

boob *n* a stupid awkward person; a blunder.

booby *n* (*pl* **boobies**) a foolish person; the loser in a game.

booby trap *n* a trap for playing a practical joke on someone; a camouflaged explosive device triggered by an unsuspecting victim.

boogie *vi* (**boogieing, boogied**) to dance to pop music or jazz. * *n* fast, rhythmic music for dancing.

boohoo *vi* (**boohooing, boohooed**) to weep noisily or to pretend to do so. * *n* (*pl* **boohoos**) the sound of noisy weeping.

book *n* a bound set of printed or blank pages; a literary composition of fact or fiction; the script or libretto of a play or musical; (*pl*) written records of transactions or accounts; a book or record of bets. * *vt* to make a reservation in advance; to note a person's name and address for an alleged offense. * *vi* to make a reservation.

bookcase *n* a piece of furniture with shelves for books.

bookish *adj* fond of reading.–**bookishness** *n.*

bookkeeping *n* the systematic recording of business accounts.–**bookkeeper** *n.*

book learning *n* theoretical, not practical, knowledge.–**book-learned** *adj.*

booklet *n* a small book, usu with a paper cover; a pamphlet.

bookmark(er) *n* a thing to mark a place in a book.

bookworm *n* an insect that feeds on books; a person who reads a lot.

boom[1] *n* a spar on which a sail is stretched; a barrier across a harbor; a long pole carrying a microphone.

boom[2] *vi* to make a deep, hollow sound. * *n* a resonant sound, as of the sea.

boom[3] *vi* to flourish or prosper suddenly. * *n* a period of vigorous growth (eg in business, sales, prices).

boomerang *n* a curved stick that, when thrown, returns to the thrower; an action that unexpectedly rebounds and harms the agent.–*also vi.*

boon[1] *n* something useful or helpful; a blessing; a favor.

boon[2] *adj* bountiful; convivial, jolly; specially friendly (*boon companion*).

boondocks *npl* (*sl*) a wild, inhospitable area; a dull, provincial region.–**boondock** *adj.*

boor *n* an ill-mannered or coarse person.–**boorish** *adj.*–**boorishly** *adv.*–**boorishness** *n.*

boost *vt* (*sales, etc*) to increase; to encourage, to improve; to push; to help by advertising or promoting. * *n* a push.

booster *n* a thing or person that increases the effectiveness of another mechanism; the first stage of a rocket, which usually breaks away after launching; a substance that increases the effectiveness of medication.

boot[1] *n* a strong covering for the foot and lower part of the leg; (*sl: with* **the**) dismissal from employment. * *vt* to kick; to get rid of by force; (*comput*) to bring a program from a disc into the memory.

boot[2] *n* (*arch*) advantage, use; **to boot** as well. * *vi* (*arch*) to avail.

bootee *n* a knitted or soft shoe for a baby.

booth *n* a stall for selling goods; a small enclosure for voting; a public telephone enclosure.

bootleg *vt* (**bootlegging, bootlegged**) to smuggle illicit alcohol; to deal in illegally made records and tapes of live music, etc.–**bootlegger** *n.*

booty *n* (*pl* **booties**) spoils obtained as plunder.

booze *vi* (*inf*) to drink alcohol excessively. * *n* alcohol.–**boozer** *n.*–**boozy** *adj.*

bop *n* a style of 1940s jazz music.–*also* **bebop**.

boracic *adj* of or yielding boron.–*also* **boric**.

boracic acid *n* a white solid acid used in manufacturing and as a mild antiseptic.

borage *n* a blue-flowered herb used in salads, etc.

borax *n* a mineral composed of the sodium salt compounded of boracic acid chiefly from the dried beds of certain lakes, used in the manufacture of glass, enamel, antiseptics, soaps, etc.

border *n* the edge, rim, or margin; a dividing line between two countries; a narrow strip along an edge. * *vi* (*with* **on**, **upon**) to be adjacent; to approach, to verge on. * *vt* to form a border.

borderline *n* a boundary. * *adj* on a boundary; doubtful, indefinite.

bore[1] *vt* to drill so as to form a hole; to weary, by being dull or uninteresting. * *n* a hole made by drilling; the diameter of a gun barrel; a dull or uninteresting person.–**boring** *adj.*

bore[2] *see* **bear**[1].

boredom *n* tedium.

boric *see* **boracic**.

born *pp* of **bear**[1]. * *adj* by birth, natural.

borne *see* **bear**[1].

boron *n* a nonmetallic element found in borax.

borough *n* a self-governing, incorporated town; an administrative area of a city, as in New York or London.

borrow *vt* to obtain (an item) with the intention of returning it; (*an idea*) to adopt as one's own; (*loan, money*) to obtain from a financial institution at definite rates of interest.–**borrower** *n.*

borscht, borsch *n* a type of soup (orig from Russia) made with beetroot.

borzoi *n* (*pl* **borzois**) a tall hound with a long, silky coat and a long head, a Russian wolfhound.

bosom *n* the breast of a human being, esp a woman; the part of a dress that covers it; the seat of the emotions. * *adj* (*friend*) very dear, intimate.

bosun *see* **boatswain**.

boss *n* (*inf*) the manager or foreman; a powerful local politician. * *vt* to domineer; to be in control.

bossy *adj* (**bossier, bossiest**) (*inf*) domineering, fond of giving orders.–**bossily** *adv.*–**bossiness** *n.*

botany *n* (*pl* **botanies**) the study of plants.–**botanical, botanic** *adj.*–**botanically** *adv.*–**botanist** *n.*

botch *n* a poorly done piece of work. * *vt* to mend or patch clumsily; to put together without sufficient care.–**botcher** *n.*

both *adj, pron* the two together; the one and the other. * *conj* together equally.–*also adv.*

bother *vt* to perplex or annoy; to take the time or trouble. * *n* worry; trouble; someone who causes problems, etc.

bottle *n* a glass or plastic container for holding liquids; its contents; (*sl*) courage, nerve. * *vt* to put in bottles; to confine as if in a bottle.

bottleneck *n* a narrow stretch of a road where traffic is held up; a congestion in any stage of a process.

bottlenose *n* a dolphin with a sharp protruding beak; a moderately large toothed whale with a prominent beak.

bottom *n* the lowest or deepest part of anything; the base or foundation; the lowest position (eg in a class); the buttocks; (*naut*) the part of a ship's hull below water; the seabed. * *vt* to be based or founded on; to bring to the bottom, to get to the bottom of. * *vi* to become based; to reach the bottom; (*with* **out**) to flatten off after dropping sharply.

bottomless *adj* very deep; without limit.

bottom line *n* the crux; the line at the bottom of a financial report that shows the net profit or loss; the final result.—**bottom-line** *adj*.

botulism *n* a type of severe food poisoning.

boudoir *n* a woman's bedroom.

bougainvillea, bougainvillaea *n* a tropical plant with large rosy or purple bracts.

bough *n* a branch of a tree.

bought *see* **buy**.

bouillon *n* a clear seasoned stock or broth.

boulder *n* a large stone or mass of rock rounded by the action of erosion.

boulevard *n* a broad, often tree-lined road.

boult *see* **bolt**[2].

bounce *vi* to rebound; to jump up suddenly; (*sl: check*) to be returned because of lack of funds; (*with* **back**) to recover easily, eg from misfortune or ill health. * *vt* to cause a ball to bounce; (*sl*) to put a (person) out by force; (*sl*) to fire from a job. * *n* a leap or springiness; capacity for bouncing; sprightliness; boastfulness, arrogance.—**bouncy** *adj*.

bouncer *n* (*sl*) a man hired to remove disorderly people from nightclubs, etc.

bound[1] *see* **bind**.

bound[2] *n* (*usu pl*) the limit or boundary. * *vt* to limit, confine or surround; to name the boundaries of.

bound[3] *n* a jump or leap. * *vi* to jump or leap.

bound[4] *adj* (*with* **for**) intending to go to, on the way to.

boundary *n* (*pl* **boundaries**) the border of an area; the limit; (*cricket*) the limit line of a field; a stroke that goes beyond the boundary line.

boundless *adj* unlimited, vast.—**boundlessly** *adv*.—**boundlessness** *n*.

bountiful *adj* generous in giving.—**bountifully** *adv*.—**bountifulness** *n*.

bounty *n* (*pl* **bounties**) generosity in giving; the gifts given; a reward or premium.

bouquet *n* a bunch of flowers; the perfume given off by wine.

bouquet garni *n* (*pl* **bouquets garnis**) herbs tied in a small bundle used for flavoring stews, soups, sauces, etc.

bourbon *n* a whiskey distilled in the US from corn mash.

bourgeois *n* (*pl* **bourgeois**) a member of the bourgeoisie or middle class; a conventional and unimaginative individual. * *adj* smug, respectable, conventional; mediocre.

bourgeoisie *n* the class between the lower and upper classes, mostly composed of professional and business people.—*also* **middle class**.

bout *n* a spell, a turn, a period spent in some activity; a contest or struggle, esp boxing or wrestling; a time of illness.

boutique *n* a small shop, usually selling fashionable clothing and accessories.

bovine *adj* relating to cattle; dull; sluggish. * *n* an ox, cow etc.

bow[1] *vi* to bend the knee or to lean the head (and chest) forward as a form of greeting or respect or shame; (*with* **before**) to accept, to submit; (*with* **out**) to withdraw or retire gracefully. * *vt* to bend downwards; to weigh down; to usher in or out with a bow. * *n* a lowering of the head (and chest) in greeting.

bow[2] *n* a weapon for shooting arrows; an implement for playing the strings of a violin; a decorative knot of ribbon, etc. * *vti* to bend, curve.

bow[3] *n* the forward part of a ship.

bowdlerize *vt* to expurgate, to remove indelicate words from.—**bowdlerism** *n*.—**bowdlerization** *n*.

bowel *n* the intestine; (*pl*) entrails; (*pl*) the deep and remote part of anything.

bower *n* an arbor, a shady recess; (*poet*) dwelling.

bowie knife *n* a long hunting knife, a sheath knife.

bowl[1] *n* a wooden ball having a bias used in bowling; (*pl*) a game played on a smooth lawn with bowls. * *vti* to play the game of bowls; (*with* **over**) to knock over; (*inf*) to astonish.

bowl[2] *n* a deep, rounded dish; the rounded end of a pipe; a sports stadium.

bow-legged *adj* having legs that curve outwards between the thigh and the ankle; bandy.

bowler[1] *n* a person who plays bowls.

bowler[2] *n* a stiff felt hat.—*also* **derby**.

bowling *n* a game in which a heavy wooden ball is bowled along a bowling alley at ten wooden skittles; the game of bowls.

bow tie *n* a necktie tied in the shape of a bow.

bow window *n* a curved bay window.

box[1] *n* a container or receptacle for holding anything; (*theatre*) a compartment with seats; (*inf*) a television set. * *vt* to put into a box; to enclose; (*with* **in**) to restrict.

box[2] *vt* to hit using the hands or fists. * *vi* to fight with the fists. * *n* a blow on the head or ear with the fist. —**boxing** *n*.

boxcar *n* an enclosed freight car.

boxer *n* a person who engages in boxing; a breed of dog with smooth hair and a stumpy tail.

boxer shorts *npl* loose underpants that resemble the pants worn by boxers.

box office *n* a theater ticket office; the popularity of a play, film, actor.—**box-office** *adj*.

boy *n* a male child; a son; a lad; a youth. * *interj* an exclamation of surprise or joy.

boycott *vt* to refuse to deal with or trade with in order to punish or coerce.—*also* *n*.

boyfriend *n* a male friend with whom a person is romantically or sexually involved.

boyhood *n* the time, or state, of being a boy.

boyish *adj* like a boy; puerile; with the appeal of a boy.—**boyishly** *adv*.—**boyishness** *n*.

Br *abbr* = British; (*chem symbol*) bromine; brother.

bra *n* a brassiere.

brace *n* a prop; a support to stiffen a framework; a hand tool for drilling; (*pl* **brace**) a pair, esp of game; (*pl*) straps for holding up trousers; a dental appliance for straightening the teeth. * *vt* to steady.

bracelet *n* an ornamental chain or band for the wrist; (*pl: sl*) handcuffs.

bracing *adj* refreshing, invigorating.—**bracingly** *adv*.

bracken *n* a large, coarse fern; a wide area of these growing on hills or moorland.

bracket *n* a projecting metal support for a shelf; a group or category of people classified according to income; (*pl*) a pair of characters (), [], {}, used in printing or writing as parentheses. * *vt* to support with brackets; to enclose by brackets; (*people*) to group together.

brackish *adj* somewhat salty; nauseating.—**brackishness** *n*.

bract *n* a modified leaf growing from a flower stem or enveloping a head of flowers.—**bracteal** *adj*.

brag *vti* (**bragging, bragged**) to boast. * *n* a boast or boastful talk.—**bragger** *n*.

braggart *n* a loud arrogant boaster.

Brahman *n* (*pl* **Brahmans**) (*Hinduism*) a member of the highest caste, formerly consisting only of priests.—**Brahmanic, Brahmanical** *adj*.

braid *vt* to interweave three or more strands (of hair, straw, etc); to make by such interweaving. * *n* a narrow band made by such interweaving for decorating clothing; a plait.—**braider** *n*.

Braille *n* printing for the blind, using a system of raised dots that can be understood by touch.—*also* *adj*.

brain *n* nervous tissue contained in the skull of vertebrates that controls the nervous system; intellectual ability; (*inf*) a person of great intelligence; (*often pl*) the chief planner of an organization or enterprise. * *vt* to shatter the skull of; (*sl*) to hit on the head.

brainchild n (pl **brainchildren**) the result of creative thought; a clever and original idea or plan.

brain drain n the loss of highly skilled scientists, technicians, academics, etc through emigration.

brainless adj (inf) stupid.–**brainlessness** n.

brainstorm n a violent mental disturbance; a brain wave.

brainwash vt to change a person's ideas or beliefs by physical or mental conditioning, usu over a long period.–**brainwasher** n.– **brainwashing** n.

brain wave n an electrical impulse in the brain; (inf) a bright idea.

brainy adj (**brainier, brainiest**) (inf) having a good mind; intelligent.–**braininess** n.

braise vt (meat, vegetables, etc) to sauté lightly and cook slowly in liquid with the lid on.

brake n a device for slowing or stopping the motion of a wheel by friction. * vt to retard or stop by a brake. * vi to apply the brake on a vehicle; to become checked by a brake.

bramble n a prickly shrub or vine, esp of blackberries and raspberries.–**brambly** adj.

bran n the husks of grain separated by sieving from the flour; a food containing these.

branch n an offshoot extending from the trunk or bough of a tree or from the parent stem of a shrub; a separately located subsidiary or office of an enterprise or business; a part of something larger, eg a road or railway. * vi to possess branches; to divide into branches; to come out (from a main part) as a branch; (with **out**) to extend or enlarge one's interests, activities, etc.

brand n an identifying mark on cattle, imprinted with hot iron; a burning piece of wood; a mark of disgrace; a trademark; a particular make (of goods). * vt to burn a mark with a hot iron; to fix in the memory; to denounce.

brandish vt (a weapon, etc) to wave or flourish in a threatening manner.–**brandisher** n.

brand name n the name by which a certain commodity is known.–**brand-name** adj.

brand-new adj entirely new and unused.

brandy n (pl **brandies**) an alcoholic liquor made from distilled wine or fermented fruit juice.

brash adj bold; loud-mouthed; reckless.–**brashly** adv.–**brashness** n.

brass n an alloy of copper and zinc; (inf) impudence; nerve; cheek; money; (often pl) the brass instruments of an orchestra or band; (sl) officers or officials of high rank.

brasserie n a bar and restaurant.

brassica n any of a group of plants that includes cabbages, turnips and mustards.–**brassicaceous** adj.

brassiere n a woman's undergarment for protecting and supporting the breasts, a bra.

brassy adj (**brassier, brassiest**) like brass; brazen; cheeky.– **brassily** adv.–**brassiness** n.

brat n an ill-mannered, annoying child.

bravado n (pl **bravadoes, bravados**) pretended confidence; swaggering.

brave adj showing courage; not timid or cowardly; fearless; handsome; of excellent appearance. * vt to confront boldly; to defy. * n a North American Indian warrior.–**bravely** adv.

bravery n (pl **braveries**) the quality of being brave; courage, fearlessness; finery, magnificence.

bravo interj well done! * n (pl **bravoes, bravos**) a cry or shout of "bravo!".

bravura n bold daring; dash; (mus) a passage requiring spirit and technical brilliance.

brawl n a loud quarrel; a noisy fight. * vi to quarrel loudly.– **brawler** n.

brawn n strong, well-developed muscles; physical strength; pickled pork.

brawny adj (**brawnier, brawniest**) muscular, tough.– **brawnily** adv.–**brawniness** n.

bray n the sound of a donkey; any harsh sound. * vi (**braying, brayed**) to make similar sounds.–**brayer** n.

brazen adj made of brass; shameless. * vt (usu with **out**) to face a situation boldly and shamelessly.–**brazenness** n.

brazier[1] n a metal container for hot coals.

brazier[2] n a worker in brass.

brazil nut n a large three-cornered nut, the seed of a tall tree of Brazil.

breach n a break or rupture; violation of a contract, promise, etc; a break in friendship. * vt to make an opening in.

bread n a dough, made from flour, yeast and milk, that is baked; nourishment; (sl) money; **bread and butter** (inf) one's livelihood. * vt to coat meat, fish, etc with breadcrumbs before cooking.

bread-and-butter adj (job) providing a basic income; (issues, etc) fundamental, basic; (letter) thanking for hospitality.

breadth n measurement from side to side, width; extent; liberality (eg of interests).

breadthways, breadthwise adv from side to side.

breadwinner n the principal wage-earner of a family.

break vb (**breaking, broke,** pp **broken**) vt to smash or shatter; to tame; (rules) to violate; to discontinue; to cause to give up a habit; (fall) to lessen the severity of; to ruin financially; (news) to impart; to decipher or solve; (with **down**) to crush or destroy; to analyse; (with **in**) to intervene; to train. * vi to fall apart; (voice) to assume a lower tone at puberty; to cut off relations with; to suffer a collapse, as of spirit; (news) to become public in a sudden and sensational way; (with **down**) to fail completely; to succumb emotionally; (with **even**) to suffer neither profit nor loss (after taking certain action); (with **in**) to force a way in; (with **out**) to appear, begin; to erupt; to throw off restraint, escape; (with **up**) to disperse; to separate; to collapse. * n a breaking; an interruption; a gap; a sudden change, as in weather; a rest or a short holiday; an escape; (snooker, billiards) a continuous run of points; (sl) a fortunate opportunity.

breakage n the action of breaking; something broken.

breakaway n secession, disassociation.

breakdown n a mechanical failure; failure of health; nervous collapse; an analysis.

breaker n a large wave that crashes onto the shore, reef, etc.

breakfast n the first meal of the morning; the food consumed. * vi to have breakfast.

break-in n the unlawful entering of premises, esp by thieves.

breakneck adj dangerously steep or fast.

breakthrough n the action of breaking through an obstruction; an important advance or discovery.

breakwater n a barrier that protects a harbor or area of coast against the force of the waves.

bream n (pl **bream**) a freshwater fish.

breast n the chest; one of the two mammary glands; the seat of the emotions. * vt to oppose, confront; to arrive at the top of; to confess (make a clean breast of).

breastbone n (anat) the flat narrow bone in the centre of the chest that connects the ribs, the sternum.

breast-feed vt (**breast-feeding, breast-fed**) to allow a baby to suck milk from the breast.

breastplate n armor covering the front of the body.

breaststroke n a swimming stroke in which both arms are brought out sideways from the chest.

breath n the inhalation and exhalation of air in breathing; the air taken into the lungs; life; a slight breeze; (scandal) a hint.

breathe vi to inhale and exhale, to respire air; to take a rest or pause; to exist or live; to speak or sing softly; to whisper. * vt to emit or exhale; to whisper or speak softly.

breather n a pause during exercise to recover one's breath.

breathing n respiration; air in gentle motion; a gentle influence; a pause; (*phonetics*) an accent (') whether an initial vowel is aspirated or not.

breathing space n a pause in which to recover, get organized or get going.

breathless adj out of breath; panting; gasping; unable to breathe easily because of emotion.–**breathlessly** adv.–**breathlessness** n.

breathtaking adj very exciting.

breathy adj (**breathier, breathiest**) (*voice*) not clear sounding.–**breathily** adv.–**breathiness** n.

bred see **breed**.

breech n the back part of a gun barrel.

breech delivery, breech birth n the birth of a baby buttocks or feet first.

breeches npl trousers extending just below the knee.

breed vb (**breeding, bred**) vt to engender; to bring forth; (*dogs*) to raise; to give rise to. * vi to produce young; to be generated. * n offspring; lineage or race; species (of animal).–**breeder** n.

breeding n the bearing of offspring; one's education and training; refined behavior.

breeze n a light gentle wind; something easy to do. * vi (*inf*) to move quickly or casually.

breezy adj (**breezier, breeziest**) windy; nonchalant; light-hearted, cheerful.–**breezily** adv.–**breeziness** n.

brethren see **brother**.

breviary n (*pl* **breviaries**) (*RC Church*) a book containing the daily offices and prayers.

brevity n (*pl* **brevities**) briefness; conciseness.

brew vt to make (beer, ale, etc) from malt and hops by boiling and fermenting; to infuse (tea, etc); to plot, scheme. * vi to be in the process of being brewed; to be about to happen. * n a brewed drink.–**brewer** n.–**brewery** n.

briar see **brier**.

bribe n money or gifts offered illegally to gain favour or influence; the gift to achieve this. * vt to offer or give a bribe to.–**bribable** adj.–**briber** n.

bribery n (*pl* **briberies**) the giving or taking of bribes.

bric-a-brac n curios, ornamental or rare odds and ends.

brick n a baked clay block for building; a similar shaped block of other material. * vt to lay or wall up with brick.

brickbat n a piece of brick, esp one used as a weapon; an unfavorable remark.

bricklayer n a person who lays bricks.

bridal adj relating to a bride or a wedding.

bride n a woman about to be married or recently married.

bridegroom n a man about to be married or recently married.

bridesmaid n a young girl or woman attending the bride during a wedding.

bridge[1] n a structure built to convey people or traffic over a river, road, railway line, etc; the platform on a ship where the captain gives directions; the hard ridge of bone in the nose; an arch to raise the strings of a guitar, etc; a mounting for false teeth.* vt to be or act as a bridge; to be a connecting link between.–**bridgeable** adj.

bridge[2] n a card game for two teams of two players based on whist.

bridle n the headgear of a horse, controlling its movements; a restraint or check; (*naut*) a mooring cable. * vt to put a bridle on (a horse); to restrain or check. * vi to draw one's head back as an expression of anger, scorn, etc.–**bridler** n.

brief n a summary of a client's case for the instruction of a barrister in a trial at law; an outline of an argument, esp that setting out the main contentions; (*pl*) men's or women's close-fitting underpants. * vt to provide with a precise summary of the facts. * adj short, concise.–**briefly** adv.–**briefness** n.

briefcase n a flat case for carrying documents, etc.

brier n a plant with a thorny or prickly woody stem; a mass of these; a tobacco pipe made from the root of the brier.–*also* **briar**.–**briery, briary** adj.

brig n a two-masted square-rigged vessel; a naval prison, esp on a ship.

brigade n an army unit, smaller than a division, commanded by a brigadier; a group of people organized to perform a particular function.

brigadier n an officer commanding a brigade and ranking next below a major general.

brigand n a bandit, usu one of a roving gang.

bright adj clear, shining; brilliant in color or sound; favorable or hopeful; intelligent, illustrious. * adv brightly.–**brightly** adv.–**brightness** n.

brighten vti to make or become brighter.–**brightener** n.

brilliance n intense radiance, lustre, splendor.

brilliant adj sparkling, bright; splendid; very intelligent.–**brilliantly** adv.

brim n the rim of a hollow vessel; the outer edge of a hat. * vti (**brimming, brimmed**) to fill or be filled to the brim; (*with* **over**) to overflow.

brimful adj completely full; overflowing.

brimstone n sulfur; a yellow butterfly.

brine n salt water; the sea.

bring vt (**bringing, brought**) to fetch, carry or convey "here" or to the place where the speaker will be; to cause to happen (eg rain, relief); to result in; to lead to an action or belief; to sell for; (*with* **about**) to induce, to effect; (*with* **down**) to cause to fall by or as if by shooting; (*with* **forth**) to give birth to; (*with* **forward**) to present something for consideration; to transfer a total figure from the bottom of a page to the top of the next page; (*with* **in**) to yield a profit or return; to return a verdict in court; to introduce (a legislative bill); to earn (an income); (*with* **off**) to achieve a success, often against odds; accomplish; (*with* **out**) to cause to appear; to produce (a play) or publish (a book); to demonstrate clearly, expose to view; to help someone with encouragement; (*with* **over**) to convince a person to change their loyalties; (*with* **round**) to convince a person to change their opinion; to get someone to agree or give support; to restore a person to consciousness, revive; (*with* **up**) to educate, rear a child; to raise (a matter) for discussion; to vomit.–**bringer** n.

brink n the verge of a steep place; the edge of the sea; the point of onset; the threshold of danger.

brinkmanship, brinksmanship n the pursuing of a policy, esp in international relations, that brings serious risk of danger in order to gain advantage.

brio n vivacity.

brisk adj alert; quick; vigorous; sharp in tone.–**briskly** adv.–**briskness** n.

brisket n meat from the breast of an animal.

bristle n a short, coarse hair. * vi to stand up, as bristles; to have the bristles standing up; to show anger or indignation; to be thickly covered (with).

bristly adj (**bristlier, bristliest**) covered with bristles; rough.–**bristliness** n.

Brit n (*inf*) a British person.

Brit. abbr = Britain; British.

British adj of or pertaining to Great Britain or its inhabitants; pertaining to the ancient Britons. * n the people of Britain; the language of the ancient Britons.–**Briton** n.

brittle adj easily cracked or broken; fragile; sharp-tempered.–**brittleness** n.

broach vt (a *topic*) to introduce for discussion; to pierce (a container) and draw out liquid.

broad adj of large extent from side to side; wide; spacious; giving an overall view or idea; (*humor*) coarse; strongly marked in

dialect or pronunciation. * n (sl) a woman.–**broadly** adv.–
broadness n.

broad bean n a plant widely grown for its large flat edible seed.

broadcast n a program on radio or television. * vti (**broadcast-ing, broadcast**) to transmit on radio or television; to make known widely; to scatter seed.–**broadcaster** n.

broaden vti to grow or make broad; to widen.

broad-minded adj tolerant; liberal in outlook.–**broad-mind-edly** adv.–**broad-mindedness** n.

broadsheet n a large sheet of paper printed on one side only; a large format newspaper.

broadside n the entire side of a ship above the waterline; a simulta-neous volley from one side of a warship; a verbal or written attack.

broad-spectrum adj efficacious against a wide range (of dis-eases, microorganisms).

brocade n a heavy fabric woven with raised patterns, orig in gold and silver. * vt to work with a raised pattern.

broccoli n (pl **broccoli**) a kind of cauliflower with loose heads of tiny green buds.

brochure n an advertising booklet.

brogue n a sturdy shoe; a dialectical accent, esp Irish.

broil vti to cook by exposure to direct heat; to grill.

broiler n a pan, grill, etc for broiling; a bird fit for broiling.

broke pt of **break**. * adj (inf) hard up, having no money.

broken pp of **break**. * adj splintered, fractured; violated; ruined; tamed; disconnected, interrupted; overwhelmed by sorrow or ill fortune; (speech) imperfect.–**brokenly** adv.–**brokenness** n.

brokenhearted adj grief-stricken; very sad.

broker n an agent who negotiates contracts of purchase and sale (as of commodities or securities); a power broker; a stockbroker.

bromide n a compound of bromine; a sedative; (sl) a bore; a trite remark.

bromine n an evil-smelling nonmetallic element related to chlo-rine and iodine.–**bromic** adj.

bronchi see **bronchus**.

bronchia npl (sing **bronchium**) the bronchial tubes, either of the two main branches of the windpipe.–**bronchial** adj.

bronchitis n inflammation of the lining of the bronchial tubes.–**bronchitic** adj.

brontosaur, brontosaurus n (pl **brontosauruses**) a large plant-eating dinosaur.–**brontosaurian** adj.

bronze n a copper and tin alloy, sometimes other elements; any object cast in bronze; a reddish-brown color. * adj made of, or like, or of the color of bronze; (skin) tanned.–**bronzy** adj.

brooch n an ornament held by a pin or a clasp.

brood vi to incubate or hatch (eggs); to ponder over or worry about. * n a group having a common nature or origin, esp the children in a family; the number produced in one hatch.

broody adj (**broodier, broodiest**) contemplative, moody; (inf) wanting to have a baby.–**broodily** adv.–**broodiness** n.

brook vt to tolerate.–**brookable** adj.

broom[1] n a bundle of fibers or twigs attached to a long handle for sweeping.

broom[2] n a shrub bearing large yellow flowers.

broomstick n the handle of a broom.

Bros abbr = Brothers.

broth n a thin or thick soup made by boiling meat, etc in water.

brothel n a house where prostitutes work.

brother n a male sibling; a friend who is like a brother; a fellow member of a group, profession or association; a lay member of a men's religious order; (pl **brethren**) used chiefly in formal address or in referring to the members of a society or sect.

brother-in-law n (pl **brothers-in-law**) the brother of a hus-band or wife; the husband of a sister.

brotherhood n the state or quality of being a brother, brotherli-ness; a fraternity, an association.

brotherly adj like a brother; kind; affectionate.–**brotherliness** n.

brought see **bring**.

brouhaha n a fuss; uproar.

brow n the forehead; the eyebrows; the top of a cliff; the jutting top of a hill.

browbeat vt (**browbeating, browbeat**, pp **browbeaten**) to intimidate with threats, to bully.

brown adj having the color of chocolate, a mixture of red, black and yellow; tanned. * n a brown color. * vti to make or become brown, esp by cooking.–**brownish** adj.–**brownness** n.

brownie n a square of flat, rich chocolate cake; a friendly helpful elf; (with cap) a member of the junior branch of the Girl Scout or Guide movement.

brownstone n a kind of sandstone; a house built of this.

browse vti to nibble, to graze; to examine (a book) at one's leisure or casually.

browser n someone that browses; a computer software package which allows the user to locate and read hypertext files.

brucellosis n an infectious disease of livestock, esp cattle, which can be passed to human beings.

bruise vt to injure and discolor (body tissue, surface of fruit) with-out breaking the skin; to break down (as leaves and berries) by pounding; to inflict psychological pain on. * vi to inflict a bruise; to undergo bruising. * n contusion of the skin; a similar injury to plant tissue; an injury, esp to the feelings.

bruiser n a tough, pugnacious man; a boxer.

brunch n breakfast and lunch combined.

brunette, brunet adj having dark-brown or black hair, often with dark eyes. * n a brunette person.

brunt n the main force or shock of a blow; the hardest part.

brush[1] n a device made of bristles set in a handle, used for groom-ing the hair, painting or sweeping; a short unfriendly meeting or exchange of words; a fox's bushy tail; a light stroke or graze, made in passing. * vt to groom or sweep with a brush; to remove with a brush; (with aside) to ignore, to regard as little account; (with up) to refresh one's memory of or skill in a subject; to wash and tidy oneself. * vi to touch lightly or graze; (with up) to smarten one's appearance.–**brusher** n.

brush[2] n brushwood.

brush-off n a curt dismissal.

brushwood n rough, close bushes; a thicket, a coppice; small wood or twigs suitable for the fire.

brushwork n a particular or characteristic style of painting.

brusque adj blunt and curt in manner.–**brusquely** adv.–**brusqueness** n.

Brussels sprout n a plant of the cabbage family with a small edi-ble green head.

brutal adj inhuman; savage, violent; severe.–**brutally** adv.–**brutality** n.

brutalize vt to treat brutally; to degrade.–**brutalization** n.

brute n any animal except man; a brutal person; (inf) an unpleas-ant or difficult person or thing. * adj (force) sheer, physical.

brutish adj brutal; stupid; savage, violent; coarse.–**brutishly** adv.–**brutishness** n.

BSc abbr = Bachelor of Science.

bubble n a film of liquid forming a ball around air or gas; a tiny ball of gas or air in a liquid or solid; a transparent dome; a scheme that collapses. * vi to boil; to rise in bubbles; to make a gurgling sound.

bubbly adj (**bubblier, bubbliest**) having bubbles, effervescent; cheerful, high-spirited. * n (inf) champagne.

bubo n (pl **buboes**) an inflamed swelling in the groin or armpit.–**bubonic** adj.

bubonic plague n a highly infectious often fatal disease con-tracted from fleas from infected rats.

buccaneer n a sea robber, a pirate. * vi to be a pirate.

buck n the male of animals such as the deer, hare, rabbit, antelope; (sl) a dollar. * vti (horse) to rear upwards quickly; (inf) to resist; (with up) (inf) to make or become cheerful; to hurry up.

bucket n a container with a handle for carrying liquid or substances in small pieces; (comput) a direct-access storage area from which data can be retrieved; (inf) a wastepaper bin. * vt to drive fast or recklessly; to pour with rain.

bucket seat n a single, contoured seat with an adjustable back as in a car, etc.

buckle n a fastening or clasp for a strap or band; a bend or bulge. * vti to fasten with a buckle; to bend under pressure, etc; (with **down**) (inf) to apply oneself diligently.

buckpasser n (inf) one who regularly shifts the blame or responsibility to someone else.

buckshee n (sl) an extra allowance, a windfall. * adj, adv free, for nothing.

buckskin n a soft leather of deerskin, etc; (pl) breeches or shoes made of this; (hist) a native American. * adj made of buckskin.

bucktooth n (pl **buckteeth**) a projecting front tooth.

buckwheat n a plant cultivated for its triangular seeds, which are ground into meal and used as a cereal.

bucolic adj pastoral; rustic. * n a pastoral poem; a rustic.–**bucolically** adv.

bud[1] n an embryo shoot, flower, or flower cluster of a plant; an early stage of development. * vi (**budding, budded**) to produce buds; to begin to develop.

bud[2] n (inf) buddy.

Buddha n one who has arrived at the state of perfect enlightenment; an image of Siddharta Gautama, founder of Buddhism.

Buddhism n a system of ethics and philosophy based on teachings of Buddha.–**Buddhist** n.

buddy n (pl **buddies**) (inf) a friend; a term of informal address; one who helps and supports another, esp an AIDS sufferer. * vi (**buddying, buddied**) to help as a buddy.

budge vti to shift or move.

budgerigar n a small Australian parrot bred as a cage bird in many varieties of different colors.–also **budgie**.

budget n an estimate of income and expenditure within specified limits of a country, a business, etc; the total amount of money for a given purpose; a stock or supply; **on a budget** restricting one's expenditure. * vb (**budgeting, budgeted**) vi to make a budget. * vt to put on a budget; to plan; (with **for**) to allow for or save money for a purpose or aim.–**budgetary** adj.

buff n a heavy, soft, brownish-yellow leather; a dull brownish yellow; (inf) a devotee, fan; (inf) a person's bare skin. * adj made of buff; of a buff color. * vt to clean or shine, orig with leather or a leather-covered wheel.

buffalo n (pl **buffalo, buffaloes** or **buffalos**) a wild ox; a bison.

buffer n anything that lessens shock, as of collision; something that serves as a protective barrier; a temporary storage area in a computer.

buffet[1] n a blow with the hand or fist. * vb (**buffeting, buffeted**) vt to hit with the hand or fist; to batter (as of the wind).

buffet[2] n a counter where refreshments are served; a meal at which guests serve themselves food.

buffoon n a clown, a jester; a silly person.–**buffoonery** n.

bug[1] n a continuing source of irritation.

bug[2] n an insect with sucking mouth parts; any insect; (inf) a germ or virus; (sl) a defect, as in a machine; (sl) a hidden microphone; an obsession, an enthusiasm. * vt (**bugging, bugged**) (sl) to plant a hidden microphone; (sl) to annoy, anger, etc.

bugbear n an object that causes great fear and anxiety.

buggy n (pl **buggies**) a light four-wheeled, one-horse carriage with one seat; a small pushchair for a baby; a small vehicle.

bugle n a valveless brass instrument like a small trumpet, used esp for military calls. * vti to signal by blowing a bugle.–**bugler** n.

build vb (**building, built**) vt to make or construct, to establish, base; (with **up**) to create or develop gradually. * vi to put up buildings; (with **up**) to grow or intensify; (health, reputation) to develop. * n the way a thing is built or shaped; the shape of a person; the physical appearance or weight or size of a person.–**builder** n.

built-in adj incorporated as an integral part of a main structure; inherent.

built-up adj made higher, stronger, etc with added parts; having many buildings on it, eg built-up area.

bulb n the underground bud of plants such as the onion and daffodil; a glass bulb in an electric light; a rounded shape.–**bulbous** adj.

bulge n a swelling; a rounded projected part; a significant rise in numbers (of population). * vti to swell or bend outward.–**bulgy** adj.

bulimia n insatiable hunger, voracity.

bulimia nervosa n an illness characterized by bouts of compulsive eating followed by self-induced vomiting.

bulk n magnitude; great mass; volume; the main part; **in bulk** in large quantities. * adj total, aggregate; (goods) not packaged.

bulkhead n a wall-like partition in the interior of a ship, aircraft or vehicle.

bulky adj (**bulkier, bulkiest**) large and unwieldy.–**bulkily** adv.–**bulkiness** adj.

bull n an adult male bovine animal; a male whale or elephant; a speculator who buys in anticipation of reselling at a profit; the bull's-eye. * adj male; rising in price.

bulldog n a variety of dog of strong muscular build, remarkable for its courage and ferocity; a short-barrelled pistol with a large caliber. * adj characterized by the courage of a bulldog; tenacious.

bulldoze vt to demolish with a bulldozer; (inf) to force.

bulldozer n an excavator with caterpillar tracks for moving earth.

bullet n a small metal missile fired from a gun or rifle.

bulletin n an announcement; a short statement of news or of a patient's progress.

bulletproof adj providing protection against bullets.

bullfight n a combat between armed men and a bull or bulls.–**bullfighting** n.–**bullfighter** n.

bullfrog n a large North American frog found in marshy places, remarkable for its loud bellowing croak.

bullion n gold or silver in mass before coinage.

bullock n a gelded bull; steer.

bullring n an arena for bullfighting.

bull's-eye n (darts, archery) the centre of a target; something resembling this; a direct hit; a large round peppermint boiled sweet.

bullwhip n a whip with a long lash for driving cattle. * vt (**bullwhipping, bullwhipped**) to whip with this.

bully n (pl **bullies**) a person, adult or child, who hurts or intimidates others weaker than himself or herself. * vb (**bullying, bullied**) vt to intimidate, oppress or hurt. * vi (with **off**) (hockey) to cross sticks in a bully-off to start a match. * adj (inf) very good, as in bully for you.

bulrush n a tall marsh plant.

bulwark n a defensive wall or rampart; (naut) a fence-like structure projecting above the deck of a ship; an object or person acting as a means of defence.

bum n (inf) a tramp; an idle person; (inf) a devotee, as of skiing or tennis. * adj broken; useless. * vti (**bumming, bummed**) to beg, to sponge; to live as a vagabond; (with **around**) to be idle, to loaf about.

bumblebee n a large, furry bee.

bummer n a worthless person who sponges on others; a low politician; an unpleasant experience, esp due to drug taking.

bump vi to knock with a jolt, or the noise of it; a lump produced by a blow. * vt to hurt by striking or knocking; (inf); (with **into**) to collide with; (inf) to meet by chance; (with **off**) (sl) to kill, murder; (with **up**) (inf) to increase prices, size or bulk. * n a jolt; a knock; the noise made by a bump or a collision; a swelling or lump; one of the bulges on the head supposedly indicating a special faculty.

bumper n a brimming glass for a toast. * adj exceptionally large.

bumpkin *n* an awkward or simple country person.

bumptious *adj* offensively conceited or self-assertive.–**bumptiously** *adv*.–**bumptiousness** *n*.

bumpy *adj* (**bumpier, bumpiest**) having many bumps; rough; jolting, jerky.–**bumpily** *adv*.–**bumpiness** *n*.

bun *n* a roll made of bread dough and currants, spices and sugar; a bun-shaped coil of hair at the nape of the neck.

bunch *n* a cluster; a number of things growing or fastened together; (*inf*) a group of people. * *vi* to group together; * *vt* to make into a bunch.–**bunchy** *adj*.–**bunchiness** *n*.

bundle *n* a number of things fastened together; a fastened package; (*sl*) a large sum of money. * *vt* to put together in bundles; to push hurriedly into.–**bundler** *n*.

bung *n* a cork or rubber stopper. * *vt* to close up with or as with a bung; (*sl*) to throw, toss.

bungalow *n* a one-story house.

bungle *n* a mistake or blunder; something carried out clumsily. * *vt* to spoil something through incompetence or clumsiness.– **bungler** *n*.–**bungling** *adj, n*.

bunion *n* a lump on the side of the first joint of the big toe.

bunk[1] *n* a narrow, shelf-like bed; a bunk bed.

bunk[2] *n* (*sl*) a hurried departure.

bunker *n* a large storage container, esp for coal; a sand pit forming an obstacle on a golf course; an underground shelter.

bunkum *n* idle or showy speech; nonsense.

bunny *n* (*pl* **bunnies**) a pet name for a rabbit.

Bunsen burner *n* a burner that mixes gas and air to produce a smokeless flame of great heat.

bunting *n* a cotton fabric used for making flags; a line of pennants and decorative flags.

buoy *n* a bright, anchored, marine float used for mooring and for making obstacles. * *vt* to keep afloat; (*usu with* **up**) to hearten or raise the spirits of; to mark with buoys.–**buoyancy** *n*.– **buoyant** *adj*.–**buoyantly** *adv*.

bur *n* a prickly seed-case of a plant; a person hard to shake off; a rough edge left after drilling or cutting; a burr. * *vt* (**burring, burred**) to pick burs off.

burden[1] *n* a load; something worrisome that is difficult to bear; responsibility. * *vt* to weigh down, to oppress.

burden[2] *n* the chorus or refrain of a song; a topic dwelt on in speech or writing.

burdensome *adj* onerous; oppressive; heavy.–**burdensomely** *adv*.

bureau *n* (*pl* **bureaus, bureaux**) a writing desk; a chest of drawers; a branch of a newspaper, magazine or wire service in an important news centre; a government department.

bureaucracy *n* (*pl* **bureaucracies**) a system of government where the administration is organized in a hierarchy; the government collectively; excessive paperwork and red tape.

bureaucrat *n* an official in a bureaucracy, esp one who adheres inflexibly to this system.–**bureaucratic** *adj*.–**bureaucratically** *adv*.

burette, buret *n* a graduated glass tube, usu with a tap, for measuring the volume of liquids.

burg *n* a town; (*formerly*) a fortified town.

burgeon *vt* to start to increase rapidly; (*plant*) to bloom copiously.

burger *n* (*inf*) hamburger.

a person who trespasses in a building with the intention of committing a crime, such as theft.

burglary *n* (*pl* **burglaries**) the act or crime of breaking into a house or any building with intent to commit a felony, esp theft.–**burglar** *n*.–**burgle, burglarize** *vti*.

burial *n* the act of burying; interment of a dead body.

burlap *n* a coarse fabric made of jute, hemp, etc, used for bagging or in upholstery.

burlesque *n* a caricature; a literary or dramatic satire. * *vti* (**burlesquing, burlesqued**) to make fun of, to caricature. * *adj* of or like burlesque; mockingly imitative.

burly *adj* (**burlier, burliest**) heavily built; sturdy.–**burliness** *n*.

burn *vb* (**burning, burned** *or* **burnt**) *vt* to destroy by fire; to injure by heat. * *vi* to be on fire; to feel hot; to feel passion; (*inf*) to suffer from sunburn; (*with* **off**) to clear ground by burning all vegetation; to get rid of (surplus gas, energy) by burning or using up; (*with* **out**) (*fire*) to go out; (*person*) to lose efficiency through exhaustion, excess or overwork. * *n* a scorch mark or injury caused by burning.

burnish *vt* to make shiny by rubbing; to polish. * *n* lustre; polish.–**burnishable** *adj*.–**burnisher** *n*.

burnt *see* **burn**.

burnt offering *n* something offered and burnt upon an altar as a sacrifice or an atonement for sin.

burnt sienna *n* an orange-reddish pigment used in painting.

burp *vi* to belch. * *vt* to pat a baby on the back to cause it to belch. * *n* a belch.

burr[1] *see* **bur**.

burr[2] *n* a whirring sound; a gruff pronunciation of the letter *r*. * *vti* to pronounce with a burr.

burrito *n* a tortilla baked with a savory filling.

burro *n* (*pl* **burros**) a donkey.

burrow *n* an underground hide or tunnel dug by a rabbit, badger or fox, etc for shelter. * *vi* to dig a burrow; to live in a burrow; to hide (oneself); to grope into the depths of one's pockets.–**burrower** *n*.

bursar *n* a treasurer; a person in charge of the finances of a college or university; a student holding a bursary.–**bursarial** *adj*.

bursary *n* (*pl* **bursaries**) a scholarship awarded to a student.– **bursarial** *adj*.

burst *vb* (**bursting, burst**) *vt* to break open; to cause to explode. * *vi* to emerge suddenly; to explode; to break into pieces; to give vent to. * *n* an explosion; a burst; a volley of shots; a sudden increase of activity; a spurt.–**burster** *n*.

bury *vt* (**burying, buried**) (*bone, corpse*) to place in the ground; to inter; to conceal, to cover; to blot out of the mind; **bury the hatchet** to make peace; to be reconciled.

bus *n* (*pl* **buses, busses**) a motor coach for public transport. * *vti* (**busing, bused** *or* **bussing, bussed**) to transport or travel by bus.

bush *n* a low shrub with many branches; a cluster of shrubs forming a hedge; woodland; (*with* **the**) uncultivated land, esp in Africa, Australia, New Zealand, Canada; a thick growth, eg of hair; a fox's tail or brush.

bushel *n* a dry measure containing 64 pints; a vessel of such a capacity; a large quantity.

bushfire *n* a fire, often widespread, in bush or scrubland.

bushy *adj* (**bushier, bushiest**) covered with bushes; (*hair*) thick.–**bushiness** *n*.

business *n* trade or commerce; occupation or profession; a firm; a factory; one's concern or responsibility; a matter; the agenda of a business meeting.

businesslike *adj* efficient, methodical, practical.

businessman *n* (**businessmen**) a person who works for an industrial or commercial company, esp as an executive.–**businesswoman** *nf* (*pl* **businesswomen**).

bust[1] *n* the chest or breast of a human being, esp a woman; a sculpture of the head and chest.

bust[2] *vti* (**busting, busted** *or* **bust**) (*inf*) to burst or break; to make or become bankrupt or demoted; to hit; to arrest. * *n* (*inf*) a failure; financial collapse; a punch; a spree; an arrest.

bustle[1] *vi* to move or act noisily, energetically or fussily. * *n* noisy activity, stir, commotion.–**bustler** *n*.–**bustling** *adj*.

bustle[2] *n* a pad placed beneath the skirt of a dress to cause it to puff up at the back.

busy *adj* (**busier, busiest**) occupied; active; crowded; full; industrious; (*painting*) having too much detail; (*room, telephone*) engaged, in use. * *vt* (**busying, busied**) to occupy; to make or keep busy (esp oneself).–**busily** *adv*.–**busyness** *n*.

busybody n (pl **busybodies**) a meddlesome person.

but prep save; except. * conj in contrast; on the contrary, other than. * adv only; merely; just. * n an objection.

butane n an inflammable gas used as a fuel.

butch adj (sl) tough; aggressively male; (often of a woman) male-looking.

butcher n a person who slaughters meat; a retailer of meat; a ruthless murderer. * vt to slaughter; to murder ruthlessly; to make a mess of or spoil.

butler n a manservant, usu the head servant of a household, etc.

butt[1] vti to strike or toss with the head or horns, as a bull, etc; (with **in**) to interfere, to enter into unasked. * n a push with the head or horns.–**butter** n.

butt[2] n a large cask for wine or beer.

butt[3] n a mound of earth behind targets; a person who is the target of ridicule or jokes; (pl) the target range.

butt[4] n the thick or blunt end; the stump; (sl) a cigarette; (sl) the buttocks. * vti to join end to end.

butter n a solidified fat made from cream by churning. * vt to spread butter on; (with **up**) (inf) to flatter.

buttercup n any of various plants with yellow, glossy, cup-shaped flowers.

butterfly n (pl **butterflies**) an insect with a slender body and four usu brightly colored wings; a swimming stroke.

buttermilk n the sour liquid that remains after separation from the cream in buttermaking.

butterscotch n a sauce made of melted butter and brown sugar; a kind of hard toffee made from this; its flavour; a brownish-yellow color.

buttery adj like or tasting of butter; insincere.

buttock n either half of the human rump.

button n a disc or knob of metal, plastic, etc used as a fastening; a badge; a small button-like sweet; an electric bell push; a knob at the point of a fencing foil. * vti to fasten with a button or buttons.

buttonhole n the slit through which a button is passed; a single flower in the buttonhole. * vt to make buttonholes; to sew with a special buttonhole stitch; (person) to keep in conversation.

buttress n a projecting structure for strengthening a wall. * vt to support or prop.

buxom adj plump and healthy; (woman) big-bosomed.–**buxomness** n.

buy vt (**buying, bought**) to purchase (for money); to bribe or corrupt; to acquire in exchange for something; (inf) to believe; (with **off**) to pay (someone) to ensure that some undesired action is not taken; (with **out**) to purchase a controlling interest in or share of; to secure the release of (e.g. a person from the army) by payment; (with **up**) to purchase the total supply of something; to acquire a controlling interest in. * n a purchase.

buyer n a person who buys; a customer; an employee who buys on behalf of his or her employer, esp a company or store.

buzz vi like an insect; to gossip; to hover (about). * vt spread gossip secretly; (inf) to telephone. * vi (with **off**) to go away. * n the humming of bees or flies; a rumor; (sl) a telephone call; (sl) a thrill, a kick.

buzzard n a large bird of prey of the hawk family.

buzzer n a device producing a buzzing sound.

buzzword n (inf) a vogue or jargon word; a word or phrase that was once a technical or specialist term and which has suddenly become popular, often used mainly for effect.–also **fuzzword**.

by prep beside; next to; via; through the means of; not later than. * adv near to; past; in reserve, aside.

bye n something subordinate or incidental; an odd man in a knockout competition.

bye-bye interj (inf) goodbye.

by-election, bye-election n an election held other than at a general election.

bygone adj past. * n (pl) past offenses or quarrels.

bylaw, bye-law n a rule or law made by a local authority or a company.

by-line n a line under a newspaper article naming its author.

bypass n a main road built to avoid a town; a channel redirecting the flow of something around a blockage; (med) an operation to redirect the flow of blood into the heart. * vt (**bypassing, bypassed**) to go around; to avoid, to act by ignoring the usual channels.

bypath n a secluded path.

byplay n action or dumb show aside from the main action.

byproduct, by-product n something useful produced in the process of making something else.

byre n a shed for cows.

byroad n an unfrequented or side road.

bystander n a chance onlooker.

byte n (comput) a set of eight bits treated as a unit.

byway n a side road; a specialist or abstruse interest or area of study.

byword n a well-known saying; a perfect example; an object of derision.

C

C abbr = Celsius, centigrade; (roman numerals) 100; (chem symbol) = carbon.

c. abbr = circa, about.

CA abbr = California; Chartered Accountant.

Ca (chem symbol) = calcium.

cab n a taxicab; the place where the driver sits in a truck, crane, etc.

cabaret n entertainment given in a restaurant or nightclub.

cabbage n a garden plant with thick leaves formed usu into a compact head, used as a vegetable.

cabin n a small house, a hut; a room in a ship; the area where passengers sit in an aircraft.

cabinet n a case or cupboard with drawers or shelves; a case containing a TV, radio, etc; (often with cap) a body of official advisers to a government; the senior ministers of a government.

cable n a strong thick rope often of wire strands; an anchor chain; an insulated cord that carries electric current; a cablegram; a bundle of insulated wires for carrying cablegrams, TV signals, etc; (naut) a cable length. * vti to send a message by cablegram.

cable car n a car drawn by a moving cable, as up a steep incline.

caboodle n (sl) a lot, a set (the whole caboodle).

caboose n the guard's car at the rear of a freight train; a kitchen on a ship's deck.

cacao n a tropical tree; its seed, from which cocoa and chocolate are obtained.

cache n a secret hiding place; a store of weapons or treasure; a store of food left for use by travelers, etc. * vt to place in a cache.

cachet n a mark of authenticity; any distinguishing mark; prestige.

cackle n the clucking sound of a hen; shrill or silly talk or laughter. * vi to utter with a cackle.

cacophony n (pl **cacophonies**) an ugly sound, a discord.–**cacophonous** adj.

cactus n (pl **cactuses, cacti**) a plant with a thick fleshy stem that stores water and is often studded with prickles.

cad n (inf) a man who behaves in an ungentlemanly or dishonorable way.–**caddish** adj.–**caddishly** adv.–**caddishness** n.

cadaver n a dead body.–**cadaveric** adj.

cadaverous adj gaunt, haggard; pallid, livid.–**cadaverousness** n.

caddie, caddy n (pl **caddies**) a person who carries a golfer's clubs.–vi (**caddying, caddied**) to perform as a caddie.

cadence n a falling of the voice; the intonation of the voice; rhythm; measured movements as in marching.

cadet n a student at an armed forces academy, police college, etc; a school pupil in a school army training corps.

cadge vti to beg or obtain by begging.–**cadger** n.

cadmium n a whitish metallic element.

Caesar n the title of Roman emperors, esp Julius Caesar (c. 100–44 BC); (without cap) any ruler.

Caesarean section, Cesarean section n the removal of a child from the womb by a surgical operation involving the cutting of the abdominal wall.

caesium see **cesium**.

cafe, café n a small restaurant, a coffee bar, a nightclub, etc.

cafeteria n a self-service restaurant.

cafetière n a usu glass coffee pot with a plunger to press down coffee grounds.

caffeine n a stimulant present in coffee and tea.–**caffeinic** adj.

caftan n a long-sleeved, full-length, voluminous garment originating in the Middle East.–also **kaftan**.

cage n a box or enclosure with bars for confining an animal, bird, prisoner, etc; a car for raising or lowering miners. * vt to shut in a cage, to confine.

cagey, cagy adj (**cagier, cagiest**) (inf) wary, secretive, not frank.–**cagily** adv.–**caginess** n.

caiman n (pl **caimans**) an alligator of South and Central America.–also **cayman**.

cairn n a stone mound placed as a monument or marker.

cajole vti to persuade or soothe by flattery or deceit.–**cajoler** n.–**cajolingly** adv.

cajolery, cajolement n (pl **cajoleries, cajolements**) the action or practice of cajoling; persuasion by false arts.

Cajun, Cajan n an inhabitant of Louisiana descended from 18th-century French-Canadian immigrants; the dialect spoken by Cajuns.

cake n a mixture of flour, eggs, sugar, etc baked in small, flat shapes or a loaf; a small block of compacted or congealed matter. * vti to encrust; to form into a cake or hard mass.

cakewalk n an elaborate step dance; a task accomplished without difficulty.

Cal abbr = California; Calorie.

cal abbr = calendar; caliber; calorie.

calamine n a zinc oxide powder used in skin lotions, etc for its soothing effect.

calamitous adj producing or resulting from calamity; disastrous.–**calamitously** adv.–**calamitousness** n.

calamity n (pl **calamities**) a disastrous event, a great misfortune; adversity.

calcify vb (**calcifying, calcified**) vt to convert into lime. * vi to harden by conversion into lime.

calcium n the chemical element prevalent in bones and teeth.

calculate vti to reckon or compute by mathematics; to suppose or believe; to plan.–**calculable** adj.

calculated adj adapted or suited (to); deliberate, cold-blooded, premeditated.–**calculatedly** adv.

calculating adj shrewd, scheming.–**calculatingly** adv.

calculation n the act of calculating; the result obtained from this; an estimate.–**calculational** adj.

calculator n a device, esp a small, electronic, hand-held one, for doing mathematical calculations rapidly; one who calculates.

calculus n (pl **calculi, calculuses**) an abnormal, stony mass in the body; (math) a mode of calculation using symbols.

caldron n a large kettle or boiling pot; a state of violent agitation.–also **cauldron**.

calendar n a system of determining the length and divisions of a year; a chart or table of months, days and seasons; a list of particular, scheduled events.

calf[1] n (pl **calves**) the young of a cow, seal, elephant, whale, etc; the leather skin of a calf.

calf[2] n (pl **calves**) the fleshy back part of the leg below the knee.

caliber, calibre n the internal diameter of a gun barrel or tube; capacity, standing, moral weight.

calibrate vt to measure the caliber of a gun; to adjust or mark units of measurement on a measuring scale or gauge.–**calibration** n.–**calibrator** n.

calico n (pl **calicoes, calicos**) a kind of cotton cloth. * adj made of this.

calif see **caliph**.

Calif. abbr = California.

caliper see **caliper**.

caliph n the former title assumed by the successors of Mohammed as rulers; title of a Turkish sultan.–also **calif**.

calisthenics npl light gymnastic exercises.–also **callisthenics**.–**calisthenic, callisthenic** adj.

calk see **caulk**.

call vi to shout or cry out; to pay a short visit; to telephone; (with in) to pay a brief or informal visit; (with on) to pay a visit; to ask, to appeal to. * vt to summon; to name; to describe as specified; to awaken; to give orders for; (with in) to summon for advice or help; to bring out of circulation; to demand payment of (a loan); (with off) to cancel; (an animal) to call away in order to stop, divert; (with out) to cry aloud; to order (workers) to come out on strike; to summon (troops) to action; (with up) to telephone; to summon to military action, as in time of war; to recall. * n a summons; the note of a bird; a vocation, esp religious; occasion; a need; a demand; a short visit; the use of a telephone; a cry, a shout.

caller n one who calls, esp by telephone; one who pays a brief visit.

calligraphy n handwriting; beautiful writing.–**calligrapher, calligraphist** n.–**calligraphic** adj.–**calligraphically** adv.

calling n the act of summoning; a summons or invitation; a vocation, trade or profession; the state of being divinely called.

calliper n a metal framework for supporting a crippled or weak leg; (pl) a two-legged measuring instrument. * vt to measure with or use callipers.–also **caliper**.

callisthenics see **calisthenics**.

callous adj (skin) hardened; (person) unfeeling.–**callously** adv.–**callousness** n.

callow adj inexperienced, undeveloped.–**callowness** n.

call-up n a summons to military service.

callus n (pl **calluses**) a hardened, thickened place on the skin.–**callused** adj.

calm adj windless; still, unruffled; quiet, peaceful. * n the state of being calm; stillness; tranquility. * vti to become or make calm.–**calmly** adv.–**calmness** n.

Calorie n a unit of heat equalling 1,000 calories.

calorie n a unit of heat; a measure of food energy.

calorific adj heat-producing; (inf) causing fat.–**calorifically** adv.

calumny n (pl **calumnies**) a slander; a lie, a false accusation.–**calumnious** adj.–**calumniously** adv.

calve vti to give birth to a calf; (glacier, iceberg) to break up and release ice.

calves see **calf**.

calypso n (pl **calypsos**) a West Indian folk song that comments on current events or personalities.

calyx n (pl **calyxes, calyces**) the outer series of leaves that form the cup from which which the petals of a flower spring.

cam n a device to change rotary to reciprocating motion.

camaraderie n friendship, comradeship.

camber n a slight upward curve in the surface of a road, etc. * vti to curve upwards slightly.–**cambered** adj.

camcorder n a portable video recorder with built-in sound recording facilities.

came see **come**.

camel n a large four-footed, long-necked animal with a humped back; a fawny-beige color.–also adj.

camellia n an oriental evergreen shrub with showy blooms.–also japonica.

cameo n (pl **cameos**) an onyx or other gem carved in relief, often showing a head in profile; an outstanding bit role, esp in a motion picture; a short piece of fine writing.

camera n the apparatus used for taking still photographs or television or motion pictures; a judge's private chamber; **in camera** in private, esp of a legal hearing excluding the public; **off camera** outside the area being filmed; **on camera** being filmed, before the camera.

cameraman n (pl **cameramen**) a film or television camera operator.

camisole n a woman or girl's loose sleeveless underbodice.

camomile see **chamomile**.

camouflage n a method (esp using coloring) of disguise or concealment used to deceive an enemy; a means of putting people off the scent. * vt to conceal by camouflage.

camp[1] n the ground on which tents or temporary accommodation is erected; the occupants of this, such as holiday-makers or troops; the supporters of a particular cause. * vi to lodge in a camp; to pitch tents.–**camping** n.–**camper** n.

camp[2] adj (sl) theatrical, exaggerated; effeminate. * vi (with **up**) to make or give an exaggerated display of camp characteristics.

campaign n a series of military operations; a series of operations with a particular objective, such as election of a candidate or promotion of a product; organized course of action. * vi to take part in or conduct a campaign.–**campaigner** n.

campanology n the art of bell ringing.–**campanologist** n.

campfire n an outdoor fire at a camp; a social gathering around such a fire.

camphor n a solid white transparent essential oil with a pungent taste and smell used to repel insects, as a stimulant in medicine, etc.–**camphoric** adj.

campsite n a camping ground, often with facilities for holiday-makers.

campus n (pl **campuses**) the grounds, and sometimes buildings, of a college or university.

Can abbr = Canada; Canadian.

can[1] vt (pt **could**) to be able to; to have the right to; to be allowed to.

can[2] n a container, usu metal, with a separate cover in which gasoline, film, etc is stored; a tin in which meat, fruit, drinks, etc are hermetically sealed; the contents of a can; (sl) jail; (sl) a lavatory; **in the can** (film) shot and edited and ready for showing; (inf) accomplished, agreed, tied up. * vti (**canning, canned**) to preserve (foods) in a can.–**canner** n.

Canadian adj of or pertaining to Canada. * n a native of Canada.

canal n an artificial waterway cut across land; a duct in the body. * vt (**canaling, canaled** or **canalling, canalled**) to provide with canals.

canapé n a small piece of pastry, bread or toast with a savory spread or topping.

canary n (pl **canaries**) a small finch, usu greenish to yellow in color, kept as a songbird.

cancan n an energetic dance performed by women, involving high kicks and the lifting of frothy petticoats.

cancel vt (**canceling, canceled** or **cancelling, cancelled**) to cross out; to obliterate; to annul, suppress; (reservation, etc) to call off; to countermand; (with **out**) to make up for.–**canceler, canceller** n.

cancelation, cancellation n the act of canceling; annulment; something that has been canceled; the mark made by canceling.

Cancer n (astron) the Crab, a northern constellation; (astrol) the 4th sign of the zodiac, operative 21 June–21 July.–**Cancerian** adj.

cancer n the abnormal and uncontrollable growth of the cells of living organisms, esp a malignant tumor; an undesirable or dangerous expansion of something.–**cancerous** adj.

candelabrum n (pl **candelabra**) a branched and ornamented candlestick or lampstand.

candid adj frank, outspoken; unprejudiced; (photograph) informal.–**candidly** adv.–**candidness** n.

candidate n a person who has nomination for an office or qualification for membership or award; a student taking an examination.–**candidacy** n.–**candidature** n.

candied adj preserved in or encrusted with sugar.

candle n a stick of wax with a wick that burns to give light. **candlelight** n the light produced by a candle or candles.

candlestick n a holder for one or more candles.

candor, candour n sincerity, openness, frankness.

candy n (pl **candies**) a solid confection of sugar or syrup with flavoring, fruit, nuts, etc, a sweet. * vb (**candying, candied**) vt to preserve by coating with candy; to encrust with crystals. * vi to become candied.

candyfloss see **cotton candy**.

cane n the slender, jointed stem of certain plants, as bamboo; a plant with such a stem, as sugar cane; strips of this used in furniture making etc or for supporting plants; a walking stick. * vt to thrash with a cane; to weave cane into; (inf) to beat, eg in a game.

canine adj of or like a dog; of the family of animals that includes wolves, dogs and foxes; pertaining to a canine tooth. * n a dog or other member of the same family of animals; in humans, a pointed tooth next to the incisors.

canister n a small box or container usu of metal for storing tea, flour, etc; a tube containing tear gas which explodes and releases its contents on impact.

canker n an erosive or spreading sore; a foot disease in horses; an ear disease in cats and dogs; a fungal disease of trees; a corrupting influence.–**cankerous** adj.

cannabis n a narcotic drug obtained from the hemp plant; the hemp plant.–also **hashish, marijuana**.–**cannabic** adj.

canned adj stored in sealed tins; recorded for reproduction; (sl) drunk.

cannelloni npl stuffed pasta tubes.

cannibal n a person who eats human flesh; an animal that feeds on its own species. * adj relating to or indulging in this practice.–**cannibalism** n.–**cannibalistic** adj.

cannibalize vti to strip (old equipment) of parts for use in other units.–**cannibalization** n.

cannon n (pl **cannon**) a large mounted piece of artillery; an automatic gun on an aircraft; (pl **cannons**) (billiards) a carom. * vi to collide with great force (with into); to rebound; (billiards) to make a carom.

cannonade n a heavy, continuous artillery attack. * vti to attack with cannon.

cannonball n the heavy, round shot fired from a cannon; (tennis) a low, fast service stroke. * vi to move along at great speed.

cannot = can not.

cannula n (pl **cannulas, cannulae**) (med) a small tube for inspecting or withdrawing fluids.

canny adj (**cannier, canniest**) knowing, shrewd; cautious, careful; thrifty.–**cannily** adv.–**canniness** n.

canoe n a narrow, light boat propelled by paddles.–also vi (**canoeing, canoed**).–**canoeist** n.

canon n a decree of the Church; a general rule or standard, criterion; a list of the books of the Bible accepted as genuine; the works of any author recognized as genuine; (mus) a round.–**canonical** adj.

canonize vt (RC Church) to declare officially (a person) a saint.–**canonization** n.

canon law n rules or laws relating to faith, morals and discipline that regulate church government, as laid down by popes and councils.

canopy n (pl **canopies**) a tent-like covering over a bed, throne, etc; any roof-like structure or projection; the transparent cover of an airplane's cockpit; the tops of trees in a forest; the sky regarded as a covering. * vt (**canopying, canopied**) to cover with or as with a canopy.

cant[1] n insincere or hypocritical speech; language specific to a group (eg thieves, lawyers); cliched talk, meaningless jargon. * vi to talk in or use cant.

cant[2] n an inclination or tilt; a slanting surface, bevel. * vti to slant, to tilt; to overturn by a sudden movement.

can't = can not.

cantaloupe, cantaloup n a variety of melon with orange flesh.

cantankerous adj ill-natured, bad-tempered, quarrelsome.—**cantankerously** adv.—**cantankerousness** n.

cantata n (mus) a composition for voices of a story or religious text.

canteen n a restaurant attached to factory, school, etc, catering for large numbers of people; a flask for carrying water; (a box containing) a set of cutlery.

canter n a horse's three-beat gait resembling a slow, smooth gallop.—also vti.

cantilever n a projecting beam that supports a balcony, etc.

canto n (pl **cantos**) a division of a long poem.

cantor n a singer of liturgical solos in a synagogue; the leader of singing in a church choir.

canvas n a strong coarse cloth of hemp or flax, used for tents, sails, etc, and for painting on; a ship's sails collectively; a tent or tents; an oil painting on canvas.

canvass vti to go through (places) or among (people) asking for votes, opinions, orders, etc.—also n.—**canvasser** n.

canyon n a long, narrow valley between high cliffs.

cap n any close-fitting headgear, visored or brimless; the special headgear of a profession, club, etc; the top of a mushroom or toadstool; a cap-like thing, as an artificial covering for a tooth; a top, a cover; a percussion cap in a toy gun; a type of contraceptive device; (sport) the head gear presented to a player chosen for a team. * vt (**capping, capped**) to put a cap on; to cover (the end of); to award a degree at a university; to seal (an oil or gas well); to equal, outdo or top; to limit the level of a tax increase, etc; (sport) to choose a player for a team.

capability n (pl **capabilities**) the quality of being capable; an undeveloped faculty.

capable adj able or skilled to do; competent, efficient; susceptible (of); adapted to.—**capably** adv.

capacious adj able to hold a great deal; roomy.—**capaciousness** n.

capacitance n (a measure of) the ability of a system to store an electric charge.

capacitor n a device for storing electric charge.

capacity n (pl **capacities**) the power of holding or grasping; cubic content; mental ability or power; character; the position held; legal competence; the greatest possible output or content.

cape[1] n a headland and promontory running into the sea.

cape[2] n a sleeveless garment fastened at the neck and hanging over the shoulders and back.

caper[1] vi to skip about playfully, to frolic. * n a playful leap or skip; (sl) an escapade; (sl) a criminal activity.

caper[2] n a low, prickly Mediterranean shrub; its pickled flower buds, used in cooking (eg caper sauce).

capillary adj of or as fine as a hair; (tube, pipe) of a hair-like caliber; (anat) of the capillaries. * n (pl **capillaries**) one of the very fine blood vessels connecting arteries and veins.

capital[1] adj of or pertaining to the head; (offense) punishable by death; serious; chief, principal; leading, first-class; of, or being the seat of government; of capital or wealth; relating to a large letter, upper case; (inf) excellent. * n a city that is the seat of government of a country; a large letter; accumulated wealth used to produce more; stock or money for carrying on a business; a city, town, etc pre-eminent in some special activity.—**capitally** adv.

capital[2] n the head or top part of a column or pillar.

capitalism n the system of individual ownership of wealth; the dominance of such a system.

capitalist n a person who has money invested in business for profit; a supporter of capitalism. * adj of or favoring capitalism.—**capitalistic** adj.

capitalize vti (with **on**) to use (something) to one's advantage; to convert into money or capital; to provide with capital; to write in or print in capital letters.—**capitalization** n.

capitulate vi to surrender on terms; to give in.—**capitulation** n.—**capitulator** n.—**capitulatory** adj.

capo n (pl **capos**) a device attached across the fingerboard of a guitar to raise the pitch of the strings.

capon n a castrated cockerel fattened for eating.

cappuccino n (pl **cappuccinos**) frothy, milky coffee usu served sprinkled with chocolate powder.

caprice n a passing fancy; an impulsive change in behavior, opinion, etc; a whim.—**capricious** adj.—**capriciously** adv.—**capriciousness** n.

unstable, inconstant; unreliable.

Capricorn n (astron) the Goat, a southern constellation; (astrol) the tenth sign of the zodiac, operative 21 December–19 January.—**Capricornian** adj.

capsicum n a tropical plant with bell-shaped fruits containing hot or mild seeds; the fruit of this plant used as a vegetable.—also **red** or **green pepper**.

capsize vti to upset or overturn.

capstan n an upright drum around which cables are wound to haul them in; the spindle in a tape recorder that winds the tape past the head.

capsule n a small gelatin case enclosing a drug to be swallowed; a metal or plastic container; (bot) a seed case; the orbiting and recoverable part of a spacecraft.—**capsular** adj.

captain n a chief, leader; the master of a ship; the pilot of an aircraft; a rank of army, naval and marine officer; the leader of a team, as in sports; a leading employer in industry; a policeman responsible for a precinct. * vt to be captain of.—**captaincy** n.

caption n a heading in a newspaper, to a chapter, etc; a legend or title describing an illustration; a subtitle. * vti to provide with a caption.

captious adj ready to find fault or take offense; carping, quibbling.—**captiously** adv.

captivate vt to fascinate; to charm.—**captivating** adj.—**captivation** n.—**captivator** n.

captive n one kept confined; a prisoner; a person obsessed by an emotion. * adj taken or kept prisoner; unable to avoid being addressed (a captive audience); unable to refuse (a product) through a lack of choice (a captive market); captivated.—**captivity** n.

captor n a person or animal who takes a prisoner.

capture vt to take prisoner; (fortress, etc) to seize; to catch; to gain or obtain by skill, attraction, etc, to win. * n the act of taking a prisoner or seizing by force; anything or anyone so taken.

car n a self-propelled motor vehicle, an automobile, a motorcar; the passenger compartment of a train, airship, lift, cable railway, etc; a railway carriage.

carafe n an open-topped bottle for serving water or wine at table.

caramel n burnt sugar, used in cooking to color or flavor; a type of sweet tasting of this.

caramelize vti to turn or be turned into caramel.

carat n a measure of weight for precious stones; a measure of the purity of gold.—also **karat**.

caravan n (esp Brit) a trailer; a band of merchants traveling together for safety. * vi (**caravanning, caravanned**) to travel with a caravan, esp on holiday.

caraway n a biennial plant with pungent aromatic seeds used as a flavoring.

carbide n a compound of carbon with another element, esp calcium carbide.

carbine n a light, semiautomatic or automatic rifle.

carbohydrate n a compound of carbon, hydrogen and oxygen, esp in sugars and starches as components of food. * npl starchy foods.

carbon n a nonmetallic element, a constituent of all organic matter; a duplicate made with carbon paper.

carbonate n a salt of carbonic acid. * vt to treat with carbon dioxide, as in making soft, fizzy drinks.–**carbonated** adj.

carbon copy n a copy of typed or written material made by using carbon paper; (inf) an exact copy of something or someone.

carbon dating n a scientific method of dating material by measuring the amount of carbon-14 it contains.

carbon dioxide n a gas formed by combustion and breathing and absorbed by plants.

carboniferous adj coal-bearing, yielding carbon; (with cap) of or relating to strata of the Paleozoic Age from which coal is derived.

carbon monoxide n a colorless, odorless, highly poisonous gas.

carbuncle n a red, knob-shaped gemstone, esp a garnet; a large inflamed boil; a pimple.–**carbuncular** adj.

carburetor n a device in an internal-combustion engine for making an explosive mixture of air and fuel vapor.

carcass n the dead body of an animal; a framework, skeleton or shell.

carcinogen n a substance that produces cancer.–**carcinogenic** adj.

carcinoma n (pl **carcinomas, carcinomata**) a tumor caused by a cancer.

card[1] n a small piece of cardboard; a piece of this with a figure or picture for playing games or fortune-telling; a membership card; a piece of card with a person or firm's name, address or with an invitation, greeting, message, etc; a small piece of plastic identifying a person for banking purposes, eg a check card, credit card; (pl) card games; (pl) card playing; (pl) employees insurance and tax documents held by the employer.

card[2] n a toothed instrument for combing cotton, wool or flax fibers off. * vt (wool, etc) to comb.

cardamum, cardamom, cardamon n a tropical Asian plant the seed pods of which are used as a spice.

cardboard n thick stiff paper, often with a clay coating, for boxes, cartons, etc. * adj made of this; lacking substance; makeshift.

cardiac adj relating to the heart. * n a person suffering a disorder of the heart; a drug to stimulate the heart.

cardigan n a knitted sweater fastening up the front.

cardinal adj of chief importance, fundamental; of a bright red. * n an official appointed by the Pope to his councils; bright red.–**cardinally** adv.

cardinal numbers npl numbers that express how many (1, 2, 3, 4 etc).

cardinal points npl the four chief points of the compass: north, south, east, west.

cardiogram n an electrocardiogram.

cardiograph n a device for recording heart movements; an electrocardiograph.

cardiology n the branch of medicine concerned with the heart and its diseases.–**cardiological** adj.–**cardiologist** n.

cardiovascular adj of or pertaining to the heart and the blood vessels.

care n anxiety; concern; serious attention, heed; consideration; charge, protection; the cause or object of concern or anxiety. * vt to feel concern; to agree, like, or be willing (to do something); **care of** at the address of, c/o. * vi (usu with **for** or **about**) to feel affection or regard; to have a desire (for); to provide for, have in one's charge.–**caring** adj.

careen vt to bring (a ship) over on one side for calking, cleansing, or repairing. * vi to incline to one side, as a ship under press of sail.

career n progress through life; a profession, occupation, esp with prospects for promotion. * vi to rush rapidly or wildly.

careerist n a person who is ambitious to advance in a chosen profession.

carefree adj without cares, lively, light-hearted.

careful adj painstaking; cautious; thoughtful.–**carefully** adv.–**carefulness** n.

careless adj not careful; unconcerned, insensitive; carefree.–**carelessly** adv.–**carelessness** n.

carer n one who takes on (professionally) the care of a dependent person.

caress n any act or expression of affection; an embrace. * vt to touch or stroke lovingly.–**caresser** n.–**caressingly** adv.

caret n a mark (^) showing where something omitted in text is to be inserted.

caretaker n a person put in charge of a place or thing; (government) one temporarily in control.

careworn adj showing signs of stress, worry.

cargo n (pl **cargoes, cargos**) the load carried by a ship, truck, aircraft, etc; freight.

caribou n (pl **caribou, caribous**) a large North American reindeer.

caricature n a likeness made ludicrous by exaggeration or distortion of characteristic features. * vt to make a caricature of, to parody.–**caricaturist** n.

caries n (pl **caries**) decay of bones or teeth.

carjacking n the violent hijacking and theft of a car, possibly involving the abduction or kidnapping of the driver or passenger.

carmine n a rich crimson pigment; the essential coloring principle of cochineal.

carnage n great slaughter.

carnal adj of the flesh; sexual; sensual; worldly.–**carnality** n.–**carnally** adv.

carnation n a garden flower, the clove pink.

carnival n public festivities and revelry; a traveling fair with sideshows, etc.

carnivore n a flesh-eating mammal.–**carnivorous** adj.

carob n an edible, sugary pod of a Mediterranean tree.

carol n a joyful song or hymn; a Christmas hymn. * vi (**caroling, caroled** or **carolling, carolled**) to sing carols; to sing with happiness.

Carolinian adj of or pertaining to either North or South Carolina.

carouse vi to drink and have fun.–**carousal** n.–**carouser** n.

carousel n a merry-go-round; a revolving circular platform, as in an airport baggage conveyor.

carp[1] vi to find fault, esp continually.

carp[2] n (pl **carp, carps**) a brown and yellow freshwater fish.

carpal adj pertaining to the carpus or wrist.

car park n a parking lot.

carpel n a simple pistil, or one of the parts of a compound pistil or ovary of a flower.–**carpellary** adj.

carpenter n a person skilled in woodwork, esp in house building.–**carpentry** n.

carpet n a woven fabric for covering floors; any thick covering * vt to cover with carpet; (inf) to issue a reprimand, to have on the carpet to rebuke.–**carpeting** n.

carpetbagger n an outsider, esp a nonresident who meddles in politics.

carport n an open-sided shelter for a car extending from the side of a house.

carpus n (pl **carpi**) the bones between the forearm and the hand, forming the wrist in man and the corresponding bones in other animals.

carriage n the act of carrying, transport; the cost of this; deportment, bearing; behavior; a rail coach or compartment; a wheeled coach drawn by horses; a frame with wheels to carry a gun.

carrier n one who carries or transports goods, esp for hire; a device for carrying; a person or animal transmitting an infectious disease without being affected by it; an aircraft carrier; a plastic or paper bag with handles for holding things; a portable seat for a baby, a carrycot.

carrion n the dead putrefying flesh of an animal.

carrot n a plant grown for its edible, fleshy orange root; an inducement, often illusory.

carroty adj orange-red in color.

carry vb (**carrying, carried**) vt to convey or transport; to support or bear; to involve, have as a result; to hold (oneself); to extend or prolong; to gain by force; to win over; to stock; to be pregnant; (with **away**) to delight; to arouse to extreme enthusiasm; to remove violently; (with **forward**) (book-keeping) to transfer (a total) to the next column, page, etc; (with **off**) to cause to die; to remove by force, capture; (situation) to handle successfully; (with **out**) to perform (a task, etc); to accomplish; (with **over**) to carry forward; (with **through**) to complete. * vi (with **away**) to be filled with joy or emotion; (with **on**) to persevere; to conduct a business, etc; (inf) to have an affair; (inf) to cause a fuss; (with **through**) to enable to survive; to persist.

carrycot n a baby carrier, a portable cot.

carsick adj ill or queasy from the motion of a moving vehicle.—**carsickness** n.

cart n a two-wheeled vehicle drawn by horses; any small vehicle for carrying loads. * vt to carry in a cart; (inf) to transport with effort.

carte blanche n (pl **cartes blanches**) full authority to act as one thinks best.

cartel n an association of business firms to coordinate production, prices, etc to avoid competition and maximize profits; a union of political parties to achieve common aims.

cartilage n tough, elastic tissue attached to the bones of animals; gristle.—**cartilaginous** adj.

cartography n the drawing and publishing of maps.—**cartographer** n.—**cartographic, cartographical** adj.

carton n a cardboard box or container.

cartoon n a humorous picture dealing with current events; a comic strip; an animated cartoon; a full-size preparatory sketch for reproduction on a fresco, etc.—**cartoonist** n.

cartridge n the case that contains the explosive charge and bullet in a gun or rifle; a sealed case of film for a camera; the device containing the stylus on the end of the pick-up arm of a record player.

cartwheel n an acrobatic handspring in which the body revolves with the weight on each hand in turn and the legs spread like the spokes of a wheel.

carve vt to shape by cutting; to adorn with designs; to cut up (meat, etc); (with **up**) to cut into pieces or shares; (sl) to share out illegal proceeds; to slash someone with a knife or razor.

carving n a figure or design carved from wood, stone, etc; the act of carving.

cascade n a small, steep waterfall; a shower, as of sparks, etc. * vti to fall in a cascade.

case[1] n a covering; a suitcase; its contents; the binding covering a book.

case[2] n an instance; a state of affairs; a condition, circumstance; a lawsuit; an argument for one side; (sl) a character; a person of a specific type; (med) a patient under treatment; (gram) the relationship between nouns, pronouns and adjectives in a sentence; **in case** in order to prevent, lest.

case-hardened adj with a hard surface; made callous.

casein n a protein in the curd matter of milk.

case law n law as settled by precedent.

casement n a window or its frame with a side hinge for opening.

case study n an analysis arrived at from studying more than one case history.

casework n social work based on the close monitoring of individuals or families.—**caseworker** n.

cash n money in coins or notes; immediate payment, as opposed to that by check or on credit. * vt to give or get cash for; (with **in**) to exchange something for money; (inf) to gain an advantage or seize an opportunity to profit from; (sl) to die. * vi (with **in**) to exploit for profit; to take advantage of.—**cashable** adj.

cash and carry n, adj (a policy of) selling for cash without delivery of goods.

cash crop n a crop grown for market not for consumption.

cashew n the small, edible nut of a tropical tree.

cash flow n money which is paid into and out of a business during its operations.

cashier[1] n a person in charge of the paying and receiving of money in a bank, shop, etc.

cashier[2] vt to dismiss (an officer) from military service; to discharge.

cashmere n a fine wool from Kashmir goats; a material made from this.

casing n any protective or outer covering; the material for this.

casino n (pl **casinos**) a room or building where gambling takes place.

cask n a barrel of any size, esp one for liquids; its contents.

casket n a small box or chest for jewels, etc; a coffin.

casserole n a covered dish for cooking and serving; the food so cooked and served. * vt to cook in a casserole.

cassette n a case containing magnetic tape or film for loading into a tape recorder or camera.

cassock n a long close-fitting black garment worn by certain clergy and by choristers.

cast vb (**casting, cast**) vt to throw or fling; to throw off or shed; to record; to direct; to shape in a mold; to calculate; to select actors, etc for a play; to throw a fishing line into the water. * vi to throw, hurl; (with **off**) to untie a ship from its moorings; (knitting) to loop off stitches from a needle without letting them unravel; (with **on**) to loop the first row of stitches onto a needle. * n act of casting; a throw; a plaster form for immobilizing an injured limb; a mold for casting; type or quantity; a tinge of color; the actors assigned roles in a play; the set of actors; a slight squint in the eye.

castanets npl hollow shell-shaped pieces of wood held between the fingers and rattled together, esp to accompany Spanish dancing.

castaway adj shipwrecked; discarded. * n a shipwrecked person.

cast down adj depressed.

caste n any of the Hindu hereditary social classes; an exclusive social group.

castellated adj having turrets and battlements, as a castle.

caster see **castor**.

castigate vt to chastise; to punish; to correct.—**castigation** n.

casting vote n the deciding vote used by the chairman of a meeting when the votes on each side are equal.

cast iron n an iron-carbon alloy melted and run into molds.

cast-iron adj made of cast iron; untiring; rigid, unadaptable.

castle n a fortified building; a chess piece (–also **rook**).

castoff n a rejected item; a rough estimate of the number of pages of a finished book, etc.

castor n a small container with a perforated top for sprinkling salt, sugar, etc; a small swiveled wheel on a table leg, etc.–also **caster**.

castor oil n a vegetable oil used as a cathartic and lubricant.

castrate vt to remove the testicles of, to geld.—**castration** n.—**castrator** n.

casual adj accidental, chance; unplanned; occasional; careless, offhand; unmethodical; informal. * n someone who works occasionally; (pl) informal or leisure clothing, shoes.—**casually** adv.—**casualness** n.

casualty n (pl **casualties**) a person injured or killed in a war or in an accident; something damaged or destroyed.

casuistry n (pl **casuistries**) the study or application of rules of right and wrong; sophistical or equivocal reasoning, esp on moral matters.

CAT (*acronym*) computerized axial tomography (*–also* **computer-aided** *or* **computer-assisted tomography**); the production of detailed three-dimensional images from scans of cross-sections of internal organs (**CAT scans**) using a computer-controlled X-ray machine (**CAT scanner**).

cat *n* a small, domesticated feline mammal kept as a pet; a wild animal related to this; lions, tigers, etc (*–also* **big cat**); (*inf*) a spiteful woman; (*sl*) a man.

cataclysm *n* a violent disturbance or disaster.–**cataclysmic** *adj*.

catacomb *n* (*usu pl*) an underground burial place.

catalog, catalogue *n* a list of books, names, etc in systematic order. * *vti* to list, to make a catalog of.–**cataloger, cataloguer** *n*.

catalysis *n* (*pl* **catalyses**) the acceleration or retardation of a chemical reaction by the action of a catalyst. –**catalytic** *adj*.

catalyst *n* a substance which accelerates or retards a chemical reaction without itself undergoing any permanent chemical change; a person or thing which produces change.–**catalyze** *v*.

catamaran *n* a (sailing) boat with twin hulls; a raft of logs.

catapult *n* a slingshot; a device for launching aircraft from the deck of an aircraft carrier. * *vt* to shoot forwards as from a catapult.

cataract *n* a waterfall, esp a large sheet one; a disease of the eye causing dimming of the lens and loss of vision.

catarrh *n* inflammation of a mucous membrane, esp in the nose and throat, causing a flow of mucus.–**catarrhal** *adj*.

catastrophe *n* a great disaster.–**catastrophic** *adj*.–**catastrophically** *adv*.

cat burglar *n* a burglar who enters by climbing.

catcall *n* a shrill whistle or cry used to express disapproval. * *vt* to express disapproval by a catcall.

catch *vb* (**catching, caught**) *vt* to take hold of, to grasp; to capture; to ensnare or trap; to be on time for; to detect; to apprehend; to become infected with (a disease); to attract (the eye); (*inf*) to see, hear, etc; to grasp (a meaning); (*with* **out**) (*inf*) to detect (a person) in a mistake. * *vi* to become entangled; to begin to burn; (*with* **on**) (*inf*) to become popular; to understand; (*with* **up**) to reach or come level with (eg a person ahead); to make up for lost time, deal with a backlog. * *n* the act of catching; the amount or number caught; a device for fastening; someone worth catching; a hidden difficulty.

catch-all *adj, n* (something) intended to cover all eventualities.

catching *adj* infectious; attractive.

catchment *n* the collecting or the drainage of water.

catch-22 *n* a predicament from which a victim is powerless to escape due to conditions beyond his or her control.

catchword *n* a guide word; a word or expression, briefly popular, representative of a person or point of view; a cue in the theater.

catchy *adj* (**catchier, catchiest**) easily remembered, as a tune.–**catchiness** *n*.

catechism *n* a simple summary of the principles of religion in question and answer form, used for instruction; continuous questioning.–**catechismal** *adj*.

categorical *adj* unconditional, absolute; positive, explicit.–**categorically** *adv*.

categorize *vt* to place in a category.–**categorization** *n*.

category *n* (*pl* **categories**) a class or division of things.

cater *vi* (*with* **for** *or* **to**) to provide with what is needed or desired, esp food and service, as for parties.–**caterer** *n*.

caterpillar *n* the worm-like larvae of a butterfly or moth; the ribbed band in place of wheels on a heavy vehicle; a vehicle (eg tank, tractor) equipped with such tracks.

catfish *n* (*pl* **catfish, catfishes**) a large, usu freshwater, fish with whisker-like feelers around the mouth.

catgut *n* a strong cord made from animal intestines, used for the strings of musical instruments, sports rackets, and surgical ligatures.

catharsis *n* (*pl* **catharses**) emotional relief given by art, ess tragedy; (*med*) purgation; (*psychoanal*) relief obtained by the uncovering of buried repressions, etc.–**cathartic** *adj*.

cathedral *n* the chief church of a diocese. * *adj* having or belonging to a cathedral.

catheter *n* a flexible tube inserted into the bladder for drawing off urine.

cathode *n* (*elect*) the negative terminal; the electrode by which current leaves.–**cathodal** *adj*.–**cathodic, cathodical** *adj*.

cathode ray *n* one of the electrons in a stream of electrons emitted by a cathode in a vacuum tube.

Catholic *n* a member of the Roman Catholic Church. * *adj* relating to the Roman Catholic Church; embracing the whole body of Christians.–**Catholicism** *n*.

catholic *adj* universal, all-embracing; broad-minded, liberal; general, not exclusive.

catkin *n* a hanging spike of small flowers, eg on birch, willow and hazel trees.

catmint, catnip *n* a strongly-scented plant attractive to cats.

catnap *n* a short, light or intermittent sleep, a snooze, a doze.–*also* *vi* (**catnapping, catnapped**).

cat-o'-nine-tails *n* (*pl* **cat-o'-nine-tails**) a whip with nine lashes of knotted cord, formerly used as a punishment in the army and navy.

Cat scan, Cat scanner *see* **CAT**.

cat's-eye *n* a hard semi-transparent variety of quartz.

cat's-paw *n* a person used as a tool by another, a dupe; (*naut*) a light breeze that slightly ripples the surface of the water.

cattery *n* (*pl* **catteries**) a place for boarding or breeding cats.

cattle *npl* domesticated bovine mammals such as bulls and cows.

catty *adj* (**cattier, cattiest**) (*inf*) spiteful, mean.–**cattily** *adv*.–**cattiness** *n*.

catwalk *n* a narrow, raised pathway on a stage, bridge, etc; fashion modeling (*with* **the**).

Caucasian *adj* of the light-skinned racial group of humankind; of or relating to the Caucasus Mountains. * *n* a Caucasian person.–**Caucasoid** *adj*.

caucus *n* (*pl* **caucuses**) a private meeting of leaders of a political party or faction, usu to plan strategy.

caught *see* **catch**.

caul *n* the membrane covering a fetus; part of this covering the head of some infants at birth.

cauldron *see* **caldron**.

cauliflower *n* a kind of cabbage with an edible white flowerhead used as a vegetable.

caulk *vt* to make (a boat) watertight by stopping up the seams with pitch.–*also* **calk**.–**caulker, calker** *n*.

causal *adj* forming or being a cause; involving, expressing or implying a cause.–**causally** *adv*.

causality *n* (*pl* **causalities**) the relationship between cause and effect.

causation *n* causality; the act of causing something to happen.–**causational** *adj*.

cause *n* that which produces an effect; reason, motive, purpose, justification; a principle for which people strive; a lawsuit. * *vt* to bring about, to effect; to make (to do something).–**causer** *n*.

causeway *n* a raised road across wet ground or water.

caustic *adj* burning tissue, etc by chemical action; corrosive; sarcastic, cutting. * *n* a caustic substance.–**caustically** *adv*.–**causticness, causticity** *n*.

cauterize *vt* to burn with a caustic substance or a hot iron so as to destroy dead tissue, stop bleeding, etc; to deaden.–**cauterization** *n*.

caution *n* care for safety, prudence; a warning, esp a formal one, to a suspect or accused person. * *vt* to warn (against); to admonish.–**cautionary** *adj*.

cautious *adj* careful, circumspect.–**cautiously** *adv*.–**cautiousness** *n*.

cavalcade *n* a procession of riders on horseback; a dramatic sequence or procession.

cavalier adj free and easy, careless; offhand, brusque. * n a horseman

cavalry n (pl **cavalries**) combat troops originally mounted on horseback.

cave n a hollow place inside the earth open to the surface. * vti (with **in**) to collapse or make collapse; (inf) to yield, submit.—**cave-in** n.

caveman n (pl **cavemen**) a prehistoric cave dweller; (inf) a person who acts in a primitive or crude manner.

cavern n a large cave.—**cavernous** adj.

caviar, caviare n salted roe of the sturgeon or other large fish.

cavil vi (**caviling, caviled** or **cavilling, cavilled**) to make trifling objections, to find fault. * n a trifling objection.—**caviller** n.

cavity n (pl **cavities**) a hole; a hollow place, esp in a tooth.

cavort vi to frolic, prance.

caw n the cry of the crow, rook, or raven. * vi to utter this cry.

cay n a small low island.

cayenne, cayenne pepper n a hot red pepper made from capsicum.

cayman see **caiman**.

CD abbr = compact disc.

Cd (chem symbol) = cadmium.

CD-ROM abbr = compact disc read only memory: a CD used for distributing text and images in electronic publishing, for computer software, and for permanent storage of computer data.

CDV abbr CD-video; compact video disc.

cease vti to stop, to come to an end; to discontinue.

ceasefire n a period of truce in a war, uprising, etc.

ceaseless adj without ceasing; incessant.—**ceaselessly** adv.

cedar n a large coniferous evergreen tree; its wood.—**cedarwood** n.

cede vt to yield to another, give up, esp by treaty; to assign or transfer the title of.—**ceder** n.

ceiling n the inner roof of a room; the lining of this; any upper limit; the highest altitude a particular aircraft can fly.

celebrate vt to make famous; to praise, extol; to perform with proper rites; to mark with ceremony; to keep (festival).—**celebrant** n.—**celebration** n.

celebrated adj famous.

celebrity n (pl **celebrities**) fame; a famous or well-known person.

celeriac n a variety of celery with a turnip-like root.

celerity n quickness, dispatch.

celery n (pl **celeries**) a vegetable with long juicy edible stalks.

celestial adj in or of the sky; heavenly; divine.—**celestially** adv.

celiac adj of or pertaining to the abdomen. * n a person with celiac disease.—also **coeliac**.

celiac disease n a chronic digestive disease, causing malnutrition and diarrhea. (pl **celibacies**) the unmarried state; complete sexual abstinence.

celibate n a person who remains unmarried, esp one who has taken religious vows; a person who abstains from sexual intercourse.—also adj.—**celibacy** n.

cell n a small room for one in a prison or monastery; a small cavity as in a honeycomb; a device that converts chemical energy into electricity; a microscopic unit of living matter; a small group of people bound by common aims within an organization or political party.

cellar n a basement; a stock of wines.

cellnet n a portable radio telephone used in cellular radio.

cello n (pl **cellos**) the violoncello, a large four-stringed bass instrument of the violin family, held between the knees.—**cellist** n.

cellophane n a thin transparent paper made from cellulose, used for wrapping.

cellular adj of, resembling or containing cells; (textiles) of an open texture.

cellule n a small cell or cavity.

cellulite n a form of fat on the hips, thighs and buttocks that causes puckering of the skin surface.

celluloid n a type of plastic made from cellulose nitrate and camphor; a plastic coating on film; cinema film.

cellulose n a starch-like carbohydrate forming the cell walls of plants, used in making paper, textiles, film, etc.

Celsius adj pertaining to a thermometer scale with a freezing point of 0 degrees and a boiling point of 100 degrees.

cement n a powdered substance of lime and clay, mixed with water, etc to make mortar or concrete, which hardens upon drying; any hard-drying substance. * vt to bind or glue together with or as if with cement; to cover with cement.—**cementer** n.

cemetery n (pl **cemeteries**) a place for the burial of the dead.

cenotaph n a monument to a person who is buried elsewhere.—**cenotaphic** adj.

censer n a covered cup-shaped vessel pierced with holes in which incense is burned.

censor n an official with the power to examine literature, movies, mail, etc and remove or prohibit anything considered obscene, objectionable, etc. * vt to act as a censor.—**censorable** adj.—**censorial** adj.—**censorship** n.

censorious adj expressing censure; fault-finding.—**censoriously** adv.—**censoriousness** n.

censure n an expression of disapproval or blame. * vt to condemn as wrong; to reprimand.—**censurable** adj.

census n (pl **censuses**) an official count of the population, including details of age, sex, occupation, etc; any official count.

cent n a hundredth of a dollar; (inf) a negligible amount of money.

centaur n a fabulous monster, half man, half horse; (astron) a southern constellation.

centenarian n one who is one hundred years old or more.—also adj.

centenary n (pl **centenaries**) a hundredth anniversary or its celebration. * adj of a hundred years.

centennial adj happening every hundred years. * n a centenary.

center n the approximate middle point or part of anything, a pivot; interior; point of concentration; a place where a particular activity goes on; (sport) a player at the center of the field, etc, a center-forward. * adj of or at the center. * vt (**centering, centered**) to place in the centre; to concentrate; to be fixed; (football, hockey) to kick or hit the ball into the centre of the pitch.—also **center**.

centerfold n a color illustration spread across the two facing pages in the middle of a newspaper or magazine.—also **centrefold**.

center of gravity n that point of a body through which the resultant of all the forces acting upon it in consequence of the earth's attraction will pass.

centerpiece n a central ornament or decoration.—also **centrepiece**.

centigrade adj Celsius.

centigram, centigramme n one hundredth of a gram.

centiliter, centilitre n one hundredth of a liter.

centimeter, centimetre n one hundredth of a meter.

centipede n a crawling creature with a long body divided into numerous segments each with a pair of legs.

central adj in, at, from or forming the center; main, principal; important.—**centrally** adv.—**centrality** n.

central heating n a system of heating by pipes from a central boiler or other heat source.

centralize vt to draw to the center; to place under the control of a central authority, esp government.—**centralization** n.

central nervous system n in vertebrates, the brain and spinal cord which coordinates an animal's activity.

centre see **center**.

centrifugal adj moving away from the center of rotation.—**centrifugally** adv.

centrifuge n a device used to separate milk, blood, etc, by rotating at very high speed.—**centrifugation** n.

centripetal adj tending to move towards the centre.—**centripetally** adv.

centurion n an officer commanding a hundred Roman soldiers.

century n (pl **centuries**) a period of a hundred years; a set of a hundred

ceramic adj of earthenware, porcelain, or brick. * n something made of ceramic.

ceramics n (sing) work executed wholly or partly in clay and baked; the art of pottery.–**ceramist, ceramicist** n.

cereal n a grass grown for its edible grain, eg wheat, rice; the grain of such grasses; a breakfast food made from such grains. * adj of corn or edible grain.

cerebellum n (pl **cerebellums, cerebella**) a part of the brain below and behind the cerebrum which coordinates voluntary movements.–**cerebellar** adj.

cerebral adj of or relating to the cerebrum; intellectual.–**cerebrally** adv.

cerebral palsy n a disability caused by brain damage before, during or immediately after birth resulting in poor muscle coordination.

cerebrum n (pl **cerebrums, cerebra**) the front part of the brain of vertebrates; the dominant part of the brain in man, associated with intellectual function; the brain as a whole.

ceremonious adj observant of ceremony; marked by formality; overpolite.–**ceremoniously** adv.

ceremony n (pl **ceremonies**) a sacred rite; formal observance or procedure; behavior that follows rigid etiquette.–**ceremonial** adj.

cerise n a light and clear red.–also adj.

cert abbr = certified; certificate; (sl) certainty.

certain adj sure, positive; unerring, reliable; sure to happen, inevitable; definite, fixed; some; one; unnamed, unspecified.

certainly adv without doubt; yes.

certainty n (pl **certainties**) something undoubted, inevitable; the condition of being certain.

certificate n a document formally attesting a fact; a testimonial of qualifications or character.–**certificated** adj.

certify vt (**certifying, certified**) to declare in writing or attest formally; to endorse with authority.–**certification** n.

certitude n freedom from doubt.

cervix n (pl **cervixes, cervices**) the neck of the womb.–**cervical** adj.

cesium n a rare silvery alkaline metal.–also **caesium**.

cessation n a stoppage; a pause.

cesspit, cesspool n a covered cistern for collecting liquid waste or sewage; (fig) a place of sin and depravity.

cetacean n a member of an order of aquatic, usu marine, mammals that includes whales, dolphins and porpoises. * adj belonging to this order (–also **cetaceous**).

cf. abbr = compare (Latin confer).

CFC abbr = chlorofluorocarbon.

cha-cha(-cha) n a ballroom dance orig from Latin America; the music for this.

chafe vti to restore warmth by rubbing; to make or become sore by rubbing; to irritate; to feel irritation, to fret.

chaff[1] n husks of grain separated from the seed by threshing or winnowing; cut hay or straw; worthless stuff.

chaff[2] vt to banter; to make a game of. * vi to use bantering language. * n good-natured teasing, banter.

chagrin n annoyance; vexation; disappointment.

chain n a series of connected links or rings; a continuous series; a series of related events; a bond; a group of shops, hotels, etc owned by the same company; a range of mountains; a group of islands; (pl) anything that restricts or binds; fetters. * vt to fasten with a chain or chains.

chain gang n a group of prisoners chained together.

chain saw n a power-driven saw with teeth linked as in a chain.

chain-smoke vti to smoke (cigarettes) one after the other.–**chain-smoker** n.

chair n a separate seat for one, with a back and legs; a seat of authority; a chairman; a professorship; the electric chair. * vt to preside as chairman of.

chair lift n a series of seats suspended from a cable for carrying sightseers or skiers uphill.

chairman n (pl **chairmen**) a person who presides at a meeting; the president of a board or committee.–**chairwoman** nf (pl **chairwomen**).–also **chairperson**.

chaise longue n (pl **chaise longues, chaises longues**) a couch-like chair with a long seat.

chalet n a Swiss hut; any similar building used in a holiday camp, as a ski lodge, etc.

chalice n a large cup with a base; a communion cup.

chalk n calcium carbonate, a soft white limestone; such a stone or a substitute used for drawing or writing. * vt to write, mark or draw with chalk; (with **up**) (inf) to score, get, achieve; to charge or credit.–**chalky** adj.

challenge vt to summon to a fight or contest; to call in question; to object to; to hail and interrogate; to demand proof of identity. * n the act of challenging; a summons to a contest; a calling in question; a problem that stimulates effort.–**challenger** n.–**challenging** adj.

chamber n a room, esp a bedroom; a deliberative body or a division of a legislature; a room where such a body meets; a compartment; a cavity in the body of an organism; part of a gun cylinder holding the cartridge; (pl) a judge's office.

chambermaid n a woman employed to clean bedrooms in a hotel, etc.

chamber music n music for performance by a small group, as a string quartet.

chameleon n a lizard capable of changing color to match its surroundings; a person of variable moods or behavior; an adaptable person.–**chameleonic** adj.

chamois n (pl **chamois**) a small antelope found in Europe and Asia; a piece of chamois leather.

chamomile n an aromatic plant with daisy-like flowers used medicinally.–also **camomile**.

champ[1] vti to munch noisily, chomp; **champ at the bit** to be impatient.

champ[2] n (inf) a champion.

champagne n a sparkling white wine; a pale straw color.

champion n a person who fights for another; one who upholds a cause; a competitor successful against all others. * adj first-class; (inf) excellent. * vt to defend; to uphold the cause of.

championship n the act of championing; the process of determining a champion; a contest held to find a champion.

chance n a course of events, fortune; an accident, an unexpected event; opportunity; possibility; probability; risk. * vti to risk; to happen; to come upon unexpectedly. * adj accidental, not planned.

chancel n the part of a church around the altar, for the clergy and the choir.

chancellor n a high government official, as, in certain countries, a prime minister; in some universities, the president or other executive officer.–**chancellorship** n.

chancre n a syphilitic ulcer.–**chancrous** adj.

chancy adj (**chancier, chanciest**) (inf) risky, uncertain.–**chancily** adv.

chandelier n an ornamental hanging frame with branches for holding lights.

chandler n a dealer or merchant, esp in candles, oil, soap, etc.

change vt to make different, to alter; to transform; to exchange; to put fresh clothes on. * vi to become different, to undergo alteration; to put on fresh clothes; to continue one's journey by leaving one station, etc, or mode of transport and going to and using another. * n alteration, modification; substitution; variety; a fresh set, esp clothes; money in small units; the balance of money returned when given in a larger denomination as payment.–**changer** n.

changeable adj able to be changed; altering rapidly between different conditions; inconstant.–**changeability** n.–**changeably** adv.

changeover *n* a complete change of system, method, state, attitude, etc.

channel *n* the bed or the deeper part of a river, harbor, etc; a body of water joining two larger ones; a navigable passage; a means of passing or conveying or communicating; a band of radio frequencies reserved for a particular purpose, eg television station; a path for an electrical signal; a groove or line along which liquids, etc may flow. * *vt* (**channeling, channeled** *or* **channelling, channelled**) to form a channel in; to groove; to direct.

chant *vti* to sing; to recite in a singing manner; to sing or shout (a slogan) rhythmically. * *n* sacred music to which prose is sung; sing-song intonation; a monotonous song; a rhythmic slogan, esp as sung or shouted by sports fans, etc.

chanter *n* a person who chants; the tenor or treble pipe of a bagpipe on which the melody is played.

chaos *n* utter confusion, muddle.–**chaotic** *adj.*–**chaotically** *adv.*

chap[1] *vti* (**chapping, chapped**) (*skin*) to make or become split or rough in cold weather. * *n* a chapped place in the skin.

chap[2] *n* (*inf*) a man.

chaparejos *npl* a cowboy's leather leg coverings.–*also* **chaps**.

chapel *n* a building for Christian worship, not as large as a church.

chaperon, chaperone *n* a woman who accompanies a girl at social occasions for propriety. * *vt* to attend as a chaperon.–**chaperonage** *n.*

chaplain *n* a clergyman serving in a religious capacity with the armed forces, or in a prison, hospital, etc.–**chaplaincy** *n.*

chaps *npl* chaparejos.

chapter *n* a main division of a book; the body or meeting of canons of a cathedral or members of a monastic order; a sequence of events; an organized branch of a society or association.

char *vb* (**charring, charred**) *vt* to burn to charcoal or carbon. * *vti* to scorch.

character *n* the combination of qualities that distinguishes an individual person, group or thing; moral strength; reputation; disposition; a person of marked individuality; an eccentric; (*inf*) a person; a person in a play or novel; a guise, role; a letter or mark in writing, printing, etc.

characteristic *adj* marking or constituting the particular nature (of a person or thing). * *n* a characteristic or distinguishing feature.–**characteristically** *adv.*

characterize *vt* to describe in terms of particular qualities; to designate; to be characteristic of, mark.–**characterization** *n.*

charade *n* a travesty; an absurd pretence; (*usu pl*) a game of guessing a word from the acted representation of its syllables and the whole.

charcoal *n* the black carbon matter obtained by partially burning wood and used as fuel, as a filter or for drawing.

chard *n* a type of beet with edible leaves and stalks.

charge *vt* to ask as the price; to record as a debt; to load, to fill, saturate; to lay a task or trust on; to burden; to accuse; to attack at a run; to build up an electric charge (in). * *n* a price charged for goods or service; a build-up of electricity; the amount which a receptacle can hold at one time; the explosive required to fire a weapon; trust, custody; a thing or person entrusted; a task, duty; accusation; an attack.

charger *n* a cavalry horse; a device for charging a battery.

chariot *n* a two-wheeled vehicle driven by two or more horses in ancient warfare, races, etc.–**charioteer** *n.*

charisma, charism *n* (*pl* **charismata, charisms**) personal quality enabling a person to influence or inspire others; a God-given power or gift.–**charismatic** *adj.*

charitable *adj* of or for charity; generous to the needy, benevolent; lenient in judging others, kindly.–**charitableness** *n.*–**charitably** *adv.*

charity *n* (*pl* **charities**) leniency or tolerance towards others; generosity in giving to the needy; a benevolent fund or institution.

charlatan *n* a person who pretends to be what he or she is not; one who professes knowledge dishonestly, esp of medicine.–**charlatanism, charlatanry** *n.*

charm *n* an alluring quality, fascination; a magic verse or formula; something thought to possess occult power; an object bringing luck; a trinket on a bracelet. * *vt* to delight, captivate; to influence as by magic.–**charmer** *n.*

charming *adj* delightful, attractive.–**charmingly** *adv.*

chart *n* a map, esp for use in navigation; an information sheet with tables, graphs, etc; a weather map; a table, graph, etc. * *vt* to make a chart of; to plan (a course of action).

charter *n* a document granting rights, privileges, ownership of land, etc; the hire of transportation. * *vt* to grant by charter; to hire.

charwoman *n* (*pl* **charwomen**) a woman employed to clean a house.

chary *adj* (**charier, chariest**) cautious; sparing; (*with* **of**) unwilling to risk.–**charily** *adv.*

chase *vt* to pursue; to run after; to drive (away); to hunt; (*inf: usu with* **up**) to pursue in a determined manner. * *n* pursuit; a hunt; a quarry hunted; a steeplechase.

chaser *n* a horse used in steeplechasing; a person that chases; (*inf*) a drink taken after another, as in beer after a whisky.

chasm *n* a deep cleft, an abyss, a gaping hole; a wide difference in opinions, etc.–**chasmal, chasmic** *adj.*

chassis *n* (*pl* **chassis**) the frame, wheels, engine of a car, airplane or other vehicle.

chaste *adj* pure, abstaining from unlawful sexual intercourse; virgin; modest; restrained, unadorned.–**chastely** *adv.*–**chasteness** *n.*

chasten *vt* to correct by suffering, discipline; to restrain.–**chastener** *n.*

chastise *vt* to punish; to beat; to scold.–**chastisement** *n.*

chastity *n* sexual abstinence; virginity; purity.

chat *vti* (**chatting, chatted**) to talk in an easy or familiar way; (*with* **up**) (*inf*) to talk in a flirtatious way with another person. * *n* informal conversation.–**chatty** *adj.*–**chattily** *adv.*

chateau, château *n* (*pl* **chateaus, châteaux**) a castle or large country estate in France.

chattel *n* (*usu pl*) goods, possessions; (*law*) personal property except freehold.

chatter *vi* to talk aimlessly and rapidly; (*animal, etc*) to utter rapid cries; (*teeth*) to rattle together due to cold or fear. * *n* idle rapid talk; the sound of chattering.– **chatterer** *n.*

chatterbox *n* an incessant talker.

chauffeur *n* a person who drives a car for someone else. * *vt* to drive as a chauffeur.–**chauffeuse** *nf.*

chauvinism *n* aggressive patriotism; excessive devotion to a belief, cause, etc, esp a man's belief in the superiority of men over women.–**chauvinist** *n.*–**chauvinistic** *adj.*

cheap *adj* low-priced, inexpensive; good value; of little worth, inferior; vulgar.–**cheaply** *adv.*–**cheapness** *n.*

cheapen *vti* to make or become cheap; to lower the value, worth or reputation of.

cheapskate *n* (*inf*) a mean or dishonorable person.

cheat *vti* to defraud, to swindle; to deceive; to play unfairly. * *n* a fraud, deception; a person who cheats.–**cheater** *n.*

check *vti* to bring or come to a stand; to restrain or impede; to admonish, reprove; to test the accuracy of, verify; (*with* **in**) to sign or register arrival at a hotel, work, an airport, etc; (*with* **out**) to settle the bill and leave a hotel; to investigate. * *n* repulse; stoppage; a pattern of squares; a control to test accuracy; a tick against listed items; a bill in a restaurant. (*chess*) a threatening of the king; a money order to a bank (*–also* **cheque**).

checkbook *n* a book containing blank checks to be drawn on a bank.

checker[1] n a cashier in a supermarket.

checker[2] n a pattern of squares (–also **chequer**); a flat counter used in the game of checkers (–also **draughtsman**); (pl) a game for two players who each move twelve round flat pieces over a checkerboard (–also **draughts**).

checkerboard n a draughtboard.

checkered adj marked with a variegated pattern; having a career marked by fluctuating fortunes.–also **chequered**.

checkmate n (chess) the winning position when the king is threatened and unable to move; utter defeat. * vt (chess) to place in checkmate; to defeat, foil.

checkout n a place where traffic may be halted for inspection; the place in a store where goods are paid for.

checkpoint n a place where visitors' passports or other official documents may be examined.

checkup n a thorough examination; a medical examination, usu repeated at intervals.

Cheddar n a type of hard, white or yellow cheese originally made in Cheddar, England.

cheek n the side of the face below the eye; (sl) buttock; impudence.

cheeky adj (**cheekier, cheekiest**) disrespectful, impudent.– **cheekily** adv.–**cheekiness** n.

cheep n the frail squeak of a young bird. * vi to make such a sound.

cheer n a shout of applause or welcome; a frame of mind, spirits; happiness. * vt to gladden; to encourage; to applaud.

cheerful adj in good spirits; happy.–**cheerfully** adv.–**cheerfulness** n.

cheerleader n a person who leads organized cheering, esp at a sports event.

cheers interj (inf) an expression used in offering a toast, as a form of farewell or thanks.

cheery adj (**cheerier, cheeriest**) lively, genial, merry.–**cheerily** adv.–**cheeriness** n.

cheese n the curds of milk pressed into a firm or hard mass; a boss or important person (big cheese).

cheeseburger n a hamburger with melted cheese on top.

cheesecloth n a thin cotton fabric.

cheesy adj (**cheesier, cheesiest**) like cheese.–**cheesiness** n.

cheetah n a large spotted cat, similar to a leopard.

chef n a professional cook.

chemical n a substance used in, or arising from, a chemical process. * adj of, used in, or produced by chemistry.–**chemically** adv.

chemise n a woman's undergarment; a loose-fitting dress.

chemist n a pharmacy; a manufacturer of medicinal drugs; a person skilled in chemistry.

chemistry n (pl **chemistries**) the science of the properties of substances and their combinations and reactions; chemical structure.

chemotherapy n the treatment of disease, esp cancer, by drugs and other chemical agents.

chenille n silk or worsted cord.

cheque see **check**.

chequer see **checker**.

cherish vt to tend lovingly, foster; to keep in mind as a hope, ambition, etc.–**cherisher** n.

cheroot n a cigar cut square at each end.

cherry n (pl **cherries**) a small red, pitted fruit; the tree bearing it; a bright red color.

cherub n (pl **cherubim**) an angel of the second order; a winged child or child's head; (pl **cherubs**) an angelic, sweet child.– **cherubic** adj.

chervil n an aromatic herb used for flavoring.

chess n a game played by two people with 32 pieces on a chessboard.

chessboard n a board checkered with 64 squares in two alternate colors, used for playing chess or draughts.

chessman n (pl **chessmen**) any of the 16 pieces used by each player in chess.

chest n a large strong box; the part of the body enclosed by the ribs, the thorax.

chestnut n a tree or shrub of the beech family; the edible nut of a chestnut; the wood of the chestnut; a horse with chestnut coloring; (inf) an old joke. * adj of the color of a chestnut, a deep reddish brown.

chesty adj (**chestier, chestiest**) (inf) prone to chest infections; having a large chest or bosom.–**chestily** adv.–**chestiness** n.

chevron n the V-shaped bar on the sleeve of a uniform, showing rank.

chew vt to grind between the teeth, to masticate; (with **over**) to ponder, think over; (with **up**) to spoil by chewing. * n the act of chewing; something to chew, as a sweet or tobacco.–**chewable, chewy** adj.–**chewer** n.

chewing gum n a flavored gum made from chicle, for chewing.

chez prep at the home of.

chic n elegance, style. * adj stylish.

chicane n a hand at bridge without trumps; a barrier or obstacle on a motor-racing course; chicanery.

chicanery n (pl **chicaneries**) underhand dealing, trickery; verbal subterfuge.

chick n a young bird; (sl) a young attractive woman or girl.

chickadee n the American blackcap titmouse.

chicken n a young, domestic fowl; its flesh. * adj cowardly, timorous. * vi (with **out**) (inf) to suffer a failure of nerve or courage.

chickenpox n a contagious viral disease that causes a rash of red spots on the skin.

chickpea n (the seed eaten as a vegetable of) an Asian leguminous plant.

chicle n the milky gum of a tropical American tree used to make chewing gum.

chicory n (pl **chicories**) a salad plant; its dried, ground, roasted root used to flavor coffee or as a coffee substitute.

chide vt (**chiding, chided** or **chid**; pp **chided, chid** or **chidden**) to rebuke, scold.–**chider** n.–**chidingly** adv.

chief adj principal, most important. * n a leader; the head of a tribe or clan.

chiefly adv especially; mainly; for the most part.

chieftain n the head of a Scottish clan; a chief.

chiffon n a thin gauzy material. * adj made of chiffon; (pie filling, etc) having a light fluffy texture.

chignon n a mass of hair worn in a roll at the back of the head, a bun.

Chihuahua n a tiny dog with erect ears, originally from Mexico.

chilblain n an inflamed swelling on the hands, toes, etc, due to cold.

child n (pl **children**) a young human being; a son or daughter; offspring; an innocent or immature person.

childbearing n pregnancy and childbirth.–also adj.

childbirth n the process of giving birth to children.

childhood n the period between birth and puberty in humans.

childish adj of, like or suited to a child; foolish.–**childishly** adv.– **childishness** n.

children see **child**.

child's play n an easy task.

chili n (pl **chilies**) the hot-tasting pod of some of the capsicums, dried and used as flavoring.

chill n a sensation of coldness; an illness caused by exposure to cold and marked by shivering; anything that dampens or depresses. * adj shivering with cold; feeling cold; unemotional, formal. * vti to make or become cold; to harden by cooling; to depress.

chilly adj (**chillier, chilliest**) cold; unfriendly.–**chilliness** n.

chime n the harmonious sound of a bell; accord; harmony; (pl) a set of bells or metal tubes, etc tuned in a scale; their ringing. * vi to ring (a bell); (with **in**) (inf) to join in in agreement; to interrupt a conversation; (with **with**) to agree. * vt to indicate the hour by chiming, as a clock.

chimera, chimaera n an imaginary monster; an impossible fancy.–**chimerical, chimeric** adj.

chimney n (pl **chimneys**) a passage for smoke, hot air or fumes, a funnel; a chimney stack; the vent of a volcano; a vertical crevice in rock large enough to enter and climb.

chimneypot n a pipe extending a chimney at the top.

chimp n (inf) chimpanzee.

chimpanzee n an African anthropoid ape.

chin n the part of the face below the mouth.

china n fine porcelain; articles made from this.

china clay n kaolin.

Chinatown n the Chinese quarter of any city.

chinchilla n a small South American rodent with soft gray fur; a breed of domestic cat; a breed of rabbit.

Chinese adj of or pertaining to China. * n (pl **Chinese**) an inhabitant of China.

chink[1] n a narrow opening; a crack or slit.

chink[2] n the sound of coins clinking together.

chino n (pl **chinos**) a strong, hardwearing twilled cotton; (pl) pants made of this fabric.

chinook n a warm dry southwesterly wind of the eastern slopes of the Rocky Mountains; a warm moist wind blowing onto the northwest coast of America.

chintz n a glazed cotton cloth printed with colored designs.–**chintzy** adj.

chip vt (**chipping, chipped**) to knock small pieces off; to shape or make by chipping. * n a small piece cut or broken off; a mark left by chipping; a thin strip of fried potato, french fry; a counter used in games; a tiny piece of semiconducting material, such as silicon, printed with a microcircuit and used as part of an integrated circuit.

chipboard n a thin stiff material made from compressed wood shavings and other waste pieces combined with resin.

chipmunk n a small, striped, squirrel-like animal of North America.

chipper adj active; lively, cheerful.

chiropody n the care and treatment of the feet.–**chiropodist** n.

chiropractic n the manipulation of joints, esp of the spine, to alleviate nerve pressure as a method of curing disease.–**chiropractor** n.

chirp n the sharp, shrill note of some birds or a grasshopper. * vi to make this sound.–**chirper** n.

chirpy adj (**chirpier, chirpiest**) lively, cheerful.–**chirpily** adv.–**chirpiness** n.

chisel n a tool with a square cutting end. * vt (**chiseling, chiseled** or **chiselling, chiselled**) to cut or carve with a chisel; (sl) to defraud.–**chiseler** n.

chit n a voucher or a sum owed for drink, food, etc; a note; a requisition.

chitchat n gossip, trivial talk.

chivalry n (pl **chivalries**) the medieval system of knighthood; knightly qualities, bravery, courtesy, respect for women.–**chivalric** adj.–**chivalrous** adj.–**chivalrously** adv.

chive, chives n a plant whose onion-flavored leaves are used in cooking and salads.

chivvy, chivy vt (**chivvying, chivvied** or **chivying, chivied**) to annoy, harass, nag.

chlorate n a salt of chloric acid.

chloride n any compound containing chlorine.–**chloridic** adj.

chlorinate vt to treat or combine with chlorine; to disinfect with chlorine.–**chlorination** n.

chlorine n a nonmetallic element, a yellowish-green poisonous gas used in bleaches, disinfectants, and in industry.

chlorofluorocarbon n any of various compounds containing carbon, chlorine, fluorine and hydrogen, used in refrigerants, aerosol propellants, etc, and thought to be harmful to the earth's atmosphere.

chloroform n a colorless volatile liquid formerly used as an anesthetic.

chlorophyll, chlorophyl n the green photosynthetic coloring matter in plants.

chock-a-block adj completely full.–also **chock-full**.

chocolate n a powder or edible solid made of the roasted, pounded cacao bean; a drink made by dissolving this powder in boiling water or milk; a sweet with a centre and chocolate coating. * adj flavored or coated with chocolate; dark reddish brown.–**chocolaty** adj.

choice n act of choosing; the power to choose; selection; alternative; a thing chosen; preference; the best part. * adj of picked quality, specially good.–**choicely** adv.–**choiceness** n.

choir n an organized group of singers, esp of a church; the part of a church before the altar used by them.

choke vti to stop the breath of, stifle; to throttle; to suffocate; to block (up); to check, esp emotion, to choke back or up. * n a fit of choking; a choking sound; a valve that controls the flow of air in a carburetor.

choler n bile; irascibility, anger.–**choleric** adj.

cholera n a severe, infectious intestinal disease.

cholesterol, cholesterin n a substance found in animal tissues, blood and animal fats, thought to be a cause of hardening of the arteries.

chomp vt to chew noisily and with relish, champ.

choose vb (**choosing, chose**, pp **chosen**) vt to select (one thing) rather than another. * vi to decide, to think fit.–**chooser** n.

choosy adj (**choosier, choosiest**) (inf) cautious; fussy, particular.–**choosily** adv.–**choosiness** n.

chop vt (**chopping, chopped**) to cut by striking; to cut into pieces. * n a cut of meat and bone from the rib, loin, or shoulder; a downward blow or motion; **get the chop** (sl) to be dismissed from one's employment; to be killed.

chopper n a tool for chopping; a cleaver; a small hand ax; (sl) a helicopter.

choppy adj (**choppier, choppiest**) (sea) running in rough, irregular waves; jerky.–**choppily** adv.–**choppiness** n.

chops npl the jaws or cheeks.

chopsticks n a pair of wooden or plastic sticks used in Asian countries to eat with.

choral[1] adj relating to, sung by, or written for, a choir or chorus.–**chorally** adv.

chorale, choral[2] n a slow hymn or psalm sung to a traditional or composed melody, esp by a choir.

chord n (mus) three or more notes played simultaneously; a feeling of sympathy, recognition or remembering (strike a chord).–**chordal** adj.

chore n a piece of housework; a regular or tedious task.

choreograph vt to devise the steps for a ballet, dance, etc.–**choreography** n.–**choreographer** n.–**choreographic** adj.–**choreographically** adv.

chorister n a member of a choir.

chorizo n (pl **chorizos**) a spicy pork sausage.

chortle vi to chuckle exultantly.–also n.

chorus n (pl **choruses**) a group of singers and dancers in the background to a play, musical, etc; a group of singers, a choir; music sung by a chorus; a refrain; an utterance by many at once. * vt (**chorusing, chorused**) to sing, speak or shout in chorus.

chose, chosen see **choose**.

chow n a breed of thick-coated dog, originally from China (–also **chow chow**); (sl) food.

chowder n a thick clam and potato soup.

chow mein n a Chinese-American dish of fried, crispy noodles with meat and vegetables.

christen vt to enter the Christian Church by baptism; to give a name to; (inf) to use for the first time.–**christener** n.–**christening** n.

Christendom n all Christians, or Christian countries regarded as a whole.

Christian n a person who believes in Christianity. * adj relating to, believing in, or based on the doctrines of Christianity; kind, gentle, humane.

Christianity n the religion based on the teachings of Christ.

Christian name n a name given when one is christened; (loosely) any forename.

Christmas n (pl **Christmases**) an annual festival (25 December) in memory of the birth of Christ.

chromatic adj of or in color; (mus) using tones outside the key in which the passage is written.–**chromatically** adv.–**chromaticism** n.

chromatics n (sing) the science of color.

chromatic scale n a twelve-note musical scale that proceeds by semitones.

chrome n chromium; a chromium pigment; something plated with an alloy of chromium.

chromium n a hard metallic element used in making steel alloys and electroplating to give a tough surface.

chromosome n any of the microscopic rod-shaped bodies bearing genes.

chronic adj (disease) long-lasting; regular; habitual.–**chronically** adv.–**chronicity** n.

chronicle n a record of events in chronological order; an account; a history. * vt to record in a chronicle.–**chronicler** n.

chronological, chronologic adj arranged in order of occurrence.–**chronologically** adv.

chronology n (pl **chronologies**) the determination of the order of events, eg in history; the arrangement of events in order of occurrence; a table of events listed in order of occurrence.–**chronologist** n.

chronometer n a very accurate instrument for measuring time exactly.

chrysalis n (pl **chrysalises, chrysalides**) the pupa of a moth or butterfly, enclosed in a cocoon.

chrysanthemum n a plant with a brightly colored flower head.

chubby adj (**chubbier, chubbiest**) plump.–**chubbiness** n.

chuck vt to throw, to toss; (inf) to stop, to give up. * n (usu with **the**) a giving up; dismissal.

chuckle vi to laugh softly; to gloat. * n a quiet laugh.–**chuckler** n.

chuff vi to make a puffing sound, as a steam engine. * n such a sound.

chug n the explosive sound of a car exhaust, etc. * vi (**chugging, chugged**) to make such a sound.

chum n (inf) a close friend, esp of the same sex. * vi (**chumming, chummed**) to be friendly (with); to room together.

chummy adj (**chummier, chummiest**) friendly, close to.–**chummily** adv.–**chumminess** n.

chump n (inf) a stupid person; a fool.

chunk n a short, thick piece or lump, as wood, bread, etc.

chunky adj (**chunkier, chunkiest**) short and thick; (clothing) of heavy material.–**chunkily** adv.–**chunkiness** n.

church n a building for public worship, esp Christian worship; the clerical profession; a religious service; (with cap) all Christians; (with **the**) a particular Christian denomination.

churchyard n the yard around a church often used as a burial ground.

churl n formerly one of the lowest orders of freemen; a peasant; a surly ill-bred person.–**churlish** adj.–**churlishly** adv.–**churlishness** n.

churn n a large metal container for milk; a device that can be vigorously turned to make milk or cream into butter. * vt to agitate in a churn; to make (butter) this way; to stir violently; (with **out**) (inf) to produce quickly or one after the other or without much effort.

chute n an inclined trough or a passage for sending down water, logs, rubbish, etc; a fall of water, a rapid; an inclined slide for children; a slide into a swimming pool.

chutney n a relish of fruits, spices, and herbs.

chutzpah, chutzpa n shameless audacity, presumption, or gall.

Ci (symbol) curie.

CIA abbr = Central Intelligence Agency.

ciao interj (Italian) used to express greeting or farewell.

cicada, cicala n (pl **cicadas, cicadae** or **cicalas, cicale**) a large fly-like insect with transparent wings, the male producing a loud chirp or drone.

cider n fermented apple juice as a drink.

cigar n a compact roll of tobacco leaf for smoking.

cigarette n shredded tobacco rolled in fine paper for smoking.

cinch n (sl) a firm hold, an easy job; a saddle band or girth.

cinder n a tiny piece of partly burned wood, etc; (pl) ashes from wood or coal.–**cindery** adj.

cinema n a place where motion pictures are shown; film as an industry or art form.–**cinematic** adj.–**cinematically** adv.

cinematography n the art or science of motion-picture photography.–**cinematographic** adj.–**cinematographer** n.

cinnabar n red sulphide of mercury. * adj vermilion.

cinnamon n a tree of the laurel family; its aromatic edible bark; a spice made from this; a yellowish-brown color. * adj yellowish brown.–**cinnamonic, cinnamic** adj.

cipher n the numeral 0, zero; any single Arabic numeral; a thing or person of no importance, a nonentity; a method of secret writing. * vt to convert (a message) into cipher.–also **cypher**.

circa prep about.

circle n a perfectly round plane figure; the line enclosing it; anything (built) in the form of a circle; the curved seating area above the stalls in a theater; a group, set or class (of people); extent, scope, as of influence. * vti to encompass; to move in a circle; to revolve (round); to draw a circle round.–**circler** n.

circuit n a distance round; a route or course; an area so enclosed; the path of an electric current; a visit to a particular area by a judge to hold courts; the area itself; a chain or association, eg of cinemas controlled by one management; sporting events attended regularly by the same competitors and at the same venues; a motor-racing track.–**circuital** adj.

circuitous adj roundabout, indirect.–**circuitously** adv.

circuitry n (pl **circuitries**) the plan of an electric circuit; the components of a circuit.

circular adj shaped like a circle, round; (argument) using as evidence the conclusion which it is seeking to prove; moving round a circle. * n an advertisement, etc addressed to a number of people.–**circularity, circularness** n.

circulate vti to pass from hand to hand or place to place; to spread or be spread about; to move round, finishing at the starting point.–**circulative** adj.–**circulator** n.–**circulatory** adj.

circulation n the act of circulating; a movement to and fro; the regular cycle of blood flow in the body; the number of copies sold of a newspaper, etc; currency.

circumcise vt to cut off the foreskin of (a male) or the clitoris of (a female), esp as a religious rite.–**circumcision** n.

circumference n the line bounding a circle, a ball, etc; the length of this line.–**circumferential** adj.

circumflex n an accent (^) placed over a vowel to indicate contraction, length, etc.–**circumflexion** n.

circumlocution n the use of more words than are necessary; a roundabout or evasive expression.–**circumlocutory** adj.

circumnavigate vt to sail or fly completely round (the world).–**circumnavigable** adj.–**circumnavigation** n.–**circumnavigator** n.

circumscribe vt to draw a line around; to enclose; to limit or restrict.–**circumscription** n.

circumspect adj prudent, cautious; careful; discreet.–**circumspection** n.–**circumspective** adj.

circumstance n an occurrence, an incident; a detail; ceremony; (pl) a state of affairs; condition in life.

circumstantial adj detailed; incidental; (law) strongly inferred from direct evidence.–**circumstantially** adv.

circumvent vt to evade, bypass; to outwit.–**circumventer, circumventor** n.–**circumvention** n.

circus n (pl **circuses**) a large arena for the exhibition of games, feats of horsemanship, etc; a traveling show of acrobats, clowns, etc.

cirrhosis n a hardened condition of the tissues of an organ, esp the liver.–**cirrhosed** adj.–**cirrhotic** adj.

cirrus n (pl **cirri**) thin, wispy clouds.

CIS abbr = Commonwealth of Independent States: a federation of former Soviet republics, such as Russia, Ukraine, who wish to retain voluntary links with one another.

cistern n a tank or reservoir for storing water, esp in a toilet.

citadel n a fortress in or near a city.

cite vt to summon officially to appear in court; to quote; to give as an example or authority.–**citation** n.–**citable, citeable** adj.

citizen n a member of a city, state or nation.–**citizenship** n.

citizenry n (pl **citizenries**) citizens collectively.

citrate n a salt or ester of citric acid.

citric acid n a sour acid found in fruits and used as a flavoring.

citrus n (pl **citruses**) a genus of trees including the lemon, orange, etc; the fruit of these trees. * adj of or relating to citrus trees or shrubs or their fruit.–**citric** adj.

city n (pl **cities**) an important or cathedral town; a town created a city by charter; the people of a city; business circles, esp financial services.–also adj.

civet n a cat-like animal of central Africa and South Asia; the pungent substance secreted by this animal used in perfumery.

civic adj of a city, citizen or citizenship. * npl the principles of good citizenship; the study of citizenship.–**civically** adv.

civil adj of citizens or the state; not military or ecclesiastical; polite, obliging; (law) relating to crimes other than criminal ones or to private rights.–**civilly** adv.

civil defense n the organization of civilians against enemy attack.

civil engineer n an engineer who designs and constructs roads, bridges, etc.

civilian n a person who is not a member of the armed forces.

civility n (pl **civilities**) good manners, politeness.

civilization n the state of being civilized; the process of civilizing; an advanced stage of social culture; moral and cultural refinement.

civilize vt to bring out from barbarism; to educate in arts and refinements.–**civilized** adj.–**civilizer** n.

civil rights npl the personal rights of a citizen.

civil service n those employed in the service of a state apart from the military.–**civil servant** n.

civil war n a war between citizens of the same state or country.

Cl (chem symbol) = chlorine.

cl abbr = centiliter(s).

clack vt to make a sudden, sharp sound; to chatter rapidly and continuously. * n a sudden, sharp sound as of wood striking wood.

clad[1] see **clothe**.

clad[2] vt (**cladding, clad**) to bond one material to another for protection (iron cladding).–**cladding** n.

claim vt to demand as a right; to call for; to require; to profess (to have); to assert; to declare to be true. * n the act of claiming; a title, right to something; a thing claimed, esp a piece of land for mining.–**claimable** adj.–**claimer** n.

claimant n a person who makes a claim.

clairvoyance n the power of seeing things not present to the senses, second sight.–**clairvoyant** n, adj.

clam n an edible marine bivalve mollusk. * vb (**clamming, clammed**) vt to gather clams. * vi (with **up**) (inf) to remain silent, refuse to talk.

clamber vi to climb with difficulty, using the hands as well as the feet. * n a climb performed in this way.–**clamberer** n.

clammy adj (**clammier, clammiest**) damp and sticky.–**clammily** adv.–**clamminess** n.

clamor, clamour n a loud confused noise; an uproar; an insistent demand. * vi to demand loudly; to make an uproar.–**clamorous** adj.

clamp n a device for gripping objects tightly together. * vt to grip with a clamp; to attach firmly. * vi (with **down**) to put a stop to forcefully.

clan n a group of people with a common ancestor, under a single chief; people with the same surname; a party or clique.–**clansman** n.–**clanswoman** nf.

clandestine adj done secretly; surreptitious; sly.–**clandestinely** adv.

clang n a loud metallic sound. * vti to make or cause to make a clang.

clangor, clangour n a sharp clang; repeated clanging.–**clangorous, clangourous** adj.–**clangorously, clangourously** adv.

clank n a short, harsh metallic sound. * vt to make or cause to make a clank.

clannish adj closely united and excluding others.–**clannishly** adv.

clap vti (**clapping, clapped**) to strike (the hands) together sharply; to applaud in this way; to slap; to flap (wings) loudly; to put or place suddenly or vigorously. * n the sound of hands clapping; a sudden sharp noise; a sudden sharp slap.

clapboard n a narrow, thin board used for building by overlapping each piece.

clapper n the tongue of a bell.

claret n a dry red wine of Bordeaux in France; its purple-red color.

clarify vti (**clarifying, clarified**) to make or become clear or intelligible; to free or become free from impurities.–**clarification** n.–**clarifier** n.

clarinet n an orchestral woodwind instrument.–**clarinettist** n.

clarion n a shrill trumpet formerly used in war; a rousing sound. * adj ringing.

clarity n clearness.

clash n a loud noise of striking weapons, cymbals, etc; a contradiction, disagreement; a collision. * vti to make or cause to make a clash by striking together; to conflict; to collide; to be at variance (with); (colors) to be unsuitable or not pleasing when put together.–**clasher** n.

clasp n a hold, an embrace; a catch or buckle. * vt to grasp firmly, to embrace; to fasten with a clasp.–**clasper** n.

class n a division, a group; a kind; a set of students who are taught together; a grade of merit or quality; standing in society, rank; (inf) high quality, excellence; style. * vt to put into a class.

classic adj of the highest class or rank, esp in literature; of music conforming to certain standards; traditional; authoritative. * n a work of literature, art, cinema, etc of the highest excellence; a definitive work of art.

classical adj influenced by, of or relating to ancient Roman and Greek art, literature and culture; traditional; serious; refined.–**classicality** n.–**classically** adv.

classicism, classicalism n the use of ancient Roman and Greek style.

classics n (with **the**) the study of ancient Greek and Roman literature; any literature considered to be a model of its type.–**classicist** n.

classification n the organization of knowledge into categories; a category or a division of a category into which knowledge or information has been put.–**classificational** adj.–**classificatory** adj.

classified adj arranged by a system of classification; (information) secret and restricted to a select few; (advertisements) grouped according to type.

classify vt (**classifying, classified**) to arrange in classes, to categorize; to restrict for security reasons.–**classifiable** adj.–**classifier** n.

classmate n a member of the same class in a school, college, etc.

classroom n a room where pupils or students are taught.

clatter n a rattling noise; noisy talk. * vti to make or cause a clatter.–**clattery** adj.

clause n a single article or stipulation in a treaty, law, contract, etc; (gram) a short sentence; a division of a sentence.–**clausal** adj.

claustrophobia n a morbid fear of confined spaces.–**claustrophobe** n.–**claustrophobic** adj.–**claustrophobically** adv.

clavicle n one of the two bones that connect the shoulder blades with the breast bone, the collar bone.–**clavicular** adj.

claw n the sharp hooked nail of an animal or bird; the pointed end or pincer of a crab, etc; a claw-like thing. * vti to seize or tear with claws or nails; to clutch or scratch (at); (with **back**) to recover (something) with difficulty; to get back money by taxing; to take back part of what was handed out, esp by taxation.–**clawer** n.

clay n a sticky ductile earthy material.–**clayey** adj.

clean adj free from dirt or impurities; unsoiled; morally or ceremonially pure; complete, decisive; free of errors; free of suggestive language; not carrying firearms or drugs. * adv entirely; outright; neatly. * vti to remove dirt from; (with **out**) to remove dirt out of; (sl) to take away everything from someone, esp money; (with **up**) to leave clean; (sl) to get rid of corrupt people, a system, etc; to gain a large profit.–**cleanable** adj.–**cleanness** n.–**cleaner** n.

cleanly adj (**cleanlier, cleanliest**) clean in habits or person; pure; neat. * adv in a clean manner.–**cleanliness** n.

cleanse vt to make clean or pure.–**cleansable** adj.–**cleanser** n.

clear adj bright, not dim; transparent; without blemish; easily seen or heard; unimpeded, open; free from clouds; quit (of); plain, distinct, obvious; keen, discerning; positive, sure; without debt. * adv plainly; completely; apart from. * vti to make or become clear; to rid (of), remove; to free from suspicion, vindicate; to disentangle; to pass by or over without touching; to make as a profit; (with **off**) (inf) to depart; (with **up**) to explain; to tidy up; (weather) to become fair.–**clearness** n.

clearance n the act of clearing; permission, authority to proceed; the space between two objects in motion.

clear-cut adj having a sharp, clearly defined outline, as if chiseled; straightforward and frank.

clear-headed adj showing sense, alertness, judgment.–**clear-headedly** adv.–**clear-headedness** n.

clearing n a tract of land cleared of trees, etc for cultivation.

clearly adv in a clear manner; evidently.

clearstory see **clerestory**.

cleat n a wedge; a strip of wood nailed crossways to a footing, etc; a projection for making ropes fast to.

cleavage n the way a thing splits; divergence; the hollow between the breasts.

cleave[1] vti (**cleaving, cleft, cleaved** or **clove, pp cleft, cleaved** or **cloven**) to divide by a blow; split; to sever.–**cleavable** adj.

cleave[2] vi (**cleaved, clave**) to be faithful to; to stick.

cleaver n a butcher's heavy chopper.

clef n a sign on a music stave that indicates the pitch of the notes.

cleft n a fissure or crack.

clematis n a climbing plant with large colorful flowers.

clement adj merciful, gentle; (weather) mild.–**clemency** n.

clench vt (teeth, fist) to close tightly; to grasp. * n a firm grip.

clerestory n (pl **clerestories**) the upper story, with windows, of the nave of a church.–also **clearstory**.–**clerestoried, clearstoried** adj.

clergy n (pl **clergies**) ministers of the Christian church collectively.

clergyman n (pl **clergymen**) a member of the clergy.

cleric n a member of the clergy.

clerical adj of or relating to the clergy or a clergyman; of or relating to a clerk or a clerk's work.–**clerically** adv.

clerk n an office worker who types, keeps files, etc; a layman with minor duties in a church; a public official who keeps the records of a court, town, etc.–**clerkdom** n.–**clerkship** n.

clever adj able; intelligent; ingenious; skillful, adroit.–**cleverly** adv.–**cleverness** n.

cliché n a hackneyed phrase; something that has become commonplace.–**cliché'd, clichéd** adj.

click n a slight, sharp sound. * vi to make such a sound; (inf) to establish immediate friendly relations with; to succeed; (inf) to become plain or evident; to fall into place.–**clicker** n.

client n a person who employs another professionally; a customer.–**cliental** adj.

clientele n clients, customers.

cliff n a high steep rock face.

climacteric n a critical period, a turning point, esp in the life of an individual; the male menopause. * adj forming a crisis (–also **climacterical**).

climate n the weather characteristics of an area; the prevailing attitude, feeling, atmosphere.–**climatic, climatical, climatal** adj.

climax n the highest point; a culmination; sexual orgasm; the highlight or most interesting part of a story, drama or music. * vti to reach, or bring to a climax.–**climactic, climactical** adj.

climb vti to mount with an effort; to ascend; to rise; (plants) to grow upwards by clinging onto walls, fences or other plants; (with **down**) to descend from a higher level; to retreat from a position previously held, eg in a debate or argument; to yield. * n an ascent.–**climber** n.

clinch vt (argument, etc) to confirm or drive home. * vi (boxing) to grip the opponent with the arms to hinder his punching. * n the act of clinching; (inf) an embrace.

clincher n a decisive point in an argument.

cling vi (**clinging, clung**) to adhere, to be attached (to); to keep hold by embracing or entwining.–**clinger** n.

clinic n a place where outpatients are given medical care or advice; a place where medical specialists practice as a group; a private or specialized hospital.

clinical adj of or relating to a clinic; based on medical observation; plain, simple; detached, cool, objective.–**clinically** adv.

clink n a slight metallic ringing sound. * vti to make or cause to make such a sound.

clip[1] vt (**clipping, clipped**) to cut or trim with scissors or shears; to punch a small hole in, esp a ticket; (words) to shorten or slur; (inf) to hit sharply. * n the piece clipped off; an extract from a movie; (inf) a smart blow; speed.

clip[2] vt (**clipping, clipped**) to hold firmly; to secure with a clip. * n any device that grips, clasps or hooks; a magazine for a gun; a piece of jewelry held in place by a clip.

clipboard n a writing board with a spring clip for holding paper.

clipper n a fast sailing ship.

clippers n a hand tool, sometimes electric, for cutting hair; nail clippers.

clique n a small exclusive group, a set.–**cliquey, cliquish** adj.

clitoris n a small sensitive erectile organ of the vulva.–**clitoral** adj.

cloak n a loose sleeveless outer garment; a covering; something that conceals, a pretext. * vt to cover as with a cloak; to conceal.

cloakroom n a room where overcoats, baggage, etc, may be left.

clobber vt (sl) to hit hard and repeatedly; to defeat; to criticize severely.

clock n a device for measuring time; any timing device with a dial and displayed figures. * vt (with a race, etc) using a stopwatch or other device; (inf) to register a certain speed; (with **off, out**) to stop work; (with **on, in**) to start work.

clockwise adv moving in the direction of a clock's hands.–also adj.

clockwork n the mechanism of a clock or any similar mechanism with springs and gears. * adj mechanically regular.

clod n a lump of earth or clay; a stupid person.

clog n a wooden-soled shoe. * vt (**clogging, clogged**) to cause a blockage in; to impede, obstruct.

cloisonné n enamel decoration with the colors of the pattern set in spaces partitioned off by wires. * adj inlaid with partitions; decorated in outline with bands of metal.

cloister n a roofed pillared walk, usu with one side open, in a convent, college, etc; a religious retreat. * vt to confine or keep apart as if in a convent.

cloistered adj solitary, secluded.

clone n a group of organisms or cells derived asexually from a single ancestor; an individual grown from a single cell of its parent and genetically identical to it; (inf) a person or thing that resembles another. * vt to propagate a clone from; to make a copy of.–**clonal** adj.

close[1] adj near; reticent, secret; nearly alike; nearly even or equal; dense, compact; cut short; sultry, airless; narrow; careful; restricted. * adv closely; near by. * n a courtyard; the entrance to a courtyard; the precincts of a cathedral.–**closely** adv.–**closeness** n.

close[2] vt to make closed; to stop up (an opening); to draw together; to conclude; to shut; (with down) to wind up, eg a business. * vi to come together; to complete; to finish. * n a completion, end.–**closed** adj.

closet n a small room or a cupboard for clothes, supplies, etc; a small private room. * vt to enclose in a private room for a confidential talk.

close-up n a movie or television shot taken from very close range; a close examination.

closure n closing; the condition of being closed; something that closes; (parliament, etc) a decision to end further debate and move to an immediate vote.

clot n a thickened mass, esp of blood; (sl) an idiot.* vti (**clotting, clotted**) to form into clots, to curdle, coagulate.

cloth n (pl **cloths**) woven, knitted or pressed fabric from which garments, etc are made; a piece of this; a tablecloth; clerical dress; (with **the**) the clergy.

clothe vt (**clothing, clothed** or **clad**) to cover with garments; to dress; to surround, endow (with).

clothes npl garments, apparel.–also **clothing** n.

cloud n a visible mass of water vapor floating in the sky; a mass of smoke, etc; a threatening thing. * vt to darken or obscure; to confuse; to depress.–**cloudless** adj.

cloudburst n a sudden rainstorm.

cloudy adj (**cloudier, cloudiest**) of or full of clouds; not clear; gloomy.–**cloudily** adv.–**cloudiness** n.

clout n a blow; (sl) power, influence.

clove[1] see **cleave**.

clove[2] n a segment of a bulb, as garlic.

clove[3] n the dried flower bud of a tropical tree, used as a spice.

clove hitch n a knot used to secure a rope around a spar or pole.

cloven adj divided; split.–see also **cleave**.

clover n a low-growing plant with three leaves used as fodder; a trefoil; **in clover** (inf) luxury.

clown n a person who entertains with jokes, antics, etc, esp in a circus; a clumsy or boorish person. * vi to act the clown, behave comically or clumsily.–**clownish** adj.

cloy vt to sicken with too much sweetness or pleasure.–**cloyingly** adv.

club n a heavy stick used as a weapon; a stick with a head for playing golf, etc; an association of people for athletic, social, or common purposes; its premises; a suit of playing cards with black clover-like markings. * vb (**clubbing, clubbed**) vt to beat with or use as a club. * vi to form into a club for a common purpose.

clubfoot n a congenital malformation of the foot.

clubhouse n premises used by a club.

cluck n the call of a hen. * vi to make such a noise.

clue n a guide to the solution of a mystery or problem. * vt (**cluing, clued**) (with **in, up**) to provide with helpful information.

clueless adj (inf) stupid, incompetent.

clump n a cluster of trees; a cluster of bacteria; a lump; (of hair) a handful; the sound of heavy footsteps.

clumsy adj (**clumsier, clumsiest**) unwieldy; awkward; lacking tact, skill or grace.–**clumsily** adv.–**clumsiness** n.

clung see **cling**.

clunk n a dull metallic sound. * vi to make this sound.

cluster n a bunch, esp of things growing or tied together; a swarm; a group. * vti to form or arrange in a cluster.–**clustery** adj.

clutch[1] vt to seize, to grasp tightly; to snatch at. * n a tight grip; a device for throwing parts of a machine into or out of action; the pedal operating this device; (pl) power.

clutch[2] n a nest of eggs; a brood of chicks.

clutter n a disordered mess; confusion. * vti to litter; to put into disorder.

cm abbr = centimeter.

CO abbr = Colorado; Commanding Officer.

Co. abbr = Company; County.

c/o abbr = care of.

coach n a long-distance bus; a railway carriage; a large, covered four-wheeled horse-drawn carriage; a sports instructor; a tutor in a specialized subject. * vti to teach or train.

coagulate vti to change from a liquid to partially solid state, to clot, curdle.–**coagulation** n.–**coagulant** n.–**coagulative** adj.–**coagulator** n.

coal n a black mineral used for fuel; a piece of this; an ember.

coalesce vi to come together and form one, to merge.–**coalescence** n.–**coalescent** adj.

coalition n a temporary union of parties or states.–**coalitional** adj.–**coalitionist, coalitioner** n.

coal tar n a thick opaque liquid distilled from bituminous coal and from which many rich dye colors are obtained.

coarse adj rough; large in texture; rude, crude; inferior.–**coarsely** adv.–**coarseness** n.

coarsen vti to make or become coarse.

coast n an area of land bordering the sea; the seashore. * vi to sail along a coast; to travel down a slope without power; to proceed with ease.–**coastal** adj.

coaster n a ship engaged in coastal trade; a tray for a decanter; a small mat for drinks; a roller coaster.

coastguard n an organization which monitors the coastline and provides help for ships in difficulties, prevents smuggling, etc.

coastline n the outline of the shore.

coat n a sleeved outer garment; the natural covering of an animal; a layer. * vt to cover with a layer or coating.

coating n a surface coat or layer; material for coats.

coat of arms n the heraldic bearings of a family, city, institution, etc.

coax vt to persuade gently; to obtain by coaxing; to make something work by patient effort.–**coaxer** n.–**coaxingly** adv.

cob n a sturdy riding horse; a corn cob; a round lump of coal; a male swan.

cobalt n a metallic element; a deep blue pigment made from it.

cobble[1] n a cobblestone, a rounded stone used for paving. * vt to pave with cobblestones.

cobble[2] vt to repair, to make (shoes); to put together roughly or hastily.

cobbler n a person who mends shoes; a clumsy workman.

cobra n a venomous hooded snake of Africa and India.

cobweb n a spider's web; a flimsy thing; an entanglement.–**cobwebbed** adj.–**cobwebby** adj.

coca n either of two South American shrubs; their leaves, chewed as a stimulant.

cocaine, cocain n an intoxicating addictive drug obtained from coca leaves, used in anesthesia.

coccyx n (pl **coccyges**) a small triangular bone at the base of the spine.–**coccygeal** adj.

cochineal n a scarlet dye obtained from dried insects.

cock n the adult male of the domestic fowl; the male of other birds; a tap or valve; the hammer of a gun; a cocked position. * vt to set erect, to stick up; to set at an angle; to bring the hammer (of a gun) to firing position; (*with* **up**) to make a complete mess of.–**cockup** *n*.

cockade *n* a rosette worn on the hat as a badge.

cockatoo *n* (*pl* **cockatoos**) a large crested parrot.

cockerel *n* a young cock, rooster.

cockeyed *adj* (*inf*) having a squint; slanting; daft, absurd.

cockle *n* an edible shellfish with a rounded shell.

cockpit *n* the compartment of a small aircraft for the pilot and crew, the flight deck; an arena for cock fighting; the driver's seat in a racing car.

cockroach *n* a nocturnal beetle-like insect.

cockscomb *n* a cock's crest; a vain young fop.–*also* **coxcomb**.

cocksure *adj* quite certain; over-confident.

cocktail *n* an alcoholic drink containing a mixture of spirits or other liqueurs; an appetizer, usu containing shellfish, served as the first course of a meal.

cocky *adj* (**cockier, cockiest**) cheeky; conceited; arrogant.–**cockily** *adv*.–**cockiness** *n*.

cocoa *n* a powder of ground cacao seeds; a drink made from this.

cocoa butter *n* a waxy substance derived from cocoa beans and used in perfumery, confectionery, etc.

coconut *n* the fruit of the coconut palm.

cocoon *n* a silky case spun by some insect larvae for protection in the chrysalis stage; a cosy covering. * *vt* to wrap in or as in a cocoon; to protect oneself by cutting oneself off from one's surroundings.

COD *abbr* = cash on delivery; collect on delivery.

cod *n* (*pl* **cod, cods**) a large edible fish of the North Atlantic.

coda *n* (*mus*) a passage at the end of a composition or section to give a greater sense of finality; a supplementary section at the end of a novel.

code *n* a system of letters, numbers or symbols used to transmit secret messages, or to simplify communication; a systematic body of laws; a set of rules or conventions; (*comput*) a set of program instructions. * *vt* to put into code.

codeine *n* an analgesic substance.

codeword, codename *n* a word used in planning and when referring to a secret operation.

codicil *n* an addition to a will modifying, adjusting, or supplementing its contents.–**codicillary** *adj*.

codify *vt* (**codifying, codified**) to collect or arrange (laws, rules, regulations, etc) into a system.–**codifier** *n*.–**codification** *n*.

coeducation *n* the teaching of students of both sexes in the same institution.–**coeducational** *adj*.–**coeducationally** *adv*.

coeliac *see* **celiac**.

coerce *vt* to compel; to force by threats.–**coercible** *adj*.–**coercion** *n*.

coexist *vi* to exist together at the same time; to live in peace together.–**coexistence** *n*.–**coexistent** *adj*.

coextensive *adj* extending over the same space or time; equally extensive.

coffee *n* a drink made from the seeds of the coffee tree; the seeds, or the shrub; a light-brown color.

coffee bean *n* the seed of the coffee plant.

coffee house, coffee bar, coffee shop *n* a refreshment house where coffee is served.

coffer *n* a strong chest for holding money or valuables.

coffin *n* a box for a dead body to be buried or cremated in.

cog *n* a tooth-like projection on the rim of a wheel.

cogent *adj* persuasive, convincing.–**cogently** *adv*.–**cogency** *n*.

cogitate *vi* to think deeply, to ponder.–**cogitation** *n*.–**cogitator** *n*.

cognac *n* a superior grape brandy distilled in France.

cognate *adj* having a common source or origin; kindred, related.–**cognation** *n*.

cognition *n* the mental act of perceiving; knowledge.–**cognitive** *adj*.

cognizance *n* judicial knowledge or notice; extent of knowledge; awareness, perception.–**cognizant** *adj*.

cognoscente *n* (*pl* **cognoscenti**) (*usu pl*) a connoisseur.

cogwheel *n* a wheel with a toothed rim for gearing.

cohabit *vi* to live together as husband or wife.–**cohabitant, cohabiter** *n*.–**cohabitation** *n*.

cohere *vi* to stick together; to remain united; to be consistent.

coherent *adj* cohering; capable of intelligible speech; consistent.–**coherently** *adv*.–**coherence** *n*.

cohesion *n* the act of cohering or sticking together; the force that causes this; interdependence.–**cohesive** *adj*.

cohort *n* a tenth part of a Roman legion; any group of persons banded together; a follower, a comrade.

coiffure *n* a hairstyle.

coil *vti* to wind in rings or folds; to twist into a circular or spiral shape. * *n* a coiled length of rope; a single ring of this; (*elect*) a spiral wire for the passage of current; an intrauterine contraceptive device.–**coiler** *n*.

coin *n* a piece of legally stamped metal used as money. * *vt* to invent (a word, phrase); to make into money, to mint; to make a lot of money quickly.

coincide *vi* to occupy the same portion of space; to happen at the same time; to agree exactly, to correspond.

coincidence *n* the act of coinciding; the occurrence of an event at the same time as another without apparent connection.

coincidental *adj* happening by coincidence.–**coincidentally** *adv*.

coitus, coition *n* sexual intercourse.–**coital** *adj*.

coke[1] *n* coal from which gas has been expelled. * *vt* to convert (coal) into coke.

coke[2] *n* (*sl*) cocaine.

col *n* a pass between mountain peaks; an atmospheric depression between two anticyclones.

Col. *abbr* = Colonel.

cola[1] *see* **colon**[1].

cola[2] *n* a carbonated drink flavored with extracts from the kola nut and coca leaves.–*also* **kola**.

colander *n* a bowl with holes in the bottom for straining cooked vegetables, pasta, etc.

cola nut *see* **kola nut**.

cold *adj* lacking heat or warmth; lacking emotion, passion or courage; unfriendly; dead; (*scent*) faint; (*sl*) unconscious. * *adv* (*inf*) without prior knowledge or preparation; completely. * *n* absence of heat; the sensation caused by this; cold weather; a virus infection of the respiratory tract.–**coldish** *adj*.–**coldly** *adv*.–**coldness** *n*.

cold-blooded *adj* having a body temperature that varies with the surrounding air or water, as reptiles and fish; without feeling; callous; ruthless; in cold blood.–**cold-bloodedness** *n*.

cold sore *n* one or more blisters appearing near the mouth, caused by the virus herpes simplex.

cold war *n* enmity between two nations characterized by military tension and political hostility.

coleslaw *n* raw shredded cabbage, carrots, onions in a dressing, used as a salad.

colic *n* acute spasmodic pain in the abdomen.–**colicky** *adj*.

coliseum *n* a large building, such as a stadium, used for sports events and other public entertainments; (*with cap*) the Colosseum.

colitis *n* inflammation of the colon.–**colitic** *adj*.

collaborate *vi* to work jointly or together, esp on a literary project; to side with the invaders of one's country.–**collaboration** *n*.–**collaborator** *n*.–**collaborative** *adj*.

collage *n* art made up from scraps of paper, material and other odds and ends pasted onto a hard surface.

collagen *n* a protein present in connective tissue and bones which yields gelatin when boiled.

collapse *vi* to fall down; to come to ruin, to fail; to break down physically or mentally. * *n* the act of collapsing; a breakdown, prostration.

collapsible, collapsable *adj* designed to fold compactly.—**collapsibility** *n*.

collar *n* the band of a garment round the neck; a decoration round the neck, a choker; a band of leather or chain put round an animal's neck. * *vt* to put a collar on; (*inf*) to seize; to arrest.

collate *vt* to examine and compare (manuscripts, etc); to put (pages) together in sequence.—**collator** *n*.—**collation** *n*.

collateral *n* security pledged for the repayment of a loan. * *adj* side by side; accompanying but secondary; descended from the same ancestor but not directly.—**collaterally** *adv*.

colleague *n* an associate in the same profession or office; a fellow worker.

collect *vti* to bring together, gather or assemble; to regain command of (oneself); to concentrate (thoughts, etc); to ask for or receive money or payment. * *adj* (*telephone call*) paid for by the person called.

collected *adj* self-possessed, cool.—**collectedly** *adv*.

collection *n* act of collecting; an accumulation; money collected at a meeting, etc; a group of things collected for beauty, interest, rarity or value; the periodic showing of a designer's fashions; a regular gathering of post from a postbox.

collective *adj* viewed as a whole, taken as one; combined, common; (*gram*) used in the singular to express a multitude. * *n* a collective enterprise, as a farm.—**collectively** *adv*.

collector *n* a person who collects things, eg stamps, butterflies, as a hobby or so as to inspect them, as tickets.

college *n* an institution of higher learning; a school offering specialized knowledge; the buildings housing a college; an organized body of professionals.—**collegiate, collegial** *adj*.

collide *vi* to come into violent contact (with); to dash together; to conflict; to disagree.—**collision** *n*.

collie *n* a breed of dog with a pointed muzzle and long hair, used as a sheepdog.

collocate *vt* to place together; to arrange.—**collocation** *n*.

colloid *adj* like glue or jelly; (*chem*) of a gummy noncrystalline kind. * *n* a viscid inorganic transparent substance.—**colloidal** *adj*.—**colloidality** *n*.

colloquial *adj* used in familiar but not formal talk, not literary.—**colloquially** *adv*.

colloquialism *n* a colloquial word or phrase.

collude *vi* to act together; to conspire, esp to defraud.—**collusion** *n*.—**collusive** *adj*.

cologne *n* eau-de-Cologne, a scented liquid.

colon[1] *n* (*pl* **colons, cola**) the part of the large intestine from the cecum to the rectum.—**colonic** *adj*.

colon[2] *n* (*pl* **colons**) a punctuation mark (:) between the semicolon and the full stop, usu written before an explanation or a list.

colonel *n* a commissioned officer junior to a brigadier but senior to a lieutenant colonel.—**colonelcy, colonelship** *n*.

colonial *adj* of or pertaining to a colony or colonies; (*with cap*) pertaining to the thirteen British colonies that became the US. * *n* a person who takes part in founding a colony, a settler.—**colonially** *adv*.

colonialism *n* the policy of acquiring and governing colonies.—**colonialist** *adj, n*.

colonist *n* a person who settles in a colony.

colonize *vt* to establish a colony in; to settle in a colony.—**colonization** *n*.—**colonizer** *n*.

colony *n* (*pl* **colonies**) an area of land acquired and settled by a distant state and subject to its control; a community of settlers; a group of people of the same nationality or interests living in a particular area; a collection of organisms in close association.

color *n* the eye's perception of wavelengths of light with different colors corresponding to different wavelengths; the attribute of objects to appear different according to their differing ability to absorb, emit, or reflect light of different wavelengths; color of the face or skin; pigment; dye; paint; (*pl*) a flag; a symbol of a club, team, etc. * *vt* to give color to, paint; to misrepresent; to influence. * *vi* to emit color; (*face*) to redden in anger or embarrassment; to blush; to change color, to ripen.—*also* **colour**.

colorant *n* a coloring matter.

color-blind *adj* unable to distinguish colors, esp red and green.—**color blindness** *n*.

colored *adj* possessing color; biased, not objective; of a darker skinned race. * *n* a person of a darker skinned race.—*also* **coloured**.

colorfast *adj* of a material made with non-running or non-fading colors after washing.—*also* **colourfast**.

colorful *adj* full of color; vivid.—*also* **colourful**.—**colorfully** *adv*.

coloring *n* appearance in term of color; disposition or use of color; a substance for giving color.—*also* **colouring**.

colorless *adj* lacking color; dull, uninteresting, characterless.—*also* **colourless**.—**colorlessly** *adv*.—**colorlessness** *n*.

colossal *adj* gigantic, immense; (*inf*) amazing, wonderful.—**colossally** *adv*.

colossus *n* (*pl* **colossi, colossuses**) a gigantic statue; something immense.

colostomy *n* (*pl* **colostomies**) a surgical opening into the bowl forming an artificial anus.

colt *n* a young male horse; a young, inexperienced person; an inexperienced player of a sport.

column *n* a round pillar for supporting or decorating a building; something shaped like this; a vertical division of a page; a narrow-fronted deep formation of troops; a long line of people; a feature article appearing regularly in a newspaper, etc.—**columnar** *adj*.—**columned, columnated** *adj*.

columnist *n* a journalist who contributes a regular newspaper or magazine column.

colour *see* **color**.

coma *n* (*pl* **comas**) deep prolonged unconsciousness.

comatose *adj* in a coma; lethargic, sleepy.

comb *n* a toothed instrument for separating hair, wool, etc; a part of a machine like this; the crest of a cock; a honeycomb. * *vt* to arrange (hair) or dress (wool) with a comb; to seek for thoroughly.

combat *vti* to strive against, oppose; to do battle. * *n* a contest; a fight; struggle.—**combatable** *adj*.—**combater** *n*.

combatant *adj* fighting. * *n* a person engaged in a fight or contest.

combative *adj* aggressive, keen to fight.

combination *n* the act of combining; a union of separate parts; persons allied for a purpose.

combine *vti* to join together; to unite intimately; to possess together; to cooperate; (*chem*) to form a compound with. * *n* an association formed for commercial or political purposes; a machine for harvesting and threshing grain.—**combinable** *adj*.—**combiner** *n*.

combo *n* (*pl* **combos**) a small jazz band; (*inf*) any small group.

combust *vt* to burn.—**combustible** *adj*.—**combustibility** *n*.

combustion *n* the process of burning; the process in which substances react with oxygen in air to produce heat.

come *vi* (**coming, came**, *pp* **come**) to approach; to arrive; to reach; to happen (to); to originate; to turn out (to be); to be derived or descended; to be caused; to result; (*with* **about**) to happen; (*with* **across**) to meet with unexpectedly; to communicate the intended information or impression; (*with* **along**) to make progress; (*with* **at**) to find out; to attack; (*with* **away**) to get detached; to leave with; (*with* **between**) to cause the estrangement of (two people); (*with* **by**) to obtain, esp by chance; to pass; (*with* **down**) to descend; to fall; to suffer an illness; to leave university; (*with* **down on**) to reprimand; (*with* **forward**) to offer oneself for some duty, volunteer; (*with* **in**) to enter, arrive; (*race*) to finish in a certain position; (*with* **into**) to enter; to receive as an inheritance; (*with* **of**) to result from; (*with* **off**) to become detached; to fall from; to emerge from or finish something in a specified way; to succeed; (*inf*) to have the intended effect; (*with* **on**) to advance, make progress; (*electricity, etc*) to begin functioning; (*with* **out**) to become public or be published; to go on strike; to declare oneself in public; to present oneself openly as homosexual; (*with* **over**) to change sides; to make an impression; (*inf*) to become affected with a certain feeling; (*with* **round, around**) to regain consciousness; to change one's opinion, accede to something; (*with* **to**) to regain consciousness, revive; (*total*) to amount to; (*with* **through**) to overcome; to survive; (*with* **under**) to be subjected to; to be classed among; (*with* **up**) to approach; to grow; (*sun*) to rise; to occur; to arise for discussion, etc; (*with* **upon**) to discover or meet unexpectedly; (*with* **up with**) to overtake; to put forward for discussion.

comeback *n* (*inf*) a return to a career or to popularity; (*inf*) a witty answer.

comedian *n* an actor of comic parts; an entertainer who tells jokes; a person who behaves in a humorous manner.—**comedienne** *nf*.

comedown *n* a downfall; a disappointment.

comedy *n* (*pl* **comedies**) an amusing play or movie; drama consisting of amusing plays; an amusing occurrence; humor.—**comedic** *adj*.

comely *adj* (**comelier, comeliest**) pleasing to the eye, good-looking.—**comeliness** *n*.

comestible *n* (*usu pl*) anything to eat.

comet *n* a celestial body that travels round the sun, with a visible nucleus and a luminous tail.—**cometary, cometic** *adj*.

comeuppance *n* (*inf*) a deserved retribution.

comfort *vti* to bring consolation to; to soothe; to cheer. * *n* consolation; relief; bodily ease.—**comforting** *adj*.

comfortable *adj* promoting comfort; at ease; adequate; (*inf*) financially well off.—**comfortably** *adv*.

comforter *n* one who comforts; a woolen scarf; a baby's dummy teat; a quilted bedcover.

comfy *adj* (**comfier, comfiest**) (*inf*) comfortable.

comic *adj* of comedy; causing amusement. * *n* a comedian; an entertaining person; a paper or book with strip cartoons.

comical *adj* funny, laughable; droll, ludicrous.—**comically** *adv*.

coming *adj* approaching next; of future importance or promise.

comma *n* a punctuation mark (,) that indicates a slight pause or break in a sentence or separates items in a list.

command *vti* to order; to bid; to control; to have at disposal; to evoke, compel; to possess knowledge or understanding of; to look down over; to be in authority (over), to govern. * *n* an order; control; knowledge; disposal; position of authority; something or someone commanded; an instruction to a computer.

commandant *n* an officer in command of troops or a military establishment, esp a fortress.

commandeer *vt* to seize for military purposes; to appropriate for one's own use.

commander *n* a person who commands, a leader; a naval officer ranking next below a captain.—**commandership** *n*.

commander in chief *n* the commander of a state's entire forces.

commanding *adj* in command; dominating; impressive.

commandment *n* a command; a divine law, esp one of the Ten Commandments in the Bible.

commando *n* (*pl* **commandos, commandoes**) a member of an elite military force trained to raid enemy territory.

commemorate *vt* to keep in the memory by ceremony or writing; to be a memorial of.—**commemoration** *n*.—**commemorative, commemoratory** *adj*.—**commemorator** *n*.

commence *vti* to begin.—**commencement** *n*.

commend *vt* to speak favorably of, to praise; to recommend; to entrust.—**commendable** *adj*.—**commendably** *adv*.—**commendatory** *adj*.

commendation *n* the act of commending, praise; an award.

commensurate *adj* having the same extent or measure; proportionate.—**commensuration** *n*.

comment *n* a remark, observation, criticism; an explanatory note; talk, gossip. * *vi* to make a comment (upon); to annotate.—**commenter** *n*.

commentary *n* (*pl* **commentaries**) a series of explanatory notes or remarks; a verbal description on TV or radio of an event as it happens, esp sport (*–also* **running commentary**).—**commentarial** *adj*.

commentator *n* one who reports and analyzes events, trends, etc, as on television.—**commentate** *vt*.

commerce *n* trade in goods and services on a large scale between nations or individuals.

commercial *adj* of or engaged in commerce; sponsored by an advertiser; intended to make a profit. * *n* a broadcast advertisement.—**commercially** *adv*.

commercialism *n* commercial methods or principle.—**commercialist** *n*.

commercialize *vt* to put on a business basis; to exploit for profit.—**commercialization** *n*.

commercial traveler *n* a sales representative or traveling salesman.

commingle *vti* to mix together, to mingle.

commiserate *vti* to sympathize (with); to feel pity for.—**commiseration** *n*.—**commiserator** *n*.

commissariat *n* a supply of provisions; the department in charge of this, as for an army.

commissary *n* (*pl* **commissaries**) a store, as in an army camp, where food and supplies are sold; a restaurant in a film studio, factory, etc.—**commissarial** *adj*.

commission *n* authority to act; a document bestowing this; appointment as a military officer of the rank of lieutenant or above; a body of people appointed (by government) for specified duties; a task or duty or business committed to someone; a special order for something, esp a picture or other art object; a percentage on sales paid to a salesman or agent; brokerage. * *vt* to empower or appoint by commission; to employ the service of; to authorize.—**commissional, commissionary** *adj*.

commissioner *n* a person empowered by a commission; various types of civil servant; a member of a commission.

commit *vti* (**committing, committed**) to entrust; to consign (to prison); to do, to perpetrate a crime, etc; to pledge, to involve.—**committer** *n*.

commitment *n* the act of committing; an engagement that restricts freedom; an obligation; an order for imprisonment or confinement in a mental institution (*–also* **committal**).

committed *adj* dedicated; pledged by a commitment.

committee *n* a body of people appointed from a larger body to consider or manage some matter.

commodious *adj* roomy.

commodity *n* (*pl* **commodities**) an article of trade; a useful thing; (*pl*) goods.

commodore *n* a naval officer ranking below a rear admiral and above a captain; the senior commander of a fleet.

common *adj* belonging equally to more than one; public; usual, ordinary; widespread; familiar; frequent; easily obtained, not rare; low, vulgar; (*noun*) applying to any of a class. * *n* a tract of open public land.—**commonality** *n*.—**commonly** *adv*.—**commonness** *n*.

commonplace *adj* ordinary, unremarkable. * *n* a platitude; an ordinary thing.

common sense *n* ordinary, practical good sense.—**common-sense** *adj*.

commonwealth n a political community; a sovereign state, republic; a federation of states; (with cap) an association of sovereign states and dependencies ruled or formerly ruled by Britain.

commotion n a violent disturbance; agitation; upheaval.–**commotional** adj.

communal adj of a commune or community; shared in common.–**communality** n.–**communally** adv.

commune[1] n a group of people living together and sharing possessions.

commune[2] vi to converse intimately; to communicate spiritually.

communicant n a person who receives Holy Communion.

communicate vti to impart, to share; to succeed in conveying information; to pass on; to transmit, esp a disease; to be connected.–**communicator** n.–**communicable** adj.

communication n the act of communicating; information; a connecting passage or channel; (pl) connections of transport; (pl) means of imparting information, as in newspapers, radio, television.

communicative adj inclined to talk and give information.

communion n common possession, sharing; fellowship; an emotional bond with; union in a religious body; (with cap) Holy Communion, the Christian sacrament of the Eucharist.–**communional** adj.

communiqué n an official communication, esp to the press or public.

communism n a social system under which private property is abolished and the means of production are owned by the people; (with cap) a political movement based on the writings of Karl Marx.

communist n a supporter of communism; (with cap) a member of a Communist party.–**communistic** adj.

community n (pl **communities**) an organized political or social body; a body of people in the same locality; the general public, society; any group having work, interests, etc in common; joint ownership; common character.

commute vti to travel a distance daily from home to work; to exchange (for); to change (to); to reduce (a punishment) to one less severe.–**commutable** adj.–**commutation** n.

commuter n a person who commutes to and from work.

compact[1] n an agreement; a contract, a treaty.

compact[2] adj closely packed; condensed; terse; firm; taking up space neatly. * vt to press or pack closely; to compose (of). * n a small cosmetic case, usu containing face powder and a mirror.–**compactly** adv.–**compactness** n.

compact disc n a small mirrored disc containing music (or audio-visual material) encoded digitally.

compact video disc n a laser disc, similar to an audio compact disc, which plays sound and pictures.

companion n an associate in an activity; a partner; a friend; one of a pair of matched things.–**companionship** n.

companionable adj friendly, sociable.–**companionably** adv.

companionway n a ladder or staircase on a ship.

company n (pl **companies**) any assembly of people; an association of people for carrying on a business, etc; a society; a military unit; the crew of a ship; companionship, fellowship; a guest, visitor(s).

comparable adj able or suitable to be compared (with **with**); similar.–**comparably** adv.–**comparability** n.

comparative adj estimated by comparison; relative, not absolute; (gram) expressing more.–**comparatively** adv.

compare vt to make one thing the measure of another; to observe similarity between, to liken; to bear comparison; (gram) to give comparative and superlative forms of (an adjective). * vi to make comparisons; to be equal or alike.–**comparer** n.

comparison n the act of comparing; an illustration; a likeness; (gram) the use of more or er with an adjective.

compartment n a space partitioned off; a division of a railway carriage; a separate section or category.–**compartmental** adj.–**compartmentalize** vt.

compass n a circuit, circumference; an extent, area; the range of a voice; an instrument with a magnetic needle indicating north, south, east, west; (often pl) a two-legged instrument for drawing circles, etc.–**compassable** adj.

compassion n sorrow for another's sufferings; pity.–**compassionate** adj.–**compassionately** adv.

compatible adj agreeing or fitting in (with); of like mind; consistent; (body organ) able to be transplanted successfully.–**compatibly** adv.–**compatibility** n.

compatriot n a fellow countryman.–also adj.

compel vt (**compelling, compelled**) to force, constrain; to oblige; to obtain by force.–**compeller** n.

compelling adj evoking powerful feelings, eg interest, admiration.

compendious adj containing much in a small space, succinct.

compendium n (pl **compendiums, compendia**) an abridgement; a summary; a collection; an assortment of things in one box.

compensate vti to counterbalance; to make up for; to recompense.–**compensator** n.–**compensatory, compensative** adj.

compensation n the act of compensating; a sum given to compensate, esp for loss or injury; an exaggerated display of ability in one area as a cover-up for a lack in another.

compete vi to strive; to contend; to take part in a competition, esp sporting.

competence n the quality of being capable; sufficiency; capacity; an adequate income to live on.

competent adj fit, capable; adequate; with enough skill for; legally qualified.–**competently** adv.

competition n act of competing; rivalry; a contest in skill or knowledge; a match.–**competitive** adj.–**competitively** adv.–**competitor** n.

compile vt to collect or make up from various sources; to amass; to gather data, etc for a book.–**compilation** n.–**compiler** n.

complacent adj self-satisfied.–**complacently** adv.–**complacency, complacence** n.

complain vi to find fault, to grumble; to be ill.–**complainer** n.

complainant n (law) a plaintiff.

complaint n a statement of some grievance; a cause of distress or dissatisfaction; an illness.

complaisant adj disposed to please, obliging; compliant.–**complaisance** n.

complement n something making up a whole; a full allowance (of equipment or number); the entire crew of a ship, including officers. * vt to make complete.

complementary adj completing; together forming a balanced whole.

complete adj entire; free from deficiency; finished; thorough. * vt to make complete; to finish.–**completeness** n.–**completer** n.–**completive** adj.

completely adv entirely, utterly.

completion n the act of completing; accomplishment; fulfillment.

complex adj having more than one part; intricate, not simple; difficult. * n a complex whole; a collection of interconnected parts, buildings or units; a group of mostly unconscious impulses, etc strongly influencing behavior; (inf) an undue preoccupation; a phobia.–**complexity** n (pl **complexities**).

complexion n a color, texture and look of the skin; aspect, character.

compliance, compliancy n the act of complying with another's wishes; acquiescence.–**compliant** adj.–**compliantly** adv.

complicate vt to make intricate or involved; to mix up.–**complicated** adj.

complication n a complex or intricate situation; a circumstance that makes (a situation) more complex; (med) a condition or disease following an original illness.

complicity n (pl **complicities**) partnership in wrongdoing.

compliment n a polite expression of praise, a flattering tribute; (pl) a formal greeting or expression of regard. * vt to pay a compliment to, to flatter; to congratulate (on).

complimentary adj conveying or expressing a compliment; given free of charge.

comply vi (**complying, complied**) to act in accordance (with); to yield, to agree.–**complier** n.

component adj going to the making of a whole, constituent. * n a component part.–**componential** adj.

comport vti to conduct (oneself); to be compatible, to accord (with).–**comportment** n.

compose vt to make up, to form; to construct in one's mind, to write; to arrange, to put in order; to settle; to adjust; to tranquilize; (print) to set up type * vi to create musical works, etc.– **composer** n.

composed adj calm, self-controlled.–**composedly** adv.–**composure** n.

composite adj made up of distinct parts or elements. * n a composite thing.

composition n the act or process of composing; a work of literature or music, a painting; a short written essay; the general make-up of something; a chemical compound.–**compositional** adj.

compositor n a person who puts together, or sets up, type for printing.

compos mentis adj of sound mind, sane.

compost n a mixture of decomposed organic matter for fertilizing soil.

compote n fruit preserved in syrup.

compound[1] n a substance or thing made up of a number of parts or ingredients, a mixture; a compound word made up of two or more words. * vt to combine (parts, elements, ingredients) into a whole, to mix; to intensify by adding new elements; to settle (debt) by partial payment. * vi to become joined in a compound; to come to terms of agreement. * adj compounded or made up of several parts; not simple.–**compounder** n.

compound[2] n an enclosure in which a building stands.

comprehend vt to grasp with the mind, to understand; to include, to embrace.–**comprehension** n.

comprehensible adj capable of being understood.–**comprehensibly** adv.–**comprehensibility** n.

comprehensive adj wide in scope or content, including a great deal–**comprehensively** adv.–**comprehensiveness** n.

compress vt to press or squeeze together; to bring into a smaller bulk; to condense. * n a soft pad for compressing an artery, etc; a wet or dry bandage or pad for relieving inflammation or discomfort.–**compressed** adj.–**compressible** adj.–**compressive** adj.

compression n the act of compressing; the increase in pressure in an engine to compress the gases so that they explode.–**compressional** adj.

compressor n a machine for compressing air or other gases.

comprise vt to consist of, to include.–**comprisable** adj.–**comprisal** n.

compromise n a settlement of a dispute by mutual concession; a middle course or view between two opposed ones. * vti to adjust by compromise; to lay open to suspicion, disrepute, etc.–**compromiser** n.

compulsion n the act of compelling; something that compels; an irresistible urge.

compulsive adj compelling; acting as if compelled.–**compulsively** adv.

compulsory adj enforced, obligatory, required by law, etc; involving compulsion; essential.–**compulsorily** adv.

compunction n pricking of the conscience; remorse; scruple.

compute vt to determine mathematically; to calculate by means of a computer. * vi to reckon; to use a computer.–**computability** n.–**computable** adj.–**computation** n.– **computational** adj.

computer n an electronic device that processes data in accordance with programmed instructions.

computerize vt to equip with computers; to control or perform (a process) using computers; to store or process data using a computer.–**computerization** n.

comrade n a companion; a fellow member of a Communist party.– **comradely** adj.–**comradeship** n.

con[1] vt (**conning, conned**) (inf) to swindle, trick. * n (inf) a confidence trick.

con[2] n against, as in **pro and con**.

con[3] prep with.

con[4] n (sl) a convict.

concave adj curving inwards, hollow. * n a concave line or surface.–**concavity** n (pl **concavities**).

conceal vt to hide, to keep from sight; to keep secret.–**concealment** n.

concede vt to grant; to admit to be true, to allow; to agree to be certain in outcome.–**conceder** n.

conceit n an over-high opinion of oneself; vanity; a far-fetched comparison, a quaint fancy.

conceited adj full of conceit, vain.–**conceitedly** adv.

conceivable adj capable of being imagined or believed; possible.–**conceivably** adv.

conceive vti to become pregnant (with); to form in the mind; to think out, to imagine; to understand; to express.

concentrate vt to bring or converge together to one point; to direct to a single object or purpose; to collect one's thoughts or efforts; (chem) to increase the strength of by diminishing bulk, to condense. * n a concentrated product, esp a food.–**concentrator** n.

concentration n the act or process of concentrating; the direction of attention to a single object; a drawing together of forces.– **concentrative** adj.

concentric, concentrical adj having a common centre.–**concentrically** adv.–**concentricity** n.

concept n a general idea, esp an abstract one.

conception n the act of conceiving; the fertilizing of an ovum by a sperm; a thing conceived; an idea, a notion.–**conceptional** adj.

conceptual adj of mental conception or concepts.–**conceptualize** vt.

concern vt to relate or apply to; to fill with anxiety; to interest (oneself) in; to take part, to be mixed up (in). * n a thing that concerns one; anxiety, misgiving; interest in or regard for a person or thing; a business or firm.

concerned adj troubled, worried; interested.–**concernedly** adv.

concerning prep about; regarding.

concert n a musical entertainment; harmony; agreement or union; **in concert** working together; (musicians) playing together.

concerted adj planned or arranged by mutual agreement; combined.

concertina n a hexagonal musical instrument, similar to an accordion, which produces sound by squeezing bellows which pass air over metal reeds.

concerto n (pl **concertos, concerti**) a musical composition for a solo instrument and orchestra.

concession n the act of conceding; something conceded; a grant of rights, land, etc by a government, corporation, or individual; the sole right to sell a product within an area; a reduction in price (of admission, travel, etc) for certain people.–**concessionary** adj.

conch n (pl **conchs, conches**) a tropical marine spiral shell, sometimes used as a trumpet.

conciliate vt to win over from hostility; to make friendly; to appease; to reconcile.–**conciliation** n.–**conciliator** n.–**conciliatory** adj.

concise adj brief, condensed, terse.–**concisely** adv.–**conciseness** n.–**concision** n.

conclave n a private or secret meeting.

conclude vti to bring or come to an end, to finish; to effect, to settle; to infer; to resolve.—**conclusion** n.

conclusive adj decisive; convincing, removing all doubt.—**conclusively** adv.

concoct vt to make by combining ingredients; to devise, to plan; to invent (a story).—**concocter, concoctor** n.—**concoction** n.

concomitant n an accompanying thing or circumstance.—also adj.—**concomitance** n.

concord n agreement, harmony; a treaty; grammatical agreement.—**concordant** adj.

concordance n agreement; an alphabetical index of words in a book or in the works of an author with their contexts.

concordat n a compact or agreement, esp between church and state.

concourse n a crowd; a gathering of people or things, eg events; an open space or hall where crowds gather, eg a railway or airport terminal.

concrete adj having a material existence; actual, specific (a concrete example); made of concrete. * n anything concrete; a mixture of sand, cement, etc with water, used in building. * vti to form into a mass, to solidify; to build or cover with concrete.

concretion n a solidified mass.

concubine n a secondary wife (in polygamous societies); (formerly) a mistress of a king or nobleman.—**concubinage** n.

concur vi (**concurring, concurred**) to happen together, to coincide; to cooperate; to be of the same opinion, to agree.—**concurrence** n.

concurrent adj existing or occurring at the same time.—**concurrently** adv.

concuss vt to shake violently, to agitate; to cause concussion of the brain to.

concussion n the violent shock of an impact or explosion; loss of consciousness caused by a violent blow to the head.—**concussive** adj.

condemn vt to express strong disapproval of; to find guilty; to blame or censure; to declare unfit for use.—**condemnable** adj.—**condemnation** n.—**condemnatory** adj.—**condemner** n.

condense vt to reduce to a smaller compass, to compress; to change from a gas into a liquid; to concentrate; to express in fewer words. * vi to become condensed.—**condensable, condensible** adj.—**condenser** n.—**condensation** n.

condescend vi to waive one's superiority; to deign, to stoop; to act patronizingly.—**condescension** n.—**condescending** adj.

condiment n a seasoning or relish.

condition n the state or nature of things; anything required for the performance, completion or existence of something else; physical state of health; an abnormality, illness; (pl) attendant circumstances. * vt to be essential to the happening or existence of; to stipulate; to agree upon; to make fit; to make accustomed (to); to bring about a required effect by subjecting to certain stimuli.

conditional adj depending on conditions; not absolute; (gram) expressing condition. * n a conditional clause or conjunction.—**conditionality** n.—**conditionally** adv.

conditioning n a bringing into a required state or state of fitness for an objective.

condo n (pl **condos, condoes**) (inf) a condominium.

condole vi (with **with**) to express sympathy for another.—**condolatory** adj.—**condoler** n.—**condolence, condolement** n.

condom n a sheath for the penis, used as a contraceptive and to prevent infection.

condominium n (pl **condominiums**) a block of apartments, each apartment being individually owned.

condone vt to overlook, to treat as nonexistent; to pardon an offense.

condor n a large South American vulture.

conduce vi to tend to bring about, to contribute (to).—**conducive** adj.

conduct vti to lead; to guide; to convey; to direct (an orchestra); to carry on or manage (a business); to transmit (electricity, heat); to behave (oneself). * n management, direction; behavior.—**conductible** adj.—**conductibility** n.

conduction n the conducting or transmission of heat or electricity through a medium.—**conductive** adj.—**conductivity** n.

conductor n a person who conducts an orchestra; one in charge of passengers on a train, or who collects fares on a bus; a substance that conducts heat or electricity.—**conductress** nf.

conduit n a channel or pipe that carries water, etc.

cone n a solid pointed figure with a circular or elliptical base; any cone-shaped object (an ice-cream cone); a warning bollard on roads, etc; the scaly fruit of the pine, fir, etc.

confection n candy, ice cream, preserves, etc.—**confectionery** n.

confectioner n a person who makes or sells confectionery.

confederacy n (pl **confederacies**) a union of states, an alliance; a combination of persons for illegal purposes; (with cap) the Confederate States of America.

confederate adj banded together by treaty, united in confederation. * vti to bring or come into alliance or confederacy. * n a member of a confederacy; a partner in design, an accomplice; an ally.—**confederation** n.

confer vt (**conferring, conferred**) to grant or bestow; to compare views or take counsel; to consult.—**conferment, conferral** n.

conference n a meeting for discussion or consultation.—**conferential** adj.

confess vt to acknowledge or admit; to disclose (sins) to a confessor; (priest) to hear confession of. * vi to make or hear a confession.

confession n admission or acknowledgement of a fault or sin, esp to a confessor; a thing confessed; a statement of one's religious beliefs, creed.—**confessionary** adj.

confessional n an enclosure in a church where a priest hears confessions.

confessor n a priest who hears confessions and grants absolution.

confetti npl small bits of colored paper thrown at weddings.

confidant n a person trusted with one's secrets.—**confidante** nf.

confide vti to put confidence (in); to entrust; to impart a confidence or secret.—**confider** n.

confidence n firm trust, faith; belief in one's own abilities; boldness; something revealed confidentially.

confident adj full of confidence; positive, assured.—**confidently** adv.

confidential adj spoken or written in confidence, secret; entrusted with secrets.—**confidentiality, confidentialness** n.—**confidentially** adv.

configuration n arrangement of parts; external shape, general outline; aspect; (astrol) the relative position of the planets; the make-up of a computer system.—**configurational, configurative** adj.

confine vt to restrict, to keep within limits; to keep shut up, as in prison, a sickbed, etc; to imprison. * n (pl) borderland, edge, limit.—**confinable, confineable** adj.—**confinement** n.

confirm vt to make stronger; to establish firmly; to make valid, to ratify; to corroborate; to administer rite of confirmation to.—**confirmed** adj.

confirmation n the act of confirming; convincing proof; the rite by which people are admitted to full communion in Christian churches.

confiscate vt to appropriate to the state as a penalty; to seize by authority.—**confiscation** n.—**confiscator** n.

conflagration n a massively destructive fire.

conflict n a fight; a contest; strife, quarrel; emotional disturbance. * vi to be at variance; to clash (with); to struggle.—**confliction** n.—**conflictive, conflictory** adj.

confluence, conflux n the point where two rivers meet; a coming together.

conform vi to comply, to be obedient (to); to act in accordance with. * vt to adapt; to make like.—**conformer** n.—**conformity, conformance** n.

conformist n one who conforms to established rules, standards, etc; compliance with the rites and doctrines of an established church.–**conformism** n.

confound vt to mix up, to obscure; to perplex, to astound; to overthrow; to mistake one thing for another.–**confounder** n.

confounded adj astonished; confused; annoying; (inf) damned.–**confoundedly** adv.

confront vt to stand in front of, to face; to bring face to face (with); to encounter; to oppose.–**confronter** n.

confrontation n the coming face to face with; hostility without actual warfare, esp between nations.

confuse vt to throw into disorder; to mix up; to mistake one thing for another; to perplex, to disconcert; to embarrass; to make unclear.–**confusable** adj.–**confusing** adj.–**confusingly** adv.–**confusion** n.

confute vt (argument, etc) to prove wrong; to convict of error; to overcome in argument.–**confutation** n.–**confutative** adj.–**confuter** n.

conga n a Cuban dance in which the dancers move along in a long line; music for this. * vi (**congaing, congaed**) to do this dance.

congeal vti to change from a liquid to a solid by cooling, to jell.–**congealment** n.

congenial adj of a similar disposition or with similar tastes, kindred; suited, agreeable (to).–**congenially** adv.–**congeniality, congenialness** n.

congenital adj existing or dating since birth, as in certain defects.–**congenitally** adv.

conger eel n a large marine eel.

congest vt to overcrowd. * vi (med) to affect with congestion.–**congested** adj.–**congestible** adj.

congestion n an overcrowding; (med) an excessive accumulation of blood in any organ; an accumulation of traffic causing obstruction.–**congestive** adj.

conglomerate adj stuck together in a mass. * vt to gather into a ball. * n a coarse-grained rock of embedded pebbles; a large corporation consisting of companies with varied and often unrelated interests.–**conglomeration** n.

congratulate vt to express sympathetic pleasure at success or good fortune of, to compliment; to feel satisfied or pleased with oneself.–**congratulation** n.–**congratulator** n.–**congratulatory** adj.

congratulations npl an expression of joy or pleasure.

congregate vti to flock together, to assemble; to gather into a crowd or mass.–**congregator** n.

congregation n a gathering, an assembly; a body of people assembled for worship.–**congregational** adj.

congress n an association or society; an assembly or conference, esp for discussion and action on some question; (with cap) the legislature of the US, comprising the Senate and the House of Representatives.

congressional adj of, or relating to, a congress.–**congressionalist** n.

Congressman n (pl **Congressmen**) a member of Congress.–**Congresswoman** nf (pl **Congresswomen**).

congruent adj in agreement; harmonious; (geom) having identical shape and size so that all parts correspond.–**congruence, congruency** n.

congruous adj accordant; fit.–**congruity** n.

conic, conical adj of a cone; cone-shaped.

conifer n any evergreen trees and shrubs with true cones (as pines) and others (as yews).–**coniferous** adj.

conjecture n a guess, guesswork. * vt to make a conjecture, to guess, surmise.–**conjecturer** n.–**conjecturable** adj.–**conjectural** adj.

conjoin vt to join together; to connect or associate. * vi to be joined.–**conjoinedly** adv.–**conjoiner** n.–**conjoint** adj.–**conjointly** adv.

conjugal adj of or relating to marriage.–**conjugality** n.–**conjugally** adv.

conjugate vt to give the parts of (a verb); to unite.–**conjugable** adj.–**conjugator** n.–**conjugative** adj.

conjugation n the act of conjugating; a group of verbs with the same inflections.–**conjugational** adj.

conjunction n (gram) a word connecting words, clauses or sentences; a union; a simultaneous occurrence of events; the apparent proximity of two or more planets.–**conjunctional** adj.

conjure vti to practice magical tricks; to call up (spirits) by invocation.–**conjurer, conjuror** n.

conk n (sl) the nose or head. * n a blow to the nose or head. * vt to hit, esp on the head. * vi (with out) (sl) (machine) to break down entirely; to collapse suddenly from exhaustion.

con man n (inf) a swindler, one who defrauds by means of a confidence trick.

connect vti to fasten together, to join; to relate together, to link up; (trains, buses, etc) to be timed to arrive as another leaves so that passengers can continue their journey; to establish a link by telephone; (sl) to punch or kick.–**connectible, connectable** adj.–**connector, connecter** n.

connection n the act of connecting; the state of being connected; a thing that connects; a relationship, bond; a train, bus, etc timed to connect with another; context; a link between components in an electric circuit; a relative.–**connectional** adj.

connective adj serving to connect.–**connectively** adv.

connive vi to permit tacitly; to wink (at); to plot.–**conniver** n.–**connivance** n.

connoisseur n a trained discriminating judge, esp of the fine arts.

connotation n a consequential meaning, an implication–**connotative, connotive** adj.–**connote** vt.

conquer vt to gain victory (over), to defeat; to acquire by conquest; to overcome, to master. * vi to be victor.–**conqueror** n.

conquest n conquering; the winning of a person's affection; a person or thing conquered.

conscience n the knowledge of right and wrong that affects action and behavior; the sense of guilt or virtue induced by actions, behavior, etc; an inmost thought; conscientiousness.

conscientious adj following the dictates of the conscience; scrupulous; careful, thorough.–**conscientiously** adv.–**conscientiousness** n.

conscious adj aware (of); awake to one's surroundings; (action) realized by the person who does it, deliberate.–**consciously** adv.

consciousness n the state of being conscious; perception; the whole body of a person's thoughts and feelings.

conscript adj enrolled into service by compulsion; drafted. * n a conscripted person (as a military recruit). * vt to enlist compulsorily.–**conscription** n.

consecrate vt to set apart as sacred, to sanctify; to devote (to).–**consecration** n.–**consecrator** n.–**consecratory, consecrative** adj.

consecutive adj following in regular order without a break; successive.–**consecutively** adv.

consensus n an opinion held by all or most; general agreement, esp in opinion.

consent vi to agree (to); to comply; to acquiesce * n agreement, permission; concurrence.–**consenter** n.

consequence n a result, an outcome; importance; (pl) an unpleasant result of an action.–**consequent** adj.

consequential adj pompous, self–important; resultant.–**consequentiality, consequentialness** n.–**consequentially** adv.

conservation n the act of conserving; preservation of the environment and natural resources.–**conservational** adj.–**conservationist** n.

conservatism n opposition to change; a political ideology favoring preservation and defense of tradition.

conservative *adj* traditional, conventional; cautious; moderate. * *n* a conservative person; (*with cap*) a member of the Conservative Party in Britain and other countries.–**conservatively** *adv*.

conservatory *n* (*pl* **conservatories**) a school for art or music.

conserve *vt* to keep from loss or injury; to preserve (a foodstuff) with sugar. * *n* a type of jam using whole fruit.–**conservable** *adj*.–**conserver** *n*.

consider *vti* to reflect (upon), to contemplate; to examine, to weigh the merits of; to take into account; to regard as; to be of the opinion; to act with respect; to allow for.–**considerer** *n*.

considerable *adj* a fairly large amount; worthy of respect.–**considerably** *adv*.

considerate *adj* careful of the feelings of others.–**considerately** *adv*.

consideration *n* the act of considering; deliberation; a point of importance; an inducement; thoughtfulness; deference; a payment.

considered *adj* well thought out.

considering *prep* in view of. * *adv* all in all. * *conj* seeing that.

consign *vt* to hand over, to commit; to send goods addressed (to).–**consignable** *adj*.–**consignation** *n*.–**consignment** *n*.

consist *vi* to be made up (of); to be comprised (of).

consistency *n* (*pl* **consistencies**) degree of density, esp of thick liquids; the state of being consistent.

consistent *adj* compatible, not contradictory; uniform in thought or action.–**consistently** *adv*.

consolation *n* someone or something that offers comfort in distress.–**consolatory** *adj*.

console[1] *vt* to bring consolation to, to cheer in distress.–**consolable** *adj*.–**consoler** *n*.

console[2] *n* a desk containing the controls of an electronic system; the part of an organ containing the pedals, stops, etc; an ornamental bracket supporting a shelf or table.

consolidate *vti* to solidify; to establish firmly, to strengthen; to combine into a single whole.–**consolidator** *n*.–**consolidation** *n*.

consommé *n* a clear soup made from meat stock.

consonant *n* a letter of the alphabet that is not a vowel; the sound representing such a letter. * *adj* consistent, in keeping (with).–**consonantal** *adj*.

consort *n* a husband or wife, esp of a reigning queen or king. * *vti* to associate, to keep company with (often dubious companions).–**consorter** *n*.

consortium *n* (*pl* **consortia**) an international banking or financial combination.–**consortial** *adj*.

conspicuous *adj* easily seen, prominent; outstanding, eminent.–**conspicuousness** *n*.–**conspicuously** *adv*.

conspiracy *n* (*pl* **conspiracies**) a secret plan for an illegal act; the act of conspiring.–**conspirator** *n*.–**conspiratorial,** *adj*.

conspire *vti* to combine secretly for an evil purpose; to plot, to devise.

constant *adj* fixed; unchangeable; unchanging; faithful; firm and steadfast; continual. –**constancy** *n*.

constantly *adv* continually, continuously, often.

constellation *n* a group of fixed stars; an assembly of the famous.–**constellatory** *adj*.

consternation *n* surprise and alarm; shock; dismay.

constipation *n* infrequent and difficult movement of the bowels.–**constipate** *vt*.–**constipated** *adj*.

constituency *n* (*pl* **constituencies**) a body of electors; the voters in a particular district or area.

constituent *adj* forming part of a whole, component; having the power to revise the constitution. * *n* a component part; a member of an elective body; a voter in a district.

constitute *vt* to set up by authority, to establish; to frame, to form; to appoint; to compose, to make up.–**constituter, constitutor** *n*.

constitution *n* fundamental physical condition; disposition; temperament; structure, composition; the system of basic laws and

principles of a government, society, etc; a document stating these specifically.–**constitutional** *adj*.–**constitutionally** *adv*.

constrain *vt* to compel, to force; to hinder by force; to confine, to imprison.–**constrainer** *n*.–**constraint** *n*.

constrict *vt* to draw together, to squeeze, to compress.–**constriction** *n*.–**constrictive** *adj*.

constrictor *n* a constrictive muscle; a snake that crushes its prey.

construct *vt* to make, to build, to fit together; to compose. * *n* a structure; an interpretation; an arrangement, esp of words in a sentence.–**constructible** *adj*.–**constructor, constructer** *n*.

construction *n* a constructing; anything constructed; a structure, building; interpretation, meaning; (*gram*) two or more words grouped together to form a phrase, clause or sentence.–**constructional** *adj*.

constructive *adj* helping to improve, promoting development.–**constructively** *adv*.

construe *vti* (**construing, construed**) to analyze grammatically; to take in a particular sense, to interpret.

consul *n* a government official appointed to live in a foreign city to attend to the interests of his country's citizens and business there.–**consular** *adj*.

consulate *n* the official residence of a consul; the office of a Roman consul.

consult *vti* to seek advice from, esp a doctor or lawyer; to seek information from, eg a work of reference; to deliberate, to confer.–**consulter, consultor** *n*.

consultant *n* a specialist who gives professional or technical advice; a senior physician or surgeon in a hospital; a person who consults another.–**consultancy** *n* (*pl* **consultancies**).

consultation *n* the act of consulting; a conference, esp with a professional adviser.–**consultative, consultatory, consultive** *adj*.

consume *vti* to destroy; to use up; to eat or drink up; to waste away; to utilize economic goods.

consumer *n* a person who uses goods and services, the end user.

consumerism *n* protection of the interests of consumers; encouragement to buy consumer goods.

consummate[1] *vt* to bring to perfection, to be the crown of; (*marriage*) to complete by sexual intercourse.–**consummation** *n*.–**consummative, consummatory** *adj*.–**consummator** *n*.

consummate[2] *adj* complete, perfect, highly skilled.

consumption *n* the act of consuming; the state of being consumed or used up; (*econ*) expenditure on goods and services by consumers; tuberculosis.

consumptive *adj* tending to consume; affected with consumption. * *n* a person with tuberculosis.

contact *n* touch, touching; connection; an acquaintance, esp one willing to provide help or introductions in business, etc; a connection allowing the passage of electricity; (*med*) a person who has been in contact with a contagious disease.* *vti* to establish contact with.–**contactual** *adj*.

contagion *n* the communicating of a disease by contact; a disease spread in this way; a corrupting influence.–**contagious** *adj*.–**contagiousness** *n*.

contain *vt* to hold, to enclose; to comprise, to include; to hold back or restrain within fixed limits.

container *n* a receptacle, etc designed to contain goods or substances; a standardized receptacle used to transport commodities.

containment *n* the prevention of the expansion of a hostile power.

contaminate *vt* to render impure by touch or mixing, to pollute, esp by radioactive contact.–**contaminant** *n*.–**contaminator** *n*.–**contamination** *n*.

contemplate *vti* to look at steadily; to reflect upon, to meditate; to have in view, to intend.–**contemplator** *n*.–**contemplation** *n*.–**contemplative** *adj*.

contemporaneous *adj* existing or occurring at the same time; of the same period.–**contemporaneously** *adv.*–**contemporaneity** *n.*

contemporary *adj* living or happening at the same time; of about the same age; present day; of or following present-day trends in style, art, fashion, etc. * *n* (*pl* **contemporaries**) a person living at the same time; a person of the same age.–**contemporarily** *adv.*

contempt *n* the feeling one has towards someone or something considered low, worthless etc; the condition of being despised; disregard.

contemptible *adj* deserving contempt.–**contemptibly** *adv.*–**contemptibility** *n.*

contemptuous *adj* showing or feeling contempt; disdainful.–**contemptuously** *adv.*–**contemptuousness** *n.*

contend *vti* to take part in a contest, to strive (for); to quarrel; to maintain (that), to assert or argue strongly for.–**contender** *n.*

content[1] *n* (*usu pl*) what is in a container; (*usu pl*) what is in a book; substance or meaning.

content[2] *adj* satisfied (with), not desiring more; willing (to); happy; pleased. * *n* quiet satisfaction. * *vt* to make content; to satisfy.–**contentment** *n.*–**contented** *adj.*–**contentedly** *adv.*

contention *n* contending, struggling, arguing; a point in dispute; an assertion in an argument.–**contentious** *adj.*

contest *vti* to call in question, to dispute; to fight to gain, to compete for; to strive. * *n* a struggle, an encounter; a competition; a debate; a dispute.–**contestable** *adj.*–**contestation** *n.*–**contester** *n.*

contestant *n* a competitor in a contest; a person who contests.

context *n* the parts of a written work or speech that precede and follow a word or passage, contributing to its full meaning; associated surroundings, setting.–**contextual** *adj.*–**contextually** *adv.*

contiguous *adj* touching, adjoining; near; adjacent.–**contiguity** *n.*

continent[1] *n* one of the six or seven main divisions of the earth's land; a large extent of land.–**continental** *adj.*

continent[2] *adj* able to control urination and defecation; practicing self-restraint; chaste.–**continence, continency** *n.*

continental drift *n* (*geol*) the (theoretical) gradual process of separation of the continents from their original solid land mass.

continental shelf *n* the sea bed, under relatively shallow seas, bordering a continent.

contingency *n* (*pl* **contingencies**) a possibility of a future event or condition; something dependent on a future event.

contingent *adj* possible, that may happen; chance; dependent (on); incidental (to). * *n* a possibility; a quota of troops.–**contingently** *adv.*

continual *adj* frequently repeated, going on all the time.–**continuality** *n.*–**continually** *adv.*

continuance *n* uninterrupted succession; duration.

continuation *n* a continuing; prolongation; resumption; a thing that continues something else, a sequel, a further installment.

continue *vt* to go on (with); to prolong; to extend; to resume, to carry further. * *vi* to remain, to stay; to last; to preserve.–**continuable** *adj.*–**continuer** *n.*–**continuingly** *adv.*

continuity *n* (*pl* **continuities**) continuousness; uninterrupted succession.

continuous *adj* continuing; occurring without interruption.–**continuously** *adv.*–**continuousness** *n.*

continuum *n* (*pl* **continua, continuums**) a continuous and homogeneous whole.

contort *vti* to twist out of a normal shape, to pull awry.–**contorted** *adj.*–**contortion** *n.*–**contortional** *adj.*

contortionist *n* a person who can twist his or her body into unusual postures, esp as entertainment.

contour *n* the outline of a figure, land, etc; the line representing this outline; a contour line. * *adj* made according to a shape or form (*contour chair*).

contour line *n* a line on a map that passes through all points at the same altitude.

contra *n* a thing that may be argued against.

contraband *n* smuggled goods; smuggling. * *adj* illegal to import or export.–**contrabandist** *n.*

contraception *n* the deliberate prevention of conception, birth control.

contraceptive *n* a contraceptive drug or device.–*also adj.*

contract *vt* to draw closer together; to confine; to undertake by contract; (*debt*) to incur; (*disease*) to become infected by; (*word*) to shorten by omitting letters. * *vi* to shrink; to become smaller or narrower; to make a contract; (*with* **out**) to decide not to take part in or join, eg a pension scheme. * *n* a bargain; an agreement to supply goods or perform work at a stated price; a written agreement enforceable by law.–**contractual** *adj.*

contraction *n* the act of contracting; the state of being contracted; a contracted word; a labor pain in childbirth.–**contractional** *adj.*–**contractive** *adj.*

contractor *n* a person who makes a business contract, esp a builder; something that draws together, eg a muscle.

contradict *vti* to assert the contrary or opposite of; to deny; to be at variance (with); to lack consistency.–**contradictable** *adj.*–**contradicter, contradictor** *n.*

contradiction *n* the act of contradicting; a denial.–**contradictory** *adj.*

contralto *n* (*pl* **contraltos**) a singing voice having a range between tenor and mezzo-soprano; a person having this voice.

contraption *n* (*inf*) a device, a gadget.

contrary *adj* opposed; opposite in nature; wayward, perverse. * *n* (*pl* **contraries**) the opposite. * *adv* in opposition to; in conflict with.–**contrarily** *adv.*–**contrariness** *n.*

contrast *vi* to show marked differences. * *vt* to compare so as to point out the differences. * *n* the exhibition of differences; difference of qualities shown by comparison.

contravene *vt* to infringe (a law), to transgress; to conflict with, to contradict.–**contravener** *n.*–**contravention** *n.*

contretemps *n* (*pl* **contretemps**) a confusing, embarrassing or awkward occurrence.

contribute *vti* to give to a common stock or fund; to write (an article) for a magazine or newspaper; to furnish ideas, etc.–**contributor** *n.*–**contributory** *adj.*–**contributive** *adj.*

contribution *n* the act of contributing; something contributed; a literary article; a payment into a collection.

con trick *n* (*inf*) confidence trick.

contrite *adj* deeply repentant, feeling guilt.–**contritely** *adv.*–**contrition** *n.*

contrivance *n* something contrived, esp a mechanical device, invention; inventive ability; an artificial construct; a stratagem.

contrive *vt* to plan ingeniously; to devise, to design, to manage; to achieve, esp by some ploy or trick; to scheme.–**contriver** *n.*

control *n* restraint; command, authority; a check; a means of controlling; a standard of comparison for checking an experiment; (*pl*) mechanical parts by which a car, airplane, etc is operated. * *vt* (**controlling, controlled**) to check; to restrain; to regulate; to govern; (*experiment*) to verify by comparison.

controller *n* a person who controls, esp one in charge of expenditure or finances.

controversy *n* (*pl* **controversies**) a discussion of contrary opinions; dispute, argument.–**controversial** *adj.*–**controversially** *adv.*–**controversialist** *n.*

contusion *n* a wound that does not break the skin, a bruise.–**contusioned** *adj.*

conundrum *n* a riddle involving a pun; a puzzling question.

conurbation *n* a vast urban area around and including a large city.

convalesce *vi* to recover health and strength after an illness; to get better.–**convalescence** *n.*–**convalescent** *adj, n.*

convection *n* the transmission of heat through a liquid by currents; the process whereby warmer air rises while cooler air drops.–**convectional** *adj*.–**convective** *adj*.

convector *n* a heater that circulates warm air.

convene *vti* to call together for a meeting.–**convenable** *adj*.–**convener** *n*.

convenience *n* what suits one; a useful appliance.

convenience food *n* food that is easily and quickly prepared.

convenient *adj* handy; suitable; causing little or no trouble.–**conveniently** *adv*.

convent *n* a house of a religious order, esp an establishment of nuns.

convention *n* a political or ecclesiastical assembly or meeting; an agreement between nations, a treaty; established usage, social custom.

conventional *adj* of or based on convention or social custom; not spontaneous; lacking imagination or originality; following accepted rules.–**conventionality** *n* (*pl* **conventionalities**).–**conventionally** *adv*.

converge *vti* to come or bring together.–**convergence, convergency** *n*.–**convergent** *adj*.

conversation *n* informal talk or exchange of ideas, opinions, etc between people.–**conversational** *adj*.–**conversationally** *adv*.

conversationalist, conversationist *n* a person who is good at conversation.

converse[1] *vi* to engage in conversation (with). * *n* familiar talk, conversation.–**converser** *n*.

converse[2] *adj* opposite, contrary. * *n* something that is opposite or contrary.–**conversely** *adv*.

conversion *n* change from one state, or from one religion, to another; something converted from one use to another; an alteration to a building undergoing a change in function.–**conversional, conversionary** *adj*.

convert *vt* to change from one thing, condition or religion to another; to alter; to apply to a different use. * *n* a converted person, esp one who has changed religion.–**converter, convertor** *n*.

convertible *adj* able to be converted. * *n* an automobile with a folding or detachable roof.–**convertibility** *n*.

convex *adj* curving outward like the surface of a sphere.–**convexly** *adv*.–**convexity** *n*.

convey *vt* to transport; to conduct; to transmit; to make known, to communicate; (*law*) to make over (property).–**conveyable** *adj*.–**conveyor, conveyer** *n*.

conveyance *n* the act of conveying; a means of transporting, a vehicle; (*law*) the act of transferring property.

conveyor belt *n* a continuous moving belt or linked plates for moving objects in a factory.

convict *vt* to prove or pronounce guilty. * *n* a convicted person serving a prison sentence.

conviction *n* act of convicting; a settled opinion; a firm belief.

convince *vt* to persuade by argument or evidence; to satisfy by proof.–**convincer** *n*.–**convincible** *adj*.–**convincing** *adj*.–**convincingly** *adv*.

convivial *adj* sociable, jovial.–**conviviality** *n*.–**convivially** *adv*.

convoke *vt* to call or summon together; to convene.–**convoker** *n*.–**convocation** *n*.

convolute *vt* to form into a rolled or coiled shape. * *adj* (*bot*) rolled upon itself; coiled.–**convoluted** *adj*.

convoy *n* a group of ships or vehicles traveling together for protection. * *vt* to travel thus.

convulse *vt* to agitate violently; to shake with irregular spasms. * *vi* (*inf*) to cause to shake with uncontrollable laughter.–**convulsive** *adj*.–**convulsively** *adv*.

convulsion *n* a violent involuntary contraction of a muscle or muscles; an agitation, tumult; (*pl*) a violent fit of laughter.

coo *n* the note of the pigeon; a soft murmuring sound. * *vt* (**cooing, cooed**) to utter the cry of a dove or pigeon; to speak softly; to act or murmur in a loving manner.

cook *vt* to prepare (food) by heat; (*inf*) to fake (accounts, etc); to subject to great heat. * *vi* to be a cook; to undergo cooking; (*with* **up**) to plot; to make up a story. * *n* a person who cooks; one whose job is to cook.–**cookable** *adj*.

cooker *n* an electric or gas appliance for cooking.

cookery *n* the art or practice of cooking.

cookie, cooky *n* (*pl* **cookies**) a small flat sweet cake; (*sl*) a person.

cool *adj* moderately cold; calm; indifferent; unenthusiastic; cheeky. * *vti* to make or become cool. * *n* coolness; composure.–**coolly** *adv*.–**coolness** *n*.

coolant *n* a fluid or other substance for cooling machinery.

cooler *n* that which cools; a vessel for cooling liquids, etc; a drink of spirits; (*sl*) prison.

coon *n* a raccoon.

coop *n* a small pen for poultry. * *vt* to confine as in a coop.

co-op *n* a cooperative.

cooperate *vi* to work together, to act jointly.–**cooperation** *n*.–**cooperator** *n*.

cooperative *adj* willing to cooperate; helpful. * *n* an organization or enterprise owned by, and operated for the benefit of, those using its services.–**cooperatively** *adv*.

co-opt *vt* to elect or choose as a member by the agreement of the existing members.–**co-optation, co-option** *n*.–**co-optative, co-optive** *adj*.

coordinate *vt* to integrate (different elements, etc) into an efficient relationship; to adjust to; to function harmoniously. * *n* an equal person or thing; any of a series of numbers that, in a given frame of reference, locate a point in space. * *adj* equal in degree or status.–**coordinately** *adv*.–**coordinator** *n*.

coordination *n* the act of coordinating; the state of being coordinated; balanced and harmonious movement of the body.

cop *vb* (**copping, copped**) *vt* (*sl*) to arrest, catch. * *vi* (*with* **out**) (*sl*) to fail to perform, to renege. * *n* (*sl*) capture; a policeman.

cope *vi* to deal successfully with; to contend on even terms (with).

copier *n* a copying machine, a photocopier.

coping *n* the top masonry of a wall.

copious *adj* plentiful, abundant.–**copiously** *adv*.–**copiousness** *n*.

copper *n* a reddish ductile metallic element; a bronze coin. * *adj* made of, or of the color of, copper. * *vt* to cover with copper.–**coppery** *adj*.

copper-bottomed *adj* to be trusted; financially sound.

copperplate *n* a polished plate of copper for engraving or printing; a print from this; copybook writing.

copra *n* the dried kernel of the coconut after the oil has been removed.

copse *n* a thicket of small trees and shrubs.

copter *n* a helicopter.

copulate *vi* to have sexual intercourse.–**copulation** *n*.–**copulatory** *adj*.

copy *n* (*pl* **copies**) a reproduction; a transcript; a single specimen of a book; a model to be copied; a manuscript for printing; newspaper text; text for an advertisement; subject matter for a writer. * *vt* (**copying, copied**) to make a copy of, to reproduce; to take as a model, to imitate.–**copyist** *n*.

copyright *n* the exclusive legal right to the publication and sale of a literary, dramatic, musical, or artistic work in any form. * *adj* protected by copyright.

copywriter *n* a writer of advertising or publicity copy.–**copywriting** *n*.

coquette *n* a woman who trifles with men's affections.–**coquettish** *adj*.

coracle *n* a boat with a wicker frame covered with leather.

coral n the hard skeleton secreted by certain marine polyps. * adj made of coral, esp jewelry; of the color of coral, deepish pink.

coral reef n a formation or bank of coral.

corbel n a stone or timber projection from a wall to support something. * vt (**corbeling, corbeled** or **corbelling, corbelled**) to furnish with or support by corbel.

cord n a thick string or thin rope; something that binds; a slender electric cable; a ribbed fabric, esp corduroy; (pl) corduroy pants; any part of the body resembling string or rope (spinal cord).

cordial adj hearty, warm; friendly; affectionate. * n a fruit-flavored drink.–**cordially** adv.–**cordialness** n.

cordiality n (pl **cordialities**) sincere sympathetic geniality; sincerity; heartiness.

cordite n an explosive used in bullets and shells.

cordon n a chain of police or soldiers preventing access to an area; a piece of ornamental cord or ribbon given as an award. * vt (with **off**) (area) to prevent access to.

corduroy n a strong cotton fabric with a velvety ribbed surface; (pl) pants of this.

core n the innermost part, the heart; the inner part of an apple, etc containing seeds; the region of a nuclear reactor containing the fissile material. * vt to remove the core from.–**corer** n.

coriander n a plant with aromatic seeds used for flavoring food.

cork n the outer bark of the cork oak used esp for stoppers and insulation; a stopper for a bottle, esp made of cork. * adj made of cork. * vt to stop up with a cork; to give a taste of cork to (wine).

corkage n a charge made by a restaurant for serving wine, esp when brought in by the customer from outside.

corked adj (wine) contaminated by a decayed cork.

corkscrew n a tool for drawing corks from wine bottles. * adj spiral-shaped, resembling a corkscrew.

corm n the bulb-like underground stem of the crocus, etc; a solid bulb.–**cormous** adj.

cormorant n a large voracious sea bird with dark plumage and webbed feet.

corn[1] n a grain or seed of a cereal plant; plants that yield grain; maize; (sl) something corny.

corn[2] n a small hard painful growth on the foot.

corn[3] vt to preserve or cure, as with salt.

corn(ed) beef n cooked salted beef.

corn circle see **crop circle**.

corncob n the central part of an ear of maize to which the corn kernels are attached; a corncob pipe.

cornea n (pl **corneas, corneae**) the transparent membrane in front of the eyeball.–**corneal** adj.

corner n the point where sides or streets meet; an angle; a secret or confined place; a difficult or dangerous situation; (football, hockey) a free kick from the corner of the pitch; a monopoly over the supply of a good or service giving control over the market price. * vt to force into a corner; to monopolize supplies of (a commodity). * vi to turn round a corner; to meet at a corner or angle.

cornerstone n the principal stone, esp one at the corner of a foundation; an indispensable part; the most important thing or person.

cornet n a tapering valved brass musical instrument.

cornice n a plaster molding round a ceiling or on the outside of a building.

corn pone n a type of Indian cornbread made with milk and eggs.

cornstarch n a type of corn or maize flour used for thickening sauces.–also **cornflour**.

cornucopia n a horn-shaped container overflowing with fruits, flowers, etc; great abundance, an inexhaustible store.

corny adj (**cornier, corniest**) (inf) hackneyed; banal; trite; overly sentimental.–**cornily** adv.–**corniness** n.

corolla n the inner envelope of a flower composed of two or more petals.

corollary n (pl **corollaries**) an additional inference from a proposition already proved; a result.

corona n (pl **coronas, coronae**) a top; a crown; a luminous halo or envelope round the sun or moon; the flat projecting part of a cornice.

coronary adj pertaining to the arteries supplying blood to the heart. * n (pl **coronaries**) a coronary artery; coronary thrombosis, blockage of one of the coronary arteries by a blood clot.

coronation n the act or ceremony of crowning a sovereign.

coroner n a public official who inquires into the causes of sudden or accidental deaths.–**coronership** n.

corpora see **corpus**.

corporal[1] n a noncommissioned officer below the rank of sergeant.–**corporalship** n.

corporal[2] adj of or relating to the body; physical, not spiritual.–**corporality** n.–**corporally** adv.

corporate adj legally united into a body; of or having a corporation; united.–**corporately** adv.

corporation n a group of people authorized by law to act as one individual; a city or town council.–**corporative** adj.

corporeal adj having a body or substance, material.–**corporeality, corporealness** n.–**corporeally** adv.

corps n (pl **corps**) an organized subdivision of the military establishment; a group or organization with a special function (medical corps).

corps de ballet n all the dancers in a ballet company.

corpse n a dead body.

corpulent adj fleshy, fat.–**corpulence, corpulency** n.

corpus n (pl **corpora**) a body or collection, esp of written works; the chief part of an organ.

corpuscle n a red or white blood cell.–**corpuscular** adj.

corral n a pen for livestock; an enclosure with wagons; a strong stockade. * vt (**corralling, corralled**) to form a corral; to put or keep in a corral.

correct vt to set right, to remove errors from; to reprove, to punish; to counteract, to neutralize; to adjust. * adj free from error; right, true, accurate; conforming to a fixed standard; proper.–**correctable, correctible** adj.–**correctly** adv.–**correctness** n.–**corrector** n.

correction n the act of correcting; punishment.–**correctional** adj.

corrective adj serving to correct or counteract. * n that which corrects.–**correctively** adv.

correlate vti to have or to bring into mutual relation; to correspond to one another. * n either of two things so related that one implies the other.–**correlation** n.–**correlative** adj.

correspond vi to answer, to agree; to be similar (to); to tally; to communicate by letter.

correspondence n communication by writing letters; the letters themselves; agreement.

correspondent n a person who writes letters; a journalist who gathers news for newspapers, radio or television from a foreign country. * adj similar, analogous.

corridor n a long passage into which compartments in a train or rooms in a building open; a strip of land giving a country without a coastline access to the sea.

corroborate vt to confirm; to make more certain; to verify.–**corroboration** n.–**corroborative** adj.–**corroborator** n.

corrode vti to eat into or wear away gradually, to rust; to disintegrate.–**corrodant, corrodent** n.–**corroder** n.–**corrodible** adj.–**corrosion** n.

corrosive adj causing corrosion. * n a corrosive substance, as acid.–**corrosively** adv.–**corrosiveness** n.

corrugate vt to form into parallel ridges and grooves.–**corrugated** adj.–**corrugation** n.

corrupt adj dishonest; taking bribes; depraved; rotten, putrid. * vti to make or become corrupt; to infect; to taint.–**corruptly** adv.–**corruption** n.

corruptible adj open to corruption.–**corruptibility** n.

corsage n a small bunch of flowers for pinning to a dress; the part of a woman's dress covering the bust.

corset n a close-fitting undergarment, worn to support the torso.

cortege, cortège n a train of attendants; a retinue; a funeral procession.

cortex n (pl **cortices**) an outer layer of tissue of any organ, eg the outer gray matter of the brain.–**cortical** adj.

cortisone n a hormone produced by the adrenal glands, the synthetic version of which is used to treat arthritis, allergies and skin disorders, etc.

corundum n a hard mineral of many colors used as an abrasive and as gemstones.

corvette n a fast escort warship.

cos abbr = cosine.

cosh vt (sl) to bludgeon.

cosignatory n a person signing along with another.

cosine n a trigonometrical function of an angle that in a right-angled triangle is equal to the ratio of the length of the adjacent side to the hypotenuse.

cosmetic n a preparation for improving the beauty, esp of the face. * adj beautifying or correcting faults in the appearance.–**cosmetically** adv.

cosmetic surgery n surgery carried out to improve the appearance.

cosmic, cosmical adj of or pertaining to the universe and the laws that govern it; vast in extent, intensity, or comprehensiveness.–**cosmically** adv.

cosmology n the science of the nature, origins, and development of the universe.–**cosmological, cosmologic** adj.–**cosmologist** n.

cosmonaut n a Russian astronaut.

cosmopolitan adj of all parts of the world; free from national prejudice; at home in any part of the world. * n a well-traveled person; a person without national prejudices.–**cosmopolitanism** n.

cosmos n the universe as an ordered whole; any orderly system.

cosset vt to make a pet of; to pamper.

cost vt (**costing, cost**) to involve the payment, loss, or sacrifice of; to have as a price; to estimate and fix the price of. * n a price; an expense; expenditure of time, labor, etc; a loss, a penalty; (pl) the expenses of a lawsuit.

cost-effective adj giving a satisfactory return for the amount spent on outlay.

costly adj (**costlier, costliest**) expensive; involving great sacrifice.–**costliness** n.

costume n a style of dress, esp belonging to a particular period, fashion, etc; clothes of an unusual or historical nature, as worn by actors in a play, etc; fancy dress.

cosy adj (**cosier, cosiest**) warm and comfortable; snug; friendly for an ulterior motive. * n a cover to keep a thing warm.–also **cozy**.–**cosily** adv.–**cosiness** n.

cot n a child's box-like bed; a narrow collapsible bed.

cote n a shed or shelter for animals or birds, esp doves.

coterie n a small circle of people with common interests; a social clique.

cottage n a small house, esp in the country.

cottage industry n manufacture carried out in the home, eg weaving, basketry.

cotton n soft white fiber of the cotton plant; fabric or thread made of this; thread. * vi (with **on**) (inf) to realize the meaning of, to understand; to take a liking to.–**cottony** adj.

cotton candy n a confection of spun sugar.–also **candyfloss**.

cotton wool n raw cotton that has been bleached and sterilized for use as a dressing, etc; absorbent cotton; a state of being protected.

couch n a piece of furniture, with a back and armrests, for seating several persons; a bed, esp as used by psychiatrists for patients. * vt to express in words in a particular way; to lie down.

couch grass n a kind of coarse grass that spreads rapidly.

cougar n a puma.

cough vi to expel air from the lungs with a sudden effort and noise; (with **up**) (inf) to hand over or tell unwillingly. * n the act of coughing; a disease causing a cough.

could see **can**[1].

couldn't = could not.

council n an elected or appointed legislative or advisory body; a central body uniting a group of organizations; an executive body whose members are equal in power and authority.–**councilor, councillor** n.–**councilorship, councillorship** n.

counsel n advice; consultation, deliberate purpose or design; a person who gives counsel, a lawyer or a group of lawyers; a consultant. * vb (**counseling** or **counselling, counseled** or **counselled**) vt to advise; to recommend. * vi to give or take advice.–**counselor, counsellor** n.

counseling, counselling n professional guidance for an individual or a couple from a qualified person.

count[1] n a European noble.

count[2] vt to number, to add up; to reckon; to consider to be; to call aloud (beats or time units); to include or exclude by counting; (with **against**) to have an adverse effect. * vi to name numbers or add up items in order; to mark time; to be of importance or value; to rely (upon); (with **on**) to rely on: (with **out**) (inf) to exclude, leave out. * n an act of numbering or reckoning; the total counted; a separate and distinct charge in an indictment; rhythm.

countdown n the descending count backwards to zero, eg to the moment a rocket lifts off.

countenance n the whole form of the face; appearance; support. * vt to favor, give approval to.

counter[1] n one who or that which counts; a disc used for scoring, a token; a table in a bank or shop across which money or goods are passed.

counter[2] adv contrary; adverse; in an opposite direction; in the wrong way. * adj opposed; opposite. * n a return blow or parry; an answering move. * vti to oppose; to retort; to give a return blow; to retaliate.

counteract vt to act in opposition to so as to defeat or hinder; to neutralize.–**counteraction** n.–**counteractive** adj.

counterattack n an attack in response to an attack. * vt to make a counterattack.

counterbalance n a weight balancing another. * vt to act as a counterbalance; to act against with equal power.

counterclockwise adj moving in a direction contrary to the hands of a clock as viewed from the front.–also adv.–also **anticlockwise**.

counterfeit vt to imitate; to forge; to feign, simulate. * adj made in imitation, forged; feigned, sham. * n an imitation, a forgery.–**counterfeiter** n.

counterfoil n a detachable section of a check or ticket, kept as a receipt or record; a stub.

counterintelligence n activities intended to frustrate enemy espionage and intelligence-gathering operations.

countermand vt to revoke or annul, as an order or command; to cancel the orders of another. * n a command canceling another.

counterpart n a thing exactly like another, a duplicate; a corresponding or complementary part or thing.

counterpoint n (mus) a melody added as an accompaniment to another. * vt to set in contrast.

counterproductive adj producing a contrary effect on productivity or usefulness; hindering the desired end.

countersign vt to authenticate a document by an additional signature. * n a word to be given in answer to a sentry's challenge; an additional mark.–**countersignature** n.

countess n a woman with the rank of count or earl; the wife or widow of a count.

countless adj innumerable.

country n (pl **countries**) a region or district; the territory of a nation; a state; the land of one's birth or residence; rural parts; country-and-western. * adj rural.

country-and-western n a style of white folk music of the southeastern US.–also **country music**.

country dance n a dance with the couples face to face in two lines.

countryman n (pl **countrymen**) a person who lives in the country; a person from the same country as another.–**country-woman** nf (pl **countrywomen**).

countryside n a rural district.

county n (pl **counties**) an administrative subdivision of a state.–also adj.

coup n a sudden telling blow; a masterstroke; a coup d'état.

coup d'état n (pl **coups d'état**) a sudden and unexpected bold stroke of policy; the sudden overthrow of a government.

coupé n a closed, four-seater, two-door automobile with a sloping back.

couple n two of the same kind connected together; a pair; a husband and wife; a pair of equal and parallel forces. * vt to link or join together. * vi to copulate.

coupling n a device for joining parts of a machine or two railway carriages.

coupon n a detachable certificate on a bond, presented for payment of interest; a certificate entitling one to a discount, gift, etc.

courage n bravery; fortitude; spirit.–**courageous** adj.–**courageously** adv.–**courageousness** n.

courier n a messenger, esp diplomatic; a tourist guide; a carrier of illegal goods between countries.

course n a race; a path or track; a career; a direction or line of motion; a regular sequence; the portion of a meal served at one time; conduct; behavior; the direction a ship is steered; a continuous level range of brick or masonry of the same height; a length of time; an area set aside for a sport or a race; a series of studies. * vt to hunt. * vi to move swiftly along an indicated path; to chase with greyhounds.

coursing n the sport of pursuing game with hunting dogs.

court n an uncovered space surrounded by buildings or walls; a short street; a playing space, as for tennis, etc; a royal palace; the retinue of a sovereign; (law) a hall of justice; the judges, etc engaged there. * vt to seek the friendship of; to woo; to flatter; to solicit; to risk. * vi to carry on a courtship.

courteous adj polite; obliging.–**courteously** adv.–**courteousness** n.

courtesan n (formerly) a prostitute, or mistress of a courtier.

courtesy n (pl **courtesies**) politeness and kindness; civility; a courteous manner or action.

courthouse n a public building that houses law courts.

courtier n one in attendance at a royal court.

courtly adj (**courtlier, courtliest**) well-mannered, polite; of a court.–**courtliness** n.

court martial n (pl **courts martial, court martials**) a court of justice composed of naval or military officers for the trial of disciplinary offenses.–**court-martial** vt.

courtship n the act of wooing.

courtyard n an enclosed space adjoining or in a large building.

cousin n the son or daughter of an uncle or aunt.–**cousinly** adj.–**cousinship** n.

couture n the design and manufacture of expensive fashion clothes.–**couturier** n.–**couturière** nf.

cove n a small sheltered bay or inlet in a body of water; a curved molding at the juncture of a wall and ceiling (–also **coving**).

coven n an assembly of witches.

covenant n a written agreement; a solemn agreement of fellowship and faith between members of a church; an agreement to pay annually a sum to a charity. * vt to promise by a covenant. * vi to enter into a formal agreement.–**covenantal** adj.–**covenanted** adj.

cover vt to overspread the top of anything with something else; to hide; to save from punishment; to shelter; to clothe; to understudy;

to insure against damage, loss, etc; to report for a newspaper; to include. * vi to spread over, as a liquid does; to provide an excuse or alibi (for); to work, eg as a salesman, in a certain area; to have within firing range. * n that which is laid on something else; a bedcover; a shelter; an understudy; something used to hide one's real actions, etc; insurance against loss or damage; a place laid at a table for a meal.–**covering** n.

coverage n the amount, extent, etc covered by something; the amount of reporting of an event for newspaper, television, etc.

coverall n (usu pl) a one-piece garment that completely covers and protects one's clothing.

covert adj covered; secret, concealed. * n a place that protects or shelters; a thicket; shelter for game.–**covertly** adv.

cover-up n something used to hide one's real activities, etc; a concerted effort to keep an act or situation from being made public.

covet vt to desire earnestly; to lust after; to long to possess (what belongs to another).–**coveter** n.–**covetous** adj.–**covetousness** n.

covey n a hatch or brood of birds, esp partridges.

cow[1] n the mature female of domestic cattle; the mature female of various other animals, as the whale, elephant, etc.

cow[2] vt to take the spirit out of, to intimidate.

coward n a person lacking courage; one who is afraid.

cowardice n lack of courage.

cowardly adj of, or like, a coward.–**cowardliness** n.

cowboy n a person who tends cattle or horses (–also **cowhand**).–**cowgirl** nf.

cower vi to crouch or sink down through fear, etc; to tremble.

cowl n a hood; the hooded habit of a monk; the draped neckline of a woman's dress or sweater; a chimney corner.

cowpox n a disease of cows that produces vesicles from which the vaccine for inoculation against smallpox is obtained.

cowpuncher, cowpoke n a cowboy.

cowry, cowrie n (pl **cowries**) a marine mollusk with a glossy, brightly speckled shell.

cowslip n a common wild plant with small fragrant yellow flowers.

cox n a coxswain. * vt to act as a coxswain.

coxcomb n a cockscomb; a vain conceited person, a fop.

coxswain n a person who steers a boat, esp a lifeboat or racing boat.–also **cockswain**.

coy adj playfully or provocatively demure; bashful.–**coyly** adv.–**coyness** n.

coyote n (pl **coyotes, coyote**) a small prairie wolf of North America.

coypu n (pl **coypus, coypu**) an aquatic beaver-like animal, originally from South America.

cozen vt to cheat, to beguile; to act deceitfully.–**cozenage** n.–**cozener** n.

cozy see **cosy**.

cp. abbr = compare.

Cpl abbr = Corporal.

Cr (chem symbol) chromium.

crab n any of numerous chiefly marine broadly built crustaceans. * vi (**crabbing, crabbed**) to fish for crabs; to complain.

crab-apple n a wild apple.

crabby adj bad-tempered.–**crabbily** adv.–**crabbiness** n.

crack vt to burst, break or sever; to utter a sharp, abrupt cry; to injure; (sl) to make (a joke); (inf) to break open (a safe); to decipher (a code). * vi to make a sharp explosive sound; (inf) to lose control under pressure; (with **up**) (inf) to be unable to cope. * n a chink or fissure; a narrow fracture; a sharp sound; a sharp resonant blow; a chat, gossip; a wisecrack; (inf) an attempt; an expert; (sl) the drug cocaine packaged in the form of pellets.

crackdown n repressive action to quell disorder, etc.

cracker n a firework that explodes with a loud crack; a thin, crisp biscuit; (sl) a person or thing of great ability or excellence.

cracking adj (inf) fast-moving; excellent. * n the act of hacking into computer games.

crackle vi to make a slight, sharp explosive noise. * vt to cover with a delicate network of minute cracks. * n a noise of frequent and slight cracks and reports; a surface glaze on glass or porcelain.–**crackly** adj.

crackpot n (inf) an eccentric, a crazy person. * adj (inf) crazy, unpractical.

cradle n a baby's crib or a small bed, often on rockers; infancy; birthplace or origin; a case for a broken limb; a framework of timbers, esp for supporting a boat. * vt to rock or place in a cradle; to nurse or train in infancy.

craft n manual skill; a skilled trade; the members of a skilled trade; cunning; (pl **craft**) a boat, ship, or aircraft.

craftsman n (pl **craftsmen**) a person skilled in a particular craft.–**craftsmanship** n.–**craftswoman** nf (pl **craftswomen**).

crafty adj (**craftier, craftiest**) cunning, wily.–**craftily** adv.–**craftiness** n.

crag n a rough steep rock or cliff.

craggy, cragged adj (**craggier, craggiest**) full of crags; rugged.–**cragginess** n.

cram vb (**cramming crammed**) vt to pack tightly, to stuff; to fill to overflowing; (inf) to prepare quickly for an examination. * vi to eat greedily.

cramp n a spasmodic muscular contraction of the limbs; (pl) abdominal spasms and pain; a clamp. * vt to affect with muscular spasms; to confine narrowly; to hamper; to secure with a cramp. * vi to suffer from cramps.

crampon, crampoon n a metal frame with spikes attached to boots for walking or climbing on ice.

cranberry n (pl **cranberries**) a small red sour berry; the shrub it grows on.

crane n a large wading bird with very long legs and neck, and a long straight bill; a machine for raising, shifting, and lowering heavy weights. * vti to stretch out (the neck).

cranium n (pl **craniums, crania**) the skull, esp the part enclosing the brain.–**cranial** adj.

crank n a right-angled arm attached to a shaft for turning it; (inf) an eccentric person, usu one with strange or unorthodox opinions. * vt to provide with a crank; to turn or wind; (with up) (engine) to start with a crank handle; (inf) to speed up.

crankshaft n a shaft with one or more cranks for transmitting motion.

cranky adj (**crankier, crankiest**) (inf) eccentric; shaky; cross.–**crankily** adv.–**crankiness** n.

cranny n (pl **crannies**) a fissure, crack, crevice.

craps n (sing or pl) a gambling game played with two dice.

crapshooter n a player of craps.

crash n a loud, sudden confused noise; a violent fall or impact; a sudden failure, as of a business or a computer; a collapse, as of the financial market. * adj done with great speed, suddenness or effort. * vti to clash together with violence; to make a loud clattering noise; (aircraft) to land with a crash; to involve a car in a collision with one or more other vehicles or with a hard object; to collapse, to ruin; (inf) to intrude into (a party); (with out) vi (sl) to fall asleep; to pass out.

crash helmet n a cushioned helmet worn by airmen, motorcyclists, etc for protection.

crash-land vti (aircraft) to make an emergency landing without lowering the undercarriage, or to be landed in this way.–**crash-landing** n.

crass adj gross; dense; very stupid.–**crassly** adv.–**crassness, crassitude** n.

crate n an open box of wooden slats, for shipping. * vt to pack in a crate.

crater n the mouth of a volcano; a cavity caused by the landing of a meteorite, the explosion of a bomb, shell, etc.

cravat n a neckcloth.

crave vt to have a strong desire (for); to ask humbly, to beg.–**craving** n.

craven adj spiritless, cowardly. * n a coward.

crawl vi to move along the ground on hands and knees; to move slowly and with difficulty; to creep; (inf) to seek favor by servile behavior; to swarm (with). * n the act of crawling; a slow motion; a racing stroke in swimming.–**crawler** n.

crayfish n (pl **crayfish**) any of numerous freshwater crustaceans; the spiny lobster.–also **crawfish**.

crayon n a stick or pencil of colored chalk; a drawing done with crayons. * vt to draw with a crayon.

craze n a passing infatuation; excessive enthusiasm; a crack in pottery glaze. * vt to produce cracks; to render insane.–**crazed** adj.

crazy adj (**crazier, craziest**) (inf) mad, insane; foolish; ridiculous; unsound.–**crazily** adv.–**craziness** n.

creak vi to make a shrill grating sound. * n such a sound.–**creaky** adj.

cream n the rich, fatty part of milk; the choicest part of anything; a yellowish white color; a type of face or skin preparation; any preparation of the consistency of cream (eg shoe cream). * vt to add or apply cream to; to beat into a soft, smooth consistency; to skim cream from; to remove the best part of. * vi to form cream or scum; to break into a creamy froth.

cream cheese n soft cheese made from soured milk or cream.

creamery n (pl **creameries**) a place where dairy products are made or sold.

cream of tartar n purified tartar or argol, potassium bitartrate.

creamy adj (**creamier, creamiest**) like cream.–**creaminess** n.

crease n a line made by folding; a wrinkle. * vti to make or form creases; to become creased; (sl) to find something very funny.

create vt to cause to come into existence; to form out of nothing. * vi to make something new, to originate.

creation n the act of creating; the thing created; the whole world or universe; a production of the human mind; (with cap) the universe as created by God.–**creational** adj.

creative adj of creation; having the power to create; imaginative, original, constructive.–**creatively** adv.–**creativeness** n.–**creativity** n.

creator n one who creates, esp God.

creature n a living being; a created thing; one dependent on the influence of another.–**creatural, creaturely** adj.

crèche n a day nursery for very young children.

credence n belief or trust, esp in the reports or testimony of another.

credentials npl documents proving the identity, honesty or authority of a person.

credible adj believable; trustworthy.–**credibility, credibleness** n.–**credibly** adv.

credit n belief; trust; honor; good reputation; approval; trust in a person's ability to pay; time allowed for payment; a sum at a person's disposal in a bank; the entry in an account of a sum received; the side of the account on which this is entered; (educ) a distinction awarded for good marks in an examination; (pl) a list of those responsible for a film, television programme, etc. * vt to believe; to trust; to have confidence in; to attribute to; to enter on the credit side of an account.

creditable adj worthy of praise.–**creditableness, creditability** n.–**creditably** adv.

creditor n a person to whom money is owed.

creditworthy adj worthy of being given credit as judged by the capacity to earn, repay debts promptly, etc.–**creditworthiness** n.

credo n (pl **credos**) a creed.

credulous *adj* over-ready to believe; easily imposed on.–**credulously** *adv*.–**credulity** *n*.

creed *n* a system of religious belief or faith; a summary of Christian doctrine; any set of principles or beliefs.–**creedal, credal** *adj*.

creek *n* a natural stream of water smaller than a river.

creel *n* a wicker fishing basket; a wickerwork cage.

creep *vi* (**creeping, crept**) to move slowly along the ground, as a worm or reptile; (*plant*) to grow along the ground or up a wall; to move stealthily or slowly; to fawn; to cringe. * *n* (*inf*) a dislikable or servile person.

creeper *n* a creeping or climbing plant.

creepy *adj* (**creepier, creepiest**) making one's flesh crawl; causing fear or disgust.–**creepily** *adv*.–**creepiness** *n*.

cremate *vt* to burn (a corpse) to ashes.–**cremation** *n*.–**cremationism** *n*.–**cremationist** *n*.

crematorium *n* (*pl* **crematoriums, crematoria**) a place where bodies are cremated.

crème de la crème *n* the cream of the cream, the very best.

Creole *n* a descendant of European settlers in the West Indies or South America; a white descendant of French settlers in the southern US; a person of mixed European and Negro ancestry; the language of any of these groups.

creole *n* a language combining two or more original languages, one of which is European.

creosote *n* an oily substance derived from tar used as a wood preservative. * *vt* to treat with creosote.–**creosotic** *adj*.

crepe, crêpe *n* a thin, crinkled cloth of silk, rayon, wool, etc (–*also* **crape**); thin paper like crepe; a thin pancake.

crept *see* **creep**.

crepuscular *adj* pertaining to or resembling twilight; active at twilight, as certain animals.

crescendo *adv* (*mus*) gradually increasing in loudness or intensity; moving to a climax. * *n* (*pl* **crescendos, crescendi**) a crescendo passage or effect.

crescent *n* the figure of the moon in its first or last quarter; a narrow, tapering curve; a curving street. * *adj* crescent-shaped; (*arch*) increasing.–**crescentic** *adj*.

cress *n* any of various plants with pungent leaves, used in salads.

crest *n* a plume of feathers on the head of a bird; the ridge of a wave; the summit of a hill; a distinctive device above the shield on a coat of arms. * *vti* to mount to the top of; to take the form of a crest; to provide or adorn with a crest, to crown.–**crested** *adj*.

crestfallen *adj* dejected.

cretin *n* a person suffering from mental and physical retardation due to a thyroid disorder; (*inf*) an idiot.–**cretinism** *n*.–**cretinoid, cretinous** *adj*.

crevasse *n* a deep cleft in a glacier; a deep crack.

crevice *n* a crack, a fissure.

crew *n* the people operating a ship or aircraft; a group of people working together. * *vi* to act as a member of the crew of a ship, etc.

crewcut *n* a very short hairstyle for men.

crib *n* a rack for fodder, a manger; a child's cot with high sides; a model of the manger scene representing the birth of Jesus.

cribbage *n* a card game for two to four players.

crib death *n* the sudden death of a baby during sleep from an unexplained cause.–*also* **cot death**.

crick *n* a painful stiffness of the muscles of the neck. * *vt* to produce a crick in.

cricket[1] *n* a leaping grasshopper-like insect.

cricket[2] *n* a game played with wickets, bats, and a ball, by eleven players on each side.–**cricketer** *n*.

cried *see* **cry**.

crier *n* one who cries; an officer who makes public proclamations.

crime *n* a violation of the law; an offense against morality or the public welfare; wrong-doing; (*inf*) a shame, disappointment.

criminal *adj* of the nature of, or guilty of, a crime. * *n* a person who has committed a crime.–**criminality** *n*.–**criminally** *adv*.

criminology *n* the scientific study of crime.–**criminological, criminologic** *adj*.–**criminologist** *n*.

crimp *vt* to press into small folds; to frill; to corrugate; (*hair*) to curl.–**crimper** *n*.

crimson *n* a deep-red color inclining to purple. * *adj* crimson-colored. * *vti* to dye with crimson; to blush.

cringe *vi* to shrink in fear or embarrassment; to cower; to behave with servility; to fawn.

crinkle *vt* to wrinkle; to corrugate; to crimp; to rustle. * *vi* to curl; to be corrugated or crimped. * *n* a wrinkle.–**crinkly** *adj*.

crinoline *n* a hooped skirt made to project all round; a stiff fabric for stiffening a garment.

cripple *vt* to deprive of the use of a limb; to disable. * *n* a lame or otherwise disabled person. * *adj* lame.

crippling *adj* harmful; unbearable.

crisis *n* (*pl* **crises**) a turning point; a critical point in a disease; an emergency; a time of serious difficulties or danger.

crisp *adj* dry and brittle; bracing; brisk; sharp and incisive; decided; very clean and tidy.* *vt* to make crisp.–**crisply** *adv*.–**crispness** *n*.–**crispy** *adj*.

crisscross *vti* to intersect; to mark with cross lines. * *n* an intersecting; a mark of a cross. * *adj* crossing; in cross lines. * *adv* crosswise.

criterion *n* (*pl* **criteria**) a standard, law or rule by which a correct judgment can be made.

critic *n* a person skilled in judging the merits of literary or artistic works; one who passes judgment; a fault-finder.

critical *adj* skilled in criticism; censorious; relating to the turning point of a disease; crucial.–**critically** *adv*.

criticism *n* being critical; an adverse comment; a review or analysis of a book, play, work of art, etc by a critic.

criticize *vt* to pass judgment on; to find fault with; to examine critically.

critique *n* a critical article or review.

croak *n* a deep hoarse discordant cry. * *vti* to utter a croak; (*inf*) to die, to kill.–**croakily** *adv*.–**croakiness** *n*.–**croaky** *adj*.

crochet *n* a kind of knitting done with a hooked needle. * *vti* (**crocheting, crocheted**) to do this; to make crochet articles.–**crocheter** *n*.

crock[1] *n* an earthenware pot.

crock[2] *n* a broken-down horse; (*sl*) a worn-out or unfit person. * *vti* to become or make unfit.

crockery *n* china dishes, earthenware vessels, etc.

crocodile *n* a large amphibious reptile, similar to an alligator.

crocus *n* (*pl* **crocuses**) a bulbous plant with yellow, purple, or white flowers.

croissant *n* a rich bread roll.

crone *n* a withered old woman.

crony *n* (*pl* **cronies**) an intimate friend.

crook *n* a shepherd's hooked staff; a bend, a curve; a swindler, a dishonest person.* *vti* to bend or to be bent into the shape of a hook.

crooked *adj* bent, twisted; dishonest.–**crookedly** *adv*.–**crookedness** *n*.

croon *vti* to sing in a soft gentle manner.–**crooner** *n*.

crop *n* a year's or a season's produce of any cultivated plant; harvest; any collection of things appearing at the same time; a pouch in a bird's gullet; a hunting whip; hair cut close or short. * *vti* (**cropping, cropped**) to clip short; to bite off or eat down (grass); (*land*) to yield; to sow, to plant; (*with* up) (*inf*) to occur or appear by chance or unexpectedly.

crop circle *n* a circular patch of corn in a cornfield that has been flattened by an as yet unexplained whirling movement.

croquet *n* a game played with mallets, balls and hoops. * *vt* (**croqueting, croqueted**) to drive away an opponent's ball by striking one's own placed in contact with it.

croquette *n* a ball of minced meat, fish or potato seasoned and fried brown.

cross n a figure formed by two intersecting lines; a wooden structure, consisting of two beams placed across each other; a symbol or mark (X); a focal point in a town; a burden, or affliction; a cross-shaped medal; a hybrid. * vti to pass across; to intersect; to meet and pass; to place crosswise; to mark with a cross; to make the sign of the cross over; to thwart, to oppose; to modify (a breed) by intermixture (with). * adj transverse; reaching from side to side; intersecting; out of temper, peevish.—**crosser** n.—**crossly** adv.—**crossness** n.

crossbar n a horizontal bar, as that across goal posts or a bicycle frame.

crossbow n a bow set crosswise on the stock from which bolts are shot along a groove.

crossbreed vt (**crossbreeding, crossbred**) to breed animals by mating different varieties. * n an animal produced in this way.

cross-examine vt to question closely; (law) to question (a witness) who has already been questioned by counsel on the other side.—**cross-examiner** n.—**cross-examination** n.

cross-eyed adj squinting.—**cross-eye** n.

crossfire n converging gunfire from two or more positions; animated debate or argument.

crossing n an intersection of roads or railway lines; a place for crossing a street; the crossbreeding of animals and plants.

cross-legged adj seated with one leg crossed over the other.

cross-question vt to question to elicit details or test the accuracy of an account already given.—**cross-questioning** n.

cross-reference n a note directing the reader to a different section of a book or document.

crossroad n a road crossing another; (pl) where two roads cross; (fig) the time when a decisive action has to be made.

cross section n a cutting at right angles to length; the surface then shown; a random selection of the public.—**cross-sectional** adj.

crosswind n a side or unfavorable wind.

crosswise, crossways adv in the manner of a cross.

crossword (puzzle) n a puzzle in which interlocking words to be inserted vertically and horizontally in a squared diagram are indicated by clues.

crotch n the region of the body where the legs fork, the genital area; any forked region.

crotchet n (mus) a note equal to the duration of a half-minim.—also **quarter note**.

crotchety adj peevish, ill-tempered.—**crotchetiness** n.

crouch vi to squat or lie close to the ground; to cringe, to fawn.

croup n inflammation of the windpipe causing coughing and breathing problems, esp in children.—**croupous, croupy** adj.

croupier n a person who presides at a gaming table and collects or pays out the money won or lost.

crouton n a small piece of fried or toasted bread sprinkled onto soups.

crow n any of various usu large, glossy, black birds; a cawing cry, the shrill sound of a cock. * vi (**crowing, crowed** or **crew**) to make a sound like a cock; to boast in triumph; to utter a cry of pleasure.—**crower** n.

crowbar n an iron bar for use as a lever.

crowd n a number of people or things collected closely together; a dense multitude, a throng; (inf) a set; a clique. * vti to press closely together; to fill to excess; to push, to thrust; to importune.—**crowded** adj.

crown n a wreath worn on the head; the head covering of a monarch; regal power; the sovereign; the top of the head; the top of a tree; a summit; a reward; the part of a tooth above the gum. * vt to invest with a crown; to adorn or dignify; to complete; to reward; to put an artificial crown on a tooth.

crow's-nest n a lookout or watchtower on the main topmast of a sailing vessel.

cruces see **crux**.

crucial adj decisive; severe; critical.—**crucially** adv.

crucible n a heat-resistant container for melting ores, etc.

crucifix n a cross with the sculptured figure of Christ.

crucifixion n a form of execution by being nailed or bound to a cross by the hands and feet; (with cap) the death of Christ in this manner.

cruciform adj cross-shaped.

crucify vt (**crucifying, crucified**) to put to death on a cross; to cause extreme pain to; to defeat utterly in an argument; to ridicule mercilessly.

crude adj in a natural state; unripe; raw; immature; harsh in color; unfinished, rough; lacking polish; blunt; vulgar. * n crude oil.—**crudely** adv.—**crudeness** n.

crude oil n unrefined petroleum.

crudités npl coarsely chopped raw vegetables eaten with a dip.

cruel adj (**crueller, cruellest**) disposed to give pain to others; merciless; hard-hearted; fierce; painful; unrelenting.—**cruelly** adv.—**cruelty** n.

cruet n a small glass bottle for vinegar and oil, used at the table; a set of containers holding salt, pepper, vinegar.

cruise vi to sail to and fro; to wander about; to move at the most efficient speed for sustained travel. * vt to cruise over or about. * n a voyage from place to place for military purposes or in a liner for pleasure.

cruise missile n a subsonic low-flying guided missile.

cruiser n fast warship smaller than a battleship; a pleasure yacht or motorboat.

crumb n a fragment of bread; the soft part of bread; a little piece of anything. * vi to cover food with breadcrumbs before cooking.

crumble vt to break into crumbs; to cause to fall into pieces. * vi to disappear gradually, to disintegrate.—**crumbly** adj.

crumple vti to twist or crush into wrinkles; to crease; to collapse. * n a wrinkle or crease made by crumpling.—**crumply** adj.

crunch vti to crush with the teeth; to tread underfoot with force and noise; to make a sound like this; to chew audibly. * n the sound or act of crunching.—**crunchy** adj.

crusade n a medieval Christian military expedition to recover the Holy Land; a vigorous concerted action for the defense of a cause or the advancement of an idea. * vi to engage in a crusade.—**crusader** n.

crush vt to press between two opposite bodies; to squeeze; to break by pressure; to bruise; to ruin; to quell, to defeat; to mortify. * vi to be pressed out of shape or into a smaller compass. * n a violent compression or collision; a dense crowd; (inf) a large party; a drink made from crushed fruit; (sl) an infatuation.—**crushable** adj.—**crusher** n.

crust n any hard external coating or rind; the exterior solid part of the earth's surface; a shell or hard covering. * vti to cover or become covered with a crust.—**crusty** adj (**crustier, crustiest**).—**crustily** adv.—**crustiness** n.

crustacean n any aquatic animal with a hard shell, including crabs, lobsters, shrimps, and barnacles .—also adj.—**crustaceous** adj.

crutch n a staff with a crosswise head to support the weight of a lame person; something that supports.

crux n (pl **cruxes, cruces**) a difficult problem; the essential or deciding point.

cry vb (**crying, cried**) vi to call aloud; to proclaim; to exclaim vehemently; to implore; to shed tears; (with **off**) (inf) to cancel (an agreement, arrangement, etc), to renege; (with **out**) to shout due to fear or pain. * vt to utter loudly and publicly; (with **out for**) to be in dire need of. * n (pl **cries**) an inarticulate sound; an exclamation of wonder or triumph; an outcry; clamor; an urgent appeal; a spell of weeping; a battle cry; a catchword; the particular sound made by an animal or bird.

cryogenics n (sing) the science of very low temperatures and their effects.

cryonics n (sing) the use of extreme cold to preserve living tissue (eg organs) for future use.

crypt n an underground chamber or vault, esp under a church, used as a chapel or for burial.

cryptic, cryptical adj hidden, secret; mysterious.

cryptogram n a coded message, cipher.

crystal n a solid piece, eg of quartz, geometrically shaped owing to regular arrangement of its atoms; very clear, brilliant glass; articles of such glass, as goblets.* adj made of crystal.–**crystalline** adj.

crystallize vti to form crystals; to give definite form; to express clearly the theme and content of an argument, proposition, etc.–**crystallization** n.

crystallography n the science of the forms and structure of crystals.–**crystallographer** n.–**crystallographic** adj.

CS gas n an irritant gas used in quelling riots and disturbances.

CST abbr = Central Standard Time.

CT abbr = Connecticut.

Cu (chem symbol) = copper.

cu. abbr = cubic.

cub n a young carnivorous mammal; a young, inexperienced person; (with cap) a Cub Scout. * vi (**cubbing, cubbed**) to bring forth cubs.

cubbyhole n a small or snug place; a pigeonhole.

cube n a solid body with six equal square sides or faces; a cube-shaped block; the product of a number multiplied by itself twice. * vt to raise (number) to the third power, or cube; to cut into cube-shaped pieces.

cube root n the number that gives the stated number when cubed.

cubic adj having the form or properties of a cube; three-dimensional.

cubicle n a small separate sleeping compartment in a dormitory, etc.

cubism n a style of painting in which objects are depicted as fragmented and reorganized geometrical forms.–**cubist** n.–**cubistic** adj.–**cubistically** adv.

cubit n an ancient measure of about 18 inches; the forearm from the elbow to the wrist.

cuboid adj like a cube. * n a regular solid contained by parallelograms.

cuckold n a man whose wife has committed adultery.–**cuckoldry** n.

cuckoo n a bird with a dark plumage, a curved bill and a characteristic call that lays its eggs in the nests of other birds. * adj (inf) crazy, silly.

cucumber n a long juicy fruit used in salads and as a pickle; the creeping plant that bears it.

cud n the food that a ruminating animal brings back into the mouth to chew again; **chew the cud** to consider and mull over.

cuddle vt to embrace or hug closely. * vt to nestle together. * n a close embrace.

cuddly adj (**cuddlier, cuddliest**) given to cuddling; tempting to cuddle.

cudgel n a short thick stick for beating. * vt (**cudgeling, cudgeled** or **cudgelling, cudgelled**) to beat with a cudgel.–**cudgeler, cudgeller** n.

cue[1] n the last word of a speech in a play, serving as a signal for the next actor to enter or begin to speak; any signal to do something; a hint. * vt (**cueing** or **cuing, cued**) to give a cue to.

cue[2] n a tapering rod used in snooker, billiards, and pool to strike the cue ball.

cuff[1] n a blow with the fist or the open hand. * vt to strike such a blow.

cuff[2] n the end of a sleeve; a covering round the wrist; the turn-up on a trouser leg.

cufflink n a decorative clip for fastening the ends of a shirt cuff.

cuisine n a style of cooking or preparing food; the food prepared.

cul-de-sac n (pl **culs-de-sac, cul-de-sacs**) a street blocked off at one end; a blind alley; a position, job leading nowhere.

culinary adj of or relating to cooking.

cull vt to select; to pick out, gather. * n the selection of certain animals with the intention of killing them.–**culler** n.

culminate vti to reach the highest point of altitude, rank, power, etc; (astron) to reach the meridian; to bring to a head or the highest point.–**culminant** adj.–**culmination** n.

culottes npl a women's flared trousers that resemble a skirt.

culpable adj deserving censure; criminal; blameworthy.–**culpably** adv.–**culpability** n.

culprit n a person accused, or found guilty, of an offense.

cult n a system of worship; devoted attachment to a person, principle, etc; a religion regarded as unorthodox or spurious; its body of adherents; a current fashion.–**cultic** adj.–**cultism** n.–**cultist** n.

cultivate vt to till and plant; to improve by care, labor, or study; to seek the society of; to civilize or refine.–**cultivated** adj.

cultivation n the act of cultivating; the state of being cultivated; tillage; culture.

cultural adj pertaining to culture.–**culturally** adv.

culture n appreciation and understanding of the arts; the skills, arts, etc of a given people in a given period; the entire range of customs, beliefs, social forms, and material traits of a religious, social, or racial group; the scientific cultivation of plants to improve them and find new species; improvement of the mind, manner, etc; a growth of bacteria, etc in a prepared substance.* vt to cultivate bacteria for study or use.

cultured adj educated to appreciate the arts; having good taste; artificially grown, as cultured pearls.

culvert n a drain or conduit under a road.

cum prep with.

cumber vt to hamper, to burden. * n a hindrance.

cumbersome adj inconveniently heavy or large, unwieldy.

cumin, cummin n a plant cultivated for its seeds which are used as a spice.

cummerbund n a sash worn as a waistband, esp with a man's tuxedo.

cumulative adj augmenting or giving force; growing by successive additions; gathering strength as it grows.–**cumulatively** adv.

cumulus n (pl **cumuli**) a cloud form having a flat base and rounded outlines.

cunning adj ingenious; sly; designing; subtle. * n slyness, craftiness.

cup n a small, bowl-shaped container for liquids, usu with a handle; the amount held in a cup; one of two shaped supporting parts of a brassiere; an ornamental cup used as a trophy. * vt (**cupping, cupped**) to take or put as in a cup; to curve (the hands) into the shape of a cup.

cupboard n a closet or cabinet with shelves for cups, plates, utensils, food etc.

cupidity n greed of gain; covetousness.

cupola n a dome, esp of a pointed or bulbous shape; a furnace for melting metals.–**cupolated** adj.

cupreous adj of or like copper; coppery.

cur n a mongrel dog; a despicable person.

curable adj able to be cured, remediable.–**curability** n.–**curably** adv.

curaçao n an orange-flavored liqueur.

curare, curari n a substance extracted from vines and used by South American Indians to poison arrows.

curate n an assistant of a vicar or rector.

curative adj tending to cure. * n a curative agent or drug.

curator n a superintendent of a museum, art gallery, etc.–**curatorial** adj.

curb vt to restrain; to check; to keep in subjection. * n that which checks, restrains, or subdues; a line of raised stone forming the edge of a pavement (–also **kerb**).

curbstone n the stone edge of a path.

curd n the coagulated part of soured milk, used to make cheese.–**curdy** adj.–**curdiness** n.

curdle vti to turn into curds; to coagulate; (with **the blood**) to cause terror.–**curdler** n.

cure n the act or art of healing; a remedy; restoration to health. * vt to heal; to rid of; to preserve meat or fish by drying, salting, etc.

curette, curet n a surgical instrument for scraping a body cavity. *vt (**curetting, curetted**) to scrape with this.–**curettage** n.

curfew n a fixed evening hour as a sign that everyone must be indoors; the signal or hour.

curie n a unit of radioactivity.

curio n (pl **curios**) an item valued as rare or unusual.

curiosity n (pl **curiosities**) the quality of being curious; inquisitiveness; a strange, rare or interesting object.

curious adj anxious to know; prying, inquisitive; strange, remarkable, odd.–**curiously** adv.–**curiousness** n.

curl vti to form into a curved shape, to coil; to twist into ringlets; to proceed in a curve, to bend; to play at curling; (with **up**) to rest with the body in a curved shape and the legs drawn up; to relax in a comfortable place; (inf) to give up; to be embarrassed and sickened by. * n a ringlet of hair; a spiral form, a twist; a bend or undulation.

curlew n a bird with a long curved bill and long legs.

curly adj (**curlier, curliest**) full of curls.–**curliness** n.

curmudgeon n an ill-natured churlish person; a miser.–**curmudgeonly** adj.

currant n a small variety of dried grape; a shrub that yields a red or black fruit.

currency n (pl **currencies**) the time during which a thing is current; the state of being in use; the money current in a country.

current adj generally accepted; happening now; presently in circulation. * n a body of water or air in motion, a flow; the transmission of electricity through a conductor; a general tendency.

currently adv at the present time.

curriculum n (pl **curricula, curriculums**) a prescribed course of study.–**curricular** adj.

curry[1] n (pl **curries**) a spicy dish with a hot sauce; curry seasoning. * vt (pl **currying, curried**) to flavor with curry.

curry[2] vt (**currying, curried**) to rub down and groom (a horse); to dress leather after tanning; to beat; (with **favor**) to use flattery to ingratiate.

curse n a calling down of destruction or evil; a profane oath; a swear word; a violent exclamation of anger; a scourge. * vti to invoke a curse on; to swear, to blaspheme; to afflict, to torment.

cursed adj damnable.

cursive adj running; flowing. * n a script with the letters joined, as in handwriting.

cursor n a flashing indicator on a computer screen indicating position; the transparent slide on a slide rule.

cursory adj hasty, passing; superficial, careless.–**cursorily** adv.

curt adj short; abrupt; concise; rudely brief.–**curtly** adv.–**curtness** n.

curtail vt to cut short; to reduce; to deprive of part (of).–**curtailment** n.

curtain n a cloth hung as a screen at a window, etc; the movable screen separating the stage from the auditorium. * vt to enclose in, or as with, curtains.

curtsy, curtsey n (pl **curtsies, curtseys**) a formal gesture of greeting or respect, involving bending the knees, made by women. * vi (**curtsying, curtsied** or **curtseying, curtseyed**) to make a curtsy.

curvaceous adj (inf) having an attractive body with shapely curves.

curvature n a bending; a curved form.

curve n a bending without angles; a bent form or thing; (geom) a line of which no part is straight. * vti to form into a curve, to bend.–**curvy** adj (**curvier, curviest**).

cushion n a case stuffed with soft material for resting on; the elastic border around a snooker table; the air mass supporting a hovercraft. * vt to furnish with cushions; to protect by padding; to give protection against difficulties, etc; to soften the effect of.–**cushiony** adj.

cusp n an apex or point; the point at each end of a crescent moon.

cuspid n a canine tooth.

cussed adj (sl) cursed; stubborn, perverse. –**cussedness** n.

custard n a sauce mixture of milk, eggs and sugar.

custodian n one who has the care of anything; a keeper; a caretaker.

custody n (pl **custodies**) guardianship; imprisonment; security.–**custodial** adj.

custom n a regular practice; usage; traditions of a people or a society; frequent repetition of the same act; business patronage; (pl) duties on imports.

customary adj habitual; conventional; common.–**customarily** adv.

custom-built adj made to a customer's specifications.

customer n a person who buys from a shop or business, esp regularly; (inf) a person.

custom house n an office or building where duties are paid on exported or imported goods and vessels are entered and cleared.

cut vb (**cutting, cut**) vt to cleave or separate with a sharp instrument; to make an incision in; to wound with a sharp instrument; to divide; to trim; to intersect; to abridge; to diminish; to pass deliberately without recognition; to wound the feelings deeply; to reduce or curtail; to grow a new tooth through the gum; to divide (a pack of cards) at random; to switch off (a light, an engine); (inf) to stay away from class, school, etc; (with **back**) to prune vegetation; to economize; (with **down**) to fell a tree; to reduce expenditure, consumption, etc; to kill; (with **off**) to take away by cutting or slicing; to stop abruptly, esp a telephone conversation; to sever relations; (with **out**) to delete; to cut into shapes; (inf) to force out a rival; to give up an indulgence or habit; (with **up**) to cut into pieces; to wound with a knife; (inf) to affect deeply. * vi to make an incision; to perform the work of an edged instrument; to grow through the gums; (cinema) to change to another scene, to stop photographing; (with **in**) to butt in; to drive between two vehicles, leaving insufficient space; (with **out**) (engine) to stop working. * n an incision or wound made by a sharp instrument; a gash; a sharp stroke; a sarcastic remark; a passage or channel cut out; a slice; the fashion or shape of a garment; the deliberate ignoring of an acquaintance; the division of a pack of cards; a diminution in price below another merchant; (sl) a share, as of profits. * adj divided or separated; gashed; having the surface ornamented or fashioned; not wrought or hand-made; reduced in price.

cutaneous adj pertaining to the skin.

cutback n a reduction, esp in expenditure; a flashback.

cute adj (inf) acute, shrewd; pretty or attractive, esp in a dainty way.–**cutely** adv.–**cuteness** n.

cuticle n the skin at the base of the fingernail or toe nail; epidermis.–**cuticular** adj.

cutis n (pl **cutes, cutises**) the vascular layer of the skin, below the epidermis.

cutlass n a sailor's short heavy sword.

cutlery n knives, forks, etc for eating and serving food.

cutlet n a neck chop of lamb, etc; a small slice cut off from the ribs or leg; minced meat in the form of a cutlet.

cutthroat n a murderer. * adj merciless; (razor) having a long blade in a handle.

cutting n a piece cut off or from; an incision; a newspaper clipping; a slip from a plant for propagation; a passage or channel cut out; the process of editing a film or recording; a recording. * *adj* (*wind*) sharp, biting; (*remarks*) hurtful.

cuttlefish *n* (*pl* **cuttlefish, cuttlefishes**) a marine creature with a flattened body that squirts ink when threatened.

cyan *n* a blue color, one of the primary colors.

cyanide *n* a poison.

cyberspace *n* all of the data stored on a large computer or network through which a virtual reality user can move.

cyclamen *n* a plant of the primrose family, with pink, purple or white flowers.

cycle *n* a recurring series of events or phenomena; the period of this; a body of epics or romances with a common theme; a group of songs; a bicycle, motorcycle, or tricycle. * *vi* to go in cycles; to ride a bicycle or tricycle.

cyclic, cyclical *adj* moving or recurring in cycles.–**cyclically** *adv*.

cyclist *n* a person who rides a bicycle.

cyclone *n* a violent circular storm; an atmospheric movement in which the wind blows spirally round towards a centre of low barometric pressure.–**cyclonic** *adj*.

cygnet *n* a young swan.

cylinder *n* a hollow figure or object with parallel sides and circular ends; an object shaped like a cylinder; any machine part of this shape; the piston chamber in an engine.–**cylindrical** *adj*.–**cylindrically** *adv*.

cymbal *n* (*mus*) one of a pair of two brass plates struck together to produce a ringing or clashing sound.–**cymbalist** *n*.

cynic *n* a morose, surly, or sarcastic person; a sceptic about people, motives and actions.–**cynicism** *n*.

cynical *adj* sceptical of or sneering at goodness; shameless in admitting unworthy motives.–**cynically** *adv*.

cypher *see* **cipher**.

cypress *n* an evergreen tree with hard wood.

cyst *n* a closed sac developing abnormally in the structure of plants or animals.–**cystic** *adj*.

cystic fibrosis *n* a congenital disorder in young children characterized by chronic respiratory and digestive problems.

cystitis *n* inflammation of the urinary bladder.

cytology *n* the scientific study of cells; cell structure.–**cytological** *adj*.–**cytologist** *n*.

czar, czarina *see* **tsar, tsarina**.

D

D *abbr* = (*roman numerals*) 500.

DA *abbr* = District Attorney.

dab *vt* (**dabbing, dabbed**) to touch lightly with something moist or soft. * *n* a quick light tap; a small lump of anything moist or soft.

dabble *vi* to move hands, feet, etc gently in water or another liquid; (*usu with* **at, in, with**) to do anything in a superficial or dilettante way. * *vt* to splash.–**dabbler** *n*.

dachshund *n* a breed of short-legged, long-bodied hound.

dad *n* (*inf*) father.

daddy *n* (*pl* **daddies**) (*inf*) father.

daddy longlegs *n* (*inf*) any of various spiders or insects with long, slender legs, esp a crane fly.

dado *n* (*pl* **dadoes**) the lower part of a room wall when separately paneled or decorated.

daffodil *n* a yellow spring flower, a narcissus; its pale yellow color.

daft *adj* (*inf*) silly, weak-minded; giddy; mad.–**daftly** *adv*.–**daftness** *n*.

dagger *n* a short weapon for stabbing.

daily *adj, adv* (happening) every day; constantly, progressively. * *n* (*pl* **dailies**) a newspaper published every weekday.

dainty *adj* (**daintier, daintiest**) delicate; choice; nice, fastidious. * *n* (*pl* **dainties**) a titbit, a delicacy.–**daintily** *adv*.–**daintiness** *n*.

dairy *n* (*pl* **dairies**) a building or room where milk is stored and dairy products made; a shop selling these; a company supplying them.

dairy products *npl* milk and products made from it, eg butter, cheese, yogurt.

dais *n* a low platform at one end of a hall or room.

daisy *n* (*pl* **daisies**) any of various plants with a yellow centre and white petals.

dale *n* a valley.

dalliance *n* idle or frivolous time-wasting; trifling; flirtation.

dally *vi* (**dallying, dallied**) to lose time by idleness or trifling; to play or trife (with); to flirt.–**dallier** *n*.

dalmatian *n* a large short-haired dog with black spot-like markings on a white body.

dam[1] *n* an artificial embankment to retain water; water so contained. * *vt* (**damming, dammed**) to retain (water) with such a barrier; to stem, obstruct, restrict.

dam[2] *n* the mother of a four-footed animal.

damage *n* injury, harm; loss; (*inf*) price, cost; (*pl*) (*law*) payment in compensation for loss or injury. * *vt* to do harm to, to injure.–**damageable** *adj*.–**damager** *n*.–**damaging** *adj*.

dame *n* (*sl*) a woman.

damn *vt* to condemn, censure; to ruin; to curse; to consign to eternal punishment. * *vti* to prove guilty. * *interj* (*sl*) expressing irritation or annoyance. * *n* (*sl*) something having no value. * *adj, adv* damned.

damnation *n* the state of being condemned to hell; the act of damning. * *interj* expressing annoyance, irritation, etc.

damned *adj* (*inf*) damnable; extremely.–*also adv*.

damp *n* humidity, moisture. * *adj* slightly wet, moist. * *vt* to moisten; (*with* **down**) to stifle, reduce.–**damply** *adv*.–**dampness** *n*.

dampen *vti* to make or become damp. * *vt* to stifle.–**dampener** *n*.

damper *n* a depressive influence; a metal plate in a flue for controlling combustion; (*mus*) a device for stopping vibration in stringed instruments.

dance *vti* to move rhythmically, esp to music; to skip or leap lightly; to execute (steps); to cause to dance or to move up and down. * *n* a piece of dancing; a dance performance of an artistic nature; a party with music for dancing; music for accompanying dancing.–**dancer** *n*.–**dancing** *adj, n*.

dandelion *n* a common wild plant with ragged leaves, a yellow flower and a fluffy seed head.

dandruff *n* scales of skin on the scalp, under the hair; scurf.–**dandruffy** *adj*.

dandy *n* (*pl* **dandies**) a man who likes to dress too fashionably. * *adj* (**dandier, dandiest**) (*inf*) excellent, fine.–**dandyish** *adj*.–**dandyism** *n*.

danger *n* exposure to injury or risk; a source of harm or risk.

dangerous *adj* involving danger; unsafe; perilous.–**dangerously** *adv*.–**dangerousness** *n*.

dangle *vi* to hang and swing loosely. * *vt* to carry something so that it hangs loosely; to display temptingly.–**dangler** *n*.

dank *adj* disagreeably damp.–**dankly** *adv*.–**dankness** *n*.

dapper *adj* nimble; neat in appearance, spruce.

dapple *vti* to mark with or show patches of a different color; to variegate. * *adj* marked in such a way. * *n* something so marked.

dare *vti* (**daring, dared** *or* **durst**) to be bold enough; to venture, to risk; to defy, to challenge. * *n* a challenge.–**darer** *n*.

daredevil *n* a rash, reckless person. * *adj* daring, bold; courageous.–**daredevilry** *n*.

daring *adj* fearless; courageous; unconventional. * *n* adventurous courage.–**daringly** *adv*.

dark *adj* having little or no light; of a shade of color closer to black than white; (*person*) having brown or black skin or hair; gloomy; (*inf*) secret, unknown; mysterious. * *n* a dark state or color; ignorance; secrecy.–**darkly** *adv*.–**darkness** *n*.

darken *vti* to make or become dark or darker.–**darkener** *n*.

dark horse n a competitor about whom little is known; a person of reserved character; a surprise political candidate.

darkroom n a room for processing photographs in darkness or safe light.

darling n a dearly loved person; a favorite. * adj lovable; much admired.

darn vt to mend a hole in fabric or a garment with stitches. * n an area that has been darned.–**darner** n.

dart n a small pointed missile; a sudden movement; a fold sewn into a garment for shaping it; (pl) an indoor game in which darts are thrown at a target. * vti to move rapidly; to send out rapidly.

dartboard n a circular cork or wooden target used in the game of darts.

dash vti to fling violently; to rush quickly; (hopes) to shatter; (one's spirits, etc) to depress, confound. * n a short race; a rush; a small amount of something added to food; a tinge; a punctuation mark (–); a dashboard; vigor, verve.

dashboard n an instrument panel in a car.

dashing adj debonair; spirited, stylish, dapper.–**dashingly** adv.

dastardly adj mean, cowardly; base.–**dastardliness** n.

DAT abbr = digital audio tape.

data npl (sing datum) (often used as sing) facts, statistics, or information either historical or derived by calculation or experimentation.

date[1] n a day or time of occurrence; a statement of this in a letter, etc; a period to which something belongs; a duration; an appointment, esp with a member of the opposite sex. * vt to affix a date to; to note the date of; to reckon the time of; (inf) to make a date with; (inf) to see frequently a member of the opposite sex. * vi to reckon from a point in time; to show signs of belonging to a particular period.–**datable, dateable** adj.–**dater** n.

date[2] n the sweet fruit of the date palm, a palm tree of tropical regions.

dated adj old-fashioned; out of style; bearing a date.–**datedness** n.

dateline n a line on a newspaper story giving the date and place of writing. * vt to provide with a dateline.

date line n the line running north to south along the 180-degree meridian, east of which is one day earlier than west of it.–also **International Date Line**.

datum n (pl data) a single unit of information; a thing given or taken for granted.

daub vt to smear or overlay (with clay, etc); to paint incompetently. * n a smear; a poor painting.–**dauber** n.

daughter n a female child or descendant; a female member of a family, race, etc; a woman in relation to her native country or place.

daughter-in-law n (pl **daughters-in-law**) the wife of one's son.

daunt vt to intimidate; to discourage.–**daunter** n.–**dauntingly** adv.

davenport n a large sofa, often able to be converted into a bed; a small ornamental writing desk.

dawdle vi to move slowly and waste time, to loiter.–**dawdler** n.

dawn vi (day) to begin to grow light; to begin to appear. * n daybreak; a first sign.

day n the time when the sun is above the horizon; the twenty-four hours from midnight to midnight; daylight; a particular period of success or influence; (usu pl) a period, an epoch.

daybreak n the first appearance of daylight, dawn.

daydream n a reverie. * vi to have one's mind on other things; to fantasize.–**daydreamer** n.

daylight n the light of the sun; dawn; publicity; a visible gap; the dawning of sudden realization or understanding.

daytime n the time of daylight.

day-to-day adj daily; routine.

daze vt to stun, to bewilder. * n confusion, bewilderment.–**dazedly** adv.–**dazedness** n.

dazzle vt to confuse the sight of or be partially blinded by strong light; to overwhelm with brilliance. * n the act of dazzling; a thing that dazzles; an overpoweringly strong light; bewilderment.–**dazzlement** n.–**dazzler** n.–**dazzlingly** adv.

dB, db abbr = decibels.

DC District of Columbia.

dc, DC abbr = direct current.

DDT abbr = dichlorodiphenyltrichloroethane, a chemical used as an insecticide.

deacon n (Anglican, RC churches) an ordained member of the clergy ranking below a priest; (Presbyterian churches) a lay church officer who assists the minister.–**deaconship** n.

deactivate vt (bomb) to make inactive or harmless.–**deactivation** n.–**deactivator** n.

dead adj without life; inanimate, inert; no longer used; lacking vegetation; emotionally or spiritually insensitive; without motion; (fire, etc) extinguished; (limb, etc) numb; (color, sound etc) dull; (a ball) out of play; complete, exact; unerring. * adv in a dead manner; completely; utterly. * n a dead person; the quietest time.–**deadness** n.

deaden vt to render numb or insensible; to deprive of vitality; to muffle.–**deadener** n.–**deadeningly** adv.

dead end n a cul-de-sac; a hopeless situation.

dead-end adj (job) holding no chance of advancement.

dead heat n a race in which two or more finish equal, a tie.

deadline n the time by which something must be done.

deadlock n a clash of interests making progress impossible; a standstill.–also vt.

deadly adj (**deadlier, deadliest**) fatal; implacable; (inf) tedious. * adv death-like; intensely.–**deadliness** n.

deadpan adj (inf) deliberately expressionless or emotionless.–also adv.

dead weight n a very heavy load; an oppressive burden.

deaf adj unable to hear; hearing badly; not wishing to hear.–**deafly** adv.–**deafness** n.

deafen vt to deprive of hearing.–**deafeningly** adv.

deaf-mute n a deaf and dumb person.

deal[1] vb (**dealing, dealt**) vt (a blow) to deliver, inflict; (cards, etc) to distribute; (with **with**) to do business with; (problem, task) to solve. * vi to do business (with); to trade (in). * n a portion, quantity; (inf) a large amount; a dealing of cards; a business transaction.

deal[2] n fir or pine wood.–also adj.

dealer n a trader; a person who deals cards; (sl) a seller of illegal drugs.

dealings npl personal or business transactions.

dealt see **deal**.

dean n the head of a cathedral chapter; a college fellow in charge of discipline; the head of a university or college faculty.–**deanship** n.

dear adj loved, precious; charming; expensive; a form of address in letters. * n a person who is loved. * adv at a high price.–**dearness** n.

dearly adv with great affection; at a high price or rate.

dearth n scarcity, lack.

death n the end of life, dying; the state of being dead; the destruction of something.

deathbed n the bed in which a person dies or is about to die.

deathly adj like death, pale, still; deadly. * adv in a manner causing or tending to death; to a degree resembling death; (inf) extremely (deathly quiet).–**deathliness** n.

death rate n the yearly proportion of deaths to population.–also **mortality rate**.

death row n the section of a prison housing inmates sentenced to death.

deathtrap n an unsafe place, thing or structure.

death warrant n official authorization for the execution of a person condemned to death; anything that guarantees the destruction of hope or expectation.

death wish *n* a usu unconscious wish for one's own death or that of another.

debacle *n* a sudden disastrous break-up or collapse; a break-up of river ice.

debark *vti* to land from a ship, to disembark.–**debarkation** *n*.

debase *vt* to lower in character or value; (*coinage*) to degrade.–**debasement** *n*.–**debaser** *n*.

debate *n* a formal argument; a discussion, esp in parliament. * *vt* to consider, contest. * *vi* to discuss thoroughly; to join in debate.–**debater** *n*.

debauch *vti* to corrupt, dissipate; to lead astray, to seduce.–**debaucher** *n*.

debauchery *n* (*pl* **debaucheries**) depraved over-indulgence; corruption; profligacy.

debilitate *vt* to weaken, to enervate.–**debilitation** *n*.–**debilitative** *adj*.

debility *n* (*pl* **debilities**) weakness, infirmity.

debit *n* the entry of a sum owed, opposite to the credit; the left side of a ledger used for this. * *vt* to charge to the debit side of a ledger.

debonair, debonnaire *adj* having a carefree manner; courteous, gracious, charming.–**debonairly** *adv*.

debrief *vt* (*diplomat*, *etc*) to make a report following a mission; to obtain such information.–**debriefing** *n*.

debris *n* (*pl* **debris**) broken and scattered remains, wreckage.

debt *n* a sum owed; a state of owing; an obligation.

debtor *n* a person, company, etc who owes money to another.

debug *vt* (**debugging**, **debugged**) (*inf*) (*room*, *etc*) to clear of hidden microphones; (*machine*, *program*, *plan*, *etc*) to locate and remove errors from; to remove insects from.

debunk *vt* (*inf*) (*claim*, *theory*) to expose as false.–**debunker** *n*.

debut *n* a first appearance as a public performer or in society. * *vi* to make one's debut.–**debutant** *n*.–**debutante** *nf*.

decade *n* a period of ten years; a group of ten.–**decadal** *adj*.

decadence, decadency *n* a state of deterioration in standards, esp of morality.–**decadent** *adj*.

decaffeinated *adj* (*coffee, tea, carbonated drinks, etc*) with caffeine reduced or removed.

decagon *n* a ten-sided plane figure.–**decagonal** *adj*.

decahedron *n* a solid with ten faces.–**decahedral** *adj*.

decamp *vi* to leave suddenly or secretly.–**decampment** *n*.

decant *vt* (*wine, etc*) to pour from one vessel to another, leaving sediment behind.–**decantation** *n*.

decanter *n* an ornamental bottle (usu glass) for holding wines, etc.

decapitate *vt* to behead.–**decapitation** *n*.–**decapitator** *n*.

decathlon *n* a track-and-field contest consisting of ten events.–**decathlete** *n*.

decay *vti* to rot, to decompose; to deteriorate, to wither. * *n* the act or state of decaying; a decline, collapse.

decease *n* death. * *vi* to die.

deceased *adj* dead. * *n* the dead person.

deceit *n* the act of deceiving; cunning; treachery; fraud.

deceitful *adj* treacherous; insincere; misleading.–**deceitfully** *adv*.–**deceitfulness** *n*.

deceive *vt* to cheat; to mislead; to delude; to impose upon.–**deceivable** *adj*.–**deceiver** *n*.–**deceivingly** *adv*.

decelerate *vt, vi* to reduce speed.–**deceleration** *n*.–**decelerator** *n*.

December *n* the twelfth and last month of the year with 31 days.

decency *n* (*pl* **decencies**) being decent; conforming to accepted standards of proper behavior.

decent *adj* respectable, proper; moderate; not obscene; (*inf*) quite good; (*inf*) kind, generous.–**decently** *adv*.

decentralize *vt* (*government, organization*) to divide among local centres.–**decentralist** *adj, n*.–**decentralization** *n*.

deception *n* the act of deceiving or the state of being deceived; illusion; fraud.

deceptive *adj* apt to mislead; ambiguous; unreliable.–**deceptively** *adv*.–**deceptiveness** *n*.

decibel *n* a unit for measuring sound level.

decide *vti* to determine, to settle; to give a judgment on; to resolve.–**decidable** *adj*.

decided *adj* unhesitating; clearly marked.

decidedly *adv* definitely, certainly.

decider *n* a deciding round, a final heat.

deciduous *adj* (*trees, shrubs*) shedding all leaves annually, at the end of the growing season.–**deciduousness** *n*.

deciliter, decilitre *n* a unit equal to one-tenth of a liter.

decimal *adj* of tenths, of numbers written to the base 10. * *n* a tenth part; a decimal fraction.–**decimally** *adv*.

decimal fraction *n* a fraction whose denominator is ten or a power of ten, indicated by figures after a decimal point.

decimal point *n* a dot written before the numerator in a decimal fraction (e.g. $0.5 = 1/2$).

decimate *vt* to kill every tenth person; to reduce by one-tenth; to kill a great number.–**decimation** *n*.–**decimator** *n*.

decimeter, decimetre *n* a measure of length, one tenth of a meter.

decipher *vt* to decode; to make out (indistinct writing, meaning, etc).–**decipherable** *adj*.–**decipherer** *n*.–**decipherment** *n*.

decision *n* a settlement; a ruling; a judgment; determination, firmness.

decisive *adj* determining the issue, positive; conclusive, final.–**decisively** *adv*.–**decisiveness** *n*.

deck *n* the floor on a ship, aircraft, bus or bridge; a pack of playing cards. * *vt* to cover; to adorn.

declaim *vti* to state dramatically; to recite.–**declaimer** *n*.

declamation *n* the art of declaiming according to rhetorical rules; impassioned oratory; distinct and correct enunciation of words in vocal music.

declaration *n* the act of declaring or proclaiming; that which is declared; an assertion; publication; a statement reduced to writing.

declare *vt* to affirm, to proclaim; to admit possession of (dutiable goods). * *vi* (*law*) to make a statement; (*with* **against, for**) to announce one's support.–**declarable** *adj*.

declension *n* (*gram*) variation in the form of a noun and its modifiers to show case and number; a complete set of such variations of a noun, etc.–**declensional** *adj*.

decline *vi* to refuse; to move down; to deteriorate, fall away; to fail; to diminish; to draw to an end; to deviate. * *vt* to reject, to refuse; (*gram*) to give the cases of a declension. * *n* a diminution; a downward slope; a gradual loss of physical and mental faculties.–**declinable** *adj*.–**decliner** *n*.

decode *vt* to translate a code into plain language.

décolleté *adj* having a low neckline.–**décolletage** *n*.

decompose *vti* to separate or break up into constituent parts, esp as part of a chemical process; to resolve into its elements. * *vi* to decay.–**decomposable** *adj*.–**decomposition** *n*.

decompress *vt* to decrease the pressure on, esp gradually; to return (a diver, etc) to a condition of normal atmospheric pressure.–**decompression** *n*.–**decompressive** *adj*.–**decompressor** *n*.

decongestant *n* a medical preparation that relieves congestion, eg catarrh.

decontaminate *vt* to free from (radioactive, etc) contamination.–**decontamination** *n*.–**decontaminator** *n*.

décor, decor *n* general decorative effect, eg of a room; scenery and stage design.

decorate *vt* to ornament; to paint or wallpaper; to honor with a badge or medal.–**decoration** *n*.–**decorator** *n*.

decorative *adj* ornamental, pretty to look at.–**decoratively** *adv*.–**decorativeness** *n*.

decorum *n* what is correct in outward appearance, propriety of conduct, decency.–**decorous** *adj*.

decoy vt to lure into a trap. * n anything intended to lure into a snare.–**decoyer** n.

decrease vti to make or become less. * n a decreasing; the amount of diminution.–**decreasingly** adv.

decree n an order, edict or law; a judicial decision. * vt (**decreeing, decreed**) to decide by sentence in law; to appoint.–**decreeable** adj.–**decreer** n.

decrepit adj worn out by the infirmities of old age; in the last stage of decay.–**decrepitly** adv.–**decrepitude** n.

decry vt (**decrying, decried**) to disparage, to censure as worthless.–**decrial** n.–**decrier** n.

dedicate vt to consecrate (to some sacred purpose); to devote wholly or chiefly; to inscribe (to someone).–**dedicatee** n.–**dedicator** n.–**dedicatory, dedicative** adj.–**dedication** n.

dedicated adj devoted to a particular cause, profession, etc; single-minded; assigned to a particular function.

deduce vt to derive (knowledge, a conclusion) from reasoning; infer.–**deducible** adj.

deduct vt to take (from); to subtract.

deduction n deducting; the amount deducted; deducing; a conclusion that something is true because it necessarily follows from a set of general premises known to be valid.–**deductive** adj.–**deductively** adv.

deed n an act; an exploit; a legal document recording a transaction.

deem vti to judge; to think, to believe.

deep adj extending or placed far down or far from the outside; fully involved; engrossed; profound, intense; heartfelt; penetrating; difficult to understand; secret; cunning; sunk low; low in pitch; (color) of high saturation and low brilliance. * adv in a deep manner; far in, into. * n that which is deep; the sea.–**deeply** adv.–**deepness** n.

deepen vt to make deeper in any sense; to increase. * vi to become deeper.–**deepener** n.

deepfreeze n a refrigerator in which food is frozen and stored.–**deep-freeze** vt.

deep-fry vt (**deep-frying, deep-fried**) to fry food in deep fat in order to cook or brown it without turning.–**deep-fryer** n.

deep-seated adj having its seat far beneath the surface; deep-rooted.

deer n (pl **deer, deers**) a four-footed animal with antlers, esp on the males, including stag, reindeer, etc.

deerhound n a large rough-haired greyhound.–also **Scottish deerhound**.

deface vt to disfigure; to obliterate.–**defaceable** adj.–**defacement** n.–**defacer** n.

defamation n the act of injuring someone's good name or reputation without justification, either orally or in writing; the condition of being defamed.–**defamatory** adj.

defame vt to destroy the good reputation of; to speak evil of.–**defamer** n.

default n neglect to do what duty or law requires; failure to fulfill a financial obligation; (comput) a basic setting or instruction to which a program reverts. * vi to fail in one's duty (as honoring a financial obligation, appearing in court).

defeat vt to frustrate; to win a victory over; to baffle. * n a frustration of plans; overthrow, as of an army in battle; loss of a game, race, etc.–**defeater** n.

defeatism n disposition to accept defeat.–**defeatist** n, adj.

defecate vi to empty the bowels.

defect n a deficiency; a blemish, fault. * vi to desert one's country or a cause, transferring one's allegiance (to another).–**defector** n.

defection n desertion of duty or allegiance.

defective adj having a defect; faulty; incomplete. * n a person defective in physical or mental powers.–**defectively** adv.–**defectiveness** n.

defend vt to guard or protect; to maintain against attack; (law) to resist, as a claim; to contest (a suit).–**defendable** adj.–**defender** n.

defendant n a person accused or sued in a lawsuit.

defense, defence n resistance or protection against attack; a means of resisting an attack; protection; vindication; (law) a defendant's plea; the defending party in legal proceedings; (sport) defending (the goal, etc) against the attacks of the opposing side; the defending players in a team.–**defenseless, defenceless** adj.–**defenselessness, defencelessness** n.–**defensible** adj.

defensive adj serving to defend; in a state or posture of defence.–**defensively** adv.–**defensiveness** n.

defer[1] vt (**deferring, deferred**) to put off to another time; to delay.–**deferrable, deferable** adj.–**deferrer** n.

defer[2] vi (**deferring, deferred**) to yield to another person's wishes, judgment or authority.–**deference** n.–**deferential** adj.

defiance n the act of defying; wilful disobedience; a challenge.–**defiant** adj.–**defiantly** adv.

deficient adj insufficient, lacking.–**deficiently** adv.–**deficiency** n.

deficit n the amount by which an amount falls short of what is required; excess of expenditure over income, or liabilities over assets.

defile vt to pollute or corrupt.–**defilement** n.–**defiler** n.

define vt to fix the bounds or limits of; to mark the limits or outline of clearly; to describe accurately; to fix the meaning of.–**definable** adj.–**definer** n.

definite adj defined; having distinct limits; fixed; exact; clear.–**definiteness** n.

definitely adv certainly; distinctly. * interj used to agree emphatically.

definition n a description of a thing by its properties; an explanation of the exact meaning of a word, term, or phrase; sharpness of outline.

definitive adj defining or limiting; decisive, final.–**definitively** adv.–**definitiveness** n.

deflate vt to release gas or air from; to reduce in size or importance; to reduce the money supply, restrict credit, etc to reduce inflation in the economy.–**deflation** n.–**deflationary** adj.–**deflationist** adj, n.

deflect vti to turn or cause to turn aside from a line or proper course.–**deflective** adj.–**deflector** n.

deflection n the action of deflecting or the state of being deflected from a straight line or regular path; deviation; the turning of a magnetic needle away from its zero; the amount of this.

defoliate vt to strip (a plant or tree) of its leaves.–**defoliation** n.–**defoliator** n.

deforest vt to clear of trees.–**deforestation** n.–**deforester** n.

deform vt to spoil the natural form of; to put out of shape.–**deformer** n.–**deformed** adj.

deformity n (pl **deformities**) the condition of being deformed; a deformed part of the body; a defect.

defraud vt to remove (money, rights, etc) from a person by cheating or deceiving.–**defraudation** n.–**defrauder** n.

defrost vt to unfreeze; to free from frost or ice. * vi to become unfrozen.

deft adj skillful, adept; nimble.–**deftly** adv.–**deftness** n.

defunct adj no longer being in existence or function or in use.

defuse vt to disarm an explosive (bomb or mine) by removing its fuse; to decrease tension in a (crisis) situation.

defy vt (**defying, defied**) to resist openly and without fear; to challenge; to resist attempts at, to elude.–**defier** n.

degenerate adj having declined in physical or moral qualities; sexually deviant. * vi to become or grow worse. * n a degenerate person.–**degeneracy** n.–**degenerative** adj.

degeneration n the act, state, or process of growing worse; degeneracy; decline; the morbid impairment of any structural tissue or organ.

degradable adj capable of being broken down by biological or chemical action.

degrade vt to reduce in rank or status; to disgrace; to decompose; to be lowered by erosion.–**degradation** n.

degree n a step in an ascending or descending series; a stage in intensity; the relative quantity in intensity; a unit of measurement in a scale; an academic title awarded as of right or as an honor.

dehumanize vt to remove human qualities from; to deprive of personality or emotion, to render mechanical.–**dehumanization** n.

dehydrate vt to remove water from. * vi to lose water, esp from the bodily tissues.–**dehydration** n.–**dehydrator** n.

de-ice vt to prevent the formation of or to remove ice from a surface.–**de-icer** n.

deify vt (**deifying, deified**) to make into a god; to worship as a god, glorify.–**deification** n.–**deifier** n.

deign vi to condescend; to think it worthy to do (something).

deity n (pl **deities**) a god or goddess; the rank or essence of a god; (**with cap and the**) God.

déjà vu n the illusion that you have already experienced the present situation.

dejected adj depressed; low in spirits.–**dejectedly** adv.–**dejection** n.

delay vt to postpone; to detain, obstruct. * vi to linger. * n a delaying or being delayed; the time period during which something is delayed.

delectable adj delightful, delicious.–**delectably** adv.

delegate vt to appoint as a representative; to give powers or responsibilities to (an agent or assembly). * n a deputy or an elected representative.

delegation n the act of delegating; a group of people empowered to represent others.

delete vt to strike out (something written or printed); to erase.–**deletion** n.

deleterious adj harmful or destructive.

delft, delftware n a type of blue-glazed earthenware, originally from Delft in Holland.

deli n (pl **delis**) (inf) a delicatessen.

deliberate vt to consider carefully. * vi to discuss or debate thoroughly; to consider. * adj well thought out; intentional; cautious.–**deliberately** adv.–**deliberateness** n.–**deliberator** n.

deliberation n careful consideration; thorough discussion; caution.

delicacy n (pl **delicacies**) delicateness; sensibility; a luxurious food.

delicate adj fine in texture; fragile, not robust; requiring tactful handling; of exquisite workmanship.–**delicately** adv.–**delicateness** n.

delicatessen n a store selling prepared foods, esp imported delicacies.

delicious adj having a pleasurable effect on the senses, esp taste; delightful.–**deliciously** adv.

delight vt to please greatly. * vi to have or take great pleasure (in). * n great pleasure; something that causes this.

delightful adj giving great pleasure.–**delightfully** adv.–**delightfulness** n.

delimit vt to fix or mark the boundaries of.–**delimitation** n.

delineate vt to describe in great detail; to represent by drawing.–**delineation** n.–**delineative** adj.

delinquency n (pl **delinquencies**) neglect of or failure in duty; a misdeed; a fault; antisocial or illegal behavior, esp by young people (–also **juvenile delinquency**).–**delinquent** adj, n.

delirium n (pl **deliriums, deliria**) a state of mental disorder, esp caused by a feverish illness; wild enthusiasm.–**delirious** adj.

deliver vt (goods, letters, etc) to transport to a destination; to distribute regularly; to liberate, to rescue; to give birth; to assist at a birth; (blow) to launch; (baseball) to pitch; (speech) to utter.–**deliverable** adj.–**deliverer** n.–**delivery** n.

deliverance n the act of rescuing or liberating.

dell n a small hollow, usu with trees.

delta n the fourth letter of the Greek alphabet; an alluvial deposit at the mouth of a river.–**deltaic** adj.

deltoid adj of the shape of the letter delta; triangular * n (anat) a muscle that lifts the upper arm.

delude vt to mislead, to deceive.–**deluder** n.

deluge n a flood; anything happening in a heavy rush. * vt to inundate.

delusion n a false belief; a persistent false belief that is a symptom of mental illness.–**delusional** adj.

deluxe adj luxurious, of superior quality.

delve vti to search deeply; to dig.–**delver** n.

demagogue, demagog n a political orator who derives power from appealing to popular prejudices.

demand vt to ask for in an authoritative manner. * n a request or claim made with authority for what is due; an urgent claim; desire for goods and services shown by consumers.–**demandable** adj.–**demander** n.

demanding adj constantly making demands; requiring great skill, concentration or effort.–**demandingly** adv.

demarcate vt to delimit; to define or mark the bounds of.–**demarcator** n.

demarcation, demarkation n the act of marking off a boundary or setting a limit to; a limit; the strict separation of the type of work done by members of different trade unions.

demean vt to lower in dignity.–**demeaning** adj.

demeanor, demeanour n behavior; bearing.

demented adj insane, mad.–**dementedly** adv.

dementia n the failure or loss of mental powers.

demigod n a being that is part mortal part god; a god-like individual.–**demigoddess** nf.

demijohn n a large bottle, often in a wicker case.

demise n (formal) death; termination, end. * vt to give or grant by will. * vi to pass by bequest or inheritance.

demo n (pl **demos**) (inf) a demonstration.

demob vt (**demobbing, demobbed**) (inf) to demobilize. * n (inf) demobilization.

demobilize vt to discharge from the armed forces.–**demobilization** n.

democracy n (pl **democracies**) a form of government by the people through elected representatives; a country governed by its people; political, social or legal equality.–**democratic** adj.–**democratically** adv.

democrat n a person who believes in or promotes democracy; (with cap) a member of the Democratic Party in the US.

democratize vt to make democratic. * vi to become democratic.–**democratization** n.

demolish vt (a building) to pull down or knock down; (an argument) to defeat; (inf) to eat up.–**demolisher** n.–**demolition** n.

demon n an evil spirit; a cruel person; someone who is very skilled, energetic, hard-working, etc.–**demonic** adj.–**demonically** adv.

demonize vt to make into or represent as a demon.

demonstrate vt to indicate or represent clearly; to provide certain evidence of, prove; to show how something (a machine, etc) works. * vi to show one's support for a cause, etc by public parades and protests; to act as a demonstrator of machinery, etc.–**demonstrable** adj.–**demonstrably** adv.

demonstration n proof by evidence; a display or exhibition; a display of feeling; a public manifestation of opinion, as by a mass meeting, march, etc; a display of armed force.

demonstrative *adj* displaying one's feelings openly and unreservedly; indicative; conclusive; (*gram*) describing an adjective or pronoun indicating the person or thing referred to.—**demonstratively** *adv.*—**demonstrativeness** *n.*

demonstrator *n* a person who shows consumer goods to the public; one who or that which shows how a machine, etc works; a person who takes part in a public protest.

demoralize *vt* to lower the morale of, discourage.—**demoralization** *n.*—**demoralizer** *n.*

demote *vt* to reduce in rank or position.—**demotion** *n.*

demur *vi* (**demurring, demurred**) to raise objections.—**demurral** *n.*

demure *adj* modest, reserved; affectedly quiet and proper; coy.—**demurely** *adv.*—**demureness** *n.*

demystify *vt* (**demystifying, demystified**) to remove the mystery from; clarify.—**demystification** *n.*

den *n* a cave or lair of a wild beast; a place where people gather for illegal activities; a room in a house for relaxation or study.

denial *n* the act of denying; a refusal of a request, etc; a refusal or reluctance to admit the truth of something.

denier *n* a unit of weight used to measure the fineness of silk, nylon or rayon fiber, esp as used in women's pantyhose, etc.

denigrate *vt* to disparage the character of; to belittle.—**denigration** *n.*—**denigrator** *n.*

denim *n* a hard-wearing cotton cloth, esp used for jeans; (*pl*) denim trousers or jeans.

denizen *n* an inhabitant, resident; an animal or plant established in a region where it is not native.

denomination *n* a name or title; a religious group comprising many local churches, larger than a sect; one of a series of related units, esp monetary.

denominator *n* the part of a fractional expression written below the fraction line.

denote *vt* to indicate, be the sign of; to mean.

denouement, dénouement *n* the resolution of a plot or story; the solution, the outcome.

denounce *vt* to condemn or censure publicly; to inform against; to declare formally the ending of (treaties, etc).—**denouncement** *n.*—**denouncer** *n.*

dense *adj* difficult to see through; massed closely together; dull-witted, stupid.—**densely** *adv.*—**denseness** *n.*

density *n* (*pl* **densities**) the degree of denseness or concentration; stupidity; the ratio of mass to volume.

dent *n* a depression made by pressure or a blow. * *vti* to make a dent or become dented.

dental *adj* of or for the teeth.—**dentally** *adv.*

dentin, dentine *n* the hard, bone-like substance forming the main part of teeth.

dentist *n* a person qualified to treat tooth decay, gum disease, etc.—**dentistry** *n.*

denture *n* (*usu pl*) a set of artificial teeth.

denude *vt* to make naked; to deprive, strip.—**denudation** *n.*—**denuder** *n.*

denunciation *n* the act of denouncing; a threat.—**denunciator** *n.*—**denunciatory** *adj.*

deny *vt* (**denying, denied**) to declare to be untrue; to repudiate; to refuse to acknowledge; to refuse to assent to a request, etc.

deodorant *n* a substance that removes or masks unpleasant odors.—**deodorize** *vt.*

depart *vi* to go away, leave; to deviate (from).

departed *adj* (*time, etc*) long past; (*person*) recently dead.

department *n* a unit of specialized functions into which an organization or business is divided; a province; a realm of activity.—**departmental** *adj.*

department store *n* a large store divided into various departments selling different types of goods.

departure *n* a departing; a deviating from normal practice; a new venture, course of action, etc.

depend *vi* to be determined by or connected with anything; to rely (on), put trust (in); to be reliant on for support, esp financially.

dependable *adj* able to be relied on.—**dependably** *adv.*—**dependability** *n.*

dependant[1], **dependent** *n* a person who is dependent on another, esp financially.

dependant[2], **dependent** *adj* relying on another person, thing, etc for support, money, etc; contingent; subordinate.

dependence, dependance *n* the state of being dependent; reliance, trust; a physical or mental reliance on a drug, person, etc.

dependency *n* (*pl* **dependencies**) dependence; a territory controlled by another country.

depersonalize *vt* to eliminate the individual character from a person, organization, etc; to make impersonal.—**depersonalization** *n.*

depict *vt* to represent pictorially; to describe.—**depicter, depictor** *n.*—**depiction** *n.*

depilatory *n* (*pl* **depilatories**) a substance for removing superfluous hair. * *adj* removing hair.

deplete *vt* to use up a large quantity of.—**depletion** *n.*—**depletive** *adj.*

deplorable *adj* shocking; extremely bad.—**deplorably** *adv.*

deplore *vt* to regret deeply; to complain of; to deprecate.—**deplorer** *n.*—**deploringly** *adv.*

deploy *vt* (*military forces*) to distribute and position strategically. * *vi* to adopt strategic positions within an area.—**deployment** *n.*

depopulate *vt* to reduce the population of.—**depopulation** *n.*—**depopulator** *n.*

deport *vt* to expel (an undesirable person) from a country; to behave (in a certain manner).—**deportation** *n.*

deportee *n* a deported person.

deportment *n* manners; bearing; behavior.

depose *vt* to remove from power; to testify, esp in court.—**deposable** *adj.*—**deposer** *n.*

deposit *vt* to place or lay down; to pay money into a bank or other institution for safekeeping, to earn interest, etc; to pay as a first installment; to let fall, leave. * *n* something deposited for safekeeping; money put in a bank; money given in part payment or security; material left in a layer, eg sediment.

deposition *n* the act of depositing or deposing; a being removed from office or power; a sworn testimony, esp in writing.

depository *n* (*pl* **depositories**) a place where anything is deposited.

depot *n* a warehouse, storehouse; a place for storing military supplies; a military training centre; a bus or railway station.

deprave *vt* to pervert; to corrupt morally.—**depraved** *adj.*—**depravity** *n.*

deprecate *vt* to criticize, esp mildly or politely; to belittle.—**deprecation** *n.*—**deprecative** *adj.*—**deprecator** *n.*

depreciate *vti* to make or become lower in value.—**depreciation** *n.*—**depreciator** *n.*—**depreciatory, depreciative** *adj.*

depress *vt* to push down; to sadden, dispirit; to lessen the activity of.—**depressing** *adj.*—**depressingly** *adv.*

depressant *adj* causing depression. * *n* a substance that reduces the activity of the nervous system; a drug that acts as a depressant.

depressed *adj* cast down in spirits; lowered in position; flattened from above, or vertically.

depression *n* excessive gloom and despondency; an abnormal state of physiological inactivity; a phase of the business cycle characterized by stagnation, widespread unemployment, etc; a falling in or sinking; a lowering of atmospheric pressure, often signalling rain.

depressive adj depressing; tending to suffer from mental depression.–**depressively** adv.

deprive vt to take a thing away from; to prevent from using or enjoying.–**deprivation** n.

deprived adj lacking the essentials of life, such as adequate food, shelter, education, etc.

dept. abbr = department.

depth n deepness; the distance downward or inward; the intensity of emotion or feeling; the profundity of thought; intensity of color; the mid point of the night or winter; the lowness of sound or pitch; the quality of being deep.

deputation n a person or group appointed to represent others.

depute vt to appoint as one's representative; to delegate.

deputize vi to act as deputy.–**deputization** n.

deputy n (pl **deputies**) a delegate, representative, or substitute.

derail vti (train) to cause to leave the rails.–**derailment** n.

derange vt to throw into confusion; to disturb; to make insane.–**deranged** adj.–**derangement** n.

derby n (pl **derbies**) a bowler hat.

deregulate vt to remove (eg government) regulations or controls from (an industry, etc).–**deregulation** n.

derelict adj abandoned, deserted and left to decay; negligent. * n a person abandoned by society; a wrecked ship or vehicle.–**dereliction** n.

deride vt to scorn, mock.–**derision** n.

de rigueur adj required by fashion or etiquette.

derisory adj showing or deserving of derision.

derivation n the tracing of a word to its root; origin; descent.

derivative adj derived from something else; not original. * n something that is derived; a word formed by derivation.–**derivatively** adv.

derive vt to take or receive from a source; to infer, deduce (from). * vi to issue as a derivative (from).

dermatitis n inflammation of the skin.

derogatory adj disparaging; deliberately offensive.–**derogatorily** adv.

derrick n any crane-like apparatus; a tower over an oil well, etc, holding the drilling machinery.

derring-do n bravery, reckless valor.

dervish n a member of a Muslim religious order vowing chastity and poverty, noted for frenzied, whirling dancing.

descant n a musical accompaniment sung or played in counterpoint to the main melody.–also vi.

descend vi to come or climb down; to pass from a higher to a lower place or condition; (with **on, upon**) to make a sudden attack upon, or visit unexpectedly; to sink in morals or dignity; to be derived. * vt to go, pass, or extend down.

descendant n a person who is descended from an ancestor; something derived from an earlier form.

descent n a descending; a downward motion or step; a way down; a slope; a raid or invasion; lineage, ancestry.

describe vt to give a verbal account of; to trace out.–**describable** adj.–**describer** n.

description n a verbal or pictorial account; a sort, a kind.–**descriptive** adj.

desecrate vt to violate a sacred place by destructive or blasphemous behavior.–**desecration** n.–**desecrator, desecrater** n.

desegregate vt to abolish (racial or sexual) segregation in.–**desegregation** n.

desert[1] n (often pl) a deserved reward or punishment.

desert[2] vt to leave, abandon, with no intention of returning; to abscond from the armed forces without permission.–**deserter** n.–**desertion** n.

desert[3] n a dry, barren region, able to support little or no life; a place lacking in some essential quality.

deserve vt to merit or be suitable for (some reward, punishment, etc).–**deserved** adj.–**deservedly** adv.–**deservedness** n.

deserving adj worthy of support, esp financially.

desiccate vti to dry or become dried up; to preserve (food) by drying.–**desiccation** n.

design vt to plan; to create; to devise; to make working drawings for; to intend. * n a working drawing; a mental plan or scheme; the particular form or disposition of something; a decorative pattern; purpose; (pl) dishonest intent.

designate vt to indicate, specify; to name; to appoint to or nominate for a position, office. * adj (after noun) appointed to office but not yet installed.–**designator** n.

designation n the act of designating; nomination; a distinguishing name or title.

designer n a person who designs things; a person who is renowned for creating high-class fashion clothes. * adj (inf) trendy, of the latest, esp expensive, fashion.

designing adj crafty, scheming. * n the art or practice of making designs.

desirable adj arousing (sexual) desire; advisable or beneficial; worth doing.–**desirability** n.–**desirably** adv.

desire vt to long or wish for; to request, ask for. * n a longing for something regarded as pleasurable or satisfying; a request; something desired; sexual craving.

desirous adj desiring; craving.

desist vi to stop (doing something).–**desistance** n.

desk n a piece of furniture with a writing surface and usu drawers; a counter behind which a cashier, etc sits; the section of a newspaper responsible for a particular topic.

desolate adj solitary, lonely; devoid of inhabitants; laid waste; forlorn, disconsolate; overwhelmed with grief. * vt to depopulate; to devastate, lay waste; to make barren or unfit for habitation; to leave alone, forsake, abandon; to overwhelm with grief.–**desolation** n.

despair vi to have no hope. * n utter loss of hope; something that causes despair.

despatch see **dispatch**.

desperado n (pl **desperadoes, desperados**) a violent criminal.

desperate adj (almost) hopeless; reckless through lack of hope; urgently requiring (money, etc); (remedy) extreme, dangerous.–**desperately** adv.–**desperation** n.

despise vt to regard with contempt or scorn; to consider as worthless, inferior.–**despicable** adj.–**despicably** adv.

despite prep in spite of.

despoil vt to plunder, rob.–**despoiler** n.–**despoliation** n.

despond vi to lose hope, to be dejected.–**despondency, despondence** n.–**despondent** adj.–**despondently** adv.

despot n a ruler possessing absolute power; a tyrant.–**despotic, despotical** adj.–**despotically** adv.

dessert n the sweet course at the end of a meal.

dessertspoon n a spoon in between a teaspoon and a tablespoon in size, used for eating desserts.

destination n the place to which a person or thing is going.

destine vt to set aside for some specific purpose; to predetermine; intend.

destiny n (pl **destinies**) the power supposedly determining the course of events; the future to which any person or thing is destined; a predetermined course of events.

destitute adj (with **of**) lacking some quality; lacking the basic necessities of life, very poor.

destitution n extreme poverty.

destroy vt to demolish, ruin, to put an end to; to kill.

destroyer n one who or that which destroys; a fast small warship.

destruction n the act or process of destroying or being destroyed; ruin.

destructive adj causing destruction; (with **of** or **to**) ruinous; (criticism) intended to discredit, negative.–**destructively** adv.

desultory adj going aimlessly from one activity or subject to another, not methodical.–**desultorily** adv.–**desultoriness** n.

detach vt to release; to separate from a larger group; (mil) to send off on special assignment.–**detachable** adj.–**detachability** n.

detached adj separate; free from bias or emotion; (house) not joined to another; aloof.

detachment n indifference; freedom from emotional involvement or bias; the act of detaching; a thing detached; a body of troops detached from the main body and sent on special service.

detail vt to describe fully; (mil) to set apart for a particular duty. * n an item; a particular or minute account; (art) treatment of smaller parts; a reproduction of a smaller part of a picture, statue, etc; a small detachment for special service.

detain vt to place in custody or confinement; to delay.–**detainment** n.

detect vt to discover the existence or presence of; to notice.–**detectable** adj.–**detectability** n.

detection n a discovery or being discovered; the job or process of detecting.

detective n a person or a police officer employed to find evidence of crimes.

detector n a device for detecting the presence of something.

détente, detente n relaxation of tension between countries.

detention n the act of detaining or withholding; a being detained; confinement; the act of being kept in (school after hours) as a punishment.

deter vt (**deterring, deterred**) to discourage or prevent (from acting).–**determent** n.

detergent n a cleaning agent, esp one made from a chemical compound rather than fats, as soap. * adj having cleaning power.

deteriorate vt to make or become worse.–**deterioration** n.–**deteriorative** adj.

determinate adj definitely bounded in time, space, position, etc; fixed; clearly defined; distinct; resolute, decisive.–**determinately** adv.–**determinateness** n.

determination n the act or process of making a decision; a decision resolving a dispute; firm intention; resoluteness.

determine vt to fix or settle officially; to find out; to regulate; to impel. * vi to come to a decision.

determined adj full of determination, resolute.–**determinedly** adv.–**determinedness** n.

deterrent n something that deters; a nuclear weapon that deters attack through fear of retaliation. * adj deterring.–**deterrence** n.

detest vt to dislike intensely.–**detestation** n.

dethrone vt to remove from a throne, to depose.–**dethronement** n.

detonate vti to explode or cause to explode rapidly and violently.–**detonation** n.

detonator n a device that sets off an explosion.

detour n a deviation from an intended course, esp one serving as an alternative to a more direct route. * vti to make or send by a detour.

detoxify vt (**detoxifying, detoxified**) to extract poison or toxins from.–**detoxification** n.

detract vt to take away. * vi to take away (from).–**detractor** n.

detraction n defamation; slander; depreciation.–**detractive** adj.–**detractively** adv.

detriment n (a cause of) damage or injury.–**detrimental** adj.–**detrimentally** adv.

detrition n a wearing down by rubbing or friction.

detritus n debris; loose matter, esp formed by rubbing away or erosion of a larger mass (eg a rock).–**detrital** adj.

deuce[1] n a playing card or dice with two spots; (tennis) the score of forty-all.

deuce[2] interj (inf) the devil!–an exclamation of surprise or annoyance.

devalue vt (**devaluing, devalued**) to reduce the exchange value of (a currency).–**devaluation** n.

devastate vt to lay waste; to destroy; to overwhelm.–**devastatingly** adv.–**devastation** n.–**devastator** n.

develop vt to evolve; to bring to maturity; to show the symptoms of (eg a habit, a disease); to treat a photographic film or plate to reveal an image; to improve the value of. * vi to grow (into); to become apparent.

developer n a person who develops; a person or organization that develops property; a reagent for developing photographs.

development n the process of growing or developing; a new situation that emerges; a piece of land or property that has been developed.–**developmental** adj.

deviant adj that which deviates from an accepted norm. * n a person whose behavior deviates from the accepted standards of society.–**deviance, deviancy** n.

deviate vi to diverge from a course, topic, principle, etc.–**deviator** n.

deviation n a deviating from normal behavior, official ideology, etc; deflection of a compass needle by magnetic disturbance.

device n a machine, implement, etc for a particular purpose; an invention; a scheme, a plot.

devil n (with cap) in Christian and Jewish theology, the supreme spirit of evil, Satan; any evil spirit; an extremely wicked person; (inf) a reckless, high-spirited person. * vb (**deviling, deviled** or **devilling, devilled**) vt to cook food with a hot seasoning.

devilish adj fiendish; mischievous. * adv (inf) very.–**devilishly** adv.–**devilishness** n.

devil-may-care adj audacious, contemptuous of authority.

devil's advocate n a person who advocates an opposing cause, esp for the sake of argument.

devious adj indirect; not straightforward; underhand, deceitful.–**deviously** adv.–**deviousness** n.

devise vt to invent, contrive; to plan; (law) to leave (real estate) by will. * n (law) a bequest (of real estate); property so bequeathed.–**deviser** n.

devoid adj (with of) lacking; free from.

devolution n a transfer of authority, esp from a central government to regional governments; a passing on from one person to another.

devolve vti to hand on or be handed on to a successor or deputy.–**devolvement** n.

devote vt to give or use for a particular activity or purpose.–**devoted** adj.–**devotedly** adv.–**devotedness** n.

devotee n (with of or to) a person who is enthusiastically or fanatically devoted to something; a religious zealot.

devotion n given to religious worship; piety; strong affection or attachment (to); ardor; (pl) prayers.–**devotional** adj.

devour vt to eat up greedily; to consume; to absorb eagerly by the senses or mind.

devout adj very religious, pious; sincere, dedicated.–**devoutly** adv.–**devoutness** n.

dew n air moisture, deposited on a cool surface, esp at night.

dewlap n a flap of skin hanging under the throat of some animals, eg cows; loose skin on the throat of an elderly person.

dexterity n manual skill, adroitness.

dexterous adj possessing manual skill; quick, mentally or physically; adroit; clever.–**dexterously** adv.–**dexterousness** n.

dextrose n a form of glucose found in fruit, honey and animal tissues.

dextrous adj dexterous.

diabetes n a medical disorder marked by the persistent and excessive discharge of urine.

diabetic adj of or suffering from diabetes. * n a person with diabetes.

diabolic, diabolical adj devilish; cruel, wicked.–**diabolically** adv.–**diabolicalness** n.

diabolism n devil worship; witchcraft.–**diabolist** n.

diaeresis see **dieresis**.

diagnose vt to ascertain by diagnosis.–**diagnosable, diagnoseable** adj.

diagnosis n (pl **diagnoses**) the identification of a disease from its symptoms; the analysis of the nature or cause of a problem.–**diagnostician** n.

diagnostic adj of or aiding diagnosis; characteristic * n a symptom distinguishing a disease; a characteristic; (pl: used as sing) the art of diagnosing.–**diagnostically** adv.

diagonal adj slanting from one corner to an opposite corner of a polygon. * n a straight line connecting opposite corners.–**diagonally** adv.

diagram n a figure or plan drawn in outline to illustrate the form or workings of something. * vt (**diagraming, diagramed** or **diagramming, diagrammed**) to demonstrate in diagram form.

dial n the face of a watch or clock; a graduated disk with a pointer used in various instruments; the control on a radio or television set indicating wavelength or station. * vt (**dialling, dialled** or **dialing, dialed**) to measure or indicate by a dial; to make a telephone connection by using a dial or numbered keypad.

dialect n the form of language spoken in a particular region or social class.–**dialectal** adj.–**dialectally** adv.

dialog n a conversation, esp in a play or novel; an exchange of opinions, negotiation.–also **dialogue**.

dial tone n a sound heard over the telephone indicating that the line is clear.

dialysis n (pl **dialyses**) the removal of impurities from the blood by filtering it through a membrane.–**dialytic** adj.–**dialytically** adv.

diamanté adj glittering with rhinestones, sequins or imitation jewels. * n a material ornamented in this way.

diameter n a straight line bisecting a circle; the length of this line.

diametric, diametrical adj of or along a diameter; completely opposed.–**diametrically** adv.

diamond n a valuable gem, a crystallized form of pure carbon; (baseball) the playing field, esp the infield; a suit of playing cards denoted by a red lozenge. * adj composed of, or set with diamonds; shaped like a diamond; denoting the 60th (or 75th) anniversary of an event.

diaper n a square of absorbent material arranged between a baby's legs and fastened at its waist to absorb excrement.

diaphragm n the midriff, a muscular structure separating the chest from the abdomen; any thin dividing membrane; a device for regulating the aperture of a camera lens; a contraceptive cap covering the cervix.–**diaphragmatic** adj.

diarist n one who keeps a diary; the author of a diary.

diarrhea, diarrhoea n excessive looseness of the bowels.– **diarrheal, diarrhoeal, diarrheic, diarrhoeic** adj.

diary n (pl **diaries**) a daily record of personal thoughts, events, or business appointments; a book for keeping a daily record.

diatribe n a lengthy and abusive verbal attack.

dice n (the pl of **die**[2] but used as sing) a small cube with numbered sides used in games of chance. * vt to gamble using dice; to cut (food) into small cubes.

dicey adj (**dicier, diciest**) (inf) risky.

dichotomy n (pl **dichotomies**) a division into two parts.– **dichotomous, dichotomic** adj.

dicta see **dictum**.

dictate vt to say or read for another person to write or for a machine to record; to pronounce, order with authority. * vi to give dictation; to give orders (to). * n an order, rule, or command; (usu pl) an impulse, ruling principle.

dictation n the act of dictating words to be written down by another; the thing dictated; an authoritative utterance.

dictator n a ruler with absolute authority, usu acquired by force.–**dictatorial** adj.–**dictatorially** adv.

dictatorship n the office or government of a dictator; a country governed by a dictator; absolute power.

diction n a way of speaking, enunciation; a person's choice of words.

dictionary n (pl **dictionaries**) a reference book containing the words of a language or branch of knowledge alphabetically arranged, with their meanings, pronunciation, origin, etc.

dictum n (pl **dictums, dicta**) an authoritative pronouncement.

did see **do**.

diddle vi (sl) to cheat.–**diddler** n.

didn't = did not.

die[1] vb (**dying, died**) vi to cease existence; to become dead; to stop functioning; to feel a deep longing; (with **out**) to become extinct. * vi to experience a particular form of death.

die[2] n a dice.

die[3] n (pl **dies**) an engraved stamp for pressing coins; a casting mold; a tool used in cutting the threads of screws or bolts, etc.

diehard n a person who prolongs futile resistance, usu an extreme conservative.

dieresis n (pl **diereses**) a sign (¨) placed over the second of two separate vowels to show that each has a separate sound in pronunciation, as Zo'; a division in a line of verse.–also **diaeresis**.–**dieretic, diaeretic** adj.

diesel n a vehicle driven by a diesel engine.

diesel oil n a form of petroleum for diesel engines, ignited by the heat of compression.

diet n food selected to adjust weight, to control illness, etc; the food and drink usually consumed by a person or animal. * vt to put on a diet. * vi to eat according to a special diet.–**dieter** n.

dietary adj pertaining to a diet.

dietetics n (used as sing) the scientific study of diet and nutrition.–**dietitian, dietician** n.

differ vi to be unlike, distinct (from); to disagree.

difference n the act or state of being unlike; disparity; a distinguishing feature; the amount or manner of being different; the result of the subtraction of one quantity from another; a disagreement or argument.

different adj distinct, separate; unlike, not the same; unusual.– **differently** adv.

differential adj of or showing a difference. * n something that marks the difference between comparable things; the difference in wage rates for different types of labor, esp within an industry.–**differentially** adv.

differentiate vt to make different; to become specialized; to note differences.–**differentiation** n.

difficult adj hard to understand; hard to make, do, or carry out; not easy to please.–**difficulty** n.

diffident adj shy, lacking self-confidence, not assertive.–**diffidently** adv.–**diffidence** n.

diffraction n the breaking up of a ray of light into colored bands of the spectrum, or into a series of light and dark bands.–**diffract** vti.–**diffractive** adj.

diffuse vt to spread widely in all directions. * vti (gases, fluids, small particles) to intermingle. * adj spread widely, not concentrated; wordy, not concise.–**diffusely** adv.–**diffusion** n.

dig vt (**digging, dug**) to use a tool or hands, claws, etc in making a hole in the ground; to unearth by digging; to excavate; to investigate; to thrust (into); to nudge; (sl) to understand, approve. * n (sl) a thrust; an archaeological excavation; a cutting remark.

digest[1] vt to convert (food) into assimilable form; to reduce (facts, laws, etc) to convenient form by classifying or summarizing; to form a clear view of (a situation) by reflection. * vi to become digested.

digest[2] n an abridgment of any written matter; a periodical synopsis of published or broadcast material.

digestion n the act or process of digesting.–**digestional** adj.

digestive adj pertaining to, performing, or aiding, digestion. * n a thing that aids digestion; a sweet wholemeal biscuit.

digger n an implement or machine for digging.

digit n any of the basic counting units of a number system, including zero; a human finger or toe.

digital adj of, having or using digits; using numbers rather than a dial to display measurements; of or pertaining to a digital computer or digital recording.–**digitally** adv.

digital audio tape n a magnetic tape capable of being used in digital recording, giving high-quality audio reproduction.

digital computer n a computer that processes information in the form of characters and digits in electronic binary code.

digital recording n the conversion of sound into discrete electronic pulses (representing binary digits) for recording.

dignify vt (**dignifying, dignified**) to confer dignity; to exalt; to add the appearance of distinction (to something).—**dignified** adj.

dignitary n (pl **dignitaries**) a person in a high position or rank.

dignity n (pl **dignities**) noble, serious, or formal manner and appearance; sense of self-respect, worthiness; a high rank, eg in the government.

digress vi to stray from the main subject in speaking or writing.—**digression** n.

dike n an embankment to prevent flooding or form a barrier to the sea; a ditch; a causeway.—also **dyke**.

dilapidate vt to bring into partial ruin by neglect or misuse. * vi to become dilapidated.—**dilapidated** adj.—**dilapidation** n.

dilate vti to make wider or larger; to increase the width of; to expand, amplify, enlarge; to extend in time, protract, prolong, lengthen. * vi to become wider or larger; to spread out, widen, enlarge, expand; to discourse or write at large; to enlarge.—**dilatable** adj.—**dilatability** n.

dilation n the action or process of dilating; something dilated.

dilatory adj tardy; causing or meant to cause delay.—**dilatorily** adv.—**dilatoriness** n.

dilemma n a situation where each of two alternative courses is undesirable; any difficult problem or choice.—**dilemmatic** adj.

dilettante n (pl **dilettantes, dilettanti**) a person who dabbles in a subject for amusement only.

diligence n careful attention; assiduity; industry.—**diligent** adj.—**diligently** adv.

dill n a yellow-flowered herb whose leaves and seeds are used for flavoring and in medicines.

dillydally vi (**dillydallying, dillydallied**) (inf) to dawdle, loiter.

dilute vt to thin down, esp by mixing with water; to weaken the strength of. * adj diluted.—**diluter, dilutor** n.—**diluteness** n.

dilution n the act of diluting; a weak liquid.

dim adj (**dimmer, dimmest**) faintly lit; not seen, heard, understood, etc clearly; gloomy; unfavorable; (inf) stupid. * vti (**dimming, dimmed**) to make or cause to become dark.—**dimly** adv.—**dimness** n.

dime n a US or Canadian coin worth ten cents.

dimension n any linear measurement of width, length, or thickness; extent; size.

diminish vti to make or become smaller in size, amount, or importance.—**diminishable** adj.—**diminishment** n.

diminution n act or process of being made smaller.

diminutive adj very small. * n a word formed by a suffix to mean small (eg duckling) or to convey affection (eg Freddie).

dimmer n a switch for reducing the brightness of an electric light.

dimple n a small hollow, usu on the cheek or chin. * vti to make or become dimpled; to reveal dimples.—**dimply** adj.

din n a loud persistent noise. * vt (**dinning, dinned**) to make a din; (with **into**) to instill by continual repetition.

dine vi to eat dinner. * vt to entertain to dinner.

diner n a person who dines; a dining car on a train; a small, cheap eating place.

ding-dong n the sound of a metallic body produced by blows, as a bell; (inf) a violent argument. * adj characterized by a rapid succession of blows; (insults, etc) vigorously maintained. * vi to ring as or like a bell. * vt to assail with constant repetition; to repeat with mechanical regularity.

dinghy n (pl **dinghies**) a small open boat propelled by oars or sails; a small inflatable boat.

dingo n (pl **dingoes**) an Australian wild dog.

dingy adj (**dingier, dingiest**) dirty-looking, shabby.—**dingily** adv.—**dinginess** n.

dinner n the principal meal of the day; a formal meal in honor of a person or occasion.

dinner jacket n a tuxedo.

dinosaur n any of an order of extinct reptiles, typically enormous in size; (inf) a person or thing regarded as outdated.

diocese n the district over which a bishop has authority.

diode n a semiconductor device for converting alternating to direct current; a basic thermionic valve with two electrodes.

dioxide n an oxide with two molecules of oxygen to one molecule of the other constituents.

dip vt (**dipping, dipped**) to put (something) under the surface (as of a liquid) and lift quickly out again; to immerse (as a sheep in an antiseptic solution). * vi to go into water and come out quickly; to suddenly drop down or sink out of sight; to read superficially; to slope downward. * n a dipping of any kind; a sudden drop; a mixture in which to dip something.

diphtheria n an acute infectious disease causing inflammation of the throat and breathing difficulties.—**diphtherial** adj.

diphthong n the union of two vowel sounds pronounced in one syllable; a ligature.—**diphthongal** adj.

diploma n (pl **diplomas**) a certificate given by a college or university to its graduating students; the course of study leading to a diploma; (pl often **diplomata**) an official document, a charter.

diplomacy n (pl **diplomacies**) the management of relations between nations; skill in handling affairs without arousing hostility.—**diplomat** n.—**diplomatic, diplomatical** adj.—**diplomatically** adv.

dipper n a ladle; any of various diving birds.

dippy adj (**dippier, dippiest**) (sl) eccentric; crazy.

dipsomania n a compulsive craving for alcohol.

dipsomaniac n a person with an uncontrollable craving for alcohol. * adj of or having dipsomania.

dipstick n a rod with graduated markings to measure fluid level.

dire adj dreadful; ominous; desperately urgent.—**direly** adv.—**direness** n.

direct adj straight; in an unbroken line, with nothing in between; frank; truthful. * vt to manage, to control; to tell or show the way; to point to, to aim at; (a letter or parcel) to address; to carry out the organizing and supervision of; to train and lead performances; to command. * vi to determine a course; to act as a director.—**directness** n.

direct current n an electric current that flows in one direction only.

direction n management, control; order, command; a knowing or telling what to do, where to go, etc; any way in which one may face or point; (pl) instructions.—**directional** adj.

directive adj directing; authoritatively guiding or ruling. * n an order, instruction.

directly adv in a direct manner; immediately; in a short while.

director n person who directs, esp the production of a show for stage or screen; one of the persons directing the affairs of a company or an institution.—**directorial** adj.—**directorship** n.

directorate n a board of directors; the position of a director (–also **directorship**).

directory n (pl **directories**) an alphabetical or classified list, as of telephone numbers, members of an organization, charities, etc.

dirge n a song or hymn played or sung at a funeral; a slow, mournful piece of music.

dirndl n a woman's full skirt with a tight waistband.

dirt n filth; loose earth; obscenity; scandal. * adj made of dirt.

dirty adj (**dirtier, dirtiest**) filthy; unclean; dishonest; mean; (weather) stormy; obscene. * vti (**dirtying, dirtied**) to make or become dirty.—**dirtily** adv.—**dirtiness** n.

disability n (pl **disabilities**) a lack of physical, mental or social fitness; something that disables, a handicap.

disable vt to make useless; to cripple; (law) to disqualify.–**disablement** n.

disabuse vt to free from a mistaken impression.

disadvantage n an unfavorable condition or situation; loss, damage. * vt to put at a disadvantage.

disadvantaged adj deprived or discriminated against in social and economic terms.

disadvantageous adj causing disadvantage; unfavorable.–**disadvantageously** adv.

disaffected adj discontented, no longer loyal.–**disaffectedly** adv.–**disaffection** n.

disagree vi (**disagreeing, disagreed**) to differ in opinion; to quarrel; (with **with**) to have a bad effect on.–**disagreement** n.

disagreeable adj nasty, bad tempered.–**disagreeableness** n.–**disagreeably** adv.

disallow vt to refuse to allow or to accept the truth or value of.–**disallowance** n.

disappear vi to pass from sight completely; to fade into nothing.–**disappearance** n.

disappoint vt to fail to fulfil the hopes of (a person).–**disappointed** adj.–**disappointing** adj.–**disappointingly** adv.

disappointment n the frustration of one's hopes; annoyance due to failure; a person or thing that disappoints.

disapprobation n disapproval, condemnation.

disapprove vti to express or have an unfavorable opinion (of).–**disapprovingly** adv.–**disapproval** n.

disarm vt to deprive of weapons or means of defence; to defuse (a bomb); to conciliate. * vi to abolish or reduce national armaments.

disarmament n the reduction or abolition of a country's armed forces and weaponry.

disarming adj allaying opposition, conciliating; ingratiating; endearing.–**disarmingly** adv.

disarray n disorder, confusion; undress. * vt to put into disorder.

disaster n a devastating and sudden misfortune; utter failure.–**disastrous** adj.–**disastrously** adv.

disavow vt to deny, disclaim; to repudiate.–**disavowal** n.–**disavower** n.

disband vt to disperse; to break up and separate.–**disbandment** n.

disbelieve vt to believe to be a lie. * vi to have no faith (in).–**disbeliever** n.–**disbelief** n.

disburse vt to pay out.–**disbursement** n.–**disburser** n.

disc see disk.

discard vti to cast off, get rid of; (cards) to throw away a card from one's hand. * n something discarded; (cards) a discarded card.

discern vt to perceive; to see clearly.–**discernible** adj.–**discernibly** adv.–**discerning** adj.–**discernment** n.

discharge vt to unload; to send out, emit; to release, acquit; to dismiss from employment; to shoot a gun; to fulfill, as duties. * vi to unload; (gun) to be fired; (fluid) to pour out. * n the act or process of discharging; something that is discharged; an authorization for release, acquittal, dismissal, etc.

disciple n a person who believes in and helps to spread another's teachings, a follower; (with cap) one of the twelve apostles of Christ.–**discipleship** n.

disciplinarian n a person who insists on strict discipline.

discipline n a field of learning; training and conditioning to produce obedience and self-control; punishment; the maintenance of order and obedience as a result of punishment; a system of rules of behavior. * vt to punish to enforce discipline; to train by instruction; to bring under control.–**disciplinary** adj.

disclaim vi to deny connection with; to renounce all legal claim to.

disclaimer n a denial of legal responsibility; a written statement embodying this.

disclose vt to bring into the open, to reveal.–**disclosure** n.

disco n (pl **discos**) (inf) a discotheque.

discolor, discolour vti to ruin the color of; to fade, stain.–**discoloration** n.

discomfit vt to defeat; to rout; to frustrate; to thwart; to disconcert.–**discomfiture** n.

discompose vt to disturb the calmness of; to ruffle.–**discomposure** n.

disconcert vt to confuse; to upset; to embarrass.–**disconcerting** adj.–**disconcertingly** adv.

disconnect vt to separate or break the connection of.–**disconnection** n.

disconsolate adj miserable; dejected.–**disconsolately** adv.–**disconsolation** n.

discontent n lack of contentment, dissatisfaction (–also **discontentment**). * adj not content; dissatisfied; discontented. * vt to deprive of contentment; to dissatisfy.

discontinue vti to stop or come to a stop; to give up, esp the production of something; (law) to terminate (a suit).

discord n lack of agreement, strife; (mus) a lack of harmony; harsh clashing sounds.

discordant adj at variance; inharmonious; jarring; incongruous.–**discordance, discordancy** n.–**discordantly** adv.

discotheque, discothèque n an occasion when people gather to dance to recorded pop music; a club or party, etc where this takes place; equipment for playing such music.

discount n a reduction in the amount or cost; the percentage charged for doing this. * vt to deduct from the amount, cost; to allow for exaggeration; to disregard; to make less effective by anticipation. * vi to make and give discounts.–**discountable** adj.–**discounter** n.

discourage vt to deprive of the will or courage (to do something); to try to prevent; to hinder.–**discouragement** n.–**discouragingly** adv.

discourse n a formal speech or writing; conversation. * vi to talk or write about.

discourteous adj lacking in courtesy, rude.–**discourteously** adv.–**discourtesy** n.

discover vt to see, find or learn of for the first time.–**discoverable** adj.–**discoverer** n.

discovery n (pl **discoveries**) the act of discovering or state of being discovered; something discovered; (law) a process obliging on the parties to an action to disclose relevant facts or documents.

discredit n damage to a reputation; doubt; disgrace; lack of credibility. * vt to damage the reputation of; to cast doubt on the authority or credibility of.

discreet adj wisely cautious, prudent; unobtrusive.–**discreetly** adv.–**discreetness** n.

discrepancy n (pl **discrepancies**) difference; a disagreement, as between figures in a total.

discrete adj individually distinct; discontinuous.–**discretely** adv.–**discreteness** n.

discretion n the freedom to judge or to choose; prudence; wise judgment; skill.

discretionary adj left to or done at one's own discretion.

discriminate vi to be discerning in matters of taste or judgment; to make a distinction; to treat differently, esp unfavorably due to prejudice.–**discrimination** n.

discriminatory adj discriminating; showing prejudice or favoritism; biased.–**discriminatorily** adv.

discursive adj wandering from one subject to another; digressive.–**discursively** adv.–**discursiveness** n.

discus n (pl **discuses, disci**) a heavy disk with a thickened middle, thrown by athletes.

discuss vt to talk over; to investigate by reasoning or argument.–**discussion** n.

disdain vt to scorn, treat with contempt. * n scorn; a feeling of contemptuous superiority.–**disdainful** adj.–**disdainfully** adv.

disease n an unhealthy condition in an organism caused by infection, poisoning, etc; sickness; a harmful condition or situation.–**diseased** adj.

disembark vti to land from a ship, debark.–**disembarkation** n.

disembarrass vt to free from embarrassment; to relieve (of); to disentangle.–**disembarrassment** n.

disembody vi (**disembodying, disembodied**) to free (a soul, spirit, etc) from the body.–**disembodiment** n.

disembowel vt (**disemboweling, disemboweled** or **disembowelling, disembowelled**) to remove the entrails of; to remove the substance of.–**disembowelment** n.

disenchant vt to disillusion.–**disenchantment** n.

disengage vt to separate or free from engagement or obligation; to detach, to release.–**disengaged** adj.–**disengagement** n.

disentangle vt to untangle; to free from complications.–**disentanglement** n.

disfavor, disfavour n dislike; disapproval. * vt to treat with disfavor.

disfigure vt to spoil the beauty or appearance of.–**disfigurer** n.

disfigurement, disfiguration n the act of disfiguring; a disfigured state; a thing that disfigures; a blemish, a defect.

disgorge vt to emit violently from the throat, to vomit; to empty; to surrender (eg stolen property).–**disgorgement** n.

disgrace n a loss of trust, favor, or honor; something that disgraces. * vt to bring disgrace or shame upon.–**disgraceful** adj.–**disgracefully** adv.

disgruntled adj dissatisfied, resentful.–**disgruntlement** n.

disguise vt to hide what one is by appearing as something else; to hide what (a thing) really is. * n the use of a changed appearance to conceal identity; a false appearance.–**disguisedly** adv.–**disguiser** n.

disgust n sickening dislike; repugnance; aversion. * vt to cause disgust in.–**disgustedly** adv.

dish n any of various shallow concave vessels to serve food in; the amount of food served in a dish; the food served; a shallow concave object, as a dish aerial. * vt (with **out**) (inf) to distribute freely; (with **up**) to serve food at mealtimes.

dish antenna, dish aerial n a microwave antenna used in radar, telescopes, telecommunications, etc having a concave reflector.

disharmony n (pl **disharmonies**) a lack of harmony between sounds; discord; a discordant situation, etc.–**disharmonious** adj.

dishearten vt to discourage.–**dishearteningly** adv.–**disheartenment** n.

disheveled, dishevelled adj rumpled, untidy.–**dishevelment** n.

dishonest adj not honest.–**dishonestly** adv.–**dishonesty** n.

dishonor, dishonour n loss of honor; disgrace, shame. * vt to bring shame on, to disgrace; to refuse to pay, as a check.–**dishonorable, dishonourable** adj.–**dishonorably, dishonourably** adv.

dishwasher n an appliance for washing dishes; a person employed to wash dishes.

dishy adj (**dishier, dishiest**) (inf) physically attractive, good-looking.

disillusion vt to free from (mistaken) ideals or illusions. * n the state of being disillusioned.–**disillusionment** n.

disincentive n a discouragement to action or effort.

disinclined adj unwilling.

disinfect vt to destroy germs.–**disinfection** n.

disinfectant n any chemical agent that inhibits the growth of or destroys germs.

disinformation n false information given out by intelligence agencies to mislead foreign spies.

disingenuous adj insincere, not candid or straightforward.–**disingenuously** adv.–**disingenuousness** n.

disinherit vt to deprive of the right to an inheritance.–**disinheritance** n.

disintegrate vti to break or cause to break into separate pieces.–**disintegration** n.–**disintegrator** n.

disinter vt (**disinterring, disinterred**) to take out of a grave; to bring out from obscurity, to unearth.–**disinterment** n.

disinterested adj impartial; objective.–**disinterestedly** adv.–**disinterestedness** n.

disjoint vt to dislocate; to take to pieces.–**disjointed** adj incoherent, muddled, esp of speech or writing.–**disjointedly** adv.–**disjointedness** n.

disk n any flat, thin circular body; something resembling this, as the sun; (comput) a storage device in a computer, either floppy or hard; a cylindrical pad of cartilage between the vertebrae; a gramophone record.–also **disc**.

disk drive n (comput) a mechanism that allows a computer to read data from, and write data to, a disk.

dislike vt to consider unpleasant. * n aversion, distaste.–**dislikable, dislikeable** adj.

dislocate vt to put (a joint) out of place, to displace; to upset the working of.–**dislocation** n.

dislodge vt to force or move out of a hiding place, established position, etc.–**dislodgment, dislodgement** n.

disloyal adj unfaithful; false to allegiance, disaffected.–**disloyally** adv.–**disloyalty** n.

dismal adj gloomy, miserable, sad; (inf) feeble, worthless. –**dismally** adv.

dismantle vt to pull down; to take apart.–**dismantlement** n.

dismay n apprehension, discouragement. * vt to fill with dismay.

dismember vt to cut or tear off the limbs from; to cut or divide into pieces.–**dismemberment** n.

dismiss vt to send away; to remove from an office or employment; to stop thinking about; (law) to reject a further hearing (in court).–**dismissible** adj.–**dismissal** n.

dismissive adj rejecting; offhand.–**dismissively** adv.

dismount vti to alight from a horse or bicycle; to remove from a mount or setting.

disobedience n the withholding of obedience; a refusal to obey; violation of a command by omitting to conform to it, or of a prohibition by acting in defiance of it; an instance of this.–**disobedient** adj.–**disobediently** adv.

disobey vt (**disobeying, disobeyed**) to refuse to follow orders.

disorder n lack of order; untidiness; a riot; an illness or interruption of the normal functioning of the body or mind. * vt to throw into confusion; to upset.–**disorderliness** n.–**disorderly** adj.

disorganize vt to confuse or disrupt an orderly arrangement.–**disorganization** n.

disorient, disorientate vt to cause the loss of sense of time, place or identity; to confuse.–**disorientation** n.

disown vt to refuse to acknowledge as one's own.

disparage vt to belittle.–**disparagement** n.–**disparagingly** adv.

disparate adj unequal, completely different.–**disparately** adv.–**disparity** n.

dispassionate adj unemotional; impartial.–**dispassionately** adv.–**dispassionateness** n.

dispatch vt to send off somewhere; to perform speedily; to kill. * n a sending off (of a letter, a messenger etc); promptness; haste; a written message, esp of news.–also **despatch**.–**dispatcher** n.

dispel vt (**dispelling, dispelled**) to drive away and scatter.

dispensable adj able to be done without; unimportant.–**dispensability** n.

dispensary n (pl **dispensaries**) a place in a hospital, a chemist shop, etc where medicines are made up and dispensed; a place where medical treatment is available.

dispensation *n* the act of distributing or dealing out; exemption from a rule, penalty, etc.

dispense *vt* to deal out, distribute; to prepare and distribute medicines; to administer.

disperse *vt* to scatter in different directions; to cause to evaporate; to spread (knowledge); to separate (light, etc) into different wavelengths. * *vi* to separate, become dispersed.—**dispersion** *n*.

dispirited *adj* depressed, discouraged.—**dispiritedly** *adv*.

displace *vt* to take the place of, to oust; to remove from a position of authority.—**displacement** *n*.

display *vt* to show, expose to view; to exhibit ostentatiously. * *n* a displaying; an eye-catching arrangement, exhibition; a computer monitor for presenting visual information.

displease *vt* to cause offense or annoyance to.

displeasure *n* a feeling of being displeased; dissatisfaction.

disport *vt* to amuse or divert (oneself) * *vi* to display gaily.

disposable *adj* designed to be discarded after use; available for use. * *n* something disposable, eg a baby's diaper.

disposal *n* a disposing of something; order, arrangement.

dispose *vt* to place in order, arrange; to influence. * *vi* to deal with or settle; to give, sell or transfer to another; to throw away.

disposition *n* a natural way of behaving toward others; tendency; arrangement.—**dispositional** *adj*.

dispossess *vt* to deprive, rid (of); to eject.—**dispossession** *n*.—**dispossessor** *n*.

disproportion *n* a lack of symmetry, a being out of proportion. * *vt* to render or make out of due proportion.—**disproportionate** *adj*.—**disproportionately** *adv*.

disprove *vt* to prove (a claim, etc) to be incorrect.—**disprovable** *adj*.

disputable *adj* likely to cause dispute, arguable.—**disputability** *n*.—**disputably** *adv*.

disputant *n* a person involved in a dispute.

disputatious *adj* fond of argument, contentious.—**disputatiously** *adv*.—**disputatiousness** *n*.

dispute *vt* to make the subject of an argument or debate; to query the validity of. * *vi* to argue. * *n* an argument; a quarrel.

disqualify *vt* (**disqualifying, disqualified**) to make ineligible because of a violation of rules; to make unfit or unsuitable, to disable.—**disqualification** *n*.—**disqualifier** *n*.

disquiet *vt* to trouble, disturb; to make uneasy or restless. * *n* disturbance; uneasiness, anxiety, worry; restlessness. * *adj* restless; uneasy; disturbed.—**disquieting** *adj*.

disregard *vt* to pay no attention to; to consider as of little or no importance. * *n* lack of attention, neglect.

disrepair *n* a worn-out condition through neglect of repair.

disreputable *adj* of bad reputation; not respectable; discreditable.—**disreputably** *adv*.

disrepute *n* disgrace, discredit.

disrespect *n* lack of respect, rudeness.—**disrespectful** *adj*.—**disrespectfully** *adv*.

disrobe *vt* to undress; to uncover.

disrupt *vti* to break up; to create disorder or confusion; to interrupt.—**disruption** *n*.—**disruptive** *adj*.—**disruptively** *adv*.

dissatisfactory *adj* unsatisfactory.

dissatisfy *vt* (**dissatisfying, dissatisfied**) to fail to please, to make discontented.—**dissatisfaction** *n*.

dissect *vt* to cut apart (a plant, an animal, etc) for scientific examination; to analyse and interpret in fine detail.—**dissection** *n*.—**dissector** *n*.

dissemble *vti* to pretend or to conceal (eg true feelings) by pretence.—**dissemblance** *n*.—**dissembler** *n*.

disseminate *vt* to spread or scatter (ideas, information, etc) widely.—**dissemination** *n*.—**disseminator** *n*.

dissension *n* disagreement, esp when resulting in conflict.

dissent *vi* to hold a different opinion; to withhold assent. * *n* a difference of opinion.—**dissenter** *n*.

dissertation *n* a written thesis, esp as required for a university degree, etc.

disservice *n* an ill turn, a harmful action.

dissident *adj* disagreeing. * *n* a person who disagrees strongly with government policies, esp one who suffers harassment or imprisonment as a result.—**dissidence** *n*.

dissimilar *adj* unlike, different.—**dissimilarly** *adv*.—**dissimilarity** *n*.

dissimulate *vt* to dissemble.—**dissimulation** *n*.—**dissimulator** *n*.

dissipate *vt* to scatter, dispel; to waste, squander (money, etc). * *vi* to separate and vanish.—**dissipater, dissipator** *n*.

dissipated *adj* dissolute, indulging in excessive pleasure; scattered, wasted.—**dissipatedly** *adv*.—**dissipatedness** *n*.

dissipation *n* dispersion; wastefulness; frivolous or dissolute living.

dissociate *vti* to separate or cause to separate the association of (people, things, etc) in consciousness; to repudiate a connection with.—**dissociation** *n*.

dissoluble *adj* soluble.—**dissolubility** *n*.

dissolute *adj* lacking moral discipline, debauched.—**dissolutely** *adv*.—**dissoluteness** *n*.

dissolution *n* separation into component parts; the dissolving of a meeting or assembly (eg parliament); the termination of a business or personal relationship; death; the process of dissolving.

dissolve *vt* to cause to pass into solution; to disperse (a legislative assembly); to melt; (*partnership, marriage*) to break up legally, annul. * *vi* to become liquid; to fade away.

dissonance *n* a harsh or inharmonious sound; discord; lack of agreement; (*mus*) an incomplete or unfulfilled chord requiring resolution into harmony.—**dissonant** *adj*.

dissuade *vt* to prevent or discourage by persuasion.—**dissuasion** *n*.—**dissuasive** *adj*.

distance *n* the amount of space between two points or things; a distant place or point; remoteness, coldness of manner. * *vt* to place at a distance, physically or emotionally; to outdistance in a race, etc.

distant *adj* separated by a specific distance; far-off in space, time, place, relation, etc; not friendly, aloof.—**distantly** *adv*.

distaste *n* aversion; dislike.—**distasteful** *adj*.—**distastefully** *adv*.

distemper *n* an infectious and often fatal disease of dogs and other animals; a type of paint made by mixing color with egg or glue instead of oil; a painting made with this.

distend *vti* to swell or cause to swell, esp from internal pressure.

distill, distil *vti* (**distills** *or* **distils, distilling, distilled**) to treat by, or cause to undergo, distillation; to purify; to extract the essence of; to let or cause to fall in drops.

distillation *n* the conversion of a liquid into vapor by heat and then cooling the vapor so it condenses again, separating out the liquid's constituents or purifying it in the process; a distillate.—**distillatory** *adj*.

distiller *n* an individual or organization that distils, eg a brewery.

distillery *n* (*pl* **distilleries**) a place where distilling, esp of alcoholic spirits, is carried on.

distinct *adj* different, separate (from); easy to perceive by the mind or senses.—**distinctive** *adj*.—**distinctly** *adv*.—**distinctness** *n*.

distinction *n* discrimination, separation; a difference seen or made; a distinguishing mark or characteristic; excellence, superiority; a mark of honor.

distinguish *vt* to see or recognize as different; to mark as different, characterize; to see or hear clearly; to confer distinction on; to make eminent or known. * *vi* to perceive a difference.—**distinguishable** *adj*.

distinguished *adj* eminent, famous; dignified in appearance or manners.

distort *vt* to pull or twist out of shape; to alter the true meaning of, misrepresent.—**distortion** *n*.

distract vt to draw (eg the mind or attention) to something else; to confuse.–**distractingly** adv.

distraction n something that distracts the attention; an amusement; perplexity; extreme agitation.–**distractive** adj.–**distractively** adv.

distraught adj extremely distressed.

distress n physical or emotional suffering, as from pain, illness, lack of money, etc; a state of danger, desperation. * vt to cause distress to.–**distressingly** adv.

distribute vt to divide and share out; to spread, disperse throughout an area.–**distributable** adj.

distribution n a distributing or a being distributed; allotment; a thing distributed; diffusion; the geographical range or occurrence of an organism; classification; (law) the apportioning of an estate among the heirs; (commerce) the marketing of goods to customers, their handling and transport; (statistics) the way numbers denoting characteristics in a statistical population are distributed.–**distributional** adj.

distributor n an agent who sells goods, esp wholesale; a device for distributing current to the spark plugs in an engine.

district n a territorial division defined for administrative purposes; a region or area with a distinguishing character.

district attorney n in US a lawyer who is the state's prosecutor in a judicial district.

distrust n suspicion, lack of trust. * vt to withhold trust or confidence from; to suspect.–**distrustful** adj.–**distrustfully** adv.–**distrustfulness** n.

disturb vt to interrupt; to cause to move from the normal position or arrangement; to destroy the quiet or composure of.–**disturbance** n.

disuse n the state of being neglected or unused.–**disused** adj.

ditch n any long narrow trench dug in the ground. * vt to make a ditch in; (sl) to drive (a car) into a ditch; (sl) to make a forced landing of (an aircraft); (sl) to get rid of.

dither vi to hesitate, vacillate. * n a state of confusion; uncertainty.–**ditherer** n.

ditto n (pl **dittos**) the same again, as above–used in written lists and tables to avoid repetition. * vt (**dittoing, dittoed**) to repeat.

ditto marks npl two small marks (") placed under an item repeated.

ditty n (pl **ditties**) a simple song.

diuretic n a substance or drug that acts to increase the discharge of urine.–also adj.

diva n (pl **divas, dive**) an accomplished female opera singer; a prima donna.

divan n a long couch without back or sides; a bed of similar design.

dive vi (**diving, dived** or **dove, dived**) to plunge headfirst into water; (aircraft) to descend or fall steeply; (diver, submarine) to submerge; to plunge (eg the hand) suddenly into anything; to dash headlong, lunge. * n a headlong plunge; a submerging of a submarine, etc; a sharp descent; a steep decline; (sl) a disreputable public place.

diver n a person who dives; a person who works or explores underwater from a diving bell or in a diving suit; any of various aquatic birds.

diverge vi to branch off in different directions from a common point; to differ in character, form, etc; to deviate from a path or course.–**divergence** n.–**divergent** adj.

diverse adj different; assorted, various.–**diversely** adv.–**diverseness** n.

diversify vb (**diversifying, diversified**) vt to vary; to invest in a broad range of securities to lessen risk of loss. * vi to engage in a variety of commercial operations to reduce risk.–**diversification** n.

diversity n (pl **diversities**) the condition or quality of being diverse; unlikeness; a difference, distinction; variety.

divert vt to turn aside from one course onto another; to entertain, amuse.–**diversion** n.–**diversionary** adj.

divest vt to strip of clothing, equipment, etc; to deprive of rights, property, power, etc.–**divestiture, divestment** n.

divide vt to break up into parts; to distribute, share out; to sort into categories; to cause to separate from something else; to separate into opposing sides; (parliament) to vote or cause to vote by division; (math) to ascertain how many times one quantity contains another. * vi to become separated; to diverge; to vote by separating into two sides. * n a watershed; a split.–**dividable** adj.

dividend n a number which is to be divided; the money earned by a company and divided among the shareholders; a bonus derived from some action.

divider n something that divides; a screen, furniture or plants, etc used to divide up a room; (pl) measuring-compasses.

divination n the art of foretelling the future or discovering hidden knowledge by supernatural means; intuitive perception.–**divinatory** adj.

divine adj of, from, or like God or a god; (inf) excellent. * n a clergyman; a theologian. * vt to foretell the future by supernatural means; to discover intuitively; to dowse. * vi to practice divination.–**divinely** adv.–**diviner** n.

diving board n a platform or springboard for diving from.

diving suit n a watertight suit with a helmet and air supply, used by divers.

divinity n (pl **divinities**) any god; theology; the quality of being God or a god.

divisible adj able to be divided.–**divisibility** n.

division n a dividing or being divided; a partition, a barrier; a portion or section; a military unit; separation; a disagreement; (math) the process of dividing one number by another.–**divisional** adj.

divisive adj creating disagreement or disunity.–**divisively** adv.–**divisiveness** n.

divorce n the legal dissolution of marriage; separation. * vt to terminate a marriage by divorce; to separate.

divorcé, divorcee n a divorced person.–**divorcée** nf.

divot n a lump of turf dug from the ground while making a golf swing, etc.

divulge vt to tell or reveal.–**divulgence** n.

Dixie n the southern States of the US.

Dixieland n Dixie; a New Orleans jazz style.

dizzy adj (**dizzier, dizziest**) confused; causing giddiness or confusion; (sl) silly; foolish. * vt to make dizzy; to confuse.–**dizzily** adv.–**dizziness** n.

DNA abbr = deoxyribonucleic acid, the main component of chromosomes that stores genetic information.

do vt (pres t **does, doing, did**, pp **done**) to perform; to work; to end, to complete; to make; to provide; to arrange, to tidy; to perform; to cover a distance; to visit; (sl) to serve time in prison; (sl) to cheat, to rob; (sl) to assault; (with **in**) (inf) to kill; to tire out. * vi to act or behave; to be satisfactory; to manage. * n (pl **dos, do's**) (inf) a party; (inf) a hoax. Do has special uses where it has no definite meaning, as in asking questions (Do you like milk?), emphasizing a verb (I do want to go), and standing for a verb already used (My dog goes where I do).

DOA abbr = dead on arrival.

doc n (inf) doctor.

docile adj easily led; submissive.–**docilely** adv.–**docility** n.

dock[1] vt (an animal's tail) to cut short; (wages, etc) to deduct a portion of.

dock[2] n a wharf; an artificial enclosed area of water for ships to be loaded, repaired, etc; (pl) a dockyard. * vt to come or bring into dock; to join (spacecraft) together in space.

dock[3] n an enclosed area in a court of law reserved for the accused.

docker n a laborer who works at the docks.–also **longshoreman** n.

docket n a list of lawsuits to be tried by a court. * vt to enter on a docket.

dockyard n an area with docks and facilities for repairing and refitting ships.

doctor n a person qualified to treat diseases or physical disorders; the highest academic degree; the holder of such a degree. * vt to treat medically; (machinery, etc) to patch up; to tamper with, falsify; (inf) to castrate or spay.–**doctoral** adj.

doctorate n the highest degree in any discipline given by a university, conferring the title of doctor.

doctrinaire adj obsessed by theory rather than by experience. * n a person so obsessed.–**doctrinairism** n.

doctrine n a principle of belief.–**doctrinal** adj.–**doctrinally** adv.

document n a paper containing information or proof of anything. * vt to provide or prove with documents.–**documental** adj.–**documentation** n.

documentary adj consisting of documents; presenting a factual account of an event or activity. * n (pl **documentaries**) a nonfiction film.

dodder vi to tremble or shake through old age or weakness; to walk slowly and shakily.–**dodderer** n.–**doddery** adj.

dodge vi to move quickly in an irregular course. * vt to evade (a duty) by cunning; to avoid by a sudden movement or shift of position; to trick. * n a sudden movement; (inf) a clever trick.–**dodger** n.

dodo n (pl **dodos, dodoes**) a large, clumsy bird, now extinct.

doe n (pl **does, doe**) a female deer, rabbit, or hare.

doer n a person who acts, as opposed to thinking or talking; an active energetic person.

does see **do**.

doesn't = does not.

doff vt to take off (esp one's hat) in greeting or as a sign of respect.

dog n a canine mammal of numerous breeds, commonly kept as a domestic pet; the male of the wolf or fox; a despicable person; a device for gripping things. * vt (**dogging, dogged**) to pursue relentlessly.–**dog-like** adj.

dog collar n a collar for a dog; (inf) a clerical collar.

dog-eared adj worn, shabby; (book) having the corners of the pages turned down.–**dog-ear** vt.

dogfight n (loosely) a fiercely disputed contest; combat between two fighter planes, esp at close quarters.

dogfish n (pl **dogfish, dogfishes**) any of various small shark-like fish.

dogged adj tenacious.–**doggedly** adv.–**doggedness** n.

dogma n (pl **dogmas, dogmata**) a belief taught or held as true, esp by a church; a doctrine; a belief.

dogmatic, dogmatical adj pertaining to a dogma; forcibly asserted as if true; overbearing.–**dogmatically** adv.

do-gooder n a well-meaning person, esp if naive or ineffectual.–**do-gooding** n.

dog rose n a prickly wild rose.

dogsbody n (pl **dogsbodies**) (inf) a drudge.

doily n (pl **doilies**) a small ornamented mat, laid under food on dishes, eg cakes.–also **doyley**.

doing n an action or its result; (pl) things done; actions.

do-it-yourself n domestic repairs, woodwork, etc undertaken as a hobby or to save money.–also adj.–**do-it-yourselfer** n.

doldrums npl inactivity; depression; boredom; the regions of the ocean about the equator where there is little wind.

dole n (inf) money received from the state while unemployed; a small portion. * vt to give (out) in small portions.

doleful adj sad, gloomy.–**dolefully** adv.–**dolefulness** n.

doll n a toy in the form of a human figure; a ventriloquist's dummy; (sl) a woman.

dollar n the unit of money in the US, Canada, Australia and many other countries.

dollop n (inf) a soft mass or lump; a portion, serving.

dolly n (pl **dollies**) (inf) a child's word for a doll; a wheeled platform for a camera. * vi (**dollying, dollied**) to maneuver a camera dolly.

dolour, dolor n grief, sorrow, distress.–**dolorous** adj.–**dolorously** adv.

dolphin n a marine mammal with a beak-like snout, larger than a porpoise but smaller than a whale.

dolt n a dull or stupid person.–**doltish** adj.–**doltishly** adv.–**doltishness** n.

domain n an area under the control of a ruler or government; a field of thought, activity, etc.

dome n a large, rounded roof; something high and rounded.–also vt.

domestic adj belonging to the home or family; not foreign; (animals) tame. * n a servant in the home.–**domestically** adv.

domesticate vt to tame; to make home-loving and fond of household duties.–**domestication** n.

domesticity n (pl **domesticities**) home life; being domestic.

domicile n a house; a person's place of residence. * vt to establish, to settle permanently.–**domiciliary** adj.

dominant adj commanding, prevailing over others; overlooking from a superior height. * n (mus) the fifth note of a diatonic scale.–**dominance** n.–**dominantly** n.

dominate vt to control or rule by strength; to hold a commanding position over; to overlook from a superior height.–**domination** n.–**dominator** n.

domineer vti to act in an arrogant or tyrannical manner.–**domineeringly** adv.

dominion n a territory with one ruler or government; the power to rule; authority.

domino n (pl **dominoes, dominos**) a flat oblong tile marked with up to six dots; (pl) a popular game usu using a set of 28 dominoes; a loose cloak, usu worn with an eye mask, at masquerades.

don vt (**donning, donned**) to put on; to invest with; to assume.

donate vt to give as a gift or donation, esp to a charity.–**donator** n.–**donation** n.

done[1] see **do**.

done[2] adj completed; cooked sufficiently; socially acceptable; (with **for**) (sl) doomed; dead; exhausted; discarded.

donkey n (pl **donkeys**) a small animal resembling a horse.

donor n a person who donates something, a donator; a person who gives their blood, organs, etc for medical use.

don't = do not.

donut n (sl) a doughnut.

doodle vi to scribble aimlessly. * vt to draw (something) absentmindedly. * n a meaningless drawing or scribble.–**doodler** n.

doom n a grim destiny; ruin. * vt condemn to failure, destruction, etc.

door n a movable barrier to close an opening in a wall; a doorway; a means of entry or approach.

doorman n (pl **doormen**) a uniformed attendant stationed at the entrance to large hotels, offices, etc.

doorpost n the straight vertical side-post of a door, jamb.

doorway n an opening in a wall, etc filled by a door.

dope n a thick pasty substance used for lubrication; (inf) any illegal drug, such as cannabis or narcotics; (sl) a stupid person; (sl) information. * vt to treat with dope. * vi to take addictive drugs.

dopey, dopy adj (**dopier, dopiest**) (sl) stupid; (inf) half asleep.–**dopiness** n.

doppelgänger, doppelganger n a ghostly double of a living person.

dormant adj sleeping; quiet, as if asleep; inactive.–**dormancy** n.

dormer n an upright window that projects from a sloping roof.

dormitory n (pl **dormitories**) a large room with many beds, as in a boarding school.

dormouse n (pl **dormice**) a small mouse-like creature that hibernates in winter.

dorsal adj of, on, or near the back.–**dorsally** adv.

dory n (pl **dories**) an edible yellow seafish.–also **John Dory**.

dosage n the administration of a medicine in doses; the size of a dose; the operation of dosing.

dose n the amount of medicine, radiation, etc administered at one time; a part of an experience. * vt to administer a dose (of medicine) to.

dossier n a collection of documents about a subject or person, a file.

dot n a small round speck, a point; the short signal in Morse code. * vt (**dotting, dotted**) to mark with a dot; to scatter (about).–**dotter** n.

dotage n weakness and infirmity caused by old age.

dotard n a person in their dotage.

dote vi (with **on** or **upon**) to show excessive affection.–**doter** n.

dotted see dot.

dotty adj (**dottier, dottiest**) (inf) eccentric, slightly mad.–**dottily** adv.–**dottiness** n.

double adj twice as large, as strong, etc; designed or intended for two; made of two similar parts; having two meanings, characters, etc; (flowers) having more than one circle of petals. * adv twice; in twos. * n a number or amount that is twice as much; a person or thing identical to another; (film) a person closely resembling an actor and who takes their place to perform stunts, etc; (pl) a game between two pairs of players. * vti to make or become twice as much or as many; to fold, to bend; to bend sharply backward; to sail around; to have an additional purpose.–**doubly** adv.

double bass n the largest instrument of the violin family.–**double bassist** n.

double-cross vt to betray an associate, to cheat. * **double cross** n.–**double-crosser** n.

double-dealing n treachery, deceit.–**double-dealer** n.

double entendre n a word or phrase with two meanings, one of which is usu indecent.

double-jointed adj having joints which allow the limbs, figures, etc an unusual degree of flexibility.

doubt vi to be uncertain or undecided. * vt to hold in doubt; to distrust; to be suspicious of. * n uncertainty; (often pl) lack of confidence in something, distrust.–**doubter** n.

doubtful adj feeling doubt; uncertain; suspicious.–**doubtfully** adv.–**doubtfulness** adv.

doubtless adv no doubt; probably. * adj assured; certain.–**doubtlessly** adv.–**doubtlessness** n.

douche n a jet of water directed on or into a part of the body; a device for applying this. * vt to cleanse or treat with a douche.

dough n a mixture of flour and water, milk, etc used to make bread, pastry, or cake; (inf) money.

doughnut n a small, fried, usu ring-shaped, cake.–also **donut**.

douse vt to plunge into or soak with water; to put out, extinguish.

dove[1] see **dive**.

dove[2] n a small bird of the pigeon family; (politics, diplomacy) an advocate of peace or a peaceful policy.

dovecote, dovecot n a shelter and breeding place for domesticated pigeons.

dovetail n a wedge-shaped joint used in woodwork. * vt to fit or combine together.

dowager n a widow possessing property or title from her husband; (inf) a dignified elderly woman.

dowdy adj (**dowdier, dowdiest**) poorly dressed, not stylish.–**dowdily** adv.–**dowdiness** n.

down[1] n soft fluffy feathers or fine hairs.

down[2] adv toward or in a lower physical position; to a lying or sitting position; toward or to the ground, floor, or bottom; to a source or hiding place; to or in a lower status or in a worse condition; from an earlier time; in cash; to or in a state of less activity. * adj occupying a low position, esp lying on the ground; depressed, dejected. * prep in a descending direction in, on, along, or through. * n a low period (as in activity, emotional life, or fortunes); (inf) a dislike, prejudice. * vti to go or cause to go or come down; to defeat; to swallow.

down[3] n (usu pl) a tract of bare hilly land used for pasturing sheep; banks or rounded hillocks of sand.

downcast adj dejected; (eyes) directed downward.

downfall n a sudden fall (from power, etc); a sudden or heavy fall of rain or snow.

downgrade n a descending slope. * vt to reduce or lower in rank or position; to disparage.

downpour n a heavy fall of rain.

downright adj frank; absolute. * adv thoroughly.

downside n the less appealing or advantageous aspect of something.

downsize vt to produce a smaller version of (eg a car); to reduce the numbers in a workforce by means of redundancy.

downstairs adv to or on a lower floor. * adj on the ground floor or a lower floor. * n (used as sing or pl) the lower part of a house, the ground floor.

downtown n the main business district of a town or city.–also adj.

downtrodden adj oppressed, trampled underfoot.

downturn n a decline in (economic) activity or prosperity.

downward adj moving from a higher to a lower level, position or condition. * adv toward a lower place, position, etc; from an earlier time to a later (–also **downwards**).

downwind adv in the direction the wind is blowing.–also adj.

downy adj (**downier, downiest**) like, covered with, or made of, down.

dowry n (pl **dowries**) the money or possessions that a woman brings to her husband at marriage.

dowse vi to search for water, treasure, etc with a divining rod.–**dowser** n.

doyen n a senior member of a group; an expert in a field; the oldest example of a category.–**doyenne** nf.

doyley see **doily**.

doze vi to sleep lightly. * n a light sleep, a nap.–**dozer** n.

dozen n a group of twelve.–**dozenth** adj.

dozy adj (**dozier, doziest**) drowsy; (inf) stupid.–**dozily** adv.–**doziness** n.

Dr abbr = Doctor.

drab adj (**drabber, drabbest**) dull, uninteresting; of a dull brown color. * n a dull yellowy brown color; cloth of this color.–**drably** adv.–**drabness** n.

draconian adj (laws, etc) very cruel, severe.

draft n a rough plan, preliminary sketch; an order for the payment of money by a bank; a smaller group selected from a larger for a specific task; conscription. * vt to draw a rough sketch or outline of; to select for a special purpose; to conscript. n a current of air, esp in an enclosed space; the pulling of a load using an animal, etc; something drawn; a dose of medicine or liquid; an act of swallowing; the depth of water required to float a ship; beer, wine, etc stored in bulk in casks.–also **draught**.

draftsman n a person who makes detailed drawings or plans.–also **draughtsman**.–**draftsmanship, draughtsmanship** n.

drafty adj letting in or exposed to drafts of air.–also **draughty**.–**draftiness, draughtiness** n.

drag vb (**dragging, dragged**) vt to pull along by force; to draw slowly and heavily; to search (in water) with a dragnet or hook. * vi to trail on the ground; to move slowly and heavily; (sl) to draw on a cigarette. * n something used for dragging, a dragnet, a heavy harrow; something that retards progress; a braking device; (sl) something boring or tedious; (sl) women's clothes worn by a man; (sl) a draw at a cigarette.

dragnet n a net for scouring a riverbed, pond, etc to search for anything; a coordinated hunt for an escaped criminal, etc.

dragon *n* a mythical winged reptile; an authoritarian or grim person, esp a woman.

dragonfly *n* (*pl* **dragonflies**) an insect with a long slender abdomen, large eyes and iridescent wings.

dragoon *vt* to force into submission by bullying commands.

drain *vt* to draw off liquid gradually; to make dry by removing liquid gradually; to exhaust physically or mentally; to drink the entire contents of a glass * *vi* to flow away gradually; to become dry as liquid trickles away. * *n* a sewer, pipe, etc by which water is drained away; something that causes exhaustion or depletion.–**drainer** *n*.

drainage *n* a draining; a system of drains; something drained off.

drainpipe *n* a pipe that carries waste liquid, sewage, etc out of a building.

drake *n* a male duck.

drama *n* a play for the stage, radio or television; dramatic literature as a genre; a dramatic situation or a set of events.

dramatic *adj* of or resembling drama; exciting, vivid.–**dramatically** *adv*.

dramatics *n* (*used as sing or pl*) the producing or performing of plays; (*used as sing*) exaggerated behaviour, histrionics.

dramatist *n* a person who writes plays.

dramatize *vt* to write or adapt in the form of a play; to express in an exaggerated or dramatic form.–**dramatization** *n*.–**dramatizer** *n*.

drank *see* **drink**.

drape *vt* to cover or hang with cloth; to arrange in loose folds; to place loosely or untidily. * *n* a hanging cloth or curtain; (*pl*) curtains.

drapery *n* (*pl* **draperies**) fabrics or curtains, esp as arranged in loose folds; the trade of a draper.

drastic *adj* acting with force and violence.–**drastically** *adv*.

draw *vti* (**drawing, drew,** *pp* **drawn**) to haul, to drag; to cause to go in a certain direction; to pull out; to attract; to delineate, to sketch; to receive (as a salary); to bend (a bow) by pulling back the string; to leave (a contest) undecided; to write up, to draft (a will); to produce or allow a current of air; to draw lots; to get information from; (*ship*) to require a certain depth to float; (*with* **on**) to approach; to use (a resource); to withdraw (money) from (an account, etc); to put on (clothes); (*with* **out**) to extract; to prolong, extend; to cause (someone) to speak freely; to take (money) from an account; (*with* **up**) to bring or come to a standstill; to draft (a document); to straighten oneself; to form soldiers into an array. * *n* the act of drawing; (*inf*) an event that attracts customers, people; the drawing of lots; a drawn game.

drawback *n* a hindrance, handicap.

drawer *n* a person who draws; a person who draws a check; a sliding box-like compartment (as in a table, chest, or desk); (*pl*) knickers, underpants.

drawing *n* a figure, plan, or sketch drawn by using lines.

drawl *vt* to speak slowly and with elongated vowel sounds. * *n* drawling speech.–**drawler** *n*.–**drawlingly** *adv*.

drawn[1] *see* **draw**.

drawn[2] *adj* looking strained because of tiredness or worry.

dread *n* great fear or apprehension. * *vt* to fear greatly.

dreadful *adj* full of dread; causing dread; extreme (*dreadful tiredness*); (*sl*) bad, disagreeable.–**dreadfully** *adv* –**dreadfulness** *n*.

dream *n* a stream of thoughts and images experienced during sleep; a day-dreaming state, a reverie; an ambition; an ideal. * *vb* (**dreaming, dreamt** *or* **dreamed**) *vi* to have a dream during sleep; to fantasize. * *vt* to dream of; to imagine as a reality; (*with* **up**) to devise, invent.–**dreamer** *n*.

dreamy *adj* (**dreamier, dreamiest**) given to dreaming, unpractical; (*inf*) attractive, wonderful.–**dreamily** *adv*.–**dreaminess** *n*.

dreary *adj* (**drearier, dreariest**) dull; cheerless.–**drearily** *adv*.–**dreariness** *n*.

dredge[1] *n* a device for scooping up material from the bottom of a river, harbour, etc. * *vt* to widen, deepen, or clean with a dredge; to scoop up with a dredge; (*with* **up**) (*inf*) to discover, reveal, esp through effort.

dredge[2] *vt* to coat (food) by sprinkling.

dredger[1] *n* a vessel fitted with dredging equipment.

dredger[2] *n* a container with a perforated lid for sprinkling.

dregs *npl* solid impurities that settle on the bottom of a liquid; residue; (*inf*) a worthless person or thing.

drench *vt* to soak, saturate.

dress *n* clothing; a one-piece garment worn by women and girls comprising a top and skirt; a style or manner of clothing. * *vt* to put on or provide with clothing; to decorate; (*wound*) to wash and bandage; (*animal*) to groom; to arrange the hair; to prepare food (eg poultry, fish) for eating by cleaning, gutting, etc; (*with* **up**) to attire in best clothes; to improve the appearance of. * *vi* to put on clothes; to put on formal wear for an occasion; (*with* **up**) to put on fancy dress, etc.

dressage *n* the training of a horse in deportment and obedience.

dresser *n* a person who assists an actor to dress; a type of kitchen sideboard.

dressing *n* a sauce or stuffing for food; manure spread over the soil; dress or clothes; the bandage, ointment, etc applied to a wound.

dressy *adj* (**dressier, dressiest**) stylish; elaborate; showy.–**dressily** *adv*.–**dressiness** *n*.

drew *see* **draw**.

dribble *vi* to flow in a thin stream or small drips; to let saliva trickle from the mouth. * *n* the act of dribbling; a thin stream of liquid.–**dribbler** *n*.

dried *see* **dry**.

drier *see* **dry, dryer**.

drift *n* a heap of snow, sand, etc deposited by the wind; natural course, tendency; the general meaning or intention (of what is said); the extent of deviation (of an aircraft, etc) from a course; an aimless course; the action or motion of drifting. * *vt* to cause to drift. * *vi* to be driven or carried along by water or air currents; to move along aimlessly; to be piled into heaps by the wind.

drifter *n* a person who wanders aimlessly.

drill *n* an implement with a pointed end that bores holes; the training of soldiers, etc; repetitious exercises or training as a teaching method; (*inf*) correct procedure or routine. * *vt* to make a hole with a drill; to instruct or be instructed by drilling.

drily *see* **dry**.

drink *vb* (**drinking, drank,** *pp* **drunk**) *vt* to swallow (a liquid); to take in, absorb; to join in a toast. * *vi* to consume alcoholic liquor, esp to excess. * *n* liquid to be drunk; alcoholic liquor; (*sl*) the sea.–**drinker** *n*.

drip *vti* (**dripping, dripped**) to fall or let fall in drops. * *n* a liquid that falls in drops; the sound of falling drops; (*med*) a device for administering a fluid slowly and continuously into a vein; (*inf*) a weak or ineffectual person.–**dripper** *n*.

drive *vb* (**driving, drove,** *pp* **driven**) *vt* to urge, push or force onward; to direct the movement or course of; to convey in a vehicle; to carry through strongly; to impress forcefully; to propel (a ball) with a hard blow. * *vi* to be forced along; to be conveyed in a vehicle; to work, to strive (at). * *n* a trip in a vehicle; a stroke to drive a ball (in golf, etc); a driveway; a military attack; an intensive campaign; dynamic ability; the transmission of power to machinery.

drive-in *n* a cinema, restaurant, etc, where customers are served in their cars.–*also adj*.

drivel *n* nonsense. * *vi* (**driveling, driveled** *or* **drivelling, drivelled**) to talk nonsense.–**driveler, driveller** *n*.

driven *see* **drive**.

driver *n* one who or that which drives; a chauffeur.

driveway *n* a road for vehicles, often on private property.

drizzle n fine light rain.–also vi.–**drizzly** adj.

droll adj oddly amusing; whimsical.–**drollness** n.–**drolly** adv.

dromedary n (pl **dromedaries**) a one-humped camel.

drone n a male honey-bee; a lazy person; a deep humming sound; a monotonous speaker or speech; an aircraft piloted by remote control. * vi to make a monotonous humming sound; to speak in a monotonous manner.

drool vi to slaver, dribble; to show excessive enthusiasm for.

droop vi to bend or hang down; to become weak or faint. * n the act or an instance of drooping.–**droopy** adj.

drop n a small amount of liquid in a roundish shape; something shaped like this, as a sweet; a tiny quantity; a sudden fall; the distance down; (pl) liquid medicine, etc dispensed in small drops. * vb (**dropping, dropped**) vi to fall in drops; to fall suddenly; to go lower, to sink; to come (in); (with **in**) to visit (with) informally; (with **out**) to abandon or reject (a course, society, etc). * vt to let fall, to cause to fall; to lower or cause to descend; to set down from a vehicle; to mention casually; to cause (the voice) to be less loud; to give up (as an idea).–**dropper** n.

dropout n a student who abandons a course of study; a person who rejects normal society.

dropsy n an unnatural accumulation of serious fluid in any cavity of the body or its tissues.–**dropsical** adj.

dross n a surface scum on molten metal; rubbish, waste matter.

drought n a long period of dry weather.–**droughty** adj.

drove[1] see **drive**.

drove[2] n a group of animals driven in a herd or flock, etc; a large moving crowd of people.

drown vti to die or kill by suffocation in water or other liquid. * vt to flood; to drench; to become deeply immersed in some activity; to blot out (a sound) with a louder noise; to remove (sorrow, etc) with drink.

drowse vi to be nearly asleep.–**drowsily** adv.–**drowsiness** n.–**drowsy** adj.

drudge vi to do boring or very menial work. * n a person who drudges, esp a servant.

drudgery n (pl **drudgeries**) dull, boring work.

drug n any substance used in medicine; a narcotic. * vt (**drugging, drugged**) to administer drugs to; to stupefy.

druggist n a pharmacist.

drugstore n a retail store selling medicines and other miscellaneous articles such as cosmetics, film, etc.

drum n a round percussion instrument, played by striking a membrane stretched across a hollow cylindrical frame; the sound of a drum; anything shaped like a drum, as a container for liquids. * vb (**drumming, drummed**) vi to play a drum; to beat or tap rhythmically. * vt (with **in**) to instill (knowledge) into a person by constant repetition; (with **up**) to summon as by drum; to create (business, etc) by concerted effort; to originate.

drummer n a person who plays a drum; (inf) a traveling salesman.

drumstick n a stick for beating a drum; the lower part of a cooked leg of poultry.

drunk[1] see **drink**.

drunk[2] adj intoxicated with alcohol. * n a drunk person.

drunkard n an habitual drunk.

drunken adj intoxicated; caused by excessive drinking.–**drunkenly** adv.–**drunkenness** n.

dry adj (**drier, driest**) free from water or liquid; thirsty; marked by a matter-of-fact, ironic or terse manner of expression; uninteresting, wearisome; (bread) eaten without butter, etc; (wine) not sweet; not selling alcohol. * vti (**drying, dried**) to make or become dry; (with **out**) to be treated for alcoholism or drug addiction.–**drily, dryly** adv.–**dryness** n.

dry-clean vt to clean with solvents as opposed to water.–**dry-cleaner** n.–**dry-cleaning** n.

dryer n a device for drying, as a tumble-drier; a clothes horse.–also **drier**.

dry ice n solid carbon dioxide.

DTP abbr = desktop publishing.

dual adj double; consisting of two.

dub[1] vt (**dubbing, dubbed**) to nickname.

dub[2] vt (**dubbing, dubbed**) to replace the soundtrack of (a movie), eg with one in a different language; to add sound effects or music to (a movie, broadcast, etc); to transfer (a recording) to a new tape.

dubiety n (pl **dubieties**) doubtfulness, uncertainty; a matter of doubt.

dubious adj doubtful (about, of); uncertain as to the result; untrustworthy.–**dubiously** adv.–**dubiousness** n.

duchess n the wife or widow of a duke; a woman having the same rank as a duke in her own right.

duck[1] vt to dip briefly in water; to lower the head suddenly, esp to avoid some object; to avoid, dodge. * vi to dip or dive; to move the head or body suddenly; to evade a duty, etc. * n a ducking movement.

duck[2] n (pl **ducks, duck**) a water bird related to geese and swans; the female of this bird; its flesh used as food.

duckling n a young duck.

duct n a channel or pipe for fluids, electric cable, etc; a tube in the body for fluids to pass through.

ductile adj malleable; yielding.

dud adj (sl) worthless. * n (sl) anything worthless; an ineffectual person.

dude n a dandy; a city person on holiday in a ranch.

due adj owed as a debt; immediately payable; fitting, appropriate; appointed or expected to do or arrive. * adv directly, exactly. * n something due or owed; (pl) fees.

duel n combat with weapons between two persons over a matter of honor, etc; conflict of any kind between two people, sides, ideas, etc. * vi (**dueling, dueled** or **duelling, duelled**) to fight in a duel.–**duelist, duellist** n.

duet n a musical composition for two performers.–**duettist** n.

dug see **dig**.

dugout n a boat made from the hollowed out tree trunk; a rough underground shelter.

duke n the highest order of British nobility.

dull adj not sharp or pointed; not bright or clear; stupid; boring; not active. * vti to make or become dull.–**dully** adv.–**dullness** n.

dullard n a slow-witted person.

duly adv properly; suitably.

dumb adj not able to speak; silent; (inf) stupid.–**dumbly** adv.–**dumbness** n.

dumbbell n one of a pair of heavy weights used for muscular exercise; (sl) a fool.

dumbfound, dumfound vti to astonish, surprise.

dummy n (pl **dummies**) a figure of a person used to display clothes; (sl) a soother or pacifier for a baby; a stupid person; an imitation.

dump vt to drop or put down carelessly in a heap; to deposit as rubbish; to abandon or get rid of; to sell goods abroad at a price lower than the market price abroad; (with **on**) (sl) to censure strongly the words or actions of others. * n a place for refuse; a temporary store; (inf) a dirty, dilapidated place; (pl) (inf) despondency, low spirits.–**dumper** n.

dumpling n a rounded piece of dough cooked by boiling or steaming; a short, fat person.

dumpster n a large garbage can.

dumpy adj (**dumpier, dumpiest**) short and thick.–**dumpily** adv.–**dumpiness** n.

dunce n a person who is stupid or slow to learn.

dune n a hill of sand piled up by the wind.

dung n excrement; manure; filth. * vt to spread with manure.–**dungy** adj.

dungaree n a coarse cotton cloth; (pl) overalls or trousers made from this.

dungeon *n* an underground cell for prisoners.

dunk *vti* to dip (cake, etc) into liquid, eg coffee.

duo *n* (*pl* **duos, dui**) a pair of performers; (*inf*) two persons connected in some way.

duodenum *n* (*pl* **duodena, duodenums**) the first part of the small intestine.–**duodenal** *adj*.

dupe *n* a person who is cheated. * *vt* to deceive; to trick.–**dupable** *adj*.–**duper** *n*.–**dupery** *n*.

duplex *adj* having two parts, double. * *n* a flat or apartment on two floors.–**duplexity** *n*.

duplicate *adj* in pairs, double; identical; copied exactly from an original. * *n* one of a pair of identical things; a copy. * *vt* to make double; to make an exact copy of; to repeat.–**duplicable** *adj*.–**duplication** *n*.

duplicity *n* (*pl* **duplicities**) treachery; deception.–**duplicitous** *adj*.

durable *adj* enduring, resisting wear, etc.–**durability** *n*.–**durably** *adv*.

duration *n* the time in which an event continues.

duress *n* compulsion by use of force or threat; unlawful constraint; imprisonment.

during *prep* throughout the duration of; at a point in the course of.

dusk *n* (the darker part of) twilight.

dusky *adj* (**duskier, duskiest**) having a dark color.–**duskily** *adv*.–**duskiness** *n*.

dust *n* fine particles of solid matter. * *vt* to free from dust; to sprinkle with flour, sugar, etc.

dust bowl *n* a drought area subject to dust storms.

duster *n* a cloth for dusting; a device for dusting; a duster coat; a light housecoat.

dusty *adj* (**dustier, dustiest**) covered with dust.–**dustily** *adv*.–**dustiness** *n*.

dutiful *adj* performing one's duty; obedient.–**dutifully** *adv*.–**dutifulness** *n*.

duty *n* (*pl* **duties**) an obligation that must be performed for moral or legal reasons; respect for one's elders or superiors; actions and responsibilities arising from one's business, occupation, etc; a tax on goods or imports, etc.

duty-free *adj* free from tax or duty.

DVD *abbr* digital video disc.

dwarf *n* (*pl* **dwarfs, dwarves**) a person, animal or plant of abnormally small size. * *vt* to stunt; to cause to appear small.–**dwarfish** *adj*.

dwell *vi* (**dwelling, dwelt** *or* **dwelled**) to live (in a place); (*with* **on**) to focus the attention on; to think, talk, or write at length about.–**dweller** *n*.

dwelling *n* the house, etc where one lives, habitation.

dwindle *vi* to shrink, diminish; to become feeble.

dye *vt* (**dyeing, dyed**) to give a new color to. * *n* a coloring substance, esp in solution; a color or tint produced by dyeing.–**dyer** *n*.

dying *see* **die**[1].

dyke *see* **dike**.

dynamic *adj* relating to force that produces motion; (*person*) forceful, energetic.–**dynamically** *adv*.

dynamics *n* (*used as sing*) the branch of science that deals with forces and their effect on the motion of bodies.

dynamism *n* dynamic influence or power.

dynamite *n* a powerful explosive; a potentially dangerous situation; (*inf*) an energetic person or thing. * *vt* to blow up with dynamite.–**dynamiter** *n*.

dynamo *n* (*pl* **dynamos**) a device that generates electric current.

dynasty *n* (*pl* **dynasties**) a line of hereditary rulers or leaders of any powerful family or similar group.–**dynastic** *adj*.–**dynastically** *adv*.

dysentery *n* painful inflammation of the large intestine with associated diarrhea.–**dysenteric** *adj*.

dysfunction *n* a failure in normal functioning.–**dysfunctional** *adj*.

dyslexia *n* impaired ability in reading or spelling.–**dyslexic** *adj, n*.

dyspepsia *n* indigestion, esp chronic.

dystrophy *n* various hereditary disorders causing progressive weakening of the muscles (*muscular dystrophy*).–**dystrophic** *adj*.

E

E. *abbr* = east; eastern.

each *adj* every one of two or more.

eager *adj* enthusiastically desirous (of); keen (for); marked by impatient desire or interest.–**eagerly** *adv*.–**eagerness** *n*.

eagle *n* a bird of prey with keen eyes and powerful wings; (*golf*) a score of two strokes under par.

ear[1] *n* (the external part of) the organ of hearing; the sense or act of hearing; attention; something shaped like an ear.

ear[2] *n* the part of a cereal plant (eg corn, maize) that contains the seeds.

eardrum *n* the membrane within the ear that vibrates in response to sound waves.

earl *n* a member of the British nobility ranking between a marquis and a viscount.–**countess** *nf*.

early *adj* (**earlier, earliest**) before the expected or normal time; of or occurring in the first part of a period or series; of or occurring in the distant past or near future.–*also adv*.–**earliness** *n*.

earmark *vt* to set aside for a specific use; to put an identification mark on. * *n* a distinguishing mark.

earn *vt* to gain (money, etc) by work or service; to acquire; to deserve; to earn interest (on money invested, etc).

earnest *adj* sincere in attitude or intention.–**earnestly** *adv*.–**earnestness** *n*.

earnings *npl* wages or profits; something earned.

earphone *n* a device held to or worn over the ear, through which sound is transmitted; a headphone.

earpiece *n* a telephone earphone.

earplug *n* a piece of wadding or wax inserted in the ear to prevent noise or water penetration.

earring *n* an ornament worn on the ear lobe.

earshot *n* hearing distance.

earth *n* the world that we inhabit; solid ground, as opposed to sea; soil; the burrow of a badger, fox, etc; a connection between an electric device or circuit with the earth. * *vt* to cover with or bury in the earth; to connect an electrical circuit or device to earth.

earthen *adj* composed of earth; made of baked clay.

earthenware *n* pottery, etc made from baked clay.

earthly *adj* (**earthlier, earthliest**) of the earth; material, worldly.–**earthliness** *n*.

earthquake *n* a violent tremor of the earth's crust.

earthworm *n* any of various common worms that live in the soil.

earthy *adj* (**earthier, earthiest**) of or resembling earth; crude.–**earthiness** *n*.

ease *n* freedom from pain, discomfort or disturbance; rest from effort or work; effortlessness; lack of inhibition or restraint, naturalness. * *vt* to relieve from pain, trouble, or anxiety; to relax, make less tight, release; to move carefully and gradually. * *vi* (*often with* **off**) to become less active, intense, or severe.

easel *n* a supporting frame, esp one used by artists to support their canvases while painting.

easily *adv* with ease; by far; probably.

east *n* the direction of the sunrise; the compass point opposite west; (*with cap preceded by* **the**) the area of the world east of Europe. * *adj, adv* in, towards, or from the east.

Easter n the Christian festival observed on a Sunday in March or April in commemoration of the resurrection of Christ.

easterly adj situated towards or belonging to the east, coming from the east. * n (pl **easterlies**) a wind from the east.

eastern adj of or in the east.

easterner n someone from the east.

eastward adj towards the east.—**eastwards** adv.

easy adj (**easier, easiest**) free from pain, trouble, anxiety; not difficult or requiring much effort; (manner) relaxed; lenient; compliant; unhurried; (inf) open to all alternatives. * adv with ease.—**easiness** n.

easygoing adj placid, tolerant, relaxed.

eat vt (**eating, ate,** pp **eaten**) to take into the mouth, chew and swallow as food; to have a meal; to consume, to destroy bit by bit; (also with **into**) to corrode; (inf) to bother, cause anxiety to; (with **up**) to consume completely. * vi (with **out**) to eat away from home, esp in a restaurant. * n (pl: inf) food.—**eater** n.

eatable adj suitable for eating; fit to be eaten. * n (pl) food.

eating disorder n a psychological disorder identified by unusual or abnormal eating patterns.

eaves npl the overhanging edge of a roof.

eavesdrop vi (**eavesdropping, eavesdropped**) to listen secretly to a private conversation.—**eavesdropper** n.

ebb n the flow of the tide out to sea; a decline. * vi (tide water) to flow back; to become lower, to decline.

ebony n (pl **ebonies**) a hard heavy wood. * adj black as ebony.

ebullient adj exuberant, enthusiastic; boiling.—**ebullience, ebulliency** n.—**ebulliently** adv.

eccentric adj deviating from a usual or accepted pattern; unconventional in manner or appearance, odd; (circles) not concentric; off centre; not precisely circular. * n an eccentric person.—**eccentrically** adv.

eccentricity n (pl **eccentricities**) strangeness of behavior; an eccentric or unusual habit.

ecclesiastic, ecclesiastical adj of or relating to the Christian Church or clergy.—**ecclesiastically** adv.

ECG abbr = electrocardiogram.

echelon n a stepped formation of troops, ships, or aircraft; a level (of authority) in a hierarchy.

echo n (pl **echoes**) a repetition of sound caused by the reflection of sound waves; imitation; the reflection of a radar signal by an object. * vb (**echoing, echoed**) vi to resound; to produce an echo. * vt to repeat; to imitate; to send back (a sound) by an echo.

éclair n a small oblong shell of choux pastry covered with chocolate and filled with cream.

eclectic adj selecting from or using various styles, ideas, methods, etc; composed of elements from a variety of sources. * n a person who adopts an eclectic method.—**eclectically** adv.—**eclecticism** n.

eclipse n the obscuring of the light of the sun or moon by the intervention of the other; a decline into obscurity, as from overshadowing by others. * vt to cause an eclipse of; to overshadow, darken; to surpass.—**eclipser** n.

ecology n (the study of) the relationships between living things and their environments.—**ecological** adj.—**ecologist** n.

economic adj pertaining to economics or the economy; (business, etc) capable of producing a profit.

economical adj thrifty.—**economically** adv.

economics n (sing) the social science concerned with the production, consumption and distribution of goods and services; (pl) financial aspects.

economist n an expert in economics.

economize vti to spend money carefully; to save; to use prudently.—**economization** n.

economy n (pl **economies**) careful use of money and resources to minimize waste; an instance of this; the management of the finances and resources, etc of a business, industry or organization; the economic system of a country.

ecosystem n (ecology) a system comprising a community of living organisms and its surroundings.

ecstasy n (pl **ecstasies**) intense joy.—**ecstatic** adj.—**ecstatically** adv.

ecumenical adj of the whole Christian Church; seeking Christian unity worldwide.—**ecumenicalism, ecumenicism** n.—**ecumenically** adv.

eczema n inflammation of the skin causing itching and the formation of scaly red patches.—**eczematous** adj.

eddy n (pl **eddies**) a swiftly revolving current of air, water, fog, etc. * vi (**eddying, eddied**) to move round and round.

edelweiss n a small white-flowered alpine herb.

edema n (pl **edemata**) a swelling in a body or plant caused by excess fluid.—also **oedema.**—**edematous** adj.

Eden n (Bible) the garden where Adam and Eve lived after the creation; a paradise.

edge n the border, brink, verge, margin; the sharp cutting side of a blade; sharpness, keenness; force, effectiveness. * vt to supply an edge or border to; to move gradually.

edgeways, edgewise adv with the edge forwards; sideways.

edgy adj (**edgier, edgiest**) irritable.—**edgily** adv.—**edginess** n.

edible adj fit or safe to eat.—**edibility, edibleness** n.

edict n a decree; a proclamation.

edifice n a substantial building; any large or complex organization or institution.

edify vt (**edifying, edified**) to improve the moral character or mind of (a person).—**edification** n.—**edifier** n.—**edifyingly** adv.

edit vt to prepare (text) for publication by checking facts, grammar, style, etc; to be in charge of a publication; (cinema) to prepare a final version of a film by selection and arrangement of photographed sequences.—**editor** n.—**editorship** n.

edition n a whole number of copies of a book, etc printed at a time; the form of a particular publication.

editorial adj of or produced by an editor. * n an article expressing the opinions of the editor or publishers of a newspaper or magazine.—**editorialist** n.—**editorially** adv.

educate vt to train the mind, to teach; to provide schooling for.—**educator** n.

education n the process of learning and training; instruction as imparted in schools, colleges and universities; a course or type of instruction; the theory and practice of teaching.—**educational** adj.—**educationally** adv.

educationalist, educationist n an expert in education.

eel n a snake-like fish.

eerie adj (**eerier, eeriest**) causing fear; weird.—**eerily** adv.—**eeriness** n.

efface vt to rub out, obliterate; to make (oneself) humble or inconspicuous.—**effaceable** adj.—**effacement** n.—**effacer** n.

effect n the result of a cause or action by some agent; the power to produce some result; the fundamental meaning; an impression on the senses; an operative condition; (pl) personal belongings; (pl: theater, cinema) sounds, lighting, etc to accompany a production. * vt to bring about, accomplish.—**effecter** n.— **effectible** adj.

effective adj producing a specified effect; forceful, striking in impression; actual, real; operative.—**effectively** adv.—**effectiveness** n.

effectual adj able to produce the desired effect.—**effectuality, effectualness** n.—**effectually** adv.

effeminate adj (man) displaying what are regarded as feminine qualities.—**effeminacy, effeminateness** n.

effervesce vt (liquid) to froth and hiss as bubbles of gas escape; to be exhilarated.—**effervescence** n.—**effervescent** adj.—**ffervescible** adj.

effete adj decadent, weak.—**effeteness** n.

efficacious adj achieving the desired result.—**efficacy, efficaciousness** n.

efficient adj achieving results without waste of time or effort; competent.–**efficiently** adv.–**efficiency** n (pl **efficiencies**).

effigy n (pl **effigies**) a sculpture or portrait; a crude figure of a person, esp for exposure to public contempt and ridicule.

effluent adj flowing out. * n that which flows out, esp sewage.

effort n exertion; an attempt, try; a product of great exertion.–**effortful** adj.

effortless adj done with little effort, or seemingly so.–**effortlessly** adv.–**effortlessness** n.

effrontery n (pl **effronteries**) impudent boldness, insolence.

effusion n a pouring out; an unrestrained outpouring, as of emotion; something poured out.–**effusive** adj.–**effusiveness** n.

e.g., eg, eg. abbr = for example (Latin exempli gratia).

egalitarian adj upholding the principle of equal rights for all.–also n.–**egalitarianism** n.

egg[1] n the oval hard-shelled reproductive cell laid by birds, reptiles and fish; the egg of the domestic poultry used as food; ovum.–**eggy** adj.

egg[2] vt (with on) to incite (someone to do something).

eggnog n a drink made from egg, beaten up with hot milk, sugar and brandy.

eggplant n a plant producing a smooth, dark-purple fruit.

eggshell n the hard outer covering of an egg. * adj fragile; (paint) having a slight sheen.

egis see **aegis**.

ego n (pl **egos**) the self; self-image, conceit.

egocentric adj self-centered.–**egocentricity** n.

egoism n self-concern; self-centeredness.–**egoist** n.–**egoistic, egoistical** adj.–**egoistically** adv.

egotism n excessive reference to oneself; conceit.–**egotist** n.–**egotistic, egotistical** adj.–**egotistically** adv.

ego trip n (inf) an activity undertaken to boost one's own self-esteem or importance in the eyes of others.–**ego-trip** vi.

egregious adj outstandingly bad.–**egregiousness** n.

egress n the way out, exit.

egret n a type of heron.

eider n a large marine duck, the down of which has commercial value as a filling for quilts etc.

eiderdown n the down of the eider duck used for stuffing quilts, etc; a thick quilt with a soft filling.

eight n, adj one more than seven; the symbol for this (8, VIII, viii); (the crew of) an eight-oared rowing boat.

eighteen n, adj one more than seventeen; the symbol for this (18, XVIII, xviii).–**eighteenth** adj.

eightfold adj, adv consisting of eight units; being eight times as great or many.

eighth adj, n one after seventh; one of eight equal parts.

eighty n (pl **eighties**) eight times ten; the symbol for this (80, LXXX, lxxx); (pl) the numbers from 80 to 89.–**eightieth** adj, n.

either adj, n the one or the other of two; each of two. * conj correlative to or.

ejaculate vti to emit a fluid (as semen); to exclaim.–**ejaculation** n.–**ejaculator** n.–**ejaculatory** adj.

eject vt to turn out, to expel by force. * vi to escape from an aircraft or spacecraft using an ejector seat.–**ejection** n.–**ejector** n.

eke vt (with out) to supplement; to use (a supply) frugally; to make (a living) with difficulty.

elaborate adj highly detailed; planned with care and exactness. * vt to work out or explain in detail.–**elaborateness** n.–**elaboration** n.–**elaborative** adj.–**elaborator** n.

elapse vi (time) to pass by.

elastic adj returning to the original size and shape if stretched or squeezed; springy; adaptable. * n fabric, tape, etc incorporating elastic thread.–**elastically** adv.–**elasticity** n.

elasticated adj made elastic by the use of elastic thread.

elate vt to fill with happiness or pride.–**elated** adj.–**elatedness** n.–**elation** n.

elbow n the joint between the forearm and upper arm; the part of a piece of clothing covering this; any sharp turn or bend, as in a pipe. * vt to shove away rudely with the elbow; to jostle.

elbowroom n space to move, scope.

elder[1] n a tree or shrub with flat clusters of white or pink flowers.

elder[2] n an older person; an office bearer in certain churches.–**eldership** n.

elderberry n (pl **elderberries**) (the fruit of) an elder.

elderly adj quite old.–**elderliness** n.

eldest n oldest, first born.

elect vti to choose by voting; to make a selection (of); to make a decision on. * adj chosen for an office but not installed.–**elective** adj.–**elector** n.

election n the public choice of a person for office, esp a politician.

electioneer vi to work on behalf of a candidate for election.–**electioneering** n.

electorate n the whole body of qualified electors.

electric adj of, producing or worked by electricity; exciting, thrilling. * npl electric fittings.–**electrical** adj.–**electrically** adv.

electrician n a person who installs and repairs electrical devices.

electricity n a form of energy comprising certain charged particles, such as electrons and protons; an electric current.

electrify vt (**electrifying, electrified**) to charge with electricity; to modify or equip for the use of electric power; to astonish or excite.–**electrifiable** adj.–**electrification** n.–**electrifier** n.

electrocardiogram n the tracing made by an electrocardiograph.

electrocardiograph n a device for recording the electrical activity of the heart.–**electrocardiographic, electrocardiographical** adj.–**electrocardiography** n.

electrocute vt to kill or execute by electricity.–**electrocution** n.

electrode n a conductor through which an electric current enters or leaves an electrolyte, gas discharge tube or thermionic valve.

electrolysis n the passage of an electric current through an electrolyte to effect chemical change; the destruction of living tissue, esp hair roots, by the use of an electric current

electrolyte n a solution that conducts electricity.

electrolyze vt to cause to undergo electrolysis.–**electrolyzation** n.–**electrolyzer** n.

electromagnet n a metal core rendered magnetic by the passage of an electric current through a surrounding coil–**electromagnetic** adj. –**electromagnetically** adv. –**electromagnetism** n.

electron n a negatively charged elementary particle that forms the part of the atom outside the nucleus.

electronic adj of or worked by streams of electrons flowing through semiconductor devices, vacuum or gas; of or concerned with electrons or electronics.–**electronically** adv.

electronic mail n messages, etc, sent and received via computer terminals.

electronic publishing n the publication of information on CD-ROM, magnetic disks, on-line databases, etc, for access by computer.

electronics n (sing) the study, development and application of electronic devices; (pl) electronic circuits.

electroplate vt to plate or cover with metal (eg silver) by electrolysis. * n electroplated objects.–**electroplater** n.

elegant adj graceful; refined; dignified and tasteful in manner and appearance.–**elegance, elegancy** n.–**elegantly** adv.

elegy n (pl **elegies**) a slow mournful song or poem.–**elegiac** adj.

element n a constituent part; any of the 105 known substances composed of atoms with the same number of protons in their nuclei; a favourable environment for a plant or animal; a wire that produces heat in an electric cooker, kettle, etc; any of the four substances (earth, air, fire, water) that in ancient and medieval thought were believed to constitute the universe; (*pl*) atmospheric conditions (wind, rain, etc); (*pl*) the basic principles, rudiments.

elemental *adj* of elements or primitive natural forces.–**elementally** *adv*.

elementary *adj* concerned with the basic principles of a subject.–**elementariness** *n*.

elephant *n* (*pl* **elephants, elephant**) a large heavy mammal with a long trunk, thick skin, and ivory tusks.–**elephantoid** *adj*.

elephantine *adj* of or like elephants; very big or clumsy.

elevate *vt* to lift up; to raise in rank; to improve in intellectual or moral stature.–**elevated** *adj*.

elevation *n* a raised place; the height above the earth's surface or above sea level; the angle to which a gun is aimed above the horizon; a drawing that shows the front, rear, or side view of something.

elevator *n* a cage or platform for moving something from one level to another; a moveable surface on the tailplane of an aircraft to produce motion up and down; a lift; a building for storing grain.

eleven *adj, n* one more than ten; the symbol for this (11, XI, xi); (*soccer, etc*) a team of eleven players.–**eleventh** *adj, n*.

elf *n* (*pl* **elves**) a mischievous fairy.–**elfin** *adj*.–**elfish, elvish** *adj*.

elicit *vt* to draw out (information, etc).–**elicitable** *adj*.–**elicitation** *n*.–**elicitor** *n*.

eligible *adj* suitable to be chosen, legally qualified; desirable, esp as a marriage partner.–**eligibility** *n*.–**eligibly** *adv*.

eliminate *vt* to expel, get rid of; to eradicate completely; (*sl*) to kill; to exclude (eg a competitor) from a competition, usu by defeat.–**eliminable** *adj*.–**elimination** *n*.–**eliminative, eliminatory** *adj*.–**eliminator** *n*.

elite, élite *n* a superior group.

elitism *n* leadership or rule by an elite; advocacy of such a system.–**elitist** *n*.

elixir *n* any medicine claimed as a cure-all; a sweet syrup containing a medicine.

elk *n* (*pl* **elks, elk**) the largest existing deer of Europe and Asia.

ellipse *n* (*geom*) a closed plane figure formed by the plane section of a right-angled cone; a flattened circle.

ellipsis *n* (*pl* **ellipses**) the omission of words needed to complete the grammatical construction of a sentence; the mark (...) used to indicate such omission.

elliptic, elliptical *adj* of or like an ellipse; having a part understood.–**elliptically** *adv*.

elm *n* a tall deciduous shade tree with spreading branches and broad top; its hard heavy wood.

elocution *n* skill in public speaking.–**elocutionary** *adj*.–**elocutionist** *n*.

elongate *vti* to make or become longer.–**elongation** *n*.

elope *vi* to run away secretly with a lover, esp to get married.–**elopement** *n*.–**eloper** *n*.

eloquence *n* skill in the use of words; speaking with fluency, power or persuasiveness.–**eloquent** *adj*.

else *adv* besides; otherwise.

elsewhere *adv* in another place.

elucidate *vt* to make clear, to explain.–**elucidation** *n*.–**elucidative, elucidatory** *adj*.–**elucidator** *n*.

elude *vt* to avoid stealthily; to escape the understanding or memory of a person.–**eluder** *n*.–**elusion** *n*.

elusive *adj* escaping; baffling; solitary, difficult to contact.–**elusiveness** *n*.

elves, elvish *see* elf.

emaciate *vti* to make or become very thin and weak.–**emaciated** *adj*.–**emaciation** *n*.

email, e-mail *n* short for electronic mail.

emanate *vi* to issue from a source.–**emanation** *n*.**emancipate** *vt* to liberate, esp from bondage or slavery.–**emancipative** *adj*.–**emancipator** *n*.–**emancipatory** *adj*.

emancipation *n* the act of freeing; freedom, liberation.–**emancipationist** *n*.

emasculate *vt* to castrate; to deprive of vigor, strength, etc.–**emasculation** *n*.–**emasculative, emasculatory** *adj*.–**emasculator** *n*.

embalm *vt* to preserve (a dead body) with drugs, chemicals, etc.–**embalmer** *n*.–**embalmment** *n*.

embankment *n* an earth or stone mound made to hold back water or to carry a roadway.

embargo *n* (*pl* **embargoes**) an order of a government forbidding ships to enter or leave its ports; any ban or restriction on commerce by law; a prohibition, ban. * *vt* (**embargoing, embargoed**) to lay an embargo on; to requisition.

embark *vti* to put or go on board a ship or aircraft to begin a journey; to make a start in any activity or enterprise.–**embarkation** *n*.–**embarkment** *n*.

embarrass *vt* to make (a person) feel confused, uncomfortable or disconcerted.–**embarrassing** *adj*.–**embarrassment** *n*.

embassy *n* (*pl* **embassies**) a person or group sent to a foreign government as ambassadors; the official residence of an ambassador.

embattle *vt* to arrange troops for battle; to prepare for battle.–**embattled** *adj*.

embed *vt* (**embedding, embedded**) to fix firmly in surrounding matter.–**embedment** *n*.

embellish *vt* to decorate, to adorn.–**embellisher** *n*.–**embellishment** *n*.

ember *n* a piece of glowing coal or wood in a fire; (*pl*) the smouldering remains of a fire.

embezzle *vt* to steal (money, securities, etc entrusted to one's care).–**embezzlement** *n*.–**embezzler** *n*.

embitter *vt* to cause to feel bitter.–**embitterment** *n*.

emblazon *vt* to make bright with color; to ornament with heraldic devices.–**emblazonment** *n*.

emblem *n* a symbol; a figure adopted and used as an identifying mark.–**emblematic, emblematical** *adj*.–**emblematically** *adv*.

embody *vt* (**embodying, embodied**) to express in definite form; to incorporate or include in a single book, law, system, etc.–**embodiment** *n*.

embolden *vt* to inspire with courage; to make bold.

emboss *vt* to ornament with a raised design.–**embosser** *n*.–**embossment** *n*.

embrace *vt* to take and hold tightly in the arms as a sign of affection; to accept eagerly (eg an opportunity); to adopt (eg a religious faith); to include. * *n* the act of embracing, a hug.–**embraceable** *adj*.–**embracement** *n*.

embroider *vt* to ornament with decorative stitches; to embellish (eg a story).–**embroiderer** *n*.–**embroidery** *n*.

embroil *vt* to involve (a person) in a conflict, argument, or problem.–**embroiler** *n*.–**embroilment** *n*.

embryo *n* (*pl* **embryos**) an animal during the period of its growth from a fertilized egg up to the third month; a human product of conception up to about the second month of growth; a thing in a rudimentary state.–**embryonic** *adj*.

emend *vt* to correct mistakes in written material.–**emendable** *adj*.–**emendation** *n*.

emerald *n* a rich green gemstone; its color.

emerge *vi* to appear up out of, to come into view; to be revealed as the result of investigation.–**emergence** *n*.–**emergent** *adj*.

emergency *n* (*pl* **emergencies**) an unforeseen situation demanding immediate action; a serious medical condition requiring instant treatment.

emery *n* a hard granular mineral used for grinding and polishing; a hard abrasive powder.

emetic *n* a medicine that induces vomiting.–*also adj*.–**emetically** *adv*.

emigrate *vi* to leave one's country for residence in another.–**emigration** *n*.–**emigrant** *n*.

eminence *n* (*pl* **eminences**) high rank or position; a person of high rank or attainments.–**eminent** *adj*.–**eminently** *adv*.

emissary *n* (*pl* **emissaries**) a person sent on a mission on behalf of another, esp a government.

emit *vt* (**emitting, emitted**) to send out (light, heat, etc); to put into circulation; to express, to utter.–**emission** *n*.–**emissive** *adj*.–**emitter** *n*.

emollient *adj* softening and soothing, esp the skin. * *n* a preparation used for skin care.–**emollience** *n*.

emote *vi* to display emotion theatrically.

emotion *n* a strong feeling of any kind.–**emotional** *adj*.–**emotionally** *adv*.

emotive *adj* characterized by or arousing emotion.–**emotiveness, emotivity** *n*.

empathize *vi* to treat with or feel empathy.

empathy *n* the capacity for participating in and understanding the feelings or ideas of another.–**empathic, empathetic** *adj*.

emperor *n* the sovereign ruler over an empire.

emphasis *n* (*pl* **emphases**) particular stress or prominence given to something; force or vigor of expression; clarity of form or outline.–**emphatic** *adj*.–**emphatically** *adv*.

emphasize *vt* to place stress on.

empire *n* a large state or group of states under a single sovereign, usu an emperor; nations governed by a single sovereign state; a large and complex business organization.

empirical *adj* based on observation, experiment or experience only, not theoretical.–**empirically** *adv*.

employ *vt* to give work and pay to; to make use of.–**employable** *adj*.

employee *n* a person who is hired by another person for wages.

employer *n* a person, business, etc that employs people.

employment *n* an employing; a being employed; occupation or profession.

empower *vt* to give official authority to.–**empowerment** *n*.

empress *n* the female ruler of an empire; the wife or widow of an emperor.

empty *adj* (**emptier, emptiest**) containing nothing; not occupied; lacking reality, substance, or value; hungry. * *vb* (**emptying, emptied**) *vt* to make empty; to transfer or discharge (the contents of something) by emptying. * *vi* to become empty; to discharge contents. * *n* (*pl* **empties**) empty containers or bottles.–**emptily** *adv*.–**emptiness** *n*.

emu *n* a fast-running Australian bird, related to the ostrich.

emulate *vt* to try to equal or do better than; to imitate; to rival or compete.–**emulation** *n*.–**emulative** *adj*.–**emulator** *n*.

emulsion *n* a mixture of mutually insoluble liquids in which one is dispersed in droplets throughout the other; a light-sensitive substance on photographic paper or film.–**emulsive** *adj*.

enable *vt* to give the authority or means to do something; to make easy or possible.–**enabler** *n*.

enact *vt* to make into law; to act (a play, etc).–**enactive** *adj*.–**enactment** *n*.–**enactor** *n*.–**enactory** *adj*.

enamel *n* a glass-like substance used to coat the surface of metal or pottery; the hard outer layer of a tooth; a usu glossy paint that forms a hard coat. * *vt* (**enameling, enameled** *or* **enamelling, enamelled**) to cover or decorate with enamel.–**enameler, enameller, enamelist, enamellist** *n*.–**enamelwork** *n*.

enamor, enamour *vt* to inspire with love.–**enamored, enamoured** *adj*.

encapsulate *vt* to enclose or be enclosed in, as a capsule; to summarize.–**encapsulation** *n*.

encase *vt* to enclose (as if) in a case.–**encasement** *n*.

enchant *vt* to bewitch, to delight.–**enchanter** *n*.–**enchantment** *n*.–**enchantress** *nf*.

encircle *vt* to surround; to move or pass completely round.–**encirclement** *n*.

enclose *vt* to shut up or in; to put in a wrapper or parcel, usu together with a letter.–**enclosable** *adj*.–**encloser** *n*.

enclosure *n* an enclosing; an enclosed area; something enclosed with a letter, in a parcel, etc.

encompass *vt* to encircle or enclose; to include.–**encompassment** *n*.

encore *interj* once more! * *n* a call for the repetition of a performance.–*also vt*.

encounter *vt* to meet, esp unexpectedly; to fight, engage in battle with; to be faced with (problems, etc). * *n* a meeting; a conflict, battle.

encourage *vt* to inspire with confidence or hope; to urge, incite; to promote the development of.–**encouragement** *n*.–**encourager** *n*.–**encouragingly** *adv*.

encroach *vi* to infringe another's territory, rights, etc; to advance beyond an established limit.–**encroacher** *n*.–**encroachingly** *adv*.–**encroachment** *n*.

encrust *vt* to cover with a hard crust; to form a crust on the surface of; to decorate a surface with jewels.–**encrustation** *n*.

encumber *vt* to weigh down; to hinder the function or activity of.–**encumbrance** *n*.

encyclopedia, encyclopaedia *n* a book or series of books containing information on all branches of knowledge, or treating comprehensively a particular branch of knowledge, usu in alphabetical order.

encyclopedic, encyclopaedic *adj* comprehensive.–**encyclopedically, encyclopaedically** *adv*.

end *n* the last part; the place where a thing stops; purpose; result, outcome. * *vt* to bring to an end; to destroy. * *vi* to come to an end; to result (in). * *adj* final; ultimate.

endanger *vt* to put in danger.–**endangerment** *n*.

endear *vt* to make loved or more loved.–**endearing** *adj*.–**endearingly** *adv*.

endearment *n* something that endears; a word or words of affection.

endeavor, endeavour *vi*.to try or attempt (to). * *n* an attempt.

endemic *adj* (*disease*) locally prevalent.

ending *n* reaching or coming to an end; the final part.

endive *n* an annual or biennial herb widely cultivated as a salad plant; a variety of chicory used in salads.

endless *adj* unending; uninterrupted; extremely numerous.–**endlessly** *adv*.–**endlessness** *n*.

endocrine *adj* secreting internally, specifically producing secretions that are distributed in the body by the bloodstream (–*also* **endocrinal**).

endorse *vt* to write one's name, comment, etc on the back of to approve; to support.–**endorsement** *n*.

endow *vt* to give money or property to provide an income for; to provide with a special power or attribute.–**endowment** *n*.

endure *vt* to undergo, tolerate (hardship, etc) esp with patience. * *vi* to continue in existence, to last out.–**endurable** *adj*.–**endurance** *n*.

endways *adv* on end, with the end foremost.

enema *n* (*pl* **enemas, enemata**) the injection of a liquid into the rectum to void the bowels; the liquid injected.

enemy *n* (*pl* **enemies**) a person who hates or dislikes and wishes to harm another; a military opponent; something harmful or deadly.

energetic *adj* lively, active; done with energy.–**energetically** *adv*.

energize *vt* to fill with energy; to invigorate; to apply an electric current to.–**energizer** *n*.

energy *n* (*pl* **energies**) capacity of acting or being active; vigor, power; (*physics*) capacity to do work.

enervate *vt* to lessen the strength or vigor of; to enfeeble in mind and body.–**enervation** *n*.–**enervative** *adj*.–**enervator** *n*.

enfold vt to wrap up; to hug in the arms.–**enfolder** n.–**enfold-ment** n.

enforce vt to compel obedience by threat; to execute with vigor.–**enforceable** adj.–**enforcement** n.–**enforcer** n.

enfranchise vt to admit to citizenship; to grant the vote to.–**enfranchisement** n.–**enfranchiser** n.

engage vt to pledge as security; to promise to marry; to keep busy; to hire; to attract and hold, esp attention or sympathy; to cause to participate; to bring or enter into conflict; to begin or take part in a venture; to connect or interlock, to mesh.–**engagement** n.

engaged adj entered into a promise to marry; reserved, occupied or busy.

engaging adj pleasing, attractive.–**engagingly** adv.–**engagingness** n.

engender vt to bring into existence.–**engenderment** n.

engine n a machine by which physical power is applied to produce a physical effect; a locomotive.

engineer n a person trained in engineering; a person who operates an engine, etc; a member of a military group devoted to engineering work; a designer or builder of engines. * vt to contrive, plan, esp deviously.

engineering n the art or practice of constructing and using machinery; the art and science by which natural forces and materials are utilized in structures or machines.

engorge vt to congest with blood; to consume (food) greedily.–**engorgement** n.

engrave vt to produce by cutting or carving a surface; to cut to produce a representation that may be printed from; to lodge deeply (in the mind, etc).–**engraver** n.

engraving n a print made from an engraved surface.

engross vt to occupy (the attention) fully.

engulf vt to flow over and enclose; to overwhelm.–**engulfment** n.

enhance vt to increase in value, importance, attractiveness, etc; to heighten.–**enhancement** n.–**enhancer** n.

enigma n someone or something that is puzzling or mysterious.–**enigmatic, enigmatical** adj.–**enigmatically** adv.

enjoy vt to get pleasure from, take joy in; to use or have the advantage of; to experience.–**enjoyment** n.

enjoyable adj giving enjoyment.–**enjoyably** adv.

enlarge vti to make or grow larger; to reproduce (a photograph) in a larger form; to speak or write at length (on).–**enlargement** n.

enlighten vt to instruct; to inform.–**enlightening** adj.–**enlightenment** n.

enlightened adj well-informed, tolerant, unprejudiced.

enlist vt to engage for service in the armed forces; to secure the aid or support of. * vi to register oneself for the armed services.–**enlistee** n.–**enlistment** n.

enliven vt to make more lively or cheerful.–**enlivening** adj.–**enlivenment** n.

enmity n (pl **enmities**) hostility, esp mutual hatred.

enormity n (pl **enormities**) great wickedness; a serious crime; huge size, magnitude.

enormous adj extremely large.–**enormously** adv.

enough adj adequate, sufficient. * adv so as to be sufficient; very; quite. * n a sufficiency. * interj stop!

enquire see **inquire**.

enrage vt to fill with anger.–**enraged** adj.–**enragement** n.

enrich vt to make rich or richer; to ornament; to improve in quality by adding to.–**enricher** n.–**enrichment** n.

enroll, enrol vti (**enrolls** or **enrols**, **enrolling**, **enrolled**) to enter or register on a roll or list; to become a member of a society, club, etc; to admit as a member.–**enrollee** n.–**enroller** n.–**enrollment, enrolment** n.

en route adv along or on the way.

ensemble n something regarded as a whole; the general effect; the performance of the full number of musicians, dancers, etc; a complete harmonious costume.

enshrine vt to enclose (as if) in a shrine; to cherish as sacred.– also **inshrine**.–**enshrinement** n.

ensign n a flag; the lowest commissioned officer in the US Navy.

enslave vt to make into a slave; to subjugate.–**enslavement** n.–**enslaver** n.

ensnare vt to trap in, or as in, a snare.–**ensnarement** n.

ensue vi (**ensuing, ensued**) to occur as a consequence or in time.–**ensuing** adj.

ensure vt to make certain, sure, or safe.–**ensurer** n.

entail vt to involve, necessitate as a result.

entangle vt to tangle, complicate; to involve in a tangle or complications.–**entanglement** n.–**entangler** n.

enter vi to go or come in or into; to come on stage; to begin, start; (with **for**) to register as an entrant. * vt to come or go into; to pierce, penetrate; (an organization) to join; to insert; (proposal, etc) to submit; to record (an item) in a diary, etc.–**enterable** adj.–**enterer** n.

enterprise n a difficult or challenging undertaking; a business project; readiness to engage in new ventures.–**enterpriser** n.–**enterprising** adj.–**enterprisingly** adv.

entertain vt to show hospitality to; to amuse, please (a person or audience); to have in mind; to consider.–**entertainer** n.–**entertainment** n.

entertaining adj amusing; diverting.–**entertainingly** adv.

enthrall, enthral vt (**enthralls** or **enthrals, enthralling, enthralled**) to captivate.–**enthrallment, enthralment** n.

enthuse vti to fill with or express enthusiasm.

enthusiasm n intense interest or liking; something that arouses keen interest.–**enthusiastic** adj.–**enthusiastically** adv.

enthusiast n a person filled with enthusiasm for something.

entice vt to attract by offering some pleasure or reward.–**enticement** n.–**enticer** n.–**enticing** adj.

entire adj whole; complete.–**entirety** n

entirely adv fully; completely.

entitle vt to give a title to; to give a right (to).–**entitlement** n.

entity n (pl **entities**) existence, being; something that has a separate existence.

entomology n the branch of zoology that deals with insects.–**entomological, entomologic** adj.–**entomologist** n.

entourage n a retinue, group of attendants.

entrails npl the insides of the body, the intestines.

entrance[1] n the act of entering; the power or authority to enter; a means of entering; an admission fee.

entrance[2] vt to put into a trance; to fill with great delight.–**entrancement** n.–**entrancing** adj.

entrant n a person who enters (eg a competition, profession).

entrap vt (**entrapping, entrapped**) to catch, as if in a trap; to lure into a compromising or incriminatory situation.–**entrapment** n.–**entrapper** n.

entreat vt to request earnestly; to implore, beg.–**entreaty** n (pl **entreaties**).

entrée, entree n the principal dish of a meal; the right or power of admission.

entrench vt to dig a trench as a defensive perimeter; to establish (oneself) in a strong defensive position.–**entrencher** n.–**entrenchment** n.

entrepreneur n a person who takes the commercial risk of starting up and running a business enterprise.–**entrepreneurial** adj.–**entrepreneurship** n.

entrust vt (usu with **with**) to confer as a responsibility, duty, etc; (usu with **to**) to place something in another's care.–**entrustment** n.

entry n (pl **entries**) the act of entering; a place of entrance; an item recorded in a diary, journal, etc; a person or thing taking part in a contest.

entwine vt to twine together or around.–**entwinement** n.

enumerate vt to count; to list.–**enumeration** n.–**enumerator** n.

enunciate vt to state definitely; to pronounce clearly.–**enunciation** n.–**enunciator** n.–**enunciative** adj.

envelop vt to enclose completely (as if) with a covering.–**envelopment** n.

envelope n something used to wrap or cover, esp a gummed paper container for a letter.

enviable adj causing envy; fortunate.–**enviably** adv.

environment n external conditions and surroundings, esp those that affect the quality of life of plants, animals and human beings.–**environmental** adj.–**environmentally** adv.

environmentalist n a person who is concerned with improving the quality of the environment.–**environmentalism** n.

environs npl the surrounding area or outskirts of a district or town.

envisage vt to have a mental picture of.–**envisagement** n.

envoy n a diplomatic agent; a representative.

envy n (pl **envies**) resentment or discontent at another's achievements, possessions, etc; an object of envy. * vt (**envying, envied**) to feel envy of.–**envious** adj.–**enviously** adv.

enzyme n a complex protein, produced by living cells, that induces or speeds chemical reactions in plants and animals.

eon see **aeon**.

epaulet, epaulette n a piece of ornamental fabric or metal worn on the shoulder, esp on a uniform.

ephemeral adj existing only for a very short time. * n an ephemeral thing or organism.–**ephemerality, empheralness** n.

epic n a long poem narrating the deeds of a hero; any literary work, film, etc in the same style. * adj relating to or resembling an epic.

epicenter, epicentre n the area of the earth's surface directly above the focus of an earthquake.–**epicentral** adj.

epicure n a person who has cultivated a refined taste in food, wine, literature, etc.–**epicurism, epicureanism** n.–**epicurean** adj.

epidemic adj, n (a disease) attacking many people at the same time in a community or region.

epidermis n an outer layer, esp of skin.–**epidermal, epidermic, epidermoid** adj.

epigram n a short witty poem or saying.–**epigrammatic** adj.–**epigrammatically** adv.

epigraph n a quotation at the beginning of a book or chapter; an inscription on a building or monument.–**epigraphic, epigraphical** adj.

epilepsy n a disorder of the nervous system marked typically by convulsive attacks and loss of consciousness.–**epileptic** adj, n.

epilogue n the concluding section of a book or other literary work; a short speech addressed by an actor to the audience at the end of a play.

epiphany n (pl **epiphanies**) a moment of sudden revelation or insight; (with cap) a festival of the Christian Church in commemoration of the coming of the Magi to Christ.

episcopacy n (pl **episcopacies**) the system of church government by bishops.–**episcopal** adj.–**episcopalian** adj, n.–**episcopalianism** n.

episode n a piece of action in a dramatic or literary work; an incident in a sequence of events.

episodic, episodical adj happening at irregular intervals; digressive.–**episodically** adv.

epistemology n the science of the processes and grounds of knowledge.

epistle n (formal) a letter.–**epistolary** adj.

epitaph n an inscription in memory of a dead person, usu on a tombstone.

epithet n a descriptive word or phrase added to or substituted for a person's name (Vlad the Impaler).

epitome n a typical example; a paradigm; personification; a condensed account of a written work.–**epitomize** vt.

epoch n a date in time used as a point of reference; an age in history associated with certain characteristics; a unit of geological time.–**epochal** adj.

eponym n a person after whom something is named; a name so derived.–**eponymous, eponymic** adj.–**eponymy** n.

EPOS abbr = electronic point of sale.

epoxy resin n a strong synthetic resin, used in laminates and adhesives.

epsilon n the 5th letter of the Greek alphabet.

equable adj level, uniform; (climate) free from extremes of hot and cold; even-tempered.–**equability, equableness** n.–**equably** adv.

equal adj the same in amount, size, number, or value; impartial, regarding or affecting all objects in the same way; capable of meeting a task or situation. * n a person that is equal. * vt (**equaling, equaled** or **equalling, equalled**) to be equal to, esp to be identical in value; to make or do something equal to.–**equally** adv.

equality n (pl **equalities**) being equal.

equalize vti to make or become equal; (games) to even the score.–**equalization** n.–**equalizer** n.

equate vt to make, treat, or regard as comparable. * vi to correspond as equal.

equation n an act of equaling; the state of being equal; a usu formal statement of equivalence (as in logical and mathematical expressions) with the relations denoted by the sign = .

equator n an imaginary circle passing round the globe, equidistant from the North and South poles.–**equatorial** adj.

equestrian adj pertaining to horses and riding; on horseback. * n a skilled rider.–**equestrienne** nf.–**equestrianism** n.

equidistant adj at equal distances.–**equidistance** n.

equilateral adj having all sides equal.

equilibrium n (pl **equilibriums, equilibria**) a state of balance of weight, power, force, etc.

equine adj of or resembling a horse.

equinox n the two times of the year when night and day are equal in length (around 21 March and 23 September).–**equinoctial** adj.

equip vt (**equipping, equipped**) to provide with all the necessary tools or supplies.–**equipper** n.

equipment n the tools, supplies and other items needed for a particular task, expedition, etc.

equitable adj just and fair; (law) pertaining to equity as opposed to common or statute law.–**equitableness** n.–**equitably** adv.

equity n (pl **equities**) fairness; (law) a legal system based on natural justice developed into a body of rules supplementing the common law; (pl) ordinary shares in a company.

equivalence, equivalency n (pl **equivalences, equivalencies**) equality of value or power.–**equivalent** adj, n.

equivocal adj ambiguous; uncertain; questionable; arousing suspicion.**equivocate** vi to use ambiguous language, esp in order to confuse or deceive.–**equivocation** n.

era n an historical period typified by some special feature; a chronological order or system of notation reckoned from a given date as a basis.

eradicate vt to obliterate.–**eradicable** adj.–**eradication** n.–**eradicator** n.

erase vt to rub out, obliterate; to remove a recording from magnetic tape; to remove data from a computer memory or storage medium.–**erasable** adj.–**erasion** n.

eraser n a piece of rubber, etc for rubbing out marks or writing.

erect adj upright; not leaning or lying down; (sexual organs) rigid and swollen with blood from sexual stimulation. * vt to construct, set up.–**erectable** adj.–**erecter, erector** n.–**erectness** n.

erectile adj (penis, clitoris, etc) able to become enlarged and rigid through sexual stimulation.–**erectility** n.

erection n construction; something erected, as a building; swelling, esp of the penis, due to sexual excitement.

ergo *adv* therefore.

ergonomics *n* (*sing*) the study of the interaction between people and their working environment with the aim of improving efficiency.–**ergonomic** *adj*.–**ergonomically** *adv*.–**ergonomist** *n*.

ermine *n* (*pl* **ermines**, **ermine**) the weasel in its winter coat; the white fur of the winter coat.

erode *vt* to eat or wear away gradually.–**erosion** *n*.–**erosive** *adj*.

erogenous *adj* sexually arousing; sensitive to sexual stimulation.

erotic *adj* of sexual love; sexually stimulating.–**erotically** *adv*.–**eroticism** *n*.

err *vi* to be or do wrong.

errand *n* a short journey to perform some task, usu on behalf of another; the purpose of this journey.

errant *adj* going astray, esp doing wrong; moving aimlessly.

erratic *adj* capricious; irregular; eccentric, odd.–**erratically** *adv*.

erroneous *adj* incorrect; mistaken.–**erroneously** *adv*.

error *n* a mistake, an inaccuracy; a mistaken belief or action.

ersatz *adj* made in imitation; synthetic.

erstwhile *adv* formerly. * *adj* former.

erudite *adj* scholarly, having great knowledge.–**eruditely** *adv*.–**erudition** *n*.

erupt *vi* to burst forth; to break out into a rash; (*volcano*) to explode, ejecting ash and lava into the air.–**eruption** *n*.

escalate *vi* to increase rapidly in magnitude or intensity.–**escalation** *n*.

escalator *n* a motorized set of stairs arranged to ascend or descend continuously.

escalope *n* a thin cut of meat, esp veal.

escapade *n* a wild or mischievous adventure.

escape *vt* to free oneself from confinement, etc; to avoid, remain unnoticed; to be forgotten. * *vi* to achieve freedom; (*gas, liquid*) to leak. * *n* an act or instance of escaping; a means of escape; a leakage of liquid or gas; a temporary respite from reality.–**escapable** *adj*.–**escaper** *n*.

escapee *n* a person who has escaped, esp a prisoner.

escapism *n* the tendency to avoid or retreat from reality into fantasy.–**escapist** *n*, *adj*.

escapologist *n* a performer who escapes from handcuffs, locked boxes, etc.–**escapology** *n*.

escargot *n* a snail prepared as food.

escarpment *n* a steep side of a ridge or plateau.

eschew *vt* to avoid as habit, esp on moral grounds.–**eschewal** *n*.

escort *n* a person, group, ship, aircraft, etc accompanying a person or thing to give protection, guidance, or as a matter of courtesy; a person who accompanies another on a social occasion. * *vt* to attend as escort.

esophagus *n* (*pl* **esophagi**) that part of the alimentary canal that takes food, etc, from the pharynx to the stomach.–*also* **oesophagus**.

esoteric *adj* intended for or understood by a select few; secret; private.–**esoterically** *adv*.–**esotericism** *n*.

esp. *abbr* = especially.

espadrille *n* a flat shoe usu having a fabric upper and rope soles.

especial *adj* notably special, unusual; particular to one person or thing.–**especially** *adv*.

espionage *n* spying or the use of spies to obtain information.

esplanade *n* a level open space for walking or driving, esp along a shore.

espouse *vt* to adopt or support a cause.–**espousal** *n*.–**espouser** *n*.

espresso *n* (*pl* **espressos**) coffee brewed by forcing steam through finely ground darkly roasted coffee beans; an apparatus for making espresso.

espy *vt* (**espying**, **espied**) to catch sight of.–**espial** *n*.–**espier** *n*.

esquire *n* a general courtesy title used instead of Mr in addressing letters.

essay *n* a short prose work usu dealing with a subject from a limited or personal point of view; an attempt. * *vt* (**essaying**, **essayed**) to try, to attempt.

essence *n* that which makes a thing what it is; a substance distilled or extracted from another substance and having the special qualities of the original substance; a perfume.

essential *adj* of or containing the essence of something; indispensable, of the greatest importance. * *n* (*often pl*) indispensable elements or qualities.–**essentiality, essentialness** *n*.–**essentially** *adv*.

establish *vt* to set up (eg a business) permanently; to settle (a person) in a place or position; to get generally accepted; to place beyond dispute, prove as a fact.–**establisher** *n*.

establishment *n* the act of establishing; a commercial organization or other large institution; the staff and resources of an organization; a household; (*with cap*) those people in institutions such as the government, civil service and commerce who use their power to preserve the social, economic and political status quo.

estate *n* landed property; a large area of residential or industrial development; a person's total possessions, esp at their death; a social or political class.

esteem *vt* to value or regard highly; to consider or think. * *n* high regard, a favorable opinion.

ester *n* (*chem*) a compound of acid and alcohol.

esthete, esthetics, estheticism *see* **aesthete, aesthetics, aestheticism**.

estimable *adj* worthy of esteem; calculable.

estimate *vt* to judge the value, amount, significance of; to calculate approximately. * *n* an approximate calculation; a judgment or opinion; a preliminary calculation of the cost of a particular job.–**estimation** *n*.

estrange *vt* to alienate the affections or confidence of.–**estranged** *adj*.–**estrangement** *n*.

estrogen *n* a hormone that develops and maintains female characteristics of the body.–*also* **oestrogen**.

estuary *n* (*pl* **estuaries**) an arm of the sea at the mouth of a river.

et al *abbr* = et alii, and others.

etc, etc. *abbr* = et cetera, and so forth.

etch *vti* to make lines on (metal, glass) usu by the action of acid; to produce (as a design) by etching; to delineate clearly.–**etcher** *n*.–**etching** *n*.

eternal *adj* continuing forever without beginning or end, everlasting; unchangeable; (*inf*) seemingly endless.–**eternally** *adv*.

eternity *n* (*pl* **eternities**) infinite time; the timelessness thought to constitute life after death; (*inf*) a very long time.

ethane *n* a colorless gaseous hydrocarbon found in natural gas and used esp as fuel.

ether *n* (*chem*) a light flammable liquid used as an anesthetic or solvent; the upper regions of space, the invisible elastic substance formerly believed to be distributed evenly through all space.–**etheric** *adj*.

ethereal *adj* delicate; spiritual; celestial.–**ethereality, etherealness** *n*.–**ethereally** *adv*.

ethic *n* a moral principle or set of principles.

ethical *adj* of or pertaining to ethics; conforming to the principles of proper conduct, as established by society, a profession, etc.–**ethically** *adv*.–**ethicalness, ethicality** *n*.

ethics *n* (*sing*) the philosophical analysis of human morality and conduct; system of conduct or behavior, moral principles.–**ethicist** *n*.

ethnic, ethnical *adj* of races or large groups of people classed according to common traits and customs.–**ethnically** *adv*.

ethos *n* the distinguishing character, sentiment, moral nature, or guiding beliefs of a person, group, or institution.

ethyl *n* the radical from which common alcohol and ether are derived.

etiquette n the form of conduct or behavior prescribed by custom or authority to be observed in social, official or professional life.

etymology n (pl **etymologies**) the study of the source and meaning of words; an account of the source and history of a word.—**etymological, etymologic** adj.—**etymologist** n.

eucalyptus, eucalypt n (pl **eucalyptuses, eucalypti** or **eucalypts**) any of a genus of mostly Australian evergreen trees cultivated for their resin, oil, and wood; a type of oil obtained from its leaves.

Eucharist n the Christian sacrament of communion in which bread and wine are consecrated.

eulogy n (pl **eulogies**) a speech or piece of writing in praise or celebration of someone or something.—**eulogize** vt.

eunuch n a castrated man.

euphemism n a mild or inoffensive word substituted for a more unpleasant or offensive term; the use of such inoffensive words.—**euphemistic** adj.—**euphemistically** adv.

euphony n (pl **euphonies**) a pleasing sound, esp words.—**euphonious** adj.

euphoria n a feeling of elation.—**euphoric** adj.—**euphorically** adv.

Eurasian adj of Europe and Asia (Eurasia) taken as one continent; of mixed European and Asian descent.—also n.

eureka interj used to express triumph on a discovery.

euro n the name for the European unit of currency.

euthanasia n the act or practice of killing painlessly, esp to relieve incurable suffering.

evacuate vti to move (people, etc) from an area of danger to one of safety; to leave or make empty; to discharge wastes from the body.—**evacuation** n.—**evacuative** adj.—**evacuator** n.

evacuee n an evacuated person.

evade vt to manage to avoid, esp by dexterity or slyness.—**evadable** adj.—**evader** n.

evaluate vt to determine the value of; to assess.—**evaluation** n.—**evaluator** n.

evangelical adj of or agreeing with Christian teachings, esp as presented in the four Gospels; pertaining to various Christian sects that believe in salvation through personal conversion and faith in Christ.—**evangelicalism** n.

evangelism n preaching the Christian gospel; missionary zeal.

evangelist n a person who preaches the gospel; one of the writers of the four Gospels.—**evangelistic** adj.—**evangelistically** adv.

evaporate vti to change into a vapor; to remove water from; to give off moisture; to vanish; to disappear.—**evaporable** adj.—**evaporation** n.—**evaporative** adj.—**evaporator** n.

evasion n the act of evading; a means of evading, esp an equivocal reply or excuse.—**evasive** adj.—**evasively** adv.—**evasiveness** n.

eve n the evening or the whole day, before a festival; the period immediately before an event.

even adj level, flat; smooth; regular, equal; balanced; exact; divisible by two. * vti to make or become even; (with **up**) to balance (debts, etc). * adv exactly; precisely; fully; quite; at the very time; used as an intensive to emphasize the identity of something (he looked content, even happy), to indicate something unexpected (she refused even to look at him), or to stress the comparative degree (she did even better).—**evenly** adv.—**evenness** n.

evening n the latter part of the day and early part of the night.

event n something that happens; a social occasion; contingency; a contest in a sports programme.

eventful adj full of incidents; momentous.

eventual adj happening at some future unspecified time; ultimate.—**eventually** adv.

eventuality n (pl **eventualities**) a possible occurrence.

ever adv always, at all times; at any time; in any case.

evergreen adj (plants, trees) having foliage that remains green all year.—also n.

everlasting adj enduring forever.—**everlastingly** adv.

evermore adv forever.

every adj being one of the total.

everybody, everyone pron every person.

everyday adj happening daily; commonplace; worn or used on ordinary days.

everything pron all things, all; something of the utmost importance.

everywhere adv in every place.

evict vt to expel from land or from a building by legal process; to expel.—**eviction** n.—**evictor** n.

evidence n an outward sign; proof, testimony, esp matter submitted in court to determine the truth of alleged facts. * vt to demonstrate clearly; to give proof or evidence for.—**evidential** adj.—**evidentially** adv.

evident adj easy to see or understand.—**evidently** adv.

evil adj wicked; causing or threatening distress or harm. * n a sin; a source of harm or distress.—**evilly** adv.—**evilness** n.

evildoer n a wicked person.—**evildoing** n.

evince vt to indicate that one has (eg a quality); to demonstrate.—**evincible** adj.—**evincive** adj.

eviscerate vt to take out the intestines of, disembowel.—**evisceration** n.—**eviscerator** n.

evocative adj serving to evoke.—**evocatively** adv.

evoke vt to call forth or up.—**evocable** adj.—**evocation** n.—**evoker** n.

evolution n a process of change in a particular direction; the process by which something attains its distinctive characteristics; a theory that existing types of plants and animals have developed from earlier forms.—**evolutionary, evolutional** adj.

evolve vi to develop by or as if by evolution.—**evolvable** adj.—**evolvement** n.

ewe n a female sheep.

ewer n a large pitcher or jug with a wide spout.

exacerbate vt to make more violent, bitter, or severe.—**exacerbatingly** adv.—**exacerbation** n.

exact adj without error, absolutely accurate; detailed. * vt to compel by force, to extort; to require.—**exactable** adj.—**exactness** n.—**exactor, exacter** n.—**exaction** n.

exacting adj greatly demanding; requiring close attention and precision.

exactitude n (the state of) being exact.

exactly adv in an exact manner; precisely. * interj quite so!

exaggerate vt to enlarge (a statement, etc) beyond what is really so or believable.—**exaggeration** n.**exalt** vt to raise up, esp in rank, power, or dignity.—**exalted** adj.—**exaltation** n.

exam n (inf) an examination.

examination n an examining, close scrutiny; a set of written or oral questions designed as a test of knowledge; the formal questioning of a witness on oath.

examine vt to look at closely and carefully, to investigate; to test, esp by questioning.—**examinable** adj.—**examiner** n.

example n a representative sample; a model to be followed or avoided; a problem to be solved in order to show the application of some rule; a warning to others.

exasperate vt to annoy intensely.—**exasperating** adj.—**exasperation** n.

excavate vt to form a hole or tunnel by digging; to unearth; to expose to view (historical remains, etc) by digging away a covering.—**excavation** n.—**excavator** n.

exceed vt to be greater than or superior to; to go beyond the limit of.—**exceedable** adj.—**exceeder** n.

exceedingly adv very, extremely.

excel vb (**excelling, excelled**) vt to outdo, to be superior to. * vi (with **in, at**) to do better than others.

excellence n that in which one excels; superior merit or quality; (with cap) a title of honor given to certain high officials.—**excellent** adj.—**excellently** adv.

except vt to exclude, to take or leave out. * prep not including; other than.—**exceptable** adj.

exception n the act of excepting; something excepted; an objection.

exceptional adj unusual, forming an exception; superior.—**exceptionally** adv.

excerpt n an extract from a book, movie, etc. * vt to select or quote (a passage from a book).—**excerptible** adj.—**excerption** n.

excess n the exceeding of proper established limits; the amount by which one thing or quantity exceeds another; (pl) overindulgence in eating or drinking; unacceptable conduct.—**excessive** adj.—**excessively** adv.

exchange vt to give and take (one thing in return for another); to give to and receive from another person. * n the exchanging of one thing for another; the thing exchanged; the conversion of money in one currency into a sum of equivalent value in another currency; a place where things and services are exchanged, esp a marketplace for securities.—**exchangeable** adj.—**exchangeability** n.—**exchanger** n.

excise[1] n a tax on the manufacture, sale, or use of certain articles within a country.—**excisable** adj.

excise[2] vt to remove by cutting out.—**excision** n.

excitation n the act of exciting; the state of excitement.

excite vt to arouse the feelings of, esp to generate feelings of pleasurable anticipation; to cause to experience strong emotion; to stir up, agitate; to rouse to activity.—**excitable** adj.—**excitability** n.

excitement n a feeling of strong, esp pleasurable, emotion; something that excites.—**excited** adj.—**excitedly** adv.—**exciting** adj.—**excitingly** adv.

exclaim vti to shout out or utter suddenly and with strong emotion.—**exclamation** n.

exclamation point, exclamation mark n the punctuation mark (!) placed after an exclamation.

exclude vt to shut out, to keep out; to reject or omit; to eject.—**excluder** n.—**exclusion** n.

exclusive adj excluding all else; reserved for particular persons; snobbishly aloof; fashionable, high-class, expensive; unobtainable or unpublished elsewhere; sole, undivided.—**exclusively** adv.—**exclusiveness** n.—**exclusivity** n.

excommunicate vt to bar from association with a church; to exclude from fellowship.—**excommunication** n. **excrement** n waste matter discharged from the bowels.—**excremental** adj.

excrescence n an outgrowth, esp abnormal, from a plant or animal; a disfigurement.

excreta npl waste matter discharged from the body, feces, urine.—**excrete** vt.—**excretion** n.

excruciate vt to inflict severe pain upon; to torture.—**excruciating** adj.—**excruciatingly** adv.

excursion n a pleasure trip; a short journey.

excusable adj able to be excused.—**excusably** adv.

excuse vt to pardon; to forgive; to give a reason or apology for; to be a reason or explanation of; to let off. * n an apology, a plea in extenuation.

execute vt to carry out, put into effect; to perform; to produce (eg a work of art); to make legally valid; to put to death by law.—**executable** adj.—**executer** n.—**execution** n.

executioner n a person who executes a death sentence upon a condemned prisoner.

executive n a person or group concerned with administration or management of a business or organization; the branch of government with the power to put laws, etc into effect. * adj having the power to execute decisions, laws, decrees, etc.

executor n a person appointed by a testator to see the terms of a will implemented.—**executorial** adj.—**executorship** n.

exemplar n a model; a typical instance or example.

exemplary adj deserving imitation; serving as a warning.—**exemplarily** adv.—**exemplariness** n.

exemplify vt (**exemplifying, exemplified**) to illustrate by example; to be an instance or example of.—**exemplification** n.—**exemplifier** n.

exempt adj not liable, free from the obligations required of others. * vt to grant immunity (from).—**exemptible** adj.—**exemption** n.

exercise n the use or application of a power or right; regular physical or mental exertion for health, amusement or acquisition of some skill; something performed to develop or test a specific ability or skill; (often pl) maneuvers carried out for military training and discipline. * vt to use, exert, employ; to engage in regular physical activity to strengthen the body, etc; to train (troops) by means of drills and maneuvers; to engage the attention of; to perplex.—**exercisable** adj.

exert vt to bring (eg strength, influence) into use.—**exertion** n.

exhale vt to breathe out.—**exhalation** n.

exhaust vt to use up completely; to make empty; to use up, tire out; (subject) to deal with or develop completely. * n the escape of waste gas or steam from an engine; the device through which these escape.—**exhausted** adj.—**exhauster** n.—**exhaustible** adj.—**exhausting** adj.

exhaustion n the act of exhausting or being exhausted; extreme weariness.

exhaustive adj comprehensive, thorough.—**exhaustively** adv.

exhibit vt to display, esp in public; to present to a court in legal form. * n an act or instance of exhibiting, something exhibited; something produced and identified in court for use as evidence.—**exhibitor** n.—**exhibitory** adj.

exhibition n a showing, a display; a public show; an allowance made to a student.

exhibitionism n an excessive tendency to show off one's abilities; a compulsion to expose oneself indecently in public.—**exhibitionist** n.

exhilarate vt to make very happy; to invigorate.—**exhilarating** adj.—**exhilaration** n.

exhort vt to urge or advise strongly.—**exhortation** n.—**exhortative, exhortatory** adj.

exhume vt to dig up (a dead person) for detailed examination.—**exhumation** n.

exigency, exigence n (pl **exigencies, exigences**) a pressing need; emergency.

exile n prolonged absence from one's own country, either through choice or as a punishment; an exiled person. * vt to banish, to expel from one's native land.

exist vi to have being; to just manage a living; to occur in a specific place under specific conditions.—**existence** n.—**existent** adj.

exit n a way out of an enclosed space; death; a departure from a stage. * vi to leave, withdraw; to go offstage.

exodus n the departure of many people; (with cap) the departure of the Israelites from Egypt led by Moses.

exonerate vt to absolve from blame; to relieve from a responsibility, obligation.—**exoneration** n.—**exonerative** adj.—**exonerator** n.

exorbitant adj (prices, demands, etc) unreasonable, excessive.—**exorbitance** n.

exorcize, exorcise vt to expel an evil spirit (from a person or place) by ritual and prayer.—**exorcizer, exorciser** n.—**exorcism** n.—**exorcist** n.

exotic adj foreign; strange; excitingly different or unusual.—**exotically** adv.—**exoticism** n.—**exoticness** n.

exotica npl exotic items, esp as a collection.

expand vt to increase in size, bulk, extent, importance; to describe in fuller detail. * vi to become larger; to become more genial and responsive.—**expandable, expandible** adj.—**expander** n.—**expansion** n.—**expansionary** adj.

expanse n a wide area of land, etc; the extent of a spread-out area.

expansive adj able to or having the capacity to expand or cause expansion; comprehensive; (person) genial, communicative.—**expansively** adv.—**expansiveness** n.

expatriate adj living in another country; self-exiled or banished. * n an expatriate person. * vti to exile (oneself) or banish (another person). —**expatriation** n.

expect vt to anticipate; to regard as likely to arrive or happen; to consider necessary, reasonable or due; to think, suppose.—**expectant** adj.—**expectantly** adv.

expectation n the act or state of expecting; something that is expected to happen; (pl) prospects for the future, esp of inheritance.

expediency, expedience n (pl **expediencies, expediences**) fitness, suitability; an inclination towards expedient methods.—**expediential** adj.

expedient adj suitable or desirable under the circumstances. * n a means to an end; a means devised or used for want of something better.—**expediently** adv.

expedite vt to carry out promptly; to facilitate.—**expediter, expeditor** n.

expedition n a journey to achieve some purpose, as exploration, etc; the party making this journey; speedy efficiency, promptness.

expeditious adj speedy; efficient.—**expeditiously** adv.

expel vt (**expelling, expelled**) to drive out, to eject; to banish.

expend vt to spend (money, time, energy, etc); to use up, consume.

expendable adj able to be consumed, not worth keeping; available for sacrifice to achieve some objective.—**expendability** n.

expenditure n the act or process of expending money, etc; the amount expended.

expense n a payment of money for something, expenditure; a cause of expenditure; (pl) money spent on some activity (eg traveling on business); reimbursement for this.

expensive adj causing or involving great expense; costly.—**expensively** adv.—**expensiveness** n.

experience n observation or practice resulting in or tending towards knowledge; knowledge gained by seeing and doing; a state of being affected from without (as by events); an affecting event. * vt to have experience of.

experienced adj wise or skilled through experience.

experiment n any test or trial to find out something; a controlled procedure carried out to discover, test, or demonstrate something. * vi to carry out experiments.—**experimentation** n.—**experimenter** n.

experimental adj of, derived from, or proceeding by experiment; empirical; provisional.—**experimentalism** n.—**experimentally** adv.

expert adj thoroughly skilled; knowledgeable through training and experience. * n a person with special skills or training in any art or science.—**expertly** adv.—**expertise** n.

expiate vt to pay the penalty for; to make amends for.—**expiation** n.—**expiator** n.—**expiatory** adj.

expire vti to come to an end; to lapse or become void; to breathe out; to die.—**expiration** n.—**expiry** n.

explain vt to make plain or clear; to give a reason for, account for.—**explainable** adj.—**explanation** n.—**explanatory** adj.

expletive n a violent exclamation or swearword.

explicit adj clearly stated, not merely implied; outspoken, frank; graphically detailed.—**explicitly** adv.—**explicitness** n.

explode vti to burst or cause to blow up with a loud noise, as in the detonation of a bomb; (emotions) to burst out; (population) to increase rapidly; to expose (a theory, etc) as false.—**explosive** adj, n.—**explosively** adv.

exploit n a bold achievement. * vt to utilize, develop (raw materials, etc); to take unfair advantage of, esp for financial gain.—**exploitable** adj.—**exploitation** n.—**exploitative** adj.

explore vti to examine or inquire into; to travel through (a country) for the purpose of (geographical) discovery; to examine minutely.—**exploration** n.—**explorer** n.—**exploratory, explorative** adj.

explosion n an act or instance of exploding; a sudden loud noise caused by this; an outburst of emotion; a rapid increase or expansion.

exponent n a person who explains or interprets something; a person who champions, advocates, or exemplifies.

export vt to send out (goods) of one country for sale in another. * n the act of exporting; the article exported.—**exportable** adj.—**exportation** n.—**exporter** n.

expose vt to deprive of protection or shelter; to subject to an influence (as light, weather); to display, reveal; to uncover or disclose.—**exposable** adj.—**exposal** n.—**exposure** n.

exposé n a revelation of crime, dishonesty, etc.

exposed adj open to view; not shielded or protected.—**exposedness** n.

exposition n a public show or exhibition; a detailed explanation; a speech or writing explaining a process, thing, or idea.—**expositional** adj.

expostulate vi to argue with, esp to dissuade.—**expostulation** n.—**expostulator** n.—**expostulatory, expostulative** adj.

expound vt to explain or set forth in detail.—**expounder** n.

express vt to represent in words; to make known one's thoughts, feelings, etc; to represent by signs, symbols, etc; to squeeze out. * adj firmly stated, explicit; (train, bus, etc) traveling at high speed with few or no stops. * adv at high speed, by express service. * n an express train, coach, etc; a system or company for sending freight, etc at rates higher than standard.

expression n an act of expressing, esp by words; a word or phrase; a look; intonation; a manner of showing feeling in communicating or performing (eg music).—**expressionless** adj.—**expressive** adj.—**expressively** adv.

expressionism n a style of art, literature, music, etc that seeks to depict the subjective emotions aroused in the artist by objects and events, not objective reality.—**expressionist** n.—**expressionistic** adj.

expressly adv explicitly; for a specific purpose.

expressway n a high-speed divided highway with partially or totally controlled access.

expropriate vt to remove (property) from its owner, to dispossess.—**expropriable** adj.—**expropriation** n.—**expropriator** n.

expulsion n the act of expelling or being expelled.—**expulsive** adj.

expunge vt to obliterate, to erase.—**expunction** n.—**expunger** n.

expurgate vt to cut from a book, play, etc any parts supposed to be offensive or erroneous.—**expurgation** n.—**expurgator** n.—**expurgatory, expurgatorial** adj.

exquisite adj very beautiful, refined; sensitive, showing discrimination; acutely felt, as pain or pleasure.—**exquisitely** adv.

extant adj still existing.

extemporaneous, extemporary adj spoken, acted, etc without preparation.—**extemporaneously, extemporarily** adv.

extemporize vi to do something extemporaneously.—**extemporization** n.

extend vt to stretch or spread out; to stretch fully; to prolong in time; to cause to reach in distance, etc; to enlarge, increase the scope of; to hold out (eg the hand); to accord, grant; to give, offer, (eg sympathy). * vi to prolong in distance or time; to reach in scope.

extension n the act of extending or state of being extended; extent, scope; an added part, eg to a building; an extra period; a programme of extramural teaching provided by a college, etc; an additional telephone connected to the principal line.

extensive *adj* large; having a wide scope or extent.–**extensively** *adv.*–**extensiveness** *n.*

extent *n* the distance over which a thing is extended; the range or scope of something; the limit to which something extends.

extenuate *vt* to make (guilt, a fault, or offense) seem less.–**extenuating** *adj.*–**extenuator** *n.*–**extenuatory** *adj.*

extenuation *n* an extenuating or being extenuated, partial justification; something that extenuates, an excuse.

exterior *adj* of, on, or coming from the outside; external; (*paint, etc*) suitable for use on the outside. * *n* the external part or surface; outward manner or appearance.

exterminate *vt* to destroy completely.–**exterminable** *adj.*–**extermination** *n.*–**exterminatory** *adj.*

external *adj* outwardly perceivable; of, relating to, or located on the outside or outer part. * *n* an external feature.–**externally** *adv.*

externalize *vt* to make external; to attribute an external existence to; to express (feelings, etc) esp in words.–**externalization** *n.*

extinct *adj* (*animals*) not alive, no longer existing; (*fire*) not burning, out; (*volcano*) no longer active.–**extinction** *n.*

extinguish *vt* to put out (a fire, light, etc); to bring to an end.–**extinguishable** *adj.*–**extinguishment** *n.*

extinguisher *n* a device for putting out a fire.

extirpate *vt* to destroy totally, as by uprooting.–**extirpation** *n.*–**extirpative** *adj.*–**extirpator** *n.*

extoll, extol *vt* (**extolls** *or* **extols, extolling, extolled**) to praise highly.–**extoller** *n.*–**extollment, extolment** *n.*

extort *vt* to obtain (money, promises, etc) by force or improper pressure.–**extorter** *n.*–**extortive** *adj.*

extortion *n* the act or practice of extorting; the criminal instance of this; oppressive or unjust exaction.–**extortionary** *adj.*–**extortioner, extortionist** *n.*

extortionate *adj* exorbitant; excessively high in price.–**extortionately** *adv.*

extra *adj* additional. * *adv* unusually; in addition. * *n* something extra or additional, esp a charge; a special edition of a newspaper; a person who plays a non-speaking role in a film.

extract *vt* to take or pull out by force; to withdraw by chemical or physical means; to abstract, excerpt. * *n* the essence of a substance obtained by extraction; a passage taken from a book, play, movie, etc.–**extractable, extractible** *adj.*–**extractability, extractibility** *n.*

extraction *n* the act of extracting; lineage; something extracted.

extractor *n* a thing that extracts; a device for extracting stale air or fumes from a room (–*also* **extractor fan**).

extracurricular *adj* not part of the regular school timetable; beyond one's normal duties or activities.

extradite *vt* to surrender (an alleged criminal) to the country where the offense was committed.–**extraditable** *adj.*–**extradition** *n.*

extramarital *adj* occurring outside marriage, esp sexual relationships.

extraneous *adj* coming from outside; not essential.–**extraneously** *adv.*

extraordinary *adj* not usual or regular; remarkable, exceptional.–**extraordinarily** *adv.*–**extraordinariness** *n.*

extravagant *adj* lavish in spending; (*prices*) excessively high; wasteful; (*behavior, praise, etc*) lacking in restraint, flamboyant, profuse.–**extravagantly** *adv.*–**extravagance** *n.*

extravaganza *n* an elaborate musical production; a spectacular show, play, movie, etc.

extravert *see* **extrovert**.

extreme *adj* of the highest degree or intensity; excessive, immoderate, unwarranted; very severe, stringent; outermost. * *n* the highest or furthest limit or degree; (*often pl*) either of the two points marking the ends of a scale or range.–**extremely** *adv.*–**extremeness** *n.*

extremist *n* a person of extreme views, esp political.–**extremism** *n.*

extremity *n* (*pl* **extremities**) the utmost point or degree; the most remote part; the utmost violence, vigor, or necessity; the end; (*pl*) the hands or feet.

extricate *vt* to release from difficulties; to disentangle.–**extrication** *n.*

extrovert *n* a person more interested in the external world than his own thoughts and feelings.–*also* **extravert**.–**extroverted, extraverted** *adj.*

exuberant *adj* lively, effusive, high-spirited; profuse.–**exuberance** *n.*–**exuberantly** *adv.*

exude *vt* to cause or allow to ooze through pores or incisions, as sweat, pus; to display (confidence, emotion) freely.

exult *vi* to rejoice greatly.–**exultation** *n.*–**exultant** *adj.*–**exultantly** *adv.*

eye *n* the organ of sight; the iris; the faculty of seeing; the external part of the eye; something resembling an eye, as the hole in a needle, the leaf-bud on a potato, etc. * *vt* (**eyeing** *or* **eying, eyed**) to look at; to observe closely.

eyeball *n* the ball of the eye. * *vt* (*sl*) to stare at.

eyebrow *n* the hairy ridge above the eye.

eyeglasses *npl* spectacles.

eyelash *n* the fringe of fine hairs along the edge of each eyelid.

eyelet *n* a small hole for a rope or cord to pass through, as in sails, garments, etc.

eyelid *n* the lid of skin and muscle that moves to cover the eye.

eye-opener *n* something that comes as a shock or surprise.

eyeshot *n* seeing distance.

eyesight *n* the faculty of seeing.

eyesore *n* anything offensive to the sight.

eyetooth *n* (*pl* **eyeteeth**) a canine tooth in the upper jaw.

eye-witness *n* a person who sees an event, such as an accident or a crime, and can describe what happened.

eyrie *n* the nest of an eagle or other bird of prey; any high inaccessible place or position.–*also* **aerie**.

F

F *abbr* = Fahrenheit; (*chem symbol*) fluorine.

fable *n* a story, often with animal characters, intended to convey a moral; a lie, fabrication; a story involving mythical, legendary or supernatural characters or events.–**fabled** *adj.*

fabric *n* cloth made by knitting, weaving, etc; framework, structure.

fabricate *vt* to construct, manufacture; to concoct (eg a lie); to forge.–**fabrication** *n.*–**fabricator** *n.*

fabulous *adj* told in fables; incredible, astonishing; (*inf*) very good.–**fabulously** *adv.*

façade, facade *n* the main front or face of a building; an outward appearance, esp concealing something hidden.

face *n* the front part of the head containing the eyes, nose, mouth, chin, etc; facial expression; the front or outer surface of anything; external show or appearance; dignity, self respect; impudence; effrontery; a coal face. * *vt* to be confronted by (a problem, etc); to deal with (an opponent, problem, etc) resolutely; to be opposite to; to turn (a playing card) face upwards; to cover with a new surface. * *vi* to turn the face in a certain direction; to be situated in or have a specific direction.

faceless *adj* lacking a face; anonymous.

face-lift *n* plastic surgery to smooth and firm the face; an improvement or renovation, esp to the outside of a building.

facet *n* a small plane surface (as on a cut gem); an aspect of character, a problem, issue, etc.

facetious *adj* joking, esp in an inappropriate manner.–**facetiously** *adv.*–**facetiousness** *n*.

face value *n* the value indicated on the face of (e.g. a coin or share certificate); apparent worth or significance.

facia *see* **fascia**.

facial *adj* of or pertaining to the face. * *n* a beauty treatment for the face.–**facially** *adv*.

facile *adj* easy to do; superficial.

facilitate *vt* to make easier; to help forward.–**facilitator** *n*.–**facilitation** *n*.

facility *n* (*pl* **facilities**) the quality of being easily done; aptitude, dexterity; something, eg a service or equipment, that makes it easy to do something.

facing *n* a lining at the edge of a garment; a covering on a surface for decoration or protection.

facsimile *n* an exact copy of a book, document, etc; a method of transmitting printed matter (text and graphics) through the telephone system.–*also* **fax**.

fact *n* a thing known to have happened or to exist; reality; a piece of verifiable information; (*law*) an event, occurrence, etc as distinguished from its legal consequences.–**factual** *adj*.

faction *n* a small group of people in an organization working together in a common cause against the main body; dissension within a group or organization.–**factional** *adj.*–**factionally** *adv.*–**factious** *adj*.

factor *n* any circumstance that contributes towards a result; (*math*) any of two or more numbers that, when multiplied together, form a product; a person who acts for another.

factory *n* (*pl* **factories**) a building or buildings where things are manufactured.

factotum *n* a person employed to do all kinds of work.

facts of life *npl* knowledge of human sexual reproduction.

faculty *n* (*pl* **faculties**) any natural power of a living organism; special aptitude; a teaching department of a college or university, or the staff of such a department.

fad *n* a personal habit or idiosyncrasy; a craze.–**faddish, faddy** *adj.*–**faddism** *n.*–**faddist** *n*.

fade *vi* to lose vigor or brightness of color gradually; to vanish gradually. * *vt* to cause (an image or a sound) to increase or decrease in brightness or intensity gradually.–*also* *n.*–**fading** *n*.

faeces *see* **feces**.

fag *vti* (**fagging, fagged**) to become or cause to be tired by hard work.

Fahrenheit *adj* of, using, or being a temperature scale with the freezing point of water marked at 32° and the boiling point at 212°.

fail *vi* to weaken, to fade or die away; to stop operating; to fall short; to be insufficient; to be negligent in duty, expectation, etc; (*exam, etc*) to be unsuccessful; to become bankrupt. * *vt* to disappoint the expectations or hopes of; to be unsuccessful in an exam, etc; to leave, to abandon; to grade (a candidate) as not passing a test, etc. * *n* failure in an examination.

failing *n* a fault, weakness. * *prep* in default or absence of.

fail-safe *adj* designed to operate safely even if a fault develops; foolproof.

failure *n* failing, non-performance, lack of success; the ceasing of normal operation of something; a deficiency; bankruptcy; an unsuccessful person or thing.

faint *adj* dim, indistinct; weak, feeble; timid; on the verge of losing consciousness. * *vi* to lose consciousness temporarily from a decrease in the supply of blood to the brain, as from shock. * *n* an act or condition of fainting.–**faintly** *adv.*–**faintness** *n*.

fair[1] *adj* pleasing to the eye; clean, unblemished; (*hair*) light-colored; (*weather*) clear and sunny just and honest; according to the rules; moderately large; average. * *adv* in a fair manner; squarely.–**fairness** *n*.

fair[2] *n* a gathering for the sale of goods, esp for charity; a competitive exhibition of farm, household, or manufactured goods; a fun-fair.

fairground *n* an open area where fairs are held.

fairly *adv* in a fair manner; justly; moderately.

fair play *n* justice, honesty; impartiality.

fairway *n* a navigable channel; the mowed part of a golf course between the tee and the green.

fairy *n* (*pl* **fairies**) an imaginary supernatural being, usu in human form.

fairy story, fairy tale *n* a story about fairies; an incredible story; a fabrication.

fait accompli *n* (*pl* **faits accomplis**) something already done; an irreversible act.

faith *n* trust or confidence in a person or thing; a strong conviction, esp a religion; any system of religious belief; fidelity to one's promises, sincerity.

faithful *adj* loyal; true; true to the original, accurate.–**faithfully** *adv.*–**faithfulness** *n*.

faithless *adj* treacherous, disloyal; untrustworthy.–**faithlessly** *adv.*–**faithlessness** *n*.

fake *vt* to make (an object) appear more real or valuable in order to deceive; to pretend, simulate. * *n* a faked article, a forgery; an impostor. * *adj* counterfeit, not genuine.–**faker** *n*.

fakir *n* a Muslim or Hindu religious mendicant or ascetic.

falcon *n* a type of hawk trained for use in hunting.–**falconry** *n*.

fall *vi* (**falling, fell**, *pp* **fallen**) to descend by force of gravity; to come as if by falling; to collapse; to drop to the ground; to become lower, weaker, less; to lose power, status, etc; to lose office; to slope in a downward direction; to be wounded or killed in battle; (*with* **back**) to retreat; (*with* **behind**) to fail to keep up with; to become in arrears with; (*with* **for**) to fall in love with; to be fooled by (a lie, trick, etc); (*with* **out**) to quarrel; to leave one's place in a military formation; (*with* **through**) to fail to happen. * *n* act or instance of falling; something which falls; the amount by which something falls; a decline in status, position; overthrow; a downward slope; a decrease in size, quantity, value; autumn.

fallacy *n* (*pl* **fallacies**) a false idea; a mistake in reasoning.–**fallacious** *adj.*–**fallaciously** *adv*.

fallen *adj* sunk to a lower state or condition; overthrown.

fallible *adj* liable to make mistakes.–**fallibly** *adv.–* **fallibility** *n*.

fall-out *n* a deposit of radioactive dust from a nuclear explosion; a by-product.

fallow *adj* (*land*) plowed and left unplanted for a season or more.

fallow deer *n* a small European deer with a brownish-yellow coat which becomes spotted with white in summer.

false *adj* wrong, incorrect; deceitful; artificial; disloyal, treacherous; misleading, fallacious.–**falsely** *adv.*–**falseness** *n*.

falsehood *n* a being untrue; the act of deceiving; a lie.

falsetto *n* (*pl* **falsettos**) an artificial tone higher in key than the natural compass of the voice.

falsify *vt* (**falsifying, falsified**) to misrepresent; to alter (a document, etc) fraudulently; to prove false.–**falsification** *n*.

falsity *n* (*pl* **falsities**) the quality of being false; an error, a lie.

falter *vi* to move or walk unsteadily, to stumble; to hesitate or stammer in speech; to be weak or unsure, to waver.–**faltering** *adj.*–**falteringly** *adv*.

fame *n* the state of being well known; good reputation.–**famed** *adj*.

familiar *adj* well-acquainted; friendly; common, well-known; too informal, presumptuous. * *n* a spirit or demon supposed to aid a witch, etc; an intimate.–**familiarly** *adv.*–**familiarity** *n.*–**familiarize** *vt*.

family *n* (*pl* **families**) parents and their children; a person's children; a set of relatives; the descendants of a common ancestor; any group of persons or things related in some way; a group of related plants or animals; a unit of a crime syndicate (as the Mafia).

family tree *n* a genealogical diagram.

famine n an acute scarcity of food in a particular area; an extreme scarcity of anything.

famish vti to make or be very hungry.

famous adj renowned; (inf) excellent.–**famously** adv.

fan[1] n a handheld or mechanical device used to set up a current of air. * vt (**fanning, fanned**) to cool, as with a fan; to ventilate; to stir up, to excite; to spread out like a fan.

fan[2] n an enthusiastic follower of some sport, hobby, person, etc.

fanatic n a person who is excessively enthusiastic about something.–**fanatical** adj.–**fanatically** adv.–**fanaticism** n.

fanciful adj not factual, imaginary; indulging in fancy; elaborate or intricate in design.–**fancifully** adv.

fancy n (pl **fancies**) imagination; a mental image; a whim; fondness. * adj (**fancier, fanciest**) not based on fact, imaginary; elegant or ornamental. * vt (**fancying, fancied**) to imagine; to have a fancy or liking for; (inf) to be sexually attracted to.

fandango n (pl **fandangos**) a Spanish dance, music for this dance, tomfoolery.

fanfare n a flourish of trumpets.

fang n a long sharp tooth, as in a canine; the long hollow tooth through which venomous snakes inject poison.

fanlight n a semicircular window with radiating bars like the ribs of a fan.

fantasia n an improvised musical or prose composition.

fantasize vt to imagine in an extravagant way. * vi to daydream.

fantastic adj unrealistic, fanciful; unbelievable; imaginative; (inf) wonderful.–**fantastically** adv.

fantasy n (pl **fantasies**) imagination; a product of the imagination, esp an extravagant or bizarre notion or creation; an imaginative poem, play or novel.

far adj (**farther, farthest** or **further, furthest**) remote in space or time; long; (political views, etc) extreme * adv very distant in space, time, or degree; to or from a distance in time or position, very much.–**farness** n.

faraway adj distant, remote; dreamy.

farce n a style of light comedy; a drama using such comedy; a ludicrous situation.–**farcical** adj.–**farcically** adv.

fare n money paid for transportation; a passenger in public transport; food. * vi to be in a specified condition.

Far East n the countries of East and Southeast Asia including China, Japan, North and South Korea, Indochina, eastern Siberia and adjacent islands.

farewell interj goodbye.–also n.

far-fetched adj unlikely.

farm n an area of land (with buildings) on which crops and animals are raised. * vt to grow crops or breed livestock; to cultivate, as land; to breed fish commercially; (with **out**) to put out (work, etc) to be done by others, to subcontract.

farmer n a person who manages or operates a farm.

farm hand n a worker on a farm.

farmhouse n a house on a farm.

farming adj pertaining to, or engaged in, agriculture. * n the business or practice of agriculture.

farmstead n a farm with the buildings belonging to it.

farmyard n a yard close to or surrounded by farm buildings.

far-reaching adj having serious or widespread consequences.

farrow n a litter of pigs. * vti to give birth to (pigs).

farther adj at or to a greater distance. * adv to a greater degree.

farthest adj at or to the greatest distance. * adv to the greatest degree.

fascia n (pl **fasciae**) the instrument panel of a motor vehicle, the dashboard; the flat surface above a shop front, with the owner's name, etc.–also **facia**.

fascinate vt to hold the attention of, to attract irresistibly.–**fascination** n.

fascinating adj having great interest or charm.

Fascism n a system of government characterized by dictatorship, belligerent nationalism, racism, and militarism.–**Fascist** n, adj.

fashion n the current style of dress, conduct, speech, etc; the manner or form of appearance or action. * vt to make in a particular form; to suit or adapt.–**fashioner** n.

fashionable adj conforming to the current fashion; attracting or frequented by people of fashion.–**fashionably** adv.

fast[1] adj swift, quick; (clock) ahead of time; firmly attached, fixed; (color, dye) non-fading. * adv firmly, thoroughly, rapidly, quickly.

fast[2] vi to go without all or certain foods. * n a period of fasting.

fasten vti to secure firmly; to attach; to fix or direct (the eyes, attention) steadily.

fastener, fastening n a clip, catch, etc for fastening.

fast food n food, such as hamburgers, kebabs, pizzas, etc prepared and served quickly.

fastidious adj hard to please; daintily refined; over-sensitive.–**fastidiously** adv.–**fastidiousness** n.

fast track n a hectic and competitive lifestyle or career.–**fast-track** adj.

fat adj (**fatter, fattest**) plump; thick; fertile; profitable. * n an oily or greasy material found in animal tissue and plant seeds; the richest or best part of anything; a superfluous part.–**fatness** n.

fatal adj causing death; disastrous (to); fateful.–**fatally** adv.

fatalism n belief that all events are predetermined by fate and therefore inevitable; acceptance of this doctrine.–**fatalist** n.–**fatalistic** adj.

fatality n (pl **fatalities**) a death caused by a disaster or accident; a person killed in such a way; a fatal power or influence.

fate n the ultimate power that predetermines events, destiny; the ultimate end, outcome; misfortune, doom, death.–**fated** adj.

fateful adj having important, usu unpleasant, consequences.–**fatefully** adv.

father n a male parent; an ancestor; a founder or originator; (with cap) God; a title of respect applied to monks, priests, etc. * vt to be the father of; to found, originate.–**fatherhood** n.

father-in-law n (pl **fathers-in-law**) the father of one's husband or wife.

fatherland n one's native country.

fatherless adj without a living father.

fatherly adj pertaining to a father; kind, affectionate, as a father. * adv like a father.

fathom n a nautical measure of 6 feet (1.83 m). * vt to measure the depth of; to understand.

fatigue n tiredness from physical or mental effort; the tendency of a material to break under repeated stress; (pl) the clothing worn in the field. * vti (**fatiguing, fatigued**) to make or become tired.

fatten vt to make fat or fleshy; to make abundant.–**fattening** adj.

fatty adj (**fattier, fattiest**) resembling or containing fat. * n (pl **fatties**) (inf) a fat person.

fatuous adj foolish, idiotic.–**fatuously** adv.–**fatuousness** n.–**fatuity** n.

fatwa, fatwah n a decision by a mufti or Muslim judge.

faucet n a fixture for draining off liquid (as from a pipe or cask); a device controlling the flow of liquid through a pipe or from a container (–also **tap**).

fault n a failing, defect; a minor offence; (tennis, etc) an incorrect serve or other error; a fracture in the earth's crust causing displacement of strata. * vt to find fault with, blame. * vi to commit a fault.

fault-finding adj censorious, critical.–**fault-finder** n.

faultless adj without fault; perfect; blameless.–**faultlessly** adv.–**faultlessness** n.

faulty adj (**faultier, faultiest**) imperfect; defective; wrong.–**faultily** adv.–**faultiness** n.

fauna n (pl **faunas, faunae**) the animals of a region, period, or specific environment.

faux pas n (pl **faux pas**) an embarrassing social blunder.

favor, favour n goodwill; approval; a kind or helpful act; partiality; a small gift given out at a party; (usu pl) a privilege granted or conceded, esp sexual. * vt to regard or treat with favor; to show support for; to oblige (with); to afford advantage to, facilitate.

favorable, favourable adj expressing approval; pleasing; propitious; conducive (to).—**favorably, favourably** adv.

favorite, favourite n a favored person or thing; a competitor expected to win. * adj most preferred.

favoritism, favouritism n the showing of unfair favor.

fawn[1] n a young deer; a yellowish-brown color. * adj fawn-colored.

fawn[2] vi (dogs, etc) to crouch, etc in a show of affection; to flatter in an obsequious manner.—**fawner** n.—**fawning** n.

fax n a document sent by facsimile transmission; a device for sending faxes. * vt to send (a document) by facsimile transmission.

faze vt (inf) to disturb; to discompose, to disconcert; to daunt.

FBI abbr = Federal Bureau of Investigation.

Fe (chem symbol) iron.

fear n an unpleasant emotion excited by danger, pain, etc; a cause of fear; anxiety; deep reverence. * vt to feel fear, be afraid of; to be apprehensive, anxious; to be sorry. * vi to be afraid or apprehensive.—**fearless** adj.—**fearlessly** adv.—**fearlessness** n.

fearful adj causing intense fear; timorous; apprehensive (of); (inf) very great, very bad.—**fearfully** adv.

fearless adj brave, intrepid.—**fearlessly** adv.—**fearlessness** n.

fearsome adj causing fear, frightful.

feasible adj able to be done or implemented, possible.—**feasibly** adv.—**feasibility** n.

feast n an elaborate meal prepared for some special occasion; something that gives abundant pleasure; a periodic religious celebration. * vi to have or take part in a feast. * vt to entertain with a feast.

feat n an action of remarkable strength, skill, or courage.

feather n any of the light outgrowths that form the covering of a bird, consisting of a hollow central shaft with a vane of fine barbs on each side; a plume. * vt to ornament with feathers.—**feathering** n.—**feathery** adj.

feature n any of the parts of the face; a characteristic trait of something; a special attraction or distinctive quality of something; a prominent newspaper article, etc; the main movie in a theater program. * vti to make or be a feature of (something).

featureless adj lacking prominent or distinctive features.

febrile adj of fever; feverish.

February n (pl **Februaries**) the second month of the year, having 28 days (or 29 days in leap years).

feces npl excrement.—also **faeces**.—**fecal, faecal** adj.

feckless adj incompetent, untrustworthy.—**fecklessly** adv.—**fecklessness** n.

fecund adj fertile, prolific.—**fecundity** n.

fed see **feed**.

federal adj designating, or of a union of states, etc, in which each member surrenders some of its power to a central authority; of a central government of this type.—**federalism** n.—**federalist** n.—**federally** adv.

federation n a union of states, groups, etc, in which each subordinates its power to a central authority; a federated organization.—**federate** vti, adj.

fedora n a soft felt hat with a curled brim and a crown creased lengthways.

fee n the price paid for the advice or service of a professional; a charge for some privilege, as membership of a club; (law) an inheritance in land.

feeble adj weak, ineffective.—**feebly** adv.—**feebleness** n.

feed vb (**feeding, fed**) vt to give food to; to give as food to; to supply with necessary material; to gratify. * vi to consume food. * n food for animals; material fed into a machine; the part of a machine supplying this material.

feedback n a return to the input of part of the output of a system; information about a product, service, etc returned to the supplier for purposes of evaluation.

feeder n a person or thing that feeds; a baby's feeding-bottle; a device for supplying material to a machine; a subsidiary road, railway, etc acting as a link with the central transport network.

feel vb (**feeling, felt**) vt to perceive or explore by the touch; to find one's way by cautious trial; to be conscious of, experience; to have a vague or instinctual impression of; to believe, consider. * vi to be able to experience the sensation of touch; to be affected by; to convey a certain sensation when touched. * n the sense of touch; feeling; a quality as revealed by touch.

feeler n a tactile organ (as a tentacle or antenna) of an animal; a tentative approach or suggestion to test another person's reactions.

feeling n the sense of touch; mental or physical awareness; a physical or mental impression; a state of mind; sympathy; emotional sensitivity; a belief or opinion arising from emotion; (pl) emotions, sensibilities.

feet see **foot**.

feign vt to invent; to pretend.

feint n a pretended attack, intended to take the opponent off his guard, as in boxing.—also vi.**felicitate** vt to congratulate.—**felicitation** n.

felicity n (pl **felicities**) happiness; apt and pleasing style in writing, speech, etc.

feline adj of cats; cat-like.—**felinity** n.

fell[1] see **fall**.

fell[2] vt to cut, beat, or knock down; to kill, to sew (a seam) by folding one raw edge under the other.

fell[3] n a skin, hide, pelt.

fellow n an associate; a comrade; an equal in power, rank, or position; the other of a pair, a mate; a member of a learned society; (inf) a man or boy. * adj belonging to the same group or class.

fellowship n companionship; a mutual sharing; a group of people with the same interests.

felon n a person guilty of a felony.

felony n (pl **felonies**) (formerly) a grave crime.—**felonious** adj.

felt[1] see **feel**.

felt[2] n a fabric made from woolen fibers, often mixed with fur or hair, pressed together. * vti to make into or become like felt.

female adj of the sex that produces young; of a woman or women. * n a female animal or plant.

feminine adj of, resembling, or appropriate to women; (gram) of that gender to which words denoting females belong.—**femininity** n.—**feminize** vti.

feminism n the movement to win political, economic and social equality for women.—**feminist** adj, n.

femme fatale n (pl **femmes fatales**) a dangerously seductive woman.

femur n (pl **femurs, femora**) the thighbone.—**femoral** adj.

fen n an area of low-lying marshy or flooded land.

fence n a barrier put round land to mark a boundary, or prevent animals, etc from escaping. * vt to surround with a fence; to keep (out) as by a fence. * vi to practice fencing; to make evasive answers.—**fencer** n.

fencing n fences; material for making fences; the art of fighting with foils or other types of sword.

fend vi (with **for**) to provide a livelihood for.

fender n anything that protects or fends off something else, as old tires along the side of a vessel, or the part of a car body over the wheel.

fennel n a European herb of the carrot family grown for its foliage and aromatic seeds; a herb grown for its edible bulbous stem tasting of aniseed.

feral, ferine adj wild, untamed; like a wild beast.

ferment *n* an agent causing fermentation, as yeast; excitement, agitation. * *vti* to (cause to) undergo fermentation; to (cause to) be excited or agitated.—**fermentable** *adj*.—**fermenter** *n*.

fermentation *n* the breakdown of complex molecules in organic components caused by the influence of yeast or other substances.

fern *n* any of a large class of nonflowering plants having roots, stems, and fronds, and reproducing by spores.—**ferny** *adj*.

ferocious *adj* savage, fierce.—**ferociously** *adv*.—**ferocity, ferociousness** *n*.

ferret *n* a variety of the polecat, used in unearthing rabbits. * *vt* to drive out of a hiding-place; (*with* **out**) to reveal by persistent investigation. * *vi* to hunt with ferrets.—**ferreter** *n*.—**ferrety** *adj*.

ferric *adj* of or containing iron.

Ferris wheel *n* a large upright revolving wheel with suspended seats, popular in amusement parks.

ferrous *adj* containing iron.

ferry *vt* (**ferrying, ferried**) to convey (passengers, etc) over a stretch of water; to transport from one place to another, esp along a regular route. * *n* (*pl* **ferries**) a boat used for ferrying; a ferrying service; the location of a ferry.—**ferryman** *n* (*pl* **ferrymen**).

fertile *adj* able to bear offspring; (*land*) easily supporting plants and vegetation; (*animals*) capable of breeding; (*eggs*) able to grow and develop; prolific; (*mind, brain*) inventive.—**fertility, fertileness** *n*.

fertilize *vt* to make (soil) fertile by adding nutrients; to impregnate; to pollinate.—**fertilization** *n*.

fertilizer *n* natural organic or artificial substances used to enrich the soil.

fervent, fervid *adj* passionate; zealous.—**fervently, fervidly** *adv*.

fervor, fervour *n* intensity of feeling; zeal; warmth.

fester *vti* to become or cause to become infected; to suppurate; to rankle.

festival *n* a time of celebration; performances of music, plays, etc given periodically.

festive *adj* merry, joyous.—**festively** *adv*.—**festivity** *n*.

festoon *n* a decorative garland of flowers, etc hung between two points. * *vt* to adorn as with festoons.—**festoonery** *n*.

fetch *vt* to go for and bring back; to cause to come; (*goods*) to sell for (a certain price); (*inf*) to deal (a blow, slap, etc); (*with* **up**) to come to stand, arrive at.—**fetcher** *n*.

fetching *adj* attractive.—**fetchingly** *adv*.

fête, fete *n* a festival; a usu outdoor sale, bazaar or entertainment in aid of charity. * *vt* to honor or entertain (as if) with a fête.

fetid *adj* stinking.—*also* **foetid**.

fetish *n* an object believed by primitive peoples to have magical properties; any object or activity regarded with excessive devotion.

fetlock, fetterlock *n* the joint on a horse's leg behind and above the hoof.

fetter *n* (*usu pl*) a shackle for the feet; anything that restrains. * *vt* to put into fetters; to impede, restrain.

fettle *n* good condition or repair.

fetus *n* (*pl* **fetuses**) the unborn young of an animal, esp in its later stages; in humans, the offspring in the womb from the fourth month until birth.—*also* **foetus** (*pl* **foetuses**).—**fetal, foetal** *adj*.

feud *n* a state of hostilities, esp between individuals, families, or clans; a dispute.—*also* *vi*.

feudalism *n* the economic and social system in medieval Europe, in which land, worked by serfs, was held by vassals in exchange for military and other services to overlords.—**feudal** *adj*.

fever *n* an abnormally increased body temperature; any disease marked by a high fever; a state of restless excitement.—**fevered, feverish** *adj*.—**feverishly** *adv*.—**feverishness** *n*.

few *adj, n* a small number, not many.

fez *n* (*pl* **fezzes**) a red brimless high cap, usu with black tassel, worn esp by men in eastern Mediterranean countries.

ff *abbr* = and the following pages; (*mus*) fortissimo–very loud.

fiancé *n* a person engaged to be married.—**fiancée** *nf*.

fiasco *n* (*pl* **fiascos, fiascoes**) a complete and humiliating failure.

fib *n* a lie about something unimportant. * *vi* (**fibbing, fibbed**) to tell a fib.—**fibber** *n*.

fiber, fibre *n* a natural or synthetic thread, eg from cotton or nylon, which is spun into yarn; a material composed of such yarn; texture; strength of character; a fibrous substance, roughage.—**fibrous** *adj*.

fiberglass, fibreglass *n* glass in fibrous form, often bonded with plastic, used in making various products.

fiber optics, fibre optics *n* (*sing*) the transmission of information in the form of light signals along thin transparent fibers of glass.—**fiber-optic, fibre-optic** *adj*.**fibula** *n* (*pl* **fibulae, fibulas**) the outer of the two bones of the lower leg.—**fibular** *adj*.

fickle *adj* inconstant; capricious.—**fickleness** *n*.

fiction *n* an invented story; any literary work with imaginary characters and events, as a novel, play, etc; such works collectively.—**fictional**.—**fictionally** *adv*.

fictitious *adj* imaginary, not real; feigned.—**fictitiously** *adv*.

fiddle *n* (*inf*) a violin. * *vt* (*inf*) to play on a violin. * *vi* to handle restlessly, to fidget.—**fiddler** *n*.

fidelity *n* (*pl* **fidelities**) faithfulness, loyalty; truthfulness; accuracy in reproducing sound.

fidget *vi* to (cause to) move restlessly. * *n* nervous restlessness; a fussy person.—**fidgetingly** *adv*.—**fidgety** *adj*.

field *n* an area of land cleared of trees and buildings, used for pasture or crops; an area rich in a natural product (eg gold, coal); a battlefield; a sports ground; an area affected by electrical, magnetic or gravitational influence, etc; the area visible through an optical lens; a division of activity, knowledge, etc; all competitors in a contest. * *vt* (*baseball*) to catch or stop and return the ball as a fielder; to put (eg. a team) into the field to play; (*inf*) to handle (eg questions) successfully.—**fielder** *n*.

field event *n* (*usu pl*) an athletic competition involving jumping or throwing, as opposed to running.

field glasses *npl* small, portable binoculars for use outdoors.

fieldwork *n* research done outside the laboratory or place of work by scientists, archaeologists, social workers, etc.—**fieldworker** *n*.

fiend *n* an evil spirit; an inhumanly wicked person; (*inf*) an avid fan.—**fiendish** *adj*.—**fiendishly** *adv*.

fierce *adj* ferociously hostile; angry, violent; intense; strong, extreme.—**fiercely** *adv*.—**fierceness** *n*.

fiery *adj* (**fierier, fieriest**) like or consisting of fire; the color of fire; intensely hot; spicy; passionate, ardent; impetuous; irascible.—**fierily** *adv*.—**fieriness** *n*.

fiesta *n* a religious celebration, a festival, esp in Spain and Latin America.

fife *n* a type of small flute with a shrill sound used esp in military music to accompany drums.—**fifer** *n*.

fifteen *adj, n* one more than fourteen; the symbol for this (15, XV, xv); the first point scored by a side in a game of tennis; a rugby football team.—**fifteenth** *adj, n*.

fifth *adj, n* last of five; (being) one of five equal parts; (*mus*) an interval of three tones and a semitone.—**fifthly** *adv*.

fifty *adj, n* (*pl* **fifties**) five times ten; the symbol for this (50, L, l).—**fiftieth** *adj*.

fig *n* a tree yielding a soft, pear-shaped fruit; a thing of little or no importance.

fight *vb* (**fighting, fought**) *vi* to engage in battle in war or in single combat; to strive, struggle (for). * *vt* to engage in or carry on a conflict with; to achieve (one's way) by fighting; to strive to overcome; (*with* **off**) to repel; to ward off or repress through effort. * *n* fighting; a struggle or conflict of any kind; a boxing match.–**fighting** *n*.–**fighter** *n*.

figment *n* something imagined or invented.

figurative *adj* metaphorical, not literal; using or full of figures of speech; emblematic; pictorial.–**figuratively** *adv*.

figure *n* a character representing a number; a number; value or price; bodily shape or form; a graphic representation of a thing, person or animal; a design; a geometrical form; a statue; appearance; a personage; (*dancing, skating*) a set of steps or movements; (*pl*) arithmetic. * *vt* to represent in a diagram or outline; to imagine; (*inf*) to consider; (*inf*) to believe; (*with* out) (*inf*) to solve. * *vi* to take a part (in), be conspicuous (in); to calculate.– **figurer** *n*.

figurehead *n* a carved figure on the bow of a ship; a nominal head or leader.

figurine *n* a statuette.

filagree *see* **filigree**.

filament *n* a slender thread or strand; a fiber; the fine wire in an electric light bulb that is made incandescent by current.–**filamentary, filamentous** *adj*.

filch *vt* to steal (something of little value), to pilfer.–**filcher** *n*.

file[1] *n* a container for keeping papers, etc, in order; an orderly arrangement of papers; a line of persons or things; (*comput*) a collection of related data under a specific name. * *vt* to dispatch or register; to put on public record. * *vi* to move in a line; to apply.– **filer** *n*.

file[2] *n* a tool, usu steel, with a rough surface for smoothing or grinding. * *vt* to cut or smooth with, or as with, a file; to polish, improve.–**filer** *n*.

filial *adj* of, or expected from, a son or daughter.–**filially** *adv*.–**filialness** *n*.

filigree *n* a kind of lace-like ornamental work in precious metal. * *vt* (**filigreeing, filigreed**) to decorate with filigree.–*also* **filagree**.

filing *n* a particle rubbed off with a file.

fill *vt* to put as much as possible into; to occupy wholly; to put a person into (a position or job, etc); to supply the things called for (in an order, etc); to close or plug (holes, etc); (*with* in) to complete (a form, design, etc) by writing or drawing; (*inf*) to provide with the latest news or facts; (*with* out) to make fuller or heavier; to fill in (a form, etc). * *vi* to become full; (*with* in) to act as a substitute for; (*with* out) to become fuller or heavier. * *n* enough to make full or to satisfy; anything that fills.

filler *n* one who or that which fills; a substance used to plug a hole or increase the bulk of something.

fillet *n* a thin boneless strip of meat or fish; a ribbon, etc worn as a headband. * *vt* to bone and slice (fish or meat).

filling *n* a substance used to fill a tooth cavity; the contents of a sandwich, pie, etc. * *adj* (*meal, etc*) substantial.

filly *n* (*pl* **fillies**) a young female horse, usu less than four years.

film *n* a fine, thin skin, coating, etc; a flexible cellulose material covered with a light-sensitive substance used in photography; a haze or blur; a motion picture. * *vti* to cover or be covered as with a film; to photograph or make a film (of).–**filmic** *adj*.

film star *n* a leading movie actor or actress.

filmy *adj* (**filmier, filmiest**) gauzy, transparent; blurred, hazy.–**filmily** *adv*.–**filminess** *n*.

filter *n* a device or substance straining out solid particles, impurities, etc, from a liquid or gas; a device for removing or minimizing electrical oscillations; or sound or light waves, of certain frequencies; a traffic signal at certain road junctions that allows vehicles to turn left or right while the main lights are red. * *vti* to pass through or as through a filter; to remove with a filter.–**filterable, filtrable** *adj*.

filth *n* dirt; obscenity.–**filthy** *adj*.–**filthily** *adv*.

fin *n* an organ by which a fish, etc steers itself and swims; a rubber flipper used for underwater swimming; any fin-shaped object used as a stabilizer, as on an aircraft or rocket. * *vb* (**finning, finned**) *vi* (*fish, whale. etc*) to agitate the fins. * *vt* to furnish with fins.

final *adj* of or coming at the end; conclusive. * *n* (*often pl*) the last of a series of contests; a final examination.–**finally** *adv*.–**finality** *n*.–**finalize** *vt*.

finale *n* the concluding part of any public performance; the last section in a musical composition.

finalist *n* a contestant in a final.

finally *adv* at last; lastly; completely.

finance *n* the management of money; (*pl*) money resources. * *vt* to supply or raise money for.–**financial** *adj*.–**financially** *adv*.–**financier** *n* a person skilled in finance.

find *vb* (**finding, found**) *vt* to discover by chance; to come upon by searching; to perceive; to recover (something lost); to reach, attain; to decide and declare to be; (*with* out) to discover; to solve; to detect in an offence. * *vi* to reach a decision (as by a jury). * *n* a discovery, something found.–**finder** *n*.

finding *n* a discovery; the conclusion reached by a judicial enquiry.

fine[1] *adj* very good; with no impurities, refined; (*weather*) clear and bright; not heavy or coarse; very thin or small; sharp; subtle; elegant. * *adv* in a fine manner; (*inf*) very well.–**finely** *adv*.–**fineness** *n*.

fine[2] *n* a sum of money imposed as a punishment. * *vt* to punish by a fine.–**finable, fineable** *adj*.

fine arts *npl* painting, sculpture, engraving, etc valued for their aesthetic qualities.

finery *n* (*pl* **fineries**) elaborate clothes, jewelry, etc.

finesse *n* delicacy or subtlety of performance; skillfulness, diplomacy in handling a situation. * *vt* to achieve by finesse.

fine-tooth(ed) comb *n* a comb with closely set fine teeth for trapping nits, etc.

fine-tune *vt* to make fine adjustments to something in order to improve its effectiveness.

finger *n* one of the digits of the hand, usu excluding the thumb; anything shaped like a finger; (*inf*) the breadth of a finger. * *vt* to touch with fingers; (*mus*) to use the fingers in a certain way when playing; to mark this way on music; (*sl*) to inform against.–**fingerer** *n*.

fingerboard *n* the part of a violin, guitar, etc against which the strings are pressed by the fingers.

fingerprint *n* the impression of the ridges on a fingertip, esp as used for purposes of identification. –*also vt*.

finicky, finicking *adj* too particular, fussy.

finish *vt* to bring to an end, to come to the end of; to consume entirely; to perfect; to give a desired surface effect to. * *vi* to come to an end. * *n* the last part, the end; anything used to finish a surface; the finished effect; means or manner of completing or perfecting; polished manners, speech, etc.–**finisher** *n*.

finite *adj* having definable limits; (*verb form*) having a distinct grammatical person and number.–**finitely** *adv* –**finiteness** *n*.

fiord *see* **fjord**.

fir *n* a kind of evergreen, cone-bearing tree; its timber.

fire *n* the flame, heat and light of combustion; something burning; burning fuel in a grate to heat a room; an electric or gas fire; a destructive burning; a strong feeling; a discharge of firearms. * *vti* to ignite; to supply with fuel; to bake (bricks, etc) in a kiln; to excite or become excited; to shoot (a gun, etc); to hurl or direct with force; to dismiss from a position.–**fireable** *adj*.–**firer** *n*.

fire alarm *n* a device that uses a bell, hooter, etc to warn of a fire.

firearm *n* a handgun.

fireball *n* a ball of fire; a meteor; the hot gas cloud created by a nuclear explosion.

firebrand *n* a piece of burning wood; a person who starts trouble.

fire brigade *n* an organized body specially trained and equipped for fighting fires.

firecracker *n* a small explosive firework.

fire engine *n* a vehicle equipped for fire-fighting.

fire escape *n* a means of exit from a building, esp a stairway, for use in case of fire.

fire extinguisher *n* a container with a spray nozzle, holding water or chemicals for putting out a fire

firefighter *n* a person who fights fires, esp a member of a fire department; fireman.

firefly *n* (*pl* **fireflies**) a winged nocturnal beetle whose abdomen glows with a soft intermittent light.

fireguard *n* a protective grating placed in front of a fire.

fireman *n* (*pl* **firemen**) a member of a fire brigade; firefighter; a person employed to tend furnaces.

fireplace *n* a place for a fire, esp a recess in a wall; the area surrounding this.

fireproof *adj* not easily destroyed by fire. * *vt* to make fireproof.

fireside *n* the area in a room nearest the fireplace; home.

fire station *n* a building where firemen and fire-fighting equipment are based.–*also* **firehouse, station house**.

firewood *n* wood for fuel.

firework *n* a device packed with explosive and combustible material used to produce noisy and colorful displays; (*pl*) such a display; (*pl*) a fit of temper, an outburst of emotions.

firing *n* baking in intense heat, esp of clay; fuel; the act of discharging a firearm; the act of adding fuel to a fire.

firing line *n* the front line of a military position; the forefront of any activity.

firing squad *n* a detachment with the task of firing a salute at a military funeral or carrying out an execution.

firm[1] *adj* securely fixed; solid, compact; steady; resolute; definite. * *vti* to make or become firm.–**firmly** *adv.*–**firmness** *n*.

firm[2] *n* a business partnership; a commercial company.

firmament *n* the sky, viewed poetically as a solid arch or vault.–**firmamental** *adj*.

first *adj* before all others in a series; 1st; earliest; foremost, as in rank, quality, etc. * *adv* before anyone or anything else; for the first time; sooner. * *n* any person or thing that is first; the beginning; the winning place, as in a race; low gear; the highest award in a university degree.

first aid *n* emergency treatment for an injury, etc, before regular medical aid is available.

first-born *adj* eldest. * *n* the eldest child in a family.

first-class *adj* of the highest quality, as in accommodation, travel. * *n* the best accommodation on a plane, train, etc; the highest class in an examination, etc.

firsthand *adj* obtained directly from a source.

firstly *adv* in the first place.

first-rate *adj, adv* of the best quality; (*inf*) excellent.

fiscal *adj* of or relating to public revenue; financial. * *n* a prosecuting official in some countries.

fish *n* (*pl* **fish, fishes**) any of a large group of cold-blooded animals living in water, having backbones, gills for breathing and fins; the flesh of fish used as food. * *vi* to catch or try to catch fish; (*with* **for**) to try to obtain by roundabout methods. * *vt* (*often with* **out**) to grope for, find, and bring to view.–**fisher** *n*.

fisherman *n* (*pl* **fishermen**) a person who fishes for sport or for a living; a ship used in fishing.

fishery *n* (*pl* **fisheries**) the fishing industry; an area where fish are caught.

fishing *n* the art, sport or business of catching fish.

fishing rod *n* a wooden, metal or fiberglass rod used with a line to catch fish.

fishy *adj* (**fishier, fishiest**) like a fish in odor, taste, etc; (*inf*) creating doubt or suspicion.–**fishily** *adv.*–**fishiness** *n*.

fissile *adj* capable of undergoing nuclear fission; easily split.–**fissility** *n*.

fission *n* a split or cleavage; the reproductive division of biological cells; the splitting of the atomic nucleus resulting in the release of energy, nuclear fission.–**fissionable** *adj*.

fissure *n* a narrow opening or cleft. * *vti* to split.

fist *n* the hand when tightly closed or clenched.

fisticuffs *npl* a fight with the fists.

fit[1] *adj* (**fitter, fittest**) suited to some purpose, function, etc; proper, right; healthy; (*sl*) inclined, ready. * *n* the manner of fitting. * *vb* (**fitting, fitted**) *vt* to be suitable to; to be the proper size, shape, etc, for; to adjust so as to fit; (*with* **out**) to equip, to outfit. * *vi* to be suitable or proper; to have the proper size or shape.–**fittable** *adj.*–**fitly** *adv.*–**fitness** *n*.

fit[2] *n* any sudden, uncontrollable attack, as of coughing; an outburst, as of anger; a short period of impulsive activity; a seizure involving convulsions or loss of consciousness.

fitful *adj* marked by intermittent activity; spasmodic.–**fitfully** *adv.*–**fitfulness** *n*.

fitment *n* a piece of equipment, esp fixed furniture.

fitter *n* a person who specializes in fitting clothes; a person skilled in the assembly and operation of a particular piece of machinery.

fitting *adj* appropriate; suitable, right. * *n* an act of one that fits, esp a trying on of altered clothes; a small often standardized electrical part.–**fittingly** *adv.*–**fittingness** *n*.

five *adj, n* one more than four; the symbol for this (5, V, v).

fivefold *adj, adv* having five units or members; being five times as great or as many.

fix *vt* to fasten firmly; to set firmly in the mind; to direct (one's eyes) steadily at something; to make rigid; to make permanent; to establish (a date, etc) definitely; to set in order; to repair; to prepare (food or meals); (*inf*) to influence the result or action of (a race, jury, etc) by bribery; (*inf*) to punish. * *vi* to become fixed; (*inf*) to prepare or intend. * *n* the position of a ship, etc, determined from the bearings of two known positions; (*inf*) a predicament; (*inf*) a situation that has been fixed; (*inf*) something whose supply becomes continually necessary or greatly desired, as a drug, entertainment, activity, etc.–**fixable** *adj*.

fixated *adj* having a fixation.

fixation *n* (*psychol*) an unhealthy obsession, esp one leading to arrested emotional development.

fixative *n* a substance used to fix things in position; a substance that prevents (colors, perfumes, etc) fading or evaporating.

fixed *adj* firm; not moving; lasting; intent.–**fixedly** *adv.*–**fixedness** *n*.

fixer *n* a chemical that fixes photographs, making the image permanent; (*sl*) a person who fixes something, esp by illegal means.

fixings *npl* trimmings.

fixture *n* what is fixed to anything, as to land or to a house; a fixed article of furniture; a firmly established person or thing; a fixed or appointed time or event.

fizz *vi* to make a hissing or sputtering sound. * *n* this sound; any effervescent drink.–**fizzy** *adj.*–**fizziness** *n*.

fizzle *vi* to make a weak fizzing sound; (*with* **out**) (*inf*) to end feebly, die out, esp after a promising start.

fjord *n* a long, narrow inlet of the sea between high cliffs, esp in Norway.–*also* **fiord**.

flab *n* (*inf*) fat.

flabby *adj* (**flabbier, flabbiest**) fat and soft; weak and ineffective.–**flabbily** *adv.*–**flabbiness** *n*.

flaccid *adj* not firm or stiff; limp, weak.–**flaccidity** *n*.

flag[1] *vi* (**flagging, flagged**) to grow limp; to become weak, listless.

flag[2] *n* a piece of cloth, usu with a design, used to show nationality, party, a particular branch of the armed forces, etc, or as a signal. * *vt* (**flagging, flagged**) to decorate with flags; to signal to (as if) with a flag; (*usu with* **down**) to signal to stop.

flagon *n* a pottery or metal container for liquids with a handle and spout and often a lid.

flagrant adj conspicuous, notorious.–**flagrancy, flagrance** n.–**flagrantly** adv.

flagship n the ship that carries the admiral and his flag; the most important vessel of a shipping line; the chief or leading item of a group or collection.

flail n a tool for threshing by hand. * vt to beat with a flail. * vi (usu with **about**) to wave (the arms, etc) wildly.

flair n natural ability, aptitude; discernment; (inf) stylishness, sophistication.

flak n shells fired by anti-aircraft guns; criticism, opposition.

flake n a small piece of snow; a small thin layer chipped from a larger mass of something. * vt to form into flakes. * vi (with out) (inf) to collapse or fall asleep from exhaustion.

flamboyant adj brilliantly colored; ornate; strikingly elaborate; dashing, exuberant.–**flamboyance, flamboyancy** n.–**flamboyantly** adv.

flame n the burning gas of a fire, appearing as a tongue of light; the state of burning with a blaze; a thing like a flame; an intense emotion; (inf) a sweetheart. * vi to burst into flame; to become bright red with emotion.–**flaming** adj.–**flamingly** adv.

flamenco n (pl **flamencos**) a type of vigorous Spanish dance and music of gypsy origin.

flamingo n (pl **flamingos, flamingoes**) any of several wading birds with rosy-pink plumage and long legs and neck.

flammable adj easily set on fire.–**flammability** n.

flan n an open case of pastry or sponge cake with a sweet or savoury filling.

flange n a raised edge, as on a wheel rim to keep it on a rail; a projecting rib. * vt to provide with a flange.–**flanged** adj.

flank n the fleshy part of the side from the ribs to the hip; the side of anything; the right or left side of a formation of troops. * vt to attack the flank of; to skirt the side of; to be situated at the side of.

flannel n a soft light cotton or woolen cloth.

flap vi (**flapping, flapped**) to move up and down, as wings; to sway loosely and noisily, as curtains in the wind, etc; to move or hang like a flap. * n the motion or noise of a flap; anything broad and flexible, either hinged or hanging loose; a light blow with a flat object.

flapjack n a kind of pancake; a cake made with oats and syrup.

flare vi to burn with a sudden, bright, unsteady flame; to burst into emotion, esp anger; to widen out gradually. * n an unsteady flame; a sudden flash; a bright light used as a signal or illumination; a widened part or shape.

flare-up n a sudden burst of fire; (inf) a sudden burst of emotion.

flash n a sudden, brief light; a brief moment; a sudden brief display; (TV, radio) a sudden brief news item about an important event; (photog) a device for producing a brief intense light; a sudden onrush of water. * vi to send out a sudden, brief light; to sparkle; to come or pass suddenly. * vt to cause to flash; to send (news, etc) swiftly.

flashback n an interruption in the continuity of a story, etc, by telling or showing an earlier episode.

flash flood n a sudden brief flood caused by a heavy rainfall.

flashlight n a small electric light; a flash of electric light used to take photographs in dark conditions.

flashpoint n the lowest temperature at which vapor, as from oil, will ignite with a flash; the point where a situation will erupt into violence.

flashy adj (**flashier, flashiest**) pretentious; showy, gaudy.–**flashily** adv.–**flashiness** n.

flask n a slim-necked bottle; a vacuum flask.

flat adj (**flatter, flattest**) having a smooth level surface; lying spread out; broad, even, and thin; not fluctuating; (tire) deflated; dull, tedious; (drink) not fizzy; (battery) drained of electric current. * adv in a flat manner or position; exactly; (mus) below true pitch. * n anything flat, esp a surface, part, or expanse; a flat tire; a set of rooms on one floor of a building (–also **apartment**).–**flatly** adv.–**flatness** n.

flatfish n (pl **flatfish, flatfishes**) any of an order of marine fishes that as adults have both eyes on one side.

flatfoot n a condition in which the arch of the instep is flattened.–**flat-footed** adj.

flatten vti to make or become flat.–**flattener** n.

flatter vt to praise excessively or insincerely, esp out of self-interest or to win favor; to display to advantage; to represent as more attractive, etc than reality; to gratify the vanity of; to encourage falsely.–**flatterer** n.–**flattering** adj.–**flatteringly** adv.–**flattery** n.

flatulence, flatulency n wind in the stomach; windiness, verbosity; pomposity.

flatulent adj causing or affected with intestinal gas; pretentious, vain.–**flatulently** adv.

flaunt vi to move or behave ostentatiously; (flag) to wave in the wind. * vt to display.–**flaunter** n.–**flauntingly** adv.

flavor, flavour n the taste of something in the mouth; a characteristic quality. * vt to give flavor to.–**flavorer, flavourer** n.–**flavorsome, flavoursome**. adj.

flavoring, flavouring n any substance used to give flavor to food.

flaw n a defect; a crack. * vti to make or become flawed.

flawless adj perfect.–**flawlessly** adv.–**flawlessness** n.

flax n a blue-flowered plant cultivated for its fiber and seed; the fiber of this plant.

flaxen, flaxy adj made of flax; pale yellow.

flay vt to strip off the skin; to berate, criticize severely.–**flayer** n.

flea n a small wingless jumping bloodsucking insect.

fleck n a spot or speckle of color; a tiny particle. * vt to mark with flecks.

fled see **flee**.

fledgling, fledgeling n a young bird just fledged; an inexperienced person, a trainee.

flee vti (**fleeing, fled**) to run away from danger, etc; to pass away quickly, to disappear.

fleece n the woolen coat of sheep or similar animal. * vt to remove wool from; to defraud.–**fleecy** adj.

fleet[1] n a number of warships under one command; (often with cap) a country's navy; any group of cars, ships, buses, etc, under one control.

fleet[2] adj swift moving; nimble.–**fleetly** adv.–**fleetness** n.

fleeting adj brief, transient.–**fleetingly** adv.

flesh n the soft substance of the body, esp the muscular tissue; the pulpy part of fruits and vegetables; meat; the body as distinct from the soul; all mankind; a yellowish-pink color. * vt (usu with out) to give substance to.

fleshly adj (**fleshlier, fleshliest**) having to do with the body and its desires, material, sensual.–**fleshliness** n.

fleshy adj (**fleshier, fleshiest**) of or resembling flesh; plump; succulent; sensual.–**fleshiness** n.

flew see **fly**.

flex vti to bend (a limb or joint, etc); to contract (a muscle).

flexible adj easily bent, pliable; adaptable, versatile; docile.–**flexibility** n.–**flexibly** adv.

flextime n the staggering of working hours to enable each employee to work the full quota of time but at periods most convenient for the individual.

flick n a light stroke or blow; (inf) a motion picture. * vt to strike or propel with a flick; a flicking movement.

flicker vi to burn unsteadily, as a flame; to move quickly to and fro. * n a flickering moment of light or flame; a flickering movement.–**flickeringly** adv.–**flickery** adj.

flier see **flyer**.

flies see **fly**.

flight[1] n the act, manner, or power of flying; distance flown; a group of creatures or things flying together; an aircraft scheduled to fly a certain trip; a trip by aircraft; a set of stairs, as between landings; a mental act of soaring beyond the ordinary; a set of feathers on a dart or arrow.

flight[2] n an act or instance of fleeing.

flight-deck n the cockpit of an aircraft.

flighty adj (**flightier, flightiest**) irresponsible, capricious, frivolous.–**flightily** adv.–**flightiness** n.

flimsy adj (**flimsier, flimsiest**) weak, insubstantial; light and thin; (excuse etc) unconvincing.–**flimsily** adv.–**flimsiness** n.

flinch vi to draw back, as from pain or fear; to wince.–**flincher** n.–**flinchingly** adv.

fling vb (**flinging, flung**) vt to cast, throw aside, esp with force; to put or send suddenly or without warning. * vi to kick out violently; to move or rush quickly or impetuously. * n the act of flinging; a lively dance; a period of pleasurable indulgence.–**flinger** n.

flint n a very hard rock that produces sparks when struck with steel; an alloy used for producing a spark in lighters.

flip vb (**flipping, flipped**) vt to toss with a quick jerk, to flick; to snap (a coin) in the air with the thumb; to turn or turn over. * vi to move jerkily; (inf) to burst into anger.

flippant adj impertinent; frivolous.–**flippancy** n.–**flippantly** adv.

flipper n a limb adapted for swimming; a flat rubber shoe expanded into a paddle, used in underwater swimming.

flirt vi to make insincere amorous approaches; to trifle or toy (eg with an idea). * n a person who toys amorously with the opposite sex.–**flirtation** n.–**flirter** n.–**flirtingly** adv.

flirtatious adj fond of flirting, coquettish.–**flirtatiously** adv.

flit vi (**flitting, flitted**) to move lightly and rapidly.

flitter vi to flit about; to flicker, flutter.

float vi to rest on the surface of or be suspended in a liquid; to move lightly; to wander aimlessly. * vt to cause to float; to put into circulation; to start up a business, esp by offering shares for sale. * n anything that floats; a cork or other device used on a fishing line to signal that the bait has been taken; a low flat vehicle decorated for exhibition in a parade; a small sum of money available for cash expenditures.–**floatable** adj.

floatation see **flotation**.

flock n a group of certain animals as birds, sheep, etc, living and feeding together; a group of people or things. * vi to assemble or travel in a flock or crowd.

floe n a sheet of floating ice.

flog vt (**flogging, flogged**) to beat harshly with a rod, stick or whip.–**flogging** n.

flood n an overflowing of water on an area normally dry; the rising of the tide; a great outpouring, as of words. * vt to cover or fill, as with a flood; to put too much water, fuel, etc on or in. * vi to gush out in a flood; to become flooded.–**floodable** adj.

floodgate n a gate for controlling the flow of water, a sluice.

floodlight n a strong beam of light used to illuminate a stage, sports field, stadium, building exterior, etc. * vt (**floodlighting, floodlit**) to illuminate with floodlights.

floor n the inside bottom surface of a room, flooring; the bottom surface of anything, as the ocean; a story in a building; the area in a legislative assembly where the members sit and debate; the lower limit, the base. * vt to provide with a floor; to knock down (a person) in a fight; (inf) to defeat; (inf) to shock, to confuse.

floorboard n one of the boards making up a floor.

floozy, floozie, floosie n (pl **floozies, floosies**) (sl) a disreputable woman.

flop vi (**flopping, flopped**) to sway or bounce loosely; to move in a heavy, clumsy or relaxed manner; (inf) to fail. * n a flopping movement; a collapse; (inf) a complete failure.

floppy adj (**floppier, floppiest**) limp, hanging loosely. * n (pl **floppies**) a floppy disk.–**floppily** adv.–**floppiness** n.

floppy disk n (comput) a flexible magnetic disk in a protective casing used for data storage and retrieval.

flora n (pl **floras, florae**) the plants of a region or a period.

floral adj pertaining to flowers.–**florally** adv.

floret n one of the small flowers forming the head of a plant.

florid adj flowery; elaborate; (complexion) ruddy.–**floridity** n.–**floridly** adv.

florist n a person who sells or grows flowers and ornamental plants.

floss n a mass of short silky fibers, as from the rough outside of the silkworm's cocoon; fine silk used in embroidery; dental floss.

flotation n the act or process of floating; the launching of a business venture.–also **floatation**.

flotilla n a small fleet of ships.

flotsam n wreckage or debris found floating in the sea.

flounce[1] vi to move in an emphatic or impatient manner.* n the act of flouncing, a plunge.

flounce[2] n a frill of material sewn to the skirt of a dress. * vt to add flounces to.

flounder[1] vi to move awkwardly and with difficulty; to be clumsy in thinking or speaking.

flounder[2] n (pl **flounder, flounders**) a small flatfish used as food.

flour n the finely ground powder of wheat or other grain. * vt to sprinkle with flour.–**floury** adj.

flourish vi (plants) to grow luxuriantly; to thrive, prosper; to live and work at a specified time. * vt to brandish dramatically. * n embellishment; a curve made by a bold stroke of the pen; a sweeping gesture; a musical fanfare.

flout vt to treat with contempt, to disobey openly.

flow vi (liquids) to move (as if) in a stream; (tide) to rise; to glide smoothly; (conversation, etc) to continue effortlessly; to be characterized by smooth and easy movement; to hang free or loosely; to be plentiful. * n a flowing; the rate of flow; anything that flows; the rising of the tide.

flower n the seed-producing structure of a flowering plant, blossom; a plant cultivated for its blossoms; the best or finest part. * vt to cause to bear flowers. * vi to produce blossoms; to reach the best stage.

flowery adj full of or decorated with flowers; (language) full of elaborate expressions.–**floweriness** n.

flown see **fly**.

fl. oz. abbr = fluid ounce.

flu n (inf) influenza.

fluctuate vi (prices, etc) to be continually varying in an irregular way.–**fluctuation** n.

flue n a shaft for the passage of smoke, hot air, etc, as in a chimney.

fluent adj able to write and speak a foreign language with ease; articulate, speaking and writing easily and smoothly; graceful.–**fluency** n.–**fluently** adv.

fluff n soft, light down; a loose, soft mass, as of hair; (inf) a mistake, bungle. * vt to pat or shake until fluffy; (inf) to forget, to bungle.

fluffy adj (**fluffier, fluffiest**) like fluff; soft and downy; feathery.–**fluffily** adv.–**fluffiness** n.

fluid n a substance able to flow freely, as a liquid or gas does. * adj able to flow freely; able to change rapidly or easily.–**fluidity** n.–**fluidly** adv.

fluid ounce n a unit of capacity equal to one sixteenth of a pint.

fluke n a stroke of luck. * vti to make or score by a fluke.

flume n a channel for water; a ravine with a stream; a chute with a flow of water into a swimming pool. * vt to transport or divert by a flume.

flung see **fling**.

flunk vti (sl) to fail, as in school work.

flunky, flunkey n (pl **flunkies, flunkeys**) a servile person, toady; a person who does menial work; a liveried servant.

fluorescence n the property of producing light when acted upon by radiant energy; light so produced.–**fluorescent** adj.–**fluoresce** vi.

fluoridate vt to add fluoride to drinking water to reduce tooth decay.–**fluoridation** n.

fluoride n any of various compounds of fluorine.

fluorine, fluorin n a chemical element, a pale greenish-yellow corrosive gas.

flurry n (pl **flurries**) a sudden gust of wind, rain, or snow; a sudden commotion. * vti (**flurrying, flurried**) to (cause to) become flustered.

flush[1] n a rapid flow, as of water; sudden, vigorous growth; a sudden excitement; a blush; a sudden feeling of heat, as in a fever. * vi to flow rapidly; to blush or glow; to be washed out by a sudden flow of water. * vt to wash out with a sudden flow of water; to cause to blush; to excite. * adj level or in one plane with another surface; (inf) abundant, well-supplied, esp with money.–**flusher** n.

flush[2] n (poker, etc) a hand of cards all of the same suit.

fluster vti to make or become confused. * n agitation or confusion.

flute n an orchestral woodwind instrument in the form of a straight pipe (with finger holes and keys) held horizontally and played through a hole located near one end; a decorative groove. * vi to play or make sounds like a flute; to cut grooves in.–**fluty** adj.–flutist.

flutter vi (birds) to flap the wings; to wave about rapidly; (heart) to beat irregularly or spasmodically. * vt to cause to flutter. * n rapid, irregular motion; nervous excitement; commotion, confusion.–**flutterer** n.–**fluttery** adj.

flux n a continual flowing or changing; a substance used to help metals fuse together, as in soldering.

fly[1] n (pl **flies**) a two-winged insect; a natural or imitation fly attached to a fish-hook as bait.

fly[2] vb (**flying, flew,** pp **flown**) vi to move through the air, esp on wings; to travel in an aircraft; to control an aircraft; to take flight, flee; to pass quickly; (inf) to depart quickly. * vt to cause to fly, as a kite; to escape, flee from; to transport by aircraft. * n a flap that conceals buttons, a zipper, etc on pants; material forming the outer roof of a tent; a device for regulating machinery, a flywheel.–**flyable** adj.

fly[3] adj (inf) sly, astute.

flyaway adj (hair etc) loose; (person) flighty.

fly-by-night adj (inf) unreliable, untrustworthy; transitory. * n an untrustworthy person, esp one who evades responsibilities or debts by flight.

flyer n something that flies or moves very fast; a pilot.–also **flier**.

flying fish n any of numerous fishes of warm seas with winglike fins used in gliding through the air.

flying squad n a small detachment of police officers mobilized for swift action.

flyleaf n (pl **flyleaves**) the blank leaf at the beginning or end of a book.

flytrap n any of various insect-eating plants; a device for catching flies.

foal n the young of the horse or a related animal. * vti to give birth to a foal.

foam n froth or fine bubbles on the surface of liquid; something like foam, as frothy saliva; a rigid or springy cellular mass made from liquid rubber, plastic, etc. * vi to cause or emit foam.–**foamy** adj.

fob n the chain or ribbon for attaching a watch to a waistcoat; any object attached to a watch chain; a small pocket in a waistcoat for a watch.

focal adj of or pertaining to a focus.–**focally** adv.

fo'c's'le, fo'c'sle see **forecastle**.

focus n (pl **focuses, foci**) a point where rays of light, heat, etc meet after being bent by a lens, curved mirror, etc; correct adjustment of the eye or lens to form a clear image; a center of activity or interest. * vt (**focusing, focused** or **focussing, focussed**) to adjust the focus of; to bring into focus; to concentrate.–**focusable** adj.–**focuser** n.

fodder n dried food for cattle, horses, etc.

foe n an enemy, an adversary.

foetid see **fetid**.

foetus see **fetus**.

fog n (a state of poor visibility caused by) a large mass of water vapor condensed to fine particles just above the earth's surface; a state of mental confusion; (photog) cloudiness on a developed photograph. * vti (**fogging, fogged**) to make or become foggy.–**foggy** adj.

fogey, fogy n (pl **fogeys, fogies**) a person of old-fashioned or eccentric habits.–**fogeyish, fogyish** adj.

foghorn n a horn (in a ship, etc) sounded in a fog as a warning.

fogy see **fogey**.

foible n a slight weakness or failing; an idiosyncrasy; the weakest part of the blade of a sword.

foil[1] vt to defeat; to frustrate; to trample a trail to spoil scent. * n (arch) the trail of hunted game.–**foilable** adj.

foil[2] n a very thin sheet of metal; a backing for a mirror or gem; anything that sets off or enhances another by contrast. * vt to cover, back or adorn with foil; to set off.

foist vt (with **in** or **into**) to introduce stealthily or without permission; (with **off** or **on**) to pass off as genuine.

fold[1] vt to cover by bending or doubling over so that one part covers another; to wrap up, envelop; to interlace (one's arms); to clasp (one's hands); to embrace; to incorporate (an ingredient) into a food mixture by gentle overturnings. * vi to become folded; to fail completely; to collapse, esp to go out of business. * n something folded, as a piece of cloth; a crease or hollow made by folding.–**foldable** adj.

fold[2] n a pen for sheep; a group of people or institutions having a common belief, activity, etc. * vt to pen in a fold.

folder n a folded cover or large envelope for holding loose papers.

foliage n leaves, as of a plant or tree.

folic acid n a B-complex vitamin used in treating anemia.

folio n (pl **folios**) a large sheet of paper folded once to make two leaves of a book; a book of sheets in this size, the largest commonly used; the number of a page in a book. * vt (**folioing, folioed**) to number the pages of.

folk n (pl **folk, folks**) a people of a country or tribe; people in general, esp those of a particular area; relatives; folk music. * adj of or originating among the ordinary people.–**folkish** adj.

folklore n the traditional beliefs, customs, legends, etc of a people; the study of these.–**folkloric, folkloristic** adj.–**folklorist** n.

folk music n traditional music.

folk song n a traditional song.

folksy adj (**folksier, folksiest**) (inf) simple, plain; friendly.–**folksiness** n.

follicle n any small sac, cavity, or gland.–**follicular, folliculate, folliculated** adj.

follow vt to go or come after; to pursue; to go along (a path, road, etc); to copy; to obey; to adopt, as an opinion; to watch fixedly; to focus the mind on; to understand the meaning of; to monitor the progress of; to come or occur after in time; to result from; (with **through**) to pursue (an aim) to a conclusion; (with **up**) to pursue a question, inquiry, etc, that has been started. * vi to go or come after another; to result; (with **on**) (cricket) to take a second innings immediately after a first; (with **suit**) to play a card of the same suit; to do the same thing; (with **through**) (sport) to continue a stroke or motion of a bat, club, etc after the ball has been struck; (with **up**) to pursue steadily; to supplement.–**followable** adj.

follower n a disciple or adherent; a person who imitates another.

following n a body of adherents or believers. * adj next after; now to be stated.

follow-up n the continuing after a beginning; a steady pursuit.

folly n (pl **follies**) a lack of sense; a foolish act or idea; an extravagant and fanciful building which serves no practical purpose.

foment vt to stir up (trouble); to bathe with warm water or lotions.–**fomenter** n.

fond adj loving, affectionate; doting, indulgent; (with **of**) having a liking for.–**fondly** adv.– **fondness** n.

fondle vt to caress.–**fondler** n.–**fondlingly** adv.

fondue n melted cheese used as a dip with small pieces of bread.

font n a receptacle for baptismal water; a receptacle for holy water; a set of printing type or characters of one style and size.

food n any substance, esp a solid, taken in by a plant or animal to enable it to live and grow; anything that nourishes.

foodstuff n a substance used as food.

fool n a person lacking wisdom or common sense; (Middle Ages) a jester; a dupe. * vt to deceive, make a fool of. * vi to act jokingly; to spend time idly; to tease or meddle with.–**foolish** adj.–**foolishly** adv.–**foolishness** n.

foolhardy adj (**foolhardier, foolhardiest**) foolishly bold; rash.–**foolhardiness** n.

foolproof adj proof against failure; easy to understand; easy to use.

foot n (pl **feet**) the end part of the leg, on which one stands; anything a resembling foot, as the lower part of a chair, table, etc; the lower part or edge of something, bottom; a measure of length equal to 12 inches (30.48 cm); a group of syllables serving as a unit of meter in verse. * vi to dance. * vt to walk, dance over or on; to pay the entire cost of (a bill).

foot-and-mouth disease n a contagious disease of cattle.

football n a field game played with an inflated leather ball by two teams; the ball used.–**footballer** n.

foothill n a hill at the foot of higher hills.

foothold n a ledge, etc for placing the foot when climbing, etc; a place from which further progress may be made.

footing n the basis upon which something rests; status, relationship; a foothold.

footlights npl a row of lights in front of a stage floor.

footnote n a note or comment at the foot of a page.

footpath n a narrow path for pedestrians.

footprint n the impression left by a foot.

footstool n a stool for the feet of a seated person.

footwear n shoes and socks, etc.

footwork n skillful use of the feet in boxing, football, dancing, etc.

fop n someone obsessed with fashion and appearance.–**foppish** adj.

for prep because of, as a result of; as the price of, or recompense of; in order to be, to serve as; appropriate to, or adapted to; in quest of; in the direction of; on behalf of; in place of; in favor of; with respect to; notwithstanding, in spite of; to the extent of; throughout the space of; during. * conj because.

forage n food for domestic animals, esp when taken by browsing or grazing; a search for provisions. * vi to search for food.–**forager** n.

foray n a sudden raid. * vti to plunder.–**forayer** n.

forbad, forbade see **forbid**.

forbear vb (**forbearing, forbore**, pp **forborne**) vi to endure, to avoid. * vt to hold oneself back from.–**forbearer** n.–**forbearingly** adv.

forbearance n patience; self-control.

forbid vt (**forbidding, forbad** or **forbade**, pp **forbidden** or **forbid**) to command (a person) not to do something; to render impossible, prevent.

forbidding adj unfriendly, solemn, strict.–**forbiddingly** adv.

forbore, forborne see **forbear**.

force n strength, power, effort; (physics) (the intensity of) an influence that causes movement of a body or other effects; a body of soldiers, police, etc prepared for action; effectiveness; violence, compulsion; legal or logical validity. * vt to compel or oblige by physical effort, superior strength, etc; to achieve by force; to press or drive against resistance; to produce with effort; to break open, penetrate; to impose, inflict.–**forceable** adj.– **forcer** n.

forced adj compulsory; strained.–**forcedly** adv.–**forcedness** n.

force-feed vt (**force-feeding, force-fed**) to compel a person to swallow food.

forceful adj powerful, effective.–**forcefully** adv.–**forcefulness** n.

forceps n (pl **forceps, forcipes**) an instrument for grasping and holding firmly, or exerting traction upon objects, esp by jewelers and surgeons.

ford n a shallow crossing place in a river, stream, etc. * vt to wade across.–**fordable** adj.

fore adj in front. * n the front. * adv in, at or towards the front.

forearm n the arm between the elbow and the wrist.

forebear n (usu pl) an ancestor.

forebode vt to be a sign or warning (of trouble, etc) in advance; to have a premonition of (an event).–**foreboding** n.

forecast vt (**forecasting, forecast** or **forecasted**) to predict (an event, the weather, etc) through rational analysis; to serve as a forecast of. * n a prediction, esp of weather; foresight.–**forecaster** n.

forecastle n the forward part of a ship containing the crew's quarters.–also **fo'c's'le, fo'c'sle**

forefather n (usu pl) an ancestor.

forefinger n the finger next to the thumb.

forefoot n (pl **forefeet**) a front foot of an animal.

forefront n the very front, vanguard.

forego[1] see **forgo**.

forego[2] vt (**foregoing, forewent**, pp **foregone**) to precede.–**foregoer** n.

foregone conclusion n an inevitable result, easily predictable.

foreground n the part of a picture or view nearest the spectator's vision.

forehand n (tennis, etc) a stroke made with the hand facing forwards. * adj (tennis stroke) made with the palm leading.

forehead n the part of the face above the eyes.

foreign adj of, in, or belonging to another country; involving other countries; alien in character; introduced from outside.

foreigner n a person from another country; a stranger.

foreleg n a front leg of an animal.

forelock n the lock of hair growing above the forehead.

foreman n (pl **foremen**) a person who supervises workers in a factory, etc; the spokesperson of a jury.–**forewoman** nf (pl **forewomen**).

foremost adj first in importance; most advanced in rank or position. * adv in the first place.

forensic adj of, belonging to or used in courts of law.–**forensicality** n.–**forensically** adv.

forensic medicine n the application of medical expertise to legal and criminal investigations.

foreplay n mutual sexual stimulation before intercourse.

forerun vt (**forerunning, foreran**, pp **forerun**) to precede, to foreshadow.–**forerunner** n.

foresee vt (**foreseeing, foresaw**, pp **foreseen**) to be aware of beforehand.–**foreseeable** adj.–**foreseer** n.

foreshadow vt to represent or indicate beforehand.–**foreshadower** n.

foresight n foreseeing; the power to foresee; prudent provision for the future.–**foresighted** adj.–**foresightedness** n.

foreskin n the loose skin that covers the end of the penis.

forest n a thick growth of trees, etc covering a large tract of land; something resembling a forest. * vt to plant with trees; to make into forest.–**forestal, forestial** adj.

forestall vt to prevent by taking action beforehand; to anticipate.

forestry n the science of planting and cultivating forests.

foretaste n partial experience in advance; anticipation. * vt to taste before possession; to have a foretaste of.

foretell vt (**foretelling, foretold**) to forecast, to predict.–**foreteller** n.

forethought n thought for the future; provident care.–**fore-thoughtful** adj.

for ever, forever adv for all future time; continually.

for evermore, forevermore adv for ever.

forewarn vt to warn beforehand.–**forewarner** n.–**forewarningly** adv.

forewent see **forego**[2].

forewoman n (pl **forewomen**) a person who supervises workers in a factory, etc; the spokesperson of a jury.

foreword n an introduction to a book to explain its purpose, often by someone other than the author.

forfeit n something confiscated or given up as a penalty for a fault; (pl) a game in which a player redeems a forfeit by performing a ludicrous task. * vt to lose or be penalized by forfeiture.–**forfeiter** n.–**forfeiture** n.

forgave see **forgive**.

forge n (a workshop with) a furnace in which metals are heated and shaped.* vt to shape (metal) by heating and hammering; to counterfeit (eg a signature). * vi to commit forgery.–**forgeable** adj.–**forger** n.

forgery n (pl **forgeries**) fraudulently copying; a forged copy; a spurious thing.

forget vti (**forgetting, forgot,** pp **forgotten**) to be unable to remember; to overlook or neglect; **forget oneself** to lose self-control; to act unbecomingly.–**forgettable** adj.

forgetful adj apt to forget, inattentive.–**forgetfully** adv.–**forgetfulness** n.

forget-me-not n a plant with bright-blue or white flowers.

forgive vt (**forgiving, forgave,** pp **forgiven**) to cease to feel resentment against (a person); to pardon. * vi to be merciful or forgiving.–**forgivable** adj.–**forgiveness** n.–**forgiving** adj.

forgo vt (**forgoing, forwent,** pp **forgone**) to give up, abstain from.–also **forego**.–**forgoer** n.

forgot, forgotten see **forget**.

fork n a small, usu metal, instrument with two or more thin prongs set in a handle, used in eating and cooking; a pronged agricultural or gardening tool for digging, etc; anything that divides into prongs or branches; one of the branches into which a road or river divides; the point of separation. * vi to divide into branches; to follow a branch of a fork in a road, etc. * vt to form as a fork; to dig, lift, etc with a fork; (with **out**) (sl) to pay or hand over (money, goods, etc).–**forked** adj.

fork-lift n a vehicle with power-operated prongs for raising and lowering loads.

forlorn adj alone; wretched.–**forlornly** adv.

form n general structure; the figure of a person or animal; a mold; a particular mode, kind, type, etc; arrangement; a way of doing something requiring skill; a conventional procedure; a printed document with blanks to be filled in; condition of mind or body; a chart giving information about racehorses; changed appearance of a word to show inflection; (sl) a criminal record. * vt to shape; to train; to develop (habits); to constitute. * vi to be formed.–**formable** adj.

formal adj in conformity with established rules or habits; regular; relating to the outward appearance only; ceremonial; punctilious; stiff.–**formally** adv.–**formality** n.

formaldehyde n a colorless pungent gas used in solution as a disinfectant and preservative.

formalize vt to make formal; to clothe with legal formality.–**formalization** n.

format n the size, form, shape in which books, etc are issued; the general style or presentation of something, eg a television programme; (comput) the arrangement of data on magnetic disk, etc for access and storage. * vt (**formatting, formatted**) to arrange in a particular form, esp for a computer.

formation n form of making or producing; that which is formed; structure; regular array or prearranged order.–**formational** adj.

formative adj pertaining to formation and development; shaping.–**formatively** n.

former adj of or occurring in a previous time; the first mentioned (of two).–**formerly** adv.

formidable adj causing fear or awe; difficult to defeat or overcome; difficult to handle.–**formidability** n.–**formidably** adv.

formless adj without distinct form, shapeless.–**formlessness** n.

formula n (pl **formulas, formulae**) a set of symbols expressing the composition of a substance; a general expression in algebraic form for solving a problem; a prescribed form; a formal statement of doctrines; a list of ingredients, as for a prescription or recipe; a fixed method according to which something is to be done; a prescribed recipe for baby food.–**formulaic** adj.

formulate vt to express in a formula; to devise.–**formulation** n.–**formulator** n.

forsake vt (**forsaking, forsook,** pp **forsaken**) to desert; to give up, renounce.–**forsaker** n.

forswear vb (**forswearing, forswore,** pp **forsworn**) vt to reject, renounce; to deny; to perjure (oneself).

fort n a fortified place for military defense.

forte n something at which a person excels.

forth adv forwards; onwards; out; into view; **and so forth** and the like.

forthcoming adj about to appear; readily available; responsive.–**forthcomingness** n.

forthright adj frank, direct, outspoken; decisive.–**forthrightly** adv.–**forthrightness** n.

fortification n the act or process of fortifying; a wall, barricade, etc built to defend a position.

fortify vt (**fortifying, fortified**) to strengthen physically, emotionally, etc; to strengthen against attack, as with forts; to support; (wine, etc) to add alcohol to; (milk) to add vitamins to.–**fortifiable** adj.–**fortifier** n.

fortitude n courage in adversity; patient endurance, firmness.–**fortitudinous** adj.

fortress n a strong fort or fortified town.

fortuitous adj happening by chance.–**fortuitously** adv.–**fortuitousness** n.

fortunate adj having or occurring by good luck.–**fortunately** adv.

fortune n the supposed arbitrary power that determines events; luck; destiny; prosperity, success; vast wealth.

fortune-teller n a person who claims to foretell a person's future.–**fortune-telling** n.

forty n (pl **forties**) four times ten, the symbol for this (40, XL, xl).–also adj.–**fortieth** adj.

forum n (pl **forums, fora**) an assembly or meeting to discuss topics of public concern; a medium for public debate, as a magazine; the marketplace and center of public affairs in ancient Rome.

forward adj at, toward, or of the front; advanced; onward; prompt; bold; presumptuous; of or for the future. * vt to promote; to send on. * n (sport) an attacking player in various games. * adv toward the front; ahead.–**forwardness** n.

forwent see **forgo**.

fossil n the petrified remains of an animal or vegetable preserved in rock. * adj of or like a fossil; dug from the earth.–**fossilize** vti.–**fossilization** n.

foster vt to encourage; to bring up (a child that is not one's own). * adj affording, giving, sharing or receiving parental care although not related.–**fosterer** n.

fought see **fight**.

foul adj stinking, loathsome; extremely dirty; indecent; wicked; (language) obscene; (weather) stormy; (sports) against the rules. * adv unfairly. * vt to make filthy; to dishonor; to obstruct; to entangle (a rope, etc); to make a foul against, as in a game; (with **up**) to contaminate; to ruin, bungle; to cause to become blocked or entangled. * *vi* to be or become fouled; (*with* **up**) to become blocked or entangled. * *n* (*sports*) a hit, blow, move, etc that is foul.–**foully** *adv*.–**foulness** *n*.

foul-mouthed *adj* using abusive or obscene language.

foul play *n* fouls in sport; violent crime, murder.

found[1] *see* **find**.

found[2] *vt* to bring into being; to establish (as an institution) often with provision for future maintenance.–**founder** *n*.

found[3] *vt* to melt and pour (metal) into a mold to produce castings.–**founder** *n*.–**foundry** *n*.

foundation *n* an endowment for an institution; such an institution; the base of a house, wall, etc; a first layer of cosmetic applied to the skin; an underlying principle, etc.–**foundational** *adj*.–**foundationary** *adj*.

founder *vi* (*ship*) to fill with water and sink; to collapse; to fail.

foundling *n* a deserted child whose parents are unknown.

fount *n* a source.

fountain *n* a natural spring of water; a source; an artificial jet or flow of water; the basin where this flows; a reservoir, as for ink. * *vti* to (cause to) flow or spurt like a fountain.

four *n* one more than three; the symbol for this (4, IV, iv) ; the fourth in a series or set; something having four units as members (as a four-cylinder engine).–*also adj*.

fourfold *adj* having four units or members; being four times as great or as many.–*also adv*.

fourscore *n* eighty.

foursome *n* a group or set of four; (*golf*) a game between two pairs in which each pair has one ball.

fourteen *n*, *adj* four and ten; the symbol for this (14, XIV, xiv).–**fourteenth** *adj*.

fourth *adj* next after third. * *n* one of four equal parts of something.–**fourthly** *adv*.

fourth estate *n* journalists or the press in general.

fowl *n* any of the domestic birds used as food, as the chicken, duck, etc; the flesh of these birds. * *vi* to hunt or snare wildfowl.–**fowler** *n*.–**fowling** *n*.

fox *n* (*pl* **foxes, fox**) any of various small, alert wild mammals of the dog family; the fur of the fox; a sly, crafty person. * *vt* to deceive by cunning. * *vi* (*inf*) to bemuse, puzzle.

foxglove *n* a tall plant with spikes of purple or white flowers.

foxtrot *n* a dance for couples in 4/4 time. * *vi* (**foxtrotting, foxtrotted**) to dance the foxtrot.

foxy *adj* (**foxier, foxiest**) reddish-brown; crafty; resembling a fox; physically attractive.–**foxily** *adv*.–**foxiness** *n*.

foyer *n* an anteroom; an entrance hallway, as in a hotel or theater.

fracas *n* (*pl* **fracas, fracases**) uproar; a noisy quarrel.

fraction *n* a small part, amount, etc; (*math*) a quantity less than a whole, expressed as a decimal or with a numerator and denominator.–**fractionary** *adj*.

fractious *adj* quarrelsome; peevish.–**fractiously** *adv*.–**fractiousness** *n*.

fracture *n* the breaking of any hard material, esp a bone. * *vti* to break; to cause or suffer a fracture.–**fracturable** *adj*.–**fractural** *adj*.

fragile *adj* easily broken; frail; delicate.–**fragilely** *adv*.–**fragility, fragileness** *n*.

fragment *n* a piece broken off or detached; an incomplete portion. * *vti* to break or cause to break into fragments.–**fragmentation** *n*.–**fragmentary** *adj*.

fragrance *n* a pleasant scent, a perfume.–**fragrant** *adj*.–**fragrantly** *adv*

frail *adj* physically or morally weak; fragile.–**frailty** *n*.

frame *vt* to form according to a pattern; to construct; to put into words; to enclose (a picture) in a border; (*sl*) to falsify evidence against (an innocent person). * *n* something composed of parts fitted together and united; the physical make-up of an animal, esp a human body; the framework of a house; the structural case

enclosing a window, door, etc; an ornamental border, as around a picture.–**framable, frameable** *adj*.–**framer** *n*.

frame-up *n* (*sl*) a conspiracy to have someone falsely accused of a crime.

framework *n* a structural frame; a basic structure (as of ideas); frame of reference.

franchise *n* the right to vote in public elections; authorization to sell the goods of a manufacturer in a particular area. * *vt* to grant a franchise.–**franchisement** *n*.

frank *adj* free and direct in expressing oneself; honest, open. * *vt* to mark letters, etc with a mark denoting free postage. * *n* a mark indicating free postage.–**frankly** *adv*.–**frankness** *n*.

frankfurter *n* a type of smoked sausage.

frankincense *n* a fragrant gum resin.

frantic *adj* violently agitated; furious, wild.–**frantically, franticly** *adv*.

fraternal *adj* of or belonging to a brother or fraternity; friendly, brotherly.–**fraternalism** *n*.–**fraternally** *adv*.

fraternity *n* (*pl* **fraternities**) brotherly feeling; a society of people with common interests.

fraternize *vt* to associate in a friendly manner.–**fraternization** *n*.

fratricide *n* the murder of a brother; a person guilty of this.–**fratricidal** *adj*.

fraud *n* deliberate deceit; an act of deception; (*inf*) a deceitful person; an impostor.

fraudulent *adj* deceiving or intending to deceive; obtained by deceit.–**fraudulence, fraudulency** *n*.–**fraudulently** *adv*.

fraught *adj* filled or loaded (with); (*inf*) anxious; difficult.

fray *vti* (*fabric, etc*) to (cause to) wear away into threads, esp at the edge of; (*nerves, temper*) to make or become irritated or strained.

frazzle *vt* to exhaust; to fray, tatter. * *n* (*inf*) a state of exhaustion.

freak *n* an unusual happening; any abnormal animal, person, or plant; (*inf*) a person who dresses or acts in a notably unconventional manner; an ardent enthusiast. * *vi* (*with* **out**) (*inf*) to hallucinate under the influence of drugs; to experience intense emotional excitement.–**freakish** *adj*.

freakish *adj* very unusual; changing suddenly.–**freakishly** *adv*.–**freakishness** *n*.

freckle *n* a small, brownish spot on the skin. * *vti* to make or become spotted with freckles.–**freckled, freckly** *adj*.

free *adj* (**freer, freest**) not under the control or power of another; having social and political liberty; independent; able to move in any direction; not burdened by obligations; not confined to the usual rules; not exact; generous; frank; with no cost or charge; exempt from taxes, duties, etc; clear of obstruction; not fastened. * *adv* without cost; in a free manner. * *vt* (**freeing, freed**) to set free; to clear of obstruction, etc.–**freely** *adv*.

freebie *n* (*sl*) something provided free of charge.

freedom *n* being free; exemption from obligation; unrestricted use; a right or privilege.

free-for-all *n* (*inf*) a disorganized fight or brawl involving as many participants as are willing.

free hand *n* freedom to act as desired.

freehand *adj* (*drawing, etc*) drawn by the hand without the aid of instruments.

freelance *n* a person who pursues a profession without long-term commitment to any employer (–*also* **freelancer**). * *vt* to work as a freelance.

freespoken *adj* outspoken, blunt.–**freespokenness** *n*.

freestyle *n* a swimming competition in which the competitor chooses the stroke.

freethinker *n* a person who rejects authority in religion, etc; a sceptic.

free verse *n* verse without a fixed metrical pattern.

freeway *n* an expressway with controlled access, a fast road, a toll-free highway.

freewheel n a device for temporarily disconnecting and setting free the back wheel of a bicycle from the driving gear. * vi to ride a bicycle with the gear disconnected; to drive a car with the gear in neutral.–**freewheeler** n.

free will n voluntary choice or decision; freedom of human beings to make choices that are not determined by prior causes or by divine intervention.

freeze vb (**freezing, froze,** pp **frozen**) vi to be formed into, or become covered by ice; to become very cold; to be damaged or killed by cold; to become motionless; to be made speechless by strong emotion; to become formal and unfriendly. * vt to harden into ice; to convert from a liquid to a solid with cold; to make extremely cold; to act towards in a stiff and formal way; to act on usu destructively by frost; to anesthetize by cold; to fix (prices, etc) at a given level by authority; to make (funds, etc) unavailable to the owners by authority.–**freezable** adj.

freeze-frame n a frame of a motion picture or television film that is repeated to give the illusion of a static picture.

freezer n a compartment or container that freezes and preserves food for long periods.

freezing adj very cold.

freezing point n the temperature at which a liquid solidifies.

freight n the transport of goods by water, land, or air; the cost for this; the goods transported. * vt to load with freight; to send by freight.

French fries, french fries npl thin strips of potato fried in oil, etc, chips.

French horn n an orchestral brass instrument with a narrow conical tube wound twice in a circle, a funnel shaped mouthpiece, and a flaring bell.

frenetic adj frantic, frenzied.–**frenetically** adv.

frenzy n (pl **frenzies**) wild excitement; violent mental derangement. * vt (**frenzying, frenzied**) to infuriate, to madden.–**frenzied** adj.–**frenziedly** adv.

frequency n (pl **frequencies**) repeated occurrence; the number of occurrences, cycles, etc in a given period.

frequent adj coming or happening often. * vi to visit often; to resort to.–**frequenter** n.–**frequently** adv.

fresco n (pl **frescos, frescoes**) a picture painted on walls covered with damp freshly laid plaster. * vt (**frescoing, frescoed**) to paint in fresco.

fresh adj recently made, grown, etc; not salted, pickled, etc; not spoiled; lively, not tired; not worn, soiled, faded, etc; new, recent; inexperienced; cool and refreshing; (wind) brisk; (water) not salt; (inf) presumptuous, impertinent. * adv newly.–**freshly** adv.–**freshness** n.

freshman n (pl **freshmen**) a first year student at university, college or high school.

fret[1] vti (**fretting, fretted**) to make or become worried or anxious; to wear away or roughen by rubbing.

fret[2] n any of a series of metal ridges along the finger-board of a guitar, banjo, etc used as a guide for depressing the strings.

fretful adj troubled; peevish; irritable; impatient.–**fretfully** adv.–**fretfulness** n.

friar n a member of certain Roman Catholic religious orders.

friary n (pl **friaries**) a monastery of friars.

fricassee n a dish made of stewed poultry, rabbit, etc in a white sauce. * vt (**fricasseeing, fricasseed**) to cook in this way.

friction n a rubbing of one object against another; conflict between differing opinions, ideas, etc; the resistance to motion of things that touch.–**frictional** adj.

Friday n the sixth day of the week.

fridge n (inf) a refrigerator.

fried see **fry**1.

friend n a person whom one knows well and is fond of; an ally, supporter, or sympathizer.–**friendless** adj.–**friendship** n.

friendly adj (**friendlier, friendliest**) like a friend; kindly; favorable. * n a sporting game played for fun, not in competition.–**friendlily** adv.–**friendliness** n.

frieze n a decorative band along the top of the wall of a room.

frigate n a warship smaller than a destroyer used for escort, anti-submarine, and patrol duties.

fright n sudden fear; a shock; (inf) something unsightly or ridiculous in appearance.

frighten vt to terrify, to scare; to force by frightening.–**frightener** n.–**frighteningly** adv.

frightful adj terrible, shocking; (inf) extreme, very bad.–**frightfully** adv.–**frightfulness** n.

frigid adj extremely cold; not warm or friendly; unresponsive sexually.–**frigidity** n.–**frigidly** adv.

frill n a piece of pleated or gathered fabric used for edging; something superfluous, an affectation. * vt to decorate with a frill or frills.–**frilled** adj.–**frilly** adj.

fringe n a decorative border of hanging threads; hair hanging over the forehead; an outer edge; a marginal or minor part. * vt to be or make a fringe for. * adj at the outer edge; additional; minor; unconventional.

frisk vi to leap playfully. * vt (inf) to search (a person) by feeling for concealed weapons, etc. * n a gambol, dance, or frolic.–**frisker** n.

frisky adj (**friskier, friskiest**) lively, playful.–**friskily** adv.–**friskiness** n.

fritter[1] n a slice of fruit or meat fried in batter.

fritter[2] vt (with **away**) to waste; to break into tiny pieces.–**fritterer** n.

frivolous adj irresponsible; trifling; silly.–**frivolously** adv.–**frivolity** n.

frizz vti (hair) to (cause to) form into small tight curls. * n hair that is frizzed.–**frizzy** adj.–**frizziness** n.

fro adv away from; backward; **to and fro** back and forward.

frock n a dress; a smock; a loose wide-sleeved gown worn by a monk. * vt to put on a frock; to invest with the office of priest.

frog n a small tailless web-footed jumping amphibian.

frogman n (pl **frogmen**) a person who wears rubber suit, flippers, oxygen supply, etc and is trained in working underwater.

frolic n a lively party or game; merriment, fun. * vi (**frolicking, frolicked**) to play happily.–**frolicker** n.

from prep beginning at, starting with; out of; originating with; out of the possibility or use of.

frond n a large leaf with many divisions, esp of a palm or fern.

front n outward behavior; (inf) an appearance of social standing; etc; the part facing forward; the first part; a forward or leading position; the advanced battle area in warfare; a person or group used to hide another's activity; an advancing mass of cold or warm air. * adj at, to, in, on, or of the front. * vti to face; to stand or be situated opposite to or over against; to serve as a front (for); to have the front turned in a particular direction.–**frontal** adj.–**frontally** adv.

frontier n the border between two countries; the limit of existing knowledge of a subject.

frontispiece n an illustration opposite the title page of a book.

frontrunner n the favorite to win a race, election, etc.

frontwards, frontward adj, adv towards the front.

frost n temperature at or below freezing point; a coating of powdery ice particles; coldness of manner. * vt to cover (as if) with frost or frosting; to give a frost-like opaque surface to (glass).

frostbite n injury to a part of the body by exposure to cold.–**frostbitten** adj.

frosting n icing for a cake.

frosty adj (**frostier, frostiest**) cold with frost; cold or reserved in manner, chilly, distant.–**frostily** adv.–**frostiness** n.

froth n foam; foaming saliva; frivolity. * vi to emit or gather foam.

frothy adj (**frothier, frothiest**) full of or composed of froth; frivolous; insubstantial.–**frothily** adv.–**frothiness** n.

frown vi to contract the brow as in anger or thought; (with **upon**) to regard with displeasure or disapproval. * n a wrinkled brow; a stern look.–**frowner** n.–**frowningly** adv.

froze see **freeze**.

frozen[1] see **freeze**.

frozen[2] adj formed into or covered by ice; damaged or killed by cold; (food, etc) preserved by freezing; motionless; made speechless by strong emotion; formal and unfriendly; extremely cold; (prices, wages, etc) fixed at a given level; (funds, etc) unrealizable.

fructose n a type of sugar found in ripe fruit and honey.

frugal adj economical, thrifty; inexpensive, meager.–**frugality** n.–**frugally** adv.

fruit n the seed-bearing part of any plant; the fleshy part of this used as food; the result or product of any action. * vti to bear or cause to bear fruit.

fruitful adj producing lots of fruit; productive.–**fruitfully** adv.–**fruitfulness** n.

fruition n a coming to fulfillment, realization.

fruitless adj unproductive; pointless; useless.–**fruitlessly** adv.–**fruitlessness** n.

fruit machine n a coin-operated gambling machine, using symbols of fruit to indicate a winning combination.

fruit salad n a dish of various fruits sliced and mixed.

fruity adj (**fruitier, fruitiest**) like, or tasting like, fruit; (inf) (voice) mellow.–**fruitiness** n.

frump n a drab and dowdy woman.–**frumpish, frumpy** adj.

frustrate vt to prevent from achieving a goal or gratifying a desire; to discourage, irritate, tire; to disappoint.–**frustrater** n.–**frustratingly** adv.–**frustration** n.

fry[1] vti (**frying, fried**) to cook over direct heat in hot fat. * n (pl **fries**) a dish of things fried.

fry[2] n (pl **fries**) recently hatched fishes; the young of a frog, etc.

ft. abbr = foot or feet.

fuchsia n any of a genus of decorative shrubs with purplish-red flowers.

fuddle vt to make drunk; to make confused.

fuddy-duddy n (pl **fuddy-duddies**) a person with old-fashioned or staid views.

fudge n a soft sweet made of butter, milk, sugar, flavoring, etc; a made-up story. * vi to refuse to commit oneself; to cheat; to contrive by imperfect or improvised means. * vt to fake; to fail to come to grips with; to make or do anything in a bungling, careless manner.

fuel n material burned to supply heat and power, or as a source of nuclear energy; anything that serves to intensify strong feelings. * vti (**fueling, fueled** or **fuelling, fuelled**) to supply with or obtain fuel.–**fueler, fueller** n.

fugitive n a person who flees from danger, pursuit, or duty. * adj fleeing, as from danger or justice; fleeting, transient; not permanent.–**fugitively** adv.

fugue n a polyphonic musical composition with its theme taken up successively by different voices.–**fugal** adj.–**fugally** adv.

fulcrum n (pl **fulcrums, fulcra**) the fixed point on which a lever turns; a critical factor determining an outcome.

fulfill, fulfil vt (**fulfills** or **fulfils, fulfilling, fulfilled**) to carry out (a promise, etc); to achieve the completion of; to satisfy; to bring to an end, complete.–**fulfiller** n.–**fulfillment, fulfilment** n.

full adj having or holding all that can be contained; having eaten all one wants; having a great number (of); complete; having reached to greatest size, extent, etc. * n the greatest amount, extent etc. * adv completely, directly, exactly.

full-blown adj in full bloom; matured, fully developed.

full-bodied adj (flavor) characterized by richness and fullness.

full-fledged adj (bird) mature; having full status.

full house n (theater, etc) a performance for which all seats are sold.

fullness n the state of being full; **fullness of time** the proper or destined time.–also **fulness**.

full-stop n (gram) a period.

fully adv thoroughly, completely; at least.

fulness see **fullness**.

fulsome adj excessively praising, obsequious.–**fulsomely** adv.–**fulsomeness** n.

fumble vi to grope about. * vt to handle clumsily; to say or act awkwardly; to fail to catch (a ball) cleanly. * n an awkward attempt.–**fumbler** n.–**fumblingly** adv.

fume n (usu pl) smoke, gas or vapor, esp if offensive or suffocating. * vi to give off fumes; to express anger. * vt to subject to fumes.–**fumer** n.–**fumingly** adv.

fumigate vt to disinfect or exterminate (pests, etc) using fumes.–**fumigation** n.–**fumigator** n.

fun n (what provides) amusement and enjoyment. * vi (**funning, funned**) to joke.

function n the activity characteristic of a person or thing; the specific purpose of a certain person or thing; an official ceremony or social entertainment. * vi to perform a function; to act, operate.

functional adj of a function or functions; practical, not ornamental; (disease) affecting the functions only, not organic.–**functionally** adv.

functionary n (pl **functionaries**) a person in an official capacity.

fund n a supply that can be drawn upon; a sum of money set aside for a purpose; (pl) ready money. * vt to provide funds for; to convert (a debt) into stock; to place in a fund.

fundamental adj basic; essential. * n that which serves as a groundwork; an essential.–**fundamentality, fundamentalness** n.–**fundamentally** adv.

fundamentalism n belief in the literal truth of the Bible, Koran etc.–**fundamentalist** adj, n.–**fundamentalistic** adj.

funeral n the ceremony associated with the burial or cremation of the dead; a procession accompanying a coffin to a burial.

funereal adj suiting a funeral, dismal, mournful.–**funereally** adv.

fungal adj of or pertaining to a fungus; caused by a fungus.

fungicide n a substance that destroys fungi.–**fungicidal** adj.

fungus n (pl **fungi, funguses**) any of a major group of lower plants, as mildews, mushrooms, yeasts, etc, that lack chlorophyll and reproduce by spores.–**fungic** adj.

funk n (inf) panic, fear; a coward; funky music. * vti (inf) to show fear; to shirk.–**funker** n.

funky adj (**funkier, funkiest**) (inf) (pop, jazz music, etc) soulful, bluesy; fashionable.–**funkiness** n.

funnel n an implement, usually a cone with a wide top and tapering to a narrow tube, for pouring fluids, powders, into bottles, etc; a metal chimney for the escape of smoke, steam, etc. * vti (**funneling, funneled** or **funnelling, funnelled**) to pour or cause to pour through a funnel.

funny adj (**funnier, funniest**) causing laughter; puzzling, odd; (inf) unwell, queasy.–**funnily** adv.–**funniness** n.

funny bone n the part of the elbow where a sensitive nerve rests close to the bone, producing a tingling sensation if struck.

fur n the short, soft, fine hair on the bodies of certain animals; their skins with the fur attached; a garment made of fur; a fabric in imitation of fur; a fur-like coating, as on the tongue. * vti (**furring, furred**) to cover or become covered with fur.–**furry** adj.

furious adj full of anger; intense; violent, impetuous.–**furiously** adv.–**furiousness** n.

furl vt to roll up (a sail, flag, etc) tightly and make secure; to fold up, close.–**furlable** adj.–**furler** n.

furlough n leave of absence from duty, esp for military personnel. * vt to grant a furlough to.

furnace n an enclosed chamber in which heat is produced to burn refuse, smelt ore, etc.

furnish vt to provide (a room, etc) with furniture; to equip with what is necessary; to supply. –**furnisher** n.

furnishings npl furniture, carpets, etc.

furniture n the things in a room, etc that equip it for living, as chairs, beds, etc; equipment.

furor n fury, indignation; widespread enthusiasm.

furrow n the groove in the earth made by a plough; a groove or track resembling this; a wrinkle. * vti to make furrows in; to wrinkle.–**furrower** n.–**furrowy** adj.

further adv at or to a greater distance or degree; in addition. * adj more distant, remote; additional. * vt to help forward, promote.–**furtherer** n.

furtherance n a helping forward.

furthermore adv moreover, besides.

furthest adj at or to the greatest distance.

furtive adj stealthy; sly.–**furtively** adv.–**furtiveness** n.

fury n (pl **furies**) intense rage; a frenzy; a violently angry person.

fuse see **fuse**.

fuselage n the body of an aircraft.

fusillade n a firing of shots in continuous or rapid succession; an outburst, as of criticism. * vt to attack or shoot down by fusillade.

fusion n the act of melting, blending or fusing; a product of fusion; union, partnership; nuclear fusion.

fuss n excited activity, bustle; a nervous state; (inf) a quarrel; (inf) a showy display of approval. * vi to worry over trifles; to whine, as a baby.–**fusser** n.

fussy adj (**fussier, fussiest**) worrying over details; hard to please; fastidious; over-elaborate.–**fussily** adv.–**fussiness** n.

futile adj useless; ineffective.–**futilely** adv.–**futility** n.

futon n a light cotton mattress.

future adj that is to be; of or referring to time yet to come. * n the time to come; future events; likelihood of eventual success; (gram) the future tense; (pl) commodities purchased at a prescribed price for delivery at some future date.

futuristic adj forward-looking in design, appearance, intention, etc.–**futuristically** adv.

fuze vti to join or become joined by melting; to (cause to) melt by the application of heat; to equip a plug, circuit, etc with a fuse; to (cause to) fail by blowing a fuse. * n a tube or wick filled with combustible material for setting off an explosive charge; a piece of thin wire that melts and breaks when an electric current exceeds a certain level.–also **fuse**.

fuzz n fine light particles of fiber (as of down or fluff); a blurred effect; fluff. * vi to fly off in minute particles; to become blurred.

fuzzy adj (**fuzzier, fuzziest**) like fuzz; fluffy; blurred.–**fuzzily** adv.–**fuzziness** n.

G

GA, Ga. abbr = Georgia.

gab vi (**gabbing, gabbed**) (inf) to talk in a rapid or thoughtless manner, chatter. * n (inf) idle talk.–**gabber** n.

gabardine n a firm cloth of wool, rayon, or cotton; gaberdine.

gabble vti to talk or utter rapidly or incoherently; to utter inarticulate or animal sounds.–**gabbler** n.

gable n the triangular upper part of a wall enclosed by the sloping ends of a pitched roof.–**gabled** adj.

gad vi (**gadding, gadded**) (usu with **about**) to wander restlessly or idly in search of pleasure.–**gadder** n.

gadget n a small, often ingenious, mechanical or electronic tool or device.–**gadgety** adj.

gaff n a pole with a sharp hook for landing large fish; (naut) a high boom or yard for hoisting a sail aft of a mast. * vt to land (a fish) with a gaff.

gaffe n a social blunder.

gag n something put over or into the mouth to prevent talking; any restraint of free speech; a joke. * vb (**gagging, gagged**) vt to cause to retch; to keep from speaking, as by stopping the mouth of. * vi to retch; to tell jokes.

gage see **gauge**.

gaggle n a flock of geese when not in flight; (inf) a disorderly collection of people.

gaiety n (pl **gaieties**) happiness, liveliness; colorful appearance.

gaily adv in a cheerful manner; with bright colors.

gain vt to obtain, earn, esp by effort; to win in a contest; to attract; to get as an addition (esp profit or advantage); to make an increase in; to reach. * vi to make progress; to increase in weight. * n an increase esp in profit or advantage; an acquisition.

gainful adj profitable.–**gainfully** adv.–**gainfulness** n.

gait n a manner of walking or running.

gal, gall. abbr = gallon.

gala n a celebration, festival.

galaxy n (pl **galaxies**) any of the systems of stars in the universe; any splendid assemblage; (with cap) the galaxy containing the Earth's solar system; the Milky Way.–**galactic** adj.

gale n a strong wind, specifically one with an average speed of 42 mph (67.6 kph) and gusts in excess of 50 mph (80.5 kph); an outburst.

gall[1] n bile; bitter feeling; (inf) impudence.

gall[2] n a skin sore caused by rubbing. * vt to chafe or hurt by rubbing; to irritate.

gallant adj dignified, stately; brave; noble; (man) polite and chivalrous to women.–**gallantly** adv.–**gallantness** n.–**gallantry** n (pl **gallantries**).

gall bladder n a membranous sac attached to the liver in which bile is stored.

galleon n a large sailing ship of the 15th–18th centuries.

gallery n (pl **galleries**) a covered passage for walking; a long narrow outside balcony; a balcony running along the inside wall of a building; (the occupants of) an upper area of seating in a theater; a long narrow room used for a special purpose, eg shooting practice; a room or building designed for the exhibition of works of art; the spectators at a golf tournament, tennis match, etc.–**galleried** adj.

galley n a long, usu low, ship of ancient or medieval times, propelled by oars; the kitchen of a ship, aircraft.

galling adj irritating, exasperating.

gallivant vi (inf) to go about in search of amusement.

gallon n a unit of liquid measure comprising 4 quarts or 3.78 liters (in UK, 4.54 liters); (pl) (inf) a large amount.

gallop n the fastest gait of a horse, etc; a succession of leaping strides; a fast pace. * vti to go or cause to go at a gallop; to move swiftly.–**galloper** n.

gallows n (pl **gallowses, gallows**) a wooden frame used for hanging criminals.

gallstone n a small solid mass in the gall bladder.

galore adv in great quantity; in plentiful supply.

galvanic adj producing electricity by chemical action; stimulating (people) into action.–**galvanically** adv.

galvanize vt to apply an electric current to; to startle; to excite; to plate (metal) with zinc.–**galvanization** n.–**galvanizer** n.

gambit n (chess) an opening in which a piece is sacrificed to gain an advantage; any action to gain an advantage.

gamble vi to play games of chance for money; to take a risk for some advantage. * vt to risk in gambling, to bet. * n a risky venture; a bet.–**gambler** n.–**gambling** n.

gambol vi (**gamboling, gamboled** or **gambolling, gambolled**) to jump and skip about in play; to frisk. * n a caper, a playful leap.

game n any form of play, amusement; activity or sport involving competition; a scheme, a plan; wild birds or animals hunted for sport or food, the flesh of such animals. * vi to play for a stake. * adj (inf) brave, resolute; (inf) willing.–**gamely** adv.–**gameness** n.

gamekeeper n a person who breeds and takes care of game birds and animals, as on an estate.–**gamekeeping** n.

gamesmanship n (inf) the art of winning games by questionable acts just short of cheating.

gamete n a reproductive cell that unites with another to form the cell that develops into a new individual.–**gametal, gametic** adj.

gamine n a boyish girl or woman with impish appeal.

gaming n the act of playing games for stakes; gambling.–also adj.

gamma n the third letter of the Greek alphabet.

gamma radiation, gamma rays n short-wave electromagnetic radiation from a radioactive substance.

gammon n cured or smoked ham; meat from the hindquarters of a side of bacon.

gamut n a complete range or series; (mus) the whole range of notes of a voice or instrument.

gander n an adult goose; (inf) a quick look.

gang n a group of persons, esp laborers, working together; a group of persons acting or associating together, esp for illegal purposes. * vti to form into or act as a gang.–**ganged** adj.

gangland n the criminal fraternity.

gangling, gangly adj tall, thin and awkward in appearance and movement.

ganglion n (pl **ganglia, ganglions**) a mass of nerve cells from which nerve impulses are transmitted.–**ganglionic** adj.

gangplank n a moveable ramp by which to board or leave a ship.

gangrene n death of body tissue when the blood supply is obstructed.–**gangrenous** adj.

gangsta n a variant of rap music with its source the US West Coast with lyrics focussed on gang culture; a performer of this style of music. * adj belonging to gangsta music.

gangster n a member of a criminal gang.

gangway n a passageway, esp an opening in a ship's side for loading, etc; a gangplank.

ganja n marijuana.

gannet n any of various large voracious fish-eating sea birds.

gantry n (pl **gantries**) a metal framework, often on wheels, for a traveling crane; a wheeled framework with a crane, platforms, etc for servicing a rocket to be launched.

gap n a break or opening in something, as a wall or fence; an interruption in continuity, an interval; a mountain pass; a divergence, disparity. * vt (**gapping, gapped**) to make a gap in.–**gappy** adj.

gape vi to open the mouth wide; to stare in astonishment, esp with the mouth open; to open widely. * n the act of gaping; a wide opening.–**gaping** adj.–**gapingly** adv.

garage n an enclosed shelter for motor vehicles; a place where motor vehicles are repaired and serviced, and fuel sold. * vt to put or keep in a garage.

garb n clothing, style of dress. * vt to clothe.

garbage n food waste; unwanted or useless material; rubbish; (comput) useless data.

garble vt to distort (a message, story, etc) so as to mislead.–**garbler** n.

garden n an area of ground for growing herbs, fruits, flowers, or vegetables; a yard; a fertile, well-cultivated region; a public park or recreation area, usu laid-out with plants and trees. * vi to make, or work in, a garden.–**gardener** n.–**gardening** n.

gardenia n a tree or shrub with beautiful fragrant white or yellow flowers.

gargantuan adj colossal, prodigious.

gargle vti to rinse the throat by breathing air from the lungs through liquid held in the mouth. * n a liquid for this purpose; the sound made by gargling.–**gargler** n.

gargoyle n a grotesquely carved face or figure, usu acting as a spout to drain water from a gutter; a person with an ugly face.–**gargoyled** adj.

garish adj crudely bright, gaudy.–**garishly** adv.–**garishness** n.

garland n a wreath of flowers or leaves worn or hung as decoration. * vt to decorate with a garland.

garlic n a bulbous herb cultivated for its compound bulbs used in cookery; its bulb.–**garlicky** adj.

garment n an item of clothing.

garner vt to gather, store.

garnet n a semiprecious stone, red, yellow or green in color.

garnish vt to decorate; to decorate (food) with something that adds color or flavor. * n something used to garnish food.–**garnisher** n.–**garniture** n.

garret n an attic.

garrison n troops stationed at a fort; a fortified place with troops. * vt to station (troops) in (a fortified place) for its defense.

garrulous adj excessively talkative.–**garrulously** adv.–**garrulousness, garrulity** n.

garter n an elasticated band used to support a stocking or sock.

gas n (pl **gases, gasses**) an air-like substance with the capacity to expand indefinitely and not liquefy or solidify at ordinary temperatures; gasoline; any mixture of flammable gases used for lighting or heating; any gas used as an anesthetic; any poisonous substance dispersed in the air, as in war; (inf) empty talk. * vt (**gases** or **gasses, gassing, gassed**) to poison or disable with gas; (inf) to talk idly and at length.–**gaseous** adj.

gas chamber n an airtight room where animals or people are killed by poisonous gas.

gash n a long, deep, open cut. * vt to cut deep.

gasket n a piece or ring of rubber, metal, etc sandwiched between metal surfaces to act as a seal.

gasoline, gasolene n a liquid fuel or solvent distilled from petroleum.–**gasolinic** adj.

gasp vi to draw in the breath suddenly and audibly, as from shock; to struggle to catch the breath. * vt to utter breathlessly. * n the act of gasping.–**gaspingly** adv.

gassy adj (**gassier, gassiest**) impregnated with or like a gas; given to pretentious talk; inflated.

gastric adj of, in, or near the stomach.

gastric juice n digestive fluid secreted by glands in the stomach lining.

gastric ulcer n an ulcer of the lining of the stomach.

gastritis n inflammation of the stomach.–**gastritic** adj.

gastroenteritis n inflammation of the mucous membrane of the stomach and intestines.–**gastroenteritic** adj.

gastronomy n the art and science of good eating.–**gastronomic, gastronomical** adj.–**gastronomically** adj.

gastropod n any of a large class of mollusks (as snails) with a flattened foot for moving and usu with stalk-like sense organs.–**gastropodan** adj, n.–**gastropodous** adj.

gasworks n sing a place where gas is manufactured.

gate n a movable structure controlling passage through an opening in a fence or wall; a gateway; a movable barrier; a structure controlling the flow of water, as in a canal; a device (as in a computer) that outputs a signal when specified input conditions are met; the total amount or number of paid admissions to a football match, etc. * vt to supply with a gate; to keep within the gates (of a university) as a punishment.

gate-crasher n a person who attends a party, etc without being invited.–**gatecrash** vi.

gatepost n a post on which a gate is hung, or to which it is attached when closed.

gateway n an opening for a gate; a means of entrance or exit.

gather vt to bring together in one place or group; to get gradually; to collect (as taxes); to harvest; to draw (parts) together; to pucker fabric by pulling a thread or stitching; to understand, infer. * vi to come together in a body; to cluster around a focus of attention.–**gatherable** adj.–**gatherer** n.

gathering n the act of gathering or assembling together; an assembly; folds made in a garment by gathering.

gauche adj socially inept; graceless, tactless.–**gauchely** adv.–**gaucheness** n.

gaucho n (pl **gauchos**) a cowboy of the pampas of South America.

gaudy adj (**gaudier, gaudiest**) excessively ornamented; tastelessly bright.–**gaudily** adv.–**gaudiness** n.

gauge n measurement according to some standard or system; any device for measuring; the distance between rails of a railway; the size of the bore of a shotgun; the thickness of sheet metal, wire, etc. * vt to measure the size, amount, etc of.–also **gage**.–**gaugeable, gagable** adj.–**gauger, gager** n.

gaunt adj excessively thin as from hunger or age; looking grim or forbidding.–**gauntness** n.

gauntlet[1] n a knight's armored glove; a long glove, often with a flaring cuff.

gauntlet[2] n (formerly) a type of military punishment in which a victim was forced to run between two lines of men who struck him as he passed.

gauze n thin often transparent fabric.–**gauzy** adj.

gave see **give**.

gavel n a hammer used by a chairman, auctioneer, judge, etc to command proceedings.

gawk vi to stare at stupidly.

gawky adj (**gawkier, gawkiest**) clumsy, awkward, ungainly.–**gawkily** adv.–**gawkiness** n.

gay adj joyous and lively; colorful; homosexual. * n a homosexual.–**gayness** n.

gaze vi to look steadily. * n a steady look.–**gazer** n.

gazelle n (pl **gazelles, gazelle**) any of numerous small swift Asian or African antelopes.

gazette n a newspaper, now mainly in newspaper titles; an official publication listing government appointments, legal notices, etc.

gazetteer n an index of geographical place names.

gazpacho n a Spanish soup of tomatoes and other vegetables, served cold.

GB abbr = Great Britain.

GDP abbr = Gross Domestic Product.

gear n clothing; equipment, esp for some task or activity; a toothed wheel designed to mesh with another; (often pl) a system of such gears meshed together to transmit motion; a specific adjustment of such a system; a part of a mechanism with a specific function. * vt to connect by or furnish with gears; to adapt (one thing) to conform with another.

gearbox n a metal case enclosing a system of gears.

gearshift n a lever used to engage or change gear, esp in a motor vehicle.

gearwheel n a cogwheel.

gecko n (pl **geckos, geckoes**) a small lizard of warm regions that feeds on insects.

gee vi (**geeing geed**) (often with **up**) to make a horse go faster. * interj a mild oath.

geese see **goose**.

geisha n (pl **geisha, geishas**) a Japanese girl trained as an entertainer to serve as a hired companion to men.

gel n a jelly-like substance, as that applied to style and sculpt hair before drying it. * vti (**gelling, gelled**) to become or cause to become a gel.–also **jell**.

gelatin, gelatine n a tasteless, odorless substance extracted by boiling bones, hoofs, etc and used in food, photographic film, medicines, etc.

gelatinous adj of or like gelatin; jelly-like in consistency.

geld vt (**gelding, gelded** or **gelt**) to castrate, esp a horse.

gelding n a castrated horse.

gem n a precious stone, esp when cut and polished for use as a jewel; a person or thing regarded as extremely valuable or beloved. * vt (**gemming, gemmed**) to decorate or set with gems.

Gemini n the third sign of the zodiac, represented by the twins Castor and Pollux, operative 21 May–20 June.–**Geminian** adj.

gemstone n a mineral or substance used as a gem.

gender n the classification by which words are grouped as feminine, masculine, or neuter; (inf) the sex of a person.

gene n any of the complex chemical units in the chromosomes by which hereditary characteristics are transmitted.

genealogy n (pl **genealogies**) a recorded history of one's ancestry, relating to or covering family descent; lineage.–**genealogical** adj.–**genealogist** n.

genera see **genus**.

general adj not local, special, or specialized; of or for a whole genus, relating to or covering all instances or individuals of a class or group; widespread, common to many; not specific or precise; holding superior rank, chief. * n something that involves or is applicable to the whole; a commissioned officer above a lieutenant general; a leader, commander; the title of the head of some religious orders.–**generalness** n.

general anesthetic n an anesthetic effecting the whole body and producing unconsciousness.

general election n a national election to choose representatives in every constituency.

generalization n general inference; induction; a general notion formed by attributing the characteristic(s) of a particular part or member (of a class, community etc) to the whole.

generalize vti to form general conclusions from specific instances; to talk (about something) in general terms.–**generalization** n.–**generalizer** n.

generally adv widely; popularly; usually; not specifically.

general strike n a strike of all workers in a city, region or country.

generate vt to bring into existence; to produce.–**generative** adj.

generation n the act or process of generating; a single succession in natural descent; people of the same period; production, as of electric current.

generation gap n the difference in attitudes and understanding between one generation and another.

generator n one who or that which generates; a machine that changes mechanical energy to electrical energy.

generic adj of a whole class, kind, or group.–**generically** adv.

generosity n (pl **generosities**) the quality of being generous; liberality; munificence; a generous act.

generous adj magnanimous; of a noble nature; willing to give or share; large, ample.–**generously** adv.–**generousness** n.

genesis n (pl **geneses**) the beginning, origin; (with cap) the first book of the Old Testament.

genetic, genetical adj of or relating to the origin, development or causes of something; of or relating to genes or genetics.–**genetically** adv.

genetic code n the order of genetic information in a cell, which determines hereditary characteristics.

genetic engineering n the modification of genetic information in the cell of a plant or animal to improve yield, performance, etc.

genetics n sing the branch of biology dealing with heredity and variation in plants and animals.–**geneticist** n.

genial adj kindly, sympathetic and cheerful in manner; mild, pleasantly warm.–**geniality, genialness** n.–**genially** adv.

genie n (pl **genies, genii**) (fairy tales) a spirit with supernatural powers which can fulfil your wishes.

genital adj of reproduction or the sexual organs.

genitals, genitalia npl the (external) sexual organs.–**genitalic** adj.

genius n (pl **geniuses**) a person possessing extraordinary intellectual power; (with **for**) natural ability, strong inclination.

genocide n the systematic killing of a whole race of people.–**genocidal** adj.

genre n a distinctive type or category, esp of literary composition; a style of painting in which everyday objects are treated realistically.

genteel adj polite or well-bred; affectedly refined.–**genteelly** adv.–**genteelness** n.

gentile n a person who is not a Jew.–also adj.

gentility n (pl **gentilities**) refinement, good manners.

gentle adj belonging to a family of high social station; refined, courteous; generous; kind; kindly; patient; not harsh or rough.– **gentleness** n.–**gently** adv.

gentleman n (pl **gentlemen**) a man of good family and social standing; a courteous, gracious and honorable man; a polite term of address.–**gentlemanly** adj.

gentlewoman n (pl **gentlewomen**) a woman of noble or gentle birth; a lady.

gentrify vt (**gentrifying, gentrified**) to convert a working-class house or district to more expensive middle-class tastes.– **gentrification** n.

gentry n people of high social standing; (formerly) landed proprietors not belonging to the nobility.

genuflect vi to act in a servile way; to bend the knee in worship or respect.–**genuflection** n.–**genuflector** n.

genuine adj not fake or artificial, real; sincere.–**genuinely** adv.– **genuineness** n.

genus n (pl **genera**) (biol) a taxonomic division of plants and animals below a family and above a species; a class of objects divided into several subordinate species.

geography n (pl **geographies**) the science of the physical nature of the earth, such as land and sea masses, climate, vegetation, etc, and their interaction with the human population; the physical features of a region.–**geographer** n.–**geographical, geographic** adj.–**geographically** adv.

geology n the science relating to the history and structure of the earth's crust, its rocks and fossils.–**geological, geologic** adj.–**geologically** adv.–**geologist, geologer** n.

geometry n the branch of mathematics dealing with the properties, measurement, and relationships of points, lines, planes, and solids.–**geometric, geometrical** adj.–**geometrically** adv.

geophysics n sing the physics of the earth.–**geophysical**.– adj.–**geophysicist** n.

georgette n a thin silk fabric.

geranium n a garden plant with red, pink or white flowers.

gerbil, gerbille n a type of burrowing desert rodent of Asia and Africa.–also **jerbil**.

geriatric adj relating to geriatrics or old people; (inf) old, decrepit. * n an aged person.

geriatrics n sing a branch of medicine dealing with the diseases and care of old people.–**geriatrician, geriatrist** n.

germ n a simple form of living matter capable of growth and development into an organism; any microscopic, disease-causing organism; an origin or foundation capable of growing and developing.

germane adj relevant.–**germanely** adv.–**germaneness** n.

German measles n (sing) a mild contagious disease similar to measles.–also **rubella**.

German shepherd n any of a breed of large smooth-haired dogs often used by the police and for guarding property.–also **Alsatian**.

germ cell n a reproductive cell.

germicide n a substance used to destroy germs.–**germicidal** adj.

germinate vti to start developing; to sprout, as from a seed.– **germinable, germinative** adj.–**germination** n.–**germinator** n.

germ warfare n the use of disease-causing bacteria against enemy forces.

gestate vt to carry (young) in the womb during pregnancy; to develop (a plan, etc) gradually in the mind.–**gestational, gestative** adj.–**gestatory** adj.

gestation n the act or period of carrying young in the womb; pregnancy.

gesticulate vi to make expressive gestures, esp when speaking.– **gesticulation** n.–**gesticulative** adj.–**gesticulator** n.

gesture n movement of part of the body to express or emphasize ideas, emotions, etc. * vi to make a gesture.–**gestural** adj.– **gesturer** n.

get vb (**getting, got**, pp **got, gotten**) vt to obtain, gain, win; to receive; to acquire; to go and bring; to catch; to persuade; to cause to be; to prepare; (inf) (with vb aux **have** or **has**) to be obliged to; to possess; (inf) to strike, kill, baffle; defeat, etc; (inf) to understand; (with **across**) to cause to be understood; (with **in**) to bring in; (with **off**) to acquit, to secure favorable treatment of; (with **out**) to cause to leave or escape; to cause to become known or published; (with **out of**) to avoid doing; (with **over**) to communicate effectively. * vi to come; to go; to arrive; to come to be; to manage or contrive; (with **about, around**) to be up and on one's feet, esp after being unwell; to be socially active; (news, gossip) to become circulated; (with **across**) to be understood; (with **at**) to reach; (inf) to mean, imply; to irritate, pester relentlessly; (inf) to criticize; (inf) to corrupt, bribe, influence illegally; (with **away**) to escape; (with **by**) (inf) to manage, to survive; (with **in**) (vehicle, etc) to enter; to arrive; (with **off**) to come off, down, or out of; to be acquitted; to escape the consequences of; to begin, depart; (with **on**) to go on or into; to put on; to proceed; to grow older; to become late; to manage; to succeed; (with **on with**) to establish a friendly relationship; (with **out**) to go out or away; to leave or escape; to take out; to become known or published; (with **over**) to overcome; to recover from; to forget; (with **round, around**) to evade, circumvent; to coax, cajole; (with **through**) to use up, spend, consume; to finish; to manage to survive; (examination, test) to succeed or pass; to contact by telephone; (with **up**) to rise to one's feet; to get out of bed; (inf) to organize; (inf) to dress in a certain style; (inf) to be involved in (mischief, etc).

get-at-able adj accessible.

getaway n the act of escaping; a start in a race, etc.

get-together n (inf) an informal social gathering or meeting.

get-up n (inf) dress, costume.

get-up-and-go n (inf) energy, enthusiasm.

geyser n a natural spring from which columns of boiling water and steam gush into the air at intervals; a water heater.

ghastly adj (**ghastlier, ghastliest**) terrifying, horrible; (inf) intensely disagreeable; pale, unwell looking.–**ghastliness** n.

gherkin n a small cucumber used for pickling.

ghetto n (pl **ghettos, ghettoes**) a section of a city in which members of a minority group live, esp because of social, legal or economic pressure.

ghost n the supposed disembodied spirit of a dead person, appearing as a shadowy apparition; a faint trace or suggestion; a false image in a photographic negative. * vt to ghostwrite.

ghostly adj (**ghostlier, ghostliest**) of or like a ghost.–**ghostliness** n.

ghostwrite vt (**ghostwriting, ghostwrote**, pp **ghostwritten**) to writes books, speeches, articles, etc for another who professes to be the author.–**ghostwriter** n.

ghoul n (Muslim folklore) an evil spirit that robs graves and feeds on the dead; a person with macabre tastes or interests.– **ghoulish** adj.–**ghoulishly** adv.

GHQ abbr = General Headquarters.

GI n (pl **GI's, GIs**) (inf) a private soldier in the US Army.

giant n a huge legendary being of great strength; a person of great size, strength, intellect, etc. * adj incredibly large.–**giantess** nf.

gibberish n unintelligible talk, nonsense.

gibbon n a small tailless ape of southeastern Asia and the East Indies.

gibe n a taunt, sneer. * vti to jeer, scoff (at).–also **jibe**.–**giber, jiber** n.–**gibingly, jibingly** adv.

giblets npl the edible internal organs of a bird.

giddy adj (**giddier, giddiest**) frivolous, flighty; having a feeling of whirling around as if about to lose balance and fall; causing giddiness. * vti (**giddying, giddied**) to make giddy, to become giddy.—**giddily** adv.—**giddiness** n.

gift n something given; the act of giving; a natural ability. * vt to present with or as a gift.—**giftedness** n.

gifted adj having great natural ability.

gig n (inf) a single booking for a jazz or pop band, etc; a single night's performance. * vi (**gigging, gigged**) to perform a gig.

gigantic adj exceedingly large.—**gigantically** adv.—**giganticness** n.

giggle vi to laugh in a nervous or silly manner. * n a laugh in this manner; (inf) a prank, a joke.—**giggler** n.—**giggly** adj.

gigolo n (pl **gigolos**) a man paid to be a woman's escort.

gild[1] see **guild**.

gild[2] vt (**gilding, gilded** or **gilt**) to coat with gold leaf; to give a deceptively attractive appearance to.—**gilder** n.—**gilding** n.

gill n an organ, esp in fish, for breathing in water.

gilt[1] see **gild**[2].

gilt[2] n gilding; a substance used for this.

gimmick n a trick or device for attracting notice, advertising or promoting a person, product or service.—**gimmickry** n.—**gimmicky** adj.

gin[1] n an alcoholic spirit distilled from grain and flavored with juniper berries.

gin[2] n a trap for catching small animals; a type of crane; a machine for separating the seeds from raw cotton. * vt (**ginning, ginned**) to trap with a gin; to separate seeds from cotton.

ginger n a tropical plant with fleshy roots used as a flavoring; the spice prepared by drying and grinding; (inf) vigour; a reddish-brown.—**gingery** adj.

gingerbread n a cookie flavored with ginger.

gingerly adv with care or caution. * adj cautious.—**gingerliness** n.

gingham n a cotton fabric with stripes or checks.

gingivitis n inflammation of the gums.

ginseng n a plant found in China and North America; its root, said to have an invigorating effect on the mind and body.

gip see **gyp**.

Gipsy see **Gypsy**.

giraffe n (pl **giraffes, giraffe**) a large cud-chewing mammal of Africa, with very long legs and neck.

gird vt (**girding, girded** or **girt**) to encircle or fasten with a belt; to surround; to prepare (oneself) for action.

girder n a large steel beam for supporting joists, the framework of a building, etc.

girdle n a belt for the waist.

girl n a female child; a young woman; (inf) a woman of any age.—**girlhood** n.—**girlish** adj.

girlfriend n a female friend, esp with whom one is romantically involved.

girlish adj of or like a girl.—**girlishly** adv.—**girlishness** n.

girt see **gird**.

girth n the thickness round something; a band put around the belly of a horse, etc to hold a saddle or pack.

gist n the principal point or essence of anything.

give vb (**giving, gave,** pp **given**) vt to hand over as a present; to deliver; to hand over in or for payment; to pass (regards etc) along; to act as host or sponsor of; to supply; to yield; (advice) to offer; (punishment, etc) to inflict; to sacrifice; to perform; (with **away**) to make a gift of; to give (the bride) to the bridegroom; to sell cheaply; to reveal, betray; (with **in**) to deliver, hand in (a document, etc); (with **off**) to emit (fumes, etc); (with **out**) to discharge; to emit; to distribute; (with **up**) to hand over; to stop, renounce; to cease; to resign (a position); to stop trying; to despair of; to surrender; to devote oneself completely (to). * vi to bend, move, etc from force or pressure; (inf) to be happening; (with **in**) to concede, admit defeat; (with **out**) to become used up or

exhausted; to fail. * n capacity or tendency to yield to force or strain; the quality or state of being springy; (with **in**) to submit; (with **out**) to become worn out; (with **up**) to accept defeat or failure to do something, to surrender.—**givable, giveable** adj.

give-and-take n mutual concessions; free-flowing exchange of ideas and conversation.

giveaway n (inf) an unintentional revelation; a free gift to encourage sales; a freesheet.

given[1] see **give**.

given[2] adj accustomed (to) by habit, etc; specified; assumed; granted.

gizzard n the second stomach of a bird, used for grinding food.

glacial adj extremely cold; of or relating to glaciers or a glacial epoch.—**glacially** adv.

glaciate vti to subject to glacial action; to cover or become covered with glaciers.—**glaciation** n.

glacier n a large mass of snow and ice moving slowly down a mountain.

glad adj (**gladder, gladdest**) happy; causing joy; very willing; bright.—**gladly** adv.—**gladness** n.

glade n an open space in a wood or forest.

gladiator n (ancient Rome) a person trained to fight with men or beasts in a public arena.—**gladiatorial** adj.

gladiolus n (pl **gladiolus, gladioli**) any of a genus of the iris family with sword-like leaves and tall spikes of funnel-shaped flowers.

glamor, glamour n charm, allure; attractiveness, beauty.—**glamorous, glamourous** adj.—**glamorousness, glamourousness** n.

glamorize, glamourize vt to make glamorous.—**glamorization, glamourization** n.—**glamorizer, glamourizer** n.

glance vi to strike obliquely and go off at an angle; to flash; to look quickly. * n a glancing off; a flash; a quick look.—**glancingly** adv.

gland n an organ that separates substances from the blood and synthesizes them for further use in, or for elimination from, the body.

glandular adj of, having or resembling glands.

glare n a harsh uncomfortably bright light, esp painfully bright sunlight; an angry or fierce stare. * vi to shine with a steady, dazzling light; to stare fiercely.

glaring adj dazzling; obvious, conspicuous.—**glaringly** adv.—**glaringness** n.

glass n a hard brittle substance, usu transparent; glassware; a glass article, as a drinking vessel; (pl) spectacles or binoculars; the amount held by a drinking glass. * adj of or made of glass. * vt to equip, enclose, or cover with glass.

glassware n objects made of glass, esp drinking vessels.

glassy adj (**glassier, glassiest**) resembling glass; smooth; expressionless, lifeless.—**glassily** adv.—**glassiness** n.

glaucoma n a disease of the eye caused by pressure.—**glaucomatous** adj.

glaze vt to provide (windows etc) with glass; to give a hard glossy finish to (pottery, etc); to cover (foods, etc) with a glossy surface. * vi to become glassy or glossy. * n a glassy finish or coating.

glazier n a person who fits glass in windows.

glazing n a glaze; the operation of setting glass or applying a glaze; windowpanes; glass; semi-transparent colors passed thinly over other colors to tone down their effect.

gleam n a subdued or moderate beam of light; a brief show of some quality or emotion, esp hope. * vi to emit or reflect a beam of light.—**gleaming** adj.

glean vti to collect (grain left by reapers); to gather (facts, etc) gradually.—**gleanable** adj.—**gleaner** n.

glee n joy and gaiety; delight; (mus) a song in parts for three or more male voices.—**gleeful** adj.—**gleefully** adv.—**gleefulness** n.

glen n a narrow valley.

glib adj (**glibber, glibbest**) speaking or spoken smoothly, to the point of insincerity; lacking depth and substance.—**glibly** adv.—**glibness** n.

glide vti to move smoothly and effortlessly; to descend in an aircraft or glider with little or no engine power. * n a gliding movement.—**glidingly** adv.

glider n an engineless aircraft carried along by air currents.

glimmer vi to give a faint, flickering light; to appear faintly. * n a faint gleam; a glimpse, an inkling.

glimpse n a brief, momentary view. * vt to catch a glimpse of.—**glimpser** n.

glint n a brief flash of light; a brief indication. * vti to (cause to) gleam brightly.

glisten vi to shine, as light reflected from a wet surface.—**glisteningly** adv.

glitch n a malfunction in a, usu electronic, system.

glitter vi to sparkle; (usu with **with**) to be brilliantly attractive. * n a sparkle; showiness, glamor; tiny pieces of sparkling material used for decoration.—**glittering** adj.—**glittery** adj.

gloat vi to gaze or contemplate with wicked or malicious satisfaction.—**gloater** n.—**gloatingly** adv.

global adj worldwide; comprehensive.—**globally** adv.

global warming n the process caused by a blanket of 'greenhouse gases' building up around the earth trapping heat from the sun. Carbon dioxide, released by burning fossil fuels is one of the main causes.—see **greenhouse effect**.

globe n anything spherical or almost spherical; the earth, or a model of the earth.

globule n a small spherical particle; a drop, pellet; a blood corpuscle.—**globular** adj.

glockenspiel n an orchestral percussion instrument with tuned metal bars, played with hammers.

gloom n near darkness; deep sadness. * vti to look sullen or dejected; to make or become cloudy or murky.—**gloomy** adj.—**gloomily** adv.

glorify vt (**glorifying, glorified**) to worship; to praise, to honor; to cause to appear more worthy, important, or splendid than in reality.—**glorifiable** adj.—**glorification** n.—**glorifier** n.

glory n (pl **glories**) great honor or fame, or its source; adoration; great splendor or beauty; heavenly bliss. * vi (**glorying, gloried**) (with **in**) to exult, rejoice proudly.—**glorious** adj.—**gloriously** adv.

gloss[1] n the luster of a polished surface; a superficially attractive appearance. * vt to give a shiny surface to; (with **over**) to hide (an error, etc) or make seem right or inconsequential.—**glossy** adj.

gloss[2] n an explanation of an unusual word (in the margin or between the lines of a text); a misleading explanation; a glossary. * vt to provide with glosses; to give a misleading sense of.—**glosser** n.

glossary n (pl **glossaries**) a list of specialized or technical words and their definitions.—**glossarial** adj.—**glossarist** n.

glottis n (**glottises, glottides**) the opening between the vocal cords in the larynx.

glove n a covering for the hand; a baseball player's mitt; a boxing glove. * vt to cover (as if) with a glove.

glow vi to shine (as if) with an intense heat; to emit a steady light without flames; to be full of life and enthusiasm; to flush or redden with emotion. * n a light emitted due to intense heat; a steady, even light without flames; a reddening of the complexion; warmth of emotion or feeling.

glower vi to scowl; to stare sullenly or angrily. * n a scowl, a glare.—**gloweringly** adv.

glucose n a crystalline sugar occurring naturally in fruits, honey, etc.

glue n a sticky, viscous substance used as an adhesive. * vt (**gluing, glued**) to join with glue.—**gluey** adj.

glum adj (**glummer, glummest**) sullen; gloomy.—**glumly** adv.—**glumness** n.

glut vt (**glutting, glutted**) to over-supply (the market). * n a surfeit, an excess of supply.

gluten n a sticky elastic protein substance, esp of wheat flour, that gives cohesiveness to dough.—**glutenous** adj.

glutinous adj resembling glue, sticky.—**glutinousness, glutinosity** n.

glutton n a person who eats and drinks to excess; a person who has a tremendous capacity for something (eg for work).—**gluttonous** adj.—**gluttony** n.

glycerin, glycerine n the popular and commercial name for glycerol.

glycerol n a colorless, syrupy liquid made from fats and oils, used in making skin lotions, explosives, etc.—**glyceric** adj.

gm abbr = gram(s).

gnarled adj (tree trunks) full of knots; (hands) rough, knobbly; crabby in disposition.

gnash vti to grind (the teeth) in anger or pain. * n a grinding of the teeth.

gnat n any of various small, two-winged insects that bite or sting.

gnaw vti (**gnawing, gnawed**, pp **gnawed** or **gnawn**) to bite away bit by bit; to torment, as by constant pain.—**gnawable** adj.—**gnawer** n.

gnocchi npl small dumplings made from flour, semolina or potatoes.

gnome n (folklore) a dwarf who dwells in the earth and guards its treasure.

GNP abbr = Gross National Product.

gnu n (pl **gnus, gnu**) either of two large African antelopes with an ox-like head.—also **wildebeest**.

go vb (**going, went**, pp **gone**) vi to move on a course; to proceed; to work properly; to act, sound, as specified; to result; to become; to be accepted or valid; to leave, to depart; to die; to be allotted or sold; to be able to pass (through); to fit (into); to be capable of being divided (into); to belong; (with **about**) to handle (a task, etc) efficiently; to undertake (duties, etc); (sailing) to change tack; (with **into**) to enter; to become a member of; to examine or investigate; to discuss; (with **off**) to explode; to depart; (food, etc) to become stale or rotten; to fall asleep; to proceed, occur in a certain manner; to take place as planned; to stop liking (something or someone); (with **on**) to continue; to happen; to talk effusively; to nag; to enter on stage; (with **out**) to depart; (light, fire, etc) to become extinguished; to cease to be fashionable; to socialize; (radio or TV show) to be broadcast; to spend time with, esp a person of the opposite sex; (with **over**) to change one's loyalties (to); to be received or regarded in a certain way; to examine and repair (something); (with **round**) to circulate; to be sufficient for everyone; (with **slow**) to work at a slow rate as part of an industrial dispute; (with **through**) to continue to the end (with); to be approved; to use up completely; to experience (an illness, etc); to search thoroughly; (with **together**) to match, to be mutually suited; (inf) to associate frequently, esp as lovers; (with **with**) to match; to accompany; to associate frequently, esp as lovers; (with **without**) to be deprived of or endure the lack of (something). * vt to travel along; (inf) to put up with. * n (pl **goes**) a success; (inf) a try; (inf) energy.

goad n a sharp-pointed stick for driving cattle, etc; any stimulus to action. * vt to drive (as if) with a goad; to irritate, nag persistently.

go-ahead n (inf) permission to proceed. * adj (inf) enterprising, ambitious.

goal n the place at which a race, trip, etc is ended; an objective; the place over or into which the ball or puck must go to score in some games; the score made.

goalkeeper n a player who defends the goal.—**goalkeeping** n.

goat n a mammal related to the sheep that has backward curving horns, a short tail, and usu straight hair.

goatee n a small pointed beard.

gobble vt to eat greedily; (often with **up**) to take, accept or read eagerly. * vi to make a throaty gurgling noise, as a male turkey.

gobbledygook, gobbledegook n (sl) nonsense, pretentious jargon.

go-between n a messenger, an intermediary.

goblet n a large drinking vessel with a base and stem but without a handle.

goblin n an evil or mischievous elf.

go-cart n a small cart for children to play in or pull; a stroller; a handcart.

god n any of various beings conceived of as supernatural and immortal, esp a male deity; an idol; a person or thing deified; (with cap) in monotheistic religions, the creator and ruler of the universe.

godchild n (pl **godchildren**) the child a godparent sponsors.

goddaughter n a female godchild.

goddess n a female deity; a woman of superior charms or excellence.

godfather n a male godparent; the head of a Mafia crime family or other criminal organization.

god-fearing adj religious.

godforsaken adj desolate, wretched.

godless adj irreligious; wicked.–**godlessly** adv.–**godlessness** n.

godlike adj like a god, divine.

godly adj (**godlier, godliest**) religious; holy; devout; devoted to God.–**godliness** n.

godmother n a female godparent.

godparent n a person who sponsors a child, as at baptism or confirmation, taking responsibility for its faith.

godsend n anything that comes unexpectedly and when needed or desired.

godson n a male godchild.

gofer n (inf) a person who runs errands, as in an office.

go-getter n (inf) an ambitious person.

goggle vi to stare with bulging eyes. * npl large spectacles, sometimes fitting snugly against the face, to protect the eyes.

going n an act or instance of going, a departure; the state of the ground, eg for walking, horse-racing; rate of progress. * adj that goes; commonly accepted; thriving; existing.

goings-on npl events or actions, esp when disapproved of.

goiter, goitre n an abnormal enlargement of the thyroid gland.–**goitrous** adj.

gold n a malleable yellow metallic element used esp for coins and jewellery; a precious metal; money, wealth; a yellow color. * adj of, or like, gold.

gold-digger n a person who mines gold; (inf) a woman who uses feminine charms to extract money or gifts from men.–**gold-digging** adj.

golden adj made of or relating to gold; bright yellow; priceless; flourishing.–**goldenly** adv.–**goldenness** n.

golden age n the fabled early age of innocence and perfect human happiness; the flowering of a nation's civilization or art.

golden eagle n a large eagle of the Northern hemisphere.

golden rule n a guiding principle.

goldfield n a district containing gold deposits and diggings.

goldfish n (pl **goldfish, goldfishes**) a small gold-colored fish of the carp family, kept in ponds and aquariums.

gold leaf n gold beaten into very thin sheets, used for gilding.

gold mine n a mine where gold is extracted; (inf) a source of wealth.

gold plate n vessels of gold; a thin covering of gold.–**gold-plated** adj.

gold rush n a rush to a new gold field, as to the Yukon in 1897.

goldsmith n a worker in gold; a dealer in gold plate.

gold standard n a monetary standard in which the basic currency unit equals a specified quantity of gold.

golf n an outdoor game in which the player attempts to hit a small ball with clubs around a turfed course into a succession of holes in the smallest number of strokes.–**golfer** n.

golf ball n a hard dimpled ball used in golf.

golf club n a club with a wooden or metal head used in golf; a golf association or its premises.

golf course, golf links n a tract of land laid out for playing golf.

gonad n a primary sex gland that produces reproductive cells, such as an ovary or testis.–**gonadal, gonadic** adj.

gondola n a long, narrow, black boat used on the canals of Venice; a cabin suspended under an airship or balloon; an enclosed car suspended from a cable used to transport passengers, esp skiers up a mountain.

gondolier n a person who propels a gondola with a pole.

gone[1] see **go**1.

gone[2] adj departed; dead; lost; (inf) in an excited state.

goner n (sl) a person or thing that is ruined, dead, or about to die.

gong n a disk-shaped percussion instrument struck with a usu padded hammer; (sl) a medal. * vi to sound a gong.

gonorrhea, gonorrhoea n a venereal disease causing a discharge of mucous and pus from the genitals.–**gonorrheal, gonorrhoeal, gonorrheic, gonorrhoeic** adj.

goo n (sl) sticky matter; sickly sentimentality.–**gooey** adj.

good adj (**better, best**) having the right or proper qualities; beneficial; valid; healthy or sound; virtuous, honorable; enjoyable, pleasant, etc; skilled; considerable. * n something good; benefit; something that has economic utility; (with **the**) good persons; (pl) personal property; commodities; (pl) the desired or required articles. * adv (inf) well; fully.–**goodish** adj.

goodbye interj a concluding remark at parting; farewell.–also n.

good-for-nothing adj useless, worthless. * n a worthless person.

Good Friday n the Friday before Easter, commemorating the Crucifixion of Christ.

good-humored adj genial, cheerful.–**good-humoredly** adv.–**good-humoredness** n.

good-looking adj handsome.

goodly adj (**goodlier, goodliest**) considerable; ample.–**goodliness** n.

good-natured adj amiable, easy-going.–**good-naturedly** adv.–**good-naturedness** n.

goodness n the state of being good; the good element in something; kindness; virtue. * interj an exclamation of surprise.

good turn n a favor; an act of kindness.

goodwill n benevolence; willingness; the established custom and reputation of a business.

goody n (pl **goodies**) something pleasant or sweet; a goody-goody. * interj an expression (usu used by a child) signifying pleasure.

goody-goody adj insufferably virtuous. * n (pl **goody-goodies**) a goody-goody person.

goof n (sl) a stupid person; a blunder. * vi (sl) to bungle.

goofy adj (**goofier, goofiest**) (sl) silly, stupid.–**goofily** adv.–**goofiness** n.

goon n (sl) a thug; a stupid person.

goose n (pl **geese**) a large, long-necked, web-footed bird related to swans and ducks; its flesh as food; a female goose as distinguished from a gander; (inf) a foolish person.

gooseberry n (pl **gooseberries**) the acid berry of a shrub related to the currant and used esp in jams and pies.

goose bumps, goose pimples, goose flesh n a roughening of the skin caused usu by cold or fear.

goose step n a stiff-legged marching step used by some armies when passing in review.–**goose-step** vi.

gopher n a North American burrowing, rat-like rodent; a ground squirrel; a burrowing tortoise.

gore[1] n (clotted) blood from a wound.

gore[2] vt to pierce or wound as with a tusk or horns.

gorge n a ravine. * vt to swallow greedily; to glut. * vi to feed gluttonously.–**gorgeable** adj.–**gorger** n.

gorgeous adj strikingly attractive; brilliantly colored; (inf) magnificent.–**gorgeously** adv.–**gorgeousness** n.

gorilla *n* an anthropoid ape of western equatorial Africa related to the chimpanzee but much larger.

gorse *n* a spiny yellow-flowered European shrub.

gory *adj* (**gorier, goriest**) bloodthirsty; causing bloodshed; covered in blood.–**gorily** *adv.*–**goriness** *n.*

gosh *interj* an exclamation of surprise.

gosling *n* a young goose.

go-slow *n* a deliberate slowing of the work rate by employees as a form of industrial action.

gospel *n* the life and teachings of Christ contained in the first four books of the New Testament; (*with cap*) one of these four books; anything proclaimed or accepted as the absolute truth.

gossamer *n* very fine cobwebs; any very light and flimsy material. * *adj* light as gossamer.

gossip *n* one who chatters idly about others; such talk. * *vi* to take part in or spread gossip.–**gossiper** *n.*–**gossipingly** *adv.*–**gossipy** *adj.*

got *see* **get**.

Gothic *adj* of a style of architecture with pointed arches, steep roofs, elaborate stonework, etc.

gotten *see* **get**.

gouge *n* a chisel with a concave blade used for cutting grooves. * *vt* to scoop or force out (as if) with a gouge.

goulash *n* a rich stew made with beef or veal seasoned with paprika.

gourd *n* any trailing or climbing plant of a family that includes the squash, melon, pumpkin, etc; the fruit of one species or its dried, hollowed-out shell, used as a cup, bowl, etc or ornament.

gourmand *n* a person who likes good food and drink, often to excess.–**gourmandism** *n.*

gourmet *n* a person who likes and is an excellent judge of fine food and drink.

gout *n* a disease causing painful inflammation of the joints; esp of the great toe.–**gouty** *adj.*–**goutiness** *n.*

govern *vti* to exercise authority over; to rule, to control; to influence the action of; to determine.–**governable** *adj.*–**governability, governableness** *n.*

governess *n* a woman employed in a private home to teach and train the children.

government *n* the exercise of authority over a state, organization, etc; a system of ruling, political administration, etc; those who direct the affairs of a state, etc.–**governmental** *adj.*

governor *n* a person appointed to govern a province, etc; the elected head of any state of the US; the director or head of a governing body of an organization or institution; a mechanical device for automatically controlling the speed of an engine.– **governorship** *n.*

Govt, govt *abbr* = government.

gown *n* a loose outer garment, specifically a woman's formal dress, a nightgown, a long, flowing robe worn by clergymen, judges, university teachers, etc; a type of overall worn in the operating room. * *vt* to dress in a gown, to supply with a gown.

goy *n* (*pl* **goyim, goys**) (*sl*) Jewish for Gentile.

grab *vt* (**grabbing, grabbed**) to take or grasp suddenly; to obtain unscrupulously; (*inf*) to catch the interest or attention of. * *n* a sudden clutch or attempt to grasp; a mechanical device for grasping and lifting objects.–**grabber** *n.*

grace *n* beauty or charm of form, movement, or expression; good will; favor; a delay granted for payment of an obligation; a short prayer of thanks for a meal. * *vt* to decorate; to dignify.

graceful *adj* having beauty of form, movement, or expression.–**gracefully** *adv.*–**gracefulness** *n.*

graceless *adj* unattractive; lacking sense of what is proper; clumsy.–**gracelessly** *adv.*–**gracelessness** *n.*

grace note *n* (*mus*) an ornamental note.

gracious *adj* having or showing kindness, courtesy, etc; compassionate; polite to supposed inferiors; marked by luxury, ease, etc.–**graciously** *adv.*–**graciousness** *n.*

gradation *n* a series of systematic steps in rank, degree, intensity, etc; arranging in such stages; a single stage in a gradual progression; progressive change.–**gradational** *adj.*

grade *n* a stage or step in a progression; a year of school; a degree in a scale of quality, rank, etc; a group of people of the same rank, merit, etc; the degree of slope; a sloping part; a mark or rating in an examination, etc. * *vt* to arrange in grades; to give a grade to; to make level or evenly sloping.

grade school *n* elementary school.

gradient *n* a sloping road or railway; the degree of slope in a road, railway, etc.

gradual *adj* taking place by degrees.–**gradually** *adv.*–**gradualness** *n.*

graduate *n* a person who has completed a course of study at a school, college, or university; a receptacle marked with figures for measuring contents. * *adj* holding an academic degree or diploma; of or relating to studies beyond the first or bachelor's degree.–**graduator** *n.*

graduation *n* graduating or being graduated; the ceremony at which degrees are conferred by a college or university; an arranging or marking in grades or stages.

graffiti *npl* (*sing* **graffito**) inscriptions or drawings, often indecent, on a wall or other public surface.

graft *n* a shoot or bud of one plant inserted into another, where it grows permanently; the transplanting of skin, bone, etc; the getting of money or advantage dishonestly.–**grafter** *n.*–**grafting** *n.*

grain *n* the seed of any cereal plant, as wheat, corn, etc; cereal plants; a tiny, solid particle, as of salt or sand; a unit of weight, 0.0648 gram; the arrangement of fibers, layers, etc of wood, leather, etc; the markings or texture due to this; natural disposition. * *vt* to form into grains; to paint in imitation of the grain of wood, etc. * *vi* to become granular.–**grainer** *n.*

grainy *adj* (**grainier, grainiest**) resembling grains in form or texture.–**graininess** *n.*

gram *n* the basic unit of weight in the metric system, equal to one thousandth of a kilogram (one twenty-eighth of an ounce).

grammar *n* the study of the forms of words and their arrangement in sentences; a system of rules for speaking and writing a language; a grammar textbook; the use of language in speech or writing judged with regard to correctness of spelling, syntax, etc.–**grammatical** *adj.*

grammarian *n* one who studies grammar; the author of a grammar.

granary *n* (*pl* **granaries**) a building for storing grain.

grand *adj* higher in rank than others; most important; imposing in size, beauty, extent, etc; distinguished; illustrious; comprehensive; (*inf*) very good; delightful. * *n* a grand piano; (*inf*) a thousand dollars.–**grandly** *adv.*–**grandness** *n.*

grandchild *n* (*pl* **grandchildren**) the child of a person's son or daughter.

granddad *n* (*inf*) grandfather; an old man.

granddaughter *n* the daughter of a person's son or daughter.

grandeur *n* splendor; magnificence; nobility; dignity.

grandfather *n* the father of a person's father or mother.

grandfather clock *n* a large clock with a pendulum in a tall, upright case.

grandiose *adj* having grandeur; imposing; pompous and showy.–**grandiosely** *adv.*–**grandiosity** *n.*

grand jury *n* a jury in the US that examines evidence in a case to determine whether an indictment should be made.

grandma *n* (*inf*) grandmother.

grandmother *n* the mother of a person's father or mother.

grandpa, grandpapa *n* (*inf*) grandfather.

grandparent *n* a grandfather or grandmother.

grand piano *n* a large piano with a horizontal harp-shaped case.

grand slam n (tennis, golf) a winning of all the major international championships in a season; (baseball) a home run hit when there is a runner on each base.

grandson n the son of a person's son or daughter.

grandstand n the main structure for seating spectators at a sporting event.

granite n a hard, igneous rock consisting chiefly of feldspar and quartz; unyielding firmness of endurance.—**granitic, granitoid** adj.

granny n (pl **grannies**) (inf) a grandmother.

grant vt to consent to; to give or transfer by legal procedure; to admit as true. * n the act of granting; something granted, esp a gift for a particular purpose; a transfer of property by deed; the instrument by which such a transfer is made.

granulate vt to form or crystallize into grains or granules. * vi to collect into grains or granules; to become roughened and grainy in surface texture.—**granulation** n.—**granulative** adj.—**granulator, granulater** n.

granule n a small grain or particle.—**granular** adj.

grape n a small round, juicy berry, growing in clusters on a vine; a dark purplish red.—**grapey, grapy** adj.

grapefruit n (pl **grapefruit, grapefruits**) a large, round, sour citrus fruit with a yellow rind.

grapevine n a type of woody vine on which grapes grow; an informal means of communicating news or gossip.

graph n a diagram representing the successive changes in the value of a variable quantity or quantities. * vt to illustrate by graphs.

graphic, graphical adj described in realistic detail; pertaining to a graph, lettering, drawing, painting, etc.—**graphically** adv.—**graphicness** n.

graphic arts npl the fine and applied arts involving design, illustration and printing.

graphics n sing or pl the use of drawings and lettering; the drawings, illustrations, etc used in a newspaper, magazine, television programme, etc; information displayed in the form of diagrams, illustrations and animation on a computer monitor.

graphite n a soft, black form of carbon used in pencils, for lubricants, etc.—**graphitic** adj.

graphology n the study of handwriting, esp as a clue to character.—**graphological** adj.—**graphologist** n.

grapple vt to seize or grip firmly. * vi to struggle hand-to-hand with; to deal or contend with. * n a grapnel; an act of grappling, a wrestle; a grip.—**grappler** n.

grasp vt to grip, as with the hand; to seize; to understand. * vi to try to clutch, seize; (with **at**) to take eagerly. * n a firm grip; power of seizing and holding; comprehension.—**graspable** adj.—**grasper** n.

grasping adj greedy, avaricious.—**graspingly** adv.—**graspingness** n.

grass n any of a large family of plants with jointed stems and long narrow leaves including cereals, bamboo, etc; such plants grown as lawn; pasture; (sl) marijuana.—**grassy** adj.

grasshopper n any of a group of plant-eating, winged insects with powerful hind legs for jumping.

grass roots npl (inf) the common people, the ordinary members of a political or other organization; the basic level, the essentials. (**grassier, grassiest**) abounding in, covered with, or like, grass.—**grassiness** n.

grate[1] n a frame of metal bars for holding fuel in a fireplace; a fireplace; a grating.

grate[2] vt to grind into particles by scraping; to rub against (an object) or grind (the teeth) together with a harsh sound; to irritate. * vi to rub or rasp noisily; to cause irritation.

grateful adj appreciative; welcome.—**gratefully** adv.—**gratefulness** n.

grater n a metal implement with a jagged surface for grating food.

gratify vt (**gratifying, gratified**) to please; to indulge.—**gratification** n.—**gratifier** n.—**gratifying** adj.—**gratifyingly** adv.

grating[1] n a open framework or lattice of bars placed across an opening.

grating[2] adj harsh; irritating.—**gratingly** adv.

gratis adj, adv free of charge.

gratitude n a being thankful for favors received.

gratuitous adj given free of charge; done without cause, unwarranted.—**gratuitously** adv.—**gratuitousness** n.

gratuity n (pl **gratuities**) money given for a service, a tip.

grave[1] n a hole dug in the ground for burying the dead; any place of burial, a tomb.

grave[2] adj serious, important; harmful; solemn, sombre; (sound) low in pitch. * n an accent (') over a vowel.—**gravely** adv.—**graveness** n.

gravel n coarse sand with small rounded stones. * vt (**graveling, graveled** or **gravelling, gravelled**) to cover or spread with gravel.—**gravelish** adj.

graven adj engraved; fixed indelibly.

gravestone n a stone marking a grave, usu inscribed with the name and details of the deceased.

graveyard n a burial-ground, cemetery.

gravitate vi to move or tend to move under the force of gravitation.—**gravitater** n.

gravitation n a natural force of attraction that tends to draw bodies together.—**gravitational** adj.—**gravitationally** adv.

gravity n (pl **gravities**) importance, esp seriousness; weight; the attraction of bodies toward the centre of the earth, the moon, or a planet.

gravy n (pl **gravies**) the juice given off by meat in cooking; the sauce made from this juice; (sl) money easily obtained.

gray n any of a series of neutral colors ranging between black and white; something (as an animal, garment, cloth, or spot) of a gray color. * adj gray in color; having gray-colored hair; darkish; dreary; vague, indeterminate.—also **grey**.—**grayish** adj.—**grayness** n.

gray matter n gray-colored nerve tissue of the brain and spinal cord; (inf) brains, intelligence.

graze[1] vi to feed on growing grass or pasture. * vt to put (animals) to feed on growing grass or pasture.—**grazer** n.

graze[2] vt to touch lightly in passing; to scrape, scratch. * n an abrasion, esp on the skin, caused by scraping on a surface.—**grazingly** adv.

grazing n pasture; the crops, plants, etc, growing on this for animals to feed from.

grease n melted animal fat; any thick, oily substance or lubricant. * vt to smear or lubricate with grease.—**greasy** adj.—**greasily** adv.—**greasiness** n.

great adj of much more than ordinary size, extent, etc; much above the average; intense; eminent; most important; more distant in a family relationship by one generation; (often with **at**) (inf) skillful; (inf) excellent; fine. * n (inf) a distinguished person.—**greatly** adv.—**greatness** n.

great-aunt n a parent's aunt.

Great Dane n a breed of very large smooth-haired dogs.

great-nephew n a nephew's or niece's son.

great-niece n a nephew's or niece's daughter.

great-uncle n a parent's uncle.

grebe n any of a family of swimming and diving birds.

greed n excessive desire, esp for food or wealth.

greedy adj (**greedier, greediest**) wanting more than one needs or deserves; having too strong a desire for food and drink.—**greedily** adv.—**greediness** n.

green adj of the color green; covered with plants or foliage; having a sickly appearance; unripe; inexperienced, naive; not fully processed or treated; concerned with the conservation of natural resources; (inf) jealous. * n a color between blue and yellow in the spectrum; the color of growing grass; something of a green color; (*pl*) green leafy vegetables, as spinach, etc; a grassy plot, esp the end of a golf fairway.–**greenish** *adj*.–**greenly** *adv*.–**greenness** *n*.–**greeny** *adj*.

greenback *n* a legal-tender note of US currency.

green bean *n* any of various beans with narrow edible pods.

greenery *n* (*pl* **greeneries**) green vegetation.

green-eyed *adj* jealous.

greenhorn *n* an inexperienced person; a person easily duped.

greenhouse *n* a heated building, mainly of glass, for growing plants.

greenhouse effect *n* action of radiant heat from the sun passing through the glass of greenhouses etc., warming the contents inside, where such heat is thus trapped; application of the same effect to a planet's atmosphere.–*see* **global warming**.

green light *n* permission to proceed with a plan, etc.

green thumb *n* gardening expertise.

greet *vt* to address with friendliness; to meet (a person, event, etc) in a specified way; to present itself to.–**greeter** *n*.

greeting *n* the act of welcoming with words or gestures; an expression of good wishes; (*pl*) a message of regards.

gregarious *adj* (*animals*) living in flocks and herds; (*people*) sociable, fond of company.–**gregariously** *adv*.–**gregariousness** *n*.

gremlin *n* an imaginary creature blamed for disruption of any procedure or of malfunction of equipment, esp in an aircraft.

grenade *n* a small bomb thrown manually or projected (as by a rifle or special launcher).

grew *see* **grow**.

grey *see* **gray**.

greyhound *n* any of a breed of tall and slender dogs noted for its great speed and keen sight.

grid *n* a gridiron, a grating; an electrode for controlling the flow of electrons in an electron tube; a network of squares on a map used for easy reference.

griddle *n* a flat metal surface for cooking.

gridiron *n* a framework of iron bars for cooking; anything resembling this, as a field used for American football.

gridlock *n* a traffic jam that halts all traffic at a street crossing; the breakdown of an organization or a system.

grief *n* extreme sorrow caused as by a loss; deep distress.

grief-stricken *adj* full of sorrow.

grievance *n* a circumstance thought to be unjust and cause for complaint.

grieve *vti* to feel or cause to feel grief.–**griever** *n*.–**grieving** *adj, n*.

grievous *adj* causing or characterized by grief; deplorable; severe.–**grievously** *adv*.–**grievousness** *n*.

grill *vt* to broil by direct heat using a grill or gridiron; (*inf*) to question relentlessly. * *n* a device on a cooker that radiates heat downward for broiling or grilling; a gridiron; broiled or grilled food; a grille; a grillroom.–**griller** *n*.

grille, grill *n* an open grating forming a screen.

grim *adj* (**grimmer, grimmest**) hard and unyielding, stern; appearing harsh, forbidding; repellent, ghastly in character.–**grimly** *adv*.–**grimness** *n*.

grimace *n* a contortion of the face expressing pain, anguish, humor, etc. * *vi* to contort the face in pain, etc.–**grimacer** *n*.–**grimacingly** *adv*.

grime *n* soot or dirt, rubbed into a surface, as the skin. * *vt* to dirty, soil with grime.

grimy *adj* (**grimier, grimiest**) dirty, soiled.–**griminess** *n*.

grin *vi* (**grinning, grinned**) to smile broadly as in amusement; to show the teeth in pain, scorn, etc. * *n* a broad smile.–**grinner** *n*.

grind *vb* (**grinding, ground**) *vt* to reduce to powder or fragments by crushing; to wear down, sharpen, or smooth by friction; to rub (the teeth) harshly together; to oppress, tyrannize; to move

or operate by a crank. * *vi* to be crushed, smoothed, or sharpened by grinding; to jar or grate; to work monotonously; to rotate the hips in an erotic manner. * *n* the act or sound of grinding; hard monotonous work.

grip *n* a secure grasp; the manner of holding a bat, club, racket, etc; the power of grasping firmly; mental grasp; mastery; a handle; a small traveling bag. * *vt* (**gripping, gripped**) to take firmly and hold fast.

gripe *vt* to cause sharp pain in the bowels of; (*sl*) to annoy. * *vi* (*sl*) to complain.–**griper** *n*.–**gripingly** *adv*.

grisly *adj* (**grislier, grisliest**) terrifying; ghastly; arousing horror.–**grisliness** *n*.

grist *n* grain that is to be or has been ground; matter forming the basis of a story or analysis.

gristle *n* cartilage, esp in meat.–**gristly** *adj*.–**gristliness** *n*.

grit *n* rough particles, as of sand; firmness of spirit; stubborn courage. * *vt* (**gritting, gritted**) to clench or grind together (eg the teeth); to spread grit on (eg an icy road).–**gritty** *adj*.

grits *npl* oats, hulled and coarsely ground; coarsely ground maize, boiled in water or milk as a food (–*also* **hominy grits**).

grizzled *adj* streaked with gray; gray-haired.

grizzly *adj* (**grizzlier, grizzliest**) grayish; grizzled. * *n* (*pl* **grizzlies**) the grizzly bear.

grizzly bear *n* a large powerful bear of North America.

groan *vi* to utter a deep moan; to make a harsh sound (as of creaking) under sudden or prolonged strain. * *n* a deep moan; a creaking sound.–**groaner** *n*.–**groaningly** *adv*.

grocer *n* a dealer in food and household supplies.

grocery *n* (*pl* **groceries**) a grocer's shop; (*pl*) goods, esp from a grocer.

grog *n* rum diluted with water, often spiced and served hot.

groggy *adj* (**groggier, groggiest**) (*inf*) weak and unsteady, usu through illness, exhaustion or alcohol.–**groggily** *adv*.–**grogginess** *n*.

groin *n* the fold marking the junction of the lower abdomen and the thighs; the location of the genitals.

grommet *n* a plastic or rubber ring used to protect wire, a cable, etc passing through a hole; a ring formed of a strand of rope laid round, used in pipe joints or sails.

groom *n* a person employed to care for horses; a bridegroom. * *vt* to clean and care for (animals); to make neat and tidy; to train (a person) for a particular purpose.–**groomer** *n*.–**grooming** *n*.

groove *n* a long, narrow channel; a spiral track in a gramophone record for the stylus; a settled routine. * *vt* to make a groove in.

grope *vi* to search about blindly as in the dark; to search uncertainly for a solution to a problem. * *vt* to find by feeling. * *n* the act of groping.–**groper** *n*.–**gropingly** *adv*.

gross *adj* fat and coarse-looking; flagrant, dense, thick; lacking in refinement; earthy; obscene; total, with no deductions. * *n* (*pl* **grosses**) an overall total; (*pl* **gross**) twelve dozen. * *vt* to earn as total revenue.–**grossly** *adv*.–**grossness** *n*.

gross domestic product *n* the total value of goods and services produced by a country in one year.

grotesque *adj* distorted or fantastic in appearance, shape, etc; ridiculous; absurdly incongruous. * *n* a grotesque person or thing; a decorative device combining distorted plant, animal and human forms.–**grotesquely** *adv*.–**grotesqueness** *n*.

grotto *n* (*pl* **grottoes, grottos**) a cave, esp one with attractive features.

grouch *vi* (*inf*) to grumble or complain. * *n* (*inf*) a grumble; a person who grumbles.–**groucher** *n*.–**grouchy** *adj*.

ground *n* the solid surface of the earth; soil; the background, as in design; the connection of an electrical conductor with the earth; (*pl*) a basis for belief, action, or argument; the area about and relating to a building; a tract of land; sediment. * *vti* to set on the ground; to run aground or cause to run aground; to base, found, or establish; to instruct in the first principles of; to prevent (aircraft) from flying.

ground beef *n* finely chopped beef.

ground control *n* the communications and tracking equipment and staff that monitor aircraft and spacecraft in flight and during takeoff and landing.

groundhog *n* a woodchuck.

grounding *n* basic general knowledge of a subject.

groundless *adj* without reason.—**groundlessly** *adv*.

groundnut *n* a climbing plant of North America with an underground nut; a peanut.

ground rule *n* a fundamental rule or principle.

groundswell *n* a large rolling wave; a wave of popular feeling.

group *n* a number of persons or things considered as a collective unit; a small musical band of players or singers; a number of companies under single ownership; two or more figures forming one artistic design. * *vti* to form into a group or groups.

grouper *n* (*pl* **grouper, groupers**) an edible sea fish.

groupie *n* a devoted fan.

grouse[1] *n* (*pl* **grouse, grouses**) a game bird; its flesh as food.

grouse[2] *vi* (*inf*) to complain.—**grouser** *n*.

grout *n* a thin mortar used as between tiles. * *vt* to fill with grout.—**grouter** *n*.

grove *n* a small wood, generally without undergrowth.

grovel *vi* (**groveling, groveled** *or* **grovelling, grovelled**) to lie and crawl in a prostrate position as a sign of respect, fear or humility.—**groveller, groveler** *n*.—**grovellingly, grovelingly** *adv*.

grow *vb* (**growing, grew**, *pp* **grown**) *vi* to come into being; to be produced naturally; to develop, as a living thing; to increase in size, quantity, etc; (*with* **on**) to become more accustomed or acceptable to; (*with* **up**) to mature; to arise, develop. * *vt* to cause or let grow; to raise, to cultivate.—**growable** *adj*.—**grower** *n*.

growl *vi* to make a rumbling, menacing sound such as an angry dog makes. * *vt* to express in a growling manner. * *n* a growling noise; a grumble.—**growler** *n*.

grown-up *n* a fully grown person, an adult. * *adj* mature, adult; fit for an adult.

growth *n* the act or process of growing; progressive increase, development; something that grows or has grown; an abnormal formation of tissue, as a tumor.

grub *vb* (**grubbing, grubbed**) *vi* to dig in the ground; to work hard. * *vt* to clear (ground) of roots; to uproot. * *n* the worm-like larva of a beetle; (*sl*) food.

grubby *adj* (**grubbier, grubbiest**) dirty.—**grubbily** *adv*.—**grubbiness** *n*.

grudge *n* a deep feeling of resentment or ill will. * *vt* to be reluctant to give or admit something.—**grudger** *n*.—**grudging** *adj*.—**grudgingly** *adv*.

gruel *n* a thin porridge cooked in water or milk.

grueling, gruelling *adj* severely testing, exhausting.

gruesome *adj* causing horror or loathing.

gruff *adj* rough or surly; hoarse.—**gruffly** *adv*.—**gruffness** *n*.

grumble *vti* to mutter in discontent; to make a rumbling sound. * *n* a complaint; a grumbling sound.—**grumbler** *n*.—**grumblingly** *adv*.

grumpy *adj* (**grumpier, grumpiest**) bad-tempered, peevish.—**grumpily** *adv*.—**grumpiness** *n*.

grunt *vi* to make a gruff guttural sound like a pig; to say or speak in such a manner. * *n* a low gruff sound; (*sl*) a US infantry man.

G-string *n* a string or strip worn round the waist and between the legs.

guarantee *n* a pledge or security for another's debt or obligation; a pledge to replace something if it is substandard, etc; an assurance that something will be done as specified; something offered as a pledge or security; a guarantor. * *vt* (**guaranteeing, guaranteed**) to give a guarantee for; to promise.

guarantor *n* a person who gives a guaranty or guarantee.

guaranty *n* (*pl* **guaranties**) (*law*) a guarantee.

guard *vt* to watch over and protect; to defend; to keep from escape or trouble; to restrain. * *vi* to keep watch (against); to act as a guard. * *n* defense; protection; a posture of readiness for defense; any device to protect against injury or loss; a person or group that guards.—**guardable** *adj*.—**guarder** *n*.

guarded *adj* discreet; cautious.—**guardedly** *adv*.—**guardedness** *n*.

guardian *n* a custodian; a person legally in charge of a minor or someone incapable of taking care of their own affairs.—**guardianship** *n*.

guardrail *n* a railing, eg at the side of a road, to prevent falling; a short metal rod placed inside the rails to keep a train's wheels on the track.

guava *n* a tropical American shrubby tree widely cultivated for its sweet acid yellow fruit.

guerrilla, guerilla *n* a member of a small force of irregular soldiers, making surprise raids.—*also adj*.

guess *vt* to form an opinion of or state with little or no factual knowledge; to judge correctly by doing this; to think or suppose. * *n* an estimate based on guessing.—**guessable** *adj*.—**guesser** *n*.

guesstimate *n* (*inf*) an estimate based mainly on guesswork.

guesswork *n* the process or result of guessing.

guest *n* a person entertained at the home, club, etc of another; any paying customer of a hotel, restaurant, etc; a performer appearing by special invitation.

guffaw *n* a crude noisy laugh. * *vi* to laugh boisterously.

guidance *n* leadership; advice or counsel.

guide *vt* to point out the way for; to lead; to direct the course of; to control. * *n* a person who leads or directs others; a person who exhibits and explains points of interest; something that provides a person with guiding information; a device for controlling the motion of something; a book of basic instruction.—**guidable** *adj*.—**guider** *n*.—**guiding** *adj, n*.

guidebook *n* a book containing directions and information for tourists.

guideline *n* a principle or instruction which determines conduct or policy.

guild *n* a club, society; an association of people with common interests.—*also* **gild**.

guile *n* craftiness, deceit.—**guileful** *adj*.—**guilefully** *adv*.—**guilefulness** *n*.

guillotine *n* an instrument for beheading by a heavy blade descending between grooved posts. * *vt* to execute (someone) by guillotine.—**guillotiner** *n*.

guilt *n* the fact of having done a wrong or committed an offense; a feeling of self-reproach from believing one has done a wrong.—**guilty** *adj*.—**guiltily** *adv*.

guinea pig *n* a rodent-like animal commonly kept as a pet, and often used in scientific experiments; a person or thing subject to an experiment.

guise *n* an external appearance, aspect; an assumed appearance or pretence.

guitar *n* a stringed musical instrument with a long, fretted neck, and a flat body, which is plucked with a plectrum or the fingers.—**guitarist** *n*.

gulch *n* a deep, narrow ravine.

gulf *n* a large area of ocean reaching into land; a wide, deep chasm; a vast separation.

gull *n* any of numerous long-winged web-footed sea birds.

gullet *n* the esophagus; the throat.

gullible *adj* easily deceived.—**gullibility** *n*.—**gullibly** *adv*.

gully *n* (*pl* **gullies**) a narrow trench cut by running water after rain; (*cricket*) a fielding position between the slips and point. * *vt* (**gullying, gullied**) to make gullies in.

gulp vt to swallow hastily or greedily; to choke back as if swallowing. * n a gulping or swallowing; a mouthful.—**gulper** n.—**gulpingly** adv.

gum[1] n the firm tissue that surrounds the teeth.

gum[2] n a sticky substance found in certain trees and plants; an adhesive; chewing gum. * vb (**gumming, gummed**) vt to coat or unite with gum. * vi to become sticky or clogged; (with **up**) (inf) to mess up, prevent from working properly.

gumbo n (pl **gumbos**) a rich soup thickened with okra.

gumboil n an abscess in the gum.

gummy adj (**gummier, gummiest**) sticky; revealing the gums, toothless.—**gummily** adv.—**gumminess** n.

gumption n (inf) shrewd practical common sense; initiative.

gumtree n a eucalyptus, or one of various other trees that yield gum.

gun n a weapon with a metal tube from which a projectile is discharged by an explosive; the shooting of a gun as a signal or salute; anything like a gun. * vb (**gunning, gunned**) vi to shoot or hunt with a gun; (with **for**) to search out in order to hurt or kill. * vt (inf) to shoot (a person).

gunboat n a small armed ship.

gunfire n repeated and consecutive gunshots; the use of guns, etc, rather than other military options.

gunk n (inf) dirty, greasy, matter; gunge.

gunman n (pl **gunmen**) an armed gangster; a hired killer.

gunnel see **gunwale**.

gunner n a soldier, etc who helps fire artillery; a naval warrant officer in charge of a ship's guns.

gunpoint n the muzzle of a gun; the threat of being shot.

gunpowder n an explosive powder used in guns, for blasting, etc.

gunrunning n the smuggling of firearms into a country.—**gunrunner** n.

gunshot n the range of a gun; the instance of shooting a gun or the shot fired from it.

gunslinger n (sl) a gunman or gunfighter.

gunwale n the upper edge of a ship's or boat's side.—also **gunnel**.

guppy n (pl **guppies**) a small vividly-colored fish of South America and the West Indies popular for aquariums.

gurgle vi (liquid) to make a low bubbling sound; to utter with this sound. * n a bubbling sound.—**gurglingly** adv.

guru n (pl **gurus**) a Hindu or Sikh spiritual teacher; an influential leader or teacher, esp of a religious cult.

gush vi to issue plentifully; to have a sudden flow; to talk or write effusively. * vt to cause to gush. * n a sudden outpouring.—**gushingly** adv.

gusher n an effusive person; an oil well from which oil spouts forth.

gushy adj (**gushier, gushiest**) expressing excessive admiration.—**gushily** adv.—**gushiness** n.

gust n a sudden brief rush of wind; a sudden outburst. * vi to blow in gusts.—**gusty** adj.

gusto n great enjoyment, zest.

gut n (often pl) the bowels or the stomach; the intestine; tough cord made from animal intestines; (pl) (sl) daring; courage. * vt (**gutting, gutted**) to remove the intestines from; to destroy the interior of.

gutless adj (inf) cowardly, lacking determination.—**gutlessness** n.

gutsy adj (**gutsier, gutsiest**) (sl) brave, courageous; passionate; greedy.

gutter n a channel for carrying off water, esp at a roadside or under the eaves of a roof; the lowest condition of human life. * adj marked by extreme vulgarity or indecency.

guttural adj formed or pronounced in the throat; harsh-sounding.—**gutturally** adv.—**gutturalness, gutturality, gutturalism** n.

guy[1] n a rope, chain, etc, for fixing or steadying anything. * vt to fix or steady with a guy.

guy[2] n (inf) a man or boy; (pl) (inf) men or women. * vt to tease.

guzzle vti to gulp down food or drink greedily.—**guzzler** n.

gym n (inf) a gymnasium.

gymnasium n (pl **gymnasiums, gymnasia**) a room or building equipped for physical training and sports.

gymnast n a person skilled in gymnastics.

gymnastics n sing training in exercises devised to strengthen the body; (pl) gymnastic exercises; (pl) feats of dexterity or agility.—**gymnastic** adj.

gynecology, gynaecology n the branch of medicine that deals with the diseases and disorders of the female reproductive system.—**gynecological, gynaecological, gynecologic, gynaecologic** adj.—**gynecologist, gynaecologist** n.

gyp vt (**gypping, gypped**) (sl) to cheat (someone). * n a swindle.—also **gip**.

gypsum n a chalk-like mineral used to make plaster of Paris and fertilizer.—**gypseous, gypsiferous** adj.

Gypsy n (pl **Gypsies**) a member of a travelling people, orig from India, now spread throughout Europe and North America; (without cap) a person who looks or lives like a Gypsy.—also **Gipsy** (pl **Gipsies**).

gyrate vi to revolve; to whirl or spiral.—**gyration** n.—**gyratory** adj.

gyroscope n a wheel mounted in a ring so that its axis is free to turn in any direction, so that when spinning rapidly it keeps its original plane of rotation.—**gyroscopic** adj.

H

H (chem symbol) hydrogen.

ha interj used to express surprise, triumph, etc.—also **hah**.

habit n a distinctive costume, as of a nun, etc; a thing done often and hence easily; a usual way of doing things; an addiction, esp to narcotics.

habitat n the normal environment of an animal or plant.

habitation n the act of inhabiting; a dwelling or residence.—**habitational** adj.

habitual adj having the nature of a habit; regular.—**habitually** adv.—**habitualness** n.

habituate vt to accustom.—**habituation** n.

hacienda n (in Spanish-speaking countries) a large estate or ranch; the main house on such an estate.

hack[1] vt to cut or chop (at) violently; to clear (vegetation) by chopping; (comput) to gain illegal access to confidential data. * n a gash or notch; a harsh, dry cough.

hack[2] n a riding horse for hire; an old worn-out horse; a mediocre or unexceptional writer. * vti to ride a horse cross-country.

hacker n (inf) (comput) a person who uses computers as a hobby, esp one who uses a personal computer to gain illegal access to the computer systems of government departments or large corporations.

hackneyed adj made trite or banal through overuse.

had see **have**.

haddock n (pl **haddocks, haddock**) an important Atlantic food fish related to the cod.

hadn't = had not.

haft n the handle of a weapon or tool.

hag n an ugly or unpleasant old woman; a witch.—**haggish** adj.—**haggishness** n.

haggard adj having an exhausted, untidy look.—**haggardly** adv.—**haggardness** n.

haggle vi to bargain; barter; to dispute over terms; to cavil. * n the act of haggling.—**haggler** n.

hah see **ha**.

ha-ha *interj* an exclamation of mockery; an outburst of laughter.–*also* **haw-haw**.

haiku *n* (*pl* **haiku**) a Japanese verse form of three lines.

hail[1] *vt* to greet; to summon by shouting or signaling, as a taxi; to welcome with approval, to acclaim. * *vi* (*with* **from**) to come from. * *interj* an exclamation of tribute, greeting, etc. * *n* a shout to gain attention; a distance within which one can be heard calling.–**hailer** *n*.

hail[2] *n* frozen raindrops; something, as abuse, bullets, etc, sent forcefully in rapid succession. * *vti* to pour down like hail.

hailstorm *n* a sudden storm of hail.

hair *n* a threadlike growth from the skin of mammals; a mass of hairs, esp on the human head; a threadlike growth on a plant.

hairdo *n* (*pl* **hairdos**) a particular style of hair after cutting, etc.

hairdresser *n* a person who cuts, styles, colors, etc, hair.–**hairdressing** *n*.

hairline *n* a very thin line; the outline of the hair on the head.

hairpiece *n* a wig or toupee; an additional piece of hair attached to a person's real hair.

hairpin *n* a U-shaped pin used to hold hair in place.

hair-raising *adj* terrifying, shocking.

hairsplitting *adj* making petty distinctions; quibbling. * *n* the act of making petty distinctions.–**hairsplitter** *n*.

hairstyle *n* the way in which hair is arranged.–**hairstylist** *n*.

hairy *adj* (**hairier, hairiest**) covered with hair; (*inf*) difficult, dangerous.–**hairiness** *n*.

hake *n* (*pl* **hake, hakes**) a marine food fish related to the cod.

halal *n* meat from animals butchered according to Muslim law. * *adj* of or pertaining to such meat.–*also* **hallal**.

halcyon *adj* calm, gentle, peaceful.

half *n* (*pl* **halves**) either of two equal parts of something. * *adj* being a half; incomplete; partial. * *adv* to the extent of a half; (*inf*) partly.

half-baked *adj* (*inf*) poorly planned or thought-out; (*inf*) stupid.

half-brother *n* a brother through one parent only.

half-hearted *adj* with little interest, enthusiasm, etc.–**half-heartedly** *adv*.–**half-heartedness** *n*.

half-life *n* the time taken for half the atoms in a radioactive substance to decay.

half-measure *n* (*often pl*) an inadequate action; a compromise.

half-moon *n* the moon at its phase when half the disc is illuminated; something shaped like this. * *adj* in the shape of a half-moon.

half-sister *n* a sister through one parent only.

half-time *n* (*sport*) an interval between two halves of a game.

halfway *adj* midway between two points, etc.

halfwit *n* a stupid or silly person; a mentally retarded person.–**halfwitted** *adj*.–**halfwittedly** *adv*.–**halfwittedness** *n*.

halibut *n* (*pl* **halibut, halibuts**) a large marine flatfish used as food.

halitosis *n* bad-smelling breath.

hall *n* a public building with offices, etc; a large room for exhibits, gatherings, etc; the main house on a landed estate; a college building, esp a dining room; a vestibule at the entrance of a building; a hallway.

hallal *see* **halal**.

hallelujah, halleluiah *interj* an exclamation of praise to God. * *n* a praising of God; a musical composition having this as its theme.

hallmark *n* a mark used on gold, silver or platinum articles to signify a standard of purity, weight, date of manufacture; a mark or symbol of high quality; a characteristic feature. * *vt* to stamp with a hallmark.

hallo *see* **hello**.

hallow *vt* to make or regard as holy.–**hallowed** *adj*.–**hallowedness** *n*.–**hallower** *n*.

Hallowe'en, Halloween *n* the eve of All Saints' Day, October 31.

hallucinate *vti* to have or cause to have hallucinations.–**hallucinator** *n*.

hallucination *n* the apparent perception of sights, sounds, etc, that are not actually present; something perceived in this manner.–**hallucinational, hallucinative** *adj*.–**hallucinatory** *adj*.

halo *n* (*pl* **haloes, halos**) a circle of light, as around the sun; a symbolic ring of light around the head of a saint in pictures; the aura of glory surrounding an idealized person or thing. * *vt* (**haloing, haloed**) to surround with a halo.

halt[1] *n* a temporary interruption or cessation of progress; a minor station on a rail line. * *vti* to stop or come to a stop.

halt[2] *vi* to falter; to hesitate.–**halting** *adj*.

halter *n* a rope or strap for tying or leading an animal; a style of women's dress top tied behind the neck and waist leaving the back and arms bare. * *vt* to put a halter on (a horse, etc).

halve *vt* to divide equally into two; to reduce by half; (*golf*) to play one hole in the same number of strokes as one's opponent.

halves *see* **half**.

ham *n* the upper part of a pig's hind leg, salted, smoked, etc; the meat from this area; (*inf*) the back of the upper thigh; (*inf*) an actor who overacts; (*inf*) a licenced amateur radio operator. * *vti* (**hamming, hammed**) to speak or move in an exaggerated manner, to overact.

hamburger *n* ground beef; a cooked patty of such meat, often in a bread roll with pickle, etc.

ham-handed, ham-fisted *adj* (*inf*) clumsy.

hamlet *n* a very small village.

hammer *n* a tool for pounding, driving nails, etc, having a heavy head and a handle; a thing like this in shape or use, as the part of the gun that strikes the firing pin. * *vti* to strike repeatedly, as with a hammer; to drive, force, or shape, as with hammer blows; (*inf*) to defeat utterly.–**hammerer** *n*.

hammerhead *n* a shark with a mallet-shaped head.

hammock *n* a length of strong cloth or netting suspended by the ends and used as a bed.

hamper[1] *vt* to hinder; to interfere with; to encumber.–**hamperer** *n*.

hamper[2] *n* a large, usu covered, basket for storing or transporting food and crockery, etc.

hamster *n* a small short-tailed rodent with cheek pouches.

hamstring *n* any of the tendons at the back of the thigh that flex and rotate the leg. * *vt* (**hamstringing, hamstrung**) to cripple by severing the hamstring of; to render useless, to thwart.

hand *n* the part of the arm below the wrist, used for grasping; a side or direction; possession or care; control; an active part; a promise to marry; skill; one having a special skill; handwriting; applause; help; a hired worker; a source; one of a ship's crew; anything like a hand, as a pointer on a clock; the breadth of a hand, four inches when measuring the height of a horse; the cards held by a player at one time; a round of card play; (*inf*) applause. * *adj* of, for, or controlled by the hand. * *vt* to give as with the hand; to help or conduct with the hand. * *vi* (*with* **on**) to pass to the next.

handbook *n* a book containing useful instructions.

handcuff *n* (*usu pl*) either of a pair of connected steel rings for shackling the wrists of a prisoner. * *vt* to manacle.

handful *n* as much as will fill the hand; a few; (*inf*) a person who is difficult to handle or control.

handicap *n* a mental or physical impairment; a contest in which difficulties are imposed on, or advantages given to, contestants to equalize their chances; such a difficulty or advantage; any hindrance. * *vt* (**handicapping, handicapped**) to give a handicap to; to hinder.–**handicapper** *n*.

handicraft *n* a skill involving the hands, such as basketwork, pottery, etc; an item of pottery, etc made by hand.

handiwork n handmade work; something done by a person or thing.

handkerchief n a small cloth for blowing the nose, etc.

handle vt to touch, hold, or move with the hand; to manage or operate with the hands; to manage, deal with; to buy and sell (goods). * vi to react in a specified way. * n a part of anything designed to be held or grasped by the hand.–**handleable** adj.–**handling** n.

handler n a person who trains or controls animals, such as a police dog.

handmade adj made by hand, carefully crafted.

hand-out n an item of food, clothing, etc, given free to the needy; a statement given to the press to replace or supplement an oral presentation.

hand-picked adj carefully selected.

handshake n a grasping and shaking of a person's hand as a greeting or when concluding an agreement.

handsome adj good-looking; dignified; generous; ample.–**handsomely** adv.–**handsomeness** n.

hands-on adj involving active participation and operating experience.

handstand n the act of supporting the body on the hands with the feet in the air.

hand-to-mouth adj having barely enough food or money to survive.–also adv.

handwriting n writing done by hand; a style of such writing.–**handwritten** adj.

handy adj (**handier, handiest**) convenient, near; easy to use; skilled with the hands.–**handily** adv.–**handiness** n.

handyman n (pl **handymen**) a person who does odd jobs.

hang vb (**hanging, hung**) vt to support from above, esp by a rope, chain, etc, to suspend; (door, etc) to attach by hinges to allow to swing freely; to decorate with pictures, or other suspended objects; to exhibit (works of art); to prevent (a jury) from coming to a decision; (pt, pp **hanged**) to put to execute or kill by suspending by the neck. * vi to be suspended, so as to dangle loosely; (clothing, etc) to fall or flow in a certain direction; to lean, incline, or protrude; to depend; to remain in the air; to be in suspense; to fall or droop; (pt, pp **hanged**) to die by hanging; (with **about, around**) to loiter; (with **back**) to hesitate, be reluctant; (with **out**) to meet regularly at a particular place. * n the way in which anything hangs.

hangar n a large shelter where aircraft are built, stored or repaired.–also vt.

hangdog adj abject or ashamed in appearance or manner.

hanger n a device on which something is hung; one who hangs things.

hanger-on n (pl **hangers-on**) a sycophantic follower.

hanging n the act of executing a person by suspending them by the neck; something hung, as a picture; (pl) decorative draperies hung on walls. * adj suspended in the air; undecided; overhanging; situated on a steep slope.

hangman n (pl **hangmen**) a person who executes prisoners by hanging them.

hangnail n a thin strip of torn skin at the root of a fingernail.

hangout n a favorite meeting place.

hangover n the unpleasant after-effects of excessive consumption of alcohol; something surviving from an earlier time.

hang-up n an emotional preoccupation with something.

hank n a coiled or looped bundle of wool, rope, etc.

hanker vi (with **after, for**) to desire longingly.–**hankerer** n.–**hankering** n.

hanky, hankie n (pl **hankies**) (inf) a handkerchief.

hanky-panky n (inf) foolish behavior; dishonesty; illicit sexual relations.

haphazard adj not planned; random. * adv by chance.–**haphazardly** adv.–**haphazardness** n.

hapless adj unfortunate, unlucky.–**haplessness** n.

happen vi to take place; to be, occur, or come by chance.

happening n an occurrence; an improvisation.

happy adj (**happier, happiest**) fortunate; having, expressing, or enjoying pleasure or contentment; pleased; appropriate, felicitous.–**happily** adv.–**happiness** n.

happy-go-lucky adj irresponsible; carefree.

happy medium n a middle course between extremes.

harangue n a tirade; a lengthy, forceful speech. * vti to make a harangue, to address vehemently.–**haranguer** n.

harass vt to annoy, to irritate; to trouble (an enemy) by constant raids and attacks.–**harasser** n.–**harassment** n.

harbinger n a person or thing that announces or presages the arrival of another, a forerunner.

harbor, harbour n a protected inlet for anchoring ships; any place of refuge. * vt to shelter or house; (grudge, etc) to keep in the mind secretly. * vi to take shelter.–**harborer, harbourer** n.

hard adj firm, solid, not easily cut or punctured; difficult to comprehend; difficult to accomplish; difficult to bear, painful; severe, unfeeling, ungenerous; indisputable, intractable; (drugs) addictive and damaging to health; (weather) severe; (currency) stable in value; (news) definite, not speculative; (drink) very alcoholic; (water) having a high mineral content that prevents lathering with soap; (color, sound) harsh. * adv with great effort or intensity; earnestly, with concentration; so as to cause hardness; with difficulty; with bitterness or grief; close, near by.–**hardness** n.

hardback n a book bound with a stiff cover.–also adj.

hardboard n a stiff board made of compressed wood chips.

hard-boiled adj (eggs) boiled until solid; (inf) unfeeling.

hard copy n output (as from microfilm or a computer) on paper.

hard core n the stubborn inner group in an organization that is resistant to change; the heavy foundation material for a road.–**hard-core** adj.

hard disk n (comput) a rigid magnetic disk in a sealed unit capable of much greater storage capacity than a floppy disk.

harden vti to make or become hard.–**hardener** n.

hard-headed adj shrewd and unsentimental; practical.–**hard-headedly** adv.–**hard-headedness** n.

hardhearted adj unfeeling; cruel.–**hardheartedly** adv.–**hardheartedness** n.

hard-hitting adj forcefully effective.

hard line n an aggressive, unyielding policy.–**hard-line** adj.–**hardliner** n.

hardly adv scarcely; barely; with difficulty; not to be expected.

hard sell n an aggressive selling technique.

hardship n something that causes suffering or privation.

hard-up adj (inf) short of money.

hardware n articles made of metal as tools, nails, etc; (comput) the mechanical and electronic components that make up a computer system.

hardy adj (**hardier, hardiest**) bold, resolute; robust; vigorous; able to withstand exposure to physical or emotional hardship.–**hardily** adv.–**hardiness** n.

hare n (pl **hare, hares**) any of various timid, swift, long-eared mammals, resembling but larger than the rabbit.

harebrained adj flighty; foolish.

harelip n a congenital deformity of the upper lip in the form of a vertical fissure.–**harelipped** adj.

harem n the usu secluded part of a Muslim household where the women live; the women in a harem.

haricot n a type of French bean with an edible light-colored seed.

hark vi to listen; (with **back**) to retrace a course; to revert (to).

harlequin n the performer in a pantomime who wears parti-colored garments and carries a wand. * adj fantastic or full of trickery; colorful.

harlot n (formerly) a prostitute.–**harlotry** n.

harm n hurt; damage; injury. * vt to inflict hurt, damage, or injury upon.–**harmful** adj.–**harmfully** adv.

harmless adj not likely to cause harm.–**harmlessly** adv.–**harmlessness** n.

harmonic adj (mus) of or in harmony. * n an overtone; (pl) the science of musical sounds.–**harmonically** adv.

harmonica n a small wind instrument that produces tones when air is blown or sucked across a series of metal reeds; a mouth-organ.

harmonious adj fitting together in an orderly and pleasing manner; agreeing in ideas, interests, etc; melodious.–**harmoniously** adv.

harmonize vi to be in harmony; to sing in harmony. * vt to make harmonious.–**harmonization** n.

harmony n (pl **harmonies**) a pleasing agreement of parts in color, size, etc; agreement in action, ideas, etc; the pleasing combination of musical tones in a chord.

harness n the leather straps and metal pieces by which a horse is fastened to a vehicle, plow, etc; any similar fastening or attachment, eg for a parachute, hang-glider. * vt to put a harness on; to control so as to use the power of.–**harnesser** n.

harp n a stringed musical instrument played by plucking. * vi (with **on** or **upon**) to talk persistently (on some subject).– **harpist, harper** n.

harpoon n a barbed spear with an attached line, for spearing whales, etc. * vt to strike with a harpoon.–**harpooner** n.

harpsichord n a musical instrument resembling a grand piano whose strings are plucked by a mechanism rather than struck.–**harpsichordist** n.

harpy n (pl **harpies**) a grasping, vicious person.

harrow n a heavy frame with spikes, spring teeth, or disks for breaking up and leveling plowed ground. * vt to draw a harrow over (land); to cause mental distress to.–**harrower** n.–**harrowing** adj, n.–**harrowment** n.

harry vt (**harrying, harried**) to torment or harass.

harsh adj unpleasantly rough; jarring on the senses or feelings; rigorous; cruel.–**harshly** adv.–**harshness** n.

hart n (pl **hart, harts**) a male deer.

harvest n (the season of) gathering in the ripened crops; the yield of a particular crop; the reward or product of any exertion or action. * vti to gather in (a crop). * vt to win by achievement.–**harvester** n.–**harvesting** n.

has see **have**.

has-been n (inf) a person or thing that has lost its former popularity or celebrity status.

hash[1] n a chopped mixture of reheated cooked meat and vegetables. * vt to chop up (meat or vegetables) for hash; to mix or mess up.

hash[2] n (inf) hashish.

hashish n resin derived from the leaves and shoots of the hemp plant, smoked or chewed as an intoxicant.

hasn't = has not.

hasp n a hinged fastening for a door, etc, esp a metal piece fitted over a staple and fastened as by a bolt or padlock.

hassock n a firm cushion used as a footstool or seat.

haste n quickness of motion; urgency.

hasten vt to accelerate; to cause to hurry. * vi to move or act with speed.–**hastener** n.

hasty adj (**hastier, hastiest**) done in a hurry; rash, precipitate.–**hastily** adv.–**hastiness** n.

hat n a covering for the head. * vt (**hatting, hatted**) to cover with a hat.

hatch[1] n a small door or opening (as on an aircraft or spaceship); an opening in the deck of a ship or in the floor or roof of a building; a lid for such an opening; a hatchway.

hatch[2] vt to produce (young) from the egg, esp by incubating; to devise (eg a plot). * vi to emerge from the egg; to incubate.–**hatchable** adj.–**hatcher** n.

hatchet n a small ax with a short handle.

hate vt to feel intense dislike for. * vi to feel hatred; to wish to avoid. * n a strong feeling of dislike or contempt; the person or thing hated.–**hater** n.

hateful adj deserving or arousing hate.–**hatefully** adv.–**hatefulness** n.

hatred n intense dislike or enmity.

haughty adj (**haughtier, haughtiest**) having or expressing arrogance.–**haughtily** adv.–**haughtiness** n.

haul vt to move by pulling; to transport by truck, etc. * n the act of hauling; the amount gained, caught, etc, at one time; the distance over which something is transported.

haulage n the transport of commodities; the charge for this.

haunch n the part of the body around the hips; the leg and loin of a deer, sheep, etc.–**haunched** adj.

haunt vt to visit often or continually; to recur repeatedly to. * vi to linger; to appear habitually as a ghost. * n a place often visited.–**haunter** n.

have vt (**has, having**, pp **had**) to have in one's possession; to possess as an attribute; to hold in the mind; to experience; to give birth to; to allow, or tolerate; to arrange or hold; to engage in; to cause, compel, or require to be; to to be obliged; to be pregnant with; (inf) to hold at a disadvantage; (inf) to deceive; to accept or receive; to consume food, drink, etc; to show some quality; to perplex.

haven n a place where ships can safely anchor; a refuge.

haven't = have not.

havoc n widespread destruction or disorder. * vt (**havocking, havocked**) to lay waste.

hawk[1] n any of numerous birds of prey; a person who advocates aggressive or intimidatory action. * vti to hunt with a hawk; to strike like a hawk.–**hawkish** adj.–**hawkishly** adv.

hawk[2] vt to offer goods for sale, as in the street; to spread gossip. * vi to peddle.

hawser n (naut) a heavy rope for towing, mooring, etc.

hawthorn n any of a genus of spring-flowering spiny shrubs or trees with white or pink flowers and red fruit.

hay n grass cut and dried for fodder.

hay fever n an allergic reaction to pollen, causing irritation of the nose and eyes.

haystack, hayrick n a pile of stacked hay ready for storing.

haywire adj (inf) out of order; disorganized.

hazard n a risk; a danger; an obstacle on a golf course. * vt to risk; to venture.–**hazardous** adj.

haze n a thin vapor of fog, smoke, etc. in the air; slight vagueness of mind.–**hazy** adj.–**hazily** adv.–**haziness** n.

hazel n a tree with edible nuts; a light-brown color. * adj light-brown.

hazelnut n the edible nut of the hazel.

H-bomb n a hydrogen bomb.

He (chem symbol) helium.

he pron the male person or animal named before; a person (male or female). * n a male person or animal.

head n the part of an animal or human body containing the brain, eyes, ears, nose and mouth; the top part of anything; the foremost part; the chief person; (pl) a unit of counting; the striking part of a tool; mind; understanding; the topic of a chapter, etc; crisis, conclusion; pressure of water, steam, etc; the source of a river, etc; froth, as on beer. * adj at the head, top or front; coming from in front; chief, leading. * vt to command; to lead; to cause to go in a specified direction; to set out; to travel (in a particular direction); to strike (a football) with the head.–**headless** adj.

headache n a continuous pain in the head; (inf) a cause of worry or trouble.–**headachy** adj.

headband n a ribbon or band worn around the head.

headdress n a decorative covering for the head.

headed adj having (a specified kind of) head; having a heading.

headfirst *adj* with the head in front; recklessly.–*also adv.*

headgear *n* a covering for the head, a hat, cap, etc.

head-hunt *vt* to cut off and preserve the heads of enemies as trophies; a person who recruits executive personnel.–**head-hunter** *n.*–**head-hunting** *n.*

heading *n* something forming the head, top, or front; the title, topic, etc of a chapter, etc; the direction in which a vehicle is moving.

headland *n* a promontory; unplowed land at the ends of a furrow.

headless *adj* being without a head; leaderless.

headlight *n* a light at the front of a vehicle.

headline *n* printed lines at the top of a newspaper article giving the topic; a brief news summary. * *vt* to give featured billing or publicity to.

headlong *adj, adv* with the head first; with uncontrolled speed or force; rashly.

headmaster, headmistress *n* the principal of a school.–**headmastership, headmistress-ship** *n.*

head-on *adj, adv* with the head or front foremost; without compromise.

head over heels *adv* as if somersaulting; completely, utterly, deeply.

headphone *n* one of two radio receivers held to the head by a band.

headquarters *n* the centre of operations of one in command, as in an army; the main office in any organization.

headrest *n* a support for the head.

headroom *n* space overhead, as in a doorway or tunnel.

headstone *n* a marker placed at the head of a grave.

headstrong *adj* determined to do as one pleases; obstinate.

headway *n* forward motion; progress.

headwind *n* a wind blowing against the direction of a ship or aircraft.

heady *adj* (**headier, headiest**) (*alcoholic drinks*) intoxicating; invigorating, exciting; impetuous.–**headily** *adv.*–**headiness** *n.*

heal *vti* to make or become healthy; to cure; (*wound, etc*) to repair by natural processes.–**healable** *adj.*–**healer** *n.*–**healingly** *adv.*

health *n* physical and mental well-being; freedom from disease, etc; the condition of body or mind; a wish for one's health and happiness, as in a toast.–**healthy** *adj.*–**healthily** *adv.*

health foods *npl* foods that are organically grown, unprocessed and additive-free.

healthful *adj* healthy.–**healthfully** *adv.*–**healthfulness** *n.*

heap *n* a mass or pile of jumbled things; (*pl*) (*inf*) a large amount. * *vt* to throw in a heap; to pile high; to fill (a plate, etc) full or to overflowing.–**heaper** *n.*

hear *vb* (**hearing, heard**) *vt* to perceive by the ear; to listen to; to conduct a hearing of (a law case, etc); to be informed of; to learn. * *vi* to be able to hear sounds; (*with* **of** *or* **about**) to be told.–**hearable** *adj.*–**hearer** *n.*

hearing *n* the sense by which sound is perceived by the ear; an opportunity to be heard; the distance over which something can be heard, earshot.

hearing aid *n* a small electronic amplifier worn behind the ear to improve hearing.

hearsay *n* rumor, gossip.

hearse *n* a vehicle for transporting a coffin to a funeral.

heart *n* the hollow, muscular organ that circulates the blood; the central, vital, or main part; the human heart as the centre of emotions, esp sympathy, courage, etc; a conventional design representing a heart; one of a suit of playing cards marked with such a symbol in red.

heartache *n* sorrow or grief.

heart attack *n* a sudden instance of abnormal heart functioning, esp coronary thrombosis.

heartbeat *n* the rhythmic contraction and dilation of the heart.

heartbreak *n* overwhelming sorrow or grief.–**heartbreaker** *n.*–**heartbreaking** *adj.*

heartbroken *adj* overcome by sorrow or grief.–**heartbrokenly** *adv.*–**heartbrokenness** *n.*

heartburn *n* a burning sensation in the lower chest.

heart failure *n* the inability of the heart to supply enough blood to the body; a cessation of heart activity leading to death.

heartfelt *adj* deeply felt; sincere.

hearth *n* the floor of a fireplace and surrounding area; this as symbolic of house and home.

heartily *adv* in a vigorous or enthusiastic way; sincerely.

heartless *adj* lacking compassion; unfeeling.–**heartlessly** *adv.*–**heartlessness** *n.*

heart-throb *n* (*inf*) the object of a person's infatuation; a heartbeat.

heart-to-heart *n* an intimate conversation. * *adj* intimate; candid.

hearty *adj* (**heartier, heartiest**) warm and friendly; (*laughter, etc*) unrestrained; strong and healthy; nourishing and plentiful.–**heartiness** *n.*

heat *n* energy produced by molecular agitation; the quality of being hot; the perception of hotness; hot weather or climate; strong feeling, esp ardor, anger, etc; a single bout, round, or trial in sports; the period of sexual excitement and readiness for mating in female animals; (*sl*) coercion. * *vti* to make or become warm or hot; to make or become excited.

heated *adj* made hot; excited, impassioned.–**heatedly** *adv.*–**heatedness** *n.*

heater *n* a device that provides heat.

heath *n* an area of uncultivated land with scrubby vegetation; any of various shrubby plants that thrive on sandy soil, eg heather.

heathen *n* (*pl* **heathens, heathen**) anyone not acknowledging the God of Christian, Jew, or Muslim belief; a person regarded as irreligious, uncivilized, etc. * *adj* of or denoting a heathen; irreligious; pagan.–**heathendom** *n.*–**heathenish** *adj.*–**heathenishly** *adv.*–**heathenishness** *n.*

heather *n* a common evergreen shrub of northern and alpine regions with small sessile leaves and tiny usu purplish pink flowers.–**heathery** *adj.*

heating *n* a system of providing heat, as central heating; the warmth provided.

heat wave *n* a prolonged period of unusually hot weather.

heave *vb* (**heaving, heaved**) *vt* to lift or move, esp with great effort; to utter (a sigh, etc) with effort; (*inf*) to throw. * *vi* to rise and fall rhythmically; to vomit; to pant; to gasp; to haul; (**heaving, hove**) (*with* **to**) (*ship*) to come to a stop. * *n* the act or effort of heaving.–**heaver** *n.*

heaven *n* (*usu pl*) the visible sky; (*sometimes cap*) the dwelling place of God and his angels where the blessed go after death; any place or state of great happiness; (*pl*) *interj* an exclamation of surprise.

heavenly *adj* of or relating to heaven or heavens; divine; (*inf*) excellent, delightful.–**heavenliness** *n.*

heavy *adj* (**heavier, heaviest**) hard to lift or carry; of more than the usual, expected, or defined weight; to an unusual extent; hard to do; stodgy, hard to digest; cloudy; (*industry*) using massive machinery to produce basic materials, as chemicals and steel; (*ground*) difficult to make fast progress on; clumsy; dull; serious. * *n* (*pl* **heavies**) (*theater*) a villain; (*sl*) a person hired to threaten violence, a thug.–**heavily** *adv.*–**heaviness** *n.*

heavy duty *adj* made to withstand heavy strain or rough usage.

heavy-handed *adj* clumsy; tactless; oppressive.–**heavy-handedly** *adv.*–**heavy-handedness** *n.*

heck *interj* an expression of surprise or grief.

heckle *vti* to harass (a speaker) with questions or taunts.–**heckler** *n.*

hectare *n* a metric measure of area, equivalent to 10,000 square meters (2.47 acres).

hectic *adj* involving intense excitement or activity.–**hectically** *adv.*

hector *vt* to bully; to annoy. * *n* a bully.

he'd = he had, he would.

hedge n a fence consisting of a dense line of bushes or small trees; a barrier or means of protection against something, esp financial loss; an evasive or noncommittal answer or statement. * vt to surround or enclose with a hedge; to place secondary bets as a precaution. * vi to avoid giving a direct answer in an argument or debate.—**hedger** n.—**hedgy** adj.

hedgehog n a small insectivorous mammal with sharp spines on the back.

hedonism n the doctrine that personal pleasure is the chief good.—**hedonistic** adj.—**hedonist** n.

heed vt to pay close attention (to). * n careful attention.—**heedful** adj.—**heedfully** adv.

heedless adj inattentive; thoughtless.—**heedlessly** adv.—**heedlessness** n.

heehaw n (an imitation of) the bray of a donkey, a crude laugh. * vi to bray like a donkey.

heel n the back part of the foot, under the ankle; the part covering or supporting the heel in stockings, socks, etc, or shoes; a solid attachment forming the back of the sole of a shoe; (inf) a despicable person. * vt to furnish with a heel; to follow closely; (inf) to provide with money, etc. * vi to follow along at the heels of someone.—**heelless** adj.

hefty adj (**heftier, heftiest**) (inf) heavy; large and strong; big.—**heftily** adv.—**heftiness** n.

heifer n a young cow that has not calved.

height n the topmost point; the highest limit; the distance from the bottom to the top; altitude; a relatively great distance above a given level; an eminence; a hill.

heighten vti to make or come higher or more intense.—**heightener** n.

heinous adj outrageously evil; wicked.—**heinously** adj.—**heinousness** n.

heir n a person who inherits or is entitled to inherit another's property, title, etc.—**heirless** adj.

heiress n a woman or girl who is an heir, esp to great wealth.

heirloom n any possession handed down from generation to generation.

heist n (sl) a robbery. * vt (sl) to steal.—**heister** n.

held see **hold**[1].

helicopter n a kind of aircraft lifted and moved, or kept hovering, by large rotary blades mounted horizontally.

heliport, helipad n a landing and takeoff place for a helicopter.

helium n a light nonflammable gaseous element.

helix n (pl **helices, helixes**) a spiral line, as a line coiled round; (zool) a snail or its shell; (anat) the folded rim of the external ear; (archit) a small volute on a capital.—**helical** adj.

hell n (Christianity) the place of punishment of the wicked after death; the home of devils and demons; any place or state of supreme misery or discomfort; (inf) a cause of this. * interj (inf) an exclamation of anger, surprise, etc.

he'll = he will.

hellbent adj (inf) rashly determined.

hellish adj of, pertaining to, or resembling hell; very wicked; (inf) very unpleasant.—**hellishly** adv.—**hellishness** n.

hello interj an expression of greeting. * n (pl **hellos**) the act of saying "hello."—also **hallo, hullo** (pl **hallos, hullos**).

helm n (naut) the tiller or wheel used to steer a ship; any position of control or direction, authority. * vt to steer; to control.

helmet n protective headgear worn by soldiers, policemen, divers, etc.—**helmeted** adj.

helmsman n (pl **helmsmen**) a person who steers.—**helmswoman** nf (pl **helmswomen**).

help vt to make things better or easier for; to aid; to assist; to remedy; to keep from; to serve or wait on. * vi to give aid; to be useful.—interj used to ask for assistance. * n the action of helping; aid; assistance; a remedy; a person that helps, esp a hired person.—**helper** n.

helpful adj giving help; useful.—**helpfully** adv.—**helpfulness** n.

helping n a single portion of food.

helpless adj unable to manage alone, dependent on others; weak and defenceless.—**helplessly** adv.—**helplessness** n.

helter-skelter adv in confused haste. * adj disorderly. * n a tall spiral slide usu found in an amusement park.

hem n the edge of a garment, etc, turned back and stitched or fixed. * vt (**hemming, hemmed**) to finish (a garment) with a hem; (with **in**) toenclose, confine.—**hemmer** n.

hematite n native ferric oxide, an important iron ore.—also **haematite**.

hematology n the branch of medicine dealing with blood and its diseases.—**hematologic, hematological** adj.—**hematologist** n.

hemisphere n half of a sphere or globe; any of the halves (northern, southern, eastern, or western) of the earth.— **hemispheric, hemispherical** adj.—**hemispherically** adv.

hemline n the bottom edge of a skirt or dress.

hemlock n a poisonous plant with small white flowers; a poison made from this plant.

hemoglobin n the oxygen-carrying red coloring matter of the red blood corpuscles.

hemophilia n a hereditary condition in which the blood fails to clot normally.—**hemophiliac, hemophile** n.—**hemophilic** adj.

hemorrhage n the escape of blood from a blood vessel; heavy bleeding. * vi to bleed heavily.—**hemorrhagic** adj.

hemorrhoids npl swollen or bleeding veins around the anus.—also **piles**.—**hemorrhoidal** adj.

hemp n a widely cultivated Asian herb of the mulberry family; its fiber, used to make rope, sailcloth, etc; a narcotic drug obtained from different varieties of this plant (–also **cannabis, marijuana**).—**hempen** adj.

hen n the female of many birds, esp the chicken.

hence adv from here; from this time; from this reason.

henceforth, henceforward adv from now on.

henchman n (pl **henchmen**) a trusted helper or follower.

henna n a tropical plant; a reddish-brown dye extracted from its leaves used to tint the hair or skin. * vt to dye with henna.

henpeck vt to nag and domineer over (one's husband).—**henpecked** adj.

hepatitis n inflammation of the liver.

her pron the objective and possessive case of the personal pronoun **she**. * adj of or belonging to a female.

herald n a person who conveys news or messages; a forerunner, harbinger. * vt to usher in; to proclaim.

heraldry n (pl **heraldries**) the study of genealogies and coats of arms; ceremony; pomp.—**heraldic** adj.

herb n any seed plant whose stem withers away annually; any plant used as a medicine, seasoning, etc.

herbaceous adj of or like herbs; green and leafy.

herbal adj of herbs. * n a book listing and describing plants with medicinal properties.

herbalist n a person who practices healing by using herbs; a person who grows or deals in herbs.

herbivore n a plant-eating animal.—**herbivorous** adj.—**herbivorousness** n.

herculean adj of extraordinary strength, size, or difficulty.

herd n a large number of animals, esp cattle, living and feeding together. * vi to assemble or move animals together. * vt to gather together and move as if a herd; to tend, as a herdsman.—**herder** n.

here adv at or in this place; to or into this place; now; on earth.

hereabout, hereabouts adv in this area.

hereafter adv after this, in some future time or state. * n (with **the**) the future, life after death.

hereby adv by this means.

heredity n (pl **heredities**) the transmission of genetic material that determines physical and mental characteristics from one generation to another.–**hereditary** adj.

heresy n (pl **heresies**) a religious belief regarded as contrary to the orthodox doctrine of a church; any belief or opinion contrary to established or accepted theory.

heretic n a dissenter from an established belief or doctrine.–**heretical** adj.–**heretically** adv.

hereupon adv (formal) on this matter, issue, etc; immediately after this.

herewith adv (formal) with this.

heritage n something inherited at birth; anything deriving from the past or tradition; historical sites, traditions, practices, etc regarded as the valuable inheritance of contemporary society.

hermaphrodite n an animal or organism with both male and female reproductive organs; a plant with stamens and pistils in the same floral envelope.–**hermaphroditic** adj.–**hermaphroditically** adv.

hermetic, hermetical adj perfectly closed and airtight; of alchemy, magical.–**hermetically** adv.

hermit n a person who lives in complete solitude, esp for religious reasons; a recluse.–**hermitic, hermitical** adj.–**hermitically** adv.

hermitage n the dwelling place of a hermit; a secluded retreat.

hernia n (pl **hernias, herniae**) the protrusion of an organ, esp part of the intestine, through an opening in the wall of the cavity in which it sits; a rupture.–**hernial** adj.–**herniated** adj.

hero n (pl **heroes**) a person of exceptional bravery; a person admired for superior qualities and achievements; the central male character in a novel, play, etc.

heroic adj of, worthy of, or like a hero; having the qualities of a hero; daring, risky; (poetry) of or about heroes and their deeds, epic; (language) grand, high-flown. * n heroic verse; (pl) melodramatic talk or behavior.–**heroically** adv.

heroin n a powerfully addictive drug derived from morphine.

heroine n a woman with the attributes of a hero; the leading female character in a novel, film or play.

heroism n the qualities or conduct of a hero; bravery.

heron n a slim wading bird with long legs and neck.

herpes n any of several virus diseases marked by small blisters on the skin or mucous membranes.–**herpetic** adj.

herring n (pl **herrings, herring**) a small food fish of commercial importance.

herringbone n a kind of cross-stitch; a zigzag pattern used in brickwork.

hers pron something or someone belonging to her.

herself pron the reflexive form of **she** or **her**.

he's = he is; he has.

hesitant adj hesitating; indecisive; reluctant; shy.–**hesitantly** adv.–**hesitancy** n.

hesitate vi to be slow in acting due to uncertainty or indecision; to be reluctant (to); to falter or stammer when speaking.–**hesitater** n.–**hesitatingly** adv.–**hesitation** n.

hessian n a coarse cloth made of jute.

heterodox adj contrary to established beliefs or opinions; unorthodox; heretical.

heterogeneous adj opposite or dissimilar in character, quality structure, etc; not homogeneous; disparate.–**heterogeneity** n.–**heterogeneously** adv.

heterosexual adj sexually attracted to the opposite sex. * n a heterosexual person.–**heterosexuality** n.–**heterosexually** adv.

hew vb (**hewing, hewed**, pp **hewed, hewn**) vt to strike or cut with blows using an ax, etc; to shape with such blows. * vi to conform (to a rule, principle, etc).–**hewer** n.

hex vt to bewitch; to bring bad luck. * n a magic spell; a curse; a witch.

hexagon n a polygon having six sides and six angles.–**hexagonal** adj.–**hexagonally** adv.

hey interj an expression of joy, surprise or to call attention.

heyday n a period of greatest success, happiness, etc.

hi interj an exclamation of greeting.

hiatus n (pl **hiatuses, hiatus**) a break in continuity; a lacuna; (med) an aperture; (phonetics) the concurrence of two vowels in two successive syllables.–**hiatal** adj.

hibernate vi to spend the winter in a dormant condition like deep sleep; to be inactive.–**hibernation** n.–**hibernator** n.

hiccup n a sudden involuntary spasm of the diaphragm followed by inhalation and closure of the glottis producing a characteristic sound; (inf) a minor setback. * vt (**hiccuping, hiccuped** or **hiccupping, hiccupped**) to have hiccups.

hick n (inf) an unsophisticated person, esp from a rural area.

hickory n (pl **hickories**) a North American tree of the walnut family; its wood; its smooth-shelled edible nut.

hid see **hide**[1].

hidden adj concealed or obscured.

hide[1] vb (**hiding, hid**, pp **hidden, hid**) vt to conceal, put out of sight; to keep secret; to screen or obscure from view. * vi to conceal oneself. * n a camouflaged place of concealment used by hunters, bird-watchers, etc.–**hider** n.

hide[2] n the raw or dressed skin of an animal; (inf) the human skin.

hide-and-seek n a children's game in which one player must find the others, who have hidden themselves.

hideous adj visually repulsive; horrifying.–**hideously** adv.–**hideousness** n.

hiding n concealment.

hierarchy n (pl **hierarchies**) a group of persons or things arranged in order of rank, grade, etc.–**hierarchical, hierarchic** adj.–**hierarchically** adv.

hieroglyph n a character used in a system of hieroglyphic writing.

hieroglyphic n a sacred character or symbol; (pl) the picture writings of the ancient Egyptians and others. * adj pertaining to hieroglyphs; emblematic.–**hieroglyphically** adv.

high adj lofty, tall; extending upward a (specified) distance; situated at or done from a height; above others in rank, position, etc; greater in size, amount, cost, etc than usual; raised or acute in pitch; (inf) intoxicated; (inf) under the influence of drugs. * adv in or to a high degree, rank, etc. * n a high level, place, etc; (inf) a euphoric condition induced by alcohol or drugs.

highbrow n (inf) an intellectual. * adj (inf) interested in things requiring learning.

high-class adj of good quality.

higher education n education at college or university level.

high-flown adj extravagantly ambitious; bombastic.

high-handed adj overbearing, arbitrary.–**high-handedly** adv.– **high-handedness** n.

highjack, highjacker see hijack.

high jump n an athletic event in which a competitor jumps over a high bar.

highland adj of or in mountains. * n a region with many hills or mountains; (pl) mountainous country.

highlander n a person who lives in a highland area.

highlight n the lightest area of a painting, etc; the most interesting or important feature. * vt to bring to special attention.

highly adv highly, very much; favorably; at a high level, wage, rank, etc.

high-minded adj having high ideals, etc.–**high-mindedness** n.

highness n the state or quality of being high; (with cap and poss pron) a title used in speaking to or of royalty.

high-pitched adj (sound) shrill; (roof) steep.

high-powered, high-power adj (lens, etc) producing great magnification; energetic; powerful; highly competent.

high priest n a chief priest, esp the principal priest of the Jewish hierarchy; an unofficial leader of fashion, etc.

high roller n a gambler; an extravagant person; a leader of fashion.–**high rolling** adj, n.

high school n a secondary school.

high seas npl open ocean waters outside the territorial limits of any nation.

high-spirited adj courageous; lively.–**high-spiritedness** n.

high-strung adj strung to a high pitch; extremely sensitive; highly strung.

high tide n the tide at its highest level; the time of this; an acme.

highway n a public road; a main thoroughfare.

highwayman n (pl **highwaymen**) one who robs travelers on a highway.

hijack vt to steal (goods in transit) by force; to force (an aircraft) to make an unscheduled flight. * n an act of hijacking.–also **highjack**.–**hijacker, highjacker** n.

hike vi to take a long walk. * vt (inf) to pull up, to increase. * n a long walk; a tramp.–**hiker** n.

hilarious adj highly amusing.–**hilariously** adv.–**hilarity** n.

hill n a natural rise of land lower than a mountain; a heap or mound; an slope in a road, etc. vt to bank up; to draw earth around (plants) in mounds.–**hilly** adj.

hillbilly n (pl **hillbillies**) (inf) a person from the mountainous areas of southeastern US; country music.–also adj.

hillock n a small hill.–**hillocked, hillocky** adj.

hilt n the handle of a sword, dagger, tool, etc.

him pron the objective case of **he**.

himself pron the reflexive (he killed himself) or emphatic (he himself was lucky) form of **he, him**.

hind[1] adj (**hinder, hindmost** or **hindermost**) situated at the back; rear.

hind[2] n (pl **hinds, hind**) a female deer.

hinder vt to obstruct, delay or impede. * vi to impose instructions or impediments. * adj belonging to or constituting the back or rear of anything.–**hindrance** n.

hindmost, hindermost adj farthest behind.

hindquarters npl the hind legs and accompanying parts of a quadruped.

hindsight n understanding an event after it has occurred.

hinge n a joint or flexible part on which a door, lid, etc turns; a natural joint, as of a clam. * vti to attach or hang by a hinge; to depend.

hint n an indirect or subtle suggestion; a slight mention; a little piece of practical or helpful advice. * vt to suggest or indicate indirectly. * vi to give a hint.

hinterland n the land behind that bordering a coast or river; a remote area.

hip[1] n either side of the body below the waist and above the thigh.

hip[2] adj (sl) stylish, up-to-date.

hippie, hippy n (pl **hippies**) (sl) a person who adopts an alternative lifestyle, eg involving mysticism, psychedelic drugs, or communal living, to express alienation from conventional society.

hippopotamus n (pl **hippopotamuses, hippopotami**) a large African water-loving mammal with thick dark skin, short legs, and a very large head and muzzle.

hire vt to pay for the services of (a person) or the use of (a thing). * n the payment for the temporary use of anything; the fact or state of being hired.–**hirable, hireable** adj.–**hirer** n.

hirsute adj covered in hair; of or pertaining to hair.–**hirsuteness** n.

his poss pron of or belonging to him.–also adj.

Hispanic adj of or derived from Spain, Spanish or Spanish-speaking countries. * n a person of Hispanic descent, esp in the US.

hiss vi to make a sound resembling a prolonged s; to show disapproval by hissing. * vt to say or indicate by hissing. * n the act or sound of hissing.–**hisser** n.

histamine n a substance released by the tissues in allergic reactions, acting as an irritant.–**histaminic** adj.

historian n a person who writes or studies history.

historic adj (potentially) important or famous in history.

historical adj belonging to or involving history or historical methods; concerning actual events as opposed to myth or legend; based on history.–**historically** adv.–**historicalness** n.

history n (pl **histories**) a record or account of past events; the study and analysis of past events; past events in total; the past events or experiences of a specific person or thing; an unusual or significant past.

histrionic, histrionical adj of actors or the theater; melodramatic.–**histrionically** adv.

histrionics n (used as sing or pl) the art of theatrical representation; melodramatic behavior or tantrums to attract attention.

hit vti (**hitting, hit**) to come against (something) with force; to give a blow (to), to strike; to strike with a missile; to affect strongly; to arrive at; (with **on**) to discover by accident or unexpectedly. * n a blow that strikes its mark; a collision; a successful and popular song, book, etc; (inf) an underworld killing; (sl) a dose of a drug.

hit-and-run n a motor vehicle accident in which the driver leaves the scene without stopping or informing the authorities.

hitch vt to move, pull, etc with jerks; to fasten with a hook, knot, etc; to obtain a ride by hitchhiking. * vi to hitchhike. * n a tug; a hindrance, obstruction; a kind of knot used for temporary fastening; (inf) a ride obtained from hitchhiking.–**hitcher** n.

hitchhike vt to travel by asking for free rides from motorists along the way.–**hitchhiker** n.

hither adv (formal) to or towards this place.

hitherto adv (formal) until this time.

hit man n a hired assassin.

HIV abbr = human immunodeficiency virus, the virus that causes Aids.

hive n a shelter for a colony of bees; a beehive; the bees of a hive; a crowd of busy people; a place of great activity. * vt to gather (bees) into a hive. * vi to enter a hive; (with **off**) to separate from a group.

hives n (used as sing or pl) a rash on the skin often caused by an allergy; nettle rash.

hiya interj an exclamation of greeting.

hoard n an accumulation of food, money, etc, stored away for future use. * vti to accumulate and store away.–**hoarder** n.

hoarfrost n a covering of minute ice crystals.–also **white frost**.

hoarse adj (voice) rough, as from a cold; (person) having a hoarse voice.–**hoarsely** adv.–**hoarseness** n.

hoary adj (**hoarier, hoariest**) white or gray with age; having whitish or grayish hairs; (joke, etc) ancient, hackneyed.–**hoarily** adv.

hoax n a deception; a practical joke. * vt to deceive by a hoax.–**hoaxer** n.

hob n a ledge near a fireplace for keeping kettles, etc hot; a flat surface on a cooker incorporating hot plates or burners.

hobble vi to walk unsteadily, to limp. * vt to fasten the legs of (horses, etc) loosely together to prevent straying. * n a limp; a rope, etc, used to hobble a horse.–**hobbler** n.

hobby n (pl **hobbies**) a spare-time activity carried out for personal amusement.–**hobbyist** n.

hobgoblin n a mischievous goblin.

hobnail n a short nail with a wide head, used on the soles of heavy shoes.–**hobnailed** adj.

hobnob vi (**hobnobbing, hobnobbed**) to spend time with in a friendly manner.

hobo n (pl **hoboes, hobos**) a migrant laborer; a tramp.–**hoboism** n.

hockey n an outdoor game played by two teams of 11 players with a ball and clubs curved at one end (–also **field hockey**); ice hockey.

hod n a trough on a pole for carrying bricks or mortar on the shoulder; a coal scuttle.

hodgepodge n a jumble.

hoe n a long-handled tool for weeding, loosening the earth, etc. * vti (**hoeing, hoed**) to dig, weed, till, etc, with a hoe.

hog n a domesticated male pig raised for its meat; (inf) a selfish, greedy, or filthy person. * vt (**hogging, hogged**) to take more than one's due; to hoard greedily.

hogwash n swill fed to pigs; rubbishy or nonsensical writing or speech.

hoist vt to raise aloft, esp with a pulley, crane, etc. * n a hoisting; an apparatus for lifting to a higher flower; a lift, elevator.–**hoister** n.

hold[1] vb (**holding, held**) vt to take and keep in one's possession; to grasp; to maintain in a certain position or condition; to retain; to contain; to own, to occupy; to support, sustain; to remain firm; to carry on, as a meeting; to regard; to believe, to consider; to bear or carry oneself; (with **back**) to withhold; to restrain; (with **down**) to restrain; (inf) to manage to retain one's job, etc; (with **forth**) to offer (eg an inducement); (with **off**) to keep apart; (with **up**) to delay; to hinder; to commit an armed robbery. * vi to go on being firm, loyal, etc; to remain unbroken or unyielding; to be true or valid; to continue; (with **back**) to refrain; (with **forth**) to speak at length; (with **off**) to wait; to refrain; (with **on**) to maintain a grip on; to persist; (inf) to keep a telephone line open. * n the act or manner of holding; grip; a dominating force on a person.–**holdable** adj.–**holder** n.

hold[2] n the storage space in a ship or aircraft used for cargo.

hold-up n a delay; an armed robbery.

hole n a hollow place; a cavity; a pit; an animal's burrow; an aperture; a perforation; a small, squalid, dingy place; (inf) a difficult situation; (golf) a small cavity into which the ball is hit; the tee, the fairway, etc leading to this. * vti to make a hole in (something); to drive into a hole; (with **up**) to hibernate; (inf) to hide oneself.–**holey** adj.

holiday n (esp Brit) a period away from work, school, etc for travel, rest or recreation, a vacation; a day of freedom from work, etc, esp one set aside by law. * vi to spend a holiday.–also **vacation**.

holiday-maker n a vacationer.

holiness n sanctity; (with cap and poss pron) the title of the Pope.

hollow adj having a cavity within or below; recessed, concave; empty or worthless. * n a hole, cavity; a depression, a valley.* vti to make or become hollow.–**hollowly** adv.–**hollowness** n.

hollow-eyed adj with the eyes deep-set or sunken from tiredness, etc.

holly n (pl **hollies**) an evergreen shrub with prickly leaves and red berries.

hollyhock n a tall-stemmed plant with spikes of large flowers.

holocaust n a great destruction of life, esp by fire; (with cap and **the**) the mass extermination of European Jews by the Nazis 1939–45.–**holocaustal, holocaustic** adj.

hologram n an image made without the use of a lens on photographic film by means of interference between two parts of a laser beam, the result appearing as a meaningless pattern until suitably illuminated, when it shows as a three-dimensional image.

holster n a leather case attached to a belt for a pistol.–**holstered** adj.

holy adj (**holier, holiest**) dedicated to religious use; without sin; deserving reverence. * n (pl **holies**) a holy place, innermost shrine.

homage n a public demonstration of respect or honor towards someone or something.

home n the place where one lives; the city, etc where one was born or reared; a place thought of as home; a household and its affairs; an institution for the aged, orphans, etc. * adj of one's home or country; domestic. * adv at, to, or in the direction of home; to the point aimed at. * vi (birds) to return home; to be guided onto a target; to head for a destination; to send or go home.

home-grown adj grown or produced at home or nearby; characteristic of a particular locale.

homeland n the country where a person was born.

homely adj (**homelier, homeliest**) simple, everyday; crude; not good-looking, plain.–**homeliness** n.

homeopathy n the system of treating disease by small quantities of drugs that cause symptoms similar to those of the disease.–**homeopath, homeopathist** n.–**homeopathic** adj.–**homeopathically** adv.

homer n (baseball) a home run.

home run n (baseball) a hit that allows the batter to touch all bases and score a run.

homesick adj longing for home.–**homesickness** n.

homestead n a farmhouse with land and buildings.–**homesteader** n

home stretch, home straight n the part of a race track between the last turn and the finish line; the final part.

homeward adj going towards home. * adv homewards.

homewards adv towards home.

homework n work, esp piecework, done at home; schoolwork to be done outside the classroom; preliminary study for a project.

homey adj (**homier, homiest**) cosy, home-like.–**homeyness** n.

homicide n the killing of a person by another; a person who kills another.–**homicidal** adj.–**homicidally** adv.

homily n (pl **homilies**) a sermon; moralizing talk or writing.–**homilist** n.

hominy (**grits**) n ground maize boiled in water to make a thin porridge.

homo n any member of the genus Homo that includes modern man.

homogeneous adj composed of parts that are of identical or a similar kind or nature; of uniform structure.–**homogeneity, homogeneousness** n.

homologous adj corresponding in relative position, structure, and descent.

homophobia n fear and hatred of homosexuals; persecution of homosexuals.–**homophobe** n.–**homophobic** adj.

Homo sapiens n the species designating mankind.

homosexual adj sexually attracted towards a person of the same sex. * n a homosexual person.–**homosexuality** n.–**homosexually** adv.

hone n a stone for sharpening cutting tools. * vt to sharpen (as if) on a hone.

honest adj truthful; trustworthy; sincere or genuine; gained by fair means; frank, open.–**honestness** n.

honestly adv in an honest manner; really.

honesty n (pl **honesties**) the quality of being honest.

honey n (pl **honeys**) a sweet sticky yellowish substance that bees make as food from the nectar of flowers; sweetness; its color; (inf) darling. * adj of, resembling honey; much loved.

honeybee n the common bee of the genus that produces honey.

honeycomb n the structure of six-sided wax cells made by bees to hold their honey, eggs, etc; anything arranged like this. * vt to fill with holes like a honeycomb.

honeydew n a sugary deposit on leaves secreted by aphids; a variety of melon with yellowish skin and pale green flesh.–**honeydewed** adj

honeyed, honied adj flattering; of, containing, or resembling honey.–**honeyedly, honiedly** adv.

honeymoon n the vacation spent together by a newly married couple.–also vi.–**honeymooner** n.

honeysuckle n a climbing shrub with small fragrant flowers.

honk n (a sound resembling) the call of the wild goose; the sound made by an old-fashioned motor horn. * vti to cry like a goose; to sound (a motor horn); (sl) to be sick.

honor, honour n high regard or respect; glory; fame; good reputation; integrity; chastity; high rank; distinction; (with cap) the title of certain officials, as judges; cards of the highest value in certain card games. * *vt* to respect greatly; to do or give something in honor of; to accept and pay (a check when due, etc).–**honorer, honourer** *n*.

honorable, honourable *adj* worthy of being honored; honest; upright; bringing honor.–**honorably, honourably** *adv*.

honorary *adj* given as an honor; (*office*) voluntary, unpaid.

hood[1] *n* a loose covering to protect the head and back of the neck; any hood-like thing as the (folding) top of a car, etc; the hinged metal covering over an automobile engine–also **bonnet**.

hood[2] *n* (*inf*) a hoodlum.

hoodlum *n* a gangster; a young hooligan.–**hoodlumism** *n*.

hoodwink *vt* to mislead by trickery.–**hoodwinker** *n*.

hoof *n* (*pl* **hoofs, hooves**) the horny covering on the ends of the feet of certain animals, as horses, cows, etc.

hook *n* a piece of bent or curved metal to catch or hold anything; a fishhook; something shaped like a hook; a strike, blow, etc, in which a curving motion is involved. * *vt* to seize, fasten, hold, as with a hook.

hookah *n* an oriental tobacco-pipe with a long tube connected to a container of water, which cools the smoke as it is drawn through.

hooked *adj* shaped like a hook; (*sl*) addicted.–**hookedness** *n*.

hooky *n* truancy from school.

hooligan *n* a lawless young person.–**hooliganism** *n*.

hoop *n* a circular band of metal or wood; an iron band for holding together the staves of barrels; anything like this, as a child's toy or ring in a hoop skirt. * *vt* to bind (as if) with hoops.–**hooped** *adj*.

hooray, hoorah see **hurrah**.

hoot *n* the sound that an owl makes; a similar sound, as made by a train whistle; a shout of scorn; (*inf*) laughter; (*inf*) an amusing person or thing. * *vi* to utter a hoot; to blow a whistle, etc. * *vt* to express (scorn) of (someone) by hooting.–**hooter** *n*.

hooves see **hoof**.

hop[1] *vi* (**hopping, hopped**) to jump up on one leg; to leap with all feet at once, as a frog, etc; (*inf*) to make a quick trip. * *n* a hopping movement; (*inf*) an informal dance; a trip, esp in an aircraft.

hop[2] *n* a climbing plant with small cone-shaped flowers; (*pl*) the dried ripe cones, used for flavoring beer.

hope *n* a feeling that what is wanted will happen; the object of this; a person or thing on which one may base some hope. * *vt* to want and expect. * *vi* to have hope (for).–**hoper** *n*.

hopeful *adj* filled with hope; inspiring hope or promise of success. * *n* a person who hopes to or looks likely to be a success.–**hopefulness** *n*.

hopefully *adv* in a hopeful manner; it is hoped.

hopeless *adj* without hope; offering no grounds for hope or promise of success; impossible to solve; (*inf*) incompetent.–**hopelessly** *adv*.–**hopelessness** *n*.

hopscotch *n* a children's game in which the players hop through a sequence of squares drawn on the ground.

horde *n* a crowd or throng; a swarm.

horizon *n* the apparent line along which the earth and sky meet; the limit of a person's knowledge, interest, etc.

horizontal *adj* level; parallel to the plane of the horizon.–**horizontally** *adv*.–**horizontalness** *n*.

hormone *n* a product of living cells formed in one part of the organism and carried to another part, where it takes effect; a synthetic compound having the same purpose.–**hormonal** *adj*.

horn *n* a bony outgrowth on the head of certain animals; the hard substance of which this is made; any projection like a horn; a wind instrument, esp the French horn or trumpet; a device to sound a warning. * *vt* to wound with a horn; (*with* **in**) to intrude.

horned *adj* having horns.

hornet *n* a large wasp with a severe sting.

hornpipe *n* a lively dance, formerly associated with British sailors; the music for such a dance; an obsolete wind instrument

horology *n* the science of measuring time; the art of making clocks, watches, etc.–**horologic, horological** *adj*.–**horologist, horologer** *n*.

horoscope *n* a chart of the zodiacal signs and positions of planets, etc, by which astrologers profess to predict future events, esp in the life of an individual.

horrendous *adj* horrific; (*inf*) disagreeable.–**horrendously** *adv*.

horrible *adj* arousing horror; (*inf*) very bad, unpleasant, etc.–**horribleness** *n*.–**horribly** *adv*.

horrid *adj* terrible; horrible.–**horridly** *adv*.–**horridness** *n*. arousing horror; horrible.

horrify *vt* (**horrifying, horrified**) to fill with horror; to shock.–**horrification** *n*.–**horrifyingly** *adv*.–**horrific** *adj*.–**horrifically** *adv*.

horror *n* the strong feeling caused by something frightful or shocking; strong dislike; a person or thing inspiring horror. * *adj* (*movie, story, etc*) designed to frighten.

hors d'oeuvre *n* (*pl* **hors d'oeuvre, hors d'oeuvres**) an appetizer served at the beginning of a meal.

horse *n* a four-legged, solid-hoofed herbivorous mammal with a flowing mane and a tail, domesticated for carrying loads or riders, etc; cavalry; a vaulting horse; a frame with legs to support something.

horsehair *n* hair from the mane or the tail of a horse, used for padding, etc.

horseman *n* (*pl* **horsemen**) a person skilled in the riding or care of horses.–**horsemanship** *n*.

horseplay *n* rough, boisterous fun.

horsepower *n* (*pl* **horsepower**) a unit for measuring the power of engines, etc, equal to 746 watts or 33,000 foot-pounds per minute.

horseradish *n* a tall herb of the mustard family; a sauce or relish made with its pungent root.

horseshoe *n* a flat U-shaped, protective metal plate nailed to a horse's hoof; anything shaped like this.

horsewoman *n* (*pl* **horsewomen**) a woman skilled at riding.

horsy, horsey *adj* (**horsier, horsiest**) of or resembling a horse; preoccupied with horses, horse racing, etc.–**horsily** *adv*.–**horsiness** *n*.

horticulture *n* the art or science of growing flowers, fruits, and vegetables.–**horticultural** *adj*.–**horticulturally** *adv*.–**horticulturist** *n*.

hosanna, hosannah *interj* an exclamation of praise to God. * *n* the cry of hosanna; a shout of praise.

hose[1] *n* a flexible tube used to convey fluids. * *vt* to spray with a hose.

hose[2] *n* (*pl* **hose, hosen**) stockings, socks collectively.

hospice *n* a home for the care of the terminally ill; a place of rest and shelter for travelers.

hospitable *adj* offering a generous welcome to guests or strangers; sociable.–**hospitableness** *n*.–**hospitably** *adv*.

hospital *n* an institution where the sick or injured are given medical treatment.

hospitality *n* (*pl* **hospitalities**) the act, practice, or quality of being hospitable.

hospitalize *vt* to place in a hospital.–**hospitalization** *n*.

host[1] *n* a person who receives or entertains a stranger or guest at his house; an animal or plant on or in which another lives; a compere on a television or radio program. * *vti* to act as a host (to a party, television program, etc).

host[2] *n* a very large number of people or things.

host[3] *n* the wafer of bread used in the Eucharist or Holy Communion.

hostage *n* a person given or kept as security until certain conditions are met.

hostel *n* a lodging place for the homeless, travelers, or other groups.–**hosteler, hosteller** *n*.–**hosteling, hostelling** *n*.

hostess n a woman acting as a host; a woman who entertains guests at a nightclub, etc.

hostile adj of or being an enemy; unfriendly.–**hostilely** adv.

hostility n (pl **hostilities**) enmity, antagonism; (pl) deliberate acts of warfare.

hot adj (**hotter, hottest**) of high temperature; very warm; giving or feeling heat; causing a burning sensation on the tongue; full of intense feeling; following closely; electrically charged; (inf) recent, new; (inf) radioactive; (inf) stolen. * adv in a hot manner.–**hotly** adv.–**hotness** n.

hot air n (sl) empty talk.

hotbed n a bed of heated earth enclosed by low walls and covered by glass for forcing plants; ideal conditions for the growth of something, esp evil.

hot-blooded adj easily excited.–**hot-bloodedness** n.

hot dog n a sausage, esp a frankfurter, served in a long soft roll.

hotel n a commercial establishment providing lodging and meals for travelers, etc.

hotelier n the owner or manager of a hotel.

hothead n an impetuous person.–**hot-headed** adj.–**hot-headedly** adv.–**hot-headedness** n.

hothouse n a heated greenhouse for raising plants; an environment that encourages rapid growth.

hot line n a direct telephone link between heads of government for emergency use.

hotplate n a heated surface for cooking or keeping food warm; a small portable heating device.

hot seat n (inf) a dangerous position; (sl) the electric chair.

hound n a dog used in hunting. * vt to hunt or chase as with hounds; to urge on by harassment.–**hounder** n.

hour n a period of 60 minutes, a 24th part of a day; the time for a specific activity; the time; a special point in time; the distance covered in an hour; (pl) the customary period for work, etc.

hourglass n an instrument for measuring time by trickling sand in a specified period.

hourly adj occurring every hour; done during an hour; frequent. * adv at every hour; frequently.

house n a building to live in, esp by one person or family; a household; a family or dynasty including relatives, ancestors and descendants; the audience in a theater; a business firm; a legislative assembly; house music. * vt to provide accommodation or storage for; to cover, encase.

house arrest n detention in one's own house, as opposed to prison.

houseboat n a boat furnished and used as a home.

housebound adj confined to the house through illness, injury, etc.

housefly n (pl **houseflies**) a common fly found in houses, which is attracted by food and can spread disease.

household n all those people living together in the same house. * adj pertaining to running a house and family; domestic; familiar.

householder n the person who owns or rents a house.

housekeeper n a person who runs a home, esp one hired to do so.

housekeeping n the daily running of a household; (inf) money used for domestic expenses; routine maintenance of equipment, records, etc in an organization.

housemaid n a female servant employed to do housework.

houseman n (pl **housemen**) an intern.

house plant n an indoor plant.

house warming n a party given to celebrate moving into a new house.

housewife n (pl **housewives**) the woman who keeps house.–**housewifely** adj.–**housewifeliness** n.–**housewifery** n.

housework n the cooking, cleaning, etc, involved in running a home.–**houseworker** n.

housing n houses collectively; the provision of accommodation; a casing enclosing a piece of machinery, etc; a slot or groove in a piece of wood, etc, to receive an insertion.

hove see **heave**.

hovel n a small miserable dwelling. * vt (**hoveling, hoveled** or **hovelling, hovelled**) to shelter in a hovel.

hover vi (bird, etc) to hang in the air stationary; to hang about, to linger.–**hoverer** n.–**hoveringly** adv.

how adv in what way or manner; by what means; to what extent; in what condition.

how do you do interj a formal greeting, esp when meeting for the first time.

however adv in whatever way or degree; still, nevertheless.

howitzer n a short cannon that fires shells at a steep trajectory.

howl vi to utter the long, wailing cry of wolves, dogs, etc; to utter a similar cry of anger, pain, etc; to shout or laugh in pain, amusement, etc. * vt to utter with a howl; to drive by howling. * n the wailing cry of a wolf, dog, etc; any similar sound.

HQ abbr = headquarters.

hr abbr = hour.

hub n the center part of a wheel; a centre of activity. **hubbub** n a confused noise of many voices; an uproar.

hubcap n a metal cap that fits over the hub of a car wheel.

hubris n arrogance, presumption.–**hubristic** adj.

huckleberry n (pl **huckleberries**) a North American shrub with dark-blue berries; the fruit of this plant.

huddle vti to crowd together in a confined space; to curl (oneself) up. * n a confused crowd or heap.–**huddler** n.

hue n color; a particular shade or tint of a color.–**hued** adj.

huff n a state of smoldering resentment. * vi to blow; to puff.

huffy adj (**huffier, huffiest**) disgruntled, moody.–**huffily** adv.–**huffiness** n.

hug vb (**hugging, hugged**) vt to hold or squeeze tightly with the arms; to cling to; to keep close to. * vi to embrace one another. * n a strong embrace.–**huggable** adj.–**hugger** n.

huge adj very large, enormous.–**hugely** adv.–**hugeness** n.

hulk n the body of a ship, esp if old and dismantled; a large, clumsy person or thing.

hulking, hulky adj unwieldy, bulky.

hull n the outer covering of a fruit or seed; the framework of a ship. * vt to remove the hulls of; to pierce the hull of (a ship, etc).–**huller** n.–**hull-less** adj.

hullabaloo, hullaballoo n (pl **hullabaloos, hullaballoos**) a loud commotion, uproar.

hullo see **hello**.

hum vb (**humming, hummed**) vi to make a low continuous vibrating sound; to hesitate in speaking and utter an inarticulate sound; (inf) to be lively, busy. * vt to sing with closed lips. * n a humming sound; a murmur.

human adj of or relating to human beings; having the qualities of humans as opposed to animals; kind, considerate. * n a human being.–**humanness** n.

human being n a member of the races of Homo sapiens; a man, woman or child.

humane adj kind, compassionate, merciful.–**humanely** adv.–**humaneness** n.

human immunodeficiency virus, HIV n either of two strains of a virus that inhibits the body from developing resistance to diseases and can lead to the development of AIDS.

humanism n belief in the promotion of human interests, intellect and welfare.

humanist n one versed in the knowledge of human nature; a student of the humanities.–**humanistic** adj.

humanitarian adj concerned with promoting human welfare. * n a humanitarian person.–**humanitarianism** n.–**humanitarianist** n.

humanity n (pl **humanities**) the human race; the state or quality of being human or humane; philanthropy; kindness; (pl) the study of literature and the arts, as opposed to the sciences.

humankind n the human species; humanity.

humanly adv in a way characteristic of humans; within the limits of human capabilities.

humanoid adj resembling a human being in appearance or character. * n a humanoid thing.

humble adj having a low estimation of one's abilities; modest, unpretentious; servile. * vt to lower in condition or rank; to humiliate.–**humbleness** n.–**humbly** adv.

humbug n fraud hoax.

humdrum adj dull, ordinary, boring.–**humdrumness** n.

humerus n (pl **humeri**) the bone extending from the shoulder to the elbow in humans.–**humeral** adj.

humid adj (air) moist, damp.–**humidly** adv.–**humidness** n.

humidifier n a device employed to increase the amount of water vapor in a room.

humidify vt (**humidifying, humidified**) to make humid.–**humidification** n.

humidity n (a measure of the amount of) dampness in the air.

humiliate vt to cause to feel humble; to lower the pride or dignity of.–**humiliatingly** adv.–**humiliator** n.–**humiliatory** adj.

humiliation n the act of humiliation; the state of being humiliated; mortification; abasement.

humility n (pl **humilities**) the state of being humble; modesty.

hummingbird n a tiny brightly coloured tropical bird with wings that vibrate rapidly, making a humming sound.

hummock n a hillock.–**hummocky** adj.

humor, humour n the ability to appreciate or express what is funny, amusing, etc; the expression of this; temperament, disposition; state of mind. * vt to indulge; to gratify by conforming to the wishes of.

humorist n a person who writes or speaks in a humorous manner.–**humoristic** adj.

humorless, humourless adj done or said without humor; lacking a sense of humor.–**humorlessness, humourlessness** n.

humorous adj funny, amusing; causing laughter.–**humorously** adv.–**humorousness** n.

hump n a rounded protuberance; a fleshy lump on the back of an animal (as a camel or whale); a deformity causing curvature of the spine. * vt to hunch; to arch.

humpback n a hunchback.–**humpbacked** adj.

humph interj expressing annoyance.

hunch n a hump; (inf) an intuitive feeling. * vt to arch into a hump. * vi to move forward jerkily.

hunchback n a person with curvature of the spine.

hundred adj, n (pl **hundreds, hundred**) ten times ten; the symbol for this (100, C, c); the hundredth in a series or set.

hundredfold adj, adv one hundred times as great or many.

hundredth adj the last of a hundred.

hundredweight n (pl **hundredweight, hundredweights**) a unit of weight, equal to 110 pounds in US and 112 pounds in the UK.

hung see **hang.hunger** n (a feeling of weakness or emptiness from) a need for food; a strong desire. * vi to feel hunger; to have a strong desire (for).

hunger strike n refusal to take food as a protest.

hung-over adj (sl) suffering from a hangover.

hungry adj (**hungrier, hungriest**) desiring food; craving for something; greedy.–**hungrily** adv.–**hungriness** n.

hunk n (inf) a large piece, lump, etc; (sl) a sexually attractive man.–**hunky** adj.

hunker vi to squat, crouch down. * npl the haunches or buttocks.

hunt vti to seek out to kill or capture (game) for food or sport; to search (for); to chase. * n a chase; a search; a party organized for hunting.

hunter n a person who hunts; a horse used in hunting.–**huntress** nf.

hunting n the art or practice of one who hunts; a pursuit; a search.

hurdle n a portable frame of bars for temporary fences or for jumping over by horses or runners; an obstacle. (pl) a race over hurdles.–**hurdler** n.

hurl vt to throw violently; to utter vehemently. * n a violent throw; a ride in a car.–**hurler** n.

hurrah interj an exclamation of approval or joy.–also **hooray, hoorah.**

hurricane n a violent tropical cyclone with winds of at least 74 miles (119 kilometers) per hour.

hurried adj performed with great haste.–**hurriedly** adv.–**hurriedness** n.

hurry n (pl **hurries**) rush; urgency; eagerness to do, go, etc. * vb (**hurrying, hurried**) vt to cause to move or happen more quickly. * vi to move or act with haste.–**hurryingly** adv.

hurt vb (**hurting, hurt**) vt to cause physical pain to; to injure, damage; to offend. * vi to feel pain; to cause pain.

hurtful adj causing hurt, mischievous.–**hurtfully** adv.–**hurtfulness** n.

hurtle vti to move or throw with great speed and force.

husband n a man to whom a woman is married. * vt to conserve; to manage economically.–**husbander** n.

husbandry n management of resources; farming.

hush vti to make or become silent. * n a silence or calm.

hush-hush adj (inf) secret.

husk n the dry covering of certain fruits and seeds; any dry, rough, or useless covering. * vt to strip the husk from.

husky[1] adj (**huskier, huskiest**) (voice) hoarse; rough-sounding; hefty, strong.–**huskily** adv.–**huskiness** n.

husky[2] n (pl **huskies**) an Arctic sled dog.

hussy n (pl **hussies**) a cheeky woman; a promiscuous woman.

hustle vt to jostle or push roughly or hurriedly; to force hurriedly; (sl) to obtain by rough or illegal means. * vi to move hurriedly. * n an instance of hustling.–**hustler** n.

hut n a very plain or crude little house or cabin.

hutch n a pen or coop for small animals; a hut.

hyacinth n a plant of the lily family with spikes of bell-shaped flowers; the orange gemstone jacinth; a light violet to moderate purple.–**hyacinthine** adj.

hybrid n the offspring of two plants or animals of different species; a mongrel. * adj crossbred.–**hybridism** n.–**hybridity** n.

hybridize vti to produce hybrids; to interbreed.–**hybridizable** adj.–**hybridization** n.–**hybridizer** n.

hydrant n a large pipe with a valve for drawing water from a water main; a fireplug.

hydrate n a chemical compound of water with some other substance. * vt to (cause to) combine with or absorb water.–**hydration** n.–**hydrator** n.

hydraulic adj operated by water or other liquid, esp by moving through pipes under pressure; of hydraulics.–**hydraulically** adv.

hydraulics n sing the science dealing with the mechanical properties of liquids, as water, and their application in engineering.

hydrocarbon n any organic compound containing only hydrogen and carbon.

hydrochloric acid n a strong, highly corrosive acid that is a solution of the gas hydrogen chloride in water.

hydrochloric adj composed of hydrogen and chlorine.

hydrodynamics n sing the science of the mechanical properties of fluids.–**hydrodynamic** adj.–**hydrodynamically** adv.

hydroelectricity n electricity generated by water power.–**hydroelectric** adj.

hydrogen n a flammable, colorless, odorless, tasteless, gaseous chemical element, the lightest substance known.

hydrogenate vt to combine with or treat with hydrogen.–**hydrogenation** n.–**hydrogenator** n.

hydrogen bomb n a powerful bomb that produces explosive energy through the fusion of hydrogen nuclei.

hydrophobia n a morbid fear of water; rabies.–**hydrophobic** adj.

hydroplane n a light motor boat that skims through the water at high speed with its hull raised out of the water; a fin that directs the vertical movement of a submarine; an attachment to an aircraft that enables it to glide along the surface of water. * vi (of a boat) to rise out of the water in the manner of a hydroplane.

hydroponics n sing the growing of plants in chemical nutrients without soil.–**hydroponically** adv.

hydrotherapy n (pl **hydrotherapies**) the treatment of certain diseases and physical conditions by the external application of water.–**hydrotherapist** n.

hyena n a nocturnal, carnivorous, scavenging mammal like a wolf.–also **hyaena**.

hygiene n the principles and practice of health and cleanliness.–**hygienic** adj.–**hygienically** adv.

hygienist n a person skilled in the practice of hygiene.

hymen n the mucous membrane partly closing the vaginal orifice–**hymenal** adj.

hymn n a song of praise to God or other object of worship.

hymnal n a hymn book.

hymn book n a book of hymns.

hype n (sl) deception; aggressive or extravagant publicity. * vt to publicize or promote a product, etc in this manner.

hyped-up adj aggressively publicized; (sl) stimulated as if by injection of a drug.

hyperactive adj abnormally active.–**hyperactivity** n.

hyperbole n a figure of speech using absurd exaggeration.–hyperbolic, **hyperbolical** adj.

hypercritical adj excessively critical.–**hypercritically** adv.–**hypercriticism** n.

hypersensitive adj extremely vulnerable; abnormally sensitive to a drug, pollen, etc.–**hypersensitivity** n.

hypertension n abnormally high blood pressure.–**hypertensive** adj.

hyphen n a punctuation mark (-) used to join two syllables or words, or to divide words into parts.

hyphenate vt to join by a hyphen.–**hyphenation** n.

hypnosis n (pl **hypnoses**) a relaxed state resembling sleep in which the mind responds to external suggestion.

hypnotherapy n the use of hypnosis in treatment of emotional and psychological disorders.

hypnotic adj of or producing hypnosis. * n a drug causing sleep.–**hypnotically** adv.

hypnotism n the act of inducing hypnosis; the study and use of hypnosis.–**hypnotist** n.

hypnotize vt to put in a state of hypnosis; to fascinate.–**hypnotizer** n.

hypochondria n chronic anxiety about health, often with imaginary illnesses.

hypochondriac n a person suffering from hypochondria. * adj pertaining to or affected with hypochondria.–**hypochondriacally** adv.

hypocrisy n (pl **hypocrisies**) falsely pretending to possess virtues, beliefs, etc; an example of this.–**hypocritical** adj.–**hypocritically** adv.

hypocrite n a person who pretends to be what he or she is not.

hypodermic adj injected under the skin. * n a hypodermic needle, syringe or injection.

hypodermic syringe n a syringe with a hollow (hypodermic) needle through which blood samples can be drawn.

hypotenuse n the side opposite to the right angle in a right-angled triangle .

hypothermia n an abnormally low body temperature.

hypothesis n (pl **hypotheses**) something assumed for the purpose of argument; a theory to explain some fact that may or may not prove to be true; supposition; conjecture.–**hypothetical** adj.–**hypothetically** adv.

hypothesize vti to form or assume as a hypothesis.

hysterectomy n (pl **hysterectomies**) surgical removal of the womb.

hysteria n a mental disorder marked by excitability, anxiety, imaginary organic disorders, etc; frenzied emotion or excitement.

hysterical adj caused by hysteria; suffering from hysteria; (inf) extremely funny.–**hysterically** adv.

hysterics n fits of hysteria; (inf) uncontrollable laughter.

I[1] pron the person who is speaking or writing, used in referring to himself or herself.

I[2] (chem symbol) iodine.

ice n water frozen solid; a sheet of this; a portion of ice cream or water ice; (sl) diamonds; * vti (often with **up** or **over**) to freeze; to cool with ice; to cover with icing.

ice age n a period when much of the earth's surface was covered in glaciers.

iceberg n a great mass of mostly submerged ice floating in the sea.

icebox n a compartment in a refrigerator for making ice.

icecap n a mass of slowly spreading glacial ice.

ice cream n a sweet frozen food, made from flavored milk or cream.

ice hockey n an indoor or outdoor hockey game played on ice by two teams of six skaters with curved sticks and a flat disk called a puck.

ice pack n a cloth or small bag filled with crushed ice for soothing sores and swellings on the body.

ice pick n a pointed awl with a handle for chipping or breaking up ice.

ice skate n a boot with a steel blade fixed to the sole for skating on ice.–also vi.–**ice skater** n.

icicle n a hanging tapering length of ice formed when dripping water freezes.–**icicled** adj.

icily adv in an icy manner, coldly.

icing n a semi-solid sugary mixture used to cover cakes, etc.–also **frosting**.

icon n an image; (Eastern Church) a sacred image, usu on a wooden panel.–also **ikon.**–**iconic, iconical** adj.

iconoclast n a person who attacks revered or traditional beliefs, opinions, etc.–**iconoclasm** n.–**iconoclastic** adj.–**iconoclastically** adv.

icy adj (**icier, iciest**) full of, made of, or covered with ice; slippery or very cold; cold in manner.

id n (psychoanal) the primitive psychological instincts in the unconscious which are the source of psychic activity.

ID abbr = identification.

I'd = I had; I should; I would.

ID card n an identity card.

idea n a mental impression of anything; a vague impression, notion; an opinion or belief; a scheme; a supposition; a person's conception of something; a significance or purpose.

ideal adj existing in the mind or as an idea; satisfying an ideal, perfect. * n the most perfect conception of anything; a person or thing regarded as perfect; a standard for attainment or imitation; an aim or principle.–**ideally** adv.–**idealness** n.

idealism n the pursuit of high ideals; the conception or representation of things in their ideal form as against their reality.–**idealist** n.–**idealistic** adj.–**idealistically** adv.

idealize vt to consider or represent as ideal.–**idealization** n.–**idealizer** n.

identical adj exactly the same; having the same origin.–**identically** adv.–**identicalness** n.

identifiable adj able to be identified.–**identifiableness** n.

identify vt (**identifying, identified**) to consider to be the same, equate; to establish the identity of; to associate closely; to regard (oneself) as similar to another.–**identification** n.

identity n (pl **identities**) the state of being exactly alike; the distinguishing characteristics of a person, personality; the state of being the same as a specified person or thing.

identity card n a card carrying personal details, a photograph, etc of an individual as carried by staff of an organization, journalists, etc.

ideology n (pl **ideologies**) the doctrines, beliefs or opinions of an individual, social class, political party, etc.–**ideological, ideologic** adj.

idiocy n (pl **idiocies**) mental deficiency; stupidity, imbecility; something stupid or foolish.

idiom n an accepted phrase or expression with a different meaning from the literal; the usual way in which the words of a language are used to express thought; the dialect of a people, region, etc; the characteristic style of a school of art, literature, etc–**idiomatic, idiomatical** adj.–**idiomatically** adv.

idiosyncrasy n (pl **idiosyncrasies**) a type of behavior or characteristic peculiar to a person or group; a quirk, eccentricity.–**idiosyncratic** adj.–**idiosyncratically** adv.

idiot n a severely mentally retarded adult; (inf) a foolish or stupid person.–**idiotic** adj.–**idiotically** adv.

idle adj not employed, unoccupied; not in use; averse to work; useless; worthless. * vt to waste or spend (time) in idleness. * vi to move slowly or aimlessly; (engine) to operate without transmitting power.–**idleness** n.–**idler** n.–**idly** adv.

idol n an image or object worshiped as a god; a person who is intensely loved, admired or honored.

idolatry n the worship of idols; excessive admiration or devotion.–**idolatrous** adj.–**idolater** n.

idolize vt to make an idol of, for worship; to love to excess.–**idolization** n.–**idolizer** n.

idyll, idyl n a short simple poem, usu evoking the romance and beauty of rural life; a romantic or picturesque event or scene; a romantic or pastoral musical composition.–**idyllic** adj.

i.e. abbr = that is (Latin id est).

if conj on condition that; in the event that; supposing that; even though; whenever; whether.

igloo n (pl **igloos**) an Eskimo house built of blocks of snow and ice.

igneous adj of fire; (rocks) produced by volcanic action or intense heat beneath the earth's surface.

ignite vti to set fire to; to catch fire; to burn or cause to burn.–**ignitable** adj.

ignition n an act or instance of igniting; the starting of an internal combustion engine; the mechanism that ignites an internal combustion engine.

ignoble adj dishonorable, despicable; base, of low birth.–**ignobly** adv.

ignominious adj bringing disgrace or shame; humiliating, degrading.–**ignominiously** adv.

ignoramus n (pl **ignoramuses**) an ignorant person.

ignorant adj lacking knowledge; uninformed, uneducated; resulting from or showing lack of knowledge.–**ignorance** n.–**ignorantly** adv.

ignore vt to disregard; to deliberately refuse to notice someone.–**ignorable** adj.–**ignorer** n.

iguana n any of a family of large lizards of tropical America.–**iguanian** adj, n.

ikon see **icon**.

ilk n a type or sort.

ill adj (**worse, worst**) not in good health; harmful; bad; hostile; faulty; unfavorable. * adv badly, wrongly; hardly, with difficulty. * n trouble; harm; evil.

I'll = I shall; I will.

ill-advised adj unwise.

illegal adj against the law.–**illegality** n.–**illegally** adv.

illegible adj impossible to read.–**illegibility, illegibleness** n.–**illegibly** adv.

illegitimate adj born of parents not married to each other; contrary to law, rules, or logic.–**illegitimacy, illegitimateness** n.–**illegitimately** adv.

illiberal adj narrow-minded; mean.–**illiberality, illiberalness** n.–**illiberally** adv.

illicit adj improper; unlawful.–**illicitly** adv.

illiterate adj uneducated, esp not knowing how to read or write. * n an illiterate person.–**illiteracy** n.–**illiterately** adv.

illness n a state of ill-health; sickness.

illogical adj not logical or reasonable.–**illogicality, illogicalness** n.–**illogically** adv.

ill-treat vt to treat unkindly, unfairly, etc.–**ill-treatment** n.

illuminate vt to give light to; to light up; to make clear; to inform; to decorate as with gold or lights.–**illumination** n.–**illuminative** adj.–**illuminator** n.

illumination n a supply of light; the act of illuminating; the state of being illuminated.

illusion n a false idea or conception; an unreal or misleading image or appearance.–**illusional, illusionary** adj.

illusionist n a magician or conjuror.–**illusionism** n.

illusory, illusive adj deceptive; based on illusion.–**illusorily** adv.–**illusoriness** n.

illustrate vt to explain, as by examples; to provide (books, etc) with explanatory pictures, charts, etc; to serve as an example.–**illustratable** adj.–**illustrative** adj.–**illustrator** n.

illustration n the act of illustrating; the state of being illustrated; an example that explains or corroborates; a picture or diagram in a book, etc.–**illustrational** adj.

illustrious adj distinguished, famous. –**illustriousness** n.

ill-will n antagonism, hostility.

I'm = I am.

image n a representation of a person or thing; the visual impression of something in a lens, mirror, etc; a copy; a likeness; a mental picture; the concept of a person, product, etc held by the public at large. * vt to make a representation of; to reflect; to imagine.

imagery n (pl **imageries**) the work of the imagination; mental pictures; figures of speech; images in general or collectively.

imaginable adj able to be imagined.–**imaginably** adv.

imaginary adj existing only in the imagination.–**imaginarily** adv.

imagination n the image-forming power of the mind, or the power of the mind that modifies the conceptions, esp the higher form of this power exercised in art and poetry; creative ability; resourcefulness in overcoming practical difficulties, etc.

imaginative adj having or showing imagination; produced by imagination.–**imaginatively** adv.

imagine vt to form a mental image of; to believe falsely; (inf) to suppose; to guess. * vi to employ the imagination.–**imaginer** n.

imbalance n a lack of balance, as in proportion, emphasis, etc.

imbecile n an adult with a mental age of a three- to eight-year-old child; an idiotic person. * adj stupid or foolish.

imbibe vti to drink, esp alcoholic liquor; to absorb mentally.–**imbiber** n.

imitate vt to try to follow as a pattern or model; to mimic humorously, impersonate; to copy, reproduce.–**imitator** n.

imitation n an act or instance of imitating; a copy; an act of mimicking or impersonation.–**imitational** adj.

immaculate adj spotless; flawless; pure, morally unblemished.–**immaculacy, immaculateness** n.–**immaculately** adv.

immaterial adj spiritual as opposed to physical; unimportant.–**immateriality** n.

immature adj not mature.–**immaturity** n.

immeasurable adj not able to be measured; immense, limitless.–**immeasurably** adv.

immediate adj acting or occurring without delay; next, nearest, without intervening agency; next in relationship; in close proximity, near to; directly concerning or touching a person or thing.–**immediacy, immediateness** n.

immediately adv without delay; directly; near, close by. * conj as soon as.

immemorial adj existing in the distant past, beyond the reach of memory.–**immemorially** adv.

immense adj very large in size or extent; limitless; (inf) excellent.–**immensely** adv.

immensity n (pl **immensities**) the character of being immense; immeasurableness; infinite space; vastness in extent or bulk.

immerse vt to plunge into a liquid; to absorb or engross; to baptize by total submergence.–**immersible** adj.–**immersion** n.

immigrant n a person who immigrates; a person recently settled in a country but not born there.

immigrate vi to come into a new country, esp to settle permanently.–**immigration** n.–**immigrator** n.–**immigratory** adj.

imminent adj about to happen; impending.–**imminence** n.–**imminently** adv.

immobile adj not able to be moved; motionless.–**immobility** n.

immobilize vt to make immobile.–**immobilization** n.

immoderate adj excessive, unrestrained.–**immoderately** adv.–**immoderation, immoderateness** n.

immodest adj lacking in modesty or decency.–**immodestly** adv.–**immodesty** n.

immoral adj against accepted standards of proper behavior; sexually degenerate; corrupt; wicked.–**immorally** adv.–**immorality** n.

immortal adj living for ever; enduring; having lasting fame. * n an immortal being or person; (pl) the gods of classical mythology.–**immortality** n.–**immortally** adv.

immortalize vt to render immortal; to bestow lasting fame upon.–**immortalization** n.

immovable adj firmly fixed; impassive, unyielding; (property) land, buildings, etc.–**immovability, immovableness** n.–**immovably** adv.

immune adj not susceptible to a specified disease through inoculation or natural resistance; conferring immunity; exempt from a certain obligation, tax, duty, etc.–**immunity** n.

immunize vt to make immune, esp against infection.–**immunization** n.

immutable adj not capable of change; unalterable.–**immutability, immutableness** n.–**immutably** adv.

imp n a mischievous child; a little devil.

impact n violent contact; a shocking effect; the force of a body colliding with another. * vt to force tightly together. * vi to hit with force.–**impaction** n.

impair vt to make worse, less, etc.–**impairer** n.–**impairment** n.

impala n (pl **impalas, impala**) a type of African antelope.

impale vt to fix on, or pierce through, with something pointed.–**impalement** n.–**impaler** n.

impalpable adj not able to be sensed by touch; difficult to apprehend or grasp with the mind.–**impalpability** n.–**impalpably** adv.

imparity n (pl **imparities**) inequality; disproportion; disparity.

impart vt to give, convey; to reveal, disclose.–**imparter** n.

impartial adj not favoring one side more than another, unbiased.–**impartiality, impartialness** n.–**impartially** adv.

impassable adj (roads, etc) incapable of being traveled through or over.–**impassability, impassableness** n.–**impassably** adv.

impasse n a situation from which there is no escape; a deadlock.

impassioned adj passionate; ardent.–**impassionedly** adv.

impassive adj not feeling or showing emotion; imperturbable.–**impassively** adv.–**impassiveness, impassivity** n.

impatient adj lacking patience; intolerant of delay, etc; restless.–**impatience** n.–**impatiently** adv.

impeach vt to question a person's honesty; to try (a public official) on a charge of wrongdoing.–**impeachable** adj.–**impeacher** n.–**impeachment** n.

impeccable adj without defect or error; faultless.–**impeccability** n.–**impeccably** adv.

impede vt to obstruct or hinder the progress of.–**impeder** n.–**impedingly** adv.

impediment n something that impedes; an obstruction; a physical defect, as a stammer that prevents fluency of speech.–**impedimental** adj.

impel vt (**impelling, impelled**) to urge or force into doing something; to propel.–**impeller** n.

impend vi to be imminent; to threaten.–**impending** adj.

impenetrable adj unable to be pierced or penetrated; incomprehensible; unable to be seen through.–**impenetrability** n.–**impenetrably** adv.

impenitent adj not sorry or feeling guilty; unrepentant.–**impenitence, impenitency** n.

imperative adj urgent, pressing; authoritative; obligatory; designating or of the mood of a verb that expresses a command, entreaty, etc. * n a command; (gram) the imperative mood of a verb.

imperceptible adj not able to be detected by the mind or senses; slight, minute, gradual.–**imperceptibility** n.–**imperceptibly** adv.

imperfect adj having faults, flaws, mistakes, etc; defective; incomplete.–**imperfection** n.

imperial adj of an empire, emperor, or empress; majestic; of great size or superior quality.–**imperially** adv.

imperialism n the policy of forming and maintaining an empire, as by subjugating territories, establishing colonies, etc.–**imperialist** n.–**imperialistic** adj.–**imperialistically** adv.

imperil vt (**imperiling, imperiled** or **imperilling, imperilled**) to put in peril, to endanger.

imperious adj tyrannical; arrogant.–**imperiously** adv

impermeable adj not allowing fluids to pass through; impervious.–**impermeability** n.

impersonal adj not referring to any particular person; cold, unfeeling; not existing as a person; (verb) occurring only in the third person singular, usu with "it" as subject.–**impersonally** adv.

impersonate vt to assume the role of another person as entertainment or for fraud.–**impersonation** n.–**impersonator** n.

impertinent adj impudent; insolent; irrelevant.–**impertinence** n.–**impertinently** adv.

imperturbable adj not easily disturbed; calm; impassive.–**imperturbability** n.–**imperturbably** adv.–**imperturbation** n.

impervious adj incapable of being penetrated, as by water; not readily receptive (to) or affected (by).

impetuous adj acting or done suddenly with impulsive energy.–**impetuosity** n.–**impetuously** adv.

impetus n (pl **impetuses**) the force with which a body moves against resistance; driving force or motive.

impinge vi (with **on, upon**) to have an impact; to encroach.–**impingement** n.–**impinger** n.

impious adj showing lack of reverence; wicked.–**impiously** adv.

impish adj of or like an imp.–**impishly** adv.–**impishness** n.

implacable adj not able to be appeased or pacified; inflexible, inexorable.–**implacability** n.–**implacably** adv.

implant vt to plant firmly; to fix (ideas, etc) firmly in the mind. * n something implanted in tissue surgically.–**implantation** n.–**implanter** n.

implausible adj not plausible.–**implausibility** n.–**implausibly** adv.

implement n something used in a given activity. * vt to carry out, put into effect.–**implemental** adj.–**implementation** n.–**implementer, implementor** n.

implicate vt to show to have a part, esp in a crime; to imply.

implication n an implicating or being implicated; that which is implied; an inference not expressed but understood; deduction.

implicit adj implied rather than stated explicitly; unquestioning, absolute.–**implicitly** adv.–**implicitness, implicity** n.

implode *vi* to collapse inwards.

implore *vt* to request earnestly; to plead, entreat.–**imploration** *n*.–**implorer** *n*.–**imploringly** *adv*.

imply *vt* (**implying, implied**) to hint, suggest indirectly; to indicate or involve as a consequence.

impolite *adj* not polite, rude.–**impolitely** *adv*.–**impoliteness** *n*.

imponderable *adj* not able to be weighed or measured. * *n* something difficult to measure or assess.–**imponderability** *n*.–**imponderably** *adv*.

import *vt* to bring (goods) in from a foreign country for sale or use; to mean; to signify. * *vi* to be of importance, to matter. * *n* something imported; meaning; importance.–**importable** *adj*.–**importer** *n*.

important *adj* having great significance or consequence; (*person*) having power, authority, etc.–**importance** *n*.–**importantly** *adv*.

importation *n* the act or business of importing; imported goods.

importune *vt* to ask urgently and repeatedly.–**importunate** *adj*.–**importunity** *n*.

impose *vt* to put (a burden, tax, punishment) on or upon; to force (oneself) on others. * *vi* (*with* **on** *or* **upon**) to take advantage of; to cheat or defraud.–**imposition** *n*.

imposing *adj* impressive because of size, appearance, dignity, etc.–**imposingly** *adv*.

impossible *adj* not capable of existing, being done, or happening; (*inf*) unendurable, outrageous.–**impossibly** *adv*.–**impossibility** *n*.

impostor, imposter *n* a person who acts fraudulently by impersonating another.

impotent *adj* lacking in necessary strength, powerless; (*man*) unable to engage in sexual intercourse.–**impotence, impotency** *n*.–**impotently** *adv*.

impound *vt* to take legal possession of; to shut up (an animal) in a pound.–**impoundage, impoundment** *n*.–**impounder** *n*.

impoverish *vt* to make poor; to deprive of strength.–**impoverishment** *n*.

impracticable *adj* not able to be carried out, not feasible.–**impracticability** *n*.

impractical *adj* not practical; not competent in practical skills.–**impracticality** *n*.

imprecise *adj* not precise; ill-defined.–**imprecisely** *adv*.–**imprecision** *n*.

impregnable *adj* secure against attack, unyielding.–**impregnability** *n*.–**impregnably** *adv*.

impregnate *vt* to cause to become pregnant, to fertilize; to saturate, soak (with); to imbue, pervade.–**impregnation** *n*.–**impregnator** *n*.

impresario *n* (*pl* **impresarios**) the manager of an opera, a concert series, etc.

impress *vt* to make a strong, usu favorable, impression on; to fix deeply in the mind; to stamp with a mark; to imprint. * *n* an imprint.

impression *n* the effect produced in the mind by an experience; a mark produced by imprinting; a vague idea, notion; the act of impressing or being impressed; a notable or strong influence on the mind or senses; the number of copies of a book printed at one go (*–also* **printing**); an impersonation or act of mimicry.–**impressional** *adj*.

impressionable *n* easily impressed or influenced.–**impressionability** *n*.–**impressionably** *adv*.

impressionism *n* painting, writing, etc in which objects are painted or described so as to reproduce only their general effect or impression without selection or elaboration of details.–**impressionist** *adj, n*.–**impressionistic** *adj*.

impressive *adj* tending to impress the mind or emotions; arousing wonder or admiration.–**impressiveness** *n*.

imprint *vt* to stamp or impress a mark on, etc; to fix firmly in the mind. * *n* a mark made by imprinting; a lasting effect.

imprison *vt* to put in a prison; to confine, as in a prison.–**imprisoner** *n*.–**imprisonment** *n*.

improbable *adj* unlikely to be true or to happen.–**improbability** *n*.–**improbably** *adv*.

impromptu *adj, adv* unrehearsed, unprepared. * *n* something impromptu, as a speech.

improper *adj* lacking propriety, indecent; incorrect; not suitable or appropriate.–**improperly** *adv*.

impropriety *n* (*pl* **improprieties**) the quality of being improper; indecency; an improper act, etc.

improve *vt* to make or become better.–**improvable** *adj*.–**improver** *n*.–**improvingly** *adv*.

improvement *n* the act of improving or being improved; an alteration that improves or adds to the value of something.

improvident *adj* lacking foresight or thrift; wanting care to provide for the future; careless.–**improvidence** *n*.

improvisation *n* the act of improvising; the act of composing poetry, music, etc, extemporaneously; an impromptu.–**improvisational** *adj*.

improvise *vti* to compose, perform, recite, etc without preparation; to make or do with whatever is at hand.–**improviser** *n*.

imprudent *adj* rash, lacking discretion; unwise.–**imprudence** *n*.–**imprudently** *adv*.

impudent *adj* disrespectfully bold; impertinent.–**impudence** *n*.–**impudently** *adv*.

impulse *n* a sudden push or thrust; a stimulus transmitted through a nerve or a muscle; a sudden instinctive urge to act.–**impulsive** *adj*.–**impulsively** *adv*.–**impulsiveness** *n*.

impunity *n* (*pl* **impunities**) exemption or freedom from punishment or harm.

impure *adj* unclean; adulterated.

impurity *n* (*pl* **impurities**) a being impure; an impure substance or constituent.

in. *abbr* = inch(es).

in *prep* inside; within; at; as contained by; during; at the end of; not beyond; affected by; being a member of; wearing; using; because of; into. * *adv* to or at a certain place; so as to be contained by a certain space, condition, etc; (*games*) batting, in play. * *adj* that is in power; inner; inside; gathered, counted, etc; (*inf*) currently smart, fashionable, etc.

inability *n* (*pl* **inabilities**) lack of ability.

inaccessible *adj* not accessible, unapproachable.–**inaccessibility** *n*.–**inaccessibly** *adv*.

inaccurate *adj* not accurate, imprecise.–**inaccuracy** *n*.–**inaccurately** *adv*.

inaction *n* idleness, inertia.

inactive *adj* not active.–**inactively** *adv*.–**inactivity** *n*.

inadequate *adj* not adequate; not capable.–**inadequacy** *n*.–**inadequately** *adv*.

inadmissible *adj* not admissible, esp as evidence.–**inadmissibility** *n*.–**inadmissibly** *adv*.

inadvertent *adj* not attentive or observant, careless; due to oversight.–**inadvertence, inadvertency** *n*.–**inadvertently** *adv*.

inadvisable *adj* not advisable; inexpedient.–**inadvisability** *n*.–**inadvisably** *adv*.

inane *adj* lacking sense, silly.–**inanely** *adv*.–**inanity** *n*.

inanimate *adj* not animate; showing no signs of life; dull.–**inanimately** *adv*.–**inanimateness, inanimation** *n*.

inapplicable *adj* not applicable.–**inapplicability** *n*.

inappropriate *adj* unsuitable.–**inappropriately** *adv*.–**inappropriateness** *n*.

inarticulate *adj* not expressed in words; incapable of being expressed in words; incapable of coherent or effective expression of ideas, feelings, etc.–**inarticulately** *adv*.

inattentive *adj* not attending; neglectful.–**inattention** *n*.

inaudible *adj* unable to be heard.–**inaudibility** *n*.–**inaudibly** *adv*.

inaugural adj of or pertaining to an inauguration. * n a speech made at an inauguration.

inaugurate vt to admit ceremonially into office; to open (a building, etc) formally to the public; to cause to begin, initiate.–**inauguration** n.–**inaugurator** n.

inauspicious adj ill-starred; unlucky; unfavorable; unfortunate.

inboard adv, adj towards the center or within an aircraft, ship, etc.

inborn adj present from birth; hereditary.

inbred adj innate; produced by inbreeding.

inbreed vti (**inbreeding, inbred**) to breed by continual mating of individuals of the same or closely related stocks.

in-built adj built in.

Inc. abbr = Incorporated.

incalculable adj beyond calculation; unpredictable.–**incalculability** n.–**incalculably** adv.

incandescent adj glowing or luminous with intense heat.–**incandescence** n.

incantation n words chanted in magic spells or rites.–**incantational, incantatory** adj.

incapable adj lacking capability; not able or fit to perform an activity.–**incapability** n.–**incapably** adv.

incapacitate vt to weaken, to disable; to make ineligible.–**incapacitation** n.

incapacity n (pl **incapacities**) lack of power or strength, inability; ineligibility.

incarcerate vt to put in prison, to confine.–**incarceration** n.–**incarcerator** n.

incarnate adj endowed with a human body; personified. * vt to give bodily form to; to be the type or embodiment of.–**incarnation** n.

incendiary adj pertaining to arson; (bomb) designed to start fires; tending to stir up or inflame. * n (pl **incendiaries**) a person that sets fire to a building, etc maliciously, an arsonist; an incendiary substance (as in a bomb); a person who stirs up violence, etc.

incense[1] vt to make extremely angry.

incense[2] n a substance that gives off a fragrant odor when burned; the fumes so produced; any pleasant odor.

incentive n a stimulus; a motive. * adj serving as a stimulus to action.

inception n the beginning of something.

incessant adj never ceasing; continual, constant.–**incessancy** n.–**incessantly** adv.

incest n sexual intercourse between persons too closely related to marry legally.–**incestuous** adj.

inch n a measure of length equal to 1/12 foot (2.54 cm); a very small distance or amount. * vti to move very slowly, or by degrees.

incidence n the degree or range of occurrence or effect.

incident adj likely to happen as a result; falling upon or affecting. * n something that happens; an event, esp a minor one; a minor conflict.

incidental adj happening in connection with something more important; happening by chance. * npl miscellaneous items, minor expenses.

incidentally adv in passing, as an aside.

incinerate vt to reduce to ashes.–**incineration** n.

incinerator n a furnace for burning refuse.

incise vt to cut or carve into a surface; to engrave.–**incised** adj.

incision n incising; a cut made into something, esp by a surgeon into a body.

incisive adj keen, penetrating; decisive; biting.–**incisively** adv.–**incisiveness** n.

incisor n any of the front cutting teeth at the front of the mouth.

incite vt to urge to action; to rouse.–**incitement** n.–**inciter** n.–**incitingly** adv.

incivility n (pl **incivilities**) lack of civility or courtesy; impoliteness.

inclement adj (weather) rough, stormy; lacking mercy; harsh.

inclination n a propensity or disposition, esp a liking; a deviation from the horizontal or vertical; a slope; inclining or being inclined; a bending movement, a bow.

incline vi to lean, to slope; to be disposed towards an opinion or action. * vt to cause to bend (the head or body) forwards; to cause to deviate, esp from the horizontal or vertical. * n a slope.

include vt to enclose, contain; to comprise as part or a larger group, amount, etc.–**inclusion** n.

inclusive adj comprehensive; including the limits specified.–**inclusively** adv.

incognito adj, adv under an assumed name or identity. * n (pl **incognitos**) a person appearing or living incognito; the name assumed by such a person.–**incognita** nf (pl **incognitas**).

incoherent adj lacking organization or clarity; inarticulate in speech or thought.–**incoherence** n.–**incoherently** adv.

income n the money etc received for labor or services, or from property, investments, etc.

incomer n one who comes in; one who succeeds, as a tenant

income tax n a tax levied on the net income of a person or business.

incoming adj coming; accruing.

incommunicado adj not allowed to communicate with others.

incomparable adj beyond comparison, matchless; not amenable to comparison.–**incomparability** n.–**incomparably** adv.

incompatible adj not able to exist together in harmony; antagonistic; inconsistent.–**incompatibility** n.–**incompatibly** adv.

incompetent adj lacking the necessary ability, skill, etc. * n an incompetent person.–**incompetence** n.–**incompetently** adv.

incomplete adj unfinished; lacking a part or parts.–**incompletely** adv.–**incompleteness, incompletion** n.

incomprehensible adj not to be understood or grasped by the mind; inconceivable.–**incomprehensibility** n.–**incomprehensibly** adv.

inconceivable adj impossible to comprehend; (inf) unbelievable.–**inconceivably** adv.

inconclusive adj leading to no definite result; ineffective; inefficient.–**inconclusively** adv.–**inconclusiveness** n.

incongruous adj lacking harmony or agreement of parts; unsuitable; inappropriate.–**incongruously** adv.–**incongruity** n.

inconsequential adj not following logically; irrelevant.–**inconsequence** n.–**inconsequentiality** n.–**inconsequentially** adv.

inconsiderable adj trivial.–**inconsiderably** adv.

inconsiderate adj uncaring about others; thoughtless.–**inconsiderately** adv.–**inconsideration** n.

inconsistent adj not compatible with other facts; contradictory; irregular, fickle.–**inconsistently** adv.–**inconsistency** n.

inconsolable adj not able to be comforted.–**inconsolability** n.–**inconsolably** adv.

inconspicuous adj not conspicuous.–**inconspicuously** adv.–**inconspicuousness** n.

inconstant adj subject to change; unstable; variable; fickle; capricious.–**inconstancy** n.

incontestable adj not admitting of question or doubt; incontrovertible.–**incontestability** n.–**incontestably** adv.

incontinent adj unable to control the excretion of bodily wastes; lacking self-restraint.–**incontinence** n.

incontrovertible adj not admitting of controversy; indisputable.–**incontrovertibility** n.–**incontrovertibly** adv.

Inconvenience n want of convenience; unfitness; that which incommodes; disadvantage. * vt to put to inconvenience; to annoy.–**inconvenient** adj.

incorporate vt to combine; to include; to embody; to merge; to form into a corporation. * vi to unite into one group or substance; to form a corporation. * adj united; formed into a corporation.–**incorporation** n.–**incorporative** adj.–**incorporator** n.

incorrect adj faulty; inaccurate; improper.–**incorrectly** adv.–**incorrectness** n.

incorrigible adj not able to be corrected, reformed or altered.–**incorrigibility** n.–**incorrigibly** adv.

increase vti to make or become greater in size, quality, amount, etc. * n increasing or becoming increased; the result or amount by which something increases.–**increasingly** adv.

incredible adj unbelievable; (inf) wonderful.–**incredibility** n.–**incredibly** adv.

incredulous adj not able or willing to accept as true; unbelieving.–**incredulously** adv.–**incredulity** n.

increment n (the amount of) an increase; an addition.–**incremental** adj.

incriminate vt to involve in or indicate as involved in a crime or fault.–**incrimination** n.–**incriminator** n.–**incriminatory** adj.

incubate vti to sit on and hatch (eggs); to keep (eggs, embryos, etc) in a favorable environment for hatching or developing; to develop, as by planning.–**incubation** n.–**incubative, incubatory** adj.

incubator n an apparatus in which eggs are hatched by artificial heat; an apparatus for nurturing premature babies until they can survive unaided.

incumbent adj resting (on or upon) one as a duty or obligation; currently in office. * n the holder of an office, etc.

incur vt (**incurring, incurred**) to bring upon oneself (something undesirable).

incurable adj incapable of being cured; beyond the power of skill or medicine; lacking remedy; incorrigible. * n a person diseased beyond cure.–**incurability** n.–**incurably** adv.

incursion n an invasion or raid into another's territory, etc.–**incursive** adj.

indebted adj in debt; obliged; owing gratitude.–**indebtedness** n.

indecent adj offending against accepted standards of decent behavior.–**indecently** adv.–**indecency** n.

indecision n not able to make a decision; hesitation.

indecisive adj inconclusive; irresolute.–**indecisively** adv.

indeed adv truly, certainly. * interj expressing irony, surprise, disbelief, etc.

indefatigable adj tireless.–**indefatigability** n.–**indefatigably** adv.

indefensible adj unable to be defended or justified.–**indefensibility** n.–**indefensibly** adv.

indefinite adj not certain, undecided; imprecise, vague; having no fixed limits.–**indefiniteness** n.–**indefinitely** adv.

indelible adj not able to be removed or erased; (pen, ink, etc) making an indelible mark.–**indelibility** adv.–**indelibly** adv.

indelicate adj improper; rough, crude; tactless.–**indelicacy** n.–**indelicately** adv.

indemnify vt (**indemnifying, indemnified**) to insure against loss, damage, etc; to repay (for damage, loss, etc).–**indemnification** n.–**indemnifier** n.

indemnity n (pl **indemnities**) compensation for damage or loss; insurance against future loss or injury.

indent vt to make notches in; to begin (a line of text) farther in from the margin than the rest. * vi to form an indentation. * n a dent or notch.–**indentor** n.

indentation n a being indented; a notch, cut, inlet, etc; a dent; a spacing in from the margin (–also **indention, indent**).

independence n the state of being independent.

Independence Day n the anniversary of the adoption of the American Declaration of Independence on 4 July 1776.

independent adj freedom from the influence or control of others; self-governing; self-determined; not adhering to any political party; not connected with others; not depending on another for financial support. * n a person who is independent in thinking, action etc.–**independently** adv.

in-depth adj detailed, thorough.

indescribable adj unable to be described; too beautiful, horrible, intense, etc for words.–**indescribability** n.–**indescribably** adv.

indestructible adj not able to be destroyed.–**indestructibility** n.–**indestructibly** adv.

indeterminate adj vague, uncertain; not defined or fixed in value.–**indeterminacy, indetermination** n.–**indeterminately** adv.

index n (pl **indexes, indices**) an alphabetical list of names, subjects, items, etc mentioned in a printed book, usu listed alphabetically at the end of the text; a figure showing ratio or relative change, as of prices or wages; any indication or sign; a pointer or dial on an instrument; the exponent of a number. * vt to make an index of or for.–**indexer** n.

index finger n the forefinger.

indicate vt to point out; to show or demonstrate; to be a sign or symptom of; to state briefly, suggest.–**indication** n.–**indicatory** adj.

indicative adj serving as a sign (of).

indicator n a thing that indicates or points; a measuring device with a pointer, etc; an instrument showing the operating condition of a piece of machinery, etc; a device giving updated information, such as a departure board in a train station or airport; a flashing light used to warn of a change in direction of a vehicle.

indices see **index**.

indict vt to charge with a crime; to accuse.

indictment n a formal written statement framed by a prosecuting authority charging a person of a crime.

indifferent adj showing no concern, uninterested; unimportant; impartial; average; mediocre.–**indifference** n.–**indifferently** adv.

indigenous adj existing naturally in a particular country, region, or environment; native.

indigent adj poor, needy.–**indigence** n.

indigestion n a pain caused by difficulty in digesting food.

indignation n anger at something regarded as unfair, wicked, etc.–**indignant** adj.–**indignantly** adv.

indignity n (pl **indignities**) humiliation; treatment making one feel degraded, undignified.

indigo n (pl **indigos, indigoes**) a deep blue dye or color.

indirect adj not straight; roundabout; secondary; dishonest.–**indirectly** adv.–**indirectness** n.

indiscreet adj not discreet; tactless.–**indiscreetly** adv.–**indiscretion** n.

indiscriminate adj not making a careful choice; confused; random; making no distinctions.–**indiscriminately** adv.

indispensable adj absolutely essential.–**indispensability** n.–**indispensably** adv.

indisposed adj ill or sick; reluctant; disinclined.–**indisposition** n.

indisputable adj unquestionable; certain.–**indisputability** n.–**indisputably** adv.

indissoluble adj permanent; not able to be dissolved or destroyed.–**indissolubility** n.–**indissolubly** adv.

indistinct adj not clearly marked; dim; not distinct.–**indistinctly** adv.–**indistinctness** n.

indistinguishable adj not distinguishable; lacking identifying characteristics.–**indistinguishability** n.–**indistinguishably** adv.

individual adj existing as a separate thing or being; of, by, for, or relating to a single person or thing. * n a single thing or being; a person.

individuality n (pl **individualities**) the condition of being individual; separate or distinct existence; distinctive character.

individualize vt to mark as distinct, particularize; to distinguish individually.–**individualization** n.

individually *adv* in a distinctive manner; one by one; separately; personally.

indivisible *adj* not divisible.–**indivisibility** *n*.–**indivisibly** *adv*.

indoctrinate *vt* to systematically instruct in doctrines, ideas, beliefs, etc.–**indoctrination** *n*.–**indoctrinator** *n*.

indolent *adj* idle; lazy.–**indolence** *n*.–**indolently** *adv*.

indomitable *adj* not easily discouraged or defeated.– **indomitability** *n*.–**indomitably** *adv*.

indoor *adj* done, used, or situated within a building.

indoors *adv* in or into a building.

indubitable *adj* not capable of being doubted.–**indubitability** *n*.–**indubitably** *adv*.

induce *vt* to persuade; to bring on; to draw (a conclusion) from particular facts.

inducement *n* something that induces; a stimulus; a motive.

induct *vt* to place formally in an office, a society, etc; to enroll (esp a draftee) in the armed forces.

induction *n* the act or an instance of inducting, eg into office; reasoning from particular premises to general conclusions.

indulge *vt* to satisfy (a desire); to gratify the wishes of; to humor. * *vi* to give way to one's desire.–**indulgent** *adj*.–**indulgently** *adv*.–**indulger** *n*.

indulgence *n* indulging or being indulged; a thing indulged in; a favor or privilege.

industrial *adj* relating to or engaged in industry; used in industry; having many highly developed industries.–**industrially** *adv*.

industrialist *n* a person who owns or manages an industrial enterprise.

industrialize *vti* to make or become industrial.–**industrialization** *n*.

industrious *adj* hard-working.–**industriously** *adv*.–**industriousness** *n*.

industry *n* (*pl* **industries**) organized production or manufacture of goods; manufacturing enterprises collectively; a branch of commercial enterprise producing a particular product; any large-scale business activity; the owners and managers of industry; diligence.

inebriate *vt* to intoxicate, esp with alcoholic drink. * *n* a drunkard. * *adj* inebriated.–**inebriated** *adj*.–**inebriation** *n*.

inedible *adj* not fit to be eaten.–**inedibility** *n*.

ineffable *adj* too intense or great to be spoken; unutterable; too sacred to be spoken.–**ineffability** *n*.–**ineffably** *adv*.

inefficient *adj* not efficient.–**inefficiency** *n*.–**inefficiently** *adv*.

ineligible *adj* not eligible.–**ineligibility** *n*.

inept *adj* unsuitable; unfit; foolish; awkward; clumsy.–**ineptitude** *n*.–**ineptly** *adv*.

inequality *n* (*pl* **inequalities**) lack of equality in size, status, etc; unevenness.

inert *adj* without power to move or to resist; inactive; dull; slow; with few or no active properties.–**inertly** *adv*.–**inertness** *n*.

inertia *n* (*physics*) the tendency of matter to remain at rest (or continue in a fixed direction) unless acted on by an outside force; disinclination to act.

inescapable *adj* which cannot be escaped, inevitable.

inessential *adj* not essential.

inestimable *adj* not to be estimated; beyond measure or price; incalculable; invaluable.–**inestimably** *adv*.

inevitable *adj* sure to happen; unavoidable. * *n* something that is inevitable.–**inevitability** *n*.–**inevitably** *adv*.

inexact *adj* not strictly true or correct.–**inexactitude** *n*.–**inexactly** *adv*.

inexcusable *adj* without excuse; unpardonable.–**inexcusably** *adv*.

inexhaustible *adj* not to be exhausted or spent; unfailing; unwearied.–**inexhaustibility** *n*.–**inexhaustibly** *adv*.

inexorable *adj* unable to be persuaded by persuasion or entreaty; relentless.–**inexorability** *n*.–**inexorably** *adv*.

inexpensive *adj* cheap.–**inexpensively** *adv*.

inexperience *n* want of experience or of the knowledge that comes by experience.–**inexperienced** *adj*.

inexplicable *adj* not to be explained, made plain, or intelligible; not to be interpreted or accounted for.–**inexplicability** *n*.–**inexplicably** *adv*.

infallible *adj* incapable of being wrong; dependable; reliable.–**infallibility** *n*.–**infallibly** *adv*.

infamous *adj* having a bad reputation; notorious; causing a bad reputation; scandalous.–**infamy** *n*.

infancy *n* (*pl* **infancies**) early childhood; the beginning or early existence of anything.

infant *n* a very young child; a baby.

infantile *adj* of infants; like an infant, babyish.

infantry *n* (*pl* **infantries**) soldiers trained to fight on foot

infatuate *vt* to inspire with intense, foolish, or short-lived passion.–**infatuated** *adj*.–**infatuatedly** *adv*.–**infatuation** *n*.

infect *vt* to contaminate with disease-causing microorganisms; to taint; to affect, esp so as to harm.–**infective** *adj*.–**infection** *n*.–**infectious** *adj*.

infer *vt* (**inferring, inferred**) to conclude by reasoning from facts or premises; to accept as a fact or consequence.–**inferable** *adj*.–**inference** *n*.–**inferential** *adj*.

inferior *adj* lower in position, rank, degree, or quality. * *n* an inferior person.–**inferiority** *n*.

infernal *adj* of hell; hellish; fiendish; (*inf*) irritating, detestable.–**infernally** *adv*.

inferno *n* (*pl* **infernos**) hell; intense heat; a devastating fire.

infertile *adj* not fertile.–**infertility** *n*.

infest *vt* to overrun in large numbers, usu so as to be harmful; to be parasitic in or on.–**infestation** *n*.–**infester** *n*.

infidel *n* a person who does not believe in a certain religion; a person who has no religion.

infidelity *n* (*pl* **infidelities**) unfaithfulness, esp in marriage.

infield *n* (*baseball*) the area of the field enclosed by the baselines.

infielder *n* (*baseball, cricket*) a player in an infield position.

infighting *n* intense competition within an organization.

infiltrate *vti* to filter or pass gradually through or into; to permeate; to penetrate (enemy lines, etc) gradually or stealthily, eg as spies.–**infiltration** *n*.–**infiltrator** *n*.

infinite *adj* endless, limitless; very great; vast.–**infinitely** *adv*.

infinitesimal *adj* immeasurably small.–**infinitesimally** *adv*.

infinitive *n* (*gram*) the form of a verb without reference to person, number or tense.–**infinitival** *adj*.

infinity *n* (*pl* **infinities**) the condition or quality of being infinite; an unlimited number, quantity, or time period.

infirm *adj* physically weak, esp from old age or illness; irresolute.–**infirmity** *n*.

infirmary *n* (*pl* **infirmaries**) a hospital or place for the treatment of the sick.

inflame *vti* to arouse, excite, etc, or to become aroused, excited, etc; to undergo or cause to undergo inflammation.–**inflamingly** *adv*.–**inflammatory** *adj*.

inflammable *adj* able to catch fire, flammable; easily excited.–**inflammability** *n*.

inflammation *n* an inflaming or being inflamed; redness, pain, heat, and swelling in the body, due to injury or disease.

inflate *vti* to fill or become filled with air or gas; to puff up with pride; to increase beyond what is normal, esp the supply of money or credit.–**inflatable** *adj*.–**inflatedly** *adv*.–**inflater, inflator** *n*.

inflation *n* an inflating or being inflated; an increase in the currency in circulation or a marked expansion of credit, resulting in a fall in currency value and a sharp rise in prices.

inflexible *adj* not flexible; stiff, rigid; fixed; unyielding.–**inflexibility** *n*.–**inflexibly** *adv*.

inflict *vt* to impose (pain, a penalty, etc) on a person or thing.–**inflicter, inflictor** *n.*–**infliction** *n.*

influence *n* the power to affect others; the power to produce effects by having wealth, position, ability, etc; a person with influence. * *vt* to have influence on.–**influential** *adj.*–**influentially** *adv.*

influenza *n* a contagious feverish virus disease marked by muscular pain and inflammation of the respiratory system.–**influenzal** *adj.*

influx *n* a sudden inflow of people or things to a place.

info *n* (*sl*) information.

inform *vt* to provide knowledge of something to. * *vi* to give information to the police; to inform.

informal *adj* not formal; not according to fixed rules or ceremony, etc; casual.–**informally** *adv.*

informality *n* (*pl* **informalities**) the lack of regular, customary, or legal form; an informal act.

informant *n* a person who gives information.

information *n* something told or facts learned; news; knowledge; data stored in or retrieved from a computer.–**informational** *adj.*

information technology *n* (the study of) the collection, retrieval, use, storage and communication of information using computers and microelectronic systems.

informative *adj* conveying information, instructive.–**informatively** *adv.*

informer *n* a person who informs on another, esp to the police for a reward.

infrared *adj* (*radiation*) having a wavelength longer than light but shorter than radio waves; of, pertaining to, or using such radiation.

infrastructure *n* the basic structure of any system or organization; the basic installations, such as roads, railroads, factories, etc that determine the economic power of a country.

infrequent *adj* seldom occurring; rare.–**infrequence, infrequency** *n.*–**infrequently** *adv.*

infringe *vt* to break or violate, esp an agreement or a law.–**infringement** *n.*

infuriate *vt* to enrage; to make furious.–**infuriating** *adj.*–**infuriatingly** *adv.*

infuse *vt* to instill or impart (qualities, etc); to inspire; to steep (tea leaves, etc) to extract the essence.–**infusion** *n.*

ingenious *adj* clever, resourceful, etc; made or done in an original or clever way.–**ingeniously** *adv.*–**ingeniousness** *n.*

ingenuity *n* (*pl* **ingenuities**) skill in contriving or inventing; resourcefulness.

ingenuous *adj* naive, innocent; candid.–**ingenuously** *adv.*–**ingenuousness** *n.*

ingest *vt* to take (as food) into the body.–**ingestion** *n.*–**ingestive** *adj.*

inglorious *adj* disgraceful, shameful; obscure.

ingot *n* a brick-shaped mass of cast metal, esp gold or silver.

ingrained *adj* (*habits, feelings, etc*) firmly established; (*dirt*) deeply embedded.–**ingrain** *vt.*

ingrate *n* an ungrateful person.

ingratiate *vt* to bring oneself into another's favor.–**ingratiating, ingratiatory** *adj.*–**ingratiation** *n.*

ingratitude *n* absence of gratitude; insensibility to kindness.

ingredient *n* something included in a mixture; a component.

ingrowing *adj* (*toe nail, etc*) growing abnormally into the flesh.

inhabit *vt* to live in; to occupy; to reside.

inhabitable *adj* fit for habitation.–**inhabitability** *n.*–**inhabitation** *n.*

inhabitant *n* a person or animal inhabiting a specified place.–**inhabitancy, inhabitance** *n.*

inhalant *n* a medicine, etc that is inhaled.

inhale *vti* to breathe in.–**inhalation** *n.*

inhaler *n* a device that dispenses medicines in a fine spray for inhalation.

inherent *adj* existing as an inseparable part of something.–**inherence, inherency** *n.*–**inherently** *adv.*

inherit *vt* to receive (property, a title, etc) under a will or by right of legal succession; to possess by genetic transmission. * *vi* to receive by inheritance; to succeed as heir.–**inheritor** *n.*

inheritance *n* the action of inheriting; something inherited.

inhibit *vt* to restrain; to prohibit.–**inhibitor, inhibiter** *n.*

inhibition *n* an inhibiting or being inhibited; a mental process that restrains or represses an action, emotion, or thought.

inhospitable *adj* not hospitable; affording no shelter; barren; cheerless.–**inhospitably** *adv.*–**inhospitality** *n.*

in-house *adj* within an organization.

inhuman *adj* lacking in the human qualities of kindness, pity, etc; cruel, brutal, unfeeling; not human.

inhumane *adj* not humane; inhuman.

inhumanity *n* (*pl* **inhumanities**) the quality of being inhuman; cruelty.

inimical *adj* hostile; adverse, unfavorable.–**inimically** *adv.*

inimitable *adj* impossible to imitate; matchless.–**inimitably** *adv.*

iniquity *n* (*pl* **iniquities**) wickedness; great injustice.–**iniquitous** *adj.*

initial *adj* of or at the beginning. * *n* the first letter of each word in a name; a large letter at the beginning of a chapter, etc. * *vt* (**initialing, initialed** *or* **initialling, initialled**) to sign with initials.–**initialer, initialler** *n.*–**initially** *adv.*

initialize *vt* (*comput*) to format (a disk) to suit a particular processor.–**initialization** *n.*

initiate *vt* to bring (something) into practice or use; to teach the fundamentals of a subject to; to admit as a member into a club, etc, esp with a secret ceremony. * *n* an initiated person.–**initiation** *n.*–**initiator** *n.*–**initiatory** *adj.*

initiative *n* the action of taking the first step; ability to originate new ideas or methods.

inject *vt* to force (a fluid) into a vein, tissue, etc, esp with a syringe; to introduce (a remark, quality, etc), to interject.–**injectable** *adj.*

injection *n* an injecting; a substance that is injected.–**injective** *adj.*

injunction *n* a command; an order; a court order prohibiting or ordering a given action.–**injunctive** *adj.*

injure *vt* to harm physically or mentally; to hurt, do wrong to.–**injurer** *n.*

injury *n* (*pl* **injuries**) physical damage; harm.–**injurious** *adj.*

injury time *n* (*sport*) time added to compensate for stoppages through injuries to players.

injustice *n* the state or practice of being unfair; an unjust act.

ink *n* a colored liquid used for writing, printing, etc; the dark protective secretion of an octopus, etc. * *vt* to cover, mark, or color with ink.

inkling *n* a hint; a vague notion.

inky *adj* (**inkier, inkiest**) like very dark ink in color; black; covered with ink.–**inkiness** *n.*

inlaid *see* **inlay.**

inland *adj* of or in the interior of a country. * *n* an inland region. * *adv* into or toward this region.–**inlander** *n.*

in-law *n* a relative by marriage.

inlay *vt* (**inlaying, inlaid**) to decorate a surface by inserting pieces of metal, wood, etc. * *n* inlaid work; material inlaid.–**inlaid** *adj.*

inlet *n* a narrow strip of water extending into a body of land; an opening; a passage, pipe, etc for liquid to enter a machine, etc. * *vt* (**inletting, inletted**) to inlay; to insert.

inmate *n* a person confined with others in a prison or institution.

inn *n* a small hotel; a restaurant or tavern, esp in the countryside.

innards npl (inf) the stomach and intestines, internal organs.

innate adj existing from birth; inherent; instinctive.–**innately** adv.

inner adj further within; inside, internal; private, exclusive. * n (archery) the innermost ring on a target.

inner city n the central area of a city, esp as affected by over-crowding and poverty.

innermost adj furthest within.

inning n (baseball) a team's turn at bat.

innkeeper n a person who owns or manages an inn.

innocence n the condition or quality of being innocent.

innocent adj not guilty of a particular crime; free from sin; blameless; harmless; inoffensive; simple, credulous, naive. * n an innocent person, as a child.–**innocence** n.–**innocently** adv.

innocuous adj harmless.–**innocuously** adv.–**innocuousness** n.

innovate vi to introduce new methods, ideas, etc; to make changes.–**innovation** n.–**innovative, innovatory** adv.

innovator n one who introduces, or seeks to introduce, new things.

innuendo n (pl **innuendos, innuendoes**) a hint or sly remark, usu derogatory; an insinuation.

Innuit see **Inuit**.

inobservance n inattention; failure to observe (law, etc).–**inobservant** adj.

inoculate vt to inject a serum or a vaccine into, esp in order to create immunity; to protect as if by inoculation.–**inoculation** n.–**inoculative** adj.

inoffensive adj harmless, not offensive.

inoperable adj not suitable for surgery.–**inoperability** n.

inoperative adj not working; producing no effect.

inopportune adj unseasonable; untimely.–**inopportuneness, inopportunity** n.

inordinate adj excessive.–**inordinately** adv.

inorganic adj not having the structure or characteristics of living organisms; denoting a chemical compound not containing carbon.–**inorganically** adv.

inpatient n a patient being treated while remaining in hospital.

input n what is put in, as power into a machine, data into a computer, etc. * vt (**inputting, input** or **inputted**) to put in; to enter (data) into a computer.

inquest n a judicial inquiry, esp into a case of violent or unexplained death; (inf) any detailed inquiry or investigation.

inquire vi to request information about; (usu with **into**) to investigate. * vt to ask about.–also **enquire**.–**inquirer, enquirer** n.

inquiry n (pl **inquiries**) the act of inquiring; a search by questioning; an investigation; a question; research.–also **enquiry**.

inquisition n a detailed examination or investigation; (with cap and **the**) (RC Church) formerly the tribunal for suppressing heresy.–**inquisitor** n.–**inquisitorial** adj.

inquisitive adj eager for knowledge; unnecessarily curious; prying.–**inquisitively** adv.–**inquisitiveness** n.

inroad n a raid into enemy territory; an encroachment or advance.

insane adj not sane, mentally ill; of or for insane people; very foolish.–**insanely** adv.–**insanity** n.

insanitary adj unclean, likely to cause infection or ill-health.–**insanitariness, insanitation** n.

insatiable adj not easily satisfied; greedy.–**insatiability** n.–**insatiably** adv.

inscribe vt to mark or engrave (words, etc) on (a surface); to add (a person's name) to a list; to dedicate (a book) to someone; to autograph; to fix in the mind.–**inscribable** adj.

inscription n an inscribing; words, etc inscribed on a tomb, coin, stone, etc.–**inscriptional** adj.

inscrutable adj hard to understand, incomprehensible; enigmatic.–**inscrutability** n.–**inscrutably** adv.

insect n any of a class of small arthropods with three pairs of legs, a head, thorax, and abdomen and two or four wings.

insecticide n a substance for killing insects.–**insecticidal** adj.

insectivore n an order of mammals that are small, nocturnal, and feed on insects or other invertebrates; any insect-eating plant or animal.–**insectivorous** adj.

insecure adj not safe; feeling anxiety; not dependable.–**insecurely** adv.–**insecurity** n.

inseminate vt to fertilize; to impregnate.–**insemination** n.–**inseminator** n.

insensible adj unconscious; unaware; indifferent; imperceptible.–**insensibility** n.–**insensibly** adv.

insensitive adj not sensitive, unfeeling.

inseparable adj not able to be separated; closely attached, as romantically.–**inseparability** n.–**inseparably** adv.

insert vt to put or fit (something) into something else. * n something inserted.–**insertion** n.

inset n something inserted within something larger; an insert. * vt (**insetting, inset**) to set in, insert.

inside n the inner side, surface, or part; (pl: inf) the internal organs, stomach, bowels. * adj internal; known only to insiders; secret. * adv on or in the inside; within; indoors. * prep in or within.

inside out adj reversed; with the inner surface facing the outside.

insider n a person within a place or group; a person with access to confidential information.

insidious adj marked by slyness or treachery; more dangerous than seems evident.–**insidiously** adv.–**insidiousness** n.

insight n the ability to see and understand clearly the inner nature of things, esp by intuition; an instance of such understanding.–**insightful** adj.

insignia n (pl **insignias, insignia**) a mark or badge of authority; a distinguishing characteristic.

insignificant adj having little or no importance; trivial; worthless; small, inadequate.–**insignificance, insignificancy** n.–**insignificantly** adv.

insincere adj not sincere; hypocritical.–**insincerely** adv.–**insincerity** n.

insinuate vt to introduce or work in slowly, indirectly, etc; to hint.–**insinuator** n.–**insinuation** n.

insipid adj lacking any distinctive flavor; uninteresting, dull.–**insipidity, insipidness** n.–**insipidly** adv.

insist vi (often with **on** or **upon**) to take and maintain a stand. * vt to demand strongly; to declare firmly.–**insister** n.

insistent adj insisting or demanding.–**insistence, insistency** n.–**insistently** adv.

insole n the inner sole of a shoe, etc; a thickness of material used as a inner sole.

insolent adj disrespectful; impudent, arrogant, rude.–**insolence** n.–**insolently** adv.

insoluble adj incapable of being dissolved; impossible to solve or explain.–**insolubility** n.–**insolubly** adv.

insolvent adj unable to pay one's debts; bankrupt.–**insolvency** n.

insomnia n abnormal inability to sleep.

insomniac n a person who suffers from insomnia.

inspect vt to look at carefully; to examine or review officially.–**inspection** n.–**inspectional** adj.–**inspective** adj.

inspector n an official who inspects in order to ensure compliance with regulations, etc; a police officer ranking below a superintendent.–**inspectoral, inspectorial** adj.–**inspectorship** n.

inspectorate n the office, district or rank of an inspector; a body of inspectors.

inspire vt to stimulate, as to some creative effort; to motivate by divine influence; to arouse (a thought or feeling) in (someone); to cause.–**inspiration** n.–**inspirational** adj.–**inspiring** adj.–**inspiringly** adv.

inst. abbr = instant (this month).

instability n (pl **instabilities**) lack of stability; inconstancy.

install, instal vt (**installs** or **instals, installing, installed**) to formally place in an office, rank, etc; to establish in a place; to settle in a position or state.–**installer** n.

installation n the act of installing or being installed; machinery, equipment, etc that has been installed.

installment, instalment n a sum of money to be paid at regular specified times; any of several parts, as of a magazine story or television serial.

instance n an example; a step in proceeding; an occasion. * vt to give as an example.

instant adj immediate; (food) concentrated or precooked for quick preparation. * n a moment; a particular moment.

instantaneous adj happening or done very quickly.–**instantaneously** adv.–**instantaneousness, instantaneity** n.

instantly adv immediately.

instead adv in place of the one mentioned.

instep n the upper part of the arch of the foot, between the ankle and the toes.

instigate vt to urge on, goad; to initiate.–**instigation** n.–**instigator** n.

instill, instil vt (**instills** or **instils, instilling, instilled**) to put (an idea, etc) in or into (the mind) gradually.–**instillation** n.–**instiller** n.

instinct n the inborn tendency to behave in a way characteristic of a species; a natural or acquired tendency; a knack.–**instinctive, instinctual** adj.–**instinctively, instinctually** adv.

institute vt to organize, establish; to start, initiate. * n an organization for the promotion of science, art, etc; a school, college, or department of a university specializing in some field.–**institutor, instituter** n.

institution n an established law, custom, etc; an organization having a social, educational, or religious purpose; the building housing it; (inf) a long-established person or thing.

institutional adj of or resembling an institution; dull, routine.

institutionalize vt to make or become an institution; to place in an institution; to make a person dependent on an institutional routine and unable to cope on their own.–**institutionalization** n.

instruct vt to provide with information; to teach; to give instructions to; to authorize.–**instructible** adj.–**instructor** n.–**instructress** nf.

instruction n an order, direction; the act or process of teaching or training; knowledge imparted; (pl) orders, directions; detailed guidance.–**instructional** adj.

instructive adj issuing or containing instructions; giving information, educational.–**instructively** adv.

instrument n a thing by means of which something is done; a tool or implement; any of various devices for indicating, measuring, controlling, etc; any of various devices producing musical sound; a formal document. * vt to orchestrate.

instrumental adj serving as a means of doing something; helpful; of, performed on, or written for a musical instrument or instruments.–**instrumentality** n.–**instrumentally** adv.

instrumentalist n a person who plays a musical instrument.

insubordinate adj not submitting to authority; rebellious.–**insubordination** n.

insubstantial adj unreal, imaginary; weak or flimsy.–**insubstantiality** n.–**insubstantially** adv.

insufferable adj intolerable; unbearable.–**insufferably** adv.

insufficient adj not sufficient.–**insufficiency, insufficience** n.–**insufficiently** adv.

insular adj of or like an island or islanders; narrow-minded; illiberal.–**insularity, insularism** n.

insulate vt to set apart; to isolate; to cover with a nonconducting material in order to prevent the escape of electricity, heat, sound, etc.–**insulation** n.–**insulator** n.

insulin n a hormone that controls absorption of sugar by the body, secreted by islets of tissue in the pancreas.

insult vt to treat with indignity or contempt; to offend. * n an insulting remark or act.–**insulter** n.

insuperable adj unable to be overcome.–**insuperability** n.–**insuperably** adv.

insurance n insuring or being insured; a contract purchased to guarantee compensation for a specified loss by fire, death, etc; the amount for which something is insured; the business of insuring against loss.

insure vt to take out or issue insurance on; to ensure. * vi to contract to give or take insurance.

insurgent adj rebellious, rising in revolt. * n a person who fights against established authority, a rebel.–**insurgence** n.–**insurgency** n.

insurmountable adj which cannot be overcome, insuperable.

insurrection n a rising or revolt against established authority.–**insurrectional** adj.–**insurrectionary** n, adj.–**insurrectionism** n.–**insurrectionist** n.

intact adj unimpaired; whole.

intake n the place in a pipe, etc where a liquid or gas is taken in; a thing or quantity taken in, as students, etc; the process of taking in.

intangible adj that cannot be touched, incorporeal; representing value but without material being, as good will; indefinable. * n something that is intangible.–**intangibility** n.–**intangibly** adv.

integer n any member of the set consisting of the positive and negative whole numbers and zero, such as $-5, 0, 5$.

integral adj necessary for completeness; whole or complete; made up of parts forming a whole. * n the result of a mathematical integration.–**integrally** adv.

integrate vti to make whole or become complete; to bring (parts) together into a whole; to remove barriers imposing segregation upon (racial groups); to abolish segregation.–**integration** n.–**integrative** adj.

integrity n honesty, sincerity; completeness, wholeness; an unimpaired condition.

intellect n the ability to reason or understand; high intelligence; a very intelligent person.–**intellectual** adj, n.–**intellectually** adv.

intelligence n the ability to learn or understand; the ability to cope with a new situation; news or information; those engaged in gathering secret, esp military, information.

intelligent adj having or showing intelligence; clever, wise, etc.–**intelligently** adv.

intelligentsia n intellectuals collectively.

intelligible adj able to be understood; clear.–**intelligibility** n.–**intelligibly** adv.

intemperate adj indulging excessively in alcoholic drink; unrestrained; (climate) extreme.–**intemperance** n.–**intemperately** adv.

intend vt to mean, to signify; to propose, have in mind as an aim or purpose.–**intender** n.

intended adj planned. * n (inf) a fiancé or fiancée.

intense adj very strong, concentrated; passionate, emotional.–**intensely** adv.–**intensity** n.

intensify vti (**intensifying, intensified**) to make or become more intense.–**intensification** n.

intensive adj of or characterized by intensity; thorough; denoting careful attention given to patients right after surgery, etc.–**intensively** adv.

intent adj firmly directed; having one's attention or purpose firmly fixed. * n intention; something intended; purpose or meaning.–**intently** adv.–**intentness** n.

intention n a determination to act in a specified way; anything intended.–**intentional** adj.–**intentionally** adv.

inter vt (**interring, interred**) to bury.

interact vi to act upon each other.–**interaction** n.–**interactional** adj.

interactive adj interacting; allowing two-way communication between a device, such as a computer or compact video disk, and its user.–**interactivity** n.

intercede vi to intervene on another's behalf; to mediate.—**interceder** n.

intercept vt to stop or catch in its course. * n a point of intersection of two geometric figures; interception by an interceptor.—**interception** n.—**interceptive** adj.

interchange vt to give and receive one thing for another; to exchange, to put (each of two things) in the place of the other; to alternate. * n an interchanging; a junction on a freeway designed to prevent traffic intersecting.

interchangeable adj able to be interchanged.—**interchangeability** n.—**interchangeably** adv.

intercom n (inf) a system of intercommunicating, as in an aircraft.

intercommunicate vi to have mutual communication; to have passage to each other.—**intercommunicable** adj.—**intercommunication** n.

interconnect vti to connect by reciprocal links.—**interconnection** n.

intercontinental adj between continents.

intercourse n a connection by dealings or communication between individuals or groups; sexual intercourse, copulation.

interdependence, interdependency n dependence on each other.—**interdependent** adj.

interdict vt to prohibit (an action); to restrain from doing or using something. * n an official prohibition.—**interdiction** n.—**interdictory** adj.

interest n a feeling of curiosity about something; the power of causing this feeling; a share in, or a right to, something; anything in which one has a share; benefit; money paid for the use of money; the rate of such payment. * vt to excite the attention of; to cause to have a share in; to concern oneself with.

interested adj having or expressing an interest; affected by personal interest, not impartial.—**interestedly** adv.

interesting adj engaging the attention.

interface n a surface that forms the common boundary between two things; an electrical connection between one device and another, esp a computer. * vt (elect) to modify the input and output configurations of (devices) so that they may connect and communicate with each other; to connect using an interface; to be interactive (with).—**interfacial** adj.—**interfacially** adv.

interfere vi to clash; to come between; to intervene; to meddle; to obstruct.—**interfering** adj.

interference n an interfering; (radio, TV) the interruption of reception by atmospherics or by unwanted signals.

interferon n a protein, produced by cells in response to a virus, which then prevents the virus from growing.

intergalactic adj occurring or existing between galaxies.

interim n an intervening period of time. * adj provisional, temporary. * adv meanwhile.

interior adj situated within; inner; inland; private. * n the interior part, as of a room, country, etc.

interject vt to throw in between; to interrupt with.—**interjector** n.—**interjectory** adj.

interjection n an interjecting; an interruption; an exclamation.—**interjectional** adj.—**interjectionally** adv.

interlock vti to lock or become locked together; to join with one another.

interlope vi to intrude in a matter in which one has no real concern.—**interloper** n.

interlude n anything that fills time between two events, as music between acts of a play.

intermarry vi (**intermarrying, intermarried**) (different races, religions, etc) to become connected by marriage; to marry within one's close family.—**intermarriage** n.

intermediary n (pl **intermediaries**) a mediator. * adj acting as a mediator; intermediate.

intermediate adj in the middle; in between.

interment n burial.

interminable adj lasting or seeming to last forever; endless.—**interminably** adv.

intermission n an interval of time between parts of a performance.

intermittent adj stopping and starting again at intervals; periodic.—**intermittence, intermittency** n.—**intermittently** adv.

intern[1] vt to detain and confine within an area, esp during wartime.—**internment** n.

intern[2] n a doctor serving in a hospital, usu just after graduation from medical school, a houseman.

internal adj of or on the inside; of or inside the body; intrinsic; domestic.—**internality** n.—**internally** adv.

internal combustion engine n an engine producing power by the explosion of a fuel-and-air mixture within the cylinders.

international adj between or among nations; concerned with the relations between nations; for the use of all nations; of or for people in various nations. * n a sporting competition between teams from different countries; a member of an international team of players.—**internationality** n.—**internationally** adv.

International Date Line n the line running north to south along the 180-degree meridian, east of which is one day earlier than west of it.

internationalism n an attitude, belief, or policy favoring the promotion of cooperation and understanding between nations.—**internationalist** n.

internecine adj extremely destructive to both sides.

Internet n the worldwide system of linked computer networks.

interplanetary adj between or among planets.

interplay n the action of two things on each other, interaction.

interpolate vt to change (a text) by inserting new material; to insert between or among others; (math) to estimate a value between two known values.—**interpolator** n.—**interpolation** n.

interpose vti to place or come between; to intervene (with); to interrupt (with).—**interposer** n.—**interposition** n.

interpret vt to explain; to translate; to construe; to give one's own conception of, as in a play or musical composition. * vi to translate between speakers of different languages.—**interpretation** n.—**interpretative, interpretive** adj.

interpreter n a person who translates orally for persons speaking in different languages.

interracial adj between or among races.

interrogate vti to question, esp formally.—**interrogation** n.—**interrogational** adj.—**interrogator** n.

interrupt vt to break into (a discussion, etc) or break in upon (a speaker, worker, etc); to make a break in the continuity of. * vi to interrupt an action, talk, etc.—**interrupter** n.—**interruption** n.—**interruptive** adj.

intersect vti to cut or divide by passing through or crossing; (lines, roads, etc) to meet and cross each other.—**intersection** n.

intersperse vt to scatter or insert among other things; to diversify with other things scattered here and there.—**interspersion** n.

interstate adj between or among different states of a federation.

interstellar adj between or among stars.

interstice n a crack; a crevice; a minute space.

intertwine vti to twine or twist closely together.

interval n a space between things; the time between events; (mus) the difference of pitch between two notes.

intervene vi to occur or come between; to occur between two events, etc; to come in to modify, settle, or hinder some action, etc.—**intervener, intervenor** n.—**intervention** n.—**interventional** adj.

interview n a meeting in which a person is asked about his or her views, etc, as by a newspaper or television reporter; a published account of this; a formal meeting at which a candidate for a job is questioned and assessed by a prospective employer. * vt to have an interview with.–**interviewer** n.

interweave vti (**interweaving, interwove** or **interweaved,** pp **interwoven** or **interweaved**) to weave together, interlace; to intermingle.

intestate adj having made no will. * n a person who dies intestate.– **intestacy** n.

intestine n the lower part of the alimentary canal between the stomach and the anus.–**intestinal** adj.

intimacy n (pl **intimacies**) close or confidential friendship; familiarity; sexual relations.

intimate adj most private or personal; very close or familiar, esp sexually; deep and thorough. * n an intimate friend. * vt to indicate; to make known; to hint or imply.–**intimately** adv.

intimation n the act of intimating; a notice, announcement.

intimidate vt to frighten; to discourage, silence, etc esp by threats.– **intimidation** n.–**intimidator** n.

into prep to the interior or inner parts of; to the middle; to a particular condition; (inf) deeply interested or involved in.

intolerable adj unbearable.–**intolerably** adv.

intolerance n lack of toleration of the opinions or practices of others; inability to bear or endure.–**intolerant** adj.

intonation n intoning; variations in pitch of the speaking voice; an accent.–**intonational** adj.

intone vti to speak or recite in a singing tone; to chant.–**intoner** n.

intoxicant n something that intoxicates, esp a drug or an alcoholic drink.–also adj.

intoxicate vt to make drunken; to elate; to poison.–**intoxicatingly** adv.–**intoxication** n.

intractable adj unmanageable, uncontrollable; (problem, illness, etc) difficult to solve, alleviate, or cure.–**intractability** n.–**intractably** adv.

intransigent adj unwilling to compromise, irreconcilable.– **intransigence** n.–**intransigently** adv.

intransitive adj (gram) denoting a verb that does not take a direct object.–**intransitively** adv.

intrauterine adj inside the uterus.

intrauterine device n a small loop or coil inserted into the uterus as a contraceptive.

intravenous adj into a vein.–**intravenously** adv.

in-tray n a tray holding documents, etc, awaiting attention.

intrepid adj bold; fearless; brave.–**intrepidity** n.–**intrepidly** adv.

intricate adj difficult to understand; complex, complicated; involved, detailed.–**intricacy** n.–**intricately** adv.

intrigue n a secret or underhand plotting; a secret or underhanded plot or scheme; a secret love affair. * vb (**intriguing, intrigued**) vi to carry on an intrigue. * vt to excite the interest or curiosity of.

intrinsic adj belonging to the real nature of a person or thing; inherent.–**intrinsically** adv.

intro n (pl **intros**) (inf) introduction.

introduce vt to make (a person) acquainted by name (with other persons); to bring into use or establish; to present (legislation, etc) for consideration or approval; to present a radio or television program; to bring into or insert.–**introducer** n.

introduction n an introducing or being introduced; the presentation of one person to another; preliminary text in a book; a preliminary passage in a musical composition.–**introductory** adj.

introspection n examination of one's own mind and feelings, etc.–**introspect** vi.–**introspective** adj.

introvert vt to turn or direct inward. * vi to produce introversion in. * n a person who is more interested in his or her own thoughts, feelings, etc than in external objects or events. * adj characterized by introversion.–**introversion** n.–**introversive** adj.– **introverted** adj.

intrude vti to force (oneself) upon others unasked.–**intruder** n.–**intrudingly** adv.–**intrusion** n.–**intrusive** adj.

intuition n a perceiving of the truth of something immediately without reasoning or analysis; a hunch, an insight.–**intuitional** adj.–**intuitionally** adv.

intuitive adj perceiving or perceived by intuition.–**intuitively** adv.

Inuit n (pl **Inuit, Inuits**) an Eskimo from Greenland or North America.–also **Innuit**.

inundate vt to cover as with a flood; to deluge.–**inundation** n.– **inundator** n.

inure vt to accustom to, esp to something unpleasant.–also **enure**.–**inurement** n.

invade vt to enter (a country) with hostile intentions; to encroach upon; to penetrate; to crowd into as if invading.–**invader** n.– **invasion** n.–**invasive** adj.

invalid[1] adj not valid.

invalid[2] n a person who is ill or disabled. * vt to cause to become an invalid; to disable; to cause to retire from the armed forces because of ill-health or injury.

invalidate vt to render not valid; to deprive of legal force.–**invalidation** n.

invalidity n (pl **invalidities**) a lack of validity; a state of illness or disability.

invaluable adj too valuable to be measured in money.–**invaluably** adv.

invariable adj never changing; constant.–**invariability** n.– **invariably** adv.

invective n the use of violent or abusive language or writing.

inveigle vt to entice or trick into doing something.–**inveiglement** n.–**inveigler** n.

invent vt to think up; to think out or produce (a new device, process, etc); to originate; to fabricate (a lie, etc).–**invention** n.–**inventive** adj.–**inventiveness** n.–**inventor** n.

inventory n (pl **inventories**) an itemized list of goods, property, etc, as of a business; the store of such goods for such a listing; a list of the property of an individual or an estate. * vt (**inventorying, inventoried**) to make an inventory of; to enter in an inventory.–**inventorial** adj.

inverse adj reversed in order or position; opposite, contrary. * n an inverse state or thing.–**inversely** adv.

invert vt to turn upside down or inside out; to reverse in order, position or relationship.–**inversion** n.–**invertible** adj.

invertebrate adj without a backbone (–also **invertebral**). * n an animal without a backbone.

inverted comma n a quotation mark.

invest vt to commit (money) to property, stocks and shares, etc for profit; to devote effort, time, etc on a particular activity; to install in office with ceremony; to furnish with power, authority, etc. * vi to invest money.

investigate vti to search (into); to inquire, examine.–**investigation** n.–**investigative, investigatory** adj.

investigator n one who investigates, esp a private detective.

investiture n the act or right of giving legal possession; the ceremony of investing a person with an office, robes, title, etc.

investment n the act of investing money productively; the amount invested; an activity in which time, effort or money has been invested.

investor n a person who invests money.

inveterate adj firmly established, ingrained; habitual.–**inveteracy** n.–**inveterately** adv.

invidious adj tending to provoke ill-will, resentment or envy; (decisions, etc) unfairly discriminating.–**invidiously** adv.– **invidiousness** n.

invigorate vt to fill with vigor and energy; to refresh.–**invigorating** adj.–**invigoration** n.–**invigorative** adj.–**invigorator** n.

invincible adj unconquerable.–**invincibility** n.–**invincibly** adv.

inviolable adj not to be broken or harmed.–**inviolability** n.– **inviolably** adv.

inviolate adj not violated; unbroken, unharmed.–**inviolacy** n.

invisible adj unable to be seen; hidden.–**invisibility** n.–**invisibly** adv.

invitation n a message used in inviting.

invite vt to ask to come somewhere or do something; to ask for; to give occasion for; to tempt; to entice. * n (inf) an invitation.

inviting adj attractive, enticing.–**invitingly** adv.

in vitro adv, adj (biological experiments, etc) occurring outside the living body and in an artificial environment.

invocation n the act of invoking; a formula used in invoking.–**invocatory** adj.

invoice n a document listing goods dispatched, usu with particulars of their price and quantity; to demand due settlement. * vt to submit an invoice for or to.

invoke vt to call on (God, etc) for help, blessing, etc; to resort to (a law, etc) as pertinent; to implore.

involuntary adj not done by choice; not consciously controlled.–**involuntarily** adv.–**involuntariness** n.

involve vt to affect or include; to require; to occupy, to make busy; to complicate; to implicate.–**involvement** n.

invulnerable adj not capable of being wounded or hurt in any way.–**invulnerability** n.

inward adj situated within or directed to the inside; relating to or in the mind or spirit. * adv inwards.

inwardly adv within; in the mind or spirit; towards the inside or center.

inwards adv towards the inside or interior; in the mind or spirit.

iodine n a nonmetallic element, found in seawater and seaweed, whose compounds are used in medicine and photography.

ion n an electrically charged atom or group of atoms formed through the gain or loss of one or more electrons.

ionize vti to change or become changed into ions.–**ionization** n.

ionosphere n the series of ionized layers high in the stratosphere from which radio waves are reflected.–**ionospheric** adj.

iota n the ninth letter of the Greek alphabet; a very small quantity; a jot.

IOU n (pl **IOUs**) a written note promising to pay a sum of money to the holder.

IQ abbr = Intelligence Quotient.

irascible adj easily angered; hot-tempered.–**irascibility** n.–**irascibly** adv.

irate adj enraged, furious.–**irately** adv.

ire n anger; wrath.

iridescent adj exhibiting a spectrum of shimmering colors, which change as the position is altered.–**iridescence** n.

iris[1] n (pl **irises, irides**) the round, pigmented membrane surrounding the pupil of the eye.

iris[2] n (pl **irises**) a perennial herbaceous plant with sword-shaped leaves and brightly colored flowers.

irk vt to annoy, irritate.

irksome adj tedious; tiresome.

iron n a metallic element, the most common of all metals; a tool, etc of this metal; a heavy implement with a heated flat underface for pressing cloth; (pl) shackles of iron; firm strength; power. * adj of iron; like iron, strong and firm. * vti to press with a hot iron; (with out) to correct or settle a problem through negotiation or similar means.–**ironer** n.

Iron Age n the period when most tools and weapons were made of iron, following the Bronze Age in around 1100BC.

iron curtain n the name of the physical and ideological barrier which once separated the former Soviet Union and Communist Eastern Europe from the rest of Europe.

ironic, ironical adj of or using irony.–**ironically** adv.

ironing n the act of ironing; items of clothing, etc, for ironing.

ironing-board n a narrow flat surface to iron clothes on.

ironworks n (pl or sing) a factory where iron is smelted, cast, or wrought.

irony n (pl **ironies**) an expression in which the intended meaning of the words is the opposite of their usual sense; an event or result that is the opposite of what is expected.

irradiate vt to shine upon; to light up; to enlighten; to radiate; to expose to X-rays or other radiation. * vi to emit rays; to shine.–**irradiation** n.–**irradiative** adj.–**irradiator** n.

irrational adj not rational, lacking the power of reason; senseless; unreasonable; absurd.–**irrationality** n.–**irrationally** adv.

irreconcilable adj not able to be brought into agreement; incompatible.–**irreconcilability** n.–**irreconcilably** adv.

irredeemable adj not able to be redeemed.–**irredeemably** adv.

irrefutable adj unable to deny or disprove; indisputable.–**irrefutability** n.–**irrefutably** adv.

irregular adj not regular, straight or even; not conforming to the rules; imperfect; (troops) not part of the regular armed forces.–**irregularity** n.–**irregularly** adv.

irrelevant adj not pertinent; not to the point.–**irrelevance, irrelevancy** n.–**irrelevantly** adv.

irreligion n lack of religious belief; disregard for, or hostility towards, religion.–**irreligious** adj.

irreparable adj that cannot be repaired, rectified or made good.–**irreparably** adv.

irrepressible adj unable to be controlled or restrained.–**irrepressibly** adv.

irresistible adj not able to be resisted; overpowering; fascinating; very charming, alluring.–**irresistibility** adv.–**irresistibly** adv.

irresolute adj lacking resolution, uncertain, hesitating.–**irresolutely** adv.–**irresoluteness, irresolution** n.

irrespective adj (with of) regardless.–**irrespectively** adv.

irresponsible adj not showing a proper sense of the consequences of one's actions; unable to bear responsibility.–**irresponsibility** n.–**irresponsibly** adv.

irretrievable adj that cannot be recovered; irreparable.–**irretrievability** n.–**irretrievably** adv.

irreverent, irreverential adj not reverent, disrespectful.–**irreverence** n.–**irreverently** adv.

irreversible adj not able to be reversed; unable to be revoked or altered.–**irreversibility** n.–**irreversibly** adv.

irrevocable adj unable to be revoked, unalterable.–**irrevocability** n.–**irrevocably** adv.

irrigate vt to supply (land) with water as by means of artificial ditches, pipes, etc; (med) to wash out (a cavity, wound, etc).–**irrigable** adj.–**irrigation** n.–**irrigative** adj.–**irrigator** n.

irritable adj easily annoyed, irritated, or provoked; (med) excessively sensitive to a stimulus.–**irritability** n.–**irritably** adv.

irritant adj irritating; causing irritation. * n something that causes irritation.

irritate vt to provoke to anger; to annoy; to make inflamed or sore.–**irritative** adj.–**irritator** n.

irritation n the act of irritating; the state of being irritated; someone who, or something which, irritates.

is see **be**.

Islam n the Muslim religion, a monotheistic religion founded by Mohammed; the Muslim world.–**Islamic** adj.

island n a land mass smaller than a continent and surrounded by water; anything like this in position or isolation.

islander n a native or inhabitant of an island.

isle n an island, esp a small one.

isn't = is not.

isobar n a line on a map connecting places of equal barometric pressure.–**isobaric** adj.–**isobarism** n.

isolate vt to set apart from others; to place alone; to quarantine a person or animal with a contagious disease; to separate a constituent substance from a compound.–**isolation** n.–**isolator** n.

isosceles adj denoting a triangle with two equal sides.

isotope n any of two or more forms of an element having the same atomic number but different atomic weights.–**isotopic** adj.–**isotopically** adv.

issue *n* an outgoing; an outlet; a result; offspring; a point under dispute; a sending or giving out; all that is put forth at one time (an issue of bonds, a periodical, etc). * *vb* (**issuing, issued**) *vi* to go or flow out; to result (from) or end (in); to be published. * *vt* to let out; to discharge; to give or deal out, as supplies; to publish.–**issuance** *n*.

isthmus *n* (*pl* **isthmuses, isthmi**) a narrow strip of land having water at each side and connecting two larger bodies of land.–**isthmoid** *adj*.

it *pron* the thing mentioned; the subject of an impersonal verb; a subject or object of indefinite sense in various constructions. * *n* the player, as in tag, who must catch another.

italic *adj* denoting a type in which the letters slant upward to the right (*this is italic type*). * *n* (*usu pl*) italic type or handwriting.

italicize *vi* to write in italics. * *vt* to underline a word to indicate italics.–**italicization** *n*.

itch *n* an irritating sensation on the surface of the skin causing a need to scratch; an insistent desire. * *vi* to have or feel an irritating sensation in the skin; to feel a restless desire.–**itchiness** *n*.–**itchy** *adj*.

item *n* an article; a unit; a separate thing; a bit of news or information.

itemize *vt* to specify the items of; to set down by items.–**itemization** *n*.

itinerant *adj* traveling from place to place. * *n* a traveller.

itinerary *n* (*pl* **itineraries**) a route; a record of a journey; a detailed plan of a journey.

it'll = it will; it shall.

its *poss pron* relating to or belonging to **it**.

it's = it is; it has.

itself *pron* the reflexive and emphatic form of **it**.

I've = I have

IVF *abbr* = in vitro fertilization: a technique for helping infertile couples to have children, in which a woman's eggs are fertilized by the father's sperm in a laboratory and then re-implanted in the womb.

ivory *n* (*pl* **ivories**) the hard, creamy-white substance forming the tusks of elephants, etc; any substance like ivory; creamy white. * *adj* of or like ivory; creamy white.

ivy *n* (*pl* **ivies**) a climbing or creeping vine with a woody stem and evergreen leaves.–**ivied** *adj*.

J

jab *vti* (**jabbing, jabbed**) to poke or thrust roughly; to punch with short, straight blows. * *n* a sudden thrust or stab; (*inf*) an injection with a hypodermic needle.

jack *n* any of various mechanical or hydraulic devices used to lift something heavy. * *vt* (*with* **up**) to raise (a vehicle) by means of a jack; to increase (prices, etc).

jackal *n* (*pl* **jackals, jackal**) any of various wild dogs of Africa and Asia.

jackass *n* a male donkey; a fool.

jacket *n* a short coat; an outer covering, as the removable paper cover of a book. * *vt* to cover with a jacket or cover.–**jacketed** *adj*.

jack-in-the-box *n* a toy consisting of a box from which a figure on a spring pops out when the lid is lifted.

jackknife *n* (*pl* **jackknives**) a pocket-knife; a dive in which the diver touches his feet with knees straight and then straightens out. * *vi* to dive in this way; (*articulated truck*) to lose control so that the trailer and cab swing against each other.

jack-of-all-trades *n* (*pl* **jacks-of-all-trades**) a person who does many different types of work.

jackpot *n* the accumulated stakes in certain games, as poker; **hit the jackpot** (*sl*) to win; to gain an enormous amount.

jack rabbit *n* a large hare with long ears, common in North America.

Jacuzzi *n* (*trademark*) a device that swirls water in a bath; a bath containing such a device.

jade *n* a hard, ornamental semiprecious stone; its light green color.

jaded *adj* tired, exhausted; satiated.–**jadedly** *adv*.–**jadedness** *n*.

jag *n* a sharp, tooth-like notch or projection. * *vt* (**jagging, jagged**) to cut into notches; to prick.

jagged *adj* having sharp notches or projecting points; notched or ragged.–**jaggedly** *adv*.–**jaggedness** *n*.

jaguar *n* (*pl* **jaguars, jaguar**) a large American black-spotted yellow wild cat similar to the leopard.

jail *n* a prison; imprisonment. * *vt* to send to or confine in prison.

jailer, jailor *n* a person in charge of prisoners in a jail.

jam[1] *n* a preserve made from fruit boiled with sugar until thickened.

jam[2] *vb* (**jamming, jammed**) *vt* to press or squeeze into a confined space; to crowd full with people or things; to cause (machinery) to become wedged and inoperable; to cause interference to a radio signal rendering it unintelligible. * *vi* to become stuck or blocked; (*sl*) to play in a jam session. * *n* a crowded mass or congestion in a confined space; a blockage caused by jamming; (*inf*) a difficult situation.–**jammer** *n*.

jamb *n* the straight vertical side-post of a door, fireplace, etc.

jamboree *n* a large party or spree; a large, usu international, gathering of Scouts.

jam-packed *adj* filled to capacity.

jam session *n* (*sl*) an unrehearsed performance by jazz, rock or other musicians, usu for their own enjoyment.

jangle *vi* to make a harsh or discordant sound, as bells. * *vt* to cause to jangle; to irritate.–*also n*.

janitor *n* a person who looks after a building, doing routine maintenance, etc.–**janitorial** *adj*.

January *n* (*pl* **Januaries**) the first month of the year, having 31 days.

jar[1] *vb* (**jarring, jarred**) *vi* to make a harsh, discordant noise; to have an irritating effect (on one); to vibrate from an impact; to clash. * *vt* to jolt. * *n* a grating sound; a vibration due to impact; a jolt.

jar[2] *n* a short cylindrical glass vessel with a wide mouth.

jargon *n* the specialized or technical vocabulary of a science, profession, etc; obscure and usu pretentious language. * *vi* to talk in jargon.–**jargonistic** *adj*.

jasmine, jasmin *n* any of a genus of climbing shrubs with fragrant white or yellow flowers.

jaundice *n* a condition characterized by yellowing of the skin, caused by excess of bile in the bloodstream; bitterness; resentment; prejudice.

jaundiced *adj* affected with jaundice; jealous, envious, disillusioned.

jaunt *n* a short journey, usu for pleasure. * *vi* to make such a journey.

jaunty *adj* (**jauntier, jauntiest**) sprightly or self-confident in manner.–**jauntily** *adv*.–**jauntiness** *n*.

javelin *n* a light spear, esp one thrown some distance in a contest.

jaw *n* one of the bones in which teeth are set; either of two movable parts that grasp or crush something, as in a vice. * *vi* (*sl*) to talk boringly and at length.

jay *n* any of several birds of the crow family with raucous voices, roving habits, and destructive behavior to other birds.

jaywalk *vi* to walk across a street carelessly without obeying traffic rules or signals.–**jaywalker** *n*.

jazz *n* a general term for American popular music, characterized by syncopated rhythms and embracing ragtime, blues, swing, jive, and bebop; (*sl*) pretentious or nonsensical talk or actions. * *vt* (*with* **up**) (*inf*) to play (a piece of music) in a jazz style; to enliven, add color to.–**jazzy** *adj*.

jealous *adj* apprehensive of or hostile toward someone thought of as a rival; envious of, resentful; anxiously vigilant or protective.–**jealously** *adv*.–**jealousness** *n*.–**jealousy** *n*.

jeans *npl* pants made from hardwearing twilled cotton cloth or denim.

jeep *n* a small robust vehicle with heavy duty tires and four-wheel drive for use on rough terrain, esp by the military.

jeer *vt* to laugh derisively. * *vi* to scoff (at). * *n* a jeering remark.–**jeerer** *n*.–**jeeringly** *adv*.

Jehovah *n* (*Bible*) God.

jell *vti* to become or make into jelly; to crystallize, as a plan.–*also* **gel**.

jello *n* a sweet edible gelatin.

jelly *n* (*pl* **jellies**) a soft, gelatinous food made from fruit syrup or meat juice; any substance like this. * *vt* (**jellying, jellied**) to turn into jelly, to congeal.–**jellied** *adj*.

jellyfish *n* (*pl* **jellyfish, jellyfishes**) a sea creature with a nearly transparent body and long tentacles.

jeopardize *vt* to endanger, put at risk.–**jeopardy** *n*.

jerbil *see* **gerbil**.

jerk[1] *n* a sudden sharp pull or twist; a sudden muscular contraction or reflex; (*inf*) a stupid person. * *vti* to move with a jerk; to pull sharply; to twitch.–**jerkily** *adv*.–**jerkiness** *n*.–**jerky** *adj*.

jerk[2] *vt* to preserve (meat) by cutting it into long strips and drying it in the sun. * *n* jerked meat (–*also* **jerky**).

jerkin *n* a close-fitting sleeveless jacket.

jerky *see* **jerk**[2].

jerry-built *adj* cheaply and flimsily constructed.–**jerry-builder** *n*.–**jerry-building** *n*.

jersey *n* (*pl* **jerseys**) any plain machine-knitted fabric of natural or artificial fibers; a knitted sweater.

jest *n* a joke; a thing to be laughed at. * *vi* to jeer; to joke.

jester *n* a person who makes jokes, esp an entertainer employed in a royal household in the Middle Ages.

Jesus (**Christ**) *n* the Jewish religious teacher and founder of Christianity.

jet[1] *n* a hard black compact mineral that can be polished and is used in jewelry; a lustrous black.–**jet-black** *adj*.

jet[2] *n* a stream of liquid or gas suddenly emitted; a spout for emitting a jet; a jet-propelled aircraft. * *vti* (**jetting, jetted**) to gush out in a stream; (*inf*) to travel or convey by jet.

jet engine *n* an engine, such as a gas turbine, producing jet propulsion.

jet lag *n* fatigue caused by disruption of the daily bodily rhythms, associated with crossing time zones at high speed.–**jet-lagged** *adj*.

jet propulsion *n* propulsion of aircraft, boats, etc, by the discharge of gases from a rear vent.–**jet-propelled** *adj*.

jetsam *n* cargo thrown overboard from a ship in distress to lighten it, esp such cargo when washed up on the shore.

jet set *n* the wealthy and fashionable social elite who travel widely for pleasure.–**jetsetter** *n*.

jet stream *n* the jet of exhaust gases from a jet engine; high-altitude winds.

jettison *vt* to abandon, to throw overboard.

jetty *n* (*pl* **jetties**) a wharf; a small pier.

Jew *n* a person descended, or regarded as descended, from the ancient Israelites; a person whose religion is Judaism.–**Jewish** *adj*.

jewel *n* a precious stone; a gem; a piece of jewelry; someone or something highly esteemed; a small gem used as a bearing in a watch. * *vt* (**jeweling, jeweled** *or* **jewelling, jewelled**) to adorn or provide with jewels.

jeweler, jeweller *n* a person who makes, repairs or deals in jewelry, watches, etc.

jewelry, jewellery *n* jewels such as rings, brooches, etc, worn for decoration.

jib *n* a triangular sail extending from the foremast in a ship. * *vti* (**jibbing, jibbed**) to pull (a sail) round to the other side; (*sail*) to swing round.–**jibber** *n*.

jiffy *n* (*pl* **jiffies**) (*inf*) a very short time.

jig *n* a lively springing dance; the music for this; a device used to guide a tool. * *vt* (**jigging, jigged**) to dance in lively manner, as in a jig; to jerk up and down rapidly.

jiggle *vt* to jerk; to move (something) up and down lightly. * *n* a jerky movement.

jigsaw *n* a saw with a narrow fine-toothed blade for cutting irregular shapes. * *vt* to cut with a jigsaw.

jigsaw (puzzle) *n* a picture mounted on wood or stiff cardboard and then cut up into irregular pieces, which are then assembled for amusement.

jihad *n* a holy war waged by Muslims against nonbelievers; a crusade for or against a cause.

jilt *vt* to discard (a lover) unfeelingly, esp without warning.–**jilter** *n*.

jingle *n* a metallic tinkling sound like a bunch of keys being shaken together; a catchy verse or song with easy rhythm, simple rhymes, etc. * *vti* (to cause) to make a light tinkling sound.–**jingler** *n*.

jingoism *n* advocacy of an aggressive foreign policy.–**jingoist** *adj*, *n*.–**jingoistic** *adj*.–**jingoistically** *adv*.

jinx *n* (*inf*) someone or something thought to bring bad luck.

jitters *npl* (*inf*) (*with* **the**) an uneasy nervous feeling; fidgets.–**jittery** *adj*.

jive *n* improvised jazz played at a fast tempo; dancing to this music; (*sl*) foolish, exaggerated, or insincere talk. * *vti* to dance the jive.

job *n* a piece of work done for pay; a task; a duty; the thing or material being worked on; work; employment; (*sl*) a criminal enterprise; (*inf*) a difficult task. * *adj* hired or done by the job. * *vti* (**jobbing, jobbed**) to deal in (goods) as a jobber; to sublet (work, etc).

jobless *adj* unemployed. * *n* unemployed people collectively.–**joblessness** *n*.

jock *n* (*inf*) a male athlete.

jockey *n* (*pl* **jockeys**) a person whose job is riding horses in races. * *vti* (**jockeying, jockeyed**) to act as a jockey; to maneuver for a more advantageous position; to swindle or cheat.

jockstrap *n* a support for the genitals worn by men participating in sport, an athletic supporter.

jocose *adj* playful, humorous.–**jocosely** *adv*.–**jocoseness** *n*.–**jocosity** *n*.

jocular *adj* joking; full of jokes.–**jocularity** *n*.–**jocularly** *adv*.

jodhpurs *npl* riding breeches cut loose at the hips but close-fitting from knee to ankle.

jog *vb* (**jogging, jogged**) *vt* to give a slight shake or nudge to; to rouse, as the memory. * *vi* to move up and down with an unsteady motion; to run at a relaxed trot for exercise; (*horse*) to run at a jogtrot. * *n* a slight shake or push; a nudge; a slow walk or trot.–**jogger** *n*.

joggle *vti* to move or shake slightly. * *n* a slight jolt.

John Dory *n* an edible yellow seafish, the dory.

joie de vivre *n* great enjoyment of life.

join *vti* to bring and come together (with); to connect; to unite; to become a part or member of (a club, etc); to participate (in a conversation, etc); (*with* **up**) to enlist in the armed forces; to unite, connect. * *n* a joining; a place of joining.

joint *n* a place where, or way in which, two things are joined; any of the parts of a jointed whole; the parts where two bones move on one another in an animal; a division of an animal carcass made by a butcher; (*sl*) a cheap bar or restaurant; (*sl*) a gambling or drinking den; (*sl*) a cannabis cigarette. * *adj* common to two or more; sharing with another. * *vt* to connect by a joint or joints; to divide (an animal carcass) into parts for cooking.

jointly *adv* in common; together.

joist *n* any of the parallel beams supporting floorboards or the laths of a ceiling.

joke n something said or done to cause laughter; a thing done or said merely in fun; a person or thing to be laughed at. * vi to make jokes.—**jokingly** adv.

joker n a person who jokes; (sl) a person; an extra playing card made use of in certain games.

jokey, joky adj (**jokier, jokiest**) full, or fond, of jokes.

jolly adj (**jollier, jolliest**) merry; full of fun; delightful; (inf) enjoyable.

jolt vt to give a sudden shake or knock to; to move along jerkily; to surprise or shock suddenly. * n a sudden jar or knock; an emotional shock.—**joltingly** adv.—**jolty** adj.

josh vi (sl) to tease gently. * n (sl) friendly teasing; a teasing joke.— **josher** n.—**joshingly** adv.

jostle vti to shake or knock roughly; to collide or come into contact (with); to elbow for position. * n a jostling; a push.

jot n a very small amount. * vt (**jotting, jotted**) to note (down) briefly.—**jotter** n.

jotting n something noted down, esp a memorandum.

journal n a daily record of happenings, as a diary; a newspaper or periodical.

journalism n the work of gathering news for or producing a newspaper, magazine or news broadcast.

journalist n a person who writes for or edits a newspaper, etc; one who keeps a diary.—**journalistic** adj.—**journalistically** adv.

journey n (pl **journeys**) a traveling or going from one place to another; the distance covered when traveling. * vi (**journeying, journeyed**) to make a journey.—**journeyer** n.

journeyman n (pl **journeymen**) a person whose apprenticeship is completed and who is employed by another; a reliable workman.

joust n a fight on horseback between two knights with lances. * vi to engage in a joust, to run at the tilt.—**jouster** n.

jovial adj full of cheerful good humor.—**joviality** n.—**jovially** adv.

jowl n the lower jaw; (usu pl) the cheek.

jowly adj (**jowlier, jowliest**) having heavy jowls.—**jowliness** n.

joy n intense happiness; something that causes this; its expression.

joyful adj filled with, expressing, or causing joy, glad.—**joyfully** adv.—**joyfulness** n.

joyless adj not occasioning joy, unhappy; bleak.—**joylessly** adv.—**joylessness** n.

joyous adj joyful, very happy.—**joyously** adv.—**joyousness** n.

joyride n (inf) a car ride, often in a stolen vehicle and at reckless speed, just for pleasure.—**joy-rider** n.—**joyriding** n.

joystick n (inf) the control lever of an aircraft; (comput) a device for controlling cursor movement on a monitor usu for computer games.

Jr., jr abbr = Junior.

jubilant adj triumphant; expressing joy; rejoicing.—**jubilance** n.—**jubilantly** adv.

jubilee n a 50th or 25th anniversary; a time of rejoicing.

Judaism n the religion of the Jews, based on the Old Testament and the Talmud.—**Judaist** n.—**Judaistic** adj.

judge n a public official with authority to hear and decide cases in a court of law; a person chosen to settle a dispute or decide who wins; a person qualified to decide on the relative worth of anything. * vti to hear and pass judgment (on) in a court of law; to determine the winner of (a contest) or settle (a dispute); to form an opinion about; to criticize or censure; to suppose, think.—**judgeable** adj.—**judgingly** adv.

judgment, judgement n a judging; a deciding; a legal decision; an opinion; the ability to come to a wise decision; censure.

judgmental, judgemental adj of or depending on judgment; tending to make moral or personal judgments.—**judgmentally, judgementally** adv.

Judgment Day n (Christianity) the time of God's final judgment of mankind; (without cap) a final judgment; a day of reckoning.

judicature n a court or courts of justice; the power of dispensing justice by legal trial and judgment; jurisdiction; a body of judges; a tribunal.

judicial adj of judges, courts, or their functions.—**judicially** adv.

judiciary adj of judges or courts. * n (pl **judiciaries**) the part of government that administers justice; a system of courts in a country; judges collectively.

judicious adj possessing or characterized by sound judgment.—**judiciously** adv.—**judiciousness** n.

judo n a Japanese system of unarmed combat, adapted as a competitive sport from jujitsu.—**judoist** n.

jug n a vessel for holding and pouring liquids, with a handle and curved lip; a pitcher.—**jugful** n.

juggernaut n a terrible, irresistible force; a large heavy truck.

juggle vi to toss up balls, etc and keep them in the air. * vt to manipulate skillfully; to manipulate so as to deceive. * n the act of juggling; manipulation.—**juggler** n.—**jugglery** n.

jugular adj (anat) of the neck or throat. * n a jugular vein.

juice n the liquid part of fruit, vegetables or meat; liquid secreted by a bodily organ; (inf) vitality; (inf) electric current.

juicer n a mechanical or electrical device for extracting juice from fruit and vegetables.

juicy adj (**juicier, juiciest**) full of juice; (inf) very interesting; (inf) highly profitable.—**juicily** adv.—**juiciness** n.

jujitsu n a traditional Japanese system of unarmed defence in which an opponent's strength is used against him.

jukebox n a coin-operated automatic record or CD player.

julep n a tall drink of bourbon or brandy and sugar over crushed ice, garnished with mint.

July n (pl **Julies**) the seventh month of the year, having 31 days.

jumble vt (often with **up**) to mix together in a disordered mass. * n items mixed together in a confused mass.—**jumbly** adj.

jumbo n (pl **jumbos**) something very large of its kind. * adj very large.

jumbo jet n a very large jet airliner.

jump vi to spring or leap from the ground, a height, etc; to jerk; to pass suddenly, as to a new topic; to rise suddenly, as prices; (sl) to be lively; (often with **at**) to act swiftly and eagerly; (with **at**) to accept or agree too eagerly; (with **on**) (inf) to reprimand or criticize harshly. * vt to leap or pass over (something); to leap upon; to cause (prices, etc) to rise; to fail to turn up (for trial when out on bail); (inf) to attack suddenly; (inf) to react to prematurely; (sl) to leave suddenly. * n a jumping; a distance jumped; a sudden transition; an obstacle; a nervous start.

jumper[1] n a person or thing that jumps

jumper[2] n a sleeveless dress for wearing over a blouse, etc.

jumper cable n one of two cables for transferring electric charge from one battery to another, used to start a car with a flat battery by using the battery of another vehicle.

jump jet n (inf) a jet aircraft that can take off and land vertically.

jump rope n a rope used for skipping

jump-start vt to start a motor vehicle by pushing it in low gear so the engine turns over or by using jump leads; (inf) to set (a sluggish system, etc) in motion.

jumpsuit n a one-piece garment, as worn by paratroopers.

jumpy adj (**jumpier, jumpiest**) moving in jerks, etc; apprehensive; easily startled.—**jumpily** adv.—**jumpiness** n.

junction n a place or point where things join; a place where roads or railway lines, etc meet, link or cross each other.—**junctional** adj.

juncture n a junction; a point of time; a crisis.

June n the sixth month of the year, having 30 days.

jungle n an area overgrown with dense tropical trees and other vegetation, etc; any scene of wild confusion, disorder, or of ruthless competition for survival.

junior adj younger in age; of more recent or lower status; of juniors. * n a person who is younger, of lower rank, etc; a young person employed in minor capacity in an office; a student in the third year of college or school; (inf) (with cap) the younger son, often used after the name if the same as the father's.

juniper n an evergreen shrub that yields purple berries.

junk[1] n a flat-bottomed sailing vessel prevalent in the China Seas.

junk[2] n discarded useless objects; (inf) rubbish, trash; (sl) any narcotic drug, such as heroin. * vt (inf) to scrap. * adj cheap, worthless; showy but without substance.

junket n a picnic; an excursion, esp one by an official at public expense. * vi to go on a junket.

junk food n a snack or fast food with little nutritional value.

junkie, junky n (pl **junkies**) (sl) an addict of a particular activity, food, etc; a drug addict.

junk mail n unsolicited mail, eg advertising leaflets.

junta n a group of people, esp military, who assume responsibility for the government of a country following a coup d'état or revolution.

jurisdiction n the right or authority to apply the law; the exercise of such authority; the limits of territory over which such authority extends.–**jurisdictional** adj.–**jurisdictionally** adv.

jurisprudence n the science or philosophy of law; a division of law.–**jurisprudential** adj.–**jurisprudentially** adv.

juror n a member of a jury; a person who takes an oath.

jury n (pl **juries**) a body of usu 12 people sworn to hear evidence and to deliver a verdict on a case; a committee or panel that decides winners in a contest.

juryman n (pl **jurymen**) a male juror.

jurywoman n (pl **jurywomen**) a female juror.

just adj fair, impartial; deserved, merited; proper, exact; conforming strictly with the facts. * adv exactly; nearly; only; barely; a very short time ago; immediately; (inf) really; justly, equitably; by right.–**justly** adv.–**justness** n.

justice n justness, fairness; the use of authority to maintain what is just; the administration of law; a judge.

justice of the peace n a magistrate who summarily tries minor cases within his or her jurisdiction.

justiciary n (pl **justiciaries**) an officer who administers justice. * adj of or pertaining to the administration of justice.

justifiable adj capable of being justified or defended.–**justifiability** n.–**justifiably** adv.

justification n the act of justifying; vindication or defence; a showing adequate reason; absolution; (print) the spacing out of type to the full length of a line.

justify vt (**justifying, justified**) to prove or show to be just or right; to vindicate; to space out (a line of type) so that it fills the required length.

jut vti (**jutting, jutted**) to project; to stick out. * n a part that projects.

jute n the fiber of either of two tropical plants used for making sacking, etc.

juvenile adj young; immature; of or for young persons. * n a young person.

juvenile delinquency n (pl **delinquencies**) antisocial or illegal behaviour by young people usu under 18.–**juvenile delinquent** n.

juxtapose vt to place side by side, esp for comparison.–**juxtaposition** n.

K

K abbr = one thousand; (comput) 1024 words, bits or bytes.

Kaiser n (formerly) the title of the emperors of Germany and Austria.

kale, kail n a variety of cabbage with crinkled leaves.

kaleidoscope n a small tube containing bits of colored glass reflected by mirrors to form symmetrical patterns as the tube is rotated; anything that constantly changes.–**kaleidoscopic** adj.–**kaleidoscopically** adv.

kamikaze n (World War II) a Japanese aircraft packed with explosives for making a suicidal crashing attack; the pilot of such an aircraft.

kangaroo n (pl **kangaroos**) an Australian marsupial with short forelegs and strong, large hind legs for jumping.

kaolin n a white clay used in porcelain, etc.

kappa n the tenth letter of the Greek alphabet.

kaput adj (sl) broken, ruined.

karaoke n a CD music system that plays recordings of popular songs with the vocal part removed to allow amateurs to sing along.

karat n a measure of weight for precious stones; a measure of the purity of gold.–also **carat**.

karate n a Japanese system of unarmed combat using sharp blows of the feet and hands.

karma n (Buddhism, Hinduism) the sum of a person's actions during one of their existences, held to determine their destiny in the next; (inf) a certain aura that a person or place is felt to possess.–**karmic** adj.

kayak n an Eskimo canoe made of skins on a wooden frame.

kazoo n (pl **kazoos**) a small tube-shaped musical instrument through which one hums to vibrate a membrane-covered hole at the end or side

KB abbr = kilobyte.

kcal abbr = kilocalorie.

kebab n small cubes of grilled meat and vegetables, usu served on a skewer.

keel n one of the main structural members of a ship extending along the bottom from stem to stern to which the frame is attached; any structure resembling this. * vti (to cause) to turn over.

keen adj eager, enthusiastic; intellectually acute, shrewd; having a sharp point or fine edge; (senses) perceptive, penetrating; extremely cold and piercing; intense; (prices) very low so as to be competitive.–**keenly** adv.–**keenness** n.

keep vb (**keeping, kept**) vt to celebrate, observe; to fulfill; to protect, guard; to take care of; to preserve; to provide for; to make regular entries in; to maintain in a specified state; to hold for the future; to hold and not let go; (with **at**) to harass (a person) into continuing (some task, etc); (with **back**) to refuse to disclose; to restrain; (with **down**) to repress; to subdue; (with **from**) to abstain or restrain from; to preserve as a secret (from someone); (with **to**) to cause to adhere strictly to; (with **up**) to persist in; to continue; to maintain in good condition. * vi to stay in a specified condition; to continue, go on; to refrain or restrain oneself; to stay fresh, not spoil; (with **at**) to persist; (with **away**) to prevent from approaching; (with **down**) to stay hidden; (with **on**) to talk or nag continuously; (with **to**) to (cause to) adhere strictly to; (with **up**) to maintain the same pace, level of knowledge, etc as another; to stay informed; to continue relentlessly. * n food and shelter; care and custody; the inner stronghold of a castle.

keeper n one who guards, watches, or takes care of persons or things.

keeping n care, charge; observance; agreement, conformity.

keepsake n something kept in memory of the giver.

keg n a small barrel.

kelp n a large brown seaweed.

kelvin n a unit of temperature of the Kelvin scale.

Kelvin scale n temperature on a scale where absolute zero (−273.15° Celsius) is taken as zero degrees.

ken n understanding; view; sight. * vt (**kenning, kenned** or **kent**) to know; to recognize at sight.

kennel n a small shelter for a dog, a doghouse; (often pl) a place where dogs are bred or kept. * vt (**kenneling, kenneled** or **kennelling, kennelled**) to keep in a kennel.

kept see **keep**.

kerb see **curb**.

kerchief n a piece of square cloth worn on the head.

kernel n the inner edible part of a fruit or nut; the essential part of anything.

kerosene, kerosine n a fuel oil distilled from petroleum.

ketch n a small two-masted sailing vessel.

ketchup n any of various thick sauces, esp one made from puréed tomato, for meat, fish, etc.

ketone n a class of chemical compounds, the simplest being acetone.

kettle n a container with a handle and spout for boiling water.

kettledrum n a musical instrument consisting of a hollow metal body with a parchment head, the tension of which controls the pitch and is adjusted by screws.

key[1] n a device for locking and unlocking something; a thing that explains or solves, as the legend of a map, a code, etc; a controlling position, person, or thing; one of a set of parts or levers pressed in a keyboard; (mus) a system of related tones based on a keynote and forming a given scale; style or mood of expression; a roughened surface for improved adhesion of plaster, etc; an electric circuit breaker. * vt to furnish with a key; to bring into harmony. * adj controlling; important.

key[2] n a low island or reef.

keyboard n a set of keys in a piano, organ, microcomputer, etc.

keyhole n an opening (in a lock) into which a key is inserted.

keyhole surgery n surgery performed through small incisions in the body using fiber-optic tubes both for internal examination and as conduits for tiny surgical instruments.

keynote n the basic note of a musical scale; the basic idea or ruling principle. * vt to give the keynote of; to give the keynote speech at.

keypad n a small usu hand-held keyboard of numbered buttons used to tap in a telephone number, operate a calculator, etc.

keystone n the middle stone at the top of an arch, holding the stones or other pieces in place.

keystroke n the depressing of a key on a typewriter, computer keyboard, etc.

kg abbr = kilogram(s).

khaki adj dull yellowish-brown. * n (pl **khakis**) strong, twilled cloth of this color; (often pl) a khaki uniform or trousers.

khan n the title of a ruler, prince, or governor in Asia.

kHz abbr = kilohertz.

kibbutz n (pl **kibbutzim**) an agricultural commune in Israel.

kick vt to strike with the foot; to drive, force, etc as by kicking; to score (a goal, etc) by kicking; (with **about, around**) (inf) to abuse physically or mentally; to discuss or analyze (a problem, etc) in a relaxed unsystematic manner; (with **out**) (inf) to eject, dismiss; (with **up**) (inf) to cause (trouble, etc). * vi to strike out with the foot; to recoil, as a gun; (inf) to complain; (with **about, around**) (inf) to wander idly; to be unused or forgotten; (with **off**) (football) to give the ball the first kick to start play; (inf) to start. * n an act or method of kicking; a sudden recoil; (inf) a thrill; (inf) an intoxicating effect.—**kicker** n.

kickback n a recoil; (inf) a returning of part of a sum of money received in payment.

kickoff n (football) a kick putting the ball into play; the beginning or start of proceedings, eg a discussion.

kid n a young goat; soft leather made from its skin; (inf) a child. * vti (**kidding, kidded**) (inf) to tease or fool playfully; (goat) to bring forth young.—**kidder** n.

kiddy, kiddie n (pl **kiddies**) (inf) a child.

kidnap vt (**kidnaping, kidnaped** or **kidnapping, kidnapped**) to seize and hold to ransom, as of a person.—**kidnaper, kidnapper** n.

kidney n (pl **kidneys**) either of a pair of glandular organs excreting waste products from the blood as urine; an animal's kidney used as food.

kidney bean n any of various cultivated beans, esp a large dark red bean seed.

kidney stone n a hard mineral deposit in the kidney.

kill vt to cause the death of; to destroy; to neutralize (a color); to spend (time) on trivial matters; to turn off (an engine, etc); (inf) to cause severe discomfort or pain to. * n the act of killing; an animal or animals killed.—**killer** n.

killer whale n a carnivorous black-and-white toothed whale.

killing adj (inf) tiring; very amusing; causing death, deadly. * n the act of killing, murder; (inf) a sudden (financial) success.—**killingly** adv.

kiln n a furnace or large oven for baking or drying (lime, bricks, etc).

kilo n (pl **kilos**) kilogram; kilometer.

kilobyte n 1024 bytes.

kilocalorie n a Calorie.

kilocycle n a kilohertz.

kilogram n a unit of weight and mass, equal to 1000 grams or 2.2046 pounds.

kilohertz n one thousand cycles per second, 1000 hertz.

kiloliter n one thousand liters.

kilometer n a unit of length equal to 1000 meters or 0.62 mile.—**kilometric** adj.

kilowatt n a unit of electrical power, equal to 1000 watts.

kilt n a knee-length skirt made from tartan material pleated at the sides, worn as part of the Scottish Highland dress for men and women.

kilter n good working order; good condition (out of kilter).

kimono n (pl **kimonos**) a loose Japanese robe.

kin n relatives; family.—see **kith**.

kind[1] n sort; variety; class; a natural group or division; essential character.

kind[2] adj sympathetic; friendly; gentle; benevolent.—**kindness** n.

kindergarten n a class or school for very young children.

kind-hearted adj benevolent; kind, warm.—**kind-heartedly** adv.

kindle vt to set on fire; to excite (feelings, interest, etc). * vi to catch fire; to become aroused or excited.

kindly adj (**kindlier, kindliest**) kind; gracious; agreeable; pleasant. * adv in a kindly manner; favorably.—**kindliness** n.

kindred n a person's family or relatives; family relationship; resemblance. * adj related; like, similar.

kinetic adj of or produced by movement.—**kinetically** adv.

king n the man who rules a country and its people; a man with the title of ruler, but with limited power to rule; man supreme in a certain sphere; something best in its class; the chief piece in chess; a playing card with a picture of a king on it, ranking above a queen; (drafts) a piece that has been crowned.

kingdom n a country headed by a king or queen; a realm, domain; any of the three divisions of the natural world: animal; vegetable, mineral.

kingfisher n a short-tailed diving bird that feeds chiefly on fish.

kingpin n (sl) the chief person in a company, group, etc; the pin in a car, etc that attaches the stub axle to the axle beam and allows limited movement to the stub axle; the foremost pin in tenpin bowling; the central pin in ninepins; the crux of an argument.

king-size, king-sized adj larger than standard size.

kink n a tight twist or curl in a piece of string, rope, hair, etc; a painful cramp in the neck, back, etc; a minor problem in some course of action; a personality quirk; a bright, original idea. * vt to form kinks.

kinky adj (**kinkier, kinkiest**) (inf) eccentric.—**kinkiness** n.

kinsfolk n blood relations.

kinship n blood relationship; close connection.

kinsman, kinswoman n (pl **kinsmen, kinswomen**) a relative, esp by blood.

kiosk *n* a small open structure used for selling newspapers, confectionery, etc.

kipper *n* a kippered herring, etc. * *vt* to cure (fish) by salting and drying or smoking.

kiss *vti* to touch with the lips as an expression of love, affection or in greeting; to touch the lips with those of another person as a sign of love or desire; to touch lightly. * *n* an act of kissing; a light, gentle touch.–**kissable** *adj.*

kiss-and-tell *adj* (*inf*) pertaining to the publication of memoirs that reveal hitherto secret details.

kiss of life *n* mouth-to-mouth resuscitation.

kit *n* clothing and personal equipment, etc; tools and equipment for a specific purpose; a set of parts with instructions ready to be assembled. * *vt* (**kitting, kitted**) (*usu with* **out** *or* **up**) to provide with kit.

kitchen *n* a place where food is prepared and cooked.

kitchen garden *n* a garden where vegetables are grown for domestic use.

kite *n* a bird of prey with long narrow wings and a forked tail; a light frame covered with a thin covering for flying in the wind.

kith *n* friends and relations, now only in **kith and kin**.

kitsch *n* art, literature, etc regarded as pretentious, inferior, or in poor taste.–*also adj.*–**kitschy** *adj.*

kitten *n* a young cat; the young of other small mammals. * *vti* to give birth to kittens.

kittenish *adj* like a kitten, playful; (*woman*) flirtatious.

kitty *n* (*pl* **kitties**) the stakes in a game of poker or other gambling game; a shared fund of money; affectionate name for a cat or kitten.

kiwi *n* (*pl* **kiwis**) a flightless bird of New Zealand; (*inf*) a New Zealander.

kl *abbr* = kiloliter.

kleptomania *n* an uncontrollable impulse to steal.–**kleptomaniac** *n.*

km *abbr* = kilometer(s).

knack *n* an ability to do something easily; a trick; a habit.

knapsack *n* a bag for carrying equipment or supplies on the back.

knave *n* (*formerly*) a tricky or dishonest man; the jack in a pack of playing cards.–**knavish** *adj.*–**knavishly** *adv.*

knead *vt* to squeeze and press together (dough, clay, etc) into a uniform lump with the hands; to make (bread, etc) by kneading; to squeeze and press with the hands.–**kneader** *n.*

knee *n* the joint between the thigh and the lower part of the human leg; anything shaped like a bent knee. * *vt* (**kneeing, kneed**) to hit or touch with the knee.

kneecap *n* the small bone covering and protecting the front part of the knee-joint. * *vt* (**kneecapping, kneecapped**) to maim by shooting into the kneecap.

knee-deep *adj* deep enough to cover the knees; deeply involved.

knee jerk *n* an involuntary jerk when the tendon below the knee is tapped.

kneejerk *adj* responding automatically.

kneel *vi* (**kneeling, kneeled** *or* **knelt**) to go down on one's knee or knees; to remain in this position.–**kneeler** *n.*

knell *n* the sound of a bell rung slowly and solemnly at a death or funeral; a warning of death, failure, etc. * *vi* (*bell*) to ring a knell; to summon, announce, etc (as if) by a knell.

knelt *see* **kneel**.

knew *see* **know**.

knickers *npl* pants gathered at the knee.

knickknack *n* a small ornament or trinket.–*also* **nicknack**.

knife *n* (*pl* **knives**) a flat piece of steel, etc, with a sharp edge set in a handle, used to cut or as a weapon; a sharp blade forming part of a tool or machine. * *vt* to cut or stab with a knife.

knife edge *n* the sharp edge of a knife; anything resembling this, such as the blade of an ice skate; a sharp wedge used as a pivot for a balance; a critical or precarious situation.

knight *n* (*Middle Ages*) a medieval mounted soldier; a man who for some achievement is given honorary rank entitling him to use "Sir" before his given name; a chessman shaped like a horse's head. * *vt* to make (a man) a knight.–**knightly** *adj.*–**knightliness** *n.*

knighthood *n* the character, rank, or dignity of a knight; the order of knights.

knit *vb* (**knitting, knitted** *or* **knit**) *vt* to form (fabric or a garment) by interlooping yarn using knitting needles or a machine; to cause (eg broken bones) to grow together; to link or join together closely; to draw (the brows) together. * *vi* to make knitted fabric from yarn by means of needles; to grow together; to become joined or united. * *n* a knitted garment or fabric.–**knitter** *n.*

knitting *n* work being knitted.

knitting needle *n* a long thin eyeless needle, usu made of plastic or steel, used in knitting.

knives *see* **knife**.

knob *n* a rounded lump or protuberance; a handle, usu round, of a door, drawer, etc.

knock *vi* to strike with a sharp blow; to rap on a door; to bump, collide; (*engine*) to make a thumping noise; (*with* **off**) (*inf*) to finish work; (*with* **up**) (*tennis, etc*) to practise before a match. * *vt* to strike; (*inf*) to criticize; (*with* **about, around**) to wander around aimlessly; to treat roughly; (*with* **back**) (*inf*) to drink, swallow quickly; to reject, refuse; (*with* **down**) to indicate a sale at an auction; (*with* **down** *or* **off**) to hit so as to cause to fall; (*with* **off**) (*inf*) to do or make hastily and without effort; to reduce in price; to discontinue, esp work; (*sl*) to kill;; (*with* **out**) to make unconscious or exhausted; to eliminate in a knock-out competition; (*inf*) to amaze; (*with* **up**) (*inf*) to make or arrange hastily; to rouse. * *n* a knocking, a hit, a rap.

knocker *n* a device hinged against a door for use in knocking.

knock-kneed *adj* having inward-curving legs.

knockout *n* a punch or blow that produces unconsciousness; a contest in which competitors are eliminated at each round; (*inf*) an attractive or extremely impressive person or thing.

knoll *n* a small round hill.

knot *n* a lump in a thread, etc formed by a tightened loop or tangling; a fastening made by tying lengths of rope, etc; an ornamental bow; a small group, cluster; a hard mass of wood where a branch grows out from a tree, which shows as a roundish, cross-grained piece in a board; a unit of speed of one nautical mile per hour; something that ties closely, esp the bond of marriage. * *vti* (**knotting, knotted**) to make or form a knot (in); to entangle or become entangled.–**knotter** *n.*

knotty *adj* (**knottier, knottiest**) full of knots; hard to solve; puzzling.–**knottiness** *n.*

know *vt* (**knowing, knew**, *pp* **known**) to be well informed about; to be aware of; to be acquainted with; to recognize or distinguish.–**knowable** *adj.*

know-how *n* practical skill, experience.

knowing *adj* having knowledge; shrewd; clever; implying a secret understanding.–**knowingly** *adv.*–**knowingness** *n.*

know-it-all *n* a person who acts as if they know about everything.

knowledge *n* what one knows; the body of facts, etc accumulated over time; fact of knowing; range of information or understanding; the act of knowing.

knowledgeable *adj* having knowledge or intelligence; well-informed.–**knowledgeably** *adv.*

known *see* **know**.

knuckle *n* a joint of the finger, esp at the roots of the fingers; the knee of an animal used as food. * *vi* (*with* **down**) (*inf*) to apply oneself in earnest (to some task, duty, etc); (*with* **under**) to submit, to give in.

koala *n* an Australian tree-dwelling marsupial with thick, grey fur.

kohl *n* a fine powder, as of antimony, used for darkening the eyelids.

kohlrabi n (pl **kohlrabies**) a variety of cabbage with a thick stem, used as a vegetable.

kola nut n the seed of either of two tropical trees which has stimulant properties and is chewed or used in making sweet drinks.—also **cola nut**.

kooky, kookie adj (**kookier, kookiest**) (inf) crazy; eccentric.

Koran n the sacred book of the Muslims.—**Koranic** adj.

kosher adj (Judaism) clean or fit to eat according to dietary laws; (inf) acceptable, genuine. * n kosher food.

kowtow vi to show exaggerated respect (to) by bowing.

kremlin n a Russian citadel; (with cap and **the**) the citadel in Moscow, housing the former palace, cathedrals, and the Russian government; (with cap) the central government of Russia.

krypton n a colorless, odorless gas used in fluorescent lights and lasers.

kudos n (used as sing) (inf) fame, glory, prestige.

kumquat n a small fruit like an orange with a sweet rind.

kung fu n a Chinese system of unarmed combat.

kw. abbr = kilowatt(s).

L

l abbr = liter(s).

lab n (inf) laboratory.

label n a slip of paper, cloth, metal, etc attached to anything to provide information about its nature, contents, ownership, etc; a term of generalized classification. * vt (**labeling, labeled** or **labelling, labelled**) to attach a label to; to designate or classify (as).—**labeler, labeller** n.

labor, labour n work, physical or mental exertion; a specific task; all wage-earning workers; workers collectively; the process of childbirth. * vi to work; to work hard; to move with difficulty; to suffer (delusions, etc); to be in childbirth. * vt to develop in unnecessary detail.

laboratory n (pl **laboratories**) a room or building where scientific work and research is carried out.

Labor Day n the first Monday in September in US and Canada, a legal holiday honoring labor.

labored, laboured adj done with effort; strained.—**laboredly, labouredly** adv.

laborer, labourer n a person who labors, esp a person whose work requires strength rather than skill.

laborious adj requiring much work; hard-working; labored.—**laboriously** adv.—**laboriousness** n.

labor union or **labour union** n an organized association of employees of any trade or industry for the protection of their income and working conditions.

labour see **labor**.

Labrador retriever n a breed of large, smooth-coated sporting dog.

labyrinth n a structure containing winding passages through which it is hard to find one's way; a maze.—**labyrinthine** adj.

lace n a cord, etc used to draw together and fasten parts of a shoe, a corset, etc; a delicate ornamental fabric of openwork design using fine cotton, silk, etc. * vt to fasten with a lace or laces; to intertwine, weave; to fortify (a drink, etc) with a dash of spirits.

lacerate vt to tear jaggedly; to wound (feelings, etc).—**laceration** n.

lachrymose adj tending to shed tears; sad.—**lachrymosity** n.

lack n the fact or state of not having any or not having enough; the thing that is needed. * vti to be deficient in or entirely without.

lackadaisical adj showing lack of energy or interest; listless.—**lackadaisically** adv.

lackey n a male servant of low rank; a servile hanger-on.

lackluster, lacklustre adj lacking in brightness or vigor; dull.

laconic adj using few words; concise.—**laconically** adv.—**laconicism** n.

lacquer n a glossy varnish. * vt to coat with lacquer, to make glossy.

lacrosse n a game played by two teams of 10 players with the aim of throwing a ball through the opponents' goal using a long stick topped with a netted pouch for catching and carrying the ball.

lactate vi (mammals) to secrete milk.—**lactation** n.—**lactational** adj.

lactic adj of or relating to milk; obtained from sour milk or whey; involving the production of lactic acid.

lactic acid n an organic acid normally present in sour milk.

lactose n a sugar present in milk.

lacuna n (pl **lacunas, lacunae**) a gap, esp a missing portion in a text.—**lacunary** adj.

lacy adj (**lacier, laciest**) resembling lace.—**lacily** adv.—**laciness** n.

lad n a boy; a young man; a fellow, chap.

ladder n a portable metal or wooden framework with rungs between two vertical supports for climbing up and down; something that resembles a ladder in form or use.

laden adj loaded with cargo; burdened.

ladies' room n a public lavatory for women.

ladle n a long-handled, cup-like spoon for scooping liquids; a device like a ladle in shape or use. * (with **out**) (inf) to give (money, etc) generously.—**ladleful** n.

lady n (pl **ladies**) a polite term for any woman; (with cap) a title of honor given to various ranks of women in the British peerage.

ladybug, ladybird n a small, usu brightly colored beetle.

ladylike adj like or suitable for a lady; refined, polite.

lag vi (**lagging, lagged**) to fall behind, hang back; to fail to keep pace in movement or development; to weaken in strength or intensity. * n a falling behind; a delay.

laggard n a person who lags behind; a loiterer. * adj backward, slow.—**laggardly** adv.

lagoon n a shallow lake or pond, esp one connected with a larger body of water; the water enclosed by a circular coral reef.

laid see **lay**[2].

laid-back adj relaxed, easy-going.

lain see **lie**[2].

lair n the dwelling or resting place of a wild animal; (inf) a secluded place, a retreat.

laissez-faire, laisser-faire n the policy of non-interference with individual freedom, esp in economic affairs.—**laissez-faireism, laisser-faireism** n.

laity n laymen, as opposed to clergymen.

lake n a large inland body of water.

lamb n a young sheep; its flesh as food; (inf) an innocent or gentle person. * vi to give birth to a lamb; to tend (ewes) at lambing time.

lambast, lambaste vt (inf) to beat or censure severely.

lambda n the Greek letter L.

lame adj disabled or crippled, esp in the feet or legs; stiff and painful; weak, ineffectual. * vt to make lame.—**lamely** adv.—**lameness** n.

lamé n a fabric interwoven with metallic threads.

lame duck n a weak, ineffectual person; an elected official serving between the end of his or her term and the inauguration of a successor.

lament vti to feel or express deep sorrow (for); to mourn. * n a lamenting; an elegy, dirge, etc mourning some loss or death.—**lamenter** n.

lamentable adj distressing, deplorable.—**lamentably** adv.

lamentation n a lamenting; a lament, expression of grief.

laminate vt to cover with one or more thin layers; to make by building up in layers. * n a product made by laminating. * adj laminated.—**laminator** n.—**lamination** n.

lamp n any device producing light, either by electricity, gas, or by burning oil, etc; a holder or base for such a device; any device for producing therapeutic rays.

lampoon n a piece of satirical writing attacking someone. * vt to ridicule maliciously in a lampoon.–**lampooner** n.–**lampoonery** n.

lamprey n (pl **lamprey, lampreys**) an animal resembling an eel but having a jawless, round sucking mouth.

LAN (acronym) local area network: a number of computers in close proximity linked together in order to transfer information and share peripherals such as printers.

lance n a long wooden spear with a sharp iron or steel head. * vt to pierce (as if) with a lance; to open a boil, etc with a lancet.

lancet n a small, usu two-edged, pointed surgical knife.

land n the solid part of the earth's surface; ground, soil; a country and its people; property in land. * vt to set (an aircraft) down on land or water; to put on shore from a ship; to bring to a particular place; to catch (a fish); to get or secure (a job, prize, etc); to deliver (a blow). * vi to go ashore from a ship; to come to port; to arrive at a specified place; to come to rest.

landfill n a large pit in which refuse is buried between layers of soil.–also adj.

landing n the act of coming to shore or to the ground; the place where persons or goods are loaded or unloaded from a ship; a platform at the end of a flight of stairs.

landing craft n a small military vessel designed for landing troops and equipment ashore.

landing gear n the undercarriage of an aircraft.

landing stage n a platform for landing goods or people from a ship.

landlocked adj surrounded by land.

landlord n a man who owns and rents property.

landlubber n a person who has had little experience of the sea.

landmark n any prominent feature of the landscape distinguishing a locality; an important event or turning point.

landmass n a large expanse of land.

land mine n an explosive charge shallowly buried in the ground, usu detonated by stepping or driving on it.

landscape n an expanse of natural scenery seen in one view; a picture of natural, inland scenery. * vt to make (a plot of ground) more attractive, as by adding lawns, bushes, trees, etc.

landslide n the sliding of a mass of soil or rocks down a slope; an overwhelming victory, esp in an election.

landward adv, adj toward the land.–**landwards** adv.

lane n a narrow road, path, etc; a path or strip specifically designated for ships, aircraft, cars, etc; one of the narrow strips dividing a running track, swimming pool, etc for athletes and swimmers.

language n human speech or the written symbols for speech; any means of communicating; a special set of symbols used for programming a computer; the speech of a particular nation, etc; the particular style of verbal expression characteristic of a person, group, profession, etc.

languid adj lacking energy or vitality; apathetic; drooping, sluggish.–**languidly** adv.–**languidness** n.

languish vi to lose strength and vitality; to pine; to suffer neglect or hardship; to assume a pleading or melancholic expression.–**languisher** n.–**languishment** n.

languor n physical or mental fatigue or apathy; dreaminess; oppressive stillness.–**languorous** adj.

lank adj tall and thin; long and limp.–**lankly** adv.–**lankness** n.

lanky adj (**lankier, lankiest**) lean, tall, and ungainly.–**lankily** adv.–**lankiness** n.

lanolin, lanoline n wool grease used in cosmetics, ointments, etc.

lantern n a portable transparent case for holding a light.

lanyard n a rope used for fastening things on board a ship; a cord worn round the neck to hold a knife, whistle, etc.

lap[1] vti (**lapping, lapped**) to take in (liquid) with the tongue; (waves) to flow gently with a splashing sound.

lap[2] n the flat area from waist to knees formed by a person sitting; the part of the clothing covering this.

lap[3] n an overlapping; a part that overlaps; one complete circuit of a race track. * vb (**lapping, lapped**) vt to fold (over or on); to wrap. * vi to overlap; to extend over something in space or time.

lapdog n a dog small and docile enough to be held on the lap.

lapel n a part of a suit, coat, jacket, etc folded back and continuous with the collar.–**lapelled** adj.

lapidary adj of or relating to stones; inscribed on stone; concise, like an inscription. * n (pl **lapidaries**) a cutter or engraver of gems.–**lapidarian** adj.

lapis lazuli n an azure, opaque, semi-precious stone.

lap of honor n a ceremonial circuit of the field by a winning person or team.

lapse n a small error; a decline or drop to a lower condition, degree, or state; a moral decline; a period of time elapsed; the termination of a legal right or privilege through disuse. * vi to depart from the usual or accepted standard, esp in morals; to pass out of existence or use; to become void or discontinued; (time) to slip away.–**lapsable, lapsible** adj.–**lapser** n.

laptop n a small portable computer that can comfortably be used on the lap.

larceny n (pl **larcenies**) the theft of someone else's property.–**larcenist, larcener** n.–**larcenous** adj.

larch n a cone-bearing tree of the pine family.

lard n melted and clarified pig fat. * vt to insert strips of bacon or pork fat (in meat) before cooking; to embellish.

larder n a room or cupboard where food is stored.

large adj great in size, amount, or number; bulky; big; spacious; bigger than others of its kind; operating on a big scale.–**largeness** n.

largely adv much, in great amounts; mainly, for the most part.

large-scale adj drawn on a big scale to reveal much detail; extensive.

largess, largesse n the generous distribution of money, gifts, favors, etc; generosity.

lariat n a rope for tethering grazing horses; a lasso.

lark[1] n any of a family of songbirds.

lark[2] n a playful or amusing adventure; a harmless prank. * vi (usu with **about**) to have fun, frolic.–**larky** adj.

larva n (pl **larvae**) the immature form of many animals after emerging from an egg before transformation into the adult state, eg a caterpillar.–**larval** adj.

laryngitis n inflammation of the larynx.–**laryngitic** adj.

larynx n (pl **larynxes, larynges**) the structure at the upper end of the windpipe, containing the vocal cords.

lasagna, lasagne n pasta formed in thin wide strips; a dish of lasagne baked in layers with cheese, minced meat and tomato sauce.

lascivious adj lecherous, lustful; arousing sexual desire.–**lasciviously** adv.–**lasciviousness** n.

laser n a device that produces an intense monochromatic beam of coherent light or other electromagnetic radiation.

laser printer n a computer printer that uses a laser beam and photoconductive drum to produce high quality text output.

lash vt to strike forcefully (as if) with a lash; to fasten or secure with a cord, etc; to attack with criticism or ridicule. * vi to move quickly and violently; (rain, waves, etc) to beat violently against; (with **out**) to attack suddenly either physically or verbally; (inf) to spend extravagantly (on). * n the flexible part of a whip; an eyelash; a stroke (as if) with a whip.–**lasher** n.

lass n a young woman or girl.

lassitude n weariness.

lasso n (pl **lassos, lassoes**) a long rope or leather thong with a running noose for catching horses, cattle, etc. * vt (**lassoes** or **lassos, lassoing, lassoed**) to catch (as if) with a lasso.–**lassoer** n.

last[1] n a shoemaker's model of the foot on which boots and shoes are made or repaired. * vt to shape with a last.

last[2] vi to remain in existence, use, etc; to endure. * vt to continue during; to be enough for.

last[3] *adj* being or coming after all the others in time or place; only remaining; the most recent; least likely; conclusive. * *adv* after all the others; most recently; finally. * *n* the one coming last.—**lastly** *adv*.

last-ditch *adj* being a final effort to avoid disaster.

lasting *adj* enduring.—**lastingly** *adv*.

lastly *adv* at the end, in the last place, finally.

last-minute *adj* at the last possible time when something can be done.

last rites *npl* the sacraments prescribed for a person near death.

latch *n* a fastening for a door, gate, or window, esp a bar, etc that fits into a notch. * *vti* to fasten with a latch.

late *adj, adv* after the usual or expected time; at an advanced stage or age; near the end; far on in the day or evening; just prior to the present; deceased; not long past; until lately; out of office.—**lateness** *n*.

latecomer *n* a person or thing that arrives late.

lately *adv* recently, in recent times.

latent *adj* existing but not yet visible or developed.—**latency** *n*.—**latently** *adv*.

later *adv* subsequently; afterwards.—*also compar of* **late**.

lateral *adj* of, at, from, toward the side.—**laterally** *adv*.

lateral thinking *n* a solving of problems by employing unorthodox thought processes.

latest *adj* most recent or fashionable. * *n* (*inf*: *with* **the**) the most up-to-date fashion, news, etc.—*also superl of* **late**.

latex *n* (*pl* **latexes, latices**) the milky juice produced by certain plants, used in the manufacture of rubber.

lath *n* (*pl* **laths**) a thin narrow strip of wood used in constructing a framework for plaster, etc.

lathe *n* a machine that rotates wood, metal, etc for shaping.

lather *n* a foam made by soap or detergent mixed with water; frothy sweat; a state of excitement or agitation. * *vti* to cover with or form lather.—**lathery** *adj*.

latitude *n* the distance from north or south of the equator, measured in degrees; a region with reference to this distance; extent; scope; freedom from restrictions on actions or opinions.—**latitudinal** *adj*.—**latitudinally** *adv*.

latrine *n* a lavatory, as in a military camp.

latter *adj* later; more recent; nearer the end; being the last mentioned of two.

latter-day *adj* present-day; modern.—**latterly** *adv*.

lattice *n* a network of crossed laths or bars.—**latticed** *adj*.

laud *vt* to praise; to extol.—**laudable** *adj*.—**laudably** *adv*.

laugh *vi* to emit explosive inarticulate vocal sounds expressive of amusement, joy or derision. * *vt* to utter or express with laughter; (*with* **off**) to dismiss as of little importance, make a joke of. * *n* the act or sound of laughing; (*inf*) an amusing person or thing.—**laugher** *n*.—**laughing** *adj, n*.—**laughingly** *adv*.

laughable *adj* causing laughter; ridiculous.—**laughably** *adv*.

laughing stock *n* an object of ridicule.

laughter *n* the act or sound of laughing.

launch[1] *vt* to throw, hurl or propel forward; to cause (a vessel) to slide into the water; (*rocket, missile*) to set off; to put into action; to put a new product onto the market. * *vi* to involve oneself enthusiastically. * *n* the act or occasion of launching.

launch[2] *n* an open, or partly enclosed, motor boat.

launch pad, launching pad *n* a platform from which a spacecraft is launched.

launder *vti* to wash and iron clothes. * *vt* to legitimize (money obtained from criminal activity) by passing it through foreign banks, or investing in legitimate businesses, etc.—**launderer** *n*.

Laundromat *n* (*trademark*) an establishment equipped with coin-operated washing machines and driers for public use.

laundry *n* (*pl* **laundries**) a place where clothes are washed and ironed; clothes sent to be washed and ironed.

laurel *n* an evergreen shrub with large, glossy leaves; the leaves used by the ancient Greeks as a symbol of achievement.

lava *n* molten rock flowing from a volcano; the solid substance formed as this cools.

lavatory *n* (*pl* **lavatories**) a sanitary device for the disposal or feces and urine; a room equipped with this.—*also* **bathroom, toilet**.

lavender *n* the fragrant flowers of a perennial shrub dried and used in sachets; a pale purple.

lavish *vt* to give or spend freely. * *adj* abundant, profuse; generous; extravagant.—**lavishly** *adv*.—**lavishness** *n*.

law *n* all the rules of conduct in an organized community as upheld by authority; any one of such rules; obedience to such rules; the study of such rules, jurisprudence; the seeking of justice in courts under such rules; the profession of lawyers, judges, etc; (*inf*) the police; a sequence of events occurring with unvarying uniformity under the same conditions; any rule expected to be observed.

law-abiding *adj* obeying the law.

lawful *adj* in conformity with the law; recognized by law.—**lawfully** *adv*.—**lawfulness** *n*.

lawless *adj* not regulated by law; not in conformity with law, illegal.—**lawlessly** *adv*.—**lawlessness** *n*.

lawn[1] *n* a fine sheer cloth of linen or cotton.

lawn[2] *n* land covered with closely cut grass, esp around a house.

lawn mower *n* a hand-propelled or power-driven machine to cut lawn grass.

lawsuit *n* a suit between private parties in a law court.

lawyer *n* a person whose profession is advising others in matters of law or representing them in a court of law.

lax *adj* slack, loose; not tight; not strict or exact.—**laxly** *adv*.—**laxity** *n*.—**laxness** *n*.

laxative *n* a substance that promotes emptying of the bowels.—*also adj*.

lay[1] *see* **lie**[2].

lay[2] *vt* (**laying, laid**) to put down; to allay or suppress; to place in a resting position; to place or set; to place in a correct position; to produce (an egg); to devise; to present or assert; to stake a bet; (*with* **down**) to put down; to surrender, relinquish; to begin to build; to establish (guidelines, rules, etc); to store, esp wine; to record tracks in a music studio; (*with* **in**) to store, to stockpile; (*with* **off**) to suspend from work temporarily or permanently; (*with* **on**) to supply, provide; to install (electricity, etc); (*with* **out**) to plan in detail; to arrange for display; to prepare (a corpse) for viewing; (*inf*) to spend money, esp lavishly; (*with* **up**) to store for future use; to disable or confine through illness. * *vi* (*inf*) to leave (a person or thing) alone; (*with* **into**) to attack physically or verbally. * *n* a way or position in which something is situated.

lay[3] *n* a simple narrative poem, esp as intended to be sung; a ballad.

lay[4] *adj* of or pertaining to those who are not members of the clergy; not belonging to a profession.

layabout *n* a loafer, lazy person.

layer *n* a single thickness, fold, etc; the runner of a plant fastened down to take root; a hen that lays. * *vti* to separate into layers; to form by superimposing layers.

layman *n* (*pl* **laymen**) a person who is not a member of the clergy; a non-specialist, someone who does not possess professional knowledge.—**laywoman** *nf* (*pl* **laywomen**).

layoff *n* a period of involuntary unemployment.

layout *n* the manner in which anything is laid out, esp arrangement of text and pictures on the pages of a newspaper or magazine, etc; the thing laid out.

laze *vti* to idle or loaf.

lazy *adj* (**lazier, laziest**) disinclined to work or exertion; encouraging or causing indolence; sluggishly moving.—**lazily** *adv*.—**laziness** *n*.

lazybones *n* a lazy person.

lb *abbr* = pound(s) weight.

leach vt to wash (soil, ore, etc) with a filtering liquid; to extract (a soluble substance) from some material. * vi to lose soluble matter through a filtering liquid.–**leacher** n.

lead[1] vb (**leading, led**) vt to show the way, esp by going first; to direct or guide on a course; to direct by influence; to be head of (an expedition, orchestra, etc); to be ahead of in a contest; to live, spend (one's life); (with **on**) to lure or entice, esp into mischief. * vi to show the way, as by going first; (with **to**) to tend in a certain direction; to be or go first. * n the role of a leader; first place; the amount or distance ahead; anything that leads, as a clue; the leading role in a play, etc; the right of playing first in cards or the card played.

lead[2] n a heavy, soft, bluish-gray, metallic element; a weight for sounding depths at sea, etc; bullets; a stick of graphite, used in pencils. * adj of or containing lead. * vt (**leading, leaded**) to cover, weight, or space out with lead.

leaden adj made of lead; very heavy; dull gray; gloomy.–**leadenly** adv.

leader n the person who goes first; the principle first violin-player in an orchestra; the director of an orchestra; the inspiration or head of a movement, such as a political party; a person whose example is followed; the leading editorial in a newspaper; the leading article.

leadership n the act of leading; the ability to be a leader; the leaders of an organization or movement collectively.

lead time n the period between the design of a product and its manufacture.

leaf n (pl **leaves**) any of the flat, thin (usu green) parts growing from the stem of a plant; a sheet of paper; a very thin sheet of metal; a hinged or removable part of a table top. * vi to bear leaves; (with **through**) to turn the pages of.

leaflet n a small or young leaf; a sheet of printed information (often folded), esp advertising matter distributed free. * vi to distribute leaflets (to).

leafy adj (**leafier, leafiest**) having many or broad leaves; resembling leaves.–**leafiness** n.

league n an association of nations, groups, etc for promoting common interests; an association of sports clubs that organizes matches between members; any class or category. * vti (**leaguing, leagued**) to form into a league.

leak n a crack or hole through which liquid or gas may accidentally pass; the liquid or gas passing through such an opening; confidential information made public deliberately or accidentally. * vi to (let) escape through an opening; to disclose information surreptitiously.–**leaker** n.

leaky adj (**leakier, leakiest**) leaking or likely to leak.–**leakiness** n.

lean[1] adj thin, with little flesh or fat; spare; meager. * n meat with little or no fat.–**leanness** n.

lean[2] vb (**leaning, leaned** or **leant**) vi to bend or slant from an upright position; to rest supported (on or against); to rely or depend for help (on). * vt to cause to lean.

leaning n inclination, tendency.

leant see **lean**[2].

leap vb (**leaping, leaped** or **leapt**) vi to jump; (with **at**) to accept something offered eagerly. * vt to pass over by a jump; to cause to leap. * n an act of leaping; bound; space passed by leaping; an abrupt transition.–**leaper** n.

leapfrog n a game in which one player vaults over another's bent back. * vi (**leapfrogging, leapfrogged**) to vault in this manner; to advance in alternate jumps.

leap year n a year with an extra day (29 February) occurring every fourth year.

learn vti (**learning, learned** or **learnt**) to gain knowledge of or skill in; to memorize; to become aware of, realize.–**learner** n.

learned adj having learning; erudite; acquired by study, experience, etc.–**learnedly** adv.

lease n a contract by which an owner lets land, property, etc to another person for a specified period. * vt to grant by or hold under lease.–**leaseable** adj.–**leaser** n.

leash n a cord, strap, etc by which a dog is held in check. * vt to hold or restrain on a leash.

least adj smallest in size, degree, etc; slightest. * adv to the smallest degree. * n the smallest amount.

leather n material made from the skin of an animal prepared by removing the hair and tanning; something made of leather. * vt to cover with leather; to thrash.–**leathery** adj.

leave[1] n permission to do something; official authorization to be absent; the period covered by this.

leave[2] vb (**leaving, left**) vt to depart from; to cause or allow to remain in a specified state; to cause to remain behind; to refrain from consuming or dealing with; to have remaining at death, to bequeath; to have as a remainder; to allow to stay or continue doing without interference; to entrust or commit to another; to abandon. * vi to depart; (with **off**) to stop, desist.–**leaver** n.

leaven n a substance to make dough rise, esp yeast; something that changes or enlivens. * vt to raise with leaven; to modify, to enliven.–**leavening** n.

leaves see **leaf**.

leave-taking n a departure, farewell.

leavings npl leftovers; remnants; refuse.

lechery n (pl **lecheries**) unrestrained sexuality; debauchery.–**lecher** n.–**lecherous** adj.

lecithin n any of a group of fatty compounds found in plant and animal tissues, used as an emulsifier and antioxidant.

lectern n a reading stand in a church; any similar reading support.

lecture n an informative talk to a class, etc; a lengthy reprimand. * vti to give a lecture (to); to reprimand.–**lecturer** n.

led see **lead**[1].

ledge n a narrow horizontal surface resembling a shelf projecting from a wall, rock face, etc; an underwater ridge of rocks.

ledger n a book in which a record of debits, credits, etc is kept.

lee n a shelter; the side or part away from the wind.

leech n a blood-sucking worm; a person who clings to or exploits another.

leek n a vegetable that resembles a greatly elongated green onion.

leer n a sly, oblique or lascivious look. * vi to look with a leer.–**leeringly** adv.

leery adj (**leerier, leeriest**) (with **of**) suspicious, wary.

lees npl sediment in the bottom of a wine bottle, etc.

leeward adj, n (naut) (in) the quarter toward which the wind blows.

leeway n the distance a ship or aircraft has strayed sideways of its course; freedom of action as regards expenditure of time, money, etc.

left[1] see **leave**[2].

left[2] adj of or on the side that is toward the west when one faces north; worn on the left hand, foot, etc. * n the left side; (often cap) of or relating to the left in politics; the left hand.

left-hand adj of or toward the left side of a person or thing; for use by the left hand.

left-handed adj using the left hand in preference to the right; done or made for use with the left hand; ambiguous, backhanded. * adv with the left hand.–**left-handedly** adv.–**left-handedness** n.

leftovers npl unused portions of something, esp uneaten food.

left-wing adj of or relating to the liberal faction of a political party, organization, etc.–**left-winger** n.

leg n one of the limbs on which humans and animals support themselves and walk; the part of a garment covering the leg; anything shaped or used like a leg; a branch or limb of a forked object; a section, as of a trip; any of a series of games or matches in a competition.

legacy n (pl **legacies**) money, property, etc left to someone in a will; something passed on by an ancestor or remaining from the past.

legal *adj* of or based on law; permitted by law; of or for lawyers.– **legally** *adv*.

legality *n* (*pl* **legalities**) conformity with the law.

legalize *vt* to make lawful.–**legalization** *n*.

legal tender *n* a currency which a creditor is legally bound to accept in payment of a debt.

legate *n* an envoy, esp from the Pope; an official emissary.–**legatine** *adj*.

legation *n* a diplomatic minister and staff; the headquarters of a diplomatic minister.–**legationary** *adj*.

legend *n* a story handed down from the past; a notable person or the stories of his or her exploits; an inscription on a coin, etc; a caption; an explanation of the symbols used on a map.–**legendary** *adj*.

legerdemain *n* trickery, sleight of hand.

leggings *npl* protective outer coverings for the lower legs; a leg-hugging fashion garment for women.

leggy *adj* (**leggier, leggiest**) having long and shapely legs.–**legginess** *n*.

legible *adj* able to be read.–**legibility** *n*.–**legibly** *adv*.

legion *n* an infantry unit of the ancient Roman army; a large body of soldiers; a large number, a multitude.

legionnaire *n* a member of certain military forces or associations.

legislate *vi* to make or pass laws * *vt* to bring about by legislation.–**legislation** *n*.–**legislative** *adj*.

legislator *n* a member of a legislative body.

legislature *n* the body of people who have the power of making laws.

legitimate *adj* lawful; reasonable, justifiable; conforming to accepted rules, standards, etc; (*child*) born of parents married to each other.–**legitimacy** *n*.–**legitimately** *adv*.

legume *n* any of a large family of plants having seeds growing in pods, including beans, peas, etc; the pod or seed of such a plant used as food.–**leguminous** *adj*.

lei *n* a garland of flowers worn around the neck, given as a token of affection in Hawaii.

leisure *n* ease, relaxation, esp freedom from employment or duties. * *adj* free and unoccupied.–**leisured** *adj*.

leisurely *adj* relaxed, without hurry.

leitmotif, leitmotiv *n* a dominant theme.

lemming *n* a small arctic rodent; one of a group wilfully heading on a course for destruction.

lemon *n* (a tree bearing) a small yellow oval fruit with an acid pulp; pale yellow; (*sl*) a person or thing considered disappointing or useless.–**lemony** *adj*.

lemonade *n* a lemon-flavored drink.

lemon grass *n* a tropical grass with lemon-scented leaves used in cooking and which yields an aromatic oil.

lend *vb* (**lending, lent**) *vt* to give the use of something temporarily in expectation of its return; to provide (money) at interest; to give, impart. * *vi* to make loans.–**lender** *n*.

length *n* the extent of something from end to end, usu the longest dimension; a specified distance or period of time; something of a certain length taken from a larger piece; a long expanse; (*often pl*) the degree of effort put into some action.–**lengthen** *vti*.

lengthwise, lengthways *adv* in the direction of the length.

lengthy *adj* (**lengthier, lengthiest**) long, esp too long.–**lengthily** *adv*.–**lengthiness** *n*.

lenient *adj* not harsh or severe; merciful.–**leniency, lenience** *n*.–**leniently** *adv*.

lens *n* a curved piece of transparent glass, plastic, etc used in optical instruments to form an image; any device used to focus electromagnetic rays, sound waves, etc; a similar transparent part of the eye that focuses light rays on the retina.

Lent *n* the forty weekdays from Ash Wednesday to Easter, observed by Christians as a period of fasting and penitence.–**Lenten** *adj*.

lent *see* **lend**.

lentil *n* any of several leguminous plants with edible seeds; their seed used for food.

Leo *n* (*astrol*) the fifth sign of the zodiac, in astrology operative July 22–August 21; (*astron*) the Lion, a constellation in the northern hemisphere.

leonine *adj* of or like a lion.

leopard *n* a large tawny feline with black spots found in Africa and Asia.–*also* **panther**.–**leopardess** *nf*.

leotard *n* a skintight one-piece garment worn by dancers and others engaged in strenuous exercise.

leper *n* a person with leprosy.

leprechaun *n* (*Irish folklore*) a fairy.

leprosy *n* a chronic infectious bacterial disease of the skin, often resulting in disfigurement.–**leprous** *adj*.

lesbian *n* a female homosexual. * *adj* of or characteristic of lesbians.–**lesbianism** *n*.

lesion *n* any change in an organ or tissue caused by injury or disease; an injury.

less *adj* not so much, not so great, etc; fewer; smaller. * *adv* to a smaller extent. * *n* a smaller amount. * *prep* minus.

lessen *vti* to make or become less.

lesser *adj* less in size, quality or importance.

lesson *n* something to be learned or studied; something that has been learned or studied; a unit of learning or teaching; (*pl*) a course of instruction.

lest *conj* in order, or for fear, that not; that.

let¹ *n* a stoppage; (*tennis*) a minor obstruction of the ball that requires a point to be replayed.

let² *vb* (**letting, let**) *vt* to allow, permit; to rent; to assign (a contract); to cause to run out, as blood; as an auxiliary in giving suggestions or commands (*let us go*); (*with* **down**) to lower; to deflate; to disappoint; to untie; to lengthen; (*with* **off**) to allow to leave (a ship, etc); to cause to explode or fire; to release, excuse from (work, etc); to deal leniently with, refrain from punishing; to allow (gas, etc) to escape; (*with* **out**) to release; to reveal; to rent out; to make a garment larger; (*with* **up**) to relax; to cease. * *vi* to be rented; (*with* **on**) (*inf*) to pretend; (*inf*) to reveal (a secret, etc); to pretend. * *n* the letting of property or accommodation.

let-down *n* a disappointment.

lethal *adj* deadly.–**lethality** *n*.–**lethally** *adv*.

lethargy *n* (*pl* **lethargies**) an abnormal drowsiness; sluggishness; apathy.–**lethargic** *adj*.–**lethargically** *adv*.

let's = let us.

letter *n* a symbol representing a phonetic value in a written language; a character of the alphabet; a written or printed message; (*pl*) literature; learning; knowledge; literal meaning. * *vt* to mark with letters.

letterhead *n* a name, address, etc printed as a heading on stationery; stationery printed with a heading.

lettering *n* the act or process of inscribing with letters; letters collectively; a title; an inscription.

lettuce *n* a plant with succulent leaves used in salads.

letup *n* a relaxation of effort.

leukemia, leukaemia *n* a chronic disease characterized by an abnormal increase in the number of white blood cells in body tissues and the blood.

leukocyte *n* a white blood cell.

levee *n* an embankment beside a river.

level *n* a horizontal line or plane; a position in a scale of values; a flat area or surface; an instrument for determining the horizontal. * *adj* horizontal; having a flat surface; at the same height, rank, position, etc; steady. * *vti* (**leveling, leveled** *or* **levelling, levelled**) to make or become level; to demolish; to raise and aim (a gun, criticism, etc).–**levelly** *adv*.

level-headed *adj* having an even temper and sound judgment.–**level-headedly** *adv*.

lever n a bar used for prising or moving something; a means to an end; a device consisting of a bar turning about a fixed point; any device used in the same way, eg to operate machinery. * vt to raise or move (as with) a lever.

leverage n the action of a lever; the mechanical advantage gained by the use of a lever; power, influence.

leviathan n something huge.

levitate vti to rise or cause to rise into the air and float without support.—**levitation** n.

levity n (pl **levities**) excessive frivolity; lack of necessary seriousness.

levy vt (**levying, levied**) to collect by force or authority, as a tax, fine, etc; an amount levied; to enrol or conscript troops; to prepare for or wage war. * n (pl **levies**) a levying; the amount levied.—**levier** n.

lewd adj indecent; lustful; obscene.—**lewdly** adv.—**lewdness** n.

lexicography n the process of writing or compiling a dictionary; the principles and practices of dictionary making.—**lexicographer** n.—**lexicographic, lexicographical** adj.—**lexicographically** adv.

lexicon n a dictionary; a special vocabulary, as of a specific language, branch of knowledge, etc.

liability n (pl **liabilities**) a being liable; something for which one is liable; (inf) a handicap, disadvantage; (pl) debts, obligations, disadvantages.

liable adj legally bound or responsible; subject to; likely (to).

liaise vi to form a connection and retain contact with.

liaison n intercommunication as between units of a military force; an illicit love affair.

liar n a person who tells lies.

libation n the act of pouring wine or oil on the ground, as a sacrifice; the liquid so poured out; a drink.

libel n any written or printed matter tending to injure a person's reputation unjustly; (inf) any defamatory or damaging assertion about a person. * vt (**libeling, libeled** or **libelling, libelled**) to utter or publish a libel against.—**libeler, libeller** n.—**libelous, libellous** adj.

liberal adj ample, abundant; not literal or strict; tolerant; (education) contributing to a general broadening of the mind, non-specialist; favoring reform or progress. * n a person who favors reform or progress.—**liberally** adv.

liberalism n liberal opinions, principles or politics.

liberate vt to set free from foreign occupation, slavery, etc.—**liberator** n.

liberation n the act of liberating; the state of being liberated; the pursuit of social, political or economic equality by or on behalf of those being discriminated against.

libertine n a dissolute person; a freethinker. * adj unrestrained, morally or socially; licentious.—**libertinism, libertinage** n.

liberty n (pl **liberties**) freedom from slavery, captivity, etc; the right to do as one pleases, freedom; a particular right, freedom, etc granted by authority; an impertinent attitude; authorized leave granted to a sailor.

libidinous adj lustful, lascivious.

libido n (pl **libidos**) the sexual urge.—**libidinal** adj.

Libra n (astrol) the 7th sign of the zodiac, operative 24 September–23 October; a constellation represented as a pair of scales.—**Libran** n, adj.

librarian n a person in charge of a library or trained in librarianship.

librarianship, library science n the profession of organizing collections of books, etc for reference by others.

library n (pl **libraries**) a collection of books, tapes, records, photographs, etc for reference or borrowing; a room, building or institution containing such a collection.

libretto n (pl **libretti, librettos**) the text to which an opera, oratorio, etc is set.—**librettist** n.

lice see **louse**.

license n a formal or legal permission to do something specified; a document granting such permission; freedom to deviate from rule, practice, etc; excessive freedom, an abuse of liberty (–also **licence**). *vt to grant a license to or for; to permit.—**licenser, licensor** n.

licensee n a person who is granted a license.

license plate n a plate on the front or rear of a motor vehicle that displays itsregistration number.–also **numberplate**.

licentious adj morally unrestrained; lascivious.—**licentiousness** n.

lichen n any of various small plants consisting of an alga and a fungus living in symbiotic association, growing on stones, trees, etc.

lick vt to draw the tongue over, esp to taste or clean; (flames, etc) to flicker around or touch lightly; (inf) to thrash; (inf) to defeat. * n a licking with the tongue; (inf) a sharp blow; (inf) a short, rapid burst of activity.

licking n (inf) a severe beating; a defeat.

licorice n a black extract made from the root of a European plant, used in medicine and confectionery; a licorice-flavored sweet.–also **liquorice**.

lid n a removable cover as for a box, etc; an eyelid.—**lidded** adj.

lie[1] n an untrue statement made with intent to deceive; something that deceives or misleads. * vi (**lying, lied**) to speak untruthfully with an intention to deceive; to create a false impression.

lie[2] vi (**lying, lay,** pp **lain**) to be or put oneself in a reclining or horizontal position; to rest on a support in a horizontal position; to be in a specified condition; to be situated; to exist. * n the way in which something is situated.

lie detector n a polygraph device used by police and security services that monitors sharp fluctuations in involuntary physiological responses as evidence of stress, guilt, etc when deliberately lying.

lien n (law) a right to keep another's property pending payment of a debt due to the holder.

lieu n place; stead (esp in lieu of, in place of, instead of).

lieutenant n a commissioned army officer ranking below a captain; a naval officer next below a lieutenant commander; a deputy, a chief assistant to a superior.—**lieutenancy** n.

life n (pl **lives**) that property of plants and animals (ending at death) that enables them to use food, grow, reproduce, etc; the state of having this property; living things collectively; the time a person or thing exists; one's manner of living; one's animate existence; vigor, liveliness; (inf) a life sentence; a biography. * adj of animate being; lifelong; using a living model; of or relating to or provided by life insurance.

lifeblood n the blood necessary to life; a vital element.

lifeboat n a small rescue boat carried by a ship; a specially designed and equipped rescue vessel that helps those in distress along the coastline.

life buoy n a ring-shaped buoyant device to keep a person afloat.

life cycle n a sequence of stages through which a living being passes during its lifetime

lifeguard n an expert swimmer employed to prevent drownings.

life jacket n a sleeveless jacket or vest of buoyant material to keep a person afloat.

lifeless adj dead; unconscious; dull.—**lifelessly** adv.—**lifelessness** n.

lifelike adj resembling a real life person or thing.

lifeline n a rope for raising or lowering a diver; a rope for rescuing a person, eg as attached to a lifebelt; a vitally important channel of communication or transport.

lifelong adj lasting one's whole life.

lifesaving adj something (as drugs) designed to save lives. * n the skill or practice of saving lives, esp from drowning.—**lifesaver** n.

life science *n* a science dealing with living organisms and life processes, such as biology, zoology, etc.

life sentence *n* imprisonment for life, or a long period, as punishment for a grave offense.

life-size, life-sized *adj* of the size of the original.

lifestyle *n* the particular attitudes, living habits, etc of a person.

lifetime *n* the length of time that a person lives or something lasts.

lift *vt* to bring to a higher position, raise; to raise in rank, condition, etc; (*sl*) to steal; to revoke. * *vi* to exert oneself in raising something; to rise; to go up; (*fog, etc*) to disperse; (*with* **off**) (*rocket, etc*) to take off. * *n* act or fact of lifting; distance through which a thing is lifted; elevation of mood, etc; elevated position or carriage; a ride in the direction in which one is going; help of any kind; upward air pressure maintaining an aircraft in flight.–**lifter** *n*.

liftoff *n* the vertical thrust of a spacecraft, etc at launching; the time of this.

ligament *n* a band of tissue connecting bones; a unifying bond.

ligature *n* a tying or binding together; a tie, bond, etc; two or more printed letters joined together, as œ; a thread used to suture a blood vessel, etc in surgery.

light[1] *n* the agent of illumination that stimulates the sense of sight; electromagnetic radiation such as ultraviolet, infrared or X-rays; brightness, illumination; a source of light, as the sun, a lamp, etc; daylight; a thing used to ignite something; a window; knowledge, enlightenment; aspect or appearance. * *adj* having light; bright; pale in color. * *adv* palely. * *vt* (**lighting, lit** *or* **lighted**) to ignite; to cause to give off light; to furnish with light; to brighten, animate.

light[2] *adj* having little weight; not heavy; less than usual in weight, amount, force, etc; of little importance; easy to bear; easy to digest; happy; dizzy, giddy; not serious; moderate; moving with ease; producing small products. * *adv* lightly. * *vi* (**lighting, lit** *or* **lighted**) to come to rest after travelling through the air; to dismount, to alight; to come or happen on or upon; to strike suddenly, as a blow.–**lightly** *adv*.–**lightness** *n*.

lighten[1] *vti* to make or become light or lighter; to shine, flash.–**lightener** *n*.

lighten[2] *vti* to make or become lighter in weight; to make or become more cheerful; to mitigate.–**lightener** *n*.

lighter *n* a small device that produces a naked flame to light cigarettes.

light-headed *adj* dizzy; delirious.–**light-headedly** *adv*.

light-hearted *adj* carefree.–**light-heartedly** *adv*.

lighthouse *n* a tower with a bright light to guide ships.

lighting *n* the process of giving light; equipment for illuminating a stage, television set, etc; the distribution of light on an object, as in a work of art.

lightning *n* a discharge or flash of electricity in the sky. * *adv* fast, sudden.

lightning conductor *or* **rod** *n* a metal rod placed high on a building and grounded to divert lightning from the structure.

lightweight *adj* of less than average weight; trivial, unimportant. * *n* a person or thing of less than average weight; a person of little importance or influence.

light-year *n* the distance light travels in one year.

likable, likeable *adj* attractive, pleasant, genial, etc.–**likably, likeably** *adv*.

like[1] *adj* having the same characteristics; similar; equal. * *adv* (*inf*) likely. * *prep* similar to; characteristic of; in the mood for; indicative of; as for example. * *conj* (*inf*) as; as if. * *n* an equal; counterpart.

like[2] *vt* to be pleased with; to wish. * *vi* to be so inclined.

likelihood *n* probability.

likely *adj* (**likelier, likeliest**) reasonably to be expected; suitable; showing promise of success.* *adv* probably.–**likeliness** *n*.

like-minded *adj* sharing the same tastes, ideas, etc.–**like-mindedness** *n*.

liken *vt* to compare.

likeness *n* a being like; something that is like, as a copy, portrait, etc; appearance, semblance.

likewise *adv* the same; also.

liking *n* fondness; affection; preference.

lilac *n* a shrub with large clusters of tiny, fragrant flowers; a pale purple. * *adj* lilac colored.

lilt *n* a light rhythmic song or tune; a springy motion. * *vi* (*music, song*) to have a lilt; to move buoyantly.–**lilting** *adj*.

lily *n* (*pl* **lilies**) a bulbous plant having typically trumpet-shaped flowers; its flower.

lily-livered *adj* cowardly.

lima bean *n* a kind of bean that produces flat, edible pale green seeds; its edible seed.

limb *n* a projecting appendage of an animal body, as an arm, leg, or wing; a large branch of a tree; a participating member, agent; an arm of a cross.–**limbless** *adj*.

limber *adj* flexible, able to bend the body easily. * *vt* to make limber. * *vi* to become limber; (*with* **up**) to stretch and warm the muscles in readiness for physical exercise.

limbo *n* (*pl* **limbos**) (*Christianity*) the abode after death assigned to unbaptized souls; a place for lost, unwanted, or neglected persons or things; an intermediate stage or condition between extremes.

lime[1] *n* a white calcium compound used for making cement and in agriculture. * *vt* to treat or cover with lime.

lime[2] *n* a small yellowish-green fruit with a juicy, sour pulp; the tree that bears it; its color.

limelight *n* intense publicity; a type of lamp, formerly used in stage lighting, in which lime was heated to produce a brilliant flame.

limerick *n* a type of humorous verse consisting of five lines.

limestone *n* a type of rock composed mainly of calcium carbonate.

limit *n* a boundary; (*pl*) bounds; the greatest amount allowed; (*inf*) as much as one can tolerate. * *vt* to set a limit to; to restrict.– **limitable** *adj*.

limitation *n* the act of limiting or being limited; a hindrance to ability or achievement.

limited *adj* confined within bounds; lacking imagination or originality.

limo *n* (*inf*) a limousine.

limousine *n* (*n*) a large luxury car.

limp[1] *vi* to walk with or as with a lame leg. * *n* a lameness in walking.–**limper** *n*.–**limpingly** *adv*.

limp[2] *adj* not firm; lethargic; wilted; flexible.–**limply** *adv*.–**limpness** *n*.

limpet *n* a mollusk with a low conical shell that clings to rocks.

limpid *adj* perfectly clear; transparent.–**limpidity** *n*.

linchpin *n* a pin passed through an axle to keep a wheel in position; a person or thing regarded as vital to an organization, project, etc.

linden *n* a tree with deciduous heart-shaped leaves and small fragrant yellow flowers.

line[1] *vt* (**lining, lined**) to put, or serve as, a lining in.

line[2] *n* a length of cord, rope, or wire; a cord for measuring, making level; a system of conducting fluid, electricity, etc; a thin threadlike mark; anything resembling such a mark, as a wrinkle; edge, limit, boundary; border, outline, contour; a row of persons or things, as printed letters across a page; a succession of persons; lineage; a connected series of things; the course a moving thing takes; a course of conduct, actions, etc; a whole system of transportation; a person's trade or occupation; a field of experience or interest; a verse; the forward combat position in warfare; fortifications, trenches or other defences used in war; a stock of goods; a piece of information; a short letter, note; (*pl*) all the speeches of a character in a play. * *vb* (**lining, lined**) *vt* to mark with lines; to form a line along; to cover with lines; to arrange in a line. * *vi* to align.

lineage n direct descent from an ancestor; ancestry.

linear adj of, made of, or using a line or lines; narrow and long; in relation to length only.–**linearity** n.–**linearly** adv.

linen n thread or cloth made of flax; household articles (sheets, cloths, etc) made of linen or cotton cloth.

liner n a large passenger ship or aircraft traveling a regular route.

lineup n an arrangement of persons or things in a line, eg for inspection.

linger vi to stay a long time; to delay departure; to dawdle or loiter; to dwell on in the mind; to remain alive though on the point of death.–**lingerer** n.–**lingering** adj.–**lingeringly** adv.

lingerie n women's underwear and nightclothes.

lingo n (pl **lingoes**) (inf) a dialect, jargon, etc.

lingua franca n (pl **lingua francas, linguae francae**) a language used for communication between speakers of different languages.

linguist n a person who is skilled in speaking foreign languages.

linguistic adj of or pertaining to language or linguistics.–**linguistically** adv.

linguistics n (used as sing) the science of language.

liniment n a soothing medication, usu applied to the skin.

lining n a material used to cover the inner surface of a garment, etc; any material covering an inner surface.

link n a single loop or ring of a chain; something resembling a loop or ring or connecting piece; a person or thing acting as a connection, as in a communication system, machine or organization. * vti to connect or become connected.

lino n (inf) (pl **linos**) linoleum.

linoleum n a floor covering of coarse fabric backing with a smooth, hard decorative coating.

linseed n the seed of flax, from which linseed oil is made.

lint n scraped and softened linen used to dress wounds; fluff.

lintel n the horizontal crosspiece spanning a doorway or window.

lion n a large, flesh-eating feline mammal with a shaggy mane in the adult male; a person of great courage or strength.–**lioness** nf.

lionhearted adj extremely brave.

lionize vt to treat as or make famous.–**lionization** n.–**lionizer** n.

lip n either of the two fleshy flaps that surround the mouth; anything like a lip, as the rim of a jug; (sl) insolent talk. * vt (**lipping, lipped**) to touch with the lips; to kiss; to utter.

liposuction n cosmetic surgery involving the removal of fat from under the skin of the thighs, stomach, etc using a suction device inserted through an incision.

lip-read vt (**lip-reading, lip-read**) to understand another's speech by watching their lip movements.

lip service n support expressed but not acted upon.

lipstick n a small stick of cosmetic for coloring the lips; the cosmetic itself.

liquefy vti (**liquefying, liquefied**) to change to a liquid.–**liquefaction** n.–**liquefier** n.

liqueur n a sweet and variously flavored alcoholic drink.

liquid n a substance that, unlike a gas, does not expand indefinitely and, unlike a solid, flows readily. * adj in liquid form; clear; limpid; flowing smoothly and musically, as verse; (assets) readily convertible into cash.–**liquidity** n.

liquidate vt to settle the accounts of; to close a (bankrupt) business and distribute its assets among its creditors; to convert into cash; to eliminate, kill.–**liquidation** n.–**liquidator** n.

liquidize vt to make liquid.

liquidizer n a domestic appliance for liquidizing and blending foods.

liquor n an alcoholic drink; any liquid, esp that in which food has been cooked.

liquorice n see **licorice**.

lisp vi to substitute the sounds th (as in thin) for s or th (as in then) for z; a speech defect or habit involving such pronunciation; to utter imperfectly. * vt to speak or utter with a lisp.–also n.– **lisper** n.

lissom adj lithe; supple; agile, etc.–**lissomness** n.

list[1] n a series of names, numbers, words, etc written or printed in order. * vt to make a list of; to enter in a directory, etc.

list[2] vti to tilt to one side, as a ship. * n such a tilting.

listen vi to try to hear; to pay attention, take heed; (with **in**) to intercept radio or telephone communications; to tune into a radio broadcast; to eavesdrop.

listing n a list, or an individual entry therein; the act of making a list; (pl) a guide giving details of events, eg music, theater, taking place in a particular area, published in a newspaper or magazine.

listless adj lacking energy or enthusiasm because of illness, dejection, etc; languid.–**listlessly** adv.–**listlessness** n.

lit see **light**[1], **light**[2].

litany n (pl **litanies**) a type of prayer in which petitions to God are recited by a priest and elicit set responses by the congregation; any tedious or automatic recital.

liter, litre n a measure of liquid capacity in the metric system, equivalent to 1.76 pints.

literacy n the ability to read and write.

literal adj in accordance with the exact meaning of a word or text; in a basic or strict sense; prosaic, unimaginative; real.–**literalness, literality** n.–**literally** adv.

literary adj of or dealing with literature; knowing much about literature.–**literarily** adv.–**literariness** n.

literate adj able to read and write; educated.–also n.

literati npl educated people.

literature n the writings of a period or of a country, esp those valued for their excellence; of style or form; all the books and articles on a subject; (inf) any printed matter.

lithe adj supple, flexible.–**litheness** n.

lithium n the lightest metallic element.

lithography n printing from a flat stone or metal plate, parts of which have been treated to repel ink.–**lithograph** n.–**lithographer** n.–**lithographic** adj.

litigant n a person engaged in a lawsuit.

litigate vti to bring or contest in a lawsuit.–**litigation** n.–**litigator** n.

litigious adj of or causing lawsuits; fond of engaging in lawsuits; contentious.–**litigiousness** n.

litmus n a coloring material obtained from certain lichens that turns red in acid solutions and blue in alkaline solutions.

litre see **liter**.

litter n rubbish scattered about; young animals produced at one time; straw, hay, etc used as bedding for animals; a stretcher for carrying a sick or wounded person. * vt to make untidy; to scatter about carelessly.

litterbug n a person who drops refuse in public places.

little adj not great or big, small in size, amount, degree, etc; short in duration; small in importance or power; narrow-minded. * n small in amount, degree, etc. * adv less, least, slightly; not much; not in the least.

liturgy n (pl **liturgies**) the prescribed form of service of a church.–**liturgical** adj.–**liturgically** adv.

live[1] vi to have life; to remain alive; to endure; to pass life in a specified manner; to enjoy a full life; to reside; (with **in, out**) (employee) to reside at (or away from) one's place of work; (with **together**) (unmarried couple) to cohabit. * vt to carry out in one's life; to spend; pass; (with **down**) to survive or efface the effects of (a crime or mistake) by waiting until it is forgotten or forgiven.

live[2] adj having life; of the living state or living beings; of present interest; still burning; unexploded; carrying electric current; broadcast during the actual performance.

livelihood n employment; a means of living.

lively adj (**livelier, liveliest**) full of life; spirited; exciting; vivid; keen. * adv in a lively manner.–**liveliness** n.

liven *vti* to make or become lively.–**livener** *n*.

liver *n* the largest glandular organ in vertebrate animals, which secretes bile, etc and is important in metabolism; the liver of an animal used as food; a reddish-brown color.

livery *n* (*pl* **liveries**) an identifying uniform, as that worn by a servant.

lives *see* **life**.

livestock *n* (farm) animals raised for use or sale.

livid *adj* (skin) discolored, as from bruising; grayish in color; (*inf*) extremely angry.–**lividly** *adv*.–**lividness, lividity** *n*.

living *adj* having life; still in use; true to life, vivid; of life, for living in. * *n* a being alive; livelihood; manner of existence.

living room *n* a room in a house used for general entertainment and relaxation.

lizard *n* a reptile with a slender body, four legs, and a tapering tail.

llama *n* a South American animal, related to the camel, used for carrying loads and as a source of wool.

load *n* an amount carried at one time; something borne with difficulty; a burden; (*often pl*) (*inf*) a great amount. * *vt* to put into or upon; to burden; to oppress; to supply in large quantities; to alter, as by adding a weight to dice or an adulterant to alcoholic drink; to put a charge of ammunition into (a firearm); to put film into (a camera); (*comput*) to install a program in memory. * *vi* to take on a load.–**loader** *n*.

loaded *adj* (*sl*) having plenty of money; drunk; under the influence of drugs.

loaf[1] *n* (*pl* **loaves**) a mass of bread of regular shape and standard weight; food shaped like this.

loaf[2] *vi* to pass time in idleness.–**loafer** *n*.

loam *n* rich and fertile soil.

loan *n* the act of lending; something lent, esp money. * *vti* to lend.–**loanable** *adj*.–**loaner** *n*.

loath *adj* unwilling.–*also* **loth**.

loathe *vt* to dislike intensely; to detest.–**loather** *n*.–**loathing** *n*.

loathsome *adj* giving rise to loathing; detestable.–**loathsomeness** *n*.

loaves *see* **loaf**[1].

lob *vti* (**lobbing, lobbed**) to toss or hit (a ball) in a high curve. * *n* a high-arching throw or kick.

lobby *n* (*pl* **lobbies**) an entrance hall of a public building; a person or group that tries to influence legislators. * *vti* (**lobbying, lobbied**) to try to influence (legislators) to support a particular cause or take certain action.

lobbyist *n* someone employed to lobby.

lobe *n* a rounded projection, as the lower end of the ear; any of the divisions of the lungs or brain.

lobotomy *n* (*pl* **lobotomies**) surgical incision into the lobe of an organ.

lobster *n* (*pl* **lobsters, lobster**) any of a family of edible sea crustaceans with four pairs of legs and a pair of large pincers.

local *adj* of or belonging to a particular place; serving the needs of a specific district; of or for a particular part of the body. * *n* an inhabitant of a specific place.–**locally** *adv*.–**localness** *n*.

locale *n* a place or area, esp in regard to the position or scene of some event.

locality *n* (*pl* **localities**) a neighborhood or a district; a particular scene, position, or place.

localize *vt* to limit, confine, or trace to a particular place.–**localization** *n*.

locate *vt* to determine or indicate the position of something; to set in or assign to a particular position.

location *n* a specific position or place; a locating or being located; a place outside a studio where a film is (partly) shot.

lock[1] *n* a fastening device on doors, etc, operated by a key or combination; part of a canal, dock, etc in which the level of the water can be changed by the operation of gates; the part of a gun by which the charge is fired; a controlling hold, as used in wrestling;

* *vt* to fasten with a lock; to shut; to fit, link; to jam together so as to make immovable. * *vi* to become locked; to interlock.–**lockable** *adj*.

lock[2] *n* a curl of hair; a tuft of wool, etc.

locker *n* a small cupboard, chest, etc that can be locked, esp one for storing possessions in a public place.

locket *n* a small ornamental case, usu holding a lock of hair, photograph or other memento, hung from the neck.

lockjaw *n* tetanus.

lockout *n* the exclusion of employees from a workplace by an employer, as a means of coercion during an industrial dispute.

locksmith *n* a person who makes and repairs locks and keys.

locomotion *n* motion, or the power of moving, from one place to another.

locomotive *n* an electric, steam, or diesel engine on wheels, designed to move a railway train. * *adj* of locomotion.

locust *n* a type of large grasshopper often traveling in swarms and destroying crops; a type of hard-wooded leguminous tree.

lode *n* an ore deposit.

lodestone *n* a magnetic oxide of iron; a piece of this oxide, used as a magnet or a crude compass.

lodge *n* a small house at the entrance to a park or stately home; a country house for seasonal leisure activities; a resort hotel or motel; the local chapter or hall of a fraternal society; a beaver's lair. * *vt* to house temporarily; to shoot, thrust, etc firmly (in); to bring before legal authorities; to confer upon. * *vi* to live in a place for a time; to live as a paying guest; to come to rest and stick firmly (in).

lodger *n* a person who lives in a rented room in another's home.

lodging *n* a temporary residence; (*pl*) accommodation rented in another's house.

lodgment, lodgement *n* the act of lodging; the state of being lodged; an accumulation of something deposited; (*mil*) a foothold in enemy territory.

loft *n* a space under a roof; a storage area under the roof of a barn or stable; a gallery in a church or hall.

lofty *adj* (**loftier, loftiest**) (*objects*) of a great height, elevated; (*person*) noble, haughty, superior in manner.–**loftily** *adv*.–**loftiness** *n*.

log[1] *n* a section of a felled tree; a device for ascertaining the speed of a ship; a record of speed, progress, etc, esp one kept on a ship's voyage or aircraft's flight. * *vb* (**logging, logged**) *vt* to record in a log; to sail or fly (a specified distance). * *vi* (*with* **on, off**) (*comput*) to establish or disestablish communication with a mainframe computer from a remote terminal in a multi-user system.–**logger** *n*.

log[2] *n* a logarithm.

logarithm *n* the exponent of the power to which a fixed number (the base) is to be raised to produce a given number, used to avoid multiplying and dividing when solving mathematical problems.–**logarithmic** *adj*.–**logarithmically** *adv*.

logbook *n* an official record of a ship's or aircraft's voyage or flight; an official document containing details of a vehicle's registration.

loggerhead *n* a type of turtle; (*pl*) a dispute, confrontation (*to be at loggerheads with someone*).

logging *n* the business of cutting down timber.

logic *n* correct reasoning, or the science of this; way of reasoning; what is expected by the working of cause and effect.–**logical** *adj*.–**logically** *adv*.–**logician** *n*.

logistics *n* (*used as sing*) the science of the organization, transport and supply of military forces; the planning and organization of any complex activity.–**logistic** *adj*.–**logistically** *adv*.

log jam *n* a blockage of logs floating in a watercourse; a deadlock, standstill.

logo *n* (*pl* **logos**) (*inf*) a printed symbol representing a corporation, product, etc; a trademark, emblem.

loin n (usu pl) the lower part of the back between the hipbones and the ribs; the front part of the hindquarters of an animal used for food.

loincloth n a cloth worn around the loins.

loiter vi to linger or stand about aimlessly.–**loiterer** n.

loll vi to lean or recline in a lazy manner, to lounge; (tongue) to hang loosely.–**loller** n.

lollipop n a flat boiled sweet at the end of a stick.

lollop vi to run or walk with an ungainly, bouncing rhythm.

lone adj by oneself; isolated; without companions, solitary.–**loneness** n.

lonely adj (**lonelier, loneliest**) isolated; unhappy at being alone; (places) remote, rarely visited.–**loneliness** n.

loner n a person who avoids the company of others.

lonesome adj having or causing a lonely feeling.–**lonesomely** adv.

long[1] adj measuring much in space or time; having a greater than usual length, quantity, etc; tedious, slow; far-reaching; well-supplied. * adv for a long time; from start to finish; at a remote time.

long[2] vi to desire earnestly, esp for something not likely to be attained.

long-distance adj traveling or communicating over long distances.

longevity n long life.

longhand n ordinary handwriting, as opposed to shorthand.

longhorn n a breed of long-horned cattle.

longing n an intense desire.–**longingly** adv.

longitude n distance east or west of the prime meridian, expressed in degrees or time.–**longitudinal** adj.

long johns npl (inf) warm underpants with long legs.

long jump n an athletic event consisting of a horizontal running jump.

long-lived adj having or tending to live a long time.

long-range adj reaching over a long distance or period of time.

longshoreman n (pl **longshoremen**) a person who loads and unloads ships at a port.

long shot n a wild guess; a competitor, etc who is unlikely to win; a project that has little chance of success.

long-sighted adj only seeing distant objects clearly.–**long-sightedly** adv.

long-standing adj having continued for a long time.

long-suffering adj enduring pain, provocation, etc patiently.

long-term adj of or extending over a long time.

long wave n a radio wave of a frequency less than 300 kHz.

longways, longwise adv in the direction of the length (of something), lengthways.

long-winded adj speaking or writing at great length; tiresome.–**long-windedly** adv.–**long-windedness** n.

look vi to try to see; to see; to search; to appear, seem; to be facing in a specified direction; (with **in**) to pay a brief visit; (with **up**) to improve in prospects. * vt to direct one's eyes on; to have an appearance befitting. * n the act of looking; a gaze, glance; appearance; aspect; (with **after**) to take care of; (with **over**) to examine; (with **up**) to research (for information, etc) in book; to visit.

look-alike n a person that looks like another.

lookout n a place for keeping watch; a person assigned to watch.

loom[1] n a machine or frame for weaving yarn or thread. * vt to weave on a loom.

loom[2] vi to come into view indistinctly and often threateningly; to come ominously close, as an impending event.

loon n a large fish-eating diving bird.

loony, looney n (pl **loonies**) (sl) a lunatic. * adj (**loonier, looniest**) (sl) crazy, demented.–**looniness** n.

loop n a figure made by a curved line crossing itself; a similar rounded shape in cord, rope, etc crossed on itself; anything forming this figure; (comput) a set of instructions in a program that are executed repeatedly; a segment of film or magnetic tape. *

vt to make a loop of; to fasten with a loop. * vi to form a loop or loops.

loophole n a means of evading an obligation, etc; a slit in a wall for looking or shooting through.

loose adj free from confinement or restraint; not firmly fastened; not tight or compact; not precise; inexact; (inf) relaxed. * vt to release; to unfasten; to untie; to detach; (bullet) to discharge. * vi to become loose.– **loosely** adv.–**looseness** n.

loose-leaf adj having pages or sheets that can easily be replaced or removed.

loosen vti to make or become loose or looser.–**loosener** n.

loot n goods taken during warfare, civil unrest, etc; (sl) money. * vti to plunder, pillage.–**looter** n.

lop vt (**lopping, lopped**) to sever the branches or twigs from a tree; to cut off or out as superfluous.

lope vi to move or run with a long bounding stride.–also n.–**loper** n.

lopsided adj having one side larger in weight, height, or size than the other; badly balanced.–**lopsidedly** adv.–**lopsidedness** n.

loquacious adj talkative.–**loquaciously** adv.–**loquacity** n.

lord n a ruler, master or monarch; a male member of the nobility; (with cap and **the**) God; (Brit) a form of address used to certain peers, bishops and judges.

lordly adj (**lordlier, lordliest**) noble; haughty; arrogant.–**lordliness** n.

lordship n the rank or authority of a lord; rule, dominion; (with **his** or **your**) a title used in speaking of or to a lord.

lore n knowledge; learning, esp of a traditional nature; a particular body of tradition.

lose vb (**losing, lost**) vt to have taken from one by death, accident, removal, etc; to be unable to find; to fail to keep, as one's temper; to fail to see, hear, or understand; to fail to have, get, etc; to fail to win; to cause the loss of; to wander from (one's way, etc); to squander. * vi to suffer (a) loss.–**losable** adj.–**loser** n.

loss n a losing or being lost; the damage, trouble caused by losing; the person, thing, or amount lost.

lost adj no longer possessed; missing; not won; destroyed or ruined; having wandered astray; wasted.

lot n an object, such as a straw, slip of paper, etc drawn from others at random to reach a decision by chance; the decision thus arrived at; one's share by lot; fortune; a plot of ground; a group of persons or things; an item or set of items put up for auction; (often pl) (inf) a great amount; much; (inf) sort. * vt (**lotting, lotted**) to divide into lots.

loth see **loath**.

lotion n a liquid for cosmetic or external medical use.

lottery n (pl **lotteries**) a system of raising money by selling numbered tickets that offer the chance of winning a prize; an enterprise, etc which may or may not succeed.

lotus n a type of water lily; (Greek legend) a plant whose fruit induced contented forgetfulness.

lotus position n an erect sitting position in yoga with the legs crossed close to the body.

louche adj untrustworthy, shady.

loud adj characterized by or producing great noise; emphatic; (inf) obtrusive or flashy.–**loudly** adv.–**loudness** n.

loudspeaker n a device for converting electrical energy into sound.

lounge vi to move, sit, lie, etc in a relaxed way; to spend time idly. * n a room with comfortable furniture for sitting, as a waiting room at an airport, etc; a comfortable sitting room in a hotel or private house.

lounger n a comfortable couch or chair for relaxing on; a person who lounges.

louse n (pl **lice**) any of various small wingless insects that are parasitic on humans and animals; any similar but unrelated insects that are parasitic on plants; (inf) (pl **louses**) a mean, contemptible person.

lousy adj (**lousier, lousiest**) infested with lice; (sl) disgusting, of poor quality, or inferior; (sl) well supplied (with).–**lousily** adv,– **lousiness** n.

lout n a clumsy, rude person.–**loutish** adj.

louver, louvre n one of a set of slats in a door or window set parallel and slanted to admit air but not rain.–**louvered, louvred** adj.

lovable adj easy to love or feel affection for.–**lovability** n.–**lovably** adv.

love n a strong liking for someone or something; a passionate affection for another person; the object of such affection; (tennis) a score of zero. * vti to feel love (for).

love affair n a romantic or sexual relationship between two people.

loveless adj without love; not feeling or receiving love.–**lovelessly** adv.

lovelorn adj pining from love.

lovely adj (**lovelier, loveliest**) beautiful; (inf) highly enjoyable.–**loveliness** n.

lovemaking n sexual activity, esp intercourse, between lovers.

lover n a person in love with another person; a person, esp a man, having an extramarital sexual relationship; (pl) a couple in love with each other; someone who loves a specific person or thing.

loving adj affectionate.–**lovingly** adv.–**lovingness** n.

low[1] n the sound a cow makes, a moo. * vi to make this sound.

low[2] adj not high or tall; below the normal level; less in size, degree, amount, etc than usual; deep in pitch; depressed in spirits; humble, of low rank; vulgar, coarse; not loud. * adv in or to a low degree, level, etc. * n a low level, degree, etc; a region of low barometric pressure.

lowbrow n (inf) a person regarded as uncultivated and lacking in taste.–also adj.

lowdown n (sl: with the) the true, pertinent facts.

lower[1] adj below in place, rank, etc; less in amount, degree, etc. * vt to let or put down; to reduce in height, amount, etc; to bring down in respect, etc. * vi to become lower.–**lowerable** adj.

lower case n small letters (not capitals) used for printing.

low frequency n a radio frequency between 300 and 30 kilohertz.

low-key, low-keyed adj of low intensity, subdued.

lowland n low-lying land; (pl) a flat region. * adj of or pertaining to lowlands.–**lowlander** n.

lowlife n (pl **lowlifes**) (sl) a criminal.

lowly adj (**lowlier, lowliest**) humble, of low status; meek.– **lowliness** n.

low spirited adj unhappy, depressed.

low technology n unsophisticated technology limited to the provision of basic human needs.–**low-tech** adj.

low tide n (the time of) the tide when it is at its lowest level; a low point.

loyal adj firm in allegiance to a person, cause, country, etc, faithful; demonstrating unswerving allegiance.–**loyally** adv.–**loyalty** n.

loyalist n a person who supports the established government, esp during a revolt.–**loyalism** n.

lozenge n a four-sided diamond-shaped figure; a cough drop, sweet, etc, originally diamond-shaped.

LP n a long-playing record, usu 12 inches (30.5 cm) in diameter and played at a speed of 33 1/3 revolutions per minute.

LSD n a powerful hallucinatory drug (lysergic acid diethylamide).

Lt abbr = lieutenant.

lubricant n a substance that lubricates.

lubricate vt to coat or treat (machinery, etc) with oil or grease to lessen friction; to make smooth, slippery, or greasy. * vi to act as a lubricant.–**lubrication** n.

lucerne see **alfalfa**.

lucid adj easily understood; sane.–**lucidly** adv.–**lucidity** n.

luck n chance; good fortune.–**luckily** adv.–**lucky** adj.

luckless n unfortunate, unlucky.–**lucklessly** adv.–**lucklessness** n.

lucrative adj producing wealth or profit; profitable.–**lucratively** adv.–**lucrativeness** n.

ludicrous adj absurd, laughable.–**ludicrously** adv.

lug vt (**lugging, lugged**) to pull or drag along with effort.

luggage n the suitcases and other baggage containing the possessions of a traveler.

lugubrious adj mournful, dismal.–**lugubriously** adv.

lukewarm adj barely warm, tepid; lacking enthusiasm.

lull vt to soothe, to calm; to calm the suspicions of, esp by deception. * n a short period of calm.

lullaby n (pl **lullabies**) a song to lull children to sleep.

lumbago n rheumatic pain in the lower back.

lumbar adj of or in the loins.

lumber[1] n timber, logs, beams, boards, etc, roughly cut and prepared for use; articles of unused household furniture that are stored away; any useless articles. * vi to cut down timber and saw it into lumber. * vt to clutter with lumber; to heap in disorder.

lumber[2] vi to move heavily or clumsily.–**lumberer** n.–**lumbering**[1] adj.–**lumberingly** adv.

lumberjack n a person employed to fell trees and transport and prepare timber.

luminary n (pl **luminaries**) a body that gives off light, such as the sun; a famous or notable person.

luminous adj emitting light; glowing in the dark; clear, easily understood.–**luminously** adv.–**luminosity** n.

lump n a small, compact mass of something, usu without definite shape; an abnormal swelling; a dull or stupid person. * adj in a lump or lumps. * vt to treat or deal with in a mass. * vi to become lumpy.

lump sum n a sum of money (esp cash) paid as a whole and not in installments.

lumpy adj (**lumpier, lumpiest**) filled or covered with lumps.–**lumpily** adv.–**lumpiness** n.

lunacy n (pl **lunacies**) insanity; utter folly.

lunar adj of or like the moon.

lunar eclipse n an eclipse when the earth passes between the sun and the moon.

lunatic adj insane; utterly foolish. * n an insane person.

lunch n a light meal, esp between breakfast and dinner. * vi to eat lunch.–**luncher** n.

luncheon n lunch, esp a formal lunch.

lung n either of the two sponge-like breathing organs in the chest of vertebrates.

lunge n a sudden forceful thrust, as with a sword; a sudden plunge forward. * vti to move, or cause to move, with a lunge.–**lunger** n.

lurch vi to lean or pitch suddenly to the side. * n a sudden roll to one side.–**lurchingly** adv.

lure n something that attracts, tempts or entices; a brightly colored fishing bait; a device used to recall a trained hawk; a decoy for wild animals. * vt to entice, attract, or tempt.–**luringly** adv.

lurid adj vivid, glaring; shocking; sensational.–**luridly** adv.– **luridness** n.

lurk vi to lie hidden in wait; to loiter furtively.–**lurker** n.

luscious adj delicious; richly sweet; delighting any of the senses.–**lusciously** adv.–**lusciousness** n.

lush[1] adj tender and juicy; of or showing abundant growth.– **lushly** adv.–**lushness** n.

lush[2] n (sl) an alcoholic.

lust n strong sexual desire (for); an intense longing for something. * vi to feel lust.–**lustful** adj.–**lustfully** adv.

luster, lustre n gloss; sheen; brightness; radiance; brilliant beauty or fame; glory; a chandelier with pendants of cut glass; a fabric with a lustrous surface; a substance used to give luster to an object; a metallic glaze on pottery; the quality and intensity of light reflected from the surface of minerals.–**lusterless** adj.– **lustrous** adj.

lusty adj (**lustier, lustiest**) strong; vigorous; healthy.–**lustily** adv.–**lustiness** n.

lute n an old, round-backed stringed musical instrument plucked with the fingers.

luxuriant *adj* profuse, abundant; ornate; fertile.–**luxuriance** *n*.

luxuriate *vi* to enjoy immensely, to revel (in).–**luxuriation** *n*.

luxurious *adj* constituting luxury; indulging in luxury; rich, comfortable.–**luxuriously** *adv*.–**luxuriousness** *n*.

luxury *n* (*pl* **luxuries**) indulgence and pleasure in sumptuous and expensive food, accommodation, clothes, etc; (*often pl*) something that is costly and enjoyable but not indispensable. * *adj* relating to or supplying luxury.

Lycra *n* (*trademark*) an elastic synthetic material used for tight-fitting garments, such as bicycle shorts and swimwear.

lye *n* an alkaline solution.

lying *see* **lie**[1], **lie**[2].

lymph *n* a clear, yellowish body fluid, found in intercellular spaces and the lymphatic vessels.–**lymphatic** *adj*.

lymphoid *adj* relating to lymph glands; resembling lymph.

lymphoma *n* (*pl* **lymphomata**) a tumor of the lymphoid tissue.

lynch *vt* to murder (an accused person) by mob action, without lawful trial, as by hanging.–**lyncher** *n*.–**lynching** *n*.

lynx *n* (*pl* **lynxes, lynx**) a wild feline of Europe and North America with spotted fur.

lyre *n* an ancient musical instrument of the harp family.

lyric *adj* denoting or of poetry expressing the writer's emotion; of, or having a high voice with a light, flexible quality. * *n* a lyric poem; (*pl*) the words of a popular song.

lyrical *adj* lyric; (*inf*) expressing rapture or enthusiasm.–**lyrically** *adv*.

lyricist *n* a person who writes lyrics, esp for popular songs.

lysergic acid *see* **LSD**.

M

m *abbr* = meter(s); mile(s); million(s).

MA *abbr* = Master of Arts; Massachusetts.

ma'am *n* madam (used as a title of respect).

macabre *adj* gruesome; grim; of death.

macadam *n* a road surface composed of successive layers of small stones compacted into a solid mass.

macadamia *n* an Australian tree bearing white flowers and an edible seed (**macadamia nut**).

macaroni *n* (*pl* **macaronis, macaronies**) a pasta made chiefly of fine wheat flour and made into tubes.

macaroon *n* a small cake or cookie made with sugar, egg whites and ground almonds or coconut.

macaw *n* a large parrot with brightly colored plumage.

mace[1] *n* a staff used as a symbol of authority by certain institutions.

mace[2] *n* an aromatic spice made from the external covering of the nutmeg.

Mach *see* **Mach number**.

machete *n* a large knife used for cutting, or as a weapon.

machination *n* (*usu pl*) an artifice; an intrigue; a plot; the act of plotting or intriguing.–**machinate** *vti*.

machine *n* a structure of fixed and moving parts, for doing useful work; an organization functioning like a machine; the controlling group in a political party; a device, as the lever, etc that transmits, or changes the application of energy. * *vt* to shape or finish by machine-operated tools. * *adj* of machines; done by machinery.

machine gun *n* an automatic gun, firing a rapid stream of bullets.–*also vt*.

machinery *n* machines collectively; the parts of a machine; the framework for keeping something going.

machinist *n* one who makes, repairs, or operates machinery.

machismo *n* strong or assertive masculinity; virility.–**macho** *adj*.

Mach number *n* the ratio of the speed of a body in a particular medium to the speed of sound in the same medium. Mach 1 is equal to the speed of sound.

mackerel *n* (*pl* **mackerel, mackerels**) a common oily food fish.

macramé *n* (the art of) knotting or weaving coarse thread to produce ornamental work.

macrobiotic *adj* (*diet*) composed of an extremely restricted range of foods, usu vegetables and whole grains.

macrocosm *n* the universe; any complex system.–**macrocosmic** *adj*.

mad *adj* (**madder, maddest**) insane; frantic; foolish and rash; infatuated; (*inf*) angry.

madam *n* a polite term of address to a woman; a woman in charge of a brothel.

madame *n* (*pl* **mesdames**) the title of a married French woman; used as a title equivalent to Mrs.

madcap *adj* reckless, impulsive.–*also n*.

madden *vti* to make or become insane, angry, or wildly excited.–**maddening** *adj*.–**maddeningly** *adv*.

made *see* **make**.

mademoiselle *n* (*pl* **mesdemoiselles**) the title of an unmarried French girl or woman; used as a title equivalent to Miss; a French teacher or governess.

madhouse *n* (*inf*) as mental institution; a state of uproar or confusion.

madly *adv* in an insane manner; at great speed, force; (*inf*) excessively.

madman *n* (*pl* **madmen**) an insane person.–**madwoman** *nf*.

madness *n* insanity; foolishness; excitability.

Madonna *n* the Virgin Mary, esp as seen in pictures or statues.

madrigal *n* a 16th-century love song or pastoral poem in the form of an unaccompanied part-song; 14th-century Italian song derived from a pastoral poem.–**madrigalist** *n*.

maelstrom *n* a whirlpool; a state of turbulence or confusion.

maestro *n* (*pl* **maestros**) a master of an art, esp a musical composer, conductor, or teacher.

Mafia *n* a secret society composed chiefly of criminal elements, originating in Sicily.

mafioso *n* (*pl* **mafiosos, mafiosi**) a member of the Mafia.

magazine *n* a military store; a space where explosives are stored, as in a fort; a supply chamber, as in a camera, a rifle, etc; a periodical publication containing articles, fiction, photographs, etc.

magenta *n* a purplish-red dye; purplish red.–*also adj*.

maggot *n* a wormlike larva, as of the housefly.–**maggoty** *adj*.–**maggotiness** *n*.

magic *n* the use of charms, spells, etc to supposedly influence events by supernatural means; any mysterious power; the art of producing illusions by sleight of hand, etc. * *adj* of or relating to magic; possessing supposedly supernatural powers; (*inf*) wonderful. * *vt* (**magicking, magicked**) to influence, produce or take (away) by or as if by magic.–**magical** *adj*.–**magically** *adv*.

magician *n* one skilled in magic; a conjurer.

magistrate *n* a public officer empowered to administer the law.–**magistrateship, magistrature** *n*.

magma *n* (*pl* **magmas, magmata**) a stratum of hot molten rock within the earth's crust, which solidifies on the surface as lava.

magnanimous *adj* noble and generous in conduct or spirit, not petty.–**magnanimity** *n*.–**magnanimously** *adv*.

magnate *n* a very wealthy or influential person.

magnesia *n* a magnesium compound used as a mild laxative.

magnesium *n* a white metallic element that burns very brightly.

magnet *n* any piece of iron or steel that has the property of attracting iron; anything that attracts.–**magnetic** *adj*.

magnetic needle *n* a thin piece of magnetized iron, steel, etc, used in a compass and other instruments, that indicates the direction of a magnetic field.

magnetic north *n* the northerly direction of the earth's magnetic field, as pointed to by a compass needle.

magnetic pole *n* either of the two variable points in the regions of the earth's northern and southern poles to which a magnetic needle points.

magnetic tape n a thin plastic ribbon with a magnetized coating for recording sound, video signals, computer data, etc.

magnetism n the property, quality, or condition of being magnetic; the force to which this is due; personal charm.

magnetize vt to make magnetic; to attract strongly.–**magnetization** n.–**magnetizer** n.

magnification n magnifying or being magnified; the degree of enlargement of something by a lens, microscope, etc.

magnificent adj splendid, stately or sumptuous in appearance; superb, of very high quality.–**magnificence** n.–**magnificently** adv.

magnify vt (**magnifying, magnified**) to exaggerate; to increase the apparent size of (an object) as (with) a lens.–**magnifiable** adj.–**magnifier** n.

magnitude n greatness of size, extent, etc; importance; (astron) the apparent brightness of a star.

magnolia n a spring-flowering shrub or tree with evergreen or deciduous leaves and showy flowers.

magnum n (pl **magnums**) a wine bottle that holds twice the normal quantity.

magnum opus n (pl **magna opera**) the great or chief work of an artist or author.

magpie n a black and white bird of the crow family; a person who chatters; an acquisitive person.

maharajah, maharaja n the former title of an Indian prince.

maharani, maharanee n the wife of a maharajah.

mahjong, mah-jongg n an orig Chinese game for four people played with decorative tiles.

mahogany n (pl **mahoganies**) the hard, reddish-brown wood of a tropical tree; a reddish-brown color.

maid n a maiden; a woman servant.

maiden n a girl or young unmarried woman. * adj unmarried or virgin; untried; first.–**maidenhood** n.–**maidenly** adj.

maidenhair (**fern**) n a delicate-leafed fern with small light green leaflets.

maiden name n the surname of a woman before marriage.

maid of honor n the principal unmarried attendant of a bride.

maidservant n a female servant.

mail[1] n a body armor made of small metal rings or links.

mail[2] n letters, packages, etc transported and delivered by the post office; a postal system. * vt to send by mail.–**mailable** adj.

mailman n (pl **mailmen**) a person who collects or delivers mail.–also **postman**.

mail order n an order for goods to be sent by post.

maim vt to cripple; to mutilate.

main adj chief in size, importance, etc; principal. * n (often pl but used as sing) a principal pipe in a distribution system for water, gas, etc; the essential point.

mainframe n a large computer that can handle multiple tasks concurrently.

mainland n the principal land mass of a continent, as distinguished from nearby islands.

mainly adv chiefly, principally.

mainstay n a chief support.

mainstream n a major trend, line of thought, etc.–also adj.

maintain vt to preserve; to support, to sustain; to keep in good condition; to affirm.–**maintainable** adj.–**maintainer** n.

maintenance n upkeep; (financial) support, esp of a spouse after a divorce.

maître d'hôtel n (pl **maîtres d'hôtel**) n a head waiter; a hotel manager or owner; a house steward.

maize n corn; a light yellow color.

majesty n (pl **majesties**) grandeur; (with cap) a title used in speaking to or of a sovereign.–**majestic** adj.

major adj greater in size, importance, amount, etc; (surgery) very serious, life-threatening; (mus) higher than the corresponding minor by half a tone. * vi to specialize (in a field of study). * n in

US, an officer ranking just above a captain, in UK, a lieutenant-colonel; (mus) a major key, chord or scale.

majority n (pl **majorities**) the greater number or part of; the excess of the larger number of votes cast for a candidate in an election; full legal age; the military rank of a major.

make vb (**making, made**) vt to cause to exist, occur, or appear; to build, create, produce, manufacture, etc; to prepare for use; to amount to; to have the qualities of; to acquire, earn; to understand; to do, execute; to cause or force; to arrive at, reach; (with **believe**) to imagine, pretend; (with **good**) to make up for, pay compensation; (with **out**) to write out; to complete (a form, etc) in writing; to attempt to understand; to discern, identify; (with **up**) to invent, fabricate, put together; to deceive; to prepare; to make complete; to put together; to settle differences between. * vi (with **do**) to manage with what is available; (with **for**) to go in the direction of; to bring about; (with **good**) to become successful or wealthy; (with **off**) to leave in haste; (with **out**) to pretend; to fare, manage; (with **up**) to become reconciled; to compensate for; to put on make-up for the stage. * n style, brand, or origin; manner of production.–**maker** n.

make-believe adj imagined, pretended.–also n.

makeshift adj being a temporary substitute.–also n.

make-up n the cosmetics, etc used by an actor; cosmetics generally; the way something is put together, composition; nature, disposition.

maladjusted adj poorly adjusted, esp to the social environment.–**maladjustment** n.

maladministration n corrupt or incompetent management of public affairs.–**maladminister** vb.

maladroit adj clumsy.–**maladroitness** n.

malady n (pl **maladies**) a disease, illness.

malaise n a feeling of discomfort or of uneasiness.

malapropism n a ludicrous misuse of words.–**malapropian** adj.

malaria n an infectious disease caused by mosquito bites, and characterized by recurring attacks of fevers and chills.–**malarial** adj.

malcontent adj discontented and potentially rebellious.–also n.

male adj denoting or of the sex that fertilizes the ovum; of, like, or suitable for men and boys; masculine. * n a male person, animal or plant.–**maleness** n.

malevolent adj ill-disposed toward others; spiteful, malicious.–**malevolence** n.–**malevolently** adv.

malformation n faulty or abnormal formation of a body or part.–**malformed** adj.

malfunction n faulty functioning. * vi to function wrongly.

malice n active ill will, intention to inflict injury upon another.–**malicious** adj.–**maliciously** adv.–**maliciousness** n.

malign adj harmful; evil. * vt to slander; to defame.–**malignity** n.–**malignly** adv.

malignant adj having a wish to harm others; injurious; (disease) rapidly spreading, resistant to treatment, esp of a tumor.–**malignancy** n.–**malignantly** adv.

malinger vi to feign illness in order to evade work, duty.–**malingerer** n.

mall n a shaded avenue, open to the public; an enclosed shopping center.

mallard n (pl **mallard, mallards**) a common wild duck, the ancestor of domestic breeds of duck.

malleable adj pliable; capable of being shaped.–**malleability** n.

mallet n a small, usu wooden-headed, short-handled hammer; a long-handled version for striking the ball in the games of polo and croquet.

malnutrition n lack of nutrition.

malodorous adj having a foul smell, bad-smelling.–**malodorously** adv.–**malodorousness** n.

malpractice n professional misconduct, esp by a medical practitioner.

malt n a cereal grain, such as barley, which is soaked and dried and used in brewing.–**malty** adj.

maltreat vt to treat roughly or badly.–**maltreatment** n.

mama n (inf) mother.–also **mamma**.

mamba n a partly tree-living green or black poisonous snake of tropical and southern Africa.

mamma see **mama**.

mammal n any member of a class of warm-blooded vertebrates that suckle their young with milk.–**mammalian** adj.

mammary adj relating to the milk-secreting organ of female mammals, such as the udder of a cow, or breast of a woman.

mammoth n an extinct elephant with long, curved tusks. * adj enormous.

man n (pl **men**) a human being, esp an adult male; the human race; an adult male with manly qualities, eg courage, virility; an individual person; a person with specific qualities for a task, etc; an ordinary soldier, as opposed to an officer; a member of a team, etc; a piece in games such as chess, checkers, etc; a husband. * vt (**manning, manned**) to provide with men for work, defense, etc.

manacle n (usu pl) a handcuff. * vt to handcuff; to restrain.

manage vt to control the movement or behavior of; to have charge of; to direct; to succeed in accomplishing. * vi to carry on business; to contrive to get along.–**manageable** adj.

management n those carrying out the administration of a business; the managers collectively; the technique of managing or controlling.

manager n a person who manages a company, organization, etc; an agent who looks after the business affairs of an actor, writer, etc; a person who organizes the training of a sports team; a person who manages efficiently.

managerial adj of or pertaining to a manager or management.–**managerially** adv.

mandarin n (formerly) a high-ranking bureaucrat of the Chinese empire; any high-ranking official, esp one given to pedantic sometimes obscure public pronouncements; (with cap) the Beijing dialect that is the official pronunciation of the Chinese language; the fruit of a small spiny Chinese tree that has been developed in cultivation (–also **tangerine**).

mandate n an order or command; the authority to act on the behalf of another, esp the will of constituents expressed to their representatives in legislatures. * vt to entrust by mandate.

mandatory adj of, containing, or having the nature of a mandate; required by mandate; compulsory; (nation) holding a mandate.–**mandatorily** adv.

mandible n the lower jaw of a vertebrate; the mouth parts of an insect; either jaw of a beaked animal.–**mandibular** adj.

mandolin n a stringed instrument similar to a lute, with four or five pairs of strings.

mandrake n a plant of the nightshade family with narcotic properties that, in folklore, shrieked when uprooted.

mane n long hair that grows on the back of the neck of the horse, lion, etc.

man-eater n an animal that eats human flesh.

maneuver n a planned and controlled movement of troops, warships, etc; a skillful or shrewd move; a stratagem. * vt to perform or cause to perform maneuvers; to manage or plan skillfully; to move, get, make, etc by some scheme.–also **manoeuvre**.–**maneuverable, manoeuvrable** adj.–**maneuverer, manoeuvrer** n.

manful adj showing courage and resolution.–**manfully** adv.

manganese n a hard brittle metallic element; its oxide.

mange n a skin disease affecting mainly domestic animals, which causes itching.

manger n a trough in a barn or stable for livestock fodder.

mangle vt to crush, mutilate; to spoil, ruin.

mango n (pl **mangoes**) a yellow-red fleshy tropical fruit with a firm central stone.

mangrove n a tropical tree or shrub with root-forming branches.

mangy adj (**mangier, mangiest**) having mange; scruffy, shabby.–**manginess** n.

manhandle vt to handle roughly; to move by human force.

manhole n a hole through which one can enter a sewer, drain, etc.

manhood n the state or time of being a man; virility; courage, etc.

manhunt n a hunt for a fugitive.–**manhunter** n.

mania n a mental disorder displaying sometimes violent behavior and great excitement; great excitement or enthusiasm; a craze.

maniac n a madman; a person with wild behavior; a person with great enthusiasm for something.–**maniacal** adj.

manic adj affected with, characterized by, or relating to mania.

manic-depressive adj of a mental disorder characterized by alternating periods of mania and deep depression. * n a person suffering from this.

manicure n trimming, polishing etc of fingernails.–also vt.–**manicurist** n.

manifest adj obvious, clearly evident. * vt to make clear; to display, to reveal. * n a list of a ship's or aircraft's cargo; a list of passengers on an aircraft.–**manifestation** n.–**manifestly** adv.

manifesto n (pl **manifestoes, manifestos**) a public printed declaration of intent and policy issued by a government or political party.

manifold adj having many forms, parts, etc; of many sorts. * n a pipe (eg in an engine) with many inlets and outlets.

manila, manilla n a strong, buff-colored paper originally made from hemp from the Philippines.

manipulate vt to work or handle skillfully; to manage shrewdly or artfully, often in an unfair way.–**manipulation** n.–**manipulative** adj.–**manipulator** n.

mankind n the human race.

manly adj (**manlier, manliest**) appropriate in character to a man; strong; virile.–**manliness** n.

man-made adj manufactured or created by man; artificial, synthetic.

manna n (Bible) the food miraculously given to the ancient Israelites in the wilderness; any help that comes unexpectedly.

manned adj performed by a person; (spacecraft, etc) having a human crew.

mannequin n a life-size model of the human body, used to fit or display clothes.

manner n a method of way of doing something; behavior; type or kind; habit; (pl) polite social behavior.

mannerism n an idiosyncrasy; an affected habit or style in dress, behavior or gesture.

mannerly adj polite; respectful. * adv politely; respectfully.–**mannerliness** n.**man-of-war** n (pl **men-of-war**) a (sailing) warship.

manor n a landed estate; the main house on such an estate; (sl) a police district.–**manorial** adj.

manpower n power furnished by human strength; the collective availability for work of people in a given area.

manqué adj potential; unsuccessful, failed.

manservant n (pl **menservants**) a male servant, esp a valet.

mansion n a large, imposing house.

manslaughter n the killing of a human being by another, esp when unlawful but without malice.

mantel n the facing above a fireplace; the shelf above a fireplace.–also **mantelpiece**.

mantilla n a scarf, usu of lace, worn as a headdress in Spain and South America; a woman's light cloak or hood.

mantis n (pl **mantises, mantes**) an insect that preys on other insects.–also **praying mantis**.

mantle n a loose cloak; anything that envelops or conceals. * vt to cover as with a mantle. * vi to be or become covered.

mantra n (Hinduism, Buddhism) a devotional incantation used in prayer, meditation and in certain forms of yoga.

manual adj of the hands; operated, done, or used by the hand; involving physical skill or hard work rather than the mind. * n a handy book for use as a guide, reference, etc; a book of instructions.–**manually** adv.

manufacture vt to make, esp on a large scale, using machinery; to invent, fabricate. * n the production of goods by manufacturing.–**manufacturer** n.

manure n animal dung used to fertilize soil. * vt to spread manure on.

manuscript n a book or document that is handwritten or typewritten as opposed to printed; an author's original handwritten or typewritten copy as submitted to a publisher before typesetting and printing.

many adj (**more, most**) numerous. * n a large number of persons or things.

map n a representation of all or part of the earth's surface, showing either natural features as continents and seas, etc or man-made features as roads, railroads etc. * vt (**mapping, mapped**) to make a map of.

maple n a tree with two-winged fruits, grown for shade, wood, or sap; its hard light-colored wood; the flavor of the syrup or sugar made from the sap of the sugar maple.

mar vt (**marring, marred**) to blemish, to spoil, to impair.

maraschino n a strong sweet liqueur made from a type of wild cherry.

marathon n a foot race of 26 miles, 385 yards (42.195 km); any endurance contest.

maraud vi to roam in search of plunder.–**marauder** n.–**marauding** adj.

marble n a hard limestone rock that takes a high polish; a block or work of art made of marble; a little ball of stone, glass, etc; (pl) a children's game played with such balls; (pl) (sl) wits. * adj of or like marble.–**marbly** adj.

March n the third month of the year having 31 days.

march vi to walk with regular steps, as in military formation; to advance steadily. * vt to make a person or group march. * n a steady advance; a regular, steady step; the distance covered in marching; a piece of music for marching.–**marcher** n.

marching orders npl official orders for infantry to move to a particular destination; (inf) a notice of dismissal.

marchioness n the wife or widow of a marquess; a woman of the rank of marquess.

Mardi Gras n the last day before Lent, Shrove Tuesday, a day of carnival in some cities, esp New Orleans.

mare n a mature female horse, mule, donkey.

margarine n a butter substitute made from vegetable and animal fats, etc.

margin n a border, edge; the blank border of a printed or written page; an amount beyond what is needed; provision for increase, error, etc; (commerce) the difference between cost and selling price.

marginal adj written in the margin; situated at the margin or border; close to the lower limit of acceptability; very slight, insignificant.–**marginally** adv.

marginalize vt to transfer someone away from the center of affairs in order to render them powerless.

marigold n a plant with a yellow or orange flower.

marijuana, marihuana n a narcotic obtained by smoking the dried flowers and leaves of the hemp plant.–also **cannabis, pot**.

marina n a small harbor with pontoons, docks, services, etc for yachts and pleasure craft.

marinade n a seasoning liquid in which meat, fish, etc is soaked to enhance flavor or to tenderize it before cooking. * vt to soak in a marinade.–also **marinate**.

marine adj of, in, near, or relating to the sea; maritime; nautical; naval. * n a soldier trained for service on land or sea; naval or merchant ships.

mariner n a seaman, sailor.

marionette n a little jointed doll or puppet moved by strings or wires.

marital adj of marriage, matrimonial.

maritime adj on, near, or living near the sea; of navigation, shipping, etc.

marjoram n a fragrant herb used in cooking and salads.

mark n a spot, scratch, etc on a surface; a distinguishing sign or characteristic; a cross made instead of a signature; a printed or written symbol, as a punctuation mark; a brand or label on an article showing the maker, etc; an indication of some quality, character, etc; a grade for academic work; a standard of quality; impression, influence, etc; a target.* vt to make a mark or marks on; to identify as by a mark; to show plainly; to heed; to grade, rate.–**marker** n.

marked adj having a mark or marks; noticeable; obvious.–**markedly** adv.

market n a meeting of people for buying and selling merchandise; a space or building in which a market is held; the chance to sell or buy; demand for (goods, etc); a region where goods can be sold; a section of the community offering demand for goods. * vti to offer for sale; to sell, buy domestic provisions.–**marketability** n.–**marketable** adj.

marketing n act of buying or selling; all the processes involved in moving goods from the producer to the consumer.

marketplace n a market in a public square; the world of economic trade and activity; a sphere in which ideas, opinions, etc compete for acceptance.

market research n the gathering of factual information from consumers concerning their preferences for goods and services.

marking n the conferring of a mark or marks; the characteristic arrangement of marks, as on fur or feathers.

marksman n (pl **marksmen**) one who is skilled at shooting.–**marksmanship** n.

markup n a selling at an increased price; the amount of increase.–also vt.

marmalade n a jam-like preserve made from oranges, sugar and water.

marmoset n a small monkey of South and Central America.

maroon[1] n a dark brownish red (–also adj).

maroon[2] vt to abandon alone, esp on a desolate island; to leave helpless and alone.

marquee n a large tent used for entertainment; a canopy over an entrance, as to a theater.

marquess n in UK, a title of nobility ranking between a duke and an earl.

marquis n (pl **marquises, marquis**) (Europe) a nobleman equivalent in rank to a British marquess.

marriage n the legal contract by which a woman and man become wife and husband; a wedding, either religious or civil; a close union.

marrow n the fatty tissue in the cavities of bones.

marry vb (**marrying, married**) vt to join as wife and husband; to take in marriage; to unite. * vi to get married.

marsh n an area of boggy, poorly drained land.–**marshiness** n.–**marshy** adj.

marshal n in some armies, a general officer of the highest rank; an officer in charge of a city's police or firefighting department; an official in charge of ceremonies, parades, etc. * vt (**marshaling, marshaled** or **marshalling, marshalled**) (ideas, troops) to arrange in order; to guide.–**marshaler** n.

marshmallow n a soft spongy confection made of sugar, gelatin, etc.

marsupial adj of an order of mammals that carry their young in a pouch. * n an animal of this kind, as a kangaroo, opossum.

marten n (pl **martens, marten**) a carnivorous tree-dwelling weasel-like mammal.

martial adj warlike; military.–**martially** adv.

martial arts npl systems of self-defense, usu from the Orient, practiced as sports, as karate or judo.

martial law n rule by military authorities over civilians, as during a war or political emergency.

Martian adj of or relating to the planet Mars. * n an inhabitant of Mars.

martin n one of various types of bird similar to the swallow, with a characteristic shape of tail; the house martin.

martinet n one who exerts strong discipline.–**martinetish, martinettish** adj.

martyr n a person tortured for a belief or cause; a person who suffers from an illness. * vt to kill as a martyr; to make a martyr of.–**martyrdom** n.

marvel n anything wonderful; a miracle. * vti (**marveling, marveled** or **marvelling, marvelled**) to become filled with wonder, surprise, etc.–**marvelous, marvellous** adj.

Marxism n the theory and practice developed by Karl Marx and Friedrich Engels advocating public ownership of the means of production and the dictatorship of the proletariat until the establishment of a classless society.–**Marxist** adj, n.

mascara n a cosmetic for darkening the eyelashes.

mascot n a person, animal or thing thought to bring good luck.

masculine adj having characteristics of or appropriate to the male sex; (gram) of the male gender.–**masculinity** n.

mash n any soft, pulpy mass; crushed malt and hot water for brewing; (inf) mashed potatoes. * vt to crush into a mash.

mask n a covering to conceal or protect the face; a moulded likeness of the face; anything that conceals or disguises; a respirator placed over the nose and mouth to aid or prevent inhalation of a gas; (surgery) a protective gauze placed over the nose and mouth to prevent the spread of germs. * vt to cover or conceal as with a mask; to disguise one's intentions or character.– **masked** adj.

masochism n abnormal pleasure, esp sexual, obtained from having physical or mental pain inflicted on one by another person.–**masochist** n.–**masochistic** adj.

mason n a person skilled in working or building with stone; (with cap) a Freemason.

masonic adj (often cap) relating to Freemasonry.

masonry n (pl **masonries**) stonework.

masquerade n a ball or party at which fancy dress and masks are worn; a pretense, false show. * vi to take part in a masquerade; to pretend to be what one is not.–**masquerader** n.

Mass. abbr = Massachusetts.

Mass n (RC Church) the celebration of the Eucharist.

mass n (pl **masses**) a quantity of matter of indefinite shape and size; a large quantity or number; bulk; size; the main part; (physics) the property of a body expressed as a measure of the amount of material contained in it; (pl) the ordinary people. * adj of or for the masses or for a large number. * vti to gather or form into a mass.

massacre n the cruel and indiscriminate killing of many people or animals. * vt to kill in large numbers.

massage n a kneading and rubbing of the muscles to stimulate the circulation of the blood. * vt to give a massage to.

masseur n a man who gives a massage professionally.–**masseuse** nf.

massive adj big, solid, or heavy; large and imposing; relatively large in comparison to normal; extensive.– **massively** adv.–**massiveness** n.

mass media npl newspapers, radio, television, and other means of communication with large numbers of people.

mass production n quantity production of goods, esp by machinery and division of labor.–**mass-produce** vt.

mast n a tall vertical pole used to support the sails on a ship; a vertical pole from which a flag is flown; a tall structure supporting a television or radio antenna.

mastectomy n (pl **mastectomies**) the removal of a breast by surgery.

master n a man who rules others or has control over something; an employer; an owner of an animal or slave; a male teacher in a private school; an expert craftsman; a writer or painter regarded as great; an original from which a copy can be made, esp a phonograph record or magnetic tape; (with cap) one holding an advanced academic degree. * adj being a master; chief; main; controlling. * vt to be for become master of; (in art, etc) to become expert.–**mastership** n.

masterful adj acting the part of a master; domineering; expert; skillful.–**masterfully** adv.–**masterfulness** n.

masterly adj expert; skillful.–**masterliness** n.

mastermind n a very clever person, esp one who plans or directs a project. * vt to be the mastermind of.

masterpiece n a work done with extraordinary skill; the greatest work of a person or group.

mastery n control as by a master; victory; expertise.

masticate vt to chew food before swallowing; to reduce to a pulp.–**mastication** n.–**masticator** n.

mastiff n a breed of large, thickset dogs used chiefly as watchdogs.

mastitis n an inflammation of a female breast or an udder.

masturbate vi to manually stimulate one's sexual organs to achieve orgasm without sexual intercourse.–**masturbation** n.

mat[1] n a piece of material of woven fibers, etc, used for protection, as under a vase, etc, or on the floor; a thick pad used in wrestling, gymnastics, etc; anything interwoven or tangled into a thick mass. * vti (**matting, matted**) to cover as with a mat; to interweave or tangle into a thick mass.

mat[2] adj without luster, dull.–also **matt**.

matador n the bullfighter who kills the bull with a sword.

match[1] n a thin strip of wood or cardboard tipped with a chemical that ignites under friction.

match[2] n any person or thing equal or similar to another; two persons or things that go well together; a contest or game; a mating or marriage. * vt to join in marriage; to put in opposition (with, against); to be equal or similar to; (one thing) to suit to another. * vi to be equal, similar, suitable, etc.

matchbox n a small box for holding matches.

matchless adj unequaled.–**matchlessly** adv.

mate n an associate or colleague; (inf) a friend; one of a matched pair; a marriage partner; the male or female of paired animals; an officer of a merchant ship, ranking below the master. * vti to join as a pair; to couple in marriage or sexual union.

material adj of, derived from, or composed of matter, physical; of the body or bodily needs, comfort, etc, not spiritual; important, essential, etc. * n what a thing is, or may be made of; elements or parts; cloth, fabric; (pl) tools, etc needed to make or do something; a person regarded as fit for a particular task, position, etc.

materialism n concern with money and possessions rather than spiritual values; the doctrine that everything in the world, including thought, can be explained only in terms of matter.–**materialist** n.–**materialistic** adj.

materialize vt to give material form to. * vi to become fact; to make an unexpected appearance.–**materialization** n.

maternal adj of, like, or from a mother; related through the mother's side of the family.–**maternally** adv.

maternity n motherhood; motherliness. * adj relating to pregnancy.

math n (inf) mathematics.

mathematical, mathematic adj of, like or concerned with mathematics; exact and precise.–**mathematically** adv.

mathematics n (used as sing) the science dealing with quantities, forms, space, etc and their relationships by the use of numbers and symbols; (sing or pl) the mathematical operations or processes used in a particular problem, discipline, etc.–**mathematician** n.

matinée n a daytime, esp an afternoon performance of a play, etc.

matins n sing or pl (Anglican Church) a morning prayer; (RC Church) one of the canonical hours of prayer.

matriarch n a woman who heads or rules her family or tribe.

matriarchy n (pl **matriarchies**) form of social organization in which the mother is the ruler of the family or tribe and in which descent is traced through the mother.–**matriarch** n.–**matriarchal, matriarchic** adj.

matrices see **matrix**.

matricide n a person who kills his (her) mother; the killing of one's mother.–**matricidal** adj.

matriculate vti to enroll, esp as a student.–**matriculation** n.

matrimony n (pl **matrimonies**) the act or rite of marriage; the married state.–**matrimonial** adj.–**matrimonially** adv.

matrix n (pl **matrices, matrixes**) the place, substance, etc from which something originates; a mold; the connective intercellular substance in bone, cartilage, or other tissue; (math) a rectangular grid of quantities in rows and columns used in solving certain problems.

matron n a wife or widow, esp one of mature appearance and manner; a woman in charge of domestic and nursing arrangements in a school, hospital or other institution.–**matronly** adj.

matt see **mat**[2].

matter n what a thing is made of; material; whatever occupies space and is perceptible to the senses; any specified substance; content of thought or expression; a quantity; a thing or affair; significance; trouble, difficulty; pus. * vi to be of importance.

matter-of-fact adj relating to facts, not opinions, imagination, etc.

mattress n a casing of strong cloth filled with cotton, foam rubber, coiled springs, etc, used on a bed.

maturation n the process of ripening or coming to maturity.

mature adj mentally and physically well-developed, grown-up; (fruit, cheese, etc) ripe; (bill) due; (plan) completely worked out. * vti to make or become mature; to become due.–**maturely** adv.–**matureness** n.

maturity n the state of being mature; full development; the date a loan becomes due.

maudlin adj foolishly sentimental; tearfully drunk.

maul vt to bruise or lacerate; to paw.

mausoleum n (pl **mausoleums, mausolea**) a large tomb.

mauve n any of several shades of pale purple. * adj of this color.

maverick n an independent-minded or unorthodox individual; an unbranded animal, eg a stray calf.

mawkish adj maudlin; insipid.–**mawkishly** adv.–**mawkishness** n.

max. abbr = maximum.

maxim n a concise rule of conduct; a precept.

maximize vt to increase to a maximum.–**maximization** n.

maximum n (pl **maxima, maximums**) the greatest quantity, number, etc. * adj highest; greatest possible reached.–**maximal** adj.

May n the fifth month of the year having 31 days.

may vb aux (past **might**) expressing possibility; permission; wish or hope.

maybe adv perhaps.

May Day n the first day of May, celebrated as a traditional spring festival; observed in many countries as a labor holiday.

Mayday n the international radio-telephone signal indicating a ship or aircraft in distress.

mayhem n violent destruction, confusion.

mayn't = may not.

mayonnaise n a salad dressing made from egg yolks whisked with oil and lemon juice or vinegar.

mayor n the chief administrative officer of a municipality.–**mayoral** adj.–**mayoralty** n.

maze n a confusing, intricate network of pathways, esp one with high hedges in a garden; a labyrinth; a confused state.–adj **mazelike**.

MB abbr = megabyte.

MBA abbr = Master of Business Administration.

MD abbr = Maryland; Doctor of Medicine; Managing Director.

MDMA abbr = methylene dioxymethamphetamine, a synthetic drug used as the stimulant Ecstasy.

me pers pron the objective case of I.

ME[1] abbr = myalgic encephalomyelitis.

ME[2], **Me** abbr = Maine.

mead n a wine made from a fermented solution of honey and spices.

meadow n a piece of land where grass is grown for hay; low, level, moist grassland.

meadowlark n one of two North American yellow-breasted songbirds related to the Baltimore oriole; any of several birds of South, Central and North America.

meager, meagre adj thin, emaciated; lacking in quality or quantity.–**meagerly, meagrely** adv.–**meagerness, meagreness** n.

meal[1] n any of the times for eating, as lunch, dinner, etc; the food served at such a time.

meal[2] n any coarsely ground edible grain; any substance similarly ground.–**mealiness** n.–**mealy** adj.

mean[1] adj selfish, ungenerous; despicable; shabby; bad-tempered; (sl) difficult; (sl) expert.–**meanly** adv.–**meanness** n.

mean[2] adj halfway between extremes; average. * n what is between extremes.

mean[3] vb (**meaning, meant**) vt to have in mind; to intend; to intend to express; to signify. * vi to have a (specified) degree of importance, effect, etc.

meander n a winding path esp a labyrinth; a winding of a stream or river. * vi (river) to wind; to wander aimlessly.–**meandering** adj.

meaning n sense; significance; import. * adj significant.–**meaningful** adj.–**meaningless** adj.

means npl that by which something is done; resources; wealth.

meant see **mean**[3].

meantime, meanwhile adv in or during the intervening time; at the same time. * n the intervening time.

measles n (used as sing) an acute, contagious viral disease, characterized by small red spots on the skin.

measly adj (**measlier, measliest**) (inf) slight, worthless; having measles.

measure n the extent, dimension, capacity, etc of anything; a determining of this, measurement; a unit of measurement; any standard of valuation; an instrument for measuring; a definite quantity measured out; a course of action; a statute, law; a rhythmical unit. * vt to find out the extent, dimensions etc of, esp by a standard; to mark off by measuring; to be a measure of. * vi to be of specified measurements.–**measurable** adj.–**measurably** adv.

measurement n a measuring or being measured; an extent or quantity determined by measuring; a system of measuring or of measures.

meat n animal flesh; food as opposed to drink; the essence of something.–**meaty** adj.

meatball n a small ball of ground meat usu mixed with breadcrumbs and spices; (inf) a stupid or foolish person.

mecca n a place of pilgrimage or a goal of aspiration; a resort or attraction that is visited by a large number of people; (with cap) Islam's holiest city, the birthplace of Muhammed (c. AD570) (–also **Makkah**).

mechanic n a person skilled in maintaining or operating machines, cars, etc.

mechanical adj of or using machinery or tools; produced or operated by machinery; done as if by a machine, lacking thought or emotion; of the science of mechanics.–**mechanically** adv.

mechanics n (used as sing) the science of motion and the action of forces on bodies; knowledge of machinery; (pl) the technical aspects of something.

mechanism n the working parts of a machine; any system of interrelated parts; any physical or mental process by which a result is produced.

mechanize vt to make mechanical; to equip with machinery or motor vehicles.–**mechanization** n.–**mechanized** adj.

medal n a small, flat piece of inscribed metal, commemorating some event or person or awarded for some distinction.–**medallic** adj.

medalist, medallist n one awarded a medal.

medallion n a large medal; a design, portrait, etc shaped like a medal; a medal worn on a chain around the neck.

meddle vi to interfere in another's affairs.–**meddler** n.–**meddlesome** adj.

media see **medium**.

median adj middle; intermediate. * n a median number, point, line, etc.

mediate vt to intervene (in a dispute); to bring about agreement. * vi to be in an intermediate position; to be an intermediary. * adj involving an intermediary, not direct or immediate.–**mediately** adv.–**mediation** n.–**mediative** adj.

mediator n one who or that which mediates; a person who acts as an intermediary; an intercessor.–**mediatory** adj.

medic n (inf) a medical student; (inf) a physician or surgeon.

medical adj relating to the practice or study of medicine. * n (inf) a medical examination.–**medically** adv.

medicate vt to treat with medicine; to impregnate (soap, shampoo, etc) with medication.–**medication** n.–**medicative** adj.

medicine n any substance used to treat or prevent disease; the science of preventing, treating or curing disease.–**medicinal** adj.–**medicinally** adv.

medieval adj of or like the Middle Ages.–also **mediaeval**.

medievalism n the spirit, esp in religion and art, customs, etc, characteristic of the Middle Ages; a study of these; any one of these extant since the Middle Ages, or a contemporary imitation of it.–also **mediaevalism**.–**medievalist, mediaevalist** n.

mediocre adj average; ordinary; inferior.–**mediocrity** n.

meditate vi to think deeply; to reflect; to empty the mind in order to concentrate on nothing or on one thing, esp as a religious exercise.–**meditation** n.–**meditator** n.

Mediterranean n the Mediterranean Sea. * adj of, or relating to (the area around) the Mediterranean Sea; (climate) characterized by hot, dry summers and warm, wet winters.

medium n (pl **media, mediums**) the middle state or condition; a substance for transmitting an effect; any intervening means, instrument, or agency; (pl **media**) a means of communicating information (eg newspapers, television, radio); (pl **mediums**) a person claiming to act as an intermediary between the living and the dead. * adj midway; average.

medley n (pl **medleys**) a miscellany; a musical piece made up of various tunes or passages.

meek adj patient, long-suffering; submissive.–**meekly** adv.–**meekness** n.

meet vb (**meeting, met**) vt to encounter, to come together; to make the acquaintance of; to contend with, deal with; to experience; to be perceived by (the eye, etc); (demand, etc) to satisfy; (bill, etc) to pay. * vi to come into contact with; to be introduced. * n a meeting for an athletics competition.

meeting n a coming together; a gathering.

megabyte n (comput) a unit of information, approximately equal to one million bytes.

megahertz n a unit of frequency equal to one million hertz.

megalith n a huge stone, esp part of a prehistoric monument.–**megalithic** adj.

megalomania n a mental illness characterized by delusions of grandeur; (inf) a lust for power.–**megalomaniac** n, adj.–**megalomaniacal** adj.

megaphone n a device to amplify and direct the voice.

megaton n a unit of explosive force equivalent to one million tons of TNT.

megawatt n one million watts.

melancholy n gloominess or depression; sadness. * adj sad; depressed.–**melancholia** n.–**melancholic** adj.

melanin n a dark brown pigment in the skin, hair, and eyes of humans and animals.

melanoma n (pl **melanomas, melanomata**) a skin tumor composed of darkly pigmented cells.

melee, mêlée n a confused, noisy struggle.

mellifluous, mellifluent adj (voice, sounds) sweetly flowing, smooth.–**mellifluously** adv.–**mellifluousness** n.

mellow adj (fruit) sweet and ripe; (wine) matured; (color, light, sound) soft, not harsh; kind-hearted and understanding. * vti to soften through age; to mature.–**mellowness** n.

melodrama n a play, movie, etc filled with overdramatic emotion and action; drama of this genre; sensational events or emotions.–**melodramatic** adj.–**melodramatically** adv.–**melodramatist** n.

melody n (pl **melodies**) a tune; a pleasing series of sounds.–**melodic** adj.–**melodious** adj.

melon n the large juicy many-seeded fruit of trailing plants, as the watermelon, cantaloupe.

melt vti (**melting, melted**, pp **molten**) to make or become liquid; to dissolve; to fade or disappear; to soften or be softened emotionally.–**melting** adj.–**meltingly** adv.

meltdown n the melting of the fuel core of a nuclear reactor; the drastic collapse of almost anything.

melting pot n a place, situation, or product of mixing many different races, traditions, cultures, etc.

member n a person belonging to a society or club; a part of a body, such as a limb; a representative in a legislative body; a distinct part of a complex whole.

membership n the state of being a member; the number of members of a body; the members collectively.

membrane n a thin pliable sheet or film; the fibrous tissue that covers or lines animal organs.–**membranous, membranaceous** adj.

memento n (pl **mementos, mementoes**) a reminder, esp a souvenir.

memo n (pl **memos**) a memorandum.

memoir n an historical account based on personal experience; (pl) an autobiographical record.

memorabilia npl (sing **memorabile**) things worthy of remembrance or record; clothing, letters, manuscripts, notes, etc, once belonging to or written by famous people or connected with famous events and thought worthy of collection.

memorable adj worth remembering; easy to remember.–**memorably** adv.

memorandum n (pl **memorandums**) an informal written communication as within an office; (pl **memoranda**) a note to help the memory.

memorial adj serving to preserve the memory of the dead. * n a remembrance; a monument.

memorize vt to learn by heart, to commit to memory.–**memorization** n.

memory n (pl **memories**) the process of retaining and reproducing past thoughts and sensations; the sum of things remembered; an individual recollection; commemoration; remembrance; the part of a computer that stores information (–also **store**).

men see **man**.

menace n a threat; (inf) a nuisance. * vt to threaten.–**menacing** adj.–**menacingly** adv.

menagerie n a place where wild animals are kept for exhibition; a collection of wild animals.

mend vt to repair; (manners, etc) to reform, improve. * vi to become better. * n the act of mending; a repaired area in a garment, etc.

mendacity n (pl **mendacities**) telling lies; a falsehood.–**mendacious** adj.–**mendaciously** adv.

menial adj consisting of work of little skill; servile. * n a domestic servant; a servile person.

meninges npl (sing **meninx**) the three membranes covering and protecting the brain and the spinal cord.–**meningeal** adj.

meningitis n inflammation of the membranes enveloping the brain or spinal cord.

menopause n the time of life during which a woman's menstrual cycle ceases permanently.–**menopausal** adj.

menstruation n the monthly discharge of blood from the uterus.–**menstrual** adj.–**menstruate** vi.

mental adj of, or relating to the mind; occurring or performed in the mind; having a psychiatric disorder; (inf) crazy, stupid.–**mentally** adv.

mentality n (pl **mentalities**) intellectual power; disposition, character.

menthol n peppermint oil.–**mentholated** adj.

mention n a brief reference to something in speech or writing; an official recognition or citation. * vt to refer to briefly; to remark; to honor officially.–**mentionable** adj.

mentor n a wise and trusted adviser.

menu n the list of dishes served in a restaurant; a list of options on a computer display.

meow n the cry of a cat.–also vi.

mercantile adj of merchants or trade.

mercenary adj working or done for money only. * n (pl **mercenaries**) a soldier hired to fight for a foreign army.–**mercenarily** adv.–**mercenariness** n.

merchandise n commercial goods. * vti to sell, to trade; to promote sales by display or advertising.–**merchandiser** n.

merchandising n the display of goods in a store, etc; the exploitation of a fictional character, pop group, etc, by the production of goods with their image, name, etc.

merchant n a trader; a retailer; (sl) a person fond of a particular activity.

merciful adj compassionate, humane.–**mercifulness** n.

mercifully adv in a merciful way; (inf) thank goodness.

merciless adj cruel, pitiless; without mercy.–**mercilessly** adv.–**mercilessness** n.

mercurial adj of, containing, or caused by mercury; lively, sprightly; volatile.–**mercurially** adv.

mercury n a heavy silvery liquid metallic element used in thermometers etc.

mercy n clemency; compassion; kindness; pity.

mere adj nothing more than; simple, unmixed.–**merely** adv.

merge vti to blend or cause to fuse together gradually; to (cause to) combine, unite.

merger n a combining together, esp of two or more commercial organizations.

meridian n the imaginary circle on the surface of the earth passing through the north and south poles.

meringue n a mixture of egg whites beaten with sugar and baked; a small cake or shell made from this, usu filled with cream.

merino n (pl **merinos**) a breed of sheep with fine silky wool; the wool or the cloth made from it.

merit n excellence; worth; (pl) (of a case) rights and wrongs; a deserving act. * vt to be worthy of, to deserve.–**meritorious** adj.–**meritoriously** adv.

meritocracy n (pl **meritocracies**) rule by those most skilled or talented; a social system or government based on this; the most talented group in a society.

mermaid n (legend) a woman with a fish's tail.–**merman** nm (pl **mermen**).

merry adj (**merrier, merriest**) cheerful; causing laughter; lively; (inf) slightly drunk.–**merrily** adv.–**merriment** n.

merry-go-round n a revolving platform of hobbyhorses, etc, a carousel.

merrymaking n festivity, fun.–**merrymaker** n.

mesa n a rocky plateau with steep sides usu found in arid regions.

mesdames see **madame**.

mesdemoiselles see **mademoiselle**.

mesh n an opening between cords of a net, wires of a screen, etc; a net; a network; a snare; (geared wheels, etc) engagement. * vt to entangle, ensnare. * vi to become entangled or interlocked.

mesmerism n hypnotism.–**mesmerist** n.

mesmerize vt to hypnotize; to fascinate.–**mesmeric** adj.–**mesmerizer** n.

mess n a state of disorder or untidiness, esp if dirty; a muddle; an unsightly or disagreeable mixture; a portion of soft and pulpy or semi-liquid food; a building where service personnel dine; a communal meal. * vti to make a mess (of), bungle; to eat in company; to potter (about).

message n any spoken, written, or other form of communication; the chief idea that the writer, artist, etc seeks to communicate in a work.

messenger n a person who carries a message.

Messiah n the promised savior of the Jews; Jesus Christ.–**Messianic** adj.

messieurs see **monsieur**.

Messrs pl of Mr.

messy adj (**messier, messiest**) dirty; confused; untidy.–**messily** adv.–**messiness** n.

met see **meet**.

metabolism n the total processes in living organisms by which tissue is formed, energy produced and waste products eliminated.–**metabolic** adj.

metabolize vt to process by metabolism; to assimilate.

metacarpus n (pl **metacarpi**) the bones of that part of the hand that is between the wrist and the fingers, or the corresponding part in other animals.–**metacarpal** adj, n.

metal n any of a class of chemical elements which are often lustrous, ductile solids, and are good conductors of heat, electricity, etc, such as gold, iron, copper, etc; any alloy of such elements as brass, bronze, etc; anything consisting of metal.–**metallic** adj.

metallurgy n the science of separating metals from their ores and preparing them for use by smelting, refining, etc.–**metallurgical** adj.–**metallurgist** n.

metamorphosis n (pl **metamorphoses**) a complete change of form, structure, substance, character, appearance, etc; transformation; the marked change in some animals at a stage in their growth, eg chrysalis to butterfly.–**metamorphic** adj.–**metamorphose** vi.

metaphor n a figure of speech in which a word or phrase is used for another of which it is an image.–**metaphoric, metaphorical** adj.–**metaphorically** adv.

metaphysical adj of or pertaining to metaphysics; abstruse, abstract; supernatural.–**metaphysically** adv.

metaphysics n sing the branch of philosophy that seeks to explain the nature of being and reality; speculative philosophy in general.–**metaphysician** n.

metastasis n (pl **metastases**) a change or shift in the location of a disease, often used of the spreading of cancer cells; a transformation or change.–**metastatic** adj.

metatarsus n (pl **metatarsi**) (anat) in humans, the instep, the middle part of the foot between the tarsus and the toes; in other animals, the part corresponding to this.–**metatarsal** adj, n.

mete vt to allot; to portion (out).

meteor n a small particle of matter which travels at great speed through space and becomes luminous through friction as it enters the earth's atmosphere; a shooting star.

meteoric adj of or relating to a meteor; dazzling, transitory.

meteorite n a meteor that has fallen to earth without being completely vaporized.–**meteoritic** adj.

meteorology n a study of the earth's atmosphere, particularly weather and climate.–**meteorological** adj.–**meteorologist** n.

meter[1] *n* a device for measuring and recording a quantity of gas, water, time, etc supplied; a parking meter. * *vt* to measure using a meter.

meter[2] *n* rhythmic pattern in verse, the measured arrangement of syllables according to stress; rhythmic pattern in music.–*also* **metre**.

meter[3] *n* the basic unit of length in the metric system, consisting of 100 centimeters and equal to 39.37 inches.–*also* **metre**.

methane *n* a colorless, odorless, flammable gas formed by the decomposition of vegetable matter, as in marshes.

method *n* the mode or procedure of accomplishing something; orderliness of thought; an orderly arrangement or system.

methodical *adj* orderly, systematic.–**methodically** *adv*.

methodology *n* (*pl* **methodologies**) the methods and procedures used by a science or discipline; the philosophical analysis of method and procedure.

methyl alcohol, methanol *n* a volatile flammable poisonous liquid.

meticulous *adj* very precise about small details.–**meticulously** *adv*.–**meticulousness** *n*.

metre[1] *see* **meter**[2].

metre[2] *see* **meter**[3].

metric *adj* based on the meter as a standard of measurement; of, relating to, or using the metric system.

metrication *n* conversion of an existent system of units into the metric system.

metric system *n* a decimal system of weights and measures based on the meter, liter and the kilogram.

metronome *n* an instrument that beats musical tempo.–**metronomic** *adj*.

metropolis *n* the main city, often a capital of a country, state, etc; any large and important city.–**metropolitan** *adj*.

mettle *n* courage, spirit.–**mettlesome** *adj*.

mezzanine *n* an intermediate story between others; a theater balcony.

mezzo *adv* (*mus*) moderately; quite. * *n* (*pl* **mezzos**) a mezzo-soprano.

mezzo-soprano *n* (*pl* **mezzo-sopranos**) (*mus*) a singer, or a part, between soprano and contralto.

Mg (*chem symbol*) magnesium.

mg *abbr* = milligram.

MHR *abbr* = Member of the House of Representatives.

MHz *abbr* = megahertz.

MI *abbr* = Michigan; military intelligence; myocardial infarction.

MIA *abbr* = missing in action.

mice *see* **mouse**.

Mich. *abbr* = Michigan.

micro *n* (*pl* **micros**) a microwave oven; (*comput*) a microcomputer, a microprocessor.

microbe *n* a microscopic organism, esp a disease-causing bacterium.–**microbial, microbic** *adj*.

microchip *n* a small wafer of silicon, etc, containing electronic circuits.–*also* **chip**.

microcircuit *n* a miniature electronic circuit, esp an integrated circuit.–**microcircuitry** *n*.

microcosm *n* a miniature universe or world.–**microcosmic, microcosmical** *adj*.–**microcosmically** *adv*.

microdot *n* a photographic reproduction of a document, plan, etc reduced to a tiny dot, esp for reasons of espionage.

micrometer, micrometre *n* a unit of length of one thousandth of a millimeter, a micron.

micron *n* (*pl* **microns, micra**) one millionth of a meter, a micrometer.

microorganism *n* an organism visible only through a microscope.

microphone *n* an instrument for transforming sound waves into electric signals, esp for transmission, or recording.–**microphonic** *adj*.

microprocessor *n* a computer processor contained on one or more integrated circuits.

microscope *n* an optical instrument for making magnified images of minute objects by means of a lens or lenses.–**microscopy** *n*.

microscopic *adj* of, with, like, a microscope; visible only through a microscope; very small.–**microscopically** *adv*.

microwave *n* an electromagnetic wave between 1 and 100 centimeters in length; (*inf*) a microwave oven. * *vt* to cook (food) in a microwave oven.–**microwavable, microwaveable** *adj*.

microwave oven *n* a cooker in which food is cooked or heated by microwaves.

mid *adj* middle. * *prep* amid.

midday *n* the middle of the day, noon.

middle *adj* halfway between two given points, times, etc; intermediate; central. * *n* the point halfway between two extremes; something intermediate; the waist. * *vt* to put in the middle.

middle age *n* the time between youth and old age, c.40–60.–**middle-aged** *adj*.

Middle Ages *npl* the period of European history between about AD 500 and 1500.

middle class *n* the class between the lower and upper classes, mostly composed of professional and business people.–**middle-class** *adj*.

middleman *n* (*pl* **middlemen**) a dealer between producer and consumer; an intermediary.

middle-of-the-road *adj* avoiding extremes, esp political extremes.–**middle-of-the-roader** *n*.

middling *adj* of medium quality, size, etc; second-rate. * *adv* moderately.–**middlingly** *adv*.

midget *n* a very small person, a dwarf; something small of its kind.–*also adj*.

midlife *n* (*pl* **midlives**) middle age.–*also adj*.

midnight *n* twelve o'clock at night.

midrib *n* the principal central vein of a leaf.

midriff *n* the middle part of the torso between the abdomen and the chest.–*also adj*.

midshipman *n* (*pl* **midshipmen**) in some navies, a noncommissioned officer ranking immediately below a sublieutenant; a student naval officer.

midst *n* middle. * *prep* amidst, among.

midsummer *n* the middle of summer.–*also adj*.

midway *adv* halfway. * *n* a middle course of action; the area of a carnival where the sideshows are.

midwife *n* (*pl* **midwives**) a person trained to assist women before, during, and after childbirth.–**midwifery** *n*.

mien *n* the expression of the face; demeanor.

miff *n* (*inf*) a petty quarrel, a tiff; a sulky mood. * *vti* to take offense; to offend.

might[1] *see* **may**.

might[2] *n* power, bodily strength.

mightn't = might not.

mighty *adj* (**mightier, mightiest**) powerful, strong; massive; (*inf*) very.–**mightily** *adv*.–**mightiness** *n*.

migraine *n* an intense, periodic headache, usu limited to one side of the head.

migrant *n* a person or animal that moves from one region or country to another; an itinerant agricultural laborer. * *adj* migrating.

migrate *vi* to settle in another country or region; (*birds, animals*) to move to another region with the change in season.–**migration** *n*.–**migratory** *adj*.

mike *n* (*inf*) a microphone. * *vt* to provide with a microphone; to transmit by microphone.

milage *see* **mileage**.

mild *adj* (*temper*) gentle; (*weather*) temperate; bland; feeble.–**mildly** *adv*.–**mildness** *n*.

mildew n a fungus that attacks some plants or appears on damp cloth, etc as a whitish coating. * vti to affect or be affected with mildew.–**mildewy** adj.

mile n a unit of linear measure equal to 5,280 feet (1.61 km); the nautical mile is 6,075 feet (1.85 km).

mileage n total miles traveled; an allowance per mile for traveling expenses; the average number of miles that can be traveled, as per liter of fuel.–also **milage**.

milestone n a stone marking the number of miles to a place; an important event in life, history, etc.

milieu n (pl **milieus, milieux**) environment, esp social setting.

militant adj ready to fight, esp to win some cause; combative.–also n.–**militance, militancy** n.–**militantly** adv.

militarism n military spirit; a policy of aggressive military preparedness.–**militarist** n.–**militaristic** adj.

military adj relating to soldiers or to war; warlike. * n (pl **militaries**) the armed forces.

militate vt to have influence or force; to produce an effect or change.

militia n an army composed of civilians called out in time of emergency.–**militiaman** n (pl **militiamen**).

milk n a white nutritious liquid secreted by female mammals for feeding their young. * vt to draw milk from; to extract money, etc, from; to exploit.–**milker** n.–**milky** adj.

milkman n (pl **milkmen**) a person who sells or delivers milk to homes.

milk tooth n any of the first teeth of a mammal.

mill n an apparatus for grinding by crushing between rough surfaces; a building where grain is ground into flour; a factory. * vt to produce or grind in a mill; (coins) to put a raised edge on. * vi to move around confusedly.–**miller** n.

millennium n (pl **millennia, millenniums**) a period of a thousand years; (Christianity) a period of a thousand years of holiness preceding or following the Second Coming of Christ; a coming time of happiness.–**millennial** adj.–**millennially** adv.

millepede see millipede.

millet n a cereal grass used for grain and fodder.

milligram n a thousandth of a gram.

milliliter, millilitre n a thousandth (.001) of a liter.

millimeter, millimetre n a thousandth (.001) of a meter.

milliner n a designer or seller of women's hats.–**millinery** n.

million n (pl **million, millions**) a thousand thousands, the number one followed by six zeros: 1,000,000; (inf) a very large number.–**millionth** n.

millionaire n a person who owns at least a million of money; one who is extremely rich.

millipede n a wormlike arthropod with many legs and a segmented body.–also **millepede**.

millstone n a stone used for grinding corn; a heavy burden.

mime n a theatrical technique using action without words; a mimic. * vi to act or express using gestures alone; (singers, musicians) to perform as if singing or playing live to what is actually a prerecorded piece of music.–**mimer** n.

mimic n a person who imitates, esp an actor skilled in mimicry. * adj related to mimicry; make-believe; sham. * vt (**mimicking, mimicked**) to imitate or ridicule.–**mimicker** n.

mimicry n (pl **mimicries**) practice, art, or way of mimicking; (biol) the resemblance of an animal to its environment, another animal, etc, to provide protection from predators, mimesis.

mimosa n any of a genus of leguminous plants, usu with clustered yellow flowers, whose leaves and stems fold when touched or when exposed to light; the sensitive plant; any of several related or similar plants.

min. abbr = minimum; minute(s).

minaret n a high, slender tower on a mosque from which the call to prayer is made.

mince vt to chop or cut up into small pieces; to diminish or moderate one's words. * vi to speak or walk with affected daintiness.–**mincer** n.–**mincing** adj.–**mincingly** adv.

mincemeat n a mixture of chopped apples, raisins, etc, used as a pie filling; finely chopped meat.

mind n the faculty responsible for intellect, thought, feelings, speech; memory; intellect; reason; opinion; sanity. * vt to object to, take offense to; to pay attention to; to obey; to take care of; to be careful about; to care about. * vi to pay attention; to be obedient; to be careful; to object.

mind-boggling adj (inf) astonishing, bewildering.–**mind-boggler** n.

minder n a person who looks after or protects another.

mind-expanding adj producing awareness; psychedelic, distorting.

mindful adj heedful, not forgetful.–**mindfully** adv.–**mindfulness** n.

mindless adj unthinking, stupid; requiring little intellectual effort.–**mindlessly** adv.–**mindlessness** n.

mindset n attitude, esp when fixed or rigid; a habit.

mind's eye n the visual memory or imagination.

mine[1] poss pron belonging to me.

mine[2] n an excavation from which minerals are dug; an explosive device concealed in the water or ground to destroy enemy ships, personnel, or vehicles that pass over or near them; a rich supply or source. * vt to excavate; to lay explosive mines in an area. * vi to dig or work a mine.

mine detector n a device for indicating the whereabouts of explosive mines.–**mine detection** n.

minefield n an area sown with explosive mines; a situation containing hidden problems.

minelayer n a ship or aircraft for laying mines.

miner n a person who works in a mine.

mineral n an inorganic substance, found naturally in the earth; any substance neither vegetable nor animal. * adj relating to or containing minerals.

mineralogy n the science of minerals.–**mineralogical** adj.–**mineralogically** adv.–**mineralogist** n.

mineral water n water containing mineral salts or gases, often with medicinal properties.

minestrone n a soup of vegetables with pieces of pasta.

minesweeper n a ship for clearing away explosive mines.–**minesweeping** n.

mingle vti to mix; to combine.–**mingler** n.

mini n (pl **minis**) something smaller than others of its type; a miniskirt.

miniature adj minute, on a small scale. * n a painting or reproduction on a very small scale.–**miniaturist** n.

miniaturize vt to greatly reduce the size of.–**miniaturization** n.

minibar n a small refrigerator in a hotel bedroom, stocked with alcoholic drinks.

minibus n (pl **minibuses, minibusses**) a small bus for carrying up to twelve passengers.

minima see minimum.

minimal adj very minute; least possible.–**minimality** n.–**minimally** adv.

minimalism n a style in the creation of art, music, etc, that uses the fewest possible elements to achieve the greatest effect.–**minimalist** n, adj.

minimize vt to reduce to or estimate at a minimum.–**minimization** n.

minimum n (pl **minimums, minima**) the least possible amount; the lowest degree or point reached.

mining n the act, process, or industry of excavating from the earth; (mil) the laying of explosive mines.

minion n a servile flatterer or dependant; an obsequious person acting on behalf of or carrying out the wishes of another. * adj dainty, graceful.

miniseries n (pl **miniseries**) (TV) the dramatization of a novel, etc, shown in several episodes; (sport) a short series.

miniskirt n a very short skirt.

minister n a clergyman serving a church; an official heading a government department; a diplomat. * vi to serve as a minister in a church; to give help (to).—**ministerial** adj.—**ministerially** adv.

ministration n the act or process of giving aid; the act of ministering religiously.

ministry n (pl **ministries**) the act of ministering; the clergy; the profession of a clergyman; a government department headed by a minister; the building housing a government department.

mink n (pl **mink, minks**) any of several carnivorous weasel-like mammals valued for its durable soft fur.

Minn. abbr = Minnesota.

minnow n (pl **minnow, minnows**) a small, slender freshwater fish.

minor adj lesser in size, importance, degree, extent; etc; (mus) lower than the corresponding major by a half step. * n (law) a person under full legal age; (education) a secondary area of study requiring fewer credits; (mus) a minor key, interval, or scale; (sport) a minor league, esp in baseball. * vi (with **in**) to take a subject requiring fewer credits.

minority n (pl **minorities**) the smaller part or number; a political or racial group smaller than the majority group; the state of being under age.

minstrel n a traveling entertainer and musician in the Middle Ages; a performer in a minstrel show.

minstrel show n a variety show with performers singing and dancing wearing black face make-up.

mint[1] n the place where money is coined; a large amount of money; a source of supply. * adj unused, in perfect condition. * vt (coins) to imprint; to invent.—**minter** n.

mint[2] n an aromatic plant whose leaves are used for flavoring.—**minty** adj.

minuet n (the music for) a slow, graceful dance in triple time.

minus prep less; (inf) without. * adj involving subtraction; negative; less than. * n a sign (−), indicating subtraction or negative quantity.

minute[1] n the sixtieth part of an hour or a degree; a moment; (pl) an official record of a meeting. * vt to record or summarize the proceedings (of).

minute[2] adj tiny; detailed; exact.—**minutely** adv.—**minuteness** n.

minuteman n (pl **minutemen**) (sometimes cap) a member of the militia in the War of American Independence, ready to fight at a minute's notice.

minutiae npl (sing **minutia**) small or unimportant details.

miracle n an extraordinary event attributed to the supernatural; an unusual or astounding event; a remarkable example of something.—**miraculous** adj.

mirage n an optical illusion in which a distant object or expanse of water seems to be nearby, caused by light reflection from hot air; anything illusory or fanciful.

mire n an area of wet, soggy, or muddy ground. * vt to sink in mire; to dirty; to embroil in difficulties.

mirror n a smooth surface that reflects images; a faithful depiction. * vt (**mirroring, mirrored**) to reflect or depict faithfully.

mirth n merriment, esp with laughter.—**mirthful** adj.—**mirthfully** adv.

mirthless adj lacking laughter; miserable.—**mirthlessly** adv.—**mirthlessness** n.

misanthrope, misanthropist n a person who hates or distrusts mankind.—**misanthropic** adj.—**misanthropically** adv.—**misanthropy** n.

misapprehend vt to misunderstand; to misconceive.—**misapprehension** n.

misappropriate vt to appropriate wrongly or dishonestly; to use illegally; to embezzle.—**misappropriation** n.

misbehave vi to behave badly. * vt to behave (oneself) badly.—**misbehavior, misbehaviour** n.

miscalculate vti to calculate wrongly.—**miscalculation** n.

miscarriage n the spontaneous expulsion of a fetus prematurely; mismanagement or failure.—**miscarry** vi.

miscellaneous adj consisting of various kinds; mixed.—**miscellaneously** adv.—**miscellaneousness** n.

miscellany n (pl **miscellanies**) a mixed collection; a book comprising miscellaneous writings, etc.

mischief n wayward behavior; damage.

mischievous adj harmful, prankish.—**mischievously** adv.—**mischievousness** n.

misconceive vt to conceive wrongly; to misjudge; to misapprehend; to misunderstand.—**misconceiver** n.

misconception n a mistaken idea; misunderstanding.

misconduct n dishonest management; improper behavior. * vt to conduct (oneself) badly; to manage dishonestly.

misconstrue vt (**misconstruing, misconstrued**) to misinterpret.—**misconstruction** n.

miscreant n an unscrupulous villain.

misdeed n a wrong or wicked act; crime; sin, etc.

misdemeanor, misdemeanour n (law) a minor offense, a misdeed.

miser n a greedy, stingy person who hoards money for its own sake.—**miserliness** n.—**miserly** adj.

miserable adj wretched; unhappy; causing misery; bad, inadequate; pitiable.—**miserableness** n.—**miserably** adv.

misery n (pl **miseries**) extreme pain, unhappiness, or poverty; a cause of such suffering.

misfit n something that fits badly; a maladjusted person.

misfortune n ill luck; trouble; a mishap; bad luck.

misgiving n a feeling of misapprehension, mistrust.

misguided adj foolish; mistaken.—**misguidedly** adv.

mishap n an unfortunate accident.

misinform vt to supply with wrong information.—**misinformant, misinformer** n.—**misinformation** n.

misjudge vt to judge wrongly, to form a wrong opinion.—**misjudgment** n.

mislay vt (**mislaying, mislaid**) to lose something temporarily; to put down or install improperly.—**mislayer** n.

mislead vt (**misleading, misled**) to deceive; to give wrong information to; to lead into wrongdoing.—**misleader** n.

misnomer n an incorrect or unsuitable name or description.—**misnomered** adj.

misogynist n a hater or distruster of women.—**misogynistic** adj.—**misogyny** n.

misplace vt to put in a wrong place; (trust, etc) to place unwisely.—**misplacement** n.

misprint vt to print incorrectly. * n an error in printing.

mispronounce vt to pronounce wrongly.—**mispronunciation** n.

misquote vt to quote wrongly.—**misquotation** n.

misread vt (**misreading, misread**) to read or to interpret wrongly.

miss[1] n (pl **misses**) a girl; (with cap) a title used before the surname of an unmarried woman or girl.

miss[2] vt to fail to reach, hit, find, meet, hear; to omit; to fail to take advantage of; to regret or discover the absence or loss of. * vi to fail to hit; to fail to be successful; to misfire, as an engine. * n a failure to hit, reach, obtain, etc.

Miss. abbr = Mississippi.

missal n a book containing the prayers for Mass.

misshapen adj badly shaped; deformed.

missile n an object, as a rock, spear, rocket, etc, to be thrown, fired, or launched.

missing adj absent; lost; lacking.

mission n a group of people sent by a church, government, etc to carry out a special duty or task; the sending of an aircraft or spacecraft on a special assignment; a vocation. * adj of a mission.

missionary n (pl **missionaries**) a person who tries to convert unbelievers to his or her religious faith, esp abroad; one sent on a mission. * adj of a religious mission; tending to propagandize.

mission control n a command center that controls space flights from the ground.

missive n (formal) a letter or message, often official. * adj (rare) sent specially, or intended to be sent.

misspent adj wasted, frittered away.

mist n a large mass of water vapor, less dense than a fog; something that dims or obscures. * vti to cover or be covered, as with mist.–**mistily** adv.–**mistiness** n.–**misty** adj.

mistake vb (**mistaking, mistook**, pp **mistaken**) * vt to misunderstand; to misinterpret; * vi to make a mistake. * n a wrong idea, answer, etc; an error of judgment; a blunder; a misunderstanding.–**mistakable** adj.–**mistakably** adv.

mistaken adj erroneous, ill-judged.–**mistakenly** adv.

mister n (inf) sir; (with cap) the title used before a man's surname.

mistletoe n an evergreen parasitic plant with white berries used as a Christmas decoration.

mistreat vt to treat wrongly or badly.–**mistreatment** n.

mistress n a woman who is head of a household; a woman with whom a man is having a prolonged affair.

mistrust n lack of trust. * vti to doubt; to suspect.–**mistrustful** adj.–**mistrustfully** adv

misunderstand vt (**misunderstanding, misunderstood**) to fail to understand correctly.

misunderstanding n a mistake as to sense; a quarrel or disagreement.

misunderstood adj not fully understood; not appreciated properly.

misuse vt to use for the wrong purpose or in the wrong way; to ill-treat, abuse. * n improper or incorrect use.

mite n any of numerous very small parasitic or free-living insects; (money, etc) a very small amount.

miter, mitre n the headdress of a bishop; a diagonal joint between two pieces of wood to form a corner. * vt to join with a miter corner.–**miterer** n.

mitigate vti to become or make less severe.–**mitigable** adj.–**mitigation** n.–**mitigator** n.

mitosis n (pl **mitoses**) n a process by which plant or animal cells divide, in which the nucleus of a somatic cell splits into nuclei, each with the same number of chromosomes as there were in the orig cell.–**mitotic** adj, adv.

mitre see **miter**.

mitt n a baseball glove.

mitten n a glove with a thumb but no separate fingers.

mix vt to blend together in a single mass; to make by blending ingredients, as a cake; to combine; (with **up**) to make into a mixture; to make disordered; to confuse or mistake. * vi to be mixed or blended; to get along together. * n a mixture.–**mixable** adj.

mixer n a device that blends or mixes; a person considered in terms of their ability (good or bad) to get on with others; a soft drink added to an alcoholic beverage.

mixture n the process of mixing; a blend made by mixing.

mix-up n a mistake; confusion, muddle; (inf) a fight.

ml abbr = mile; milliliter.

mm abbr = millimeter.

MN abbr = Minnesota.

Mn (chem symbol) manganese.

mnemonic adj of or aiding memory.–n a device to aid the memory.–**mnemonically** adv.

MO abbr = Missouri.

moan n a low mournful sound as of sorrow or pain. * vti to utter a moan; to complain.–**moaner** n.–**moaningly** adv.

moat n a deep ditch surrounding a fortification or castle, usu filled with water.

mob n a disorderly or riotous crowd; a contemptuous term for the masses; (sl) a gang of criminals. * vt (**mobbing, mobbed**) to attack in a disorderly group; to surround.–**mobbish** adj.

mobile adj movable, not fixed; easily changing; characterized by ease in change of social status; capable of moving freely and quickly; (inf) having transport. * n a suspended structure of wood, metal, etc with parts that move in air currents.–**mobility** n.

mobilize vt to prepare for action, esp war by readying troops for active service; to organize for a particular reason; to put to use.–**mobilization** n.

mobster n (sl) a gangster.

moccasin n a flat shoe based on Amerindian footwear; any soft, flexible shoe resembling this.

mock vt to imitate or ridicule; to behave with scorn; to defy; (with **up**) to make a model of. * n ridicule; an object of scorn. * adj false, sham, counterfeit.–**mocker** n.–**mockery** n.–**mockingly** adv.

mockingbird n a gray American bird with the ability to imitate with exactness the call of other birds.

modal adj of mode or form, not substance; (mus) of or composed in a mode.–**modality** n.–**modally** adv.

mode n a way of acting, doing or existing; a style or fashion; form; (mus) any of the scales used in composition; (statistics) the predominant item in a series of items.

model n a pattern; an ideal; a standard worth imitating; a representation on a smaller scale, usu three-dimensional; a person who sits for an artist or photographer; a person who displays clothes by wearing them. * adj serving as a model; representative of others of the same style. * vb (**modeling, modeled** or **modelling, modelled**) vt (with **after, on**) to create by following a model; to display clothes by wearing. * vi to serve as a model for an artist, etc.–**modeler, modeller** n.

modem n a device that links two computers via the telephone network for transmitting data.

moderate vti to make or become moderate; to preside over. * adj having reasonable limits; avoiding extremes; mild, calm; of medium quality, amount, etc. * n a person who holds moderate views.–**moderately** adv.–**moderation** n.

moderator n a mediator; one who presides at a court, assembly, etc.

modern adj of the present or recent times; up-to-date.–**modernity** n.–**modernly** adv.

modernism n modern view, methods or usage; the theory or practice of modern art, literature, etc; (Christianity) rationalistic theology.–**modernist** adj, n.–**modernistic** adj.–**modernistically** adv.

modernize vti to make or become modern.–**modernization** n.

modest adj decent or seemly; having a humble opinion of oneself; unpretentious.–**modestly** adv.–**modesty** n.

modicum n (pl **modicums, modica**) a small quantity.

modification n a modifying or being modified; the result of this; a modified form; an adjustment, alteration.–**modificator** n.–**modificatory, modificative** adj.

modifier n one who or that which modifies; (gram) a word, clause or phrase that qualifies or limits the meaning of another word, etc, a qualifier.

modify vt (**modifying, modified**) to lessen the severity of; to change or alter slightly; (gram) to limit in meaning, to qualify.–**modifiable** adj.–**modifiability** n.

modish adj fashionable, stylish.–**modishly** adv.–**modishness** n.

modulate vti to adjust; to regulate; to vary the pitch, intensity, frequency, etc, of.–**modulation** n.–**modulator** n.–**modulatory** adj.

module n a unit of measurement; a self-contained unit, esp in a spacecraft.–**modular** adj.

modus operandi n (pl **modi operandi**) a method of operating, procedure.

mogul, moghul n (inf) an important person, a magnate; (with cap) a ruler of the former Moghul Empire in India.

mohair n the long, fine hair of the Angora goat; the silk cloth made from it.

moist adj damp; slightly wet.–**moistly** adv.–**moistness** n.

moisten *vti* to make or become moist.–**moistener** *n*.

moisture *n* liquid in a diffused, absorbed, or condensed state.

moisturize *vt* (*skin, air, etc*) to add moisture to.–**moisturizer** *n*.

molar *n* a back tooth, used for grinding food.

molasses *n* (*pl* **molasses**) the thick brown sugar that is produced during the refining of sugar; treacle.

mold[1] *n* a fungus producing a furry growth on the surface of organic matter.–*also* **mould**.–**moldy** *adj*.

mold[2] *n* a hollow form in which something is cast; a pattern; something made in a mold; distinctive character. * *vt* to make in or on a mold; to form, shape, guide.–*also* **mould**.–**moldable** *adj*.–**molder** *n*.

molder *vi* to decay to rot, to crumble to dust.

molding *n* anything made in a mold; a shaped strip of wood or plaster, as around the upper walls of a room.–*also* **moulding**.

mole[1] *n* a spot on the skin, usu dark-colored and raised.

mole[2] *n* a small burrowing insectivore with soft dark fur; a spy within an organization. of or inherent in molecules.

molecule *n* the simplest unit of a substance, retaining the chemical properties of that substance; a small particle.–**molecular** *adj*.

molehill *n* a mound of earth thrown up by a burrowing mole.

moleskin *n* the fur of a mole; a twilled cotton cloth with a soft surface resembling a mole's fur, used for work clothes; (*pl*) pants made of moleskin.

molest *vt* to annoy; to attack or assault, esp sexually.–**molestation** *n*.–**molester** *n*.

mollify *vt* (**mollifying, mollified**) to make less severe or violent; to soften.–**mollification** *n*.–**mollifier** *n*.–**mollifyingly** *adv*.

mollusk, mollusc *n* an invertebrate animal usu enclosed in a shell, as oysters, etc.–**molluskan, molluscan** *adj, n*.

molt *vi* to shed hair, skin, horns, etc prior to replacement of new growth. * *n* a moulting.–*also* **moult**.–**molter** *n*.

molten *adj* melted by heat.

mom *n* (*inf*) mother.

moment *n* an indefinitely brief period of time; a definite point in time; a brief time of importance.

momentarily *adv* for a short time; in an instant; at any moment.

momentary *adj* lasting only for a moment.–**momentariness** *n*.

momentous *adj* very important.–**momentously** *adv*.–**momentousness** *n*.

momentum *n* (*pl* **momenta, momentums**) the impetus of a moving object, equal to the product of its mass and its velocity.

mommy *n* (*pl* **mommies**) (*inf*) mother.

monarch *n* a sovereign who rules by hereditary right; a powerful or dominant thing or person.–**monarchal, monarchic, monarchical** *adj*.–**monarchically** *adv*.

monarchism *n* the principles of, or devotion to, monarchy.–**monarchist** *n*, *adj*.–**monarchistic** *adj*.

monarchy *n* (*pl* **monarchies**) a government headed by a monarch; a kingdom.

monastery *n* (*pl* **monasteries**) the residence of a group of monks, or nuns.–**monasterial** *adj*.

monastic, monastical *adj* of monks or monasteries. * *n* a monk; a recluse.–**monastically** *adv*.–**monasticism** *n*.

Monday *n* the second day of the week.

monetarism *n* (*economics*) the theory that control of the money supply is the key to achieving low inflation and economic growth.–**monetarist** *n, adj*.

monetary *adj* of the coinage or currency of a country; of or relating to money.–**monetarily** *adv*.

money *n* (*pl* **moneys, monies**) coins or paper notes authorized by a government as a medium of exchange; property; wealth.

moneyed *adj* rich.–*also* **monied**.

mongoose *n* (*pl* **mongooses**) a small predatory mammal of Africa and Asia.

mongrel *n* an animal or plant of mixed or unknown breed, esp a dog. * *adj* of mixed breed or origin.–**mongrelism** *n*.–**mongrelly** *adj*.

monied *see* **moneyed**.

monies *see* **money**.

monitor *n* a student chosen to help the teacher; any device for regulating the performance of a machine, aircraft, etc; a screen for viewing the image being produced by a television camera; a display screen connected to a computer. * *vti* (*TV or radio transmissions, etc*) to observe or listen to for political or technical reasons; to watch or check on; to regulate or control, a machine, etc.–**monitorial** *adj*.

monk *n* a male member of a religious order living in a monastery.

monkey *n* any of the primates except man and the lemurs, esp the smaller, long-tailed primates. * *vi* (**monkeying, monkeyed**) (*inf*) to play, trifle, or meddle.

monkey business *n* (*inf*) mischief; underhand dealings.

monochrome *n* a painting, drawing, or print in a single color. * *adj* in one color or shades of one color; black and white.–**monochromatic** *adj*.

monocle *n* a single eyeglass held in place by the face muscles.–**monocled** *adj*.

monogamy *n* the practice of being married to only one person at a time.–**monogamist** *n*.–**monogamous** *adj*.

monogram *n* the embroidered or printed initials of one's name on clothing, stationery, etc.–**monogrammed** *adj*.–**monogrammatic** *adj*.

monolith *n* a single large block of stone; any massive, unyielding structure.–**monolithic** *adj*.–**monolithically** *adv*.

monologue, monolog *n* a long speech; a soliloquy, a skit, etc for one actor only.–**monologuist, monologist** *n*.

monoplane *n* an airplane with a single pair of wings.

monopolize *vt* to get, have, or exploit a monopoly of; to get full control of.–**monopolization** *n*.–**monopolizer** *n*.

monopoly *n* (*pl* **monopolies**) exclusive control in dealing in a particular commodity or supplying a service; exclusive use or possession; that which is exclusively controlled; such control granted by a government.–**monopolism** *n*.–**monopolist** *n*.–**monopolistic** *adj*.–**monopolistically** *adv*.

monorail *n* a single track railroad, often with suspended carriages.

monosodium glutamate *n* a chemical additive used to give food a meaty taste.

monosyllable *n* a word of one syllable.–**monosyllabic** *adj*.

monotheism *n* the doctrine of or belief in the existence of only one God.–**monotheist** *n*.–**monotheistic** *adj*.–**monotheistically** *adv*.

monotone *n* an utterance or musical tone without a change in pitch; a tiresome sameness of style, color, etc.–**monotonic** *adj*.–**monotonically** *adv*.

monotonous *adj* unvarying in tone; with dull uniformity, wearisome.–**monotonously** *adv*.–**monotony** *n*.

monoxide *n* an oxide with one oxygen atom in each molecule.

monsieur *n* (*pl* **messieurs**) the French equivalent of sir in address and of Mr with a name.

Monsignor *n* (*pl* **Monsignors, Monsignore**) (*RC Church*) a title given, usu by the Pope, to some prelates or offices.

monsoon *n* a seasonal wind of southern Asia; the rainy season.

monster *n* any greatly malformed plant or animal; an imaginary beast; a very wicked person; a very large animal or thing. * *adj* very large, huge.

monstrosity *n* (*pl* **monstrosities**) the state or quality of being monstrous; an ugly, unnatural or monstrous thing or person.

monstrous *adj* abnormally developed; enormous; horrible.–**monstrously** *adv*.–**monstrousness** *n*.

montage *n* a rapid sequence of film shots, often superimposed; the art or technique of assembling various elements, esp pictures or photographs; such an assemblage.

month n any of the twelve divisions of the year; a calendar month.

monthly adj continuing for a month; done, happening, payable, etc every month. * n a monthly periodical. * adv once a month; every month.

monument n an obelisk, statue or building that commemorates a person or an event; an exceptional example.–**monumental** adj.–**monumentally** adv.

moo n the long deep sound made by a cow. * vi (cattle) to low; to make a deep long noise like a cow.

mood n a temporary state of mind or temper; a gloomy feeling; a predominant feeling or spirit; (gram) that form of a verb indicating mode of action; (mus) mode.

moody adj (**moodier, moodiest**) gloomy; temperamental.–**moodily** adv.–**moodiness** n.

moon n the natural satellite that revolves around the earth and shines by reflected sunlight; any natural satellite of another planet; something shaped like the moon. * vi to behave in an idle or abstracted way.

moonbeam n a ray of moonlight.

moonlight n the light of the moon. * vi (inf) to have a secondary (usu night-time) job.–**moonlighter** n.

moonlit adj lit by the moon.

moonshine n moonlight; (inf) nonsense, foolish talk; (sl) illegally distilled spirits.

moor[1] n a tract of open wasteland, usu covered with heather and often marshy.

moor[2] vti (a ship) to secure or be secured by cable or anchor.

mooring n the act of mooring; the place where a ship is moored; (pl) the lines, cables, etc by which a ship is moored.

moorland n a stretch of moors.

moose n (pl **moose**) the largest member of the deer family, native to North America.

moot adj debatable; hypothetical.

mop n a rag, sponge, etc fixed to a handle for washing floors or dishes; a thick or tangled head of hair. * vt (**mopping, mopped**) to wash with a mop.

mope vi to be gloomy and apathetic. * n a person who mopes, a moper.–**moper** n.–**mopey** adj.–**mopingly** adv.

moped n a light, motor-assisted bicycle.

moraine n a mass of earth, stones, etc, deposited by a glacier.–**morainal, morainic** adj.

moral adj of or relating to character and human behavior, particularly as regards right and wrong; virtuous, esp in sexual conduct; capable of distinguishing right from wrong; probable, although not certain; psychological, emotional. * n a moral lesson taught by a fable, event, etc; (pl) principles; ethics.

morale n moral or mental condition with respect to courage, discipline, confidence, etc.

moralist n a teacher or student of morals; one for whom morality needs no religious sanction; one concerned with the morals of others.–**moralistic** adj.–**moralistically** adv.

morality n (pl **moralities**) virtue; moral principles; a particular system of moral principles.

moralize, moralise vt to explain or interpret morally; to give a moral direction to. * vi to make moral pronouncements.–**moralization, moralisation** n.–**moralizer, moraliser** n.

morally adv in a moral manner, ethically; virtually, practically.

moral philosophy n ethics.

morass n a bog, marsh.

moratorium n (pl **moratoria, moratoriums**) a legally authorized delay in the payment of money due; an authorized delay or suspension of any activity.–**moratory** adj.

morbid adj diseased, resulting as from a diseased state of mind; gruesome.–**morbidly** adv.–**morbidness** n.

morbidity n the state of being morbid; the relative incidence of disease.

mordant adj biting, caustic; corrosive. * n a chemical fixative; a corrosive substance.–**mordancy** n.–**mordantly** adv.

more adj (superl **most**) greater; further; additional (–also compar of **many, much**). * adv to a greater extent or degree; again; further.

moreover adv in addition to what has been said before; besides.

mores npl customs so fundamentally established that they have the force of law.

morgue n a place where the bodies of unknown dead or those dead of unknown causes are temporarily kept prior to burial; a collection of reference materials, eg newspaper clippings.

moribund adj in a dying state; near death.–**moribundity** n.

morning n the part of the day from midnight or dawn until noon; the early part of anything. * adj of or in the morning.

morning sickness n a period of nausea and vomiting in the early stages of pregnancy.

moron n an adult mentally equal to a 8 to 12-year-old child; (inf) a very stupid person.–**moronic** adj.–**moronically** adv.–**moronism, moronity** n.

morose adj sullen, surly; gloomy.–**morosely** adv.–**moroseness** n.

morphine, morphia n an alkaloid derived from opium, used as an anesthetic and sedative.–**morphinic** adj.

Morse code n a code in which letters are represented by dots and dashes or long and short sounds, and are transmitted by visual or audible signals.

morsel n a small quantity of food; a small piece of anything.

mortal adj subject to death; causing death, fatal; hostile; very intense. * n a human being.–**mortality** n.–**mortally** adv.

mortality rate n the yearly proportion of deaths to population.–also **death rate**.

mortar n a mixture of cement or lime with sand and water used in building; an artillery piece that fires shells at low velocities and high trajectories; a bowl in which substances are pounded with a pestle.

mortarboard n a small square board for holding mortar; a square black college or university cap with a tassel.

mortgage n a transfer of rights to a piece of property usu as security for the payment of a loan or debt that becomes void when the debt is paid. * vt to make over as a security or pledge; to put an advance claim on.

mortician n a person who manages funerals.

mortify vti (**mortifying, mortified**) to subdue by repression or penance; to humiliate or shame; to become gangrenous.–**mortification** n.–**mortifier** n.–**mortifyingly** adv.

mortuary n (pl **mortuaries**) a place of temporary storage for dead bodies.

mosaic n a surface decoration made by inlaying small pieces (of glass, stone, etc) to form figures or patterns; a design made in mosaic. * adj of or made of mosaic. * vt (**mosaicking, mosaicked**) to adorn with or make into mosaic.–**mosaicist** n.

mosey vi (inf) (often with **along, on down**) to go, to saunter, to amble.

Moslem see **Muslim**.

mosque n a place of worship for Muslims.

mosquito n (pl **mosquitoes, mosquitos**) a small two-winged bloodsucking insect.

moss n a very small green plant that grows in clusters on rocks, moist ground, etc.–**mossy** adj.

most adj (compar **more**) greatest in number; greatest in amount or degree; in the greatest number of instances (–also superl of **many, much**). * adv in or to the greatest degree or extent. * n the greatest amount or degree; (with pl) the greatest number (of).

mostly adv for the most part; mainly, usually.

motel n an hotel for motorists with adjacent parking.

moth n a four-winged chiefly night-flying insect related to the butterfly.

mothball n a small ball of camphor or naphthalene used to protect stored clothes from moths.

moth-eaten adj eaten into by moths; dilapidated; outmoded.

mother n a female who has given birth to offspring; an origin or source. * adj of or like a mother; native. * vt to be the mother of or a mother to.

motherhood n the state of being a mother; the qualities of feelings of being a mother; mothers collectively.

mother-in-law n (pl **mothers-in-law**) the mother of one's spouse.

motherland n a person's native land or the country of a person's forebears.

motherly adj of, proper to a mother; like a mother.–**motherliness** n.

mother-of-pearl n the iridescent lining of the shell of the pearl oyster.

motif n a recurrent theme in a musical composition.–also **motive**.

motion n activity, movement; a formal suggestion made in a meeting, law court, or legislative assembly; evacuation of the bowels. * vti to signal or direct by a gesture.

motionless adj not moving, still.–**motionlessness** n.

motion picture n a film, movie.

motivate vt to supply a motive to; to instigate.–**motivation** n.–**motivator** n.

motive n something (as a need or desire) that causes a person to act; a motif in music. * adj moving to action; of or relating to motion.–**motiveless** adj.–**motivity** n.

motley adj multicolored; composed of diverse elements.

motor n anything that produces motion; a machine for converting electrical energy into mechanical energy; a motor car. * adj producing motion; of or powered by a motor; of, by or for motor vehicles; of or involving muscular movements. * vi to travel by car.

motorbike n a motorcycle.

motorboat n a boat propelled by an engine or motor.

motorcade n a procession of motor vehicles.

motorcar n a usu four-wheeled vehicle powered by an internal combustion engine.–also **automobile**.

motorcycle n a two-wheeled motor vehicle.–**motorcyclist** n.

motorist n a person who drives a car.

motorize vt to equip with a motor; to equip with motor vehicles.–**motorization** n.

mottle vt to mark with colored blotches or spots, to variegate. * n a pattern of colored blotches of spots, as on marble; one of the colored blotches in such a pattern.

motto n (pl **mottoes, mottos**) a short saying adopted as a maxim or ideal.

mould see **mold**[1], **mold**[2].

moulder see **molder**.

moulding see **molding**.

mouldy see **moldy**.

moult see **molt**.

mound n an artificial bank of earth or stones; a heap or bank of earth. * vt to form into a mound.

mount[1] n a high hill.

mount[2] vi to increase. * vt to climb, ascend; to get up on (a horse, platform, etc); to provide with horses; (a jewel) to fix on a support; (a picture) to frame. * n a horse for riding; (for a picture) a backing.–**mountable** adj.–**mounter** n.

mountain n a land mass higher than a hill; a vast number or quantity. * adj of or in mountains.–**mountainous** adj.

mountaineer n one who climbs mountains.–**mountaineering** n.

mounted adj seated on horseback or on a bicycle, etc; serving on horseback, as a policeman; placed on a suitable support.

mourn vti (someone dead) to grieve for; (something regrettable) to feel or express sorrow for.–**mourner** n.

mournful adj expressing grief or sorrow; causing sorrow.–**mournfully** adv.–**mournfulness** n.

mourning adj grieving. * n the expression of grief; dark clothes worn by mourners.

mouse n (pl **mice**) a small rodent with a pointed snout, long body and slender tail; a timid person; a hand-held device used to position the cursor and control software on a computer screen.

mousse n a chilled dessert made of fruit, eggs, and whipped cream; a similar savory dish made with meat or fish; a foamy substance applied to the hair to help it keep its style.

moustache see **mustache**.

mousy, mousey adj (**mousier, mousiest**) mouse-like; gray-brown in color; quiet, stealthy; timid, retiring.–**mousily** adv.–**mousiness** n.

mouth n (pl **mouths**) the opening in the head through which food is eaten, sound uttered or words spoken; the lips; opening, entrance, as of a bottle, etc. * vt to say, esp insincerely; to form words with the mouth without uttering sound. * vi to utter pompously; to grimace.–**mouther** n.

mouthful n (pl **mouthfuls**) as much (food) as fills the mouth; a word or phrase that is difficult to say correctly.

mouthpiece n the part of a musical instrument placed in the mouth; a person, periodical, etc that expresses the views of others.

mouthwash n a flavored, often antiseptic liquid for rinsing the mouth.

mouthwatering adj appetizing; tasty.

movable, moveable adj that may be moved. * npl personal property.–**movably** adv.–**movability** n.

move vt (**moving, moved**) to shift or change place; to set in motion; to rouse the emotions; to put (a motion) formally. * vi to go from one place to another; to walk, to carry oneself; to change place; to evacuate the bowels; to propose a motion as in a meeting; to change residence; (chess, checkers, etc) to change the position of a piece on the board. * n the act of moving; a movement, esp in board games; one's turn to move; a premeditated action.

movement n act of moving; the moving part of a machine, esp a clock; the policy and activities of a group; a trend, eg in prices; a division of a musical work; tempo.

mover n one who moves; (inf) a driving force, an innovator; a proposer of a motion.

movie n a cinema film, motion picture; (pl) the showing of a motion picture; the motion-picture medium or industry.

moving adj arousing the emotions; changing position; causing motion.–**movingly** adv.

mow vti (**mowing, mowed**, pp **mowed** or **mown**) (grass, etc) to cut from with a sickle or lawn mower; (with **down**) to cause to fall like cut grass.–**mower** n.

mph abbr = miles per hour.

Mr n (pl **Messrs**) used as a title before a man's name or an office he holds.

Mrs n (pl **Mrs** or **Mesdames**) used as a title before a married woman's name.

MS abbr = (pl **MSS**) manuscript; multiple sclerosis.

Ms n the title used before a woman's name instead of Miss or Mrs.

MT abbr = Montana.

Mt abbr = mount.

much adj (compar **more**, superl **most**) plenty. * adv considerably; to a great extent.

muck n moist manure; black earth with decaying matter; mud, dirt, filth.–**mucky** adj.

mucous membrane n the mucus-secreting lining of body cavities.

mucus n the slimy secretion that keeps mucous membranes moist.–**mucous** adj.

mud n soft, wet earth. * vt (**muds, mudding, mudded**) to muddy; to throw mud at; to vilify.

muddle vt to confuse; to mix up. * n confusion, mess.

muddy adj (**muddier, muddiest**) like or covered with mud; not bright or clear; confused. * vti (**muddying, muddied**) to make or become dirty or unclear.–**muddily** adv.–**muddiness** n.

muezzin n a Muslim official who proclaims from the minaret of a mosque the hour of prayer, and summons the faithful to worship.

muff n a warm soft fur cover for warming the hands.

muffin n a baked yeast roll.

muffle vt to wrap up for warmth or to hide; (sound) to deaden by wrapping up.

mug n a cylindrical drinking cup, usu of metal or earthenware; its contents; (sl) the face; (sl) a fool. * vb (**mugging, mugged**) vt to assault, usu with intent to rob.

mugger n a person who assaults with intent to rob.

muggy adj (**muggier, muggiest**) (weather) warm, damp and close.–**mugginess** n.

mulberry n (pl **mulberries**) a tree on whose leaves silkworms feed; its berry.

mulch n loose, organic, strawy dung providing a protective covering around the roots of plants. * vt to spread mulch.

mule[1] n the offspring of a male donkey and a female horse; a machine for spinning cotton; an obstinate person.–**mulish** adj.–**mulishly** adv.–**mulishness** n.

mule[2] n a slipper without a heel.

mull[1] vti (inf) to ponder (over).

mull[2] vt (wine, etc) to heat, sweeten and spice.–**mulled** adj.

mullah, mulla n (formerly) a Muslim theologian or teacher; a Muslim title of respect.

mullet n (pl **mullets, mullet**) any of various types of food fish.

multicolored, multicoloured adj many-colored.

multifarious adj multiform; diversified, of great variety; manifold.–**multifariously** adv.–**multifariousness** n.

multilingual adj speaking or in more than two languages.–**multilingually** adv.

multimillionaire n a person with two or more millions of money.

multinational n a business operating in several countries.–also adj.

multiple adj of many parts; manifold; various; complex. * n (math) a number exactly divisible by another.

multiple sclerosis n a disease of the nervous system with loss of muscular coordination, etc.

multiplex adj (radio, telecommunications) the use of a single channel of communication to transmit more than one signal; manifold, multiple. * n a movie theater with several auditoria. * vi to transmit messages or send signals in a multiplex system. * vt to send (several signals) simultaneously on one frequency.

multiplication n the act of multiplying; the process of repeatedly adding a quantity to itself a certain number of times, or any other process which has the same result.–**multiplicational** adj.

multiplicity n (pl **multiplicities**) a great number or variety (of).

multiplier n a thing or person that multiplies; the number by which another is to be multiplied.

multiply vti (**multiplying, multiplied**) to increase in number, degree, etc; to find the product (of) by multiplication.

multitude n a large number (of people).

mum adj silent, not speaking.

mumble vti to speak indistinctly, mutter. * n a mumbled utterance.–**mumbler** n.–**mumblingly** adv.

mumbo jumbo n (pl **mumbo jumbos**) meaningless ritual, talk, etc.

mummify vt (**mummifying, mummified**) to embalm (a body) as a mummy; to shrivel, to desiccate.–**mummification** n.

mummy n (pl **mummies**) a carefully preserved dead body, esp an embalmed corpse of ancient Egypt.

mumps n sing or pl an acute contagious virus disease characterized by swelling of the salivary glands.

munch vti to chew steadily.–**muncher** n.

mundane adj routine, everyday; banal; worldly.–**mundanely** adv.

municipal adj of or concerning a city, town, etc or its local government.–**municipally** adv.

municipality n (pl **municipalities**) a city or town having corporate status and powers of self-government; the governing body of a municipality.

munificent adj extremely generous, bountiful.–**munificence** n.–**munificently** adv.

munition vt to equip with arms. * n (pl) war supplies, esp weapons and ammunition.

mural adj relating to a wall. * n a picture or design painted directly onto a wall.–**muralist** n.

murder n the intentional and unlawful killing of one person by another; (inf) something unusually difficult or dangerous to do or deal with. * vti to commit murder (upon), to kill; to mangle, to mar.–**murderer** n.–**murderess** nf.

murderous adj capable of or bent on murder; deadly.–**murderously** adv.–**murderousness** n.

murk n indistinct gloom, darkness.–**murky** adj.

murmur n a continuous low, indistinct sound; a mumbled complaint; (med) an abnormal sound made by the heart. * vti to make a murmur; to say in a murmur.–**murmurer** n.–**murmurous** adj.

muscatel, muscadel n a sweet wine made from muscat grapes.

muscle n fibrous tissue that contracts and relaxes, producing bodily movement; strength; brawn; power. * vi (inf) to force one's way (in).–**muscular** adj.–**muscularity** n.

muscle-bound adj having some of the muscles abnormally enlarged and lacking in elasticity as from too much exercise; inflexible, rigid.

muscovado, muscavado n raw sugar left after the molasses has evaporated from sugar cane.

musculature n the entire system of muscles in a living thing; the system of muscles in an organ or a part of this system.

muse vti to ponder, meditate; to be lost in thought. * n a fit of abstraction.–**muser** n.

museum n a building for exhibiting objects of artistic, historic or scientific interest.

mush n a thick porridge of boiled meal; any thick, soft mass; (inf) sentimentality.–**mushy** adj.

mushroom n a fleshy fungus with a capped stalk, some varieties of which are edible. * vi to gather mushrooms; to spread rapidly, to increase.

music n the art of combining tones into a composition having structure and continuity; vocal or instrumental sounds having rhythm, melody or harmony; an agreeable sound.

musical adj of or relating to music or musicians; having the pleasant tonal qualities of music; having an interest in or talent for music. * n a play or movie incorporating dialogue, singing and dancing.–**musicality** n.–**musically** adv.

musician n one skilled in music, esp a performer.–**musicianly** adj.–**musicianship** n.

musicology n the study of the history, forms, etc of music.–**musicological** adj.–**musicologist** n.

musing adj meditative; lost in thought.–**musingly** adv.

musk n an animal secretion with a strong odor, used in perfumes; the odor of musk; a plant with a similar odor.–**musky** adj.–**muskiness** n.

musket n a long-barreled, smoothbore shoulder gun formerly used by infantrymen.

muskrat n (pl **muskrats, muskrat**) a large North American aquatic rodent, related to the vole, that emits a musky secretion; the fur from this.

Muslim n an adherent of Islam. * adj of Islam, its adherents and culture.–also **Moslem**.

muslin n a fine cotton cloth.

muss vt (often with **up**) (inf) to disarrange, to rumple. * n a state of disorder.

mussel n an edible marine bivalve shellfish.

must aux vb expressing: necessity; probability; certainty. * n (inf) something that must be done, had, etc.

mustache n the hair on the upper lip.–also **moustache**.

mustang n a small hardy semi-wild horse of the American prairies.

mustard n the powdered seeds of the mustard plant used as a condiment; a brownish-yellow color.

muster vt to assemble or call together, as troops for inspection or duty; to gather. * vi to be assembled, as troops. * n gathering; review; assembly.

musty adj (**mustier, mustiest**) moldy, damp; stale.—**mustily** adv.—**mustiness** n.

mutant n a mutation; an organism whose structure has undergone mutation. * adj mutating.

mutate vti to experience or cause to experience change or alteration.

mutation n the act or process of mutating; alteration; (biol) a sudden change in some inheritable characteristic of a species; (linguistics) a change in a vowel sound when assimilated with another, esp an umlaut.—**mutational** adj.

mute adj silent; dumb. * n a person who is unable to speak; a device that softens the sound of a musical instrument. * vt to lessen the sound of a musical instrument.—**mutely** adv.—**muteness** n.

mutilate vt to maim; to damage by removing an essential part of.—**mutilation** n.—**mutilative** adj.—**mutilator** n.

mutineer n a person who takes part in a mutiny.

mutiny vi (**mutinying, mutinied**) to revolt against authority, esp in military service. * n (pl **mutinies**) a rebellion against authority, esp by soldiers and sailors against officers.—**mutinous** adj.

mutt n a mongrel dog.

mutter vti to utter in a low tone or indistinctly; to grumble.—**mutterer** n.—**mutteringly** adv.

mutton n the edible flesh of sheep.

mutual adj given and received in equal amount; having the same feelings one for the other; shared in common.—**mutuality** n.—**mutually** adv.

muzzle n the projecting nose or mouth of an animal; a strap fitted over the jaws to prevent biting; the open end of a gun barrel. * vt to put a muzzle on; to silence or gag.—**muzzler** n.

muzzy adj (**muzzier, muzziest**) confused, dazed; dizzy; blurred; dull.—**muzzily** adv.—**muzziness** n.

MW abbr = medium wave; megawatt.

my poss adj of or belonging to me.

myalgia n pain, stiffness or cramp in the voluntary muscles or in one muscle.

myalgic encephalomyelitis n a viral condition affecting the nervous system, characterized by fatigue and muscle pains.—also **post-viral syndrome**.

myna (bird) n any of several Asian birds resembling the starling, some species of which can imitate speech.

myopia n short-sightedness.—**myopic** adj.—**myopically** adv.

myriad n a great number of persons or things. * adj innumerable.

myrrh n a fragrant gum resin used in perfume, incense, etc.

myrtle n an evergreen shrub with fragrant leaves; a trailing periwinkle.

myself pron emphatic and reflexive form of I; in my normal state.

mystery n (pl **mysteries**) something unexplained and secret; a story about a secret crime, etc; secrecy.—**mysterious** adj.—**mysteriously** adv.—**mysteriousness** n.

mystic n one who seeks direct knowledge of God or spiritual truths by self-surrender. * adj mystical.

mystical adj having a meaning beyond normal human understanding; magical.—**mystically** adv.

mysticism n the beliefs or practices of a mystic; belief in a reality accessible by intuition, not the intellect; obscurity of thought or doctrine.

mystify vt (**mystifying, mystified**) to puzzle, bewilder, to confuse.—**mystification** n.—**mystifier** n.—**mystifyingly** adv.

myth n a fable; a fictitious event; a traditional story of gods and heroes, taken to be true.—**mythic** adj.

mythical adj imaginary, unreal, untrue; having to do with myths, mythic.—**mythically** adv.

mythology n (pl **mythologies**) myths collectively; the study of myths.—**mythological** adj.

N

N (chem symbol) nitrogen. * abbr = North.

Na (chem symbol) sodium.

nab vt (**nabbing, nabbed**) (sl) to catch, arrest.

nacho n a Mexican snack consisting of a tortilla chip often served grilled with melted cheese, chilli, etc.

nadir n the point opposite the zenith; the lowest point; the depths of despair.

nag[1] vti (**nagging, nagged**) to scold constantly; to harass; to be felt persistently. * n a person who nags.

nag[2] (inf) a horse.

nail n a horny plate covering the end of a human finger or toe; a thin pointed metal spike for driving into wood as a fastening or hanging device. * vt to fasten with nails; to fix, secure; (inf) to catch or hit; (inf) to arrest.

nailfile n a small metal file or strip of cardboard coated with emery used for trimming and shaping the nails.

nail polish n a lacquer for giving a clear or colored shiny surface to nails.

naive, naïve adj inexperienced; unsophisticated; (argument) simple.—**naively, naïvely** adv.

naiveté, naïveté, naivety n natural, unaffected simplicity or ingenuousness.

naked adj bare, without clothes; without a covering; without addition or ornament; (eye) without optical aid.—**nakedness** n.

name n a word or term by which a person or thing is called; a title; reputation; authority. * vt to give a name to; to call by name; to designate; to appoint to an office; (a date, price, etc) to specify.

name-calling n verbal abuse, esp in place of reasoned debate.

name-dropping n the practice of mentioning the names of famous or important people as if they were friends, in order to impress others.—**name-dropper** n.

nameless adj without a name; obscure; anonymous; unnamed; indefinable; too distressing or horrifying to be described.

namely adv that is to say.

namesake n a person or thing with the same name as another.

nanny n (pl **nannies**) a child's nurse.

nap[1] n a short sleep, doze. * vi (**napping, napped**) to take a nap.

nap[2] n a hairy surface on cloth or leather; such a surface.

napalm n a substance added to petrol to form a jelly-like compound used in firebombs and flame-throwers. * vt to attack or burn with napalm.

nape n the back of the neck.

naphtha n a clear, volatile, inflammable bituminous liquid hydrocarbon exuding from the earth or distilled from coal tar, etc; rock oil.

napkin n a square of cloth or paper for wiping fingers or mouth or protecting clothes at table, a serviette.

narcissism n excessive interest in one's own body or self.—**narcissistic** adj.

narcissus n (pl **narcissi, narcissuses**) a spring-flowering bulb plant, esp the daffodil.

narcosis n (pl **narcoses**) a state of unconsciousness or drowsiness produced by narcotics.

narcotic adj inducing sleep. * n a drug, often addictive, used to relieve pain and induce sleep.

narrate vt (a story) to tell, relate; to give an account of; (film, TV) to provide a spoken commentary for.

narration n the act of narrating; a statement, written or verbal.

narrative n a spoken or written account of a sequence of events, experiences, etc; the art or process of narration.–*also adj.*

narrator n one who narrates.

narrow *adj* small in width; limited; with little margin; (*views*) prejudiced or bigoted. * n (*usu pl*) the narrow part of a pass, street, or channel. * *vti* to make or grow narrow; to decrease; to contract.–**narrowly** *adv.*–**narrowness** n.

narrow gauge *adj* denoting the distance of less than standard gauge (4 feet, 8.5 inches/1.44 meters) between rail metals.

narrow-minded *adj* prejudiced, bigoted; illiberal.–**narrow-mindedness** n.

NASA *abbr* = National Aeronautics and Space Administration.

nasal *adj* of the nose; sounded through the nose. * n a sound made through the nose.–**nasally** *adv.*

nasturtium n an ornamental garden plant with bright flowers, a pungent odor, and edible leaves.

nasty *adj* (**nastier, nastiest**) unpleasant; offensive; ill-natured; disagreeable; (*problem*) hard to deal with; (*illness*) serious or dangerous.–**nastily** *adv.*–**nastiness** n.

nation n people of common territory, descent, culture, language, or history; people united under a single government.

national *adj* of a nation; common to a whole nation, general. * n a citizen or subject of a specific country.–**nationally** *adv.*

national anthem n a patriotic song or hymn adopted officially by a nation for ceremonial and public occasions.

National Guard n in US, state militia that can be called into federal service.

nationalism n patriotic sentiments, principles, etc; a policy of national independence or self-government; fanatical patriotism, chauvinism.–**nationalist** n.–**nationalistic** *adj.*

nationality n (*pl* **nationalities**) the status of belonging to a nation by birth or naturalization; a nation or national group.

nationalize *vt* to make national; to convert into public or government property.–**nationalization** n.

native *adj* inborn; natural to a person; innate; (*language, etc*) of one's place of birth; relating to the indigenous inhabitants of a country or area; occurring naturally. * n a person born in the place indicated; a local inhabitant; an indigenous plant or animal; an indigenous inhabitant.

nativity n (*pl* **nativities**) birth; a horoscope at the time of one's birth; (*with cap*) the birth of Christ.

NATO *abbr* = North Atlantic Treaty Organization.

natural *adj* of or produced by nature; not artificial; innate, not acquired; true to nature; lifelike; normal; at ease; (*mus*) not flat or sharp. * n (*inf*) a person or thing considered to have a natural aptitude (for) or to be an obvious choice (for); (*inf*) a certainty; (*mus*) a natural note or a sign indicating one.–**naturalness** n.

natural gas n gas trapped in the earth's crust, a combustible mixture of methane and hydrocarbons extracted for fuel.

natural history n the study of nature, esp the animal, mineral, and vegetable world.

naturalism n (*art, literature*) the theory or practice of describing nature, character, etc in realistic detail.–**naturalistic** *adj.*

naturalist n a person who studies natural history; a person who advocates or practices naturalism.

naturalize *vt* to confer citizenship upon (a person of foreign birth); (*plants*) to become established in a different climate. * *vi* to become established as if native.

naturally *adv* in a natural manner, by nature; of course.

nature n the phenomena of physical life not dominated by man; the entire material world as a whole, or forces observable in it; the essential character of anything; the innate character of a person, temperament; kind, class; vital force or functions; natural scenery.

naughty *adj* (**naughtier, naughtiest**) mischievous or disobedient; titillating.–**naughtily** *adv.*–**naughtiness** n.

nausea n a desire to vomit; disgust.–**nauseous** *adj.*

nauseate *vti* to arouse feelings of disgust; to feel nausea or revulsion.–**nauseating** *adj.*

nautical *adj* of ships, sailors, or navigation.

nautical mile n an international unit of measure for air and sea navigation equal to 6,075 feet (1.85 km).

nautilus n (*pl* **nautiluses, nautili**) a genus of cephalopods, including those furnished with a chambered spinal univalve shell; a shellfish with webbed arms once supposed to sail upon the sea; a kind of diving bell.

naval *adj* of the navy; of ships.

nave n the central space of a church, distinct from the chancel and aisles.

navel n the small scar in the abdomen caused by severance of the umbilical cord; a central point.

navigable *adj* (*rivers, seas*) that can be sailed upon or steered through.–**navigability** n.–**navigably** *adv.*

navigate *vti* to steer or direct a ship, aircraft, etc; to travel through or over (*water, air, etc*) in a ship or aircraft; to find a way through, over, etc, and to keep to a course.

navigation n the act, art or science of navigating; the method of calculating the position of a ship, aircraft, etc.–**navigational** *adj.*

navigator n one who navigates; one skilled in the science of navigation.

navy n (*pl* **navies**) (*often with cap*) the warships of a nation; a nation's entire sea force, including ships, men, stores, etc; navy blue.

navy blue n an almost black blue.

nay *adv* (*arch*) no; not only so; yet more; or rather, and even. * n a refusal or denial.

Nazi n (*pl* **Nazis**) a member of the German National Socialist party (1930s).–*also adj.*

NB *abbr* = note well (Latin *nota bene*); New Brunswick.

NBC *abbr* = National Broadcasting Company.

NC *abbr* = North Carolina.

NCO *abbr* = noncommissioned officer.

ND *abbr* = North Dakota.

NE *abbr* = Nebraska; northeast, northeastern.

near *adj* (**nearer, nearest**) close, not distant in space or time; closely related, intimate; approximate, (*escape, etc*) narrow. * *adv* to or at a little distance; close by; almost. * *prep* close to. * *vti* to approach; to draw close to.–**nearness** n.

nearby *adj* neighboring; close by in position.

nearly *adv* almost, closely.

near-sighted *adj* short-sighted, myopic.–**near-sightedness** n.

neat *adj* clean and tidy; skillful; efficiently done; well made; (*alcoholic drink*) undiluted; (*sl*) nice, pleasing, etc.–**neatly** *adv.*–**neatness** n.

neaten *vt* to make tidy and neat.

nebula n (*pl* **nebulae, nebulas**) a gaseous mass or star cluster in the sky appearing as a hazy patch of light.–**nebular** *adj.*

nebulous *adj* indistinct; formless.

necessarily *adv* as a natural consequence.

necessary *adj* indispensable; required; inevitable. * n (*pl* **necessaries**) something necessary; (*pl*) essential needs.

necessitate *vt* to make necessary; to compel.

necessitous *adj* urgent; pressing; needy.

necessity n (*pl* **necessities**) a prerequisite; something that cannot be done without; compulsion; need.

neck n the part of the body that connects the head and shoulders; that part of a garment nearest the neck; a neck-like part, esp a narrow strip of land; the narrowest part of a bottle; a strait. * *vti* (*sl*) to kiss and caress.

neckerchief n a cloth square worn around the neck.

necklace n a string or band, often of precious stones, beads, or pearls, worn around the neck.

neckline n the line traced by the upper edge of a garment below the neck.

necktie n a man's tie.

necropolis n (pl **necropolises, necropoleis**) a cemetery.

necrosis n mortification and death of a bone; gangrene; a disease in plants, characterized by small black spots.–**necrotic** adj.

nectar n a sweetish liquid in many flowers, used by bees to make honey; any delicious drink.

nectarine n a smooth-skinned peach.

nee, née adj (literally) born: indicating the maiden name of a married woman.

need n necessity; a lack of something; a requirement; poverty. * vt to have a need for; to require; to be obliged.

needful adj necessary, required, vital. * n (inf) what is required, esp money.–**needfulness** n.

needle n a small pointed piece of steel for sewing; a larger pointed rod for knitting or crocheting; a stylus; the pointer of a compass, gauge, etc; the thin, short leaf of the pine, spruce, etc; the sharp, slender metal tube at the end of a hypodermic syringe. * vt to goad, prod, or tease.

needlepoint n a type of embroidery worked on canvas; point lace.

needless adj not needed, unnecessary; uncalled for, pointless.–**needlessly** adv.–**needlessness** n.

needlework n sewing, embroidery.

needn't = need not.

needy adj (**needier, neediest**) in need, very poor.

nefarious adj wicked, evil.

negate vt to nullify; to deny.

negation n a negative statement, denial; the opposite or absence of something; a contradiction.

negative adj expressing or meaning denial or refusal; lacking positive attributes; (math) denoting a quantity less than zero, or one to be subtracted; (photog) reversing the light and shade of the original subject, or having the colours replaced by complementary ones; (elect) of the charge carried by electrons; producing such a charge. * n a negative word, reply, etc; refusal; something that is the opposite or negation of something else; (in debate, etc) the side that votes or argues for the opposition; (photog) a negative image on transparent film or a plate. * vt to refuse assent, contradict; to veto.–**negatively** adv.

neglect vt to pay little or no attention to; to disregard; to leave uncared for; to fail to do something. * n disregard; lack of attention or care.–**neglectful** adj.–**neglectfully** adv.

negligee n a woman's loosely fitting dressing gown.

negligent adj careless, heedless.–**negligence** n.–**negligently** adv.

negligible adj that need not be regarded; unimportant; trifling.

negotiable adj able to be legally negotiated; (bills, drafts, etc) transferable.–**negotiability** n.

negotiate vti to discuss, bargain in order to reach an agreement or settlement; to settle by agreement; (fin) to obtain or give money value for (a bill); (obstacle, etc) to overcome.–**negotiation** n.–**negotiator** n.

Negro n (pl **Negroes**) a member of the dark-skinned, indigenous peoples of Africa; a member of the Negroid group; a person with some Negro ancestors.–also adj.–**Negress** nf.

Negroid adj denoting, or of, one of the major groups of humankind, including most of the peoples of Africa south of the Sahara.

neigh vi (**neighing, neighed**) to whinny; to make a sound like the cry of a horse. * n the cry of a horse; a whinny.

neighbor, neighbour n a person who lives near another; a person or thing situated next to another; a fellow human being. * vt to be near, to adjoin.–**neighboring, neighbouring** adj.

neighborhood, neighbourhood n a particular community, area, or district; the people in an area.

neighborly, neighbourly adj characteristic of a neighbor, friendly. * adv in a neighborly or social manner.–**neighborliness, neighbourliness** n.

neither adj, pron not one or the other (of two); not either. * conj not either; also not.

nemesis n (pl **nemeses**) retribution; just punishment; an agent of defeat.

neologism n a new word; the coining of new words, neology; the introduction of new doctrines.–**neologistic, neological** adj.

neon n an inert gaseous element that gives off a bright orange glow, used in lighting and advertisements.

neophyte n a novice; one recently baptized; a convert. * adj recently entered.

nephew n the son of a brother or sister.

nephritis n inflammation of the kidneys.

nepotism n undue favoritism shown to relatives, esp in securing jobs.

nerd n (sl) a boring, straight-laced person; a creep.

nerve n any of the fibers or bundles of fibers that transmit impulses of sensation or of movement between the brain and spinal cord and all parts of the body; courage, coolness in danger; (inf) audacity, boldness; (pl) nervousness, anxiety. * vt to give strength, courage, or vigor to.

nerve cell n a cell transmitting impulses in nerve tissue.–also **neuron, neurone**.

nerve center, nerve centre n a group of closely connected cells; (mil, etc) a center of control from which instructions are sent out.

nerve gas n a poison gas that affects the nervous system.

nerveless adj calm, cool; weak, feeble.–**nervelessly** adv.

nerve-racking, nerve-wracking adj straining the nerves, stressful.

nervous adj excitable, highly strung; anxious, apprehensive; affecting or acting on the nerves or nervous system.

nervous breakdown n a (usu temporary) period of mental illness resulting from severe emotional strain or anxiety.

nervous system n the brain, spinal cord, and nerves collectively.

nervy adj (**nervier, nerviest**) (inf) anxious, agitated; (inf) impudent, cheeky.

nest n a structure or place where birds, fish, mice, etc, lay eggs or give birth to young; a place where young are nurtured; a swarm or brood; a lair; a cosy place; a set of boxes, tables, etc of different sizes, designed to fit together. * vi to make or occupy a nest.

nest egg n money put aside as a reserve or to establish a fund.

nestle vti to rest snugly; to lie snugly, as in a nest; to lie sheltered or half-hidden.

net[1] n an openwork material of string, rope, or twine knotted into meshes; a piece of this used to catch fish, to divide a tennis court, etc; a snare. * vti (**netting, netted**) to snare or enclose as with a net; to hit (a ball) into a net or goal.

net[2], **nett** adj clear of deductions, allowances or charges. * n a net amount, price, weight, profit, etc. * vt (**netting, netted**) to clear as a profit.

nether adj lower or under.

nether world n the underworld, hell.

netting n netted fabric.

nettle n a wild plant with stinging hairs. * vt to irritate, annoy.

network n an arrangement of intersecting lines; a group of people who co-operate with each other; a chain of interconnected operations, computers, etc; (radio, TV) a group of broadcasting stations connected to transmit the same program simultaneously. * vt to broadcast on a network; (comput) to interconnect systems so that information, software, and peripheral devices, such as printers, can be shared.

networking n the making of contacts and trading information as for career advancement; the interconnection of computer systems.

neural adj of or pertaining to the nerves.

neuralgia n pain along a nerve.–**neuralgic** adj.

neurology n the branch of medicine studying the nervous system and its diseases.–**neurological** adj.–**neurologist** n.

neuron, neurone see **nerve cell**.

neurosis n (pl **neuroses**) a mental disorder with symptoms such as anxiety and phobia.

neurosurgery n the branch of surgery dealing with the nervous system.–**neurosurgical** adj.

neurotic adj suffering from neurosis; highly strung; of or acting upon the nerves. * n someone with neurosis.

neuter adj (gram) of gender, neither masculine nor feminine; (biol) having no sex organs; having undeveloped sex organs in the adult. * n a neuter person, word, plant, or animal. * vt to castrate or spay.

neutral adj nonaligned; not taking sides with either party in a dispute or war; having no distinctive characteristics; (color) dull; (chem) neither acid nor alkaline; (physics) having zero charge. * n a neutral state, person, or color; a position of a gear mechanism in which power is not transmitted.

neutrality n the state of being neutral.

neutralize vt to render ineffective; to counterbalance; to declare neutral.–**neutralization** n.–**neutralizer** n.

neutrally adv in a neutral manner.

neutron n an elementary particle with no electric charge and the same mass approximately as a proton.

neutron bomb n a nuclear bomb with a small blast that releases neutrons, destroying life but leaving property undamaged.

never adv at no time, not ever; not at all; in no case; (inf) surely not.

nevertheless adv all the same, notwithstanding; in spite of, however.

new adj recently made, discovered, or invented; seen, known, or used for the first time; different, changed; recently grown, fresh; unused; unaccustomed; unfamiliar; recently begun. * adv again; newly; recently.

new blood n a recent arrival in an organization expected to bring new ideas and revitalize the system.

newborn adj newly born; reborn.

newcomer n a recent arrival.

newfangled adj (contemptuous) new; novel, very modern.

newly adv recently, lately.

newlywed n a recently married person.

new moon n the moon when first visible as a crescent.

news npl current events; recent happenings; the mass media's coverage of such events; a program of news on television or radio; information not known before.

newscast n radio or television news broadcast.–**newscaster** n.

newsdealer, newsagent n a retailer of newspapers, magazines, etc.

newsflash n an important news item broadcast separately and often interrupting other programs.

newsletter n a bulletin regularly distributed among the members of a group, society, etc, containing information and news of activities, etc.

newspaper n a printed periodical containing news published daily or weekly.

newsprint n an inexpensive paper on which newspapers are printed.

newsworthy adj timely and important or interesting.

newt n any of various small amphibious lizard-like creatures.

New Testament n the second part of the Bible including the story of the life and teachings of Christ.

newton n the SI unit of force that when acting for 1 second on a mass of 1 kilogram imparts an acceleration of 1 meter per second.

New Year's (Day) n the first day of a new year; 1 January, a legal holiday in many countries.

New Year's Eve n the evening of the last day of the year; 31 December..

next adj nearest; immediately preceding or following; adjacent. * adv in the nearest time, place, rank, etc; on the first subsequent occasion.

next of kin n the nearest relative of a person.

NH abbr = New Hampshire.

Ni (chem symbol) nickel.

nib n a pen point. * vt (**nibbing, nibbed**) to furnished with a nib; to cut or insert a pen nib.

nibble vti to take small bites at (food, etc); to bite (at) lightly and intermittently.–**nibbler** n.

nice adj pleasant, attractive, kind, good, etc; particular, fastidious; delicately sensitive.–**nicely** adv.–**niceness** n.

nice-looking adj pretty, handsome.

nicety n (pl **niceties**) a subtle point of distinction; refinement.

niche n a shallow recess in a wall for a statue, etc; a place, use, or work for which a person or thing is best suited.

nick n a small cut, chip, etc, made on a surface. * vt to make a nick in; to wound superficially.

nickel n a silvery-white metallic element used in alloys and plating; a US or Canadian coin worth five cents.

nicknack see **knickknack**.

nickname n a substitute name, often descriptive, given in fun; a familiar form of a proper name. * vt to give as a nickname.

nicotine n a poisonous alkaloid present in tobacco.

niece n the daughter of a brother or sister.

nifty adj (**niftier, niftiest**) (sl) neat, stylish.–**niftily** adv.–**niftiness** n.

niggard adj meanly covetous; parsimonious; miserly; niggardly. * n one who is meanly covetous; a stingy person, a miser.–**niggardliness** n.–**niggardly** adj.

niggling adj finicky, fussy; petty; gnawing, irritating.–**nigglingly** adv.

nigh adj, adv, prep near.

night n the period of darkness from sunset to sunrise; nightfall; a specified or appointed evening.

night blindness n poor vision in near darkness.

nightclub n a place of entertainment for drinking, dancing, etc, at night.

nightdress n a loose garment worn in bed by women and girls.

nightfall n the close of the day.

nightingale n a songbird celebrated for its musical song at night.

night life n social entertainment at night, esp in towns.

night-light n a dim light kept burning at night.

nightlong adj lasting through the night.

nightly adj, adv done or happening by night or every night.

nightmare n a frightening dream; any horrible experience.–**nightmarish** adj.

night owl n (inf) a person who stays up late at night.

nightspot n (inf) a nightclub.

night watchman n the person who guards a building at night.

nihilism n the belief that nothing has real existence, skepticism; the rejection of customary beliefs in morality, religion, etc.

nihilist n a supporter of nihilism.–**nihilisitic** adj.

nil n nothing.

nimble adj agile; quick.–**nimbly** adv.

nimbus n (pl **nimbi, nimbuses**) (art) the halo or cloud of light surrounding the heads of divinities, saints, and sovereigns; a rain cloud.

nine adj, n one more than eight. * n the symbol for this (9, IX, ix); the ninth in a series or set; something having nine units as members.

ninepins see **skittles**.

nineteen adj, n one more than eighteen. * n the symbol for this (19, XIX, xix).–**nineteenth** adj.

nineteenth adj being one of 19 equal parts. * n a nineteenth part.

ninetieth adj next after 89. * n a ninetieth part.

ninety adj, n nine times ten. * n the symbol for this (90, XC, xc); (in pl) **nineties**; the numbers from 90 to 99; the same numbers in a life or century.

ninny n (pl **ninnies**) a person of weak character or mind, a simpleton.

ninth adj, n next after eighth; one of nine equal parts of a thing.

niobium n a metallic element used in alloys.

nip vt (**nipping, nipped**) to pinch, pinch off; to squeeze between two surfaces; (dog) to give a small bite; to prevent the growth of; (plants) to have a harmful effect on because of cold. * n a pinch; a sharp squeeze; a bite; severe frost or biting coldness.

nipper n a person or thing that nips; the pincer of a crab or lobster; (pl) pliers, pincers, etc.

nipple n the small protuberance on a breast or udder through which the milk passes, a teat; a teat-like rubber part on the cap of a baby's bottle; a projection resembling a nipple.

nippy adj (**nippier, nippiest**) (weather) frosty.

nirvana n (Buddhism) the highest religious state, when all desire of existence and worldly good is extinguished, and the soul is absorbed into the Deity.

nit n the egg of a louse or other parasitic insect.

niter n potassium nitrate, saltpeter.—also **nitre**.

nit-picking n (inf) concern with petty details in order to find fault.—also adj.

nitrate n a salt of nitric acid; a fertilizer made of this.—**nitration** n.

nitre see **niter**.

nitric adj containing nitrogen.

nitric acid n a corrosive, caustic liquid used to make explosives, fertilizers, etc.

nitrogen n a gaseous element forming nearly 78 per cent of air.—**nitrogenous** adj.

nitroglycerin, nitroglycerine n a powerful explosive made by adding glycerin to a mixture of nitric and sulphuric acids.

nitrous adj resembling, obtained from, or impregnated with, niter.

nitty-gritty n (sl) basic elements; harsh realities; practical details.

NJ abbr = New Jersey.

NM abbr = New Mexico.

No, no abbr = number.

no adv (used to express denial or disagreement) not so, not at all, by no amount. * adj not any; not a; not one, none; not at all; by no means. * n (pl **noes, nos**) a denial; a refusal; a negative vote or voter.

nobility n (pl **nobilities**) nobleness of character, mind, birth, or rank; the class of people of noble birth.

noble adj famous or renowned; excellent in quality or character; of high rank or birth. * n a person of high rank in society.—**nobly** adv.

nobleman n (pl **noblemen**) a peer.—**noblewoman** nf (pl **noblewomen**).

nobody n (pl **nobodies**) a person of no importance. * pron no person.

nocturnal adj of, relating to, night; active by night.—**nocturnally** adv.

nocturne n a picture of a night scene; a musical composition appropriate to the night; a lullaby.

nod vti (**nodding, nodded**) to incline the head quickly, esp in agreement or greeting; to let the head drop, be drowsy; to indicate by a nod; (with **off**) (inf) to fall asleep. * n a quick bob of the head; a sign of assent or command.

node n a knob; a knot; a point of intersection; (med) a swelling; (bot) the joint of a stem and leaf or leaves; (astron) two points at which the orbit of a planet intersects the ecliptic; (math) the point at which a curve crosses itself; the point of rest in a vibrating body.—**nodal** adj.

nodule n a small lump or tumor.—**nodular** adj.

Noel, No'l n Christmas, esp in carols.

no-go area n an area that certain individuals or groups are forbidden to enter.

nohow adv in no way, by no means.

noise n a sound, esp a loud, disturbing or unpleasant one; a din; unwanted fluctuations in a transmitted signal; (pl) conventional sounds, words, etc made in reaction, such as sympathy. * vt to make public.

noisome adj harmful, noxious; foul-smelling.

noisy adj (**noisier, noisiest**) making much noise; turbulent, clamorous.—**noisily** adv. **noisiness** n.

nomad n one of a people or tribe who move in search of pasture; a wanderer.—**nomadic** adj.

no-man's-land n an unclaimed piece of land; a strip of land, esp between armies, borders; an ambiguous area, subject, etc.

nom de plume n (pl **noms de plume**) a pseudonym.

nomenclature n a system of names, terminology, used in a science, etc, or for parts of a device, etc.

nominal adj of or like a name; existing in name only; having minimal real worth, token.

nominally adv in name only.

nominate vt to appoint to an office or position; (candidate) to propose for election.—**nomination** n.—**nominator** n.

nominee n a person who is nominated.

nonalcoholic adj (drinks, etc) containing little or no alcohol.

nonaligned adj not in alliance with any side, esp in power politics.

nonchalant adj calm; cool, unconcerned, indifferent.—**nonchalantly** adv.—**nonchalance** n.

noncombatant n a member of the armed forces whose duties do not include fighting, as a doctor or chaplain; a civilian during wartime.

noncommissioned officer n (mil) a subordinate officer, as a corporal, sergeant, etc, appointed from the ranks.

noncommittal adj not revealing one's opinion.—**noncommittally** adv.

nonconformist n a person who does not conform to prevailing attitudes, behavior, etc.–also adj.

nondescript adj hard to classify, indeterminate; lacking individual characteristics. * n a nondescript person or thing.

none pron no one; not anyone; (pl verb) not any; no one. * adv not at all.

nonentity n (pl **nonentities**) a person or thing of no significance.

nonetheless conj nevertheless.

nonevent n an event or experience that is unexpectedly disappointing.

nonferrous adj containing no iron.

nonflammable adj not easily set on fire.

nonpareil adj without an equal; (person or thing) unrivaled, matchless, unsurpassed. * n unequaled excellence.

nonplus vt (**nonpluses, nonplusing, nonplused** or **nonplusses, nonplussing, nonplussed**) to cause to be so perplexed that one cannot, go, speak, act further. * n (pl **nonpluses**) a state of perplexity, a standstill.

nonproliferation n, adj (placing) restriction on the acquisition or production of, esp nuclear weapons.

nonsense n words, actions, etc, that are absurd and have no meaning.—also adj. * interj absurd!—**nonsensical** adj.—**nonsensically** adv.

non sequitur n a statement that has no relevance to what has preceded it.

nonstarter n a person who is unlikely to succeed; (horse, racing car, etc) withdrawn at the last moment.

nonstick adj (saucepans) coated with a surface that prevents food from sticking.

nonstop adj (train, plane, etc) not making any intermediate stops; not ceasing. * adv without stopping or pausing.

nonviolence n the abstaining from physical force to achieve civil rights.—**nonviolent** adj.

noodle n (often pl) pasta formed into a strip.

nook n a secluded corner, a retreat; a recess.

noon n midday; twelve o'clock in the day. * adj pertaining to noon.

no one pron nobody.

noose n a loop of rope with a slipknot, used for hanging, snaring, etc. * vt to tie in a noose; to make a noose in or of.

nor conj and not; not either.

norm n a standard or model, esp the standard of achievement of a large group.–**normative** adj.

normal adj regular; usual; stable mentally. * n anything normal; the usual state, amount, etc.–**normalcy** n.–**normality** n.–**normally** adv.

normalize vti to make or become normal.–**normalization** n.

north n one of the four points of the compass, opposite the sun at noon, to the right of a person facing the sunset; the direction in which a compass needle points; (often with cap) the northern part of one's country or the earth. * adj in, of, or toward the north; from the north. * adv in or toward the north.

northeast adj, n (of) the direction midway between north and east.

northeaster n a northeast wind.

northeasterly adj toward or coming from the northeast. * n (pl **northeasterlies**) a northeast wind or storm.

northeastern adj belonging to the northeast, or in that direction.

northeastward adj toward or in the northeast.–also adv.–**northeastwards** adv.

northerly adj in, from, or toward the north. * n (pl **northerlies**) a northerly wind.

northern adj of or in the north.

northerner n a native or inhabitant of the north.

northern lights npl the aurora borealis.

North Pole n the northern end of the axis of the earth at a latitude of 90 degrees north.

north star n the polar star.

northward adj toward or in the north.–also adv.–**northwards** adv.

northwest adj, n (of) the direction midway between north and west.

northwester n a northwest wind.

northwesterly adj toward or coming from the northwest. * n (pl **northwesterlies**) a northwest wind or storm.

northwestern adj belonging to the northwest, or in that direction.

northwestward adj toward or in the northwest.–also adv.–**northwestwards** adv.

nose n the part of the face above the mouth, used for breathing and smelling, having two nostrils; the sense of smell; anything like a nose in shape or position. * vt to discover as by smell; to nuzzle; to push (away, etc) with the front forward. * vi to sniff for; to inch forwards; to pry.

nosebleed n a bleeding from the nose.

nose dive n a swift downward plunge of an aircraft, nose first; any sudden sharp drop, as in prices.–**nose-dive** vi.

nosegay n a bouquet.

nose job n (sl) cosmetic plastic surgery to reshape the nose.

nosey see **nosy**.

nostalgia n yearning for past times or places.–**nostalgic** adj.–**nostalgically** adv.

nostril n one of the two external openings of the nose for breathing and smelling.

nostrum n a quack remedy, patent medicine.

nosy adj (**nosier, nosiest**) (inf) inquisitive, snooping.–**nosily** adv.–**nosiness** n.–also **nosey**.

not adv expressing denial, refusal, or negation.

notability n (pl **notabilities**) the quality of being notable; a notable person or thing.

notable adj worthy of being noted or remembered; remarkable, eminent. * n an eminent or famous person.–**notably** adv.

notation n a system of symbols or signs to represent quantities, etc, esp in mathematics, music, etc.

notch n a V-shaped cut in an edge or surface; (inf) a step, degree; a narrow pass with steep sides. * vt to cut notches in.

note n a brief summary or record, written down for future reference; a memorandum; a short letter; notice, attention; an explanation or comment on the text of a book; a musical sound of a particular pitch; a sign representing such a sound; a piano or organ key; the vocal sound of a bird. * vt to notice, observe; to write down; to annotate.

notebook n a book with blank pages for writing in.

noted adj celebrated, well-known.

note paper n paper for writing letters.

noteworthy adj outstanding; remarkable.

nothing n no thing; not anything; nothingness; a zero; a trifle; a person or thing of no importance or value. * adv in no way, not at all.

notice n an announcement; a warning; a placard giving information; a short article about a book, play, etc; attention, heed; a formal warning of intention to end an agreement at a certain time. * vt to observe; to remark upon. * vi to be aware of.

noticeable adj easily noticed or seen.–**noticeably** adv.

notifiable adj (infectious diseases) that must be reported to health authorities.

notify vt (**notifying, notified**) to inform; to report, give notice of.–**notification** n.

notion n a general idea; an opinion; a whim.

notional adj hypothetical, abstract; imaginary.

notorious adj widely known, esp unfavorably.–**notoriety** n.–**notoriously** adv.

notwithstanding prep in spite of. * adv nevertheless. * conj although.

nougat n a chewy sweet consisting of sugar paste with nuts.

noun n (gram) a word that names a person, a living being, an object, action etc; a substantive.

nourish vt to feed; to encourage the growth of; to raise, bring up.–**nourishing** adj.

nourishment n food; the act of nourishing.

nouveau riche n (pl **nouveaux riches**) the new rich, a parvenu.–also adj.

nova n (pl **novas, novae**) a new star that explodes into bright luminosity before subsiding.

novel n a relatively long prose narrative that is usually fictitious and in the form of a story. * adj new and unusual.

novelist n a writer of novels.

novella n (pl **novellas, novelle**) a short novel.

novelty n (pl **novelties**) a novel thing or occurrence; a new or unusual thing; (pl) cheap, small objects for sale.

November n the eleventh month, having 30 days.

novice n a person on probation in a religious order before taking final vows; a beginner.

now adv at the present time; by this time; at once; nowadays. * conj since; seeing that. * n the present time. * adj of the present time.

nowadays adv in these days; at the present time.

noway adv not at all. * interj (**no way**) used to express emphatic denial or refusal.

nowhere adv not in, at, or to anywhere.

noxious adj harmful, unhealthy.–**noxiously** adv.–**noxiousness** n.

nozzle n the spout at the end of a hose, pipe, etc.

NT abbr = New Testament.

-n't = not.

nth adj (maths) of or having an unspecified number; (inf) utmost, extreme.

nuance n a subtle difference in meaning, color, etc.

nub n a lump or small piece; (inf) the central point or gist of a matter.

nubile adj (girl) marriageable; attractive.

nuclear adj of or relating to a nucleus; using nuclear energy; having nuclear weapons.

nuclear bomb n a bomb whose explosive power derives from uncontrolled nuclear fusion or fission.

nuclear energy n energy released as a result of nuclear fission or fusion.

nuclear family n father, mother and children.

nuclear fission n the splitting of a nucleus of an atom either spontaneously or by bombarding it with particles.

nuclear fusion n the combining of two nuclei into a heavier nucleus, releasing energy in the process.

nuclear power n electrical or motive power produced by a nuclear reactor.

nuclear reactor n a device in which nuclear fission is maintained and harnessed to produce energy.

nuclear waste n radioactive waste.

nucleic acid n DNA, RNA or similar complex acid present in all living cells.

nucleus n (pl **nuclei, nucleuses**) the central part of core around which something may develop, or be grouped or concentrated; the centrally positively charged portion of an atom; the part of an animal or plant cell containing genetic material.

nude adj naked; bare; undressed. * n a naked human figure, esp in a work of art; the state of being nude.–**nudity** n.

nudge vt to touch gently with the elbow to attract attention or urge into action; to push slightly. * n a gentle touch, as with the elbow.

nudism n the practice of going nude, esp in groups at designated places and times.–**nudist** n, adj.

nugget n a small lump, esp of gold in its natural state.

nuisance n a person or thing that annoys or causes trouble.

nuke vt (sl) to attack and destroy with a nuclear weapon; (sl) to cook or heat (food) in microwave oven. * n a nuclear weapon.

null adj without legal force; invalid.

nullify vt (**nullifying, nullified**) to make null, to cancel out.–**nullification** n.

numb adj deadened; having no feeling (due to cold, shock, etc.). * vt to make numb.–**numbness** n.

number n a symbol or word indicating how many; a numeral identifying a person or thing by its position in a series; a single issue of a magazine; a song or piece of music, esp as an item in a performance; (inf) an object singled out; a total of persons or things; (gram) the form of a word indicating singular or plural; a telephone number; (pl) arithmetic; (pl) numerical superiority. * vti to count; to give a number to; to include or be included as one of a group; to limit the number of; to total.

number one n the first in a list, series, etc; (inf) oneself or one's own interests; (inf) the most important person or thing; (inf) a best-selling pop record. * adj most important, urgent, etc.

numbskull see **numskull**.

numeral n a symbol or group of symbols used to express a number (eg two = 2 or II, etc).

numerate adj having a basic understanding of arithmetic. * vt to reckon or enumerate; to point or read, as figures.

numerator n the number above the line in a fraction.

numerical, numeric adj of or relating to numbers; expressed in numbers.

numerology n the study of the supposed occult meaning of numbers.

numerous adj many, consisting of many items.

numismatics n (used as sing) the study of coins, medals, etc.– also **numismatology**.–**numismatic** adj.

numismatist n one skilled in numismatics; a student of coins.

numskull n a dolt, a blockhead.–also **numbskull**.

nun n a woman belonging to a religious order.

nunnery n (pl **nunneries**) a convent of nuns.

nuptial adj relating to marriage. * npl a wedding ceremony; marriage.

nurse n a person trained to care for the sick, injured or aged; a person who looks after another person's child or children. * vt to tend, to care for; (baby) to feed at the breast; (hatred) to foster; to tend with an eye to the future.

nursemaid n a woman in charge of children, a nanny.

nursery n (pl **nurseries**) a room set aside for children; a place where children may be left in temporary care; a place where young trees and plants are raised for transplanting.

nursery rhyme n a short traditional poem or song for children.

nursery school n a school for young children, usu under five.

nursing n the profession of a nurse.

nursing home n an establishment providing care for convalescent, chronically ill, or disabled people.

nurture vt to feed; to bring up, educate. * n the act of bringing up a child; nourishment.

nut n a kernel (sometimes edible) enclosed in a hard shell; a usu metallic threaded block screwed on the end of a bolt; (sl) a mad person; (sl) a devotee, fan. * vt (**nutting, nutted**) to gather nuts.

nut-brown adj colored like a ripe hazelnut.

nutcracker n (usu pl) a tool for cracking nuts; a bird with speckled plumage.

nutmeg n the aromatic kernel produced by a tree, grated and used as a spice.

nutrient n a substance that nourishes. * adj promoting growth.

nutrition n the act or process by which plants and animals take in and assimilate food in their systems; the study of the human diet.–**nutritional** adj.

nutritionist n a specialist who studies and advises on the human diet.

nutritious adj efficient as food; health-giving, nourishing.

nuts adj (inf) very angry.

nutshell n the hard covering of a nut; a tiny receptacle; a compact way of expression.

nutty adj (**nuttier, nuttiest**) tasting of or containing nuts; (sl) very enthusiastic; (sl) crazy.

nuzzle vti to push (against) or rub with the nose or snout; to nestle, snuggle.

NV abbr = Nevada.

NW abbr = northwest, northwestern.

NY abbr = New York.

nylon n any of numerous strong, tough, elastic, synthetic materials used esp in plastics and textiles; (pl) stockings made of nylon.

nymph n (myth) a spirit of nature envisaged as a maiden; the chrysalis of an insect.–**nymphean** adj.

nympho n (pl **nymphos**) (inf) a nymphomaniac.

nymphomania n uncontrollable sexual desire in women.–**nymphomaniac** adj, n.–**nymphomaniacal** adj.

O

O (chem symbol) oxygen. * interj an exclamation of wonder, pain, etc.

oaf n (pl **oafs**) a loutish or stupid person.–**oafish** adj.–**oafishly** adv

oak n a tree with a hard durable wood, having acorns as fruits.

oar n a pole with a flat blade for rowing a boat; an oarsman.

oasis n (pl **oases**) a fertile place in a desert; a refuge.

oatcake n a thin broad cake of oatmeal.

oath n (pl **oaths**) a solemn declaration to a god or a higher authority that one will speak the truth or keep a promise; a swear word; a blasphemous expression.

oatmeal n ground oats; a porridge of this; a pale grayish-brown color.

oats npl a cereal grass widely cultivated for its edible grain; the seeds.

obdurate adj hard-hearted; unyielding, stubborn.–**obduracy** n.–**obdurately** adv.

obedient adj obeying; compliant; submissive to authority, dutiful.–**obedience** n.–**obediently** adv.

obeisance n a bow or curtsey; an act of reverence or homage.

obelisk n a four-sided tapering pillar usu with a pyramidal top; a reference mark used in printing ( ) (–also **dagger**).

obese adj very fat.–**obesity** n.

obey *vti* (**obeying, obeyed**) to carry out (orders, instructions); to comply (with); to submit (to).

obfuscate *vt* to bewilder or confuse, to darken.–**obfuscation** *n*.

obituary *n* (*pl* **obituaries**) an announcement of a person's death, often with a short biography.–**obituarist** *n*.

object *n* something that can be recognized by the senses; a person or thing toward which action, feeling, etc, is directed; a purpose or aim; (*gram*) a noun or part of a sentence governed by a transitive verb or a preposition. * *vti* to state or raise an objection; to oppose; to disapprove.–**objector** *n*.

objectify *vt* (**objectifying, objectified**) to render objective; to embody; to materialize.–**objectification** *n*.

objection *n* the act of objecting; a ground for, or expression of, disapproval.

objectionable *adj* causing an objection; disagreeable.–**objectionably** *adv*.

objective *adj* relating to an object; not influenced by opinions or feelings; impartial; having an independent existence of its own, real; (*gram*) of, or appropriate to an object governed by a verb or a preposition. * *n* the thing or placed aimed at; (*gram*) the objective case.–**objectively** *adv*.–**objectivity** *n*.

object lesson *n* a convincing practical illustration of some principle.

objet d'art *n* (*pl* **objets d'art**) a small decorative object.

obligate *vt* to bind by a contract, promise, sense of duty, etc.

obligation *n* the act of obligating; a moral or legal requirement; a debt; a favor; a commitment to pay a certain amount of money; the amount owed under such an obligation.

obligatory *adj* binding, not optional; compulsory.

oblige *vt* to compel by moral, legal, or physical force; (*person*) to make grateful for some favour; to do a favor for.–**obliging** *adj*.–**obligingly** *adv*.

oblique *adj* slanting, at an angle; diverging from the straight; indirect, allusive. * *n* an oblique line.–**obliquely** *adv*.

oblique angle *n* an angle greater or less than a right angle.

obliterate *vt* to wipe out, to erase, to destroy.–**obliteration** *n*.

oblivion *n* a state of forgetting or being forgotten; a state of mental withdrawal.

oblivious *adj* forgetful, unheeding; unaware (of).

oblong *adj* rectangular. * *n* any oblong figure.

obloquy *n* (*pl* **obloquies**) reproachful language, detraction; calumny; slander, disgrace.

obnoxious *adj* objectionable; highly offensive.–**obnoxiously** *adv*.–**obnoxiousness** *n*.

oboe *n* an orchestral woodwind instrument having a mouthpiece with a double reed.–**oboist** *n*.

obscene *adj* indecent, lewd; offensive to a moral or social standard.–**obscenely** *adv*.–**obscenity** *n*.

obscure *adj* not clear; dim; indistinct; remote, secret; not easily understood; inconspicuous; unimportant, humble. * *vt* to make unclear, to confuse; to hide.–**obscurely** *adv*.–**obscurity** *n*.

obsequious *adj* subservient; fawning.–**obsequiously** *adv*.

observance *n* the observing of a rule, duty, law, etc; a ceremony or religious rite.

observant *adj* watchful; attentive, mindful.–**observantly** *adv*.

observation *n* the act or faculty of observing; a comment or remark; careful noting of the symptoms of a patient, movements of a suspect, etc prior to diagnosis, analysis or interpretation.–**observational** *adj*.–**observationally** *adv*.

observatory *n* (*pl* **observatories**) a building for astronomical observation; an institution whose primary purpose is making such observations.

observe *vt* to notice; to perceive; (*a law, etc*) to keep to or adhere to; to arrive at as a conclusion; to examine scientifically. * *vi* to take notice; to make a comment (on).–**observable** *adj*.–**observably** *adv*.

observer *n* a person who observes; a delegate who attends a formal meeting but may not take part; an expert analyst and commentator in a particular field.

obsess *vt* to possess or haunt the mind of; to preoccupy.–**obsessive** *adj*, *n*.–**obsessively** *adv*.

obsession *n* a fixed idea, often associated with mental illness; a persistent idea or preoccupation; the condition of obsessing or being obsessed.

obsolescent *adj* becoming obsolete, going out of date.–**obsolescence** *n*.

obsolete *adj* disused, out of date.

obstacle *n* anything that hinders something; an obstruction.

obstetrics *n sing* the branch of medicine concerned with the care and treatment of women during pregnancy and childbirth.–**obstetric, obstetrical** *adj*.–**obstetrician** *n*.

obstinate *adj* stubborn, self-willed; intractable; persistent.–**obstinacy** *n*.–**obstinately** *adv*.

obstreperous *adj* unruly, turbulent, noisy.

obstruct *vt* to block with an obstacle; to impede; to prevent, hinder; to keep (light, etc) from.–**obstruction** *n*.–**obstructive** *adj*.–**obstructively** *adv*.–**obstructiveness** *n*.

obtain *vt* to get, to acquire, to gain. * *vi* to be prevalent, hold good.–**obtainable** *adj*.–**obtainment** *n*.

obtrude *vti* to push (an opinion, oneself) on others uninvited; to intrude.–**obtruding** *adj*.–**obtrusion** *n*.

obtrusive *adj* apt to obtrude, pushy; protruding, sticking out.–**obtrusively** *adv*.–**obtrusiveness** *n*.

obtuse *adj* mentally slow; not pointed; dull, stupid; (*geom*) greater than a right angle.–**obtusely** *adv*.–**obtuseness** *n*.

obverse *n* the front or top side; (*coin*) the head; a counterpart. * *adj* facing the viewer; with the top wider than the base.–**obversely** *adv*.

obviate *vt* to make unnecessary; (*danger, difficulty*) to prevent, clear away.–**obviation** *n*.

obvious *adj* easily seen or understood; evident.–**obviously** *adv*.–**obviousness** *n*.

ocarina *n* an egg-shaped wind instrument played like a flute.

occasion *n* a special occurrence or event; a time when something happens; an opportunity; reason or grounds; a subsidiary cause. * *vt* to cause; to bring about.

occasional *adj* infrequent, not continuous; intermittent; produced for an occasion; (*a cause*) incidental.

occasionally *adv* intermittently; now and then; infrequently.

occident *n* the west; (*with cap*) specifically Europe and America; the countries west of Asia and Turkey in Europe.–**Occidental, occidental** *adj*.

occlude *vti* to shut out or in; to stop up, close; (*chem*) to absorb and retain.–**occlusion** *n*.

occult *adj* supernatural, magical; secret.–*also n*.

occultism *n* mysticism, spiritualism, theosophy, etc.–**occultist** *n*.

occupancy *n* (*pl* **occupancies**) the act of taking and holding in possession; the time of possession.

occupant *n* a person who occupies, resides in, holds a position or place, etc.

occupation *n* the act of occupying; the state of being occupied; employment or profession; a pursuit.–**occupational** *adj*.

occupational therapy *n* therapy by means of work in the arts and crafts, to aid recovery from disease or injury.–**occupational therapist** *n*.

occupier *n* an occupant.

occupy *vt* (**occupying, occupied**) to live in; (*room, office*) to take up or fill; (*a position*) to hold; to engross (one's mind); (*city, etc*) to take possession of.

occur *vi* (**occurring, occurred**) to happen; to exist; to come into the mind of.

occurrence *n* a happening, an incident, an event; the act or fact of occurring.

ocean *n* a large stretch of sea, esp one of the earth's five oceans; a huge quantity or expanse.–**oceanic** *adj*.

oceanography n the study of the oceans including their physical and chemical make-up, marine biology, and their exploitation.– **oceanographer** n.

ocelot n a medium-sized spotted wildcat of North and South America.

ocher, ochre n a yellow to orange-colored clay used as a pigment.

o'clock adv indicating the hour; indicating a relative direction or position, twelve o'clock being directly ahead or above.

octagon n a plane figure having eight equal sides.–**octagonal** adj.

octane n a hydrocarbon found in petrol.

octave n (mus) the eighth full tone above or below a given tone, the interval of eight degrees between a tone and either of its octaves, or the series of tones within this interval.

octet, octette n a group of eight (performers, lines of a sonnet); a composition for eight instruments or voices.

October n the tenth month of the year, having 31 days.

octogenarian n a person who is in his or her eighties.

octopus n (pl **octopuses, octopi**) a mollusk having a soft body and eight tentacles covered with suckers.

ocular adj of, by, or relating to the eye; resembling an eye in form or function.

OD n (inf) an overdose of a drug, esp a narcotic. * vi (**OD'ing, OD'd**) to take an overdose.

odd adj eccentric; peculiar; occasional; not divisible by two; with the other of the pair missing; extra or left over. * npl probability; balance of advantage in favor of one against another; excess of one number over another, esp in betting; likelihood; disagreement; strife; miscellaneous articles, scraps.–**oddly** adv.–**oddness** n.

oddball n (sl) an eccentric person. * adj bizarre.

oddity n (pl **oddities**) the state of being odd; an odd thing or person; peculiarity.

odd man out n a person left when others pair off.

oddment n an odd piece left over, esp of fabric.

odds and ends npl miscellaneous articles, scraps.

ode n a lyric poem marked by lofty feeling and dignified style.

odious adj causing hatred or offense; disgusting.–**odiously** adv.–**odiousness** n.

odium n general dislike.

odometer n an instrument attached to the axle of a vehicle to measure the distance it travels.

odor n smell; scent; aroma; a characteristic or predominant quality.–also **odour**.–**odorous** adj.

odoriferous adj diffusing fragrance; (sl) smelly.

odorless adj without odor.

odour see **odor**.

odyssey n (pl **odysseys**) a long adventurous journey; an intellectual or spiritual quest.

oedema see **edema**.

Oedipus complex n (psychoanal) a complex arising from the relationship of a son to his parents.

oesophagus see **esophagus**.

oestrogen see **estrogen**.

oeuvre n a work of art, literature, music, etc; the life's work of an artist, writer or composer.

of prep from; belonging or relating to; concerning; among; by; during; owing to.

off adv away, from; detached, gone; unavailable; disconnected; out of condition; entirely. * prep away from; not on. * adj distant; no longer operating; canceled; (food or drink) having gone bad; on the right-hand side; (runners, etc) having started a race.

offal n the entrails of an animal eaten as food.

offbeat adj unconventional, eccentric.

off-color adj unwell; risqué.

offend vt to affront, displease; to insult. * vi to break a law.–**offender** n.

offense, offence n an illegal action, crime; a sin; an affront, insult; a cause of displeasure or anger.

offensive adj causing offense; repulsive, disagreeable; insulting; aggressive. * n an attack; a forceful campaign for a cause, etc.–**offensively** adv.–**offensiveness** n.

offer vt to present for acceptance or rejection; to show willingness (to do something); to present for consideration; to bid; (a prayer) to say. * vi to present itself; to declare oneself willing. * n something offered; a bid or proposal.

offering n a gift, present; a sacrifice.

offertory n (pl **offertories**) a church collection; the part of the service when it is taken.

offhand adv impromptu; without thinking. * adj inconsiderate; curt, brusque; unceremonious.

office n a room or building where business is carried out; the people there; (with cap) the location, staff, of authority of a Government department, etc; a task or function; a position of authority; a duty; a religious ceremony, rite.

officer n an official; a person holding a position of authority in a government, business, club, military services, etc; a policeman.

official adj of an office or its tenure; properly authorized; formal. * n a person who holds a public office.–**officially** adv.

officialdom n a body of officials.

officialese n the jargon of official documents or as expressed by officials.

officiate vi to conduct a ceremony; to act in an official capacity; to perform the functions of a priest, minister, rabbi, etc.

officious adj interfering, meddlesome; offering unwanted advice.–**officiously** adv.–**officiousness** n.

offing n the near or foreseeable future.

off-key adj sung or played in the wrong key; out of tune; out of step.

off-line adj (comput) not connected to the central processor; disconnected.

off-load vt to unload; to get rid off.

off-piste adj pertaining to skiing in areas away from the normal runs.

offprint n a separately printed copy or part of a publication.

off-putting adj discouraging, daunting.

offset vt (**offsetting, offset**) to compensate for, counterbalance.

offshoot n a branch or shoot growing from the main stem; something derivative.

offshore adv at sea some distance from the shore.

offspring n a child, progeny; a result.

offstage adj, adv out of sight of the audience; behind the scenes.

off-the-wall adj (sl) innovative, unusual, unexpected.

off-white n, adj white tinged with yellow or gray.

often adv many times, frequently.

ogee n an architectural wave-like molding shaped like an S.

ogle vti (**ogling, ogled**) to gape at; to make eyes at; to look at lustfully.–**ogler** n.

ogre n a man-eating giant; a hideous person.

OH abbr = Ohio.

oh interj expressing surprise, delight, pain, etc.

ohm n a unit of electrical resistance.

ohmmeter n an instrument for measuring electrical resistance.

oil n any of various greasy, combustible liquid substances obtained from animal, vegetable, and mineral matter; petroleum; an oil painting; (pl) paint mixed by grinding a pigment in oil * vt to smear with oil, lubricate.–**oiled** adj.

oilcloth n a waterproof fabric impregnated with oil or synthetic resin.

oil painting n a painting in oils; the art of painting in oils.

oil rig n a drilling rig for extracting oil or natural gas.

oilskin n fabric made waterproof by treatment with oil; a waterproof garment of oilskin or a plastic-coated fabric.

oil slick n a mass of oil floating on the surface of water.

oil well n a well from which petroleum is extracted.

oily adj (**oilier, oiliest**) like or covered with oil; greasy; too suave or smooth, unctuous.–**oiliness** n.

ointment n a fatty substance used on the skin for healing or cosmetic purposes; a salve.

OK[1] *abbr* = Oklahoma.

OK[2], **okay** *adj, adv* (*inf*) all right; correct(ly). * *n* (*pl* **OK's, okays**) approval; * *vt* (**OK'ing, OK'ed** *or* **okaying, okayed**) to approve, sanction as OK.

okay *see* OK.

okra *n* a tall annual plant yielding long seed-pods used as a vegetable.

old *adj* aged; elderly, not young; having lived or existed for a long time; long used, not new; former; of the past, not modern; experienced; worn out; of long standing.

old country *n* the birthplace of an immigrant or an immigrant's ancestors.

olden *adj* relating to a bygone era.

old-fashioned *adj* out of date; in a fashion of an older time.

old guard *n* the (original) conservative elements within a political party or other organization.

old maid *n* (*derog*) a woman, esp an older woman who has never married; a prim, prudish, fussy person.

old master *n* a painting by one of the best painters working in Europe in the 16th and 17th centuries; one of these painters.

Old Testament *n* the Christian designation for the Holy Scriptures of Judaism, the first of the two general divisions of the Christian Bible.

old-time *adj* of an earlier period; old-fashioned.

old-timer *n* an old man; a veteran; a person who has been in the same job, position, etc, for many years.

old-world *adj* traditional, quaint; antiquated.

oleaginous *adj* oily; unctuous.

oleander *n* a poisonous evergreen shrub with handsome fragrant flowers.

olfactory *adj* relating to the sense of smell. * *n* (*pl* **olfactories**) (*usu pl*) an organ of smell.

olive *n* an evergreen tree cultivated for its edible hard-stoned fruit and oil; its fruit; a yellow-green color. * *adj* of a yellow-green color.

olive branch *n* a gesture of reconciliation of desire to make peace.

olive oil *n* an edible yellow oil obtained from the fruit of the olive by pressing.

Olympic Games *n sing or pl* an ancient athletic contest revived in 1896 as an international meeting held every four years in a different country.—*also* **Olympics.**

ombudsman *n* (*pl* **ombudsmen**) an official appointed to investigate citizens' or consumers' complaints.

omega *n* the last letter of the Greek alphabet.

omelet, omelette *n* eggs beaten and cooked flat in a pan.

omen *n* a sign or warning of impending happiness or disaster.

omerta *n* a conspiracy of silence, esp as practiced by the Mafia.

ominous *adj* relating to an omen; foreboding evil; threatening.—**ominously** *adv.*

omit *vt* (**omitting, omitted**) to leave out; to neglect to do, leave undone.—**omission** *n.*

omnipotent *adj* all-powerful, almighty; having very great power.—**omnipotence** *n.*

omnipresent *adj* present everywhere, uniquitous.—**omnipresence** *n.*

omniscient *adj* knowing all things.—**omnisciently** *adv.*—**omniscience** *n.*

omnivore *n* an omnivorous animal or person.

omnivorous *adj* eating any sort of food; taking in everything indiscriminately.

on *prep* in contact with the upper surface of; supported by, attached to, or covering; directed toward; at the time of; concerning, about; using as a basis, condition or principle; immediately after; (*sl*) using; addicted to. * *adv* (so as to be) covering or in contact with something; forward; (*device*) switched on; continuously in progress; due to take place; (*actor*) on stage; on duty.

once *adv* on one occasion only; formerly; at some time. * *conj* as soon as. * *n* one time.

once-over *n* a preliminary survey.

oncology *n* the branch of medicine dealing with tumours.—**oncologist** *n.*

oncoming *adj* approaching.

one *adj* single; undivided, united; the same; a certain unspecified (time, etc). * *n* the first and lowest cardinal number; an individual thing or person; (*inf*) a drink; (*inf*) a joke. * *pron* an indefinite person, used to apply to many people; someone.

one-liner *n* (*inf*) a brief joke or witty comment.

one-night stand *n* a performance given for one night only in a certain place; (*inf*) (a partner in) a sexual liaison that lasts one night only.

onerous *adj* oppressive, burdensome; troublesome.

oneself *pron reflex form of* one.

one-sided *adj* favoring one side; unequal.

one-track *adj* with a single line of rails; with room for only one idea at a time.

one-upmanship *n* the skill of being one jump ahead of or going one better than someone or something else.

one-way *adj* (*traffic*) restricted to one direction; requiring no reciprocal action or obligation.

ongoing *adj* progressing, continuing.

onion *n* an edible bulb with a pungent taste and odor.

on-line *adj* referring to equipment that is connected to and controlled by the central processor of a computer.

onlooker *n* a spectator.

only *adj* alone of its kind; single, sole. * *adv* solely, merely; just; not more than. * *conj* except that, but.

onomatopoeia *n* the formation of a word to imitate a sound.—**onomatopoeic** *adj.*

onrush *n* a powerful rushing forwards.

onset *n* a beginning; an assault, attack.

onshore *adj, adv* towards the land; on land, not the sea.

onslaught *n* a fierce attack.

onto *prep* to a position on.

onus *n* (*pl* **onuses**) responsibility, duty; burden.

onward *adj* advancing, forward. * *adv* to the front, ahead, forward.

onwards *adv* onward.

onyx *n* a limestone similar to marble with layers of color.

oodles *npl* (*sl*) an abundance.

ooh *interj* expressing surprise, delight, pain, etc.

oops *interj* expressing surprise or apology, esp when making a mistake.

ooze *vti* to flow or leak out slowly; to seep; to exude. * *n* soft mud or slime.

opacity *n* (*pl* **opacities**) the state of being opaque; obscurity.

opal *n* a white or bluish stone with a play of iridescent colors.

opalescent *adj* resembling opal in its reflection of light, iridescent.—**opalescence** *n.*

opaque *adj* not letting light through; neither transparent nor translucent.—**opaquely** *adv.*—**opaqueness** *n.*

OPEC *abbr* = Organization of Petroleum Exporting Countries.

open *adj* not closed; accessible; uncovered, unprotected; not fenced; free from trees; spread out, unfolded; public; lacking reserve; (a *person*) forthcoming; generous; readily understood; liable (to); unrestricted; (*syllable*) ending with a vowel. * *vti* to make or become accessible; to unfasten; to begin; to expand, unfold; to come into view. * *n* a wide space; (*sport*) a competition that any player can enter.—**openness** *n.*

open air *n* outdoors.

open-and-shut *adj* easily solved; straightforward.

open-ended *adj* with no fixed limit of time or amount.

opener *n* a device for opening cans or bottles.

openhanded *adj* generous.—**openhandedness** *n.*

open-heart surgery *n* surgery on the heart whilst its function is performed temporarily by a heart-lung machine.

opening n a gap, aperture; a beginning; a chance; a job opportunity. * adj initial.

openly adv frankly; publicly.

open-minded adj unprejudiced.–**open-mindedness** n.

open secret n a supposed secret which is actually widely known.

opera n a dramatic work represented through music and song; plural form of **opus**.–**operatic** adj.

operable adj capable of being put into action, practicable; (med) capable of being operated upon.

opera house n a theater for opera.

operate vi to work, to function; to produce a desired effect; to carry out a surgical operation. * vt (a machine) to work or control; to carry on, run.–**operator** n.

operating system n the software in a computer which controls basic operations such as accepting keyboard input, printing, file handling and displaying error messages.

operation n a method of operating; a procedure; a military action; a surgical procedure.–**operational** adj.

operative adj functioning; in force, effective; of, by surgery. * n a mechanic; a secret agent; a private detective.

operetta n a light opera.

ophthalmology n the branch of medicine dealing with diseases of the eye.–**ophthalmologist** n.

opiate n a narcotic drug that contains opium; something that induces sleep or calms feelings.

opinion n a belief that is not based on proof; judgment; estimation, evaluation; a formal expert judgment; professional advice.

opinionated adj unduly confident in one's opinions, dogmatic.

opium n a narcotic drug produced from an annual Eurasian poppy.

opossum n (pl **opossums, opossum**) a small nocturnal and arboreal marsupial.

opponent n a person who opposes another; an adversary, antagonist. * adj opposing.

opportune adj well-timed; convenient.–**opportunely** adv.

opportunist n a person who forms or adapts his or her views or principles to benefit from opportunities; to seize opportunities as they may arise.–**opportunism** n.–**opportunistic** adj.

opportunity n (pl **opportunities**) chance; a favorable combination of circumstances.

oppose vt to put in front of or in the way of; to place in opposition; to resist; to fight against; to balance against.–**opposable** adj.–**opposer** n.

opposite adj placed on opposed sides of; face to face; diametrically different; contrary. * n a person or thing that is opposite; an antithesis. * prep, adv across from.

opposite number n a person in a corresponding position on the other side; a counterpart.

opposition n the act of opposing or the condition of being opposed; resistance; antithesis; hostility; a political party opposing the government.

oppress vt to treat unjustly; to subjugate; to weigh down in the mind.–**oppression** n.–**oppressor** n.

oppressive adj tyrannical; burdensome; (weather) sultry, close.–**oppressively** adv.–**oppressiveness** n.

opt vi to choose, to exercise an option; (with **in**) to choose to participate in something; (with **out**) to choose not to participate in something.

optic adj relating to the eye or sight. * n (inf) the eye; a device for dispensing a standard measure of spirits, etc.

optical adj of or relating to the eye or light; optic; aiding or correcting vision; visual.–**optically** adv.

optical fiber n thin glass fiber through which light can be transmitted.

optician n a person who makes or sells optical aids.

optics n sing the branch of physics dealing with light and vision.

optimism n a tendency to take the most cheerful view of things; hopefulness; the belief that good must ultimately prevail.–**optimist** n.–**optimistic** adj.–**optimistically** adv.

optimum n (pl **optima, optimums**) the best, most favorable condition.–also adj.–**optimal** adj.–**optimally** adv.

option n the act of choosing; the power to choose; a choice; the right to buy, sell or lease at a fixed price within a specified time.–**optional** adj.–**optionally** adv.

opulent adj wealthy; luxuriant.–**opulence** n.

opus n (pl **opuses, opera**) an artistic or literary work; a musical composition, esp any of the numbered works of a composer.

OR abbr = Oregon.

or conj denoting an alternative; the last in a series of choices.

oracle n a place in ancient Greece where a deity was consulted; the response given (often ambiguous); a wise adviser; sage advice.–**oracular** adj.

oral adj of the mouth; spoken, not written; (drugs) taken by mouth. * n a spoken examination.–**orally** adv.

oral history n the history of past events as recorded from interviews with people living at the time.

orange n a round, reddish-yellow, juicy, edible citrus fruit; the tree bearing it; its color. * adj orange-coloured.

orangeade n a drink made with the juice of oranges.

orangutan, orangoutang n a large, long-armed, herbivorous anthropoid ape.

orate vi to make an oration; (inf) to hold forth.

oration n a formal or public speech.

orator n an eloquent public speaker.–**oratorical** adj.

oratorio n (pl **oratorios**) a sacred story set to music for voices and instruments.

oratory n (pl **oratories**) the art of public speaking; eloquence; a place for prayer.

orb n a sphere or globe; an ornamental sphere surmounted by a cross, esp as carried by a sovereign at a coronation.

orbit n (astron) a curved path along which a planet or satellite moves; a field of action or influence; the eye socket; (physics) the path of an electron around the nucleus of an atom. * vti to put (a satellite, etc) into orbit; to circle round.–**orbital** adj.

orchard n an area of land planted with fruit trees.

orchestra n a group of musicians playing together under a conductor; their instruments; the space (or pit) in a theater where they sit; the stalls of a theater.–**orchestral** adj.

orchestrate vt to arrange music for performance by an orchestra; to arrange, organize to best effect.–**orchestration** n.–**orchestrator** n.

orchid n a plant with unusually shaped flowers in brilliant colors comprising three petals of uneven size.

ordain vti to confer holy orders upon; to appoint; to decree; to order, to command.–**ordainer** n.–**ordainment** n.

ordeal n a severe trial or test; an exacting experience.

order n arrangement; method; relative position; sequence; an undisturbed condition; tidiness; rules of procedure; an efficient state; a class, group, or sort; a religious fraternity; a style of architecture; an honour or decoration; an instruction or command; a rule or regulation; a state or condition, esp with regard to functioning; a request to supply something; the goods supplied; (zool) divisions between class and family or genus. * vti to put or keep (things) in order; to arrange; to command; to request (something) to be supplied.

orderly adj in good order; well-behaved; methodical. * n (pl **orderlies**) a hospital attendant; a soldier attending an officer.–**orderliness** n.

ordinal adj showing position in a series. * n an ordinal number.

ordinal number n a number denoting its order in a sequence, as first, second, etc.

ordinary adj normal, usual; common; plain, unexceptional.–**ordinarily** adv.

ordination *n* the act of ordaining or being ordained; admission to the ministry.

ordnance *n* military stores; artillery.

ordure *n* excrement; dung.

ore *n* a substance from which minerals can be extracted.

Oreg. *abbr* = Oregon.

oregano *n* an aromatic herb whose leaves, either fresh of dried, are used to flavor food.

organ *n* a usu large and complex musical wind instrument with pipes, stops, and a keyboard; a part of an animal or plant that performs a vital or natural function; the means by which anything is done; a medium of information or opinion, a periodical.

organic *adj* of or relating to bodily organs; (disease) affecting a bodily organ; of, or derived from, living organisms; systematically arranged; structural; (*chem*) of the class of compounds.that are formed from carbon; (vegetables, etc) grown without the use of artificial fertilizers or pesticides.–**organically** *adv*.

organism *n* an animal or plant, any living thing; an organized body.

organist *n* a person who plays an organ.

organization *n* the act or process of organizing; the state of being organized; arrangement, structure; an organized body or association.

organize *vt* to arrange in an orderly way; to establish; to institute; to persuade to join a cause, group, etc; to arrange for.–**organizer** *n*.

orgasm *n* the climax of sexual excitement.–**orgasmic** *adj*.

orgy *n* (*pl* **orgies**) a wild party or gathering of people, with excessive drinking and indiscriminate sexual activity; over-indulgence in any activity.–**orgiastic** *adj*.

Orient *n* the East, or Asia, esp the Far East.

orient, orientate *vti* to adjust (oneself) to a particular situation; to arrange in a direction, esp in relation to the points of the compass; to face or turn in a particular direction.–**orientation** *n*.

oriental *adj* (*often cap*) of the Orient, its people or languages.

orienteering *n* the sport of racing on foot over difficult country using a map and compass

orifice *n* an opening or mouth of a cavity.

origami *n* the Japanese art of paper folding to make complicated shapes.

origin *n* the source or beginning of anything; ancestry or parentage.

original *adj* relating to the origin or beginning; earliest, primitive; novel; unusual; inventive, creative. * *n* an original work, as of art or literature; something from which copies are made; a creative person; an eccentric.–**originality** *n*.–**originally** *adv*.

originate *vti* to initiate or begin; to bring or come into being.–**origination** *n*.–**originator** *n*.

oriole *n* kinds of yellow, black-winged bird.

ormolu *n* an imitation gold made of copper and tin alloy, used for decoration.

ornament *n* anything that enhances the appearance of a person or thing; a small decorative object. * *vt* to adorn, to decorate with ornaments.–**ornamental** *adj*.–**ornamentally** *adv*.

ornamentation *n* the act or process of ornamenting; something that decorates.

ornate *adj* richly adorned; (*style*) highly elaborate.–**ornately** *adv*.–**ornateness** *n*.

ornithology *n* the study of birds.–**ornithological** *adj*.–**ornithologically** *adv*.–**ornithologist** *n*.

orphan *n* a child whose parents are dead. * *vt* to cause to become an orphan.–*also adj*.

orphanage *n* a residential institution for the care of orphans.

orthodontics *n sing* the branch of dentistry dealing with the correction of irregularities in the teeth.–**orthodontic** *adj*.–**orthodontist** *n*.

orthodox *adj* conforming with established behavior or opinions; not heretical; generally accepted, conventional; (*with cap*) of or relating to a conservative political or religious group.

orthodoxy *n* (*pl* **orthodoxies**) the state or quality of being orthodox; an orthodox practice or belief.

orthography *n* (*pl* **orthographies**) the art of spelling and writing words with grammatical correctness; a map projection with a point of sight supposedly infinitely distant.–**orthographer** *n*.–**orthographic, orthographical** *adj*.

orthopedics, orthopaedics *n* the study and surgical treatment of bone and joint disorders.–**orthopedic** *adj*.–**orthopedist** *n*.

Oscar *n* any of several small gold statuettes awarded annually by the US Academy of Motion Picture Arts and Sciences for outstanding achievements.

oscillate *vi* to swing back and forth as a pendulum; to waver, vacillate between extremes of opinion, etc.–**oscillation** *n*.

osmosis *n* (*pl* **osmoses**) the percolation and intermixture of fluids separated by a porous membrane.–**osmotic** *adj*.–**osmotically** *adv*.

osprey *n* (*pl* **ospreys**) a large fish-eating bird of prey.

osseous *adj* pertaining to, consisting of, or like, bone.

ossify *vb* (**ossifying, ossified**) *vt* to convert into bone or into a bone-like substance; to harden. * *vi* to become bone; to grow rigid and unprogressive.–**ossification** *n*.

ostensible *adj* apparent; seeming; pretended.–**ostensibly** *adv*.

ostentation *n* a showy, pretentious display.–**ostentatious** *adj*.–**ostentatiously** *adv*.

osteoarthritis *n* painful inflammation of the joints, esp the hips, knees and others that bear weight.–**osteoarthritic** *adj*.

osteopathy *n* the treatment of disease by manipulation of the bones and muscles, often as an adjunct to medical and surgical measures.–**osteopath** *n*.

osteoporosis *n* the development of brittle bones due to a calcium deficiency in the bone matrix.–**osteoporotic** *adj*.

ostracize *vt* to exclude, banish from a group, society, etc.–**ostracism** *n*.

ostrich *n* (*pl* **ostriches, ostrich**) a large, flightless, swift-running African bird.

OT *abbr* = Old Testament.

other *adj* second; remaining; different; additional. * *pron* the other one; some other one.

otherwise *adv* if not, or else; differently.

otherworldly *adj* spiritual; unworldly.–**otherworldliness** *n*.

otiose *adj* superfluous, serving no practical purpose; futile; at leisure.–**otiosity** *n*.

otitis *n* inflammation of the ear.

otter *n* (*pl* **otters, otter**) a fish-eating mammal with smooth fur and a flat tail.

ottoman *n* an upholstered, backless chair or couch.

ouch *interj* an exclamation of pain or annoyance.

ought *aux vb* expressing obligation or duty; to be bound, to be obliged (to).

ounce *n* a unit of weight, equal to one sixteenth of a pound or 28.34 grams; one sixteenth of a pint, one fluid ounce.

our *poss adj, pron* relating or belonging to us.

ours *pron* belonging to us.

ourselves *pron* emphatic and reflexive form of we.

oust *vt* to eject, expel, esp by underhand means; to remove forcibly.

out *adv* not in; outside; in the open air; to the full extent; beyond bounds; no longer holding office; ruled out, no longer considered; loudly and clearly; no longer included (in a game, fashion, etc); in error; on strike; at an end; extinguished; into the open; published; revealed; (*radio conversation*) transmission ends. * *prep* out of; out through; outside. * *adj* external; outward. * *n* an exit; means of escape.

out-and-out *adj* thoroughgoing; absolute; complete.

outback *n* a remote area inland, esp in Australia.

outbid *vt* (**outbidding, outbid,** *pp* **outbidden** *or* **outbid**) to bid higher than.

outboard *adj* (*engine*) outside a ship, etc. * *n* an engine attached to the outside of a boat.

outbreak n a sudden eruption (of disease, strife, etc).

outbuilding n a detached subsidiary building.

outburst n a bursting out; a spurt; an explosion of anger, etc.

outcast n a person who is rejected by society.

outclass vt to surpass or excel greatly.

outcome n the result, consequence.

outcrop n an exposed rock surface. * vi (**outcropping, out-cropped**) to crop out at the surface.

outcry n (pl **outcries**) protest; uproar.

outdated adj obsolete, old-fashioned.

outdistance vt to get well ahead of.

outdo vt (**outdoing, outdid,** pp **outdone**) to surpass, to do more than, to excel.

outdoor adj existing, taking place, or used in the open air.

outdoors adv in or into the open air; out of doors. * n the open air, outside world.

outer adj further out or away.

outermost adj furthest out; most distant.

outer space n any region of space beyond the earth's atmosphere.

outfield n the outer part of a baseball field.

outfit n the equipment used in an activity; clothes worn together, an ensemble; a group of people associated in an activity. * vt (**outfitting, outfitted**) to provide with an outfit or equipment.–**outfitter** n.

outgo vt (**outgoing, outwent,** pp **outgone**) to go beyond; to surpass.

outgoing adj departing; retiring; sociable, forthcoming. * n an outlay; (pl) expenditure.

outgrow vt (**outgrowing, outgrew,** pp **outgrown**) to become too big for; to grow taller than; to grow out of.

outing n a pleasure trip; an excursion.

outlandish adj unconventional; strange; fantastic.

outlast vt to endure longer than.

outlaw vt to declare illegal. * n an outlawed person; a habitual or notorious criminal.

outlay n a spending (of money); expenditure.

outlet n an opening or release; a means of expression; a market for goods or services.

outline n a profile; a general indication; a rough sketch or draft.– also vt.

outlive vt to live longer than, outlast; to live through; to survive.

outlook n mental attitude; view; prospect.

outlying adj detached; remote, distant.

outmaneuver, outmanoeuvre vt to outwit in tactics.

outmoded adj old-fashioned.

outnumber vt to exceed in number.

out-of-date adj no longer valid, unfashionable; outmoded.

out-of-the-way adj uncommon; secluded.

outpatient n a person treated at, but not resident in, a hospital.

outpost n (mil) a post or detachment at a distance from a main force.

outpouring n an effusion, an emotional speech.

output n the quantity (of goods, etc) produced, esp over a given period; information delivered by a computer, esp to a printer; (elect) the useful voltage, current, or power delivered.–also vt.

outrage n an extremely vicious or violent act; a grave insult or offense; great anger, etc, aroused by this.–also vt.–**outrageous** adj.–**outrageously** adv.–**outrageousness** n.

outrank vt to be of a higher rank than; to be of a higher priority.

outright adj complete, downright, direct. * adv at once; without restrictions.

outrun vt (**outrunning, outran,** pp **outran**) to run faster than; to exceed, to go beyond; to escape by running.

outset n the start, beginning.

outshine vt (**outshining, outshone**) to outdo in brilliance, ability; to shine longer and brighter than.

outside n the outer part or surface, the exterior. * adj outer; outdoor; (chance, etc) slight. * adv on or to the outside. * prep on or to the exterior of; beyond.

outsider n a person or thing not included in a set, group, etc, a non-member; a contestant, esp a horse, not thought to have a chance in a race.

outsize adj of a larger than usual size.

outskirts npl districts remote from the center, as of a city.

outsmart vt to outwit.

outspoken adj candid in speech, frank, blunt.

outstanding adj excellent; distinguished; prominent; unpaid; unresolved, still to be done.

outstrip vt (**outstripping, outstripped**) to surpass; to go faster than.

outvote vt to defeat by a higher number of votes.

outward adj directed toward the outside; external; clearly apparent. * adv toward the outside.

outwardly adv externally.

outwards adv outward.

outweigh vt to count for more than, to exceed in value, weight, or importance.

outwit vt (**outwitting, outwitted**) to get the better of, defeat, by wit or cunning.

ouzo n a Greek aniseed-flavoured spirit.

ova see **ovum**.

oval adj egg-shaped; elliptical. * n anything oval.

ovary n (pl **ovaries**) one of the two female reproductive organs producing eggs.–**ovarian** adj.

ovate adj (bot) oval, egg-shaped.

ovation n enthusiastic applause or public welcome.

oven n an enclosed, heated compartment for baking or drying.

oven-ready adj (food) prepared for immediate cooking in the oven.

over prep higher than; on top of; across; to the other side of; above; more than; concerning. * adv above; across; in every part; completed; from beginning to end; up and down; in addition; too. * adj upper; excessive; surplus; finished; remaining. * n (cricket) the number of balls bowled before changing ends.

overact vti to act in an exaggerated manner, to overdo a part.

overactive adj abnormally or excessively active.–**overactivity** n.

overall adj including everything. * adv as a whole; generally. * n a loose protective garment; (pl) a one-piece protective garment covering body and legs.

overarm adj, adv (sport) bowled, thrown, performed, etc with the arm raised above the shoulder.

overawe vt to restrain by awe, daunt.

overbalance vti to fall over; to upset; to outweigh. * n a surplus.

overbearing adj domineering; overriding.–**overbearingly** adv.

overblown adj excessive, pretentious.

overboard adv over the side of a ship, etc; (inf) to extremes of enthusiasm.

overburden vt to load too heavily.

overcame see **overcome**.

overcast adj clouded over.

overcharge vt (battery) to overload; to fill to excess; to demand too high a price (from). * n an excessive or exorbitant charge or load.

overcoat n a warm, heavy topcoat.

overcome vti (**overcoming, overcame,** pp **overcome**) to get the better of, to prevail; to render helpless or powerless, as by tears, laughter, emotion, etc; to be victorious; to surmount obstacles, etc.

overcompensation n (psychoanal) an excess of compensation, often resulting in an overbearing manner.–**overcompensatory** adj.

overcrowd *vti* to make or become too crowded.

overdo *vt* (**overdoing, overdid,** *pp* **overdone**) to do to excess; to overact; to cook (food) too much.–**overdone** *adj*.

overdose *n* an excessive dose –*also vti*.

overdraft *n* an overdrawing, an amount overdrawn, at a bank.

overdraw *vti* (**overdrawing, overdrew,** *pp* **overdrawn**) to draw in excess of a credit balance; to exaggerate in describing; to make an overdraft.

overdrive *n* a high gear in a motor vehicle to reduce wear for traveling at high speed. * *vt* (**overdriving, overdrove,** *pp* **overdriven**) to drive too hard, overtax.

overdue *adj* past the time for payment, return, performance, etc; in arrears; delayed.

overeat *vi* (**overeating, overate,** *pp* **overeaten**) to eat too much.

overestimate *vt* to set too high an estimate on or for. * *n* an excessive estimate.–**overestimation** *n*.

overexpose *vt* (*photog*) to expose (a film) to light for too long.–**overexposure** *n*.

overflow *vti* (**overflowing, overflowed,** *pp* **overflown**) to flow over, flood; to exceed the bounds (of); to abound (with emotion, etc). * *n* that which overflows; surplus, excess; an outlet for surplus water, etc.

overgrown *adj* grown beyond the normal size; rank; ungainly.

overhand *adj, adv* (*sport*) bowled, thrown, performed, etc with the hand above the shoulder.

overhang *vti* (**overhanging, overhung**) to hang or project over. * *n* a projecting part.

overhaul *vt* to examine for, or make, repairs; to overtake.–*also n*.

overhead *adj, adv* above the head; in the sky. * *n* (often *pl*) the general, continuing costs of a business, as of rent, light, etc.

overhear *vt* (**overhearing, overheard**) to hear without the knowledge of the speaker.

overheat *vti* to make or become excessively hot; to stimulate unduly.

overjoyed *adj* highly delighted.

overkill *n* the capability to employ more weapons, etc than are necessary to destroy an enemy; excess capacity for a task.

overland *adj, adv* by, on, or across land.

overlap *vt* (**overlapping, overlapped**) to extend over (a thing or each other) so as to coincide in part.–*also n*.

overlay *vt* (**overlaying, overlaid**) to cover with a coating, to spread over. * *n* a coating.

overleaf *adv* on the other side of the leaf of a book.

overload *vt* to put too great a burden on; (*elect*) to charge with too much current.

overlook *vt* to fail to notice; to look at from above; to excuse.

overman *vt* (**overmanning, overmanned**) to supply with too many workers.

overnight *adv* for the night; in the course of the night; suddenly. * *adj* done in the night; lasting the night.

overpass *n* a road crossing another road, path, etc, at a higher level; the upper level of such a crossing. * *vt* (**overpassing, overpassed,** *pp* **overpast**) to pass beyond, to overstep; to surpass.

overpower *vt* to overcome by superior force, to subdue; to overwhelm.–**overpowering** *adj*.

overqualified *adj* having more qualifications or experience that required for a particular job.

overrate *vt* to value or assess too highly.

overreact *vi* to show an excessive reaction to something.

override *vt* (**overriding, overrode,** *pp* **overridden**) to ride over; to nullify; to prevail.

overrule *vt* to set aside by higher authority; to prevail over.

overrun *vt* (**overrunning, overran,** *pp* **overrun**) to attack and defeat; to swarm over; to exceed (a time limit, etc).

overseas *adj, adv* across or beyond the sea; abroad.

oversee *vt* (**overseeing, oversaw,** *pp* **overseen**) to supervise; to superintend.–**overseer** *n*.

overshadow *vt* to throw a shadow over; to appear more prominent or important than.

overshoot *vt* (**overshooting, overshot**) to shoot or send beyond (a target, etc); (*aircraft*) to fly or taxi beyond the end of a runway when landing or taking off.–*also n*.

oversight *n* a careless mistake or omission; supervision.

oversize, oversized *adj* of larger than average size.

oversleep *vi* (**oversleeping, overslept**) to sleep beyond the intended time.

overspend *vt* (**overspending, overspent**) to spend more than necessary; to wear out, tire. * *vi* to spend more than one can afford.

overstate *vt* to state too strongly, to exaggerate.–**overstatement** *n*.

overstay *vt* to remain longer than or beyond the limits of.

overstep *vt* (**overstepping, overstepped**) to exceed; (a *limit*) to step beyond.

oversubscribe *vt* to apply for more shares in (an issue) than can be allotted.

overt *adj* openly done, unconcealed; (*law*) done with evident intent, deliberate.–**overtly** *adv*.

overtake *vt* (**overtaking, overtook,** *pp* **overtaken**) to catch up with and pass; to come upon suddenly.

overtax *vt* to make too great demands on; to tax too heavily.

overthrow *vt* (**overthrowing, overthrew,** *pp* **overthrown**) to throw over, overturn; (*government, etc*) to bring down by force.–*also n*.

overtime *adv* beyond regular working hours. * *n* extra time worked; payment for this.

overtone *n* an additional subtle meaning; an implicit quality.

overtook *see* **overtake**.

overture *n* an initiating of negotiations; a formal offer, proposal; (*mus*) an instrumental introduction to an opera, etc.

overturn *vti* to upset, turn over; to overthrow.

overview *n* a general survey.

overweening *adj* arrogant, presumptuous, conceited.

overweight *adj* weighing more than the proper amount. * *n* excess weight.

overwhelm *vt* to overcome totally; to submerge; to crush; to overpower with emotion.–**overwhelming** *adj*.

overwork *vti* to work or use too hard or too long.

overwrought *adj* over-excited; too elaborate.

ovine *adj* pertaining to sheep.

oviparous *adj* producing young by eggs.–**oviparity** *n*.

ovoid *adj* egg-shaped.

ovulate *vi* to discharge or produce eggs from an ovary.–**ovulation** *n*.

ovum *n* (*pl* **ova**) an unfertilized female egg cell.

owe *vti* to be in debt; to be obliged to pay; to feel the need to give, do, etc, as because of gratitude.

owing *adj* due, to be paid; owed; (*with* **to**) because of, on account of.

owl *n* a nocturnal bird of prey with a large head and eyes; a person of nocturnal habits, solemn appearance, etc.–**owlish** *adj*.

owlet *n* a young owl.

own[1] *vti* to possess; to acknowledge, admit; to confess to.

own[2] *adj* belonging to oneself or itself, often used reflexively (*my own, their own*).

owner *n* one who owns, a possessor, a proprietor.–**ownership** *n*.

ox *n* (*pl* **oxen**) a cud-chewing mammal of the cattle family; a castrated bull.

oxidation *n* the operation of converting into an oxide.

oxide *n* a compound of oxygen with another element.

oxidize *vti* to cause to undergo a chemical reaction with oxygen; to rust.–**oxidization** *n*.

oxtail *n* the tail of an ox, esp skinned and used for stews, soups, etc.

oxyacetylene *n* a mixture of oxygen with acetylene used in a blowlamp to cut or weld metal.–*also adj.*

oxygen *n* a colorless, odorless, tasteless, highly reactive gaseous element forming part of air, water, etc, and essential to life and combustion.–**oxygenic, oxygenous** *adj.*

oxygenate *vt* to combine or supply with oxygen.–**oxygenation** *n.*

oxygenize *vt* to oxygenate.–**oxygenizer** *n.*

oxygen tent *n* a canopy over a hospital bed, etc, within which a supply of oxygen is maintained.

oxymoron *n* (*pl* **oxymora**) a figure of speech combining contradictory words, e.g. "faith unfaithful kept him falsely true."

oyster *n* an edible marine bivalve shellfish.

oz *abbr* = ounce(s).

ozone *n* a condensed form of oxygen; (*inf*) bracing seaside air.–**ozonic, ozonous** *adj.*

ozone layer *n* a layer of ozone in the stratosphere that absorbs ultraviolet rays from the sun.

P

p *abbr* = page.

PA *abbr* = Panama; Pennsylvania; personal assistant; public address (system).

pace *n* a single step; the measure of a single stride; speed of movement. * *vti* to measure by paces; to walk up and down; to determine the pace in a race; to walk with regular steps.–**pacer** *n.*

pacemaker *n* a person who sets the pace in a race; an electronic device inserted in the heart, used to regulate heartbeat.

pachyderm *n* any large thick-skinned mammal, esp an elephant.–**pachydermatous** *adj.*

pacifier *n* a person or thing that pacifies; a small rubber or plastic nipple for a baby to suck or chew on.

pacifism *n* opposition to the use of force under any circumstances, specifically the refusal to participate in war.–**pacifist** *n.*

pacify *vt* (**pacifying, pacified**) to soothe; to calm; to restore peace to.–**pacification** *n.*

pack *n* a load or bundle (esp one carried on the back); a set of playing cards; a group or mass; a number of wild animals living together; an organized troop; a compact mass (as of snow); a small package used as a container for goods for sale. * *vt* to put together in a bundle or pack; (*suitcase*) to fill; to crowd; to press tightly so as to prevent leakage; to carry in a pack; to send (off); (*sl: gun, etc*) to carry; (*sl: punch*) to deliver with force. * *vi* (*snow, ice*) to form into a hard mass; to assemble one's belongings in suitcases or boxes. * *adj* used for carrying packs, loads, etc.–**packer** *n.*

package *n* a parcel, a wrapped bundle; several items, arrangements, etc offered as a unit. * *vt* to make a parcel of; to group together several items, etc.–**packager** *n.*

package store *n* a place where alcohol is sold for consumption off the premises.

packaging *n* the wrapping round a product offered for sale; the presentation of a product.

pack animal *n* an animal, such as a mule or camel, used for carrying loads.

packet *n* a small box or package.

packing *n* material for protecting packed goods or for making airtight or watertight; the act of filling a suitcase, box, etc.

pact *n* an agreement or treaty.

pad[1] *n* the dull sound of a footstep. * *vi* (**padding, padded**) to walk, esp with a soft step.

pad[2] *n* a piece of a soft material or stuffing; several sheets of paper glued together at one edge; the cushioned thickening of an animal's sole; a piece of folded absorbent material used as a surgical dressing; a flat concrete surface. * *vt* (**padding, padded**) to stuff with soft material; to fill with irrelevant information.

padding *n* stuffing; anything unimportant or false added to achieve length or amount.

paddle *n* a short oar with a wide blade at one or both ends; a implement shaped like this, used to hit, beat or stir. * *vti* (*canoe, etc*) to propel by a paddle.–**paddler** *n.*

paddock *n* an enclosed field in which horses are exercised.

paddy *n* (*pl* **paddies**) threshed unmilled rice; a rice field.

padlock *n* a detachable lock used to fasten doors etc. * *vt* to secure with a padlock.

padre *n* a military chaplain.

pagan *n* a heathen; a person who has no religion.* *adj* irreligious; heathen, non-Christian.–**paganism** *n.*–**paganist** *adj, n.*

page[1] *n* a uniformed boy employed to run errands. * *vt* to summon by messenger, loudspeaker, etc.

page[2] *n* a sheet of paper in a book, newspaper etc. * *vt* (*a book*) to number the pages of (–*also* **paginate**).

pageant *n* a spectacular procession or parade; representation in costume of historical events; a mere show.

pageantry *n* (*pl* **pageantries**) grand or formal display; pomp.

pager *n* a device carried on a person so he or she can be summoned.–*also* **beeper**.

paginate *see* **page**[2].

pagination *n* the act of numbering the pages of a book; the arrangement and number of pages.

pagoda *n* an oriental temple in the form of a tower.

paid *see* **pay**.

pail *n* a bucket.

pain *n* physical or mental suffering; hurting; (*pl*) trouble, exertion. * *vt* to cause distress to.

painful *adj* giving pain, distressing.–**painfully** *adv.*–**painfulness** *n.*

painkiller *n* a drug that relieves pain.

painstaking *adj* very careful, laborious.–**painstakingly** *adv.*

paint *vt* (*a picture*) to make using oil pigments, etc; to depict with paints; to cover or decorate with paint; to describe. * *vi* to make a picture. * *n* a coloring pigment; a dried coat of paint.

painter *n* a person who paints, esp an artist.

pair *n* a set of two things that are equal, suited, or used together; any two persons or animals regarded as a unit. * *vti* to form a pair (of); to mate.

pajamas *npl* a loosely fitting sleeping suit of jacket and pants.–*also* **pyjamas**.

pal *n* a close friend. * *vi* (**palling, palled**) (*with* **up**) (*inf*) to make friends (with).

palace *n* the official residence of a sovereign, president or bishop; a large stately house or public building.

palatable *adj* (*taste*) pleasant; (*fig*) pleasant or acceptable.–**palatability** *n.*–**palatably** *adv.*

palate *n* the roof of the mouth; taste; mental relish.

palatial *adj* of or like a palace.–**palatially** *adv.*–**palatialness** *n.*

palaver *n* idle chatter; flattery; cajolery. * *vt* to flatter, cajole. * *vi* to talkidly.

palaeontology *see* **paleontology**.

pale[1] *n* a fence stake; a boundary.

pale[2] *adj* (*complexion*) with less colour than usual; (*colour, light*) faint, wan, dim. * *vti* to make or become pale.–**palely** *adv.*–**paleness** *n.*

paleontology *n* the study of fossils.–*also* **palaeontology**.–**paleontological** *adj.*–**paleontologist** *n.*

palette *n* a small, wooden board on which colored paints are mixed.

palette knife *n* (*pl* **palette knives**) a thin knife used for mixing colors; a round-ended, flexible knife used in cookery.

palindrome *n* a word or sentence reading the same forwards as backwards, eg "Able was I ere I saw Elba".–**palindromic** *adj.*

palisade *n* a fence made of pointed stakes driven into the ground; a pointed stake used in a fence of this kind.

pall[1] n a heavy cloth over a coffin; (of smoke) a mantle.

pall[2] vi to become boring; to become satiated.

palladium n a rare grayish-white metal found with platinum.

pallbearer n someone who carries the coffin at a funeral.

pallet[1] n a portable platform for lifting and stacking goods.

pallet[2] n a straw bed.

palliate vt to extenuate, to excuse; to alleviate without curing.–**palliation** n.–**palliative** adj, n.–**palliator** n.

pallid adj wan, pale.–**pallidness** n.

pallor n paleness, esp of the face.

palm[1] n the underside of the hand between fingers and wrist. * vt to conceal in or touch with the palm; (with **off**) to pass off by fraud, foist.

palm[2] n a tropical branchless tree with fan-shaped leaves; a symbol of victory.

palmistry n foretelling the future from lines of the hand.–**palmist** n.

Palm Sunday n the Sunday before Easter.

palm-top n a portable computer small enough to fit in the palm of the hand.

palomino n (pl **palominos**) a horse with a golden or cream-colored coat and a white mane and tail.

palpable adj tangible; easily perceived, obvious.–**palpability** n.–**palpably** adv.

palpate vt to examine by touch, esp medically.–**palpation** n.

palpitate vi (heart) to beat abnormally fast; to tremble, flutter.–**palpitation** n.

palsy n (pl **palsies**) paralysis; a condition marked by an uncontrollable tremor of a part of the body. * vt (**palsying, palsied**) to paralyze; to make helpless.

paltry adj (**paltrier, paltriest**) almost worthless; trifling.–**paltrily** adv.–**paltriness** n.

pampas npl the treeless, grassy plains of South America.

pamper vt to overindulge; to coddle, spoil.–**pamperer** n.

pamphlet n a thin, unbound booklet, esp one attacking or advocating a cause, etc; a brochure.–**pamphleteer** n.

pan[1] n a wide metal container, a saucepan; (of scales) a tray; a depression in the earth filled with water; severe criticism; the bowl of a lavatory. * vb (**panning, panned**) *vi (with **out**) (inf) to turn out, esp to turn out well; to succeed. * vt to wash gold-bearing gravel in a pan; (inf) to disparage, find fault with.

pan[2] vti (**panning, panned**) (film camera) to move horizontally to follow an object or provide a panoramic view.–also n.

panacea n a cure-all, universal remedy.–**panacean** adj.

panache n flair; sense of style.

Pan-American adj of or pertaining to North, South and Central America collectively; advocating unity among American countries.

pancake n a round, thin cake made from batter and cooked on a griddle; a thing shaped thus. * vi (aircraft) to descend vertically in a level position.

pancreas n a large gland secreting a digestive juice into the intestine and also producing insulin.–**pancreatic** adj.

panda n a large black and white bear-like herbivore (also **giant panda**); a related reddish-brown raccoon-like animal with a ringed tail (–also **lesser panda**).

pandemic adj epidemic over a large region, universal.

pandemonium n (pl **pandemoniums**) uproar; chaos.

pander n a go-between in sexual liaisons; a pimp. * vi (usu with **to**) to gratify or exploit a person's desires or weaknesses, etc.–**panderer** n.

pandit see **pundit**.

pane n a sheet of glass in a frame of a window, door, etc.–**paned** adj.

panel n a usu rectangular section or division forming part of a wall, door, etc; a board for instruments or controls; a lengthwise strip in a skirt, etc; a group of selected persons for judging, discussing, etc. * vt (**paneling, paneled** or **panelling, panelled**) to decorate with panels.

panelist, panellist n a member of a panel.

pang n a sudden sharp pain or feeling.

panhandle vi (inf) to beg, esp from passers-by. * vt (inf) to obtain by begging.–**panhandler** n.

panic n a sudden overpowering fright or terror.–also adj. * vti (**panicking, panicked**) to affect or be affected with panic.–**panicky** adj.

panic button n a switch for setting off an alarm; (sl) a frenzied response.

panoply n (pl **panoplies**) a complete array; a full suit of armor.–**panoplied** adj.

panorama n a complete view in all directions; a comprehensive presentation of a subject; a constantly changing scene.–**panoramic** adj.–**panoramically** adv.

pansy n (pl **pansies**) a garden flower of the violet family, with velvety petals.

pant vi to breathe noisily, gasp; to yearn (for or after something). * vt to speak while gasping.

pantheism n the doctrine that the universe in its totality is God; willingness to worship all, or several gods.–**pantheist** n.–**pantheistic, pantheistical** adj.

pantheon n a temple to all the gods; a building in which the famous dead of a nation are buried or remembered; a group of famous persons.

panther n (pl **panther, panthers**) a leopard, esp one with a black unspotted coat; a puma.

pantihose n women's tights.–also **panty hose**.

panties npl (inf) short underpants.

pantomime n a drama without words, using only actions and gestures; mime. * vti to mime.–**pantomimic** adj.

pantry n (pl **pantries**) a small room or cupboard for storing cooking ingredients and utensils, etc.

pants npl trousers; underpants.

panty hose see **pantihose**.

pap n soft, bland food for infants, invalids, etc; any oversimplified or insipid writing, ideas, etc.

papacy n (pl **papacies**) the office or authority of the pope; papal system of government.

papal adj of the pope or the papacy.–**papally** adv.

paparazzo n (pl **paparazzi**) a freelance photographer who pursues celebrities for sensational or candid shots for publication in newspapers and magazines.

papaya n (a West Indian tree bearing) an elongated melon-like fruit with edible yellow flesh and small black seeds.

paper n the thin, flexible material made from pulped rags, wood, etc which is used to write on, wrap in, or cover walls; a single sheet of this; an official document; a newspaper; an essay or lecture; a set of examination questions; (pl) personal documents. * adj like or made of paper. * vt to cover with wallpaper.

paperback n a book bound in a flexible paper cover. * adj pertaining to such a book or the publication of such books.

paperknife n (pl **paperknives**) a blunt knife for opening letters or cutting folded paper.

papery adj like paper in appearance or consistency.–**paperiness** n.

papier-mâché n a substance made of paper pulp mixed with size, glue, etc and molded into various objects when moist.

papoose n an American Indian young child.

paprika n a mild red condiment ground from the fruit of certain peppers.

papyrus n (pl **papyri, papyruses**) an aquatic plant; paper made from this plant, as used in ancient times.

par n the standard or normal level; the established value of a currency in foreign-exchange rates; the face value of stocks, shares, etc; (golf) the score for a hole required by an expert player; equality.

parable n a short story used to illustrate a religious or moral point.–**parabolist** n.

parabola n (pl **parabolas**) (math) the curve formed by the cutting of a cone by a plane parallel to its side.

parachute n a fabric umbrella-like canopy used to retard speed of fall from an aircraft. * vti to drop, descend by parachute.—**parachutist** n.

parade n a ceremonial procession; an assembly of troops for review; ostentatious display; public walk, promenade. * vti to march or walk through, as for display; to show off; to assemble in military order.

paradigm n a pattern or model; a list of grammatical inflexions of a word.—**paradigmatic** adj.—**paradigmatically** adv.

paradise n heaven; (Bible) the Garden of Eden; any place of perfection.

paradox n a self-contradictory statement that may be true; an opinion that conflicts with common beliefs; something with seemingly contradictory qualities or phases.—**paradoxical** adj.—**paradoxically** adv.

paraffin n a white waxy tasteless substance obtained from shale, wood, etc.—**paraffinic** adj.

paragon n a model of excellence or perfection.

paragraph n a subdivision in a piece of writing used to separate ideas, marked by the beginning of a new line; a brief mention in a newspaper. * vt to divide into paragraphs.—**paragraphic** adj.—**paragraphically** adv.

parakeet n a small parrot.

parallel adj equidistant at every point and extended in the same direction; side by side; never intersecting; similar, corresponding. * n a parallel line, surface, etc; a likeness, counterpart; comparison; a line of latitude. * vt (**paralleling, paralleled**) to make or be parallel; to compare.

parallelogram n a four-sided plane figure whose opposite sides are parallel.

paralysis n (pl **paralyses**) a partial or complete loss of voluntary muscle function or sensation in any part of the body; a condition of helpless inactivity.—**paralytic** adj, n.

paralyze, paralyse vt to affect with paralysis; to bring to a stop.—**paralysation** n.

paramedic n a person trained to provide emergency medical treatment and to support professional medical staff.

parameter n (math) an arbitrary constant, the value of which influences the content but not the structure of an expression; (inf) a limit or condition affecting action, decision, etc.—**parametric** adj.—**parametrically** adv.

paramilitary adj (forces) organized on a military pattern and ancillary to military forces.

paramount adj of great importance.

paramour n an illicit lover.

paranoia n a mental illness characterized by delusions of grandeur and persecution; (inf) unfounded fear, suspicion.—**paranoiac** adj, n.

paranoid adj of or like paranoia; (inf) highly suspicious or fearful.—also n.

paranormal adj beyond the scope of normal experience or scientific explanation.—**paranormally** adv.

parapet n a low, protective wall along the edge of a roof, balcony, or bridge, etc.—**parapeted** adj.

paraphernalia npl personal belongings; accessories.

paraphrase n expression of a passage in other words in order to clarify meaning. * vt to restate.—**paraphrastic** adj.

paraplegia n paralysis of the lower half of the body.—**paraplegic** adj.

parasite n an organism that lives on and feeds off another without rendering any service in return; a person who sponges off another.—**parasitic** adj.—**parasitically** adv.

parasol n a lightweight umbrella used as a sunshade.

paratroops npl troops dropped by parachute into the enemy area.—**paratrooper** n.

parboil vt to boil briefly as a preliminary cooking procedure.

parcel n a tract or plot of land; a wrapped bundle; a package; a collection or group of persons, animals, or things. * vt (**parceling, parceled** or **parcelling, parcelled**) to wrap up into a parcel; (with **out**) to apportion.

parch vti to make or become hot and dry, thirsty; to scorch, roast.—**parched** adj.

parchment n the skin of a sheep, etc prepared as a writing material; paper like parchment.

pardon vt to forgive; to excuse; to release from penalty. * n forgiveness; remission of penalty.—**pardonable** adj.—**pardonably** adv.

pare vt to cut or shave; to peel; to diminish.

parent n a father or a mother; an organism producing another; a source.—**parental** adj.—**parentally** adv.—**parenthood** n.

parentage n descent, extraction from parents.

parenthesis n (pl **parentheses**) an explanatory comment in a sentence contained within brackets and set in a sentence, independently of grammatical sequence; the brackets themselves ( ).—**parenthetic, parenthetical** adj.—**parenthetically** adv.

parenting n the act of being a parent; the role of a parent in relation to a child; that role in relation to someone who is not the child of a parent.

pariah n a social outcast.

parish n an ecclesiastical area with its own church and clergy; the inhabitants of a parish.

parishioner n an inhabitant of a parish.

parity n (pl **parities**) equality; equality of value at a given ratio between different kinds of money, etc; being at par.

park n land kept as a game preserve or recreation area; a piece of ground in an urban area kept for ornament or recreation; an enclosed stadium, esp for ball games; a large enclosed piece of ground attached to a country house. * vti (vehicle) to leave in a certain place temporarily; to maneuver into a parking space.

parking lot n an area reserved for parking motor vehicles.

parking meter n a coin-operated machine that registers the purchase of parking time for a motor vehicle.

parlance n a manner of speech, idiom.

parley n a conference, esp with an enemy. * vi to discuss, esp with an enemy with a view to bringing about a peace.

parliament n a legislative assembly made up of representatives of a nation or part of a nation; (with cap) the supreme governing and legislative body of various countries, esp the UK.

parlor n a room in a house used primarily for conversation or receiving guests; a room or a shop used for business.

parochial adj of or relating to a parish; narrow; provincial in outlook.—**parochially** adv.

parochialism n narrow-mindedness.

parody n (pl **parodies**) a satirical or humorous imitation of a literary or musical work or style. * vt (**parodying, parodied**) to make a parody of.—**parodic** adj.—**parodist** n.

parole n word of honor; the release of a prisoner before his sentence has expired, on condition of future good behavior. * vt to release on parole.

parolee n a person on parole.

paroxysm n a sudden attack of a disease; a violent convulsion of pain or emotion; an outburst of laughter.—**paroxysmal** adj.

parquetry n mosaic woodwork used to cover floors.

parrot n a tropical or subtropical bird with brilliant plumage and the ability to mimic human speech; one who repeats another's words without understanding. * vt to repeat mechanically.

parry vt (**parrying, parried**) to ward off, turn aside. * n (pl **parries**) a defensive movement in fencing.

parse vti (words) to classify; (sentences) to analyze in terms of grammar; to give a grammatical description of a word or group of words.

parsimony n extreme frugality; meanness, stinginess.—**parsimonious** adj.

parsley n a bright green herb used to flavor or garnish some foods.

parsnip *n* a biennial plant cultivated for its long tapered root used as a vegetable.

parson *n* an Anglican clergyman in charge of a parish; (*inf*) any, esp Protestant, clergyman.

parsonage *n* the house provided for a parson by his church.

part *n* a section; a portion (of a whole); an essential, separable component of a piece of equipment or a machine; the role of an actor in a play; a written copy of his/her words; (*mus*) one of the melodies of a harmony; the music for it; duty, share; one of the sides in a conflict; a parting of the hair; (*pl*) qualities, talent; the genitals; a region, land or territory. * *vt* to separate; to comb the hair so as to leave a parting. * *vi* to become separated; to go different ways.

partake *vi* (**partaking, partook**; *pp* **partaken**) to participate (in); (*food or drink*) to have a portion of.

partial *adj* incomplete; biased, prejudiced; (*with* **to**) having a liking or preference for.–**partiality** *n.*–**partially** *adv.*

participant *n* one who participates; a sharer.

participate *vi* to join in or take part with others (in some activity).–**participator** *n.*–**participation** *n.*–**participatory** *adj.*

participle *n* (*gram*) a verb form used in compound forms or as an adjective.–**participial** *adj.*–**participially** *adv.*

particle *n* a tiny portion of matter; a speck; a very small part.

particular *adj* referring or belonging to a specific person or thing; distinct; exceptional; careful; fastidious. * *n* a detail, single item; (*pl*) detailed information.

particularity *n* (*pl* **particularities**) the quality of being particular, as distinguished from universal; exactness; fastidiousness.

particularly *adv* very; especially; in detail.

parting *n* a departure; a breaking or separating. * *adj* departing, esp dying; separating; dividing.

partisan *n* a strong supporter of a person, party, or cause.–*also adj.*–**partisanship** *n.*

partition *n* division into parts; that which divides into separate parts; a dividing wall between rooms. * *vt* to divide.

partly *adv* in part; to some extent.

partner *n* one of two or more persons jointly owning a business who share the risks and profits; one of a pair who dance or play a game together; either member of a married or non-married couple. * *vt* to be a partner (in or of); to associate as partners.

partnership *n* a contract between two or more people involved in a joint business venture; the state of being a partner.

part of speech *n* each of the categories (eg verb, noun, adjective) into which words are divided according to their grammatical and semantic functions.

partook *see* **partake**.

part-time *adj* working fewer than the full number of hours.–**part-timer** *n.*–**part time** *adv.*

parturition *n* the act of childbirth.

party *n* (*pl* **parties**) a group of people united for political or other purpose; a social gathering; a person involved in a contract or lawsuit; a small company, detachment; a person consenting, accessory; (*inf*) an individual. * *vb* (**partying, partied**) *vi* to attend social parties. * *vt* to give a party for. * *adj* of or for a party.

parvenu *n* someone regarded as vulgar or an upstart, following a rise in his social or economic status.–**parvenue** *nf.*

pascal *n* the SI unit of pressure.

pas de deux *n* (*pl* **pas de deux**) a ballet sequence for two dancers.

pass *vb* (**passing, passed**) *vi* to go past; to go beyond or exceed; to move from one place or state to another; (*time*) to elapse; to go; to die; to happen; (*with* **for**) to be considered as; (*in exam*) to be successful; (*cards*) to decline to make a bid; (*law*) to be approved by a legislative assembly. * *vt* to go past, through, over, etc; (*time*) to spend; to omit; (*law*) to enact; (*judgment*) to pronounce; to excrete; (*in test, etc*) to gain the required marks; to approve. * *n* a narrow passage or road; a permit; (*in a test, etc*) success; transfer of (a ball) to another player; a gesture of the hand; (*inf*) an uninvited sexual approach.

passable *adj* fairly good, tolerable; (*a river, etc*) that can be crossed.–**passably** *adv.*

passage *n* act or right of passing; transit; transition; a corridor; a channel; a route or crossing; a lapse of time; a piece of text or music.

passageway *n* a narrow way, esp flanked by walls, that allows passage; a corridor.

passbook *n* a bankbook.

passé *adj* past its best; outdated.

passenger *n* a traveler in a public or private conveyance; one who does not pull his/her weight.

passer-by *n* (*pl* **passers-by**) one who happens to pass or go by.

passing *adj* transient; casual. * *n* departure, death.

passion *n* compelling emotion, such as love, hate, envy; ardent love, esp sexual desire; (*with cap*) the suffering of Christ on the cross; the object of any strong desire.–**passionless** *adj.*

passionate *adj* moved by, showing, strong emotion or desire; intense; sensual.–**passionately** *adv.*

passive *adj* acted upon, not acting; submissive; (*gram*) denoting the voice of a verb whose subject receives the action.–**passively** *adv.*–**passivity** *n.*

passive smoking *n* the involuntary inhalation of smoke from others' cigarettes.

Passover *n* (*Judaism*) a spring holiday, celebrating the liberation of the Israelites from slavery in Egypt.

passport *n* an official document giving the owner the right to travel abroad; something that secures admission or acceptance.

password *n* a secret term by which a person is recognized and allowed to pass; any means of admission; a sequence of characters required to access a computer system.

past *adj* completed; ended; in time already elapsed. * *adv* by. * *prep* beyond (in time, place, or amount). * *n* time that has gone by; the history of a person, group, etc; a personal background that is hidden or questionable.

pasta *n* the flour paste from which spaghetti, noodles, etc is made; any dish of cooked pasta.

paste *n* a soft plastic mixture; flour and water forming dough or adhesive; a fine glass used for artificial gems. * *vt* to attach with paste.

pasteboard *n* a stiff board made from sheets of paper pasted together. * *adj* flimsy.

pastel *n* a dried mixture of chalk, pigments and gum used for drawing; a drawing made with such; a soft, pale color. * *adj* delicately colored.

pasteurize *vt* (*milk, etc*) to sterilize by heat or radiation to destroy harmful organisms.–**pasteurization** *n.*

pastiche *n* (*pl* **pastiches**) a literary, musical, or artistic work in imitation of another's style, or consisting of pieces from other sources.–*also* **pasticcio** (*pl* **pasticci**).

pastime *n* a hobby; recreation, diversion.

pastor *n* a clergyman in charge of a congregation.

pastoral *adj* of shepherds or rural life; pertaining to spiritual care, esp of a congregation.–**pastorally** *adv.*

pastrami *n* highly seasoned smoked beef.

pastry *n* (*pl* **pastries**) dough made of flour, water, and fat used for making pies, tarts, etc; (*pl*) baked foods made with pastry.

pasture *n* land covered with grass for grazing livestock; the grass growing on it. * *vt* (*cattle, etc*) to put out to graze in a pasture.

pasty *adj* (**pastier, pastiest**) like paste; pallid and unhealthy in appearance.–**pastily** *adv.*–**pastiness** *n.*

pat[1] *vti* (**patting, patted**) to strike gently with the palm of the hand or a flat object; to shape or apply by patting. * *n* a light tap, usu with the palm of the hand; a light sound; a small lump of shaped butter.

pat[2] *adj* apt; exact; glib.–*also adv.*

patch *n* a piece of cloth used for mending; a scrap of material; a shield for an injured eye; a black spot of silk, etc worn on the face; an irregular spot on a surface; a plot of ground; a bandage; an area or spot. * *vt* to repair with a patch; to piece together; to mend in a makeshift way.–**patchable** *adj.*–**patcher** *n.*

patchwork *n* needlework made of pieces sewn together; something made of various bits.

patchy *adj* (**patchier, patchiest**) irregular; uneven; covered with patches.–**patchily** *adv.*–**patchiness** *n.*

pâté *n* a rich spread made of meat, fish, herbs, etc.

patella *n* (*pl* **patellae**) (*anat*) the kneecap.–**patellar** *adj.*

patent *adj* plain; apparent; open to public inspection; protected by a patent. * *n* a government document, granting the exclusive right to produce and sell an invention, etc for a certain time; the right so granted; the thing protected by such a right. * *vt* to secure a patent for.–**patentable** *adj.*

patently *adv* obviously, openly.

paternal *adj* fatherly in disposition; related through the father.–**paternally** *adv.*

paternity *n* fatherhood; origin or descent from a father.

path *n* (*pl* **paths**) a way worn by footsteps; a track for people on foot; a direction; a course of conduct.

pathetic *adj* inspiring pity; (*sl*) uninteresting, inadequate.–**pathetically** *adv.*

pathogen *n* an agent, such as a microorganism, that causes disease.–**pathogenic** *adj.*

pathological, pathologic *adj* of pathology; of the nature of, caused or altered by disease; (*inf*) compulsive.–**pathologically** *adv.*

pathologist *n* a medical specialist who diagnoses by interpreting the changes in tissue and body fluid caused by a disease.

pathology *n* (*pl* **pathologies**) the branch of medicine that deals with the nature of disease, esp its functional and structural effects; any abnormal variation from a sound condition.

pathos *n* a quality that excites pity or sadness; an expression of deep feeling.

pathway *n* a path; (*chem*) a sequence of enzyme-catalyzed reactions.

patience *n* the capacity to endure or wait calmly; a card game for one (–*also* **solitaire**).

patient *adj* even-tempered; able to wait or endure calmly; persevering. * *n* a person receiving medical, dental, etc treatment.–**patiently** *adv.*

patina *n* a green incrustation on old bronze; a surface appearance of something grown beautiful by age or use; a superficial covering or exterior.

patio *n* (*pl* **patios**) an inner, usu roofless, courtyard; a paved area adjoining a house, for outdoor lounging, dining, etc.

patriarch *n* the father and head of a family or tribe; a man of great age and dignity.–**patriarchal** *adj.*

patriarchy *n* (*pl* **patriarchies**) government by the head of a family, tribe, etc; a community ruled in this way.

patrician *adj* aristocratic; oligarchic.

patricide *n* the unlawful killing of one's father; a person who kills his or her father.–**patricidal** *adj.*

patrimony *n* (*pl* **patrimonies**) an estate or right inherited from a father or one's ancestors; an ecclesiastical endowment or estate.–**patrimonial** *adj.*

patriot *n* one who strongly supports and serves his or her country.–**patriotic** *adj.*–**patriotically** *adv.*

patriotism *n* love for or loyalty to one's country.

patrol *vti* (**patrolling, patrolled**) to walk around a building or area in order to watch, guard, inspect. * *n* the act of going the rounds; a unit of persons or vehicles employed for reconnaissance, security, or combat.–**patroller** *n.*

patrolman (*pl* **patrolmen**) a policeman who patrols a particular area.

patron *n* a regular client or customer; a person who sponsors and supports the arts, charities, etc; a protector.–**patronal** *adj.*

patronage *n* the support given or custom brought by a patron; clientele; business; trade; the power to grant political favors; such favors.

patronize *vt* to treat with condescension; to sponsor or support; to be a regular customer of.–**patronization** *n.*

patronizing *adj* condescending.–**patronizingly** *adv.*

patter[1] *vi* to make quick tapping sounds, as if by striking something; to run with light steps. * *n* the sound of tapping or quick steps.

patter[2] *vi* to talk rapidly and glibly; to mumble (prayers, etc) mechanically. * *vt* to repeat speech mechanically, to gabble. * *n* rapid speech, esp that of a salesman, comedian, etc; glib speech; chatter; jargon.

pattern *n* a decorative arrangement; a model to be copied; instructions to be followed to make something; a regular way of acting or doing; a predictable route, movement, etc. * *vt* to make or do in imitation of a pattern.–**patterned** *adj.*

patty *n* (*pl* **patties**) a small pie; a flat cake of ground meat, fish, etc, usu fried.

paucity *n* fewness; lack of; scarcity.

paunch *n* the belly, esp a potbelly.–**paunchy** *adj.*

pauper *n* a very poor person; (*formerly*) a person dependent on charity.–**pauperism** *n.*

pause *n* a temporary stop, esp in speech, action or music. * *vi* to cease in action temporarily, wait; to hesitate.

pave *vt* (a *road, etc*) to cover with concrete to provide a hard level surface; **pave the way** to prepare a smooth easy way; to facilitate development.–**paving** *n.*

pavement *n* a hard surface, esp on a road.

pavilion *n* an annex; a temporary building for exhibitions; a large ornate tent.

paw *n* a foot of a mammal with claws; (*sl*) a hand. * *vti* to touch, dig, hit, etc with paws; to maul; to handle clumsily or roughly.

pawn[1] *n* the piece of lowest value in chess; a person used to advance another's purpose.

pawn[2] *vt* to deposit an article as security for a loan; to wager or risk. * *n* a thing pawned; the state of being given as a pawn.–**pawner** *n.*

pawnbroker *n* a person licensed to lend money at interest on personal property left with him as security.–**pawnbroking** *n.*

pay *vti* (**paying, paid**) to give (money) in payment for a debt, goods or services; to give in compensation; to yield a profit; to bear a cost; to suffer a penalty; (*homage, attention*) to give. * *n* payment for services or goods; salary, wages.–**paying** *adj.*–**payer** *n.*

pay dirt *n* soil, gravel, etc worth mining for minerals; (*inf*) a source of wealth.

payee *n* one to whom money is paid.

payment *n* the act of paying; amount paid; reward.

payroll *n* a list of employees and their wages; the actual money for paying wages.

Pb (*chem symbol*) lead.

PBS *abbr* = Public Broadcasting System.

PC *abbr* = personal computer; political correctness, politically correct.

P.D. *abbr* = Police Department; postal district.

pea *n* the edible, round, green seed of a climbing leguminous annual plant.

peace *n* tranquillity, stillness; freedom from contention, violence or war; a treaty that ends a war.

peaceable *adj* inclined to peace.–**peaceably** *adv.*–**peaceableness** *n.*

peaceful *adj* having peace; tranquil; quiet.–**peacefully** *adv.*–**peacefulness** *n.*

peacemaker *n* one who makes or restores peace; one who reconciles enemies.–**peacemaking** *adj, n.*

peace offering *n* a conciliatory gift.

peach *n* a round, sweet, juicy, downy-skinned stone-fruit; the tree bearing it; a yellowish pink color.

peacock n (**peacocks, peacock**) a male peafowl with a large brilliantly colored fan-like tail; a person who is a show-off.—**pea-hen** nf.

peak n the summit of a mountain; the highest point; the pointed end of anything; maximum value; the eyeshade of a cap, visor. * vti (politician, actor, etc) to reach or cause to reach the height of power, popularity; (prices) to reach and stay at the highest level.

peaked adj drawn, emaciated; sickly.

peal n a reverberating sound as of thunder, laughter, bells, etc; a set of bells, the changes rung on them. * vti to sound in peals, ring out.

peanut n a leguminous plant with underground pods containing edible seeds; the pod or any of its seeds; (pl) (sl) a trifling thing or amount.

peanut butter n a food paste made by grinding roasted peanuts.

pear n a common juicy fruit of tapering oval shape; the tree bearing it.

pearl n the lustrous white round gem produced by oysters; mother-of-pearl; anything resembling a pearl intrinsically or physically; one that is choice and precious; a bluish medium gray. * vti to fish for pearls; to form drops (on), to bespangle.—**pearly** adj.

peasant n (inf) a countryman or countrywoman; an agricultural laborer.

peat n decayed vegetable matter from bogs, which is dried and cut into blocks for fuel or used as a fertilizer.—**peaty** adj.

pebble n a small rounded stone; an irregular, grainy surface.—**pebbled** adj.—**pebbly** adj.

pecan n a hickory tree widely grown in the US and Mexico for its edible nuts; its wood; its thin-shelled nut.

peccadillo n (pl **peccadilloes, peccadillos**) a trifling misdeed, indiscretion.

peck vt to strike with the beak or a pointed object; to pick at one's food; (inf) to kiss lightly; to nag. also n.

pecking order n a social hierarchy in groups of some birds (eg hens), characterized by the pecking of those lower in the scale and submitting to being pecked by those higher; any social hierarchy.

pectin n a carbohydrate found in fruits and vegetables, yielding a gel that is used to set jellies.—**pectic** adj.

pectoral adj of or relating to the breast, chest. * n the muscle in the chest; something worn on the breast.

peculiar adj belonging exclusively (to); special; distinct; characteristic; strange.—**peculiarly** adv.

peculiarity n (pl **peculiarities**) an idiosyncrasy; a characteristic; an oddity.

pecuniary adj of or consisting of money.—**pecuniarily** adv.

pedagogue n a schoolteacher.—**pedagogic, pedagogical** adj.

pedagogy n the art or science of teaching.

pedal n a lever operated by the foot. * vt (**pedaling, pedaled** or **pedalling, pedalled**) to operate or propel by pressing pedals with the foot.—**pedaler, pedaller** n.

pedant n a person who attaches too much importance to insignificant details.—**pedantic** adj.—**pedantically** adv.

peddle vt to go from place to place selling small items; to sell (drugs, etc) illegally.—**peddler** n.

pedestal n the base that supports a column, statue, etc. * vt to set on a pedestal; to serve as a pedestal for.

pedestrian adj on foot; dull, commonplace. * n a person who walks.

pedicure n cosmetic care of the feet, toes, and nails; a person trained to care for feet in this way.

pedigree n a line of descent of an animal; a recorded purity of breed of an individual; a genealogy; lineage; derivation. * adj having a known ancestry.—**pedigreed** adj.

pediatrics n sing the branch of medicine dealing with children and their diseases.—also **paediatrics**.—**pediatric** adj.—**pediatrician** n.

pedometer n an instrument for measuring the distance walked by recording the number of steps taken.

pedophilia n sexual attraction towards children.—also **paedophilia**.—**pedophiliac, pedophilic** adj.—**pedophile** n.

pee vi (sl) to urinate. * n urination; urine.

peek vi to look quickly or furtively.—also n.

peekaboo n a child's game in which one person hides behind his or her hands then peeps out suddenly, shouting, "peekaboo!"

peel vt to remove skin or rind from; to bare. * vi to flake off, as skin or paint. * n rind, esp that of fruit and vegetables.—**peeling** n.

peep[1] vi to make shrill noises as a young bird. * n a peeping sound.

peep[2] vi to look hastily or furtively; to look through a slit or narrow opening; to be just showing. * n a furtive or hurried glance, a glimpse; (of day) the first appearance.

peephole n a small hole, esp in a door, to spy through.

peeping Tom n a person who peeps furtively, a voyeur.

peer[1] vi to look closely; to look with difficulty; to peep out.

peer[2] n an equal in rank, ability, etc; a nobleman.—**peeress** nf.

peerage n the rank or title of a peer; peers collectively; a book with a list of peers.

peer group n a group of people of the same age, background, education, interests, etc.

peerless adj having no equal, matchless.

peeve vt (inf) to annoy.

peevish adj fretful, irritable.—**peevishly** adv.—**peevishness** n.

peg n a tapered piece (of wood) for securing or hanging things on, for marking position; a predetermined level at which (a price) is fixed; (mus) one of the movable parts for tuning the string of an instrument. * vti (**pegging, pegged**) to fasten or mark with a peg; (a price) to keep steady; (with **away at**) to work steadily, persevere.

pejorative adj (word, etc) disparaging, derogatory. * n a disparaging word.—**pejoratively** adv.

Pekingese, Pekinese n (pl **Pekingese, Pekinese**) a breed of small dog with long, silky hair, short legs, and a pug nose.

pelican n a large fish-eating waterbird with an expandable pouched bill.

pellet n a small ball of paper, bread, etc; a pill; a small ball of hair, bones, etc regurgitated by a bird of prey; a piece of shot. * vt to form into pellets.

pelmet n a canopy for a window frame to hide a curtain rail, etc; a valance.

pelt[1] vt to throw missiles, or words, at. * vi (rain) to fall heavily; to hurry, rush. * n a rush.—**pelter** n.

pelt[2] n a usu undressed skin of an animal with its hair, wool, or fur.

pelvis n (pl **pelvises, pelves**) the bony cavity that joins the lower limbs to the body; the bones forming this.—**pelvic** adj.

pemmican, pemican n a cake of dried lean meat formerly used by North American Indians; a mixture of beef and suet used as emergency rations.

pen[1] n an implement used with ink for writing or drawing. * vt (**penning, penned**) to write, compose.

pen[2] n a small enclosure for cattle, poultry, etc; a small place of confinement. * vt (**penning, penned**) to enclose in a pen, shut up.

penal adj relating to, liable to, or prescribing punishment; punitive.—**penally** adv.

penal code n a code of laws concerning crimes and offenses and their punishment.

penalize vt to impose a penalty; to put under a disadvantage.—**penalization** n.

penalty n (pl **penalties**) a punishment attached to an offense; suffering or loss as a result of one's own mistake; a disadvantage imposed for breaking a rule as in sports; a fine.

penance n voluntary suffering to atone for a sin; a sacramental rite consisting of confession, absolution, and penance. * vt to impose a penance on.

pence see **penny**.

penchant n inclination, strong liking (for).

pencil n a pointed rod-shaped instrument with a core of graphite or crayon for writing, drawing, etc; a set of convergent light rays or straight lines; a fine paintbrush. * vt (**penciling, penciled** or **pencilling, pencilled**) to write, draw, or colour with a pencil; (with **in**) to commit tentatively.–**penciler, penciller** n.

pendant, pendent n a hanging ornament, esp a jewel on a necklace, bracelet, etc; a light-fitting suspended from a ceiling. * adj (usu **pendent**) hanging; projecting; undecided.–**pendency** n.

pending adj undecided; unfinished; imminent. * prep during; until, awaiting.

pendulous adj hanging downwards and swinging freely.–**pendulously** adv.

pendulum n a weight suspended from a fixed point so as to swing freely; such a device used to regulate the movement of a clock; something that swings to and fro.

penetrate vti to thrust, force a way into or through something; to pierce; to permeate; to understand.–**penetrator** n.–**penetrative** adj.

penetrating adj acute, discerning; (voice) easily heard through other sounds.–**penetratingly** adv.

penetration n the capability, act, or action of penetrating; acute insight.

penguin n a flightless, marine bird with black and white plumage, usu found in the Antarctic.

penicillin n an antibiotic produced naturally and synthetically from molds.

peninsula n a piece of land almost surrounded by sea.–**peninsular** adj.

penis n (pl **penises, penes**) the male copulative and urinary organ in mammals.

penitent adj feeling regret for sin, repentant, contrite. * n a person who atones for sin.–**penitence** n.–**penitently** adv.

penitential adj of or expressing penance; being penitent.–**penitentially** adv.

penitentiary n (pl **penitentiaries**) a state or federal prison. * adj pertaining to penance; pertaining to the reformatory treatment of prisoners.

penknife n (pl **penknives**) a small knife, usu with one or more folding blades, that fits into the pocket.

Penn, Penna abbr = Pennsylvania.

pen name n a literary pseudonym.–also **nom de plume**.

pennant n a long tapering flag used for identifying vessels and for signaling; such a flag symbolizing a championship.

penny n (pl **pence** denoting sum, **pennies** denoting separate coins) a bronze coin of the UK worth one hundredth of a pound; (US) a one cent coin.

pen pal n a friend with whom one is in contact only through correspondence.

pension n a periodic payment to a person beyond retirement age, or widowed, or disabled; a periodic payment in consideration of past services. * vt to grant a pension to; (with **off**) to dismiss or retire from service with a pension.–**pensionable** adj.

pensioner n a person who receives a pension; a senior citizen.

pensive adj thoughtful, musing; wistful, melancholic.–**pensively** adv.–**pensiveness** n.

pentagon n (geom) a polygon with five sides; (with cap) the pentagonal headquarters of the US defense establishment; the US military leadership collectively.–**pentagonal** adj.

pentagram n a five-pointed star, often used as a magic symbol.–also **pentangle**.

pentameter n a verse of five metrical feet.

pentathlon n an athletic contest involving participation by each contestant in five different events.–**pentathlete** n.

Pentecost n a Christian festival on the seventh Sunday after Easter; Whit Sunday.

penthouse n an apartment on the roof or in the top floor of a building.

pent-up adj (emotion) repressed, confined.

penult n the penultimate syllable of a word. * adj last but one.

penultimate adj last but one.–also adj.

penurious adj grudging with money, stingy; poor; scanty.–**penuriously** adv.–**penuriousness** n.

penury n (pl **penuries**) extreme poverty; want.

peony n (pl **peonies**) a plant with large, showy, red, pink or white flowers.

people n the body of enfranchised citizens of a state; a person's family, relatives; the persons of a certain place, group, or class; persons considered indefinitely; human beings; (pl) all the persons of a racial or ethnic group, typically having a common language, institutions, homes, and culture. * vt to populate with people.

pep n (inf) energy, vigor; bounce. * vt (**pepping, pepped**) (usu with **up**) to enliven by injecting with pep.

pepper n a sharp, hot condiment made from the fruit of various plants; the fruit of the pepper plant, which can be red, yellow, or green, sweet or hot, and is eaten as a vegetable. * vt to sprinkle or flavor with pepper; to hit with small shot; to pelt; to beat.

peppercorn n a dried pepper berry.

pepper mill n hand mill for grinding peppercorns.

peppermint n a pungent and aromatic mint plant; its oil used for flavoring; a sweet flavored with peppermint.

pepperoni n a spicy beef and pork sausage.

peppery adj of, like, full of, pepper; fiery; hot-tempered.–**pepperiness** n.

pep talk n (inf) a vigorous talk made with the intention of arousing enthusiasm, increasing confidence, etc.

peptic adj of or promoting digestion; of, producing, or caused by the action of the digestive juices.

peptic ulcer n an ulcer of the stomach lining or duodenum.

per prep for or in each; through, by, by means of; (inf) according to.

per annum adv yearly; each year.

perceive vt to become aware of, apprehend, through the senses; to recognize.–**perceivable** adj.–**perceivably** adv.

per cent, percent adv in, for each hundred. * n a percentage.

percentage n rate per hundred parts; a proportion; (inf) profit, gain.

perceptible adj able to be perceived; discernible.–**perceptibility** n.–**perceptibly** adv.

perception n the act or faculty of perceiving; discernment; insight; a way of perceiving, view.–**perceptional** adj.

perceptive adj able to perceive; observant.–**perceptively** adv.–**perceptivity, perceptiveness** n.

perch[1] n (pl **perch, perches**) a spiny-finned chiefly freshwater edible fish.

perch[2] n a pole on which birds roost or alight; an elevated seat or position. * vti to alight, rest, on a perch; to balance (oneself) on; to set in a high position.

percipient adj perceiving; perceptive. * n a person who perceives.–**percipience** n.

percolate vt (liquid) to pass through a filter or pores; to brew coffee. * vi to ooze through; to spread gradually.–**percolation** n.

percolator n a coffeepot in which boiling water is forced through ground coffee beans.

percussion n impact, collision; musical instruments played by striking with sticks or hammers, eg cymbals, drums, etc; such instruments regarded as a section of an orchestra; (med) tapping the body to discover the condition of an organ by the sounds.–**percussive** adj.

percussionist n a person who plays a percussion instrument.

perdition n utter loss of the soul; eternal damnation; (arch) total destruction, ruin.

peremptory adj urgent; absolute; dogmatic; dictatorial.–**peremptorily** adv.–**peremptoriness** n.

perennial adj perpetual; lasting throughout the year. * n (bot) a plant lasting more than two years.–**perennially** adv.

perfect adj faultless; exact; excellent; complete. * n (gram) a verb form expressing completed action or designating a present state that is the result of an action in the past. * vt to improve; to finish; to make fully accomplished in anything.–**perfecter** n.–**perfectness** n.

perfection n the act of perfecting; the quality or condition of being perfect; great excellence; faultlessness; the highest degree; a perfect person or thing.

perfectionist n one who demands the highest standard.–**perfectionism** n.

perfectly adv thoroughly, completely; quite well; in a perfect manner.

perfidious adj treacherous, faithless; deceitful.–**perfidiously** adv.–**perfidiousness** n.

perfidy n (pl **perfidies**) breach of faith; treachery.

perforate vt to pierce; to make a hole or row of holes, by boring through. * adj perforated.–**perforatory** adj.–**perforator** n.

perforation n the act of perforating; the condition of being perforated; a hole; a row of holes to facilitate tearing.

perform vti to carry out, do; to put into effect; to act; to execute; to act before an audience; to play a musical instrument.–**performable** adj.–**performing** adj.

performance n the act of performing; a dramatic or musical production; an act or action; (inf) a fuss; the capabilities of a vehicle, aircraft, etc. * adj high-performance.

performer n a person who performs, esp one who entertains an audience.

perfume n a pleasing odor; fragrance; a mixture containing fragrant essential oils and a fixative. * vt to scent; to put perfume on.–**perfumer** n.

perfumery n (pl **perfumeries**) a place where perfume is sold; perfume in general.

perfunctory adj superficial, hasty; done merely as a matter of form, half-hearted; performed carelessly; indifferent.–**perfunctorily** adv.–**perfunctoriness** n.

perhaps adv possibly, maybe.

peril n danger, jeopardy; risk, hazard.–**perilous** adj.–**perilously** adv.

perimeter n a boundary around an area; (math) the curve or line bounding a closed figure; the length of this.–**perimetric** adj.–**perimetry** n.

perineum n the area between the genitals and the anus.–**perineal** adj.

period n a portion of time; menstruation; an interval of time as in an academic day, playing time in a game, etc; an age or era in history, epoch; a stage in life; (gram) the punctuation mark at the end of a sentence, a full stop (.); (astron) a planet's time of revolution.

periodic adj relating to a period; recurring at regular intervals, cyclic; intermittent.–**periodically** adv.–**periodicity** n.

periodical adj periodic. * n a magazine, etc issued at regular intervals.

periodic table n a list of chemical elements tabulated by their atomic number.

periodontics n sing the branch of dentistry dealing with disorders of the gums and tissues around the teeth.–**periodontal** adj.–**periodontist** n.

peripatetic adj itinerant; (teacher) traveling from one school to another.–also n.

peripheral adj incidental, superficial; relating to a periphery; (equipment) for connection to a computer. * n a device such as a printer, scanner, etc used with a computer.–**peripherally** adv.

periphery n (pl **peripheries**) the outer surface or boundary of an area; the outside surface of anything.

periscope n a device with mirrors that enables the viewer to see objects above or around an obstacle or above water, as from a submarine.

perish vi to be destroyed or ruined; to die, esp violently; (rubber, etc) to deteriorate, rot. * vt to cause to rot or perish.

perishable adj liable to spoil or decay. * n something perishable, esp food.–**perishability** n.

peritoneum n (pl **peritoneums, peritonea**) a membrane that lines the walls of the abdomen.–**peritoneal** adj.

peritonitis n inflammation of the peritoneum.–**peritonitic** adj.

perjury n (pl **perjuries**) (law) the crime of giving false witness under oath, swearing to what is untrue.–**perjure** vt.–**perjurer** n.

perk[1] n (usu pl) (inf) a perquisite.

perk[2] vti (usu with up) to recover self-confidence; to become lively or cheerful; to prick up, as of a dog's ears; to smarten up.

perky adj (**perkier, perkiest**) pert, cheeky; lively, jaunty.–**perkily** adv.–**perkiness** n.

perm n a straightening or curling of hair by use of chemicals or heat lasting through many washings. *vt (hair) to give a perm to.–also **permanent wave**.

permafrost n subsoil that is permanently frozen.

permanent adj lasting, or intended to last, indefinitely.–**permanence, permanency** n.–**permanently** adv.

permeable adj admitting the passage of a fluid.–**permeability** n.–**permeably** adv.

permeate vti to fill every part of, saturate; to pervade, be diffused (through); to pass through by osmosis.–**permeation** n.

permissible adj allowable.–**permissibility** n.

permission n authorization; consent.

permissive adj allowing permission; lenient; sexually indulgent.–**permissively** adv.–**permissiveness** n.

permit vti (**permitting, permitted**) to allow to be done; to authorize; to give opportunity. * n a license.–**permitter** n.

permutation n any radical alteration; a change in the order of a series; any of the total number of groupings within a group; an ordered arrangement of a set of objects.–**permutational** adj.

pernicious adj destructive; very harmful.–**perniciously** adv.–**perniciousness** n.

pernickety see **persnickety**.

peroxide n hydrogen peroxide; a colorless liquid used as an antiseptic and as a bleach.

perpendicular adj upright, vertical; (geom) at right angles (to). * n a perpendicular line, position or style.–**perpendicularity** n.–**perpendicularly** adv.

perpetrate vt (something evil, criminal, etc) to do; (a blunder, etc) to commit.–**perpetration** n.–**perpetrator** n.

perpetual adj continuous; everlasting; (plant) blooming continuously throughout the season.–**perpetually** adv.

perpetuate vt to cause to continue; to make perpetual.–**perpetuation** n.–**perpetuator** n.

perpetuity n (pl **perpetuities**) endless duration, eternity; perpetual continuance; an annuity payable forever.

perplex vt to puzzle, bewilder, confuse; to complicate.–**perplexity** n.

perquisite n an expected or promised privilege, gain, or profit incidental to regular wages or salary; a tip, gratuity; something claimed as an exclusive right.–also **perk**.

per se adv by itself; by its very nature, intrinsically.

persecute vt to harass, oppress, esp for reasons of race, religion, etc; to worry persistently.–**persecutor** n.

persecution n a persecuting or being persecuted; unfair or cruel treatment for reasons of race, religion, etc; a time of persecution.

persevere vi to persist, maintain effort, steadfastly, esp in face of difficulties.–**perseverance** n.–**perseveringly** adv.

persist vi to continue in spite of obstacles or opposition; to persevere; to last.–**persistence, persistency** n.–**persister** n.

persistent adj persevering; stubborn.–**persistently** adv.

persnickety adj (inf) fussy, fastidious; over-attentive to detail.–also **pernickety**.

person n (*pl* **persons**) a human being, individual; the body (including clothing) of a human being; (*in a play*) a character; one who is recognized by law as the subject of rights and duties; (*gram*) one of the three classes of personal pronouns and verb forms, referring to the person(s) speaking, spoken to, or spoken of.

persona n (*pl* **personae**) a person; a character in a play, etc; (*pl*) public role or image.

personable adj pleasing in personality and appearance.–**personableness** n.–**personably** adv.

personage n a distinguished person.

personal adj concerning a person's private affairs, or his or her character, habits, body, etc; done in person; (*law*) of property that is movable; (*gram*) denoting person.

personality n (*pl* **personalities**) one's individual characteristics; excellence or distinction of social and personal traits; a person with such qualities; a celebrity.

personalize vt to mark with name, initials, etc; to endow with personal characteristics; to take personally; to personify.–**personalization** n.

personally adv in person; in one's own opinion; as though directed to oneself.

personify vt (**personifying, personified**) to think of, represent, as a person; to typify.–**personification** n.–**personifier** n.

personnel n the employees of an organization or company; the department that hires them.

perspective n objectivity; the art of drawing so as to give an impression of relative distance or solidity; a picture so drawn; relation, proportion, between parts of a subject; vista, prospect. * adj of or in perspective.

perspicacious adj of clear understanding; shrewd; discerning.–**perspicaciously** adv.–**perspicacity** n.

perspiration n the salty fluid excreted on to the surface of the skin, sweat; the act of perspiring.

perspire vti to excrete (moisture) through the pores of the skin to cool the body, to sweat.–**perspiringly** adv.

persuadable, persuasible adj able to be persuaded.–**persuadability, persuasibility** n.

persuade vt to convince; to induce by argument, reasoning, advice, etc.–**persuader** n.–**persuasive** adj.–**persuasively** adv.–**persuasiveness** n.

persuasion n the act of persuading; a conviction or opinion; a system of religious beliefs; a group adhering to such a system.

pert adj impudent, cheeky; sprightly.–**pertly** adv.–**pertness** n.

pertain vi to belong to; to be appropriate to; to have reference to.

pertinacious adj persistent; unyielding; obstinate.–**pertinacity, pertinaciousness** n.

pertinent adj relevant, apposite; to the point.–**pertinence** n.–**pertinently** adv.

perturb vt to trouble; to agitate; to throw into confusion; (*astron*) to cause to undergo perturbation.–**perturbable** adj.–**perturbably** adv.–**perturbingly** adv.

perturbation n the state of being troubled, mental agitation.

peruse vt to read carefully, to examine.–**perusal** n.

pervade vt to permeate or spread through; to be rife among.–**pervasion** n.–**pervasive** adj.

perverse adj deviating from right or truth; persisting in error; wayward; contrary.–**perversely** adv.–**perverseness** n.–**perversity** n.

perversion n an abnormal way of obtaining sexual gratification, eg sadism; a perverted form or usage of something.

pervert vt to corrupt; to misuse; to distort. * n a person who is sexually perverted.–**perverter** n.–**pervertible** adj.

perverted adj wrong; harmful; unnatural; sexually deviant.–**pervertedly** adv.

pesky adj (**peskier, peskiest**) (*inf*) troublesome, annoying.

pessary n (*pl* **pessaries**) (*med*) a surgical appliance or suppository inserted into the vagina.

pessimism n a tendency to see in the world what is bad rather than good; a negative outlook that always expects the worst.–**pessimist** n.–**pessimistic** adj.–**pessimistically** adv.

pest n anything destructive, esp a plant or animal detrimental to man as rats, flies, weeds, etc; a person who pesters or annoys.

pester vt to annoy or irritate persistently.–**pesterer** n.

pesticide n any chemical for killing pests.–**pesticidal** adj.

pestilence n an outbreak of a fatal epidemic disease; anything regarded as harmful.

pestilent adj irritating; likely to cause a fatal epidemic.–**pestilently** adv.

pestilential adj of the nature of or conveying pestilence; harmful; annoying.–**pestilentially** adv.

pestle n a usu club-shaped tool for pounding or grinding substances in a mortar. * vt to beat, pound, or pulverize with a pestle.

pet n a domesticated animal kept as a companion; a person treated as a favourite. * adj kept as a pet; spoiled, indulged; favorite; particular. * vti (**petting, petted**) to stroke or pat gently; to caress; (*inf*) to kiss, embrace, etc in making love.

petal n any of the leaf-like parts of a flower's corolla.–**petaline** adj.–**petalled** adj.

peter vi (*with* **out**) to come to an end; to dwindle to nothing.

petite adj (*woman*) small and trim in figure.

petition n a formal application or entreaty to an authority; a written demand for action by a government, etc, signed by a number of people. * vti to present a petition to; to ask humbly.–**petitionary** adj.–**petitioner** n.

petrel n a dark-colored sea bird capable of flying far from land.

petrify vti (**petrifying, petrified**) to turn or be turned into stone; to stun or be stunned with fear, horror, etc.–**petrifaction, petrification** n.

petrochemical n any chemical obtained from natural gas or petroleum.

petroleum n a crude oil consisting of hydrocarbons occurring naturally in certain rock strata and distilled to yield gasoline, paraffin, etc.

petty adj (**pettier, pettiest**) trivial; small-minded; minor.–**pettily** adv.–**pettiness** n.

petty officer n a noncommissioned officer in the navy.

petulant adj showing impatience or irritation; bad-humored.–**petulance** n.–**petulantly** adv.

petunia n a plant with funnel-shaped purple or white flowers.

pew n a wooden, bench-like seat in a church, often enclosed; (*sl*) a chair.

pewter n an alloy of tin and lead with a silvery-gray color; dishes, etc, made of pewter.–**pewterer** n.

phalanx n (*pl* **phalanxes, phalanges**) a massed body or rank of people; (*pl* **phalanges**) a bone of a finger or toe.

phallus n (*pl* **phalli, phalluses**) the male reproductive organ.–**phallic** adj.

phantasmagoria, phantasmagory n a series of shifting images, like those seen in a dream.–**phantasmagoric, phantasmagorical** adj.

phantom n a specter or apparition. * adj illusionary.

pharaoh n (*also with* cap) the title of the kings of ancient Egypt.–**pharaonic** adj.

pharmaceutical adj of, relating to pharmacy or drugs. * n a medicinal drug.

pharmaceutics n sing the science of pharmacy.

pharmacist n one licensed to practice pharmacy.

pharmacology n the science dealing with the effects of drugs on living organisms.–**pharmacological** adj.–**pharmacologist** n.

pharmacy n (*pl* **pharmacies**) the preparation and dispensing of drugs and medicines; a drugstore.

pharynx n (*pl* **pharynges, pharynxes**) the cavity leading from the mouth and nasal passages to the larynx and esophagus.

phase n (pl **phases**) an amount of the moon's or a planet's surface illuminated at a given time; a characteristic period in a regularly recurring sequence of events or stage in a development. * vt to do by stages or gradually; (with **out**) (making, using, etc) to stop gradually.–**phasic** adj.

PhD abbr = Doctor of Philosophy.

pheasant n a richly colored game bird.

phenol n carbolic acid.

phenomenal adj perceptible through the senses; remarkable; outstanding.–**phenomenally** adv.

phenomenon n (pl **phenomena, phenomenons**) anything perceived by the senses as a fact; a fact or event that can be scientifically described; a remarkable thing or person.

pheromone n a molecule that functions as a chemical communication signal between individuals of the same species.

phew interj an exclamation of relief, surprise, etc.

phi n the 21st letter of the Greek alphabet.

phial n a small glass bottle; a vial.

philander vi (man) to flirt with women for amusement.–**philanderer** n.

philanthropist n a person who tries to benefit others.

philanthropy n (pl **philanthropies**) love of mankind, esp as demonstrated by benevolent or charitable actions.–**philanthropic, philanthropical** adj.–**philanthropically** adv.

philatelist n a person who collects or studies stamps.

philately n the study and collecting of postage and imprinted stamps; stamp collecting.–**philatelic** adj.–**philatelically** adv.

philharmonic adj loving music.

philistine n a person with no feeling for culture; an uncultured, conventional person. * adj uncultured.–**philistinism** n.

philology n the study, esp comparative, of languages and their history and structure.–**philological** adj.–**philologist, philologer** n.

philosopher n a person who studies philosophy; a person who acts calmly and rationally.

philosophical, philosophic adj of, relating to, or according to philosophy; serene; temperate; resigned.–**philosophically** adv.

philosophy n (pl **philosophies**) the study of the principles underlying conduct, thought, and the nature of the universe; general principles of a field of knowledge; a particular system of ethics; composure; calmness.

phlebitis n (med) an inflammation of a vein.–**phlebitic** adj.

phlegm n a thick mucus discharged from the throat, as during a cold; sluggishness; apathy.

phlegmatic, phlegmatical adj unemotional, composed; sluggish.–**phlegmatically** adv.

phobia n an irrational, excessive, and persistent fear of some thing or situation.–**phobic** adj, n.

phoenix n a mythical bird that set fire to itself and rose from its ashes every 500 years; a symbol of immortality.

phone n, vti (inf) (to) telephone.

phone book n (inf) telephone book.

phone-in n a radio program in which questions or comments by listeners are broadcast.

phonetic adj relating to, or representing, speech sounds.–**phonetically** adv.

phonetics n sing the science concerned with pronunciation and the representation of speech sounds.

phonics n sing a phonetics-based method of teaching reading.–**phonic** adj.

phony, phoney adj (**phonier, phoniest**) (inf) not genuine. * n (pl **phoneys, phonies**) a fake; an insincere person.–**phoniness, phoneyness** n.

phosphate n a compound of phosphorus.–**phosphatic** adj.

phosphorescence n the property of giving off light without noticeable heat, as phosphorus does; such light.–**phosphorescent** adj.

phosphorus n a highly reactive, poisonous nonmetallic element; a phosphorescent substance or body, esp one that glows in the dark.–**phosphorous** adj.

photo n (pl **photos**) a photograph.

photocell n a photoelectric cell.

photochemical adj of or relating to the effect of radiant energy, esp light.

photochemistry n the branch of chemistry concerned with the effect of radiant energy in producing chemical changes; photochemical properties or processes.

photocopy n (pl **photocopies**) a photographic reproduction of written or printed work. * vt (**photocopying, photocopied**) to copy in this way.–**photocopier** n.

photoelectric cell n a cell whose electrical properties are affected by light; any device in which light controls an electric circuit that operates a mechanical device, as for opening doors.– also **photocell**.

photo finish n the finish of a race where the decision on the winner has to be determined by a photograph as the contestants are so close; any race where the winning margin is small.

photogenic adj likely to look attractive in photographs.–**photogenically** adv.

photograph n an image produced by photography.–also **photo**.

photographic adj of or like a photograph; minutely accurate like a photograph; (memory) capable of retaining facts, etc, after reading for only a brief time.–**photographically** adv.

photography n the art or process of recording images permanently and visibly by the chemical action of light on sensitive material, producing prints, slides or film.–**photographer** n.

photojournalism n a form of news reporting in which the story is presented mainly through photographs.–**photojournalist** n.

photosynthesis n (bot) the process by which a green plant manufactures sugar from carbon dioxide and water in the presence of light.–**photosynthetic** adj.–**photosynthetically** adv.

phrasal adj of or consisting of a phrase or phrases.–**phrasally** adv.

phrase n a group of words that does not contain a finite verb but which expresses a single idea by itself; a pointed saying; a high-flown expression; (mus) a short, distinct musical passage. * vt to express orally, put in words; (mus) to divide into melodic phrases.

phrase book n a book containing idiomatic expressions of a foreign language and their translations.

phraseology n (pl **phraseologies**) mode of expression, wording; phrases used by a particular group.–**phraseological** adj.

phrasing n the wording of a speech or a piece of writing; (mus) the division of a melodic line, etc, into musical phrases.

phrenology n the belief that intelligence and ability may be judged from the shape of a person's skull; study of the shape of the skull based on this belief.–**phrenological** adj.–**phrenologist** n.

phylum n (pl **phyla**) a major division of the animal or plant kingdom.

physical adj relating to the world of matter and energy, the human body, or natural science. * n a general medical examination.–**physically** adv.

physical education n education in fitness and cure of the body, stressing athletics and hygiene.

physician n a doctor of medicine.

physicist n a specialist in physics.

physics n the branch of science concerned with matter and energy and their interactions in the fields of mechanics, acoustics, optics, heat, electricity, magnetism, radiation, atomic structure and nuclear phenomena; the physical processes and phenomena of a particular system.

physiognomy n (pl **physiognomies**) the art of judging character from facial features; facial expression, face; physical features generally.—**physiognomic, physiognomical** *adj.*—**physiognomist** *n.*

physiology *n* the science of the functioning and processes of living organisms.—**physiological** *adj.*—**physiologist** *n.*

physiotherapy *n* physical therapy.—**physiotherapist** *n.*

physique *n* bodily structure and appearance; build.

pi *n* the 16th letter of the Greek alphabet; (*math*) the Greek letter (_) used as a symbol for the ratio of the circumference to the diameter of a circle, approx. 3.14159.

pianist *n* a person who plays the piano.

piano *n* (*pl* **pianos**) a large stringed keyboard instrument in which each key operates a felt-covered hammer that strikes a corresponding steel wire or wires.

pianoforte *n* (*pl* **pianofortes**) a piano.

piazza *n* in Italy, a public square; a covered walkway or gallery; a veranda.

piccolo *n* (*pl* **piccolos**) a small shrill flute.

pick *n* a heavy tool with a shaft and pointed crossbar for breaking ground; a tool for picking, such as a toothpick or icepick; a plectrum; right of selection; choice; best (of). * *vti* to break up or remove with a pick; to pluck at; to nibble (at), eat fussily; to contrive; to choose; (*fruit, etc*) to gather; to steal from a pocket; (*lock*) to force open; (*with* **up**) to lift; to acquire; to call for; to recover; (*inf*) to make the acquaintance of casually; to learn gradually; to resume; to give a lift to; to increase speed.

pickax, pickaxe *n* (*pl* **pickaxes**) a pick with a long pointed head for breaking up hard ground, etc.

picket *n* a pointed stake; a patrol or group of men selected for a special duty; a person posted by strikes outside a place of work to persuade others not to enter. * *vt* (**picketing, picketed**) to tether to a picket; to post as a military picket; to place pickets, or serve as a picket (at a factory, etc).

pickle *n* vegetables preserved in vinegar; (*inf*) a plight, mess. * *vt* to preserve in vinegar.

pick-me-up *n* a tonic.

pickpocket *n* a person who steals from pockets.

pick-up *n* the act of picking up; a person or thing picked up; (*elect*) a device for picking up current; the power to accelerate rapidly.

pickup truck *n* a light truck with an enclosed cab and open body.

picnic *n* a usu informal meal taken on an excursion and eaten outdoors; an outdoor snack; the food so eaten; an easy or agreeable task. * *vi* (**picnicking, picnicked**) to have a picnic.—**picnicker** *n.*

pictorial *adj* relating to pictures, painting, or drawing; containing pictures; expressed in pictures; graphic.—**pictorially** *adv.*

picture *n* drawing, painting, photography, or other visual representation; a scene; an impression or mental image; a vivid description; a motion picture. * *vt* to portray, describe in a picture; to visualize.

picturesque *adj* striking, vivid, usually pleasing; making an effective picture.—**picturesquely** *adv.*—**picturesqueness** *n.*

piddling *adj* (*inf*) trifling, insignificant.

pidgin *n* a jargon for trade purposes, using words and grammar from two or more different languages.

pie *n* a baked dish of fruit, meat, etc, with an under or upper crust of pastry, or both.

piebald *adj* covered with patches of two colors. * *n* a piebald horse, etc.

piece *n* a distinct part of anything; a single object; a literary, dramatic, artistic, or musical composition; (*sl*) a firearm; a man in chess or checkers; an opinion, view; a short distance. * *vt* to fit together, join.—**piecer** *n.*

pièce de résistance *n* (*pl* **pièces de résistance**) the most important item or dish.

piecemeal *adv* gradually; bit by bit.

pied *adj* of mixed colors, mottled.

pier *n* a structure supporting the spans of a bridge; a structure built out over water and supported by pillars, used as a landing place, promenade, etc; a heavy column used to support weight.

pierce *vt* to cut or make a hole through; to force a way into; (*fig*) to touch or move. * *vi* to penetrate.

piercing *adj* penetrating; keen; (*cold, pain*) acute.—**piercingly** *adv.*

piety *n* (*pl* **pieties**) religious devoutness; the characteristic of being pious.

pig *n* a domesticated animal with a broad snout and fat body raised for food; a hog; a greedy or filthy person; an oblong casting of metal poured from the smelting furnace; (*sl*) a policeman. * *vi* (**pigging, pigged**) (*sow*) to give birth; (*inf*) to live in squalor.

pigeon *n* a bird with a small head and a heavy body; (*inf*) a person who is easily conned.

pigeonhole *n* a small compartment for filing papers, etc; a category usu failing to reflect actual complexities. * *vt* to file, classify; to put aside for consideration, shelve.

pigeon-toed *adj* having the toes turned inward.

piggy *n* (*pl* **piggies**) a child's name for a young or little pig. * *adj* (**piggier, piggiest**) piggish.

piggyback *n* a ride on the shoulders or back of a person. * *adv* carried on the shoulders or back; transported on top of a larger object.

piggy bank *n* a container for coins, often shaped like a pig.

pigheaded *adj* stupidly stubborn.—**pigheadedly** *adv.*—**pigheadedness** *n.*

piglet *n* a young pig.

pigment *n* paint; a naturally occurring substance used for coloring.—**pigmentary** *adj.*

pigmentation *n* (*biol*) coloration of the tissues of plants and animals caused by pigment; the depositing of pigments by cells.

pigmy *see* **pygmy.**

pigpen *n* a pen for pigs; a dirty hovel.

pigtail *n* a tight braid of hair.—**pigtailed** *adj.*

pike[1] *n* a sharp point or spike; the top of a spear. * *vt* to pierce or kill with a pike.

pike[2] *n* (*pl* **pike, pikes**) a long-snouted fish, important as a food and game fish.

pilaster *n* a rectangular pillar, usu set in a wall.

pile[1] *n* a heap or mound of objects; a large amount; a lofty building; a pyre; (*sl*) a fortune. * *vt* (*with* **up, on**) to heap or stack; to load; to accumulate. * *vi* to become heaped up; (*with* **up, out, on**) to move confusedly in a mass.

pile[2] *n* a vertical beam driven into (the ground) as a foundation for a building, etc. * *vt* to support with piles; to drive piles into.

pile[3] *n* the nap of a fabric or carpet; soft, fine fur or wool.

piledriver *n* a machine for driving in piles.

piles *npl* hemorrhoids.

pile-up *n* an accumulation of tasks, etc; (*inf*) a collision of several vehicles.

pilfer *vti* to steal in small quantities.—**pilferage** *n.*—**pilferer** *n.*

pilgrim *n* a person who makes a pilgrimage.

pilgrimage *n* a journey to a holy place as an act of devotion; any long journey; a life's journey.

pill *n* medicine in round balls or tablet form; (*with cap*) an oral contraceptive.

pillage *n* looting, plunder. * *vti* to plunder, esp during war.—**pillager** *n.*

pillar *n* a slender, vertical structure used as a support or ornament; a column; a strong supporter of a cause.

pillion *n* a seat behind the driver for a passenger on a motorcycle, etc.

pillory *n* (*pl* **pillories**) (*formerly*) stocks in which criminals were put as punishment. * *vt* (**pillorying, pilloried**) to expose to public scorn and ridicule.

pillow *n* a cushion that supports the head during sleep; something that supports to equalize or distribute pressure. * *vti* to rest on, serve as, a pillow.

pillowcase n a removable cover for a pillow.

pilot n a person who operates an aircraft; one who directs ships in and out of harbor; a guide; a television show produced as a sample of a proposed series. * vt to direct the course of, act as pilot; to lead or guide.

pilot light n a burning gas flame used to light a larger jet; an electric indicator light.

pimento n (pl **pimentos**) allspice; a pimiento.

pimiento n a sweet red pepper (capsicum) used in salads and cooked dishes.

pimp n a prostitute's agent.–also vt.

pimple n a small, raised, inflamed swelling of the skin.–**pimply** adj.

PIN abbr = personal identification number (issued by a bank to a customer to validate electronic transactions).

pin n a piece of metal or wood used to fasten things together; a small piece of pointed wire with a head; an ornament or badge with a pin or clasp for fastening to clothing. * vt (**pinning, pinned**) to fasten with a pin; to hold, fix; (with **down**) to get (someone) to commit himself or herself as to plans, etc; (a fact, etc) to establish.

pincers npl a tool with two handles and jaws used for gripping and drawing out nails, etc; a grasping claw, as of a crab.

pinch vti to squeeze or compress painfully; to press between the fingers; to nip. * n a squeeze or nip; what can be taken up between the finger and thumb, a small amount; a time of stress; an emergency.

pinched adj appearing to be squeezed; drawn by cold or stress.

pincushion n a pad for holding pins.

pine[1] n an evergreen coniferous tree with long needles and well-formed cones; a tree of the pine family; its wood.

pine[2] vi to languish, waste away through longing or mental stress; (with **for**) to yearn.

pineapple n a tropical plant; its juicy, fleshy, yellow fruit.

ping n a high-pitched ringing sound. * vti to strike with a ping, emit a ping.–**pinger** n.

ping-pong n a name for table tennis; (with caps) (trademark) table tennis equipment.

pinion n the outer joint of a bird's wing; a wing feather. * vt to cut off a pinion; to bind arms to sides, restrain.

pink n any of various garden plants with a fragrant flower, including carnations; a pale red color. * adj pink-colored.

pinkie, pinky n (pl **pinkies**) the little finger on the human hand.

pinnacle n a slender tower crowning a roof, etc; a rocky peak of a mountain; the highest point, climax.

pinpoint vt to locate or identify very exactly.

pinprick n a small puncture as made by a pin; a trivial annoyance.

pins and needles npl a tingling feeling in the fingers, toes, etc, caused by impeded blood circulation returning to normal; (with **on**) in an anxious or expectant state.

pinstripe n a very narrow stripe in suit fabrics, etc.

pint n a liquid measure equal to half a quart or one eighth of a gallon (0.47 liters); (inf) a drink of beer.

pinto n (pl **pintos**) a piebald horse.

pin-up n (sl) a photograph of a naked or partially naked person; a person who has been so photographed; a photograph of a famous person.

pioneer n a person who initiates or explores new areas of enterprise, research, etc; an explorer; an early settler; (mil) one who prepares roads, sinks mines, etc. * vti to initiate or take part in the development of; to act as a pioneer (to); to explore (a region).

pious adj devout; religious; sanctimonious.–**piously** adv.–**piousness** n.

pip[1] n the seed in a fleshy fruit, eg apple, orange.

pip[2] n a spot with a numerical value on a playing card, dice, etc; (inf) insignia on a uniform showing an officer's rank; a signal on a radar screen.

pip[3] vi (**pipping, pipped**) (bird) to chirp, to peep.

pipe n a tube of wood, metal etc for making musical sounds; (pl) the bagpipes; a stem with a bowl for smoking tobacco; a long tube or hollow body for conveying water, gas, etc. * vt to play on a pipe; (gas, water, etc) to convey by pipe; to lead, summon with the sound of a pipe(s); to trim with piping.

pipeline n a pipe (often underground) used to convey oil, gas, etc; a direct channel for information; the processes through which supplies pass from source to user.

piper n a person who plays a pipe, esp bagpipes.

pipette, pipet n a hollow glass tube into which liquids are sucked for measurement.

piping n a length of pipe, pipes collectively; a tube-like fold of material used to trim seams; a strip of icing, cream, for decorating cakes, etc; a high-pitched sound. * adj making a high-pitched sound.

piping hot adj very hot.

pipsqueak n (inf) a contemptible or insignificant person.

piquant adj strong-tasting; pungent, sharp; stimulating.–**piquancy** n.–**piquantly** adv.

pique n resentment, ill-feeling. * vt (**piquing, piqued**) to cause resentment in; to offend.

piracy n (pl **piracies**) robbery at sea; the hijacking of a ship or aircraft; infringement of copyright; unauthorized use of patented work.

piranha n a small voracious freshwater fish of tropical America with sharp teeth and a strong jaw.

pirate n a person who commits robbery at sea; a hijacker; one who infringes copyright. * vti to take by piracy; to publish or reproduce in violation of a copyright.–**piratical, piratic** adj.

pirouette n a spin on the toes in ballet.–also vi.

Pisces n the Fishes, in astrology the twelfth sign of the zodiac, operative from 19 February–20 March.–**Piscean** adj, n.

pistachio n (pl **pistachios**) a tree found in Mediterranean countries and West Asia; the edible nut of this tree.

piste n a ski trail of packed snow.

pistol n a small, short-barreled handgun. * vt (**pistoling, pistoled** or **pistolling, pistolled**) to shoot with a pistol.

piston n a disc that slides to and fro in a close-fitting cylinder, as in engines, pumps.

pit n a deep hole in the earth; a (coal) mine; a scooped-out place for burning something; a sunken or depressed area below the adjacent floor area; a space at the front of the stage for the orchestra; the area in a securities or commodities exchange in which members do the trading; the scar left by smallpox, etc; the stone of a fruit; a place where racing cars refuel. * vti (**pitting, pitted**) to set in competition; to mark or become marked with pits; to make a pit stop.

pitch[1] vti (tent, etc) to erect by driving pegs, stakes, etc, into the ground; to set the level of; (mus) to set in key; to express in a style; to throw, hurl; to fall heavily, plunge, esp forward. * n a throw; height, intensity; a musical tone; a place where a street trader or performer works; distance between threads (of a screw); amount of slope; a sound wave frequency; a sports field; sales talk.

pitch[2] n the black, sticky substance from distillation of tar, etc; any of various bituminous substances. * vt to smear with pitch.

pitch-black adj black, or extremely dark.

pitchblende n a black mineral, composed largely of uranium oxide, that also yields radium.

pitch-dark adj completely dark.

pitcher n a large water jug; (baseball) the player who pitches the ball.

pitchfork n a long-handled fork for tossing hay, etc. * vt to lift with this; to thrust suddenly or willy-nilly into.

pitfall n concealed danger; unexpected difficulty.

pith n the soft tissue inside the rind of citrus fruits; the gist, essence; importance.–**pithy** adj.–**pithily** adv.–**pithiness** n.

pitiable adj deserving pity, lamentable, wretched.–**pitiableness** n.–**pitiably** adv.

pitiful adj causing pity, touching; contemptible, paltry.–**pitifully** adv.–**pitifulness** n.

pitiless *adj* without pity, ruthless.–**pitilessly** *adv.*–**pitilessness** *n.*

pittance *n* a very small quantity or allowance of money.

pituitary *adj* of or pertaining to the pituitary gland. * *n* (*pl* **pituitaries**) the pituitary gland.

pituitary gland *n* a ductless gland at the base of the brain that affects growth and sexual development.

pity *n* (*pl* **pities**) sympathy with the distress of others; a cause of grief; a regrettable fact. * *vt* (**pitying, pitied**) to feel pity for.–**pityingly** *adv.*

pivot *n* a pin on which a part turns, fulcrum; a key person upon whom progress depends; a cardinal point or factor. * *vt* to turn or hinge (on) a pivot; to attach by a pivot. * *vi* to run on, or as if on, a pivot.–**pivotal** *adj.*

pixel *n* any of the tiny units that form an image (as on a television screen, computer monitor).

pixie, pixy *n* (*pl* **pixies**) a fairy or elf.

pizza *n* a baked dough crust covered with cheese, tomatoes, etc.

pizzeria *n* a pizza restaurant.

placard *n* a poster or notice for public display.

placate *vt* to appease; to pacify.–**placation** *n.*–**placatory** *adj.*

place *n* a locality, spot; a town or village; a building, residence; a short street, a square; space, room; a particular point, part, position, etc; the part of space occupied by a person or thing; a position or job; a seat; rank, precedence; a finishing position in a race. * *vt* to put; to put in a particular place; to find a place or seat for; to identify; to estimate; to rank; (*order*) to request material from a supplier. * *vi* to finish second or among the first three in a race.

placebo *n* (*pl* **placebos, placeboes**) something harmless given by a doctor to fool a patient into thinking he is undergoing treatment.

placement *n* a placing or being placed; location or arrangement.

place name *n* the name of a geographical locality.

placenta *n* (*pl* **placentas, placentae**) the organ in the uterus of a female mammal that nourishes the fetus.–**placental** *adj.*

placid *adj* calm, tranquil.–**placidity** *n.*–**placidly** *adv.*

plagiarism *n* the act of stealing from another author's work, literary theft; that which is plagiarized.–**plagiarist** *n.*–**plagiaristic** *adj.*

plagiarize *vt* to appropriate writings from another author.–**plagiarizer** *n.*

plague *n* a highly contagious and deadly disease; (*inf*) a person who is a nuisance. * *vt* (**plaguing, plagued**) to afflict with a plague; (*inf*) to annoy, harass.

plaid *n* a long wide piece of woolen cloth used as a cloak in Highland dress; cloth with a tartan or checkered pattern.

plain *adj* level, flat; understandable; straightforward; manifest, obvious; blunt; unadorned; not elaborate; not colored or patterned; not beautiful; ugly; pure; unmixed. * *n* a large tract of level country.–**plainness** *n.*

plain clothes *npl* ordinary clothes, not uniform, as worn by a policeman on duty.–*also adj.*

plainly *adv* clearly, intelligibly.

plaintiff *n* (*law*) a person who brings a civil action against another.

plaintive *adj* sad, mournful.–**plaintively** *adv.*–**plaintiveness** *n.*

plait *n* intertwined strands of hair, straw, etc; a pigtail. * *vti* (**plaiting, plaited**) to twist strands (of hair) together into a plait.

plan *n* a scheme or idea; a drawing to scale of a building; a diagram, map; any outline or sketch. * *vti* (**planning, planned**) to make a plan of; to design; to arrange beforehand, intend; to make plans.

plane[1] *n* a tall tree with large broad leaves.

plane[2] *n* a tool with a steel blade for smoothing level wooden surfaces. * *vt* to smooth with a plane.

plane[3] *n* any level or flat surface; a level of attainment; one of the main supporting surfaces of an airplane; an airplane. * *adj* flat or level. * *vi* to fly while keeping the wings motionless; to skim across the surface of water; to travel by airplane.

planet *n* a celestial body that orbits the sun or other star.

planetarium *n* (*pl* **planetariums, planetaria**) a machine used to exhibit the planets, their motions around the sun and their relative distances and magnitudes; a building for housing this instrument; a model of the solar system.

planetary *adj* (*astrol*) under the influence of one of the planets; terrestrial; wandering, erratic.

plank *n* a long, broad, thick board; one of the policies forming the platform of a political party. * *vt* to cover with planks.

plankton *n* the microscopic organisms that float on seas, lakes, etc.

planner *n* a person who plans; in UK, an official who plans architectural development and land use.–**planning** *n.*

plant *n* a living organism with cellulose cell walls, which synthesizes its food from carbon dioxide, water and light; a soft-stemmed organism of this kind, as distinguished from a tree or shrub; the machinery, buildings, etc of a factory, etc; (*sl*) an act of planting; (*sl*) something or someone planted. * *vt* (**seeds, cuttings**) to put into the ground to grow; to place firmly in position; to found or establish; (*sl*) to conceal something in another's possession in order to implicate.

plantain *n* a tropical broad-leaved tree yielding an edible fruit similar to the banana.

plantation *n* a large cultivated planting of trees; an estate where tea, rubber, cotton, etc, is grown, cultivated by local labor.

planter *n* a person who owns or runs a plantation; a machine that plants; a decorative container for plants.

plaque *n* an ornamental tablet or disc attached to or inserted in a surface; a film of mucus on the teeth that harbors bacteria.

plasma *n* the colourless liquid part of blood, milk, or lymph; a collection of charged particles resembling gas but conducting electricity and affected by a magnetic field.

plaster *n* an adhesive dressing for cuts; a mixture of sand, lime and water that sets hard and is used for covering walls and ceilings. * *vt* to cover as with plaster; to apply like a plaster; to make lie smooth and flat; to load to excess.–**plasterer** *n.*

plaster cast *n* a rigid dressing of gauze impregnated with plaster of Paris; a sculptor's model in plaster of Paris.

plaster of Paris *n* gypsum and water made into a quick-setting paste.

plastic[1] *adj* able to be molded; pliant; made of plastic; (*art*) relating to modeling or molding. * *n* any of various nonmetallic compounds, synthetically produced, that can be molded, cast, squeezed, drawn, or laminated into objects, films, or filaments.

plastic[2] *n* colloquial term for charge cards, store cards, credit cards etc. used to pay for goods and services instead of cash.

plasticity *n* the ability to be molded or altered; the ability to retain a shape attained by pressure deformation.

plastic surgery *n* surgery to repair deformed or destroyed parts of the body.

plate *n* a flat sheet of metal on which an engraving is cut; an illustration printed from it; a full-page illustration separate from text; a sheet of metal photographically prepared with text, etc, for printing from; a sheet of glass with sensitized film used as a photographic negative; a trophy as prize at a race; a coating of metal on another metal; a flat shallow dish from which food is eaten; a helping of food; the part of a denture that fits the palate; (*inf*) a denture. * *vt* (*a metal*) to coat with a thin film of another metal; to cover with metal plates.

plateau *n* (*pl* **plateaus, plateaux**) a flat, elevated area of land; a stable period; a graphic representation showing this.

plated *adj* coated with metal, esp silver or gold.

plate glass *n* rolled, ground, and polished sheet glass.

platelet *n* a small disk-shaped cell in the blood involved in the process of blood clotting.

platform *n* a raised floor for speakers, musicians, etc; a stage; a place or opportunity for public discussion; the raised area next to a rail line where passengers board trains; a statement of political aims.

plating n the act or process of plating; a thin coating of metal; a coating of metal plates.

platinum n a valuable, silvery-white metal used for jewelry, etc.

platinum-blond adj (hair) silvery blond. * n someone with hair of this color.–**platinum-blonde** nf.

platitude n a dull truism; a commonplace remark.–**platitudinous** adj.

platonic adj (love) spiritual and free from physical desire.–**platonically** adv.

platoon n a military unit divided into squads or sections.

platter n an oval flat serving dish.

platypus n (pl **platypuses**) a small aquatic egg-laying mammal of Australia and Tasmania, with webbed feet, a bill like a duck's, dense fur, and a broad flat tail.–also **duck-billed platypus**.

plaudit n (usu pl) a commendation; a round of applause.

plausible adj apparently truthful or reasonable.–**plausibility** n.–**plausibly** adv.

play vi to amuse oneself (with toys, games, etc); to act carelessly or trifle (with somebody's feelings); to gamble; to act on the stage or perform on a musical instrument; (light) to flicker, shimmer; (water) to discharge or direct on. * vt to participate in a sport; to be somebody's opponent in a game; to perform a dramatic production; (instrument) to produce music on; (hose) to direct; (fish) to give line to; to bet on. * n fun, amusement; the playing of, or manner of playing, a game; the duration of a game; a literary work for performance by actors; gambling; scope, freedom to move.–**playable** adj.

playact vi to behave affectedly or overdramatically; to make believe, pretend; to act in a play.–**playacting** n.–**playactor** n.

playback n the act of reproducing recorded sound or pictures, esp soon after they are made; a mechanism in an audio or video recorder for doing this.–also vt.

playboy n a person who lives for pleasure.

player n a person who plays a specified game or instrument; an actor.

playful adj full of fun; humorous; sportive; fond of sport or amusement.–**playfully** adv.–**playfulness** n.

playground n an area outdoors for children's recreation.

playhouse n a theater.

playing card n one of a set of 52 cards used for playing games, each card having an identical pattern on one side and its own symbol on the reverse.

playing field n a place for playing sport.

playmate n a friend in play.

playpen n a portable usu collapsible enclosure in which a young child may be left to play safely.

plaything n a toy; a thing or person treated as a toy.

playtime n a time for recreation, esp at a school.

playwright n a writer of plays.

plaza n a public square in a town or city.

plea n (law) an answer to a charge, made by the accused person; a request; an entreaty.

plead vti (**pleading, pleaded, plead** or **pled**) to beg, implore; to give as an excuse; to answer (guilty or not guilty) to a charge; to argue (a law case).–**pleadable** adj.–**pleader** n.

pleading n advocacy of a cause in a court of law; one of the allegations and counter allegations made alternately, usu in writing, by the parties in a legal action; the act or instance of making a plea; a sincere entreaty. * adj begging, imploring.–**pleadingly** adv.

pleasant adj agreeable; pleasing.–**pleasantly** adv.–**pleasantness** n.

pleasantry n (pl **pleasantries**) a polite or amusing remark.

please vti to satisfy; to give pleasure to; to be willing; to have the wish. * adv as a word to express politeness or emphasis in a request; an expression of polite affirmation.–**pleased** adj.–**pleasing** adj.–**pleasingly** adv.

pleasurable adj gratifying, delightful.–**pleasurably** adv.

pleasure n enjoyment, recreation; gratification of the senses; preference.

pleat n a double fold of cloth, etc pressed or stitched in place. * vt to gather into pleats.

plebeian adj relating to the common people; base, vulgar. * n one of the common people.

plebiscite n a direct vote of the electorate on a political issue such as annexation, independent nationhood, etc.

plectrum n (pl **plectra, plectrums**) a thin piece of metal, etc for plucking the strings of a guitar, etc.

pledge n a solemn promise; security for payment of a debt; a token or sign; a toast. * vt to give as security; to pawn; to bind by solemn promise; to drink a toast to.

plenary adj full, complete; (assembly, etc) attended by all the members.–**plenarily** adv.

plentiful adj abundant, copious.–**plentifully** adv.–**plentifulness** n.

plenty n an abundance; more than enough; a great number. * adv (sl) quite.

plethora n overabundance, glut; (med) an excess of red corpuscles in the blood.–**plethoric** adj.

pleurisy n inflammation of the membranes enclosing the lungs.–**pleuritic** adj.

pliable adj easily bent or molded; easily influenced.–**pliability** n. –**pliably** adv.

pliant adj easily bent or influenced; supple; flexible, yielding.–**pliancy** n.–**pliantly** adv.

pliers npl a tool with hinged arms and jaws for cutting, shaping wire.

plight[1] n a dangerous situation; a predicament.

plight[2] vt to pledge, vow solemnly. * n a pledge; an engagement.–**plighter** n.

plod vi (**plodding, plodded**) to walk heavily and slowly, to trudge; to work or study slowly and laboriously.–**plodder** n.–**ploddingly** adv.

plop vti (**plopping, plopped**) to fall into water without a splash. * n the sound of this. * adv with a plop.

plot n a small piece of land; a secret plan or conspiracy; the story in a play or novel, etc. * vt (**plotting, plotted**) to conspire; (route) to mark on a map; (points) to mark (on a graph) with coordinates.–**plotter** n.

plow, plough n a farm implement for turning up soil; any implement like this, as a snowplow. * vt to cut and turn up with a plow; to make a furrow (in), to wrinkle; to force a way through; to work at laboriously; (with **into**) to run into; (with **back**) to reinvest.

plowman, ploughman n (pl **plowmen, ploughmen**) one who plouws; a farmworker.

plowshare, ploughshare n the part of a plow which cuts the soil.

ploy n a tactic or maneuver to outwit an opponent; an occupation or job; an escapade.

pluck vt to pull off or at; to snatch; to strip off feathers; (fruit, flowers, etc) to pick; (person) to remove from one situation in life and transfer to another. * vi to make a sharp pull or twitch. * n a pull or tug; heart, courage; dogged resolution.–**plucker** n.

plucky adj (**pluckier, pluckiest**) brave, spirited.–**pluckily** adv.–**pluckiness** n.

plug n a stopper used for filling a hole; a device for connecting an appliance to an electricity supply; (inf) a free advertisement usu incorporated in other matter. * vti (**plugging, plugged**) to stop up with a plug; (inf) to seek to advertise by frequent repetition; (with **at**) (inf) to work doggedly.

plum n an oval smooth-skinned sweet stone-fruit; a tree bearing it; a reddish-purple color; a choice thing.

plumage n a bird's feathers.

plumb n a lead weight attached to a line, used to determine how deep water is or whether a wall is vertical; any of various weights. * *adj* perfectly vertical. * *adv* vertically; in a direct manner; (*inf*) entirely. * *vt* to test by a plumb line; to examine minutely and critically; to weight with lead; to seal with lead; to supply with or install as plumbing. * *vi* to work as a plumber.

plumber *n* a person who installs and repairs water or gas pipes.

plumbing *n* the system of pipes used in water or gas supply, or drainage; the plumber's craft.

plume *n* a large or ornamental bird's feather; a feathery ornament or thing; something resembling a feather in structure or density. * *vt* (*feathers*) to preen; to adorn with feathers; to indulge (oneself) with an obvious display of self-satisfaction.

plummet *n* a plumb. * *vi* (**plummeting, plummeted**) to fall in a perpendicular manner; to drop sharply and abruptly.

plump[1] *adj* rounded, chubby. * *vti* to make or become plump; to swell.–**plumply** *adv*.–**plumpness** *n*.

plump[2] *vti* to fall, drop or sink, or come into contact suddenly and heavily; (*someone, something*) to favor or give support. * *n* a sudden drop or plunge or the sound of this. * *adv* straight down, straight ahead; abruptly; bluntly.

plunder *vt* to steal goods by force, to loot. * *n* plundering; booty.–**plunderer** *n*.

plunge *vti* to immerse, dive suddenly; to penetrate quickly; to hurl oneself or rush; (*horse*) to start violently forward.

plunger *n* a solid cylinder that operates with a plunging motion, as a piston; a larger rubber suction cup used to free clogged drains.

plural *adj* more than one; consisting of or containing more than one kind or class. * *n* (*gram*) the form referring to more than one person or thing.–**plurally** *adv*.

pluralism *n* the simultaneous holding of more than one office or benefice; a theory that reality is composed of a plurality of entities; a theory that there are at least two levels of ultimate reality; the coexistence in society of people of distinct ethnic, cultural or religious groups, each preserving their own traditions; a doctrine or policy advocating this condition.–**pluralist** *n*.–**pluralistic** *adj*.–**pluralistically** *adv*.

plurality *n* (*pl* **pluralities**) being plural; a majority; a large number; another term for pluralism.

plus *prep* added to; in addition to. * *adj* indicating addition; positive. * *n* the sign (+) indicating a value greater than zero; an advantage or benefit; an extra.

plush *n* a velvet-like fabric with a nap. * *adj* made of plush; (*inf*) luxurious.

plutocracy *n* (*pl* **plutocracies**) government or rule by the wealthy; a wealthy class.–**plutocratic** *adj*.–**plutocratically** *adv*.

plutocrat *n* a person who has power through wealth; a rich person.

plutonium *n* a highly toxic transuranic element used as fuel in nuclear power stations and in nuclear weapons.

ply[1] *vti* (**plying, plied**) to work at diligently and energetically; to wield; to subject to persistently; (*goods*) to sell; to go to and fro, run regularly; to keep busy.

ply[2] *n* (*pl* **plies**) a layer or thickness, as of cloth, plywood, etc; any of the twisted strands in a yarn, etc. * *vt* (**plying, plied**) to twist together.

plywood *n* a building material consisting of several thin layers of wood glued together.

p.m. *abbr* = post meridiem.

PMS *abbr* = premenstrual syndrome.

pneumatic *adj* concerning wind, air, or gases; operated by or filled with compressed air.–**pneumatically** *adv*.

pneumatics *n sing* the science dealing with the mechanical properties of air.

pneumonia *n* acute inflammation of the lungs.–**pneumonic** *adj*.

poach[1] *vt* to cook (an egg without its shell, fish, etc) in or over boiling water.

poach[2] *vti* to catch game or fish illegally; to trespass for this purpose; to encroach on, usurp another's rights, etc; to steal another's idea, employee, etc.–**poacher** *n*.–**poaching** *n*.

pock *n* an eruptive pustule on the skin, esp as a result of smallpox.

pocket *n* a small bag or pouch, esp in a garment, for carrying small articles; an isolated or enclosed area; a deposit (as of gold, water, or gas). * *adj* small enough to put in a pocket. * *vt* to put in one's pocket, to steal; (*ball*) to put in a pocket; to envelop; to enclose; (*money*) to take dishonestly; to suppress.

pocketbook *n* a small folder or case for letters, money, credit cards, etc; a woman's purse, a handbag; monetary resources; a small esp paperback book.

pocketful *n* (*pl* **pocketfuls**) as much as a pocket holds.

pocketknife *n* (*pl* **pocketknives**) a small knife with one or more blades that fold into the handle.

pocket money *n* money for occasional expenses; a child's allowance.

pod *n* a dry fruit or seed vessel, as of peas, beans, etc; a protective container or housing; a detachable compartment on a spacecraft. * *vi* (**podding, podded**) to remove the pod from.

podium *n* (*pl* **podiums, podia**) a platform used by lecturers, etc; a low wall around the arena of an amphitheater.

poem *n* an arrangement of words, esp in meter, often rhymed, in a style more imaginative than ordinary speech; a poetic thing.

poet *n* the writer of a poem; a person with imaginative power and a sense of beauty.–**poetess** *nf*.

poetic, poetical *adj* of poets or poetry; written in verse; imaginative, romantic, like poetry.–**poetically** *adv*.

poetry *n* the art of writing poems; poems collectively; poetic quality or spirit.

pogrom *n* an organized extermination of a minority group.

poignant *adj* piercing; incisive; deeply moving.–**poignancy** *n*.–**poignantly** *adv*.

point *n* a dot or tiny mark used in writing or printing (eg a decimal point, a full stop); a location; a place in a cycle, course, or scale; a unit in scoring or judging; the sharp end of a knife or pin; a moment of time; one of thirty-two divisions of the compass; a fundamental reason or aim; the tip; a physical characteristic; a railroad switch; a unit of size in printing equal to one seventy-second of an inch; a unit used in quoting the prices of stocks, bonds and commodities; a headland or cape. * *vti* to give point to; to sharpen; to aim (at); to extend the finger (at or to); to indicate something; to call attention (to).

point-blank *adj* aimed straight at a mark; direct, blunt.–*also adv*.

pointed *adj* having a point; pertinent; aimed at a particular person or group; conspicuous.–**pointedly** *adv*.–**pointedness** *n*.

pointer *n* a rod or needle for pointing; an indicator; a breed of hunting dog.

pointless *adj* without a point; irrelevant, aimless.–**pointlessly** *adv*.–**pointlessness** *n*.

poise *vt* to balance; to hold supported without motion; (*the head*) to hold in a particular way; to put into readiness. * *vi* to become drawn up into readiness; to hover. * *n* a balanced state; self-possessed assurance of manner; gracious tact; bearing, carriage.

poison *n* a substance that through its chemical action usu destroys or injures an organism; any corrupt influence; an object of aversion or abhorrence. * *vt* to administer poison in order to kill or injure; to put poison into; to influence wrongfully.–**poisoner** *n*.

poison ivy *n* a climbing plant with ivory-colored berries and an acutely irritating oil that causes an intensely itchy skin rash; the rash caused by poison ivy.

poisonous *adj* being or containing poison; toxic; having a harmful influence; (*inf*) unpleasant.–**poisonously** *adv*.–**poisonousness** *n*.

poke *vt* to thrust (at), jab or prod; (*hole, etc*) to make by poking; (*sl*) to hit. * *vi* to jab (at); to pry or search (about or around). * *n* a jab; a prod or nudge; a thrust.

poker[1] n a metal rod for poking or stirring fire.

poker[2] n a card game in which a player bets that the value of his hand is higher than that of the hands held by others.

poker face n an expressionless face, concealing a person's thoughts or feelings.–**poker-faced** adj.

poky, pokey adj (**pokier, pokiest**) small and uncomfortable.–**pokily** adv.–**pokiness** n.

polar adj of or near the North or South Pole; of a pole; having positive and negative electricity; directly opposite.

polar bear n a large creamy-white bear that inhabits arctic regions.

polarity n (pl **polarities**) the condition of being polar; the magnet's property of pointing north; attraction towards a particular object or in a specific direction; (elect) the state, positive or negative, of a body; diametrical opposition; an instance of such opposition.

polarize vt (light waves) to cause to vibrate in a definite pattern; to give physical polarity to; to break up into opposing factions; to concentrate.–**polarizable** adj.–**polarization** n.–**polarizer** n.

Polaroid n (trademark) a transparent material used esp in sunglasses and lamps to prevent glare; a camera that produces a print in seconds.

pole[1] n a long slender piece of wood, metal, etc; a flagstaff. * vt to propel, support with a pole.

pole[2] n either end of an axis, esp of the earth; either of two opposed forces, parts, etc, as the ends of a magnet, terminals of a battery, etc; either of two opposed principles.

poleax, poleaxe n a long-handled battle ax; a type of ax used to slaughter cattle. * vt to hit or knock down with, or as if with, such an ax.

polecat n (pl **polecats, polecat**) a small, dark-brown animal, found in Europe, North Africa and Asia, related to the weasel and known for its unpleasant smell.

polemic n a controversy or argument over doctrine; strong criticism; a controversialist. * adj involving dispute; controversial (–also **polemical**).–**polemically** adv.–**polemicist** n.

polemics n sing the art of controversial debate. * adj disputatious, controversial.

pole vault n a field event in which competitors jump over a high bar using a long flexible pole.–**pole-vault** vi.–**pole-vaulter** n.

police n the government department for keeping order, detecting crime, law enforcement, etc; (pl) the members of such a department; any similar organization. * vt to control, protect, etc with police or a similar force.

policeman n (pl **policemen**) a member of a police force.–**policewoman** nf (pl **policewomen**).

police officer n a policeman or policewoman.

policy[1] n (pl **policies**) a written insurance contract.

policy[2] n (pl **policies**) political wisdom, statecraft; a course of action selected from among alternatives; a high-level overall plan embracing the general principles and aims of an organization, esp a government.

policyholder n a person who has an insurance policy.

polio n poliomyelitis.

poliomyelitis n an acute infectious virus disease marked by inflammation of nerve cells in the spinal cord, causing paralysis.

polish vti to make or become smooth and shiny by rubbing (with a cloth and polish); to give elegance or culture to; (with **off**) (inf) to finish completely. * n smoothness; elegance of manner; a finish or gloss; a substance, such as wax, used to polish.–**polisher** n.

polished adj accomplished; smoothly or professionally done or performed; (rice) having had the husk removed.

polite adj courteous; well-bred; refined.–**politely** adv.–**politeness** n.

politic adj expedient; shrewdly tactful; prudent.

political adj relating to politics or government; characteristic of political parties or politicians.–**politically** adv.

political correctness n a movement aimed at removing discrimination against women, ethnic minorities, gays and lesbians, etc by combating sexist and racist language or policies in education, the arts, media and government.–**politically correct** adj.

politician n a person engaged in politics, often used with implications of seeking personal or partisan gain, scheming, etc.

politics n (sing or pl) the science and art of government; political activities, beliefs or affairs; factional scheming for power.

polka n a lively dance; the music for this. * vi to dance the polka.

polka dot n any of a pattern of small round dots forming a pattern on cloth.

poll n a counting, listing, etc of persons, esp of voters; the number of votes recorded; an opinion survey; (pl) a place where votes are cast. * vti to receive the votes (of); to cast a vote; to canvass or question in a poll.–**poller** n.

pollen n the yellow dust, containing male spores, that is formed in the anthers of flowers.–**pollinic** adj.

pollinate vti to fertilize by uniting pollen with seed.–**pollination** n.–**pollinator** n.

pollster n a person who conducts a poll or compiles data obtained from a poll.

pollute vt to contaminate with harmful substances; to make corrupt; to profane.–**polluter** n.

pollution n the act of polluting; the state of being polluted; contamination by chemicals, noise, etc.

polo n a game played on horseback by two teams, using a wooden ball and long-handled mallets.

polo shirt n a sports shirt made of a knitted fabric.

poltergeist n a spirit believed to move heavy objects about and to make noises.

polyester n any of a number of synthetic polymeric resins used for adhesives, plastics, and textiles.

polyethylene n a light, plastic, multipurpose synthetic material resistant to moisture and chemicals.–also **polythene**.

polygamist n a person who advocates or practices polygamy.

polygamy n the practice of being married to more than one person at a time.–**polygamous** adj.–**polygamously** adv.

polyglot adj having command of many languages; composed of numerous languages; containing matter in several languages; composed of elements from different languages. * n a person who speaks several languages.

polygon n a closed plane figure bound by three or more straight lines.–**polygonal** adj.

polygraph n an instrument for detecting and measuring involuntary changes in blood pressure, breathing, etc, often used as a lie detector.–**polygraphic** adj.

polyhedron n (pl **polyhedrons, polyhedra**) a solid with many (usu more than six) plane faces.–**polyhedral** adj.

polymath n someone learned in many subjects.

polymer n (chem) a compound that has large molecules composed of many simpler molecules.–**polymeric** adj.–**polymerism** n.

polyp n a small water animal with tentacles at the top of a tube-like body; a growth on mucous membrane.–**polypoid** adj.

polystyrene n a rigid plastic material used for packing, insulating, etc.

polytheism n belief in many gods, or more than one god.–**polytheist** n.–**polytheistic** adj.

polythene see polyethylene.

polyunsaturated adj denoting any of certain plant and animal fats and oils with a low cholesterol content.

polyurethane n any of various polymers that are used esp in flexible and rigid foams, resins, etc.

pomander n an aromatic ball or powder formerly carried for its pleasant smell or as protection against infection; a container for this.

pomegranate n an edible fruit with many seeds; the widely cultivated tropical tree bearing it.

pommel n the rounded, upward-projecting front part of a saddle; a knob on the hilt of a sword. * vt (**pommeling, pommeled** or **pommelling, pommelled**) to pummel.

pomp n stately ceremony; ostentation.

pompon, pompom n an ornamental ball or tuft of fabric strands used on clothing as an ornament.

pompous adj stately; self-important.–**pomposity** n.–**pompously** adv.–**pompousness** n.

poncho n (pl **ponchos**) a blanket-like cloak with a hole in the centre for the head.

pond n a body of standing water smaller than a lake.

ponder vti to think deeply; to consider carefully.

ponderous adj heavy; awkward; dull; lifeless.–**ponderously** adv.–**ponderousness** n.

pone n corn pone; maize bread.

pontiff n the Pope; a bishop.

pontificate vi to speak sententiously, pompously or dogmatically; to officiate at a pontifical mass.–**pontificator** n.

pontoon n a boat or cylindrical float forming a support for a bridge.

pony n (pl **ponies**) a small horse, a bronco, mustang, etc; (inf) a racehorse.

ponytail n a style of arranging hair to resemble a pony's tail.

poodle n a breed of dog of various sizes with a curly coat.

pool[1] n a small pond; a puddle; a small collection of liquid; a swimming pool.

pool[2] n a game played on a billiards table with six pockets; a combination of resources, funds, supplies, people, etc for some common purpose; the parties forming such a combination. * vti to contribute to a common fund, to share.

poop n (naut) the stern of a ship; the raised deck in the stern of a ship.

poor adj having little money, needy; deserving pity, unfortunate; deficient; disappointing; inferior. * n those who have little.–**poorness** n.

poorly adv insufficiently, badly. * adj not in good health.

pop[1] n a short, explosive sound, a shot; any carbonated, nonalcoholic beverage. * vti (**popping, popped**) to make or cause a pop; to shoot; to go or come quickly (in, out, up); (corn, maize) to roast until it pops; to put suddenly; (eyes) to bulge.

pop[2] adj in a popular modern style. * n pop music; pop art; pop culture.

pop[3] n (inf)father; (inf) a name used to address an old man.

pop art n a realistic art style using techniques and subjects from commercial art, comic strips, posters, etc.

popcorn n a kind of corn or maize, which when heated pops or puffs up.

pope n the bishop of Rome, head of the RC Church.–**popedom** n.

pop-eyed adj with bulging eyes; (fig) astonished.

poplar n a slender, quick-growing tree of the willow family.

poplin n a sturdy corded fabric.

poppy n (pl **poppies**) an annual or perennial plant with showy flowers, one of which yields opium; a strong reddish color.

populace n the common people; the masses; all the people in a country, region, etc.

popular adj of the people; well liked; pleasing to many people; easy to understand.–**popularly** adv.

popularity n the condition or quality of being popular.

popularize vt to make popular; to make generally accepted or understood.–**popularization** n.–**popularizer** n.

populate vt to inhabit; to supply with inhabitants.

population n all the inhabitants or the number of people in an area.

populist n an advocate of populism; one who claims to represent the people.–**populism** n.

populous adj densely inhabited.–**populously** adv.–**populousness** n.

porcelain n a hard, white, translucent variety of ceramic ware. * adj made of porcelain.–**porcellaneous** adj.

porch n a covered entrance to a building; an open or enclosed gallery or room on the outside of a building.

porcupine n a large rodent covered with protective quills.

pore[1] n a tiny opening, as in the skin, plant leaves, stem, etc, for absorbing and discharging fluids.

pore[2] vti (with over) to look with steady attention; to study closely.

pork n the flesh of a pig used as food.

porno n (sl) pornography–also **porn**. * adj pornographic.

pornography n writings, pictures, films, etc, intended primarily to arouse sexual desire.–**pornographer** n.–**pornographic** adj.–**pornographically** adv.

porous adj having pores; able to absorb air and fluids, etc.–**porously** adv.–**porousness** n.

porphyry n (pl **porphyry**) a reddish igneous rock, containing crystals of feldspar.

porpoise n (pl **porpoise, porpoises**) any of several small whales, esp a black blunt-nosed whale of the north Atlantic and Pacific; any of several bottle-nosed dolphins.

porridge n a thick food, usu made by boiling oats or oatmeal in water or milk.

port[1] n a harbor; a town with a harbor where ships load and unload cargo; airport; a place where goods may be cleared through customs.

port[2] n a porthole; an opening, as in a valve face, for the passage of steam, etc; a hole in an armored vehicle for firing a weapon; a circuit in a computer for inputting or outputting data.

port[3] n the left of an aircraft or ship looking forward.–also adj.

port[4] n a strong, sweet, fortified dark red wine.

portable adj capable of being carried or moved about easily.–**portability** n.

portal n an impressive gate or doorway.

portend vt to give warning of, to foreshadow.

portent n an omen, warning.

portentous adj ominous; pompous, self-important.–**portentously** adv.–**portentousness** n.

porter n a person who carries baggage, etc, for hire at a station, airport, etc; a railroad attendant for passengers.

portfolio n (pl **portfolios**) a flat case for carrying papers, drawings, etc; a collection of work; a list of stocks, shares, etc.

porthole n an opening (as a window) with a cover or closure esp in the side of a ship or aircraft; a port through which to shoot; an opening for intake or exhaust of a fluid.

portico n (pl **porticoes, porticos**) a covered walkway with columns supporting the roof.

portion n a part, a share, esp an allotted part; a helping of food; destiny. * vt to share out.

portly adj (**portlier, portliest**) dignified; stout.–**portliness** n.

portrait n a painting, photograph, etc, of a person, esp of the face; (of person) a likeness; a vivid description.

portraitist n a maker of portraits by painting, photography, etc.

portraiture n the drawing of portraits; a portrait; a description in words; portraits collectively.

portray vt to make a portrait of; to depict in words; to play the part of in a play, movie, etc.–**portrayable** adj.–**portrayal** n.–**portrayer** n.

pose n a position or attitude, esp one held for an artist or photographer; an attitude deliberately adopted for effect. * vti to propound, assert; to assume an attitude for effect; to sit for a painting, photograph; to set oneself up (as).

poser n a person who poses.

posh adj (inf) elegant; fashionable.

position n place, situation; a position occupied; posture; a job; state of affairs; point of view. * vt to place or locate.

positive adj affirmative; definite; sure; marked by presence, not absence, of qualities; expressed clearly, or in a confident manner;

constructive; empirical; (*elect*) charged with positive electricity; (*math*) greater than zero, plus; (*photog*) having light, shade, color as in the original. * *n* a positive quality or quantity; a photographic print made from a negative.

positively *adv* in a positive way; decidedly.

positiveness *n* the condition or quality of being positive; confidence; certainty.

positivism *n* a philosophy recognizing only matters of fact and experience; the quality of being positive.–**positivist** *n, adj.*–**positivistic** *adj.*–**positivistically** *adv.*

posse *n* a body of people summoned by a sheriff to assist in keeping the peace, etc.

possess *vt* to own, have, keep; to dominate or control the mind of.–**possessor** *n.*–**possessory** *adj.*

possessed *adj* owned; controlled as if by a demon.

possession *n* ownership; something possessed; (*pl*) property.

possessive *adj* of or indicating possession; (*gram*) denoting a case, form or construction expressing possession; having an excessive desire to possess or dominate.–**possessively** *adv.*–**possessiveness** *n.*

possibility *n* (*pl* **possibilities**) the state of being possible; a possible occurrence, a contingency.

possible *adj* that may be or may happen; feasible, practicable.–**possibly** *adv.*

possum *n* (*inf*) an opossum.

post[1] *n* a piece of wood, metal, etc, set upright to support a building, sign, etc; the starting or finishing point of a race. * *vt* (*poster, etc*) to put up; to announce by posting notices; (*name*) to put on a posted or published list.

post[2] *n* a fixed position, esp where a sentry or group of soldiers is stationed; a position or job; a trading post; a settlement. * *vt* to station in a given place.

post[3] *vt* to send a letter or parcel; to keep informed.

postage *n* the charge for sending a letter, etc, as represented by stamps.

postcard *n* a card, usu decorative, for sending messages by post; a postal card.

postdate *vt* to write a future date on a letter or cheque.

poster *n* a usu decorative or ornamental printed sheet for advertising.

posterior *adj* later in time or order; at the rear. * *n* the buttocks.–**posteriorly** *adv.*

posterity *n* future generations; all of a person's descendants.

postgraduate *n* a person pursuing study after graduating from a high school or college. * *adj* (*study*) continued after the taking of a degree.

posthaste *adv* with all possible speed.

posthumous *adj* (*child*) born after its father's death; (*award, etc*) given after one's death.–**posthumously** *adv.*

postman *n* (*pl* **postmen**) a mailman.

postmark *n* the post office mark canceling the stamp on a letter by showing the date, place of posting.

postmaster *n* the manager of a post office.

post meridiem = p.m. (Latin for *after noon*).

postmortem *n* an examination of a corpse to determine the cause of death; an autopsy.–*also adj.*

postnatal *adj* occurring immediately after birth.

post office *n* the building where postage stamps are sold and other postal business conducted; a public department handling the transmission of mail.

postpone *vt* to put off, delay to a future date.–**postponable** *adj.*–**postponement** *n.*–**postponer** *n.*

postscript *n* a note added to a letter after completion.

postulant *n* someone making a request; a candidate for admission to a religious order.

postulate *vt* to assume to be true; to demand or claim. * *n* a position taken as self-evident; (*math*) an unproved assumption taken as basic; an axiom.–**postulation** *n.*

posture *n* a pose; a body position; an attitude of mind; an official stand or position. * *vti* to pose in a particular way; to assume a pose.–**postural** *adj.*–**posturer** *n.*

post-viral syndrome *n* the viral condition myalgic encephalomyelitis that affects the nervous system.

posy *n* (*pl* **posies**) a small bunch of flowers.

pot[1] *n* a deep, round cooking vessel; an earthenware or plastic container for plants; a framework for catching fish or lobsters; (*inf*) a large amount (as of money); (*inf*) all the money bet at a single time. * *vb* (**potting, potted**) *vt* to put or preserve in a pot. * *vi* to take a pot shot, shoot.

pot[2] *n* (*sl*) cannabis.

potash *n* potassium carbonate.

potassium *n* a soft silvery-white metallic element.–**potassic** *adj.*

potato *n* (*pl* **potatoes**) a starchy, oval tuber eaten as a vegetable.

potbelly *n* (*pl* **potbellies**) a protruding belly.–**potbellied** *adj.*

potent *adj* powerful; influential; intoxicating; (*a male*) able to have sexual intercourse.–**potency** *n.*–**potently** *adv.*

potentate *n* a person with great power; a ruler; a monarch.

potential *adj* possible, but not yet actual. * *n* the unrealized ability to do something.–**potentiality** *n.*–**potentially** *adv.*

pothole *n* a hole worn in a road by traffic; (*geol*) a deep hole or cave in rock caused by the action of water.

potion *n* a mixture of liquids, such as poison.

potpourri *n* (*pl* **potpourris**) a mixture of scented, dried flower petals; a collection; a medley or miscellany.

potsherd, potshard *n* a piece of broken earthenware.

pot shot *n* a random or easy shot.

potted *adj* in a pot; preserved (in a pot); (*version, history*) abridged.

potter *n* a person who makes earthenware vessels.

pottery *n* (*pl* **potteries**) earthenware vessels; a workshop where such articles are made.

potty *n* (*pl* **potties**) (*inf*) a chamber pot.

pouch *n* a small bag or sack; a bag for mail; a sacklike structure, as that on the abdomen of a kangaroo, etc, for carrying young.–**pouched** *adj.*

poultice *n* a hot moist dressing applied to a sore part of the body.

poultry *n* domesticated birds kept for meat or eggs.

pounce *vi* to swoop or spring suddenly (upon) in order to seize; to make a sudden assault or approach.–*also n.*

pound[1] *n* a unit of weight equal to 16 ounces; a unit of money in the UK and other countries, symbol £.

pound[2] *vt* to beat into a powder or a pulp; to hit hard. * *vi* to deliver heavy blows repeatedly (at or on); to move with heavy steps; to throb; (*with* **away**) to work hard and continuously.–**pounder** *n.*

pound[3] *n* a municipal enclosure for stray animals; a depot for holding impounded personal property until claimed; a place or condition of confinement.

pour *vti* to cause to flow in a stream; to flow continuously; to rain heavily; to serve tea or coffee.–**pourer** *n.*

pout *vti* to push out (the lips); to look sulky. * *n* a thrusting out of the lips; (*pl*) a fit of pique.

poverty *n* the condition of being poor; scarcity.

poverty-stricken *adj* very poor, impoverished.

POW *abbr* = prisoner of war.

powder *n* any substance in tiny, loose particles; a specific kind of powder, esp for medicinal or cosmetic use; fine dry light snow. * *vti* to sprinkle or cover with powder; to reduce to powder.–**powderer** *n.*

powdery *adj* like powder; easily crumbled.

power *n* ability to do something; political, social or financial control or force; a person or state with influence over others; legal force or authority; physical force; a source of energy; (*math*) the result of continued multiplication of a quantity by itself a specified number of times. * *adj* operated by electricity, a fuel engine, etc;

served by an auxiliary system that reduces effort; carrying electricity. * *vt* to supply with a source of power.–**powered** *adj*.

powerful *adj* mighty; strong; influential.–**powerfully** *adv*.–**powerfulness** *n*.

powerhouse *n* a power station; (*inf*) a strong or energetic person, team, etc.

power plant, power station *n* a building where electric power is generated.

powwow *n* an American Indian ceremony (as for invoking victory in war); (*inf*) any conference or get-together. * *vi* to confer, chat.

pox *n* a virus disease marked by pustules.

pp. *abbr* = pages.

PR *abbr* = public relations.

practicable *adj* able to be practiced; possible, feasible.–**practicability** *n*.–**practicably** *adv*.

practical *adj* concerned with action, not theory; workable; suitable; trained by practice; virtual, in effect.

practicality *n* (*pl* **practicalities**) the condition of being practical; a practical feature or aspect.

practical joke *n* a prank intended to embarrass or to cause discomfort.

practically *adv* in a practical manner; virtually.

practice *n* action; habit, custom; repetition and exercise to gain skill; the exercise of a profession. * *vti* to repeat an exercise to acquire skill; to put into practice; to do habitually or frequently; (*profession*) to work at. –**practiced** *adj* acquired by practice; proficient; experienced.

practitioner *n* a person who practices a profession.

pragmatic *adj* practical; testing the validity of all concepts by their practical results.–**pragmatically** *adv*.

pragmatism *n* the judging of events or actions by their results, esp in politics; pragmatic behavior; (*philos*) a theory that judges the truth of a doctrine by the conduct resulting from belief in it.–**pragmatist** *n*.–**pragmatistic** *adj*.

prairie *n* a large area of level or rolling land predominantly in grass; a dry treeless plateau.

prairie dog *n* a burrowing rodent related to the marmot.

praise *vt* to express approval of, to commend; to glorify, to worship. * *vi* to express praise. * *n* commendation; glorification.–**praiser** *n*.

praiseworthy *adj* deserving praise; commendable.–**praiseworthily** *adv*.–**praiseworthiness** *n*.

prance *vi* (*horse*) to spring on the hind legs, bound; (*person*) to walk or ride in a showy manner; to swagger. * *n* a prancing; a caper.–**prancer** *n*.–**prancingly** *adv*.

prank *n* a mischievous trick or joke; a ludicrous act.–**prankster** *n*.

prattle *vti* to talk in a childish manner; to babble. * *n* empty chatter.–**prattler** *n*.

prawn *n* an edible marine shrimp-like crustacean. * *vi* to fish for prawns.–**prawner** *n*.

pray *vti* to offer prayers to God; to implore.

prayer *n* supplication, entreaty, praise or thanks to God; the form of this; the act of praying; (*pl*) devotional services; something prayed for.

preach *vi* to advocate in an earnest or moralizing way. * *vt* to deliver a sermon; (*patience, etc*) to advocate.–**preacher** *n*.

preachy *adj* (**preachier, preachiest**) (*inf*) fond of moralizing or preaching.

preamble *n* an introductory part to a document, speech, or story, stating its purpose.–**preambulary** *adj*.

prearrange *vt* to arrange beforehand.–**prearrangement** *n*.

precancerous *adj* likely to become cancerous.

precarious *adj* dependent on chance; insecure; dangerous.–**precariously** *adv*.–**precariousness** *n*.

precaution *n* a preventive measure; care taken beforehand; careful foresight.–**precautionary** *adj*.

precede *vti* to be, come or go before in time, place, order, rank, or importance.

precedence *n* priority; the right of higher rank.

precedent *n* a previous and parallel case serving as an example; (*law*) a decision, etc, serving as a rule. * *adj* preceding; previous.–**precedented** *adj*.–**precedently** *adv*.

preceding *adj* coming or going before; former.

precept *n* a rule of moral conduct; a maxim; an order issued by a legally constituted authority to a subordinate.

precinct *n* a police district or a subdivision of a voting ward; (*usu pl*) an enclosure between buildings, walls, etc; a limited area; an urban area where traffic is prohibited; (*pl*) environs.

precious *adj* of great cost or value; beloved; very fastidious; affected; thoroughgoing. * *adv* (*sl*) very.–**preciously** *adv*.–**preciousness** *n*.

precious metal *n* gold, silver, or platinum.

precious stone *n* a diamond, emerald, ruby, sapphire, pearl, and sometimes black opal; a gem.

precipice *n* a cliff or overhanging rock face.

precipitate *vti* to throw from a height; to cause to happen suddenly or too soon; to rain; to fall as rain, snow, dew, etc.–**precipitately** *adv*.–**precipitateness** *n*.–**precipitator** *n*.

precipitation *n* the act of precipitating; undue haste; rain, snow, etc; the amount of this.

precipitous *adj* of or like a precipice; sheer, steep.–**precipitously** *adv*.–**precipitousness** *n*.

précis *n* (*pl* **précis**) a summary or abstract. * *vt* to make a précis of.

precise *adj* clearly defined, exact; accurate; punctilious; particular.–**precisely** *adv*.–**preciseness** *n*.

precision *n*. the quality of being precise; accuracy. * *adj* (*machines*) having a high degree of accuracy.

preclude *vt* to rule out in advance; to make impossible.–**preclusion** *n*.–**preclusive** *adj*.

precocious *adj* prematurely ripe or developed.–**precociously** *adv*.–**precociousness** *n*.

precocity *n* the condition of being precocious, precociousness; early development, esp of a child's mind.

preconceive *vt* to form an idea or opinion of before actual experience.

preconception *n* the act of preconceiving; an opinion formed without actual knowledge.

precursor *n* a predecessor; a substance from which another substance is formed.–**precursory** *adj*.

predate *vt* to antedate.

predator *n* a person who preys, plunders or devours; a carnivorous animal.–**predatory** *adj*.

predecease *vt* to die before (another).

predecessor *n* a former holder of a position or office; an ancestor.

predestine *vt* to foreordain; to destine beforehand.

predetermine *vt* to decide beforehand.–**predetermination** *n*.

predicament *n* a difficult or embarrassing situation.

predicate *vt* to state as a quality or attribute; to base (on facts, conditions etc). * *n* (*gram*) that which is stated about the subject.–**predication** *n*.

predict *vt* to foretell; to state (what one believes will happen).–**predictor** *n*.

predictable *adj* able to be predicted or anticipated; lacking originality.–**predictability** *n*.–**predictably** *adv*.

prediction *n* the act of predicting; that which is predicted; a forecast or prophecy.–**predictive** *adj*.–**predictively** *adv*.

predilection *n* partiality, liking for.

predispose *vt* to incline beforehand; (*disease, etc*) to make susceptible to.–**predisposition** *n*.

predominant *adj* ruling over, controlling; influencing.–**predominance, predominancy** *n*.

predominantly *adv* mainly.

predominate *vt* to rule over; to have influence or control over; to prevail; to be greater in number, intensity, etc.–**predomination** *n*.–**predominator** *n*.

pre-eminent, preeminent adj distinguished above others; outstanding.—**pre-eminence, preeminence** n.—**pre-eminently, preeminently** adv.

pre-empt, preempt vt to take action to check other action beforehand; to gain the right to buy (public land) by settling on it; to seize before anyone else can; to replace.—**pre-emptor, preemptor** n.—**pre-emptory, preemptory** adj.

preen vti (birds) to clean and trim the feathers; to congratulate (oneself) for achievement; to groom (oneself); to gloat.—**preener** n.

prefabricate vt (house, etc) to build in standardized sections for shipment and quick assembly; to produce artificially.—**prefabrication** n.—**prefabricator** n.

preface n an introduction or preliminary explanation; a foreword or introduction to a book; a preamble. * vt to serve as a preface; to introduce.—**prefacer** n.—**prefatory** adj.

prefect n a person placed in authority over others; a student monitor in a school; in some countries, an administrative official.—**prefectorial** adj.

prefer vt (**preferring, preferred**) to like better; to promote, advance; to put before a court, etc, for consideration.—**preferrer** n.

preferable adj deserving preference; superior; more desirable.—**preferably** adv.

preference n the act of preferring, choosing, or favoring one above another; that which is chosen or preferred; prior right; advantage given to one person, country, etc, over others.

preferential adj giving or receiving preference.—**preferentialism** n.—**preferentially** adv.

preferment n advancement; promotion to a higher post.

prefix vt to put at the beginning of or before; to put as an introduction. * n a syllable or group of syllables placed at the beginning of a word, affecting its meaning.—**prefixal** adj.—**prefixally** adv.

pregnant adj having a fetus in the womb; significant, meaningful; imaginative; filled (with) or rich (in).—**pregnancy** n.

prehensile adj capable of grasping, esp by wrapping around.—**prehensility** n.

prehistoric, prehistorical adj of the period before written records began; (inf) old-fashioned.—**prehistorically** adv.

prehistory n (pl **prehistories**) events that took place before recorded history; the study of prehistoric events; the history of the earlier background of an incident, etc.—**prehistorian** n.

prejudge vt to pass judgment on before a trial; to form a premature opinion.—**prejudger** n.—**prejudgment, prejudgement** n.

prejudice n a judgment or opinion made without adequate knowledge; bias; intolerance or hatred of other races, etc; (law) injury or disadvantage due to another's action. * vt to affect or injure through prejudice.—**prejudiced** adj.

prejudicial adj causing prejudice; detrimental, damaging.—**prejudicially** adv.

prelate n a church dignity with episcopal authority.—**prelatic** adj.

preliminary adj preparatory; introductory. * n (pl **preliminaries**) an event preceding another; a preliminary step or measure; (in school) a preparatory examination.—**preliminarily** adv.

prelude n an introductory act or event; an event preceding another of greater importance; (mus) a movement which acts as an introduction. * vti to serve as a prelude to, to usher in; to play a prelude.

premarital adj (sex) taking place before marriage.

premature adj occurring before the expected or normal time; too early, hasty.—**prematurely** adv.—**prematurity** n.

premeditate vt (crime, etc) to plan in advance.—**premeditatedly** adv.—**premeditative** adj.—**premeditator** n.

premeditation n deliberation or thought before doing something; (law) the plotting of a crime beforehand, demonstrating intent to commit it.

premier adj principal; first. * n the head of a government, a prime minister.—**premiership** n.

premiere, prèmiere n the first public performance of a play, movie, etc. * vt to give a premiere of. * vi to have a first performance; to appear for the first time as a star performer.

premise n a proposition on which reasoning is based; something assumed or taken for granted (–also **premiss**); (pl) a piece of land and its buildings. * vt to state as an introduction; to postulate; to base on certain assumptions.

premium n a reward, esp an inducement to buy; a periodical payment for insurance; excess over an original price; something given free or at a reduced price with a purchase; a high value or value in excess of expectation. * adj (goods) high quality.

premonition n a foreboding; a feeling of something about to happen.—**premonitory** adj.

prenatal adj before birth.

preoccupy vt (**preoccupying, preoccupied**) to take possession of beforehand; to engross, fill the thoughts of.—**preoccupation** n.—**preoccupied** adj.

preordain vt to ordain beforehand.—**preordination** n.

prepaid see prepay.

preparation n the act of preparing; a preparatory measure; something prepared, as a medicine, cosmetic, etc.

preparatory adj serving to prepare; introductory. * adv by way of preparation; in a preparatory manner.—**preparatorily** adv.

prepare vt to make ready in advance; to fit out, equip; to cook; to instruct, teach; to put together. * vi to make oneself ready.—**preparedly** adv.

prepay vt (**prepaying, prepaid**) to pay in advance.—**prepayment** n.

preponderant adj being greater in number, amount, importance, weight, etc; predominant.—**preponderance, preponderancy** n.—**preponderantly** adv.

preponderate vi to be greater in number, amount, influence, etc; to predominate, prevail; to weigh more.—**preponderation** n.

preposition n a word used before a noun or pronoun to show its relation to another part of the sentence.—**prepositional** adj.

prepossessing adj impressing favorably; attractive.—**prepossessingly** adv.

preposterous adj ridiculous; laughable; absurd.—**preposterously** adv.—**preposterousness** n.

prepuce n the loose skin at the end of the penis.–also **foreskin**.

prerecord vt (radio, TV program) to record in advance for later broadcasting.—**prerecorded** adj.

prerequisite n a condition, etc, that must be fulfilled prior to something else. * adj required beforehand.

prerogative n a special privilege or right.

presage n a foreboding or presentiment; an omen. * vt to foretell; to have a presentiment of.

preschool adj of or for a child between infancy and school age.

prescience n foreknowledge.—**prescient** adj.

prescribe vt to designate; to ordain; (rules) to lay down; (medicine, treatment) to order, advise.—**prescriber** n.

prescription n act of prescribing; (med) a written instruction by a physician for the preparation of a drug.

prescriptive adj prescribing, ordering, advising; based on long use, traditional.—**prescriptively** adv.

presence n being present; immediate surroundings; personal appearance and bearing; impressive bearing, personality, etc; something (as a spirit) felt or believed to be present.

presence of mind n readiness of resource in an emergency, etc; the ability to say the right thing.

present[1] adj being at the specified place; existing or happening now; (gram) denoting action or state now or action that is always true. * n the time being; now; the present tense.

present[2] n a gift.

present[3] vt to introduce someone, esp socially; (a play, etc) to bring before the public, exhibit; to make a gift or award; to show; to perform; (law) to lay a charge before a court; (weapon) to point in a particular direction. * *vi* to present a weapon; to become manifest; to come forward as a patient.

presentable *adj* of decent appearance; fit to go into company.–**presentability** *n*.–**presentably** *adv*.

presentation *n* act of presenting; a display or exhibition; style of presenting; something offered or given; a description or persuasive account.–**presentational** *adj*.

presenter *n* a person who presents someone or something; (*radio, TV*) a person who introduces a show, an announcer.

presentiment *n* a premonition, apprehension, esp of evil.

presently *adv* in a short while, soon.

preservation *n* the act of preserving or securing; a state of being preserved or repaired.

preservationist *n* someone who undertakes or advocates preservation (as of a biological species or a historic landmark).

preservative *adj* preserving. * *n* something that preserves or has the power of preserving, esp an additive.

preserve *vt* to keep safe from danger; to protect; (*food*) to can, pickle, or prepare for future use; to keep or reserve for personal or special use. * *vi* to make preserves; to raise and protect game for sport. * *n* (*usu pl*) fruit preserved by cooking in sugar; an area restricted for the protection of natural resources, esp one used for regulated hunting, etc; something regarded as reserved for certain persons.–**preservable** *adj*.–**preserver** *n*.

preset *vt* (**presetting, preset**) to set (the controls of an electrical device) in advance.

preside *vi* to take the chair or hold the position of authority; to take control or exercise authority.–**presider** *n*.

president *n* the head of state of a republic; the highest officer of a company, club, etc.–**presidency** *n*.–**presidential** *adj*.–**presidentially** *adv*.

press *vt* to act on with steady force or weight; to push against, squeeze, compress, etc; to squeeze the juice, etc from; (*clothes, etc*) to iron; to embrace closely; to force, compel; to entreat; to emphasize; to trouble; to urge on. * *vi* to weigh down; to crowd closely; to go forward with determination. * *n* pressure, urgency, etc; a crowd; a machine for crushing, stamping, etc; a machine for printing; a printing or publishing establishment; the gathering and distribution of news and those who perform these functions; newspapers collectively; any of various pressure devices.

press conference *n* a group interview given to members of the press by a politician, celebrity, etc.

pressing *adj* urgent; calling for immediate attention; importunate. * *n* a number of records made at one time from a master.–**pressingly** *adv*.

press secretary *n* a person officially in charge of relations with the press for a usu prominent public figure.

press-up *n* an exercise involving raising and lowering the body with the arms.

pressure *n* the act of pressing; a compelling force; a moral force; compression; urgency; constraint; (*physics*) force per unit of area. * *vt* to pressurize.

pressure cooker *n* a strong, sealed pan in which food can be cooked quickly by steam under pressure; (*inf*) a situation beset with emotional or social pressure.

pressure group *n* a group of people organized to alert public opinion, legislators, etc, to a particular area of interest.

pressurize *vt* to keep nearly normal atmospheric pressure inside an aircraft, etc, as at high altitudes; to exert pressure on; to attempt to compel, press.–**pressurization** *n*.–**pressurizer** *n*.

prestidigitation *n* sleight of hand.–**prestidigitator** *n*.

prestige *n* standing in the eyes of people; commanding position in people's minds.–**prestigious** *adj*.

presumable *adj* that may be presumed or taken to be true.

presumably *adv* as may be presumed.

presume *vt* to take for granted, suppose. * *vi* to assume to be true; to act without permission; to take liberties; (*with on,* **upon**) to take advantage of.–**presumedly** *adv*.–**presumer** *n*.

presuming *adj* venturing without permission; presumptuous.–**presumingly** *adv*.

presumption *n* a supposition; a thing presumed; a strong probability; effrontery.

presumptive *adj* assumed in the absence of contrary evidence; probable.–**presumptively** *adv*.

presumptuous *adj* tending to presume; bold; forward.–**presumptuously** *adv*.–**presumptuousness** *n*.

presuppose *vt* to assume beforehand; to involve as a necessary prior condition.–**presupposition** *n*.

pretend *vti* to claim, represent, or assert falsely; to feign, make believe; to lay claim (to).

pretended *adj* feigned; ostensible; untrue; insincerely asserted or claimed.–**pretendedly** *adv*.

pretender *n* a person who makes a pretense; a claimant to a title.

pretense, (*Brit*) **pretence** *n* the act of pretending; a hypocritical show; a fraud, a sham.

pretension *n* a false claim; affectation; assumption of superiority.

pretentious *adj* claiming great importance; ostentatious.–**pretentiously** *adv*.–**pretentiousness** *n*.

pretext *n* a pretended reason to conceal a true one; an excuse.

pretty *adj* (**prettier, prettiest**) attractive in a dainty, graceful way. * *adv* (*inf*) fairly, moderately. * *vt* (**prettying, prettied**) (*with* **up**) (*inf*) to make pretty.–**prettily** *adv*.–**prettiness** *n*.

pretzel *n* a hard, brittle, salted biscuit, often formed in a loose knot.

prevail *vi* to overcome; to predominate; to be customary or in force.

prevailing *adj* generally accepted, widespread; predominant.–**prevailingly** *adv*.

prevalent *adj* current; predominant; widely practiced or experienced.–**prevalence** *n*.–**prevalently** *adv*.

prevaricate *vi* to make evasive or misleading statements.–**prevarication** *n*.–**prevaricator** *n*.

prevent *vt* to keep from happening; to hinder.–**preventable, preventible** *adj*.–**preventably, preventibly** *adv*.–**preventer** *n*.

prevention *n* a preventing or being prevented; a hindrance; a preventive.

preventive, preventative *adj* serving to prevent, precautionary. * *n* something used to prevent disease.–**preventively** *adv*.–**preventiveness** *n*.

preview *n* an advance, restricted showing, as of a movie; a showing of scenes from a movie to advertise it. * *vt* to view or show in advance of public presentation; to give a preliminary survey.

previous *adj* coming before in time or order; prior, former.–**previously** *adv*.–**previousness** *n*.

prewar *adj* before a war.

prey *n* an animal killed for food by another; a victim. * *vi* (*with* **on, upon**) to seize and devour prey; (*person*) to victimize; to weigh heavily on the mind.

price *n* the amount, usu in money, paid for anything; the cost of obtaining some benefit; value, worth. * *vt* to set the price of something; to estimate a price; (*with* **out of the market**) to deprive by raising prices excessively.

priceless *adj* very expensive; invaluable; (*inf*) very amusing, odd, or absurd.–**pricelessly** *adv*.

pricey *adj* (**pricier, priciest**) (*inf*) expensive.–*also* **pricy**.

prick *n* a sharp point; a puncture or piercing made by a sharp point; the wound or sensation inflicted; a qualm (of conscience). * *vti* to affect with anguish, grief, or remorse; to pierce slightly; to cause a sharp pain to; to goad, spur; (*the ears*) to erect.

prickle *n* a thorn, spine or bristle; a pricking sensation. * *vti* to feel or cause to feel a pricking sensation.–**prickly** *adj*.

pride *n* feeling of self-worth or esteem; excessive self-esteem; conceit; a sense of one's own importance; a feeling of elation due to success; the cause of this; splendor; a herd (of lions). * *vti* (*reflex*) (*with* **in** or **on**) to be proud of; to take credit for.–**prideful** *adj*.

priest *n* in various churches, a person authorized to perform sacred rites; an Anglican, Eastern Orthodox, or Roman Catholic clergyman ranking below a bishop.

priestess *n* a priest who is a woman; a woman regarded as a leader (as of a movement).

priesthood *n* the office of priest; priests collectively.

prig *n* a smug, self-righteous person.–**priggish** *adj*.–**priggishly** *adv*.–**priggishness** *n*.

prim *adj* (**primmer, primmest**) proper, formal and precise in manner; demure.–**primly** *adv*.–**primness** *n*.

prima ballerina *n* (*pl* **prima ballerinas**) the principal female dancer in a ballet company.

primacy *n* (*pl* **primacies**) the office of primate; the state of being first.

prima donna *n* (*pl* **prima donnas**) the leading female singer in an opera; (*inf*) a temperamental person.

primal *adj* primeval; original; primitive; fundamental.

primarily *adv* mainly.

primary *adj* first; earliest; original; first in order of time; chief; elementary. * *n* (*pl* **primaries**) a person or thing that is highest in rank, importance, etc; a preliminary election at which candidates are chosen for the final election.

primary color *n* one of the three colors from which all others except black can be obtained: red, blue, and yellow.

primary school *n* a school for children up to the third or fourth grade of elementary school and sometimes kindergarten.

primate[1] *n* any of the highest order of mammals, including man.–**primatial** *adj*.

primate[2] *n* an archbishop or the highest ranking bishop in a province, etc.–**primateship** *n*.

prime[1] *adj* first in rank, importance, or quality; chief; (*math*) of a number, divisible only by itself and 1. * *n* the best time; the height of perfection; full maturity; full health and strength.–**primeness** *n*.

prime[2] *vt* to prepare or make something ready; to pour liquid into (a pump) or powder into (a firearm); to paint on a primer.

prime minister *n* the head of the government in a parliamentary democracy.

primer[1] *n* a simple book for teaching; a small introductory book on a subject.

primer[2] *n* a detonating device; a first coat of paint or oil.

prime time *n* (*radio, TV*) the hours when the largest audience is available.

primeval *adj* of the first age of the world; primitive.

primitive *adj* of the beginning or the earliest times; crude; simple; basic. * *n* a primitive person or thing.–**primitively** *adv*.–**primitiveness** *n*.

primordial *adj* earliest; primeval; fundamental; primitive.–**primordially** *adv*.

primrose *n* a perennial plant with pale yellow flowers.

prince *n* the son of a sovereign; a ruler ranking below a king; the head of a principality; any pre-eminent person.–**princedom** *n*.–**princely** *adj*.

princess *n* a daughter of a sovereign; the wife of a prince; one outstanding in a specified respect.

principal *adj* first in rank or importance; chief. * *n* a principal person; a person who organizes; the head of a college or school; the leading player in a ballet, opera, etc; a capital sum lent or invested.–**principalship** *n*.

principality *n* (*pl* **principalities**) the position of responsibility of a principal; the rank and territory of a prince.

principally *adv* mainly.

principle *n* a basic truth; a law or doctrine used as a basis for others; a moral code of conduct; a chemical constituent with a characteristic quality; a scientific law explaining a natural action; the method of a thing's working.

principled *adj* having, or acting in line with, moral principles.

print *vti* to stamp (a mark, letter, etc) on a surface; to produce (on paper, etc) the impressions of inked type, etc; to produce (a book, etc); to write in letters resembling printed ones; to make (a photographic print). * *n* a mark made on a surface by pressure; the impression of letters, designs, etc, made from inked type, a plate, or block; an impression made by a photomechanical process; a photographic copy, esp from a negative.

printer *n* a person engaged in printing; a machine for printing from; a device that produces printout.

printing *n* the activity, skill, or business of producing printed matter; a style of writing using capital letters; the total number of books, etc, printed at one time (–*also* **impression**).

printout *n* the printed output of a computer.

prior[1] *adj* previous; taking precedence (as in importance).–**priority** *n*.

prior[2] *n* the superior ranking below an abbot in a monastery; the head of a house or group of houses in a religious community.–**prioress** *nf*.–**priory** *n*.

prism *n* (*geom*) a solid whose ends are similar, equal, and parallel plane figures and whose sides are parallelograms; a transparent body of this form usu with triangular ends used for dispersing or reflecting light.

prison *n* a building used to house convicted criminals for punishment and suspects remanded in custody while awaiting trial; a penitentiary or jail.

prisoner *n* a person held in prison or under arrest; a captive; a person confined by a restraint.

prisoner of war *n* a member of a military force taken prisoner by the enemy during combat.

pristine *adj* pure; in an original, unspoiled condition.

privacy *n* (*pl* **privacies**) being private; seclusion; secrecy; one's private life.

private *adj* of or concerning a particular person or group; not open to or controlled by the public; for an individual person; not holding public office; secret. * *n* (*pl*) the genitals; an enlisted man of the lowest military rank in the army.–**privately** *adv*.

privateer *n* a privately owned ship commissioned by a government to seize and plunder enemy vessels; a captain or crew member of such a ship.

privation *n* being deprived; want of comforts or necessities; hardship.

privatize *vt* to restore private ownership by buying back publicly owned stock in a company.

privilege *n* a right or special benefit enjoyed by a person or a small group; a prerogative. * *vt* to bestow a privilege on.–**privileged** *adj*.

privy *adj* private; having access to confidential information. * *n* (*pl* **privies**) a latrine.–**privily** *adv*.

prize *n* an award won in competition or a lottery; a reward given for merit; a thing worth striving for. * *adj* given as, rewarded by, a prize. * *vt* to value highly.

prizefight *n* a professional boxing match.–**prizefighter** *n*.

pro[1] *adv*, *prep* in favor of. * *n* (*pl* **pros**) an argument for a proposal or motion.

pro[2] *adj* professional. * *n* (*pl* **pros**) a professional.

probable *adj* likely; to be expected.–**probability** *n*.–**probably** *adv*.

probate *n* the validating of a will; the certified copy of a will.

probation *n* testing of character or skill; release from prison under supervision by a probation officer; the state or period of being on probation.–**probationary, probational** *adj*.

probationer *n* a person (as a newly admitted student nurse or teacher) whose fitness is being tested during a trial period; a convicted offender on probation.

probation officer *n* an official who watches over prisoners on probation.

probe n a flexible surgical instrument for exploring a wound; a device, as an unmanned spacecraft, used to obtain information about an environment; an investigation. * vt to explore with a probe; to examine closely; to investigate.–**prober** n.

probity n honesty, integrity, uprightness.

problem n a question for solution; a person, thing or matter difficult to cope with; a puzzle; (math) a proposition stating something to be done; an intricate unsettled question.–**problematical, problematic** adj.–**problematically** adv.

proboscis n (pl **proboscises, proboscides**) an elephant's trunk; a long snout; an insect's sucking organ; (humorous) a (large) nose.

procedure n an established mode of conducting business, esp in law or in a meeting; a practice; a prescribed or traditional course; a step taken as part of an established order of steps.–**procedural** adj.–**procedurally** adv.

proceed vi to go on, esp after stopping; to come from; to continue; to carry on; to issue; to take action; to go to law.

proceeding n an advance or going forward; (pl) steps, action, in a lawsuit; (pl) published records of a society, etc.

proceeds npl the total amount of money brought in; the net amount received.

process n a course or state of going on; a series of events or actions; a method of operation; forward movement; (law) a court summons; the whole course of proceedings in a legal action. * vt to handle something following set procedures; (food, etc) to prepare by a special process; (law) to take action; (film) to develop.

procession n a group of people marching in order, as in a parade.–**processional** adj.

processor n one who or that which processes; (comput) a central processing unit.

pro-choice adj supporting a woman's right to choose whether or not to have an abortion.

proclaim vt to announce publicly and officially; to tell openly; to praise.–**proclamation** n.–**proclamatory** adj.–**proclaimer** n.

procrastinate vti to defer action, to delay.–**procrastination** n.–**procrastinator** n.

procreate vt to bring into being, to engender offspring.–**procreation** n.–**procreant, procreative** adj.–**procreator** n.

procure vt to obtain by effort; to get and make available for sexual intercourse; to bring about. * vi to procure women.–**procurable** adj.–**procurement** n.

prod vt (**prodding, prodded**) to poke or jab, as with a pointed stick; to rouse into activity. * n the action of prodding; a sharp object; a stimulus.–**prodder** n.

prodigal adj wasteful; extravagant; open-handed. * n a wastrel; a person who squanders money.–**prodigality** n.–**prodigally** adv.

prodigious adj enormous, vast; amazing.–**prodigiously** adv.–**prodigiousness** n.

prodigy n (pl **prodigies**) an extraordinary person, thing or act; a gifted child.

produce vt to bring about; to bring forward, show; to yield; to cause; to manufacture, make; to give birth to; (play, movie) to put before the public. * vi to yield something. * n that which is produced, esp agricultural products.–**producible** adj.–**producibility** n.

producer n someone who produces, esp a farmer or manufacturer; a person who finances or supervises the putting on of a play or making of a movie; an apparatus or plant for making gas.

product n a thing produced by nature, industry or art; a result; an outgrowth; (math) the number obtained by multiplying two or more numbers together.

production n the act of producing; a thing produced; a work presented on the stage or screen or over the air.–**productional** adj.

productive adj producing or capable of producing; fertile.–**productively** adv.–**productiveness** n.

productivity n the state of being productive; the ratio of the output of a manufacturing business to the input of materials, labor, etc.

profane adj secular, not sacred; showing no respect for sacred things; irreverent; blasphemous; not possessing esoteric or expert knowledge. * vt to desecrate; to debase by a wrong, unworthy or vulgar use.–**profanation** n.–**profanely** adv.–**profaneness** n.–**profaner** n.–**profanity** n.

profess vt to affirm publicly, declare; to claim to be expert in; to declare in words or appearance only.–**professed** adj.–**professedly** adv.

profession n an act of professing; avowal, esp of religious belief; an occupation requiring specialized knowledge and often long and intensive academic preparation; the people engaged in this; affirmation; entry into a religious order.

professional adj of or following a profession; conforming to the technical or ethical standards of a profession; earning a livelihood in an activity or field often engaged in by amateurs; having a specified occupation as a permanent career; engaged in by persons receiving financial return; pursuing a line of conduct as though it were a profession. * n one who follows a profession; a professional sportsman; one highly skilled in a particular occupation or field.–**professionally** adv.

professionalism n the methods of professionals; the pursuit of an activity, eg a sport, for financial gain.

professor n a teacher of the highest rank at an institution of higher education; a teacher.–**professorial** adj.–**professorship** n.

proffer vt to offer, usu something intangible.

proficient adj skilled, competent.–**proficiency** n.–**proficiently** adv.

profile n a side view of the head as in a portrait, drawing, etc; a biographical sketch; a graph representing a person's abilities. * vt to represent in profile; to produce (as by writing, drawing, etc) a profile of.

profit n gain; the excess of returns over expenditure; the compensation to entrepreneurs resulting from the assumption of risk; (pl) the excess returns from a business; advantage, benefit. * vti to be of advantage (to), benefit; to gain.–**profitability** n.–**profitable** adj.–**profitably** adv.–**profitless** adj.

profiteer vi to make exorbitant profits, esp in wartime. * n a person who profiteers.–**profiteering** n.

profit sharing n a system by which employees share in the profits of a business.–**profit-sharing** adj.

profligate adj dissolute; immoral; extravagant. * n a profligate person, a libertine.–**profligacy** n.–**profligately** adv.

profound adj at great depth; intellectually deep; abstruse, mysterious.–**profoundly** adv.–**profundity** n.

profuse adj abundant; generous; extravagant.–**profusely** adv.–**profusion** n.

progenitor n an ancestor.

progeny n (pl **progenies**) offspring; descendants; outcome.

prognosis n (pl **prognoses**) a prediction; (med) a forecast of the course of a disease.

program n a printed list containing details of a ceremony, of the actors in a play, etc; a scheduled radio or television broadcast; a curriculum or syllabus for a course of study; a plan or schedule; a sequence of instructions fed into a computer. * vti (**programming, programmed** or **programing, programed**) to prepare a plan or schedule; to prepare a plan or schedule to feed a program into a computer; to write a program.–**programmable** adj.–**programmer, programer** n.–**programmatic** adj.

progress n a movement forward or onward, advance; satisfactory growth or development; a tour from place to place in stages. * vi to move forward, advance; to improve. * vt (project) to take to completion.

progression n progress; advancement by degrees; (math) a series of numbers, each differing from the succeeding according to a fixed law; (*mus*) a regular succession of chords.–**progressional** *adj*.

progressive *adj* advancing, improving; proceeding by degrees; continuously increasing; aiming at reforms. * *n* a person who believes in moderate political change, esp social improvement by government action.–**progressively** *adv*.–**progressiveness** *n*.–**progressivism** *n*.

prohibit *vt* to forbid by law; to prevent.–**prohibitive, prohibitory** *adj*.–**prohibitively** *adv*.

prohibition *n* the act of forbidding; an order that forbids; a legal ban on the manufacture and sale of alcoholic drinks; (*with cap*) the period (1920–33) when there was a legal ban of alcohol in the US.

prohibitionist *n* an advocate of legally prohibiting the sale of alcohol; (*with cap*) a member of the Prohibition Party in the US.

project *n* a plan, scheme; an undertaking; a task carried out by students, etc, involving research. * *vt* to throw forward; (*light, shadow, etc*) to produce an outline of on a distance surface; to make objective or externalize; (*one's voice*) to make heard at a distance; (*feeling, etc*) to attribute to another; to imagine; to estimate, plan, or figure for the future. * *vi* to jut out; to come across vividly; to make oneself heard clearly.

projectile *n* a missile; something propelled by force. * *adj* throwing forward; capable of being thrown forward.

projection *n* the act of projecting or the condition of being projected; a thing projecting; the representation on a plane surface of part of the earth's surface; a projected image; an estimate of future possibilities based on a current trend; a mental image externalized; an unconscious attribution to another of one's own feelings and motives.–**projectional** *adj*.

projectionist *n* a person who operates a projector.

projector *n* an instrument that projects images from transparencies or film; an instrument that projects rays of light.

prolapse *vi* (*med*) to fall or slip out of place. * *n* a prolapsed condition.

proletariat *n* the lowest social or economic class of a community; wage earners; the industrial working class.–**proletarian** *adj*, *n*.

proliferate *vi* to grow or reproduce rapidly.–**proliferation** *n*.–**proliferative** *adj*.

prolific *adj* producing abundantly; fruitful.–**prolificacy** *n*.–**prolifically** *adv*.

prologue, prolog *n* the introductory lines of a play, speech, or poem; the reciter of these; a preface; an introductory event. * *vt* (**prologuing, prologued** *or* **prologing, prologed**) to provide with a prologue; to usher in.

prolong *vt* to extend or lengthen in space or time; to spin out.–**prolongation** *n*.–**prolonger** *n*.

prom *n* a dance for a high school or college class.

promenade *n* an esplanade; a ball or dance; a leisurely walk. * *vti* to take a promenade (along or through).–**promenader** *n*.

prominent *adj* jutting, projecting; standing out, conspicuous; widely and favorably known; distinguished.–**prominence** *n*.–**prominently** *adv*.

promiscuous *adj* indiscriminate, esp in sexual liaisons.–**promiscuity** *n*.–**promiscuously** *adv*.

promise *n* a pledge; an undertaking to do or not to do something; an indication, as of a successful future. * *vti* to pledge; to undertake; to give reason to expect.–**promiser** *n*.

promising *adj* likely to turn out well; hopeful.

promontory *n* (*pl* **promontories**) a peak of high land that juts out into a body of water.

promote *vt* to encourage; to advocate; to raise to a higher rank; (*employee, student*) to advance from one grade to the next higher grade; (*product*) to encourage sales by advertising, publicity, or discounting.–**promotable** *adj*.–**promoter** *n*.

promotion *n* an elevation in position or rank; the furtherance of the sale of merchandise through advertising, publicity, or discounting.–**promotional** *adj*.

prompt *adj* without delay; quick to respond; immediate; of or relating to prompting actors. * *vt* to urge; to inspire; (*actor*) to remind of forgotten words, etc (as in a play). * *n* something that reminds; a time limit for payment of an account; the contract by which this time is fixed.–**promptly** *adv*.–**promptness** *n*.

prompter *n* one that prompts, esp a person who sits offstage and reminds actors of forgotten lines.

prone *adj* face downwards; lying flat, prostrate; inclined or disposed (to).–**pronely** *adv*.–**proneness** *n*.

prong *n* a spike of a fork or other forked object.–**pronged** *adj*.

pronoun *n* a word used to represent a noun (eg *I, he, she, it*).

pronounce *vt* to utter, articulate; to speak officially, pass (judgment); to declare formally.–**pronounceable** *adj*.–**pronouncement** *n*.–**pronouncer** *n*.

pronounced *adj* marked, noticeable.–**pronouncedly** *adv*.

pronto *adv* (*inf*) quickly.

pronunciation *n* articulation; the way a word is pronounced.

proof *n* evidence that establishes the truth; the fact, act, or process of validating; test; demonstration; a sample from type, etc, for correction; a trial print from a photographic negative; the relative strength of an alcoholic liquor. * *adj* resistant; impervious, impenetrable. * *vt* to make proof against (water).

proofread *vti* (**proofreading, proofread**) to read and correct (printed proofs).–**proofreader** *n*.

prop[1] *vt* (**propping, propped**) to support by placing something under or against. * *n* a rigid support; a thing or person giving support.

prop[2] *see* **property**.

propaganda *n* the organized spread of ideas, doctrines, etc, to promote a cause; the ideas, etc, so spread.–**propagandism** *n*.–**propagandist** *n*, *adj*.

propagate *vti* to cause (a plant or animal) to reproduce itself; (*plant or animal*) to reproduce; (*ideas, customs, etc*) to spread.–**propagation** *n*.–**propagative** *adj*.

propane *n* a colorless flammable gas obtained from petroleum and used as a fuel.

propel *vt* (**propelling, propelled**) to drive or move forward.

propellant, propellent *n* a thing that propels; an explosive charge; rocket fuel; the gas that activates an aerosol spray.

propeller, propellor *n* a mechanism to impart drive; a device having two or more blades in a revolving hub for propelling a ship or aircraft.

propensity *n* (*pl* **propensities**) a natural inclination; disposition, tendency.

proper *adj* own, individual, peculiar; appropriate, fit; correct, conventional; decent, respectable; in the most restricted sense; (*sl*) thorough.

properly *adv* in the right way; justifiably; (*sl*) thoroughly.

proper noun *n* the name of a particular person, place, etc.

property *n* (*pl* **properties**) a quality or attribute; a distinctive feature or characteristic; one's possessions; real estate, land; a movable article used in a stage setting (–*also* **prop**).

prophecy *n* (*pl* **prophecies**) a message of divine will and purpose; prediction.

prophesy *vti* (**prophesying, prophesied**) to predict with assurance or on the basis of mystic knowledge; to foretell.–**prophesier** *n*.

prophet *n* a religious leader regarded as, or claiming to be, divinely inspired; one who predicts the future.–**prophetess** *nf*.–**prophetic, prophetical** *adj*.–**prophetically** *adv*.

propinquity *n* nearness of time, place or relationship.

propitiate *vt* to appease, conciliate.–**propitiation** *n*.–**propitiator** *n*.

propitious *adj* favorable, encouraging; auspicious, opportune.–**propitiously** *adv*.–**propitiousness** *n*.

proponent *n* someone who makes a proposal, or proposition.

proportion n the relationship between things in size, quantity, or degree; ratio; symmetry, balance; comparative part or share; (*math*) the equality of two ratios; a share or quota; (*pl*) dimensions. * vt to put in proper relation with something else; to make proportionate (to).–**proportionment** n.–**proportionable** adj.

proportional adj of proportion; aiming at due proportion; proportionate.–**proportionality** n.–**proportionally** adv.

proportionate adj in due proportion, corresponding in amount. * vt to make proportionate.–**proportionately** adv.

propose vt to present for consideration; to suggest; to intend; to announce the drinking of a toast to; (*person*) to nominate; to move as a resolution. * vi to make an offer (of marriage).–**proposal** n.–**proposer** n.

proposition n a proposal for consideration; a plan; a request for sexual intercourse; (*inf*) a proposed deal, as in business; (*inf*) an undertaking to be dealt with; (*math*) a problem to be solved.–**propositional** adj.

propound vt to put forward (a question, suggestion, etc).

proprietary adj characteristic of a proprietor; privately owned and managed and run as a profit-making organization; (*drug*) made and distributed under a tradename. * n (*pl* **proprietaries**) proprietors collectively; a drug protected by secrecy, patent, or copyright against free competition.

proprietor n one with legal title to something; an owner.–**proprietorial** adj.–**proprietorially** adv.

propriety n (*pl* **proprieties**) correctness of conduct or taste; fear of offending against rules of behavior, esp between the sexes; (*pl*) the customs and manners of polite society.

propulsion n the act of propelling; something that propels.–**propulsive, propulsory** adj.

prosaic adj commonplace, matter-of-fact, dull.–**prosaically** adv.–**prosaicness** n.

proscribe vt to outlaw; to denounce; to prohibit the use of.–**proscriber** n.–**proscription** n.–**proscriptive** adj.–**proscriptively** adv.

prose n ordinary language, as opposed to verse. * adj in prose; humdrum, dull.

prosecute vt to bring legal action against; to pursue. * vi to institute and carry on a legal suit or prosecution.–**prosecutable** adj.–**prosecution** n.–**prosecutor** n.

prospect n a wide view, a vista; (*pl*) measure of future success; future outlook; expectation; a likely customer, candidate, etc. * vti to explore or search (for).

prospective adj likely; anticipated; expected.–**prospectively** adv.

prospector n one who prospects for gold, etc.

prospectus n (*pl* **prospectuses**) a printed statement of the features of a new work, enterprise, etc; something (as a condition or statement) that forecasts the course or nature of a situation.

prosper vi to thrive; to flourish; to succeed.

prosperity n (*pl* **prosperities**) success; wealth.

prosperous adj successful, fortunate, thriving; favorable.–**prosperously** adv.

prostate n (*also* **prostate gland**) a gland situated around the neck of a man's bladder.–**prostatic** adj.

prosthesis n (*pl* **prostheses**) (*med*) the replacement of a lost limb, tooth, etc with an artificial one.–**prosthetic** adj.

prostitute n a person who has sexual intercourse for money; (*fig*) one who deliberately debases his or her talents (as for money). * vt to offer indiscriminately for sexual intercourse, esp for money; to devote to corrupt or unworthy purposes.–**prostitution** n.–**prostitutor** n.

prostrate adj lying face downward; helpless; overcome; lying prone or supine. * vt to throw oneself down; to lie flat; to humble oneself.–**prostration** n.

protagonist n the main character in a drama, novel, etc; a supporter of a cause.

protect vt to defend from danger or harm; to guard; to maintain the status and integrity of, esp through financial guarantees; to foster or shield from infringement or restriction; to restrict competition through tariffs and trade controls.–**protector** n.

protection n the act of protecting; the condition of being protected; something that protects; shelter; defence; patronage; the taxing of competing imports to foster home industry; the advocacy or theory of this (–*also* **protectionism**); immunity from prosecution or attack obtained by the payment of money.

protectionist n a person who advocates the protection of home trade by taxing competitive imports. * adj serving to protect.–**protectionism** n.

protective adj serving to protect, defend, shelter.–**protectively** adv.–**protectiveness** n.

protectorate n the administration of a weaker state by a powerful one; a state so controlled.

protégé n a person guided and helped in his career by another person.–**protégée** nf.

protein n a complex organic compound containing nitrogen that is an essential constituent of food.

protest vi to object to; to remonstrate. * vt to assert or affirm; to execute or have executed a formal protest against; to make a statement or gesture in objection to. * n public dissent; an objection; a complaint; a formal statement of objection.–**protester, protestor** n.–**protestingly** adv.

Protestant n a member or adherent of one of the Christian churches deriving from the Reformation; a Christian not of the Orthodox or Roman Catholic Church, who adheres to the principles of the Reformation.–**Protestantism** n.

protestation n a solemn declaration; a strong protest.

protocol n a note, minute or draft of an agreement or transaction; the ceremonial etiquette accepted as correct in official dealings, as between heads of state or diplomatic officials; the formatting of data in an electronic communications system; the plan of a scientific experiment or treatment.

proton n an elementary particle in the nucleus of all atoms, carrying a unit positive charge of electricity.

protoplasm n a semi-fluid viscous colloid, the essential living matter of all plant and animal cells.–**protoplasmic** adj.

prototype n an original model or type from which copies are made.–**prototypal, prototypic, prototypical** adj.

protozoan, protozoon n (*pl* **protozoans, protozoa**) a microscopic animal consisting of a single cell or a group of cells.

protract vt to draw out or prolong; to lay down the lines and angles of with scale and protractor; to extend forward and outward.–**protractible** adj.–**protraction** n.

protractor n an instrument for measuring and drawing angles; a muscle that extends a limb.

protrude vti to thrust outward or forward; to obtrude; to jut out, project.–**protrusion** n.

protuberant adj bulging out, prominent.–**protuberance, protuberancy** n.–**protuberantly** adv.

proud adj having too high an opinion of oneself; arrogant, haughty; having proper self-respect; satisfied with one's achievements.–**proudly** adv.–**proudness** n.

prove vti (**proving, proved** or **proven**) to try out, test, by experiment; to establish or demonstrate as true using accepted procedures; to show (oneself) to be worthy or capable; to turn out (to be), esp after trial or test; to rise.–**provable** adj.–**provably** adv.–**prover** n.

provenance n place of origin, source.

proverb n a short traditional saying expressing a truth or moral instruction; an adage.–**proverbial** adj.–**proverbially** adv.

provide vti to arrange for; to supply; to prepare; to afford (an opportunity); to make provision for (financially).–**provider** n.

provided, providing conj on condition (that).

providence n foresight, prudence; God's care and protection.–**providential** adj.–**providentially** adv.

provident adj providing for the future; far-seeing; thrifty.–**providently** adv.

province n an administrative district or division of a country; (pl) the parts of a country removed from the main cities; a department of knowledge or activity.

provincial adj of a province or provinces; having the way, speech, etc of a certain province; country-like; rustic; unsophisticated. * n an inhabitant of the provinces or country areas; a person lacking sophistication.–**provinciality** n.–**provincially** adv.

provision n a requirement; something provided for the future; a stipulation, condition; (pl) supplies of food, stores. * vt to supply with stores.–**provisioner** n.

provisional, provisionary adj temporary; conditional.–**provisionally** adv.

proviso n (pl **provisos, provisoes**) a condition, stipulation; a limiting clause in an agreement, etc.

provisory adj conditional; making provision; temporary.–**provisorily** adv.

provoke vt to anger, infuriate; to incite, to arouse; to give rise to; to irritate, exasperate.–**provocation** n.–**provocative** adj.–**provocatively** adv.–**provocativeness** n.

provoking adj annoying, exasperating.–**provokingly** adv.

prow n the forward part of a ship, bow.

prowess n bravery, gallantry; skill.

prowl vi to move stealthily, esp in search of prey.–also n.

prowler n one that moves stealthily, esp an opportunist thief.

proximity n nearness in place, time, series, etc.

proxy n (pl **proxies**) the authority to vote or act for another; a person so authorized.–also n.

prude n a person who is overly modest or proper in behavior, speech, attitudes to sex, etc.–**prudery** n.–**prudish** adj.–**prudishly** adv.–**prudishness** n.

prudent adj cautious; sensible; managing carefully; circumspect.–**prudence** n.–**prudently** adv.

prune[1] n a dried plum.

prune[2] vti (plant) to remove dead or living parts from; to cut away what is unwanted or superfluous.–**pruner** n.

prurient adj tending to excite lust; having lewd thoughts.–**prurience** n.–**pruriently** adv.

pry[1] vi (**prying, pried**) to snoop into other people's affairs; to inquire impertinently. * n (pl **pries**) close inspection; impertinent peeping; a highly inquisitive person.

pry[2] vt (**prying, pried**) to raise with a lever.

PS abbr = postscript.

psalm n a sacred song or hymn, esp one from the Book of Psalms in the Bible.

pseudo adj false, pretended.

pseudonym n a false name adopted as by an author.–**pseudonymity** n.

psoriasis n a chronic skin disease marked by red scaly patches.–**psoriatic** adj.

psyche n the spirit, soul; the mind, esp as a functional entity governing the total organism and its interactions with the environment.

psychedelic adj of or causing extreme changes in the conscious mind; of or like the auditory or visual effects produced by drugs (as LSD). * n a psychedelic drug.–**psychedelically** adv.

psychiatrist n a specialist in psychiatric medicine.

psychiatry n the branch of medicine dealing with disorders of the mind, including psychoses and neuroses.–**psychiatric** adj.–**psychiatrically** adv.

psychic adj of the soul or spirit; of the mind; having sensitivity to, or contact with, forces that cannot be explained by natural laws (–also **psychical**). * n a person apparently sensitive to non-physical forces; a medium; psychic phenomena.

psychoanalysis n a method of treating neuroses, phobias, and some other mental disorders by analyzing emotional conflicts, repressions, etc.–**psychoanalytic, psychoanalytical** adj.

psychoanalyst n a specialist in psychoanalysis.

psychoanalyze, psychoanalyse vt to analyze and treat by psychoanalysis.

psychological adj of or relating to psychology; of, relating to or coming from the mind or emotions; able to affect the mind or emotions.–**psychologically** adv.

psychologist n a person trained in psychology.

psychology n (pl **psychologies**) the science that studies the human mind and behavior; mental state.

psychopath n a person suffering from a mental disorder that results in antisocial behavior and lack of guilt.–**psychopathic** adj.

psychosis n (pl **psychoses**) a mental disorder in which the personality is very seriously disorganized and contact with reality is usu impaired.

psychosomatic adj of physical disorders that have a psychological or emotional origin.–**psychosomatically** adv.

psychotherapy n the treatment of mental disorders by psychological methods. **psychotherapeutic** adj. **psychotherapist** n.

psychotic adj of or like a psychosis; having a psychosis. * n a person suffering from a psychosis.–**psychotically** adv.

pt abbr = pint.

PTA abbr = Parent-Teacher Association.

PTO abbr = please turn over.

pub n a public house, a bar.

puberty n the stage at which the reproductive organs become functional.–**pubertal** adj.

pubescent adj arriving at or having reached puberty; of or relating to puberty; covered with fine soft short hairs.–**pubescence** n.

pubis n (pl **pubes**) the front part of the bones composing either half of the pelvis.–**pubic** adj.

public adj of, for, or by the people generally; performed in front of people; for the use of all people; open or known to all; acting officially for the people. * n the people in general; a particular section of the people, such as an audience, body of readers, etc; open observation.

publication n public notification; the printing and distribution of books, magazines, etc; something published as a periodical, book, etc.

publicist n a person who publicizes, esp one whose business it is; a political journalist.

publicity n any information or action that brings a person or cause to public notice; work concerned with such promotional matter; notice by the public.

publicize vt to give publicity to.

publicly adv in a public manner; openly; by the public; with the consent of the public.

public relations n relations with the general public of a company, institution, etc, as through publicity.

public school n a school maintained by public money and supervised by local authorities.

publish vt to make generally known; to announce formally; (book) to issue for sale to the public. * vi to put out an edition; to have one's work accepted for publication.–**publishable** adj.

publisher n a person or company that prints and issues books, magazines, etc.

publishing n the business of the production and distribution of books, magazines, recordings, etc.

pucker vti to draw together in creases, to wrinkle; (with **up**) to contract the lips ready to kiss. * n a wrinkle or fold.

pudding n a dessert; a steamed or baked dessert; a suet pie.

puddle n a small pool of water, esp stagnant, spilled, or muddy water; a rough cement of kneaded clay. * vti to dabble in mud, to make muddy; to make or line with puddle; to stir (molten iron) to free it from carbon.–**puddler** n.

pudendum *n* (*pl* **pudenda**) (*usu pl*) the external reproductive organs, esp of a woman.–**pudendal** *adj*.

pudgy *adj* (**pudgier, pudgiest**) short and fat, squat.–**pudginess** *n*.

pueblo *n* an Indian settlement in Mexico and the South West United States.

puerile *adj* juvenile; childish.–**puerilely** *adv*.–**puerility** *n*.

puff *n* a sudden short blast or gust; an exhalation of air or smoke; a light pastry; a pad for applying powder. * *vti* to emit a puff; to breathe hard, pant; to put out of breath; to swell; to blow, smoke, etc, with puffs.–**puffily** *adv*.–**puffiness** *n*.–**puffy** *adj*.

pug *n* a breed of small dog with a face and nose like a bulldog.

pugilist *n* a boxer; a prizefighter.–**pugilism** *n*.–**pugilistic** *adj*.–**pugilistically** *adv*.

pugnacious *adj* fond of fighting, belligerent.–**pugnacity, pugnaciousness** *n*.

puke *vti* (*inf*) to vomit.–*also n*.

pulchritude *n* beauty.

pull *vt* to tug at; to pluck; to move or draw towards oneself; to drag; to rip; to tear; (*muscle*) to strain; (*inf*) to carry out, perform; (*inf*) to restrain; (*inf: gun, etc*) to draw out; (*inf*) to attract. * *vi* to carry out the action of pulling something; to be capable of being pulled; to move (away, ahead, etc). * *n* the act of pulling or being pulled; a tug; a device for pulling; (*inf*) influence; (*inf*) drawing power.

pullet *n* a young hen.

pulley *n* a wheel with a grooved rim for a cord, etc, used to raise weights by downward pull or change of direction of the pull; a group of these used to increase applied force; a wheel driven by a belt.

pullover *n* a buttonless garment with or without sleeves pulled on over the head.

pulmonary *adj* of, relating to or affecting the lungs; having lungs; denoting the artery that conveys deoxygenated blood directly to the lungs from the right ventricle of the heart.

pulp *n* a soft, moist, sticky mass; the soft, juicy part of a fruit or soft pith of a plant stem; ground-up, moistened fibers of wood, rags, etc, used to make paper; a book or magazine printed on cheap paper and often dealing with sensational material. * *vti* to make or become pulp or pulpy; to produce or reproduce (written matter) in pulp form.

pulpit *n* a raised enclosed platform, esp in a church, from which a clergyman preaches; preachers as a group.

pulsar *n* any of several very small stars that emit radio pulses at regular intervals.

pulsate *vi* to beat or throb rhythmically; to vibrate, quiver.–**pulsation** *n*.–**pulsative** *adj*.

pulse[1] *n* a rhythmic beat or throb, as of the heart; a place where this is felt; an underlying opinion or sentiment or an indication of it; a short radio signal. * *vti* to throb, pulsate.

pulse[2] *n* the edible seeds of several leguminous plants, such as beans, peas and lentils; the plants producing them.

pulverize *vti* to reduce to a fine powder; to demolish, smash; to crumble.–**pulverization** *n*.–**pulverizer** *n*.

puma *n* a mountain lion.

pumice *n* a light, porous volcanic rock, used for scrubbing, polishing, etc.–**pumiceous** *adj*.

pummel *vt* (**pummeling, pummeled** *or* **pummelling, pummelled**) to strike repeatedly with the fists, to thump.

pump[1] *n* a device that forces a liquid or gas into, or draws it out of, something. * *vti* to move (fluids) with a pump; to remove water, etc, from; to drive air into with a pump; to draw out, move up and down, pour forth, etc, as a pump does; (*inf*) to obtain information through questioning.

pump[2] *n* a light low shoe or slipper; a rubber-soled shoe.

pumpernickel *n* a coarse rye bread.

pumpkin *n* a large, round, orange fruit of the gourd family widely cultivated as food.

pun *n* a play on words of the same sound but different meanings, usu humorous. * *vi* (**punning, punned**) to make a pun.–**punningly** *adv*.

punch[1] *vt* to strike with the fist; to prod or poke; to stamp, perforate with a tool; (*cattle*) to herd. * *n* a blow with the fist; (*inf*) vigor; a machine or tool for punching.

punch[2] *n* a hot, sweet drink made with fruit juices, often mixed with wine or spirits.

punch line *n* the last line of a joke or story, that conveys its humor or point.

punctilious *adj* very formal in conduct; scrupulously exact.

punctual *adj* being on time; prompt.–**punctuality** *n*.–**punctually** *adv*.

punctuate *vt* to use certain standardized marks in (written matter) to clarify meaning; to interrupt; to emphasize. * *vi* to use punctuation marks.–**punctuation** *n*.–**punctuator** *n*.

punctuation mark *n* one of the standardized symbols used in punctuation, as the period, colon, semicolon, comma, etc.

puncture *n* a small hole made by a sharp object; the deflation of a tire caused by a puncture. * *vt* to make useless or ineffective as if by a puncture; to deflate. * *vi* to become punctured.–**puncturable** *adj*.

pundit *n* a learned person; an expert; a critic, esp one who writes in a daily newspaper.–*also* **pandit**.

pungent *adj* having an acrid smell or a sharp taste; caustic; bitter.–**pungency** *n*.–**pungently** *adv*.

punish *vt* to subject a person to a penalty for a crime or misdemeanor; to chastise; to handle roughly.–**punisher** *n*.

punishable *adj* liable to legal punishment.–**punishability** *n*.

punishing *adj* causing retribution; (*inf*) arduous, grueling, exhausting.–**punishingly** *adv*.

punishment *n* a penalty for a crime or misdemeanor; rough treatment; the act of punishing or being punished.

punitive, punitory *adj* involving the inflicting of punishment.–**punitively** *adv*.–**punitiveness** *n*.

punk *n* a young gangster; a follower of punk rock.

punk rock *n* an aggressive form of rock music usu performed in a coarse, offensive way.

punt[1] *n* a long flat-bottomed square-ended river boat usu propelled with a pole. * *vti* to propel or convey in a punt.

punt[2] *vt* to kick a dropped ball before it reaches the ground. * *n* such a kick.

punter *n* a person who gambles; (*sl*) a consumer; a customer.

puny *adj* (**punier, puniest**) of inferior size, strength, or importance; feeble.–**puniness** *n*.

pup *n* a young dog, a puppy; a young fox, seal, rat, etc. * *vi* (**pupping, pupped**) to give birth to pups.

pupa *n* (*pl* **pupae, pupas**) an insect at the quiescent stage between the larva and the adult.–**pupal** *adj*.

pupil[1] *n* a child or young person taught under the supervision of a teacher or tutor; a person who has been taught or influenced by a famous or distinguished person.

pupil[2] *n* the round, dark opening in the centre of the iris of the eye through which light passes.

puppet *n* a doll moved by strings attached to its limbs or by a hand inserted in its body; a person controlled by another. * *adj* of or relating to puppets; acting in response to the controls of another while appearing independent.

puppeteer *n* a person who controls and entertains with puppets.

puppetry *n* the art of making and entertaining with puppets; stilted presentation.

puppy *n* (*pl* **puppies**) a young domestic dog less than a year old.–**puppyhood** *n*.–**puppyish** *adj*.

purchase *vt* to buy; to obtain by effort or suffering. * *n* the act of purchasing; an object bought; leverage for raising or moving loads; means of achieving advantage.–**purchasable** *adj*.–**purchaser** *n*.

pure *adj* clean; not contaminated; not mixed; chaste, innocent; free from taint or defilement; mere; that and that only; abstract and theoretical.–**pureness** *n*.

purée *n* cooked food sieved or pulped in a blender; a thick soup of this. * *vt* (**puréeing, puréed**) to prepare food in this way.

purely *adv* in a pure way; solely, entirely.

purgative *adj* purging, cleansing; * *n* a drug or agent that purges the bowels.

purgatory *n* a place of suffering or purification; (*with cap: RC church*) the intermediate place between death and heaven, where venial sins are purged.

purge *vt* to cleanse, purify; (*nation, party, etc*) to rid of troublesome people; to clear (oneself) of a charge; to clear out the bowels of. * *n* the act or process of purging; a purgative; the removal of persons believed to be disloyal from an organization, esp a political party.–**purger** *n*.

purify *vti* (**purifying, purified**) to make or become pure; to cleanse; to make ceremonially clean; to free from harmful matter.–**purification** *n*.–**purificatory** *adj*.–**purifier** *n*.

purist *n* someone who is a stickler for correctness in language, style, etc.–**purism** *n*.–**puristic** *adj*.–**puristically** *adv*.

puritan *adj* a person who is extremely strict in religion or morals. * *adj* of or like a puritan.–**puritanical** *adj*.–**puritanically** *adv*.–**puritanism** *n*.

purity *n* the state of being pure.

purl *vti* to knit a stitch by drawing its base loop from front to back of the fabric. * *n* a stitch made in this way.

purloin *vt* to steal.–**purloiner** *n*.

purple *n* a dark, bluish red; crimson cloth or clothing, esp as a former emblem of royalty. * *adj* purple-colored; royal; (*writing style*) over-elaborate. * *vti* to make or become purple.

purport *vt* to claim to be true; to imply; to be intended to seem. * *n* significance; apparent meaning.–**purportedly** *adv*.

purpose *n* objective; intention; aim; function; resolution, determination. * *vti* to intend, design.–**purposeful** *adj*.–**purposefully** *adv*.–**purposeless** *adj*.–**purposelessly** *adv*.

purposely *adv* deliberately; on purpose.

purr *vi* (*cat*) to make a low, murmuring sound of pleasure.–**purring** *n*.

purse *n* a small pouch or bag for money; finances, money; a sum of money for a present or a prize; a woman's handbag. * *vt* to pucker, wrinkle up.

purser *n* an officer on a passenger ship in charge of accounts, tickets, etc; an airline official responsible for the comfort and welfare of passengers.

pursue *vb* (**pursuing, pursued**) *vt* to follow; to chase; to strive for; to seek to attain; to engage in; to proceed with. * *vi* to follow in order to capture.–**pursuer** *n*.

pursuit *n* the act of pursuing; an occupation; a pastime.

purvey *vti* to procure and supply (provisions).–**purveyance** *n*.–**purveyor** *n*.

pus *n* a yellowish fluid produced by infected sores.

push *vti* to exert pressure so as to move; to press against or forward; to impel forward, shove; to urge the use, sale, etc, of; (*inf*) to sell drugs illegally; to make an effort * *n* a thrust, shove; an effort; an advance against opposition; (*inf*) energy and drive.

push button *n* a knob that activates an electrical switch which opens or closes a circuit to operate a radio, bell, etc.

pusher *n* that which pushes; (*inf*) a person who sells illegal drugs.

pushover *n* (*inf*) something easily done, as a victory over an opposing team; (*inf*) a person easily taken advantage of.

pushy *adj* (**pushier, pushiest**) (*inf*) assertive; forceful; aggressively ambitious.–**pushily** *adv*.–**pushiness** *n*.

pusillanimous *adj* faint-hearted, cowardly.–**pusillanimity** *n*.

pussycat *n* (*inf*) a cat; an amiable person.

pussyfoot *vi* to move stealthily; to be evasive.–**pussyfooter** *n*.

pustule *n* a blister or swelling containing pus.–**pustular** *adj*.–**pustulation** *n*.

put *vti* (**putting, put**) to place, set; to cast, throw; to apply, direct; to bring into a specified state; to add (to); to subject to; to submit; to estimate; to stake; to express; to translate; to propose; (*a weight*) to hurl; (*with* **about**) to change the course of (a ship); to worry; (*with* **across**) to effect successfully; (*with* **away**) to remove; to lay by; (*sl*) to consume; (*with* **back**) to replace; to return to land; (*with* **by**) to thrust aside; to store up; (*with* **down**) to suppress; to silence; to kill or have killed; to write or enter; to reckon; to assign; (*with* **forth**) to exert; to bud or shoot; to set out; (*with* **in**) to interpose; to spend (time); to apply (for); to call (at); (*with* **off**) to doff, discard; to postpone; to evade; to get rid of; to discourage, repel; to foist (upon); to leave shore; (*with* **on**) to don; to assume, pretend; to increase; to add; to advance; (*with* **out**) to eject; to extend; to exert; to dislocate; to quench; to publish; to place (money) at interest; to disconcert, to anger; to leave shore; (*with* **over**) to succeed in, to carry through; (*with* **up**) to rouse; to offer (prayer); to propose as a candidate; to pack; to sheathe; to lodge; (*with* **up with**) to endure, to tolerate; (*with* **upon**) to impose upon; (*with* **wise**) to disabuse, to enlighten. * *adj* fixed.

putrefy *vti* (**putrefying, putrefied**) to make or become putrid; to rot, decompose.–**putrefaction** *n*.–**putrefactive** *adj*.–**putrefier** *n*.

putrid *adj* rotten or decayed and foul-smelling.–**putridity** *n*.–**putridly** *adv*.

putt *vti* (*golf*) to hit (a ball) with a putter. * *n* in golf, a stroke to make the ball roll into the hole.

putter[1] *n* (*golf*) a straight-faced club used in putting.

putter[2] *n* to busy oneself idly; to spend time.–**putterer** *n*.

putty *n* (*pl* **putties**) a soft, plastic mixture of powdered chalk and linseed oil used to fill small cracks, fix glass in window frames, etc. * *vt* (**puttying, puttied**) to fix or fill with putty.

puzzle *vt* to bewilder; to perplex. * *vi* to be perplexed; to exercise one's mind, as over a problem. * *n* bewilderment; a difficult problem; a toy or problem for testing skill or ingenuity; a conundrum.–**puzzlement** *n*.–**puzzler** *n*.

puzzling *adj* perplexing, bewildering, inexplicable.–**puzzlingly** *adv*.

PVC *abbr* = polyvinyl chloride.

pygmy *n* (*pl* **pygmies**) an undersized person.–*also* **pigmy** (*pl* **pigmies**).

pyjamas *see* **pajamas**.

pylon *n* a tower-like structure supporting electric power lines.

pyramid *n* (*geom*) a solid figure having a polygon as base, and whose sides are triangles sharing a common vertex; a huge structure of this shape, as a royal tomb of ancient Egypt; an immaterial structure built on a broad supporting base and narrowing gradually to an apex.–**pyramidal, pyramidical, pyramidic** *adj*.–**pyramidally, pyramidically** *adv*.

pyre *n* a pile of wood for cremating a dead body.

pyromania *n* (*psychol*) an uncontrollable urge to set things on fire.

pyrotechnics *n sing* the art of making or setting off fireworks; (*sing or pl*) a fireworks display; a brilliant display of virtuosity.–**pyrotechnic, pyrotechnical** *adj*.

Pyrrhic *adj* (*victory*) so costly as to be equal to defeat.

python *n* a large, nonpoisonous snake that kills by constriction.–**pythonic** *adj*.

Q

qt *abbr* = quart.

quack[1] *n* the cry of a duck. * *vi* to make a sound like a duck.

quack[2] *n* an untrained person who practices medicine fraudulently; a person who pretends to have knowledge and skill he does not have.–*also adj*.

quad n quadrangle; quadruplet.

quadrangle n (geom) a plane figure with four sides and four angles, a rectangle; a court enclosed by buildings.–**quadrangular** adj.

quadrant n (geom) a quarter of the circumference of a circle; an arc of 90 degrees; an instrument with such an arc for measuring angles, altitudes, or elevations; a curved street.–**quadrantal** adj.

quadraphonic adj using four channels to record and reproduce sound.–**quadraphonics, quadraphony** n.

quadratic adj square; (math) involving the square but no higher power * n a quadratic equation.

quadratic equation n an equation in which the highest power of the unknown is the square.

quadrilateral adj having four sides. * n (geom) a plane figure of four sides; a combination or group that involves four parts or individuals.

quadrille n a square dance for four or more couples; the music for this.

quadriplegia n paralysis of all four limbs.–**quadriplegic** adj, n.

quadruped n a four-footed animal.–**quadrupedal** adj.

quadruple adj four times as much or as many; made up of or consisting of four; having four divisions or parts. * vti to make or become four times as many.

quadruplet n one of four children born at one birth.

quadruplicate vt to multiply by four; to make four copies of. * adj fourfold.–**quadruplication** n.

quaff vti to take large drinks (of), drain.–**quaffer** n.

quagmire n soft, wet ground; a difficult situation.

quail[1] vi to cower, to shrink back with fear.

quail[2] n (pl **quails, quail**) a small American game bird.

quaint adj attractive or pleasant in an odd or old-fashioned style.–**quaintly** adv.–**quaintness** n.

quake vi to tremble or shiver, esp with fear or cold; to quiver. * n a shaking or tremor; (inf) an earthquake.

qualifiable adj that may be qualified.

qualification n qualifying; a thing that qualifies; a quality or acquirement that makes a person fit for a post, etc; modification; limitation; (pl) academic achievements.

qualify vti (**qualifying, qualified**) to restrict; to describe; to moderate; to modify, limit; to make or become capable or suitable; to fulfill conditions; to pass a final examination; (gram) to limit the meaning of.–**qualificatory** adj.–**qualifier** n.–**qualifyingly** adv.

qualitative adj of or depending on quality; determining the nature, not the quality, of components.–**qualitatively** adv.

quality n (pl **qualities**) a characteristic or attribute; degree of excellence; high standard. * adj of high quality.

qualm n a doubt; a misgiving; a scruple; a sudden feeling of faintness or nausea.–**qualmish** adj.

quandary n (pl **quandaries**) a predicament; a dilemma.

quango n (pl **quangos**) (acronym) quasi-autonomous non-governmental organization.

quantify vt (**quantifying, quantified**) to express as a quantity; to determine the amount of.–**quantifiable** adj. –**quantification** n.

quantity n (pl **quantities**) an amount that can be measured, counted or weighed; a large amount; the property by which a thing can be measured; a number or symbol expressing this property.–**quantitative** adj.–**quantitatively** adv.

quantum n (pl **quanta**) a quantity, share or portion; a fixed, elemental unit of energy. * adj large, significant.

quantum leap n an abrupt transition from one energy state to another; a sudden or noticeable change or increase.–also **quantum jump.**

quarantine n a period of isolation imposed to prevent the spread of disease; the time or place of this. * vt to put or keep in quarantine.

quark n (physics) a hypothetical elementary particle.

quarrel n an argument; an angry dispute; a cause of dispute. * vi (**quarreling, quarreled** or **quarrelling, quarrelled**) to argue violently; to fall out (with); to find fault (with).–**quarreler, quarreller** n.–**quarrelsome** adj.

quarry[1] n (pl **quarries**) an excavation for the extraction of stone, slate, etc; a place from which stone is excavated; a source of information, etc. * vti (**quarrying, quarried**) to excavate (from) a quarry; to research.

quarry[2] n (pl **quarries**) a hunted animal, prey.

quart n a liquid measure equal to a quarter of a gallon or two pints; a dry measure equal to two pints.

quarter n a fourth of something; one fourth of a year; one fourth of an hour; 25 cents, or a coin of this value; any leg of a four-legged animal with the adjoining parts; a particular district or section; (pl) lodgings; a particular source; an unspecified person or group; a compass point other than the cardinal points; mercy. * vti to share or divide into four; to provide with lodgings; to lodge; to range over (an area) in search (of). * adj constituting a quarter.

quarterback n (American football) a player directly behind forwards and the centre, who directs play. * vt to direct the attacking play of (a football team); to manage, direct. * vi to play quarterback.

quarterfinal n one of four matches held before the semifinals in a tournament.–also adj.

quarterly adj occurring, issued, or spaced at three-month intervals; (her) divided into quarters. * adv once every three months; (her) in quarters. * n (pl **quarterlies**) a publication issued four times a year.

quartermaster n (mil) an officer in charge of stores; (naut) a petty officer in charge of steering, etc.

quarter note n (mus) a note having one fourth the duration of a whole note.

quarters npl lodgings, esp for soldiers; action stations, esp used in reference to each member of the crew of a battleship.

quartet, quartette n a set or group of four; a piece of music composed for four instruments or voices; a group of four instrumentalists or voices.

quarto n (pl **quartos**) a page size, approx 9 by 12 inches; a book of this size of page.

quartz n a crystalline mineral, a form of silica, usu colorless and transparent.

quasar n a distant, starlike, celestial object that emits much light and powerful radio waves.

quash vt (rebellion etc) to put down; to suppress; to make void.

quasi adv seemingly; as if. * prefix almost, apparently.

quaternary adj consisting of, arranged in, or by, fours; of the number 4; (chem) an atom bound to four other atoms or groups, or containing such an atom; (math) with four variables.

quaver vi to tremble, vibrate; to speak or sing with a quivering voice. * n a trembling sound or note; (mus) an eighth note.–**quaveringly** adv.–**quavery** adj.

quay n a loading wharf or landing place for vessels.

queasy adj (**queasier, queasiest**) nauseous; easily upset; overscrupulous.–**queasily** adv.–**queasiness** n.

queen n a female sovereign and head of state; the wife or widow of a king; a woman considered pre-eminent; the egg-laying female of bees, wasps, etc; a playing card with a picture of a queen; (chess) the most powerful piece. * vi (with it) to act like a queen, esp to put on airs.–**queenly** adj.–**queenliness** n.

queer adj strange, odd, curious; (inf) eccentric. *vt (sl) to spoil the success of.–**queerness** n.

quell vt to suppress; to allay.–**queller** n.

quench vt (thirst) to satisfy or slake; (fire) to put out, extinguish; (steel) to cool; to suppress.–**quenchable** adj.–**quencher** n.

querulous adj complaining, fretful, peevish.–**querulously** adv. n.

query n (pl **queries**) a question; a question mark; doubt. * vti (**querying, queried**) to question; to doubt the accuracy of.

quest n a search, seeking, esp involving a journey. * vti to search (about) for, seek.–**quester** n.–**questingly** adv.

question n an interrogative sentence; an inquiry; a problem; a doubtful or controversial point; a subject of debate before an assembly; a part of a test or examination. * vti to ask questions (of); to interrogate intensively; to dispute; to subject to analysis.–**questioner** n.

questionable adj doubtful; not clearly true or honest.–**questionability** n. –**questionably** adv.

question mark n a punctuation mark (?) used at the end of a sentence to indicate a question, or to express doubt about something; something unknown.

questionnaire n a series of questions designed to collect statistical information; a survey made by the use of questionnaire.

queue n a line of people, vehicles, etc awaiting a turn. * vi (**queuing, queued**) to wait in turn.

quibble n a minor objection or criticism. * vi to argue about trifling matters.–**quibbler** n.–**quibblingly** adv.

quiche n a savory tart filled with onions and a cheese and egg custard.

quick adj rapid, speedy; nimble; prompt; responsive; alert; eager to learn. * adv (inf) in a quick manner. * n the sensitive flesh below a fingernail or toenail; the inmost sensibilities.–**quickly** adv.–**quickness** n.

quicken vti to speed up or accelerate; to make alive; to come to life; to invigorate.–**quickener** n.

quickie n (inf) anything done rapidly or in haste.

quicksand n loose wet sand easily yielding to pressure in which persons, animals, etc may be swallowed up.

quicksilver n mercury.

quickstep n a ballroom dance in quick time; the music for this. * vi (**quickstepping, quickstepped**) to do this dance.

quick-tempered adj easily angered.

quick-witted adj mentally alert; quick in repartee.–**quick-wittedness** n.

quid pro quo n (pl **quid pro quos**) something equivalent given in exchange for something else.

quiet adj silent, not noisy; still, not moving; gentle, not boisterous; unobtrusive, not showy; placid, calm; monotonous, uneventful; undisturbed. * n stillness, peace, repose; an undisturbed state. * vti to quieten.–**quietly** adv.–**quietness** n.

quieten vti to make or become quiet; to calm, soothe.

quietude n repose; tranquillity.

quill n the hollow stem of a feather; anything made of this, as a pen; a stiff, hollow spine of a hedgehog or porcupine.

quilt n a thick, warm bedcover; a bedspread; a coverlet of two cloths sewn together with padding between. * vti to stitch together like a quilt; to make a quilt.–**quilter** n.–**quilting** n.

quince n a hard-fleshed yellow Asian fruit used in preserves; the tree it grows on.

quint n a quintuplet.

quintessence n the purest form or most typical representation of anything, the embodiment.–**quintessential** adj.–**quintessentially** adv.

quintet, quintette n a set or group of five; a piece of music composed for five instruments or voices; a group of five instrumentalists or voices.

quintuple adj fivefold; having five divisions or parts; five times as much or as many. * vti to multiply by five. * n a number five times greater than another.

quintuplet n one of five offspring produced at one birth.

quip n a witty remark; a gibe. * vt (**quipping, quipped**) to make a clever or sarcastic remark.–**quipster** n.

quirk n an unexpected turn or twist; a peculiarity of character or mannerism.–**quirky** adj.

quit vti (**quitting, quitted** or **quit**) to leave; to stop or cease; to resign; to free from obligation; to admit defeat. * adj free from; released from.–**quitter** n.

quite adv completely; somewhat, fairly; really.

quits adj even; on equal terms by payment or revenge.

quiver[1] vi to shake; to tremble, shiver. * n a shiver, vibration.–**quiveringly** adv.–**quivery** adj.

quiver[2] n a case for holding arrows.–**quiverful** n.

quixotic, quixotical adj chivalrous or romantic to extravagance; unrealistically idealistic.–**quixotically** adv.

quiz n (pl **quizzes**) a form of entertainment where players are asked questions of general knowledge; a short written or oral test. * vt (**quizzing, quizzed**) to interrogate; to make fun of.–**quizzer** n.

quiz show n an entertainment program on television or radio in which contestants answer questions to win prizes.

quizzical adj humorous and questioning.–**quizzicality** n.–**quizzically** adv.

quoit n a ring of metal, plastic, etc thrown in quoits; (pl) a game in which rings are thrown at or over a peg.

quorum n the minimum number that must be present at a meeting or assembly to make its proceedings valid.

quota n a proportional share; a prescribed amount; a part to be contributed.

quotation n the act of quoting; the words quoted; an estimated price.

quotation mark n a punctuation mark to indicate the beginning (' or ") and the end (' or ") of a quoted passage.

quote vt to cite; to refer to; to repeat the words of a novel, play, poem, speech, etc exactly; to adduce by way of authority; to set off by quotation marks; to state the price of (something). * n (inf) something quoted; a quotation mark.

quotient n (math) the result obtained when one number is divided by another.

qwerty, QWERTY n (inf) a standard typewriter or computer keyboard.

R

rabbi n (pl **rabbis**) the religious and spiritual leader of a Jewish congregation.

rabbit n a small burrowing mammal of the hare family with long ears, a short tail, and long hind legs; their flesh as food; their fur.

rabble n a disorderly crowd, a mob; the common herd.

rabid adj infected with rabies; raging; fanatical.

rabies n an acute, infectious, viral disease transmitted by the bite of an infected animal.–also **hydrophobia**.

raccoon n a small nocturnal carnivore of North America that lives in trees; its yellowish gray fur.

race[1] n any of the divisions of humankind distinguished esp by color of skin; any geographical, national, or tribal ethnic grouping; a subspecies of plants or animals; distinctive flavor or taste.

race[2] n a contest of speed, as in running, swimming, cycling, etc; a rapid current or channel of water. * vi to run at top speed or out of control; to compete in a race; (engine) to run without a working load or with the transmission disengaged. * vt to cause to race; to contest against.–**racer** n.

racecourse n a track over which races are run, esp an oval track for racing horses.–also **racetrack**.

racehorse n a horse bred and trained for racing.

race relations npl the relationship between different races in a community or nation; the sociological study of such relations.

racetrack see **racecourse**

racial adj of or relating to any of the divisions of humankind distinguished by color, etc.

racism, racialism n a belief in the superiority of some races over others; prejudice against or hatred of other races; discriminating behavior toward people of another race.–**racist** n.

rack n a framework for holding or displaying articles; an instrument for torture by stretching; the triangular frame for setting up balls in snooker; a toothed bar to engage with the teeth of a wheel pinion or worm gear; extreme pain or anxiety. * vt (*person*) to stretch on a rack; to arrange in or on a rack; to torture, torment; to move parts of machinery with a toothed rack.

racket[1] n a bat strung with nylon, for playing tennis, etc. (*pl*) a game for two or four players played in a four-walled court (*–also* **racquet**).

racket[2] n noisy confusion; din; an obtaining of money illegally; any fraudulent business.

racketeer n a person who extorts money by threat or engages in an illegal profit-making enterprise.

raconteur n a person who excels in relating anecdotes.

racquet see **racket**[1].

racy adj (**racier, raciest**) lively, spirited; risqué.–**racily** adv.

radar n a system or device for detecting objects such as aircraft by using the reflection of radio waves.

radial adj like a radius; branching from a common center.

radiance n the condition of being radiant; brilliant light; dazzling beauty.

radiant adj shining; beaming with happiness; sending out rays; transmitted by radiation.–**radiantly** adv.

radiate vt (*light, heat, etc*) to emit in rays; (*happiness, love, etc*) to give forth. * vi to spread out as if from a center; to shine; to emit rays.

radiation n radiant particles emitted as energy; rays emitted in nuclear decay; (*med*) treatment using a radioactive substance.

radiator n an apparatus for heating a room; a cooling device for a vehicle engine.

radical adj of or relating to the root or origin; fundamental; favoring basic change. * n a person who advocates fundamental political or social change.–**radicalism** n. –**radically** adv.

radicchio n (*pl* **radicchios**) a type of Italian chicory with white-veined purple leaves eaten raw in salads.

radii see **radius**.

radio n the transmission of sounds or signals by electromagnetic waves through space, without wires, to a receiving set; such a set; broadcasting by radio as an industry, entertainment, etc. * adj of, using, used in, or sent by radio. * vti to transmit, or communicate with, by radio.

radioactive adj giving off radiant energy in the form of particles or rays caused by the disintegration of atomic nuclei.–**radioactivity** n.

radio astronomy n astronomy dealing with radio waves in space in order to obtain information about the universe.

radiocarbon n a radioisotope of carbon used in carbon dating.

radiocarbon dating n carbon dating.

radio frequency n a frequency intermediate between audio frequencies and infrared frequencies used esp in radio and television transmission.

radiography n the production of X-ray photographs for use in medicine, industry, etc.–**radiographer** n.

radiology n a branch of medicine concerned with the use of radiant energy (as X-rays and radium) in the diagnosis and treatment of disease.–**radiologist** n.

radiotherapy n the medical treatment of disease, esp cancer, by X-rays or other radioactive substances.–**radiotherapist** n.

radish n a pungent root eaten raw as a salad vegetable.

radium n a highly radioactive metallic element.

radius n (*pl* **radii**) (*geom*) a straight line joining the center of a circle or sphere to its circumference; a thing like this, a spoke; a sphere of activity; (*anat*) the thicker of the two bones of the forearm.

radon n a gaseous radioactive element.–*also* **niton**.

raffia n a kind of palm; fiber from its leaves used in basket-making, etc.

raffle n a lottery with prizes. * vt to offer as a prize in a raffle.

raft n a platform of logs, planks, etc strapped together to float on water.

rafter n one of the inclined, parallel beams that support a roof.

rag n a torn or waste scrap of cloth; a shred; (*inf*) a sensationalist newspaper; (*pl*) tattered or shabby clothing.

ragamuffin n an unkempt dirty person, esp a child.

rage n violent anger; passion; frenzy; fashion, craze. * vi to behave with violent anger; to storm; to spread rapidly; to be prevalent.

ragged adj jagged; uneven; irregular; worn into rags; tattered.– **raggedly** adv.–**raggedness** n.

raging adj violent; intense.

raglan n a type of loose sleeve cut in one piece with the shoulder of a garment.

ragout n a stew of meat and vegetables, highly seasoned.

ragtime n quick tempo jazz piano music.

raid n a sudden attack to assault or seize. * vt to make a raid on; to steal from.–**raider** n.

rail n a horizontal bar extending from one post to another, as in a fence, etc; one of a pair of parallel steel lines forming a track for the wheels of a train; a railroad.

railing n a fence of rails and posts; rails collectively.

railroad n a track of parallel steel rails along which carriages are drawn by locomotive engines; a complete system of such tracks * vt to force unduly; (*bill, etc*) to push forward fast; to imprison hastily, esp unjustly.

railway n railroad.

rain n water that falls from the clouds in the form of drops; a shower; a large quantity of anything falling like rain; (*pl*) the rainy season in the tropics. * vti (*of rain*) to fall; to fall like rain; (*rain, etc*) to pour down.–**rainy** adj.

rainbow n the arc containing the colors of the spectrum formed in the sky by the refraction of the sun's rays in falling rain or in mist. * adj many-colored.

rain check n a ticket stub allowing future admission to an event in the case of it being rained off; the postponement of acceptance of an offer or invitation.

raincoat n a waterproof coat.

rainfall n a fall of rain; the amount of rain that falls on a given area in a specified time.

rain forest n a dense, evergreen forest in a tropical area with much rainfall.

rainproof adj rain-resisting.

raise vt to elevate; to lift up; to set or place upright; to stir up; rouse; to increase in size, amount, degree, intensity, etc; to breed, bring up; (*question, etc*) to put forward; to collect or levy; (*siege*) to abandon. * n a rise in wages.

raisin n a sweet, dried grape.

raison d'être n (*pl* **raisons d'être**) reason for existence; justification.

rake[1] n a tool with a row of teeth and a handle for gathering together, scraping (leaves, hay, etc) or for smoothing gravel, etc. * vt to scrape, gather as with a rake; to sweep with gaze or gunshot; (*with* **in**: *money, etc*) to gather a great amount rapidly; (*with* **up**: *past misdemeanors, etc*) to bring to light.

rake[2] n a dissolute, debauched man, a libertine.

rakish adj jaunty, dashing; dissolute.–**rakishly** adv.–**rakishness** n.

rally vti (**rallying, rallied**) to bring or come together; to recover strength, revive; to take part in a motor rally; (*with* **round**) to help (a person); to support financially or morally. * n (*pl* **rallies**) a large assembly of people for a political purpose; a recovery (after illness); (*stock exchange*) a sharp increase in price after a decline; (*tennis*) a lengthy exchange of shots; a competitive test of driving and navigational skills.

ram n a male sheep; a battering device; a piston; (*with cap*) Aries, the first sign of the zodiac. * vt (**ramming, rammed**) to force or drive; to crash; to cram; to thrust violently.

ramble vi to wander or stroll about for pleasure; (*plant*) to straggle; to write or talk aimlessly. * n a leisurely walk in the countryside.–**rambler** n.–**rambling** adj.

ramification n a branching out; an offshoot; a consequence.

ramp n a sloping walk or runway joining different levels; a wheeled staircase for boarding a plane; a sloping runway for launching boats, as from trailers.

rampage n angry or violent behavior. * vi to rush about in an angry or violent manner.

rampant adj dominant; luxuriant, unrestrained; violent; rife, prevalent; (her) (of a beast) standing on its hind legs.

rampart n an embankment surrounding a fortification; a protective wall.

ramrod n a rod for ramming home a charge in a muzzle-loading gun. * adj denoting a stiff, inflexible person.

ramshackle adj dilapidated.

ran see **run**.

ranch n a large farm for raising cattle, horses, or sheep; a style of house with all the rooms on one floor. * vi to own, manage, or work on a ranch.–**rancher** n.

rancid adj having an unpleasant smell and taste, as stale fats or oil.–**rancidity, rancidness** n.

rancor, rancour n bitter hate or spite.–**rancorous** adj.–**rancorously** adv.

random adj haphazard; left to chance.

rang see **ring**².

range n a row; a series of mountains, etc; scope, compass; the distance a ship, aircraft, or motor vehicle can travel without refueling; the distance a gun, etc can fire, a projectile can be thrown, or from gun to target; fluctuation; a large open area for grazing livestock; a place for testing rockets in flight; a place for shooting or golf practice; a cooking stove. * vt to place in order or a row; to establish the range of; (livestock) to graze on a range. * vi to be situated in a line; to rank or classify; (gun) to point or aim; to vary (inside limits).

ranger n a forest or park warden.

rank¹ n a line of objects; a line of soldiers standing abreast; high standing or position; status; (pl) ordinary members of the armed forces. * vti to arrange in a line; to have a specific position in an organization or on a scale; to outrank; (with **with**) to be counted among.

rank² adj growing uncontrollably; utter, flagrant; offensive in odor or flavor.

rank and file n ordinary soldiers; ordinary members, as distinguished from their leaders.

rankle vi to fester; to cause continuous resentment or irritation.

ransack vt to plunder, to search thoroughly.

ransom n the release of a captured person or thing; the price paid for this. * vt to secure release of by payment.

rant vi to speak loudly or violently; to preach noisily. * n loud, pompous talk.

rap¹ n a sharp blow; a knock; (inf) talk, conversation; (sl) arrest for a crime; (sl) rap music. * vti (**rapping, rapped**) to strike lightly or sharply; to knock; (sl) to criticize sharply; (with **out**) to utter abruptly; (sl) to speak in a fast and rhythmic manner to a musical backing.

rap² n a style of popular music in which (usu rhyming) words and phrases are spoken in a rhythmic chant over an instrumental backing.–**rapper** n.

rapacious adj grasping; extortionate.–**rapaciously** adv.–**rapacity** n.

rape¹ n the act of forcing a person to have sexual intercourse against his or her will; the plundering (of a city, etc) as in warfare. * vti to commit rape (upon).

rape² n a bright yellow plant of the mustard family grown for its leaves and oily seeds.

rapid adj at great speed; fast; sudden; steep. * npl a part of a river where the current flows swiftly.–**rapidity** n.–**rapidly** adv.

rapier n a straight, two-edged sword with a narrow pointed blade.

rapine n plunder, pillage.

rapist n a person who commits rape.

rapport n a sympathetic relationship; accord.

rapt adj carried away, enraptured; absorbed, intent.

rapture n the state of being carried away with love, joy, etc; intense delight, ecstasy.–**rapturous** adj.–**rapturously** adv.

rare¹ adj unusual; seldom seen; exceptionally good; (gas) of low density, thin. adv.–**rareness** n.

rare² adj not completely cooked, partly raw; underdone.

rarefy vti (**rarefying, rarefied**) to make or become less dense; to thin out; to expand without the addition of matter; to make more spiritual, abstruse or refined.–**rarefied** adj.

rarely adv almost never, seldom; exceptionally, unusually.

raring adj (inf) eager, enthusiastic.

rarity n (pl **rarities**) rareness; a rare person or thing.

rascal n a rogue; a villain; a mischievous person.

rase see **raze**.

rash¹ adj reckless; impetuous.–**rashly** adv.–**rashness** n.

rash² n a skin eruption of spots, etc.

rasp n a coarse file; a grating sound. * vt to scrape with a rasp. * vi to produce a grating sound.

raspberry n (pl **raspberries**) a shrub with white flowers and red berry-like fruits; the fruit produced; (inf) a sound of dislike or derision.

rat n a long-tailed rodent similar to a mouse but larger; (sl) a sneaky, contemptible person, esp an informer; a scab. * vi (**ratting, ratted**) to hunt or catch rats; to betray or inform on someone; to work as a scab.

ratchet n a device with a toothed wheel that moves in one direction only.

rate n the amount, degree, etc of something in relation to units of something else; price, esp per unit; degree. * vt to fix the value of; to rank; to regard or consider; (sl) to think highly of. * vi to have value or status.

rather adv more willingly; preferably; somewhat; more accurately; on the contrary; (inf) yes, certainly.

ratify vt (**ratifying, ratified**) to approve formally; to confirm.

rating n an assessment; an evaluation, an appraisal, as of credit worthiness; classification by grade, as of military personnel; (radio, TV) the relative popularity of a program according to sample polls.

ratio n (pl **ratios**) the number of times one thing contains another; the quantitative relationship between two classes of objects; proportion.

ration n (food, etc) a fixed amount or portion; (pl) food supply. * vt to supply with rations; (food, etc) to restrict the supply of.

rational adj of or based on reason; reasonable; sane.–**rationally** adv.

rationale n the reason for a course of action; an explanation of principles.

rationalize vti to make rational; to justify one's reasons for an action; to cut down on personnel or equipment; to substitute a natural for a supernatural explanation.–**rationalization** n.

rational number n a number that can be expressed as the ratio of two integers.

rat race n continual hectic competitive activity.

rattle vi to clatter. * vt to make a series of sharp, quick noises; to clatter; to recite rapidly; to chatter; (inf) to disconcert, fluster. * n a rattling sound; a baby's toy that makes a rattling sound; a voluble talker; the rings on the tail of a rattlesnake.

rattlesnake n a venomous American snake with a rattle in its tail.

ratty adj (**rattier, rattiest**) like or full of rats; (sl) angry, irritable, snappish.

raucous adj hoarse and harsh-sounding; loud and rowdy.

raunchy adj (**raunchier, raunchiest**) (sl) coarse, earthy; careless, slovenly; cheap, inferior.

ravage vt to ruin, destroy; to plunder, lay waste. * n destruction; ruin; (pl) the effects of this.

rave vi to speak wildly or as if delirious; (inf) to enthuse. * n enthusiastic praise.–**raving** adj.

raven n a large crow-like bird with glossy black feathers. * adj of the color or sheen of a raven.

ravenous adj famished; voracious.–**ravenously** adv.

ravine n a deep, narrow gorge, a large gully.

ravioli n small cases of pasta filled with highly seasoned chopped meat or vegetables.

ravish vt to violate; to rape; to enrapture.–**ravishing** adj.

raw adj uncooked; unrefined; in a natural state, crude; untrained, inexperienced; sore, skinned; damp, chilly; (inf) harsh or unfair.–**rawness** n.

ray[1] n a beam of light that comes from a bright source; any of several lines radiating from a centre; a beam of radiant energy, radioactive particles; a tiny amount.

ray[2] n any of various fishes with a flattened body and the eyes on the upper surface.

rayon n a textile fiber made from a cellulose solution; a fabric of such fibers.

raze vt to demolish; to erase; to level to the ground.–also **rase**.

razor n a sharp-edged instrument for shaving.

razzle-dazzle, razzmatazz n (inf) exciting, exuberant or colorful activity or atmosphere.

RC abbr = Roman Catholic.

Rd abbr = road.

re prep concerning, with reference to.

reach vti to arrive at; to extend as far as; to make contact with; to pass, hand over; to attain, realize; to stretch out the hand; to extend in influence, space, etc; to carry, as sight, sound, etc; to try to get. * n the act or power of reaching; extent; mental range; scope; a continuous extent, esp of water.

react vi to act in response to a person or stimulus; to have a mutual or reverse effect; to revolt; (chem) to undergo a chemical reaction.

reaction n an action in response to a stimulus; a revulsion of feeling; exhaustion after excitement, etc; opposition to new ideas; (chem) an action set up by one substance in another.

reactionary adj, n (a person) opposed to political or social change.

reactor n a person or substance that undergoes a reaction; (chem) a vessel in which a reaction occurs; a nuclear reactor.

read vti (**reading, read**) to understand something written; to speak aloud (from a book); to study by reading; to interpret, divine; to register, as a gauge; to foretell; (of a computer) to obtain (information) from; (sl) to hear and understand (a radio communication, etc); (with **about, of**) to learn by reading; to be phrased in certain words. * adj well-informed.–**reader** n.

readership n all the readers of a certain publication, author, etc.

readily adv in a ready manner; willingly, easily.

read-only memory n a small computer memory that cannot be changed by the computer and that contains a special-purpose program.

ready adj (**readier, readiest**) prepared; fit for use; willing; inclined, apt; prompt, quick; handy. * n the state of being ready, esp the position of a firearm aimed for firing. * vt (**readying, readied**) to make ready.–**readiness** n.

reagent n (chem) a substance used to detect, measure, or react with other substances.

real adj existing, actual, not imaginary; true, genuine, not artificial; (law) immovable, consisting of land or houses. * adv (sl) very; really.

real estate n property; land.

realism n practical outlook; (art, literature) the ability to represent things as they really are without concealment; (philos) the doctrine that the physical world has an objective existence; the doctrine that general ideas have an objective existence.–**realist** n.

realistic adj matter-of-fact, not visionary; lifelike; of or relating to realism.–**realistically** adv.

reality n (pl **realities**) the fact or condition of being real; an actual fact or thing; truth.

realization n the action of realizing; something comprehended or achieved.

realize vt to become fully aware of; (ambition, etc) to make happen; to cause to appear real; to convert into money, be sold for.

really adv in fact, in reality; positively, very. * interj indeed.

realm n a kingdom, country; domain, region; sphere.

real number n any rational or irrational number.

realtor n a person whose business is selling and leasing property, an estate agent.

ream n a quantity of paper varying from 480 to 516 sheets; (pl: inf) a great amount.

reap vti to harvest; to gain (a benefit).–**reaper** n.

rear[1] n the back part or position, esp of an army; (sl) the rump. * adj of, at, or in the rear.

rear[2] vt to raise; (children) to bring up; to educate, nourish, etc. * vi (horse) to stand on the hind legs.

rear admiral n a naval officer next below in rank to a vice admiral.

rear guard n a military detachment assigned to guard the rear of a body of troops. * adj relating to determined defensive resistance.

rearm vti to arm or become armed again, esp with better weapons.–**rearmament** n.

rearward adj, adv at or toward the rear.–**rearwards** adv.

reason n motive or justification (of an action or belief); the mental power to draw conclusions and determine truth; a cause; moderation; sanity; intelligence. * vti to think logically (about); to analyze; to argue or infer.

reasonable adj able to reason or listen to reason; rational; sensible; not expensive; moderate, fair.–**reasonableness** n.–**reasonably** adv.

reassure vt to hearten; to give confidence to; to free from anxiety.–**reassurance** n.

rebate n a refund of part of an amount paid; discount.

rebel n a person who refuses to conform with convention. * vi (**rebeling, rebeled** or **rebelling, rebelled**) (army) to rise up against the authorities or the government; to dissent.

rebellion n armed resistance to an established government, insurrection; defiance of authority.

rebellious adj of or engaged in rebellion; tending to rebel; stubborn.–**rebelliously** adv.

rebirth n a second or new birth; a revival, renaissance; spiritual regeneration.

rebound vi to spring back after impact; to bounce back; to recover. * n a recoil; an emotional reaction.

rebuff vt to snub, repulse; to refuse unexpectedly.–also n.

rebuke vt to reprimand, chide. * n a reproof, reprimand.

rebut vt (**rebutting, rebutted**) to disprove or refute by argument, etc.–**rebuttal** n.

recalcitrant adj refusing to obey authority, etc; actively disobedient.–**recalcitrance** n.

recall vt to call back; to bring back to mind, remember; to revoke. * n remembrance; a summons to return; the removal from office by popular vote.

recant vti to repudiate or retract a former opinion, declaration, or belief.–**recantation** n.

recap vti (**recapping, recapped**) to recapitulate. * n (inf) recapitulation.

recapitulate vt to restate the main points of, to summarize.–**recapitulation** n.

recede vi to move back; to withdraw, retreat; to slope backwards; to grow less; to decline in value.–**receding** adj.

receipt n the act of receiving; a written proof of this; (pl) amount received from business. * vt to acknowledge and mark as paid; to write a receipt for.

receive vt to acquire, be given; to experience, be subjected to; to admit, allow; to greet on arrival; to accept as true; (stolen goods) to take in; to transfer electrical signals. * vi to be a recipient; to convert radio waves into perceptible signals.

received *adj* accepted, recognized.

receiver *n* a person who receives; equipment that receives electronic signals, esp on a telephone; (*law*) a person appointed to manage or hold in trust property in bankruptcy or pending a lawsuit.–**receivership** *n*.

recent *adj* happening lately, fresh; not long established, modern.–**recently** *adv*.

receptacle *n* a container.

reception *n* the act of receiving or being received; a welcome; a social gathering, often to extend a formal welcome; a response, reaction; the quality of the sound or image produced by a radio or television set.

receptionist *n* a person employed to receive visitors to an office, hotel, hospital, etc.

receptive *adj* able or quick to take in ideas or impressions.

recess *n* a temporary halting of work, a vacation; a hidden or inner place; an alcove or niche. * *vti* to place in a recess; to form a recess in; to take a recess.

recession *n* the act of receding; a downturn in economic activity; an indentation.

recharge *vi* to renew the electric charge in (a battery, etc) to recover one's energies.

recipe *n* a list of ingredients and directions for preparing food; a method for achieving an end.

recipient *n* a person who receives.

reciprocal *adj* done by each to the other; mutual; complementary; interchangeable. * *n* (*math*) an expression so related to another that their product is 1.–**reciprocally** *adv*.–**reciprocity** *n*.

reciprocate *vti* to give in return; to repay; (*mech*) to move alternately backwards and forwards.–**reciprocating** *adj*.–**reciprocation** *n*.

recital *n* the act of reciting; a detailed account, narrative; a statement of facts; (*mus*) a performance given by an individual musician.

recitation *n* the act of reciting; something recited, as a poem, etc.

recite *vti* to repeat aloud from memory, declaim; to recount, enumerate; to repeat (a lesson).

reckless *adj* rash, careless, incautious.–**recklessly** *adv*.–**recklessness** *n*.

reckon *vti* to count; to regard or consider; to think; to calculate; (*with* **with**) to take into account.

reckoning *n* a calculation; the settlement of an account.

reclaim *vt* to recover, win back from a wild state or vice; (*wasteland*) to convert into land fit for cultivation; (*plastics, etc*) to obtain from waste materials.–**reclaimable** *adj*.–**reclamation** *n*.

recline *vti* to cause or permit to lean or bend backwards; to lie down on the back or side.–**reclinable** *adj*.

recluse *n* a person who lives in solitude; a hermit.

recognition *n* the act of recognizing; identification; acknowledgment, admission.

recognize *vt* to know again, identify; to greet; to acknowledge formally; to accept, admit.–**recognizable** *adj*.

recoil *vti* to spring back, kick, as a gun; to shrink or flinch. * *n* the act of recoiling, a rebound.

recollect *vti* to recall; to remind (oneself) of something temporarily forgotten; to call something to mind.

recollection *n* the act of recalling to mind; a memory, impression; something remembered; tranquility of mind; religious contemplation.

recommend *vt* to counsel or advise; to commend or praise; to introduce favorably.–**recommendable** *adj*.–**recommendation** *n*.

recompense *n* to reward or pay an equivalent; to compensate. * *n* reward; repayment; compensation.

reconcile *vt* to re-establish friendly relations; to bring to agreement; to make compatible; to resolve; to settle; to make resigned (to); (*financial account*) to check with another account for accuracy.–**reconcilable** *adj*.–**reconciliation** *n*.

recondition *vt* to repair and restore to good working order.

reconnaissance *n* a survey of an area, esp for obtaining military information about an enemy.

reconnoiter, reconnoitre *vti* to make a reconnaissance (of).

reconsider *vt* to consider afresh, review; to modify.–**reconsideration** *n*.

reconstitute *vt* (*a dried or condensed substance*) to constitute again, esp to restore to its original form by adding water.–**reconstitution** *n*.

reconstruct *vt* to build again; to build up, as from remains, an image of the original; to supply missing parts by conjecture.–**reconstruction** *n*.

record *vt* to preserve evidence of; to write down; to chart; to register, enrol; to register permanently by mechanical means; (*sound or visual images*) to register on a disc, tape, etc for later reproduction; to celebrate; to make a recording. * *vi* to record something. * *adj* being the best, largest, etc. * *n* a written account; a register; a report of proceedings; the known facts about anything or anyone; an outstanding performance or achievement that surpasses others previously recorded; a grooved vinyl disc for playing on a record player; (*comput*) data in machine-readable form.

recorder *n* an official who keeps records; a machine or device that records; a tape recorder; a wind instrument of the flute family.

recording *n* what is recorded, as on a disc or tape; the record.

recount[1] *vt* to narrate the details of; to narrate.

recount[2] *vt* to count again * *n* a second counting of votes at an election.

recoup *vti* to make good (financial losses); to regain; to make up for something lost.

recourse *n* a resort for help or protection when in danger; that to which one turns when seeking help.

recover *vti* to regain after losing; to reclaim; to regain health or after losing emotional control.–**recoverable** *adj*.–**recovery** *n*.

recreation *n* relaxation of the body or mind; a sport, pastime or amusement.–**recreational** *adj*.

recriminate *vi* to return an accusation, make a countercharge.–**recrimination** *n*.–**recriminatory** *adj*.

recruit *n* a soldier newly enlisted; a member newly joined; a beginner. * *vti* to enlist (military personnel); to enlist (new members) for an organization; to increase or maintain the numbers of; to restore, reinvigorate.–**recruitment** *n*.

rectangle *n* a parallelogram with all its angles right angles.–**rectangular** *adj*.

rectify *vt* (**rectifying, rectified**) to put right, correct; to amend.–**rectifiable** *adj*.

rectitude *n* moral uprightness; probity; a being correct in judgment or procedure.

rector *n* in some churches, a clergyman in charge of a parish; the head of certain schools, colleges, etc.–**rectorial** *adj*.

rectum *n* (*pl* **rectums, recta**) the part of the large intestine leading to the anus.–**rectal** *adj*.

recumbent *adj* leaning, resting; lying down.

recuperate *vti* to get well again; to recover (losses, etc).–**recuperation** *n*.

recur *vi* (**recurring, recurred**) to be repeated in thought, talk, etc; to occur again or at intervals.–**recurrence** *n*.–**recurrent** *adj*.

recycle *vti* (*a substance*) to pass through a process again; (*used matter*) to process to regain re-usable material; to save from loss and restore to usefulness.–**recyclable** *adj*.

red *adj* (**redder, reddest**) of the color of blood; politically leftwing. * *n* the color of blood; any red pigment; a communist.

red carpet *n* a strip of red carpet for dignitaries to walk on; a grand or impressive welcome or entertainment.

Red Cross *n* a red cross on a white ground, the symbol of the International Red Cross, a society for the relief of suffering in time of war and disaster.

redden *vti* to make or become red; to blush.

redeem vt to recover by payment; to regain; to deliver from sin; to pay off; to restore to favor; to make amends for.–**redeemable** adj.–**redeemer** n.

redemption n the act of redeeming or the state of being redeemed; recovery; repurchase; salvation.

redeploy vt (troops, workers) to assign to new positions or activities.–**redeployment** n.

red-handed adj caught in the act of committing a crime.

redhead n a person having red hair.–**redheaded** adj.

red herring n a herring cured to a dark brown color; something that diverts attention from the real issue.

red-hot adj glowing with heat; extremely hot; very excited, angry, etc; very new.

red-light adj (of a district) containing brothels.

redneck n (derog) a poor white farm laborer in the US South. * adj racist, reactionary.

redo vt (**redoing, redid,** pp **redone**) to do again; to redecorate.

redolent adj having a strong scent, fragrant; reminiscent (of).–**redolence** n.

redoubtable adj formidable.

redound vi to have a directly positive or negative effect (on); to rebound (on or upon).

redress vt to put right, adjust; to compensate, make up for. * n remedy; compensation.

red tape n rigid adherence to bureaucratic routine and regulations, causing delay.

reduce vt to diminish or make smaller in size, amount, extent, or number; to lower in price; to simplify; to make thin; to subdue; to bring or convert (to another state or form).–**reducible** adj.

reduction n the act or process of reducing or being reduced; something reduced; the amount by which a thing is reduced.–**reductional** adj.–**reductive** adj.

redundant adj surplus to requirements; (words) unnecessary to the meaning.–**redundancy** n.

reduplicate vt to make double, to repeat. * adj doubled, repeated.–**reduplication** n.–**reduplicative** adj.

redwood n an important timber tree of California that can reach a height of 360 feet; any of various trees yielding a red dye or reddish wood.

reed n a tall grass found in marshes; a thin piece of cane in the mouthpiece of a musical instrument.

reef n a ridge of rocks, sand, or coral at or just below the surface of water; a hazardous obstruction; a lode or vein of ore.

reef knot n a symmetrical double knot.

reek n a strong smell. * vi to give off smoke, fumes or a strong or offensive smell.

reel[1] n a winding device; a spool or bobbin; thread wound on this; a length of film, about 300m (1,000ft). * vt to wind on to a reel; (with **in**) to draw in by means of a reel; (with **off**) to tell, write, etc with fluency; (with **out**) to unwind from a reel.

reel[2] vi to stagger or sway about; to be dizzy or in a whirl. * n a staggering motion.

reel[3] n a lively Scottish or Irish dance; the music for it. * vi to dance a reel.

ref n (inf) a referee.

refer vti (**referring, referred**) to attribute, assign (to); (with **to**) to direct, have recourse (to); to relate to; to mention or allude to; to direct attention (to).–**referable** adj.–**referral** n.

referee n an adjudicator, arbitrator; an umpire; a judge.

reference n the act of referring; a mention or allusion; a testimonial; a person who gives a testimonial; a direction to a passage in a book; a passage in a book referred to.

referendum n (pl **referendums, referenda**) the submission of an issue directly to the vote of the electorate, a plebiscite.

refill vt to fill again. * n a replacement pack for an empty permanent container; a providing again.

refine vti to purify; to make free from impurities or coarseness; to make or become cultured.–**refinement** n.

refinery n (pl **refineries**) a plant where raw materials, eg sugar, oil, are refined.

refit vti (**refitting, refitted**) to make or become functional again by repairing, re-equipping, etc.–also n.

reflect vt (light, heat, etc) to throw back; to bend aside or back; to show an image of, as a mirror; to express. * vi to reproduce to the eye or mind; to mirror; to meditate; (with **upon**) to ponder; (with **on**) to discredit, disparage.

reflection n a reflecting back, turning aside; the action of changing direction when a ray strikes and is thrown back; reflected heat, light or color; a reflected image; meditation, thought; reconsideration; reproach.

reflective adj meditative; concerned with ideas.–**reflectively** adv.–**reflectiveness** n.

reflector n a disc, instrument, strip or other surface that reflects light or heat.

reflex n an involuntary response to a stimulus. * adj (angle) of more than 180 degrees; (camera) with a full-size viewfinder using the main lens.

reflexology n (alternative medicine) a technique of applying pressure to specific points on the hands and feet to stimulate the blood supply to other areas of the body and help relieve stress.–**reflexologist** n.

reform vti to improve; to make or become better by the removal of faults; to amend; to abolish abuse. * n improvement or transformation, esp of an institution; removal of social ills.–**reformation** n.–**reformed** adj.–**reformer** n.

refraction n the bending of a ray or wave of light, heat, or sound as it passes from one medium into another.–**refract** vt.

refractory adj obstinate; (disease, etc) resistant to treatment

refrain[1] vi to abstain (from).

refrain[2] n recurring words in a song or poem, esp at the end of a stanza; a chorus.

refresh vt to revive; to give new energy to; to make cool; to take a drink.

refresher n something that refreshes, esp a drink; a reminder; a training course to renew one's skill or knowledge.

refreshing adj invigorating, reviving; pleasing because unsophisticated.

refreshment n the act of refreshing; a restorative; (pl) food and drink; a light meal.

refrigerate vti to make, become, or keep, cold; to preserve by keeping cold.–**refrigeration** n.

refrigerator n something that refrigerates; a chamber for keeping food, etc, cool; an apparatus for cooling.–also **fridge, icebox.**

refuel vti (**refueling, refueled** or **refuelling, refuelled**) to supply with or take on fresh fuel.

refuge n a protection or shelter from danger; a retreat, sanctuary.

refugee n a person who flees to another country to escape political or religious persecution.

refund vti to repay; to reimburse. * n a refunding or the amount refunded.

refurbish vt to renovate or re-equip.–**refurbishment** n.

refuse[1] n garbage, waste, rubbish.

refuse[2] vt to decline, reject; to withhold, deny. * vi (horse) to decline to jump.–**refusal** n.

refute vt to rebut; to disprove.–**refutable** adj.–**refutably** adv.–**refutation** n.

regain vt to get back, recover; to reach again.

regal adj royal; relating to a king or queen.

regale vt to entertain, as with a feast; to delight.

regalia npl royal insignia or prerogatives; the insignia of an order, office, or membership; finery.

regard vt to gaze at, observe; to hold in respect; to consider; to heed, take into account. * n a look; attention; reference; respect, esteem; (pl) good wishes, greetings.

regarding prep with reference to, about.

regardless *adj* having no regard to. * *adv* (*inf*) in spite of everything; without heeding the cost, consequences, etc.

regenerate *vti* to renew, give new life to; to be reborn spiritually; to reorganize; to produce anew.–**regeneration** *n*.

regent *n* a person who rules or administers a country during the sovereign's minority, absence, or incapacity; a member of a governing board (as of a university).–**regency** *n*.

reggae *n* a strongly accented West Indian musical form with four beats to the bar.

regime, régime *n* a political or ruling system.

regiment *n* a military unit, smaller than a division, consisting usu of a number of battalions. * *vt* to organize in a strict manner; to subject to order or conformity.–**regimental** *adj*.

region *n* a large, indefinite part of the earth's surface; one of the zones into which the atmosphere is divided; an administrative area of a country; a part of the body.–**regional** *adj*.

register *n* an official list; a written record, as for attendance; the book containing such a record or list; a tone of voice; a variety of language appropriate to a subject or occasion. * *vti* to record; to enter in or sign a register; to correspond exactly; to express emotion facially; to make or convey an impression.

registrar *n* a person who keeps records, esp one in an educational institution in charge of student records.

registration *n* the act of registering; the condition of having registered.

registry *n* (*pl* **registries**) registration; a place where records are kept; an official record book.

regress *vi* to move backwards; to revert to a former condition.–**regression** *n*.–**regressive** *adj*.–**regressively** *adv*.

regret *vt* (**regretting, regretted**) to feel sorrow, grief, or loss; to remember with longing; (*with* **that**) to repent of. * *n* disappointment; sorrow; grief; (*pl*) polite refusal.–**regretful** *adj*.–**regretfully** *adv*.–**regrettable** *adj*.

regular *adj* normal; habitual, not casual; at fixed intervals; according to rule, custom, or the accepted practice; uniform, consistent; symmetrical; fully qualified; belonging to a standing army; (*inf*) thorough, complete; (*inf*) pleasant, friendly. * *n* a professional soldier; (*inf*) a person who attends regularly.–**regularity** *n*.–**regularly** *adv*.

regulate *vt* to control according to a rule; to cause to conform to a standard or needs; to adjust so as to put in good order.–**regulator** *n*.–**regulatory** *adj*.

regulation *n* the act of regulating or state of being regulated; a prescribed rule, ordinance. * *adj* normal, standard.

regurgitate *vti* to pour back, cast up again, esp from the stomach to the mouth.–**regurgitation** *n*.

rehabilitate *vt* (*prisoner etc*) to help adapt to society after a stay in an institution; to put back in good condition; to restore to rights or privileges; (*sick person etc*) to help to adjust to normal conditions after illness.–**rehabilitation** *n*.

rehash *n* old materials put in a new form. * *vt* to dish up again.

rehearse *vti* to practice repeatedly before public performance; to recount, narrate in detail.–**rehearsal** *n*.

reign *n* the rule of a sovereign; the period of this; influence; domination. * *vi* to rule; to prevail.

reimburse *vt* to repay; to refund (for expense or loss).–**reimbursable** *adj*.–**reimbursement** *n*.

rein *n* the strap of a bridle for guiding or restraining a horse; (*pl*) a means of control or restraint. * *vt* to control with the rein; to restrain.

reincarnation *n* the incarnation of the soul after death in another body.–**reincarnate** *adj*, *vt*.

reindeer *n* a large deer with branched antlers found in northern regions.

reinforce *vt* (*army etc*) to strengthen with fresh troops; (*a material*) to add to the strength of.–**reinforcement** *n*.

reinstate *vt* to restore to a former position, rank, or condition.–**reinstatement** *n*.

reiterate *vt* to repeat; to say or do again or many times.–**reiteration** *n*.

reject *vt* to throw away, to discard; to refuse to accept, to decline; to rebuff. * *n* a thing or person rejected.–**rejection** *n*.

rejoice *vi* to feel joyful or happy.

rejoin *vt* to join again; to return to.

rejoinder *n* a retort, a reply.

rejuvenate *vt* to give youthful vigor to.–**rejuvenation** *n*.

relapse *vi* to fall back into a worse state after improvement; to return to a former vice, to backslide. * *n* the recurrence of illness after apparent recovery.

relate *vt* to narrate, recount; to show a connection (between two or more things). * *vi* to have a formal relationship (with).

relation *n* the way in which one thing stands in respect to another, footing; reference, regard; connection by blood or marriage; a relative; a narration, a narrative; (*pl*) the connections between or among persons, nations, etc; (*pl*) one's family and in-laws.

relationship *n* the tie or degree of kinship or intimacy; affinity; (*inf*) an affair.

relative *adj* having or expressing a relation; corresponding; pertinent; comparative, conditional; respective; meaningful only in relationship; (*gram*) referring to an antecedent. * *n* a person related by blood or marriage.–**relatively** *adv*.

relativity *n* the state of being relative; the relation between one thing and another; (*physics*) the theory of the relative, rather than absolute, character of motion, velocity, mass, etc, and the interdependence of time, matter, and space.

relax *vti* to slacken; to make or become less severe or strict; to make (the muscles) less rigid; to take a rest.–**relaxation** *n*.

relay *n* a team of fresh horses, men, etc to relieve others; a race between teams, each member of which goes a part of the distance; a relayed broadcast. * *vt* (**relaying, relayed**) (*news, etc*) to spread in stages; to broadcast signals.

release *vt* to set free; to let go; to relinquish; (*film, etc*) to issue for public exhibition; (*information*) to make available. * *n* a releasing, as from prison, work, etc; a device to hold or release a mechanism; a news item, etc, released to the public.

relegate *vt* to move to an inferior position; to demote; to banish.–**relegation** *n*.

relent *vi* to soften in attitude; to become less harsh or severe.

relentless *adj* pitiless; unremitting.

relevant *adj* applying to the matter in hand, pertinent; to the point.–**relevance, relevancy** *n*.

reliable *adj* dependable, trustworthy.–**reliability** *n*.–**reliably** *adv*.

reliance *n* trust; dependence; a thing relied on.–**reliant** *adj*.

relic *n* an object, fragment, or custom that has survived from the past; part of a saint's body or belongings; (*pl*) remains of the dead.

relief *n* the sensation following the easing or lifting of discomfort or stress; release from a duty by another person; a person who takes the place of another on duty; that which relieves; aid; assistance to the needy or victims of a disaster; the projection of a carved design from its ground; distinctness, vividness. * *adj* providing relief in disasters etc.

relieve *vt* to bring relief or assistance to; to release from obligation or duty; to ease; (*with* **oneself**) to empty the bladder or bowels. * *vi* to give relief; to break the monotony of; to bring into relief, to stand out.

religion *n* a belief in God or gods; a system of worship and faith; a formalized expression of belief.

religious *adj* of or conforming to religion; devout, pious; scrupulously and conscientiously faithful.–**religiously** *adv*.

relinquish *vt* to give up; to renounce or surrender.–**relinquishment** *n*.

relish *n* an appetizing flavor; a distinctive taste; enjoyment of food or an experience; a spicy accompaniment to food; gusto, zest. * *vt* to like the flavor of; to enjoy, appreciate.

reluctant adj unwilling, loath; offering resistance.–**reluctance** n.–**reluctantly** adv.

rely vi (**relying, relied**) to depend on; to trust.

remain vi to stay behind or in the same place; to continue to be; to survive, to last; to be left over. * npl anything left after use; a corpse.

remainder n what is left, the rest; (math) the result of subtraction; the quantity left over after division; unsold stock, esp of books.

remark vti to notice; to observe; to pass a comment (upon). * n a brief comment.

remarkable adj unusual; extraordinary; worthy of comment.– **remarkably** adv.

remedial adj providing a remedy; corrective; relating to the teaching of people with learning difficulties.

remedy n a medicine or any means to cure a disease; anything that puts something else to rights. * vt (**remedying, remedied**) to cure; to put right.

remember vti to recall; to bear in mind; to mention (a person) to another as sending regards; to exercise or have the power of memory.

remembrance n a reminiscence; a greeting or gift recalling or expressing friendship or affection; the extent of memory; an honoring of the dead or a past event.

remind vt to cause to remember.

reminder n a thing that reminds, esp a letter from a creditor.

reminisce vi to think, talk, or write about past events.

reminiscence n the recalling of a past experience; (pl) memoirs.

reminiscent adj reminding, suggestive (of); recalling the past.

remiss adj negligent, slack.

remission n the act of remitting; the reduction in length of a prison term; the lessening of the symptoms of a disease; pardon, forgiveness.

remit vti (**remitting, remitted**) to forgive; to refrain from inflicting (a punishment) or exacting (a debt); to abate, moderate; to send payment (by mail). * n the act of referring; an area of authority.

remittance n the sending of money or a payment (by mail); the payment or money sent.

remnant n a small remaining fragment or number; an oddment or scrap; a trace; an unsold or unused end of piece goods.

remodel vt (**remodeling, remodeled** or **remodelling, remodelled**) to fashion afresh; to recast.

remonstrate vi to protest, to make a complaint (against).– **remonstrance** n.

remorse n regret and guilt for a misdemeanor; compassion.– **remorseful** adj.–**remorsefully** adv.

remorseless adj ruthless, cruel; relentless.–**remorselessly** adv.–**remorselessness** n.

remote adj far apart or distant in time or place; out of the way; not closely related; secluded; aloof; vague, faint.–**remotely** adv.

remote control n the control of a device or activity from a distance, usu by means of an electric circuit or the making or breaking of radio waves.

remove vti to take away and put elsewhere; to dismiss, as from office; to get rid of; to kill; to go away. * n a stage in gradation; a degree in relationship.–**removable** adj.–**removal** n.

remunerate vt to pay for a service; to reward.–**remuneration** n.

renaissance n a rebirth or revival; (with cap) the revival of European art and literature under the influence of classical study during the 14th–16th centuries.–also adj.

rend vti (**rending, rent**) to tear, to wrench (apart); to be torn apart.

render vt (payments, accounts, etc) to submit, as for approval; to give back; to pay back; to perform; to represent as by drawing; to translate, interpret; to cause to be; (fat) to melt down.

rendezvous n (pl **rendezvous**) an arranged meeting; a place to meet; a popular haunt; the process of bringing two spacecraft together. * vi to meet by appointment.

rendition n an interpretation; performance.

renegade n a deserter; a person who is faithless to a principle, party, religion, or cause.

renege vti to go back on, or fail to keep, a promise or agreement.

renew vti to restore to freshness or vigor; to begin again; to make or get anew; to replace; to grant or obtain an extension of.– **renewable** adj.–**renewal** n.

renounce vt to abandon formally; to give up; to disown.

renovate vt to renew; to restore to good condition; to do up, repair.–**renovation** n.–**renovator** n.

renown n fame, celebrity.–**renowned** adj.

rent[1] see **rend**.

rent[2] n regular payment to another for the use of a house, machinery, etc. * vti to occupy as a tenant; to hire; to let for rent.

rental n an amount paid or received as rent; a house, car, etc, for rent; an act of renting; a business that rents something.

renunciation n the act of renouncing; formal abandonment; repudiation.

repair vt to mend; to restore to good working order; to make amends for. * n the act of repairing; a place repaired; condition as to soundness.

reparation n amends; (pl) compensation, as for war damage.

repartee n a witty reply; skill in making such replies.

repatriate vt to send back or restore to one's country of origin or citizenship.–**repatriation** n.

repay vt (**repaying, repaid**) to pay back; to refund.– **repayable** adj.–**repayment** n.

repeal vt to annul, to rescind; to revoke.–also n.

repeat vti to say, write, or do again; to reiterate; to recite after another or from memory; to reproduce; to recur. * n a repetition, encore; anything said or done again, as a re-broadcast of a television program; (mus) a passage to be repeated; the sign for this.–**repeatable** adj.–**repeated** adj.

repeatedly adv many times, over and over again.

repel vt (**repelling, repelled**) to drive back; to beat off, repulse; to reject; to hold off; to cause distaste; (water, dirt) to be resistant to.

repellent adj distasteful, unattractive; capable of repelling; impermeable. * n a substance that repels, esp a spray for protection against insects.

repent vi to wish one had not done something; to feel remorse or regret (for); to regret and change from evil ways.–**repentance** n.–**repentant** adj.

repercussion n a rebound; a reverberation; a far-reaching, often indirect reaction to an event.

repertoire n the stock of plays, songs, etc, that a company, singer, etc, can perform.

repetition n the act of repeating; something repeated, a copy.– **repetitive** adj.

repetitious adj full of repetition; boring.–**repetitiously** adv.– **repetitiousness** n.

replace vt to put back; to take the place of, to substitute for; to supersede.–**replaceable** adj.–**replacement** n.

replenish vt to stock again, refill.–**replenishment** n.

replete adj filled, well provided; stuffed, gorged.

replica n an exact copy; a reproduction.

reply vti (**replying, replied**) to answer, respond; to give as an answer. * n an answer.

report vti to give an account of; to tell as news; to take down and describe for publication; to make a formal statement of; to complain about or against; to inform against; to present oneself (for duty). * n an account of facts; the formal statement of the findings of an investigation; a newspaper, radio or television account of an event; a rumor; a sharp, loud noise, as of a gun.

reporter n a person who gathers and reports news for a newspaper, radio or television.

repose n rest, sleep; stillness, peace; composure, serenity. * vti to lie down or lay at rest; to place (trust, etc) in someone; to rest; to lie dead.

repository n (pl **repositories**) a receptacle; a storehouse, warehouse; a confidant.

repossess vt to possess again; to restore possession of (property), esp for nonpayment of debt.–**repossession** n.

reprehensible adj blameworthy, culpable.

represent vt to portray; to describe; to typify; to stand for, symbolize; to point out; to perform on the stage; to act as an agent for; to deputize for; to serve as a specimen, example, etc, of.–**representable** adj.–**representation** n.

representative adj typical; portraying; consisting of or based on representation of the electorate by delegates. * n an example or type; a person who acts for another; a member of a house of legislature; a delegate, agent, salesman, etc.

repress vt to suppress, restrain; (emotions) to keep under control; to exclude involuntarily from the conscious mind.–**repression** n.–**repressive** adj.–**represser, repressor** n.

reprieve vt to postpone or commute the punishment of; to give respite to.–also n.

reprimand n a formal rebuke. * vt to reprove formally.

reprisal n an act of retaliation for an injury done.

reproach vt to accuse of a fault; to blame. * n a reproof; a source of shame or disgrace.–**reproachful** adj.

reprobate n a depraved person; a hardened sinner; a scoundrel.

reproduce vti to make a copy, duplicate, or likeness of; to propagate; to produce offspring; to multiply.–**reproduction** n.–**reproductive** adj.

reproof n a rebuke, blame.

reprove vt to rebuke, censure.–**reprovingly** adv.

reptile n any of a class of cold-blooded, air-breathing vertebrates with horny scales or plates, as turtles, crocodiles, snakes, lizards, etc; a grovelling or despised person.–**reptilian** adj.

republic n a government in which the people elect the head of state, usu called president, and in which the people and their elected representatives have supreme power; a country governed in this way; a body of persons freely engaged in a specified activity.

republican adj of, characteristic of, or supporting a republic. * n an advocate of republican government; (with cap) a member of the US Republican party.–**republicanism** n.

repudiate vt to reject, disown; to refuse to acknowledge or pay; to deny; (a treaty, etc) to disavow.–**repudiation** n.

repugnant adj distasteful, offensive; contradictory; incompatible.–**repugnance** n.

repulse vt to drive back; to repel; to reject. * n a rebuff, rejection; a defeat, check.–**repulsion** n.

repulsive adj disgusting; loathsome; exercising repulsion.–**repulsively** adv.

reputable adj of good repute, respectable.–**reputably** adv.

reputation n the estimation in which a person or thing is held; good name, honor.

repute vt to consider to be, to deem. * n reputation.

request n an asking for something; a petition; a demand; the thing asked for. * vt to ask for earnestly.

requiem n a mass for the dead; music for this.

require vt to demand; to need, call for; to order, command.–**requirement** n.

requisite adj needed; essential, indispensable. * n something required or indispensable.

requisition n a formal request, demand, or order, as for military supplies; the taking over of private property, etc, for military use. * vt to order; to take by requisition.

rerun vt to run (a race, etc) again; to show a television program, movie, etc again.–also n.

rescue vt to save (a person, thing) from captivity, danger, or harm; to free forcibly from legal custody.–also n.–**rescuer** n.

research n a diligent search; a systematic and careful investigation of a particular subject; a scientific study. * vi to carry out an investigation; to study.–**researcher** n.

resemble vt to be like, to have a similarity to.–**resemblance** n.

resent vt to be indignant about; to begrudge; to take badly.–**resentful** adj.–**resentfully** adv.–**resentment** n.

reservation n the act of reserving; (of tickets, accommodation, etc) a holding until called for; a limitation or proviso; (pl) doubt, skepticism; land set aside for a special purpose.

reserve vt to hold back for future use; to retain; to have set aside; (tickets, hotel room, etc) to book. * n something put aside for future use; land set aside for wild animals; (sport) a substitute; (mil) a force supplementary to a regular army; a restriction or qualification; reticence of feelings; caution.

reserved adj set apart, booked; uncommunicative, lacking cordiality.–**reservedly** adv.

reservoir n a tank or artificial lake for storing water; an extra supply or store.

reside vi to live in a place permanently; to be vested or present in.

residence n the act of living in a place; the period of residing; the house where one lives permanently; the status of a legal resident; a building used as a home.–**residential** adj.

resident adj residing; domiciled; living at one's place of work. * n a permanent inhabitant; a doctor who is training at a hospital.

residue n a remainder; a part left over; what is left of an estate after payment of debts and legacies.–**residual** adj.

resign vti to give up (employment, etc); to relinquish; to yield to; to reconcile (oneself).–**resignation** n.

resigned adj submissive, acquiescent; accepting the inevitable.

resilient adj elastic, springing back; buoyant; (person) capable of carrying on after suffering hardship.

resin n a sticky substance exuded in the sap of trees and plants and used in medicines, varnishes, etc; rosin; a similar synthetic substance used in plastics.–**resinous** adj.

resist vti to fight against; to be proof against; to oppose or withstand.

resistance n the act of resisting; the power to resist, as to ward off disease; opposition, esp to an occupying force; hindrance; (elect) non-conductivity, opposition to a steady current.

resistant adj capable of resisting; (with **to**) immune to.

resolute adj determined; firm of purpose, steadfast.–**resolutely** adv.–**resoluteness** n.

resolution n the act of resolving or the state of being resolved; determination; a fixed intention; the formal decision or opinion of a meeting; analysis, disintegration; the picture definition in a TV.

resolve vt to break into component parts, dissolve; to convert or be converted (into); to analyze; to determine, make up one's mind; to solve, settle; to vote by resolution; to dispel (doubt); to explain; to conclude. * n a fixed intention; resolution; courage.

resonance n resounding quality, vibration.–**resonant** adj.

resort n a popular holiday location; a source of help, support, etc; recourse. * vi to have recourse to; to turn (to) for help, etc.

resound vti to echo; to reverberate; to go on sounding; to be much talked of; to spread (fame).

resounding adj echoing; notable; thorough.

resource n source of help; an expedient; the ability to cope with a situation; a means of diversion; (pl) wealth; assets; raw materials.–**resourceful** adj.–**resourcefulness** n.

respect n esteem; consideration; regard; (pl) good wishes; reference; relation. * vt to feel or show esteem or regard to; to treat considerately.–**respectful** adj.–**respectfully** adv.

respectable adj worthy of esteem; well-behaved; proper, correct, well-conducted; of moderate quality or size.–**respectability** n.–**respectably** adv.

respecting prep concerning.

respective adj proper to each, several.

respectively adv in the indicated order.

respiration n the act or process of breathing.–**respiratory** adj.–**respire** vti.

respirator n an apparatus to maintain breathing by artificial means; a device or mask to prevent the inhalation of harmful substances.

respite n a temporary delay; a period of rest or relief; a reprieve.

resplendent adj dazzling, shining brilliantly; magnificent.

respond vti to answer; to reply; to show a favorable reaction; to be answerable; (with **to**) to react.

response n an answer; a reaction to stimulation.–**responsive** adj.

responsible adj having control (over); (with **for**) accountable (for); capable of rational conduct; trustworthy; involving responsibility.–**responsibility** n.–**responsibly** adv.

rest[1] n stillness, repose, sleep; inactivity; the state of not moving; relaxation; tranquillity; a support or prop; a pause in music, meter, etc; a place of quiet. * vti to take a rest; to give rest to; to be still; to lie down; to relax; to be fixed (on); to lean, support or be supported; to put one's trust (in).

rest[2] n the remainder; the others. * vi to remain.

restaurant n a place where meals can be bought and eaten.

restaurateur n the keeper of a restaurant.

restful adj peaceful.–**restfully** adv.–**restfulness** n.

restitution n the restoring of something to its owner; a reimbursement, as for loss.

restless adj unsettled; agitated.–**restlessly** adv.–**restlessness** n.

restorative adj tending to restore health and strength. * n a medicine or food that reinvigorates.

restore vt to give or put back; to re-establish; to repair; to renovate; to bring back to the original condition.–**restoration** n.–**restorer** n.

restrain vt to hold back; to restrict; (person) to deprive of freedom.

restraint n the ability to hold back; something that restrains; control of emotions, impulses, etc.

restrict vt to keep within limits, circumscribe.–**restriction** n.–**restrictive** adj.

restroom n a room equipped with toilets, washbowls, etc for the use of the public.

result vi to have as a consequence; to terminate in. * n a consequence; an outcome; a value obtained by mathematical calculation; (sport) the final score; (pl) a desired effect.

resume vti to begin again; to continue after a stop or pause; to proceed after interruption.–**resumption** n.

résumé n a summary, esp of employment experience; a curriculum vitae.

resurgence n a revival; a renewal of activity.–**resurgent** adj.

resurrect vt to bring back into use; (a custom) to revive; to restore to life.

resurrection n a revival; a rising from the dead; (with cap) the rising of Christ from the dead.

resuscitate vti to revive when apparently dead or unconscious.–**resuscitation** n.

retail n selling directly to the consumer in small quantities. * adv at a retail price. * vti to sell or be sold by retail.–also adj.–**retailer** n.

retain vt to keep possession of; to keep in the mind, to remember; to keep in place, support; to hire the services of.

retainer n that which returns; (formerly) a servant to a family, a dependant; a fee to retain the services of.

retaliate vti to revenge oneself, usu by returning like for like; to strike back; to cast back (an accusation).–**retaliation** n.–**retaliatory** adj.

retard vti to slow down, to delay; to make slow or late.–**retardation** n.

retch vi to heave as if to vomit.

retention n the act of retaining; the capacity to retain; memory; (med) the abnormal retaining of fluid in a body cavity.

reticent adj reserved in speech; uncommunicative.–**reticence** n.

retina n (pl **retinas, retinae**) the innermost part of the eye, on which the image is formed.

retinue n a body of attendants.

retire vi to give up one's work when pensionable age is reached; to withdraw; to retreat; to go to bed. * vt (troops) to withdraw from use; to compel to retire from a position, work, etc.–**retirement** n.

retiring adj unobtrusive; shy.

retort vi to reply sharply or wittily. * n a sharp or witty reply; a vessel with a funnel bent downward used in distilling; a receptacle used in making gas and steel.

retrace vt to go back over; to trace back to a source.–**retraceable** adj.

retract vti to draw in or back; to withdraw (a statement, opinion, etc); to recant.–**retractable** adj.–**retraction** n.

retreat vi to withdraw, retire; to recede. * n a withdrawal, esp of troops; a sign for retiring; a quiet or secluded place, refuge; seclusion for religious devotion.

retribution n deserved reward; something given or exacted in compensation, esp punishment.

retrieve vt to recover; to revive; (a loss) to make good; (comput) to obtain information from data stored in a computer. * vi (dogs) to retrieve game.–**retrievable** adj.–**retrieval** n.

retriever n any of several breeds of dogs capable of being trained for retrieving.

retroactive adj having an effect on things that are already past.

retrograde adj going backwards; passing from better to worse.

retrospect n a looking back; a mental review of the past.–**retrospection** n.–**retrospective** adj.–**retrospectively** adv.

retrovirus n any of various viruses that use RNA to synthesize DNA, reversing the normal process in cells of transcription from DNA to RNA, which includes HIV.

return vi to come or go back; to reply; to recur. * vt to give or send back; to repay; to yield; to answer; to elect. * n something returned; a recurrence; recompense; (pl) yield, revenue; a form for computing (income) tax.

reunion n a meeting following separation; a social gathering of former colleagues.

reunite vt to unite again; to reconcile. * vi to become reunited.

Rev. abbr = Reverend.

rev vt (**revving, revved**) (inf) (with **up**) to increase the speed of an engine. * n revolution per minute.

revamp vt to renovate, to rework, remodel; to transform. * n the process of revamping; something revamped.

reveal vt (something hidden or secret) to make known; to expose; to make visible.

reveille n a morning bugle call to wake soldiers.

revel vi (**reveling, reveled** or **revelling, revelled**) (with **in**) to take pleasure or delight in; to make merry. * n (pl) merrymaking; entertainment.–**reveler, reveller** n.–**revelry** n.

revelation n the act of revealing; the disclosure of something secret; a communication from God to man; an illuminating experience.

revenge vt to inflict punishment in return for; to satisfy oneself by retaliation; to avenge. * n the act of revenging; retaliation; a vindictive feeling.–**revenger** n.

revenue n the total income produced by taxation; gross income from a business or investment.

reverberate vi to rebound, recoil; to be reflected in; to resound, to echo.–**reverberation** n.

revere vt to regard with great respect or awe; to venerate.–**reverence** n.–**reverent** adj.–**reverently** adv.

reverend adj worthy of reverence; of or relating to the clergy; (with cap) a title for a member of the clergy.

reverie n a daydream.

reverse vti to turn in the opposite direction; to turn outside in, upside down, etc; to move backward; (law) to revoke or annul. * n the contrary or opposite of something; the back, esp of a coin; a setback; a mechanism for reversing. * adj opposite, contrary; causing movement in the opposite direction.–**reversal** n.

reversible adj with both sides usable; wearable with either side out; able to undergo a series of changes either backward or forward. * n a reversible cloth or article of clothing.

revert vi to go back (to a former state); to take up again (a former subject).–**revertible** adj.

review n an evaluation; a survey; a reconsideration; a critical assessment, a critique; a periodical containing critical essays; an official inspection of ships or troops. * vt to re-examine; to inspect formally; to write a critique on.

reviewer n a person who writes a review, esp for a newspaper, a critic.

revile vti to use abusive language (to or about).

revise vt to correct and amend; to prepare a new, improved version of; to study again (for an examination).–**revision** n.

revival n the act of reviving; recovery from a neglected or depressed state; renewed performance (of a play); renewed interest in; religious awakening.

revive vti to return to life; to make active again; to take up again.–**reviver** n.

revoke vt to cancel; to rescind. * vi (cards) to fail to follow suit.–**revocable** adj.–**revocation** n.

revolt vi to rebel; to overturn; to shock. * vi to feel great disgust. * n rebellion; uprising; loathing.

revolution n the act of revolting; a motion round a centre or axis; a single completion of an orbit or rotation; a great change; an overthrow of a government, social system, etc.–**revolutionary** adj, n.

revolve vt to travel or cause to travel in a circle or orbit; to rotate.

revolver n a handgun with a magazine that revolves to reload.

revue n a musical show with skits, dances, etc, often satirizing recent events.

revulsion n disgust; aversion; a sudden change or reversal of feeling, esp withdrawal with a sense of utter distaste.

reward n something that is given in return for something done; money offered, as for the capture of a criminal. * vt to give a reward.

rewarding adj (experience, activity, etc) pleasing, profitable.

rework vt to use again in a different form; to rewrite; to remodel.

rhapsody n (pl **rhapsodies**) an enthusiastic speech or writing; (mus) an irregular instrumental composition of an epic, heroic or national character.

rhesus factor n a substance usually present in the red blood cells of humans and higher animals.

rhesus monkey n a type of southern Asian macaque with light brown fur.

rhesus negative adj lacking the rhesus factor in the blood.

rhesus positive adj containing the rhesus factor in the blood.

rhetoric n the art of effective speaking and writing; skill in using speech; insincere language.–**rhetorical** adj.–**rhetorically** adv.

rhetorical question n a question asked for effect, to which no answer is expected.

rheumatism n a disorder causing pain in muscles and joints.–**rheumatic** adj, n.

rheumatoid adj of or like rheumatism.

rheumatoid arthritis n a usu chronic disease characterized by inflammation, pain, and swelling of the joints.

rhinestone n a colorless imitation precious stone made from paste, glass, or quartz.

rhino n (pl **rhinos, rhino**) (inf) a rhinoceros.

rhinoceros n (pl **rhinoceroses, rhinoceros**) a large, thick-skinned mammal with one or two horns on the nose.

rhododendron n an evergreen shrub with large flowers.

rhombus n (pl **rhombuses, rhombi**) a diamond shape.

rhubarb n a plant with large leaves and edible (when cooked) pink stalks; (inf) a noisy quarrel.

rhyme n the repetition of sounds usu at the ends of lines in verse; such poetry or verse; a word corresponding with another in end sound. * vti to form a rhyme (with); to versify, put into rhyme.

rhythm n a regular recurrence of beat, accent or silence in the flow of sound, esp of words and music; a measured flow; cadence.–**rhythmic, rhythmical** adj.–**rhythmically** adv.

RI abbr = Rhode Island.

rib n one of the curved bones of the chest attached to the spine; any rib-like structure; a leaf vein; a vein of an insect's wing; a ridge or raised strip, as of knitting; a ridge of a mountain. * vt (**ribbing, ribbed**) to provide with ribs; to form vertical ridges in knitting; (inf) to tease or ridicule.

ribald adj irreverent; humorously vulgar.

ribbon n silk, satin, velvet, etc, woven into a narrow band; a piece of this; a strip of cloth, etc, inked for use, as in a typewriter; (pl) torn shreds.

rib cage n the bony framework of ribs enclosing the wall of the chest.

ribonucleic acid n any of a group of nucleic acids found in all living cells, where they are essential to protein development.–**RNA** abbr.

rice n an annual cereal grass cultivated in warm climates; its starchy food grain.

rich adj having much money, wealthy; abounding in natural resources, fertile; costly, fine; (food) sweet or oily, highly flavored; deep in color; (inf) full of humor. * n wealthy people collectively; (pl **riches**) wealth, abundance.–**richly** adv.–**richness** n.

rickets n a children's disease marked by softening of the bones, caused by vitamin D deficiency.

rickety adj shaky, unsteady.

rickshaw, ricksha n a light, two-wheeled man-drawn vehicle, orig used in Japan.

ricochet vi (**ricocheting, ricocheted** or **ricochetting, ricochetted**) (bullet) to rebound or skip along ground or water. * n a rebound or glancing off; (bullet) a hit made after ricocheting.

rid vt (**ridding, rid** or **ridded**) to free from; to dispose (of).–**riddance** n.

ridden see ride.

riddle n a puzzling question; an enigma; a mysterious person or thing.

ride vb (**riding, rode**, pp **ridden**) vti to be carried along or travel in a vehicle or on an animal, bicycle, etc; to be supported or move on the water; to lie at anchor; to travel over a surface; to move on the body; (inf) to continue undisturbed. * vt (horse, bicycle etc); to sit on and control; to oppress, dominate; (inf) to torment. * n a trip or journey in a vehicle or on horseback, on a bicycle, etc; a thing to ride at a fairground.

rider n a person who rides; an addition to a document, amending a clause; an additional statement; something used to move along another piece.

ridge n a narrow crest or top; the ploughed earth thrown up between the furrows; a line where two slopes meet; (of land etc) a raised strip or elevation; a range of hills. * vti to form into ridges, wrinkle.–**ridged** adj.

ridicule n mockery, derision. * vt to make fun of, to mock.

ridiculous adj deserving ridicule; preposterous, silly.–**ridiculously** adv.–**ridiculousness** n.

rife adj widespread; prevalent.

riffle vt to leaf or flick rapidly through (pages, files, etc); to shuffle cards by dividing the deck and then flicking the corners together with the thumbs. * vi to flick cursorily (through). * n (the sound of) an act or instance of riffling.

rifle[1] n a shoulder gun with a spirally grooved bore.

rifle[2] vti to steal; to look through (a person's papers or belongings).

rift n a split; a cleft; a fissure. * vti to split.

rig vt (**rigging, rigged**) (naut) to equip with sails and tackle; to set up in working order; to manipulate fraudulently. * n the way sails, etc, are rigged; equipment or gear for a special purpose, such as oil drilling; a type of truck.

right adj correct, true; just or good; appropriate; fit, recovered; opposite to left; conservative; designating the side meant to be seen. * *adv* straight; directly; completely, exactly; correctly, properly; to or on the right side. * *n* that which is just or correct; truth; fairness; justice; privilege; just or legal claim; (*pl*) the correct condition. * *vti* to set or become upright; to correct; to redress.—**rightness** *n*.

right angle *n* an angle of 90 degrees.

righteous *adj* moral, virtuous.—**righteously** *adv*.—**righteousness** *n*.

rightful *adj* legitimate; having a just claim.—**rightfully** *adv*.—**rightfulness** *n*.

right-hand *adj* of or toward the right side of a person or thing; for use by the right hand.

right-handed *adj* using the right hand; done or made for use with the right hand. * *adv* with the right hand.

rightly *adv* in truth; in the right; with good reason; properly.

right-wing *adj* of or relating to the conservative faction of a political party, organization, etc.—**right-winger** *n*.

rigid *adj* stiff, inflexible; severe, strict.—**rigidity** *n*.—**rigidly** *adv*.—**rigidness** *n*.

rigmarole *n* nonsense; a foolishly involved procedure.

rigor *n* harsh inflexibility; severity; strictness.—*also* **rigour**.—**rigorous** *adj*.—**rigorously** *adv*.—**rigorousness** *n*.

rigor mortis *n* the stiffening of the body after death.

rigour *see* **rigor**.

rile *vt* (*inf*) to irritate, to annoy, to anger.

rim *n* a border or raised edge, esp of something circular; the outer part of a wheel. * *vt* (**rimming, rimmed**) to supply or surround with a rim; to form a rim.

rind *n* crust; peel; bark.

ring[1] *n* a circular band, esp of metal, worn on the finger, in the ear, etc; a hollow circle; a round enclosure; an arena for boxing, etc; a group of people engaged in secret or criminal activity to control a market, etc. * *vt* (**ringing, ringed**) to encircle, surround; to fit with a ring.

ring[2] *vti* (**ringing, rang** or **rung, pp rung**) to emit a bell-like sound; to resound; to peal; to sound a bell; to telephone; (*with* **up**) to total and record esp by means of a cash register; to achieve. * *n* a ringing sound; a resonant note; a set of church bells.

ringleader *n* a person who takes the lead in mischievous or unlawful behavior.

ringlet *n* a curling lock of hair.

ringworm *n* a contagious skin infection.

rink *n* an expanse of ice for skating; a smooth floor for roller skating.

rinse *vt* to wash lightly; to flush under clean water to remove soap. * *n* the act of rinsing; a preparation for tinting the hair.

riot *n* violent public disorder; uproar; unrestrained profusion; (*inf*) something very funny. * *vi* to participate in a riot.—**rioter** *n*.—**rioting** *n*.—**riotous** *adj*.—**riotously** *adv*.—**riotousness** *n*.

RIP *abbr* = rest in peace.

rip *vti* (**ripping, ripped**) to cut or tear apart roughly; to split; (*with* **off, out**) to remove in a violent or rough manner; (*inf*) to rush, speed; (*with* **into**) to attack, esp verbally. * *n* a tear; a split.

ripe *adj* ready to be eaten or harvested; fully developed; mature.—**ripely** *adv*.—**ripen** *vt*.—**ripeness** *n*.

ripple *n* a little wave or undulation on the surface of water; the sound of this. * *vti* to have or form little waves on the surface (of).

rise *vi* (**rising, rose, pp risen**) to get up; to stand up; to ascend; to increase in value or size; to swell; to revolt; to be provoked; to originate; to tower; to slope up; (*voice*) to reach a higher pitch; to ascend from the grave; (*fish*) to come to the surface. * *n* an ascent; origin; an upward slope.

rising *n* a revolt, insurrection. * *adj* ascending; approaching.

risk *n* chance of loss or injury; hazard; danger, peril. * *vt* to expose to possible danger or loss; to take the chance of.—**risky** *adj*.

risotto *n* (*pl* **risottos**) a dish of onions, rice, butter, etc, cooked in meat stock.

risqué *adj* verging on indecency; slightly offensive.

rite *n* a ceremonial practice or procedure, esp religious.

ritual *adj* relating to rites or ceremonies. * *n* a fixed (religious) ceremony.—**ritually** *adv*.

ritzy *adj* (**ritzier, ritziest**) (*sl*) luxurious, smart.

rival *n* one of two or more people, organizations or teams competing with each other for the same goal. * *adj* competing; having comparable merit or claim. * *vt* (**rivaling, rivaled**) to strive to equal or excel; to be comparable to; to compete.—**rivalry** *n*.

river *n* a large natural stream of fresh water flowing into an ocean, lake, etc; a copious flow.

rivet *n* a short, metal bolt for holding metal plates together, the headless end being hammered flat. * *vt* to join with rivets; to fix one's eyes upon immovably; to engross one's attention.

rivulet *n* a little stream.

RNA *abbr* = ribonucleic acid.

roach *n* a small silvery freshwater fish.

road *n* a track, surfaced with tarmac or concrete, made for traveling; a highway; a street; a way or route; an anchorage for ships.

road block *n* a barrier erected across a road to halt traffic.

roadie *n* (*inf*) a person with responsibility for transporting and setting up stage equipment for a rock group, etc on tour.

road-test *vt* to test (a vehicle) under practical operating conditions.—**road test** *n*.

roam *vti* to wander about, to rove.

roan *adj* having a base color thickly sprinkled with white or gray. * *n* a horse with a roan coat, esp when the base color is red.

roar *vti* to make a loud, full, growling sound, as a lion, wind, fire, the sea; to utter loudly, as in a rage; to bellow; to guffaw.—*also* **n**.

roast *vti* (*meat, etc*) to cook with little or no moisture, as before a fire or in an oven; (*coffee, etc*) to process by exposure to heat; to expose to great heat; (*inf*) to criticize severely; to undergo roasting. * *n* roasted meat; a cut of meat for roasting; a picnic at which food is roasted.

rob *vb* (**robbing, robbed**) *vt* to seize forcibly; to steal from; to plunder. * *vi* to commit robbery.—**robber** *n*.

robbery *n* (*pl* **robberies**) theft from a person by intimidation or by violence.

robe *n* a long flowing outer garment; the official dress of a judge, academic, etc; a bathrobe or dressing gown; a covering or wrap; (*pl*) ceremonial vestments. * *vti* to put on or dress in robes.

robin *n* a songbird with a dull red breast.

robot *n* a mechanical device that acts in a seemingly human way; a mechanism guided by automatic controls.

robotics *n* (*used as sing*) the science of designing and using robots.

robust *adj* strong, sturdy; vigorous.—**robustly** *adv*.—**robustness** *n*.

rock[1] *n* a large stone or boulder; a person or thing providing foundation or support; (*inf*) a diamond, ice.

rock[2] *vti* to move to and fro, or from side to side; to sway strongly; to shake. * *n* a rocking motion; rock-and-roll.

rock-and-roll *n* popular music that incorporates country and blues elements and is usu played on electronic instruments with a heavily accented beat.

rock bottom *n* the lowest or most fundamental part or level. * *adj* very lowest.

rocket *n* any device driven forward by gases escaping through a rear vent, such as a firework, distress signal, or the propulsion mechanism of a spacecraft. * *vi* to move in or like a rocket; to soar.

rocky *adj* (**rockier, rockiest**) having many rocks; like rock; rugged, hard; shaky, unstable.

rod *n* a stick; a thin bar of metal or wood; a staff of office; a wand; a fishing rod; (*sl*) a pistol.

rode *see* **ride**.

rodent *n* any of several relatively small gnawing animals with two strong front teeth.

rodeo *n* (*pl* **rodeos**) the rounding up of cattle; a display of cowboy skill.

roe n the eggs of fish.

rogue n a scoundrel; a rascal; a mischievous person; a wild animal that lives apart from the herd.–**roguish** adj.–**roguishly** adv.

role, rôle n a part in a movie or play taken by an actor; a function.

role model n a person who inspires others to emulate him or her.

roll n a scroll; anything wound into cylindrical form; a list or register; a turned-over edge; a rolling movement; a small cake of bread; a trill of some birds; an undulation; the sound of thunder; the beating of drumsticks. * vi to move by turning over or from side to side; to move like a wheel; to curl; to move in like waves; to flow. * vt to cause to roll; to turn on its axis; to move on wheels; to press with a roller; (dice) to throw; to beat rapidly, as a drum.

roll call n the reading aloud of a list of names to check attendance.

roller n a revolving cylinder used for spreading paint, flattening surfaces, moving paper, etc; a large wave.

roller coaster n an elevated amusement ride in which small cars move on tracks that curve and dip sharply.

roller skate n a four-wheeled skate strapped on to shoes.–**roller skating** n.

ROM abbr (comput) = read-only memory.

Roman Catholic adj belonging to the Christian church that is headed by the Pope.–also n.

romance n a prose narrative; a medieval tale of chivalry; a series of unusual adventures; a novel dealing with this; an atmosphere of awe or wonder; a love story; a love affair; a picturesque falsehood. * vi to write romantic fiction; to exaggerate.

Roman numerals n the letters I, V, X, L, C, D, and M used to represent numbers in the manner of the ancient Romans.

romantic adj of or given to romance; strange and picturesque; imaginative; sentimental; (art, literature) preferring passion and imagination to proportion and finish, subordinating form to content.–**romantically** adv.

romanticize vt to imbue (a person, concept, etc) with a romantic character. * vi to have romantic ideas.–**romanticization** n.

romp vi to play boisterously. * n a noisy game; a frolic; an easy win.

roof n (pl **roofs**) the upper covering of a building; the top of a vehicle; an upper limit. * vt to provide with a roof, to cover.

rook[1] n a crow-like bird.

rook[2] n (chess) a piece with the power to move horizontally or vertically, a castle.

rookie n (sl) an inexperienced army recruit; any novice.–also adj.

room n space; unoccupied space; adequate space; a division of a house, a chamber; scope or opportunity; those in a room; (pl) lodgings. * vi to lodge.

roommate n a person with whom one shares a room or rooms.

roomy adj (**roomier, roomiest**) having ample space; wide.–**roominess** n.

roost n a bird's perch or sleeping-place; a place for resting. * vi to rest or sleep on a roost; to settle down, as for the night.

rooster n an adult male domestic fowl, a cockerel.

root[1] n the part of a plant, usu underground, that anchors the plant, draws water from the soil, etc; the embedded part of a tooth, a hair, etc; a supporting or essential part; something that is an origin or source; (math) the factor of a quantity which multiplied by itself gives the quantity; (pl) plants with edible roots. * vti to take root; to become established; (with **out**) to tear up, to eradicate.

root[2] vti to dig up with the snout; to search about, rummage; (with **for**) (inf) to encourage a team by cheering.

root beer n a carbonated drink flavored with extracts of certain roots and barks.

rope n a thick cord or thin cable made of twisted fibers or wires; a string or row of things braided, intertwined or threaded together. * vt to tie, bind, divide or enclose with a rope; to lasso.–**ropy** adj.

rosary n (pl **rosaries**) a string of beads for keeping count of prayers; a series of prayers.

rose[1] see **rise**.

rose[2] n a prickly-stemmed plant with fragrant flowers of many delicate colors; its flower; a rosette; a perforated nozzle; a pinkish red or purplish red.

rosemary n a fragrant shrubby mint used in cookery and perfumery.

rosette n a rose-shaped bunch of ribbon; a carving, etc, in the shape of a rose.

roster n a list or roll, as of military personnel; a list of duties.

rostrum n (pl **rostrums, rostra**) a platform or stage for public speaking.

rosy adj (**rosier, rosiest**) of the color of roses; having pink, healthy cheeks; optimistic, hopeful.

rot vti (**rotting, rotted**) to decompose; to decay; to become degenerate. * n decay; corruption; several different diseases affecting timber or sheep; (inf) nonsense.

rotary adj revolving; turning like a wheel.

rotate vti to turn around an axis like a wheel; to follow a sequence.–**rotation** n.

rotten adj decayed, decomposed; corrupt; (inf) bad, nasty.–**rottenness** n.

rotund adj rounded; spherical; plump.

rouge n a red cosmetic for coloring the cheeks; a red powder for polishing jewelry, etc. * vt to color (the face) with rouge.

rough adj uneven; not smooth; ill-mannered; violent, rude, unpolished; shaggy; coarse in texture; unrefined; violent, boisterous; stormy; wild; harsh, discordant; crude, unfinished; approximate; (inf) difficult. * n rough ground; (golf) any part of a course with grass, etc, left uncut; a first sketch. * vt to make rough; to sketch roughly; (with **up**) (inf) to injure violently, beat up. * adv in a rough manner.–**roughly** adv.–**roughness** n.

roughage n rough or coarse food or fodder, as bran, etc.

rough-and-tumble n a scuffle; confusion.

roulette n a gambling game played with a revolving disc and a ball; a toothed wheel for making dots or perforations.

round adj circular, spherical, or cylindrical in form; curved; plump; (math) expressed to the nearest ten, hundred, etc, not fractional; considerable; candid; (style) flowing, balanced. * adv circularly; on all sides; from one side to another; in a ring; by indirect way; through a recurring period of time; in circumference; in a roundabout way; about; near; here and there; with a rotating movement; in the opposite direction; around. * prep encircling; on every side of; in the vicinity of; in a circuit through; around. * n anything round; a circuit; (shots) a volley; a unit of ammunition; a series or sequence; a bout, turn; (golf) a circuit of a course; a stage of a contest; (mus) a kind of canon. * vt to make or become round or plump; (math) to express as a round number; to complete; to go or pass around. * vi to make a circuit; to turn; to reverse direction.–**roundly** adv.–**roundness** n.

roundabout adj indirect, circuitous.

round trip n a journey to a place and back again.

roundup n a driving together of livestock; (inf) the detention of several prisoners; a summary, as of news.

rouse vti to provoke; to stir up; to awaken; to wake up; to become active.

rout n a noisy crowd, a rabble; a disorderly retreat. * vt to defeat and put to flight.

route n a course to be taken; the roads traveled on a journey. * vt to plan the route of; to send (by a specified route).

routine n a procedure that is regular and unvarying; a sequence of set movements, as in a dance, skating, etc.–also adj.

rove vti to wander about, roam (over).–**rover** n.

row[1] n a line of persons or things; a line of seats (in a theater, etc).

row[2] vti to propel with oars; to transport by rowing. * n an act or instance of rowing.–**rower** n.

row[3] n a noisy quarrel or dispute; a scolding; noise, disturbance. * vi to quarrel; to scold.

rowdy adj (**rowdier, rowdiest**) rough and noisy, disorderly. * n (pl **rowdies**) a rowdy person, a hooligan.–**rowdiness, rowdyism** n.

royal adj relating to or fit for a king or queen; regal; under the patronage of a king or queen; founded by a king or queen; of a kingdom, its government, etc. * n (inf) a member of a royal family.–**royally** adv.

royalty n (pl **royalties**) the rank or power of a king or queen; a royal person or persons; a share of the proceeds from a patent, book, song, etc, paid to the owner, author, composer, etc.

rpm abbr = revolutions per minute.

RSVP abbr = répondez s'il vous pla"t.

rub vti (**rubbing, rubbed**) to move (a hand, cloth, etc) over the surface of with pressure; to wipe, scour; to clean or polish; (with **away, off, out**) to remove or erase by friction; to chafe, grate; to fret; to take a rubbing of; (with **along**) to manage somehow; (with **down**) to rub vigorously with a towel; to smooth down. * n the act or process of rubbing; a drawback, difficulty.

rubber n an elastic substance made synthetically or from the sap of various tropical plants.

rubberneck n (sl) a person who gapes, esp intrusively; a sight-seer.–also vi.

rubber-stamp vt (inf) to give automatic approval without investigation.

rubbish n refuse; garbage, trash; nonsense.–**rubbishy** adj.

rubble n rough broken stone or rock; builders' rubbish.

rubella n a mild contagious viral disease that may cause damage to an unborn child; German measles.

ruby n (pl **rubies**) a deep red, transparent, valuable precious stone. * adj of the color of a ruby.

ruckus n (inf) a disturbance, a row, uproar.

rudder n a flat vertical piece of wood or metal hinged to the stern of a ship or boat or the rear of an aircraft to steer by; a guiding principle.

ruddy adj (**ruddier, ruddiest**) reddish pink; (complexion) of a healthy, red color.

rude adj uncivil, ill-mannered; uncultured, coarse; harsh, brutal; crude, roughly made; in a natural state, primitive; vigorous, hearty.–**rudely** adv.–**rudeness** n.

rudiment n a first stage; a first slight beginning of something; an imperfectly developed organ; (pl) elements, first principles.–**rudimentary** adj.

rue vti (**rueing, rued**) to feel remorse for (a sin, fault, etc); to regret (an act, etc).

rueful adj regretful; dejected; showing good-humored self-pity.–**ruefully** adv.

ruff n a pleated collar or frill worn round the neck; a fringe of feathers or fur round the neck of a bird or animal.

ruffian n a brutal lawless person; a villain.

ruffle vti to disturb the smoothness of, disarrange; to irritate; to agitate; to upset; to swagger about; to be quarrelsome; to flutter. * n pleated material used as a trim; a frill; a bird's ruff; a dispute, quarrel.

rug n a thick heavy fabric used as a floor covering; a thick woolen wrap or coverlet.

rugby n a football game for two teams of 15 players played with an oval ball.

rugged adj rocky; rough, uneven; strong; stern; robust.–**ruggedly** adv.–**ruggedness** n.

ruin n destruction; downfall, wrecked state; the cause of this; a loss of fortune; (pl) the remains of something destroyed, decayed, etc. * vti to destroy; to spoil; to bankrupt; to come to ruin.–**ruinous** adj.

rule n a straight-edged instrument for drawing lines and measuring; government; the exercise of authority; a regulation, an order; a principle, a standard; habitual practice; the code of a religious order; a straight line. * vti to govern, to exercise authority over; to manage; to draw (lines) with a ruler; (with **out**) to exclude, to eliminate; to make impossible.

ruler n a person who governs; a strip of wood, metal, etc, with a straight edge, used in drawing lines, measuring, etc.

rum n a spirit made from sugar cane.

rumble vti to make a low heavy rolling noise (as thunder); to move with such a sound; (sl) to see through, find out. * n the dull deep vibrant noise of thunder, etc.

ruminant n a cud-chewing animal, such as cattle, deer, camels, etc. * adj chewing the cud; thoughtful.

ruminate vi to regurgitate food after it has been swallowed, chew cud; to ponder deeply, muse (on).

rummage n odds and ends; a search by ransacking. * vti to search thoroughly; to ransack; to fish (out).

rummy n a card game whose object is to form sets and sequences.

rumor, rumour n hearsay, gossip; common talk not based on definite knowledge; an unconfirmed report, story. * vt to report by way of rumor.

rump n the hindquarters of an animal's body; the buttocks; the back end.

rumple n a crease or wrinkle. * vti to crease; to disarrange, tousle.

rumpus n (pl **rumpuses**) a commotion; a din.

run vi (**running, ran** or **run**, pp **run**) to go by moving the legs faster than in walking; to hurry; to flee; to flow; to operate; to be valid; to compete in a race, election, etc; (colors), to merge; (with **across**) to meet by accident; (with **around**) vi (inf) to associate (with); to behave evasively or promiscuously; (with **away**) vi to take flight, escape; to go out of control; (with **away with**) to abscond, elope; to steal; to win easily; (with **down**) (engine, etc) to cease to operate through lack of power; to become tired or exhausted; (with **off**) to leave hastily; to decide (a race) with a run-off; (with **through**) to use up (money, etc) completely; to read quickly. * vt (a car, etc) to drive; (a business, etc) to manage; (a story) to publish in a newspaper; (with **down**) to knock down with a moving vehicle; to collide with and cause to sink; to chase and capture; to tire, exhaust; to investigate, find; to criticize persistently; (engine, etc) to allow to gradually lose power; to reduce in quantity; (with **in**) to run a new car engine gently to start with; (inf) to arrest; (with **off**) to compose and talk glibly; to produce quickly, as copies on a photocopier; (liquid) to drain off; (with **out**) to exhaust a supply; (inf) to desert; (with **over**) (vehicle) to knock down a person or animal; to overflow; to exceed a limit; to rehearse quickly; (with **through**) to pierce with a sword or knife; to rehearse; (with **up**) to incur or amass. * n an act of running; a trip; a flow; a series; prevalence; a trend; an enclosure for chickens, etc; free and unrestricted access to all parts.

run-around n deceitful or evasive behavior towards someone.

runaway n a person or thing that runs away; a fugitive. * adj out of control; (inflation) rising uncontrollably; (race, etc) easily won.

run-down adj dilapidated; ill; tired.

rundown n a brief summary; the process of going into a decline.

rung[1] see **ring**[2].

rung[2] n the step of a ladder; the crossbar of a chair.

runner n an athlete; a person who runs; a smuggler; a groove or strip on which something glides.

runner-up n (pl **runners-up**) the competitor who finishes second in a race, contest, etc.

running mate n the candidate in a US election standing for the less important of two positions in a linked office.

runny adj (**runnier, runniest**) tending to flow.

run-of-the-mill adj average, mediocre.

runt n an unusually small animal, esp the smallest of a litter of pigs; a person of small stature.

run-up n a preliminary period.

runway n a landing strip for aircraft.

rupture n a breach; a severance, quarrel; the act of bursting or breaking; hernia. * vti to cause or suffer a rupture.

rural adj relating to the country or agriculture, rustic.—**rurally** adv.

ruse n a trick or stratagem.

rush[1] vti to move, push, drive, etc, swiftly or impetuously; to make a sudden attack (on); to do with unusual haste; to hurry. * adj marked by or needing extra speed or urgency. * n a sudden surge; a sudden demand; a press, as of business, requiring unusual haste; an unedited film print.

rush[2] n a marsh plant; its slender pithy stem; a worthless thing.

rush hour n the time at the beginning and end of the working day when traffic is at its heaviest.

russet adj reddish-brown. * n a russet color; a winter apple with a rough russet skin; a homespun russet cloth.

rust n a reddish oxide coating formed on iron or steel when exposed to moisture; a reddish brown color; a red mould on plants; the fungus causing this. * vti to form rust (on); to deteriorate, as through disuse.

rustic n pertaining to or characteristic of the country; rural; simple, unsophisticated. * n a person from the country; a simple country dweller.

rustle n a crisp, rubbing sound as of dry leaves, paper, etc. * vti to make or move with a rustle; to hustle; to steal (cattle); (with **up**) (inf) to collect or get together.

rusty adj (**rustier, rustiest**) coated with rust; rust-colored, faded; out of practice; antiquated.—**rustiness** n.

rut n a track worn by wheels; an undeviating mechanical routine. * vt (**rutting, rutted**) to mark with ruts.

ruthless adj cruel; merciless.—**ruthlessly** adv.—**ruthlessness** n.

rye n a hardy annual grass; its grain, used for making flour and whiskey; a whiskey made from rye.

S

S abbr = South, Southern.

Sabbath n a day of rest and worship observed on a Saturday by Jews, Sunday by Christians and Friday by Muslims.

sabbatical n a year's leave from a teaching post, often paid, for research or travel.

saber n a cavalry sword with a curved blade; a light fencing sword.

sable n a carnivorous mammal of arctic regions valued for its luxuriant dark brown fur; its fur.

sabotage n deliberate damage of machinery, or disruption of public services, by enemy agents, disgruntled employees, etc, to prevent their effective operation. * vt to practise sabotage on; to spoil, disrupt.

saboteur n a person who engages in sabotage.

sac n a bag-like part or cavity in a plant or animal.

saccharin n a non-fattening sugar substitute.

saccharine adj containing sugar; excessively sweet.

sachet n a sealed envelope or packet; a small perfumed bag or pad used to perfume clothes.

sack[1] n a large bag made of coarse cloth used as a container; the contents of this; a loose-fitting dress or coat; (baseball) a bag serving as a base; (sl: with **the**) dismissal. * vt to put into sacks; (sl) to dismiss.

sack[2] n the plunder or destruction of a place. * vt to plunder or loot.

sacrament n a religious ceremony forming outward and visible sign of inward and spiritual grace, esp baptism and the Eucharist; the consecrated elements in the Eucharist, esp the bread; a sacred symbol or pledge.

sacred adj regarded as holy; consecrated to a god or God; connected with religion; worthy of or regarded with reverence, sacrosanct.

sacred cow n (inf) a person or thing regarded as above criticism.

sacrifice n the act of offering ceremonially to a deity; the slaughter of an animal (or person) to please a deity; the surrender of something valuable for the sake of something more important or worthy; loss without return; something sacrificed, an offering. * vt to slaughter or give up as a sacrifice; to give up for a higher good; to sell at a loss.—**sacrificial** adj.

sacrilege n violation of anything holy or sacred.—**sacrilegious** adj.—**sacrilegiously** adv.

sacrosanct adj inviolable; very holy.

sad adj (**sadder, saddest**) expressing grief or unhappiness; sorrowful; deplorable.—**sadly** adv.—**sadness** n.

sadden vti to make or become sad.

saddle n a seat, usu of leather, for a rider on a horse, bicycle, etc; a ridge connecting two mountain peaks; a joint of mutton or venison consisting of the two loins; **in the saddle** mounted on a saddle; in control. * vt to put a saddle on; to burden, encumber.

sadism n sexual pleasure obtained from inflicting cruelty upon another; extreme cruelty.—**sadist** n.—**sadistic** adj.—**sadistically** adv.

sadomasochism n sexual pleasure obtained from inflicting cruelty upon oneself and receiving it from another.—**sadomasochist** n.—**sadomasochistic** adj.

s.a.e. abbr = stamped addressed envelope.

safari n (pl **safaris**) a journey or hunting expedition, esp in Africa.

safe adj unhurt; out of danger; reliable; secure; involving no risk; trustworthy; giving protection; prudent; sure; incapable of doing harm. * n a locking metal box or compartment for valuables.—**safely** adv.

safecracker n a person who opens and robs safes.—also **safebreaker**.—**safecracking** n.

safe-deposit adj (box, room, etc) designed for the protective storage of valuables, deeds, etc. * n a building with safes for renting—also **safety deposit**.

safeguard n anything that protects against injury or danger; a proviso against foreseen risks. * vt to protect.

safe house n a refuge for victims of domestic violence, sexual abuse, etc run by social welfare organizations; a clandestine place used by intelligence services, terrorists, etc as a refuge.

safekeeping n the act or process of keeping safely; protection.

safe sex n sex in which precautions are taken to lessen the risk of catching AIDS or other sexually transmitted diseases.

safety n (pl **safeties**) freedom from danger; the state of being safe.

safety belt n a belt worn by a person working at a great height to prevent falling; a seatbelt.

safety net n a net suspended beneath acrobats, etc; any protection against loss.

safety pin n a pin with a guard to cover the point.

saffron n a crocus whose bright yellow stigmas are used as a food coloring and flavoring; an orange-yellow color.

sag vi (**sagging, sagged**) to droop downward in the middle; to sink or hang down unevenly under pressure.

saga n a long story of heroic deeds.

sagacious adj mentally acute, shrewd; wise.—**sagaciously** adv.—**sagacity** n.

sage[1] adj wise through reflection and experience. * n a person of profound wisdom.—**sagely** adv.—**sagely** adv.

sage[2] n a herb with leaves used for flavoring food; sagebrush.

sagebrush n a low shrub of the alkaline plains of North America.

Sagittarius n the Archer, ninth sign of the zodiac; in astrology, operative November 22–December 20.—**Sagittarian** adj, n.

said see **say**.

sail n a piece of canvas used to catch the wind to propel or steer a vessel; sails collectively; anything like a sail; an arm of a windmill; a voyage in a sailing vessel; **under sail** with the sails set; under way. * vt to navigate a vessel; to manage (a vessel); **to set sail** to spread the sails; to begin a voyage. * vi to be moved by sails; to travel by water; to glide or pass smoothly; to walk in a stately manner.

sailor n a person who sails; one of a ship's crew.

saint n a person who is very patient, charitable, etc; a person who is canonized by the Roman Catholic Church; one of the blessed in heaven.–**sainthood** n.–**saintly** adj.–**saintliness** n.

sainted adj canonized; holy; dead; much admired.

sake[1] n behalf; purpose; benefit; interest.

sake[2], **saké, saki** n a Japanese alcoholic drink made from fermented rice and drunk warm.

salaam n a form of ceremonial greeting in Muslim countries. * vti to make a salaam (to).

salacious adj lustful; obscene.–**salaciously** adv.–**salaciousness** n.

salad n a dish, usu cold, of vegetables, fruits, meat, eggs, etc; lettuce, etc, used for this.

salad dressing n a cooked or uncooked sauce of oil, vinegar, spices, etc, to put on a salad.

salamander n any of various lizard-like amphibians; a mythical lizard-like creature that was supposedly impervious to fire.

salami n a highly seasoned Italian sausage.

salary n (pl **salaries**) fixed, regular payment for non-manual work, usu paid monthly.

sale n the act of selling; the exchange of goods or services for money; the market or opportunity of selling; an auction; the disposal of goods at reduced prices; the period of this.

salesclerk n a person who sells goods in a store.

salesman n (pl **salesmen**) a person who sells either in a given territory or in a store.–**saleswoman** nf (pl **saleswomen**).

salesperson n (pl **salespeople**) a salesman or saleswoman.

sales representative n a person who travels to sell within a given territory.

sales tax n a tax levied (usu as a percentage) on the price of an object bought by a consumer.

salient adj projecting outward; conspicuous; noteworthy; leaping, gushing.–**salience, saliency** n.–**saliently** adv.

saline adj of or impregnated with salt or salts; salty. * n a solution of salt and water.–**salinity** n.

saliva n the liquid secreted by glands in the mouth that aids digestion.–**salivary** adj.–**salivate** vi.–**salivation** n.

sallow adj (complexion) an unhealthy yellow color, a pale brown color.–**sallowness** n.

sally n (pl **sallies**) a sudden attack; an outburst; a lively remark, quip. * vi (**sallying, sallied**) to make a sally; to go (forth).

salmon n (pl **salmon, salmons**) a large silvery edible fish that lives in salt water and spawns in fresh water; salmon pink.

salmonella n (pl **salmonellae, salmonella, salmonellas**) any of a genus of bacteria that causes food poisoning and diseases of the genital tract.

salon n a large reception hall or drawing room for receiving guests; the shop of a hairdresser, beautician, or couturier; an art gallery.

saloon n a large reception room; a large cabin for the social use of a ship's passengers; a place where alcoholic drinks are sold and consumed.

salsa n (the music for) a type of Puerto Rican dance; a spicy tomato sauce.

salt n a white crystalline substance (sodium chloride) used as a seasoning or preservative; piquancy, wit; (chem) a compound of an acid and a base; (pl) mineral salt as an aperient. * adj containing or tasting of salt; preserved with salt; pungent. * vt to flavor, pickle or sprinkle with salt; to give flavor or piquancy to (as a story); (with **away**) to hoard; to keep for the future.

salty adj (**saltier, saltiest**) of, containing or tasting of salt; witty; earthy, coarse.

salubrious adj health-giving; wholesome.–**salubriously** adv.–**salubriousness** n.

salutary adj beneficial, wholesome.–**salutarily** adv.–**salutariness** n.

salutation n a greeting; the words used in it.

salute n a gesture of respect or greeting; (mil) a motion of the right hand to the head, or to a rifle; a discharge of guns, etc, as a military mark of honor. * vti to make a salute (to); to greet; to kiss; to praise or honor.

salvage n the rescuing of a ship or property from loss at sea, by fire, etc; the reward paid for this; the thing salvaged; waste material intended for further use. * vt to save from loss or danger.–**salvageable** adj.–**salvager** n.

salvation n the act of saving or the state of being saved; in Christianity, the deliverance from evil; a means of preservation.–**salvational** adj.

salve n a healing ointment or balm; a soothing influence. * vt to apply ointment to; to smooth over; to soothe.

salver n a small tray.

salvo n (pl **salvoes, salvos**) a firing of several guns or missiles simultaneously; a sudden burst; a spirited verbal attack.

sal volatile n a solution of ammonium carbonate in alcohol used as a remedy for faintness.

samba n a Brazilian dance of African origin; the music for this. * vi to dance the samba.

same adj identical; exactly similar; unchanged; uniform, monotonous; previously mentioned. * pron the same person or thing. * adv in like manner.–**sameness** n.

samosa n (pl **samosas, samosa**) an Indian savory pasty with a spicy meat or vegetable filling.

samovar n a metal urn with an internal element used for boiling water for tea, esp in Russia.

sample n a specimen; a small part representative of the whole; an instance. * vt (food, drink) to taste a small quantity of; to test by taking a sample.

sampler n a person who takes samples; something containing a representative selection (as a record, book); an assortment; a piece of ornamental embroidery showing different stitches and patterns as an example of skill.

sampling n (mus industry) the practice of extracting phrases from several recorded songs and putting them together electronically to make a new one.

samurai n (pl **samurai**) a member of an ancient Japanese warrior caste.

sanatorium see **sanitarium**.

sanctify vt (**sanctifying, sanctified**) to make holy; to purify from sin or evil; (the Church) to give official approval.–**sanctification** n.–**sanctifier** n.

sanctimonious adj pretending to be holy; hypocritically pious or righteous.–**sanctimoniously** adv.–**sanctimoniousness** n.

sanction n express permission, authorization; a binding influence; a penalty by which a law is enforced, esp a prohibition on trade with a country that has violated international law. * vt to permit; to give authority.–**sanctionable** adj.

sanctity n (pl **sanctities**) the condition of being holy or sacred; inviolability.

sanctuary n (pl **sanctuaries**) a sacred place; the part of a church around the altar; a place where one is free from arrest or violence, an asylum; a refuge; an animal reserve.

sand n very fine rock particles; (pl) a desert; a sandy beach. * vt to smooth or polish with sand or sandpaper; to sprinkle with sand. * adj reddish yellow.–**sandy** adj.

sandal n a shoe consisting of a sole strapped to the foot; a low slipper or shoe.–**sandalled, sandaled** adj.

sandalwood n the yellow, scented wood of an Asian tree; the tree.

sandbag n a bag of sand used for ballast or to protect against floodwater. * vt (**sandbagging, sandbagged**) to protect by laying sandbags; to hit with a sandbag; (inf) to coerce; (sl) to deceive.—**sandbagger** n.

sand bar n a ridge of sand built up in a river, a lake, or coastal waters by currents.

sand castle n a model of a castle moulded from damp sand, as made at the seaside by children.

sander n a power-driven tool for sanding wood or other surfaces.

sandpaper n a paper coated on one side with sand or another abrasive, used to smooth or polish. * vt to rub with sandpaper.

sandstone n a sedimentary rock of compacted sand.

sandwich n two slices of bread with meat, cheese, or other filling between; anything in a sandwich-like arrangement. * vt to place between two things or two layers; to make such a place for.

sane adj mentally sound, not mad; reasonable, sensible.—**sanely** adv.—**saneness** n.

sang see **sing**.

sanguine adj confident, hopeful; blood-red; (complexion) ruddy.—**sanguineness** n.

sanitarium n (pl **sanitariums, sanitaria**) an establishment for the treatment of convalescents or the chronically ill.—also **sanatorium**.

sanitary adj relating to the promotion and protection of health; relating to the supply of water, drainage, and sewage disposal; hygienic.—**sanitarily** adv.—**sanitariness** n.

sanitary napkin, sanitary towel n an absorbent pad worn externally during menstruation.

sanitation n the science and practice of achieving hygienic conditions; drainage and disposal of sewage.

sanitize vt to clean or sterilize; to make (language, etc) more respectable or acceptable.

sanity n the condition of being sane; mental health; common sense.

sank see **sink**.

sap[1] n the vital juice of plants; energy and health; (inf) a fool. * vt (**sapping, sapped**) to drain of sap; to exhaust the energy of.

sap[2] n a narrow or covered siege trench; the digging of this, undermining. * vti (**sapping, sapped**) to attack by or dig a sap; to undermine insidiously.

sapling n a young tree; a youth.

sapphire n a transparent blue precious stone; a deep pure blue.—also adj.

sarcasm n a scornful or ironic remark; the use of this.—**sarcastic** adj.—**sarcastically** adv.

sarcoma n (pl **sarcomas, sarcomata**) a malignant tumor of connective tissue.—**sarcomatous** adj.

sarcophagus n (pl **sarcophagi, sarcophaguses**) a large stone coffin or tomb.

sardine n (pl **sardines, sardine**) a small, edible seafish.

sardonic adj (smile, etc) derisive, mocking, maliciously jocular.—**sardonically** adv.

sari, saree n a Hindu woman's principal garment, consisting of a long piece of cloth wrapped around the waist and across the shoulder.

sarong n a long strip of cloth wrapped around the lower body, worn esp in the Malay archipelago and the Pacific Islands.

sartorial adj of or relating to the making of men's clothing.—**sartorially** adv.

sash[1] n a band of satin or ribbon worn around the waist or over the shoulder, often as a badge of honor.

sash[2] n a frame for holding the glass of a window, esp one that slides vertically.

sashay vi (inf) to walk in a casual manner, saunter; to swagger.

sassafras n a North American tree of the laurel family; the aromatic dried root of this used as a flavoring.

sassy adj (**sassier, sassiest**) (sl) rude; cheeky.

sat see **sit**.

Satan n the devil, the adversary of God.

satanic, satanical adj of or relating to Satan, devilish; marked by viciousness or cruelty.—**satanically** adv.

satchel n a bag with shoulder straps for carrying school books, etc.

sate vt to satisfy to repletion, to satiate.

satellite n a planet orbiting another; a man-made object orbiting the earth, moon, etc, to gather scientific information or for communication; a nation economically dependent on a more powerful one.

satellite broadcasting, satellite television n the transmission of television programs via an orbiting satellite to subscribers in possession of a receiving satellite dish aerial.

satiate vt to provide with more than enough so as to weary or disgust; to gorge.—**satiation** n.

satiety n the state of being sated; a feeling of having had too much.

satin n a fabric of woven silk with a smooth, shiny surface on one side. * adj of or resembling satin.—**satiny** adj.

satire n a literary work in which folly or evil in people's behavior are held up to ridicule; trenchant wit, sarcasm.—**satirical** adj.—**satirically** adv.

satirist n a writer of satires.

satirize vt to attack with satire.—**satirizer** n.

satisfaction n the act of satisfying or the condition of being satisfied; that which satisfies; comfort; atonement, reparation.—**satisfactory** adj.—**satisfactorily** adv.

satisfy vb (**satisfying, satisfied**) vi to be enough for; to fulfill the needs or desires of. * vt to give enough to; (hunger, desire etc.) to appease; to please; to gratify; to comply with; (creditor) to discharge, to pay in full; to convince; to make reparation to; (guilt, etc) to atone for.

saturate vt to soak thoroughly; to fill completely.—**saturation** n.—**saturator** n.

Saturday n the seventh and last day of the week.

saturnine adj sullen, morose.—**saturninely** adv.

satyr n (Greek myth) a woodland god in human form but with goat's ears, tail, and legs; a man with strong sexual appetites.—**satyric** adj.

sauce n a liquid or dressing served with food to enhance its flavor; stewed or preserved fruit eaten with other food or as a dessert. * vt to season with sauce; to make piquant.

saucepan n a deep cooking pan with a handle and lid.

saucer n a round shallow dish placed under a cup; a shallow depression; a thing shaped like a saucer.

saucy adj (**saucier, sauciest**) rude, impertinent; sprightly.—**saucily** adv.—**sauciness** n.

sauerkraut n a German dish of chopped pickled cabbage.

sauna n exposure of the body to hot steam, followed by cold water; the room where this is done.

saunter vi to walk in a leisurely or idle way. * n a stroll.—**saunterer** n.

sausage n minced seasoned meat, esp pork, packed into animal gut or other casing.

sauté adj fried quickly and lightly. * vt (**sautéing, sautéed**) to fry in a small amount of oil or fat. * n a sautéed dish.

savage adj fierce; wild; untamed; uncivilized; ferocious; primitive. * n a member of a primitive society; a brutal, fierce person or animal.—**savagely** adv.—**savageness** n.

savagery n (pl **savageries**) the state of being a savage; an act of violence or cruelty; an uncivilized state.

savanna, savannah n a treeless plain; an area of tropical or subtropical grassland.

save[1] vt to rescue from harm or danger; to keep, to accumulate; to set aside for future use; to avoid the necessity of; (energy etc) to prevent waste of; (theol) to deliver from sin. * vi to avoid waste, expense, etc; to economize; to store up money or goods; (sports) to keep an opponent from scoring or winning. * n (sports) the act of preventing one's opponent from scoring.—**savable, saveable** adj.

save[2] conj, prep except, but.

saveloy n a type of highly-seasoned smoked sausage.

saving[1] *adj* thrifty, economical; (*clause*) containing a reservation; redeeming. * *n* what is saved; (*pl*) money saved for future use.

saving[2] *prep* except; with apology to.

savings and loan association *n* a company that pays interest on deposits and issues loans to enable people to buy their own houses, a building society.

savior, saviour *n* a person who saves another from harm or danger; (*with cap*) Jesus Christ.

savor, savour *n* the flavor or smell of something; a distinctive quality. * *vti* to season; to enjoy; to have a specified taste or smell; to smack (of); to appreciate critically.–**savorer, savourer** *n*.

savory, savoury *adj* having a good taste or smell; spicy, not sweet; reputable. * *n* (*pl* **savories, savouries**) a savory dish at the beginning or end of dinner; (*pl*) snacks served with drinks.–**savorily, savourily** *adv*.–**savoriness, savouriness** *n*.

saw[1] *see* **see**[1]

saw[2] *n* a tool with a toothed edge for cutting wood, etc. * *vti* (**sawing, sawed,** *pp* **sawed** or **sawn**) to cut or shape with a saw; to use a saw; to make a to-and-fro motion.–**sawer** *n*.

sawdust *n* fine particles of wood caused by sawing.

sawn *see* **saw**[2].

sax *n* saxophone.

saxophone *n* a brass wind instrument with a single reed and about twenty finger-keys.–**saxophonic** *adj*.–**saxophonist** *n*.

say *vb* (**says, saying, said**) *vt* to speak, to utter; to state in words; to affirm, declare; to recite; to assume. * *vi* to tell; to express in words. * *n* (*pl* **says**) the act of uttering; the right or opportunity to speak; a share in a decision. * *adv* for example. * *interj* expressing admiration, surprise, etc.

saying *n* a common remark; a proverb or adage.

say-so *n* (*inf*) an unfounded assertion; an authorization; the right to authorize.

SC *abbr* = South Carolina; Supreme Court.

scab *n* a dry crust on a wound or sore; a plant disease characterized by crustaceous spots; a worker who refuses to join a strike or who replaces a striking worker. * *vi* (**scabbing, scabbed**) to form a scab; to be covered with scabs; to work as a scab.–**scabby** *adj*.

scabbard *n* a sheath for a sword or dagger. * *vt* to sheathe.

scabies *n* a contagious, itching skin disease.

scaffold *n* a raised platform for the execution of a criminal; capital punishment; scaffolding.

scaffolding *n* a temporary framework of wood and metal for use by workmen constructing a building, etc; materials for a scaffold.

scalawag *n* (*inf*) a rascal; a scamp.–*also* **scallawag, scallywag**.

scald *vt* to burn with hot liquid or steam; to heat almost to boiling point; to immerse in boiling water (to sterilize). * *n* an injury caused by hot liquid or steam.

scale[1] *n* (*pl*) a machine or instrument for weighing; one of the pans or the tray of a set of scales; (*pl*) (*with cap*) Libra, the seventh sign of the zodiac. * *vti* to weigh in a set of scales; to have a specified weight on a set of scales.

scale[2] *n* one of the thin plates covering a fish or reptile; a flake (of dry skin); an incrustation on teeth, etc. * *vti* to remove the scales from; to flake off.–**scaly** *adj*.–**scaliness** *n*.

scale[3] *n* a graduated measure; an instrument so marked; (*math*) the basis for a numerical system, 10 being that in general use; (*mus*) a series of tones from the keynote to its octave, in order of pitch; the proportion that a map, etc, bears to what it represents; a series of degrees classified by size, amount, etc; relative scope or size. * *vt* (*wall*) to go up or over; (*model*) to make or draw to scale; to increase or decrease in size.

scalene *adj* (*geom*) having three sides of unequal length. * *n* a scalene triangle.

scallawag, scallywag *see* **scalawag**.

scallop *n* an edible shellfish with two fluted, fan-shaped shells; one of a series of curves in an edging. * *vt* to cut into scallops.–**scalloped** *adj*.

scalp *n* the skin covering the skull, usu covered with hair. * *vti* to cut the scalp from; to criticize sharply; (*inf*) (*tickets, etc*) to buy and resell at higher prices.

scalpel *n* a short, thin, very sharp knife used esp for surgery.

scamp *n* a rascal; a mischievous child.

scamper *vi* to run away quickly or playfully. * *n* a brisk or playful run or movement.

scan *vb* (**scanning, scanned**) *vt* (*page etc*) to look through quickly; to scrutinize; (*med*) to examine with a radiological device; (*TV*) to pass an electronic beam over; (*radar*) to detect with an electronic beam; (*poem*) to conform to a rhythmical pattern; to check for recorded data by means of a mechanical or electronic device; (*human body*) to make a scan of in a scanner. * *vi* to analyze the pattern of verse. * *n* the act of scanning or an instance of being scanned.

scandal *n* a disgraceful event or action; talk arising from immoral behavior; a feeling of moral outrage; the thing or person causing this; disgrace; malicious gossip.–**scandalous** *adj*.–**scandalously** *adv*.

scandalize *vt* to shock the moral feelings of; to defame.–**scandalization** *n*.–**scandalizer** *n*.

scanner *n* a person or thing that scans; an electronic device that monitors or scans; a device for receiving or transmitting radar signals; a device for scanning the human body to obtain an image of an internal part.

scant *adj* limited; meager; insufficient; scanty; grudging.

scanty *adj* (**scantier, scantiest**) barely adequate; insufficient; small.–**scantily** *adv*.–**scantiness** *n*.

scapegoat *n* a person who bears the blame for others; one who is the object of irrational hostility.

scar *n* a mark left after the healing of a wound or sore; a blemish resulting from damage or wear. * *vti* (**scarring, scarred**) to mark with or form a scar.

scarce *adj* not in abundance; hard to find; rare.–**scarceness** *n*.

scarcely *adv* hardly, only just; probably not or certainly not.

scarcity *n* (*pl* **scarcities**) the state of being scarce; a dearth, deficiency.

scare *vti* to startle; to frighten or become frightened; to drive away by frightening. * *n* a sudden fear; a period of general fear; a false alarm.

scarecrow *n* a wooden figure dressed in clothes for scaring birds from crops; a thin or tattered person; something frightening but harmless.

scarf *n* (*pl* **scarves**) a rectangular or square piece of cloth worn around the neck, shoulders or head for warmth or decoration.

scarlet *n* a bright red with a tinge of orange; scarlet cloth or clothes. * *adj* scarlet colored; immoral or sinful.

scarlet fever *n* an acute contagious disease marked by a sore throat, fever, and a scarlet rash.

scarp *n* a low steep slope; the inner face of a ditch in a fortification.

scarves *see* **scarf**.

scary *adj* (**scarier, scariest**) frightening, alarming.–**scariness** *n*.

scathing *adj* bitterly critical; cutting, withering.–**scathingly** *adv*.

scatter *vti* to throw loosely about; to sprinkle; to dissipate; to put or take to flight; to disperse; to occur at random. * *n* a scattering or sprinkling.

scatterbrain *n* a frivolous, heedless person.–**scatterbrained** *adj*.

scattered *adj* dispersed widely, spaced out; straggling.

scattering *n* a small amount spread over a large area; a dispersion.

scavenge *vi* to gather things discarded by others; (*animal*) to eat decaying matter.–**scavenger** *n*.

scenario *n* (*pl* **scenarios**) an outline of events, real or imagined; the plot or script of a movie, etc.

scene *n* the place in which anything occurs; the place in which the action of a play or a story occurs; a section of a play, a division of an act; the stage of a theater; a painted screen, etc, used on this; an unseemly display of strong emotion; a landscape; surroundings; a place of action; (*inf*) an area of interest or activity (eg *the music scene*).

scenery n (pl **sceneries**) painted screens, etc, used to represent places, as in a play, movie, etc; an aspect of a landscape, esp of beautiful or impressive countryside.

scenic adj relating to natural scenery; picturesque; of or used on the stage.–**scenically** adv.

scent n a perfume; an odor left by an animal, by which it can be tracked; the sense of smell; a line of pursuit or discovery. * vt to recognize by the sense of smell; to track by smell; to impart an odor to, to perfume; to get wind of, to detect.–**scented** adj.

scepter, sceptre n the staff of office held by a monarch on a ceremonial occasion; sovereignty.

schedule n a list, inventory or tabulated statement; a timed plan for a project; a timetable. * vt to make a schedule; to plan.

scheme n a plan; a project; a systematic arrangement; a diagram; an underhand plot. * vti to devise or plot.–**schematic** adj.–**schematically** adv.

scheming adj cunning; intriguing.

schism n a division or separation into two parties, esp of a church; the sin of this; discord, disharmony.

schizo n (pl **schizos**) (inf) a schizophrenic person. * adj schizophrenic.

schizoid adj mildly schizophrenic.–also n.

schizophrenia n a mental disorder characterized by withdrawal from reality and deterioration of the personality; the presence of mutually contradictory qualities or parts.–**schizophrenic** adj, n.

schmaltz, schmalz n overly sentimental music, art, movie, etc.–**schmaltzy, schmalzy** adj.

scholar n a pupil, a student; a learned person; the holder of a scholarship.

scholarly adj learned, erudite, academic.

scholarship n an annual grant to a scholar or student, usu won by competitive examination; learning, academic achievement.

scholastic adj of or relating to schools, scholars, or education; academic.–**scholastically** adv.

school[1] n a shoal of porpoises, whales, or other aquatic animals of one kind swimming together.

school[2] n an educational establishment; its teachers and students; a regular session of teaching; formal education, schooling; a particular division of a university; a place or means of discipline; a group of thinkers, artists, writers, holding similar principles. * vt to train; to teach; to control or discipline.

schoolboy n a boy who attends school.

schoolchild n (pl **schoolchildren**) a child who attends school.

schoolgirl n a girl who attends school.

schoolteacher n a person who teaches in school.

schooner n a sailing ship with two or more masts rigged with fore-and-aft sails; a large drinking glass for sherry or beer.

science n knowledge gained by systematic experimentation and analysis, and the formulation of general principles; a branch of this; skill or technique.

science fiction n highly imaginative fiction typically involving actual or projected scientific phenomena.

science park n an area where scientific discoveries are translated into commercial products and applications.

scientific adj of or concerned with science; based on or using the principles and methods of science; systematic and exact; having or showing expert skill.–**scientifically** adv.

scientist n a specialist in a branch of science, as in chemistry, etc.

sci-fi n science fiction.

scintillate vti to give off sparks; to sparkle.–**scintillation** n.

scintillating adj sparkling; amusing.

scion n a shoot for grafting; a young member of a family, a descendant.

scissor vt to cut with scissors, to clip. * npl a tool for cutting paper, hair, etc, consisting of two fastened pivoted blades whose edges slide past each other; a gymnastic feat in which the leg movements resemble the opening and closing of scissors.

sclerosis n a pathological hardening of body tissue; a disease marked by this.

scoff vti to jeer (at) or mock. * n an expression or object of derision; mocking words, a taunt.

scold vi to reprove angrily; to tell off.

scone n a small, round cake made from flour and fat which is baked and spread with butter, etc.

scoop n a small shovel-like utensil as for taking up flour, ice cream, etc; the bucket of a dredge, etc; the act of scooping or the amount scooped up at one time; (inf) a piece of exclusive news; (inf) the advantage gained in being the first to publish or broadcast this. * vt to shovel, lift or hollow out with a scoop; (inf) to obtain as a scoop; (inf: rival newspaper etc) to forestall with a news item.

scoot vti to run quickly; to hurry (off).

scooter n a child's two-wheeled vehicle with a footboard and steering handle; a motor scooter.

scope n the opportunity to use one's abilities; extent; range; an instrument for viewing.

scorch vti to burn or be burned on the surface; to wither from over-exposure to heat; to singe; (inf) to drive or cycle furiously.

scorching adj (inf: weather) very hot; scathing.

score n the total number of points made in a game or examination; a notch or scratch; a line indicating deletion or position; a group of twenty; a written copy of a musical composition showing the different parts; the music composed for a film; a grievance for settling; a reason or motive; (inf) the real facts; a bill or reckoning; (pl) an indefinite, large number. * vt to mark with cuts; (mus) to arrange in a score, to orchestrate; to gain or record points, as in a game; to evaluate in testing. * vi to make points, as in a game; to keep the score of a game; to gain an advantage, a success, etc; (sl) to be successful in seduction; (with off) to get the better of someone.–**scorer** n.

scoreboard n a large manually or electronically operated board showing the score in a game or match.

scorecard n (golf, etc) a card on which scores are recorded.

scorn n extreme contempt or disdain; the object of this. * vt to treat with contempt, to despise; to reject or refuse as unworthy.–**scornful** adj.–**scornfully** adv.

Scorpio n the eighth sign of the zodiac in astrology, operative October 23–November 21.–**Scorpionic** adj.

scorpion n a small, tropical, insect-like animal with pincers and a jointed tail with a poisonous sting.

scotch vt (a rumor) to stamp out.

Scotch n whisky made in Scotland.

scot-free adj without penalty or injury.

scoundrel n a rascal; a dishonest person.

scour[1] vt to clean by rubbing with an abrasive cloth; to flush out with a current of water; to purge. * n the act or process of scouring; a place scoured by running water; scouring action (as of a glacier); damage done by scouring action.

scour[2] vt to hasten over or along, to range over, esp in search or pursuit.

scourge n a whip; a means of inflicting punishment; a person who harasses and causes widespread and great affliction; a pest. * vt to flog; to punish harshly.

scout n a person, plane, etc, sent to observe the enemy's strength, etc; a person employed to find new talent or survey a competitor, etc; (with cap) a member of the Scouting Association, an organization for young people. * vti to reconnoiter; to go in search of (something).

Scouting Association n (formerly Boy Scouts, Girl Guides) an organization for young people.

scowl n a contraction of the brows in an angry or threatening manner, a sullen expression. * vi to make a scowl; to look sullen.

scrabble vi to scratch or grope about; to struggle; to scramble. * n a repeated scratching or clawing; a scramble; a scribble.

scraggy *adj* (**scraggier, scraggiest**) thin and bony, gaunt.

scram *vi* (**scramming, scrammed**) (*sl*) to get out, to go away at once.

scramble *vi* to move or climb hastily on all fours; to scuffle or struggle for something; to move with urgency or panic. * *vt* to mix haphazardly; to stir (slightly beaten eggs) while cooking; (*transmitted signals*) to make unintelligible in transit. * *n* a hard climb or advance; a disorderly struggle; a rapid emergency take-off of fighter planes; a motorcycle rally over rough ground.– **scrambler** *n*.

scrap[1] *n* a small piece; a fragment of discarded material; (*pl*) bits of food. * *adj* in the form of pieces, leftovers, etc; used and discarded. * *vt* (**scrapping, scrapped**) to make into scraps.

scrap[2] *n* (*inf*) a fight or quarrel. * *vi* (**scrapping, scrapped**) to have a scrap.

scrapbook *n* a book for pasting clippings, etc, in.

scrape *vt* to rub with a sharp or abrasive object so as to clean, smooth or remove; to eke out or to be economical; to amass in small portions; to draw along with a grating or vibration; to get narrowly past; to draw back the foot in making a bow; (*with* **together**) to save or collect with difficulty. * *vi* (*with* **through**) to manage or succeed with difficulty or by a slim margin. * *n* the act of scraping; a grating sound; an abrasion, scratch; an awkward predicament.

scrapheap *n* a pile of discarded material or things.

scratch *vt* to mark with a sharp point; to scrape with the nails or claws; to rub to relieve an itch; to chafe; to write awkwardly; (*writing etc*) to strike out; to withdraw from a race, etc. * *vi* to use nails or claws to tear or dig. * *n* the act of scratching; a mark or sound made by this; a slight injury; a starting line for a race; a scribble. * *adj* taken at random, haphazard, impromptu; without a handicap.

scrawl *n* careless or illegible handwriting; a scribble. * *vti* to draw or write carelessly.

scrawny *adj* (**scrawnier, scrawniest**) skinny; bony.–**scrawniness** *n*.

scream *vti* to utter a piercing cry, as of pain, fear, etc; to shout; to shriek. * *n* a sharp, piercing cry; (*inf*) a very funny person or thing.

screech *n* a harsh, high-pitched cry. * *vti* to utter a screech, to shriek.

screen *n* a movable partition or framework to conceal, divide, or protect; a shelter or shield from heat, danger or view; an electronic display (as in a television set, computer terminal, etc); a surface on which films, slides, etc are projected; the motion picture industry; a coarse wire mesh over a window or door to keep out insects; a sieve. * *vt* to conceal or shelter; to grade by passing through a screen; to separate according to skill, etc; (*a film*) to show on a screen.

screenplay *n* a story written in a form suitable for a movie.

screenwriter *n* a person who writes screenplays.

screw *n* a metal cylinder or cone with a spiral thread around it for fastening things by being turned; any spiral thing like this; a twist or turn of a screw; a twist of paper; pressure; a propeller with revolving blades on a shaft. * *vt* to fasten, tighten etc with a screw; to oppress; to extort; to cheat out of something due; (*with* **up**) to gather (courage, etc). * *vi* to go together or come apart by being turned like a screw; to twist or turn with a writhing movement; (*with* **up**) to bungle.

screwball *n* (*sl*) an odd or eccentric person. * *adj* whimsical, zany.

screwdriver *n* a tool like a blunt chisel for turning screws; a drink of vodka and orange juice.

screwy *adj* (**screwier, screwiest**) (*sl*) eccentric, odd.–**screwiness** *n*.

scribble *vti* to draw or write hastily or carelessly, to scrawl; to be a writer. * *n* hasty writing, a scrawl.–**scribbler** *n*.

scribe *n* a person who copies (documents); an author or journalist. * *vt* to draw a line on by cutting with a pointed instrument.

scrimp *vti* to be sparing or frugal (with); to make too small, to skimp.

script *n* handwriting; a style of writing; the text of a stage play, screenplay or broadcast; a plan of action; (*print*) type that resembles handwriting. * *vt* to write a script (for).

scripture *n* any sacred writing; (*with cap, often pl*) the Jewish Bible or Old Testament; the Christian Bible or Old and New Testaments. * *adj* contained in or quoted from the Bible.–**scriptural** *adj*.

scriptwriter *n* a writer of screenplays for movies, TV, etc; a screenwriter.–**scriptwriting** *n*.

scroll *n* a roll of parchment or paper with writing on it; an ornament like this; a list. * *vti* (*comput*) to move text across a screen; to decorate with scrolls.

scrotum *n* (*pl* **scrota, scrotums**) the pouch of skin containing the testicles.

scrounge *vti* (*inf*) to seek or obtain (something) for nothing.–**scrounger** *n*.

scrub[1] *n* an arid area of stunted trees and shrubs; such vegetation; anything small or mean. * *adj* small, stunted, inferior, etc.

scrub[2] *vti* (**scrubbing, scrubbed**) to clean vigorously, to scour; to rub hard; (*inf*) to remove, to cancel. * *n* the act of scrubbing.

scrubby *adj* (**scrubbier, scrubbiest**) stunted; paltry; unkempt.–**scrubbily** *adv*.–**scrubbiness** *n*.

scruff *n* the back of the neck, the nape.

scruffy *adj* (**scruffier, scruffiest**) shabby; unkempt.–**scruffily** *adv*.–**scruffiness** *n*.

scrumptious *adj* (*inf*) delicious; very pleasing.–**scrumptiously** *adv*.–**scrumptiousness** *n*.

scrunch *vti* to crumple, esp the hair when drying; to crunch; to be crumpled or crunched. * *n* a crunching sound; the act of scrunching.

scruple *n* (*usu pl*) a moral principle or belief causing one to doubt or hesitate about a course of action. * *vti* to hesitate owing to scruples.

scrupulous *adj* careful; conscientious; thorough.–**scrupulously** *adv*.–**scrupulousness** *n*.

scrutiny *n* (*pl* **scrutinies**) a careful examination; a critical gaze; an official inspection of votes cast in an election.–**scrutinize** *vti*.–**scrutinizer** *n*.

scuba *n* a diver's apparatus with compressed-air tanks for breathing underwater.

scud *vti* (**scudding, scudded**) to go along swiftly; to be driven before the wind. * *n* an act of scudding; light clouds, etc, driven by wind; a type of missile.

scuff *vti* to drag the feet, to shuffle; to wear or mark the surface of by doing this.

scuffle *n* a confused fight; the sound of shuffling. * *vi* to fight confusedly; to move by shuffling.

scull *n* an oar worked from side to side over the stern of a boat; a light rowing boat for racing. * *vti* to propel with a scull.

scullery *n* (*pl* **sculleries**) a room for storage or kitchen work, such as washing dishes, etc.

sculpt *vt* to carve, to sculpture.

sculptor *n* a person skilled in sculpture.

sculpture *n* the art of carving wood or forming clay, stone, etc, into figures, statues, etc; a three-dimensional work of art; a sculptor's work. * *vt* to carve, adorn or portray with sculptures; to shape, mould or form like sculpture.–**sculptural** *adj*.

scum *n* a thin layer of impurities on top of a liquid; refuse; despicable people.

scurf *n* small flakes of dead skin (as dandruff); any scaly coating.

scurrilous *adj* abusive; grossly offensive.

scurry *vi* (**scurrying, scurried**) to hurry with quick, short steps, to scamper. * *n* (*pl* **scurries**) a bustle; a flurry (as of snow).

scurvy *n* a disease caused by a deficiency of vitamin C.

scuttle *vi* to run quickly; to hurry away. * *n* a short swift run; a hurried pace.

scythe *n* a two-handed implement with a large curved blade for cutting grass, etc. * *vti* to cut with a scythe; to mow down.

SD *abbr* = South Dakota.

SE *abbr* = southeast(ern).

sea *n* the ocean; a section of this; a vast expanse of water; a heavy wave, the swell of the ocean; something like the sea in size; the seafaring life. * *adj* marine, of the sea.

seaboard *n, adj* (land) bordering on the sea.

seafaring *n* traveling by sea, esp the work of a sailor.–*also adj.–* **seafarer** *n*.

seafood *n* edible fish or shellfish from the sea.

seagoing *adj* (*ship*) made for use on the open sea.

seagull *n* a gull.

sea horse *n* a small bony-plated fish with a horselike head and neck and a long tail, that swims in an upright position; in fable, a horse with the tail of a fish.

seal[1] *n* an engraved stamp for impressing wax, lead, etc; wax, lead, etc, so impressed; that which authenticates or pledges; a device for closing or securing tightly. * *vt* to fix a seal to; to close tightly or securely; to shut up; to mark as settled, to confirm.

seal[2] *n* an aquatic mammal with four webbed flippers; the fur of some seals; a dark brown. * *vi* to hunt seals.

sealant *n* a thing that seals, as wax, etc; a substance for stopping a leak, making watertight, etc.

sea lion *n* a large seal of the Pacific Ocean that has a loud roar and, in the male, a mane.

seam *n* the line where two pieces of cloth are stitched together; (*geol*) a stratum of coal, oil, etc, between thicker ones; a line or wrinkle. * *vt* to join with a seam; to furrow.

seaman *n* (*pl* **seamen**) a sailor; a naval rank.

seamstress *n* a woman who sews for a living.

seamy *adj* (**seamier, seamiest**) unpleasant or sordid.

seance, séance *n* a meeting of spiritualists to try to communicate with the dead.

seaplane *n* an airplane with floats that allow it to take off from and land on water.

sear *vt* to burn or scorch the surface of; to brand with a heated iron; to wither up.

search *vi* to look around to find something; to explore. * *vt* to examine or inspect closely; to probe into. * *n* the act of searching; an investigation; a quest.–**searcher** *n*.

searchlight *n* a powerful ray of light projected by an apparatus on a swivel; the apparatus.

search party *n* a group of people organized to locate a missing person or thing.

search warrant *n* a legal document that authorizes a police search.

seashell *n* the discarded or empty shell of a marine mollusc.

seasick *adj* affected with nausea brought on by the motion of a ship.–**seasickness** *n*.

season *n* one of the four equal parts into which the year is divided: spring, summer, autumn, or winter; a period of time; a time when something is plentiful or in use; a suitable time; (*inf*) a season ticket. * *vt* (*food*) to flavor by adding salt, spices, etc; to make mature or experienced; (*wood*) to dry until ready for use. * *vi* to become experienced.

seasonal *adj* of or relating to a particular season.–**seasonally** *adv*.

seasoning *n* salt, spices, etc, used to enhance the flavor of food; the process of making something fit to use.

season ticket *n* a ticket or set of tickets valid for a number of concerts, games, journeys, etc, during a specified period.

seat *n* a piece of furniture for sitting on, such as a chair, bench, etc; the part of a chair on which one sits; the buttocks, the part of the trousers covering them; a way of sitting (on a horse, etc); the chief location, or centre; a part at or forming a base. * *vt* to place on a seat; to provide with seats; to settle.

seatbelt *n* an anchored strap worn in a car or aeroplane to secure a person to a seat.

sea urchin *n* a small marine animal with a round body enclosed in a shell covered with sharp spines.

seaweed *n* a mass of plants growing in or under water; a sea plant, esp a marine alga.

seaworthy *adj* fit to go to sea; able to withstand sea water, watertight.–**seaworthiness** *n*.

sebaceous *adj* of, secreting, containing, or producing oily or fatty matter.

sec *n* (*inf*) a second.

secateurs *npl* a pair of small shears with curved blades for pruning, etc.

secede *vi* to withdraw formally one's membership from a society or organization.–**seceder** *n*.–**secession** *n*.

seclude *vt* to keep (a person, etc) separate from others; to remove or screen from view.–**seclusion** *n*.

second *adj* next after first; alternate; another of the same kind; next below the first in rank, value, etc. * *n* a person or thing coming second; another; an article of merchandise not of first quality; an aid or assistant, as to a boxer, duellist; the gear after low gear; one sixtieth of a minute of time or of an angular degree; (*pl*) (*inf*) another helping of food. * *adv* in the second place, group, etc. * *vt* to act as a second (to); (*a motion, resolution, etc*) to support; (*mil*) to place on temporary service elsewhere.

secondary *adj* subordinate; second in rank or importance; in the second stage; derived, not primary; relating to secondary school. * *n* (*pl* **secondaries**) that which is secondary; a delegate, a deputy.–**secondarily** *adv*.

second best *adj* next to the best; inferior. * *adv* in second place. * *n* next to the best; an inferior alternative.

second class *n* the class next to the first in a classification. * *adj* (second-class) relating to a second class; inferior, mediocre; (*seating, accommodation*) next in price and quality to first class; (*mail*) less expensive and handled more slowly (than first class).

second hand *n* the moving pointer in a clock or watch that indicates the seconds.

second-hand *adj* bought after use by another; derived, not original.–*also adv*.

secondly *adv* in the second place.

second nature *n* a long-established habit, etc, deeply fixed in a person's nature.

second-rate *adj* of inferior quality.

second sight *n* the supposed faculty of seeing events before they occur.

second wind *n* a return to regular breathing after a bout of exercise; renewed energy or enthusiasm.

secret *adj* not made public; concealed from others; hidden; private; remote. * *n* something hidden; a mystery; a hidden cause.–**secrecy** *n*.

secret agent *n* a spy.

secretariat *n* an administrative office or staff, as in a government.

secretary *n* (*pl* **secretaries**) a person employed to deal with correspondence, filing, telephone calls of another or of an association; the head of a state department.–**secretarial** *adj*.

secretary of state *n* (*with caps*) in the US, the minister in charge of foreign affairs; in the UK, any of various ministers in charge of government departments.

secrete *vt* to conceal; to hide; (*cell, gland, etc*) to produce and release (a substance) out of blood or sap.

secretion *n* the process of secreting; a substance secreted by an animal or plant.

secretive *adj* given to secrecy; uncommunicative, reticent.–**secretively** *adv*.–**secretiveness** *n*.

secretly *adv* in a secret way; unknown to others.

secret service *n* a government agency that gathers intelligence, infiltrates terrorist or subversive organizations, conducts espionage, etc in the interests of national security.

sect *n* a religious denomination; a group of people united by a common interest or belief; a faction.

sectarian *adj* of or confined to a religious sect; bigoted. * *n* a member or adherent of a sect.

sectarianism *n* devotion to a sect; religious narrowness.

section *n* the act of cutting; a severed or separable part; a division; a distinct portion; a slice; a representation of anything cut through to show its interior; (*geom*) the cutting of a solid by a plane; a plane figure formed by this. * *vti* to cut or separate into sections; to represent in sections; to become separated or cut into parts.

sectional *adj* of a section; made up of several sections; local rather than general in character.–**sectionally** *adv*.

sector *n* (*geom*) a space enclosed by two radii of a circle and the arc they cut off; a distinctive part (as of an economy); a subdivision; (*mil*) an area of activity .

secular *adj* having no connection with religion or the church; worldly.–**secularly** *adv*.

secure *adj* free from danger, safe; stable; firmly held or fixed; confident, assured (of); reliable. * *vt* to make safe; to fasten firmly; to protect; to confine; to fortify; to guarantee; to gain possession of, to obtain.–**securely** *adv*.

security *n* (*pl* **securities**) the state of being secure; a financial guarantee, surety; a pledge for repayment, etc; a protection or safeguard; a certificate of shares or bonds.

security guard *n* a person employed to protect public buildings, banks, offices, etc and to transport large sums of money.

sedan *n* a car with no division between driver and passengers; a covered chair for one person with poles carried by two bearers.

sedate[1] *adj* calm; composed; serious and unemotional.–**sedately** *adv*.–**sedateness** *n*.

sedate[2] *vti* to calm or become calm by the administration of a sedative.–**sedation** *n*.

sedative *n* a drug with a soothing, calming effect. * *adj* having a soothing, calming effect.

sedentary *adj* requiring a sitting position; inactive; not migratory.

sediment *n* matter that settles at the bottom of a liquid; (*geol*) matter deposited by water or wind.–**sedimentary** *adj*.

sedition *n* incitement to rebel against the government.–**seditious** *adj*.–**seditiously** *adv*.

seduce *vt* to lead astray; to corrupt; to entice into unlawful sexual intercourse.–**seducer** *n*.

seduction *n* the act of seducing; temptations; attraction.–**seductive** *adj*. –**seductively** *adv*.

see[1] *vt* (**seeing**, **saw**, *pp* **seen**) to perceive with the eyes; to observe; to grasp with the intelligence; to ascertain; to take care (that); to accompany; to visit; to meet; to consult; (*guests*) to receive; (*with* **through**) to persist or endure to the end; to assist (eg a friend) during a crisis, difficulty, etc. * *vi* to have the faculty of sight; to make inquiry; to consider, to reflect; to understand; (*with* **about**) to deal with; to consider in detail; (*with* **off**) to be present when someone leaves on a journey, etc; (*inf*) to repel, get rid of; (*with* **through**) *vi* to recognize the true character of.

see[2] *n* the diocese of a bishop.

seed *n* the small, hard part (ovule) of a plant from which a new plant grows; such seeds collectively; the source of anything; sperm or semen; descendants; (*tennis*) a seeded tournament player. * *vti* to sow (seed); to produce or shed seed; to remove seeds from; (*tennis*) to arrange (a tournament) so that the best players cannot meet until later rounds.

seedling *n* a young plant raised from seed, not from a cutting; a young tree before it is a sapling.

seedy *adj* (**seedier**, **seediest**) full of seeds; out of sorts, indisposed; shabby; rundown.–**seedily** *adv*.–**seediness** *n*.

seek *vti* (**seeking**, **sought**) to search for; to try to find, obtain, or achieve; to resort to; (*with* **to**) to try to, to endeavor; (*with* **out**) to search for and locate a person or thing; to try to secure the society of.–**seeker** *n*.

seem *vi* to appear (to be); to give the impression of; to appear to oneself.

seeming *adj* that seems real, true; ostensible, apparent.–**seemingly** *adv*.

seen *see* **see**[1].

seep *vi* to ooze gently, to leak through.–**seepage** *n*.

seer *n* a person who sees visions, a prophet.

seersucker *n* a light, usu cotton, fabric with a puckered surface.

seesaw *n* a plank balanced across a central support so that it is tilted up and down by a person sitting on each end; an up-and-down movement like this; vacillation. * *vi* to move up and down; to fluctuate. * *adj*, *adv* alternately rising and falling.

seethe *vi* to be very angry inwardly; to swarm (with people).

segment *n* a section; a portion; one of the two parts of a circle or sphere when a line is drawn through it. * *vti* to cut or separate into segments.–**segmentation** *n*.

segregate *vti* to set apart from others, to isolate; to separate racial or minority groups.

segregation *n* the act of segregating or the condition of being segregated; the policy of compelling racial groups to live apart.

seismic *adj* of or caused by earthquakes.–**seismically** *adv*.

seismology *n* the scientific study of earthquakes.–**seismologic, seismological** *adj*.–**seismologist** *n*.

seize *vt* to grasp; to capture; to take hold of suddenly or forcibly; to attack or afflict suddenly. * *vi* (*machinery*) to become jammed.–**seizable** *adj*.

seizure *n* the act of seizing; what is seized; a sudden attack of illness, an apoplectic stroke.

seldom *adv* not often, rarely.

select *vti* to choose or pick out. * *adj* excellent; choice; limited (eg in membership); exclusive.–**selective** *adj*.–**selectively** *adv*.

selection *n* the act of selecting; what is or are selected; the process by which certain animals or plants survive while others are eliminated, natural selection.

self *n* (*pl* **selves**) the identity, character, etc, of any person or thing; one's own person as distinct from all others; one's own interests or advantage. * *adj* (*color*) matching, uniform.

self-centered, self-centred *adj* preoccupied with one's own affairs.–**self-centeredly, self-centredly** *adv*.–**self-centeredness, self-centredness** *n*.

self-colored, self-coloured *adj* of a single color.

self-confessed *adj* according to one's own testimony.

self-conscious *adj* embarrassed or awkward in the presence of others, ill at ease.–**self-consciously** *adv*.–**self-consciousness** *n*.

self-contained *adj* complete in itself; showing self-control; uncommunicative.–**self-containment** *n*.

self-defense, self-defence *n* the act of defending oneself; (*law*) a plea for the justification for the use of force.

self-denial *n* abstention from pleasure, etc; unselfishness.

self-esteem *n* confidence and respect for oneself; an exaggerated opinion of oneself.

self-help *n* the provision of means to help oneself, instead of relying on others.

self-image *n* one's sense of oneself or one's importance.

self-importance *n* an exaggerated estimate of one's own worth; pompousness.–**self-important** *adj*.

self-indulgence *n* undue gratification of one's desires, appetites, or whims.–**self-indulgent** *adj*.

self-interest *n* regard to one's own advantage.

selfish *adj* chiefly concerned with oneself; lacking in consideration for others.–**selfishly** *adv*.–**selfishness** *n*.

selfless *adj* with no thought of self, unselfish.–**selflessly** *adv*.–**selflessness** *n*.

self-made *adj* having achieved status or wealth by one's own efforts.

self-possessed *adj* cool and collected.

self-respect *n* proper respect for oneself, one's standing and dignity.–**self-respecting** *adj*.

self-righteous *adj* thinking oneself better than others; priggish.–**self-righteousness** *n*.

self-rising *adj* (*flour*) containing a raising agent.

self-sacrifice *n* the sacrifice of one's own interests, welfare, etc, to secure that of others.

selfsame adj identical, the very same.

self-service adj serving oneself in a cafe, store, filling station, etc.

self-styled adj called by oneself; pretended.

self-sufficient adj independent; supporting oneself (eg in growing food) without the help of others.**–self-sufficiency** n.

sell vb (**selling, sold**) vt to exchange (goods, services, etc) for money or other equivalent; to offer for sale; to promote; to deal in; (with **up**) to sell all the goods of (a debtor) to clear the debt. * vi (with **off**) to clear out (stock) at bargain prices; (with **out**) to sell off, to betray for money or reward; (inf) to disappoint, to trick; to make sales; to attract buyers; (with **up**) to sell one's house, business, etc. * n an act or instance of selling; (inf) a disappointment, a trick, a fraud.**–seller** n.

sellout n a show, game, etc, for which all the tickets are sold; (inf) a betrayal.

selvage, selvedge n the edge of cloth so finished as to prevent unraveling.

selves see **self**.

semantic adj relating to the meaning of words. * npl the study of word meanings and changes.

semaphore n a system of visual signaling using the operator's arms, flags, etc; a signaling device consisting of a post with movable arms.

semblance n likeness, resemblance; an outward, sometimes deceptive appearance.

semen n the fluid that carries sperm in men and male animals.

semester n an academic or school half-year.

semi n (pl **semis**) (inf) a semifinal.

semicircle n half of a circle.**–semicircular** adj.

semicolon n the punctuation mark (;) of intermediate value between a comma and a full stop.

semiconductor n a substance in a transmitter, as silicon, used to control the flow of current.

semifinal adj, n (the match or round) before the final in a knockout tournament.**–semifinalist** n.

seminal adj of, relating to, or containing semen; promising or contributing to further development; original, influential.**–seminally** adv.

seminar n a group of students engaged in study or research under supervision; any group meeting to pool and discuss ideas.

seminary n (pl **seminaries**) a training college for priests, ministers, etc.

semiprofessional adj taking part in sport for pay, but not on a fulltime basis.**–semiprofessionally** adv.

semitone n (mus) an interval equal to half a tone.

semolina n coarse particles of grain left after the sifting of wheat.

senate n a legislative or governing body; (with cap) the upper branch of a two-body legislature in France, the US, etc; the governing body of some universities.

senator n a member of a senate.**–senatorial** adj.

send vti (**sending, sent**) to cause or enable to go; to have conveyed, to dispatch (a message or messenger); to cause to move, to propel; to grant; to cause to be; (sl) to move (a person) to ecstasy; (with **down**) to expel from university; (with **for**) to order to be brought, to summon; (with **up**) (inf) to send to prison; to imitate or make fun of.**–sender** n.

send-off n a friendly demonstration at a departure; a start given to someone or something.

senile adj of or relating to old age; weakened, esp mentally, by old age.**–senility** n.

senior adj higher in rank; of or for seniors; longer in service; older (when used to distinguish between father and son with the same first name). * n one's elder or superior in standing; a person of advanced age; a student in the last year of college or high school.

senior citizen n an elderly person, esp a retired one.

seniority n (pl **seniorities**) the condition of being senior; status, priority, etc, in a given job.

sensation n awareness due to stimulation of the senses; an effect on the senses; a thrill; a state of excited interest; the cause of this.**–sensational** adj.**–sensationally** adv.

sensationalism n the use of sensational writing, language, etc; the doctrine that all knowledge is obtained from sense impressions.**–sensationalist** adj.

sense n one of the five human and animal faculties by which objects are perceived: sight, hearing, smell, taste, and touch; awareness; moral discernment; soundness of judgment; meaning, intelligibility; (pl) conscious awareness. * vt to perceive; to become aware of; to understand; to detect.

senseless adj stupid, foolish; meaningless, purposeless; unconscious.**–senselessly** adv.**–senselessness** n.

sensibility n (pl **sensibilities**) the capacity to feel; over-sensitiveness; susceptibility; (pl) sensitive awareness or feelings.

sensible adj having good sense or judgment; reasonable; practical; perceptible by the senses, appreciable; conscious (of); sensitive.**–sensibleness** n.**–sensibly** adv.

sensitive adj having the power of sensation; feeling readily and acutely, keenly perceptive; (skin) delicate, easily irritated; (wound etc) still in a painful condition; easily hurt or shocked, tender, touchy; highly responsive to slight changes; sensory; (photog) reacting to light.**–sensitively** adv.**–sensitiveness** n.

sensitivity n (pl **sensitivities**) the condition of being sensitive; awareness of changes or differences; responsiveness to stimuli or feelings, esp to excess.

sensitize vt to make or become sensitive; (person) to render sensitive to an antigen, etc; (photog: paper etc) to render sensitive to light.**–sensitization** n.**–sensitizer** n.

sensor n a device for detecting, recording, or measuring physical phenomena, as heat, pulse, etc; a sense organ.

sensory adj of or relating to the senses, sensation, or the sense organs; conveying nerve impulses to the brain.

sensual adj bodily, relating to the senses rather than the mind; arousing sexual desire.**–sensuality** n.**–sensually** adv.

sensuous adj giving pleasure to the mind or body through the senses.**–sensuously** adv.**–sensuousness** n.

sent see **send**.

sentence n a court judgment; the punishment imposed; (gram) a series of words conveying a complete thought. * vt (a convicted person) to pronounce punishment upon; to condemn (to).

sententious adj terse, pithy; making frequent use of axioms and maxims; exhibiting a pompous, moralizing tone.**–sententiously** adv.**–sententiousness** n.

sentient adj making use of the senses, conscious.**–sentiently** adv.

sentiment n a feeling, awareness, or emotion; the thought behind something; an attitude of mind; a tendency to be swayed by feeling rather than reason; an exaggerated emotion.

sentimental adj of or arising from feelings; foolishly emotional; nostalgic.**–sentimentality** n.**–sentimentally** adv.

sentinel n a sentry or guard.

sentry n (pl **sentries**) a soldier on guard to give warning of danger and to prevent unauthorized access.

se-or n (pl **se-ores, se-ors**) the title of a Spanish-speaking man, equivalent to Mr or sir.

se-ora n (pl **se-oras**) the title of a Spanish-speaking married woman, equivalent to Mrs or madam.

se-orita n (pl **se-oritas**) the title of a Spanish-speaking unmarried woman, equivalent to Miss or madam.

sepal n any of the individual parts of the calyx of a flower.

separate vt to divide or part; to sever; to set or keep apart; to sort into different sizes. * vi to go different ways; to cease to live together as man and wife. * adj divided; distinct, individual; not shared. * n (pl) articles of clothing designed to be interchangeable with others to form various outfits.**–separately** adv.**–separateness** n.**–separation** n.

separatist n a person who advocates or practices separation from an organization, church, or government; a person who advocates racial or political separation.–also adj.–**separatism** n.

sepia adj, n dark reddish brown.

September n the ninth month of the year, having 30 days.

septic adj infected by microorganisms; causing or caused by putrefaction.–**septically** adv.–**septicity** n.

septicemia, septicaemia n a disease caused by poisonous bacteria in the blood.–**septicemic, septicaemic** adj.

septic tank n an underground tank in which sewage is decomposed by the action of bacteria.

septuplet n one of seven offspring produced at one birth.

sepulchral adj of or like a sepulcher; dismal, funereal; (sound) deep and hollow.

sepulcher, sepulchre n a tomb, a burial vault.

sequel n something that follows, the succeeding part; a consequence; the continuation of a story begun in an earlier literary work, film, etc.

sequence n order of succession; a series of succeeding things; a single, uninterrupted episode, as in a film.–**sequential** adj.–**sequentially** adv.

sequester vt to place apart; to retire in seclusion; (law) to remove from one's possession until the claims of one's creditors are satisfied.

sequin n a shiny round piece of metal or foil sewn on clothes for decoration.

sequoia n a lofty coniferous Californian tree.

sera see serum.

seraph n (pl **seraphs, seraphim**) (theol) a member of the highest order of angels.–**seraphic** adj.

serenade n music sung or played at night beneath a person's window, esp by a lover. * vt to entertain with a serenade.

serendipity n the faculty of making fortunate finds by chance.

serene adj calm; untroubled; tranquil; clear and unclouded; (with cap) honored (used as part of certain royal titles).–**serenely** adv.–**serenity** n.

serf n (pl **serfs**) a laborer in feudal service who was bound to, and could be sold with, the land he worked; a drudge.–**serfdom** n.

serge n a hard-wearing twilled woolen fabric.

sergeant n a noncommissioned officer ranking above a corporal in the army, air force, and marine corps; a police officer ranking above a constable.

sergeant major n a noncommissioned officer in the army, air force, marine corps serving as chief administrative assistant in a headquarters.

Sergt. abbr = Sergeant.

serial adj of or forming a series; published, shown or broadcast by installments at regular intervals. * n a story presented in regular installments with a connected plot.

serialize vt to arrange, publish or broadcast in serial form.–**serialization** n.

serial killer n a person who murders people one at a time over a period of time.

serial number n one of a series of numbers given for identification.

series n sing, pl a succession of items or events; a succession of things connected by some likeness; a sequence, a set; a radio or television serial whose episodes have self-contained plots; a set of books issued by one publisher; (math) a progression of numbers or quantities according to a certain law.

serious adj grave, solemn, not frivolous; meaning what one says, sincere, earnest; requiring close attention or thought; important; critical.–**seriously** adv.–**seriousness** n.

sermon n a speech on religion or morals, esp by a clergyman; a long, serious talk of reproof, esp a tedious one.

sermonize vti to compose sermons; to preach at or to at length.–**sermonizer** n.

serpent n a snake; a venomous or treacherous person.–**serpentine** adj.

serrated adj having an edge notched like the teeth of a saw.

serum n (pl **serums, sera**) the watery part of bodily fluid, esp liquid that separates from the blood when it coagulates; such fluid taken from the blood of an animal immune to a disease, used as an antitoxin.

servant n a personal or domestic attendant; one in the service of another.

serve vt to work for; to do military or naval service (for); to be useful to; to meet the needs (of); to suffice; (a customer) to wait upon; (food, etc) to hand round; (a sentence) to undergo; to be a soldier, sailor, etc; (of a male animal) to copulate with; (law) to deliver (a summons, etc); (tennis) to put (the ball) into play. * vi to be employed as a servant; to be enough. * n the act of serving in tennis, etc.

service n the act of serving; the state of being a servant; domestic employment; a department of state employ; the people engaged in it; military employment or duty; work done for others; use, assistance; attendance in a hotel, etc; a facility providing a regular supply of trains, etc; a set of dishes; any religious ceremony; an overhaul of a vehicle; (tennis) the act or manner of serving; (pl) friendly help or professional aid; a system of providing a utility, as water, gas, etc. * vt to provide with assistance; to overhaul.

serviceable adj useful; durable.–**serviceably** adv.–**serviceableness** n.

serviceman n (pl **servicemen**) a member of the armed services; a person whose work is repairing something.–**servicewoman** n (pl **servicewomen**).

servile adj of or like a slave; subservient; submissive; menial.–**servilely** adv.–**servility** n.

serving n a portion of food or drink.

servitude n slavery, bondage; work imposed as punishment for a crime.

sesame n an Asian plant that yields oil-bearing seeds; its seeds, also used for flavoring.

session n the meeting of a court, legislature, etc; a series of such meetings; a period of these; a period of study, classes, etc; a university year; a period of time passed in an activity.

set vb (**setting, set**) vt to put in a specified place, condition, etc; (trap for animals) to fix; (clock etc) to adjust; (table) to arrange for a meal; (hair) to fix in a desired style; (bone) to put into normal position, etc; to make settled, rigid, or fixed; (gems) to mount; to direct; to furnish (an example) for others; to fit (words to music or music to words); (type) to arrange for printing; (with against) to weigh up, compare; to cause to be opposed to; (with aside) to discard; to reserve for a particular reason; (with down) to place (something) on a surface; to record, put in writing; to regard; to attribute (to); to allow to alight from (a vehicle); (with out) to present or display; to explain in detail; to plan, lay out. * vi to become firm, hard or fixed; to begin to move (out, forth, off, etc); (sun) to sink below the horizon; (with about) to begin; to abuse physically or verbally; (with in) to stitch (a sleeve) within a garment; to become established; (with off) to show up by contrast; to set in motion; to cause to explode; (with on) to urge (as a dog) to attack or pursue; to go on, advance; (with out) to begin a journey, career, etc; (with to) to start working, esp eagerly; to start fighting; (with up) to erect; to establish, to found; (with upon) to attack, usu with violence. * adj fixed, established; intentional; rigid, firm; obstinate; ready. * n a number of persons or things classed or belonging together; a group, a clique; the way in which a thing is set; direction; the scenery for a play, film, etc; assembled equipment for radio or television reception, etc; (math) the totality of points, numbers, or objects that satisfy a given condition; (tennis) a series of games forming a unit of a match; a rooted cutting of a plant ready for transplanting; a badger's burrow (–also **sett**).

setback n misfortune; a reversal.

set-square *n* a flat triangular instrument for drawing angles.

setter *n* a large breed of gundog trained to stand rigid when spotting game.

setting *n* a background, scene, surroundings, environment; a mounting, as for a gem; the music for a song, etc.

settle *vti* to put in order; to pay (an account); to clarify; to decide, to come to an agreement; to make or become quiet or calm; to make or become firm; to establish or become established in a place, business, home, etc; to colonize (a country); to take up residence; to come to rest; (*dregs*) to fall to the bottom; to stabilize; to make or become comfortable (for resting); (*bird*) to alight; to bestow legally for life; (*with* **for**) to be content with.

settlement *n* the act of settling; a sum settled, esp on a woman at her marriage; an arrangement; a small village; a newly established colony; subsidence (of buildings).

settler *n* a person who settles; an early colonist.

set-up *n* the plan, makeup, etc, of equipment used in an organization; the details of a situation, plan, etc; (*inf*) a contest, etc, arranged to result in an easy win.

seven *adj, n* one more than six. * *n* the symbol for this (7, VII, vii); the seventh in a series or set; something having seven units as members.

seventeen *adj, n* one more than sixteen. * *n* the symbol for this (17, XVII, xvii).—**seventeenth** *adj*.

seventh *adj, n* next after sixth; one of seven equal parts of a thing. * *n* (*mus*) an interval of seven diatonic degrees; the leading note.

seventy *adj, n* seven times ten. * *n* the symbol for this (70, LXX, lxx); (in *pl*) **seventies** (70s) the numbers for 70 to 79; the same numbers in a life or century.—**seventieth** *adj*.

sever *vti* to separate, to divide into parts; to break off.—**severance** *n*.

several *adj* more than two but not very many; various; separate, distinct; respective. * *pron* (*with pl vb*) a few. * *n* (*with pl vb*) a small number (of).

severe *adj* harsh, not lenient; very strict; stern; censorious; exacting, difficult; violent, not slight; (*illness*) critical; (*art*) plain, not florid.—**severely** *adv*.—**severity** *n*.

sew *vti* (**sewing, sewn** *or* **sewed**) to join or stitch together with needle and thread; to make, mend, etc, by sewing; (*with* **up**) to get full control of; (*inf*) to make sure of success in.—**sewing** *n*.

sewage *n* waste matter carried away in a sewer.

sewer *n* an underground pipe or drain for carrying off liquid waste matter, etc; a main drain.

sewerage *n* a system of drainage by sewers; sewage.

sewing machine *n* a machine for sewing or stitching usu driven by an electric motor.

sewn *see* **sew**.

sex *n* the characteristics that distinguish male and female organisms on the basis of their reproductive function; either of the two categories (male and female) so distinguished; males or females collectively; the state of being male or female; the attraction between the sexes; (*inf*) sexual intercourse.

sex appeal *n* what makes a person sexually desirable.

sexism *n* exploitation and domination of one sex by the other, esp of women by men.—**sexist** *adj, n*.

sexless *adj* without sexual intercourse; sexually unappealing.—**sexlessly** *adv*.—**sexlessness** *n*.

sex object *n* a person regarded solely in terms of their sexual attractiveness.

sextant *n* a navigator's instrument for measuring the altitude of the sun, etc, to determine position at sea.

sextet *n* a set of six singers or players; a musical composition for six instruments or voices.

sexton *n* an officer in charge of the maintenance of church property.

sextuplet *n* one of six offspring produced at one birth.

sexual *adj* of sex or the sexes; having sex.—**sexually** *adv*.

sexual harassment *n* frequent unwelcome attention from the opposite sex in the form of suggestive remarks, fondling, etc.

sexual intercourse *n* the act of copulating.

sexuality *n* sexual activity; expression of sexual interest, esp when excessive.

sexually transmitted disease *n* any of various diseases, such as syphilis or AIDS, transmitted by sexual contact.—*also* **venereal disease**.

sexy *adj* (**sexier, sexiest**) (*inf*) exciting, or intending to excite, sexual desire; attractive, entertaining; fashionable or stylish and as a result worthwhile.—**sexily** *adv*.—**sexiness** *n*.

SF *abbr* = science fiction.

Sgt *abbr* = sergeant

shabby *adj* (**shabbier, shabbiest**) (*clothes*) threadbare, worn, or dirty; run-down, dilapidated; (*act, trick*) mean, shameful.—**shabbily** *adv*.—**shabbiness** *n*.

shack *n* a small, crudely built house or cabin; a shanty. * *vi* (*with* **up**) (*sl*) to cohabit (with); to spend the night (with), esp a person of the opposite sex.

shackle *n* a metal fastening, usu in pairs, for the wrists or ankles of a prisoner; a staple; anything that restrains freedom; (*pl*) fetters. * *vt* to fasten or join by a shackle; to hamper, to impede.

shade *n* relative darkness; dimness; the darker parts of anything; shadow; a shield or screen protecting from bright light; a ghost; a place sheltered from the sun; degree of darkness of a color, esp when made by the addition of black; a minute difference; a covering for a window; (*pl*) the darkness of approaching night; (*pl. sl*) sunglasses. * *vti* to screen from light; to overshadow; to make dark; to pass by degrees into another color; to change slightly or by degrees.

shadow *n* a patch of shade; darkness, obscurity; the dark parts of a painting, etc; shelter, protection; the dark shape of an object produced on a surface by intercepted light; an inseparable companion; a person (as a detective, etc) who shadows; an unsubstantial thing, a phantom; a mere remnant, a slight trace; gloom, affliction. * *vt* to cast a shadow over; to cloud; to follow and watch, esp in secret. * *adj* having an indistinct pattern or darker section.

shadowy *adj* full of shadows; dim, indistinct; unsubstantial.

shady *adj* (**shadier, shadiest**) giving or full of shade; sheltered from the sun; (*inf*) of doubtful honesty, disreputable.

shaft *n* a straight rod, a pole; a stem, a shank; the main part of a column; an arrow or spear, or its stem; anything hurled like a missile; a ray of light, a stroke of lightning; a revolving rod for transmitting power, an axle; one of the poles between which a horse is harnessed; a hole giving access to a mine; a vertical opening through a building, as for an elevator; a critical remark or attack; (*sl*) harsh or unfair treatment.

shaggy *adj* (**shaggier, shaggiest**) (*hair, fur, etc*) long and unkempt; rough; untidy.—**shagginess** *n*.

shah *n* the title of the former ruler of Iran.

shake *vti* (**shaking, shook, pp shaken**) to move to and fro with quick short motions, to agitate; to tremble or vibrate; to jar or jolt; to brandish; to make or become unsteady; to weaken; to unsettle; to unnerve or become unnerved; to clasp (another's hand) as in greeting; (*with* **down**) to cause to subside by shaking; to obtain makeshift accommodation; (*sl*) to extort money from; (*with* **off**) to get rid of; (*with* **out**) to empty by shaking; to spread (a sail); (*with* **up**) to shake together, to mix; to upset. * *n* the act of shaking or being shaken; a jolt; a shock; a milkshake; (*inf*) a deal; (*pl inf*) a convulsive trembling.

shake-up *n* an extensive reorganization.

shaky *adj* (**shakier, shakiest**) unsteady; infirm; unreliable.—**shakily** *adv*.—**shakiness** *n*.

shale *n* a kind of clay rock like slate but softer.

shall *vb aux* (*pt* **should**) used formally to express the future in the 1st person and determination, obligation or necessity in the 2nd and 3rd person; the more common form is **will**.

shallot n a small onion.

shallow adj having little depth; superficial, trivial. * n a shallow area in otherwise deep water.–**shallowness** n.

sham n a pretense; a person or thing that is a fraud. * adj counterfeit; fake.

shaman n a priest of shamanism believed to possess magical powers which allow him to communicate with and influence the spirit world.

shamanism n a religion of northern Asia which views the world as dominated by good and evil spirits that can be influenced only by the shamans.

shamble vi to walk with an ungainly stumbling gait.–also n.

shambles npl a scene of great disorder.

shame n a painful emotion arising from guilt or impropriety; modesty; disgrace, dishonor; the cause of this; (sl) a piece of unfairness. * vti to cause to feel shame; to bring disgrace on; to force by shame (into); to humiliate by showing superior qualities.

shamefaced adj bashful or modest; sheepish; showing shame; ashamed.–**shamefacedly** adv.–**shamefacedness** n.

shameful adj disgraceful; outrageous.–**shamefully** adv.–**shamefulness** n.

shameless adj immodest; impudent, brazen.–**shamelessly** adv.–**shamelessness** n.

shampoo n a liquid cleansing agent for washing the hair; the process of washing the hair or a carpet, etc. * vt to wash with shampoo.–**shampooer** n.

shamrock n a three-leaved cloverlike plant, the national emblem of Ireland.

shan't = shall not.

shank n the leg from the knee to the ankle, the shin; a shaft, stem, or handle.

shanty n (pl **shanties**) a crude hut built from corrugated iron or cardboard.

shape n the external appearance, outline or contour of a thing; a figure; a definite form; an orderly arrangement; a mold or pattern; (inf) condition. * vt to give shape to; to form; to model, to mold; to determine; (with **up**) to develop to a definite or satisfactory form.

shapeless adj lacking definite form; baggy.–**shapelessly** adv.–**shapelessness** n.

shapely adj (**shapelier, shapeliest**) well-proportioned.–**shapeliness** n.

shard n a fragment or broken piece, esp of pottery.

share n an allotted portion, a part; one of the parts into which a company's capital stock is divided, entitling the holder to a share of profits. * vti to distribute, to apportion (out); to have or experience in common with others; to divide into portions; to contribute or receive a share of; to use jointly.

sharecropper n a tenant farmer who hands over a portion of the crop as rent.–**sharecrop** vi.

shareholder n a holder of shares in a property, esp a company.

shark n a large voracious marine fish; an extortioner, a swindler; (sl) an expert in a given activity.

sharp adj having a keen edge or fine point; pointed, not rounded; clear-cut; distinct; intense, piercing; cutting, severe; keen, biting; clever, artful; alert, mentally acute; (mus) raised a semitone in pitch; out of tune by being too high; (sl) smartly dressed. * adv punctually, quickly; (mus) above the right pitch. * n (mus) a note that is a semitone higher than the note denoted by the same letter; the symbol for this (#).–**sharply** adv.–**sharpness** n.

sharpen vti to make or become sharp or sharper.

sharpener n something that sharpens.

sharpshooter n a marksman.

sharp-tongued adj sarcastic; quick to criticize.

shatter vti to reduce to fragments suddenly; to smash; to damage or be damaged severely.

shave vti to remove facial or body hair with a razor; to cut away thin slices, to pare; to miss narrowly, to graze. * n the act or process of shaving; a narrow escape or miss; a paring.

shaver n one who shaves; an instrument for shaving, esp an electrical one.

shaving n the act of using a razor or scraping; a thin slice of wood, metal, etc, shaved off.

shawl n a large square or oblong cloth worn as a covering for the head or shoulders or as a wrapping for a baby.

she pron (obj **her**, poss **her, hers**) the female person or thing named before or in question. * n a female person or animal.

sheaf n (pl **sheaves**) a bundle of reaped corn bound together; a collection of papers, etc, tied in a bundle.

shear vti (**shearing, sheared** or **shorn**) to clip or cut (through); to remove (a sheep's fleece) by clipping; to divest; (metal) to break off because of a heavy force or twist. * n a stress acting sideways on a rivet and causing a break, etc; a machine for cutting metal; (pl) large scissors; (pl) a tool for cutting hedges, etc.

sheath n (pl **sheaths**) a close-fitting cover, esp for a blade; a condom; a closefitting dress usu worn without a belt.

sheathe vt to put into a sheath; to encase, to protect with a casing; (cat) to withdraw its claws.

sheaves see **sheaf**.

she'd = she had; she would.

shed[1] n a hut for storing garden tools; a large roofed shelter often with one or more sides open; a warehouse.

shed[2] vt (**shedding, shed**) (tears) to let fall; (skin, etc) to lose or cast off; to allow or cause to flow; to diffuse, radiate. * n a parting in the hair.

sheen n a gloss, luster; brightness.

sheep n (pl **sheep**) a cud-chewing four-footed animal with a fleece and edible flesh called mutton; a bashful, submissive person.

sheepish adj bashful, embarrassed.–**sheepishly** adv.–**sheepishness** n.

sheepskin n the skin of a sheep, esp with the fleece; a rug, parchment, or leather made from it; a garment made of or lined with sheepskin.

sheer[1] adj pure, unmixed; downright, utter; perpendicular; extremely steep; (fabric) delicately fine, transparent. * adv outright; perpendicularly, steeply.

sheer[2] vti to deviate or cause to deviate from a course; to swerve. * n the act of sheering; the upward curve of a deck toward bow or stern; a change in a ship's course.

sheet n a broad thin piece of any material, as glass, plywood, metal, etc; a large rectangular piece of cloth used as inner bed clothes; a single piece of paper; (inf) a newspaper; a broad, flat expanse; a suspended or moving expanse (as of fire or rain).

sheet lightning n lightning that has the appearance of a broad sheet due to reflection and diffusion by the clouds and sky.

sheet music n music printed on unbound sheets of paper.

sheikh n an Arab chief.

shelf n (pl **shelves**) a board fixed horizontally on a wall or in a cupboard for holding articles; a ledge on a cliff face; a reef, a shoal.

shelf life n the length of time for which something may be stored without deterioration.

shell n a hard outside covering of a nut, egg, shellfish, etc; an explosive projectile; an external framework; a light racing boat; outward show; a cartridge. * vt to remove the shell from; to bombard (with shells); (with **out**) (inf) to pay out (money).

she'll = she will; she shall.

shellac, shellack n a resin usu produced in thin, flaky layers or shells; a thin varnish containing this and alcohol.

shellfish n an aquatic animal, esp an edible one, with a shell.

shell shock n a nervous disorder caused by the shock of being under fire.–**shell-shocked** adj.

shelter n a structure that protects, esp against weather; a place giving protection, a refuge; protection. * vti to give shelter to, to shield, to cover; to take shelter.

shelve *vti* to place on a shelf; to defer consideration, to put aside; to slope gently, to incline.

shelves *see* **shelf**.

shenanigan *n* (*often pl*) trickery, deception; mischief, boisterous high spirits.

shepherd *n* a person who looks after sheep; a pastor. * *vt* to look after, as a shepherd; to maneuver or marshal in a particular direction.–**shepherdess** *nf*.

sherbet *n* a fruit-flavored powder that can be used to make a slightly sparkling drink; a sorbet.

sheriff *n* in US, the chief law enforcement officer of a county; in Scotland, a judge in an intermediate law court; in England and Wales, the chief officer of the Crown, a ceremonial post.

sherry *n* (*pl* **sherries**) a fortified wine originally made in Spain.

she's = she is; she has.

shied *see* **shy**[1], **shy**[2].

shield *n* a broad piece of armor carried for defense, usu on the left arm; a protective covering or guard; a thing or person that protects; a trophy in the shape of a shield. * *vti* to defend; to protect; to screen.

shier, shiest *see* **shy**[1].

shift *vti* to change position (of); to contrive; to manage; to remove, to transfer; to replace by another or others; (*gears*) to change the arrangement of. * *n* a change in position; an expedient; a group of people working in relay with others; the time worked by them; a change or transfer; a straight dress.

shiftless *adj* incapable; feckless.–**shiftlessly** *adv*.–**shiftlessness** *n*.

shifty *adj* (**shiftier, shiftiest**) artful, tricky; evasive.–**shiftily** *adv*.–**shiftiness** *n*.

shillyshally *vi* (**shillyshallying, shillyshallied**) to vacillate, to hesitate. * *n* (*pl* **shillyshallies**) the inability to make up one's mind.

shimmer *vi* to glisten softly, to glimmer.–*also n*.–**shimmery** *adj*.

shimmy *n* (*pl* **shimmies**) a jazz dance involving rapid movements of the upper body; an abnormal vibration in a vehicle or aircraft. * *vi* (**shimmying, shimmied**) to dance a shimmy; to vibrate.

shin *n* the front part of the leg from the knee to the ankle; the shank. * *vi* (*with* **up**) to climb (a pole, etc) by gripping with legs and hands.

shine *vti* (**shining, shone**) to emit light; to be bright, to glow; to be brilliant or conspicuous; to direct the light of; to cause to gleam by polishing; * *n* a luster, a gloss; (*sl*) a liking.

shingle[1] *n* a thin wedge-shaped roof tile; a small signboard.

shingle[2] *n* waterworn pebbles as on a beach; an area covered with these.–**shingly** *adj*.

shingles *npl* a virus disease marked by a painful rash of red spots on the skin.

shiny *adj* (**shinier, shiniest**) glossy, polished; worn smooth.

ship *n* a large vessel navigating deep water; its officers and crew; a spacecraft. * *vti* (**shipping, shipped**) to transport by any carrier; to take in (water) over the side; to lay (oars) inside a boat; to go on board; to go or travel by ship.

shipmate *n* a fellow sailor.

shipment *n* goods shipped; a consignment.

shipper *n* an individual or company that ships goods.

shipping *n* the business of transporting goods; ships collectively.

shipwreck *n* the loss of a vessel at sea; the remains of a wrecked ship; ruin, destruction. * *vti* to destroy by or suffer shipwreck; to ruin.

shipyard *n* a yard or shed where ships are built or repaired.

shirk *vti* to neglect or avoid work; to refuse to face (duty, danger, etc).–**shirker** *n*.

shirt *n* a sleeved garment of cotton, etc, for the upper body, typically having a fitted collar and cuffs and front buttons.

shiver *vi* to shake or tremble, as with cold or fear, to shudder.–*also n*.–**shivery** *adj*.

shoal *n* a large number of fish swimming together; a large crowd. * *vi* to form shoals.

shock[1] *n* a shaggy mass of hair.

shock[2] *n* a violent jolt or impact; a sudden disturbance to the emotions; the event or experience causing this; the nerve sensation caused by an electrical charge through the body; a disorder of the blood circulation, produced by displacement of body fluids (due to injury); (*sl*) a paralytic stroke. * *vt* to outrage, horrify. * *vi* to experience extreme horror, outrage, etc.

shock absorber *n* a device, as on the springs of a car, that absorbs the force of bumps and jars.

shocking *adj* revolting; scandalous, improper; very bad.–**shockingly** *adv*.

shock wave *n* the violent effect in the vicinity of an explosion caused by the change in atmospheric pressure; the compressed wave built up when the speed of a body or fluid exceeds that at which sound can be transmitted in the medium in which it is traveling.

shod, shodden *see* **shoe**.

shoddy *adj* (**shoddier, shoddiest**) made of inferior material; cheap and nasty, trashy.–**shoddily** *adv*.–**shoddiness** *n*.

shoe *n* an outer covering for the foot not enclosing the ankle; a thing like a shoe, a partial casing; a horseshoe; a drag for a wheel; a device to guide movement, provide contact, or protect against wear or slipping; a dealing box that holds several decks of cards. * *vt* (**shoeing, shod** *or* **shoed**, *pp* **shod, shoed** *or* **shodden**) to provide with shoes; to cover for strength or protection.

shoehorn *n* a curved piece of plastic, metal, or horn used for easing the heel into a shoe.

shoelace *n* a cord that passes through eyelets in a shoe and is tied to keep the shoe on the foot.

shoestring *n* a shoelace; (*inf*) a small amount of money.

shone *see* **shine**.

shoo *interj* used to frighten (animals, people) away. * *vt* (**shooing, shooed**) to frighten away (as if) by shouting "shoo". * *vi* to cry "shoo".

shook *see* **shake**.

shoot *vb* (**shooting, shot**) *vt* to discharge or fire (a gun etc); to hit or kill with a bullet, etc; (*rapids*) to be carried swiftly over; to propel quickly; to thrust out; (*bolt*) to slide home; to variegate (with another color, etc); (*a film scene*) to photograph; (*sport*) to kick or drive (a ball, etc) at goal; (*with* **down**) to disprove (an argument); (*with* **up**) to grow rapidly, to rise abruptly. * *vi* to move swiftly, to dart; to emit; to put forth buds, to sprout; to attack or kill indiscriminately; (*sl*) to inject a narcotic into a vein. * *n* a contest, a shooting trip, etc; a new growth or sprout.

shooting star *n* a meteor.

shop *n* a building were retail goods are sold or services provided; a factory; a workshop; the details and technicalities of one's own work, and talk about these. * *vti* (**shopping, shopped**) to visit shops to examine or buy; (*with* **around**) to hunt for the best buy.

shopkeeper *n* a person who owns or runs a shop.–**shopkeeping** *n*.

shoplifting *n* stealing from a shop during shopping hours.–**shoplifter** *n*.

shopper *n* a person who shops; a bag for carrying shopping.

shopping mall *n* a large enclosed shopping center.

shoptalk *n* the specialized vocabulary of those in the same line of work or sharing an area of interest; talk about work after hours.

shore[1] *n* land beside the sea or a large body of water; beach.

shore[2] *n* a prop or beam used for support. * *vt* to prop (up), to support with a shore.

shorn *see* **shear**.

short *adj* not measuring much; not long or tall; not great in range or scope; brief; concise; not retentive; curt; abrupt; less than the correct amount; below standard; deficient, lacking; (*pastry*) crisp or flaky; (*vowel*) not prolonged, unstressed; (*drink*) undiluted, neat. * *n* something short; (*pl*) pants not covering the knee; (*pl*) an undergarment like these; a short circuit. * *adv* abruptly; concisely; without reaching the end. * *vti* to give less than what is needed; to short-change; to short-circuit.–**shortness** *n*.

shortage *n* a deficiency.

short-change *vt* to give back less than the correct change; (*sl*) to cheat.

short-circuit *n* the deviation of an electric current by a path of small resistance; an interrupted electric current. * *vti* to establish a short-circuit in; to cut off electric current; to provide with a short cut.

shortcoming *n* a defect or inadequacy.

short cut *n* a shorter route; any way of saving time, effort, etc.

shorten *vt* to make or become short or shorter; to reduce the amount of (sail) spread; to make (pastry, etc) crisp and flaky by adding fat.

shortening *n* the act of shortening; the state of becoming shortened; a fat used for making pastry, etc, crisp and flaky.

shortfall *n* (the amount or degree of) a deficit or deficiency.

shorthand *n* a method of rapid writing using signs or contractions.–*also adj*.

short-handed *adj* not having the usual number of assistants.

short list *n* a selected list of qualified applicants from which a choice must be made.–**short-list** *vt*.

shortly *adv* soon, in a short time; briefly; rudely.

short-range *adj* having a limited range in time or distance.

short-sighted *adj* not able to see well at a distance; lacking foresight.–**short-sightedly** *adv*.–**short-sightedness** *n*.

short-tempered *adj* easily annoyed.

short-term *adj* of or for a limited time.

shortwave *n* a radio wave 60 meters or less in length.

shot[1] *see* **shoot**.

shot[2] *n* the act of shooting; range, scope; an attempt; a solid projectile for a gun; projectiles collectively; small lead pellets for a shotgun; a marksman; a photograph or a continuous film sequence; a hypodermic injection, as of vaccine; a drink of alcohol.

shotgun *n* a smooth-bore gun for firing small shot at close range.

shotgun wedding *n* (*inf*) an enforced wedding, usu because the woman is pregnant.

shot put *n* a field event in which a heavy metal ball is propelled with an overhand thrust from the shoulder.–**shot-putter** *n*.

should *vb aux* used to express obligation, duty, expectation or probability, or a future condition.–*also pt of* **shall**.

shoulder *n* the joint connecting the arm with the trunk; a part like a shoulder; (*pl*) the upper part of the back; (*pl*) the capacity to bear a task or blame; a projecting part; the strip of land bordering a road. * *vti* to place on the shoulder to carry; to assume responsibility; to push with the shoulder, to jostle.

shoulder blade *n* the large flat triangular bone on either side of the back part of the human shoulder.

shouldn't = should not.

shout *n* a loud call; a yell. * *vti* to call loudly, to yell; (*with down*) to drown out or silence (a person speaking) by shouting.

shove *vti* to drive forward; to push; to jostle; (*with off*) to push (a boat) off from the shore; (*inf*) to depart, leave. * *n* a forceful push.

shovel *n* a broad tool like a scoop with a long handle for moving loose material. * *vt* (**shoveling, shoveled** *or* **shovelling, shovelled**) to move or lift with a shovel.

show *vti* (**showing, showed** *or* **shown**) to present to view, to exhibit; to demonstrate, to make clear; to prove; to manifest, to disclose; to direct, to guide; to appear, to be visible; to finish third in a horse race; (*inf*) to arrive; (*with off*) to display to advantage; to try to attract admiration; to behave pretentiously; (*with up*) to put in an appearance, to arrive; to expose to ridicule. * *n* a display, an exhibition; an entertainment; a theatrical performance; a radio or television program; third place at the finish (as a horse race).

show business, show biz *n* the entertainment industry.

showcase *n* a glass case or cabinet for displaying items in a shop or museum; a setting or situation designed to exhibit something to best advantage.–*also vt*.

showdown *n* (*inf*) a final conflict; a disclosure of cards at poker.

shower *n* a brief period of rain, hail, or snow; a similar fall, as of tears, meteors, arrows, etc; a great number; a method of cleansing in which the body is sprayed with water from above; a wash in this; a party for the presentation of gifts, esp to a bride. * *vt* to pour copiously; to sprinkle; to bestow (with gifts). * *vi* to cleanse in a shower.

showman *n* (*pl* **showmen**) a man who manages or presents a theatrical show, circus, etc; a person skilled in presentation.

shown *see* **show**.

showpiece *n* an exhibit; a perfect example of something.

showroom *n* a room where goods for sale are displayed.

showy *adj* (**showier, showiest**) bright, colorful; ostentatious.–**showily** *adv*.–**showiness** *n*.

shrank *see* **shrink**.

shrapnel *n* an artillery shell filled with small pieces of metal that scatter on impact.

shred *n* a strip cut or torn off; a fragment, a scrap. * *vt* (**shredding, shredded**) to cut or tear into small pieces.

shrewd *adj* astute, having common sense; keen, penetrating.–**shrewdly** *adv*.–**shrewdness** *n*.

shriek *n* a loud, shrill cry, a scream. * *vti* to screech, to scream.

shrill *adj* high-pitched and piercing in sound; strident.

shrimp *n* a small edible shellfish with a long tail; (*sl*) a small or unimportant person. * *vt* to fish for shrimp.

shrine *n* a container for sacred relics; a saint's tomb; a place of worship; a hallowed place.

shrink *vti* (**shrinking, shrank** *or* **shrunk**, *pp* **shrunk** *or* **shrunken**) to become smaller, to contract as from cold, wetting, etc; to recoil (from), to flinch; to cause (cloth, etc) to contract by soaking. * *n* (*sl*) a psychiatrist.–**shrinkable** *adj*.

shrinkage *n* contraction; diminution.

shrink-wrap *vt* (**shrink-wrapping, shrink-wrapped**) (*book etc*) to wrap in plastic film that is then shrunk by heat to form a tightly fitting package.

shrivel *vti* (**shriveling, shriveled** *or* **shrivelling, shrivelled**) to dry up or wither and become wrinkled; to curl up with heat, etc.

shroud *n* a burial cloth; anything that envelops or conceals; (*naut*) a supporting rope for a mast. * *vt* to wrap in a shroud; to envelop or conceal.

shrub *n* a woody plant smaller than a tree with several stems rising from the same root; a bush.–**shrubby** *adj*.

shrubbery *n* (*pl* **shrubberies**) an area of land planted with shrubs.

shrug *vti* (**shrugging, shrugged**) to draw up and contract (the shoulders) as a sign of doubt, indifference, etc; (*with off*) to brush aside; to shake off; (*a garment*) to remove by wriggling out. * *n* the act of shrugging.

shrunk *see* **shrink**.

shrunken *adj* shriveled, pinched; reduced.

shuck *n* a husk, pod or shell. * *vt* to remove the shucks from.

shudder *vi* to tremble violently, to shiver; to feel strong repugnance. * *n* a convulsive shiver of the body; a vibration.

shuffle *vt* to scrape (the feet) along the ground; to walk with dragging steps; (*playing cards*) to change the order of, to mix; to intermingle, to mix up; (*with off*) to get rid of.–*also n*.

shuffleboard *n* a game in which players propel plastic or wooden discs into numbered scoring areas marked on a large flat surface.

shun *vt* (**shunning, shunned**) to avoid scrupulously; to keep away from.

shunt *vti* to move to a different place; to put aside, to shelve; (*trains*) to switch from one track to another; (*sl*) to collide.–*also n.*

shut *vti* (**shutting, shut**) to close; to lock, to fasten; to close up parts of, to fold together; to bar; (*with* **down**) to (cause to) stop working or operating; (*with* **in**) to confine; to enclose; to block the view from; (*with* **off**) to check the flow of; to debar; (*with* **out**) to exclude; (*with* **up**) to confine; (*inf*) to stop talking; (*inf*) to silence.

shutter *n* a movable cover for a window; a flap device for regulating the exposure of light to a camera lens.

shuttle *n* a device in a loom for holding the weft thread and carrying it between the warp threads; a bus, aircraft, etc, making back-and-forth trips over a short route. * *vti* to move back and forth rapidly.

shuttlecock *n* a cork stuck with feathers, or a plastic imitation, hit with a racket in badminton.

shy[1] *adj* (**shyer, shyest** *or* **shier, shiest**) very self-conscious, timid; bashful; wary, suspicious (of); (*sl*) lacking. * *vi* (**shying, shied**) to move suddenly, as when startled; to be or become cautious, etc. * *n* (*pl* **shies**) a sudden movement.–**shyly** *adv.*–**shyness** *n.*

shy[2] *vt* (**shying, shied**) to throw (something). * *n* (*pl* **shies**) a throw; (*inf*) an attempt, try.

shyster *n* (*inf*) a person, esp a lawyer, who is manipulative and disreputable.

SI *n* (Système International d'Unités) the universally used system of units based on the metre, second, kilogram, ampere, kelvin, candela, siemens, tesla, weber and mole.

sibilant *adj* hissing. * *n* a sibilant letter, eg *s*, *z*.–**sibilance** *n.*

sibling *n* a brother or sister.

sic *adv* as written (used in text to indicate that an error or doubtful usage is reproduced from the original).

sick *adj* unhealthy, ill; having nausea, vomiting; thoroughly tired (of); disgusted by or suffering from an excess; (*inf*) of humor, sadistic, gruesome.–**sicken** *vti*.–**sickness** *n.*

sick bay *n* an area in a ship used as a hospital or dispensary; a room used for the treatment of the sick.

sickle *n* a tool with a crescent-shaped blade for cutting tall grasses; anything shaped like this.

sick leave *n* absence from work due to illness.

sickle cell anemia *n* a form of anemia that is hereditary and marked by the presence of sickle-shaped red blood cells.

sickly *adj* (**sicklier, sickliest**) inclined to be ill; unhealthy; causing nausea; mawkish; pale, feeble.–**sickliness** *n.*

side *n* a line or surface bounding anything; the left or right part of the body; the top or underneath surface; the slope of a hill; an aspect, a direction; a party or faction; a cause; a team; a line of descent; (*sl*) conceit. * *adj* toward or at the side, lateral; incidental. * *vi* to associate with a particular faction.

sideboard *n* a long table or cabinet for holding cutlery, crockery, etc.

sidecar *n* a small car attached to the side of a motor cycle; a cocktail of brandy, liqueur, and lemon juice.

side dish *n* food accompanying a main course at a meal.

side effect *n* a secondary and usu adverse effect, as of a drug or medical treatment.

sidekick *n* (*sl*) a confederate; a partner; a close friend.

sideline *n* a line marking the side limit of a playing area; a minor branch of business; a subsidiary interest.

sidelong *adj* oblique, not direct. * *adv* obliquely.

sideshow *n* a minor attraction at a fair, etc; a subsidiary event.

sidestep *vti* to take a step to one side; to avoid or dodge.–*also n.*

sideswipe *n* a glancing blow; (*inf*) an incidental jibe or criticism.

sidetrack *vt* to prevent action by diversionary tactics; to shunt aside, to shelve. * *n* a railroad siding.

sidewalk *n* a path, usu paved, at the side of a street.

sideward, sidewards *adj, adv* sideways.

sideways, sideway *adj, adv* toward or from one side; facing to the side.

siding *n* a short line beside a main railroad track for use in shunting; a covering as of boards for the outside of a frame building.

sidle *vi* to move sideways, esp to edge along.

siege *n* the surrounding of a fortified place to cut off supplies and compel its surrender; the act of besieging; a continued attempt to gain something.

sierra *n* a range of mountains with jagged peaks.

siesta *n* a midday nap, esp in hot countries.

sieve *n* a utensil with a meshed wire bottom for sifting and straining; a person who cannot keep secrets. * *vt* to put through a sieve, to sift.

sift *vti* to separate coarser parts from finer with a sieve; to sort out; to examine critically; to pass as through a sieve.

sigh *vti* to draw deep audible breath as a sign of weariness, relief, etc; to make a sound like this; to pine or lament (for); to utter with a sigh.–*also n.*

sight *n* the act or faculty of seeing; what is seen or is worth seeing, a spectacle; a view or glimpse; range of vision; a device on a gun etc to guide the eye in aiming it; aim taken with this; (*inf*) anything that looks unpleasant, odd, etc. * *vti* to catch sight of; to aim through a sight.

sight-read *vt* (**sight-reading, sight-read**) to play or sing from a piece of printed music without previous preparation. * *vi* to read at sight.

sightseeing *n* the viewing or visiting of places of interest.–**sightseer** *n.*

sign *n* a mark or symbol; a gesture; an indication, token, trace, or symptom (of); an omen; (*math*) a conventional mark used to indicate an operation to be performed; a board or placard with publicly displayed information. * *vi* to append one's signature; to ratify thus. * *vt* to engage by written contract; to write one's name on; to make or indicate by a sign; to signal; to communicate by sign language; (*with* **away**) to relinquish by signing a deed, etc; (*with* **on**) to accept employment; to register; (*with* **off**) to complete a broadcast.

signal *n* a sign, device or gesture to intimate a warning or to give information, esp at a distance; a message so conveyed; a semaphore system used by railways; in radio, etc, the electrical impulses transmitted or received; a sign or event that initiates action. * *vti* (**signaling, signaled** *or* **signalling, signalled**) to make a signal or signals (to); to communicate by signals. * *adj* striking, notable.–**signaler, signaller** *n.*

signally *adv* remarkably; notably.

signatory *n* (*pl* **signatories**) a party or state that has signed an agreement or treaty; the person who signs on behalf of their government.

signature *n* a person's name written by himself or herself; the act of signing one's own name; a characteristic mark; (*mus*) the flats and sharps after the clef showing the key; (*print*) a mark on the first pages of each sheet of a book as a guide to the binder; such a sheet when folded.

signature tune *n* a tune associated with a performer or a TV, radio program, etc.

signet *n* a small seal, esp one set in a ring; an official seal used in lieu of a signature in authenticating documents; the impression made by this.

signet ring *n* a ring with a seal set in it.

significant *adj* full of meaning, esp a special or hidden one; momentous, important; highly expressive; indicative (of).–**significance** *n.*–**significantly** *adv.*

signify *vti* (**signifying, signified**) to mean; to be a sign of; to indicate; to represent; to matter, to be important; to make a sign.–**signification** *n.*

sign language *n* a system of manual signs and gestures for conveying meaning, used esp by the deaf.

signor, signior *n* (*pl* **signors, signori**) an Italian man–equivalent to Mr.

signora n (pl **signoras, signore**) a married Italian woman–equivalent to Mrs or madam.

signorina n (pl **signorinas, signorine**) an unmarried Italian woman–equivalent to Miss.

signpost n a post with signs on it to direct travelers; a beacon, a guide.–also vt.

silence n absence of sound; the time this lasts; refusal to speak or make a sound; secrecy. * vt to cause to be silent. * interj be silent!

silent adj not speaking; taciturn; noiseless; still.–**silently** adv.

silhouette n the outline of a shape against light or a lighter background; a solid outline drawing, usu in solid black on white, esp of a profile. * vt to show up in outline; to depict in silhouette.

silica n a hard mineral, a compound of oxygen and silicon, found in quartz and flint.

silicon n a metalloid element occuring in silica and used extensively in transistors, etc, and as a compound in glass, etc. * adj of an area in which there are a number of computer software and hardware companies.

silicon chip n a microchip.

silicone n an organic polymer compound with good lubricating and insulating properties, used widely as a repellent, resin, etc.

silk n a fiber produced by silkworms; lustrous textile cloth, thread or a garment made of silk; (pl) silk garments; (pl) the colors of a racing stable, worn by a jockey, etc. *adj of, relating to or made of silk.

silkworm n a caterpillar of various moths that feeds on mulberry leaves and produces a strong fiber to construct its cocoon.

silky adj (**silkier, silkiest**) soft and smooth like silk; glossy; suave.–**silkiness** n.

sill n a heavy, horizontal slab of wood or stone at the bottom of a window frame or door.

silly adj (**sillier, silliest**) foolish, stupid; frivolous; lacking in sense or judgment; being stunned or dazed. * n (pl **sillies**) a silly person.–**silliness** n.

silo n (pl **silos**) an airtight pit or tower for storing fodder in a green compressed state; a deep pit for storing cement, coal, etc; an underground structure from which a missile can be fired.

silt n a fine-grained sandy sediment carried or deposited by water. * vti to fill or choke up with silt.

silver n a ductile, malleable, grayish-white metallic element used in jewelry, cutlery, tableware, coins, etc; a lustrous, grayish white. * adj made of or plated with silver; silvery; (hair) gray; marking the 25th in a series * vt to coat with silver or a substance resembling silver; to make or become silvery or gray.

silver paper n a metallic paper coated or laminated to resemble silver, tinfoil.

silver plate n a plating of silver; domestic utensils made of silver or of silver-plated metal.–**silver-plate** vt.

silver screen n (inf) (with **the**) the motion-picture industry; the screen on which a movie is projected.

silversmith n a worker in silver.

silver wedding n the 25th anniversary of a marriage.

silvery adj white and lustrous like silver; covered with silver; resembling silver in color; (sound) soft and clear.

simian adj of or like an ape or monkey.

similar adj having a resemblance to, like; nearly corresponding; (geom) corresponding exactly in shape if not size.–**similarity** n.–**similarly** adv.

simile n a figure of speech likening one thing to another by the use of like, as, etc.

simmer vti to boil gently; to be or keep on the point of boiling; to be in a state of suppressed rage or laughter; (with **down**) to abate. * n the state of simmering.

simper vi to smile in a silly or self-conscious way.–also n.

simple adj single, uncompounded; plain, not elaborate; clear, not complicated; easy to do, understand, or solve; artless, not sophisticated; weak in intellect; unsuspecting, credulous; sheer, mere.–**simpleness** n.

simple interest n interest paid on the principal of a loan only.

simpleton n a foolish, weak-minded person.

simplicity n (pl **simplicities**) the quality or state of being simple; absence of complications; easiness; lack of ornament, plainness, restraint; artlessness; directness; guilelessness, openness, naivety.

simplify vt (**simplifying, simplified**) to make simple or easy to understand.–**simplification** n.

simplistic adj oversimplified; uncomplicated.–**simplistically** adv.

simply adv in a simple way; plainly; merely; absolutely.

simulate vt to pretend to have or feel, to feign; (conditions) to reproduce in order to conduct an experiment; to imitate.–**simulation** n.

simulator n a device that simulates specific conditions in order to test actions or reactions.

simultaneous adj done or occurring at the same time.–**simultaneity** n.–**simultaneously** adv.

sin[1] n an offense against a religious or moral principle; transgression of the law of God; a wicked act, an offense; a misdeed, a fault. * vi (**sinning, sinned**) to commit a sin; to offend (against).

sin[2] abbr = sine.

sin bin n (ice hockey, etc) (sl) an enclosure off the playing area where players guilty of fouls are temporarily sent.

since adv from then until now; subsequently; ago. * prep during, or continously from (then) until now; after. * conj from the time that; because, seeing that.

sincere adj genuine, real, not pretended; honest, straightforward.–**sincerely** adv.–**sincerity** n.

sine n (trig) a function that in a right-angled triangle is equal to the ratio of the length of the side opposite the angle to that of the hypotenuse.

sinecure n a position or office that provides an income without involving duties.

sinew n a cord of fibrous tissue, a tendon; (usu pl) the chief supporting force, a mainstay; (pl) muscles, brawn.

sinewy adj having a lean body and strong muscles; tough, stringy.

sinful adj guilty of sin, wicked.–**sinfully** adv.–**sinfulness** n.

sing vti (**singing, sang,** pp **sung**) to utter (words) with musical modulations; (a song) to perform; to hum, to ring; to write poetry (about), to praise; (with **out**) to shout, call out.–**singer** n.–**singing** n.

singe vt (**singeing, singed**) to burn slightly; to scorch, esp to remove feathers, etc.–also n.

singing telegram n (a service that provides) a greetings message delivered in song, usu by a person in fancy dress.

single adj one only, not double; individual; composed of one part; alone, sole; separate; unmarried; for one; with one contestant on each side; simple; whole, unbroken; (tennis) played between two persons only; (ticket) for the outward journey only. * n a single ticket; a game between two players; a hit scoring one; a record with one tune on each side. * vt (with **out**) to pick out, to select.

single-breasted adj (suit, etc) fastening in the center with a single row of buttons.

single file n a single column of persons or things, one behind the other.

single-handed adj, adv without assistance, unaided.–**single-handedly** adv.–**single-handedness** n.

single-minded adj having only one aim in mind.–**single-mindedly** adv.–**single-mindedness** n.

singles bar n a bar or social club for single people only.

single ticket n a ticket for a one-way journey only.

singly adv alone; one by one.

singsong n a droning monotonous utterance; a verse with a regular, marked rhythm and rhyme; (inf) a party where everyone sings. * adj having a regular or monotonous rhythm.

singular *adj* remarkable; exceptional; unusual; eccentric; odd; (*gram*) referring to only one person or thing. * *n* (*gram*) the singular number or form of a word.

singularly *adv* unusually; exceptionally.

sinister *adj* inauspicious; ominous; ill-omened; evil-looking; malignant; wicked; left; (*her*) on the left side of the shield.

sink *vti* (**sinking, sank** *or* **sunk**, *pp* **sunk**) to go under the surface or to the bottom (of a liquid); to submerge in water; to go down slowly; (*wind*) to subside; to pass to a lower state; to droop, to decline; to grow weaker; to become hollow; to lower, to degrade; to cause to sink; to make by digging out; to invest; (*with* **in**) to penetrate; to thrust into; (*inf*) to be understood in full. * *n* a basin with an outflow pipe, usu in a kitchen; a cesspool; an area of sunken land.–**sinking** *n*.

sinker *n* a weight used to submerge a fishing line.

sinner *n* a person who sins.

sinuous *adj* curving; winding; tortuous.–**sinuously** *adv*.–**sinuousness** *n*.

sinus *n* (*pl* **sinuses**) an air cavity in the skull that opens in the nasal cavities.

sinusitis *n* inflammation of a sinus.

sip *vti* (**sipping, sipped**) to drink in small mouthfuls. * *n* the act of sipping; the quantity sipped.

siphon *n* a bent tube for drawing off liquids from a higher to a lower level by atmospheric pressure; a bottle with an internal tube and tap at the top for aerated water. * *vti* to draw off, or be drawn off, with a siphon.–*also* **syphon**.

sir *n* a title of respect used to address a man in speech or correspondence; (*with cap*) a title preceding the first name of a knight or baronet. * *vt* to address as "sir".

sire *n* a father; a male ancestor; the male parent of an animal; a form of address to a king. * *vt* (*animal*) to beget.

siren *n* a device producing a loud wailing sound as a warning signal; a fabled sea nymph who lured sailors to destruction with a sweet song; a seductive or alluring woman.

sirloin *n* the upper part of a loin of beef.

sirocco *n* a hot, oppressive wind that blows across southern Europe from North Africa.

sis *n* (*inf*) sister.

sisal *n* (a tropical agave plant whose leaves yield) a tough fiber used to make rope.

sissy *n* (*pl* **sissies**) an effeminate, feeble or cowardly boy or man.–*also adj*.

sister *n* a female sibling, a daughter of the same parents; a female member or associate of the same race, creed, trade union, etc; a member of a religious sisterhood; one of the same kind, model, etc; a senior nurse. * *adj* (*ship, etc*) belonging to the same type.

sisterhood *n* a female religious or charitable order, or loyal association; the state of being a sister.

sister-in-law *n* (*pl* **sisters-in-law**) the sister of a husband or wife; the wife of a brother.

sisterly *adj* like a sister, kind, affectionate.

sit *vti* (**sitting, sat**) to rest oneself on the buttocks, as on a chair; (*bird*) to perch; (*hen*) to cover eggs for hatching; (*legislator, etc*) to occupy a seat; (*court*) to be in session; to pose, as for a portrait; to ride (a horse); to press or weigh (upon); to be located; to rest or lie; to take an examination; to take care of a child, pet, etc, while the parents or owners are away; to cause to sit; to provide seats or seating room for; (*with* **down**) to take a seat; (*with* **in**) to attend a discussion or a musical session; to participate in a sit-in; (*with* **on**) to hold a meeting to discuss; to delay action on something; (*inf*) to suppress; to rebuke; (*with* **out**) to sit through the whole; to abstain from dancing; (*with* **up**) to straighten the back while sitting; not to go to bed; (*inf*) to be astonished.

sitcom *see* **situation comedy**.

site *n* a space occupied or to be occupied by a building; a situation; the place or scene of something. * *vt* to locate, to place.

sit-in *n* a strike in which the strikers refuse to leave the premises; civil disobedience in which demonstrators occupy a public place and refuse to leave voluntarily.

sitter *n* a person who looks after a child, dog, house, etc, while the parents or owners are away.

sitting *n* the state of being seated; a period of being seated, as for a meal, a portrait, a session, as of a court; a clutch of eggs. * *adj* that is sitting; being in a judicial or legislative seat; used in or for sitting; performed while sitting.

sitting duck, sitting target *n* (*inf*) a person or thing that is an easy target for attack, criticism, etc.

situate *vt* to place in a site, situation, or category.

situation *n* a place, a position; a state of affairs, circumstances; a job or post.

situation comedy *n* a comic television or radio series made up of episodes involving the same group of characters.–*also* **sitcom**.

sit-up *n* an exercise of sitting up from a prone position without using hands or legs.

six *adj*, *n* one more than five. * *n* the symbol for this (6, VI, vi); the sixth in a series or set; something having six units as members.

six-pack *n* a pack of six units, as of cans of beer, etc, sold together.

sixteen *adj*, *n* one more than fifteen. * *n* the symbol for this (16, XVI, xvi).–**sixteenth** *adj*, *n*.

sixteenth note *n* a musical note with a sixteenth the time value of a whole note, a semiquaver.

sixth *n* one of six equal parts of a thing; (*mus*) an interval of six diatonic degrees; the sixth tone of a diatonic scale.–*also adv*. * *adj* next after fifth.–**sixthly** *adv*.

sixth sense *n* intuitive power.

sixty *n* six times ten. * *n* (*pl* **sixties**) the symbol for this (60, LX, lx); (in *pl*) sixties (60s), the numbers for 60 to 69; the same numbers in a life or century.–**sixtieth** *adj*, *adv*.

sixty-fourth note *n* a musical note with the time value of one sixty-fourth of a whole note; a hemidemisemiquaver.

sizable, sizeable *adj* of some size; large.–**sizably, sizeably** *adv*.–**sizableness, sizeableness** *n*.

size[1] *n* magnitude; the dimensions or proportions of something; a graduated measurement, as of clothing or shoes. * *vt* to sort according to size; to measure; (*with* **up**) (*inf*) to make an estimate or judgment of; to meet requirements.

size[2] *n* a thin pasty substance used to glaze paper, stiffen cloth, etc. * *vt* to treat with size.

sizzle *vti* to make a hissing spluttering noise, as of frying; to be extremely hot; to be very angry; to scorch, sear or fry with a sizzling sound. * *n* a hissing sound.

skate *n* a steel blade attached to a boot for gliding on ice; a boot with such a runner; a roller skate. * *vi* to move on skates; (*with* **over**) to avoid dealing with (an issue, problem, etc) directly.–**skater** *n*.

skateboard *n* a short, oblong board with two wheels at each end for standing on and riding.–*also vi*.

skein *n* a folded coil of yarn, thread, etc; a tangle; a flight of wild fowl, esp geese.

skeleton *n* the bony framework of the body of a human, an animal or plant; the bones separated from flesh and preserved in their natural position; a supporting structure, a framework; an outline, an abstract; a very thin person; something shameful kept secret. * *adj* (*staff, crew, etc*) reduced to the lowest possible level.–**skeletal** *adj*.

skeleton key *n* a key with a slender bit that can open many simple locks.

skeptic *n* a person who questions opinions generally accepted; a person who doubts religious doctrines, an agnostic; an adherent of skepticism.

skeptical *adj* doubting; questioning.–**skeptically** *adv*.

skepticism *n* an attitude of questioning criticism, doubt; (*philos*) the doctrine that absolute knowledge is unattainable.

sketch n a rough drawing, quickly made; a preliminary draft; a short literary piece or essay; a short humorous item for a revue, etc; a brief outline. * vti to make a sketch (of); to plan roughly.

sketchy adj (**sketchier, sketchiest**) incomplete; vague; inadequate.–**sketchily** adv.–**sketchiness** n.

skew adj slanting, oblique, set at an angle. * adv at a slant. * vti to slant or set at a slant; to swerve.

skewer n a long wooden or metal pin on which pieces of meat and vegetables are cooked. * vt to pierce and fasten on a skewer; to transfix.

ski n (pl **skis**) a long narrow runner of wood, metal or plastic that is fastened to a boot for moving across snow; a water-ski. * vi (**skiing, skied**) to travel on skis.–**skier** n.

skid vti (**skidding, skidded**) to slide without rotating; to slip sideways; (vehicle) to slide sideways out of control; to cause (a vehicle) to skid. * n the act of skidding; a drag to reduce speed; a ship's fender; a movable support for a heavy object; a runner on an aircraft's landing gear.

skid row, skid road n (sl) a shabby district where vagrants, etc, live.

skied see **ski**.

ski jump n a long ramp surmounting a slope from which skiers jump in competition.–**ski-jump** vi.

skill n proficiency; expertness, dexterity; a developed aptitude or ability; a type of work or craft requiring specialist training.

skilled adj fully trained, expert.

skillet n a frying pan.

skillful, skilful adj having skill; proficient, adroit.–**skillfully, skilfully** adv.–**skillfulness, skilfulness** n.

skim vti (**skimming, skimmed**) to remove (cream, scum) from the surface of; to glide lightly over, to brush the surface of; to read superficially.

skim milk, skimmed milk n milk from which the cream has been removed.

skimp vti to give scant measure (of), to stint; to be sparing or frugal (with).

skimpy adj (**skimpier, skimpiest**) small in size; inadequate; scant, meager.–**skimpily** adv.–**skimpiness** n.

skin n the tissue forming the outer covering of the body; a hide; the rind of a fruit; an outer layer or casing; a film on the surface of a liquid; a vessel for water, etc, made of hide. * vti (**skinning, skinned**) to remove the skin from, to peel; to injure by scraping (the knee, etc); to cover or become covered with skin; (inf) to swindle.

skin-deep adj superficial.

skin diving n the sport of swimming underwater with scuba equipment.–**skin-diver** n.

skinflint n a stingy person.

skin graft n a piece of skin taken from one part of the body to replace damaged skin elsewhere.

skinny adj (**skinnier, skinniest**) very thin; emaciated.–**skinniness** n.

skintight adj (clothing) fitting tightly; clinging.

skip vti (**skipping, skipped**) to leap or hop lightly over; to keep jumping over a rope as it is swung under one; to make omissions, to pass over, esp in reading; (inf) to leave (town) hurriedly, to make off; (inf) to miss deliberately. * n a skipping movement; a light jump.

ski pants npl fashion pants worn tight with a strap that fits under the foot.

skipjack n (pl **skipjack, skipjacks**) any of various food fishes including two varieties of tuna, one striped (skipjack) and the other spotted (black skipjack).

ski pole n one of a pair of pointed metal sticks used by skiers to provide forward thrust and to aid stability.

skipper n the captain of a boat, aircraft, or team. * vt to act as skipper; to captain.

skirmish n a minor fight in a war; a conflict or clash. * vi to take part in a skirmish.

skirt n a woman's garment that hangs from the waist; the lower part of a dress or coat; an outer edge, a border. * vti to border; to move along the edge (of); to evade.

skirting board n a narrow panel of wood at the foot of an interior wall.

skit n a short humorous sketch, as in the theater.

skittish adj (animal) frisky, easily frightened; (person) playful, frivolous, lively.–**skittishly** adv.–**skittishness** n.

skulduggery, skullduggery n (inf) deceit, underhand dealing.

skulk vi to move in a stealthy manner; to lurk.

skull n the bony casing enclosing the brain; the cranium.

skull and crossbones n (pl **skulls and crossbones**) an image of a human skull and crossed thighbones used as a warning of danger.

skunk n a small black-and-white mammal that emits a foul-smelling liquid when frightened; its fur; (sl) an obnoxious or mean person.

sky n (pl **skies**) the apparent vault over the earth; heaven; the upper atmosphere; weather, climate.

sky-diving n the sport of parachute jumping involving free-fall maneuvres.–**sky-diver** n.

skylight n a window in the roof or ceiling.

skyline n the visible horizon; the outline, as of mountains, buildings, etc, seen against the sky.

skyrocket n a rocket. * vi to rise rapidly (eg in price, status, etc).

skyscraper n a very tall building.

skyward adj, adv toward the sky.–**skywards** adv.

slab n a flat, broad, thick piece (as of stone, wood, or bread, etc); something resembling this. * vt to cut or form into slabs; to cover or support with slabs; to put on thickly.

slack adj loose, relaxed, not tight; (business) slow, not brisk; sluggish; inattentive, careless. * n the part (of a rope, etc) that hangs loose; a dull period; a lull; (pl) trousers for casual wear. * vti to neglect (one's work, etc), to be lazy; (with **off**) to slacken (a rope, etc).–**slackness** n.

slacken vti to make or become less active, brisk, etc; to loosen or relax, as a rope; to diminish, to abate.–**slackening** n, adj.

slag n the waste product from the smelting of metals; volcanic lava.

slain see **slay**.

slake vt to quench or satisfy (thirst, etc); to mix (lime) with water.

slam vti (**slamming, slammed**) to shut with a loud noise, to bang; to throw (down) violently; (inf) to criticize severely. * n a sound or the act of slamming, a bang; (inf) severe criticism; (bridge) the taking of 12 or 13 tricks.

slander n a false and malicious statement about another; the uttering of this. * vt to utter a slander about, to defame.–**slanderous** adj.

slang n words or expressions used in familiar speech but not regarded as standard English; jargon of a particular social class, age group, etc. * adj relating to slang.

slant vti to incline, to slope; to tell in such a way as to have a bias. * n a slope; an oblique position; a bias, a point of view. * adj sloping.–**slantly** adv.

slap n a smack with the open hand; an insult; a rebuff. * vt (**slapping, slapped**) to strike with something flat; to put, hit, etc, with force. * adv directly, full.

slapdash adj impetuous; hurried; careless; haphazard. * adv carelessly.

slapstick n boisterous humor of a knockabout kind.

slash vti to cut gashes in, to slit; to strike fiercely (at) with a sword, etc; to reduce (prices) sharply. * n a cutting blow; a long slit, a gash.

slat n a thin, flat, narrow strip of wood, etc.

slate[1] vt to criticize or punish severely.

slate[2] n a fine-grained rock easily split into thin layers; a flat plate of this or other material used in roofing; a tablet (as of slate) for writing on; a list of proposed candidates. * *adj* the color of slate, a deep bluish-gray color; made of slate. * *vt* to cover with slates; to suggest as a political candidate.

slaughter *n* the butchering of animals for food; a wholesale killing, a massacre.–*also vt*.–**slaughterer** *n*.

slaughterhouse *n* a place where animals are slaughtered.

slave *n* a person without freedom or personal rights, who is legally owned by another; a person under domination, esp of a habit or vice; a person who works like a slave, a drudge. * *vti* to toil hard, as a slave.

slave driver *n* a supervisor of slaves at work; a hard taskmaster.

slaver[1] *n* a person engaged in the buying and selling of slaves.

slaver[2] *vti* to dribble, to cover with saliva; to fawn upon, to flatter.

slavery *n* the condition of being a slave; bondage; drudgery; slave-owning as an institution.

slavish *adj* servile, abject; unoriginal.–**slavishly** *adv*.–**slavishness** *n*.

slay *vti* (**slaying, slew,** *pp* **slain**) to kill in great numbers; to murder; (*sl*) to overwhelm, to affect in a powerful way.–**slayer** *n*.

sleazy *adj* (**sleazier, sleaziest**) disreputable, squalid.–**sleaziness** *n*.

sled, sledge *n* a framework on runners for traveling over snow or ice; a toboggan; a sleigh. * *vti* to go or convey by sled.

sledgehammer *n* a large, heavy hammer for two hands.

sleek *adj* smooth, glossy; having a prosperous or well-groomed appearance; plausible.

sleep *n* a natural, regularly recurring rest for the body, with little or no consciousness; a period spent sleeping; a state of numbness followed by tingling. * *vti* (**sleeping, slept**) to rest in a state of sleep; to be inactive; to provide beds for; (*with* **around**) (*inf*) to be sexually promiscuous; (*with* **in**) to sleep on the premises; to sleep too long in the morning; (*with* **on**) to have a night's rest before making a decision; (*with* **off**) to get rid of by sleeping; (*with* **over**) to pass the night in someone else's house; (*with* **with**) to have sexual relations with.

sleeper *n* a person or thing that sleeps; a horizontal beam that carries and spreads a weight; a sleeping car; something that suddenly attains prominence or value.

sleeping bag *n* a padded bag for sleeping in, esp outdoors.

sleeping car *n* a train carriage with berths.

sleeping partner *n* a partner in a business who takes no part in its management.

sleeping pill *n* a pill that induces sleep.

sleepwalker *n* a person who walks while asleep, a somnambulist.–**sleepwalking** *n*.

sleepy *adj* (**sleepier, sleepiest**) drowsy; tired; lazy, not alert.–**sleepily** *adv*.–**sleepiness** *n*.

sleet *n* snow or hail mixed with rain. * *vi* to rain in the form of sleet.

sleeve *n* the part of a garment enclosing the arm; (*mech*) a tube that fits over a part; an open-ended cover, esp a paperboard envelope for a record.

sleeveless *adj* (*garment*) without sleeves.

sleight of hand *n* manual dexterity, such as in conjuring or juggling; a deception.

slender *adj* thin; slim; slight; scanty.–**slenderly** *adv*.–**slenderness** *n*.

slept *see* **sleep**.

sleuth *n* (*inf*) a detective.

slew[1] *see* **slay**.

slew[2], **slue** *n* (*inf*) a great quantity.

slice *n* a thin flat piece cut from something (as bread, etc); a wedge-shaped piece (of cake, pie, etc); a portion, a share; a broad knife for serving fish, cheese, etc; (*golf*) a stroke that makes the ball curl to the right. * *vti* to divide into parts; to cut into slices; to strike (a ball) so that it curves.–**slicer** *n*.–**slicing** *adj, n*.

slick *adj* clever, deft; smart but unsound; insincere; wily; (*inf*) smooth but superficial, tricky, etc. * *n* a patch or area of oil floating

on water. * *vt* to make glossy; (*with* **up**) (*inf*) to make smart, neat, etc.

slide *vti* (**sliding, slid**) to move along in constant contact with a smooth surface, as on ice, to glide; to coast over snow and ice; to pass gradually (into); to move (an object) unobtrusively. * *n* the act of sliding, a glide; a strip of smooth ice for sliding on; a chute; the glass plate of a microscope; a photographic transparency; a landslide.

sliding scale *n* a schedule for automatically varying one thing (eg wages) according to the fluctuations of another thing (eg cost of living); a flexible scale.

slier, sliest *see* **sly**.

slight *adj* small, inconsiderable; trifling; slim; frail, flimsy. * *vt* to disregard as insignificant; to treat with disrespect, to snub. * *n* intentional indifference or neglect, discourtesy.–**slightly** *adv*.–**slightness** *n*.

slim *adj* slender, not stout; small in amount, degree, etc; slight. * *vti* (**slimming, slimmed**) to make or become slim; to reduce one's weight by diet, etc.–**slimness** *n*.

slime *n* a sticky, slippery, half-liquid substance; a glutinous mud; mucus secreted by various animals (eg slugs).–**slimy** *adj*.

slimmer *n* a person who controls their diet to lose weight.

sling *n* a loop of leather with a string attached for hurling stones; a rope for lifting or hoisting weights; a bandage suspended from the neck for supporting an injured arm. * *vt* (**slinging, slung**) to throw, lift, or suspend (as) with a sling; to hurl.

slingshot *n* a contraption with elastic for shooting small stones, a catapult.

slink *vi* (**slinking, slinked** *or* **slunk**) to move stealthily or furtively, to sneak.

slinky *adj* (**slinkier, slinkiest**) (*inf*) sinuous in line or movement; (*clothes*) hugging the figure.

slip[1] *vti* (**slipping, slipped**) to slide, to glide; to lose one's foothold and stumble; to go or put quietly or quickly; to let go, to release; to escape from; (*with* **up**) to make a slight mistake. * *n* the act of slipping; a mistake, a lapse; a woman's undergarment; a pillowcase; a slipway.

slip[2] *n* a small piece of paper.

slipcase *n* a protective case for one or more books with an open end to reveal the spines.

slipknot *n* a knot that slips along the rope around which it is tied; a knot that can be undone at a pull.

slip-on *adj* (*garment or shoe*) easy to put on or take off.–*also n*.

slipped disk *n* a ruptured cartilaginous disk between vertebrae.

slipper *n* a light, soft, shoe worn in the house.

slippery *adj* so smooth as to cause slipping; difficult to hold or catch; evasive, unreliable, shifty.

slipshod *adj* having the shoes down at heel; slovenly, careless.

slipstream *n* a stream of air driven astern by the engine of an aircraft; an area of forward suction immediately behind a rapidly moving racing car.

slip-up *n* (*inf*) an error, a lapse.

slit *vt* (**slitting, slit**) to cut open or tear lengthways; to slash or tear into strips. * *n* a long cut, a slash; a narrow opening.–**slitter** *n*.

slither *vi* to slide, as on a loose or wet surface; to slip or slide like a snake.–**slithery** *adj*.

sliver *n* a small narrow piece torn off, a splinter; a thin slice.

slob *n* (*sl*) a coarse or sloppy person.

slobber *vti* to drool; to run at the mouth; to smear with dribbling saliva or food. * *n* dribbling saliva; maudlin talk.

slog *vti* (**slogging, slogged**) to hit hard and wildly; to work laboriously; to trudge doggedly. * *n* a hard, boring spell of work; a strenuous walk or hike; a hard, random hit.–**slogger** *n*.

slogan *n* a catchy phrase used in advertising or as a motto by a political party, etc.

sloop *n* a small sailing vessel with one mast and a jib.

slop n a puddle of spilled liquid; unappetizing semi-liquid food; (pl) liquid kitchen refuse. * vti (**slopping, slopped**) to spill or be spilled.

slope n rising or falling ground; an inclined line or surface; the amount or degree of this. * vti to incline, to slant; (inf) to make off, to go.

sloppy adj (**sloppier, sloppiest**) slushy; (inf) maudlin, sentimental; (inf) careless, untidy.–**sloppily** adv.–**sloppiness** n.

slosh n watery snow, slush; (inf) a heavy blow; the sound of liquid splashing. * vi to walk (through) or splash (around) in liquid, mud, etc; (of liquid) to splash. * vt to throw or splash liquid, etc at someone or something; (inf) to hit somebody.

slot n a long narrow opening in a mechanism for inserting a coin, a slit. * vt (**slotting, slotted**) to fit into a slot; to provide with a slot; (inf) to place in a series.

sloth n laziness, indolence; a slow-moving South American animal.–**slothful** adj.

slouch vti to sit, stand or move in a drooping, slovenly way. * n a drooping slovenly posture or gait; the downward droop of a hat brim; (inf) a poor performer, a lazy or incompetent person.

slough[1] n a bog; deep, hopeless dejection.

slough[2] n the dead, outer skin of a snake. * vti to cast off, as a dead skin.

slovenly adj untidy, dirty; careless.–**slovenliness** n.

slow adj moving at low speed, not fast; gradual; not quick in understanding; reluctant, backward; dull, sluggish; not progressive; (clock) behind in time; tedious, boring; (surface) causing slowness. * vti (also with **up, down**) to reduce the speed (of).–**slowly** adv.–**slowness** n.

slow-motion adj moving slowly; denoting a filmed or taped scene with the original action slowed down.

slowpoke n (inf) a person who moves, works or thinks slowly.

sludge n soft mud or snow; sediment; sewage.

slue see **slew**[2].

slug[1] n a mollusk resembling a snail but with no outer shell.

slug[2] n a small bullet; a disc for inserting into a slot machine; a line of type; (inf) a hard blow; a drink of spirits. * vt (**slugging, slugged**) (inf) to hit hard with a fist or a bat.

sluggish adj slow, inactive; unresponsive.–**sluggishly** adv.–**sluggishness** n.

sluice n a gate regulating a flow of water; the water passing through this; an artificial water channel. * vti to draw off through a sluice; to wash with a stream of water; to stream out as from a sluice.

slum n a squalid, rundown house; (usu pl) an overcrowded area characterized by poverty, etc. * vi (**slumming, slummed**) to make do with less comfort.

slumber vi to sleep. * n a light sleep.

slump n a sudden fall in value or slackening in demand; (sport) a period of poor play. * vi to fall or decline suddenly; to sink down heavily; to collapse; to slouch.

slung see **sling**.

slunk see **slink**.

slur vti (**slurring, slurred**) to pronounce or speak indistinctly; (letters, words) to run together; (mus) to produce by gliding without a break; to make disparaging remarks. * n the act of slurring; a stigma, an imputation of disgrace; (mus) a curved line over notes to be slurred.

slurp vti (sl) to drink or eat noisily. * n a loud sipping or sucking sound.

slush n liquid mud; melting snow; (inf) sentimental language.–**slushy** adj.

slush fund n a fund of money used secretly to bribe, etc.

slut n a slovenly or immoral woman.–**sluttish** adj.

sly adj (**slyer, slyest** or **slier, sliest**) secretively cunning, wily; underhand; knowing.–**slyly** adv.–**slyness** n.

smack[1] n a taste; a distinctive smell or flavor; small quantity, a trace. * vi to have a smell or taste (of); to have a slight trace of something.

smack[2] vt to strike or slap with the open hand; to kiss noisily; to make a sharp noise with the lips.–also n.

smack[3] n a small fishing vessel used in coastal waters.

small adj little in size, number, importance, etc; modest, humble; operating on a minor scale; young; petty. * adv in small pieces. * n the narrow, curving part of the back.

small change n coins of low value.

small fry npl people or things of little significance.

small intestine n the section of the alimentary canal between the stomach and the colon.

small-minded adj intolerant, narrow-minded; mean, vindictive.–**small-mindedly** adv.–**small-mindedness** n.

smallpox n an acute contagious viral disease, now rare, causing the eruption of pustules which leave the skin scarred and pitted.

small-scale adj small in size or scope.

small screen n a television.

small talk n light, social conversation.

smart n a sudden, stinging pain. * vi to have or cause a sharp, stinging pain (as by a slap); to feel distress. * adj stinging; astute; clever, witty; fashionable; neatly dressed; (equipment, etc) capable of seemingly intelligent action through computer control; (bombs, missiles) guided to the target by lasers ensuring pinpoint accuracy.–**smartly** adv.–**smartness** n.

smart aleck n (inf) an annoyingly clever person, a know-all.

smart card n a credit card containing a memory chip that records transactions made with the card.

smash vti to break into pieces with noise or violence; to hit, collide, or move with force; to destroy or be destroyed. * n a hard, heavy hit; a violent, noisy breaking; a violent collision; total failure, esp in business; (inf) a popular success.

smashed adj (sl) drunk or under the influence of drugs.

smattering n a slight superficial knowledge; a small number.

smear vt to cover with anything greasy or sticky; to make a smudge; to slander. * n a smudge; a slanderous attack; a deposit of blood, secretion, etc on a glass slide for examination under a microscope.

smear test n microscopic analysis of a smear of bodily cells, esp from the cervix, for cancer.

smell n the sense by which odors are perceived with the nose; a scent, odor, or stench; a trace. * vti (**smelling, smelt** or **smelled**) to have or perceive an odor.–**smelly** adj.

smelt[1] vt to extract ore from metal by melting.

smelt[2] see **smell**.

smile vti to express amusement, friendship, pleasure, etc, by a slight turning up of the corners of the mouth. * n the act of smiling; a bright aspect.–**smilingly** adv.

smirk vi to smile in an expression of smugness or scorn. * n a smug or scornful smile.–**smirkingly** adv.

smite vb (**smiting, smote, pp smitten** or **smote**) vt (arch) to strike hard; to kill or injure; to have a powerful affect on. * vi to strike, beat or come down (on) with force.–**smiter** n.

smith n a person who works in metal; a blacksmith.

smithereens npl (inf) fragments.

smithy n (pl **smithies**) a blacksmith's workshop.

smitten see **smite**.

smock n a loose shirtlike outer garment to protect the clothes.

smog n a mixture of fog and smoke; polluted air.–**smoggy** adj.

smoke n a cloud or plume of gas and small particles emitted from a burning substance; any similar vapor; an act of smoking tobacco, etc; (inf) a cigar or cigarette. * vi to give off smoke; to (habitually) draw and exhale the smoke of tobacco, etc. * vt to fumigate; to cure food by treating with smoke; to darken (eg glass) using smoke; (with **out**) to flush out using smoke; to bring into public view.–**smokable, smokeable** adj.

smoke detector n an electrical device that sets off an alarm when smoke is detected.

smoke screen n dense smoke used to conceal military movements, etc; something designed to obscure, conceal, or disguise the truth.

smoky adj (**smokier, smokiest**) emitting smoke, esp excessively; filled with smoke; resembling smoke in appearance, flavor, smell, color, etc.–**smokily** adv.–**smokiness** n.

smolder vi to burn slowly or without flame; (feelings) to linger on in a suppressed state; to have concealed feelings of anger, jealousy, etc.–also **smoulder**.

smooch vi (sl) to kiss and cuddle, esp while dancing as a couple. * n (sl) a long kiss, an embrace.–**smoochy** adj.

smooth adj having an even or flat surface; silky; not rough or lumpy; hairless; of even consistency; calm, unruffled; gently flowing in rhythm or sound. * vti to make smooth; to calm; to make easier.–**smoothly** adv.–**smoothness** n.

smooth-tongued adj persuasive in speech.

smorgasbord, smörgåsbord n a type of buffet or hors d'œuvres of various cold dishes of cheese, fish, salads, etc, served in Scandinavia; a restaurant specializing in this.

smote see **smite**.

smother vt to stifle, to suffocate; to put out a fire by covering it to remove the air supply; to cover over thickly; to hold back, suppress. * vi to undergo suffocation.–also n.

smoulder see **smoulder**.

smudge n a dirty or blurred spot or area; a fire made to produce dense smoke. * vt to make a smudge; to smear; to blur; to produce smoke to protect against insects, etc. * vi to become smudged.–**smudgy** adj.–**smudgily** adv.

smug adj (**smugger, smuggest**) complacent, self-satisfied.–**smugly** adv.–**smugness** n.

smuggle vt to import or export (goods) secretly without paying customs duties; to convey or introduce secretly.–**smuggler** n.

smut n a speck or smudge of dirt, soot, etc; indecent talk, writing, or pictures; a fungal disease of crop plants that covers the leaves in sooty spores. * vti (**smutting, smutted**) to stain or become stained with smut; (crops, etc) to infect or become infected with smut.

smutty adj (**smuttier, smuttiest**) soiled with smuts; obscene, filthy.–**smuttily** adv.–**smuttiness** n.

snack n a light meal between regular meals.

snag n a sharp point or projection; a tear, as in cloth, made by a snag, etc; an unexpected or hidden difficulty. * vti (**snagging, snagged**) to tear, etc, on a snag; to clear of snags.

snail n a mollusk having a wormlike body and a spiral protective shell; a slow-moving or sluggish person or thing.

snail's pace n a very slow speed or rate of progress.

snake n a limbless, scaly reptile with a long, tapering body and with salivary glands often modified to produce venom; a sly, treacherous person. * vt to twist along like a snake. * vi to crawl silently and stealthily.

snake charmer n a person who entertains by appearing to mesmerize venomous snakes by playing music.

snap vti (**snapping, snapped**) to break suddenly; to make or cause to make a sudden, cracking sound; to close, fasten, etc with this sound; (with **at**) to bite or grasp suddenly; to speak or utter sharply. * adj sudden. * n a sharp, cracking sound; a fastener that closes with a snapping sound; a crisp biscuit; a snapshot; a sudden spell of cold weather; (inf) vigor, energy.

snapdragon n any of several plants of the figwort family with showy white, red or yellow flowers shaped like small jaws.

snap fastener n a press stud.

snapper n one who or that which snaps; (pl **snapper, snappers**) any of various sea fishes used as food; a snapping turtle.

snappy adj (**snappier, snappiest**) speaking sharply; brisk; lively; smart, fashionable.–**snappily** adv.–**snappiness** n.

snapshot n a photograph taken casually with a simple camera.

snare n a loop of string or wire for trapping birds or animals; something that catches one unawares, a trap; a loop of gut wound with wire stretched around a snare drum that produces a rattling sound. * vt to trap using a snare.

snarl[1] vi to growl with bared teeth; to speak in a rough, angry manner. * vt to express in a snarling manner. * n the act of snarling; the sound of this.

snarl[2] vti to make or become entangled or complicated. * n a tangle; disorder.

snatch vt to seize or grasp suddenly; to take as opportunity occurs. * n the act of snatching; a brief period; a fragment; (inf) a robbery.

snazzy adj (**snazzier, snazziest**) (inf) stylish, fashionable; flashy.

sneak vti (**sneaking, sneaked,** pp (sl) **snuck**) to move, act, give, put, take, etc, secretly or stealthily. * n a person who acts secretly or stealthily; (inf) a person who tells or informs on others. * adj without warning.

sneaker n one who or that which sneaks; a shoe with a cloth upper and soft rubber sole, worn informally.

sneaky adj (**sneakier, sneakiest**) like a sneak; furtive; underhand.–**sneakily** adv.–**sneakiness** n.

sneer vi to show scorn or contempt by curling up the upper lip. * n a derisive look or remark.–**sneerer** n.–**sneeringly** adv.

sneeze vi to expel air through the nose violently and audibly. * n the act of sneezing.–**sneezy** adj.

snicker vi to laugh furtively and slyly, to snigger; to neigh, to whinny. * n a half-suppressed laugh, a giggle.–**snickeringly** adv.

snide adj malicious; superior in attitude; sneering.–**snidely** adv.–**snideness** n.

sniff vti to inhale through the nose audibly; to smell by sniffing; to scoff; (with **at**) to express dislike or contempt for. * n the act of sniffing; the sound of this; a smell.–**sniffer** n.

sniffle vi to sniff repeatedly. * n the act or sound of sniffling.

snip vti (**snipping, snipped**) to cut or clip with a single stroke of the scissors, etc. * n a small piece cut off; the act or sound of snipping; (inf) a bargain; (inf) a certainty, cinch.

snipe n (pl **snipes, snipe**) any of various birds with long straight flexible bills. * vi to shoot snipe; to shoot at individuals from a hidden position; to make sly criticisms of.–**sniper** n.

snippet n a scrap of information.

snivel vi (**sniveling, sniveled** or **snivelling, snivelled**) to whine or whimper; to have a runny nose.–**sniveler, sniveller** n.

snob n a person who wishes to be associated with those of a higher social status, whilst acting condescendingly to those whom he or she regards as inferior.–**snobbish** adj.–**snobbishly** adv.–**snobbishness** n.

snobbery n (pl **snobberies**) snobbish behavior or attitude; a snobbish act.

snoop vi (inf) to pry about in a sneaking way. * n an act of snooping; a person who pries into other people's business.–**snooper** n.

snooty adj (**snootier, snootiest**) haughty, snobbish.–**snootily** adv.–**snootiness** n.

snooze vi (inf) to sleep lightly. * n (inf) a nap.

snore vi to breathe roughly and noisily while asleep. * n the act or sound of snoring.

snorkel n a breathing tube extending above the water, used in swimming just below the surface. * vi (**snorkeling, snorkeled**) to swim using a snorkel.–**snorkeler** n.

snort vi to exhale noisily through the nostrils, esp as an expression of contempt or scorn. * vt to inhale (a drug) through the nose.

snot n (sl) nasal mucus; (sl) a snotty person.

snotty adj (**snottier, snottiest**) covered with snot; (sl) irritatingly unpleasant; snobbish.–**snottily** adv.–**snottiness** n.

snout n the nose or muzzle of an animal.

snow n frozen water vapor in the form of white flakes; a snowfall; a mass of snow; (sl) cocaine or heroin. * vi to fall as snow; to deceive with smooth talk.

snowball n snow pressed together in a ball for throwing; a drink made with advocaat and lemonade. * vi to throw snowballs; to increase rapidly in size.

snow-blind adj temporarily blinded or dazzled by the intense glare of sunlight reflected from snow.–**snow-blindness** n.

snowboard *n* a board shaped like a large ski which a person can stand on to slide across snow.

snowcap *n* a covering of snow, as on a mountain peak.–**snow-capped** *adj*.

snowfall *n* a fall of snow; the amount of snow in a given time or area.

snowflake *n* a fragile cluster of ice crystals.

snow goose *n* a large white North American goose with black-tipped wings.

snowman *n* (*pl* **snowmen**) snow piled into the shape of a human figure.

snowplow, snowplough *n* a vehicle designed for clearing away snow.

snow tire *n* a heavy tire with deep treads for improved traction on snow and ice.

snowy *adj* (**snowier, snowiest**) covered with snow; white or pure, like snow.–**snowily** *adv*.–**snowiness** *n*.

snub *vt* (**snubbing, snubbed**) to insult by ignoring or making a cutting remark. * *n* the act of snubbing; an intentional slight.

snub-nosed *adj* having a short upturned nose; (*pistol*) having a very short barrel.

snuck *see* **sneak**.

snuff[1] *n* a powdered preparation of tobacco inhaled through the nostrils.

snuff[2] *n* the charred portion of a wick. * *vt* to extinguish (a candle flame).

snuffle *vi* to make sniffing noises, as when suffering from a cold or crying. * *n* the act of snuffling; (*pl*) a form of catarrh.

snug *adj* (**snugger, snuggest**) cosy; warm; close-fitting.–**snugly** *adv*.–**snugness** *n*.

snuggle *vi* to nestle, cuddle. * *vt* to cuddle.

so *adv* in this way; as shown; as stated; to such an extent; very; (*inf*) very much; therefore; more or less; also, likewise; then.

soak *vt* to submerge in a liquid; to take in, absorb; (*sl*) to extract large amounts of money from. * *vi* to become saturated; to penetrate. * *n* the act or process of soaking.

so-and-so *n* (*pl* **so-and-sos**) an unspecified person or thing; (*inf*) (*euphemism*) an unpleasant or disliked person or thing.

soap *n* a substance used with water to produce suds for washing; (*inf*) a soap opera. * *vt* to rub with soap.–**soapy** *adj*.

soapbox *n* a temporary platform from which to deliver informal speeches.

soap opera *n* (*inf*) a daytime radio or television serial melodrama.

soapy *adj* (**soapier, soapiest**) like or full of soap; flattering, unctuous.–**soapily** *adv*.–**soapiness** *n*.

soar *vi* to rise high in the air; to glide along high in the air; to increase; to rise in status.–**soarer** *n*.

sob *vb* (**sobbing, sobbed**) *vi* to weep with convulsive gasps. * *vt* to speak while sobbing.

sober *adj* not drunk; serious and thoughtful; realistic, rational; subdued in color. * *vt* (*often with* **up** *or* **down**) to make or become sober.–**soberly** *adv*.–**soberness** *n*.

sobriety *n* soberness; temperance; seriousness.

sob story *n* (*inf*) a tale of distress intended to arouse sympathy.

so-called *adj* commonly named or known as.

soccer *n* a football game played on a field by two teams of 11 players with a round inflated ball, association football.

sociable *adj* friendly; companionable.–**sociability** *n*.–**sociably** *adv*.

social *adj* living or organized in a community, not solitary; relating to human beings living in society; of or intended for communal activities; sociable. * *n* an informal gathering of people, such as a party.–**socially** *adv*.

social climber *n* a person who strives to attain a higher social position.

socialism *n* (a system based on) a political and economic theory advocating state ownership of the means of production and distribution.–**socialist** *n*, *adj*.–**socialistic** *adj*.–**socialistically** *adv*.

socialite *n* a person active or prominent in fashionable society.

socialize *vt* to meet other people socially.–**socialization** *n*.–**socializer** *n*.

social science *n* the study of human social organization and relationships using scientific methods.

social security *n* financial assistance for the unemployed, the disabled, etc to alleviate economic distress.

social work *n* any of various professional welfare services to aid the underprivileged in society.–**social worker** *n*.

society *n* (*pl* **societies**) the social relationships between human beings or animals organized collectively; the system of human institutional organization; a community with the same language and customs; an interest group or organization; the fashionable or privileged members of a community; companionship.–**societal** *adj*.

sociology *n* the study of the development and structure of society and social relationships.–**sociological** *adj*.–**sociologically** *adv*.–**sociologist** *n*.

sociopath *n* a person suffering from a mental disorder that results in antisocial behavior and lack of guilt.–**sociopathic** *adj*.

sock *n* a kind of short stocking covering the foot and lower leg.

socket *n* a hollow part into which something is inserted, such as an eye, a bone, a tooth, an electric plug, etc.

sod *n* a lump of earth covered with grass; turf. * *vt* (**sodding, sodded**) to cover with turf.

soda *n* sodium bicarbonate; sodium carbonate; soda water.

soda fountain *n* a counter selling soft drinks, ice cream, snacks, etc; a device that dispenses soda water.

soda siphon *n* a pressurized container that dispenses soda water.

soda water *n* a fizzy drink made by charging water with carbon dioxide under pressure.

sodden *adj* completely soaked through.–**soddenly** *adv*.

sodium *n* a metallic element.

sodium bicarbonate *n* a white soluble alkaline powder used in baking powder, fire extinguishers and in antacid medicines.

sodium chloride *n* salt.

sofa *n* an upholstered couch or settee with fixed back and arms.

soft *adj* malleable; easily cut, shaped, etc; not as hard as normal, desirable, etc; smooth to the touch; (*drinks*) nonalcoholic; mild, as a breeze; lenient; (*sl*) easy, comfortable; (*color, light*) not bright; (*sound*) gentle, low; (*drugs*) non-addictive.–**softly** *adv*.–**softness** *n*.

softball *n* a game similar to baseball, but played with a larger, softer ball.

soft-core *adj* (*pornography*) not sexually explicit.

soft drink *n* a nonalcoholic drink.

soften *vti* to make or become soft or softer.–**softener** *n*.

soft-focus *adj* (*lens*) designed to produce a slightly blurred image.

soft furnishings *npl* items such as curtains, carpets, rugs, etc.

softhearted *adj* kind; sentimental.–**softheartedly** *adv*.–**softheartedness** *n*.

soft palate *n* the fleshy area at the back of the roof of the mouth.

soft-pedal *n* a pedal on a piano for muting the tone. * *vt* (*inf*) (**soft-pedaling, soft-pedaled** *or* **soft-pedalling, soft-pedalled**) to avoid direct reference to, esp something embarrassing or unpleasant.

soft touch *n* (*inf*) a person who is easily persuaded or exploited.

software *n* the programs used in computers.

soggy *adj* (**soggier, soggiest**) soaked with water; moist and heavy.–**soggily** *adv*.–**sogginess** *n*.

soil[1] *n* the ground or earth in which plants grow; territory.

soil[2] *vt* to make or become dirty or stained.

sojourn *n* a temporary stay. * *vi* to stay for a short time.–**sojourner** *n*.

solace *n* comfort in misery; consolation. * *vt* to bring solace to.

solar *adj* of or from the sun; powered by light or heat from the sun; reckoned by the sun.

solar plexus *n* the network of nerves behind the stomach; (*inf*) the pit of the stomach.

solar system *n* the sun and those bodies moving about it under the attraction of gravity.

sold *see* **sell**.

solder *n* a metal alloy used when melted to join or patch metal parts, etc. * *vti* to join or be joined with solder.

soldering iron *n* an electrically heated tool for melting and applying solder.

soldier *n* a person who serves in an army, esp a non-commissioned officer or private. * *vi* to serve as a soldier; (*with* **on**) to continue regardless of difficulties or dangers.–**soldierly** *adj*.

sole[1] *n* the underside of the foot or shoe. * *vt* to put a new sole on (a shoe).

sole[2] *n* (*pl* **sole, soles**) a type of flatfish used as food.

sole[3] *adj* only, being the only one; exclusive.–**solely** *adv*.

solemn *adj* serious; formal; sacred; performed with religious ceremony.–**solemnly** *adv*.–**solemnness** *n*.

solemnity *n* (*pl* **solemnities**) solemness; a formal rite.

solicit *vti* to make a request or application to (a person for something); (*prostitute*) to offer sexual services for money.–**solicitation** *n*.

solicitous *adj* showing concern or attention.–**solicitously** *adv*.–**solicitousness** *n*.–**solicitude** *n*.

solid *adj* firm; compact; not hollow; strongly constructed; having three dimensions; neither liquid nor gaseous; unanimous. * *n* a solid substance (not liquid or gas); a three-dimensional figure.–**solidly** *adv*.–**solidness** *n*.

solidarity *n* (*pl* **solidarities**) unity of interest and action.

solidi *see* **solidus**.

solidify *vti* (**solidifying, solidified**) to make or become solid, compact, hard, etc.–**solidification** *n*.

solidity *n* the state of being solid; density; compactness; stability; truth; moral firmness.

solidus *n* (*pl* **solidi**) an oblique stroke (/) used to separate items of text as in dates, alternative words, lists, or the terms of fractions.

soliloquy *n* (*pl* **soliloquies**) the act of talking to oneself; an act or speech in a play that takes this form.

solitaire *n* a single gemstone, esp a diamond; a card game for one, patience.

solitary *adj* alone; only; single; living alone; lonely. * *n* (*pl* **solitaries**) a recluse.–**solitarily** *adv*.–**solitariness** *n*.

solitude *n* the state of being alone; lack of company; a lonely place.–**solitudinous** *adj*.

solo *n* (*pl* **solos**) a musical composition for one voice or instrument; a flight by a single person in an aircraft, esp a first flight. * *vi* to perform by oneself. * *adv* alone. * *adj* unaccompanied.–**soloist** *n*.

so long *interj* (*inf*) goodbye, farewell.

solstice *n* either of the two times in the year at which the sun is farthest from the equator (June 21 and December 21).–**solsticial** *adj*.

soluble *adj* capable of being dissolved (usu in water); capable of being solved or answered.–**solubility** *n*.–**solubly** *adv*.

solution *n* the act or process of answering a problem; the answer found; the dispersion of one substance in another, usu a liquid, so as to form a homogeneous mixture.

solve *vt* to work out the answer to; to clear up, resolve.

solvent *adj* capable of dissolving a substance; able to pay all debts. * *n* a liquid that dissolves substances.–**solvency** *n*.

solvent abuse *n* the deliberate inhalation of fumes from solvents (such as in glue and polish) to become intoxicated.

somber, sombre *adj* dark, gloomy or dull; dismal; sad.–**somberly, sombrely** *adv*.–**somberness, sombreness** *n*.

sombrero *n* (*pl* **sombreros**) a wide-brimmed hat with a high crown, worn esp in Spanish-speaking countries.

some *adj* certain but not specified or known; of a certain unspecified quantity, degree, etc; a little; (*inf*) remarkable, striking, etc. * *pron* a certain unspecified quantity, number, etc.

somebody *n* (*pl* **somebodies**) an unspecified person; an important person. * *pron* someone.

somehow *adv* in a way or by a method not known or stated.

someone *n* somebody.–*also pron*.

somersault *n* a forward or backward roll head over heels along the ground or in mid-air.–*also vi*.

something *n*, *pron* a thing not definitely known, understood, etc; an important or notable thing. * *adv* to some degree.

sometime *adj* former. * *adv* at some unspecified future date. * *adj* having been formerly; being so occasionally or in only some respects.

sometimes *adv* at times, now and then.

somewhat *adv* to some extent, degree, etc; a little.

somewhere, somewheres *adv* in, to or at some place not known or specified.

somnambulism *n* the practice of walking in one's sleep.–**somnambulist** *n*.–**somnambulistic** *adj*.

somnolent *adj* sleepy, drowsy.–**somnolence, somnolency** *n*.

son *n* a male offspring or descendant.

sonar *n* an apparatus that detects underwater objects by means of reflecting sound waves.

sonata *n* (*mus*) a composition for a solo instrument, usu the piano.

song *n* a piece of music composed for the voice; the act or process of singing; the call of certain birds.

song and dance *n* (*inf*) a fuss; a long involved story.

songbird *n* a bird with a musical call.

sonic *adj* of, producing, or involving sound waves.–**sonically** *adv*.

sonic barrier *n* the increase in air resistance experienced by objects traveling close to the speed of sound, the sound barrier.

son-in-law *n* (*pl* **sons-in-law**) a daughter's husband.

sonnet *n* a rhyming poem in a single stanza of fourteen lines.

sonorous *adj* giving out sound; full, rich, or deep in sound.–**sonorously** *adv*.–**sonorousness** *n*.

soon *adv* in a short time; before long; **sooner or later** at some future unspecified time, eventually.

soot *n* a black powder produced from flames.–**sooty** *adj*.

soothe *vt* to calm or comfort; to alleviate; to relieve (pain, etc).–**soothing** *adj*.–**soothingly** *adv*.

soothsayer *n* a person who predicts events.

sop *n* a piece of bread or other food dipped in liquid before being eaten; a concession, bribe offered to appease or cajole. * *vt* (**sopping, sopped**) to dip (bread, etc) into liquid. * *vi* to be soaked.

sophism *n* a clever but fallacious argument.–**sophistry** *n*.–**sophist** *n*.–**sophistic, sophistical** *adj*.

sophisticated *adj* refined; worldly-wise; intelligent; complex.–**sophistication** *n*.

sophomore *n* in US, a second-year student at college or high school.–**sophomoric** *adj*.

soporific *adj* inducing sleep; sleepy.

sopping *adj* wet through.

soppy *adj* (**soppier, soppiest**) wet; (*inf*) sickly sentimental.–**soppily** *adv*.–**soppiness** *n*.

soprano *n* (*pl* **sopranos, soprani**) the highest singing voice of females or boys; a person who sings soprano.

sorbet *n* a flavored water ice; sherbet.

sorcerer *n* person who uses magic powers; a magician or wizard.–**sorceress** *nf*.

sorcery *n* (*pl* **sorceries**) the practice of magic, esp with the assistance of evil spirits.

sordid *adj* filthy, squalid; vile; base; selfish.–**sordidly** *adv*.–**sordidness** *n*.

sore *n* a painful or tender injury or wound; an ulcer or boil; grief; a cause of distress. * *adj* painful; tender; distressed.–**soreness** *n*.

sorghum *n* any of a genus of tropical cereal grasses grown for fodder.

sorority n (pl **sororities**) a society of women university students.

sorrow n sadness; regret; an expression of grief. * vi to mourn, to grieve.–**sorrowful** adj.–**sorrowfully** adv.–**sorrowfulness** n.

sorry adj (**sorrier, sorriest**) feeling pity, sympathy, remorse or regret; pitiful; poor.–**sorrily** adv.–**sorriness** n.

sort n a class, kind, or variety; quality or type. * vt to arrange according to kind; to classify; (with **out**) to find a solution to, resolve; to disentangle; to organize, discipline; (inf) to punish, to attack violently.–**sorter** n.

sortie n a sudden attack by troops from a besieged position; one mission by a single military plane.

SOS n an international signal code of distress; an urgent call for help or rescue.

so-so adj not good but not bad, middling. * adv average, indifferently. **soufflé** n a baked dish made light and puffy by adding beaten egg whites before baking.–also adj.

sought see **seek**.

souk n an open-air market in Muslim countries.

soul n a person's spirit; the seat of the emotions, desires; essence; character; a human being. * adj characteristic of American Blacks.

soul-destroying adj extremely boring, depressing.

soulful adj expressing profound sentiment.–**soulfully** adv.–**soulfulness** n.

soulless adj devoid of emotion; bleak; dull.

soul mate n a person, such as a lover or close friend, with whom one bonds deeply.

soul music n music derived from Afro-American gospel singing marked by intensity of feeling and closely related to rhythm and blues.

soul-searching n close examination of one's conscience, motives, etc.

sound[1] adj healthy; free from injury or damage; substantial; stable; deep (as sleep) solid; thorough.–**soundly** adv.–**soundness** n.

sound[2] n a narrow channel of water connecting two seas or between a mainland and an island.

sound[3] n vibrations transmitted through the air and detected by the ear; the sensation of hearing; any audible noise; the impression given by something. * vi to make a sound; to give a summons by sound. * vt to cause to make a sound; to voice; to make a signal or order by sound; (with **off**) (inf) to complain loudly.

sound[4] vt to measure the depth of; (often with **out**) to attempt to discover the opinions and intentions of (someone).

sound barrier n the increase in air resistance experienced by objects traveling close to the speed of sound, the sonic barrier.

sound effects npl artificial sounds used for dramatic purposes in plays, television programs, movies, etc.

sounding board n a thin board placed behind a platform to direct the sound at the audience; a sound board; a person or thing used to test reaction to a new idea or plan.

soundproof adj unable to be penetrated by sound. * vt to make soundproof by insulation, etc.

soundtrack n the sound accompanying a film; the area on cinema film that carries the sound recording.

soup n a liquid food made from boiling meat, fish, vegetables, etc, in water; (inf) a difficult or embarrassing situation. * vt (with **up**) (inf) to increase the power and performance of an engine.–**soupy** adj.

sour adj having a sharp, biting taste; spoiled by fermentation; cross; bad-tempered; distasteful or unpleasant; (soil) acid in reaction. * vti to make or become sour.–**sourly** adv.–**sourness** n.

source n a spring forming the head of a stream; an origin or cause; a person, book, etc, that provides information. * vti (inf) to find a supplier; to identify a source.

sour cream n cream deliberately soured by bacteria and used in sauces, dressings, etc.

sour grapes n sing pretending to dislike something because it cannot be obtained or achieved by oneself.

souse vt to immerse in water or other liquid; to saturate; to pickle or steep in a marinade; (sl) to make drunk. * vi to become saturated or immersed. * n the act of sousing; something pickled; pickling liquid; (sl) a drunkard.

south n the direction to one's right when facing the direction of the rising sun; the region, country, continent, etc, lying relatively in that direction. * adj, adv facing toward or situated in the south.

southeast n the point on a compass midway between south and east. * adj, adv at, toward, or from the southeast.

southeasterly adj, adv toward or from the southeast. * n (pl **southeasterlies**) a wind from the southeast.

southeastern adj in, toward, or from the southeast; inhabiting or characteristic of the southeast.–**southeasterner** n.

southerly adj in, toward, or from the south. * n (pl **southerlies**) a wind from the south.

southern adj in, toward, or from the south; inhabiting or characteristic of the south.–**southernmost** adj.

southerner n an inhabitant of the south.

South Pole n the most southerly point on the earth's axis; the most southerly point on the celestial sphere; (without caps) the pole of a magnet that points south.

southward adj toward the south.–**southwards** adv.

southwest n the point on a compass midway between south and west. * adj, adv at, toward, or from the southwest.

southwester n a strong wind from the southwest.

southwesterly adj, adv toward or from the southwest. * n (pl **southwesterlies**) a wind from the southwest.

southwestern adj in, toward, or from the southwest; inhabiting or characteristic of the southwest.–**southwesterner** n.

souvenir n a keepsake, a memento.

sovereign adj supreme in authority or rank; (country, state, etc) independent. * n a supreme ruler; a monarch.–**sovereignty** n.

soviet n a workers' council in the former USSR.

sow[1] n an adult female pig.

sow[2] vt (**sowing, sowed**, pp **sown** or **sowed**) to plant or scatter seed on or in the ground; to disseminate; to implant.–**sower** n.

soya bean, soybean n a type of bean (orig from Asia) used as a source of food and oil.

soy sauce, soya sauce n a dark, salty sauce made from fermented soybeans.

spa n a mineral spring; a resort where there is a mineral spring.

space n the limitless three-dimensional expanse within which all objects exist; outer space; a specific area; an interval, empty area; room; an unoccupied area or seat. * vt to arrange at intervals.

space bar n the long bar on a typewriter or computer keyboard for inserting spaces.

spacecraft n a vehicle for travel in outer space.

spaceman n (pl **spacemen**) a person who travels in outer space; an alien.–**spacewoman** (pl **spacewomen**) nf.

space probe n an unmanned rocket equipped for exploring outer space.

spaceship n a crewed spacecraft.

space shuttle n a manned spacecraft designed as a reusable ferry between the earth and a space station.

spacesuit n a sealed and pressurized suit worn by astronauts in space.

space-time (continuum) n (physics) the four-dimensional coordinate system comprising the three spatial and one temporal coordinates which together define a continuum in which any particle or event may be located.

spacewalk n a period of time spent by an astronaut floating in space outside a spacecraft. * vi to walk in space.–**spacewalker** n.

spacious adj large in extent; roomy.–**spaciously** adv.–**spaciousness** n.

spade n a tool with a broad blade and a handle, used for digging.

spaghetti n pasta made in thin, solid strings.

spaghetti western n a type of violent cowboy film, usu shot on location in Italy or Spain, which became popular in the 1960s.

span n a unit of length equal to a hand's breadth (about 9 inches/23 cm); the full extent between any two limits, such as the ends of a bridge or arch. * vt (**spanning, spanned**) to extend across.

spangle n a sequin or other small piece of shiny decoration; any small glittering particle. * vt to decorate with spangles. * vi to sparkle with or like spangles.–**spangly** adj.

spaniel n any of various breeds of dog with large drooping ears and a long silky coat.

spank vt to slap with the flat of the hand, esp on the buttocks.– also n.

spanner n a tool with a hole or (often adjustable) jaws to grip and turn nuts or bolts, a wrench.

spar[1] n a pole supporting the rigging of a ship; one of the main structural members of the wing of an airplane.

spar[2] vi (**sparring, sparred**) to box using gentle blows, as in training; to argue.–also n.

spare vt to refrain from harming or killing; to afford; to make (something) available (eg time). * adj kept as an extra, additional; scanty. * n a spare part; a spare tyre –**sparely** adv.– **spareness** n.

sparing adj frugal, economical.–**sparingly** adv.–**sparingness** n.

spark n a fiery or glowing particle thrown off by burning material or by friction; a flash of light from an electrical discharge; a trace. * vt to stir up; to activate. * vi to give off sparks.

sparking plug n a spark plug.

sparkle n a spark; vivacity. * vi to shine; to glitter; (water, wine) to effervesce; to be lively or witty.

sparkler n a handheld firework that throws off brilliant sparks; (inf) a diamond.

spark plug n a device that produces a spark to ignite the explosive mixture in an internal combustion engine.–also **sparking plug**.

sparring partner n (boxing) a partner who stands in as an opponent for training purposes; a person with whom one regularly argues.

sparrow n any of various small brownish songbirds related to the finch.

sparse adj spread out thinly; scanty.–**sparsely** adv.–**sparseness, sparsity** n.

Spartan adj of or pertaining to Sparta in ancient Greece; rigorously severe.

spasm n a sudden, involuntary muscular contraction; any sudden burst (of emotion or activity).–**spasmodic** adj intermittent; of or like a spasm.–**spasmodically** adv.

spastic n a person who suffers from cerebral palsy. * adj affected by muscle spasm.–**spasticity** n.

spat[1] see **spit**[2].

spat[2] n a petty argument, or quarrel. * vi to have a petty argument.

spate n a large amount; a sudden outburst (as of words); a sudden flood.

spatial adj relating to space.–**spatially** adv.

spatter vti to scatter or spurt out in drops; to splash.–also n.

spatula n a tool with a broad, flexible blade for spreading or mixing foods, paints, etc.

spawn n a mass of eggs deposited by fish, frogs, or amphibians; offspring. * vti to lay eggs; to produce, esp in great quantity.

spay vt (female animals) to sterilize by removing the ovaries from.

speak vi (**speaking, spoke,** pp **spoken**) to utter words; to talk; to converse with; to deliver a speech; to be suggestive of something; to produce a characteristic sound; (with **out, up**) to speak loudly; to express an opinion frankly.–**speakable** adj.

speakeasy n (pl **speakeasies**) a club where alcoholic drink was sold illegally during the Prohibition era in the US in the 1920s.

speaker n a person who speaks, esp before an audience; the presiding official in a legislative assembly; a loudspeaker.

spear n a weapon with a long shaft and a sharp point; a blade or shoot (of grass, broccoli, etc). * vt to pierce with a spear.

spearhead n the pointed head of a spear; the leading person or group in an attack or other action. * vt to serve as a leader of.

spearmint n a common mint plant which yields an oil used for flavoring.

special adj distinguished; uncommon; designed for a particular purpose; peculiar to one person or thing.–**specially** adv.

specialist n a person who concentrates on a particular area of study or activity, esp in medicine.

speciality see **specialty**.

specialize vi to concentrate on a particular area of study or activity. * vt to adapt to a particular use or purpose.–**specialization** n.

specialty n (pl **specialties**) a special skill or interest; a special product.–also **speciality**.

species n (pl **species**) a class of plants or animals with the same main characteristics, enabling interbreeding; a distinct kind or sort.

specific adj explicit; definite; of a particular kind. * n a characteristic quality or influence; a drug effective in treating a particular disease.–**specifically** adv.–**specificity** n.

specification n a requirement; (pl) detailed description of dimensions, materials, etc of something.

specify vt (**specifying, specified**) to state specifically; to set down as a condition.–**specifier** n.

specimen n (plant, animal, etc) an example of a particular species; a sample; (inf) a person.

specious adj apparently true, but in fact false.–**speciously** adv.–**speciousness** n.

speck n a small spot; a fleck.

speckle n a small mark of a different color. * vt to mark with speckles.

spectacle n an unusual or interesting scene; a large public show; an object of derision or ridicule; (pl) a pair of glasses.–**spectacled** adj.

spectacular adj impressive; astonishing.–**spectacularly** adv.

spectator n an onlooker.

specter n an apparition or ghost; a haunting mental image.–also **spectre**.

spectra see **spectrum**.

spectral adj of or like a specter; of or produced by a spectrum.–**spectrality** adv.–**spectrally** adv.

spectre see **specter**.

spectrum n (pl **spectra**) the range of color which is produced when a white light is passed through a prism; any similar distribution of wave frequencies; a broad range.

speculate vi to theorize, to conjecture; to make investments in the hope of making a profit.–**speculation** n.–**speculative** adj.–**speculatively** adv.–**speculator** n.

speculum n (pl **specula, speculums**) a medical instrument for dilating and examining a bodily passage or cavity; a mirror used as a reflector in an optical instrument such as a telescope.

sped see **speed**.

speech n the action or power of speaking; a public address or talk; language, dialect.

speechless adj unable to speak; silent, as from shock; impossible to express in words.–**speechlessly** adv.–**speechlessness** n.

speed n quickness; rapidity or rate of motion; (photog) the sensitivity of film to light; (sl) an amphetamine drug. * vi (**speeding, sped** or **speeded**) to go quickly, to hurry; to drive (a vehicle) at an illegally high speed.–**speeding** n the driving of a vehicle at an illegally high or dangerous speed.

speedometer n an instrument in a motor vehicle for measuring its speed.

speedway n the sport of racing light motorcycles around dirt or cinder tracks; a stadium for motorcycle racing; a road reserved for fast traffic.

speedy adj (**speedier, speediest**) quick; prompt.–**speedily** adv.–**speediness** n.

spell[1] n a sequence of words used to perform magic; fascination.

spell[2] vb (**spelling, spelt** or **spelled**) vt to name or write down in correct order the letters to form a word; (letters) to form a word when placed in the correct order; to indicate; (with **out**) to read slowly and painstakingly; to explain in detail; to discern, realize the meaning of. * vi to spell words.

spell[3] n a usu indefinite period of time; a period of duty in a certain occupation or activity. * vt to relieve, stand in for.

spellbound adj entranced, enthralled.

spelling bee n a spelling contest.

spelt see **spell**[2].

spend vb (**spending, spent**) vt to pay out (money); to concentrate (one's time or energy) on an activity; to pass, as time; to use up. * vi to pay out money.–**spender** n.

spendthrift n a person who spends money wastefully or extravagantly.

spent[1] see **spend**.

spent[2] adj consumed, used up; physically drained, exhausted.

sperm n semen; the male reproductive cell.

spermatozoon n (pl **spermatozoa**) any of the male reproductive cells present in the semen.

spermicide n a substance that destroys sperm.–**spermicidal** adj.

sperm whale n a large whale with a blunt head which is hunted for its oil and spermaceti.

spew vti to vomit; to flow or gush forth. * n something spewed.

sphere n a ball, globe or other perfectly round object; a field of activity or interest; a social class.–**spherical, spheric** adj.–**spherically** adv.

sphinx n any of various massive statues with a lion's body and human head erected by the ancient Egyptians; a mysterious or enigmatic person.

spice n an aromatic vegetable substance used for flavoring and seasoning food; these substances collectively; something that adds zest or interest. * vt to flavor with spice; to add zest to.

spicy adj (**spicier, spiciest**) flavored with spice; pungent; (inf) somewhat scandalous or indecent.–**spicily** adv.–**spiciness** n.

spider n a small wingless creature (arachnid) with eight legs, and abdominal spinnerets for spinning silk threads to make webs.

spidery adj thin, and angular, like a spider's legs.

spied see **spy**.

spiel n glib talk intended to cajole or persuade.–also vi.

spigot n a small stopper or tap for a cask; a faucet.

spike n a long heavy nail; a sharp-pointed projection, as on a shoe to prevent slipping; an ear of corn, etc; a cluster of stalkless flowers arranged on a long stem. * vt to pierce with a spike.–**spiky** adj.

spill vti (**spilling, spilled** or **spilt**) to cause, esp unintentionally, to flow out of a container; to shed (blood). * n something spilled.–**spillage** n.

spilt see **spill**.

spin vb (**spinning, spun**) vt to rotate rapidly; to draw out and twist fibers into thread or yarn; (spiders, silkworm, etc) to make a web or cocoon; to draw out (a story) to a great length; (with **out**) to prolong, extend; to cause to last longer, eg money. * vi to seem to be spinning from dizziness; (wheels) to turn rapidly without imparting forward motion. * n a swift rotation; (inf) a brief, fast ride in a vehicle; an emphasis or slant imparted to information, proposals or policies.

spina bifida n a congenital abnormality in the formation of the spine causing the meninges to protrude, and associated with partial paralysis.

spinach n a plant with large, green edible leaves.

spinal adj of or relating to the spine or spinal cord.–**spinally** adv.

spinal column n the skeleton of jointed vertebrae and interconnecting cartilaginous tissue that surrounds and protects the spinal cord.–also **spine**, **backbone**.

spinal cord n the cord of nerves enclosed by the spinal column.

spindle n the notched rod by which thread is twisted in spinning; a pin around which machinery turns.

spindly adj (**spindlier, spindliest**) tall and slender; frail.

spine n a sharp, stiff projection, as a thorn of the cactus or quill of a porcupine; a spinal column; the backbone of a book.

spineless adj lacking a spine; weak-willed; irresolute.–**spinelessly** adv.–**spinelessness** n.

spinning wheel n a small household machine with a wheel-driven spindle for spinning yarn from fibre.

spin-off n a product or benefit derived incidentally from existing research and development.

spinster n an unmarried woman.

spiny adj (**spinier, spiniest**) covered with spines or thorns; troublesome.

spiral adj winding round in a continuous curve up or down a centre or pole. * n a helix; a spiral line or shape; a continuous expansion or decrease, eg in inflation. * vi (**spiraling, spiraled** or **spiralling, spiralled**) to move up or down in a spiral curve; to increase or decrease steadily.

spire n the tapering point of a steeple.

spirit n soul; a supernatural being, as a ghost, angel, etc; (pl) disposition; mood; vivacity, courage, etc; real meaning; essential quality; (usu pl) distilled alcoholic liquor. * vt to carry (away, off, etc) secretly and swiftly.

spirited adj full of life; animated.–**spiritedly** adv.–**spiritedness** n.

spirit level n a glass tube filled with liquid containing an air bubble and mounted in a frame, used for testing whether a surface is level.

spiritual adj of the soul; religious; sacred. * n an emotional religious song, originating among the Black slaves in the American South.–**spirituality** n.–**spiritually** adv.

spiritualism n the belief that the spirits of the dead can communicate with the living, as through mediums.–**spiritualist** n.

spirt see **spurt**.

spit[1] n a pointed iron rod on which meat is roasted; a long narrow strip of land projecting into the water. * vt (**spitting, spitted**) to fix as on a spit, impale.

spit[2] vb (**spitting, spat** or **spit**) vt to eject from the mouth; to utter with scorn. * vi to expel saliva from the mouth; (hot fat) to splutter; to rain lightly. * n saliva.

spite n ill will; malice. * vt to annoy spitefully, to vex.–**spiteful** adj.

spittle n saliva ejected from the mouth.

splash vti to spatter with liquid; to move with a splash; to display prominently; (with **down**) to land (a spacecraft) on water. * n something splashed; a patch of color; a small amount, esp of a mixer added to an alcoholic drink.–**splashy** adj.

splashdown n (the scheduled time of) the landing of a spacecraft on the ocean.

splatter vti to splash, spatter.–also n.

splay vti to turn out at an angle; to spread out.

spleen n a large lymphatic organ in the upper left part of the abdomen which modifies the blood structure; spitefulness; ill humor.

splendid adj brilliant; magnificent; (inf) very good.–**splendidly** adv.–**splendidness** n.

splendor, splendour n brilliance; magnificence; grandeur.–**splendorous, splendrous** adj.

splice vt to unite (two ends of a rope) by intertwining the strands; to connect (two pieces of timber) by overlapping.–also n.

splint n a rigid structure used to immobilize and support a fractured limb; a splinter of wood for lighting fires. * vt to put in splints.

splinter *n* a thin, sharp piece of wood, glass, or metal broken off. * *vti* to break off into splinters.–**splintery** *adj*.

split *vti* (**splitting, split**) to break apart (usu into two pieces); to separate into factions; to divide into shares; to burst or tear. * *n* the act or process of splitting; a narrow gap made (as if) by splitting; a dessert consisting of sliced fruit, esp banana, with ice cream, nuts, etc; (*often pl*) the act of extending the legs in opposite directions and lowering the the body to the floor. * *adj* divided; torn; fractured.

split-level *adj* (*building*) having rooms or areas in one part less than a full story higher than another that adjoins them.

split-screen *n* (*cinema, television*) a technique involving the simultaneous projection of different images onto separate areas of the screen.

split second *n* a very brief moment, an instant.–**split-second** *adj*.

splurge *vi* to spend lavishly (on); to show off. * *n* an extravagant display, esp of wealth.

splutter *vi* to spit out food or drops of liquid noisily; to utter words confusedly and hurriedly.–*also n*.

spoil *vb* (**spoiling, spoiled** *or* **spoilt**) *vt* to damage as to make useless, etc; to impair the enjoyment, etc, of; to overindulge (a child). * *vi* to become spoiled; to decay, etc, as food. * *npl* booty, valuables seized in war; the opportunities for financial gain from holding public office.

spoiler *n* a projecting structure on an aircraft wing that increases drag to reduce lift; any similar structure for increasing the stability of vehicles at high speed.

spoil-sport *n* (*inf*) a person who spoils the fun of others.

spoilt *see* **spoil**.

spoke[1], **spoken** *see* **speak**.

spoke[2] *n* any of the braces extending from the hub to the rim of a wheel.

spokesman *n* (*pl* **spokesmen**) a person authorized to speak on behalf of others.–**spokeswoman** *nf* (*pl* **spokeswomen**).

sponge *n* a plantlike marine animal with an internal skeleton of elastic interlacing horny fibers; a piece of natural or manmade sponge for washing or cleaning. * *vt* to wipe with a sponge. * *vi* (*inf*) to scrounge.–**sponginess** *n*.–**spongy** *adj*.

sponge cake *n* a sweet cake with a light porous texture.

sponsor *n* a person or organization that pays the expenses connected with an artistic production or sports event in return for advertising; in US, a business firm, etc that pays for a radio or TV programme advertising its product. * *vt* to act as sponsor for.–**sposorship** *n*.

spontaneous *adj* arising naturally; unpremeditated.–**spontaneity** *n*.–**spontaneously** *adv*.–**spontaneousness** *n*.

spontaneous combustion *n* the self-igniting of a substance through internal chemical processes such as oxidation.

spoof *n* (*sl*) a hoax or joke; a light satire.–*also vti*.

spook *n* (*inf*) a ghost; (*inf*) a spy. * *vt* to frighten.–**spooky** *adj*.

spool *n* a cylinder, bobbin, or reel, upon which thread, photographic film, etc, are wound. * *vt* to wind on a spool.

spoon *n* utensil with a shallow bowl and a handle, for eating, stirring, etc.–**spoonful** *n*.

spoonerism *n* the accidental transposition of the initial letters or opening syllables of two or more words with amusing results, e.g *half-warmed fish* for *half-formed wish*.

sporadic *adj* occurring here and there; intermittent.–**sporadically** *adv*.

spore *n* an asexual reproductive body produced by algae, fungae and ferns capable of giving rise to new individuals.

sport *n* an athletic game or pastime, often competitive and involving physical capability; good-humored joking; (*inf*) a person regarded as fair and abiding by the rules. * *vi* to play, to frolic. * *vt* (*inf*) to display, flaunt.

sportsman *n* (*pl* **sportsmen**) a person engaged in sport; a person who plays by the rules, is fair, is a good loser, etc.–**sportswoman**

nf (*pl* **sportswomen**).–**sportsmanlike, sportsmanly** *adj*.–**sportsmanship** *n*.

sporty *adj* (**sportier, sportiest**) (*inf*) fond of sport; flashy, ostentatious.–**sportily** *adv*.–**sportiness** *n*.

spot *n* a small area differing in color, etc, from the surrounding area; a stain, speck, etc; a taint on character or reputation; a small quantity or amount; a locality; (*inf*) a difficult or embarrassing situation; a place on an entertainment programme; a spotlight. * *vt* (**spotting, spotted**) to mark with spots; (*inf*) to identify or recognise; to glimpse.

spot check *n* a sudden random examination.–**spot-check** *vt*.

spotless *adj* immaculate.–**spotlessly** *adv*.–**spotlessness** *n*.

spotlight *n* a powerful light used to illuminate a small area; intense public attention. * *vt* (**spotlighting, spotlighted** *or* **spotlit**) to illuminate with a spotlight; to focus attention on.

spotty *adj* (**spottier, spottiest**) marked with spots, esp on the skin; intermittent, uneven.–**spottily** *adv*.–**spottiness** *n*.

spouse *n* (one's) husband or wife.

spout *vti* to eject in a strong jet or spurts; (*inf*) to drone on boringly. * *n* a projecting lip or tube for pouring out liquids.

sprain *n* a wrenching of a joint by sudden twisting or tearing of ligaments.–*also vt*.

sprang *see* **spring**.

sprat *n* a small food fish related to the herring; a small or young herring.

sprawl *vi* to lie down with the limbs stretched out in an untidy manner; to spread out in a straggling way. * *n* a sprawling position.

spray[1] *n* fine particles of a liquid; mist; an aerosol or atomizer. * *vti* to direct a spray (on); to apply as a spray.

spray[2] *n* a number of flowers on one branch; a decorative flower arrangement; an ornament resembling this.

spread *vt* (**spreading, spread**) to extend; to unfold or open; to disseminate; to distribute; to apply a coating (eg butter). * *vi* to expand in all directions. * *n* an expanse; (*inf*) a feast; food which can be spread on bread; a bed cover.

spread-eagle *vt* to stand or lie with the limbs outstretched.–**spread-eagled** *adj*.

spreadsheet *n* a computer program that allows easy entry and manipulation of text and figures, used for accounting and financial planning.

spree *n* (*inf*) excessive indulgence, eg in spending money, alcohol consumption, etc.

sprier *see* **spry**.

sprig *n* a twig with leaves on it.

sprightly *adj* (**sprightlier, sprightliest**) full of life or energy.–**sprightliness** *n*.

spring *vb* (**springing, sprang** *or* **sprung, *pp* sprung**) *vi* to move suddenly, as by elastic force; to arise suddenly; to originate. * *vt* to cause to spring up, to cause to operate suddenly. * *n* a leap; the season between winter and summer; a coiled piece of wire that springs back to its original shape when stretched; the source of a stream.

springboard *n* a flexible board used by divers and in gymnastics to provided added height or impetus.

springbok *n* a South African gazelle.

spring-clean *vi* to clean (a house, etc) thoroughly.–**spring clean** *n*.

springy *adj* (**springier, springiest**) elastic, resilient; light, spongy.–**springily** *adv*.–**springiness** *n*.

sprinkle *vt* to scatter in droplets or particles (on something).–*also n*.

sprinkler *n* a nozzle for spraying water; a fire-extinguishing system that operates automatically on detection of smoke or heat.

sprinkling *n* a small quantity scattered randomly.

sprint *n* a short run or race at full speed. * *vi* to go at top speed.–**sprinter** *n*.

sprite *n* an elf or imp; a dainty person.

spritzer *n* a drink made with wine, usu white, and soda water.

sprocket n a wheel with a row of teeth which engage the holes in a chain, or a reel of film, in order to turn it.

sprout n a new shoot on a plant; a small cabbage-like vegetable. * vt to put forth (shoots). * vi to begin to grow.

spruce[1] adj smart, neat, trim. * vt to smarten.

spruce[2] n an evergreen tree of the pine family with a conical head and soft light wood.

sprung see **spring**.

spry adj (**sprier**, **spriest** or **spryer**, **spryest**) vigorous, agile.– **spryly** av.–**spryness** n.

spume n foam; surf; froth.

spun see **spin**.

spunk n a spark, a match; (sl) pluck, courage.–**spunky** adj.– **spunkily** adv.

spur n a small metal wheel on a rider's heel, with sharp points for urging on the horse; encouragement, stimulus; a hard sharp projection. * vt (**spurring**, **spurred**) to urge on.

spurious adj not legitimate or genuine; false.–**spuriously** adv.–**spuriousness** n.

spurn vt to reject with disdain. * n disdainful rejection.

spurt vt to gush forth in a sudden stream or jet. * n a sudden stream or jet; a burst of activity.–also **spirt**.

sputnik n the name used for series of artificial satellites launched by the former Soviet Union in the 1950s and 1960s (Russian *travelling companion*).

sputter vi to splutter.–also n.

sputum n (pl **sputa**) saliva and mucus.

spy n (pl **spies**) a secret agent employed to collect information on rivals. * vb (**spying**, **spied**) vi to keep under secret surveillance, act as a spy (usu with **on**). * vt to catch sight of.

sq abbr = sequence; squadron; square.

squabble vi to quarrel noisily. * n a noisy, petty quarrel.–also n.

squad n a small group of soldiers which form a working unit; a section of a police force; (sport) a group of players from which a team is selected.

squadron n a unit of warships, cavalry, military aircraft, etc.

squalid adj filthy; neglected, sordid; degrading.–**squalidly** adv.–**squalidness** n.

squall vi to cry out loudly (like a baby). * n a loud cry; a violent gust of wind.

squalor n foulness; dirt, filth.

squander vt to spend extravagantly or wastefully.

square n a shape with four sides of equal length and four right angles; an open space in a town, surrounded by buildings; (inf) an old-fashioned person; an instrument for drawing right angles; the product of a number multiplied by itself. * adj square-shaped; forming a square; forming a right angle (with); (financial account) settled; fair, honest; equal in score; (inf) old-fashioned. * vt to make square; to multiply (a quantity) by itself; (with **away**) (inf) to put in order, tidy up. * vi to agree.– **squarely** adv.–**squareness** n.

square bracket n either of a pair of written or printed characters [ ] used to enclose text or in mathematical expressions.

square dance n any of various dances in which the participants join hands to form squares.–**square-dance** vi.

square root n a number that when multiplied by itself produces a given number (2 is the square root of 4).

squash[1] vt to squeeze, press, or crush; to suppress. * vi to squelch; to crowd. * n a crushed mass; a crowd of people pressed together; a fruit-flavored drink; a game played in a walled court with rackets and rubber ball.–**squashy** adj.

squash[2] n (pl **squashes**, **squash**) a marrow or gourd eaten as a vegetable.

squat vi (**squatting**, **squatted**) to crouch down upon the heels; to occupy land or property, without permission or title. * adj short and dumpy. * n the act of squatting; a house that is occupied by squatters.–**squatter** n.

squawk n a loud, raucous call or cry, as of a bird; (inf) a loud protest.–also vi.

squeak vi to make a high-pitched cry. * n a squeaky noise.– **squeaker** n.–**squeaky** adj.

squeal vi to make a shrill and prolonged cry or sound; (sl) to be an informer; to protest.

squeamish adj easily nauseated; easily shocked or disgusted.– **squeamishly** adv.–**squeamishness** n.

squeeze vt to press firmly, compress; to grasp tightly; to hug; to force (through, into) by pressing; to extract liquid, juice, from by pressure; to obtain (money, etc) by force, to harass. * n squeezing or being squeezed; a hug; a small amount squeezed from something; a crowding together; financial pressure or hardship.–**squeezable** adj.

squelch vi to walk through soft, wet ground, making a sucking noise. * vt to crush or squash completely. * n a squelching sound.

squid n (pl **squids**, **squid**) an edible mollusc, related to the cuttlefish, with a long body and ten arms.

squiggle n a short wavy line, esp handwritten. * vi to squirm; to wriggle.–**squiggly** adj.

squint vi to half close or cross the eyes; to glance sideways. * n crossed eyes, as caused by a visual disorder; a glance sideways; (inf) a look. * adj squinting; (inf) crooked.

squire n a country gentleman, esp the leading landowner in a district.

squirm vi to writhe; to wriggle; to feel embarrassed or ashamed.

squirrel n (pl **squirrels**, **squirrel**) a bushy tailed rodent with gray or reddish fur which lives in trees and feeds on nuts. * vt (**squirreling**, **squirreled** or **squirrelling**, **squirrelled**) (usu with **away**) to hoard.

squirt vt to eject liquid in a jet. * vi to spurt. * n a jet of liquid; (inf) an insignificant person.

squish vt to crush, esp so as to produce a squelching sound. * vi to make or move with a squelching sound. * n a soft squelching sound.–**squishy** adj.

Sr abbr = Senior; Se-or.

St abbr = Saint.

St. abbr = Street.

stab vt (**stabbing**, **stabbed**) to injure with a knife or pointed weapon; to pain suddenly and sharply. * vi to thrust at (as if) with a pointed weapon. * n an act or instance of stabbing; a wound made by stabbing; a sudden sensation, as of emotion, pain, etc; (inf) an attempt.

stabilize vti to make or become stable or steady.–**stabilization** n.

stabilizer n a device for stabilizing (an aircraft, ship, bicycle, etc).

stable[1] adj steady or firm; firmly established; permanent; not decomposing readily.–**stability** n.

stable[2] n a building where horses or cattle are kept; a group of racehorses belonging to one owner; a group of people working for or trained by a specific establishment, as writers, performers, etc. * vti to put, keep, or live in a stable.

staccato adj (musical notes) short, abrupt; (speech) sharp, abrupt, disconnected. * adv in a staccato manner.

stack n a large neatly arranged pile (of hay, papers, records, etc); a chimney stack; (inf) a large amount of; a number of aircraft circling an airport waiting for permission to land. * vt to pile, arrange in a stack.

stadia see **stadium**.

stadium n (pl **stadiums**, **stadia**) a sports ground surrounded by tiers of seats.

staff n (pl **staves**) a strong stick or pole; (mus) one of the five horizontal lines upon which music is written (–also **stave**); (pl **staffs**) a body of officers who help a commanding officer, or perform special duties; the workers employed in an establishment; the teachers or lecturers of an educational institution. * vt to provide with staff.

stag n a full-grown male deer. * adj (party) for men only.

stage n a degree or step in a process; a raised platform, esp for acting on; (with **the**) the theater, the theatrical calling; any field of action or setting; a portion of a journey; a propulsion unit of a space rocket discarded when its fuel is spent. * *vt* to perform a play on the stage; to plan, organize (an event).

stagecoach *n* a four-wheeled vehicle drawn by horses, that formerly carried passengers or mail.

stage fright *n* nervousness at appearing before an audience.

stage manager *n* a person responsible for the stage arrangements prior to and during the performance of a play.

stagger *vi* to walk unsteadily, to totter. * *vt* to astound; to give a shock to; to arrange so as not to overlap; to alternate.

stagnant *adj* (*water*) not flowing, standing still with a revolting smell; unchanging, dull.–**stagnancy** *n*.

stagnate *vi* to be, or become, stagnant.–**stagnation** *n*.

stag party *n* a party for men only, usu given for one who is due to be married shortly.

staid *adj* sober; sedate; old-fashioned.–**staidly** *adv*.–**staidness** *n*.

stain *vt* to dye; to discolor with spots of something which cannot be removed. * *vi* to become stained; to produce stains. * *n* a discolored mark; a moral blemish; a dye or liquid for staining materials, eg wood.

stained glass *n* colored glass used in windows.

stainless *adj* free from stain; (materials) resistant to staining.–**stainlessly** *adv*.

stainless steel *n* a type of steel resistant to tarnishing and corrosion.

stair *n* a flight of stairs; a single step; (*pl*) a stairway.

staircase *n* a flight of stairs with banisters.

stairway *n* a staircase.

stake[1] *n* a sharpened metal or wooden post driven into the ground, as a marker or fence post; a post to which persons were tied for execution by burning; this form of execution. * *vt* to support with, tie or tether to a stake; to mark out (land) with stakes; (*with* **out**) to put under surveillance.

stake[2] *vt* to bet; (*inf*) to provide with money or resources. * *n* a bet; a financial interest; (*pl*) money risked on a race; (*pl*) the prize in a race

stakeout *n* surveillance, esp by police; premises under surveillance.

stalactite *n* an icicle-like calcium deposit hanging from the roof of a cave.

stalagmite *n* a cylindrical deposit projecting upward from the floor of a cave, caused by the dripping of water and lime from the roof.

stale *adj* deteriorated from age; tainted; musty; stagnant; jaded.–**staleness** *n*.

stalemate *n* (*chess*) a situation in which a king can only be moved in and out of check, thus causing a draw; a deadlock.–*also vt*.

stalk[1] *n* the stem of a plant.

stalk[2] *vi* to stride in a stiff or angry way; to hunt (game, prey) stealthily.–**stalker** *n*.

stall[1] *n* a compartment for one animal in a stable; a table or stand for the display or sale of goods; a stalling of an engine; (*aircraft*) a loss of lift and downward plunge due to an excessive decrease in airspeed; (*pl*) (*Brit*) the seats on the ground floor of a theater. * *vti* (*vehicle engine*) to stop or cause to stop suddenly, eg by misuse of the clutch; (*aircraft*) to lose or cause to lose lift because of an excessive reduction in airspeed.

stall[2] *vti* to play for time; to postpone or delay. * *n* (*inf*) any action used in stalling.

stallion *n* an uncastrated male horse, esp one kept for breeding.

stalwart *adj* strong, sturdy; resolute; dependable. * *n* a loyal, hardworking supporter.

stamen *n* (*pl* **stamens, stamina**) the pollen-bearing part of a flower.

stamina *n* strength; staying power.

stammer *vti* to pause or falter in speaking; to stutter.–*also n*.–**stammerer** *n*.

stamp *vt* to put a mark on; to imprint with an official seal; to affix a postage stamp; (*with* **out**) to extinguish by stamping; to

suppress, eradicate, by force. * *vi* to bring the foot down heavily (on); * *n* a postage stamp; the mark canceling a postage stamp; a block for imprinting.

stampede *n* an impulsive rush of a panic-stricken herd; a rush of a crowd.–*also vti*.

stance *n* posture; the attitude taken in a given situation.

stanch see **staunch**[2].

stanchion *n* an upright post, pillar, rod or similar support. * *vt* to provide with a stanchion.

stand *vb* (**standing, stood**) *vi* to be in an upright position; to be on, or rise to one's feet; to make resistance; to remain unchanged; to endure, tolerate; to reach a deadlock; (*with* **by**) to look on without interfering; to be available for use if required; (*with* **down**) to withdraw, resign; to leave a witness box after testifying in court; (*soldier*) to go off duty; (*with* **off**) to remain at a distance; to reach a stalemate; (*with* **up**) to rise to one's feet. * *vt* to put upright; to endure, tolerate; (*with* **by**) to remain loyal to, to defend; (*with* **off**) to (cause to) keep at a distance; to lay off (employees) temporarily; (*with* **up**) to resist; to withstand criticism, close examination, etc; (*inf*) to fail to keep an appointment with. * *n* a strong opinion; a standing position; a standstill; a place for taxis awaiting hire; (*pl*) a structure for spectators; the place taken by a witness for testifying in court; a piece of furniture for hanging things from; a stall or booth for a small retail business.

standard *n* a flag, banner, or emblem; an upright pole, pillar; an authorized weight or measure; a criterion; an established or accepted level of achievement; (*pl*) moral principles. * *adj* serving as a standard; typical.

standardize *vt* to make standard; to reduce to a standard.–**standardization** *n*.–**standardizer** *n*.

stand-by *n* (*pl* **stand-bys**) a person or thing held in readiness for use in an emergency, etc.–*also adj*.

stand-in *n* a substitute; a person who takes the place of an actor during the preparation of a scene or in stunts.–*also vi*.

standing *n* status or reputation; length of service, duration. * *adj* upright; permanent; (*jump*) performed from a stationary position.

standing order *n* an instruction to a bank by a depositor to pay fixed amounts at regular intervals (for bills, etc); a regulation governing conduct, procedure, etc in an organization or assembly.

standoff *n* a deadlock, stalemate.

standpoint *n* a point of view, opinion.

standstill *n* a complete halt.

stand-up *adj* (*comedian*) telling jokes standing alone in front of an audience.

stank see **stink**.

stanza *n* a group of lines which form a division of a poem.

staple[1] *n* a principal commodity of trade or industry of a region or nation; a main constituent. * *adj* chief.

staple[2] *n* a U-shaped thin piece of wire for fastening. * *vt* to fasten with a staple.

star *n* any one of the celestial bodies, esp those visible by night which appear as small points of light, including planets, comets, meteors, and less commonly the sun and moon; a figure with five points; an exceptionally successful or skillful person; a famous actor, actress, musician, etc. * *vti* (**starring, starred**) to feature or be featured as a star.

starboard *n* the right side of a ship or aircraft when facing the bow.

starch *n* a white, tasteless, food substance found in potatoes, cereal, etc; a fabric stiffener based on this. * *vt* to stiffen with starch.–**starchy** *adj*.

stardom *n* the fame and status enjoyed by celebrities or stars.

stare *vi* to gaze fixedly, as in horror, astonishment, etc; to glare. * *n* a fixed gaze.

starfish *n* (*pl* **starfish, starfishes**) an echinoderm consisting of a central disk from which five arms radiate outward.

stark *adj* bare; plain; blunt; utter. * *adv* completely.–**starkly** *adv*.–**starkness** *n*.

starlet *n* a young actress regarded as a potential star.

starling *n* any of a family of small songbirds, esp a common European bird with black plumage tinged with green that congregates in large groups.

Stars and Stripes *n sing* (*with* **the**) the national flag of the USA consisting of 13 alternate red and white stripes and a blue square filled with white stars representing the individual states.–*also* **Star-Spangled Banner**.

Star Spangled Banner *n* (*with* **the**) the national anthem of the USA; the Stars and Stripes.

star-studded *adj* featuring many celebrities.

start *vi* to commence, begin; to jump involuntarily, from fright. * *vt* to begin. * *n* a beginning; a slight involuntary body movement; a career opening.

starter *n* a person who starts something, esp an official who signals the beginning of a race; a competitor in a race; the first course of a meal; a small electric motor used to start an internal combustion engine (–*also* **self-starter**).

startle *vti* to be, or cause to be, frightened or surprised.–**startling** *adj*.

starve *vi* to die or suffer from a lack of food. * *vt* deprive (a person) of food; to deprive (of) anything necessary.–**starvation** *n*.

stash *vt* to hide (money, etc) for future use. * *n* a hiding place; something hidden; (*sl*) drugs hidden for personal consumption.

state *n* condition; frame of mind; position in society; ceremonious style; (*with cap*) an area or community with its own government, or forming a federation under a sovereign government. * *adj* of the state or State; public; ceremonial. * *vt* to express in words; to specify, declare officially.

state department *n* the government department that handles foreign affairs; foreign office.

stateless *adj* not having a nationality.–**statelessness** *n*.

stately *adj* (**statelier, stateliest**) dignified; majestic.–**stateliness** *n*.

statement *n* a formal announcement; a declaration; a document showing one's bank balance.

state-of-the-art *adj* using the most advanced technology yet possible.

stateside *adj* of, in, or to the US.–*also adv*.

statesman *n* (*pl* **statesmen**) a well-known and experienced politician.–**statesmanship** *n*.

static *adj* fixed; stationary; at rest. * *n* electrical interference causing noise on radio or TV.

static electricity *n* electricity which is stationary as opposed to flowing in a current.

station *n* a railway or bus terminal or stop; headquarters (of the emergency services); military headquarters; (*inf*) a TV channel; position in society, standing. * *vt* to assign to a post, place, office.

stationary *adj* not moving.

stationer *n* a dealer in stationery, office supplies, etc.

stationery *n* writing materials, esp paper and envelopes.

station wagon *n* a car with extra carrying space reached through a rear door.–*also* **estate car**.

statistic *n* a fact obtained from analyzing information expressed in numbers.

statistics *n sing* the branch of mathematics dealing with the collection, analysis and presentation of numerical data.–**statistical** *adj*.–**statistician** *n*.

statue *n* a representation of a human or animal form that is carved or moulded.

statuesque *adj* like a statue.–**statuesquely** *adv*.–**statuesqueness** *n*.

statuette *n* a small statue, figurine.

stature *n* the standing height of a person; level of attainment.

status *n* (*pl* **statuses**) social or professional position or standing; prestige; condition or standing from the point of view of the law, position of affairs.

status quo *n* the existing state of affairs.

status symbol *n* a possession that indicates high social standing, wealth, etc.

statute *n* a law enacted by a legislature; a regulation.–**statutory** *adj*.

staunch[1] *adj* loyal; dependable.–**staunchly** *adv*.–**staunchness** *n*.

staunch[2] *vt* to stem the flow of, as blood. * *vi* to cease to flow.–*also* **stanch**.

stave *n* a piece of wood of a cask or barrel; (*mus*) a staff. * *vt* (**staving, staved** *or* **stove**) (*usu with* **in**) to smash or dent inward.

staves *see* **staff**.

stay[1] *n* a rope supporting a mast

stay[2] *vi* to remain in a place; to wait; to reside temporarily. * *vt* to support; to endure; to stop, restrain. * *n* a suspension of legal proceedings; a short time spent as a visitor or guest.

staying power *n* stamina.

STD *abbr* = sexually transmitted disease; subscriber trunk dialing.

steadfast *adj* firm, fixed; resolute.–**steadfastly** *adv*.–**steadfastness** *n*.

steady *adj* (**steadier, steadiest**) firm, stable; regular, constant; calm, unexcitable. * *n* (*pl* **steadies**) (*inf*) a regular boyfriend or girlfriend. * *vti* (**steadying, steadied**) to make or become steady.–**steadily** *adv*.–**steadiness** *n*.

steak *n* a slice of meat, esp beef or fish, for grilling or frying.

steakhouse *n* a restaurant that specializes in steaks.

steal *vt* (**stealing, stole,** *pp* **stolen**) to take (from someone) dishonestly; to obtain secretly. * *n* (*inf*) an unbelievable bargain.

stealth *n* a manner of moving quietly and secretly.–**stealthy** *adj*.–**stealthily** *adv*.

steam *n* the hot mist or vapor created by boiling water. * *vi* to give off steam; to move by steam power; to cook with steam; (*sl*) to take part in illegal steaming; (*with* **up**) (*glasses, windows*) to become covered in condensation. * *adj* driven by steam.

steamboat *n* a boat powered by steam.

steam engine *n* a stationary or locomotive engine powered by steam.

steamer *n* a pan with a perforated bottom for cooking by steam; a ship propelled by steam engines; (*sl*) one who takes part in steaming.

steamroller *n* a vehicle with heavy rollers for pressing down road surfaces; an overpowering person or thing. * *vt* to crush (as if) with a steamroller; to obtain or influence by overpowering force.

steamy *adj* (**steamier, steamiest**) full of steam; (*inf*) erotic.–**steamily** *adv*.–**steaminess** *n*.

steel *n* an alloy of iron and carbon; strength or courage. * *adj* of, or like, steel. * *vt* to cover with steel; to harden; to nerve (oneself).

steel band *n* a band that uses percussion instruments made from oil drums.

steel wool *n* a compact mass of steel fibers used for scouring and polishing.

steely *adj* (**steelier, steeliest**) of or like steel; hard, relentless.–**steeliness** *n*.

steep[1] *adj* sloping sharply; (*inf*) excessive, exorbitant.–**steeply** *adv*.–**steepness** *n*.

steep[2] *vti* to soak or be soaked in a liquid; to saturate; to imbue.–*also n*.

steeple *n* a tower of a church, with or without a spire; the spire alone.

steeplechase *n* a horse race across country or on a course over jumps; a track race over hurdles and water jumps.–**steeplechaser** *n*.

steer[1] *n* a castrated male of the cattle family.

steer[2] *vti* to direct (a vehicle, ship, bicycle, etc) in the correct direction of travel.

steerage *n* the cheapest berths on a passenger ship.

steering *n* the mechanism that controls the direction of a ship, vehicle, etc; the practice of maneuvering non-white house buyers or tenants away from white areas.

steering committee *n* a committee that organizes the content and order of business for a legislative assembly.

stellar *adj* of, or composed of stars.

stem[1] *n* a plant stalk; the upright slender part of anything, such as a wineglass; the root of a word. * *vi* (**stemming, stemmed**) to originate (from).

stem[2] *vt* (**stemming, stemmed**) to stop, check (the flow or tide).

stench *n* a foul odor.

stencil *n* a pierced sheet of card or metal for reproducing letters by applying paint; a design so made. * *vti* (**stenciling, stenciled** or **stencilling, stencilled**) to produce (letters, etc) or designs using a stencil.–**stenciler, stenciller** *n*.

stenography *n* shorthand.–**stenographer** *n*.

stentorian *adj* (*voice*) loud, booming.

step *n* one movement of the foot ahead in walking, running, or dancing; a pace; a grade or degree; a stage toward a goal; one tread of a stair, rung of a ladder. * *vti* (**stepping, stepped**) to take a step or a number of paces.

stepbrother *n* a son of one's step-parent from a former marriage.

stepchild *n* (*pl* **stepchildren**) a stepson or stepdaughter.

stepdaughter *n* the daughter of one's spouse from a former marriage.

stepfather *n* the husband of one's remarried mother.

stepladder *n* a short portable ladder with flat steps fixed within a frame.

stepmother *n* the wife of one's remarried father.

stepping stone *n* a stone or stones allowing a stream, puddle, etc to be crossed by foot; a means of advancing toward some end.

stepsister *n* the daughter of one's step-parent from a former marriage

stepson *n* the son of one's spouse from a former marriage

stereo *n* (*pl* **stereos**) a hi-fi or record player with two loudspeakers; stereophonic sound. * *adj* stereophonic.

stereophonic *adj* (*sound reproduction system*) using two separate channels for recording and transmission to create a spatial effect.–**stereophonically** *adv*.–**stereophony** *n*.

stereoscope *n* an optical device which blends two images viewed from a slightly different aspect into a single three-dimensional picture.–**stereoscopic** *adj*.

stereotype *n* a fixed, general image of a person or thing shared by many people.–*also vt*.

sterile *adj* unable to produce offspring, fruit, seeds, or spores; fruitless; free from germs.–**sterility** *n*.

sterilize *vt* to render incapable of reproduction; to free from germs.–**sterilization** *n*.–**sterilizer** *n*.

sterling *n* the British system of money. * *adj* of excellent character.

stern[1] *adj* severe; austere, harsh.–**sternly** *adv*.–**sternness** *n*.

stern[2] *n* the rear part of a boat or ship

sternum *n* (*pl* **sterna, sternums**) the breastbone.

steroid *n* any of a large number of compounds sharing the same chemical structure, including sterols and many hormones.

stethoscope *n* an instrument used to detect body sounds.–**stethoscopic** *adj*.

stetson *n* a man's felt hat with a broad brim and high crown.

stevedore *n* a laborer who loads and unloads ships.

stew *n* a meal of cooked meat with vegetables. * *vt* to cook slowly.

steward *n* a manager (of property); a race organizer; a person who serves food on an aircraft or ship and looks after passengers.

stewardess *n* a woman steward on an aircraft or ship.

stick[1] *vb* (**sticking, stuck**) *vt* to pierce or stab; to attach with glue, adhesive tape, etc; (*with* **up**) (*inf*) to rob at gunpoint. * *vi* to cling to, to adhere; to stay close to; to be held up; (*with* **around**) (*inf*) to wait in the vicinity, to linger; (*with* **by**) to remain faithful to; to stay close to.

stick[2] *n* a broken off shoot or branch of a tree; a walking stick; a hockey stick; a rod.

sticker *n* an adhesive label or poster.

sticking plaster *n* a thin strip of cloth with an adhesive backing for covering small cuts and abrasions.

stickler *n* a person who is scrupulous or obstinate about something.

stick-up *n* (*inf*) a robbery at gunpoint.

sticky *adj* (**stickier, stickiest**) covered with adhesive or something sweet; (*weather*) warm and humid; (*inf*) difficult.–**stickily** *adv*.–**stickiness** *n*.

stiff *adj* not flexible or supple; rigid; firm; moving with difficulty; having aching joints and muscles; formal, unfriendly; (*drink*) potent; (*breeze*) strong; (*penalty*) severe. * *n* (*sl*) a corpse. * *adv* utterly.–**stiffly** *adv*.–**stiffness** *n*.

stiffen *vti* to make or become stiff.–**stiffener** *n*.

stifle *vt* to suffocate; to smother; to suppress, hold back.

stifling *adj* excessively hot and stuffy.

stigma *n* (*pl* **stigmas, stigmata**) a social disgrace; the part of a flower that receives pollen; (*Christianity*) marks resembling the wounds of Christ thought to appear on the bodies of saintly people.

stigmatize *vt* to brand as bad or disgraceful.–**stigmatization** *n*.

stile *n* a step, or set of steps, for climbing over a wall or fence.

stiletto *n* (*pl* **stilettos**) a small slender dagger; a pointed tool for piercing holes in leather, etc; a high heel tapering to a point on a woman's shoe. * *vt* (**stilettoeing, stilettoed**) to stab with a stiletto.

still[1] *adj* motionless; calm; silent; (*drink*) not carbonated. * *n* a single photograph taken from a motion picture. * *vti* to make or become still. * *adv* continuously; nevertheless.–**stillness** *n*.

still[2] *n* an apparatus for distilling liquids, esp spirits.

stillborn *adj* born dead; (*idea, project, etc*) a failure from the start, abortive.

still life *n* (*pl* **still lifes**) a painting of inanimate objects, such as flowers, fruit, etc.

stilt *n* either of a pair of poles with footrests on which one can walk, as in a circus; a supporting column.

stilted *adj* (*speech, writing*) pompous, unnaturally formal; (*conversation*) forced, intermittent.

stimulant *n* a drug, drink, or food that increases one's heart rate and body activity.

stimulate *vt* to excite, arouse.–**stimulation** *n*.

stimulus *n* (*pl* **stimuli**) something that acts as an incentive; an agent that arouses or provokes a response in a living organism.

sting *n* a sharp pointed organ of a bee, wasp, etc, or hair on a plant, used for injecting poison; a skin wound caused by injected poison from an insect or plant; (*sl*) a swindle. * *vt* to wound with a sting; to cause to suffer mentally; to goad, incite; (*sl*) to cheat by overcharging. * *vi* to feel a sharp pain.

stingray *n* any of various rays with a whiplike tail bearing sharp venomous spines.

stingy *adj* (**stingier, stingiest**) miserly, mean.–**stingily** *adv*.–**stinginess** *n*.

stink *vi* (**stinking, stank** or **stunk**, *pp* **stunk**) to give out an offensive smell; (*sl*) to possess something in an excessive amount; (*sl*) to be extremely bad in quality. * *n* a foul smell.

stint *vt* to be frugal in the supply or allowance of something. * *vi* to be frugal, miserly. * *n* a fixed period or quantity of work; a limitation, restriction.

stipend *n* a regular payment of money as wages or for expenses, esp to a clergyman.

stipulate *vt* to specify as a condition of an agreement.–**stipulation** *n*.

stir *vb* (**stirring, stirred**) *vt* to mix, as with a spoon; to rouse; to stimulate or excite; (*with* **up**) to agitate, instigate. * *vi* to be disturbed; to move oneself; to be active. * *n* a stirring movement; tumult.

stir-fry *vt* to cook (chopped vegetables, etc) by stirring rapidly in hot oil in a wok or frying pan.

stirring *adj* rousing, exciting.–**stirringly** *adv*.

stirrup *n* a strap and flat-bottomed ring hanging from a saddle, for a rider's foot.

stitch *n* a single in-and-out movement of a threaded needle in sewing; a single loop of a yarn in knitting or crocheting; a sudden, sharp pain, esp in the side. * *vti* to sew.

stock *n* raw material; goods on hand; shares of corporate capital, or the certificates showing such ownership; lineage, family, race; a store; the cattle, horses, etc, kept on a farm; the broth obtained by boiling meat, bones, and vegetables as a foundation for soup, etc. * *vt* to supply; to keep in store. * *adj* standard; hackneyed.

stockade *n* a defensive enclosure or barrier of stakes fixed in the ground.

stockbroker *n* a person who deals in stocks.

stockholder *n* an owner of corporate stock.

stocking *n* a sock; a nylon covering for a woman's leg, supported by suspenders or a garter belt.

stock market, stock exchange *n* the market for dealing in stocks and shares.

stockpile *n* a reserve supply of essentials.–*also vt*.

stock-still *adv* motionless.

stocky *adj* (**stockier, stockiest**) short and sturdy.–**stockily** *adv*.–**stockiness** *n*.

stodgy *adj* (**stodgier, stodgiest**) (*food*) thick, heavy and indigestible; uninteresting.–**stodgily** *adv*.–**stodginess** *n*.

stoic *n* a person who suffers hardship without showing emotion.–**stoical** *adj*.–**stoically** *adv*.–**stoicism** *n*.

stoke *vt* to stir and feed (a fire) with fuel.

stole[1] *see* **steal**.

stole[2] *n* a long scarf or piece of fur worn on the shoulders.

stolen *see* **steal**.

stolid *adj* impassive; unemotional.–**stolidity** *n*.–**stolidly** *adv*.

stomach *n* the organ where food is digested; the belly. * *vt* to put up with.

stomach pump *n* a suction pump that empties the contents of the stomach through a long tube inserted orally.

stomp *vti* to walk with heavy steps; to stamp. * *n* an early jazz dance.

stone *n* a small lump of rock; a precious stone or gem; the hard seed of a fruit; (*pl* **stone**) a unit of weight (14 lb./6.35 kg). * *vt* to throw stones at; to remove stones from (fruit).

stoned *adj* (*inf*) under the influence of drink or drugs.

stone's throw *n* a short distance.

stonewall *vi* to obstruct or hinder, esp in politics and government.

stonewashed *adj* (*clothes*) made to appear worn and faded by the abrasive action of pumice particles.

stony, stoney *adj* (**stonier, stoniest**) of, like, or full of stones; unfeeling, heartless.–**stonily** *adv*.–**stoniness** *n*.

stony-broke *adj* (*inf*) completely without money.

stony-hearted *adj* unfeeling, cruel.–**stony-heartedness** *n*.

stood *see* **stand**.

stooge *n* (*sl*) a performer who feeds lines to a comedian; a person subordinate to or dominated by another; a stool pigeon. * *vi* to act as a stooge.

stool *n* a seat or a support for the back when sitting, with no back or arms; matter evacuated from the bowels.

stoop[1] *vti* to bend the body forward and downward; to degrade oneself; to deign.–*also n*.

stoop[2] *n* a porch or small landing with stairs at the entrance to a house or building.

stooped *adj* hunched.

stop *vb* (**stopping, stopped**) *vt* to halt; to prevent; to intercept; to plug or block. * *vi* to cease; to come to an end; to stay. * *n* an act or instance of stopping; an impediment; (a knob controlling)

a set of organ pipes; any of the standard settings of the aperture in a camera lens, f-stop; a regular stopping place for a bus or train; a punctuation mark, esp full stop.

stopgap *n* a temporary substitute, expedient.

stopover *n* a short break in a journey.

stoppage *n* stopping or being stopped; an obstruction; a deduction from pay; a concerted cessation of work by employees, as during a strike.

stopper *n* a cork or bung.

stopwatch *n* a watch that can be started and stopped, used for timing sporting events.

storage *n* storing or being stored; an area reserved for storing; (*comput*) the storing of data in a computer memory or on disk, tape, etc.

store *n* a large supply of goods for future use; a warehouse; a shop. * *vt* to set aside; to put in a warehouse, etc; (*comput*) to put (data) into a computer memory or onto a storage device.

store card *n* a charge card issued by a store or chain of stores for the purchase of goods there only.

stork *n* a long-necked and long-legged wading bird.

storm *n* a heavy fall of rain, snow, etc with strong winds; a violent commotion; a furore; (*mil*) an attack on a fortified place. * *vt* to rush, invade. * *vi* to be angry; to rain, snow hard.–**stormy** *adj*.

story[1] *n* (*pl* **stories**) a narrative of real or imaginary events; a plot of a literary work; an anecdote; an account; (*inf*) a lie; a news article.

story[2] *n* (*pl* **stories**) a horizontal division of a building, a storey; a set of rooms occupying this space.

storyboard *n* (*films, television*) a sequence of drawings or photographs showing the images to be shot to film for a particular story.

stout *adj* strong; short and plump; sturdy. * *n* strong dark beer.–**stoutly** *adv*.–**stoutness** *n*.

stove[1] *n* a cooker; heating apparatus.

stove[2] *see* **stave**.

stow *vt* to store, pack, in an orderly way.

stowaway *n* a person who hides on a ship, car, aircraft etc to avoid paying the fare.

straddle *vt* to have one leg or support on either side of something.

straggle *vi* to stray; to wander.–**straggler** *n*.–**straggly** *adj*.

straight *adj* (*line*) continuing in one direction, not curved or bent; direct; honest; (*sl*) heterosexual; (*alcoholic drinks*) neat, not diluted. * *adv* directly; without delay. * *n* being straight; a straight line, form, or position; a straight part of a racetrack; (*poker*) a hand containing five cards in sequence.–**straightness** *n*.

straightaway *adv* without delay.

straighten *vti* to make or become straight; (*with* **out**) to make or become less confused or entangled; to resolve.

straight face *n* a face betraying no signs of emotion, esp amusement.–**straight-faced** *adj*.

straightforward *adj* honest, open; simple; easy.–**straightfor-wardly** *adv*.–**straightforwardness** *n*.

strain[1] *vt* to tax; to stretch; to overexert; to stress; to injure (a muscle) by overstretching; (*food*) to drain or sieve. * *n* overexertion; tension; an injury from straining.

strain[2] *n* a plant or animal within a species having a common characteristic; a trait; a trace.

strainer *n* a sieve or colander used for straining liquids, pasta, tea, etc.

strait *n* a channel of sea linking two larger seas; (*usu pl*) difficulty, distress.

straitjacket *n* a coatlike device for restraining violent people; something that restricts or limits.–*also vt*.

strand[1] *vt* to run aground; to leave helpless, without transport or money.

strand[2] *n* a single piece of thread or wire twisted together to make a rope or cable; a tress of hair.–*also vt*.

strange adj peculiar; odd; unknown; unfamiliar.–**strangely** adv.–**strangeness** n.

stranger n a person who is unknown; a new arrival to a place, town, social gathering, etc; a person who is unfamiliar with or ignorant of something.

strangle vt to kill by compressing the windpipe, to choke; to stifle, suppress.–**strangler** n.

stranglehold n (wrestling) a grip that presses an opponent's windpipe; a powerful restrictive force or influence.

strap n a narrow strip of leather or cloth for carrying or holding (a bag, etc); a fastening, as on a shoe, wristwatch. * vti (**strapping, strapped**) to fasten with a strap; to beat with a strap.

strata see **stratum**.

stratagem n a clever action planned to deceive or outwit an enemy.

strategic, strategical adj of, relating to, or important in strategy; (weapons) designed to strike at the enemy's homeland, not for use on the battlefield.–**strategically** adv.

strategy n (pl **strategies**) the planning and conduct of war; a political, economic, or business policy.–**strategist** n.

stratified adj arranged or deposited in strata or layers.–**stratification** n.

stratosphere n a layer of the earth's atmosphere above 10 km (6 miles) in which temperature increases with height.–**stratospheric** adj.

stratum n (pl **strata, stratums**) a layer of sedimentary rock; a level (of society).

stratus n (pl **strati**) a continuous horizontal layer of cloud.

straw n the stalks of threshed grain; a tube for sucking up a drink.

strawberry n (pl **strawberries**) a soft red fruit used in desserts and jam.

strawberry blonde adj (hair) reddish blonde. * n a woman with hair of this color.

strawberry mark n an irregular blood-colored birth mark.

stray vi to wander; to deviate; to digress. * n a domestic animal that has become lost. * adj random.

streak n a line or long mark of contrasting color; a flash of lightning; a characteristic, a trace. * vti to mark with or form streaks; to run naked in public as a prank.–**streaker** n.

streaky adj (**streakier, streakiest**) marked with streaks; (bacon) having alternate layers of fat and lean.

stream n a small river, brook, etc; a flow of liquid; anything flowing and continuous, * vi to flow, gush.

streamer n a banner; a long decorative ribbon.

streamline vt to shape (a car, boat, etc) in a way that lessens resistance through air or water; to make more efficient, to simplify.–**streamlined** adj.

street n a public road in a town or city lined with houses; such a road with its buildings and pavements; the people living,working, etc, along a given street. * adj pertaining to urban youth culture.

streetcar n an electrically powered vehicle for public transport, which travels along rails set into the ground, a tram.

street value n the value of a commodity, esp an illegal drug, in terms of the price charged to the ultimate users.

streetwise adj (inf) experienced in surviving or avoiding the potential dangers of urban life.

strength n the state or quality of being physically or mentally strong; power of exerting or withstanding pressure, stress, force; potency; effectiveness.

strengthen vti to make or become stronger.

strenuous adj vigorous; requiring exertion.–**strenuously** adv.–**strenuousness** n.

streptococcus n (pl **streptococci**) any of a genus of spherical bacteria occurring in chains of different length.

stress n pressure; mental or physical tension or strain; emphasis; (physics) a system of forces producing or sustaining a strain. * vt to exert pressure on; to emphasize.

stretch vt to extend, to draw out. * vi to extend, spread; to extend (the limbs, body); to be capable of expanding, as in elastic material. * n the act of stretching or instance of being stretched; the capacity for being stretched; an expanse of time or space; (sl) a period of imprisonment.–**stretchy** adj.

stretcher n a portable frame for carrying the sick or injured.

strew vt (**strewing, strewed,** pp **strewn** or **strewed**) to scatter; to spread.

stricken adj suffering (from an illness); afflicted, as by something painful.

strict adj harsh, firm; enforcing rules rigorously; rigid.–**strictly** adv.–**strictness** n.

stricture n harsh criticism, censure.

stride vi (**striding, strode,** pp **stridden**) to walk with long steps. * vt to straddle.–**also** n.

strident adj loud and harsh.–**stridency** n.–**stridently** adv.

strife n a fight, quarrel; struggle.

strike vb (**striking, struck**) vt to hit; to crash into; (mil) to attack; to ignite (a match) by friction; (disease, etc) to afflict suddenly; to come upon, esp unexpectedly; to delete; (clock) to indicate by sounding; to assume (eg an attitude); to occur to; (medal, coin) to produce by stamping; (flag, tent) to lower, take down; to come upon (oil, ore, etc) by drilling or excavation; (with **down**) to afflict or cause to die suddenly; (with **off**) to delete or erase from (a list, etc); to prevent from continuing in a profession, esp due to malpractice; to sever or separate from (as if) with a blow; (with **out**) to erase or delete; (with **up**) to cause to begin, to bring about. * vi to cease work to enforce a demand (for higher wages or better working conditions). * n a stoppage of work; a military attack; (with **out**) to begin on a journey; (baseball) to be put out on strikes; (inf) to be completely unsuccessful; (with **up**) (orchestra, band) to begin to play or sing.

strike pay n money paid to workers on strike from trade union funds.

striker n a worker who is on strike; a mechanism that strikes, as in a clock; (soccer) a forward player whose primary role is to score goals.

striking adj impressive.–**strikingly** adv.

string n a thin length of cord or twine used for tying, fastening, etc; a stretched length of catgut, wire, or other material in a musical instrument; (pl) the stringed instruments in an orchestra; their players; a line or series of things. * vt (**stringing, strung**) to thread on a string; (with **up**) (sl) to kill by hanging. * vi (with **along**) (inf) to appear to agree (with); to accompany; to deceive, esp to gain time.

stringed adj (musical instruments) having strings.

stringent adj strict.–**stringently** adv.–**stringency** n.

string quartet n (a piece of music written for) a musical ensemble comprising two violins, one viola, and one cello.

stringy adj (**stringier, stringiest**) of or resembling string; (meat, etc) fibrous, chewy; (physique) sinewy.

strip vb (**stripping, stripped**) vt to peel off; to divest; to take away removable parts. * vi to undress. * n a long, narrow piece (of cloth, land, etc); an airstrip or runway.

strip cartoon n a series of drawings in a newspaper, etc which tell a story.

stripe n a narrow band of a different color from the background; a chevron worn on a military uniform to indicate rank. * vt to mark with a stripe.–**striped** adj.–**stripy** adj.

strip mining n mining by surface excavation, opencast mining.

stripper n a striptease artist; a device or solvent that removes paint.

striptease n an erotic show where a person removes their clothes slowly and seductively to music.

strive vi (**striving, strove,** pp **striven**) to endeavor earnestly, labor hard, to struggle, contend.

strobe lighting n (the equipment used to produce) high-intensity flashing light.

strode see **stride**.

stroganoff n sliced beef cooked with mushrooms and onions in a sour cream sauce.

stroke[1] n a blow or hit; (med) a seizure; the sound of a clock; (sport) an act of hitting a ball; a manner of swimming; the sweep of an oar in rowing; a movement of a pen, pencil, or paintbrush.

stroke[2] vt to caress; to do so as a sign of affection.

stroll vi to walk leisurely, to saunter. * n a leisurely walk for pleasure.

stroller n a wheeled metal and canvas chair for a small child.

strong adj physically or mentally powerful; potent; intense; healthy; convincing; powerfully affecting the sense of smell or taste, pungent. * adv effectively, vigorously.–**strongly** adv.

stronghold n a fortress; a center of strength or support.

strop n a strip of leather for sharpening a razor. * vt (**stropping, stropped**) to sharpen using a strop.

strove see **strive**.

struck see **strike**.

structure n organization; construction; arrangement of parts in an organism, or of atoms in a molecule of a substance; system, framework; order. * vt to organize, to arrange; to build up. – **structural** adj.–**structurally** adv.

strudel n very thin pastry rolled up with a fruit filling and baked.

struggle vi to move strenuously so as to escape; to strive; to fight; to exert strength; to make one's way (along, through, up, etc) with difficulty. * n a violent effort; a fight.

strum vt (**strumming, strummed**) to play on (a guitar, etc), by moving the thumb across the strings.

strung see **string**.

strung-up adj (inf) tense, anxious.

strut[1] vi (**strutting, strutted**) to walk in a proud or pompous manner.

strut[2] n a brace or structural support. * vt to brace.

strychnine n a poison used in very small quantities as a stimulant.

stub n a short piece left after the larger part has been removed or used; the counterfoil of a check, receipt, etc. * vt (**stubbing, stubbed**) to knock (one's toe or foot) painfully; to extinguish (a cigarette).

stubble n the stubs or stumps left in the ground when a crop has been harvested; any short, bristly growth, as of beard.–**stubbly** adj.

stubborn adj obstinate; persevering; determined, inflexible.–**stubbornly** adv.–**stubbornness** n.

stubby adj (**stubbier, stubbiest**) short and thick. * n (pl **stubbies**) (Austral sl) a small bottle of beer.

stucco n (pl **stuccoes, stuccos**) a type of cement or plaster used to coat and decorate outside surfaces of walls. * vt (**stuccoing, stuccoed**) to decorate or finish with stucco.

stuck see **stick**.

stuck-up adj (inf) conceited; proud; snobbish.

stud[1] n a male animal, esp a horse, kept for breeding; a collection of horses and mares for breeding; a farm or stable for stud animals.

stud[2] n a large-headed nail; an ornamental fastener. * vt (**studding, studded**) to cover with studs.

student n a person who studies or investigates a particular subject; a person who is enrolled for study at a school, college, university, etc.

studied adj carefully planned.–**studiedly** adv.–**studiedness** n.

studio n (pl **studios**) the workshop of an artist, photographer or musician; (pl) a building where motion pictures are made; a room where television or radio programs are recorded.

studio apartment n a small apartment with one main room, a kitchen and a bathroom.

studious adj given to study; careful.–**studiously** adv.–**studiousness** n.

study vt (**studying, studied**) to observe and investigate (eg phenomena) closely; to learn (eg a language); to scrutinize; to follow a course (at college, etc). * n (pl **studies**) the process of studying; a detailed investigation and analysis of a subject; the written report of a study of something; a room for studying.

stuff n material; matter; textile fabrics; cloth, esp when woolen; personal possessions generally. * vt to cram or fill.

stuffing n material used to stuff or fill anything; a seasoned mixture put inside poultry, meat, vegetables etc before cooking.

stuffy adj (**stuffier, stuffiest**) badly ventilated; lacking in fresh air; dull, uninspired.–**stuffily** adv.–**stuffiness** n.

stultify vt (**stultifying, stultified**) to make ineffectual or futile.–**stultification** n.

stumble vi to trip up or lose balance when walking; to falter; to discover by chance (with **across** or **on**). * n a trip; a blunder.

stumbling block n an obstacle to further progress.

stump n the part of a tree remaining in the ground after the trunk has been felled; the part of a limb, tooth, that remains after the larger part is cut off or destroyed. * vt (inf) to confuse, baffle; to campaign for an election.

stumpy adj (**stumpier, stumpiest**) short and thick.–**stumpiness** n.

stun vt (**stunning, stunned**) to render unconscious due to a fall or heavy blow; to surprise completely; to shock.

stung see **sting**.

stunk see **stink**.

stunning adj (inf) strikingly attractive.–**stunningly** adv.

stunt[1] vt to prevent the growth of; to dwarf.

stunt[2] n a daring or spectacular feat; a project designed to attract attention. * vi to carry out stunts.

stupefy vt (**stupefying, stupefied**) to dull the senses of.–**stupefaction** n.

stupendous adj wonderful, astonishing.–**stupendously** adv.

stupid adj lacking in understanding or common sense; silly; foolish; stunned.–**stupidity** n.–**stupidly** adv.

stupor n extreme lethargy; mental dullness.

sturdy adj (**sturdier, sturdiest**) firm; strong, robust.–**sturdily** adv.–**sturdiness** n.

sturgeon n any of various large food fishes whose roe is also eaten as caviare.

stutter vi to stammer.–also n.

sty, stye n (pl **sties**) an inflamed swelling on the eyelid.

style n the manner of writing, painting, composing music peculiar to an individual or group; fashion, elegance. * vt to design or shape (eg hair).–**styler** n.–**stylish** adj.–**stylishly** adv.

stylist n a person who writes, paints, etc, with attention to style; a designer; a hairdresser.

stylistic adj of literary or artistic style.–**stylistically** adv.

stylize vt to give a conventional style to.–**stylization** n.–**stylizer** n.

stylus n (pl **styluses, styli**) the device attached to the cartridge on the arm of a record-player that rests in the groove of a record and transmits the vibrations that are converted to sound.

stymie n (pl **stymies**) (golf) a situation in which a ball is obstructed by another ball between it and the hole. * vt (**stymieing, stymied**) to obstruct, hinder.

suave adj charming, polite.–**suavely** adv.–**suaveness** n.

sub n (inf) a submarine; a substitute; a subscription; a subeditor.

subaqua adj of or pertaining to underwater sports.

subconscious adj happening without one's awareness. * n the part of the mind that is active without one's conscious awareness.–**subconsciously** adv.–**subconsciousness** n.

subcontinent n a land mass having great size but smaller than any of the usu recognized continents.

subcontract n a secondary contract, under which work or supply of materials is let out to a firm other than the main party of the contract.–also vt.–**subcontractor** n.

subculture n a distinct group with its own customs, language, dress, etc within an existing culture.

subcutaneous adj under the skin.–**subcutaneously** adv.

subdivide vt to further divide what has already been divided. * vi to divide or be divided into parts.–**subdivision** n.

subdue vt to dominate; to render submissive; to repress (eg a desire, impulse); to soften, tone down (eg color, etc).

subeditor n a person who checks and corrects newspaper articles.–**subedit** vt.

subhead, subheading n a heading associated with a subdivision of a text.

subhuman adj (animals) lower down the evolutionary scale than mankind; less than human.

subject adj under the power of; liable. * n a person under the power of another; a citizen; a topic; a theme; the scheme or idea of a work of art. * vt to bring under control; to make liable; to cause to undergo something.–**subjection** n.

subjective adj determined by one's own mind or consciousness; relating to reality as perceived and not independent of the mind; arising from one's own thoughts and emotions, personal.–**subjectively** adv.–**subjectivity** n.

subjugate vt to overpower, to conquer.–**subjugation** n.

sublet vt (**subletting, sublet**) to let (a property which one is renting) to another.

sublime adj noble; exalted.–**sublimely** adv.–**sublimity** n.

subliminal adj beneath or beyond the conscious awareness.–**subliminally** adv.

submarine adj underwater, esp under the sea. * n a naval vessel capable of being propelled under water, esp for firing torpedoes or missiles.

submerge, submerse vt to plunge or sink under water; to cover, hide.–**submergence, submersion** n.

submersible adj capable of being submerged. * n an underwater vessel used for exploration or construction work.

submission n an act of submitting; something submitted, as an idea or proposal; the state of being submissive, compliant; the act of referring something for another's consideration, criticism, etc.–**submissive** adj.–**submissively** adv.–**submissiveness** n.

submit vb (**submitting, submitted**) vt to surrender (oneself) to another person or force; to refer to another for consideration or judgment; to offer as an opinion. * vi to yield, to surrender.

subordinate adj secondary; lower in order, rank. * n a subordinate person. * vt to put in a lower position or rank.–**subordination** n.

subpoena n a written legal order requiring the attendance of a person in court. * vt (**subpoenaing, subpoenaed**) to serve with a subpoena.

subscribe vt to pay to receive regular copies (of a magazine, etc); to donate money (to a charity, campaign); to support or agree with (an opinion, faith).–**subscriber** n.–**subscription** n.

subscript n a character written or printed below another character.–also adj.

subsequent adj occurring or following after.–**subsequently** adv.

subservient adj obsequious; servile; subordinate.–**subservience** n.–**subserviently** adv.

subside vi to sink or fall to the bottom; to settle; to diminish; to abate.–**subsidence** n.

subsidiarity n the devolution of decision making or control to the lowest effective level.

subsidiary adj secondary; supplementary; (company) owned or controlled by another. * n (pl **subsidiaries**) an accessory, an auxiliary; a business owned by another.–**subsidiarily** adv.

subsidize vt to aid or support with a subsidy.–**subsidization** n.–**subsidizer** n.

subsidy n (pl **subsidies**) government financial aid to a private person or company to assist an enterprise.

subsist vi to exist; to continue; to manage to keep oneself alive (on).–**subsistence** n.

substance n matter (such as powder, liquid); the essential nature or part; significance.

substantial adj of considerable value or size; important; strongly built.–**substantiality** n.–**substantially** adv.

substantiate vt to prove, to verify.–**substantiation** n.

substitute vt to put or act in place of another person or thing (with **for**); to replace (by). * n a person or thing that serves in place of another.–also adj.–**substitution** n.

subterfuge n a trick employed to conceal something.

subterranean adj below the surface of the earth; concealed.

subtitle n an explanatory, usu secondary, title to a book; a printed translation superimposed on a foreign language film.–also vt.

subtle adj delicate; slight; not noticeable; difficult to define, put into words; ingenious.–**subtleness** n.–**subtlety** n.–**subtly** adv.

subtotal n the sum of part of a series of figures. * vt (**subtotaling, subtotaled** or **subtotalling, subtotalled**) to sum in part.

subtract vti to take away or deduct, as one quantity from another.–**subtraction** n.

subtropical adj of, characteristic of, the regions bordering on the tropics.

suburb n a residential district on the outskirts of a large town or city.–**suburban** adj.–**suburbia** n.

subversion n the act of undermining the authority of a government, institution, etc; collapse, ruin.

subversive adj liable to subvert established authority. * n a person who engages in subversive activities.–**subversively** adv.–**subversiveness** n.

subvert vt to overthrow, to ruin (something established); to corrupt, as in morals.

subway n a passage under a street; an underground metropolitan electric railroad.

succeed vt to come after, to follow; to take the place of. * vi to accomplish what is attempted; to prosper.

success n the gaining of wealth, fame, etc; the favorable outcome (of anything attempted); a successful person or action.–**successful** adj.–**successfully** adv.

succession n following in sequence; a number of persons or things following in order; the act or process of succeeding to a title, throne, etc; the line of descent to succeed to something.–**successive** adj.–**successively** adv.

successor n a person who succeeds another, as to an office.

succinct adj clear, concise.–**succinctly** adv.–**succinctness** n.

succor, succour n (a person or thing that provides) help, support, esp in time of need. * vt to provide such help.

succulent adj juicy; moist and tasty; (plant) having fleshy tissue. * n a succulent plant (as a cactus).–**succulence, succulency** n.–**succulently** adv.

succumb vi to yield to superior strength or overpowering desire; to die.

such adj of a specified kind (eg such people, such a film); so great. * adv so; very.

suchlike adj of similar kind.

suck vt to draw (a liquid, air) into the mouth; to dissolve or roll about in the mouth (as a sweet); to draw in as if by sucking (with **in**, **up**, etc).–also n.

sucker n (sl) a person who is easily taken in or deceived; a cup-shaped piece of rubber that adheres to surfaces.

suckle vt to feed at the breast or udder.

suckling n a young animal that is not yet weaned.

sucrose n sugar.

suction n the act or process of sucking; the exertion of a force to form a vacuum.

sudden adj happening quickly and unexpectedly, abrupt.–**suddenly** adv.–**suddenness** n.

suds npl the bubbles or foam on the surface of soapy water. – **sudsy** adj.

sue vt (**suing, sued**) to bring a legal action against.

suede, suède n leather finished with a soft nap.

suet n white, solid fat in animal tissue, used in cooking.

suffer vt to undergo; to endure; to experience. * vi to feel pain or distress.–**sufferer** n.–**suffering** n.

sufferance n reluctant tolerance, tacit permission; endurance.

suffice vi to be sufficient, adequate (for some purpose).

sufficient adj enough; adequate.–**sufficiency** n.–**sufficiently** adv.

suffix n (pl **suffixes**) a letter, syllable, or syllables added to the end of a word to modify its meaning or to form a new derivative.

suffocate vti to kill or be killed by depriving of oxygen, or by inhaling a poisonous gas; to feel hot and uncomfortable due to lack of air; to prevent from developing.–**suffocation** n.

suffrage n the right to vote.

suffuse vt to spread over or fill, as with color or light.–**suffusion** n.

sugar n a sweet white, crystalline substance obtained from sugar cane and sugar beet * vi to sweeten.

sugar beet n a type of beet from which sugar is extracted.

sugar cane n a tall grass with stout canes grown as a source of sugar.

sugary adj resembling or containing sugar; cloyingly sweet in manner, content, etc.–**sugariness** n.

suggest vt to put forward for consideration; to bring to one's mind; to evoke.–**suggestion** n.

suggestible adj easily influenced by others.–**suggestibility** n.

suggestive adj evocative; rather indecent, risqué.–**suggestively** adv.–**suggestiveness** n.

suicide n a person who kills himself intentionally; the act or instance of killing oneself intentionally; ruin of one's own interests.–**suicidal** adj.–**suicidally** adv.

suit n a set of matching garments, such as a jacket and trousers or skirt; one of the four sets of thirteen playing cards; a lawsuit. * vt to be appropriate; to be convenient or acceptable to.

suitable adj fitting; convenient (to, for).–**suitably** adv.–**suitability** n.

suitcase n a portable, oblong traveling case.

suite n a number of followers or attendants; a set, esp of rooms, furniture, pieces of music.

suitor n a man who courts a woman; (law) a person who brings a lawsuit.

sulfate n a salt of sulfuric acid.–also **sulphate**.

sulfur n a yellow nonmetallic element that is inflammable and has a strong odor.–also **sulphur**.–**sulfuric, sulphuric** adj.

sulfur dioxide n a pungent toxic gas used in various industrial processes that is a major air pollutant.

sulfuric acid n a powerfully corrosive acid.

sulk vi to be sullen.

sulky adj (**sulkier, sulkiest**) bad-tempered, quiet and sullen, because of resentment.–**sulkily** adv.–**sulkiness** n.

sullen adj moody and silent; gloomy, dull.–**sullenly** adv.–**sullenness** n.

sully vt (**sullying, sullied**) to blemish, to defile the purity of. * n (pl **sullies**) a tarnish or stain.

sulphate see **sulfate**.

sulphur see **sulfur**.

sultan n a ruler, esp of a Muslim state.

sultana n a dried, white grape used in cooking; the wife or female relative of a sultan.

sultry adj (**sultrier, sultriest**) (weather) very hot, humid and close; sensual; passionate.–**sultrily** adv.–**sultriness** n.

sum n the result of two or more things added together; the total, aggregate; a quantity of money; essence, gist. * vt (**summing, summed**) to add (usu with **up**); to encapsulate; to summarize.

summarize vt to make or be a summary of.–**summarization** n.–**summarizer** n.

summary adj concise; performed quickly, without formality. * n (pl **summaries**) a brief account of the main points of something.–**summarily** adv.–**summariness** n.

summer n the warmest season of the year, between spring and autumn.–**summery** adj.

summer school n an academic course held during the summer.

summing-up n a concluding summary of the points in a speech, argument, etc; a review of the main evidence made by a judge to the jury before it considers its verdict.

summit n the highest point, the peak; a meeting of world leaders.

summon vt to order to appear, esp in court; to convene; to gather (strength, enthusiasm, etc).

summons n (pl **summonses**) a call to appear (in court). * vt to serve with a summons.

sumo n traditional Japanese wrestling.

sump n a section of the crankcase under an engine for the oil to drain into to form a reservoir.

sumptuous adj lavish; luxurious.–**sumptuously** adv.–**sumptuousness** n.

sun n the star around which the earth and other planets revolve which gives light and heat to the solar system; the sunshine. * vi (**sunning, sunned**) to expose oneself to the sun's rays.

sunbathe vi to lie in the rays of the sun or a sun lamp to get a suntan.–**sunbather** n.

sunbeam n a ray of sunlight.

sunburn n inflammation of the skin from exposure to sunlight.–also vti.

sundae n a serving of ice cream covered with a topping of fruit, syrup, nuts, etc.

Sunday n the day of the week after Saturday, regarded as a day of worship by Christians; a newspaper published on a Sunday.

sundial n a device that shows the time by casting a shadow on a graduated dial.

sundown n sunset.

sundry adj miscellaneous, various. * n (pl **sundries**) (pl) miscellaneous small things.

sunflower n a tall plant with large yellow flowers whose seeds yield oil.

sung see **sing**.

sunglasses npl tinted glasses to protect the eyes from sunlight.

sunk see **sink**.

sunny adj (**sunnier, sunniest**) (weather) bright with sunshine; (person, mood) cheerful.–**sunnily** adv.–**sunniness** n.

sunrise n dawn.

sunroof n a panel in the roof of a car that slides open.

sunset n dusk.

sunshine n the light and heat from the sun.

sunstroke n illness caused by exposure to the sun.

suntan n browning of the skin by the sun.–**suntanned** adj.

super adj (inf) fantastic, excellent; (inf) a superintendent, as in the police. * n a variety of high-octane petrol.

superannuation n regular contributions from employees' wages toward a pension scheme.

superb adj grand; excellent; of the highest quality.–**superbly** adv.

supercilious adj arrogant; haughty, disdainful.–**superciliously** adv.–**superciliousness** n.

superconductivity n (physics) the complete loss of electrical resistance exhibited by certain materials at very low temperatures.–**superconducting, superconductive** adj.–**superconduction** n.–**superconductor** n.

superego n (pl **superegos**) (psychol) the division of the unconscious mind that functions as a conscience.

superficial adj near the surface; slight, not profound; (person) shallow in nature.–**superficiality** n.–**superficially** adv.

superfluous adj exceeding what is required; unnecessary.–**superfluity** n.

superglue n an adhesive that forms strong bonds instantly.

superhuman adj surpassing normal human strength or abilities; divine.

superimpose vt to put or lay upon something else.

superintendent n a person who manages or supervises; a director; a British police officer next above the rank of inspector.

superior adj higher in place, quality, rank, excellence; greater in number, power. * n a person of higher rank.–**superiority** n.

superlative adj of outstanding quality; (gram) denoting the extreme degree of comparison of adjectives and adverbs. – **superlatively** adv.

superman n (pl **supermen**) a person of outstanding abilities and achievements.

supermarket n a large self-service store selling food and household goods.

supernatural adj relating to things that cannot be explained by nature; involving ghosts, spirits, etc.–**supernaturally** adv.

supernova n (pl **supernovae, supernovas**) a star that explodes temporarily burning with an intensity one hundred million times that of the sun.

supernumerary adj extra; beyond the usual number. * n (pl **supernumeraries**) an extra person or thing.

superpower n a nation with great economic and military strength.

superscript n a character written or printed above another character.–also adj.

supersede vt to take the place of, replace.

supersonic adj faster than the speed of sound.–**supersonically** adv.

superstar n (inf) a sporting celebrity; a famous film actor or musician.

superstition n irrational belief based on ignorance or fear.–**superstitious** adj.

superstore n a very large supermarket.

superstructure n a structure above or on something else, as above the base or foundation, as above the main deck of a ship.

supervise vti to have charge of, direct, to superintend.–**supervision** n.–**supervisor** n.–**supervisory** adj.

supine adj lying on the back; lazy, indigent.–**supinely** adv.

supper n a meal taken in the evening, esp when dinner is eaten at midday; an evening social event; the food served at a supper; a light meal served late in the evening.

supplant vt to replace; to remove in order to replace with something else.

supple adj flexible, easily bent; lithe; (mind) adaptable.–**suppleness** n.

supplement n an addition or extra amount (usu of money); an additional section of a book, periodical or newspaper. * vt to add to.–**supplemental** adj.

supply vt (**supplying, supplied**) to provide, meet (a deficiency, a need); to fill (a vacant place). * n (pl **supplies**) a stock; (pl) provisions.–**supplier** n.

support vt to hold up, bear; to tolerate, withstand; to assist; to advocate (a cause, policy); to provide for (financially). * n a means of support; maintenance.

supporter n a person who backs a political party, sports team, etc.

suppose vt to assume; to presume as true without definite knowledge; to think probable; to expect. * vi to conjecture.–**supposition** n.

supposed adj believed to be on available evidence.

supposedly adv allegedly.

suppository n (pl **suppositories**) a cone or cylinder of medicated soluble material for insertion into the rectum or vagina.

suppress vt to crush, put an end to (eg a rebellion); to restrain (a person); to subdue.–**suppression** n.–**suppressor** n.

suppurate vi to form or discharge pus.–**suppuration** n.–**suppurative** adj.

supremacist n a person who advocates the supremacy of a particular group.

supreme adj of highest power; greatest; final; ultimate. – **supremacy** n.

surcharge vt to overcharge (a person); to charge an additional sum; to overload. * n an additional tax or charge; an additional or excessive load.

sure adj certain; without doubt; reliable, inevitable; secure; safe; dependable. * adv certainly.

sure-fire adj (inf) certain to succeed.

sure-footed adj not liable to slip or fall; unlikely to make a mistake.

surely adv certainly; securely; it is to be hoped or expected that.

sure thing n (inf) something assured of success. * interj yes, of course.

surety n (pl **sureties**) a person who undertakes responsibility for the fulfillment of another's debt; security given as a guarantee of payment of a debt.

surf n the waves of the sea breaking on the shore or a reef.

surface n the exterior face of an object; any of the faces of a solid; the uppermost level of sea or land; a flat area, such as the top of a table; superficial features. * adj superficial; external. * vt to cover with a surface, as in paving. * vi to rise to the surface of water.

surfboard n a long, narrow board used in the sport of surfing.

surfeit n an excessive amount.

surfing n the sport of riding in toward shore on the crest of a wave, esp on a surfboard.

surge n the rolling of the sea, as after a large wave; a sudden, strong increase, as of power.–also vi.

surgeon n a medical specialist who practises surgery.

surgery n (pl **surgeries**) the treatment of diseases or injuries by manual or instrumental operations.–**surgical**–**surgically** adv.

surgical spirit n methylated spirit used for sterilizing.

surly adj (**surlier, surliest**) ill-tempered or rude.–**surlily** adv.–**surliness** n.

surmise n guess, conjecture. * vt to infer the existence of from partial evidence.

surmount vt to overcome; to rise above.

surname n the family name. * vt to give a surname to.

surpass vt to outdo, to outshine; to excel; to exceed.–**surpassing** adj.–**surpassingly** adv.

surplice n a loose, white, wide-sleeved clerical garment worn by clergymen and choristers.

surplus n (pl **surpluses**) an amount in excess of what is required; an excess of revenues over expenditure in a financial year.

surprise n the act of catching unawares; an unexpected gift, event; astonishment. * vt to cause to feel astonished; to attack unexpectedly; to take unawares.–**surprising** adj.–**surprisingly** adv.

surreal adj bizarre.

surrealism n a movement in art characterized by the expression of the activities of the unconscious mind and dream elements.–**surrealist** n.–**surrealistic** adj.

surrender vt to relinquish or give up possession or power. * vi to give oneself up (to an enemy).–also n.

surreptitious adj done by stealth; clandestine, secret.–**surreptitiously** adv.

surrogacy, surrogate motherhood n a practice in which a woman bears a child for a childless couple.–**surrogate mother** n.

surrogate n a person or thing acting as a substitute for another person or thing.–also adj.

surround vt to encircle on all or nearly all sides; (mil) to encircle. * n a border around the edge of something.

surroundings npl the conditions, objects, etc around a person or thing; the environment.

surveillance n a secret watch kept over a person, esp a suspect.

survey vt (**surveying, surveyed**) to take a general view of; to appraise; to examine carefully; to measure and make a map of an area. * n (pl **surveys**) a detailed study, as by gathering information and analyzing it, a general view; the process of surveying an area or a house.

surveyor *n* a person who surveys land or buildings.

survival *n* surviving; a person or thing that survives; a relic.

survive *vt* to live after the death of another person; to continue, endure; to come through alive. * *vi* to remain alive (after experiencing a dangerous situation).**–survivor** *n*.

susceptible *adj* ready or liable to be affected by; impressionable.**–susceptibility** *n*.**–susceptibly** *adv*.

sushi *n* a Japanese dish of small cakes of cold rice with various toppings, esp raw fish.

suspect *vt* to mistrust; to believe to be guilty; to think probable. * *n* a person under suspicion. * *adj* open to suspicion.

suspend *vt* to hang; to discontinue, or cease temporarily; to postpone; to debar temporarily from a privilege, etc.

suspenders *npl* supporting straps for trousers.

suspense *n* mental anxiety or uncertainty; excitement.

suspension *n* suspending or being suspended; a temporary interruption or postponement; a temporary removal from office, privileges, etc; the system of springs, shock absorbers, etc that support a vehicle on its axles; (*chem*) a dispersion of fine particles in a liquid.

suspension bridge *n* a bridge carrying a roadway suspended by cables anchored to towers at either end.

suspicion *n* act of suspecting; a belief formed or held without sure proof; mistrust; a trace.**–suspicious** *adj*.**–suspiciously** *adv*.

sustain *vt* to hold up, support; to maintain; to suffer (eg an injury); to nourish.

sustenance *n* nourishment.

suture *n* a stitch holding together a wound after surgery.**–also** *vt*.

svelte *adj* slim and elegant.

SW *abbr* = southwest(ern); short wave.

swab *n* a wad of absorbent material, usu cotton, used to clean wounds, take specimens, etc; a mop.**–also** *vt*.

swaddle *vt* to bind tightly, envelop; to wrap a baby in swaddling clothes.

swagger *vi* to strut; to brag loudly. * *n* boastfulness; swinging gait.

swallow[1] *n* a small migratory bird with long wings and a forked tail.

swallow[2] *vt* to cause food and drink to move from the mouth to the stomach; to endure; to engulf; (*inf*) to accept gullibly; (*emotion, etc*) to repress.**–also** *n*.

swam *see* swim.

swamp *n* wet, spongy land; bog. * *vt* to overwhelm; to flood as with water.**–swampy** *adj*.

swan *n* a large, usu white, bird with a very long neck that lives on rivers and lakes. * *vi* (**swanning, swanned**) (*inf*) to wander aimlessly.

swank *vi* (*inf*) to show off.**–also** *n*.**–swanky** *adj*.

swan song *n* a final appearance, performance, etc by a person facing retirement or death.

swap *vti* (**swapping, swapped**) (*inf*) to trade, barter. * *n* (*inf*) the act of exchanging one thing for another.**–also swop**.

swarm *n* a colony of migrating bees; a moving mass, crowd or throng. * *vi* to move in great numbers; to teem.

swarthy *adj* (**swarthier, swarthiest**) dark-complexioned.**–swarthiness** *n*.

swastika *n* an ancient symbol formed by a cross with the ends of the arms bent at right-angles, used by Nazi Germany.

swat *vt* (**swatting, swatted**) (*inf*) to hit with a sharp blow; to swipe.**–also** *n*.**–swatter** *n*.

swath *n* the width of one sweep of a scythe or other mowing device; a strip, row, etc, mowed; a broad strip.

swathe *vt* to bind or wrap round, as with a bandage; to envelop, enclose.

sway *vi* to swing or move from one side to the other or to and fro; to lean to one side; to vacillate in judgment or opinion. * *n* influence; control.

swear *vi* (**swearing, swore,** *pp* **sworn**) to make a solemn affirmation, promise, etc, calling God as a witness; to give evidence on oath; to curse, blaspheme or use obscene language; to vow; (*with* **off**) to promise abstinence from. * *vt* (*with* **in**) to appoint to an office by the administration of an oath.

swearword *n* a profane or obscene expression.

sweat *n* perspiration; (*inf*) hard work; (*inf*) a state of eagerness, anxiety.**–also** *vti*.**–sweaty** *adj*.

sweater *n* a knitted pullover.

sweatshirt *n* a loose, collarless, heavy cotton jersey.

sweatshop *n* a small factory or workshop where employees work long hours at low wages in poor conditions.

sweep *vb* (**sweeping, swept**) *vt* to clean with a broom; to remove (rubbish, dirt) with a brush. * *vi* to pass by swiftly. * *n* a movement, esp in an arc; a stroke; scope, range; a sweepstake.**–sweeper** *n*.

sweeping *adj* wide-ranging; indiscriminate.**–sweepingly** *adv*.

sweepstake, sweepstakes *n* a lottery in which the prize constitutes all the money staked; a horserace, etc in which the winner receives the entire prize.

sweet *adj* having a taste like sugar; pleasing to other senses; gentle; kind. * *n* a small piece of confectionery; a dessert.**–sweetly** *adv*.**–sweetness** *n*.

sweet-and-sour *adj* (*food*) cooked in a sauce containing sugar and vinegar or lemon juice.

sweetcorn *n* maize, corn on the cob.

sweeten *vti* to make or become sweet or sweeter; to mollify.

sweetener *n* a sweetening substance that contains no sugar; (*sl*) a bribe.

sweetheart *n* a lover.

sweet pepper *n* (a plant bearing) a large fruit with thick fleshy walls eaten ripe (red) or unripe (green).

sweet potato *n* (a tropical climbing plant with) a large edible tuberous root.

sweet-talk *vt* (*inf*) to flatter, cajole.**–sweet talk** *n*.

swell *vi* (**swelling, swelled,** *pp* **swollen** *or* **swelled**) to increase in size or volume; to rise into waves; to bulge out. * *n* the movement of the sea; a bulge; a gradual increase in the loudness of a musical note; (*inf*) a socially prominent person. * *adj* excellent.

swelling *n* inflammation.

swelter *vi* to suffer from heat. * *n* humid, oppressive heat.**–sweltering** *adj*.

swept *see* sweep.

swerve *vi* to turn aside suddenly from a line or course; to veer.**–also** *n*.

swift *adj* moving with great speed; rapid. * *n* a swallow-like bird.**–swiftly** *adv*.**–swiftness** *n*.

swig *vt* (**swigging, swigged**) (*inf*) to take a long drink, esp from a bottle.**–also** *n*.

swill *vti* to drink greedily; to guzzle; to rinse with a large amount of water. * *n* liquid refuse fed to pigs.

swim *vi* (**swimming, swam,** *pp* **swum**) to move through water by using limbs or fins; to be dizzy; to be flooded with. * *n* the act of swimming.**–swimmer** *n*.

swimsuit, swimming costume *n* a one-piece garment for swimming in.

swindle *vti* to cheat (someone) of money or property.**–also** *n*.**–swindler** *n*.

swine *n* (*pl* **swine**) a pig; (*inf*) an contemptible person; (*inf*) an unpleasant thing.

swing *vb* (**swinging, swung**) *vi* to sway or move to and fro, as an object hanging in the air; to pivot; to shift from one mood or opinion to another; (*music*) to have a lively rhythm; (*sl*) to be hanged. * *vt* to whirl; to play swing music; to influence; to achieve, bring about. * *n* a swinging, curving or rhythmic movement; a suspended seat for swinging in; a shift from one condition to another; a type of popular jazz played by a large band and characterized by a lively, steady rhythm.

swipe n (inf) a hard, sweeping blow. * vt (inf) to hit with a swipe; (sl) to steal.

swirl vti to turn with a whirling motion.–also n.

swish vi to move with a soft, whistling, hissing sound. * n a swishing sound. * adj (inf) smart, fashionable.

switch n a control for turning on and off an electrical device; a sudden change; a swap. * vt to shift, change, swap; to turn on or off (as of an electrical device).

switchboard n an installation in a building where telephone calls are connected.

swivel n a coupling that permits parts to rotate. * vi (**swiveling, swiveled** or **swivelling, swivelled**) to turn (as if) on a pin or pivot.

swollen see **swell**.

swoon vt to faint.–also n.

swoop vt to carry off abruptly. * vi to make a sudden attack (usu with **down**) as a bird in hunting.–also n.

swop see **swap**.

sword n a weapon with a long blade and a handle at one end.

swordfish n a large marine fish with a sword-like upper jaw.

swordsman n (pl **swordsmen**) a person skilled in the use of a sword.

swore, sworn see **swear**.

swum see **swim**.

swung see **swing**.

sycamore n a Eurasian maple tree; an American plane tree; a tree of Africa and Asia bearing a fruit resembling a fig.

sycophant n a person who flatters and praises powerful people to win their favor.–**sycophancy** n.–**sycophantic** adj.

syllabi see **syllabus**.

syllable n word or part of a word uttered in a single sound; one or more letters written to represent a spoken syllable.–**syllabic** adj.

syllabus n (pl **syllabuses, syllabi**) a summary or outline of a course of study or of examination requirements; the subjects studied for a particular course.

symbol n a representation; an object used to represent something abstract; an arbitrary or conventional sign standing for a quality, process, relation, etc as in music, chemistry, mathematics, etc.

symbolic, symbolical adj of, using, or constituting a symbol.–**symbolically** adv.

symbolism n the use of symbols; a system of symbolic representation.–**symbolist** n.

symbolize vt to be a symbol; to represent by a symbol.–**symbolization** n.–**symbolizer** n.

symmetry n (pl **symmetries**) the corresponding arrangement of one part to another in size, shape and position; balance or harmony of form resulting from this.–**symmetrical, symmetric** adj.–**symmetrically** adv.

sympathetic adj having sympathy; compassionate.–**sympathetically** adv.

sympathize vi feel sympathy for; to commiserate; to be in sympathy (with).–**sympathizer** n.–**sympathizingly** adv.

sympathy n (pl **sympathies**) agreement of ideas and opinions; compassion; (pl) support for an action or cause.

symphony n (pl **symphonies**) an orchestral composition in several movements; a large orchestra for playing symphonic works.–**symphonic** adj.–**symphonically** adv.

symptom n a bodily sensation experienced by a patient indicative of a particular disease; an indication.–**symptomatic** adj.–**symptomatically** adv.

synagogue n the building where Jews assemble for worship and religious study.

sync, synch n (inf) synchronization. * vti (inf) to synchronize.

synchronize vti to occur at the same time and speed; (watches) to adjust to show the same time.–**synchronization** n.–**synchronizer** n.

syncopate vt (mus) to modify beats (in a musical piece) by displacing the rhythmical accents from strong beats to weak ones and vice versa.–**syncopation** n.

syndicate n an association of individuals or corporations formed for a project requiring much capital; any group, as of criminals, organized for some undertaking; an organization selling articles or features to many newspapers, etc. * vt to manage as or form into a syndicate; to sell (an article, etc) through a syndicate. * vi to form a syndicate.–**syndication** n.

syndrome n a characteristic pattern of signs and symptoms of a disease.

synod n a council of members of a church that meets to discuss religious issues.

synonym n a word that has the same, or similar, meaning as another or others in the same language.–**synonymous** adj.–**synonymously** adv.

synopsis n (pl **synopses**) a summary or brief review of a subject.

syntax n (gram) the arrangement of words in the sentences and phrases of language; the rules governing this.–**syntactic** adj.–**syntactically** adv.

synth n a synthesizer.

synthesis n (pl **syntheses**) the process of combining separate elements of thought into a whole; the production of a compound by a chemical reaction.–**synthesize** vti.

synthesizer n an electronic device producing music and sounds by using a computer to combine individual sounds previously recorded.

synthetic adj produced by chemical synthesis; artificial.–**synthetically** adv.

syphilis n a contagious, infectious venereal disease.–**syphilitic** adj.

syphon see **siphon**.

syringe n a hollow tube with a plunger at one end and a sharp needle at the other by which liquids are injected or withdrawn, esp in medicine. * vt to inject or cleanse with a syringe.

syrup n a thick sweet substance made by boiling sugar with water; the concentrated juice of a fruit or plant.–**syrupy** adj.

system n a method of working or organizing by following a set of rules; routine; organization; structure; a political regime; an arrangement of parts fitting together.–**systematic** adj.–**systematically** adv.

systematize vt to arrange according to a system.–**systematization** n.–**systematizer** n.

systemic adj (poison, infection, etc) of or affecting the entire body; (insecticide, etc) designed to be taken up into the plant tissues.–**systemically** adv.

systems analysis n analysis of a particular task or operation to determine how computer hardware and software may best perform it.–**systems analyst** n.

T

tab[1] n tabulator; tablet. * vt (**tabbing, tabbed**) to tabulate.

tab[2] n a small tag, label or flap; (inf) a bill, as for expenses. * vt (**tabbing, tabbed**) to fix a tab on.

tabby n (pl **tabbies**) a domestic cat with a striped coat, esp a female; a heavy watered silk. * adj striped in brown or gray. * vt (**tabbying, tabbied**) to pattern (silk) with a wavy pattern.

tabernacle n (Bible) the portable tent carried by Jews through the desert containing their sacred writings; a place of worship.–**tabernacular** adj.

table n a piece of furniture consisting of a slab or board on legs; the people seated round a table; supply of food; a flat surface; a level area; a slab or tablet in a wall; an inscription on this; a list of facts and figures arranged in columns for reference or comparison; a folding leaf of a backgammon board; **at table** having a meal; **on the table** (legislative bill, etc) postponed,

tableau 287 **talk show**

tableau to put (an opponent) in a position of disadvantage previously held by oneself. * *vt* to submit, to put forward; to postpone indefinitely; to lay on a table. * *adj* of, on or at a table.

tableau *n* (*pl* **tableaux, tableaus**) a dramatic or graphic representation of a group or scene.

tablecloth *n* a cloth for covering a table.

table d'hôte *n* (*pl* **tables d'hôte**) a meal at a fixed price for a set number of courses.–*also adj.*

tablespoon *n* a large serving spoon; a unit of measure in cooking.

tablet *n* a pad of paper; a medicinal pill; a cake of solid substance, such as soap; a slab of stone.

table tennis *n* a game like tennis played on a table with small bats and a ball.

tableware *n* dishes, cutlery, etc for use at mealtimes.

tabloid *n* a small-format newspaper characterized by emphasis on photographs and news in condensed form.

taboo, tabu *n* (*pl* **taboos, tabus**) a religious or social prohibition of the use or practice of something; the thing prohibited. * *adj* forbidden from use, mention, etc. * *vt* (**tabooing, tabooed** *or* **tabuing, tabued**) to forbid by social or personal influence the use, practice or mention of something or contact with someone.

tabular *adj* like a table, flat; arranged in the form of a table; calculated with a table.–**tabularly** *adv.*

tabulate *vt* to arrange (written material) in tabular form.–**tabulation** *n*

tabulator *n* a device that sets stops to locate columns on a typewriter or word processor.

tachograph *n* a device in motor vehicles, esp trucks, to record speed and time of travel.

tacit *adj* implied without really being spoken; understood.–**tacitly** *adv.*–**tacitness** *n.*

taciturn *adj* habitually silent and reserved.–**taciturnity** *n.*

tack *n* a short, flat-headed nail; the course of a sailing ship; a course of action, approach; adhesiveness. * *vt* to fasten with tacks. * *vi* to change direction.

tackle *n* a system of ropes and pulleys for lifting; equipment; rigging; (*sport*) an act of grabbing and stopping an opponent. * *vt* (*task, etc*) to attend to, undertake; (*a person*) to confront; (*sport*) to challenge with a tackle.

tacky[1] *adj* (**tackier, tackiest**) (*paint, etc*) sticky.

tacky[2] *adj* (**tackier, tackiest**) (*inf*) shabby; ostentatious and vulgar; seedy.–**tackiness** *n.*

tact *n* discretion in managing the feelings of others.–**tactful** *adj.*–**tactless** *adj.*

tactics *n sing* stratagem; ploy; the science or art of maneuvering troops in the presence of the enemy.–**tactical** *adj.*–**tactician** *n.*

tactile *adj* relating to, or having a sense of touch.

tad *n* (*inf*) a tiny quantity; a bit.

tadpole *n* the larva of a frog or toad, esp at the stage when the head and tail have developed.

taffeta *n* a thin glossy fabric with a silky luster.

tag[1] *n* a strip or label for identification. * *vt* to attach a tag; to mark with a tag. * *vi* (*with* **onto, after, along**) to trail along (behind).

tag[2] *n* a children's chasing game; (*baseball*) the putting out of a runner by touching him with the ball. * *vt* (**tagging, tagged**) to touch another player in a game of tag; to put a runner out by touching him with the ball.

tagliatelle *n* pasta in narrow ribbons.

tahini *n* a thick paste of ground sesame seeds.

tail *n* the appendage of an animal growing from the rear, generally hanging loose; the rear part of anything; (*pl*) the side of a coin without a head on it; (*inf*) a person who keeps another under surveillance, esp a detective. * *vti* to follow closely, to shadow; (*with* **off, away**) to (cause to) dwindle.

tailback *n* a long queue of traffic behind an obstruction.

tailgate *n* the hinged board at the rear of a truck which can be let down or removed. * *vti* to drive dangerously close behind (another vehicle).–**tailgater** *n.*

taillight *n* a red warning light at the rear of a motor vehicle.

tailor *n* a person who makes and repairs outer garments, esp men's suits. * *vi* to work as a tailor. * *vt* to adapt to fit a particular requirement.

tailor-made *adj* specially designed for a particular purpose or person.

tailwind *n* a wind in the same direction as a ship or aircraft is traveling.

taint *vt* to contaminate; to infect. * *vi* to be corrupted or disgraced. * *n* a stain; corruption.

take *vb* (**taking, took**, *pp* **taken**) *vt* to lay hold of; to grasp or seize; to gain, win; to choose, select; (*attitude, pose*) to adopt; to understand; to consume; to accept or agree to; to lead or carry with one; to use as a means of travel; (*math*) to subtract (from); to use; to steal; to endure calmly; (*with* **apart**) to dismantle; to criticize; (*with* **back**) to retract, withdraw (a promise, etc); (*with* **down**) to write down; to dismantle; to humiliate; (*with* **for**) (*inf*) to mistakenly believe to be; (*with* **in**) to understand, perceive; to include; to make a garment smaller by altering seams, etc; to offer accommodation to; (*inf*) to swindle, deceive; (*with* **on**) to employ as labor; to assume or acquire; to agree to do (something); to fight against; (*with* **out**) to extract; to obtain, procure; to escort; (*sl*) to kill; (*with* **up**) to begin as a business or hobby; to accept an offer or invitation; to occupy (time or space); to act as a patron to; to shorten (a garment); to interrupt or criticize; to absorb. * *vi* (*plant, etc*) to start growing successfully; to become effective; to catch on; to have recourse to; to go to; (*with* **after**) to resemble in appearance, character, etc; (*with* **on**) (*inf*) to become upset or distraught; (*with* **to**) to escape to as a refuge; to acquire a liking for; to adopt as a habit; (*with* **up**) to resume, continue further. * *n* (*film, TV*) the amount of film used without stopping the camera when shooting.

taken *see* **take**.

takeoff *n* the process of an aircraft becoming airborne; (*inf*) an amusing impression or caricature of another person.

takeout, take-out *n* a cooked meal that is sold for consumption outside the premises; a shop or restaurant that provides such meals.–*also adj.*

takeover *n* the taking over of control, as in business.–*also adj.*

taking *adj* attractive, charming; (*inf*) catching, contagious. * *n* the act of one that takes; (*pl*) earnings; profits.

talcum powder *n* perfumed powdered talc for the skin.

tale *n* a narrative or story; a fictitious account, a lie; idle or malicious gossip.

talent *n* any innate or special aptitude.–**talented** *adj.*

talent scout *n* a person employed to recruit talented people for professional careers in sport, entertainment, etc.

talisman *n* (*pl* **talismans**) an object or charm supposed to ward off evil and bring good luck; an amulet.

talk *vt* to speak; to know how to speak (a language); to discuss or speak of (something); to influence by talking; (*with* **down**) to silence or override (a speaker, argument, etc) by talking loudly; to radio instructions to (an aircraft) so that it may land safely; (*with* **into**) to persuade by argument or talking; (*with* **out**) to resolve by discussion; (*with* **round**) to persuade by talking. * *vi* to converse; to discuss; to gossip; to divulge information; (*with* **back**) to reply impudently; (*with* **down**) to speak in a condescending manner (to); (*with* **round**) to discuss (a subject) without reaching any conclusion; (*with* **shop**) to discuss work, esp after working hours. * *n* a discussion; a lecture; gossip; (*pl*) negotiations.

talkative *adj* given to talking a great deal.

talkie *n* (*inf*) an early motion-picture film with sound.

talking-to *n* a reprimand, lecture.

talk show *n* a television or radio program with informal interviews and conversation, a chat show.

tall adj above average in height; (inf) (story) exaggerated.–**tallness** n.

tallboy n a high chest of drawers on legs, a highboy.

tall order n (inf) a request that is difficult to fulfill.

tallow n solid animal fat used to make soap, candles, etc.

tall ship n a square-rigged sailing vessel.

tally n (pl **tallies**) reckoning, account; one score in a game. * vi (**tallying, tallied**) to correspond; to keep score.

Talmud n the body of Jewish law.–**Talmudic** adj.

talon n a claw of an animal, esp a bird of prey.

tamarind n a tropical evergreen tree bearing a pulpy fruit used for food, in beverages and in laxative preparations.

tambourine n a percussion hand instrument made of skin stretched over a circular frame with small jingling metal discs around the edge.

tame adj (animal) not wild, domesticated; compliant; dull, uninteresting. * vt (animal) to domesticate; to subdue; to soften.

tamp vt to pack down firmly with a series of blows; to pack (a blast-hole) with sand or earth above the explosive charge.

tamper vi to meddle (with); to interfere (with).

tampon n a firm plug of cotton wool inserted in the vagina during menstruation.

tan[1] n a yellowish-brown color; suntan. * vti (**tanning, tanned**) to acquire a suntan through sunbathing; (skin, hide) to convert into leather using tannin; (inf) to thrash.

tan[2] abbr = tangent.

tandem n a bicycle for two riders, sitting one behind the other.

tandoori n an Indian method of cooking meat, vegetables and bread using a large clay oven.

tang n sharp smell or a strong taste.–**tangy** adj.

tangent n a line that touches a curve or circle at one point, without crossing it. * adj touching at one point.

tangential adj of superficial relevance; digressive.

tangerine n a small, sweet orange with a loose skin; the color of this.–also adj.

tangible adj capable of being felt, seen or noticed; substantial; real.–**tangibility** n.

tangle n a mass of hair, string or wire knotted together confusedly; a complication. * vt to intertwine in a mass, to snarl; to entangle, complicate. * vi to become tangled or complicated; (with **with**) to become involved in argument with.

tango n (pl **tangos**) a Latin American ballroom dance. * vi (**tangoing, tangoed**) to dance the tango.

tank n a large container for storing liquids or gases; an armored combat vehicle, mounted with guns and having caterpillar tracks.

tankard n a tall, one-handled drinking mug, often with a hinged lid.

tanker n a large ship or truck for transporting oil and other liquids.

tannic acid n tannin.

tannin n a yellow or brown chemical found in plants or tea, used in tanning.–**tannic** adj.

tantalize vt to tease or torment by presenting something greatly desired, but keeping it inaccessible.

tantamount adj equivalent (to) in effect; as good as.

tantrum n a childish fit of bad temper.

Taoism n a Chinese religious and philosophical system advocating a simple passive life in harmony with the natural order.

tap[1] n a quick, light blow or touch; a piece of metal attached to the heel or toe of a shoe for reinforcement or to tap-dance. * vti (**tapping, tapped**) to strike lightly; to make a tapping sound.

tap[2] n a device controlling the flow of liquid through a pipe or from a container, a faucet. * vt (**tapping, tapped**) to pierce in order to draw fluid from; to connect a secret listening device to a telephone; (inf) to ask for money from; (resources, etc) to draw on.

tap-dance vi to perform a step dance in shoes with taps.–**tap-dancer** n.–**tap-dancing** n.

tape n a strong, narrow strip of cloth, paper, etc, used for tying, binding, etc; tape measure; magnetic tape, as in a cassette or videotape. * vt to wrap with tape; to record on magnetic tape.

tape deck n a tape recorder in a hi-fi system.

tape measure n a tape marked in inches or centimeters for measuring.

taper n a long thin candle. * vti to make or become gradually narrower toward one end.–**tapering** adj.

tape recorder n a machine used for recording and reproducing sounds or music on magnetic tape, esp as part of a hi-fi system, a tape deck.

tapestry n (pl **tapestries**) a heavy fabric woven with patterns or figures, used for wall hangings and furnishings.

tapeworm n a tape-like, parasitic, intestinal worm.

tapioca n a glutinous starch extracted from the root of the cassava and used in puddings, etc.

tar n a thick, dark, viscous substance obtained from wood, coal, peat, etc., used for surfacing roads. * vt to coat with tar.–**tarry** adj.

tarantula n (pl **tarantulas, tarantulae**) a large, hairy spider with a poisonous bite that is painful but not deadly.

tardy adj (**tardier, tardiest**) slow; later than expected.–**tardily** adv.–**tardiness** n.

target n a mark to aim at, esp in shooting; an objective or ambition.

tariff n a tax on imports or exports; (in a hotel) a list of prices; the rate of charge for public services, such as gas or electricity.

Tarmac, Tarmacadam n a material for surfacing roads made from crushed stones and tar; an airport runway. * vti (**tarmacking, tarmacked**) to lay down a tarmac surface.

tarnish vi (metal) to lose its luster or discolor due to exposure to the air. * vt (reputation) to taint.–also n.

tarot n a game played with 22 pictorial cards, which are also used for fortune-telling.

tarpaulin n canvas cloth coated with a waterproof substance.

tarragon n an aromatic herb used for flavoring.

tarry vi (**tarrying, tarried**) to delay or dawdle; to linger; to wait briefly.

tarsus n (pl **tarsi**) the small bones of the ankle and the heel in vertebrates; the plate of tissue that stiffens the eyelid.–**tarsal** adj, n.

tart[1] adj having a sour, sharp taste; (speech) sharp, severe. –**tartly** adv.–**tartness** n.

tart[2] n an open pastry case containing fruit, jam or custard; (inf) a prostitute. * vt (with **up**) (inf) to dress cheaply and gaudily; to decorate, esp cheaply.

tartan n a woolen cloth with a checkered pattern, having a distinctive design for each Scottish clan.

tartar n a hard, yellow, crusty deposit which forms on the teeth; a salty deposit on the sides of wine casks.

tartar sauce n a mayonnaise sauce with chopped capers, herbs, etc, eaten esp with fish.

task n a specific amount of work to be done; a chore.

task force n a small unit with a specific mission, usu military.

tassel n an ornamental tuft of silken threads decorating soft furnishings, clothes, etc; a growth that looks like this, esp on corn. * vb (**tasseling, tasseled** or **tasselling, tasselled**) vt to decorate with tassels.

taste vt to perceive (a flavor) by taking into the mouth; to try by eating and drinking a little; to sample; to experience. * vi to try by the mouth; to have a specific flavor. * n the sense by which flavors are perceived; a small portion; the ability to recognize what is beautiful, attractive, etc; liking; a brief experience.

taste bud n any of the small projecting sensory organs on the tongue's surface by which taste is perceived.

tasteful adj showing good taste.–**tastefully** adv.–**tastefulness** n.

tasteless adj without taste, bland; in bad taste.–**tastelessly** adv.

tasty adj (**tastier, tastiest**) savory; having a pleasant flavor.

tatter n a torn or ragged piece of cloth.–**tattered** adj.

tattle vi to gossip. * vt to reveal (secrets, etc) by gossiping. * n (a) gossip.

tattoo vt (**tattooing, tattooed**) to make permanent patterns or pictures on the skin by pricking and marking with dyes. * n (pl **tattoos**) marks made on the skin in this way.

tatty adj (**tattier, tattiest**) shabby, ragged.

taught see **teach**.

taunt vt to provoke with mockery or contempt; to tease. * n an insult.

Taurus n the Bull, the second sign of the zodiac.–**Taurean** adj.

taut adj stretched tight; tense; stressed.

tauten vti to make or become taut.

tautology n (pl **tautologies**) a statement which uses different words to repeat the same thing.–**tautological, tautologous** adj.

tavern n a place licensed to sell alcoholic drinks; an inn.

tawdry adj (**tawdrier, tawdriest**) showy, cheap, and of poor quality.

tawny adj yellowish brown.

tax n a rate imposed by the government on property or persons to raise revenues; a strain. * vt to impose a tax (upon); to strain:

taxation n the act of levying taxes; the amount raised as tax.

tax exempt adj (**expenses**, etc) legitimately deducted from income before tax assessment.

tax exile n a person who lives abroad to avoid paying high taxes.

tax haven n a place where taxes are lower than average.

taxi n (pl **taxis**) a car that may be hired to transport passengers. * vi (**taxiing** or **taxying, taxied**) (aircraft) to move along the runway before takeoff or after landing.

taxidermy n the art of preparing and stuffing the skins of animals ready for exhibiting.–**taxidermist** n.

taxonomy n (the science of) the classification of living things into groups based on similarities of biological origin, design, function, etc.

tax return n a statement of a person's income for the purposes of tax assessment.

TB abbr = tuberculosis.

T-bone steak n a large sirloin steak containing a T-shaped bone.

tbs., tbsp. abbr = tablespoon.

T-cell n a lymphocyte that kills cells infected with a virus.–also **T-lymphocyte**.

tea n a shrub growing in China, India, Sri Lanka, etc; its dried, shredded leaves, which are infused in boiling water for a beverage; in UK, a light meal taken in mid-afternoon; a main meal taken in the early evening.

tea bag n a small porous bag containing tea leaves for infusing.

tea caddy n an airtight container for storing tea.

teach vb (**teaching, taught**) vt to impart knowledge to; to give lessons (to); to train; to help to learn. * vi to give instruction, esp as a profession.–**teachable** adj.

teacher n a person who instructs others, esp as an occupation.

teacup n a small cup for drinking tea.

teak n a type of hard wood from an East Indian tree.

team n a group of people participating in a sport together; a group of people working together; two or more animals pulling a vehicle. * vi (with **up**) to join in cooperative activity.

team-mate n a colleague, a fellow team member.

team spirit n willingness to work harmoniously within a group.

teamster n a truck driver.

teamwork n cooperation of individuals for the benefit of the team; the ability of a team to work together.

teapot n a vessel in which tea is made.

tear[1] n a drop of salty liquid appearing in the eyes when crying or when the eyes are smarting; anything tear-shaped.

tear[2] vb (**tearing, tore,** pp **torn**) vt to pull apart by force; to split; to lacerate; (with **down**) to destroy, demolish. * vi to move with speed; (with **into**) (inf) to attack physically or verbally. * n a hole or split.

tearful adj weeping; sad.–**tearfully** adv.

tear gas n gas that irritates the eyes and nasal passages, used in riot control.

tear-jerker n a strongly sentimental book, film, movie, etc.

tearoom n a restaurant where tea and light refreshments are served.

tease vt to separate the fibers of; to torment or irritate; to taunt playfully. * n a person who teases or torments; (inf) a flirt.– **teaser** n.

tea service, tea set n the set of cups and saucers, etc for serving tea.

teaspoon n a small spoon for use with a teacup or as a measure; the amount measured by this.–**teaspoonful** n.

teat n the nipple on a breast or udder; the mouthpiece of a baby's feeding bottle.

technical adj relating to, or specializing in practical, industrial, mechanical or applied sciences; (expression, etc) belonging to or peculiar to a particular field of activity.–**technically** adv.

technicality n (pl **technicalities**) a petty formality or technical point.

technician n a person skilled in the practice of any art, esp in practical work with scientific equipment.

technique n method of performing a particular task; knack.

technology n (pl **technologies**) the application of mechanical and applied sciences to industrial use.–**technological** adj.–**technologist** n.

teddy bear n a stuffed toy bear.

tedious adj monotonous; boring.–**tediously** adv.–**tedium** n.

tee n (golf) the place from where the first stroke is played at each hole; a small peg from which the ball is driven. * vti to position (the ball) on the tee; (with **off**) to hit a golf ball from a tee.

teem[1] vi (with **with**) to be prolific or abundant in.

teem[2] vi to pour (with rain).

teen n a teenager. * adj teenage.

teenager n (inf) a person who is in his or her teens.

teens npl the years of one's life from thirteen to nineteen.– **teenage, teenaged** adj.

teeny adj (**teenier, teeniest**) (inf) tiny.

teepee see **tepee**.

tee-shirt see **T-shirt**.

teeter vi to move or stand unsteadily.

teeth see **tooth**.

teethe vi to cut one's first teeth.

teething ring n a hard ring for a teething baby to chew on.

teething troubles npl problems encountered in the early stages of a project, etc; pain caused by growing teeth.

teetotaller, teetotaler n a person who abstains from alcoholic drinks.–**teetotal** adj.

Teflon n (trademark) polytetrafluoroethylene, a coating for pots and pans that prevents food sticking. * adj (inf) able to avoid (political) scandal by claiming ignorance or blaming others.

tel. abbr = telephone.

telecom, telecoms n short for telecommunications.

telecommunication n communication of information over long distances by telephone and radio; (pl) the technology of telephone and radio communication.

telegraph n a system for transmitting messages over long distances using electricity, wires and a code. * vt to transmit by telegraph.–**telegraphic** adj.–**telegraphy** n.

telekinesis n the movement of objects using pure thought without the application of physical force.–**telekinetic** adj.

telepathy n the communication between people's minds of thoughts and feelings, without the need for speech or proximity.– **telepathic** adj.

telephone n an instrument for transmitting speech at a distance, esp by means of electricity. * vt (someone) to call by telephone.

telephone book n a book listing the names, addresses and telephone numbers of subscribers in a given area.

telephone booth n a cubicle for paid public use of a telephone.

telephone operator, telephonist n a person who operates a telephone switchboard.

telephoto lens n a camera lens that magnifies distant objects.

telesales *npl* selling products and services by telephone.

telescope *n* a tubular optical instrument for viewing objects at a distance.–**telescopic** *adj.*–**telescopically** *adv.*

telethon *n* a long television extravaganza which encourages viewers to send in money for a charitable cause.

televangelist *n* a person, usu a minister of the Christian Pentecostal church, who conducts television shows to preach the church's message and seek donations.

televise *vt* (*a program*) to transmit by television.

television *n* the transmission of visual images and accompanying sound through electrical and sound waves; a television receiving set; television broadcasting.

tell *vb* (**telling, told**) *vt* to narrate; to disclose; to inform; to notify; to instruct; to distinguish; (*with* **off**) (*inf*) to reprimand; to count off and assign to a duty. * *vi* to tell tales, to inform on; to produce a marked effect.

teller *n* a bank clerk; a person appointed to count votes in an election.

telling *adj* having great impact.

telltale *n* a person who tells tales about others. * *adj* revealing what is meant to be hidden.

temerity *n* rashness.

temp *n* (*inf*) a temporary employee.

temper *n* a frame of mind; a fit of anger. * *vt* to tone down, moderate; (*steel*) to heat and cool repeatedly to bring to the correct hardness.

temperament *n* one's disposition.

temperamental *adj* easily irritated; erratic.–**temperamentally** *adv.*

temperance *n* moderation; abstinence from alcohol.

temperate *adj* mild or moderate in temperature; (*behaviour*) moderate, self-controlled.

temperature *n* degree of heat or cold; body heat above the normal.

tempest *n* a violent storm.

tempestuous *adj* stormy; violent; passionate.

tempi *see* **tempo**.

template *n* a pattern, gauge or mould used as a guide esp in cutting metal, stone or plastic.

temple[1] *n* a place of worship.

temple[2] *n* the region on either side of the head above the cheekbone.

tempo *n* (*pl* **tempos, tempi**) (*mus*) the speed at which music is meant to be played; rate of any activity.

temporal *adj* relating to time; secular, civil.

temporary *adj* lasting or used for a limited time only; not permanent.–**temporarily** *adv.*

tempt *vt* to entice to do wrong; to invite, attract, induce.–**tempter** *n*.–**temptress** *nf*.

temptation *n* the act of tempting or the state of being tempted; something or someone that tempts.

tempting *adj* attractive, inviting.

tempura *n* a Japanese dish of seafood or vegetables fried in batter.

ten *adj, n* the cardinal number next above nine. * *n* the symbol for this (10, X, x).

tenable *adj* capable of being believed, held, or defended.

tenacious *adj* grasping firmly; persistent; retentive; adhesive.

tenacity *n* the state or quality of being tenacious; doggedness, obstinacy; adhesiveness, stickiness.

tenancy *n* (*pl* **tenancies**) the temporary possession by a tenant of another's property; the period of this.

tenant *n* a person who pays rent to occupy a house or apartment or for the use of land or buildings; an occupant.

tend[1] *vt* to take care of; to attend (to).

tend[2] *vi* to be inclined; to move in a specific direction.

tendency *n* (*pl* **tendencies**) an inclination or leaning.

tendentious, tendencious *adj* showing bias, not impartial.–**tendentiousness, tendenciousness** *n*.

tender[1] *vt* to present for acceptance; to offer as payment. * *vi* to make an offer. * *n* an offer to provide goods or services at a fixed price.

tender[2] *adj* soft, delicate; fragile; painful, sore; sensitive; sympathetic.–**tenderly** *adv.*–**tenderness** *n*.

tenderize *vt* (*meat*) to make more tender by pounding or by adding a substance that softens.–**tenderization** *n*.–**tenderizer** *n*.

tendon *n* fibrous tissue attaching a muscle to a bone.

tendril *n* a thread-like shoot of a climbing plant by which it attaches itself for support.

tenement *n* a building divided into apartments, each occupied by a separate owner or tenant.

tenet *n* any belief or doctrine.

Tenn. *abbr* = Tennessee.

tennis *n* a game for two or four people, played by hitting a ball over a net with a racket.

tennis court *n* a court surfaced with clay, asphalt or grass on which tennis is played.

tennis elbow *n* stiffness and pain in the elbow joint due to excessive exercise, such as playing tennis.

tenor *n* a general purpose or intent; the highest regular adult male voice, higher than a baritone and lower than an alto; a man who sings tenor.

tense[1] *n* (*gram*) the verb form that indicates the time of an action or the existence of a state.

tense[2] *adj* stretched, taut; apprehensive; nervous and highly strung. * *vti* to make or become tense.–**tensely** *adv.*–**tenseness** *n*.

tension *n* the act of stretching; the state of being stretched; (*between forces, etc*) opposition; stress; mental strain.–**tensile** *adj*.

tent *n* a portable shelter of canvas, plastic or other waterproof fabric, which is erected on poles and fixed to the ground by ropes and pegs.

tentacle *n* a long, slender, flexible growth near the mouth of invertebrates, used for feeling, grasping or handling.

tentative *adj* provisional; not definite.–**tentatively** *adv.*–**tentativeness** *n*.

tenth *adj* the last of ten; being one of ten equal parts. * *n* one of ten equal parts.

tenuous *adj* slight, flimsy, insubstantial.–**tenuousness** *n*.

tenure *n* the holding of property or a position; the period of time which a position lasts; a permanent position, usu granted after holding a job for a number of years.–**tenured** *adj*.

tepee *n* a cone-shaped, North American Indian tent formed of skins; a wigwam.–*also* **teepee**.

tepid *adj* slightly warm, lukewarm.

tequila *n* a spirit distilled from a Mexican agave plant; the plant itself.

term *n* a limit; any prescribed period of time; a division of an academic year; a word or expression, esp in a specialized field of knowledge; (*pl*) mutual relationship between people; (*pl*) conditions of a contract, etc. * *vt* to call, designate.

terminal *adj* being or situated at the end or extremity; (*disease*) fatal, incurable. * *n* a bus, coach or railroad station at the end of the line; the point at which an electrical current enters or leaves a device; a device with a keyboard and monitor for inputting or viewing data from a computer.–**terminally** *adv.*

terminate *vti* to bring or come to an end.–**termination** *n*.

terminology *n* (*pl* **terminologies**) the terms used in any specialized subject.

terminus *n* (*pl* **termini, terminuses**) the final part; a limit; end of a transportation line.

termite *n* a wood-eating, white, ant-like insect.

terrace *n* a raised level area of earth, often part of a slope; an unroofed paved area adjoining a house; a row of houses; a patio or balcony. * *vt* to make into a terrace.

terracotta n a brownish-red clay used for making flower pots and statues, which is baked but not glazed; a brown-red color.

terrain n the surface features of a tract of land; (fig) field of activity.

terrestrial adj relating to, or existing on, the earth; earthly; representing the earth.

terrible adj causing great fear; dreadful; (inf) very unpleasant.

terribly adv frighteningly; (inf) very.

terrier n a type of small, active dog.

terrific adj of great size; (inf) excellent.

terrify vt (**terrifying, terrified**) to fill with terror, to frighten greatly.

territorial adj relating to or owned by a territory.

territory n (pl **territories**) an area under the jurisdiction of a city or state; a wide tract of land; an area assigned to a salesman; an area of knowledge.

terror n great fear; an object or person inspiring fear or dread.

terrorism n the use of terror and violence to intimidate.—**terrorist** n.

terrorize vt to terrify; to control by terror.—**terrorization** n.

terse adj abrupt, to the point, concise.—**tersely** adv.

tertiary adj third.

test n an examination; trial; a chemical reaction to test a substance or to test for an illness; a series of questions or exercises. * vt to examine critically.

testament n a will; proof; tribute; (with cap) one of the two main parts of the Bible.

testate adj having made and left a will.

testator n a person who leaves a will.

test ban n an agreement between nations to limit or abandon tests of nuclear weapons.

testes see **testis**.

testicle n either of the two male reproductive glands that produce sperm, a testis.

testify vb (**testifying, testified**) vi to give evidence under oath; to serve as witness (to); (with **to**) to be evidence of. * vt to be evidence of.

testimonial adj relating to a testimony. * n a recommendation of one's character or abilities.

testimony n (pl **testimonies**) evidence; declaration of truth or fact.

testis n (pl **testes**) a testicle.

testosterone n a steroid hormone secreted by the testes.

test pilot n someone who flies new types of aircraft to test their performance and characteristics.

test tube n a cylinder of thin glass closed at one end, used in scientific experiments.

testy adj (**testier, testiest**) touchy, irritable.

tetanus n an intense and painful spasm of muscles, caused by the infection of a wound by bacteria; lockjaw.

tetchy adj (**tetchier, tetchiest**) irritable, touchy.—also **techy**.—**tetchily** adv.—**tetchiness** n.

tête-à-tête n (pl **tête-à-têtes, tête-à-tête**) a private conversation between two people.

tether n a rope or chain for tying an animal; the limit of one's endurance. * vt to fasten with a tether; to limit.

tetrahedron n (pl **tetrahedrons, tetrahedra**) a solid figure enclosed by four plane faces of triangular shape.

Tex. abbr = Texas.

text n the main part of a printed work; the original or exact wording; a passage from the Bible forming the basis of a sermon; a subject or topic; a textbook.

textbook n a book used as a basis for instruction.

textile n a woven fabric or cloth. * adj relating to the making of fabrics.

textual adj of or relating to a text; contained in or based on a text; (operation, etc) exactly as planned according to theory or calculation.

texture n the characteristic appearance, arrangement or feel of a thing; the way in which threads in a material are interwoven.—**textural** adj.

thalidomide n a sedative drug withdrawn from use when it was discovered to cause malformation in unborn babies.

than conj introducing the second element of a comparison.

thank vt to express gratitude to or appreciation for. * npl an expression of gratitude.—**thankful** adj.—**thankfully** adv.

thankless adj without thanks; unappreciated; fruitless, unrewarding.—**thanklessness** n.

thanksgiving n the act of giving thanks; a prayer of gratitude to God; (with cap) Thanksgiving Day.

Thanksgiving Day n a legal holiday observed on the fourth Thursday of November in the US, and on the second Monday of October in Canada.

thank-you n an expression of gratitude.

that demons adj, pron (pl **those**) the (one) there or then, esp the latter or more distant thing. * rel pron who or which. * conj introducing noun clause or adverbial clause of purpose or consequence; because; in order that; (preceded by **so, such**) as a result.

thatch n roofing straw. * vt to cover a roof with thatch.

thaw vi to melt or grow liquid; to become friendly. *vt to cause to melt. * n the melting of ice or snow by warm weather.

the demons adj denoting a particular person or thing. * adv used before comparative adjectives or adverbs for emphasis.

theater, theatre n a building where plays and operas are performed; the theatrical world as a whole; a setting for important events; field of operations.

theatrical adj relating to the theater; melodramatic, affected.—**theatrically** adv.

thee pron the objective case of **thou**.

theft n act or crime of stealing.

their poss adj of or belonging to them; his, hers, its.

theirs poss pron of or belonging to them; his, hers, its.

them pron the objective case of **they**.

theme n the main subject of a discussion; an idea or motif in a work; a short essay; a leading melody; a style adopted for an exhibition, activity, etc.—**thematic** adj.

theme park n a leisure area in which the buildings and settings follow a particular theme, eg a period in history.

themselves pron the reflexive form of **they** or **them**.

then adv at that time; afterward; immediately; next in time. * conj for that reason; in that case.

thence adv from that time or place; for that reason.

theologian n a person who studies and interprets religious texts, etc; a teacher of theology.

theology n (pl **theologies**) the study of God and of religious doctrine and matters of divinity.—**theological, theologic** adj.—**theologically** adv.

theorem n a proposition that can be proved from accepted principles; law or principle.

theoretical, theoretic adj of or based on theory, not practical application; hypothetical; conjectural.—**theoretically** adv.

theorize vi to form theories; to speculate.—**theorist, theorizer** n.—**theorization** n.

theory n (pl **theories**) an explanation or system of anything; ideas and abstract principles of a science or art; speculation; a hypothesis.

therapeutic, therapeutical adj relating to the treatment of disease; beneficial.—**therapeutically** adv.

therapy n (pl **therapies**) the treatment of physical or mental illness.—**therapist** n.

there adv in, at or to, that place or point; in that respect; in that matter.

thereabout, thereabouts adv at or near that place or number.

thereafter adv after that; according to that.

therefore adv for that or this reason; consequently.

therm n a measurement of heat.

thermal, thermic adj generating heat; hot; warm; (underwear) of a knitted material with air spaces for insulation. * n a rising current of warm air.

thermometer n an instrument for measuring temperature.

Thermos n (trademark) a brand of vacuum bottle to keep liquids hot or cold.

thermostat n an automatic device for regulating temperatures.

thesaurus n (pl thesauri, thesauruses) a reference book of synonyms and antonyms.

these see **this**.

thesis n (pl theses) a dissertation written as part of an academic degree; a theory expressed as a statement for discussion.

thespian adj of or pertaining to drama. * n an actor or actress.

they pers pron, pl of **he**, **she** or **it**.

they'd = they would; they had.

they'll = they will; they shall.

they're = they are.

they've = they have.

thiamine, thiamin n vitamin B, present in a wide variety of plants and animals and essential for normal metabolism and nerve function.

thick adj dense; viscous; fat, broad; abundant, closely set; in quick succession; crowded; (inf) stupid. * adv closely; frequently.

thicken vti to make or become thick.–**thickener** n.

thicket n a small group of trees or shrubs growing thickly and closely together.

thickness n being thick; the dimension other than length or width; a layer.

thickset adj having a short, stocky body.

thick-skinned adj not sensitive; not easily offended.

thief n (pl thieves) a person who steals.

thieve vti to steal.

thigh n the thick fleshy part of the leg from the hip to the knee.

thimble n a cap or cover worn to protect the finger when sewing.

thin adj (thinner, thinnest) narrow; slim; lean; sparse, weak, watery; (material) fine; not dense. * vt to make thin; to make less crowded; to water down.–**thinly** adv.–**thinness** n.

thing n an inanimate object; an event; an action; (pl) possessions; (inf) an obsession.

think vb (thinking, thought) vi to exercise the mind in order to make a decision; to revolve ideas in the mind, to ponder; to remember; to consider; * vt to judge, to believe or consider; (with up) to concoct, devise; (with over) to ponder, to consider the costs and benefits of.–**thinker** n.

thin-skinned adj overly sensitive to criticism; easily offended.

third adj the last of three; being one of three equal parts. * n one of three equal parts.

third degree n the use of torture, bullying or rough questioning to obtain information.

thirdly adv in the third place; as a third point.

third person n grammatical forms, such as pronouns and verbs, used when referring to the person or thing spoken or written of, not to the person speaking or writing or to the person or persons addressed.

third-rate adj inferior.

Third World n the underdeveloped countries of the world (usu refers to Africa, Asia and South America).

thirst n a craving for drink; a longing. * vi to feel thirst; to have a longing.

thirsty adj (thirstier, thirstiest) having a desire to drink; dry, arid; longing or craving for.–**thirstily** adv.–**thirstiness** n.

thirteen adj, n three and ten.–**thirteenth** adj, n.

thirty adj, n (pl thirties) three times ten.–**thirtieth** adj, n.

this demons pron (pl these) or adj denoting a person or thing near, just mentioned, or about to be mentioned.

thistle n a wild plant with prickly leaves and a purple flower.

thither adv (arch) to or toward that place.

thong n a piece or strap of leather to lash things together; the lash of a whip; a sandal held on the foot by a thong passing between the toes and fixed to a strap passing over the top of the foot.

thorax n (pl thoraxes, thoraces) the part of the body enclosed by the ribs; the chest; (in insects) the middle one of the three chief divisions of the body.–**thoracic** adj.

thorn n a shrub or small tree having thorns, esp hawthorn; a sharp point or prickle on the stem of a plant or the branch of a tree.

thorny adj (thornier, thorniest) prickly; (problem) knotty.

thorough adj complete, very detailed and painstaking, exhaustive.–**thoroughness** n.

thoroughbred adj bred from pure stock. * n a pedigree animal, esp a horse.

thoroughfare n a way through; a public highway, road; right of passing through.

thoroughly adv completely, fully; entirely, absolutely.

those adj, pron plural of **that**.

thou pron an old-fashioned word for **you**.

though conj yet, even if; * adv however; nevertheless.

thought n the act of thinking; reasoning; serious consideration; an idea; opinions collectively; design, intention. * pt, pp of **think**.

thoughtful adj pensive; considerate.

thoughtless adj without thought; inconsiderate.

thousand adj ten times one hundred; (pl) denoting any large but unspecified number. * n the number 1000.–**thousandth** adj, n.

thrash vt to beat soundly; to defeat; (with out) to discuss thoroughly, until agreement is reached. * vi to thresh grain; to writhe.–**thrashing** n.

thread n a fine strand or filament; a long thin piece of cotton, silk or nylon for sewing; the spiral part of a screw; (of reasoning) a line. * vt to pass a thread through the eye of a needle; to make one's way (through).

threadbare adj worn, shabby.

threadworm n a long slender worm, parasitic in humans and pigs.

threat n a declaration of an intention to inflict harm or punishment upon another.

threaten vti to utter threats to; to portend.–**threatening** adj.–**threateningly** adv.

three adj, n the cardinal number next above two. * n the symbol (3, III, iii) expressing this.

three-D, 3-D n a three-dimensional effect.

three-dimensional adj having three dimensions.

three-quarter adj being three quarters of the normal size or length.

threesome n a group of three; a game for three people.

thresh vti to beat out (grain) from (husks).

threshold n the sill at the door of a building; doorway, entrance; the starting point, beginning.

threw see **throw**.

thrice adv three times.

thrift n careful management of money.–**thrifty** adj.

thrift store, thrift shop n a store that sells used clothing and other items to raise money for charity.

thrill vti to tingle with pleasure or excitement. * n a sensation of pleasure and excitement; a trembling or quiver.

thriller n a novel, movie or play depicting an exciting story of mystery and suspense.

thrive vi (thriving, thrived or throve, pp thrived or thriven) to prosper, to be successful; to grow vigorously.–**thriving** adj.

throat n the front part of the neck; the passage from the back of the mouth to the top of the tubes into the lungs and stomach; an entrance.

throaty adj (throatier, throatiest) hoarse; guttural; deep, husky.–**throatily** adv.

throb vi (**throbbing, throbbed**) to beat or pulsate rhythmically, with more than usual force; to vibrate, beat.–also n.

throes npl violent pangs or pain.

thrombosis n (pl **thromboses**) the forming of a blood clot in the heart or in a blood-vessel.

throne n a chair of state occupied by a monarch; sovereign power. * vt to place on a throne.

throng n a crowd. * vti to crowd, congregate.

throttle n a valve controlling the flow of fuel or steam to an engine. * vt to regulate the speed of (an engine) using a throttle; to choke or strangle.

through prep from one side or end to the other; into and then out of; covering all parts; from beginning to end of; by means of; in consequence of; up to and including. * adv from one end or side to the other; completely. * adj going without interruption; unobstructed.

throughout prep in every part of; from beginning to end. * adv everywhere; at every moment.

throughway see **thruway**.

throve see **thrive**.

throw vb (**throwing, threw**, pp **thrown**) vt to hurl, to fling; to cast off; (party) to hold; (inf) to confuse or disconcert; (with **off**) to cast off, discard, abandon; to distract, elude; to produce in a casual manner; to confuse, disconcert; (with **out**) to discard, reject; to dismiss or eject, esp forcibly; to emit, give forth; to construct out from a main section; to confuse, distract; (with **over**) to abandon, jilt; (with **together**) to assemble hurriedly or carelessly; to bring (people) into casual contact; (with **up**) to raise quickly; to resign from, abandon; to build hurriedly; to produce; (inf) to vomit. * vi to cast or hurl through the air (with the arm and wrist); to cast dice; (with **up**) (inf) to vomit. * n the act of throwing; the distance to which anything can be thrown; a cast of dice.

throwaway adj disposable.

throwback n a reversion to an earlier or more primitive type.

thrown see **throw**.

thru prep (sl) through.

thrush[1] n a songbird with a brown back and spotted breast.

thrush[2] n a fungal disease occurring in the mouths of babies or in women's vaginas.

thrust vti (**thrusting, thrust**) to push with force; to stab, pierce; to force into a situation. * n a forceful push or stab; pressure; the driving force of a propeller; forward movement; the point or basic meaning.

thruway n an expressway.–also **throughway**.

thud n a dull, heavy sound, caused by a blow or a heavy object falling. * vi (**thudding, thudded**) to make such a sound.

thug n a violent and rough person, esp a criminal.

thumb n the first, short, thick finger of the human hand. * vt (book) to turn (the pages) idly.

thumbtack n a flat-headed pin used for fastening paper, drawings, etc, a drawing pin.

thump n a heavy blow; a thud. * vt to strike with something heavy. * vi to throb or beat violently.

thunder n the deep rumbling or loud cracking sound after a flash of lightning; any similar sound. * vi to sound as thunder. * vt (words) to utter loudly.

thunderbolt n a flash of lightning accompanied by thunder; anything sudden and shocking.

thunderclap n a loud bang of thunder.

thunderstorm n a storm with thunder and lightning.

thunderstruck adj astonished.

Thursday n the fifth day of the week.

thus adv in this or that way; to this degree or extent; so; therefore.

thwart vt to prevent, to frustrate.

thy poss adj an old-fashioned word for **your**.

thyme n a herb with small leaves used for flavoring savory food.

thyroid n the gland in the neck affecting growth and metabolism.

tiara n a semicircular crown decorated with jewels.

tibia n (pl **tibiae, tibias**) the inner and thicker of the two bones between the knee and the ankle; the shinbone.

tic n any involuntary, regularly repeated, spasmodic contraction of a muscle.

tick[1] n a small bloodsucking insect that lives on people and animals.

tick[2] vi to make a regular series of short sounds; to beat, as a clock; (inf) to work, function; (with **over**) (engine) to idle; to function routinely. * n the sound of a clock; (sl) a moment.

tick[3] vt (often with **off**) to check off, as items in a list. * n a check mark (_) to check off items on a list or to indicate correctness.

ticket n a printed card, etc, that gives one a right of travel or entry; a label on merchandise giving size, price, etc.

tickle vt to touch lightly to provoke pleasure or laughter; to please or delight.

ticklish, tickly adj sensitive to being tickled; easily offended; difficult or delicate.

tick-tack-toe n sing a game in which two players place noughts and crosses into squares on a grid with nine spaces, the winner being the first to form a row of three noughts or crosses, noughts and crosses.

tidal wave n a large wave as a result of high winds with spring tides; a huge destructive wave caused by earthquakes; something overwhelming.

tidbit see **titbit**.

tide n the regular rise and fall of the seas, oceans, etc usu twice a day; a current of water; a tendency; a flood. * vt (with **over**) to help along temporarily.–**tidal** adj.

tidings npl news, information.

tidy adj (**tidier, tidiest**) neat; orderly. * vt to make neat; to put things in order.–**tidily** adv.–**tidiness** n.

tie vb (**tying, tied**) vt to bind; to fasten with a string or thread; to make a bow or knot in; to restrict; (with **in**) to link with something; (with **up**) to fasten tightly (as if) with cord, string, etc; to connect, link; to invest money, etc, so as to make it unavailable for alternative uses; to preoccupy, distract. * vi to score the same number of points (as an opponent); (with **in**) to be linked in a certain way; (with **up**) to dock (a vessel). * n a knot, bow, etc; a bond; a long narrow piece of cloth worn with a shirt; necktie; an equality in score.

tiebreaker, tiebreak n any means of deciding a contest which has ended in a draw, such as an extra game, hole, question, etc.

tie-in n a link or connection; a book linked to a film or TV series.

tier n a row or rank in a series when several rows are placed one above another.

tiff n a petty quarrel or disagreement. * vi to quarrel; to be in a huff.

tiger n a large, fierce carnivorous animal of the cat family, having orange and black stripes.–**tigress** nf.

tight adj taut; fitting closely; not leaky; constricted; miserly; difficult; providing little space or time for variance; (contest) close; (inf) drunk.

tighten vti to make or grow tight or tighter.

tightfisted adj miserly.

tightrope n a taut rope on which acrobats walk.

tights npl (Brit) a one-piece garment covering the legs and lower body, panty hose.

tike see **tyke**.

tile n a thin slab of baked clay used for covering roofs, floors, etc. * vt to cover with tiles.

till[1] n a drawer inside a cash register for keeping money.

till[2] prep until. * conj until.

till[3] vt (land) to cultivate for raising crops, as by ploughing.

tiller n the handle or lever for turning a rudder in order to steer a boat.

tilt *vi* to slope, incline, slant. * *vt* to raise one end of. * *n* a slope or angle.

timber *n* wood when used as building material; a beam; trees collectively. * *vt* to provide with timber or beams.

timbre *n* the quality of sound of a voice or musical instrument.

time *n* the past, present and future; a particular moment; hour of the day; an opportunity; the right moment; duration; occasion; musical beat. * *vt* to regulate as to time; to measure or record the duration of.

time bomb *n* a bomb designed to explode at a predetermined time; something with a potentially delayed reaction.

time-honored *adj* traditional, in accordance with venerable customs.

timekeeper *n* a person or instrument that records or keeps time; an employee who records the hours worked by others.–**timekeeping** *n*.

timeless *adj* eternal; ageless.

timely *adj* at the right time, opportune.–**timeliness** *n*.

time-out *n* (*sport*) a suspension of play to rest, discuss tactics, etc; a brief rest period.

timer *n* a device for measuring, recording or controlling time; a device for controlling lights, heating, etc by setting an electrical clock to regulate their operations.

timetable *n* a list of times of arrivals and departures of trains, aeroplanes, etc; a schedule showing a planned order or sequence.

time zone *n* a geographical region throughout which the same standard time is used.

timid *adj* shy; lacking confidence.–**timidity** *n*.–**timidly** *adv*.

timing *n* the control and expression of speech or actions to create the best effect, esp in the theater, etc.

timorous *adj* timid, fearful.–**timorously** *adv*.–**timorousness** *n*.

timpani *npl* a set of kettledrums.–**timpanist** *n*.–*also* **tympani, tympany**.

tin *n* a malleable metallic element; a container of tin, a can. * *adj* made of tin or tin plate. * *vt* (**tinning, tinned**) to put food into a tin.

tincture *n* an extract of a substance in a solution of alcohol for medicinal use; a color, hue, tint; a hint of flavor or aroma; an heraldic color. * *vt* to tint with a color.

tinfoil *n* baking foil for wrapping food; silver paper.

tinge *vt* to tint or color. * *n* a slight tint, color or flavor.

tingle *vi* to feel a prickling, itching or stinging sensation. * *n* a prickling sensation; a thrill.–**tinglingly** *adv*.–**tingly** *adj*.

tinker *vi* to fiddle with; to attempt to repair.

tinkle *vi* to make a sound like a small bell ringing; to clink, to jingle; to clink repeatedly. * *n* a tinkling sound; (*inf*) a telephone call.

tinnitus *n* a continuous ringing or roaring sound in the ears caused by an infection, etc.

tinny *adj* (**tinnier, tinniest**) of or resembling tin; flimsy in construction or appearance; (*food*) having a metallic taste; having a high metallic sound.

tinsel *n* a shiny Christmas decoration made of long pieces of thread wound round with thin strips of metal or plastic foil; something showy but of low value. * *adj* cheaply showy, flashy. * *vt* (**tinseling, tinseled** *or* **tinselling, tinselled**) to adorn with tinsel.

tint *n* a shade of any color, esp a pale one; a tinge; a hair dye. * *vt* to color or tinge.

tiny *adj* (**tinier, tiniest**) very small.

tip[1] *n* the pointed end of anything; the end, as of a billiard cue, etc. * *vt* (**tipping, tipped**) to put a tip on.

tip[2] *vti* (**tipping, tipped**) to tilt or cause to tilt; to overturn; to empty (out, into, etc); to give a gratuity to, as a waiter, etc; (*garbage*) to dump; to give a helpful hint or inside information to. * *n* a light tap; a gratuity; (*Brit*) a garbage dump; an inside piece of information; a helpful hint.

tip-off *n* a warning based on inside information.

tipple *vi* to drink alcohol regularly in small quantities. * *n* an alcoholic drink.

tipsy *adj* (**tipsier, tipsiest**) slightly drunk.

tiptoe *vi* (**tiptoeing, tiptoed**) to walk very quietly or carefully.

tiptop *adj* excellent. * *adv* at the peak of condition. * *n* the best; the highest point.

tirade *n* a long angry speech of censure or criticism.

tire[1] *vt* to exhaust the strength of, to weary. * *vi* to become weary; to lose patience; to become bored.

tire[2] *n* a protective, usu rubber, covering around the rim of a wheel.–*also* **tyre**.

tired *adj* weary, sleepy; hackneyed, conventional, flat; (*with* **of**) exasperated by, bored with.

tireless *adj* never wearying.–**tirelessly** *adv*.–**tirelessness** *n*.

tiresome *adj* tedious.

tiro *see* **tyro**.

tissue *n* thin, absorbent paper used as a disposable handkerchief, etc; a very finely woven fabric; a mass of organic cells of a similar structure and function.

titanic *adj* monumental; huge.

titanium *n* a strong metallic element used to make lightweight alloys.

tit for tat *n* an equivalent given in retaliation.

tithe *n* a tenth part of agricultural produce, formerly allotted for the maintenance of the clergy and other church purposes. * *vti* to pay a tithe.

titillate *vt* to tickle; to arouse or excite pleasurably.–**titillation** *n*.

title *n* the name of a book, play, piece of music, work of art, etc; the heading of a section of a book; a name denoting nobility or rank or office held, or attached to a personal name; (*law*) that which gives a legal right (to possession).–**titled** *adj*.

title page *n* the page of a book containing its title and usually the author's and publisher's names.

titter *vi* to giggle, snigger. * *n* a suppressed laugh.

titular *adj* having, or relating to, a title; existing in name or title only.

tizzy *n* (*inf*) a state of confusion or agitation.

T-lymphocyte *see* **T-cell**.

TN *abbr* = Tennessee.

TNT *abbr* = trinitrotoluene.

to *prep* in the direction of; toward; as far as; expressing the purpose of an action; indicating the infinitive; introducing the indirect object; in comparison with. * *adv* toward.

toad *n* an amphibious reptile, like a frog, but having a drier skin and spending less time in water.

toadstool *n* a mushroom, esp a poisonous or inedible one.

toady *n* (*pl* **toadies**) a person who flatters insincerely, a sycophant. * *vi* (**toadying, toadied**) (*with* **to**) to act in a servile manner.

to and fro *adv* forward and backward; here and there.–**toing and froing** *n*.

toast *vt* to brown over a fire or in a toaster; to warm; to drink to the health of. * *n* toasted bread; the sentiment or person to which one drinks.

toaster *n* a person who toasts; a thing that toasts, esp an electrical appliance for toasting.

tobacco *n* (*pl* **tobaccos, tobaccoes**) a plant whose dried leaves are used for smoking, chewing or snuff.

toboggan *n* a sled. * *vi* to slide downhill on a toboggan.–**tobogganing** *n*.

today *n* this day; the present age. * *adv* on this day; nowadays.

toddle *vi* to walk with short, unsteady, steps, as a child who is learning to walk.

toddler *n* a young child.

to-do *n* (*pl* **to-dos**) (*inf*) a fuss, commotion, quarrel.

toe *n* one of the five digits on the foot; the part of the shoe or sock that covers the toes.

toehold *n* a small ledge, crack, etc used in climbing; any slight means of support or access.

tofu *n* unfermented soya bean curd, used in cooking.

toga *n* a piece of cloth draped around the body, as worn by citizens in ancient Rome.

together *adv* in one place or group; in cooperation with; in unison; jointly.

toggle *n* a peg attached to a rope to prevent it from passing through a loop or knot; a button of this form; (*comput*) a software instruction for starting or stopping a style, etc. * *vt* to fasten with a toggle.

toil *vi* to work strenuously; to move with great effort. * *n* hard work.

toilet *n* a lavatory; the room containing a lavatory; the act of washing and dressing oneself.

toiletry *n* (*pl* **toiletries**) a lotion, perfume, etc used in washing and dressing oneself.

token *n* a symbol, sign; an indication; a metal disc for a slot machine; a souvenir; a gift voucher. * *adj* nominal; symbolic.

tokenism *n* the making of only a token effort.

told *see* **tell**.

tolerable *adj* bearable; fairly good.–**tolerably** *adv*.

tolerance *n* open-mindedness; forbearance; (*med*) ability to resist the action of a drug, etc; ability of a substance to endure heat, stress, etc without damage.

tolerant *adj* able to put up with the beliefs, actions, etc of others; broad-minded; showing tolerance to a drug, etc; capable of enduring stress, etc.

tolerate *vt* to endure, put up with, suffer.

toll[1] *n* money levied for passing over a bridge or road; a charge for a service; the number of people killed in an accident or disaster.

toll[2] *vt* (*bell*) to ring slowly and repeatedly, as a funeral bell. * *vi* to sound, as a bell. * *n* the sound of a bell when tolling.

tom *n* a male animal, esp a cat.

tomahawk *n* a light axe used by North American Indians.

tomato *n* (*pl* **tomatoes**) a plant with red pulpy fruit used as a vegetable.

tomb *n* a vault in the earth for the burial of the dead.

tomboy *n* a girl who likes rough outdoor activities.

tombstone *n* a memorial stone over a grave.

tomcat *n* a male cat.

tome *n* a large, heavy book, esp a scholarly one.

tomfoolery *n* (*pl* **tomfooleries**) foolish behavior; nonsense.

tomorrow *n* the day after today; the future.–*also adv*.

ton *n* a unit of weight equivalent to 2,000 pounds in US or 2,240 pounds in UK; (*pl*) (*inf*) a great quantity.

tone *n* the quality of a sound; pitch or inflection of the voice; color, shade; body condition. * *vti* to give tone to; to harmonize (with); (*with* **down**) to (become) moderate in tone; (*with* **up**) to make or become healthier, tighter, etc.

tone-deaf *adj* insensitive to differences in musical pitch.

toner *n* a cosmetic used on the skin for various effects; a chemical used to alter the tone of a photograph; the ink particles used in various reprographic devices such as laser printers and photocopiers.

tongs *npl* an instrument consisting of two arms that are hinged, used for grasping and lifting.

tongue *n* the soft, moveable organ in the mouth, used in tasting, swallowing, and speech; the ability to speak; a language; (*shoe*) a piece of leather under the laces; a jet of flame; the tongue of an animal served as food; the catch of a buckle.

tongue-tied *adj* speechless.

tongue-twister *n* a sequence of words that it is difficult to pronounce quickly and clearly.

tonic *n* a medicine that improves physical well-being; something that imparts vigor; a carbonated mineral water with a bitter taste. * *adj* relating to tones or sounds.

tonight *n* this night; the night or evening of the present day.–*also adv*.

tonne *n* metric ton, 1,000 kg.

tonsil *n* one of the two oval organs of soft tissue situated one on each side of the throat.

tonsillitis *n* inflammation of the tonsils.

too *adv* in addition; also, likewise; extremely; very.

took *see* **take**.

tool *n* an implement that is used by hand; a means for achieving any purpose.

tooth *n* (*pl* **teeth**) one of the white, bone-like structures arranged in rows in the mouth, used in biting and chewing; the palate; a tooth-like projection on a comb, saw, or wheel.

toothache *n* a pain in a tooth.

toothbrush *n* a small brush for cleaning teeth.

toothpaste *n* a paste for cleaning teeth, used with a toothbrush.

toothpick *n* a sliver of wood or plastic for removing food particles from between the teeth.

top[1] *n* the highest, or uppermost, part or surface of anything; the highest in rank; the crown of the head; the lid. * *adj* highest; greatest. * *vt* to cover on the top; to remove the top of or from; to rise above; to surpass; (*with* **up**) to raise up to the full capacity or amount.

top[2] *n* a child's toy, which is spun on its pointed base.

topaz *n* any of various yellow gems.

top dog *n* (*inf*) the leader, the most important person.

top hat *n* a man's tall, silk hat.

top-heavy *adj* having an upper part too heavy for the lower, causing instability.

topiary *adj* pertaining to the art or practice of trimming bushes and trees into ornamental shapes. * *n* (**topiaries**) a tree or bush shaped in this way.

topic *n* a subject for discussion; the theme of a speech or writing.–**topical** *adj*.

topless *adj* lacking a top; (*garment*) revealing the breasts; wearing such a garment.

topping *n* a top layer, esp a sauce for food.

topple *vi* to fall over. * *vt* to cause to overbalance and fall; (*government*) to overthrow.

top secret *adj* highly confidential.

topsy-turvy *adj*, *adv* turned upside down; in confusion.

torch *n* a flashlight; a device for giving off a hot flame.–**torch-light** *n*.

tore *see* **tear**.

torment *n* torture, anguish; a source of pain. * *vt* to afflict with extreme pain, physical or mental.–**tormentor, tormenter** *n*.

torn *see* **tear**[2].

tornado *n* (*pl* **tornadoes, tornados**) a violently whirling column of air seen as a funnel-shaped cloud that usu destroys everything in its narrow path.

torpedo *n* (*pl* **torpedoes**) a self-propelled submarine offensive weapon, carrying an explosive charge. * *vt* to attack, hit, or destroy with torpedo(es).

torpid *adj* lethargic, sluggish.–**torpidity** *n*.

torpor *n* a state of lethargy.

torque *n* (*physics*) a force that causes rotation around a central point, such as an axle.

torrent *n* a rushing stream; a flood of words.–**torrential** *adj*.

torrid *adj* burning, parched or scorched with heat; passionate.–**torridity, torridness** *n*.

torsi *see* **torso**.

torsion *n* a twisting effect on an object when equal forces are applied at both ends but in opposite directions.

torso *n* (*pl* **torsos, torsi**) the trunk of the human body.

tortilla *n* a round thin maize pancake usually eaten hot with a topping or filling.

tortoise *n* a slow-moving reptile with a dome-shaped shell into which it can withdraw.

tortuous *adj* full of twists, involved.–**tortuously** *adv*.

torture *n* subjection to severe physical or mental pain to extort a confession, or as a punishment. –*also vt.*–**torturer** *n*.

toss *vt* to throw up; to pitch; to fling; (*head*) to throw back; (*with* **off**) to produce, write, perform, etc, quickly and easily; to drink in one gulp. * *vi* to be tossed about; to move restlessly; (*with* **up**) to spin a coin to decide a question by the side that falls uppermost. * *n* the act of tossing or being tossed; a pitch; a fall.

toss-up *n* the throwing of a coin to decide a question; an even chance.

tot *n* anything little, esp a child; a small measure of spirits.

total *adj* whole, complete; absolute. * *n* the whole sum; the entire amount. * *vt* (**totaling, totaled** *or* **totalling, totalled**) to add up.–**totally** *adv*.

totalitarian *adj* relating to a system of government in which one political group maintains complete control, esp under a dictator.–**totalitarianism** *n*.

totality *n* (*pl* **totalities**) the whole amount.

tote *vt* to carry.

totem *n* an object regarded as a symbol and treated with respect by a particular group of people.

totem pole *n* a large pole carved with totemic symbols used in rituals by certain North American Indian tribes.

totter *vi* to walk unsteadily; to shake or sway as if about to fall.–**tottery** *adj*.

toucan *n* a fruit-eating South American bird with an immense, brightly colored beak.

touch *vt* to come in contact with, esp with the hand or fingers; to reach; to affect with emotion; to tinge or tint; to border on; (*sl*) to ask for money (from); (*with* **off**) to cause to explode, as with a lighted match; to cause (violence, a riot, etc) to start; (*with* **up**) to improve by making minor alterations or additions to. * *vi* to be in contact; to be adjacent; to allude to. * *n* the act of touching; the sense by which something is perceived through contact; a trace; understanding; a special quality or skill.

touch-and-go *adj* precarious, risky.

touchdown *n* the moment when an aircraft or spaceship lands; (*Rugby football, American football*) a placing of the ball on the ground to score.

touchy *adj* (**touchier, touchiest**) irritable; very risky.

tough *adj* strong; durable; hardy; rough and violent; difficult; (*inf*) unlucky.–**toughen** *vti*.–**toughness** *n*.

toupee *n* a wig or section of hair to cover a bald spot, esp worn by men.

tour *n* a turn, period, etc as of military duty; a long trip, as for sightseeing. * *vti* to go on a tour (through).

tourism *n* traveling for pleasure; the business of catering for people who do this; the encouragement of touring.

tourist *n* one who makes a tour, a sightseer, traveling for pleasure.–*also adj*.

tournament *n* a sporting event involving a number of competitors and a series of games.

tourniquet *n* a device for compressing a blood vessel to stop bleeding.

tousle *vt* to make untidy, ruffle, make tangled (esp hair).

tout *vti* (*inf*) to praise highly; (*inf*) to sell betting tips on (race horses); (*inf*) to solicit business in a brazen way. * *n* (*inf*) a person who does so.

tow *vt* to pull or drag with a rope. * *n* the act of towing; a towrope.

toward, towards *prep* in the direction of; concerning; just before; as a contribution to.

towel *n* an absorbent cloth for drying the skin after it is washed, and for other purposes; **to throw in the towel** to admit defeat. * *vti* (**toweling, toweled** *or* **towelling, towelled**) to rub (oneself) with a towel.

toweling, towelling *n* cloth for towels; a rubbing with a towel.

tower *n* a tall, narrow building, standing alone or forming part of another; a fortress. * *vi* (*with* **over**) to rise above; to loom.

towering *adj* immensely tall; powerful, impressive; intense.

town *n* a densely populated urban centre, smaller than a city and larger than a village; the people of a town.

town hall *n* a large building housing the offices of the town council, often with a hall for public meetings.

town house *n* a two or three-story house with a garage below, usu one of a row.

township *n* a division of a county in many US states, constituting a unit of local government; in South Africa, an urban area reserved for Blacks.

toxic *adj* poisonous; harmful; deadly.–**toxicity** *n*.

toxicology *n* the scientific study of poisons, their effects and antidotes.–**toxicologic, toxicological** *adj*.–**toxicologist** *n*.

toxin *n* a poison produced by microorganisms and causing certain diseases.

toy *n* an object for children to play with; a replica; a miniature. * *vi* to trifle; to flirt.

trace *n* a mark etc left by a person, animal or thing; a barely perceptible footprint; a small quantity. * *vt* to follow by tracks; to discover the whereabouts of; (*map, etc*) to copy by following the lines on transparent paper.

trachea *n* (*pl* **tracheae**) the air passage from the mouth to the lungs, the windpipe.

tracheotomy *n* (*pl* **tracheotomies**) an incision into the trachea, esp to bypass a blockage in the air passage.

tracing paper *n* transparent paper used for tracing.

track *vt* to follow the tracks of; (*satellite, etc*) to follow by radar and record position; (*with* **down**) to find by tracking. * *n* a mark left; a footprint; parallel steel rails on which trains run; a course for running or racing; sports performed on a track, as running, hurdling; the band on which the wheels of a tractor or tank run; one piece of music on a record; a sound track.–**tracker** *n*.

track-and-field *adj* denoting various competitive athletic events (as running, jumping, weight-throwing) performed on a track and adjacent field.

track record *n* (*inf*) a record of the past achievements or failures of someone or something.

tracksuit *n* a loose suit worn by athletes to keep warm.

tract[1] *n* an expanse of land or water; a part of a bodily system or organ.

tract[2] *n* a treatise.

tractable *adj* easily worked; easily taught; docile.

traction *n* act or state of drawing and pulling; (*med*) the using of weights to pull on a muscle, etc, to correct an abnormal condition.

tractor *n* a motor vehicle for pulling heavy loads and farming machinery.

trade *n* buying and selling (of commodities); commerce; occupation; customers; business. * *vi* to buy and sell; to exchange; (*with* **on**) to take advantage of.–**trader** *n*.

trade-in *n* a used item given in part payment when buying a replacement.

trademark *n* a name used on a product by a manufacturer to distinguish it from its competitors, esp when legally protected.–*also vt*.

trade-off *n* the exchange or substitution of one thing or priority for another, often as a compromise.

tradition *n* the handing down from generation to generation of opinions and practices; the belief or practice thus passed on; custom.–**traditional** *adj*.–**traditionally** *adv*.

traffic *n* trade; the movement or number of vehicles, pedestrians, etc, along a street, etc. * *vi* (**trafficking, trafficked**) to do business (esp. in illegal drugs).

traffic light *n* one of a set of colored lights used to control traffic at street crossings, etc.

tragedian n an actor who plays mainly tragic roles.–**tragedienne** nf.

tragedy n (pl **tragedies**) a play or drama that is serious and sad, and the climax a catastrophe; an accident or situation involving death or suffering.–**tragic** adj.–**tragically** adv.

tragicomedy n a dramatic or literary work which combines tragic and comic elements; a situation or event with tragic and comic aspects.

trail vt to drag along the ground; to have in its wake; to follow behind; to advertise a film, event or program beforehand. * vi to hang or drag loosely behind; (plant) to climb; (with **off** or **away**) to grow weaker or dimmer. * n a path or track; the scent of an animal; something left in the wake (eg a trail of smoke).

trailblazer n a person who blazes a trail; a pioneer in a particular field.

trailer n a large enclosed vehicle equipped to be lived in and able to be pulled by a car, a large vehicle designed to be towed by a truck, etc; a motor home; an advertisement for a film or television programme.

trailer park n an area available for rent to motor homes, caravans, etc, usu with electricity, water, etc, piped in.

train vt to teach, to guide; to tame for use, as animals; to prepare for racing, etc; (gun, etc) to aim. * vi to do exercise or preparation. * n a series of railroad cars pulled by a locomotive; a sequence; the back part of a dress that trails along the floor; a retinue.–**trainer** n.

trainee n a person who is being trained.

trait n a characteristic feature.

traitor n a person who commits treason or betrays his country, friends, etc.–**traitorous** adj.

trajectory n (pl **trajectories**) the path of an object, such as a bullet, moving through space.

trammel vt (**trammeling, trammeled** or **trammelling, trammelled**) to trap, catch; to hinder, restrict.

tramp vti to walk heavily; to tread or trample; to wander about as a tramp. * n a vagrant; (sl) a prostitute.

trample vti to tread under foot.

trampoline n a sheet of strong canvas stretched tightly on a frame, used in acrobatic tumbling.

trance n a state of unconsciousness, induced by hypnosis, in which some of the powers of the waking body, such as response to commands, may be retained.

tranquil adj quiet, calm, peaceful.–**tranquility, tranquillity** n.–**tranquilly** adv.

tranquilize, tranquillize vt to make tranquil, esp by administering a drug.–**tranquilization, tranquillization** n.

tranquilizer, tranquillizer n a drug that calms.

transact vt (business) to conduct or carry out.

transaction n the act of transacting; something transacted, esp a business deal; (pl) a record of the proceedings of a society.

transatlantic adj crossing the Atlantic Ocean; across, beyond the Atlantic.

transcend vt to rise above or beyond; to surpass.–**transcendent** adj.

transcendental adj beyond physical experience; surpassing; supernatural.–**transcendentally** adv.

transcendental meditation n a technique for emptying and refreshing the mind by repeating a mantra.

transcontinental adj extending or traveling across a continent.–**transcontinentally** adv.

transcribe vt to write out fully from notes or a tape recording; to make a phonetic transcription; to arrange a piece of music for an instrument other than the one it was written for.

transcript n a written or printed copy made by transcribing; an official copy of proceedings, etc.

transcription n the act of transcribing; something transcribed, esp a piece of music; a transcript; a recording made for broadcasting.

transfer vb (**transferring, transferred**) vt to carry, convey, from one place to another; (law) to make over (property) to another; (money) to move from the control of one institution to another. * vi to change to another bus, etc. * n the act of transferring; the state of being transferred; someone or something that is transferred; a design that can be moved from one surface to another.–**transferable** adj.–**transference** n.

transfix vt to impale with a sharp weapon; to paralyse with shock or horror.

transform vti to change the shape, appearance, or condition of; to convert.–**transformation** n.

transformer n a device for changing alternating current with an increase or decrease of voltage.

transfusion n the injection of blood into the veins of a sick or injured person.–**transfuse** vt.

transgress vti to break or violate (a moral law or code of behavior); to overstep (a limit).–**transgression** n.–**transgressor** n.

transient adj temporary; of short duration, momentary.–**transience** n.

transistor n a device using a semiconductor to amplify sound, as in a radio or television; a small portable radio.

transit n a passing over or through; conveyance of people or goods.

transition n passage from one place or state to another; change.–**transitional** adj.

transitive adj (gram) denoting a verb that requires a direct object; of or relating to transition.–**transitively** adv.–**transitivity** n.

translate vti to express in another language; to explain, interpret.–**translation** n.–**translator** n.

translucent adj allowing light to pass through, but not transparent.–**translucence** n.

transmission n the act of transmitting; something transmitted; a system using gears, etc, to transfer power from an engine to a moving part, esp wheels of a vehicle; a radio or television broadcast.

transmit vt (**transmitting, transmitted**) to send from one place or person to another; to communicate; to convey; (radio or television signals) to send out.

transmitter n an apparatus for broadcasting television or radio programs.

transom n a horizontal bar across a window or between a door and a window over it; a fanlight.

transparency n (pl **transparencies**) the state of being transparent; (photog) a slide.–**transparent** adj.–**transparently** adv.

transpire vti to become known, to leak out; (inf) to happen.

transplant vt (plant) to remove and plant in another place; (med) to remove an organ from one person and transfer it to another.–also n.

transport vt to convey from one place to another; to enrapture. * n the system of transporting goods or passengers; the conveyance of troops and their equipment by sea or land; a vehicle for this purpose.–**transportable** adj.–**transportation** n.

transpose vt to put into a different order; to interchange; (mus) to change the key of.–**transposition** n.

transsexual n a person born of one sex who identifies psychologically with the opposite sex.–**transsexualism** n.

transverse adj crosswise.–**transversely** adv.

transvestite n a person who gains sexual pleasure from wearing the clothes of the opposite sex.–**transvestism** n.

trap n a mechanical device or pit for snaring animals; an ambush; a trick to catch someone out; a two-wheeled horsedrawn carriage. * vt (**trapping, trapped**) to catch in a trap; to trick.

trapdoor n a hinged or sliding door in a roof, ceiling or floor.

trapeze n a gymnastic apparatus consisting of a horizontal bar suspended by two parallel ropes.

trapezium n (pl **trapeziums, trapezia**) in US, a quadrilateral in which none of the sides are parallel; a quadrilateral in which two of the sides are parallel.–**trapezial** adj.

trapper n a person who traps animals, esp for their skins.

trappings npl trimmings; additions; ornaments.

trash n nonsense; refuse; rubbish.–**trashy** adj.

trash can n a container for household refuse, a dustbin, garbage can.

trauma n an emotional shock that may cause long-term psychological damage; an upsetting experience.–**traumatic** adj.

travel vb (**traveling, traveled** or **travelling, travelled**) vi to journey or move from one place to another. * vt to journey across, through. * n journey.

travel agency n an agency through which one can book travel.–**travel agent** n.

traveler, traveller n a person who travels; a salesman who travels for a company.

traveler's check n a draft purchased from a bank, etc signed at the time of purchase and signed again at the time of cashing.

traverse n a horizontal move in rock climbing, skiing, etc. * vt to cross.

travesty n (pl **travesties**) a misrepresentation; a poor imitation; a parody.

trawl vti to fish by dragging a large net behind a fishing boat.

trawler n a boat used for trawling.

tray n a flat board, or sheet of metal or plastic, surrounded by a rim, used for carrying food or drink.

treacherous adj untrustworthy, disloyal; unstable, dangerous.

treachery n (pl **treacheries**) disloyalty, betrayal of trust.

tread vti (**treading, trod,** pp **trodden**) to step or walk on, along, in, over or across; to crush or squash (with the feet); to trample (on). * n a step, way of walking; the part of a shoe, wheel, or tyre that touches the ground.

treadle n a foot lever or pedal on a machine.

treadmill n a grind; a monotonous routine.

treason n the crime of betraying one's government or attempting to overthrow it; treachery.–**treasonable** adj.

treasure n wealth and riches hoarded up; a person or thing much valued. * vt to hoard up; to prize greatly.

treasurer n a person appointed to take charge of the finances of a society, government or city.

treasure-trove n (law) valuable items such as gold and silver found buried and of unknown ownership; any valuable find.

treasury n (pl **treasuries**) a place where valuable objects are deposited; the funds or revenues of a government.

treat vt to deal with or regard; to subject to the action of a chemical; to apply medical treatment to; to pay for another person's entertainment; to deal with in speech or writing. * n an entertainment paid for by another person; a pleasure seldom indulged; a unusual cause of enjoyment.

treatise n a formal essay in which a subject is treated systematically.

treatment n the application of drugs, etc, to a patient; the manner of dealing with a person or thing, esp in a novel or painting; behavior toward someone.

treaty n (pl **treaties**) a formal agreement between states.

treble adj triple, threefold; (mus) denoting the treble. * n the highest range of musical notes in singing. * vti to make or become three times as much.

treble clef n (mus) a clef that places G above middle C on the second line of the staff.

tree n a tall, woody, perennial plant having a single trunk, branches and leaves.

trek vi (**trekking, trekked**) to travel slowly or laboriously; (inf) to go on foot (to). * n a long and difficult journey; a migration.

trellis n a structure of latticework, for supporting climbing plants, etc.–**trelliswork** n.

tremble vi to shake, shiver from cold or fear; to quiver.–also n.

tremendous adj awe-inspiring; very large or great; (inf) wonderful; marvellous.

tremor n a vibration; an involuntary shaking.

tremulous adj quivering; agitated.

trench n a long narrow channel in the earth, used for drainage; such an excavation made for military purposes.

trenchant adj keen; incisive; effective.

trench coat n a waterproof coat.

trend n tendency; a current style or fashion.

trendy adj (**trendier, trendiest**) (inf) fashionable. * n (pl **trendies**) (inf) a person who tries to be fashionable.–**trendily** adv.–**trendiness** n.

trepidation n a state of fear or anxiety.

trespass vi to intrude upon another person's property without their permission; to encroach upon, or infringe, another's rights. * n act of trespassing.–**trespasser** n.

trestle n a wooden framework for supporting a table top or scaffold boards.

triad n a group or set of three, a trio.

trial n a test or experiment; judicial examination; an attempt; a preliminary race, game in a competition; suffering; hardship; a person causing annoyance.

trial and error n solving problems through trying various solutions and rejecting the least successful.

trial run n an opportunity to test something before purchase, as a vehicle; a rehearsal.

triangle n (math) a plane figure with three angles and three sides; a percussion instrument consisting of a triangular metal bar beaten with a metal stick.–**triangular** adj.

triathlon n an athletic event in which all contestants compete in swimming, cycling and running.

tribe n a group of people of the same race, sharing the same customs, religion, language or land.–**tribal** adj.–**tribesman** n.

tribulation n distress, difficulty, hardship.

tribunal n a court of justice; a committee that investigates and decides on a particular problem.

tributary n (pl **tributaries**) a stream or river flowing into a larger one.

tribute n a speech, gift or action to show one's respect or thanks to someone; a payment made at certain intervals by one nation to another in return for peace.

trick n fraud; deception; a mischievous plan or joke; a magical illusion; a clever feat; skill, knack; the playing cards won in a round. * adj using fraud or clever contrivance to deceive. * vt to deceive, cheat.–**trickster** n.

trickle vti to flow or cause to flow in drops or in a small stream.–also n.

trick or treat n a Halloween tradition in which children dress in costumes, call on their neighbours and threaten to do mischief if refused presents of sweets, apples, nuts, money, etc.

tricky adj (**trickier, trickiest**) complicated, difficult to handle; risky; cunning, deceitful.–**trickily** adv.–**trickiness** n.

tricycle n a three-wheeled pedal cycle, esp for children.

trident n three-pronged spear.

tried see **try**.

trifle vi to treat lightly; to dally. * n anything of little value; a dessert of whipped cream, custard, sponge cake, sherry, etc.

trifling adj insignificant.

trigger n a catch that when pulled activates the firing mechanism of a gun. * vt (with **off**) to initiate; to set (off).

trigger-happy adj too eager to resort to firearms or violence; rash, aggressive.

trigonometry n the branch of mathematics concerned with calculating the angles of triangles or the lengths of their sides.

trilateral adj having three sides.

trill *vti* to sing or play with a tremulous tone; (*a bird*) to make a shrill, warbling sound.–*also n.*

trilogy *n* (*pl* **trilogies**) any series of three related literary or operatic works.

trim *adj* (**trimmer, trimmest**) in good condition; tidy, neat; slim. * *vt* to neaten; to cut or prune; to decorate; (*ship, aircraft*) to balance the weight of cargo in. * *n* a decorative edging; a haircut that tidies.

trimester *n* a period of three months; a division of the academic year in certain North American colleges and universities.

trimming *n* decorative part of clothing; (*pl*) accompaniments.

trinity *n* (*pl* **trinities**) a group of three; (*with cap*) in Christianity, the union of Father, Son and Holy Spirit in one God.

trinket *n* a small or worthless ornament.

trio *n* (*pl* **trios**) a set of three; (*mus*) a group of three singers or instrumentalists.

trip *vb* (**tripping, tripped**) *vi* to move or tread lightly; to stumble and fall; to make a blunder. * *vt* (*often with* **up**) to cause to stumble; to activate a trip. * *n* a stumble; a journey, tour, or voyage; a slip; a mistake; a light step; a mechanical switch; (*sl*) a hallucinatory experience under the influence of a drug.

tripartite *adj* made up of or divided into three parts; involving or binding three parties.

tripe *n* the stomach lining of a ruminant, prepared for cooking; (*inf*) rubbish, nonsense.

triple *adj* threefold; three times as many. * *vti* to treble.

triple jump *n* an athletic event in which a competitor makes a hop, step and jump in succession.

triplet *n* one of three children born at one birth.

triplicate *adj* threefold.

tripod *n* a three-legged stand, as for supporting a camera.

tripwire *n* a concealed wire that sets off a bomb, booby trap, etc when tripped over.

trite *adj* dull; hackneyed.

triumph *n* a victory; success; a great achievement. * *vi* to win a victory or success; to rejoice over a victory.–**triumphal** *adj.*

triumphant *adj* feeling or showing triumph; celebratory; victorious.–**triumphantly** *adv.*

trivet *n* a three-legged metal stand for supporting hot dishes.

trivia *npl* unimportant details.–**trivial** *adj.*

trod, trodden *see* **tread**.

troglodyte *n* a cave dweller.

troll *n* a supernatural creature, dwelling in a cave, hill, etc.

trolley *n* (*pl* **trolleys**) a streetcar run on overhead electic wires.

trombone *n* brass musical wind instrument whose length is varied with a U-shaped sliding section.

troop *n* a crowd of people; a group of soldiers within a cavalry regiment; (*pl*) armed forces; soldiers. * *vi* to go in a crowd.

trophy *n* (*pl* **trophies**) a cup or shield won as a prize in a competition or contest; a memento, as taken in battle or hunting.

tropic *n* one of the two parallel lines of latitude north and south of the equator; (*pl*) the regions lying between these lines.

tropical *adj* relating to the tropics; (*weather*) hot and humid.

trot *vb* (**trotting, trotted**) *vi* (*horse*) to go, lifting the feet higher than in walking and moving at a faster rate. * *vt* (*with* **out**) (*inf*) to produce or display repeatedly, esp for others' approval; to produce in a trite or careless manner. * *n* the gait of a horse; a brisk pace.

troubadour *n* a minstrel; a poet or singer.

trouble *vti* to cause trouble to; to worry; to pain; to upset; to cause inconvenience; to take pains (to). * *n* an anxiety; a medical condition causing pain; a problem; unrest or disturbance.–**troublesome** *adj.*

troubleshooter *n* a person whose work is to locate and eliminate a source of trouble or conflict.–**troubleshooting** *n.*

trough *n* a long, narrow container for water or animal feed; a channel in the ground.

trounce *vt* to defeat completely.

troupe *n* a traveling company, esp of actors, dancers or acrobats.–**trouper** *n.*

trousers *npl* an item of clothing covering the body from waist to ankle, with two tubes of material for the legs; pants.

trout *n* (*pl* **trout**) a game fish of the salmon family living in fresh water.

trove *see* **treasure trove**.

trowel *n* a hand tool for gardening; a flat-bladed tool for spreading cement, etc.

truant *n* a pupil who is absent from school without permission. * *vi* to play truant.–*also adj.*–**truancy** *n.*

truce *n* an agreement between two armies or states to suspend hostilities.

truck *n* a heavy motor vehicle for transporting goods; a vehicle open at the back for moving goods or animals. * *vt* (*goods*) to convey by truck. * *vi* to drive a truck.

truculent *adj* sullen; aggressive.–**truculence** *n.*–**truculently** *adv.*

trudge *vti* to travel on foot, heavily or wearily. * *n* a tiring walk.

true *adj* (**truer, truest**) conforming with fact; correct, accurate; genuine; loyal; perfectly in tune. * *adv* truthfully; rightly.

truffle *n* a round, edible underground fungus; a sweet made with chocolate, butter and sugar.

truism *n* a self-evident truth.

truly *adv* completely; genuinely; to a great degree.

trump *n* (*cards*) the suit that is chosen to have the highest value in one game. * *vt* to play a trump card on; (*with* **up**) to invent maliciously, fabricate (an accusation, etc).

trumpet *n* a brass wind instrument consisting of a long tube with a flared end and three buttons. * *vti* to proclaim loudly.–**trumpeter** *n.*

truncate *vt* to cut the top end off; to shorten.–**truncation** *n.*

trundle *vt* (*an object*) to push or pull on wheels. * *vi* to move along slowly.

trunk *n* the main stem of a tree; the torso; the main body of anything; the proboscis of an elephant; a strong box or chest for clothes, etc, esp on a journey; storage space at the rear of a car; (*pl*) a man's short, light pants for swimming.

truss *n* a supporting framework for a roof or bridge; a hernia brace. * *vt* to bind (up).

trust *n* firm belief in the truth of anything, faith in a person; confidence in; custody; a financial arrangement of investing money for another person; a business syndicate. * *adj* held in trust. * *vti* to have confidence in; to believe.–**trustful** *adj.*

trustee *n* a person who has legal control of money or property that they are keeping or investing for another person, or for an organization or institution.–**trusteeship** *n.*

trustworthy *adj* reliable, dependable.

trusty *adj* (**trustier, trustiest**) trustworthy, faithful.–**trustily** *adv.*–**trustiness** *n.*

truth *n* that which is true, factual or genuine; agreement with reality.–**truthful** *adj.*–**truthfulness** *n.*

try *vb* (**trying, tried**) *vt* to test the result or effect by experiment; to determine judicially; to put strain on; (*with* **on**) to put (a garment) on to check the fit, etc; (*inf*) to attempt to deceive somebody; (*with* **out**) to test (someone) for a job, etc. * *vi* to attempt; to make an effort; (*with* **out**) to undergo a test (for a job, team, etc). * *n* (*pl* **tries**) an attempt, an effort; (*Rugby football*) a score made with a touchdown.

trying *adj* causing annoyance, exasperating.–**tryingly** *adv.*–**tryingness** *n.*

tryout *n* an experimental test; an audition for a theatrical part; (*sports, etc*) a test for a position in a team.

tsar *n* (*formerly*) the title of the emperors of Russia (until 1917) and sovereigns of certain other Slav nations; a powerful person.–*also* **czar**.

tsarina *n* the wife of a tsar; an empress.–*also* **czarina**.

tsetse fly *n* a fly that feeds on blood and transmits diseases.

T-shirt *n* a short-sleeved casual cotton top.–*also* **tee-shirt**.

tsp. *abbr* = teaspoon.

T-square *n* a T-shaped instrument for drawing and determining right angles.

tub *n* a circular container, made of staves and hoops; a bathtub.

tuba *n* a large brass instrument of bass pitch.

tubby *adj* (**tubbier, tubbiest**) plump.

tube *n* a long, thin, hollow pipe; a soft metal or plastic cylinder in which thick liquids or pastes, such as toothpaste, are stored.–**tubular** *adj*.

tuber *n* the swollen, fleshy root of a plant where reserves of food are stored up, as a potato.

tuberculosis *n* an infectious disease of the lungs.–**tubercular** *adj*.

tuck *vt* to draw or gather together in a fold; (*with* **up**) to wrap snugly. * *vi* (*inf*) (*with* **into**) to eat greedily. * *n* a fold in a garment.

Tuesday *n* the third day of the week.

tuft *n* a bunch of grass, hair or feathers held together at the base; a clump.

tug *vti* (**tugging, tugged**) to pull with effort or to drag along. * *n* a strong pull; a tugboat.

tugboat *n* a small powerful boat for towing ships.

tug of war *n* a contest in which two teams tug on opposite ends of a rope to pull the opposing team over a central line; a struggle for supremacy between two opponents.

tuition *n* teaching, instruction.

tulip *n* a highly-colored cup-shaped flower grown from bulbs.

tumble *vi* to fall over; to roll or to twist the body, as an acrobat; (*with* **to**) (*inf*) to discover (a secret, etc); to understand. * *vt* to push or cause to fall. * *n* a fall.

tumbler *n* a large drinking glass without a handle or stem; an acrobat.

tummy *n* (*pl* **tummies**) (*inf*) stomach.

tumor, tumour *n* an abnormal growth of tissue in any part of the body.

tumult *n* a commotion; an uproar.–**tumultuous** *adj*.–**tumultuously** *adv*.

tuna *n* (*pl* **tuna, tunas**) a large ocean fish of the mackerel group.

tundra *n* a vast treeless arctic plain.

tune *n* a melody; correct musical pitch; harmony. * *vt* (*musical instrument*) to adjust the notes of; (*radio, TV etc*) to adjust the resonant frequency, etc, to a particular value; (*with* **up**) to adjust an engine to improve its performance. * *vi* (*with* **up**) to adjust (musical instruments) to a common pitch before playing.–**tuneful** *adj*.–**tunefully** *adv*.

tungsten *n* a hard malleable grayish white metallic element used in lamps, etc, and in alloys with steel.

tunic *n* a hip or knee-length loose, usu belted blouse-like garment; a close-fitting jacket worn by soldiers and policemen.

tuning fork *n* a two-pronged steel fork that produces a fixed note when struck and is used to tune musical instruments or set a pitch for singing.

tunnel *n* an underground passage, esp one for cars or trains underneath a river or town center. * *vb* (**tunneling, tunneled** *or* **tunnelling, tunnelled**) *vt* to make a way through. * *vi* to make a tunnel.

tunnel vision *n* a condition in which peripheral vision is impaired; a narrowness of viewpoint due to preoccupation with a single idea, plan, etc.

turban *n* a headdress consisting of cloth wound in folds around the head worn by men; a woman's hat of this shape.

turbine *n* a machine in which power is produced when the forced passage of steam, water, etc causes the blades to rotate.

turbojet engine *n* a gas turbine that provides propulsive power from a jet of hot exhaust gases.

turboprop *n* a jet aircraft engine that also operates a turbine-driven air compressor.

turbulence *n* a state of confusion and disorder; (*weather*) instability causing gusty air currents.–**turbulent** *adj*.

tureen *n* a large dish for serving soup, etc.

turf *n* (*pl* **turfs, turves**) the surface layer of grass and its roots; (*with* **the**) horse racing; a racetrack. * *vt* to cover with turf; (*with* **out**) (*inf*) to eject forcibly, throw out.

turgid *adj* swollen; pompous, bombastic.–**turgidity** *n*.–**turgidly** *adv*.

turkey *n* (*pl* **turkeys, turkey**) a large bird farmed for its meat.

turmeric *n* a tropical Indian plant; the powdered stem of this plant used as a yellow coloring agent and curry spice.

turmoil *n* agitation; disturbance, confusion.

turn *vi* to revolve; to go in the opposite direction; to depend on; to appeal (to) for help; to direct (thought or attention) away from; to change in character; to be shaped on the lathe; (*with* **off**) to leave or deviate from a road, etc; (*with* **in**) (*inf*) to retire to bed for the night; (*with* **on**) to depend on; (*with* **to**) to begin a task; (*with* **up**) to appear, arrive; to find unexpectedly; to happen without warning. * *vt* to change the position or direction of by revolving; to reverse; to transform; (*age, etc*) to have just passed; to change or convert; to invert; (*with* **off**) to cause to cease operating (as if) by flicking a switch, turning a knob, etc; (*inf*) to cause a person to lose interest in or develop a dislike for something; (*with* **down**) to reduce the volume or intensity of (sound, brightness, etc); to refuse, decline; to fold down (sheets, a collar, etc); (*with* **in**) to deliver; to produce, record (a performance, score, etc); (*with* **on**) to cause to begin operating (as if) by flicking a switch, turning a knob, etc; (*sl*) to arouse or excite, esp sexually; (*sl*) to introduce (a person) to drugs; (*with* **up**) to discover, uncover; to increase the volume or intensity of (sound, brightness, etc). * *n* a rotation; new direction or tendency; a place in sequence; a turning point, crisis; performer's act; an act of kindness or malice; a bend.

turnaround *n* a reversal of position, opinion, attitude, etc.

turncoat *n* a deserter, renegade.

turning *n* a road, path, etc that leads off from a main way; the point where it leads off; a bend.

turning point *n* the point at which a significant change occurs.

turnip *n* a plant with a large white or yellow root, cultivated as a vegetable.

turnout *n* a gathering of people.

turnover *n* the volume of business transacted in a given period; a fruit or meat pasty; the rate of replacement of workers.

turnpike *n* a toll road, esp one that is an expressway.

turnstile *n* a mechanical gate across a footpath or entrance which admits only one person at a time.

turntable *n* a circular, horizontal revolving platform, as in a record player.

turpentine *n* an oily resin secreted by coniferous trees, used as a solvent and thinner for paints.–*also* **turps**.

turquoise *n* an opaque greenish-blue mineral, valued as a gem; the color of turquoise.–*also adj*.

turret *n* a small tower on a building rising above it; a dome or revolving structure for guns, as on a warship, tank or aeroplane.–**turreted** *adj*.

turtle *n* any of an order of land, freshwater or marine reptiles having a soft body encased in a hard shell; **to turn turtle** to turn upside down.

turtleneck *n* a high close-fitting neckline on a sweater.

tusk *n* a long, projecting tooth on either side of the mouth, as of the elephant.–**tusked** *adj*.

tussle *n* a scuffle.

tutelage *n* guardianship; guidance by a tutor.

tutor n a private teacher who instructs pupils individually; a member of staff responsible for the supervision and teaching of students in a British university. * vt to instruct; to act as a tutor.

tutorial n a period of tuition by a tutor to an individual or a small group. * adj of or pertaining to a tutor.

tutu n a short, projecting, layered skirt worn by a ballerina.

tuxedo n a man's semi-formal suit with a tailless jacket.–also **dinner jacket**.

TV abbr = television.

twang n a sharp, vibrant sound, as of a taut string when plucked; a nasal tone of voice. * vt to make a twanging sound.

tweak vt to twist, pinch or pull with sudden jerks. * n a sharp pinch or twist.

tweed n a twilled woolen fabric used in making clothes.

tweet interj an imitation of the chirp of a small bird. * vi to make this sound.

tweezers n sing small pincers used for plucking.

twelfth adj the last of twelve; being one of twelve equal parts.

twelve adj the cardinal number next after eleven. * n the symbol for this (12, XII, xii).

twenty adj, n two times ten. * n (pl **twenties**) the symbol for this (20, XX, xx).–**twentieth** adj.

twenty-twenty, 20/20 adj (vision) normal.

twice adv two times; two times as much; doubly.

twiddle vt to twirl or fiddle with idly.

twig n a small branch or shoot of a tree.–**twiggy** adj.

twilight n the dim light just after sunset and before sunrise; the final stages of something.

twill n a cloth woven in such a way as to produce diagonal lines across it.–**twilled** adj.

twin n either of two persons or animals born at the same time; one thing resembling another. * adj double; very like another; consisting of two parts nearly alike. * vt (**twinning, twinned**) to pair together.

twin bed n one of a pair of single beds.

twine n a string of twisted fibers or hemp. * vti to twist together; to wind around.

twinge n a sudden, stabbing pain; an emotional pang.

twinkle vi to sparkle; to flicker.

twinkling n a wink; an instant; the shining of the stars.

twirl vt to whirl; to rotate; to wind or twist. * vi to turn around rapidly.

twist vt to unite by winding together; to coil; to confuse or distort (the meaning of); to bend. * vi to revolve; to writhe. * n the act or result of twisting; a twist of thread; a curve or bend; an unexpected event; a wrench.

twister n a tornado.

twitch vt to pull with a sudden jerk. * vi to be suddenly jerked. * n a sudden muscular spasm.

twitter n a chirp, as of a bird. * vi to chirp.

two adj, n the cardinal number next above one. * n the symbol for this (2, II, ii).

two-dimensional adj of or having two dimensions; lacking (the illusion of) depth.

two-faced adj deceitful, hypocritical.

twofold adj multiplied by two; double. * adv doubly.

two-ply adj made of two thicknesses or strands.

twosome n a group of two; a game for two people.

two-step n (the music for) a ballroom dance in duple time.

two-time vti (sl) to be unfaithful to (a lover, etc); to double-cross.–**two-timer** n.

two-tone adj of two colors or shades of the same color; (sirens, etc) having two notes.

two-way adj allowing movement or operation in two (opposite) directions; involving two participants; involving mutual obligation; (radio, telephone) capable of transmitting and receiving messages. **TX** abbr = Texas.

tycoon n a powerful industrialist, etc.

tympani, tympany see **timpani**.

tympanum n (pl **tympanums, tympana**) the cavity of the middle ear; the tympanic membrane, eardrum.

type n a kind, class or group; sort; model; a block of metal for printing letters; style of print. * vt to write by means of a typewriter; to classify.

typecast vt (**typecasting, typecast**) (actor) to cast in the same role repeatedly because of physical appearance, etc.

typeface n the printing surface of a type character; a particular design of a set of type characters.

typescript n a typed copy of a book, document, etc.

typeset vt (**typesetting, typeset**) to set in type.–**typesetter** n.

typewriter n a keyboard machine for printing characters.

typhoid n typhoid fever. * adj of or pertaining to typhoid fever (–also **typhoidal**).

typhoid fever n an acute infectious disease acquired by ingesting contaminated food or water.

typhoon n a violent tropical cyclone originating in the western Pacific.

typhus n a highly contagious acute disease spread by body lice and characterized by fever, a rash and headache.–**typhous** adj.

typical adj representative of a particular type; characteristic.–**typicality** n.–**typically** adv.

typify vt (**typifying, typified**) to characterize.–**typification** n.

typist n a person who uses a typewriter, esp as a job.

typo n (pl **typos**) (inf) a typographical error.

typography n the way in which printed material is designed or set for printing.–**typographic, typographical** adj.

tyrannize vi to exercise power (over) in a vicious and oppressive manner. * vt to crush, oppress.–**tyrannizer** n.

tyrannosaur, tyrannosaurus n a large carnivorous dinosaur of the Cretaceous period which stood on powerful hind legs.

tyranny n (pl **tyrannies**) the government or authority of a tyrant; harshness; oppression.

tyrant n a person who uses his or her power arbitrarily and oppressively; a despot.–**tyrannical** adj.

tyre see tire.

tyro n (pl **tyros**) a novice, a beginner.–also **tiro**.

tzar n a czar.–**tzarina** nf.

U

ubiquitous adj existing, or seeming to exist everywhere at once.–**ubiquity** n.

U-boat n a German submarine.

udder n a milk-secreting organ containing two or more teats, as in cows.

UFO abbr = unidentified flying object.

ugly adj (**uglier, ugliest**) unsightly; unattractive; repulsive; ill tempered.–**ugliness** n.

ugly duckling n an initially unpromising person or thing that turns out successfully.

UHF abbr = ultrahigh frequency.

uh-huh interj used to indicate assent or agreement.

UK abbr = United Kingdom.

ukelele, ukulele n a small, four-stringed guitar.

ulcer n an open sore on the surface of the skin or a mucous membrane.–**ulcerous** adj

ulcerate vti to make or become ulcerous.

ulna n (pl **ulnas, ulnae**) the longer and thinner of the two bones in the human forearm; the corresponding bone in the forelimb of other vertebrates.–**ulnar** adj.

ulterior adj (motives) hidden, not evident; subsequent.

ultimate adj last; final; most significant; essential. * n the most significant thing.**–ultimately** adv.

ultimatum n (pl **ultimatums, ultimata**) the final proposal, condition or terms in negotiations.

ultrahigh frequency n a radio frequency in the range between 300 megahertz and 3000 megahertz.

ultramarine adj deep blue. * n a blue pigment; a vivid, deep blue.

ultrasonic adj (waves, vibrations) having a frequency beyond the human ear's audible range.

ultrasound n ultrasonic waves used in medical diagnosis and therapy.

ultraviolet adj of light waves, shorter than the wavelengths of visible light and longer than X-rays.

umber n a brown pigment. * adj dark brown.

umbilical adj of, pertaining to, near, or resembling the navel.

umbilical cord n the vascular tube connecting a fetus with the placenta through which oxygen and nutrients are passed.

umbilicus n (pl **umbilici**) the navel; a navel-shaped depression on a plant or animal.

umbrage n resentment; offense.

umbrella n a cloth-covered collapsible frame carried in the hand for protection from rain or sun; a general protection.

umpire n an official who enforces the rules in sport; an arbitrator.–also vti.

umpteen adj (inf) an undetermined large number.**–umpteenth** adj.

UN abbr = United Nations.

unable adj not able; lacking the strength, skill, power or opportunity (to do something).

unaccountable adj inexplicable, puzzling; not to be called to account for one's actions.

unaccustomed adj (with **to**) not used (to); not usual or familiar.

unadulterated adj pure, unmixed.

unaffected adj sincere, frank, without pretension; not influenced or affected.**–unaffectedly** adv.

un-American adj contrary to US customs, ideals or interests.**–unAmericanism** n.

unanimous adj showing complete agreement.**–unanimity** n.**–unanimously** adv.

unapproachable adj aloof, unfriendly; impossible to reach; not to be equaled or rivaled.

unassuming adj unpretentious; modest.

unattached adj unmarried, not engaged to be married; not belonging to a particular group, organization, etc.

unattended adj not supervised; not accompanied.

unaware adj not conscious or aware (of); ignorant (of).

unawares adv by surprise; unexpectedly, without warning.

unbalanced adj mentally unstable; having bias or over-representing a particular view, group, interest, etc; (bookkeeping) not having equal debit and credit totals.

unbearable adj intolerable, not able to be endured.**–unbearably** adv.

unbelievable adj not able to be believed; incredible.**–unbelievably** adv.

unbeliever n a person who does not believe, esp in a religion.

unbelieving adj lacking belief; sceptical.**–unbelievingly** adv.

unbiased, unbiassed adj without prejudice or bias; impartial, even-handed, disinterested.

unburden vt to reveal or confess one's troubles, secrets, etc to another in order to relieve the mind; to take off a burden.

uncalled-for adj unnecessary, unwanted, unwarranted.

uncanny adj (**uncannier, uncanniest**) odd; unexpected; suggestive of supernatural powers; unearthly.

uncertain adj not knowing accurately, doubtful; (with **of**) not confident or sure; not fixed, variable, changeable.**–uncertainty** n.

uncivilized adj not civilized, unsophisticated; remote, wild.

uncle n the brother of one's father or mother; the husband of one's aunt.

uncomfortable adj causing discomfort; feeling discomfort or unease.

uncommon adj rare, unusual; extraordinary.

uncommonly adv hardly ever; exceptionally, particularly.

unconditional adj without restrictions or conditions, absolute.

unconscionable adj unscrupulous; unreasonable.**–unconscionably** adv.

unconscious adj not aware (of); lacking normal perception by the senses, insensible; unintentional. * n the deepest level of mind containing feelings and emotions of which one is unaware and unable to control.**–unconsciously** adv.

unconstitutional adj contrary to the constitution of a country.**–unconstitutionality** n.

unconventional adj not bound by social rules or conventions.**–unconventionally** adv.

uncouth adj lacking in manners; rough; rude.**–uncouthness** n.

undaunted adj fearless; not discouraged.**–undauntedly** adv.

undecided adj doubtful, hesitant; (solution, etc) not determined.**–undecidedly** adv.

undeniable adj readily apparent, obviously true; unquestionably excellent.

under prep lower than; beneath the surface of; below; covered by; subject to; less than, falling short of. * adv beneath, below, lower down. * adj lower in position, degree or rank; subordinate.

underachieve vi to perform less well than expected given one's potential.**–underachieve**r n.

underarm adj of, for, in, or used on the area under the arm, or armpit; done with the hand below the level of the elbow or shoulder.

undercarriage n the landing gear of an aeroplane; a car's supporting framework.

underclass n those least privileged people in society who fall outside the normal social scale, characterized by poverty, unemployment, poor education, social instability, etc.

underclothes npl underwear.**–also underclothing**.

undercoat n a coat of paint, etc, applied as a base below another; a growth of hair or fur under another; a coat worn under an overcoat.

undercover adj done or operating secretly.

undercurrent n a hidden current under water; an emotion, opinion, etc, not apparent.

underdog n the loser in an encounter, contest, etc; a person in an inferior position.

underestimate vti to set too low an estimate on or for. * n too low an estimate.

undergo vt (**undergoing, underwent,** pp **undergone**) to experience, suffer, endure.

undergraduate n a student at a college or university studying for a first degree.

underground adj situated under the surface of the ground; secret; of noncommercial newspapers, movies, etc that are unconventional, radical, etc. * n a secret group working for the overthrow of the government or the expulsion of occupying forces; an underground railroad system; a subway.

undergrowth n shrubs, plants, etc growing beneath trees.

underhanded adj sly, secret, deceptive.**–underhandedly** adv.

underlie vt (**underlying, underlay,** pp **underlain**) to be situated under; to form the basis of.**–underlying** adj.

underline vt to put a line underneath; to emphasize.

undermine vt to wear away, or weaken; to injure or weaken, esp by subtle or insidious means.

underneath adv under. * adj lower. * n the underside.**–also prep.**

undernourished adj consuming or supplied with less than the minimum quantity of food necessary for normal health and growth.

underpants *npl* pants worn as an undergarment by men and boys, shorts

underpass *n* a section of road running beneath another road, a railway, etc.

underprivileged *adj* lacking the basic rights of other members of society; poor.

underrate *vt* to undervalue, to underestimate.

underscore *vt* to draw a line under; to emphasize.

undershirt *n* a sleeveless undergarment for the upper body, a vest.

underside *n* the lower surface.

undersigned *adj* signed at the end. * *n* a person who signs his or her name at the end of a document.

understand *vb* (**understanding, understood**) *vt* to comprehend; to realize; to believe; to assume; to know thoroughly (eg a language); to accept; to be sympathetic with. * *vi* to comprehend; to believe.–**understandable** *adj*.

understanding *n* comprehension; compassion, sympathy; personal opinion, viewpoint; mutual agreement. * *adj* sympathetic.

understate *vt* to state something in restrained terms; to represent as less than is the case.–**understatement** *n*.

understudy *vti* (**understudying, understudied**) to learn a role or part so as to be able to replace (the actor playing it); to act as an understudy (to).–*also n*.

undertake *vt* (**undertaking, undertook, pp undertaken**) to attempt to; to agree to; to commit oneself; to promise; to guarantee.

undertaker *n* a funeral director.

undertaking *n* enterprise; task; promise; obligation.

undertone *n* a hushed tone of voice; an undercurrent of feeling; a pale color.

under way *adv* in or into motion or progress.

underwear *n* garments worn underneath one's outer clothes, next to the skin.

underwent *see* **undergo**.

underworld *n* criminals as an organized group; (*myth*) Hades.

underwrite *vt* to agree to finance (an undertaking, etc); to sign one's name to (an insurance policy), thus assuming liability. * *vi* to work as an underwriter.–**underwriter** *n*.

undesirable *adj* not desirable; not pleasant; objectionable.–**undesirability** *n*.–**undesirably** *adv*.

undo *vt* (**undoing, undid, pp undone**) to untie or unwrap; to reverse (what has been done); to bring ruin on.

undress *vt* to remove the clothes from. * *vi* to take off one's clothes.

undue *adj* improper; excessive.

unduly *adv* too; excessively; improperly.

unearth *vt* to dig up from the earth; to discover; to reveal.

unearthly *adj* mysterious; eerie; supernatural; absurd, unreasonable.

uneasy *adj* uncomfortable; restless; anxious; disquieting.–**uneasily** *adv*.–**uneasiness** *n*.

unemployed *adj* not having a job, out of work.–**unemployment** *n*.

unequivocal *adj* unambiguous; plain; clear.–**unequivocally** *adv*.

UNESCO *abbr* = United Nations Educational, Scientific and Cultural Organization.

uneven *adj* not level or smooth; variable; not divisible by two without leaving a remainder.–**unevenness** *n*.

unfair *adj* unjust; unequal; against the rules.–**unfairly** *adv*.–**unfairness** *n*.

unfaithful *adj* disloyal; not abiding by a promise; adulterous.–**unfaithfully** *adv*.–**unfaithfulness** *n*.

unfamiliar *adj* not known, strange; (*with* **with**) not familiar.

unfasten *vt* to open or become opened; to undo or become undone; to loose, loosen.

unfavorable, unfavourable *adj* negative, disapproving; adverse.

unfeeling *adj* callous, hardhearted.–**unfeelingly** *adv*.

unfit *adj* unsuitable; in bad physical condition.

unflinching *adj* calm, steadfast.–**unflinchingly** *adv*.

unfold *vti* to open or spread out; to become revealed; to develop.

unforgettable *adj* never to be forgotten; fixed in the mind; impressive, exceptional.–**unforgettably** *adj*.

unfortunate *adj* unlucky; disastrous; regrettable. * *n* an unlucky person.–**unfortunately** *adv*.

ungainly *adj* (**ungainlier, ungainliest**) awkward; clumsy.–**ungainliness** *n*.

unhappy *adj* (**unhappier, unhappiest**) not happy or fortunate; sad; wretched; not suitable.–**unhappily** *adv*.–**unhappiness** *n*.

unhealthy *adj* (**unhealthier, unhealthiest**) not healthy or fit, sick; encouraging or resulting from poor health; harmful, degrading; dangerous.–**unhealthily** *adv*.–**unhealthiness** *n*.

unheard-of *adj* not known before; without precedent.

unholy *adj* (**unholier, unholiest**) wicked; (*inf*) outrageous, enormous.

UNICEF *abbr* = United Nations International Children's Emergency Fund, now United Nations Children's Fund.

unicorn *n* an imaginary creature with a body like a horse and a single horn on the forehead.

uniform *adj* unchanging in form; consistent; identical. * *n* the distinctive clothes worn by members of the same organization, such as soldiers, schoolchildren.–**uniformity** *n*.–**uniformly** *adv*.

unify *vt* (**unifying, unified**) to make into one; to unite.–**unification** *n*.

unilateral *adj* involving one only of several parties; not reciprocal.–**unilateralism** *n*.–**unilaterally** *adv*.

uninhibited *adj* not repressed or restrained; relaxed, spontaneous.–**uninhibitedly** *adv*.

union *n* the act of uniting; a combination of several things; a confederation of individuals or groups; marriage; a trades union.

unique *adj* without equal; the only one of its kind.–**uniquely** *adv*.

unisex *adj* of a style that can be worn by both sexes.

unison *n* accordance of sound, concord, harmony; **in unison** simultaneously, in agreement, in harmony.

unit *n* the smallest whole number, one; a single or whole entity; (*measurement*) a standard amount; an establishment or group of people who carry out a specific function; a piece of furniture fitting together with other pieces.–**unitary** *adj*.

unite *vti* to join into one, to combine; to be unified in purpose.

United Nations *n sing or pl* an international organization of nations for world peace and security formed in 1945.

unity *n* (*pl* **unities**) oneness; harmony; concord.

universal *adj* widespread; general; relating to all the world or the universe; relating to or applicable to all mankind.–**universally** *adv*.–**universality** *n* (*pl* **universalities**).

universe *n* all existing things; (*astron*) the totality of space, stars, planets and other forms of matter and energy; the world.

university *n* (*pl* **universities**) an institution of higher education which confers bachelors' and higher degrees; the campus or staff of a university.

unjust *adj* not characterized by justice; not fair.–**unjustly** *adv*.–**unjustness** *n*.

unkempt *adj* uncombed; slovenly, disheveled.

unkind *adj* lacking in kindness or sympathy; harsh; cruel.–**unkindly** *adv*.–**unkindness** *n*.

unleaded *adj* (*gasoline*) not mixed with tetraethyl lead.

unleash *vt* to release from a leash; to free from restraint.

unless *conj* if not; except that.

unlike *adj* not the same, dissimilar. * *prep* not like; not characteristic of.–**unlikeness** *n*.

unlikely *adj* improbable; unpromising.

unload *vti* to remove a load, discharge freight from a truck, ship, etc; to relieve of or express troubles, etc; to dispose of, dump; to empty, esp a gun.

unlock vt (door, lock, etc) to unfasten; to let loose; to reveal; to release.

unlucky adj (**unluckier, unluckiest**) not lucky, not fortunate; likely to bring misfortune; regrettable.

unmistakable, unmistakeable adj obvious, clear.–**unmistakably, unmistakeably** adv.

unmitigated adj unqualified, absolute.

unnatural adj abnormal; contrary to nature; artificial; affected; strange; wicked.–**unnaturally** adv.

unnecessary adj not necessary.–**unnecessarily** adv.–**unnecessariness** n.

unnerve vt to cause to lose courage, strength, confidence; to frighten.

unobtrusive adj modest, staying in the background.

unpack vti (suitcase, etc) to remove the contents of; (container, etc) to take things out of; to unload.

unparalleled adj having no equal, unmatched.

unpleasant adj not pleasing or agreeable; nasty; objectionable.–**unpleasantly** adv.–**unpleasantness** n.

unpopular adj disliked; lacking general approval.–**unpopularity** n.

unprecedented adj having no precedent; unparalleled.

unprincipled adj lacking scruples.

unprofessional adj contrary to professional etiquette.–**unprofessionally** adv.

unqualified adj lacking recognized qualifications; not equal to; not restricted, complete.

unquestionable adj certain, not disputed.–**unquestionably** adv.

unravel vt (**unraveling, unraveled** or **unravelling, unravelled**) to disentangle; to solve.

unreasonable adj contrary to reason; lacking reason; immoderate; excessive.–**unreasonably** adv.

unrelenting adj relentless; continuous.–**unrelentingly** adv.

unremitting adj incessant.

unrequited adj not reciprocated, not returned.

unreserved adj not reserved; frank, demonstrative; absolute; entire; not booked.–**unreservedly** adv.

unrest n uneasiness; anxiety; angry discontent verging on revolt.

unrivaled, unrivalled adj without equal, peerless.

unruly adj (**unrulier, unruliest**) hard to control, restrain, or keep in order; disobedient.

unsavory, unsavoury adj distasteful; disagreeable; offensive.

unscathed adj unharmed.

unscrupulous adj without principles.

unseemly adj unbecoming; inappropriate.

unselfish adj not selfish; thinking of others before oneself.–**unselfishly** adv.–**unselfishness** n.

unsettle vti to disturb, disrupt, or disorder.

unsightly adj unattractive; ugly.

unsociable n antisocial; reserved.

unsophisticated adj naïve, inexperienced; simple; pure, unadulterated.

unsound adj flimsy, not stable; defective, flawed; in poor health; not sane.–**unsoundly** adv.–**unsoundness** n.

unspeakable adj bad beyond words, indescribable.

unstable adj easily upset; mentally unbalanced; irresolute.

unsteady adj (**unsteadier, unsteadiest**) shaky, reeling; vacillating.–**unsteadily** adv.

unsubstantial adj lacking weight, flimsy; of doubtful factual validity.

unsung adj not acclaimed or celebrated.

unswerving adj not deviating; constant, unchanging.

untangle vt to rid of tangles, unravel; to sort out.

unthinkable adj inconceivable; out of the question; improbable.–**unthinkably** adv.

untidy adj (**untidier, untidiest**) not neat, disordered. * vt (**untidying, untidied**) to make untidy.–**untidily** adv.

untie vt (**untying, untied**) to undo a knot in, unfasten.

until prep up to the time of; before. * conj up to the time when or that; to the point, degree, etc that; before.

untimely adj premature; inopportune.

untoward adj unseemly; unfavorable; adverse.

untrue adj incorrect, false; not faithful, disloyal; inaccurate.–**untruthful** adj telling lies; false.

unused adj not (yet) used; (with to) not accustomed (to something).

unusual adj uncommon; rare.

unutterable adj impossible to express in words.–**unutterably** adv.

unvarnished adj not varnished; plain, direct; not embellished.

unveil vt to reveal; to disclose.

unwelcome adj not welcome, not invited; disagreeable; unpleasant.

unwell adj ill, not well; (inf) suffering from a hangover.

unwieldy adj not easily moved or handled, as because of large size; awkward.–**unwieldily** adv.–**unwieldiness** n.

unwilling adj not willing, reluctant; said or done with reluctance.–**unwillingly** adv.–**unwillingness** n.

unwind vt to untangle; to undo. * vi to relax.

unwise adj lacking wisdom; imprudent.–**unwisely** adv.

unwitting adj not knowing; unintentional.–**unwittingly** adv.

unworthy adj (**unworthier, unworthiest**) not deserving.

up adv to, toward, in or on a higher place; to a later period; so as to be even with in time, degree, etc. * prep from a lower to a higher point on or along. * adj moving or directed upward; at an end; (inf) well-informed. * vt (**upping, upped**) to raise; to increase; to take up. * n ascent; high point.

up-and-coming adj promising for the future; likely to succeed.

upbeat n (mus) an unaccented beat in the last bar. * adj (inf) cheerful, optimistic.

upbringing n the process of educating and nurturing (a child).

update vt to bring up to date.

upfront adj honest, open. * adv (money) paid in advance.

upgrade vt to improve, raise to a higher grade.

upheaval n radical or violent change.

uphill adj ascending, rising; difficult, arduous. * adv up a slope or hill; against difficulties.

uphold vt (**upholding, upheld**) to support, sustain; to defend.

upholster vt (furniture) to fit with stuffing, springs, covering, etc.–**upholsterer** n.

upholstery n (pl **upholsteries**) materials used to make a soft covering esp for a seat.

upkeep n maintenance; the cost of it.

uplift vt to raise, lift up; to improve the moral, cultural, spiritual, etc standard or condition of. * n a moral, cultural, spiritual, etc improvement.

upmarket adj of or appealing to wealthier buyers.

upon prep on, on top of.

upper adj farther up; higher in position, rank, status. * n the part of a boot or shoe above the sole.

upper class n people occupying the highest social rank.–also adj.

upper hand n the position of control, advantage.

uppermost adj at the top; highest in importance. * adv into the highest position, etc.

uppity adj (inf) snobbish, arrogant.

upright adj vertical, in an erect position; righteous, honest, just. * n a vertical post or support. * adv vertically.

uprising n a revolt; a rebellion.

uproar n a noisy disturbance; a commotion; an outcry.

uproarious adj making or marked by an uproar; extremely funny; (laughter) boisterous.–**uproariously** adv.

uproot vt to tear out by the roots; to remove from established surroundings.

upset[1] *vt* (**upsetting, upset**) to overturn; to spill; to disturb; to put out of order; to distress; to overthrow; to make physically sick.

upset[2] *n* an unexpected defeat; distress or its cause. * *adj* distressed; confused; defeated.

upshot *n* the conclusion; the result.

upside down *adj* inverted; the wrong way up; (*inf*) topsy turvy.

upstage *vt* to draw attention to oneself. * *adv* to the rear of the stage.

upstairs *adv* up the stairs; to an upper level or storey. * *n* an upper floor.

upstart *n* a person who has suddenly risen to a position of wealth and power; an arrogant person.

upstate *n* the mostly northern areas of a US state. * *adv, adj* towards, in, or pertaining to this area of a US state.

upsurge *n* a sudden rise or swell.

uptake *n* a taking up; a shaft or pipe for carrying smoke upwards; (*inf*) understanding.

uptight *adj* (*inf*) very tense, nervous, etc.

up-to-date *adj* modern; fashionable.

upward, upwards *adj* from a lower to a higher place.–*also adv.*

uranium *n* a metallic element used as a source of nuclear energy.

urban *adj* of or relating to a city.–**urbanization, urbanisation** *n.*

urbane *adj* sophisticated; refined.–**urbanity** *n.*

urchin *n* a raggedly dressed mischievous child; a sea urchin.

urethra *n* the duct carrying urine out of the bladder.

urge *vt* to drive forward; to press, plead with. * *n* an impulse, yearning.

urgency *n* (*pl* **urgencies**) the quality or condition of being urgent; compelling need; importance.

urgent *adj* impelling; persistent; calling for immediate attention.–**urgently** *adv.*

urinal *n* a bowl or trough for urination in public lavatories.

urinate *vi* to pass urine.

urine *n* a yellowish fluid excreted by the kidneys and conveyed to the bladder.–**urinary** *adj.*

urn *n* a vase or large vessel; a receptacle for preserving the ashes of the dead; a large metal container for boiling water for tea or coffee.

US *abbr* = United States.

us *pron* the objective case of **we**.

USA *abbr* = United States of America.

usage *n* customary use; practice, custom; use of language.

use[1] *vt* to put to some purpose; to utilize; to exploit (a person); to partake of (drink, drugs, tobacco, etc).–**usable, useable** *adj.*

use[2] *n* act of using or putting to a purpose; usage; usefulness; need (for); advantage; practice, custom.

used *adj* not new; second-hand.

useful *adj* able to be used to good effect; (*inf*) capable, commendable.–**usefully** *adv.*

useless *adj* having no use.–**uselessly** *adv.*–**uselessness** *n.*

user *n* one who uses; (*inf*) a drug addict.

user-friendly *adj* easy to understand and operate.

usher *n* one who shows people to their seats in a theater, church, etc; a doorkeeper in a law court. * *vt* to escort to seats, etc.

USSR *abbr* = (*formerly*) Union of Soviet Socialist Republics.

usual *adj* customary; ordinary; normal.–**usually** *adv.*

usurp *vt* to seize or appropriate unlawfully.–**usurper** *n.*

UT *abbr* = Utah.

utensil *n* an implement or container, esp one for use in the kitchen.

uterus *n* (*pl* **uteri**) the female organ in which offspring are developed until birth; the womb.–**uterine** *adj.*

utilitarian *adj* designed to be of practical use.

utility *n* (*pl* **utilities**) usefulness; a public service, such as telephone, electricity, etc; a company providing such a service.

utilize *vt* to make practical use of.–**utilization** *n.*

utmost *adj* of the greatest degree or amount; furthest. * *n* the most possible.

utopia *n* a imaginary society or place considered to be ideal or perfect.–**utopian** *adj, n.*

utter[1] *adj* absolute; complete.

utter[2] *vt* to say; to speak.–**utterance** *n.*

utterly *adv* completely.

UV *abbr* = ultraviolet.

uvula *n* (*pl* **uvulas, uvulae**) the fleshy tissue suspended in the back of the throat over the back part of the tongue.

V

V *abbr* = volt(s).

v *abbr* = against (Latin *versus*); see (Latin *vide*); verb.

VA *abbr* = Virginia.

vacancy *n* (*pl* **vacancies**) emptiness; an unoccupied job or position.

vacant *adj* empty; unoccupied; (*expression*) blank.–**vacantly** *adv.*–**vacantness** *n.*

vacate *vt* to leave empty; to give up possession of.

vacation *n* a period away from work, school etc for travel, rest or recreation; a period of the year when universities, colleges and law courts are closed. * *vi* to go on vacation.

vaccinate *vt* to inoculate with vaccine as a protection against a disease.–**vaccinator** *n.*

vaccination *n* inoculation with a vaccine; the resulting scar.

vaccine *n* a modified and hence harmless virus or other microorganism used for inoculation to give immunity from certain diseases by stimulating antibody production; cowpox virus used in this way against smallpox.

vacillate *vi* to waver, to show indecision; to fluctuate.–**vacillation** *n.*–**vacillator** *n.*

vacuous *adj* empty; lacking intelligence, mindless.–**vacuously** *adv.*–**vacuousness** *n.*

vacuum *n* (*pl* **vacuums, vacua**) a region devoid of all matter; a region in which gas is present at low pressure; a vacuum cleaner. * *vt* to clean with a vacuum cleaner. * *adj* of, having or creating a vacuum; working by suction or maintenance of a partial vacuum.

vacuum bottle, vacuum flask *n* a container for keeping liquids hot or cold.

vacuum cleaner *n* an electrical appliance for removing dust from carpets, etc, by suction.–**vacuum-clean** *vt.*

vacuum-packed *adj* sealed in an airtight packet from which the air has been removed.

vagary *n* (*pl* **vagaries**) unpredictable or erratic behavior or actions; a whim.–**vagarious** *adj.*

vagina *n* (**vaginas, vaginae**) in female mammals and humans, the canal connecting the uterus and the external sex organs.–**vaginal** *adj.*

vagrant *n* a person who has no settled home, a tramp. * *adj* wandering, roaming; wayward.–**vagrancy** *n.*–**vagrantly** *adv.*

vague *adj* unclear; indistinct, imprecise; (*person*) absentminded.–**vaguely** *adv.*–**vagueness** *n.*

vain *adj* conceited; excessively concerned with one's appearance; senseless; futile; worthless; **in vain** to no purpose.–**vainly** *adv.*–**vainness** *n.*

valance *n* a decorative cover for the base of a bed; a canopy for a window frame to hide rods, etc; a pelmet.–**valanced** *adj.*

valediction *n* a saying farewell; a taking leave; an instance of this; a speech made at this time.–**valedictory** *adj.*

valence, valency *n* (*pl* **valences, valencies**) (*chem*) the power of elements to combine; the number of atoms of hydrogen that an atom or group can combine with to form a compound.

valentine n a lover or sweetheart chosen on St Valentine's Day, February 14; a card or gift sent on that day.

valet n a manservant; a steward in a hotel or on board ship. * vt to attend (someone) as a valet. * vi to work as a valet.

valiant adj courageous; brave.–**valiance, valiancy** n.–**valiantly** adv.

valid adj based on facts; (objection, etc) sound; legally acceptable; binding.–**validity** n.–**validly** adv.

validate vt to corroborate; to legalize.–**validation** n.

valise n a small case, usu of a size large enough to carry what is needed for an overnight visit.

valley n (pl **valleys**) low land between hills or mountains usu with a river or stream flowing along its bottom; something resembling a valley, eg the angle where two sloping sides of a roof meet.

valor n courage; bravery (in battle).–also **valour**.–**valorous** adj.–**valorously** adv.

valuable adj having considerable importance or monetary worth. * n a personal possession of value, esp jewelry; (pl) valuable possessions.–**valuably** adv.

valuation n the act of valuing or valuating; an estimated price or worth; an estimation.–**valuational** adj.

value n worth, merit, importance; market value; purchasing power; relative worth; (pl) moral principles. * vt (**valuing, valued**) to estimate the worth of; to regard highly; to prize.–**valuer** n.

value judgment n a subjective or unwarranted judgment.

valueless adj without value; worthless.–**valuelessness** n.

valve n a device for controlling the flow of a gas or liquid through a pipe; (anat) a tube allowing blood to flow in one direction only.

vampire n (folklore) a dead creature that by night leaves its grave to suck the blood of living people; a person who preys on others, an extortioner; a vampire bat.–**vampiric** adj.

vampire bat n a tropical American blood-sucking bat.

van[1] n a covered motor vehicle for transporting goods, etc.

van[2] n the vanguard.

vandal n a person who wilfully or ignorantly damages property. * adj of acting like a vandal; characterized by vandalism or lack of culture.

vandalism n the ruthless destruction or spoiling of anything beautiful or venerable; barbarous, ignorant or inartistic treatment.–**vandalistic** adj.

vandalize vt to carry out an act of vandalism.–**vandalization** n.

vane n a blade at the top of a spire, etc to show wind direction; a weather vane; a blade on a windmill or propeller.

vanguard n the front part of an army; the leading position of any movement.

vanilla n extract from the orchid pod used as a flavoring.–**vanillic** adj from vanilla.

vanish vi to disappear from sight, to become invisible, esp in a rapid and mysterious manner; to fade away; to cease to exist; (math) (numbers, quantities) to become zero.–**vanisher** n.

vanity n (pl **vanities**) a fruitless endeavor; worthlessness; empty pride or conceit; love of indiscriminate admiration; an idle matter or show; a worthless or unfounded idea or statement; emptiness, lightness.

vanity case, vanity box n a small case used for carrying cosmetics, etc.

vanquish vt to conquer; to defeat; to overcome, to subdue.–**vanquisher** n.–**vanquishment** n.

vantage n a favorable position; a position allowing a clear view or understanding.

vapid adj flavorless, flat, insipid; dull, lifeless.–**vapidity** n.–**vapidly** adv.

vapor n the gaseous state of a substance normally liquid or solid; particles of water or smoke in the air; (pl) hysteria. * vi to pass off in vapor, vaporize; to boast.–also **vapour**.

vaporize vt to change into vapor.–**vaporization** n.–**vaporizer** n.

vapor trail n condensed vapor left in the wake of an aircraft exhaust appearing as a white trail in the sky.

vapour see **vapor**.

variable adj liable to change; not constant. * n (math) a changing quantity that can have different values, as opposed to a constant.–**variability** n.–**variably** adv.

variance n disagreement, dissension; variation; tendency to vary; (law) a discrepancy between two statements or documents; **at variance** in conflict.

variant adj different; differing from an accepted or normal type, text, etc. * n a variant form or reading.

variation n a varying or being varied; alteration; deviation from a standard or type; diversity; deviation of the magnetic needle from true north; the measure of this; (mus) repetition of a theme or melody with modifications.–**variational** adj.

varicose adj (veins) abnormally swollen and dilated.–**varicosis** n.–**varicosity** n.

varied adj showing variety, changing; partially changed; various; variegated.–**variedly** adv.

variegate vt to mark with different colors or tints; to dapple, streak; to cause to diversify. –**variegated** adj.

variety n (pl **varieties**) diversity; an assortment.–**varietal** adj.

various adj varied, different; several.–**variously** adv.

varnish n a sticky liquid which dries and forms a hard, glossy coating. * vt to coat with varnish.–**varnisher** n.

vary vti (**varying, varied**) to change, to diversify, modify; to become altered.–**varyingly** adv.

vascular adj (biol) of, consisting of, or containing vessels as part of a structure of animal and vegetable organisms for conveying blood, sap, etc.–**vascularity** n.

vase n a vessel for displaying flowers.

vasectomy n (pl **vasectomies**) male sterilization involving the cutting of the sperm-carrying tube.

vassal n a servant, dependant; subordinate.

vast adj immense.–**vastly** adv.–**vastness** n.

vat n a large barrel or tank. * vt (**vatting, vatted**) to put in a vat; to treat in a vat.

vaudeville n a stage show consisting of various acts, such as singing, dancing and comedy.

vault[1] n an arched ceiling or roof; a burial chamber; a strongroom for valuables; a cellar.–**vaulted** adj.

vault[2] vti to leap or jump over an obstacle. * n a leap.–**vaulter** n.

vaunt vti to display boastfully; to brag. * n a boast.–**vaunter** n.–**vauntingly** adv.

VCR abbr = video cassette recorder.

VDU abbr = video display unit.

veal n the edible flesh of a calf.

vector n (physics) a physical quantity having both direction and magnitude, eg displacement, acceleration, etc; an aircraft's or missile's course.–**vectorial** adj.

veer vi (wind) to change direction; to swing around; to change from one mood or opinion to another.–**veeringly** adv.

vegan n a strict vegetarian who consumes no animal or dairy products.

vegetable n a herbaceous plant grown for food; (inf) a person who has suffered brain damage. * adj of, relating to or derived from plants.

vegetarian n a person who consumes a diet that excludes meat and fish. * adj of vegetarians; consisting wholly of vegetables.

vegetarianism n the doctrine or practice of vegetarians; abstention from eating meat, fish, or other animal products.

vegetate vi to grow like a plant; to sprout; to lead a mentally inactive, aimless life.

vegetation n vegetable growth; plants in general.–**vegetational** adj.

vehement *adj* passionate; forceful; furious.–**vehemence, vehemency** *n*.–**vehemently** *adv*.

vehicle *n* a conveyance, such as a car, bus or truck, for carrying people or goods on land; a means of transmission for ideas, impressions, etc, a medium; (*med*) a substance in which a strong medicine can be administered palatably.–**vehicular** *adj*.

veil *n* a thin fabric worn over the head or face of a woman; a nun's headdress; anything that conceals; a velum. * *vt* to put on a veil; to cover; to conceal, dissemble.

veiled *adj* covered with or wearing a veil; shrouded in a veil; concealed, hidden; covert; not openly declared; (*sound, voice*) indistinct, muffled.

vein *n* (*anat*) one of the vessels that convey the blood back to the heart; (*geol*) a seam of a mineral within a rock; (*bot*) a branching rib in a leaf; a streak of different color, as in marble, cheese, etc; a style or mood (*serious vein*). * *vt* to streak.–**veiny** *adj*.

Velcro *n* (*trademark*) a nylon material made of matching strips of tiny hooks and pile that are easily pressed together or pulled apart.

vellum *n* fine parchment; a good quality writing paper.

velocity *n* (*pl* **velocities**) the rate of change of position of any object; speed.

velour, velours *n* a velvet-like fabric.

velvet *n* a fabric made from silk, rayon, etc with a soft, thick pile; anything like velvet in texture.

velvety *adj* soft to the touch; mellow.

venal *adj* corrupt; willing to accept bribes.–**venality** *n*.–**venally** *adv*.

vendetta *n* the taking of private vengeance; a feud.–**vendettist** *n*.

vending machine *n* a coin-operated machine which dispenses goods.

vendor, vender *n* a seller; a machine that ejects goods, etc, after a required amount of coins has been inserted.

veneer *n* an overlay of fine wood or plastic; a superficial appearance. * *vt* to cover with veneer.

venerable *adj* worthy of reverence or respect.–**venerability** *n*.–**venerably** *adv*.

venerate *vt* to revere; to respect.–**veneration** *n*.–**venerator** *n*.

venereal disease *n* any of various diseases, such as syphilis or AIDS, transmitted by sexual contact.–*also* **sexually transmitted disease**.

Venetian blind *n* a window blind formed of long thin horizontal slips of wood that can be pivoted.

vengeance *n* the act of taking revenge; retribution; **with a vengeance** to a high degree; and no mistake.

vengeful *adj* bent on vengeance; vindictive.–**vengefully** *adv*–**vengefulness** *n*.

venial *adj* (*sin*) forgivable, excusable, not very wrong; (*sin*) not entailing damnation.–**veniality** *n*.–**venially** *adv*.

venison *n* the edible flesh of the deer.

venom *n* the poison of a snake, wasp, etc; spite, malice, rancor.–**venomous** *adj*.–**venomously** *adv*.

venous *adj* pertaining to, contained in, or consisting of veins or blood.–**venously** *adv*.–**venousness** *n*.

vent *n* a small opening or slit; an outlet or flue for the escape of fumes. * *vt* to release; (*temper*) to give expression to.–**venter** *n*.

ventilate *vt* to supply with fresh air; to oxygenate (the blood); to make public, to submit to discussion.–**ventilation** *n*.–**ventilative** *adj*.

ventilator *n* an appliance for ventilating a room, etc; (*med*) a device for enabling a patient to breathe normally.

ventricle *n* a small cavity; one of the lower chambers of the heart, which pumps blood; one of the four cavities of the brain.–**ventricular** *adj*.

ventriloquism, ventriloquy *n* the act or art of speaking so that the sounds appear to come from a source other than the actual speaker.–**ventriloquial** *adj*.–**ventriloquist** *n*.–**ventriloquistic** *adj*.

venture *n* a dangerous expedition; a risky undertaking. * *vti* to risk; to dare.–**venturer** *n*.

venture capital *n* capital available for investment in risky but potentially very profitable enterprises and repayable at higher than normal interest rates, risk capital.

venue *n* the place of an action or event.

veracity *n* (*pl* **veracities**) habitual observance of the truth; correspondence with the truth or facts; a truthful statement, a truth.–**veracious** *adj*.–**veraciously** *adv*.

veranda, verandah *n* a roofed porch, supported by light pillars.

verb *n* (*gram*) the part of speech that expresses an action, a process, state or condition or mode of being.

verbal *adj* of, concerned with or expressed in words; spoken, not written; literal; (*gram*) of, pertaining to or characteristic of a verb.–**verbally** *adv*.

verbalize *vt* to put into words; to make into a verb.–**verbalization** *n*.

verbatim *adj, adv* word for word.

verbose *adj* using more words than are necessary; overloaded with words.–**verbosely** *adv*.–**verbosity** *n*.

verdant *adj* (*grass, foliage*) green and fresh; covered with grass; inexperienced, gullible.–**verdancy** *n*.–**verdantly** *adv*.

verdict *n* the decision of a jury at the end of a trial; decision, judgment.

verdure *n* green vegetation; greenness; freshness; the freshness and healthy growth of vegetation.–**verdurous** *adj*.–**verdurousness** *n*.

verge[1] *n* the brink; the extreme edge or margin; a grass border beside a road.

verge[2] *vi* to incline, descend; (*with* **on**) to border on, to be on the verge of.

verify *vt* (**verifying, verified**) to confirm the truth of; to check; to substantiate, to bear out; (law) to authenticate or support by proofs.–**verifiable** *adj*.–**verification** *n*.–**verifier** *n*.

veritable *adj* real, genuine.–**veritably** *adv*.

verity *n* (*pl* **verities**) the quality or state of being true; a truth; a true fact, reality.

vermicelli *n* a pasta similar to spaghetti but in finer strings.

vermilion, vermillion *n* a bright scarlet color. * *adj* of this color.

vermin *n* (*used as pl*) pests, such as insects and rodents; persons dangerous to society.

vermouth *n* a white wine flavoured with herbs, used in cocktails and as an aperitif.

vernacular *n* the commonly spoken language or dialect of a country or region. * *adj* native.–**vernacularly** *adv*.

vernal *adj* of, appearing in, relating to, or suggestive of the spring.–**vernally** *adv*.

verruca *n* (*pl* **verrucae, verrucas**) a wart on the hand or foot.–**verrucose, verrucous** *adj*.

versatile *adj* turning readily from one occupation to another, adaptable; talented in many different ways; variable, fickle, changeable; (*biol*) able to move or turn freely.–**versatilely** *adv*.–**versatility** *n*.

verse *n* a line of poetry; a stanza of a poem; a metrical composition, esp of a light nature; a short section of a chapter in the Bible. * *vti* to make verses (about).

versed *adj* skilled or learned in a subject.

version *n* a translation from one language into another; a particular account or description.–**versional** *adj*.

versus *prep* against; in contrast to.

vertebra *n* (*pl* **vertebrae, vertebras**) one of the interconnecting bones of the spinal column.–**vertebral** *adj*.

vertebrate *n* an animal with a backbone. * *adj* having a backbone; of the vertebrates.

vertex *n* (*pl* **vertexes, vertices**) the topmost point; apex; (*anat*) the crown of the head; (*geom*) the point at which two sides of a polygon or the planes of a solid intersect.

vertical *adj* perpendicular to the horizon; upright. * *n* a vertical line or plane.–**verticality** *adv.*–**vertically** *adv.*

vertigo *n* (*pl* **vertigoes, vertigines**) a sensation of dizziness and sickness caused by a disorder of the sense of balance.–**vertiginous** *adj.*

verve *n* enthusiasm; liveliness; energy.

very *adj* complete; absolute; same. * *adv* extremely; truly; really.

vesicle *n* a small blister; a small cyst or sac; (*anat*) a bladder-like vessel or cavity, esp one filled with serous fluid; (*geol*) a cavity in rock formed by gases during solidification; (*bot*) a small sac found in some seaweeds and aquatic plants.–**vesicular** *adj.*

vessel *n* a container; a ship or boat; a tube in the body along which fluids pass.

vest *n* a waist-length sleeveless garment worn under a jacket; a sleeveless undergarment worn next to the skin. * *vt* to place or settle (power, authority, etc.); (*with* **in**) to confer or be conferred on; to invest with a right to.

vested interest *n* a strong reason for acting in a certain way, usu for personal gain; (usu *pl*) people in such a state.

vestibule *n* an entrance hall or lobby.

vestige *n* a hint; a trace; a rudimentary survival of a former organ; a particle.–**vestigial** *adj.*–**vestigially** *adv.*

vestment *n* a garment or robe, esp that worn by a priest or official.–**vestmental** *adj.*

vestry *n* (*pl* **vestries**) a room in a church where vestments, etc, are kept and parochial meetings held; a meeting for parish business.–**vestral** *adj.*

vet *n* a veterinarian. * *vt* (**vetting, vetted**) to examine, check for errors, etc.

veteran *adj* old, experienced; having served in the armed forces. * *n* a person who has served in the armed forces; a person who has given long service in a particular activity.

veterinarian, veterinary surgeon *n* a person trained in treating sick or injured animals.

veterinary *adj* of or dealing with diseases of domestic animals.

veto *n* (*pl* **vetoes**) the right of a person or group to prohibit an action or legislation; a prohibition. * *vt* (**vetoing, vetoed**) to refuse to agree to; to prohibit.–**vetoer** *n.*

vex *vt* to annoy; to puzzle, confuse.–**vexation** *n.*–**vexer** *n.*–**vexingly** *adv.*

vexatious *adj* causing vexation; annoying; troublesome; harassing; (*litigation*) designed merely to annoy.–**vexatiously** *adv.*

vexed *adj* annoyed; (*question*) much debated.–**vexedly** *adv.*–**vexedness** *n.*

VHF *abbr* = very high frequency.

via *prep* by way of.

viable *adj* capable of growing or developing; workable; practicable.–**viability** *n.*–**viably** *adv.*

viaduct *n* a road or railroad carried by a bridge with arches over a valley, river, etc.

vial *n* a small bottle for medicines, etc; a phial.

vibes *npl* (*sl*) vibrations; vibraphone.

vibrant *adj* vibrating; resonant; bright; lively.–**vibrancy** *n.*–**vibrantly** *adv.*

vibrate *vti* to shake; to move quickly backward and forward; to quiver; to oscillate; to resound.–**vibratingly** *adv.*

vibration *n* a vibrating or being vibrated; oscillation; resonance; vacillation; (usu *pl*) an emotional reaction instinctively sensed.–**vibrational** *adj.*

vibrato *n* (*pl* **vibratos**) (*mus*) a pulsating effect obtained by rapid variation of emphasis on the same tone.

vicar *n* a parish priest; a clergyman in charge of a chapel.

vicarage *n* the residence of a vicar.

vicarious *adj* substitute; obtained second-hand by listening to or watching another person's experiences.–**vicariously** *adv.*–**vicariousness** *n.*

vice *n* an evil action or habit; a grave moral fault; great wickedness; a serious defect, a blemish.

vice admiral *n* a rank of naval officer next below admiral.

vice-chairman *n* (*pl* **vice-chairmen**) one who takes the chair in a chairman's absence.

vice president *n* a deputy or assistant president.

viceroy *n* one who rules a country or province as a representative of a king or queen.–**viceregal** *adj.*

vice versa *adv* conversely; the other way round.

vicinity *n* (*pl* **vicinities**) a nearby area; proximity.

vicious *adj* cruel; violent; malicious; ferocious.–**viciously** *adv.*–**viciousness** *n.*

vicissitude *n* a change of circumstances or fortune; (*pl*) ups and downs.–**vicissitudinary, vicissitudinous** *adj.*

victim *n* a person who has been killed or injured by an action beyond his or her control; a dupe.

victimize *vt* to make a victim of, to cause to suffer.–**victimization** *n.*–**victimizer** *n.*

victor *n* a winner; a conqueror.

victorious *adj* having won in battle or contest; emblematic of victory; triumphant.–**victoriously** *adv.*

victory *n* (*pl* **victories**) triumph in battle; success; achievement.

victual *n* (usu *pl*) food, provisions. * *vt* (**victualing, victualed** *or* **victualling, victualled**) to supply with food; to take in provisions.

video *n* (*pl* **videos**) the transmission or recording of television programs or movies, using a television set and a video recorder and tape. * *vt* (**videoing, videoed**) to record on video tape.

video cassette *n* a cassette containing video tape.

video recorder *n* the machine on which video cassettes are played or recorded.

video tape *n* a magnetic tape on which images and sounds can be recorded for reproduction on television.–**video-tape** *vt.*

vie *vi* (**vying, vied**) to contend or strive for superiority.–**vier** *n.*

view *n* sight; range of vision; inspection, examination; intention; scene; opinion. * *vt* to see; to consider; to examine intellectually.

viewer *n* a person who views, esp television; an optical device used in viewing.

viewpoint *n* opinion; a place from which something can be viewed, esp a scenic panorama.

vigil *n* keeping watch at night.

vigilant *adj* on the watch to discover and avoid danger, watchful; alert; cautious.–**vigilance** *n.*–**vigilantly** *adv.*

vigilante *n* a self-appointed law enforcer.

vigor *n* physical or mental strength; vitality.–*also* **vigour**.–**vigorous** *adj.*–**vigorously** *adv.*

vile *adj* wicked; evil; offensive; very bad.–**vilely** *adv.*–**vileness** *n.*

vilify *vt* (**vilifying, vilified**) to malign.–**vilification** *n.*–**vilifier** *n.*

villa *n* a large country or suburban house.

village *n* a collection of houses smaller than a town.

villager *n* an inhabitant of a village.

villain *n* a scoundrel; the main evil character in a play, film or novel.

villainous *adj* depraved, evil, wicked; very bad, wretched.–**villainously** *adv.*–**villainy** *n.*

vim *n* (*sl*) energy, force.

vinaigrette *n* a salad dressing made from oil, vinegar and seasoning.

vindicate *vt* to establish the existence or truth of, to justify; to clear of charges, to absolve from blame.–**vindicable** *adj.*–**vindicator** *n.*–**vindicatory** *adj.*

vindication *n* a vindicating or being vindicated; an event, fact, evidence, etc, that justifies a deed or claim.

vindictive adj vengeful; spiteful; (damages) exemplary, punitive.–**vindictively** adv.–**vindictiveness** n.

vine n any climbing plant, or its stem; a grapevine; a sphere of activity, esp spiritual or mental endeavour.

vinegar n a sour-tasting liquid containing acetic acid, used as a condiment and preservative.

vinegary adj of or like vinegar; sour; ill-tempered.

vineyard n a plantation of grapevines.

viniculture n the cultivation of vines and manufacture of wine, viticulture.–**vinicultural** adj.–**viniculturist** n.

vinous adj of, pertaining to, or having the qualities of wine; like wine; wine-colored; inspired by wine.–**vinosity** n.

vintage n the grape harvest of one season; wine, esp of good quality, made in a particular year; wine of a particular region; the product of a particular period. * adj (cars) classic; (wine) of a specified year and of good quality; (play) characteristic of the best.

vinyl n a strong plastic used in floor coverings, furniture and records, etc.

viola n a stringed instrument of the violin family, and tuned a fifth below it.

violate vt to break or infringe (an agreement); to rape; to disturb (one's privacy).–**violation** n.–**violative** adj.–**violator** n.

violence n physical force intended to cause injury or destruction; natural force; passion, intensity.

violent adj urged or driven by force; vehement; impetuous; forcible; furious; severe.–**violently** adv.

violet n a small plant with bluish-purple flowers; a bluish-purple color.

violin n a four-stringed musical instrument, played with a bow.

violinist n a person who plays the violin.

VIP abbr = Very Important Person.

viper n a common European venomous snake.–**viperine** adj.

virago n (pl **viragoes, viragos**) a bad-tempered woman.

viral adj of or caused by a virus.

virgin n a person (esp a woman) who has never had sexual intercourse; (with cap) Mary, the mother of Christ; a painting or statue of her. * adj chaste; pure; untouched.

virginal adj of or pertaining to a virgin or virginity; befitting a virgin; chaste, pure, innocent; fresh, unsullied, untouched.

virginity n the state of being a virgin; the state of being chaste, untouched, etc.

Virgo n the Virgin, the 6th sign of the zodiac.–**Virgoan** adj.

virile adj of a mature man, manly; strong, forceful; sexually potent.–**virility** n.

virtual adj in effect or essence, though not in fact or strict definition; (comput) denoting memory, making use of an external memory to increase capacity.

virtually adv to all intents and purposes, practically.

virtue n moral excellence; any admirable quality; chastity; merit.

virtuoso n (pl **virtuosos, virtuosi**) a person highly skilled in an activity, esp in playing a musical instrument. * adj skilled, masterly in technique.–**virtuosic** adj.–**virtuosity** n.

virtuous adj righteous; upright; pure.–**virtuously** adv.–**virtuousness** n.

virulent adj (disease) deadly; extremely poisonous; hostile; vicious.–**virulence** n.–**virulently** adv.

virus n (pl **viruses**) a very simple microorganism capable of replicating within living cells, producing disease; the disease caused by a virus; a harmful influence.

visa n an endorsement on a passport allowing the bearer to travel in the country of the government issuing it. * vt (**visaing, visaed**) to mark with a visa; to grant a visa to.

visage n the face; the countenance; appearance.

vis-à-vis prep opposite to; in face of. * adj, adv facing. * n the person opposite; a counterpart.

viscera npl (sing **viscus**) the large internal organs of the animal body, the entrails.

visceral adj of, pertaining to, or affecting the viscera; pertaining to or touching deeply inward feelings.–**viscerally** adv.

viscid adj (leaves) covered with a sticky layer; (fluids) thick, glutinous.–**viscidity** n–**viscidly** adv.

viscose n a form of cellulose used in making artificial silk.

viscount n in Britain, a title of nobility next below an earl.–**viscountess** nf.

viscous adj sticky, thick.–**viscosity** n.–**viscously** adv.–**viscousness** n.

viscus see **viscera**.

vise n a clamping device with jaws, used for holding objects firmly.–also **vice**.

visibility n (pl **visibilities**) clearness of seeing or being seen; the degree of clearness of the atmosphere.

visible adj able to be seen, perceptible; apparent, evident.–**visibleness** n.–**visibly** adv.

vision n the power of seeing, sight; a supernatural appearance; a revelation; foresight; imagination; a mental concept; a person, scene, etc of unusual beauty; something seen in a dream or trance.–**visional** adj.

visionary adj imaginative; having foresight; existing in imagination only, not real. * n (pl **visionaries**) an imaginative person; a dreamer; an idealist, a mystic.

visit vt to go to see; to pay a call upon a person or place; to stay with or at; to punish or reward with. * vi to see or meet someone regularly. * n the act of going to see, a call.–**visitable** adj.

visitation n a visit by a superior; a punitive act of God; an official visit; right of access of a divorced parent to his or her children.–**visitational** adj.

visitor n a person who visits; a caller; a tourist; a migratory bird pausing in transit.

visor n a movable part of a helmet protecting the face; the peak of a cap.–also **vizor**.–**visored** adj.

vista n a view, as from a high place; a mental picture.

visual adj having, producing, or relating to vision or sight; perceptible, visible; (knowledge) attained by sight or vision; (impressions, etc) based upon something seen; of the nature of, producing or conveying a picture in the mind; (physics) optical. * n a piece of graphic material used for display or to convey a concept, etc; (pl) the visual aspect of a movie, etc.–**visually** adv.

visual aid n a film, slide or overhead projector, etc used to aid teaching.

visualize vt to form a mental picture of; to make visible to the mind or imagination. * vi to construct a visual image in the mind.–**visualization** n.–**visualizer** n.

vital adj of, connected with or necessary to life; essential; lively, animated; fundamental; (wound, error) fatal. * n (pl) the bodily organs essential for life.–**vitally** adv.

vitality n (pl **vitalities**) vigor, hold on life; spirits; animation; capacity to last, durability.

vitalize vt to give life to; to animate; to make vigorous.–**vitalization** n.

vital statistics npl data recording births, deaths, marriages, etc used in compiling population statistics.

vitamin n one of several organic substances occurring naturally in foods, which are essential for good health.–**vitaminic** adj.

vitiate vt to make faulty or ineffective; to taint; to deprave; to invalidate or annul (a legal document, etc).–**vitiation** n.–**vitiator** n.

vitreous adj of like or obtained from glass; of the vitreous body.–**vitreousness** n.

vitreous body, vitreous humor n the transparent tissue of the eyeball.

vitriol n sulphuric acid; savage criticism. * vt (**vitrioling, vitrioled** or **vitriolling, vitriolled**) to throw vitriol over, to poison with vitriol.–**vitriolic** adj.

vituperate vt to berate; to abuse verbally.–**vituperation** n.–**vituperative** adj.–**vituperator** n.

viva interj long live, hurrah for.

vivacious adj lively; animated; spirited.–**vivaciously** adv.–**vivaciousness** n.

vivacity n (pl **vivacities**) vivaciousness; animation of the mind or disposition; liveliness of conception or perception; spirited conduct, manner or speech; brilliancy of light or color.

vivid adj brightly colored; graphic; lively; intense.–**vividly** adv.–**vividness** n.

vivisection n the practice of performing surgical operations on living animals for scientific research.–**vivisectional** adj.

vivisectionist n a person who practices or approves of vivisection.

vixen n a female fox; a malicious or shrewish woman.–**vixenish** adj.

viz abbr = namely (Latin videlicet).

vizor see **visor**.

vocabulary n (pl **vocabularies**) an alphabetical list of words with their meanings; the words of a language; an individual's command or use of particular words.

vocal adj of, for, endowed with, relating to, or produced by the voice; outspoken, noisy; (phonetics) having a vowel function. * n a vowel; (pl) music for the voice, not another instrument.–**vocally** adv.

vocal cords npl either of two pairs of elastic membranous folds in the larynx, esp the lower pair, which vibrate and produce sound.

vocalist n a singer.

vocalize vti to express with the voice; to articulate, utter distinctly; to use the singing voice; to sing to vowel sounds; to write with vowels or vowel points.–**vocalization** n.–**vocalizer** n.

vocation n a calling to a particular career or occupation, esp to a religious life; a sense of fitness for a particular career.

vocational adj of or relating to a vocation or occupation; providing special training for a particular career.–**vocationally** adv.

vociferous adj clamorous, noisy.–**vociferously** adv.–**vociferousness** n.

vodka n a spirit distilled from rye, potatoes, etc.

vogue n the fashion at a specified time; popularity. * adj fashionable, in vogue.–**voguish** adj.

voice n sound from the mouth; sound produced by speaking or singing; the quality of this; the power of speech; utterance; expressed opinion, vote. * vt to express; to speak.–**voicer** n.

voiced adj having a voice, esp of a specified kind, quality or tone.

voice-over n the voice of an unseen narrator, esp in a movie, TV commercial, etc.

void adj unoccupied, empty; not legally binding; having no cards of a particular suit. * n an empty space, a vacuum; vacancy, sense of loss. * vt to discharge, to emit; empty; to make invalid.–**voidable** adj.–**voider** n.

voile n a light, sheer fabric of silk, rayon, etc, used for dresses, scarves, etc.

volatile adj evaporating very quickly; changeable, fickle; unstable; light-hearted, mercurial; flighty.–**volatility** n.

volcano n (pl **volcanoes, volcanos**) a hill or mountain formed by ejection of lava, ashes, etc through an opening in the earth's crust.–**volcanic** adj.–**volcanically** adv.

volcanology n the science of volcanoes and the occurrences associated with them.–also **vulcanology**.–**volcanological, vulcanological** adj.–**volcanologist, vulcanologist** n.

volition n the exercise of the will; choice.–**volitional** adj.

volley n (pl **volleys**) the multiple discharge of many missiles or small arms; a barrage; (tennis, volleyball) the return of the ball before it reaches the ground. * vt (**volleying, volleyed**) to return (a ball) before it hits the ground.–**volleyer** n.

volleyball n a team game played by hitting a large inflated ball over a net with the hands; the ball used.

volt n the unit of measure of the force of an electrical current.

voltage n electrical energy that moves a charge around a circuit, measured in volts.

voluble adj speaking with a great flow of words, fluent; (arch) revolving, rotating; (bot) twining.–**volubility** n.–**volubly** adv.

volume n the amount of space occupied by an object; quantity, amount; intensity of sound; a book; one book of a series.–**volumed** adj.

voluminous adj of great size or bulk; (writings) capable of filling many volumes; (clothes) ample, loose.–**voluminosity** n.–**voluminously** adv.

voluntary adj spontaneous, deliberate; without remuneration; supported by voluntary effort; having free will; (law) acting gratuitously or from choice, not because of any legal compulsion or argument; (muscles) controlled by conscious effort; designed.* n (pl **voluntaries**) an organ solo, often improvised, played before or after a church service; (arch) a volunteer.–**voluntarily** adv.–**voluntariness** n.

volunteer n a person who carries out work voluntarily; a person who freely undertakes military service. * vti to offer unasked; to come forward, enlist or serve voluntarily.

voluptuous adj excessively fond of pleasure; having an attractive figure; luxurious; exciting sensual desire.–**voluptuously** adv.–**voluptuousness** n.

vomit vi to eject the contents of the stomach through the mouth, to spew. * n matter ejected from the stomach when vomiting.–**vomiter** n.

voodoo n (pl **voodoos**) a religious cult in the West Indies, based on a belief in sorcery, etc; one who practices voodoo. * vt (**voodooing, voodooed**) to affect by voodoo.

voracious adj eager to devour (food, literature etc); very greedy.–**voraciously** adv.–**voracity** n.

vortex n (pl **vortexes, vortices**) a whirlpool; a powerful eddy; a whirlwind; a whirling motion or mass.–**vortical** adj.–**vortically** adv.

votary n (pl **votaries**) a person vowed to religious service or worship; an ardent follower, a devotee of a person, religion, occupation, idea, etc (–also **votarist**). * adj ardently devoted to a deity or saint.

vote n an indication of a choice or opinion as to a matter on which one has a right to be consulted; a ballot; decision by a majority; the right to vote; franchise. * vt to cast one's vote. * vt to elect (to office).–**votable, voteable** adj.

voter n a person with a right to vote, esp one who uses it.

vouch vt to provide evidence or proof of. * vi to give assurance; to guarantee.

voucher n a written record of a transaction; a receipt; a token that can be exchanged for something else.

vouchsafe vt to give, to grant; to condescend (to).–**vouchsafement** n.

vow n a solemn or binding promise. * vt to promise; to resolve.–**vower** n.

vowel n an open speech sound produced by continuous passage of the breath; a letter representing such a sound, as a, e, i, o, u. * adj of or constituting a vowel.–**vowelless** adj.

voyage n a long journey, esp by ship or spacecraft. * vi to journey.–**voyager** n.

voyeur n a person who is sexually gratified from watching sexual acts or objects; a peeping Tom.–**voyeurism** n.–**voyeuristic** adj.

VP abbr = vice-president.

vs abbr = against (Latin versus) .

VT abbr = Vermont.

vulcanize vt to treat (rubber) with sulphur, white lead and other substances at high temperatures under pressure to improve its strength and elasticity or render it hard and non-elastic; to change the properties of (any material) in a similar way.–**vulcanization** n.

vulcanology see **volcanology**.

vulgar adj of the common people; vernacular; unrefined, in bad taste; coarse; offensive, indecent.–**vulgarly** adv.–**vulgarness** n.

vulgarity n (pl **vulgarities**) coarseness of manners or language; a vulgar phrase, expression, act, etc.

vulgarize vt to debase; to popularize.–**vulgarization** n.–**vulgarizer** n.

vulnerable adj capable of being wounded physically or mentally; open to persuasion; easily influenced; open to attack, assailable.–**vulnerability** n.–**vulnerably** adv.

vulture n a large bird of prey having no feathers on the neck or head and feeding chiefly on carrion; a rapacious person.

vulva n (pl **vulvae, vulvas**) the external genitals of human females.–**vulval, vulvar, vulvate** adj.

vying see **vie**.

W

w abbr = watt(s); west.

WA abbr = Washington.

wacky adj (**wackier, wackiest**) (sl) crazy, eccentric.–**wackily** adv.–**wackiness** n.

wad n a small, soft mass, as of cotton or paper; a bundle of paper money.

waddle vi to walk with short steps and sway from side to side, as a duck.–also n.

wade vti to walk through water; to pass (through) with difficulty.

wafer n a thin crisp cracker or cookie.

waffle n a thick, crisp pancake baked in a waffle iron.

waffle iron n a metal cooking utensil with two hinged metal parts that close and impress a square pattern on a waffle.

waft vt to drift or float through the air. * n a breath, scent or sound carried through the air.

wag[1] vti (**wagging, wagged**) to move rapidly from side to side or up and down (as of a finger, tail).–also n.

wag[2] n a joker, a wit.

wage vt to carry on, esp war. * n (often pl) payment for work or services.

wager n a bet. * vti to bet.

waggle vti to wag.–also n.

wagon n a four-wheeled vehicle pulled by a horse or tractor, for carrying heavy goods.

waif n a homeless, neglected child.

wail vi to make a long, loud cry of sorrow or grief; to howl, to moan.–also n.

waist n the narrowest part of the human trunk, between the ribs and the hips; the narrow part of anything that is wider at the ends; the part of a garment covering the waist.

waistband n a band of material (on a skirt, trousers, etc) that strengthens and completes the waist.

waistline n the narrowest part of the waist; its measurement; the seam that joins the bodice and skirt of a dress, etc; the level of this.

wait vti to stay, or to be, in expectation or readiness; to defer or to be postponed; to remain; (with **at** or **on**) to serve food at a meal. * n act or period of waiting.

waiter n a man or woman who serves at table, as in a restaurant.–**waitress** nf.

waiting n the act of remaining inactive or stationary; a period of waiting. * adj of or pertaining to a wait; in attendance.

waiting room n a room for people to wait in at a station, hospital, etc.

waive vt to refrain from enforcing; to relinquish voluntarily.

waiver n (law) a waiving of a right, claim etc.

wake[1] vb (**waking, woke,** pp **woken**) vi to emerge from sleep; to become awake. * vt to rouse from sleep. * n a watch or vigil beside a corpse, on the eve of the burial.–**wakeful** adj.–**waken** vti.

wake[2] n the waves or foamy water left in the track of a ship; a trail.

walk vi to travel on foot with alternate steps; (with **out**) to leave suddenly; to go on strike; (with **on**) to abandon, jilt. * vt to pass through or over; (a dog) to exercise; to escort on foot. * n the act of walking; distance walked over; gait; a ramble or stroll; a profession.–**walker** n.

walkie-talkie, walky-talky n (pl **walkie-talkies, walky-talkies**) a portable two-way radio transmitter and receiver.

walk-in adj (closet) large enough to enter and move around in.

walking stick n a stick used in walking, a cane.

Walkman n (trademark) a small portable cassette player (and sometimes radio) used with earphones.

walkout n a strike; a sudden departure.

walkover n an unopposed or easy victory; a horse race with only one starter.

walkway n road, path, etc, for pedestrians only.

wall n a vertical structure of brick, stone, etc for enclosing, dividing or protecting. * vt to enclose with a wall; to close up with a wall.

wallaby n (pl **wallabies, wallaby**) a small kangaroo-like animal.

wallet n a flat pocketbook for paper money, cards etc.

wallop vt (inf) to beat or defeat soundly; (inf) to strike hard. * n (inf) a hard blow.

wallow vi (animal) to roll about in mud; to indulge oneself in emotion.–also n.

wallpaper n decorated paper for covering the walls of a room.

wall-to-wall adj (carpet) covering the whole area of a room; (inf) nonstop, continuous.

walnut n a tree producing an edible nut with a round shell and wrinkled seed; its nut; its wood used for furniture.

walrus n (pl **walruses, walrus**) a large, thick-skinned aquatic animal, related to the seals, having long canine teeth and coarse whiskers.

waltz n a piece of music with three beats to the bar; a whirling or slowly circling dance. * vi to dance a waltz.

wan adj (**wanner, wannest**) pale and sickly; feeble or weak.–**wanly** adv.–**wanness** n.

wand n a magician's rod.

wander vi to ramble with no definite destination; to go astray; to lose concentration.–also n.

wanderlust n a compelling desire for travel.

wane vi to decrease, esp of the moon; to decline. * n decrease, decline.

wangle vti (inf) to achieve (something) by devious means.

wannabee n (sl) a person who wants to be someone or something else.

want n lack; poverty. * vt to need; to require; to lack; to wish (for).

wanton adj malicious; willful; sexually provocative.

war n military conflict between nations or parties; a conflict; a contest. * vi (**warring, warred**) to make war.

warble vi to sing with trills and runs; to sing like a bird.

war crime n a crime committed in wartime (such as mistreatment of prisoners) which violates conventional notions of decency.

ward n a section of a hospital; an electoral district; a division of a prison; a child placed under the supervision of a court. * vt (with **off**) to repel; to fend off.–**wardship** n.

warden n an official; a person in charge of a building or home; a prison governor.

wardrobe n one's clothes.

ware n (pl) merchandise, goods for sale; pottery.

warehouse n a building for storing goods.

warfare n armed hostilities; conflict.

warfarin n a crystalline substance used in medicine as an anticoagulant and also as a poison to kill rodents.

war game n a simulated battle or tactical exercise using models or computers for military training; a re-enactment of a battle using model soldiers.

warhead n the section of a missile containing the explosive.

warlock n a sorcerer, a magician.

warlord n a military leader or ruler of (part of) a country.

warm adj moderately hot; friendly, kind; (colors) rich; enthusiastic. * vt to make warm. * vi to become enthusiastic (about).–**warmly** adv–**warmth** n.

warm-blooded adj having a constant and relatively high temperature; passionate.

warmonger n a person who incites war, esp for personal gain; warrior, a fighting soldier.

warm-up n a period of exercise or practice before a race, etc.

warn vt to notify of danger; to caution or advise (against).–**warning** n.

warp vti to twist out of shape; to distort; to corrupt. * n the threads arranged lengthwise on a loom across which other threads are passed.

warpath n the route used by a war party of North American Indians; (with **on the**) on a hostile expedition; (with **on the**) (inf) angry.

warrant vt to guarantee; to justify. * n a document giving authorization; a writ for arrest.

warrant officer n a person in the armed services holding a rank between commissioned officers and NCOs.

warranty n (pl **warranties**) a pledge to replace something if it is not as represented, a guarantee.

warren n an area in which rabbits breed.

warrior n a soldier, fighter.

wart n a small, hard projection on the skin.–**warty** adj.

wary adj (**warier, wariest**) watchful; cautious.–**warily** adv.–**wariness** n.

was see **be**.

wash vti to cleanse with water and soap; to flow against or over; to sweep along by the action of water; to separate gold, etc, from earth by washing; to cover with a thin coat of metal or paint; (with **down**) to wash thoroughly from top to bottom; to take a drink of liquid to help in swallowing food. * n a washing; the break of waves on the shore; the waves left behind by a boat; a liquid used for washing.

washbowl, washbasin n a basin or bowl, esp a bathroom fixture, for use in washing one's hands, etc.–also **wash-hand basin**.

washed-out adj faded in color; fatigued.

washed-up adj unsuccessful, ineffective; unpromising.

washer n a flat ring of metal, rubber, etc, to give tightness to joints; a washing machine.

washroom n cloakroom, lavatory.

wasn't = was not.

wasp n a winged insect with a black and yellow striped body, which can sting.

waspish adj sharp in speech or manner, irritable.

waste adj useless; left over; uncultivated or uninhabited. * vt to ravage; to squander; to use foolishly; to fail to use. * vi to lose strength, etc as by disease. * n uncultivated or uninhabited land; discarded material, garbage, excrement.–**wasteful** adj.–**wastefully** adv.–**wastefulness** n.

wasted adj ravaged, devastated; not used to best advantage; weak, emaciated; (sl) dead, killed; (sl) showing the effects of alcohol or drug abuse.

wasteland n a piece of barren or uncultivated land; a desolate region; something (eg a period of time, relationship) lacking in moral, spiritual, emotional, etc vitality.

wastepaper n paper discarded as waste.

watch n surveillance; close observation; vigil; guard; a small timepiece worn on the wrist, etc; a period of duty on a ship * vi to look with attention; to wait for; to keep vigil. * vt to keep one's eyes fixed on; to guard; to tend; to observe closely; (chance, etc) to wait for.–**watcher** n.–**watchful** adj.–**watchfully** adv.–**watchfulness** n.

watchdog n a dog that guards property; a person or group that monitors safety, standards, etc.

watchman n (pl **watchmen**) a person who guards a building or other property.

water n the substance H_2O, a clear, thin liquid, lacking taste or smell, and essential for life; any body of it, as the ocean, a lake, river, etc; bodily secretions such as tears, urine. * vt to moisten with water; to irrigate; to dilute with water; (with **down**) to dilute; to reduce in strength or effectiveness. * vi (eyes) to smart; to salivate; to take in water.

water bed n a bed with a water-filled mattress.

watercolor, watercolour n a water-soluble paint; a picture painted with watercolors.

watercress n a plant growing in ponds and streams, used in a salad.

waterfall n a fall of water over a precipice or down a hill.

waterfront n an area alongside a body of water, esp a docks.

water ice n an iced dessert made from frozen water, sugar and a flavoring.

watering can n a container with a spout for watering plants.

water lily n any of a family of plants with large floating leaves and showy flowers.

waterlogged adj soaked or saturated with water.

watermark n a line marking the height to which water has risen; a mark impressed on paper which can only be seen when held up to the light.

watermelon n a large fruit with a hard green rind and edible red watery flesh.

water polo n a game played in water by two teams of seven swimmers with the aim of scoring by hitting a ball into the opponents' goal.

waterproof adj impervious to water; watertight.–also vt.

watershed n a turning point.

water-skiing n the sport of planing on water by being towed by a motorboat–**water-skier** n.

watertight adj not allowing water to pass through; foolproof.

waterway n a navigable channel of water.

waterworks n (as sing) an establishment that supplies water to a district; (pl: inf) the urinary system; (inf) tears.

watery adj thin, diluted.

watt n a unit of electrical power.

wattle n (material for) a framework of stakes or poles interwoven with thin branches, twigs, etc formerly used for fencing and building; a loose flap of skin hanging from the necks of certain birds and lizards. * vt to build of or with wattle; to interweave or interlace (with sticks, etc) to make a light frame.

wave n an undulation traveling on the surface of water; the form in which light and sound are thought to travel; an increase or upsurge (eg of crime); a hair curl; a movement of the hand in greeting or farewell. * vti to move freely backward and forward; to flutter; to undulate; to move the hand to and fro in greeting, farewell, etc; (with **down**) to signal (a vehicle, etc) to stop with a wave.–**wavy** adj.

wave band n a range of radio frequencies or wavelengths.

wavelength n the distance between the crests of successive waves of light or sound; radio frequency.

waver vi to hesitate; to falter.–**waverer** n.

wax[1] n beeswax; an oily substance used to make candles, polish, etc * vt to rub, polish, cover or treat with wax.

wax[2] vi to increase in strength, size, etc.

waxen adj made of wax; pale and smooth like wax.

waxy adj (**waxier, waxiest**) consisting of or like wax; adhesive.–**waxily** adv.–**waxiness** n.

way n path, route; road; distance; room to advance; direction; state; means; possibility; manner of living; (pl) habits.

waylay vt (**waylaying, waylaid**) to lie in wait for; to accost.

way-out adj (inf) unconventional, unusual; amazing.

wayward adj willful, stubborn; unpredictable.–**waywardness** n.

we pron pl of I; I and others.

weak adj lacking power or strength; feeble; ineffectual.–**weakness** n.

weaken vti to make or grow weaker.

weakling n a person who lacks strength of character.

wealth n a large amount of possessions or money; affluence; an abundance (of).–**wealthy** adj.

wean vt (baby, animal) to replace the mother's milk with other nourishment; to dissuade (from indulging a habit).

weapon n any instrument used in fighting.

weaponry n weapons collectively.

wear vb (**wearing, wore,** pp **worn**) vt to have on the body as clothing; (hair, etc) to arrange in a particular way; to display; to rub away; to impair by use; to exhaust, tire; (with **down**) to overcome gradually through persistent pressure; (with **out**) to tire or exhaust. * vi to be impaired by use or time; to be spent tediously; (with **off**) to become gradually weaker in effect; (with **out**) to make or become worthless through prolonged use. * n deterioration from frequent use; articles worn.–**wearer** n.

weary adj (**wearier, weariest**) tired; bored. * vti (**wearying, wearied**) to make or become tired.–**weariness** n.–**wearisome** adj.

weasel n a small carnivorous animal with a long slender body and reddish fur.

weather n atmospheric conditions, such as temperature, rainfall, cloudiness, etc * vt to expose to the action of the weather; to survive. * vi to withstand the weather.

weather-beaten adj worn or damaged by the weather; hardened or bronzed through exposure to the weather.

weatherman n (pl **weathermen**) a weather forecaster on radio or television who is usually also a professional meteorologist.

weather station n a meteorological post for collecting, recording and transmitting data on weather conditions.

weather vane n a device attached to a tall structure to indicate wind direction.

weave vb (**weaving, wove,** pp **woven**) vt to interlace threads in a loom to form fabric; to construct. * vi to make a way through (eg a crowd), to zigzag.–**weaver** n.

web n a woven fabric; the fine threads spun by a spider; the membrane joining the digits of birds, animals.

webbed adj (ducks, etc) having the digits connected by a fold of skin.

wed vti (**wedding, wedded** or **wed**) to marry; to join closely.

we'd = we had; we would.

wedding n marriage; the ceremony of marriage.

wedge n a v-shaped block of wood or metal for splitting or fastening; a wedge-shaped object. * vti to split or secure with a wedge; to thrust (in) tightly; to become fixed tightly.

wedlock n marriage.

Wednesday n fourth day of the week, between Tuesday and Thursday.

weed n any undesired plant, esp one that crowds out desired plants; (pl) a widow's black mourning clothes. * vt to remove weeds; (with **out**) to remove or eliminate (something superfluous or harmful).–**weedy** adj. **week** n the period of seven consecutive days, esp from Sunday to Sunday.

weekday n a day of the week other than Saturday or Sunday.

weekend, week-end n the period from Friday night to Sunday night–also adj.

weekly adj happening once a week or every week.

weep vti (**weeping, wept**) to shed tears, to cry; (wound) to ooze.

weepy adj (**weepier, weepiest**) tearful; prone to crying.–**weepily** adv.–**weepiness** n.

weevil n a beetle which feeds on plants and crops.

weft n the yarn woven across the lengthwise threads in a loom.–also **woof**.

weigh vt to measure the weight of; to consider carefully; (with **down**) to weight; to oppress; (with **up**) to assess, make a judgment about (a person, thing, etc). * vi to have weight; to be burdensome; (with **in**) (boxer, wrestler) to be weighed before a bout; (jockey) to be weighed after a race; (inf) to make a contribution to (eg an argument).

weigh-in n (sports) the checking of the weight of a contestant, esp of a jockey after a race or of a boxer before a bout.

weight n the amount which anything weighs; influence; any unit of heaviness. * vt to attach a weight to.

weightlessness n the state of having no or little reaction to gravity, esp in space travel.

weight lifting n the sport of lifting weights of a specific amount in a particular way.–**weight lifter** n.

weight training n physical exercise involving lifting heavy weights.

weight watcher n a person on a diet to lose weight.

weighty adj (**weightier, weightiest**) heavy; serious.–**weightily** adv.

weird adj unearthly, mysterious; eerie; bizarre.–**weirdly** adv.

weirdo, weirdie n (pl **weirdos, weirdies**) (inf) an eccentric person.

welcome adj gladly received; pleasing. * n reception of a person or thing. * vt to greet kindly.

weld vt to unite, as metal by heating until fused or soft enough to hammer together; to join closely. * n a welded joint.

welfare n well-being; health; assistance or financial aid granted to the poor, the unemployed, etc.

well[1] n a spring; a hole bored in the ground to provide a source of water, oil, gas, etc; the open space in the middle of a staircase * vi to pour forth.

well[2] adj (**better, best**) agreeable; comfortable; in good health. * adv in a proper, satisfactory, or excellent manner; thoroughly; prosperously; with good reason; to a considerable degree; fully. * interj an expression of surprise, etc.

we'll = we will; we shall.

well-being n condition of being well or contented; welfare.

well-bred adj well brought up; of good stock.

well-disposed adj favorable, feeling kindly (toward).

well-done adj performed with skill; thoroughly cooked, as meat.

well-groomed adj clean and tidy in dress and appearance.

well-heeled adj (inf) wealthy.

well-known adj widely known, famous; known fully.

well-meaning adj having good intentions (but often without producing good results).

well-off adj in comfortable circumstances; prosperous.

well-preserved adj well looked after; remaining youthful in appearance.

well-read adj having read widely and deeply.

well-spoken adj spoken clearly and eloquently; spoken in a pleasing manner.

well-thought-of adj having a good reputation.

well-to-do adj prosperous.

well-wisher n a person who is sympathetic to another person, cause, etc.

well-worn adj showing signs of wear; (phrase, etc) trite, hackneyed.

welsh vti to avoid paying a gambling debt; to run off without paying.–**welsher** n.

welt n a band or strip to strengthen a seam; a raised mark on the skin left by a blow with a lash.

welter vi to roll or wallow. * n a jumble.

wend vt to amble, to saunter.

went see **go**.

wept see **weep**.

were see **be**.

we're = we are.

weren't = were not.

werewolf n (pl **werewolves**) an imaginary person able to transform himself for a time into a wolf.

west n the direction of the sun at sunset; one of the four points of the compass; the region in the west of any country; (with cap) Europe and the Western Hemisphere. * adj situated in, or toward the west. * adv in or to the west.

westerly adj toward the west; blowing from the west. * n (pl **westerlies**) a wind blowing from the west.–also adv.

western adj of or in the west. * n a movie, novel, etc about the usu pre-20th century American West.

westerner n a person from the west.

westward adj toward the west.–also adv.–**westwards** adv.

wet adj (**wetter, wettest**) covered or saturated with water or other liquid; rainy; misty; not yet dry. * n water or other liquid; rain or rainy weather. * vti (**wetting, wet** or **wetted**) to soak; to moisten.–**wetness** n.

wet suit n a close-fitting suit worn by divers, etc, to retain body heat.

we've = we have.

whack vti (inf) to strike sharply, esp making a sound. * n (inf) a sharp blow.

whale n a very large sea mammal that breathes through a blow-hole, and resembles a fish in shape. * vi to hunt whales.

whalebone n a horny substance forming plates in the upper jaws of toothless whales; a piece of this formerly used for stiffening undergarments.

whaler n a person or a ship employed in hunting whales.

wham n (the sound of) a heavy blow. * vti (**whamming, whammed**) to hit or cause to hit with a loud noise.

wharf n (pl **wharfs, wharves**) a platform for loading and unloading ships in harbor.

what adj of what sort, how much, how great. * relative pron that which; as much or many as. * interj used as an expression of surprise or astonishment.

whatever pron anything that; no matter what.

whatnot n (inf) something or someone the name of which has been forgotten, is unknown or is hard to categorize.

whatsit n (inf) something or someone the name of which has been forgotten, is unknown or is hard to categorize.

wheat n a cereal grain usu ground into flour for bread.

wheat germ n the kernel of a grain of wheat, high in nutritive value.

wheatmeal adj, n (made from) brown flour with a high proportion of wheat grain.

wheedle vt to persuade, to cajole (into); to coax with flattery.

wheel n a solid disc or circular rim turning on an axle; a steering wheel; (pl) the moving forces. * vt to transport on wheels. * vi to turn round or on an axis; to move in a circular direction, as a bird.

wheelbarrow n a cart with one wheel in front and two handles and legs at the rear.

wheelchair n a chair with large wheels for invalids.

wheeler-dealer n (inf) a shrewd operator in business, politics, etc.

wheelie n a stunt in which a bicycle or motorcycle is ridden for a distance with the front wheel off the ground.

wheeze vi to breathe with a rasping sound; to breathe with difficulty.–also n.–**wheezy** adj.

whelp n the young of various animals, esp a dog. * vt to give birth to (a puppy, etc). * vi (bitch) to bring forth young.

when adv at what or which time * conj at the time at which; although. * relative pron at which.

whence adv from what place.–also conj.

whenever adv, conj at whatever time.

where adv at which or what place; to which place; from what source; relative pron in or to which.

whereabouts adv near or at what place; about where. * n approximate location.

whereas conj since; on the contrary.

whereby adv by which.–also conj.

whereupon adv at which point; upon which.

wherever adv at or to whatever place.

wherewithal n the means or resources.

whet vt (**whetting, whetted**) to sharpen by rubbing, to stimulate.

whether conj introducing an alternative possibility or condition.

whey n the watery part of milk that is separated from the curds in sour milk.

which adj what one (of) * pron which person or thing; that. * relative pron person or thing referred to.

whichever pron whatever one that; whether one or the other; no matter which.–also adj.

whiff n a sudden puff of air, smoke or odor.

while n a period of time. * conj during the time that; whereas; although. * vt to pass (the time) pleasantly.

whim n a fancy; an irrational thought.

whimper vi to make a low, unhappy cry.–also n.

whimsical adj unusual, odd, fantastic.–**whimsicality** n.

whimsy, whimsey n (pl **whimsies, whimseys**) a fanciful notion, a whim.

whine vi (dog) to make a long, high-pitched cry; (person) to complain childishly. * n a plaintive cry.

whinny vi (**whinnying, whinnied**) to neigh softly.–also n.

whip n a piece of leather attached to a handle used for punishing people or driving on animals; an officer in parliament who maintains party discipline. * vb (**whipping, whipped**) vt to move, pull, throw, etc quickly; to strike, as with a lash; (eggs, etc) to beat into a froth; (with up) to stir into action, excite; (inf) to produce in a hurry. * vi to move rapidly.

whiplash n a stroke with a whip; a neck injury when the head is jerked forward and backward.

whippoorwill n a nocturnal American bird with a distinctive call.

whir, whirr n a humming or buzzing sound. * vti (**whirring, whirred**) to revolve with a buzzing noise.

whirl n a swift turning; confusion, commotion; (inf) an attempt or try. * vti to turn around rapidly; to spin.

whirlpool n a circular current or vortex of water.

whirlwind n a whirling column of air; rapid activity.

whisk vt to make a quick sweeping movement; (eggs, cream) to beat, whip. * vi to move nimbly and efficiently. * n a kitchen utensil for whisking; (inf) a small amount.

whisker n any of the sensory bristles on the face of a cat, etc; (pl) the hair growing on a man's face, esp the cheeks.–**whiskered** adj.

whiskey n whisky distilled in the US or Ireland.

whisky n (pl **whiskies**) a spirit distilled from barley or rye.

whisper vti to speak softly; to spread a rumour. * n a hushed tone; a hint, trace.

whist n a card game for four players in two sides, each side attempting to win the greater number of the 13 tricks.

whistle vti to make a shrill sound by forcing the breath through the lips; to make a similar sound with a whistle; (wind) to move with a shrill sound; (with for) (inf) to demand or hope for in vain. * n a whistling sound; a musical instrument; a metal tube that is blown to make a shrill warning sound.

whit n the tiniest possible amount.

white adj of the color of snow; pure; bright; (skin) light-colored. * n the color white; the white part of an egg or the eye.

white-collar adj of office and professional workers.

white elephant n a thing of little use.

white feather n a symbol of cowardice.

white flag n a flag of plain white material used to signify surrender or arrange a truce.

white gold n a pale alloy of gold chiefly with platinum and palladium.

white heat n an intense heat accompanied by the emission of white light from a substance; (inf) intense excitement or emotion.

white-hot adj of a temperature so hot that white light is emitted; intensely passionate.

White House n the official residence of the president of the US; the US presidency.

white lie n a harmless lie, esp as uttered out of politeness.

whiten vti to make or become white; to bleach.

white noise n sound that contains approximately equal proportions of all the audible frequencies.

white sauce n a sauce made with butter, flour and seasonings mixed with milk, cream or stock.

white slave n a woman or girl held against her will and forced into prostitution.

whitewash n a mixture of lime and water, used for whitening walls; concealment of the truth.–also vt.

whither adv to what or which place.

whittle vt to pare or cut thin shavings from (wood); (with away or down) to reduce.

whiz, whizz vi (whizzing, whizzed) to make a humming sound. * n (pl whizzes) a humming sound; (inf) an expert.

whiz kid, whizz kid (inf) a person of extraordinary achievements given their relatively young age.

WHO abbr = World Health Organization.

who pron what or which person; that.

whoa interj a command given, esp to a horse, to slow down or come to a halt.

who'd = who would.

whodunit, whodunnit n (inf) a detective novel, play, etc.

whoever pron anyone who; whatever person.

whole adj not broken, intact; containing the total amount, number, etc.; complete. * n the entire amount; a thing complete in itself.

wholefood n unrefined food, free from additives.

wholehearted adj sincere, single-minded, enthusiastic.–**wholeheartedly** adv.

whole note n (mus) a note with a time value equal to two half notes.–also **semibreve**

whole number n a number without fractions; an integer.

wholesale n selling of goods, usu at lower prices and in quantity, to a retailer.

wholesome adj healthy; mentally beneficial.–**wholesomeness** n.

wholewheat adj (esp US flour) made from the entire wheat kernel.

who'll = who will; who shall.

wholly adv completely.

whom pron objective case of **who**.

whoop n a loud cry of excitement.

whoopee interj used to express wild excitement. * n boisterous fun.

whooping cough n an infectious disease, esp of children, causing coughing spasms.

whoops interj (inf) an exclamation of surprise or apology.

whoosh n a rushing or hissing sound. * vi to make or move with such a sound.

whopper n (inf) a large specimen.–**whopping** adj.

whore n a prostitute.

whorehouse n a brothel.

whorl n a ring of leaves or petals round a stem; a single turn of a spiral; something shaped like a spiral; the central ridges of a fingerprint forming a complete circle.

who's = who is.

whose pron the possessive case of **who** or **which**.

who's who n a reference book containing the names and brief biographical details of famous or important people.

why adv for what cause or reason? * interj exclamation of surprise. * n (pl **whys**) a cause.

WI abbr = Wisconsin; West Indies.

wick n a cord, as in a candle or lamp, that supplies fuel to the flame.

wicked adj evil, immoral, sinful.–**wickedly** adv.–**wickedness** n.

wicker n a long, thin, flexible twig; such twigs woven together, as in making baskets.–**wickerwork** n.

wicket n a small door or gate; (croquet) any of the small wire arches through which the balls must be hit.

wide adj broad; extensive; of a definite distance from side to side; (with of) far from the aim; open fully. * n (cricket) a ball bowled beyond the reach of the batsman.–**widely** adv.

wide-angle adj (photog) with an angle of view of 60 degrees or more.

wide-awake adj fully awake; ready, alert.

wide-eyed adj astonished; innocent.

widen vti to make or grow wide or wider.

widespread adj widely extended; general.

widow n a woman whose husband has died. * vt to cause to become a widow.–**widowhood** n.

widower n a man whose wife has died.

width n breadth.

wield vt (a weapon, etc) to brandish; to exercise power.

wife n (pl **wives**) a married woman.

wig n an artificial covering of real or synthetic hair for the head.

wiggle vti to move from side to side with jerky movements.

wigwam n a North American Indian conical shelter.

wild adj in its natural state; not tamed or cultivated; uncivilized; lacking control; disorderly; furious.–**wildly** adv.–**wildness** n.

wild card n (card games) a card with an arbitrary value determined by the holder; (sport) a team that has not qualified for a competition but is allowed to take part; (sl) an unpredictable element.

wilderness n an uncultivated and desolate place.

wildfire n a fire that spreads fast and is hard to put out.

wildfowl n any bird that is hunted for game, esp waterbirds such as ducks and geese.

wild-goose chase n a futile pursuit of something.

wildlife n animals in the wild.

Wild West n the western US during the lawless period of early settlement.

wile n a trick, craftiness.

wilful see **willful**.

will[1] n power of choosing or determining; desire; determination; attitude, disposition; a legal document directing the disposal of one's property after death. * vt to bequeath; to command.

will[2] aux vb used in constructions with 2nd and 3rd persons; used to show futurity, determination, obligation.

willful adj stubborn; done intentionally.–also **wilful**.–**willfully, wilfully** adv.–**willfulness, wilfulness** n.

willies npl (with **the**) nervousness, jumpiness.

willing adj ready, inclined; eager.–**willingly** adv.–**willingness** n.

willow n a tree or shrub with slender, flexible branches; the wood of the willow.

willow pattern n a traditional oriental-style design on china tableware consisting of a scene with figures and a willow tree, usu in blue on a white background.

willowy adj flexible, graceful.

willpower n the ability to control one's emotions and actions.

willy-nilly adv whether desired or not.

wilt vi to become limp, as from heat; (plant) to droop; to become weak or faint.

wily adj (**wilier, wiliest**) crafty; sly.–**wiliness** n.

wimp n (inf) a weak or ineffectual person.

win vti (**winning, won**) to gain with effort; to succeed in a contest; to gain eg by luck; to achieve influence over; (with **over**) to gain the support or affection of (someone). * n a success.

wince vi to shrink back; to flinch (as in pain).–also n.

winch n a hoisting machine. * vt to hoist or lower with a winch.

wind[1] n a current of air; breath; scent of game; (inf) flatulence; tendency; (mus) wind instrument(s). * vt (**winding, winded**) to cause to be short of breath; to perceive by scent.

wind[2] vb (**winding, wound**) vt to turn by cranking; to tighten the spring of a clock; to coil around something else; to encircle or cover, as with a bandage; (with **down**) to lower by winding a handle, etc. * vi to turn, to twist, to meander; (with **down**) to diminish in power or intensity; to slacken; to relax.

windbreak n a shelter that breaks the force of the wind, as a line of trees.

wind-chill n a measure of the effect of low temperature combined with wind.

windfall n fruit blown off a tree; any unexpected gain, esp financial.

wind instrument n a musical instrument played by blowing into it or passing an air current through it.

windlass n any of various devices for hoisting, hauling or lifting using a rope or chain wound round a motorized drum. * vt to hoist, etc using a windlass.

windmill n a machine operated by the force of the wind turning a set of sails.

window n a framework containing glass in the opening in a wall of a building, or in a vehicle, etc, for air and light.

windowdressing n the arrangement of goods in a shop window; ornamentation intended to disguise the true nature of something.

window-shopping n the occupation of looking at goods for sale without buying them.–**window-shopper** n.

windpipe n the air passage from the mouth to the lungs, the trachea.

windshield, windscreen n a protective shield of glass in the front of a vehicle.

windshield wiper, windscreen wiper n a metal blade with a rubber edge that removes rain, etc, from a windshield.

windsurfing n the sport of skimming along the surface of the water standing on a surfboard fitted with a sail.

windswept adj exposed to the wind; disheveled.

windy adj (**windier, windiest**) exposed to the winds; stormy; verbose.

wine n fermented grape juice used as an alcoholic beverage; the fermented juice of other fruits or plants.

wing n the forelimb of a bird, bat or insect, by which it flies; the main lateral surface of an airplane; a projecting part of a building; the side of a stage; a section of a political party. * vti to make one's way swiftly; to wound without killing.

wingspan, wingspread n the width of a bird or airplane between the tips of the wings.

wink vi to quickly open and close one's eye; to give a hint by winking; (with **at**) to disregard; to allow (something normally prohibited) to happen. * n the act of winking; an instant.

winner n one that wins; (inf) a person or thing that is assured of success.

winning n a victory; (pl) money won in gambling. * adj charming.

wino n (pl **winos**) (inf) a down-and-out addicted to cheap wine.

winsome adj charming, pleasing.

winter n the coldest season of the year: in the northern hemisphere from November or December to January or February. * vi to spend the winter.

wintry, wintery adj (**wintrier, wintriest**) typical of winter, cold, stormy, snowy; unfriendly, frigid.

wipe vt to rub a surface with a cloth in order to clean or dry it; (with **out**) to remove; to erase; to kill off; to destroy. * n a wiping.

wire n a flexible thread of metal; a length of this; (horse racing) the finish line of a race; a telegram. * adj formed of wire. * vt to fasten, furnish, connect, etc, with wire; to send a telegram.

wired adj (sl) wearing a hidden electronic recording or listening device; (sl) nervous or edgy, esp as a result of taking a stimulating drug.

wireless n (formerly) a radio.

wiretap vb (**wiretapping, wiretapped**) vi to connect to a telephone wire in order to listen in to a private conversation. * vt to tap (a telephone).–**wiretapper** n.

wiry adj (**wirier, wiriest**) lean, supple and sinewy.–**wiriness** n.

wisdom n the ability to use knowledge; sound judgment.

wisdom tooth n one of four teeth set at the end of each side of the upper and lower jaw in humans and grown last.

wise adj having knowledge or common sense; learned; prudent. * vti (with **up**) (inf) (to cause) to become informed or aware.–**wisely** adv.

wisecrack n (inf) a witty or sarcastic remark.–also vi.

wise guy n (inf) a person who is always making critical or sarcastic comments.

wish vti to long for; to express a desire. * n desire; thing desired.

wishbone n the forked bone at the front of the breastbone of a bird consisting of the fused clavicles.

wishful adj having a wish; hopeful.

wishful thinking n the mistaken belief that one's wishes correspond to reality.

wishy-washy adj weak, thin, feeble.

wisp n a thin strand; a small bunch, as of hay; anything slender.–**wispy** adj.

wistful adj pensive; sad; yearning.–**wistfully** adv.–**wistfulness** n.

wit n (speech, writing) the facility of combining ideas with humorous effect; a person with this ability; (pl) ability to think quickly.

witch n a woman who practises magic and is considered to a have dealings with the devil.

witchcraft n the practice of magic.

witch doctor n a man in certain tribes who appears to be able to cure sickness or cause harm to people.

witch hunt n a campaign of harassment of those with dissenting opinions; the search for and persecution of those accused of witchcraft.

with prep denoting nearness or agreement; in the company of; in the same direction as; among; by means of; possessing.

withdraw vb (**withdrawing, withdrew,** pp **withdrawn**) vt to draw back or away; to remove; to retract. * vi to retire; to retreat.–**withdrawal** n.

withdrawn adj introverted, reserved; remote.

wither vi to fade or become limp or dry, as of a plant. * vt to cause to dry up or fade.

withhold vt (**withholding, withheld**) to hold back; to deduct; to restrain; to refuse to grant.

within prep inside; not exceeding; not beyond.

without prep outside or out of; beyond; not having, lacking. * adv outside.

withstand vt (**withstanding, withstood**) to oppose or resist, esp successfully; to endure.

witless adj foolish, stupid; not witty.

witness n a person who gives evidence or attests a signing; testimony (of a fact). * vt to have first-hand knowledge of; to see; to be the scene of; to serve as evidence of; to attest a signing. * vi to testify.

witness stand, witness box n an enclosure for witnesses in a court of law.

witticism *n* a witty remark.

wittingly *adv* knowingly.

witty *adj* (**wittier, wittiest**) full of wit.–**wittily** *adv.*–**wittiness** *n*.

wives *see* **wife**.

wizard *n* a magician; a man who practises witchcraft or magic; an expert.–**wizardry** *n*.

wizened *adj* dried up, wrinkled, shriveled.

wobble *vi* to sway unsteadily from side to side; to waver, to hesitate.–**wobbly** *adj*.

woe *n* grief, misery; (*pl*) misfortune.–**woeful** *adj.*–**woefully** *adv.*

woebegone *adj* sorrowful.

wok *n* a large, metal, hemispherical pan used for Chinese-style cooking.

woke, **woken** *see* **wake**[1].

wolf *n* (*pl* **wolves**) a wild animal of the dog family that hunts in packs; a flirtatious man.

wolfram *n* tungsten.

wolverine *n* a voracious carnivorous animal of northern forests of Europe, North America and Asia with thick black fur.

wolves *see* **wolf**.

woman *n* (*pl* **women**) an adult human female; the female sex.

womanhood *n* the state of being a woman.

womanize *vi* to pursue women for sex.–**womanizer** *n*.

womankind *n* female human beings; women collectively, esp as distinct from men.

womanly *adj* having the qualities of a woman.

womb *n* the female organ in which offspring are developed until birth, the uterus; any womb-like cavity; a place where something is produced.

wombat *n* an Australian marsupial mammal resembling a small bear.

women *see* **woman**.

womenfolk *npl* women collectively; the female members of a family, group or community.

won *see* **win**.

wonder *n* a feeling of surprise or astonishment; something that excites such a feeling; a prodigy. * *vi* to feel wonder; to be curious; to speculate; to marvel.

wonderful *adj* marvellous.–**wonderfully** *adv*.

wonderland *n* a land full of marvels.

wonderment *n* astonishment, awe; curiosity.

wont *adj* accustomed; inclined. * *n* habit.

won't = will not.

woo *vt* (**wooing, wooed**) to seek to attract with a view to marriage; to court; to solicit eagerly.–**wooer** *n*.

wood *n* the hard fibrous substance under the bark of trees; trees cut or sawn, timber; a thick growth of trees.

woodchuck *n* a North American marmot with thick reddish-brown fur.–*also* **groundhog**.

wooded *adj* covered with trees.

wooden *adj* made of wood; stiff.

woodland *n* land covered with trees.

woodpecker *n* a bird that pecks holes in trees to extract insects.

woodwind *n* section of an orchestra in which wind instruments, originally made of wood, are played.

woodwork *n* carpentry.

woof[1] *n* the horizontal threads crossing the warp in a woven fabric.

woof[2] *interj* a noise like the bark of a dog. * *vi* to make this sound.

wool *n* the fleece of sheep and other animals; thread or yarn spun from the coats of sheep; cloth made from this yarn.

woolen, woollen *adj* made of wool.

wooly, woolly *adj* (**woolier, wooliest** *or* **woollier, woolliest**) of, like or covered with wool; indistinct, blurred; muddled. * *n* (*pl* **woolies** *or* **woollies**) (*inf*) a woolen garment.–**wooliness, woolliness** *n*.

woozy *adj* (**woozier, wooziest**) (*inf*) mentally confused, dazed; dizzy, nauseous.

word *n* a single unit of language in speech or writing; talk, discussion; a message; a promise; a command; information; a password; (*pl*) lyrics; (*pl*) a quarrel. * *vt* to put into words, to phrase; to flatter.

word for word *adj, adv* (*a translation, etc*) using exactly the same words, verbatim.

wording *n* the way in which words are used, esp in written form; a choice of words.

word-perfect *adj* able to repeat something without mistake.–*also* **letter-perfect**.

word processor *n* computer software that allows the input, formatting, storage and printing of text electronically; the hardware, including microprocessor, monitor, keyboard and printer, required to operate word-processing software.

wordy *adj* (**wordier, wordiest**) verbose.

wore *see* **wear**.

work *n* employment, occupation; a task; the product of work; manner of working; place of work; a literary composition; (*pl*) a factory, plant. * *vi* to be employed, to have a job; to operate (a machine, etc); to produce effects; (*with* **on**) to (attempt to) persuade by persistent effort; (*with* **out**) to undertake a regular, planned series of exercises. * *vt* to effect, to achieve; (*with* **off**) to eliminate though effort; (*with* **over**) to examine closely; (*inf*) to assault violently. –**workable** *adj.*–**worker** *n*.

workaholic *n* a person with a compulsive need to work.

workbench *n* a bench designed for woodworking, metalworking, etc.

workbook *n* an exercise book with spaces for answers to set questions.

work force *n* the number of workers who are engaged in a particular industry; the total number of workers who are potentially available.

working class *n* people who work for wages, esp manual workers; proletariat.–*also adj*.

workload *n* the amount of work done or required to be done in a particular period.

workman *n* (*pl* **workmen**) a person employed in manual labor; a person who works in a particular manner.

workmanlike *adj* skillful.

workmanship *n* technical skill; the way a thing is made, style.

work-out *n* a session of strenuous physical exercises.

workshop *n* a room or building where work is done; a seminar for specified intensive study, work, etc.

work station *n* a place in an office, esp a desk equipped with a computer terminal, where a single person works.

world *n* the planet earth and its inhabitants; mankind; the universe; a sphere of existence; the public.

world-class *adj* of the highest quality in the world.

worldly *adj* (**worldlier, worldliest**) earthly, rather than spiritual; material; experienced.

world music *n* popular music of or combining ethnic styles from various different countries around the world.

world power *n* a country that is powerful enough to influence international politics.

worldwide *adj* universal.

worm *n* an earthworm; an insect larva; the thread of a screw. * *vt* to work (oneself into a position) slowly or secretly; to extract information by slow and persistent means.

worm's-eye view *n* the view from the very bottom or humblest position.

wormwood *n* a European plant that yields a bitter oil used in making absinthe; (something causing) bitterness.

worn *see* **wear**.

worn-out *adj* (*machine, etc*) past its useful life; (*person*) depressed, tired.

worry vb (**worrying, worried**) vt to bother, pester, harass. * vi to be uneasy or anxious; to fret. * n (pl **worries**) a cause or feeling of anxiety.–**worrier** n.

worse adj (compar of **bad** and **ill**) less favorable; not so well as before. * adv with great severity.–**worsen** vti.

worship n religious adoration; a religious ritual, eg prayers; devotion. * vb (**worshiping, worshiped** or **worshipping, worshipped**) vt to adore or idolize. * vi to participate in a religious service.–**worshiper, worshipper** n.

worst adj (superl of **bad** or **ill**; see also **worse**) bad or ill in the highest degree; of the lowest quality. * adv to the worst degree. * n the least good part.

worst-case adj being, or taking account of, the worst possible situation or outcome (worst-case scenario).

worth n value; price; excellence; importance. * adj equal in value to; meriting.

worthless adj valueless; useless; of bad character.–**worthlessness** n.

worthwhile adj important or rewarding enough to justify the effort.

worthy adj (**worthier, worthiest**) virtuous; deserving. * n (pl **worthies**) a worthy person, a local celebrity.–**worthily** adv.

would see **will**².

would-be adj aspiring or professing to be.

wouldn't = would not.

wound¹ n any cut, bruise, hurt, or injury caused to the skin; hurt feelings. * vt to injure.

wound² see **wind**².

wove, woven see **weave**.

wow interj exclamation of astonishment. * n (sl) a success.

wp, WP abbr = word processing; word processor.

wrangle vi to argue; to dispute noisily. * n a noisy argument.

wrap vt (**wrapping, wrapped**) to fold (paper) around (a present, purchase etc); to wind (around); to enfold; (with **up**) to enclose in paper; (inf) to make the final arrangements for. * vi (with **up**) to put warm clothes on; (inf) to be quiet. * n a shawl.

wrapper n one who or that which wraps; a book jacket; a light dressing gown.

wrath n intense anger; rage.–**wrathful** adj.

wreak vt to inflict or exact (eg vengeance, havoc).

wreath n (pl **wreaths**) a twisted ring of leaves, flowers, etc; something like this in shape.

wreathe vti to form into a wreath; to decorate with wreaths; to move or coil in wreaths.

wreck n accidental destruction of a ship; a badly damaged ship; a run-down person or thing. * vt to destroy; to ruin.

wreckage n the process of wrecking; remnants from a wreck.

wrecked adj (sl) intoxicated by alcohol or drugs; exhausted.

wren n small brownish songbird, with a short erect tail.

wrench vt to give something a violent pull or twist; to injure with a twist, to sprain; to distort. * n a forceful twist; a sprain; a spanner; emotional upset caused by parting.

wrest vt to take with force (from); to seize; to obtain by toil.

wrestle vti to fight by holding and trying to throw one's opponent down; to struggle. * n a contest in which the opponents wrestle.–**wrestler** n.

wrestling n the skill or sport of fighting by grappling and trying to throw each other to the ground.

wretch n a miserable or pitied person; a despised and scorned person.

wretched adj very miserable; in poor circumstances; despicable.–**wretchedly** adv.–**wretchedness** n.

wrier, wriest see **wry**.

wriggle vi to move with a twisting motion; to squirm, to writhe; to use evasive tricks.–also n.–**wriggler** n.–**wriggly** adj.

wring vt (**wringing, wrung**) to twist; to compress by twisting in order to squeeze water from; to pain; to obtain forcibly.

wrinkle n a small crease or fold on a surface. * vti to make or become wrinkled.

wrist n the joint connecting the hand with the forearm.

wristband n the cuff of a sleeve that covers the wrist; a band round the wrist that absorbs sweat.

writ n (law) a written court order.

write vb (**writing, wrote**, pp **written**) vt to form letters on paper with a pen or pencil; to express in writing; to compose (a letter, music, literary work, etc); to communicate by letter; (with **off**) to cancel a bad debt as a loss; (inf) to damage (a vehicle) beyond repair; (with **down**) vt to put in writing; to harm or demean (a person) in writing; (with **up**) to describe, update, or put into finished form by writing; to praise or publicize in writing. * vi to be a writer; (with **down to** or **for**) to write in a simplified style for a less educated taste.

write-off n a debt canceled as a loss; (inf) a badly damaged car.

writer n an author; a scribe or clerk.

write-up n a published report or review, esp a favorable one.

writhe vi to twist the body violently, as in pain; to squirm (under, at).

written see **write**.

wrong adj not right, incorrect; mistaken, misinformed; immoral. * n harm; injury done to another. * adv incorrectly. * vt to do wrong to.–**wrongly** adv.

wrongdoer n a person who breaks (moral) laws.–**wrongdoing** n.

wrongful adj unwarranted, unjust.–**wrongfully** adv.

wrote see **write**.

wrought adj formed; made; (metals) shaped by hammering, etc.

wrought iron n iron that is forged or rolled, not cast.

wrung see **wring**.

wry adj (**wryer, wryest** or **wrier, wriest**) twisted, contorted; ironic.–**wryly** adv.–**wryness** n.

wt abbr = weight.

WWW abbr World Wide Web.

WY abbr = Wyoming.

WYSIWYG adj (acronym) (comput) what you see is what you get: meaning that the layout and style of text, etc, on screen will be exactly as printed out.

X

X, x symbol (math) unknown quantity; the figure 10. * n an unknown or mysterious factor.

xanthochroid adj blond and blue-eyed with fair white skin. * n an xanthochroid person.

xanthoma n (pl **xanthomas, xanthomata**) a small yellow tumor in the skin caused by deposits of lipids.–**xanthomatous** adj.

xanthophyll n (bot) an orange or yellow pigment in autumn leaves.–**xanthophyllous** adj.

xanthopsia n a disturbance in vision causing everthing to appear yellow.

xanthosis n a yellow pigmentation of the skin in diabetes, etc.

xanthous adj yellow.

x-axis n (pl **x-axes**) the reference axis of a graph along which the x coordinate is measured.

X-chromosome n one of the pair (with the Y-chromosome) of sex chromosomes that occur in females.

xenolith n (geol) a rock occuring in a system of rocks to which it does not belong.

xenomorphic adj (mineral grain) abnormal in shape owing to the pressure of adjacent minerals in rock.

xenon n a heavy inert colorless odorless gaseous element found in tiny quantities in the atmosphere.

xenophobia *n* fear or dislike of strangers or foreigners.–**xenophobe** *n*.–**xenophobic** *adj*.

Xerox *n* (*trademark*) a photocopying process using xerography; the copy produced by this. * *vt* to produce a copy in this way.

x-height *n* (*print*) the height of the letter x in lowercase.

xi *n* (*pl* **xis**) the 14th letter of the Greek alphabet.

Xmas *abbr* = Christmas.

X-ray, x-ray *n* radiation of very short wavelengths, capable of penetrating solid bodies, and printing on a photographic plate a shadow picture of objects not permeable by light rays. * *vt* to photograph by x-rays.

xylophone *n* a percussion instrument consisting of a series of wooden bars which are struck with small hammers.–**xylophonic** *adj*.

xylophonist *n* a performer on a xylophone.

Y

Y, y *symbol* (*math*) the second unknown quantity.

yacht *n* a sailing or mechanically driven vessel, used for pleasure cruises or racing. * *vi* to race or cruise in a yacht.–**yachting** *n*.–**yachtsman** *n* (*pl* **yachtsmen**).–**yachtswoman** *nf* (*pl* **yachtswomen**).

yahoo *n* (*pl* **yahoos**) a crude, vicious person.

yak[1] *n* a domesticated species of ox found in Tibet having horns and long hair.

yak[2] *n* (*sl*) persistent trivial talk or chatter. * *vi* (**yakking, yakked**) to talk in this way.

yam *n* the edible, starchy tuberous root of a tropical climbing plant; sweet potato.

yammer *vi* (*inf*) to whimper or whine constantly; (*inf*) to complain loudly and persistently. * *n* (*inf*) a whining or complaining sound.

yank *vti* to pull suddenly, to jerk. * *n* a sudden sharp pull.

Yankee *n* (*inf*) a citizen of the US, an American.

yap *vi* (**yapping, yapped**) to yelp, bark; (*sl*) to talk constantly, esp in a noisy or irritating manner.

yard[1] *n* a unit of measure of three feet and equivalent to 0.9144 meters; (*naut*) a spar hung across a mast to support a sail.

yard[2] *n* an enclosed concrete area, esp near a building; an enclosure for a commercial activity (eg a shipyard); an area of ground for growing herbs, fruits, flowers, or vegetables, usu attached to a house, a garden; an area with tracks for the making up of trains, servicing of locomotives, etc.

yardarm *n* (*naut*) either half of a yard.

yardstick *n* a standard used in judging.

yarn *n* fibers of wool, cotton etc spun into strands for weaving, knitting, etc; (*inf*) a tale or story. * *vi* to tell a yarn; to talk at length.

yashmak, yashmac *n* a veil worn by Muslim women, showing only the eyes.

yaw *vi* (*ship, aircraft*) to deviate from a course; (*aircraft*) to turn from side to side about the vertical axis. * *vt* to cause to yaw. * *n* a yawing movement or course.

yawl *n* a two-masted sailing vessel with its aftermast at the stern.

yawn *vi* to open the jaws involuntarily and inhale, as from drowsiness; to gape.–*also n*.

yawning *adj* gaping; wide-open; drowsy.–**yawningly** *adv*.

y-axis *n* (*pl* **y-axes**) the reference axis of a graph along which the y coordinate is measured.

Y-chromosome *n* one of the pair (with the X-chromosome) of sex chromosomes that occur in males.

yd., yds *abbr* = yard(s).

yeah *adv* (*inf*) yes.

year *n* a period of twelve months, or 365 or 366 days, beginning with 1 January and ending with 31 December; a period of approximately twelve months.

yearbook *n* an annual publication reviewing the events of the previous year or bringing information up to date.

yearling *n* an animal a year old or in its second year.

yearlong *adj* lasting a year.

yearly *adj* occurring every year; lasting a year. * *adv* once a year; from year to year.

yearn *vi* to feel desire (for); to long for.–**yearning** *n*.

yeast *n* a fungus that causes alcoholic fermentation, used in brewing and baking.

yell *vti* to shout loudly; to scream; to emit a yell. * *n* a loud shout; a concerted cheer by supporters, students, etc, at a game.

yellow *adj* of the color of lemons, egg yolk, etc; having a yellowish skin; (*inf*) cowardly. * *n* the color yellow. * *vi* to become or turn yellow.

yellow fever *n* an infectious tropical fever caused by a virus transmitted by certain mosquitoes.

yellow pages *npl* (part of) a telephone book that lists business subscribers under different categories according to the type of service offered.

yelp *vti* to utter a sharp, shrill cry or bark.–*also n*.

yen *n* (*inf*) a yearning, an ambition.

yeoman *n* (*pl* **yeomen**) (*formerly*) a farmer who cultivated his own land; a non-commissioned officer in the navy, marines.

yep *adv* (*inf*) yes.

yes *adv* a word of affirmation or consent.

yes man *n* a servile, fawning, sycophantic person.

yesterday *n* the day before today; the recent past. * *adv* on the day before today; recently.

yet *adv* still; so far; even. * *conj* nevertheless; however; still.

yeti *n* a mysterious animal thought to live high in the Himalayan mountains but never seen.–*also* **abominable snowman**.

yew *n* an evergreen tree or shrub with thin, sharp leaves and red berries.

Yiddish *n* a mixed German and Hebrew dialect spoken by European Jews.

yield *vt* to resign; to give forth, to produce, as a crop, result, profit, etc. * *vi* to submit; to give way to physical force, to surrender. * *n* the amount yielded; the profit or return on a financial investment.

yippee *interj* used to express exuberant delight.

yodel *vti* (**yodeling, yodeled** *or* **yodelling, yodelled**) to sing, alternating from the ordinary voice to falsetto.–**yodeler, yodeller** *n*.

yoga *n* a system of exercises for attaining bodily and mental control and well-being.–**yogic** *adj*.–**yogi** *n*

yogurt, yoghurt *n* a semi-liquid food made from milk curdled by bacteria.

yoke *n* a bond or tie; slavery; the wooden frame joining oxen to make them pull together; part of a garment that is fitted below the neck. * *vt* to put a yoke on; to join together.

yokel *n* (*derog*) a country person who is regarded as unsophisticated and simple-minded.

yolk *n* the yellow part of an egg.

yonder *adv* over there.

yore *n* time long past.

you *pron* (*gram*) 2nd person singular or plural; the person or persons spoken to.

you'd = you would; you had.

you'll = you will; you shall.

young *adj* in the early period of life; in the first part of growth; new; inexperienced. * *n* young people; offspring.

youngster *n* a young person; a youth.

your *poss adj* of or belonging to or done by you.

you're = you are.

yours *poss pron* of or belonging to you.

yourself *pron* (*pl* **yourselves**) the emphatic and reflexive form of **you**.

youth *n* the period between childhood and adulthood; young people collectively; the early stages of something; a young man or boy.–**youthful** *adj*.–**youthfully** *adv*.

you've = you have.

yowl *n* a loud mournful cry, esp from pain.–*also vi*.

yo-yo *n* (*pl* **yo-yos**) a hand-held toy made of a flat spool which can be made to wind up and down a piece of string.

yucca *n* a plant with stiff, spear-like leaves and white flowers.

yuck *interj* (*sl*) expressing disgust.–**yucky** *adj*.

yule *n* Christmas.

yuletide *n* the Christmas festival or season.

yummy *adj* (**yummier, yummiest**) (*inf*) tasty, pleasing. * *interj* yum-yum.

yum-yum *interj* used to express pleasure, esp when eating.

yup *adv* (*inf*) yes.

yuppie *n* (*inf*) any young professional regarded as affluent, ambitious, materialistic, etc.

Z

z (*symbol*) (*math*) an algebraic variable; the z-axis.

zabaglione *n* a dessert of whipped egg yolks, sugar and marsala wine.

zany *adj* (**zanier, zaniest**) comical; eccentric.–**zanily** *adv*.–**zaniness** *n*.

zap *vb* (**zapping, zapped**) *vt* to attack; to kill; to bombard; (*comput*) to get rid of data. * *vi* to rush around.

z-axis *n* the reference axis of a three-dimensional coordinate system, along which the z-coordinate is measured.

zeal *n* fervent devotion; fanaticism.

zealot *n* an extreme partisan, a fanatic.

zealous *adj* full of zeal; ardent.–**zealously** *adv*.–**zealousness** *n*.

zebra *n* (*pl* **zebras, zebra**) a black and white striped wild animal related to the horse.–**zebrine** *adj*.

Zeitgeist *n* the spirit of the time; the beliefs, attitudes, tastes, etc, of a particular period.

Zen *n* a Japanese Buddhist sect that emphasizes self-awareness and self-mastery as the means to enlightenment.

zenith *n* the point at which the sun or moon appears to be exactly overhead; peak, summit (of ambition), etc).

zephyr *n* a soft, gentle breeze; a very thin woolen material; a garment made of this.

zeppelin *n* a rigid, cigar-shaped airship.

zero *n* (*pl* **zeros, zeroes**) the symbol 0; nothing; the lowest point; freezing point, 0 degrees Celsius. * *vi* (*with* **in**) (*inf*) to focus attention on (a problem, subject, etc); (*inf*) to converge upon; (*with* **in on**) to concentrate fire (from a weapon) on a specific target.

zero gravity *n* weightlessness.

zero hour *n* the time at which something is scheduled to begin.

zest *n* the outer part of the skin of an orange or lemon used to give flavor; enthusiasm; excitement.–**zestful** *adj*.–**zestfully** *adv*.–**zestfulness** *n*.

zeta *n* the sixth letter of the Greek alphabet.

zeugma *n* a figure of speech in which a word is used with two others, to only one of which it properly applies.–**zeugmatic** *adj*.

zigzag *n* a series of short, sharp angles in alternate directions. * *adj* having sharp turns. * *vti* (**zigzagging, zigzagged**) to move or form in a zigzag.

zillion *n* (*pl* **zillion, zillions**) (*inf*) an indefinitely large number or quantity.

Zimmer *n* (*trademark*) a frame of tubular metal used by the infirm as a walking aid.

zinc *n* a bluish-white metallic element used in alloys and batteries. * *vt* (**zincing, zinced** *or* **zincking, zincked**) to coat with zinc.–**zincic** *adj*.

zing *n* (*inf*) a high-pitched buzz; (*inf*) vitality, exuberance. * *vi* (*inf*) to move with a zinging sound.

Zionism *n* a movement formerly to resettle Jews in Palestine as their national home, now concerned with the development of Israel.–**Zionist** *n, adj*.–**Zionistic** *adj*.

zip *n* a light whizzing sound of a bullet, etc; (*sl*) brisk energy; a slide fastener on clothing, bags, etc with interlocking teeth, a zipper. * *vb* (**zipping, zipped**) *vi* to move at high speed, to dart. * *vt* to fasten with a zip.

ZIP Code *n* (*trademark*) a postcode that uses digits to denote an area.

zipper *n* a zip.

zippy *adj* (**zippier, zippiest**) speedy; energetic.

zircon *n* a variously colored hard translucent mineral, some varieties of which are cut as gemstones.

zirconium *n* a metallic element found in zircon and used in alloys.

zit *n* (*sl*) a pimple, spot.

zither *n* a musical instrument with 30–45 strings over a shallow sounding box played by plucking.–**zitherist** *n*.

zodiac *n* an imaginary belt in the heavens along which the sun, moon, and chief planets appear to move, divided crosswise into twelve equal areas, called "signs of the zodiac," each named after a constellation; a diagram representing this.–**zodiacal** *adj*.

zoetrope *n* a toy with a revolving cylinder showing a series of pictures in apparent motion.

zombie, zombi *n* (*pl* **zombies**) a person who is lifeless and apathetic; an automaton.

zone *n* a region, area; a subdivision; any area with a specified use or restriction. * *vt* to divide or mark off into zones; to designate as a zone; to encircle with a zone.–**zonal** *adj*.

zonked *adj* (*sl*) intoxicated by drugs or alcohol; (*sl*) exhausted.

zoo *n* (*pl* **zoos**) a place where a collection of living wild animals is kept for public showing.

zoological garden *n* a zoo.

zoologist *n* a person who studies animals and animal behavior.

zoology *n* (*pl* **zoologies**) the study of animals with regard to their classification, structure and habits.–**zoological** *adj*.–**zoologically** *adv*.

zoom *vi* to go quickly, to speed; to climb upward sharply in an aeroplane; to rise rapidly; (*photog*) to focus in on an object using a zoom lens. * *n* the act of zooming; a zoom lens.

zoom lens *n* (*photog*) a camera lens that makes distant objects appear closer without moving the camera.

zucchini *npl n* a type of small vegetable marrow.–*also* **courgette**.